D1560853

Rosato's
Plastics Encyclopedia
and Dictionary

Dominick V. Rosato

Rosato's Plastics Encyclopedia and Dictionary

Hanser Publishers, Munich Vienna New York Barcelona

The Author: Dominick V. Rosato, 40 Karen Road, Waban, MA 02168, USA

Die Deutsche Bibliothek – CIP-Einheitsaufnahme

Rosato, Dominick V.: [Plastics encyclopedia and dictionary] Rosato's plastics encyclopedia and dictionary / Dominick V. Rosato. – Munich; Vienna; New York; Barcelona: Hanser; New York: Oxford Univ. Press, 1993
ISBN 3-446-16490-1
NE: HST

Typography and production: Charlotte Fabian, Dublin

Printed and bound in Germany by Passavia Druckerei GmbH, Passau.

PREFACE

For over a century the plastics industry has built up a language and a terminology of its own. About 11,000 of the most commonly used worldwide words and expressions are defined in this book. In many instances the words and expressions being defined are peculiar to the plastics industry. In other cases, those used by the industry may derive from words and expressions commonly used in other industries or specialty markets.

This book is unique in that it concentrates on the details of engineering, chemistry, polymer structures, designs, testing, quality control, products, and comparing plastics to other materials rather than the usual of just chemistry. It is not just a dictionary in the usual sense of an assemblage of brief descriptions, but rather a compendium of technical to business descriptive expressions on information pertaining to all facets of the plastics industry.

The prime objective of this one-source book is to provide a satisfactory reference book on the overall review of plastics and reinforced plastics. Thus, its contents make it useful to those involved with plastics and reinforced plastics as well as those contemplating its use or not familiar with these unique materials.

This book principally uses the word plastic rather than polymer, resin, etc. ▷ **plastic**. Each of these words has its individual description or definition, but it also identifies itself as a plastic. Note that (1) the plastic industry is identified by the word plastic, (2) by far most people worldwide use the term plastic, (3) by far most products, materials, shows or exhibitions, technical meetings, advertising, etc. use the term plastic, and (4) practically all people from all corners refer to the world of plastics. Also the terms "reinforced plastic" and "composite" tend to be used interchangeably. Up to the 1960s practically only reinforced plastic was used and thereafter the term composite became very popular, which is properly identified as a plastic composite. The term composite includes many different types of composites ▷ **composite**.

This comprehensive book concentrates and focuses on: (1) engineering, chemical, and other technologies, (2) the behavior of plastics and reinforced plastics, (3) the handling and processing of these materials, (4) the controls and testing of these materials, processes, and products, (5) the understanding of their advantages and limitations (disadvantages), and (6) the designing of products that meet performance requirements at the lowest cost. In order to meet these objectives, this book reviews many different categories or subdivisions that range from descriptive to quantitative to multidisciplinary sciences involved in understanding plastics and reinforced plastics. Examples of these categories and subdivisions are as follows: additives, adhesives, assemblies, auxiliary equipment, basics (engineering, polymer chemistry, computers, plastic melt behavior, etc), business (plant control, data storage, etc.), chemistry, coatings, colors, compounding, composites, computer aids, controls (materials, processes, testing, etc.), costs, decorating, designs, ecology, economics, elastomers, electrical/electronics, energy, engineering, environments, fabrication processes (extrusion, injection molding, blow molding, thermoforming, compression molding, bag molding, filament winding, casting, etc.), fabrics, facts (versus myths), feedstocks, fibers, films, flammability, foams, glasses, hazards, incineration, loadings (static, dynamic, etc.), manufacturing, markets, mixing, modeling, molds, molecular structures, moduli, morphology, nondestructive testing, nonwoven fabrics, patents, performances, plastics, polymerization, polymers, printing, processes, products, protocols, recycling, regulations, reinforced plastics, resins, rheology, rubbers, safety, standards/specifications, statistics, steels, strains, strengths, stresses, tests (tensile, creep, fatigue, impact, etc.), thermal analysis, tradenames, waste, woods, woven fabrics, zero defects, etc.

Each of these categories is individually grouped together and/or cross-referenced so that those not familiar with pertinent terms (words or expressions) in each category can easily identify them. The entries provide an explanation of what the terms mean, together with any necessary or important background, illustrations, tables, and/or cross-references to other related terms. Many examples are used such as mechanical property variables with plastic chemical structures, extruded performance with melt rheology, design influenced by environment, etc. Thus, there are entries longer than a brief description that identify this book as an encyclopedic dictionary.

The reviews are targeted to provide help in clarifying definitions. The information provided has been selected to present a balanced account of the facets involving plastics and reinforced plastics; as examples see the diagrams in the entries on ▷**design, FALLO approach, polymer chemistry terminology, reinforced plastic directional properties, testing,** and **viscoelasticity**. Some terms have more than one definition because they are used by different subdivisions of the plastics industry or by different groups such as mechanical engineers, chemical engineers, electrical engineers, production engineers, etc. Each has its own definition to meet its specific requirements. Entries have been included that are not specifically plastic terms, but have a special relevance in the context of the plastics industry. This book includes sections on: (1) *abbreviations, acronyms*, (2) *conversions* (SI metric to English) and (3) *references*.

This book has been prepared with an awareness that its usefulness will depend largely on its simplicity. The guiding premise has been to provide essential information. Words and expressions are organized to best present a methodology of those terms used with plastics and reinforced plastics.

The book will be useful to all groups of people: educational, technical (chemist, engineer, thermodynamics, etc.) and nontechnical, manufacturers of materials and equipment, new product venture groups, research and development organizations, production, marketing, purchasing, and management (all types of products). It includes both practical and theoretical viewpoints. Thus, this book is useful to those involved in either practicalities or theoretical aspects. For those who are practical, the theory will be understandable and useful. In turn, the theorist will gain an insight into limitations owing to materials and equipment; similar to situations in other industries such as steel ▷**perfection**. All have advantages and limitations which can (must) be understood and properly applied ▷**plastic bad and other myths**.

Plastics concern virtually every group of people worldwide. They occupy an important part of research, development, design, production, sales, and consumers' workload efforts in diverse industries. For over a century plastics have been used successfully and required in a myriad applications ▷**markets for plastics** and **world consumption of plastics**. Significant improvements have continually been made in plastic materials, processes, applications, and recycling, with the future to be even more spectacular in the capability of designing and manufacturing with plastics and reinforced plastics.

Because plastics are unique in their broad range of properties, they are adaptable to different products or markets. One can decide on practically any requirement and there will be a processable plastic, whereas other materials have relatively narrow capabilities compared to the present and future abundance of superior performing plastics. Recognize that there are tremendous variations in properties and performances of plastics. This book will show that there is a practical and easy approach to understanding processing and identifying plastics performances, as there is with other materials.

All information provided is only to be used as a guide. No information in this book shall be considered a recommendation for any use that may infringe on patent rights or endorsements. Obtain the latest and more complete information or data from material suppliers and different data banks that are available from various sources worldwide.

Information presented may be covered by U.S. and/or foreign patents and/or trademarks. No authorization to utilize these patents or trademarks is given or implied; they are discussed for information only. The use of general descriptive names, proprietary names, tradenames, commercial designations, or the like does not in any way imply they may be used freely. They are often legally protected by registered trademarks or other formats even if not designated as such in this book. While information presented represents useful information that can be studied or analyzed and is believed to be true and accurate, neither the author nor the publisher can accept any legal responsibility for any errors, omissions, or other factors.

In preparing this book, extensive use was made of personal worldwide industry and teaching experiences developed by the author (starting 1939) as well as information from industry and society or trade organizations, published books, articles, reports, conferences, and the like as evident from the selected bibliography. Special thanks are due to Matthew V., Drew V., Donald V. and M. Virginia Rosato for providing source previews with cross-references and helping in converting the manuscript into a formal text.

D. V. Rosato

▷ refers to cross-references

CONTENTS

LIST OF ABBREVIATIONS

This compilation provides a guide to uniform contractions of terms and recognizes that some have more than one definition because they are used by different industry groups with diverse interests.

A	Acetone, Acrylate, Acrylonitrile, Alkyl, Amide, etc.
A	Ampere
A	Angstrom (replaces Å)
A	Area
AA	Acetic Aldehyde
AA	Aluminum Assoc.
AA	Atomic Absorption
AAAS	American Academy of Arts and Science
AAAS	American Assoc. of the Advancement of Science
AAAS	Automatic Activation Analysis System
AAE	American Assoc. of Engineers
AAES	American Assoc. of Engineering Societies
AAR	Assoc. of American Railroads
AAS	Assoc. for the Advancement of Science
AAS	Atomic Absorption Spectroscopy
AATC	American Assoc. of Textile Chemists
ABA	Acrylonitrile-Butadiene-Acrylate
abbr.	Abbreviation
ABEA	Azobisformamide
ABL	Allegeny Ballistic Laboratory
abs.	Absolute
ABS	Acrylonitrile-Butadiene-Styrene
—	Acetal (see POM)
AC	Acetate
AC	Alternating Current
ACC	Automotive Composite Consortium (GM, Ford, Chrysler)
ACGIH	American Conference of Governmental Industrial Hygienists
ACM	Acrylate Rubber
ACPES	Acrylonitrile-Chlorinated Polyethylene-Styrene
ACS	American Chemical Society
A/D	Analog-to-Digital Converter (also ADC)
AD	Average Deviation
ADC	Allyl Diglycol Carbonate (see CR-39)
ADC	see A/D
ADH	Adhesive
AE	Auxiliary Equipment
AEB	Average Extent of Burning
AEC	Acrylonitrile Ethylene Styrene
AF	Air Force
AFCMA	Aluminum Foil Container Manufacturers' Assoc.
AFMA	American Furniture Manufacturers Assoc.
AGA	American Gas Assoc.
AGE	Allylglycidylether
AHMA	American Hotel and Motel Assoc.
AI	Artificial Intelligence
AIA	Aerospace Industries Assoc.
AIChE	American Institute of Chemical Engineers
AIDS	Acquired Immune Deficiency Syndrome
AIMCL	Assoc. of Industrial Metallizers, Coaters and Laminators
AIMMPE	American Institute of Mining, Metallurgical and Petroleum Engineers
AIP	American Institute of Polymers
AISI	American Iron and Steel Institute
Al	Aluminum
alc.	Alcohol
ALU	Arithmetric-Logic Unit
AMA	Adhesives Manufacturers' Assoc.
AMA	American Management Assoc.
AMA	American Medical Assoc.
AMC	Alkyd Molding Compound
AMMA	Acrylonitrile-Methyl-Methacrylate
AMS	Alpha Methyl Styrene
AN	Acrylonitrile
ANSI	American National Standard Institute
ANTEC	Annual Technical Conference (SPE)
APET	Amorphous Polyethylene Terephthalate

Abbreviations

API Addition Reaction Polyimide
API American Petroleum Institute
APM Assoc. of Plastics Manufacturers (in Europe)
approx. Approximate
aq. Aqueous
AQL Acceptable Quality Level
AR Acceptable Risk
AR Alkaline Resistant
AR Aromatic
AR Aspect Ratio
ARM Assoc. of Rotational Molders
ARP Advanced Reinforced Plastics
ASA Acrylic-Styrene-Acrylonitrile
ASA American Standard Assoc.
ASAP As Soon As Possible
ASCE American Society of Civil Engineers
ASD Adjustable Speed Drive
ASM American Society for Metals
ASME American Society of Mechanical Engineers
ASQC American Society for Quality Control
AS/RS Automated Storage and Retrieval System
Assoc. Association
ASTM American Society for Testing and Materials
ATA Air Transport Assoc.
ATB Average Time of Burning
ATC Assembly Test Chip
ATH Aluminum Trihydrate
atm. Atmosphere or Atmospheric
at. no. Atomic Number; symbol: Z
ATPE Aromatic Amine Terminated Polyether
av. Average
AWS American Welding Society
AZ Azodicarbonamide

B Benzyl, Butadiene, Butyl, Butyrate, etc.
BA Butyl Acrylate
BATF Bureau of Alcohol, Tobacco and Firearms
bbl. Barrel
BBP Benzyl Butyl Phthalate
BCB Bisbenzocyclobutene
BC Biocomputing
BCl_3 Boron Trichloride
Be Beryllium
BeCu Beryllium Copper
Bhn Brinell Hardness Number
BIF Benchmark Interface Format
bit Binary Digit
BM Back Molding
BM Bag Molding
BM Blow Molding
BMC Bulk Molding Compound
BMI Bismaleimide
BMW Broad Molecular Weight
BO Bioriented
BOA Benzyl Octyl Adipate
BOM Bill of Material
BOPP Bioriented Polypropylene
b.p. Boiling Point
BP British Petroleum
BPA Bisophenol-A
BPO Benzoyl Peroxide
Bq Becquerel
BR Blowup Ratio (see BUR)
BR Butadiene Rubber
BS British Standard
BS Butadiene Styrene
BSI British Standard Institute
BTC Bottling Technology Council
Btu British Thermal Unit
BTX Benzene-Toluene-Xylene (solvent)
Bu Informal abbreviation for Butyl
BUN Blood Urea Nitrogen
Buna Polybutadiene
BUR Blowup Ratio (preferred to BR)
BX Bureau of Export Administration

C Carbonate, Cellulose, Chloride, Cresyl, etc.
C Calorie (also cal)
C Carbon
C Celsius
c Centi (10^{-2})
C Centigrade (preference Celsius)
C Compliance
C Coulomb
C Stiffness Constant
Ca Calcium
CA Cellulose Acetate
ca. Circa (or approximate)
CAA Clean Air Act
CAB Cellulose Acetate Butyrate
$CaCO_3$ Calcium Carbonate
CAD Charged Area Development
CAD Compact Audio Disc
CAD Computer-Aided Design
CAD Computer Audio Disc
CADD Computer-Aided Design and Drafting
CAE Computer-Aided Engineering
cal Calorie (also C)
CALED Calculated
CAM Composition And Makeup
CAM Computer-Aided Manufacturing

Abbreviations

CAM Computer-Assisted Makeup
CAMG Computer-Aided Molecular Graphics
CAN Cellulose Acetate Nitrate
CAP Cellulose Acetate Propionate
CAPP Computer-Aided Process Planning
CASING Crosslinking by Activated Species of Inert Gases
CAT Computer-Aided Testing
CAT Computer-Aided Tomography
CBA Chemical Blowing Agent
CCC Computer Command Center
CCD Charge Couple Device
CCL Commodity Control List
CCM Computer Cost Modeling
CCT Cone Calorimeter Test
Cd Cadmium
cd Candela
CD Compact Disc
CDB Conjugated Diene Butyl
CD-ROM Compact Disc-Read Only Memory
CE Chemical Engineer
CEO Chief Executive Officer
CEPP Chemical Emergency Preparedness Program
CERCLA Comprehensive Environmental Response Compensation and Liability Act (or Superfund)
CF Cresol-Formaldehyde
CFC Chlorofluorocarbon
CFCC Continuous Fiber Ceramic Composite
cfm Cubic Foot per Minute
CFR Code of Federal Regulations
CFRTP Continuous Fiber Reinforced Thermoplastic
CG Computer Graphic
CGNP Current Gross National Product
CGPM Conférénce Général des Poids et Mesures (French General Conference on Weights and Measures)
Ci Curie
CIE Commission Internationale de l'Eclairage (French International Commission on Illumination)
CIIM Computer Integrated Injection Molding
CIIT Chemical Industry Institute of Toxicology
CIL Canada Industries Ltd.
CIM Computer-Integrated Machine
CIM Computer-Integrated Manufacturing
CIP Computer-Integrated Production
CIV Composite Intensive Vehicle
CL Computerized Laboratory
CLTE Coefficient of Linear Thermal Expansion
cm Centimeter
CM Chloro-Polyethylene
CM Compression Molding
CMA Chemical Manufacturers' Assoc.
CMC Carboxymethyl Cellulose
CMC Ceramic Matrix Composite
CMC Continuous Molding Compound
CMM Coordinate Measuring Machine
CMRA Chemical Marketing Research Assoc.
CN Cellulose Nitrate (Celluloid)
CNC Computer Numerical Control
CO Carbon Monoxide
CO_2 Carbon Dioxide
CO Epichorhydrin Rubber
coef. Coefficient
COPE Copolyester Elastomer
COPPE Council on Plastics and Packaging in the Environment
CP Canadian Plastics
CP Cellulose Propionate
cp Centipoise
c.p. Chemically Pure
CP Chlorinated Polyether
CP Coefficient of Permeability
CPC Continuous Process Control
CPC Critical Point Control
cpd Compound
CPE Chlorinated Polyethylene
CPET Chlorinated Polyethylene Terephthalate
CPET Crystalline Polyethylene Terephthalate
CPI Condensation Reaction Polyimide
CPRR Center for Plastics Recycling Research
cps Cycles Per Second (or c/s)
CPSA Consumer Product Safety Act
CPSC Consumer Product Safety Commission
CPU Central Processing Unit
CPVC Chlorinated Polyvinyl Chloride
CR Chloroprene Rubber
Cr Chromium
CR Compression Ratio
CR Controlled Rheology
CR-39 Diethylene Glycol Bis-Allyl Carbonate (or ADC)
CR Neoprene Rubber
CRE Constant Rate of Extension
CRI Carpet and Rug Institute

Abbreviations

CRL Constant Rate of Load
CRM Certified Reference Material
CrN Chromium Nitrate
CRS Committee on Resin Statistics (SPI)
CRT Cathode Ray Tube
CRT Constant Rate of Transverse
CS Casein
c/s Cycles per Second
CSA Canadian Standards Assoc.
CSPE Chlorosulfonated Polyethylene
CSWS Council for Solid Waste Solutions (SPI)
CT Chain Transfer
CTA Cellulose Triacetate
CTE Coefficient Thermal Expansion (see CLTE)
CTFA Cosmetic, Toiletries and Fragrance Assoc.
CTFE Chlorotrifluoroethylene
CU Computer Unit
CU Control Unit
Cu Copper
cu. Cubic
CV Cardiovascular
CV Coefficient of Variation
CVD Chemical Vapor Deposition
CVR Computerized Virtual Reality
CWA Clean Water Act

D Decyl
d Denier (preferred Den)
d Density
D Diameter
D/A Digital-to-Analog converter (or DAC)
DAC Diallyl Chlorendate
DAF Diallyl Fumarate
DAF Direct-Access File
DAIP Diallyl Isophthalate
DAM Diallyl Malcatc
DAMP Diallyl Metaphthalate
DAOP Diallyl Orthophthalate
DAP Diallyl Phthalate
DAT Digital Audio Tape
db Decibel
DBM Dip Blow Molding
DBMS Database Management System
DBP Dibutyl Phthalate
DC Design Control
DC Direct Current
DCP Dicapryl Phthalate
DCPD Dicylopentadiene
DEA Dielectric Analysis
DEC Decompose
DEHP Di (2-Ethexyl) Phthalate
Den Denier (or d)
Den/Fil Denier per Filament
DEP Diethyl Phthalate
DGA Differential Gravimetric Analysis
DHP Diheptyl Phthalate
DIBP Diisobutyl Phthalate
DIDA Diisodecyl Adipate
DIM Design Integrated Manufacturing
DIN Deutsches Institut für Normung (German Standard)
DIOA Diisooctyladipate
DIOP Diisooctyl Phthalate
distn. Distillation
DMA Direct Memory Access
DMA Dynamic Mechanical Analysis
DMC Dough Molding Compound
DMDI Diphenylmethane Diisocyanate
DMP Dimethyl Phthalate
DMR Device Master Record
DMS Dynamic Mechanical Spectroscopy
DMT Dimethyl Ester of Terephthalic Acid
DN Design News
DN Deutscher Normenausschuss
DNC Direct Numerical Control
DNP Dinonyl Phthalate
DOA Dioctyl Adipate
DOC Department of Commerce
DOD Department of Defense
DOE Department of Energy
DOP Dioctyl Phthalate
DOS Department of State
DOS Dioctyl Sebacate
DOS Disc Operating System
DOT Department of Transportation
DOT Dual-Ovenable Tray
DOZ Dioctyl Azelate
DP Degree of Polymerization
$\overline{DP}$ Average Degree of Polymerization
DP Dew Point
DPCF Diphenyl Cresyl Phosphate
DPM Discreet Polymer Modifier
DPOF Diphenyl 2-ethylhexyl Phosphate
DPSU Diphenylsulfone
DRAW Direct Read-After Write
DS Degree of Saturation
DS Degree of Substitution
DSC Differential Scanning Calorimeter
DSD Duales System Deutschland (German Recycling System)
DSMO Dimethyl Sulfoxide
DSSP Deep Submergence System Program
DST Direct Screw Transfer
DTA Differential Thermal Analysis
DTUL Deflection Temperature Under Load
DV Devolatilization

Abbreviations

DVR	Design Visual Resource
DVR	Donald Vincent Rosato
DVR	Dynamic Velocity Ratio
DWP	Designing With Plastics
DWV	Drain-Waste-Vent (piping)
E	Epoxidized, Ester, Ethyl, Ethylene, etc.
E	Modulus of Elasticity, Modulus or Young's Modulus
E_c	Modulus, Creep (apparent)
E_t	Modulus, Tensile
E_r	Modulus, Relaxation
E_s	Modulus, Secant
EA	Ethyl Acrylate
EAA	Ethylene Acrylic Acid
EB	Electron Beam
EB	Ethyl Benzene
EBA	Ethylene Butyl Acrylate
EBM	Engineered Blow Molding
EC	Ethyl Cellulose
EC	European Community
ECN	Engineering Change Notice
ECO	Epichlorhydrin Rubber
ECP	Electrical Conducting Polymer
ECPE	Extended Chain Polyethylene
ECTFE	Ethylenechlorotrifluoroethylene
EDD	Engineering Design Database
EDF	Environmental Defense Fund
EDG	Electronic Dot Generation
EDM	Electron-Discharge Machine
EDM	Engineering Data Management
E-Draw	Erasable Direct Read After Write (information disc)
E/E	Electrical and Electronic
EEA	Ethylene Ethyl Acrylate
EEC	European Economic Community
EG	Ethylene Glycol
e.g.	for example
EI	Modulus (times) Moment of Inertia (stiffness)
EIA	Electronic Industries Assoc.
ELL	Electroluminescent Lamp
ELO	Epoxidized Linseed Oil
EMA	Ethylene-Methyl Acrylate
EMAC	Ethylene-Methyl Acrylate Copolymer
EMC	Electromagnetic Compatibility
EMF	Electromagnetic Frequency
EMF	Electromotive Force
EMI	Electromagnetic Interference
EMU	Electromagnetic Unit
EP	Epoxy
E/P	Ethylene/Propylene
EPA	Enthalpimetric Analysis
EPA	Environmental Protection Agency
EPDM	Ethylene-Propylene Diene Monomer
EPF	Expandable Plastic Foam
EPIC	Environmental and Plastic Institute of Canada
EPR	Ethylene-Propylene Rubber
EPS	Expandable Polystyrene
EPT	Ethylene-Propylene Diene Terpolymer
ESA	Electrostatic Assist
ESC	Environmental Stress Cracking
ESCA	Electron Spectroscopy for Chemical Analysis
ESCR	Electron Spectroscopy for Chemical Resistance
ESD	Electrostatic Dissipation
ESO	Epoxidized Soya Bean Oil
ESR	Electron Spin Resonance
est.	Estimate
ESU	Electrostatic Unit
et al.	and others
ETE	Engineering Thermoplastic Elastomer
ETFE	Ethylenetetrafluoroethylene
ETI	Ethylene Terminated Imidothioether
ETO	Ethylene Oxide
EU	Entropy Unit
EUROMAP	European Committee of Machine Manufacturers for the Rubber and Plastics Industries (Zurich, Swiz.)
eV	Electron Volt
EVA	Ethylene-Vinyl Acetate
EVAL	Ethylene-Vinyl Alcohol (Tradename of EVAL Company of America) (see EVOH)
EVE	Ethylene-Vinyl Ether
EVOH	Ethylene-Vinyl Alcohol (used by industry) (see EVAL)
EXTR	Extruder or Extruding
F	Fluoride, Formaldehyde, Phosphate, etc.
F	Coefficient of Friction
F	Fahrenheit
F	Farad
F	Force
FAA	Federal Aviation Administration
FALLO	Follow ALL Opportunities
FAO	Food and Agriculture Organization (UN)
FAP	Fastener Accreditation Progress
FB	Fishbone
FBA	Flexible Packaging Assoc.
FBVF	Fiber (glass) Backed Vacuum Thermoforming

Abbreviations

FC Flow Casting
FC Fluorocarbon
FCC Federal Communications Commission
FCP Fatigue Crack Propagation
FDA Federal Food and Drugs Administration
FDEMS Frequency-Dependent Electromagnetic Sensor
FEA Federal Energy Agency
FEA Finite Element Analysis
FEM Finite Element Modeling
FEP Fluoronated Ethylene Propylene
FF Furan-Formaldehyde
FFF Field-Flow Fractionation
FFS Form, Fill and Seal
FHSA Federal Hazardous Substances Act
FI Factor of Ignorance
FM Formal
FMCT Fusible Metal Core Technology
FMEA Failure Mode and Effect Analysis
FML Flexible Membrane Liner
FOB Free On Board
FP Fluoroplastic
FP Freeze Point
FPVC Flexible Polyvinyl Chloride
FR Fiber Reinforced
FR Flame Retardant
FRCA Fire Retardant Chemicals Assoc.
FRP Fiber Reinforced Plastic
FS Factor of Safety
FSI Flame Spread Index
FSTS Fire, Smoke and Toxicity Standard
FT Fischer-Tropsch
FTA Fault Tree Analysis
FW Filament Winding
FWA Fluorescent Whitening Agent
FY Fiscal Year

G Gauss
G Giga (10^6)
g Gram
G Gravity
G Shear Modulus
G Torsional Modulus
GA Genetic Algorithm
GAIN Gas Assisted Injection
gal Gallon
GC Gas Chromatography
GCP Gas Counter Pressure
g/Den Gram per Denier
GDP Gross Domestic Product (European)
GD&T Geometric Dimensioning & Tolerancing
gf/Tex Gram-Force per Tex
GID Gas Internal Pressure
GIGO Garbage In—Garbage Out
GIM Gas Injection Molding
GMI Geometric Modeling System
g-mol Gram-Molecule
g-mol Gram-Mole
GMP Good Manufacturing Practice
GMTP Glass Mat Reinforced Thermoplastic
GNP Gross National Product (U.S.)
GP General Purpose
GPa Gigapascal
GPC Gel Permeation Chromatography
GPC Graphics Performance Characterization
GPD Gas Phase Deposition
GPIA General Purpose Instrumentation Bus
gpm Gallons Per Minute
GPMS General Purpose Metering Screw
GPPS General Purpose Polystyrene
GRAS Generally Recognized As Safe
GR-1 Butyl Rubber (former U.S. acronym)
GR-N Nitrile Rubber
GRP Glass Reinforced Plastic
GR-S Styrene Butadiene Rubber (former U.S. acronym)
GTR Gas Transmission Rate
Gy Gray

H Henry
H Heptyl
H_2 Hydrogen
HAF High Abrasion Furnace (black)
HALS Hindered Amine
HAO Higher Alpha Olefin
HAR High Aspect Ratio
HB Brinell Hardness Number
HCC High Color Channel (black)
HCFC Hydrochlorofluorocarbon
HCl Hydrogen Chloride
HDI Hexamethyl Diisocyanate
HDPE High Density Polyethylene
HDT Heat Deflection Temperature
HF High Frequency
Hg Mercury
HIP Hot Isotactic Pressing
HIPS High Impact Polystyrene
HK Hardness, Knoop

Abbreviations

HM	High Modulus
HMC	High Strength Molding Compound
HMW	High Molecular Weight
HMW-HDPE	High Molecular Weight-High Density Polyethylene
H-NBR	Hydrogenite Nitrile Rubber
H_2O	Water
HP	High Pressure
hp	Horsepower
HPO	Hydrogen Peroxide
HR	High Resilience
hr	Hour
HRc	Hardness Rockwell Cone
HSc	Hardness Scleroscope Number
HV	Hardness, Vickers Number
HVAC	Heating, Ventilation and Air Conditioning
Hx	Hexyl
Hz	Hertz (cycles)
I	Initiator
I	Moment of Inertia
I_{abs}	Intensity of Absorbed Light
IATA	International Air Transport Assoc. (Geneva, Switz.)
IBC	Internal Bubble Cooling
IBM	Injection Blow Molding
IC	Integrated Circuit
ICC	Interstate Commerce Commission
ICI	International Commission on Illumination (International Abbreviation CIE)
ICM	Injection-Compression Molding
ICMA	International Card Manufacturers Assoc.
ICP	Intrinsically Conductive Polymer
ICP	Intrinsically Connecting Polymer
ICR	Internal Cooling System
ICRP	International Commission on Radiological Protection
ID	Industrial Design
ID	Internal Diameter
IDSA	Industrial Designers Society of America
IDT	Intelligent Data Terminal
i.e.	that is
IEC	International Electrochemical Commission
IEEE	Institute of Electrical and Electronic Engineers
IF/F	Identification Friend/(or) Foe
IGP	Internal Gas Pressure
IIR	Butyl Rubber (Isoprene Rubber)
ILS	Interlaminar Shear
IM	Injection Molding
IMC	In-Mold Coating
IML	In-Mold Labeling
IMM	Injection Molding Machine
IMR	Internal Mold Release
in.	inch
insol.	Insoluble
I/O	Input and Output
IO	Ionomer
I_0	Intensity of Incident Light
IPDF	Isophoron Diisocyanate
IPE	Intelligent Processing Equipment
IPN	Interpenetrating Polymer Network
IPP	Institute of Packaging Professionals
ipr	Inches Per Rack
IPTS	International Practical Temperature Scale
IQI	Image Quality Indicator
IR	Infrared
IR	Isoprene Rubber (synthetic)
IRPI	Infrared Polymerization Index
IS	Injection Stamping
ISO	International Standardization Organization (or International Organization of Standardization)
ISO	Reactive Isocyanate
ISS	Ion Spectroscopy Scattering
ITAR	International Traffic in Arms Regulation
ITGA	Isothermogravimetric Analysis
ITP	Interpenetrating Thickening Process
IU	International Unit
IUPAC	International Union of Pure and Applied Chemistry
IV	Inherent Viscosity
IV	Intravenous
IV	Intrinsic Viscosity
IVD	In vitro Diagnostic
J	Joule
JIT	Just In Time
JM	Jet Molding
JND	Just Noticeable Difference
J_p	Polar Moment of Inertia
JS	Jet Spinning
JUSE	Japanese Union of Science and Engineering
K	Carbazole
κ	Kappa

Abbreviations

K	Bulk Modulus of Elasticity
K	Coefficient of Thermal Conductivity
K	Kelvin
K	Kunststoffe (German for Plastic)
KAB	Keep America Beautiful
kB	Kilobyte (1000 bytes)
kcal	Kilogram Calorie
KISS	Keep It Short and Simple
KISS	Keep it Simple and Safe
KISS	Keep It Simple Stupid
km/h	Kilometer per Hour
KO	Knockout
kPa	Kilopascal
ksi	Thousand pounds per Square Inch (psi $\times 10^3$)
kV	Kilovolt
KWIC	Keyword-In-Context
KWOC	Keyword-Out-Of-Context
L	Length
L	Linseed
L	Litre (U.S. also Liter)
LAB	Laboratory
LAN	Local Area Network
lb	Pound
lbf	Pound-Force
LC	Liquid Chromatography
LCD	Liquid Crystal Display
LCD	Lowest Common Denominator
LCM	Liquid Composite Molding
LCP	Liquid Crystal Polymer
LD	Laser Disc
L/D	Length-to-Diameter
LDPE	Low Density Polyethylene
LEC	Liquid Elastomer Connector
LED	Light Emitting Diode
LIM	Liquid Injection Molding
LLDPE	Linear Low Density Polyethylene
LLM	Low Molar-Mass
LMC	Low Pressure Molding Compound
LMC	Low Molecular Weight
ln	Logarithm (natural)
LNG	Liquified Natural Gas
LOD	Limit Of Detection
LODP	Leveling-Off Degree of Polymerization
log	Logarithm (common)
LOI	Limiting Oxygen Index
LOI	Loss On Ignition
LPE	Linear Polyethylene
LPG	Liquified Petroleum Gas
LPIM	Low Pressure Injection Molding
LS	Light Stabilizer
LSR	Liquid Silicone Rubber
LTL	Less Truck Load

LVDT	Linear Variable Differential Transformer
LWP	Lost Wax Process
lx	Lux
M	Melamine, Methyl, Methylene, etc.
M	Mega (prefix for 10^6)
m	Meter
μm	Micrometer
M	Molar (actual mass)
M_b	Bending Moment
M_c	Crosslinked Density
M_c	Molecular Weight per Crosslinked Unit
$\underline{M}_c$	Network Parameter
$\overline{M}_n$	Number-Average Molecular Weight
$\overline{M}_v$	Viscosity-Average Molecular Weight
$\overline{M}_w$	Weight-Average Molecular Weight
$\overline{M}_z$	Z-Average Molecular Weight
MA	Maleic Anhydride
MABS	Methylmethacrylate ABS
MAD	Mean Absolute Deviation
MAD	Molding Area Diagram
MAN	Methyl Acrylonitrile
MAP	Modified Atmosphere Packaging
MAP	Manufacturing Automation Protocol
max.	Maximum
MB	Megabyte (million bytes)
MBS	Methacrylate-Butadiene-Styrene
MBT	Mercaptobenzthiazole
M/C	Machine
MC	Megacycle
MC	Methyl Cellulose
MCA	Manufacturers' Chemists Assoc.
MCS	Motion Control System
MCT	Metallic-Core Technology
MD	Machine Design
MD	Machine Direction
MD	Mean Deviation
MDA	Methylene Dianiline
MD&DI	Medical Device & Diagnostic Industry
MDG	Machine Data Gathering
MDI	Methane Diisocyanate
MDPE	Medium Density Polyethylene
ME	Mechanical Engineer
MEK	Methyl Ethyl Ketone
MEKP	Methyl Ethyl Ketone Peroxide
meq	Milliequivalent
MER	Chemical Repeating Unit
MF	Melamine Formaldehyde
MFD	Micro Floppy Disc

MFI Melt Flow Index
MFR Melt Flow Rate
MH Unnamed transparent plastic from Japan Synthetic Rubber Co.
MI Melt Index
mike Microinch (10^{-6} inch)
mil One Thousandth of Inch (10^{-3} inch)
MIM Metal Injection Molding
min. Minimum
MIPS Medium Impact Polystyrene
MIPS Millions of Instructions Per Second
MIS Management Information System
misc. Miscellaneous
MIU Machine Interface Unit
MLFM Multi-Live Feed Molding
MMA Methyl Methacrylate
MMC Metal Matrix Composite
MMC Monolithic Metal Composite
MMFPA Man-Made Fiber Producers Assoc.
MMW Medium Molecular Weight
MO Magnetic-Optical (CD)
mo. Month
MODEM Modular or Demodular
MOE Metal-On-Elastomer
mol Mole, Molecule or Molecular
MOR Modulus Of Rupture
MP Melting Point
MP Modern Plastics
MPCP Molded Printed Circuit Board
MPDA M-Phenylene Diamine
MPF Melamine Phenol Formaldehyde
mph Miles Per Hour
MPPO Modified PPO
MPR Melt Processable Rubber
MQ Dimethylsilicone Elastomer
MRF Material Recovery Facility
MRI Magnetic Resonance Imaging
MRP Manufacturing Requirement Planning
MRQ Material's Requirement Planning
MS Mass Spectrometry
MSDS Material Safety Data Sheet
Msi Million Pounds per Square Inch (psi × 10^6)
MSW Municipal Solid Waste
MTO Melt Temperature Override
MUD Master Unit Die
mV Millivolt
MVD Molding Volume Diagram
MVR Molding Vapor Resistance
MVS Metal Vapor Synthesis
MVSS Motor Vehicle Safety Standard
MVT Moisture Vapor Transmission
MW Molecular Weight
MWR Molding With Rotation

N Nitrate, Nonyl, etc.
n Nano (10^{-9})
N Newton (force)
N Nitrogen
N Normal (as applied to concentration)
N Number of Cycles
NA Not Available
NACE National Assoc. of Corrosion Engineers
NAPCR National Assoc. for Plastics Container Recovery
NAS National Academy of Science
NASA National Aeronautics and Space Administration
NATEC National Technical Conference (SPE)
NBR Nitrile Butadiene Rubber, Nitrile Rubber or GR-1
NBS National Bureau of Standards (since the 1980s renamed National Institute for Science and Technology, or NIST)
NC Nitrocellulose
NC Numerical Control
NCGA National Computer Graphics Assoc.
NCO Nitrogen Carbon Monoxide
NCR Acrylonitrile Chloroprene Nitrate
NCRC National Container Recycling Coalition
NDE Nondestructive Evaluation
NDI Nondestructive Inspection
NDT Nondestructive Testing
NEAT Nothing Else Added to It
neg. Negative
NEMA National Electrical Manufacturers Assoc.
NFPA National Fire Protection Assoc.
NIH National Institute of Health
NIOSH National Institute for Occupational Safety and Health
NIR Acrylonitrile Isoprene Rubber
NIST National Institute for Science and Technology (see NBS)
NLA National Lime Assoc.
NLO Nonlinear Optic
nm Nanometer
NMI Nuclear Magnetic Image
NMW Narrow Molecular Weight
No. Number
NOL Naval Ordnance Laboratory

Abbreviations

NOL	Net Operating Loss
NOS	Not Otherwise Specified
NP	Network Polymer
NPCM	National Plastics Center and Museum
NPE	National Plastics Exhibition (SPI)
NPII	National Printing Ink Institute
NR	Natural Rubber (polyisoprene)
NRC	National Recycling Condition
NRC	National Research Council
NRDGA	National Retail Dry Goods Assoc.
NSC	National Safety Council
NSDA	National Soft Drink Assoc.
NSR	Nitrile-Silicone Rubber
NSWA	National Solid Waste Assoc.
NTMA	National Tool and Machining Assoc.
—	Nylon, see PA
NVLAP	National Voluntary Laboratory Accreditation Program
O	Octyl, Oil, Oxy, etc
O	Oriented
O-	Ortho-
O–	Oxygen denoting attachment
O_2	Oxygen
O_3	Ozone
OC	Operating Characteristic
OCR	Optical Character Recognition
OD	Optical Disc
O.D.	Outside Diameter
ODD	Optical Data Disc
ODG	Operating Data Gathering
ODP	Octyl Decyl Phthalate
ODS	Optical Data Storage
OE	Original Equipment
OEM	Original Equipment Manufacturer
OEP	Oil Extended Polymer
OES	Optical Emission Spectroscopy
OFR	Office of Federal Register
OH	Oxygen-Hydrogen
OPEC	Organization of Petroleum Exporting Countries
OPP	Oriented Polypropylene
OPR	Propylene Oxide Rubber
OPS	Oriented Polystyrene
OSA	Olefin-modified Styrene-Acrylonitrile
OSHA	Occupational Safety and Health Administration
OTC	Over The Counter
OWF	On Weight of Fiber
OWG	On Weight of Goods
Ox	Oxide
%v	Percentage by Volume (see vol%)
%w	Percentage by Weight (see wt%)
P	Load
P	Permeability
P	Phenyl
P	Poise
P	Pressure
Pa	Pascal
PA	Polyamide (nylon)
PAA	Polyacrylic Acid
PAE	Polyarylether
PAEK	Polyaryletherketone
PAH	Polycyclic Aromatic Hydrocarbon
PAI	Polyamide-Imide
PAK	Polyester Alkyd
PAMS	Polyalpha-Methylstyrene
PAN	Polyacrylonitrile
PAR	Polyarylate
PAS	Polyarylsulfone
PB	Polybutylene
PBA	Physical Blowing Agent
PBAN	Polybutadiene-Acrylonitrile
PBI	Plastic Bottle Institute (SPI)
PBI	Polybenzimidazole
PBR	Polybutadiene-Vinyl Pyridene
PBS	Polybutadiene-Styrene
PBT	Polybutadiene-Terephthalate
PBZ	Polybenzobisoxazole
PC	Plastic Composite
PC	Personal Computer
PC	Plastic Compounding
PC	Plastic-Concrete
PC	Polycarbonate
PC	Positive Collapse
PC	Process Control
PC	Programmable Circuit
PC	Programmable Controller
PCA	Polycarbonate-Acrylic
PCB	Printed Circuit Board
PCDP	Polydicyclopentadiene
pcf	Pounds per Cubic Foot
PC/PBT	Polycarbonate/Polybutylene-Terephthalate
PCR	Post-Consumer Reclaimed (or Resin)
PCT	Polycyclohexylenedimethylene-Terephthalate
PCTFE	Polychlorotrifluoroethylene
PDA	Production Data Acquisition
PDAP	Polydiallyl Phthalate
PE	Plastics Engineer
PE	Polyethylene
PE	Professional Engineer
PEA	Polyethyl Acrylate
PEBA	Polyether Block Amide
PEC	Chlorinated Polethylene (usually CPE)

Abbreviations

PEC Polyphenylene Ether Copolymer
PEEK Polyetheretherketone
PEI Polyetherimide
PEK Polyetherketone
PEKEKK Polyetherketoneetherketone-ketone
PEKK Polyetheketoneketone
PEL Permissible Exposure Limit
PEN Polyethylene Naphthalate
PEO Polyethylene Oxide
PEP Polyethylene Polymer
PEPA Polyether-Polyamide
PES Polyethersulfone
PET Polyethylene-Terephthalate
PETG Polyethylene-Terephthalate Glycol
PETS Plastic Evaluation and Trouble-shooting System
PF Phenol Formaldehyde (phenolic)
PFA Perfluoroalkoxy
PFF Phenol Furfural
PFFC Paper, Film and Foil Converter
PGE Planetary Gear Extruder
pH Negative Logarithm of the Effective Hydrogen Ion Concentration
PHE Parts Handling Equipment
PHR Parts Per Hundred
pi $\pi = 3.141593$
PI Isoprene Rubber
PI Polyimide
PIA Plastics Institute of America
PIB Polyisobutylene
PIBI Polyisobutene-Isoptene (butyl rubber)
PID Proportional-Integral-Derivative
PIR Polyisocyanurate
PITA Parison Inflation Thinning Analysis
PL Parting Line
PLASTEC Plastic Technical Evaluation Center (U.S. Army)
PLB Picture Level Benchmark
PMA Polymethyl Acrylate
PMA Premarket Approval
PMA Polyurethane Manufacturers Assoc.
PMCA Polymethyl-Chloroacylate
PMI Polymethacrylimide
PMMA Polymethyl Methacrylate (acrylic)
PMP Polymethyl Pentene
PMQ Phenylsilicone Elastomer
PMR Polymerization Monomer Reactant
PMS Paramethyl Styrene
PNF Polyfluoroalkoxyphosphazene
PO Polyolefin
POF Plastic Optical Fiber
POLY Reactive Polyols in RIM
POM Polyoxymethylene (acetal)
POP Polyoxypropylene
pos. Positive
PP Polypropylene
PPA Plastics Pioneer Assoc.
PPA Polyphthalamide
ppb Parts Per Billion
PPC Propylene Chlorinated
PPC Polystyrene Packaging Council
PPE Polyphenylene Ether
PPE/PPO Polyphenylene Ether/ Polyphenylene Oxide
PPFA Plastics Pipe and Fittings Assoc.
pph Parts Per Hour
PPI Plastics Pipe Institute (SPI)
PPI Polymer Processing Institute
ppm Parts Per Million
PPMS Polypara-Methylstyrene
PPO Polyphenylene Oxide
PPOX Polypropylene Oxide
PPP Partnership for Plastics Progress
PPS Polyphenylene Sulfide
PPSS Polyphenylene Sulfide Sulfone
PPSU Polyphenylene Sulfone
PPT Polypropylene-Terephthalate
PPT Precipitate
PPTN Precipitation
PPX Poly(P-xylylene)
PPZ Polyorganophosphazene
PR Press Release
PR Pump Ratio
PRF Plastics Recycling Foundation
PRT Pressure Reduction Time
PS Polystyrene
P/S Pressure Sensitive
PSB Polystyrene Butadiene Rubber (GR-S, SBR)
psi Pounds per Square Inch
psig Pounds per Square Inch, Gage (above atmospheric pressure)
PSU Polysulfone
PT Plastics Technology
P-T Pressure-Temperature
PTE Patent Term Expansion
PTFE Polytetrafluoroethylene
PTMG Polytetramethylene Glycol
PTO Patent and Trademark Office
PTX Pressure-Temperature-Concentration Variables
PUR Polyurethane (also PU)
P-V Pressure-Volume
PV Process Validation
PVAC Polyvinyl Acetate
PVAL Polyvinyl Alcohol
PVB Polyvinyl Butyral

PVAC	Polyvinyl Chloride Acetate
PVC	Polyvinyl Chloride
PVD	Physical Vapor Deposition
PVDC	Polyvinylidene Chloride
PVDF	Polyvinylidene Fluoride
PVFM	Polyvinyl Formal
PVIE	Polyvinyl Isobutyl Ether
PVK	Polyvinyl Carbazole
PVP	Polyvinyl Pyrrolidone
PVT	Pressure-Volume-Temperature
PW	Plastics World
PWB	Printed Wiring Board
Q	Silicone Elastomer
QA	Quality Assurance
QA	Quality Auditing
QC	Quality Control
QDS	Quality Data Statistics
QF	Quality Factor
QMC	Quick Mold Change
QPL	Qualified Products List
qual.	Qualitative
quan.	Quantitative
q.v.	Quod Vide, Which see.
R	Radius
R	Rankine
R	Rockwell (hardness)
R	Roentgen
RA	Reduction of Area
RA	Regulatory Agencies
RA	Release Agent
rad	Radian
RADOME	Radar Dome
RAF	Random Access File
RAM	Random Access Memory
RAPRA	Rubber and Plastic Research Assoc.
RC	Resistance Condenser
RCE	Return on Capital Employed
RCF	Refractory Ceramic Fiber
RCRA	Resource Conservation and Recovery Act
R&D	Research & Development
RDA	Recommended Dietary Allowance
RDF	Refuse-Derived Fuel
RDS	Rheometric Dynamic Scanning
ref.	Reference
resp.	Respectively
RETEC	Regional Technical Conference (SPE)
REX	Reactive Extrusion
RF	Radio Frequency
RF	Resorcinol Formaldehyde
RFI	Radio Frequency Interference
RGA	Residual Gas Analysis
RH	Relative Humidity
RIA	Robotic Industries Assoc.
RIM	Reaction Injection Molding
RLM	Reactive Liquid Polymer
RM	Raw Material
RMPS	Rubber Modified Polystyrene
RMS	Rheological Mechanical Spectrometer
RMS	Root Mean Square
RMSD	Root Mean Square Difference
RO	Reverse Osmosis
ROI	Return-On-Investment
ROM	Read Only Memory
RonD	Research on Design
RP	Reinforced Plastic
RPBT	Reinforced Polybutylene Terephthalate
RP/C	Reinforced Plastics/Composite
RP/CI	Reinforced Plastics/Composite Institute
rpm	Revolutions Per Minute
RPRA	Rubber and Plastics Research Assoc.
rps	Revolutions Per Second
RPVC	Rigid Polyvinyl Chloride
RRIM	Reinforced Reaction Injection Molding
RS	Reciprocating Screw
Rsec	Reciprocal Second
RSP	Reciprocating Screw Plasticator
RT	Real Time
RT	Residence Time
RT	Room Temperature
RTD	Resistance Temperature Detector
RTD	Room Temperature Dry
RTI	Relative Thermal Index
RTM	Resin Transfer Molding
RTP	Reinforced Thermoplastic
RTS	Reinforced Thermoset
RTV	Room Temperature Vulcanization
RTW	Room Temperature, Wet
s	Second
S	Siemens
SA	Shrink Allowance
SACMA	Suppliers of Advanced Composite Materials Assoc.
SAE	Society of Automotive Engineers
SAMPE	Society of the Advancement of Material and Process Engineering
SAN	Styrene-acrylonitrile
SANS	Small Angle Neutron Scattering
SARA	Superfund Amendments and Reauthorization Act
satd.	Saturated

SB	Styrene-butadiene
SBM	Stretch Blow Molding
SBR	Styrene-Butadiene Rubber
SBS	Short Beam Shear
SBS	Styrene-butadiene-styrene
scf	Standard Cubic Foot (760 mmHg, °C)
SCI	Society of the Chemical Industry
SCR	Silicone Controlled Rectifier
SCR	Styrene Chloroprene Rubber
SCT	Soluble Core Technology
SDM	Standard Deviation Measurement
SDP	Standard Depth of Penetration
SDR	Standard Dimension Ratio
SDWA	Safe Drinking Water Act
SE	Shielding Effect
SE	Sound Emission
SE	Static Electricity
sec.	Second
SEC	Size Exclusion Chromatography
SEM	Scanning Electron Microscope
S-EPDM	Sulfonated-EPDM
SF	Safety Factor
SF	Shape Factor
SF	Structural Foam
SFM	Structural Foam Molding
s.g.	Specific Gravity
SGMP	Statistical Good Manufacturing Practices
SHED	Sealed Housing For Evaporation Determining
SHIPS	Super High Impact Polystyrene
Si	Silicone
SI	International System of Units called SI per CGPM
SiC	Silicone Carbide
SIC	Standard Industrial Classification
SINEH	Sine Hyperbolic
SIR	Silicone Isoprene Rubber
SIRC	Styrene Information and Research Center
SIS	Styrene-Isoprene-Styrene
SLA	Stereolithography Apparatus
SMA	Styrene Maleic Anhydride
SMC	Sheet Molding Compound
SME	Society of Manufacturing Engineers
S/MMA	Styrene/Methyl Methacrylate
SMS	Styrene Methylstyrene
SMT	Surface Mounted Technology
S-N	Stress-Number of cycles
Sn	Tin
SO	Secondary Operation
SOC	Stress-Optical Coefficient
sol.	Soluble
SOS	Self Opening Style (bag)
SP	Saturated Polyester
SP	Softening Point
sp.	Specific
SPC	Statistical Process Control
SPE	Society of the Plastics Engineers
Spec.	Specification
SPF	Solid Phase Forming
SPF	Super Plastic Forming
SPF/DB	Super Plastic Forming/Diffusion Bonding
sp. gr.	Specific Gravity
SPI	Society of the Plastics Industry
spm	Stroke Per Minute
SPPF	Solid Phase Pressure Forming
SPRINT	Strategic Program for Innovation and Technology Transfer
sp. vol.	Specific Volume
sq.	Square
SQC	Statistical Quality Control
SR	Polysulfide Rubber
sr	Steradian (solid angle quantity)
SR	Synthetic Rubber
SRIM	Structural Reaction Injection Molding
SRM	Standard Reference Material
SRP	Styrene-Rubber Plastic
SS	Single stage
SS	Stainless Steel
S-S	Stress-Strain
SSE	Solid-State Extrusion
SST	Self-Staining Tape
SST	Step-by-Step Test
STAT	Sheet Thinning Analysis for Thermoforming
STC	Structural Thermoplastic Composite Sheet
STD	Standard
STP	Special Technical Publication (ASTM)
STP	Standard Temperature and Pressure (0°C 760 mmHg or 101.3 kPa)
Sv	Sievert
SWCC	Solid Waste Composing Council (of SPI)
sym.	Symmetrical
T	Temperature
T	Tesla
t	Thickness
T	Time
T	Torque
T_g	Glass Transition Temperature
T_h	Homogeneous Temperature

Abbreviations

T_m	Melt Temperature
T_s	Specular Transmission
T_s	Tensile Strength
TA	Terephthalic Acid
TA	Thermal Analysis
TA	Thermoanalytical
TAC	Total Area Coverage
TAC	Triallyl Cyanurate
TAPPI	Technical Association of the Pulp and Paper Industry
TC	Temperature Control
T/C	Thermocouple
TCE	Trichloroethylene
TCEF	Trichloroethyl Phosphate
TCF	Tricresyl Phosphate
TCM	Technical Cost Modeling
TCNA	Tube Council of North America
TCP	Tricresyl Phosphate
TD	Transverse Direction
TDI	Toluene Diisocyanate
TEEE	Thermoplastic Elastomer Ether-Ether
TEM	Transmission Electron Microscopy
TEO	Thermoplastic Elastomer Olefinic
tera	▷ **tera**
TES	Thermal Energy Storage
TES	Thermoplastic Elastomer Styrene
TFE	Tetrafluoroethylene
TGA	Thermogravimetric Analysis
THF	Tetrahydrofuran
Three-D	Three-Dimensional (usually 3-D)
TiO_2	Titanium Dioxide
TIR	Technical Information Release
TIR	Tooling Indicator Runout
T/L	Truck Load
TLC	Thin-Layer Chromatography
TM	Trademark
TM	Transfer Molding
TMA	Thermomechanical Analysis
TMC	Thick Molding Compound
TN	Tradename
TNR	Term Not Recommended
TOC	Tagliabue Open Cup (Flash Point)
TOF	Trioctyl Phosphate
torr	mm mercury (mmHg)
TOSCA	Toxic Substances Control Act
TP	Thermoplastic
TPA	Terephthalic Acid
TPC	Transfer Point Controller
TPE	Thermoplastic Elastomer
TPE-A	Thermoplastic Elastomer-Amide
TPE-E	Thermoplastic Elastomer-Polyester
TPE-S	Thermoplastic Elastomer-Styrene
TPI	Thermoplastic Polyimide
tpi	Turns Per Inch
TPO	Thermoplastic Polyolefin
TPP	Triphenyl Phosphate
TPS	Thermal Protection System
TPS	Toughened Polystyrene
TPU	Thermoplastic Polyurethane
TPV	Thermoplastic Vulcanizate
TPX	Polymethylpentene
TQM	Total Quality Management
TR	Torque Rheometer
TREF	Temperature Rising Elution Fraction
TS	Thermoset
TS	Troubleshooting
TSC	Thermal Stress Cracking
TSCA	Toxic Substance Control Act
TSE	Thermoset Elastomer
TSI	Thermoset Polyimide
TSSC	Toluenesulfonyl Semicarbazide
T_t	Torque
TTT	Time-Temperature-Transformation
TTU	Through-Transmission Ultrasonic
TV	Television
TVL	Tenth-Value-Layer
Two-D	Two-Dimensional (usually 2-D)
U	Urea, Uranium, Unsaturated, etc.
UD	Unidirectional
UF	Urea Formaldehyde
UHMWPE	Ultra High Molecular Weight Polyethylene
UL	Underwriters' Laboratories
ULDPE	Ultra Low Density Polyethylene
UN	United Nations
UP	Unsaturated Polyester
UPVC	Unplasticized PVC
UR	Urethane (see PUR)
USASI	United States American Standards Institute
USDA	U.S. Department of Agriculture
USP	Unique Selling Point
USP	U.S. Pharmacopeia
USPO	United States Patent Office
UT	Universal Time
UTL	Use Temperature Limit
UTS	Ultimate Tensile Strength
U.V.	Ultraviolet
UVA	Ultraviolet Absorber
UVL	Ultraviolet Light
UVI	Ultraviolet Inhibitor

V	Velocity
V	Vinyl
V	Volt
VA	Value Analysis
VA	Vinyl Acetate
VAE	Vinyl Acetate Ethylene
VB	Vented Barrel
VC	Value Creation
VC	Virtually Crosslinked
VC/E	Vinyl Chloride/Ethylene
VCM	Vinyl Chloride Monomer
VC/MA	Vinyl Chloride/Methylacrylate
VD	Vinylidene
VDC	Vinylidene Chloride
VDP	Vapor Deposition Polymerized
VDT	Video Display Terminal
VDT	Visual Display Tube
VF	Vulcanized Fiber
VFC	Voltage Frequency Converter
VG	Valve Gate
VHP	Vacuum Hot Pressing
VI	Vinyl Institute
VIM	Vented Injection Molding
VLC	Vapor-Liquid Chromatography
VLDPE	Very Low Density Polyethylene
VLS	Vapor-Liquid-Solid (process)
VMQ	Vinylsilicone Elastomer
VOC	Volatile Organic Compound
vol	Volume
vol%	Percentage by Volume (see %v)
VP	Virgin Plastic
VPE	Vulcanized Polyethylene
VPI	Vapor Phase Inhibitor
VPT	Velocity-Pressure-Transfer Point
VR	Virtual Reality (software)
vs	Versus
VST	Vicat Softening Temperature
VT	Vicat Temperature
VT	Vinyl Toluene

W	Tungsten
W	Watt
W	Width
WAD	Worst Area Difference
Wb	Weber
WCM	World Class Manufacturing
WP	Word Processing
WPC	Wood-Plastic Composite
WPE	Western Plastic Exhibition
WPI	World Patent Index
WR	Woven Roving
WRDC	Wright Research and Development Center
WSB	Water Soluble Polyester
wt%	Percentage by Weight (see %w)
WVT	Water Vapor Transmission
WVTR	Water Vapor Transmission Rate
WYSIWYG	What You See Is What You Get

X	Number of Structural Units in Polymer Molecule
$\bar{X}$	Arithmetic Mean (read 'X bar')
X_m	Number-Average Degree of Polymerization
X_w	Weight-Average Degree of Polymerization
X-axis	Axis in plane used as 0° reference
XLPE	Crosslinked Polyethylene
XMC	Extra High Strength Molding Compound
XPS	Expandable Polystyrene
XPS	X-ray Photoelectron Spectroscopy
XRF	X-Ray Fluorescence

Y-axis	Axis in the Plane Perpendicular to X-axis
YPE	Yield Point Elongation
yr	Year

Z	Atomic Number (colloquialism: at. no.)
Z	Azelate
Z	Zeta
Z-axis	Axis Normal to the Plane of the X-Y axes
ZD	Zero Defect
ZDP	Zero Defect Part
ZMS	Zero Metering Screw
Zn	Zinc
ZNC	Ziegler-Natta Catalyst
ZST	Zero-Strength Time
Z-twist	Twisting fiber direction

CONVERSION TABLES

This section provides conversion factors that meet the International System of Units (SI) which is the metric system being used worldwide. Data are based on ASTM E 380 standard publication (copyright ASTM, reprinted with permission).

(1) SI comes from the French name Le Système International d'Unités.

(2) Internationally, the SI approved spelling of metre and litre using "re". However, the U.S. DOD policy is to use "er" (meter and liter) with an option to use "re".

(3) These conversion factors are listed in two ways: alphabetically and classified by physical quantity. The classified list contains the more frequently used units for each physical quantity. Thus, for example, *to convert from* lbf/ft^2 (pound force per square foot) to Pa, *multiply by* 4.788 026 E + 01 which means: 1 lbf/ft^2 = 47.880 26 Pa.

(4) Conversion factors are presented for ready adaptation to computer readout and electronic data transmission. The factors are written as a number equal to or greater than one and less than 10 with six or fewer decimal places. This number is followed by the letter E (for exponent), a plus or minus symbol, and two digits which indicate the power of 10 by which the number must be multiplied to obtain the correct value. For example:

$$3.523\,907 \text{ E} - 02 \text{ is } 3.523\,907 \times 10^{-2}$$

or 0.035 239 07

Similarly:

$$3.386\,389 \text{ E} + 03 \text{ is } 3.386\,389 \times 10^{3}$$

or 3 386.389

(5) An asterisk (*) after the sixth decimal place indicates that the conversion factor is exact and that all subsequent digits are zero. All other conversion factors have been rounded to the figures given. Where less than six decimal places are shown, more precision is not warranted.

(6) In regard to numbers, the recommended decimal marker is a dot on the line. When writing numbers less than one, a zero should be written before the decimal marker (0.26). Outside the U.S., the comma is often used as a decimal marker. In some applications, therefore, the common practice in the U.S. of using the comma to separate digits into groups of three (as in 23,478) may cause ambiguity. To avoid this potential confusion, recommended international practice calls for separating the digits into groups of three, counting from the decimal point toward the left and the right, and using a small space to separate the groups. In numbers of four digits on either side of the decimal point the space is usually not necessary, except for uniformity in tables (examples are: 2.141 596 or 73 722 or 7372 or 0.1335). Where this practice is followed, the space should be narrow (about the width of the letter "i"), and the width of the space should be constant even if, as is often the case in printing, variable-width spacing is used between words. An exception is in certain specialized applications, such as engineering drawings and financial statements, where the practice of using a space for a separator is not customary.

(7) The conversion factors for other compound units can easily be generated from numbers given in the alphabetical list by the substitution of converted units, as follows: to find conversion factor of $oz \cdot in^2$ to $kg \cdot m^2$, *first convert* 1 oz to 0.028 349 52 kg *and* 1 in^2 to 0.000 645 16 m^2, *then substitute*: (0.028 349 52 kg) · (0.000 645 16 m^2) = 0.000 018 289 98 $kg \cdot m^2$, *thus the factor is* = 1.828 998 E − 05.

(8) Tables at the end of this section provide additional aids (ASTM E 380).

(9) ▷ **Greek alphabet** and **tera**.

(10) In Tables 1 and 2, symbols of SI units are given in parenthesis.

Conversion Tables

Table 1 Alphabetical list of units.

To convert from	to	Multiply by
abampere	ampere (A)	1.000 000*E + 01
abcoulomb	coulomb (C)	1.000 000*E + 01
abfarad	farad (F)	1.000 000*E + 09
abhenry	henry (H)	1.000 000*E − 09
abmho	siemens (S)	1.000 000*E + 09
abohm	ohm (Ω)	1.000 000*E − 09
abvolt	volt (V)	1.000 000*E − 08
acre foot	cubic metre (m^3)	1.233 489 E + 03
acre	square metre (m^2)	4.046 873 E + 03
ampere hour	coulomb (C)	3.600 000*E + 03
angstrom	metre (m)	1.000 000*E − 10
are	square metre (m^2)	1.000 000*E + 02
astronomical unit	metre (m)	1.495 979 E + 11
atmosphere, standard	pascal (Pa)	1.013 250*E + 05
atmosphere, technical (= 1 kgf/cm^2)	pascal (Pa)	9.806 650*E + 04
bar	pascal (Pa)	1.000 000*E + 05
barn	square metre (m^2)	1.000 000*E − 28
barrel (for petroleum, 42 gal)	cubic metre (m^3)	1.589 873 E − 01
board foot	cubic metre (m^3)	2.359 737 E − 03
British thermal unit (International Table)	joule (J)	1.055 056 E + 03
British thermal unit (mean)	joule (J)	1.055 87 E + 03
British thermal unit (thermochemical)	joule (J)	1.054 350 E + 03
British thermal unit (39°F)	joule (J)	1.059 67 E + 03
British thermal unit (59°F)	joule (J)	1.054 80 E + 03
British thermal unit (60°F)	joule (J)	1.054 68 E + 03
Btu (International Table) · ft/(h · ft^2 · °F) (thermal conductivity)	watt per metre kelvin [W/(m · K)]	1.730 735 E + 00
Btu (thermochemical) · ft/(h · ft^2 · °F) (thermal conductivity)	watt per metre kelvin [W/(m · K)]	1.729 577 E + 00
Btu (International Table) · in/(h · ft^2 · °F) (thermal conductivity)	watt per metre kelvin [W/(m · K)]	1.442 279 E − 01
Btu (thermochemical) · in/(h · ft^2 · °F) (thermal conductivity)	watt per metre kelvin [W/(m · K)]	1.441 314 E − 01
Btu (International Table) · in/(s · ft^2 · °F) (thermal conductivity)	watt per metre kelvin [W/(m · K)]	5.192 204 E + 02
Btu (thermochemical) · in/(s · ft^2 · °F) (thermal conductivity)	watt per metre kelvin [W/(m · K)]	5.188 732 E + 02
Btu (International Table)/h	watt (W)	2.930 711 E − 01
Btu (International Table)/s	watt (W)	1.055 056 E + 03
Btu (thermochemical)/h	watt (W)	2.928 751 E − 01
Btu (thermochemical)/min	watt (W)	1.757 250 E + 01
Btu (thermochemical)/s	watt (W)	1.054 350 E + 03
Btu (International Table)/ft^2	joule per square metre (J/m^2)	1.135 653 E + 04
Btu (thermochemical)/ft^2	joule per square metre (J/m^2)	1.134 893 E + 04
Btu (International Table)/(ft^2 · s)	watt per square metre (W/m^2)	1.135 653 E + 04
Btu (International Table)/(ft^2 · h)	watt per square metre (W/m^2)	3.154 591 E + 00
Btu (thermochemical)/(ft^2 · h)	watt per square metre (W/m^2)	3.152 481 E + 00
Btu (thermochemical)/(ft^2 · min)	watt per square metre (W/m^2)	1.891 489 E + 02
Btu (thermochemical)/(ft^2 · s)	watt per square metre (W/m^2)	1.134 893 E + 04
Btu (thermochemical)/(in^2 · s)	watt per square metre (W/m^2)	1.634 246 E + 06
Btu (International Table)/(h · ft^2 · °F) (thermal conductance)[15]	watt per square meter kelvin [W/(m^2 · K)]	5.678 263 E + 00
Btu (thermochemical)/(h · ft^2 · °F) (thermal conductance)[15]	watt per square meter kelvin [W/(m^2 · K)]	5.674 466 E + 00
Btu (International Table)/(s · ft^2 · °F)	watt per square meter kelvin [W/(m^2 · K)]	2.044 175 E + 04
Btu (thermochemical)/(s · ft^2 · °F)	watt per square meter kelvin [W/(m^2 · K)]	2.042 808 E + 04
Btu (International Table)/lb	joule per kilogram (J/kg)	2.326 000*E + 03
Btu (thermochemical)/lb	joule per kilogram (J/kg)	2.324 444 E + 03
Btu (International Table)/(lb · °F) (heat capacity)	joule per kilogram kelvin [J/(kg · K)]	4.186 800*E + 03
Btu (thermochemical)/(lb · °F) (heat capacity)	joule per kilogram kelvin [J/(kg · K)]	4.184 000*E + 03
Btu (International Table)/ft^3	joule per cubic metre (J/m^3)	3.725 895 E + 04
Btu (thermochemical)/ft^3	joule per cubic metre (J/m^3)	3.723 402 E + 04
bushel (U.S)	cubic metre (m^3)	3.523 907 E − 02
calorie (International Table)	joule (J)	4.186 800*E + 00
calorie (mean)	joule (J)	4.190 02 E + 00

Table 1 Alphabetical list of units (continued).

To convert from	to	Multiply by
calorie (thermochemical)	joule (J)	4.184 000*E + 00
calorie (15°C)	joule (J)	4.185 80 E + 00
calorie (20°C)	joule (J)	4.181 90 E + 00
calorie (kilogram, International Table)	joule (J)	4.186 800*E + 03
calorie (kilogram, mean)	joule (J)	4.190 02 E + 03
calorie (kilogram, thermochemical)	joule (J)	4.184 000*E + 03
cal (thermochemical)/cm^2	joule per square metre (J/m^2)	4.184 000*E + 04
cal (International Table)/g	joule per kilogram (J/kg)	4.186 800*E + 03
cal (thermochemical)/g	joule per kilogram (J/kg)	4.184 000*E + 03
cal (International Table)/(g · °C)	joule per kilogram kelvin [J/(kg · K)]	4.186 800*E + 03
cal (thermochemical)/(g · °C)	joule per kilogram kelvin [J/(kg · K)]	4.184 000*E + 03
cal (thermochemical)/min	watt (W)	6.973 333 E − 02
cal (thermochemical)/s	watt (W)	4.184 000*E + 00
cal (thermochemical)/(cm^2 · s)	watt per square metre (W/m^2)	4.184 000*E + 04
cal (thermochemical)/(cm^2 · min)	watt per square metre (W/m^2)	6.973 333 E + 02
cal (thermochemical)/(cm^2 · s)	watt per square metre (W/m^2)	4.184 000*E + 04
cal (thermochemical)/(cm · s · °C)	watt per metre kelvin [W/(m · K)]	4.184 000*E + 02
cd/in^2	candela per square metre (cd/m^2)	1.550 003 E + 03
carat (metric)	kilogram (kg)	2.000 000*E − 04
centimetre of mercury (0°C)	pascal (Pa)	1.333 22 E + 03
centimetre of water (4°C)	pascal (Pa)	9.806 38 E + 01
centipoise (dynamic viscosity)	pascal second (Pa · s)	1.000 000*E − 03
centistokes (kinematic viscosity)	square metre per second (m^2/s)	1.000 000*E − 06
chain	metre (m)	2.011 684 E + 01
circular mil	square metre (m^2)	5.067 075 E − 10
clo	kelvin square metre per watt (K · m^2/W)	1.55 E − 01
cup	cubic metre (m^3)	2.365 882 E − 04
curie	becquerel (Bq)	3.700 000*E + 10
darcy	square metre (m^2)	9.869 233 E − 13
day	second (s)	8.640 000*E + 04
day (sidereal)	second (s)	8.616 409 E + 04
degree (angle)	radian (rad)	1.745 329 E − 02
degree Celsius	kelvin (K)	$T_K = t_{°C} + 273.15$
degree Fahrenheit	degree Celsius (°C)	$t_{°C} = (t_{°F} - 32)/1.8$
degree Fahrenheit	kelvin (K)	$T_K = (t_{°F} + 459.67/1.8$
degree Rankine	kelvin (K)	$T_K = T_{°R}/1.8$
°F · h · ft^2/Btu (International Table) (thermal resistance)	kelvin square metre per watt (K · m^2/W)	1.761 102 E − 01
°F · h · ft/Btu (thermochemical) (thermal resistance)	kelvin square metre per watt (K · m^2/W)	1.762 280 E − 01
°F · h · ft^2/[Btu (International Table) · in] (thermal resistivity)	kelvin metre per watt (K · m/W)	6.933 471 E + 00
°F · h · ft^2/[Btu (thermochemical) · in] (thermal resistivity)	kelvin metre per watt (K · m/W)	6.938 113 E + 00
denier	kilogram per metre (kg/m)	1.111 111 E − 07
dyne	newton (N)	1.000 000*E − 05
dyne · cm	newton metre (N · m)	1.000 000*E − 07
dyne/cm^2	pascal (Pa)	1.000 000*E − 01
electronvolt	joule (J)	1.602 19 E − 19
EMU of capacitance	farad (F)	1.000 000*E + 09
EMU of current	ampere (A)	1.000 000*E + 01
EMU of electric potential	volt (V)	1.000 000*E − 08
EMU of inductance	henry (H)	1.000 000*E − 09
EMU of resistance	ohm (Ω)	1.000 000*E − 09
ESU of capacitance	farad (F)	1.112 650 E − 12
ESU of current	ampere (A)	3.335 6 E − 10
ESU of electric potential	volt (V)	2.997 9 E + 02
ESU of inductance	henry (H)	8.987 554 E + 11
ESU of resistance	ohm (Ω)	8.987 554 E + 11
erg	joule (J)	1.000 000*E − 07
erg/(cm^2 · s)	watt per square metre (W/m^2)	1.000 000*E − 03
erg/s	watt (W)	1.000 000*E − 07
faraday (based on carbon-12)	coulomb (C)	9.648 70 E + 04
faraday (chemical)	coulomb (C)	9.649 57 E + 04
faraday (physical)	coulomb (C)	9.652 19 E + 04
fathom	metre (m)	1.828 804 E + 00

Table 1 Alphabetical list of units (continued).

To convert from	to	Multiply by
fermi (femtometre)	metre (m)	1.000 000*E − 15
fluid ounce (U.S.)	cubic metre (m^3)	2.957 353 E − 05
foot	metre (m)	3.048 000*E − 01
foot (U.S. survey)	metre (m)	3.048 006 E − 01
foot of water (39.2°F)	pascal (Pa)	2.988 98 E + 03
ft^2	square metre (m^2)	9.290 304*E − 02
ft^2/h(thermal diffusivity)	square metre per second (m^2/s)	2.580 640*E − 05
ft^2/s	square metre per second (m^2/s)	9.290 304*E − 02
ft^3(volume; section modulus)	cubic metre (m^3)	2.831 685 E − 02
ft^3/min	cubic metre per second (m^3/s)	4.719 474 E − 04
ft^3/s	cubic metre per second (m^3/s)	2.831 685 E − 02
ft^4(second moment of area)	metre to the fourth power (m^4)	8.630 975 E − 03
ft/h	metre per second (m/s)	8.466 667 E − 05
ft/min	metre per second (m/s)	5.080 000*E − 03
ft/s	metre per second (m/s)	3.048 000*E − 01
ft/s^2	metre per second squared (m/s^2)	3.048 000*E − 01
footcandle	lux (lx)	1.076 391 E + 01
footlambert	candela per square metre (cd/m^2)	3.426 259 E + 00
ft · lbf	joule (J)	1.355 818 E + 00
ft · lbf/h	watt (W)	3.766 161 E − 04
ft · lbf/min	watt (W)	2.259 697 E − 02
ft · lbf/s	watt (W)	1.355 818 E + 00
ft-poundal	joule (J)	4.214 011 E − 02
g, standard free fall	metre per second squared (m/s^2)	9.806 650*E + 00
gal	metre per second squared (m/s^2)	1.000 000*E − 02
gallon (Canadian liquid)	cubic metre (m^3)	4.546 090 E − 03
gallon (U.K. liquid)	cubic metre (m^3)	4.546 092 E − 03
gallon (U.S. dry)	cubic metre (m^3)	4.404 884 E − 03
gallon (U.S. liquid)	cubic metre (m^3)	3.785 412 E − 03
gallon (U.S. liquid) per day	cubic metre per second (m^3/s)	4.381 264 E − 08
gallon (U.S. liquid) per minute	cubic metre per second (m^3/s)	6.309 020 E − 05
gallon (U.S. liquid) per hp · h (SFC, specific fuel consumption)	cubic metre per joule (m^3/J)	1.410 089 E − 09
gamma	tesla (T)	1.000 000*E − 09
gauss	tesla (T)	1.000 000*E − 04
gilbert	ampere (A)	7.957 747 E − 01
gill (U.K.)	cubic metre (m^3)	1.420 653 E − 04
gill (U.S.)	cubic metre (m^3)	1.182 941 E − 04
grade	degree (angular)	9.000 000*E − 01
grade	radian (rad)	1.570 796 E − 02
grain	kilogram (kg)	6.479 891*E − 05
grain/gal (U.S. liquid)	kilogram per cubic metre (kg/m^3)	1.711 806 E − 02
gram	kilogram (kg)	1.000 000*E − 03
g/cm^3	kilogram per cubic metre (kg/m^3)	1.000 000*E + 03
gf/cm^2	pascal (Pa)	9.806 650*E + 01
hectare	square metre (m^2)	1.000 000*E + 04
horsepower (550 ft · lbf/s)	watt (W)	7.456 999 E + 02
horsepower (boiler)	watt (W)	9.809 50 E + 03
horsepower (electric)	watt (W)	7.460 000*E + 02
horsepower (metric)	watt (W)	7.354 99 E + 02
horsepower (water)	watt (W)	7.460 43 E + 02
horsepower (U.K.)	watt (W)	7.457 0 E + 02
hour	second(s)	3.600 000*E + 03
hour (sidereal)	second (s)	3.590 170 E + 03
hundredweight (long)	kilogram (kg)	5.080 235 E + 01
hundredweight (short)	kilogram (kg)	4.535 924 E + 01
inch	metre (m)	2.540 000*E − 02
inch of mercury (32°F)	pascal (Pa)	3.386 38 E + 03
inch of mercury (60°F)	pascal (Pa)	3.376 85 E + 03
inch of water (39.2°F)	pascal (Pa)	2.490 82 E + 02
inch of water (60°F)	pascal (Pa)	2.488 4 E + 02
in^2	square metre (m^2)	6.451 600*E − 04
in^3 (volume)	cubic metre (m^3)	1.638 706 E − 05
in^3 (section modulus)	metre cubed (m^3)	1.638 706 E − 05
in^3/min	cubic metre per second (m^3/s)	2.731 177 E − 07
in^4(second moment of area)	metre to the fourth power (m^4)	4.162 314 E − 07
in/s	metre per second (m/s)	2.540 000*E − 02
in/s^2	metre per second squared (m/s^2)	2.540 000*E − 02
kayser	1 per metre (1/m)	1.000 000*E + 02

Table 1 Alphabetical list of units (continued).

To convert from	to	Multiply by
kelvin	degree Celsius (°C)	$t_{°C} = T_K - 273.$
kilocalorie (International Table)	joule (J)	4.186 800°E + 03
Kilocalorie (mean)	joule (J)	4.190 02 E + 03
kilocalorie (thermochemical)	joule (J)	4.184 000*E + 03
kilocalorie (thermochemical)/min	watt (W)	6.973 333 E + 01
kilocalorie (thermochemical)/s	watt (W)	4.184 000*E + 03
kilogram-force (kgf)	newton (N)	9.806 650*E + 00
kgf · m	newton metre (N · m)	9.806 650*E + 00
kgf · s^2/m (mass)	kilogram (kg)	9.806 650*E + 00
kgf/cm^2	pascal (Pa)	9.806 650*E + 04
kgf/m^2	pascal (Pa)	9.806 650*E + 00
kgf/mm^2	pascal (Pa)	9.806 650*E + 06
km/h	metre per second (m/s)	2.777 778 E − 01
kilopond (1 kp = 1 kgf)	newton (N)	9.806 650*E + 00
kW · h	joule (J)	3.600 000*E + 06
kip (1000 lbf)	newton (N)	4.448 222 E + 03
kip/in^2(ksi)	pascal (Pa)	6.894 757 E + 06
knot (international)	metre per second (m/s)	5.144 444 E − 01
lambert	candela per square metre (cd/m^2)	1/π *E + 04
lambert	candela per square metre (cd/m^2)	3.183 099 E + 03
langley	joule per square metre (J/m^2)	4.184 000*E + 04
light year	metre (m)	9.460 55 E + 15
litre	cubic metre (m^3)	1.000 000*E − 03
lm/ft^2	lumen per square metre (lm/m^2)	1.076 391 E + 01
maxwell	weber (Wb)	1.000 000*E − 08
mho	siemens (S)	1.000 000*E + 00
microinch	metre (m)	2.540 000*E − 08
micron (deprecated term, use micrometre)	metre (m)	1.000 000*E − 06
mil	metre (m)	2.540 000*E − 05
mile (international)	metre (m)	1.609 344*E + 03
mile (U.S. statute)	metre (m)	1.609 347 E + 03
mile (international nautical)	metre (m)	1.852 000*E + 03
mile (U.S. nautical)	metre (m)	1.852 000*E + 03
mi^2 (international)	square metre (m^2)	2.589 988 E + 06
mi^2 (U.S. statute)	square metre (m^2)	2.589 998 E + 06
mi/h (international)	metre per second (m/s)	4.470 400*E − 01
mi/h (international)	kilometre per hour (km/h)	1.609 344*E + 00
mi/min (international)	metre per second (m/s)	2.682 240*E + 01
mi/s (international)	metre per second (m/s)	1.609 344*E + 03
millibar	pascal (Pa)	1.000 000*E + 02
millimetre of mercury (0°C)	pascal (Pa)	1.333 22 E + 02
minute (angle)	radian (rad)	2.908 882 E − 04
minute	second (s)	6.000 000*E + 01
minute (sidereal)	second (s)	5.983 617 E + 01
oersted	ampere per metre (A/m)	7.957 747 E + 01
ohm centimetre	ohm metre (Ω · m)	1.000 000*E − 02
ohm circular-mil per foot	ohm metre (Ω · m)	1.662 426 E − 09
ounce (avoirdupois)	kilogram (kg)	2.834 952 E − 02
ounce (troy or apothecary)	kilogram (kg)	3.110 348 E − 02
ounce (U.K. fluid)	cubic metre (m^3)	2.841 306 E − 05
ounce (U.S fluid)	cubic metre (m^3)	2.957 353 E − 05
ounce-force	newton (N)	2.780 139 E − 01
ozf · in	newton metre (N · m)	7.061 552 E − 03
oz (avoirdupois)/gal (U.K. liquid)	kilogram per cubic metre (kg/m^3)	6.236 023 E + 00
oz (avoirdupois)/gal (U.S. liquid)	kilogram per cubic metre (kg/m^3)	7.489 152 E + 00
oz (avoirdupois)/in^3	kilogram per cubic metre (kg/m^3)	1.729 994 E + 03
oz (avoirdupois)/ft^2	kilogram per square metre (kg/m^2)	3.051 517 E − 01
oz (avoirdupois)/yd^2	kilogram per square metre (kg/m^2)	3.390 575 E − 02
parsec	metre (m)	3.085 678 E + 16
peck (U.S.)	cubic metre (m^3)	8.809 768 E − 03
pennyweight	kilogram (kg)	1.555 174 E − 03
perm (0°C)	kilogram per pascal second square metre [kg/(Pa · s · m^2)]	5.721 35 E − 11
perm (23°C)	kilogram per pascal second square metre [kg/(Pa · s · m^2)]	5.745 25 E − 11
perm · in (0°C)	kilogram per pascal second metre [kg/(Pa · s · m)]	1.453 22 E − 12
perm · in (23°C)	kilogram per pascal second metre [kg/(Pa · s · m)]	1.459 29 E − 12

Table 1 Alphabetical list of units (continued).

To convert from	to	Multiply by
phot	lumen per square metre (lm/m^2)	1.000 000*E + 04
pica (printer's)	metre (m)	4.217 518 E − 03
pint (U.S. dry)	cubic metre (m^3)	5.506 105 E − 04
pint (U.S. liquid)	cubic metre (m^3)	4.731 765 E − 04
point (printer's)	metre (m)	3.514 598*E − 04
poise (absolute viscosity)	pascal second (Pa · s)	1.000 000*E − 01
pound (lb avoirdupois)	kilogram (kg)	4.535 924 E − 01
pound (troy or apothecary)	kilogram (kg)	3.732 417 E − 01
lb · ft^2 (moment of inertia)	kilogram square metre (kg · m^2)	4.214 011 E − 02
lb · in^2 (moment of inertia)	kilogram square metre (kg · m^2)	2.926 397 E − 04
lb/ft · h	pascal second (Pa · s)	4.133 789 E − 04
lb/ft · s	pascal second (Pa · s)	1.488 164 E + 00
lb/ft^2	kilogram per square metre (kg/m^2)	4.882 428 E + 00
lb/ft^3	kilogram per cubic metre (kg/m^3)	1.601 846 E + 01
lb/gal (U.K. liquid)	kilogram per cubic metre (kg/m^3)	9.977 637 E + 01
lb/gal (U.S. liquid)	kilogram per cubic metre (kg/m^3)	1.198 264 E + 02
lb/h	kilogram per second (kg/s)	1.259 979 E − 04
lb/hp · h (SFC, specific fuel consumption)	kilogram per joule (kg/J)	1.689 659 E − 07
lb/in^3	kilogram per cubic metre (kg/m^3)	2.767 990 E + 04
lb/min	kilogram per second (kg/s)	7.559 873 E − 03
lb/s	kilogram per second (kg/s)	4.535 924 E − 01
lb/yd^3	kilogram per cubic metre (kg/m^3)	5.932 764 E − 01
poundal	newton (N)	1.382 550 E − 01
poundal/ft^2	pascal (Pa)	1.488 164 E + 00
poundal · s/ft^2	pascal second (Pa · s)	1.488 164 E + 00
pound-force (lbf)	newton (N)	4.448 222 E + 00
lbf · ft	newton metre (N · m)	1.355 818 E + 00
lbf · ft/in	newton metre per metre (N · m/m)	5.337 866 E + 01
lbf · in	newton metre (N · m)	1.129 848 E − 01
lbf · in/in	newton metre per metre (N · m/m)	4.448 222 E + 00
lbf · s/ft^2	pascal second (Pa · s)	4.788 026 E + 01
lbf · s/in^2	pascal second (Pa · s)	6.894 757 E + 03
lbf/ft	newton per metre (N/m)	1.459 390 E + 01
lbf/ft^2	pascal (Pa)	4.788 026 E + 01
lbf/in	newton per metre (N/m)	1.751 268 E + 02
lbf/in^2 (psi)	pascal (Pa)	6.894 757 E + 03
lbf/lb (thrust/weight [mass] ratio)	newton per kilogram (N/kg)	9.806 650 E + 00
quart (U.S. dry)	cubic metre (m^3)	1.101 221 E − 03
quart (U.S. liquid)	cubic metre (m^3)	9.463 529 E − 04
rad (absorbed dose)	gray (Gy)	1.000 000*E − 02
rem (dose equivalent)	sievert (Sv)	1.000 000*E − 02
rhe	1 per pascal second [1/(Pa · s)]	1.000 000*E + 01
rod	metre (m)	5.029 210 E + 00
roentgen	coulomb per kilogram (C/kg)	2.58 000*E − 04
rpm (r/min)	radian per second (rad/s)	1.047 198 E − 01
second (angle)	radian (rad)	4.848 137 E − 06
second (sidereal)	second (s)	9.972 696 E − 01
shake	second (s)	1.000 000*E − 08
slug	kilogram (kg)	1.459 390 E + 01
slug/ft · s	pascal second (Pa · s)	4.788 026 E + 01
slug/ft^3	kilogram per cubic metre (kg/m^3)	5.153 788 E + 02
statampere	ampere (A)	3.335 640 E − 10
statcoulomb	coulomb (C)	3.335 640 E − 10
statfarad	farad (F)	1.112 650 E − 12
stathenry	henry (H)	8.987 554 E + 11
statmho	siemens (S)	1.112 650 E − 12
statohm	ohm (Ω)	8.987 554 E + 11
statvolt	volt (V)	2.997 925 E + 02
stere	cubic metre (m^3)	1.000 000*E + 00
stilb	candela per square metre (cd/m^2)	1.000 000*E + 04
stokes (kinematic viscosity)	square metre per second (m^2/s)	1.000 000*E − 04
tablespoon	cubic metre (m^3)	1.478 676 E − 05
teaspoon	cubic metre (m^3)	4.928 922 E − 06
tex	kilogram per metre (kg/m)	1.000 000*E − 06
therm (European Community)	joule (J)	1.055 06 *E + 08
therm (U.S.)	joule (J)	1.054 806*E + 08
ton (assay)	kilogram (kg)	2.916 667 E − 02
ton (long, 2240 lb)	kilogram (kg)	1.016 047 E + 03
ton (metric)	kilogram (kg)	1.000 000*E + 03

Table 1 Alphabetical list of units (continued).

To convert from	to	Multiply by
ton (nuclear equivalent of TNT)	joule (J)	4.184 E + 09
ton of refrigeration (= 12 000 Btu/h)	watt (W)	3.517 E + 03
ton (register)	cubic metre (m^3)	2.831 685 E + 00
ton (short, 2000 lb)	kilogram (kg)	9.071 847 E + 02
ton (long)/yd^3	kilogram per cubic metre (kg/m^3)	1.328 939 E + 03
ton (short)/yd^3	kilogram per cubic metre (kg/m^3)	1.186 553 E + 03
ton (short)/h	kilogram per second (kg/s)	2.519 958 E − 01
ton-force (2000 lbf)	newton (N)	8.896 443 E + 03
tonne	kilogram (kg)	1.000 000*E + 03
torr (mmHg, 0°C)	pascal (Pa)	1.333 22 E + 02
unit pole	weber (Wb)	1.256 637 E − 07
W · h	joule (J)	3.600 000*E + 03
W · s	joule (J)	1.000 000*E + 00
W/cm^2	watt per square metre (W/m^2)	1.000 000*E + 04
W/in^2	watt per square metre (W/m^2)	1.550 003 E + 03
yard	metre (m)	9.144 000*E − 01
yd^2	square metre (m^2)	8.361 274 E − 01
yd^3	cubic metre (m^3)	7.645 549 E − 01
yd^3/min	cubic metre per second (m^3/s)	1.274 258 E − 02
year (365 days)	second (s)	3.153 600*E + 07
year (sidereal)	second (s)	3.155 815 E + 07
year (tropical)	second (s)	3.155 693 E + 07

Table 2 Classified list of units.

To convert from	to	Multiply by
Acceleration		
ft/s^2	metre per second squared (m/s^2)	3.048 000*E − 01
free fall, standard (*g*)	metre per second squared (m/s^2)	9.806 650*E + 00
gal	metre per second squared (m/s^2)	1.000 000*E − 02
in/s^2	metre per second squared (m/s^2)	2.540 000*E − 02
Angle		
degree	radian (rad)	1.745 329 E − 02
minute	radian (rad)	2.908 882 E − 04
second	radian (rad)	4.848 137 E − 06
grade	degree (angular)	9.000 000*E − 01
grade	radian (rad)	1.570 796 E − 02
Area		
acre	square metre (m^2)	4.046 873 E + 03
are	square metre (m^2)	1.000 000*E + 02
barn	square metre (m^2)	1.000 000*E − 28
circular mil	square metre (m^2)	5.067 075 E − 10
darcy	square metre (m^2)	9.869 233 E − 13
ft^2	square metre (m^2)	9.290 304*E − 02
hectare	square metre (m^2)	1.000 000*E + 04
in^2	square metre (m^2)	6.451 600*E − 04
mi^2 (international)	square metre (m^2)	2.589 988 E + 06
mi^2 (U.S. statute)	square metre (m^2)	2.589 998 E + 06
yd^2	square metre (m^2)	8.361 274 E − 01
Bending moment or torque		
dyne · cm	newton metre (N · m)	1.000 000*E − 07
kgf · m	newton metre (N · m)	9.806 650*E + 00
ozf · in	newton metre (N · m)	7.061 552 E − 03
lbf · in	newton metre (N · m)	1.129 848 E − 01
lbf · ft	newton metre (N · m)	1.355 818 E + 00
Bending moment or torque per unit length		
lbf · ft/in	newton metre per metre (N · m/m)	5.337 866 E + 01
lbf · in/in	newton metre per metre (N · m/m)	4.448 222 E + 00
Capacity, density, electricity and magnetism		
abampere	ampere (A)	1.000 000*E + 01
abcoulomb	coulomb (C)	1.000 000*E + 01
abfarad	farad (F)	1.000 000*E + 09
abhenry	henry (H)	1.000 000*E − 09
abmho	siemens (S)	1.000 000*E + 09
abohm	ohm (Ω)	1.000 000*E − 09
abvolt	volt (V)	1.000 000*E − 08
ampere hour	coulomb (C)	3.600 000*E + 03
EMU of capacitance	farad (F)	1.000 000*E + 09
EMU of current	ampere (A)	1.000 000*E + 01
EMU of electric potential	volt (V)	1.000 000*E − 08
EMU of inductance	henry (H)	1.000 000*E − 09
EMU of resistance	ohm (Ω)	1.000 000*E − 09
ESU of capacitance	farad (F)	1.112 650 E − 12
ESU of current	ampere (A)	3.335 6 E − 10
ESU of electric potential	volt (V)	2.997 9 E + 02
ESU of inductance	henry (H)	8.987 554 E + 11
ESU of resistance	ohm (Ω)	8.987 554 E + 11
faraday (based on carbon-12)	coulomb (C)	9.648 70 E + 04
faraday (chemical)	coulomb (C)	9.649 57 E + 04
faraday (physical)	coulomb (C)	9.652 19 E + 04
gamma	tesla (T)	1.000 000*E − 09
gauss	tesla (T)	1.000 000*E − 04
gilbert	ampere (A)	7.957 747 E − 01
maxwell	weber (Wb)	1.000 000*E − 08
mho	siemens (S)	1.000 000*E + 00
oersted	ampere per metre (A/m)	7.957 747 E + 01
ohm centimetre	ohm metre (Ω · m)	1.000 000*E − 02
ohm circular-mil per foot	ohm metre (Ω · m)	1.662 426 E − 09
statampere	ampere (A)	3.335 640 E − 10
statcoulomb	coulomb (C)	3.335 640 E − 10

Table 2 Classified list of units (continued).

To convert from	to	Multiply by
statfarad	farad (F)	1.112 650 E − 12
stathenry	henry (H)	8.987 554 E + 11
statmho	siemens (S)	1.112 650 E − 12
statohm	ohm (Ω)	8.987 554 E + 11
statvolt	volt (V)	2.997 925 E + 02
unit pole	weber (Wb)	1.256 637 E − 07
Energy (includes Work)		
British thermal unit (International Table)	joule (J)	1.055 056 E + 03
British thermal unit (mean)	joule (J)	1.055 87 E + 03
British thermal unit (thermochemical)	joule (J)	1.054 350 E + 03
British thermal unit (39°F)	joule (J)	1.059 67 E + 03
British thermal unit (59°F)	joule (J)	1.054 80 E + 03
British thermal unit (60°F)	joule (J)	1.054 68 E + 03
calorie (International Table)	joule (J)	4.186 800*E + 00
calorie (mean)	joule (J)	4.190 02 E + 00
calorie (thermochemical)	joule (J)	4.184 000*E + 00
calorie (15°C)	joule (J)	4.185 80 E + 00
calorie (20°C)	joule (J)	4.181 90 E + 00
calorie (kilogram, International Table)	joule (J)	4.186 800*E + 03
calorie (kilogram, mean)	joule (J)	4.190 02 E + 03
calorie (kilogram, thermochemical)	joule (J)	4.184 000*E + 03
electronvolt	joule (J)	1.602 19 E − 19
erg	joule (J)	1.000 000*E − 07
ft · lbf	joule (J)	1.355 818 E + 00
ft-poundal	joule (J)	4.214 011 E − 02
kilocalorie (International Table)	joule (J)	4.186 800*E + 03
kilocalorie (mean)	joule (J)	4.190 02 E + 03
kilocalorie (thermochemical)	joule (J)	4.184 000*E + 03
kW · h	joule (J)	3.600 000*E + 06
therm (European Community)	joule (J)	1.055 06 E + 08
therm (U.S.)	joule (J)	1.054 804*E + 08
ton (nuclear equivalent of TNT)	joule (J)	4.184 E + 09
W · h	joule (J)	3.600 000*E + 03
W · s	joule (J)	1.000 000*E + 00
Energy per unit area time		
Btu (International Table)/(ft^2 · s)	watt per square metre (W/m^2)	1.135 653 E + 04
Btu (International Table)/(ft^2 · h)	watt per square metre (W/m^2)	3.154 591 E + 00
Btu (thermochemical)/(ft^2 · s)	watt per square metre (W/m^2)	1.134 893 E + 04
Btu (thermochemical)/(ft^2 . min)	watt per square metre,(W/m^2)	1.891 489 E + 02
Btu (thermochemical)/(ft^2 · h)	watt per square metre (W/m^2)	3.152 481 E + 00
Btu (thermochemical)/(in^2 · s)	watt per square metre (W/m^2)	1.634 246 E + 06
cal (thermochemical)/(cm^2 · min)	watt per square metre (W/m^2)	6.973 333 E + 02
cal (thermochemical)/(cm^2 · s)	watt per square metre (W/m^2)	4.184 000*E + 04
erg/(cm^2 · s)	watt per square metre (W/m^2)	1.000 000*E − 03
W/cm^2	watt per square metre (W/m^2)	1.000 000*E + 04
W/in^2	watt per square metre (W/m^2)	1.550 003 E + 03
Flow (see Mass per unit time or Volume per unit time) and Force		
dyne	newton (N)	1.000 000*E − 05
kilogram-force	newton (N)	9.806 650*E + 00
kilopond (kp)	newton (N)	9.806 650*E + 00
kip (1000 lbf)	newton (N)	4.448 222 E + 03
ounce-force	newton (N)	2.780 139 E − 01
pound-force (lbf)	newton (N)	4.448 222 E + 00
lbf/lb (thrust/weight [mass] ratio)	newton per kilogram (N/kg)	9.806 650 E + 00
poundal	newton (N)	1.382 550 E − 01
ton-force (2000 lbf)	newton (N)	8.896 443 E + 03
Force per unit area, force per unit length		
lbf/ft	newton per metre (N/m)	1.459 390 E + 01
lbf/in	newton per metre (N/m)	1.751 268 E + 02
Heat		
Btu (International Table) · ft/(h · ft^2 · °F) (thermal conductivity)	watt per metre kelvin [W/(m · K)]	1.730 735 E + 00
Btu (thermochemical) · ft/(h · ft^2 · °F) (thermal conductivity)	watt per metre kelvin [W/(m · K)]	1.729 577 E + 00

Table 2 Classified list of units (continued).

To convert from	to	Multiply by
Heat		
Btu (International Table) · in/(h · ft^2 · °F) (thermal conductivity)	watt per metre kelvin [W/(m · K)]	1.442 279 E − 01
Btu (thermochemical) · in(h · ft^2 · °F) (thermal conductivity)	watt per metre kelvin [W/(m · K)]	1.441 314 E − 01
Btu (International Table) · in/(s · ft^2 · °F) (thermal conductivity)	watt per metre kelvin [W/(m · K)]	5.192 204 E + 02
Btu (thermochemical) · in/(s · ft^2 · °F) (thermal conductivity)	watt per metre kelvin [W/(m · K)]	5.188 732 E + 02
Btu (International Table)/ft^2	joule per square metre (J/m^2)	1.135 653 E + 04
Btu (thermochemical)/ft^2	joule per square metre (J/m^2)	1.134 893 E + 04
Btu (International Table)/(h · ft^2 · °F) (thermal conductance)	watt per square metre kelvin [W/(m^2 · K)]	5.678 263 E + 00
Btu (thermochemical)/(h · ft^2 · °F) (thermal conductance)	watt per square metre kelvin [W/(m^2 · K)]	5.674 466 E + 00
Btu (International Table)/(s · ft^2 · °F)	watt per square metre kelvin [W/(m^2 · K)]	2.044 175 E + 04
Btu (thermochemical)/(s · ft^2 °F)	watt per square metre kelvin [W/(m^2 · K)]	2.042 808 E + 04
Btu (International Table)/lb	joule per kilogram (J/kg)	2.326 000*E + 03
Btu (thermochemical)/lb	joule per kilogram (J/kg)	2.324 444 E + 03
Btu (International Table)/lb · F°) (heat capacity)	joule per kilogram kelvin [J/(kg · K)]	4.186 800*E + 03
Btu (thermochemical)/(lb · °F) (heat capacity)	joule per kilogram kelvin [J/(kg · K)]	4.184 000*E + 03
Btu (International Table)/ft^3	joule per cubic metre (J/m^3)	3.725 895 E + 04
Btu (thermochemical)/ft^3	joule per cubic metre (J/m^3)	3.723 402 E + 04
cal (thermochemical)/(cm · s · °C)	watt per metre kelvin [W/(m · K)]	4.184 000*E + 02
cal (thermochemical)/cm^2	joule per square metre (J/m^2)	4.184 000*E + 04
cal (thermochemical)/(cm^2 · min)	watt per square metre (W/m^2)	6.973 333 E + 02
cal (thermochemical)/(cm^2 · s)	watt per square metre (W/m^2)	4.184 000*E + 04
cal (International Table)/g	joule per kilogram (J/kg)	4.186 800*E + 03
cal (thermochemical)/g	joule per kilogram (J/kg)	4.184 000*E + 03
cal (International Table)/(g · °C)	joule per kilogram kelvin [J/(kg · K)]	4.186 800*E + 03
cal (thermochemical)/(g · °C)	joule per kilogram kelvin [J/(kg · K)]	4.184 000*E + 03
cal (thermochemical)/min	watt (W)	6.973 333 E − 02
cal (thermochemical)/s	watt (W)	4.184 000*E + 00
clo	kelvin square metre per watt (K · m^2/W)	1.55 E − 01
°F · h · ft^2/Btu (International Table) (thermal resistance)	kelvin square metre per watt (K · m^2/W)	1.761 102 E − 01
°F · h · ft^2/Btu (thermochemical) (thermal resistance)	kelvin square metre per watt (K · m^2/W)	1.762 280 E − 01
°F · h · ft^2/[Btu (International Table) · in] (thermal resistivity)	kelvin metre per watt (K · m/W)	6.933 471 E + 00
°F · h · ft^2/[Btu (thermochemical) · in] (thermal resistivity)	kelvin metre per watt (K · m/W)	6.938 113 E + 00
ft^2/h(thermal diffusivity)	square metre per second (m^2/s)	2.580 640*E − 05
Length		
angstrom	metre (m)	1.000 000*E − 10
astronomical unit	metre (m)	1.495 979 E + 11
chain	metre (m)	2.011 684 E + 01
fathom	metre (m)	1.828 804 E + 00
fermi (femtometre)	metre (m)	1.000 000*E − 15
foot	metre (m)	3.048 000*E − 01
foot (U.S. survey)	metre (m)	3.048 006 E − 01
inch	metre (m)	2.540 000*E − 02
light year	metre (m)	9.460 55 E + 15
microinch	metre (m)	2.540 000*E − 08
micron (deprecated term, use micrometre)	metre (m)	1.000 000*E − 06
mil	metre (m)	2.540 000*E − 05
mile (international nautical)	metre (m)	1.852 000*E + 03
mile (U.S. nautical)	metre (m)	1.852 000*E + 03
mile (international)	metre (m)	1.609 334*E + 03
mile (U.S. statute)	metre (m)	1.609 347 E + 03
parsec	metre (m)	3.085 678 E + 16
pica (printer's)	metre (m)	4.217 518 E − 03
point (printer's)	metre (m)	3.514 598*E − 04

Table 2 Classified list of units (continued).

To convert from	to	Multiply by
rod	metre (m)	5.029 210 E + 00
yard	metre (m)	9.144 000*E − 01
Light		
cd/in²	candela per square metre (cd/m²)	1.550 003 E + 03
footcandle	lux (lx)	1.076 391 E + 01
footlambert	candela per square metre (cd/m²)	3.426 259 E + 00
lambert	candela per square metre (cd/m²)	3.183 099 E + 03
lm/ft²	lumen per square metre (lm/m²)	1.076 391 E + 01
Mass		
carat (metric)	kilogram (kg)	2.000 000*E − 04
grain	kilogram (kg)	6.479 891*E − 05
gram	kilogram (kg)	1.000 000*E − 03
hundredweight (long)	kilogram (kg)	5.080 235 E + 01
hundredweight (short)	kilogram (kg)	4.535 924 E + 01
kgf · s²/m (mass)	kilogram (kg)	9.806 650*E + 00
ounce (avoirdupois)	kilogram (kg)	2.834 952 E − 02
ounce (troy or apothecary)	kilogram (kg)	3.110 348 E − 02
pennyweight	kilogram (kg)	1.555 174 E − 03
pound (lb avoirdupois)	kilogram (kg)	4.535 924 E − 01
pound (troy or apothecary)	kilogram (kg)	3.732 417 E − 01
slug	kilogram (kg)	1.459 390 E + 01
ton (assay)	kilogram (kg)	2.916 667 E − 02
ton (long, 2240 lb)	kilogram (kg)	1.016 047 E + 03
ton (metric)	kilogram (kg)	1.000 000*E + 03
ton (short, 2000 lb)	kilogram (kg)	9.071 847 E + 02
tonne	kilogram (kg)	1.000 000*E + 03
Mass per unit area		
oz/ft²	kilogram per square metre (kg/m²)	3.051 517 E − 01
oz/yd²	kilogram per square metre (kg/m²)	3.390 575 E − 02
lb/ft²	kilogram per square metre (kg/m²)	4.882 428 E + 00
Mass per unit capacity (see Mass per unit volume) and Mass per unit length		
denier	kilogram per metre (kg/m)	1.111 111 E − 07
lb/ft	kilogram per metre (kg/m)	1.488 164 E + 00
lb/in	kilogram per metre (kg/m)	1.785 797 E + 01
tex	kilogram per metre (kg/m)	1.000 000*E − 06
Mass per unit time (includes Flow)		
perm (0°C)	kilogram per pascal second square metre [kg/(Pa · s · m²)]	5.721 35 E − 11
perm (23°C)	kilogram per pascal second square metre [kg/(Pa · s · m²)]	5.745 25 E − 11
perm · in (0°C)	kilogram per pascal second metre [kg/(Pa · s · m)]	1.453 22 E − 12
perm · in (23°C)	kilogram per pascal second metre [kg/(Pa · s · m)]	1.459 29 E − 12
lb/h	kilogram per second (kg/s)	1.259 979 E − 04
lb/min	kilogram per second (kg/s)	7.559 873 E − 03
lb/s	kilogram per second (kg/s)	4.535 924 E − 01
lb/(hp · h)(SFC, specific fuel consumption)	kilogram per joule (kg/J)	1.689 659 E − 07
ton (short)/h	kilogram per second (kg/s)	2.519 958 E − 01
Mass per unit volume (includes Density and Mass Capacity)		
grain/gal (U.S. liquid)	kilogram per cubic metre (kg/m³)	1.711 806 E − 02
g/cm³	kilogram per cubic metre (kg/m³)	1.000 000*E + 03
oz (avoirdupois)/gal (U.K. liquid)	kilogram per cubic metre (kg/m³)	6.236 023 E + 00
oz (avoirdupois)/gal (U.S. liquid)	kilogram per cubic metre (kg/m³)	7.489 152 E + 00
oz (avoirdupois)/in³	kilogram per cubic metre (kg/m³)	1.729 994 E + 03
lb/ft³	kilogram per cubic metre (kg/m³)	1.601 846 E + 01
lb/in³	kilogram per cubic metre (kg/m³)	2.767 990 E + 04
lb/gal (U.K. liquid)	kilogram per cubic metre (kg/m³)	9.977 637 E + 01
lb/gal (U.S. liquid)	kilogram per cubic metre (kg/m³)	1.198 264 E + 02
lb/yd²	kilogram per cubic metre (kg/m³)	5.932 764 E − 01
slug/ft³	kilogram per cubic metre (kg/m³)	5.153 788 E + 02
ton (long)/yd³	kilogram per cubic metre (kg/m³)	1.328 939 E + 03
ton (short)/yd³	kilogram per cubic metre (kg/m³)	1.186 553 E + 03

Table 2 Classified list of units (continued).

To convert from	to	Multiply by
Power		
Btu (International Table)/h	watt (W)	2.930 711 E − 01
Btu (International Table)/s	watt (W)	1.055 056 E + 03
Btu (thermochemical)/h	watt (W)	2.928 751 E − 01
Btu (thermochemical)/min	watt (W)	1.757 250 E + 01
Btu (thermochemical)/s	watt (W)	1.054 350 E + 03
cal (thermochemical)/min	watt (W)	6.973 333 E − 02
cal (thermochemical)/s	watt (W)	4.184 000*E + 00
erg/s	watt (W)	1.000 000*E − 07
ft · lbf/h	watt (W)	3.766 161 E − 04
ft · lbf/min	watt (W)	2.259 697 E − 02
ft · lbf/s	watt (W)	1.355 818 E + 00
horsepower (550 ft · lbf/s)	watt (W)	7.456 999 E + 02
horsepower (boiler)	watt (W)	9.809 50 E + 03
horsepower (electric)	watt (W)	7.460 000*E + 02
horsepower (metric)	watt (W)	7.354 99 E + 02
horsepower (water)	watt (W)	7.460 43 E + 02
horsepower (U.K.)	watt (W)	7.457 0 E + 02
kilocalorie (thermochemical)/min	watt (W)	6.973 333 E + 01
kilocalorie (thermochemical)/s	watt (W)	4.184 000*E + 03
ton of refrigeration (= 12 000 Btu/h)	watt (W)	3.517 E + 03
Pressure or stress (force per unit area)		
atmosphere, standard	pascal (Pa)	1.013 250*E + 05
atmosphere, technical (= 1 kgf/cm²)	pascal (Pa)	9.806 650*E + 04
bar	pascal (Pa)	1.000 000*E + 05
centimetre of mercury (0°C)	pascal (Pa)	1.333 22 E + 03
centimetre of water (4°C)	pascal (Pa)	9.806 38 E + 01
dyne/cm²	pascal (Pa)	1.000 000*E − 01
foot of water (39.2°F)	pascal (Pa)	2.988 98 E + 03
gf/cm²	pascal (Pa)	9.806 650*E + 01
inch of mercury (32°F)	pascal (Pa)	3.386 38 E + 03
inch of mercury (60°F)	pascal (Pa)	3.376 85 E + 03
inch of water (39.2°F)	pascal (Pa)	2.490 82 E + 02
inch of water (60°F)	pascal (pa)	2.488 4 E + 02
kgf/cm²	pascal (Pa)	9.806 650*E + 04
kgf/m²	pascal (Pa)	9.806 650*E + 00
kgf/mm²	pascal (pa)	9.806 650*E + 06
kip/in² (ksi)	pascal (Pa)	6.894 757 E + 06
millibar	pascal (Pa)	1.000 000*E + 02
millimetre of mercury (0°C)	pascal (Pa)	1.333 22 E + 02
poundal/ft²	pascal (Pa)	1.488 164 E + 00
lbf/ft²	pascal (Pa)	4.788 026 E + 01
lbf/in²(psi)	pascal (Pa)	6.894 757 E + 03
psi	pascal (Pa)	6.894 757 E + 03
torr (mmHg, 0°C)	pascal (Pa)	1.333 22 E + 02
Radiation units		
curie	becquerel (Bq)	3.700 000*E + 10
rad	gray (Gy)	1.000 000*E − 02
rem	sievert (Sv)	1.000 000*E − 02
roentgen	coulomb per kilogram (C/kg)	2.580 000*E − 04
Speed, stress, temperature		
degree Celsius	kelvin (K)	$T_K = t_{°C} + 273.15$
degree Fahrenheit	degree Celsius (°C)	$t_{°C} = (t_{°F} - 32)/1.8$
degree Fahrenheit	kelvin (K)	$T_K = (t_{°F} + 459.67)1/8$
degree Rankine	kelvin (K)	$T_K = T_{°R}/1.8$
kelvin	degree Celsius (°C)	$t_{°C} = T_K - 273.15$
Time		
day	second (s)	8.640 000*E + 04
day (sidereal)	second (s)	8.616 409 E + 04
hour	second (s)	3.600 000*E + 03
hour (sidereal)	second (s)	3.590 170 E + 03
minute	second (s)	6.000 000*E + 01
minute (sidereal)	second (s)	5.983 617 E + 01
second (sidereal)	second (s)	9.972 696 E − 01
year (365 days)	second (s)	3.153 600*E + 07

Table 2 Classified list of units (continued).

To convert from	to	Multiply by
year (sidereal)	second (s)	3.155 815 E + 07
year (tropical)	second (s)	3.155 693 E + 07
Torque, velocity (includes Speed)		
ft/h	metre per second (m/s)	8.466 667 E − 05
ft/min	metre per second (m/s)	5.080 000*E − 03
ft/s	metre per second (m/s)	3.048 000*E − 01
in/s	metre per second (m/s)	2.540 000*E − 02
km/h	metre per second (m/s)	2.777 778 E − 01
knot (international)	metre per second (m/s)	5.144 444*E − 01
mi/h (international)	metre per second (m/s)	4.470 400*E − 01
mi/min (international)	metre per second (m/s)	2.682 240*E + 01
mi/s (international)	metre per second (m/s)	1.609 344*E + 03
mi/h (international)	kilometre per hour (km/h)	1.609 344*E + 00
rpm (r/min)	radian per second (rad/s)	1.047 198 E − 01
Viscosity		
centipoise (dynamic viscosity)	pascal second (Pa · s)	1.000 000*E − 03
centistokes (kinematic viscosity)	square metre per second (m^2/s)	1.000 000*E − 06
ft^2/s	square metre per second (m^2/s)	9.290 304*E − 02
poise	pascal second (Pa · s)	1.000 000*E − 01
poundal · s/ft^2	pascal second (Pa · s)	1.488 164 E + 00
lb/(ft · h)	pascal second (Pa · s)	4.133 789 E − 04
lb/(ft · s)	pascal second (Pa · s)	1.488 164 E + 00
lbf · s/ft^2	pascal second (Pa · s)	4.788 026 E + 01
lbf · s/in^2	pascal second (Pa · s)	6.894 757 E + 03
rhe	1 per pascal second [1/(Pa ·s)]	1.000 000*E + 01
slug/(ft · s)	pascal second (Pa · s)	4.788 026 E + 01
stokes	square metre per second (m^2/s)	1.000 000*E − 04
Volume (includes Capacity)		
acre-foot	cubic metre (m^3)	1.233 489 E + 03
barrel (oil, 42 gal)	cubic metre (m^3)	1.589 873 E − 01
board foot	cubic metre (m^3)	2.359 737 E − 03
bushel (U.S.)	cubic metre (m^3)	3.523 907 E − 02
cup	cubic metre (m^3)	2.365 882 E − 04
ounce (U.S. fluid)	cubic metre (m^3)	2.957 353 E − 05
ft^3	cubic metre (m^3)	2.831 685 E − 02
gallon (Canadian liquid)	cubic metre (m^3)	4.546 090 E − 03
gallon (U.K. liquid)	cubic metre (m^3)	4.546 092 E − 03
gallon (U.S. dry)	cubic metre (m^3)	4.404 884 E − 03
gallon (U.S. liquid)	cubic metre (m^3)	3.785 412 E − 03
gill (U.K.)	cubic metre (m^3)	1.420 653 E − 04
gill (U.S.)	cubic metre (m^3)	1.182 941 E − 04
in^3	cubic metre (m^3)	1.638 706 E − 05
litre	cubic metre (m^3)	1.000 000*E − 03
ounce (U.K. fluid)	cubic metre (m^3)	2.841 306 E − 05
ounce (U.S. fluid)	cubic metre (m^3)	2.957 353 E − 05
peck (U.S.)	cubic metre (m^3)	8.809 768 E − 03
pint (U.S. dry)	cubic metre (m^3)	5.506 105 E − 04
pint (U.S. liquid)	cubic metre (m^3)	4.731 765 E − 04
quart (U.S. dry)	cubic metre (m^3)	1.101 221 E − 03
quart (U.S. liquid)	cubic metre (m^3)	9.463 599 E − 04
stere	cubic metre (m^3)	1,000 000*E + 00
tablespoon	cubic metre (m^3)	1.478 676 E − 05
teaspoon	cubic metre (m^3)	4.928 922 E − 06
ton (register)	cubic metre (m^3)	2.831 685 E + 00
yd^3	cubic metre (m^3)	7.645 549 E − 01
Volume per unit time (includes Flow)		
ft^3/min	cubic metre per second (m^3/s)	4.719 474 E − 04
ft^3/s	cubic metre per second (m^3/s)	2.831 685 E − 02
gallon (U.S. liquid)/(hp · h)(SFC, specific fuel consumption)	cubic metre per joule (m^3/J)	1.410 089 E − 09
in^3/min	cubic metre per second (m^3/s)	2.731 177 E − 07
yd^3/m	cubic metre per second (m^3/s)	1.274 258 E − 02
gallon (U.S. liquid) per day	cubic metre per second (m^3/s)	4.381 264 E − 08
gallon (U.S. liquid) per minute	cubic metre per second (m^3/s)	6.309 020 E − 05
Work (see Energy)		

Conversion Tables

Table 3 SI prefixes.

Multiplication factor	Prefix	Symbol
1 000 000 000 000 000 000 = 10^{18}	exa	E
1 000 000 000 000 000 = 10^{15}	peta	P
1 000 000 000 000 = 10^{12}	tera	T
1 000 000 000 = 10^{9}	giga	G
1 000 000 = 10^{6}	mega	M
1 000 = 10^{3}	kilo	k
100 = 10^{2}	hecto	h
10 = 10^{1}	deka	da
0.1 = 10^{-1}	deci	d
0.01 = 10^{-2}	centi	c
0.001 = 10^{-3}	milli	m
0.000 001 = 10^{-6}	micro	μ
0.000 000 001 = 10^{-9}	nano	n
0.000 000 000 001 = 10^{-12}	pico	p
0.000 000 000 000 001 = 10^{-15}	femto	f
0.000 000 000 000 000 001 = 10^{-18}	atto	a

Table 4 Units in use with SI.

Quantity	Unit	Symbol	Definition
Time	Minute	min	1 min = 60 s
	Hour	h	1 h = 60 min = 3600 s
	Day	d	1 d = 24 h = 86 400 s
	Week, month, etc.	. . .	. . .
Plane angle	Degree	°	1° = $(\pi/180)$ rad
	Minute	′	1′ = (1/60)° = $(\pi/10\,800)$ rad
	Second	″	1″ = (1/60)′ = $(\pi/648\,000)$ rad
Volume	Litre	L	1 L = 1 dm^3 = 10^{-3} m^3
Mass	Metric ton	t	1 t = 10^3 kg
Area	Hectare	ha	1 ha = 1 hm^2 = 10^4 m^2

Table 5 Recommended pronunciation.

Prefix	Pronunciation (USA)[1]	Selected units	Pronunciation
exa	ex′ a (*a* as in *a*bout)	candela	can*dell′* a
peta	pet′ a (*e* as in pet, *a* as in *a*bout)	joule	rhyme with *tool*
tera	as in *terra* firma	kilometre	*kill′* oh metre
giga	jig′ a (*i* as in j*i*g, *a* as in *a*bout)	pascal	rhyme with rascal
mega	as in *mega*phone	siemens	same as *seamen's*
kilo	kill′ oh		
hecko	heck′ toe		
deka	deck′ a (*a* as in *a*bout)		
deci	as in *deci*mal		
centi	as in *centi*pede		
milli	as in *mili*tary		
micro	as in *micro*phone		
nano	nan′ oh (*an* as in *an*t)		
pico	peek′ oh		
femto	fem′ toe (*fem* as in *fem*inine)		
atto	as in an*ato*my		

[1] The first syllable of every prefix is accented to assure that the prefix will retain its identity. Therefore, the preferred pronunciation of kilometre places the accent on the first syllable, *not* the second.

PLASTICS CHRONOLOGY

The chronology concerning plastics is very extensive. Historically, the development of plastics worldwide is rather spectacular. The following very brief review provides a progression of developments.

1800 B.C. Reliefs on the walls of Egyptian royal tombs record the art of glass blow molding; basic technology applied to modern plastic blow molding techniques.

1700 to 1600 B.C. Egyptians further developed the art, which includes blow molds requiring the parison to be flashed outside the cavity. The excess is ground smooth.

465 B.C. Democritus was first to conceive matter in the form of particles, which he called atoms.

1492 A.D. The birth of natural rubber (elastomer) to the world dates back to when Columbus first reported that he had been intrigued on his journey through the New World to see natives playing with a ball that actually bounced.

1600 Van Helmont adopted the word gas.

1650 The hydraulic press was developed. The only one discovered since prehistoric times, a simple machine that operates on Pascal's Law; pressure applied to a unit area of a confined liquid is transmitted equally in all directions throughout the liquid.

1652 Robert Boyle (Ireland) developed Boyle's Law that concerns the behavior of gas.

1660 The term 'catalyst' refers to the nontechnical sense of dissolution or destruction.

1670 First reported record in using the word adhesive; referring to stick (ad) or cling (haes) two similar or dissimilar materials.

1675 The American iron and steel industry is considered to have begun in 1830. Such events, however, do not start at a singular point in time. Nor do they begin full-bloom. In this case, the bog iron industry was a predecessor. Working bog iron in New Jersey lasted from about 1675 to 1850. Bog iron is a porous limonite, a hydrated ferric oxide. It is formed by rainwater, soaking through fallen pine needles and other vegetable matter, taking on enough acid to leach iron from the underlying marls and greensands. This dissolved iron makes its way to the surface where it is picked up by springs and streams. On contact with the air, it oxidizes into a patch of rust brown scrum and drifts into shallow water. Layer upon layer of iron oxide is laid down along stream banks until eventually a sandstone 'composite' known as bog iron, from 2 in. (5 cm) to 2 ft (0.6 m) thick, is formed. After area is cleared of its iron, it can be naturally replenished in less than 20 yr.

1678 Robert Hooke (England) was the first to record or document the fundamental block law where the proportionality between load (stress) and deflection (strain) occurs in certain materials; becomes known as Hooke's Law.

1683 Gottfried Wilhelm (Germany) initiated the use of calculus to solve space problems (used in modern space flights); simultaneously Isaac Newton (England) also developed the use of calculus. It is the mathematical tool used to analyze changes in physical quantities (comprising differential and integral calculations). It was developed to study four major classes of scientific and mathematical problems of the time, namely, (1) find the tangent to a curve at a point, (2) find the length of a curve, the area of a region, and the volume of a solid, (3) find the maximum and minimum value of a quantity such as the distance of a planet from the sun, and (4) given a formula for the distance traveled by a body in any specified amount of time, find the velocity and acceleration of the body at any instant. These problems were attacked by the greatest minds of the 17th century, culminating in the crowning achievements of Wilhelm and Newton.

1688 The descriptive term 'calender' introduced as the major part of a calender machine.

1711 G. D. Fahrenheit introduced the use of mercury instead of alcohol in thermometers.

1736 The *Hevea brasiliensis* tree is the main source of natural rubber and its existence in the South American Amazon basin was first reported by Charles de la Condamine to the French Academy. He described to them the native methods of obtaining rubber from this tree and also methods that were used to convert it into useful products. La Condamine named this material 'cahutchu', the word being of Indian origin, and from this has come the more common name 'caoutchouc'.

1760 Enoch Noyes (U.S.'s first comb maker) began with cattle horns and tortoise shells in West Newbury, MA. The animal horn was boiled, slit, and pressed into desired shape.

1771 First synthetic dye is discovered; Woulfe prepared picric acid by the action of nitric acid on indigo and shows that it dyed silk to bright yellow shades. However, birth of the synthetic industry is considered to be in 1856.

1774 The actual derivation of the word 'rubber' is attributed to John Priestley, the chemist who discovered oxygen in 1774, and who successfully used this material for rubbing out unwanted pencil marks. He found that the crude product obtained by coagulation of latex was able to erase by rubbing.

1789 Graphite, so named by Werner (Germany), in reference to its marking ability as in pencils.

1789 Carbo (from the Latin word carbo for coal) so named by Lavoisier (French) as the chief constituent of coal.

1801 First reporting of the Greek word amorphous referring to a material that lacks crystal structure; Greek 'a' (not, without) + 'morph' (shape).

1805 The Gough-Jowle effect is discovered when rubber (elastomer) is stretched adiabatically (without heat entering or leaving the system) and it self-generates heat. This effect was originally discovered by Gough in 1805 and rediscovered by Joule in 1859.

1807 Thomas Young (England) first recorded and documented that the (tensile) modulus of elasticity relates to the slope of the straight line portion of the stress/strain curve; referred to as Young's modulus.

1807 The term organic first used by Berzelius to designate substances derived from living organisms.

1812 Humphry Davy (England) started the name aluminum.

1820 Natural rubber is used as coatings on fabrics to make water-proof clothing.

1820 Hancock invented prototype of modern rubber processing mill.

1822 Frederik Mohs establishes a measure of hardness based on a scale ranking different materials.

1823 Macintosh (Scotland) obtains a patent for his process of uniting two textile layers with a flexible cement prepared from a solution of rubber in solvent naphtha; from this the first waterproof raincoat is developed.

1823 Liebig and Wohler made isomerism of cyanates and fulminates. The term isomer introduced compounds that usually share their constituent atoms equally, though their arrangement is different.

1825 Faraday discovers benzene and hydrocarbon isomerism. He provides basis for elastomers or synthetic rubbers development by establishing the empirical formula C_5H_8 for natural rubber. The exact structure of natural rubber has been the subject of much controversy, nevertheless Faraday's work has been of great value to all scientists who carried on his work in their attempts to produce synthetic rubbers similar to and possibly better in certain specific properties than natural rubber.

1826 The term 'butyl' is introduced; from the Latin word butyrum (butter).

1826 Aniline discovered.

1826 Faraday reports the fractionation of a liquid that separates from illuminating gas under pressure. The substance is now known as butene, an isomer of ethylene.

1827 Styrene is polymerized.

1828 Dumas explains Etherin Theory where organic compounds are addition products of ethylene.

1828 Wohler produces urea from ammonium cyanate; first to synthesize the organic compound urea.

1830 Reichenbach distills crude oil.
1830 The Radical Theory explained where radicals are capable of separate existence.
1831 Earliest description of styrene reported.
1832 Ludersdorf (German) discovers that caoutchouc (natural rubber) can be cross-linked with sulphur. This discovery is thereafter completely forgotten.
1832 Liebig and Wohler describe the benzoyl radical.
1833 Liebig and Dumas explain that organic chemistry is the chemistry of radicals.
1834 Liebig first isolated melamine; became of academic interest in 1935.
1835 Pelouze nitrated cellulose.
1835 Regnault prepared vinyl chloride.
1836 Charles Goodyear (U.S.) discovered (by chance) that natural rubber could be vulcanized (crosslinked) using sulphur. Hancock (England) made a parallel discovery (See 1843). The material produced is not only highly elastic but has none of the residual tackiness characterizing natural rubber. The Goodyear process of natural rubber vulcanization by heat of a rubber-sulphur mixture is patented in 1844. In 1832 Ludersdorf discovered cross-linking natural rubber with sulphur.
1836 J. J. Berzelius classifies minerals chemically; discovers and isolates many elements (Se, Th, Si, Zn, etc.); coins the term isomer and catalyst as applied to chemistry; term catalyst describes a catalytic reaction.
1836 Acetylene (ethyne), the first member of the alkyne series, is discovered by Edmund Davy. During 1940s it became very important in the plastics industry as an intermediate in the manufacture of large volume monomers.
1837 Simeon Poisson describes the discrete distribution referred to as Poisson probability distribution.
1838 Regnault (France) prepares the first specimen of vinyl chloride and polyvinyl chloride on a laboratory scale.
1840 The term ozone introduced; bad odor characteristic of gas.
1841 U.S. Patent No. 2252 issued (Sept. 11) was the first packaging squeeze tube issued to artist John Goffe Rand to hold his oil paints. It was made by soldering two pieces of tin together and filled on a one-to-one basis. Today at least 220 tubes can be filled every minute. The tin used for nearly all tubes is now only an extremely small percent of materials presently used. Tubes are filled with many different products (toothpaste, food, medication, etc.) with 30% being metal (of which 95% are aluminum). The remaining are 30% all plastics and about 40% laminated of paper, aluminum, and/or plastic combinations.
1841 The word casein is introduced; refers to the Latin word 'caseus' for cheese, of which it was a major component.
1842 Hancock's (England) process of cross-linking natural rubber with sulphur is called vulcanization by Hancock.
1843 Hancock issued British patent for a process of vulcanization rubber-sulphur. He admitted openly that he had seen samples of sulphur-vulcanized rubber made by Goodyear (1839).
1844 Walton (England) discovers linoleum.
1844 Connection broken between organic and inorganic compounds.
1844 Cellulose acetate studied in Europe.
1844 Goodyear's discovery of natural rubber-sulphur mixture patent is issued.
1844 F. Walton produces linoleum.
1845 A. P. Critchlow develops "Florence" (shellac) compound.
1845 Schonbein (Switzerland) obtains cellulose nitrate, the starting point to reach "Celluloid".
1845 Bewley designs extruder for gutta-percha tubes.
1845 Hoffmann obtained aniline and benzene from coal-tar.
1845 Nitration of cellulose first described.
1845 Schonbein nitrates cellulose in the presence of sulfuric acid, which produces gun cotton.
1847 Berzelius made first polyester.
1847 Alkyd first coined from the words al (cohol) and acid (cid = kyd); describing their chemical derivation.
1847 Nitration of benzene occurs.
1848 Wurtz discovers amines and their relation to ammonia.
1850 A. P. Critchlow develops shellac compounds molding daguerreotype cases and started plastics molding in U.S.; Prophylactic Brush Co., Florence, MA.
1850 The term ceramic introduced; from the Greek word keramos referring to pottery and potters' clay.
1851 S. T. Armstrong's (U.S.) patent issued on improvement in making gutta-perchahollow ware. Tree producing gutta-percha is a tough natural plastic substance from the latex of several Malaysian trees.

Plastics Chronology

1851 Armstrong's U.S. patent refers to blow molding a plastic material other than glass; a tubular parison of gutta-percha that is a natural latex with thermoplastic properties. Water is used as the pressuring medium.

1851 R. Wilhelm (Germany) introduces the bunsen burner in the laboratory.

1852 Samuel Peck begins working with wood flour-shellac plastic compression molding parts such as photocases. Shellac was the pioneer natural plastic for many early reinforced (natural) plastics that were converted to phenolic (synthetic) plastic RPs in later years.

1854 First scientific recognition of the principles of fiber optics occurs by Tyndall when observing light being guided along a stream of water exiting from an orifice.

1856 Start of the synthetic dye industry.

1858 B. C. Brodie reported the first synthesis of diacyl peroxide, benzoyl peroxide. This peroxide was also the first synthetic peroxide produced commercially.

1859 Butlerov describes formaldehyde plastics.

1859 Chlorination of rubber produced hard rubber.

1859 Edwin L. Drake extracted oil with drilling equipment for the first time near Titusville, PA.

1859 Thomas Taylor (England) invents vulcanized fiber, came to U.S. in 1871, and in 1873 formed the Vulcanized Fiber Co. of Pennsylvania.

1860 Greville Williams isolated isoprene by the dry distillation of natural rubber.

1860 Berthelot and de St. Gilles prepared hydrolysis of esters.

1862 Alexander Parkes (England) at the Great Exhibition in London exhibited tiny synthetic plastic objects. They were made from "Parkesine", a cellulose nitrate-based compound machined under pressure. No industrial factory was started since material used disappeared soon after its introduction.

1862 Baldwin's compression mold patented.

1863 Caventou (France) discovered butadiene by the pyrolysis of amyl alcohol. However, the first polymerization was not carried out until 1910 by Lebedor (Russia).

1863 Lecture by Berthelot to the Chemical Society of Paris contains the first general discussion of polymerization of polymers in the literature.

1865 John C. Rockefeller (26 years old) buys oil business for $72,500 in Cleveland, OH; five years later Rockefeller establishes Standard Oil Co. and becomes the world's first oil giant.

1865 Parke's main patent for the Parkesine process issued (England).

1865 Schutzenberger (France) develops in the laboratory cellulose acetate.

1866 Synthetic method of preparing styrene is in existence by M. Berthelot; styrene is synthesized.

1867 George A. Waters (U.S.) produced the first laminated boat 13 ft. (4 m) long fabricated from manilla paper and glue. Four such boats were purchased by the U.S. Naval Academy in 1868.

1868 John Wesley Hyatt (Albany, NY, printer) eventually mixed pyroxylin and nitric acid with camphor to create cellulose nitrate, which he named "Celluloid". It is recognized as the first commercial plastic in the U.S. It was developed as a substitute for ivory in billiard balls, which in turn provided Hyatt with a £10,000 award sponsored by a billiard ball manufacturer.

1869 Term valence introduced; referring to the building strength of interatomic attraction.

1870 Establishment of Hyatt's Albany Dental Plate Co., later to become the Celluloid Manufacturing Co.

1870 Hyatt's basic Celluloid patent issued (to John W. Hyatt, Jr. and Isaiah S. Hyatt).

1870 Haldie Nicholson, a horn expert, arrived in Leominster (MA) from England to begin making Celluloid combs and cutlery handles.

1871 The word gasoline was introduced; reportedly coined from 'gas-oil', a heavy petroleum fraction from which the first gasoline was made.

1872 Baumann reported polymerization of vinyl chloride.

1872 von Baeyer (Germany) reported reaction between phenols and aldehydes; however, acid-catalyzed condensation of phenol with formaldehyde becomes commercially productive with "Bakelite" in 1909.

1872 Celluloid registered as U.S. trademark by Hyatt.

1872 Vinyl bromide obtained from acetylene and hydrogen bromine by Reboul.

1872 Hyatt brothers patented the first plastics (ram) injection molding machine derived from metal die casting presses.

1873 Caspery and Tollens prepared various acrylate esters.

1873 Liquid polymers of isobuty-lene were described by Butlerov and Gorianov. The actual polymerization of poly-isobutylene to form solid polymers did not follow until 60 yr later. The development of solid polyisobutylene rubber was a result of a joint research venture by Standard Oil Development Co. U.S. and I. G. Farbenindustrie (Germany).

1873 Osborne Reynolds (England) identified the phenomenon of cavitation erosion on ships. By the turn of the century it is called 'cavitation' by R. E. Froude, director of the British Admiralty Ship Model Testing Laboratories.

1875 Obediah Hills set up a plastic comb making business in Leominster, MA. Between 1800 and 1850, Leominster produced two-thirds of all combs manufactured in U.S.

1875 Baumann observed the exposure of vinyl bromide and vinyl chloride monomer to sunlight in sealed tubes, converted the liquids to polyvinyl chloride powdered-solid plastics.

1875 Bouchardat prepared an elastic-rubber-like solid by the treatment of isoprene; obtained by the destructive distillation of rubber with hydrochloric acid; not commercially important.

1876 Henry Wickham (England) collected many thousands of seeds used for growing rubber trees in South America (against the law in SA; punishable by death), and shipped them to Kew Gardens, England. Many of these rubber-tree seeds grew into healthy young plants, some of which were sent to Ceylon. A few years later, Henry Ridley, who was at that time a director of Singapore Gardens, against strong opposition, planted rubber trees in Malaysia. Today, because of this action, this country is the leading producer of raw natural rubber.

1876 L. Boltzmann developed the kinetic theory of gases (and others) summarized in Boltzmann's Law. Law applicable today in many disciplines such as the behavior of reinforced plastics.

1877 The word flocculation introduced referring to the appearance of aggregates; from the Latin word 'floccus' for a tuft of wool.

1877 Daniel Spill (England) manufactured cellulose nitrate which he called "Xylonite". Spill's greatest fame was as an unsuccessful plaintiff in the 8-year patent action against Hyatt.

1878 Hyatt manufactures the first multi-impression injection mold.

1878 Rhein Gummi- and Celluloidfabrik were the first manufacturers of Celluloid in Germany.

1879 M. Gray (England) granted patent for first screw extruder; employed an archimedian screw.

1879 Francis Shaw, Ltd. (England) produces the first commercial screw type extruder.

1879 Polymerization of isoprene into rubber compound. Bouchardat obtained a mass resembling natural rubber by heating isoprene with hydrochloric acid in a sealed tube.

1880 Kahlbaum polymerizes methylacrylate.

1880 John Royle & Sons, Inc. (U.S.) produced the first commercial screw type extruder in the U.S.; processed rubber tubing.

1880 It was theorized that glass drawn into fine fibers would be suitable for use in various textile applications. Although experimental glass fibers blended with silk fibers were woven into novel dresses and gowns in the U.S. and France, commercial glass fiber did not become a reality until 1939.

1880 Carbon fibers based on rayon (or cellulose) were first investigated. It was during this year that Thomas Edison first patented his incandescent lamp (after years of trial and error with literally thousands of materials). The fila-ments that he used in the lamp were made of carbon and had been produced by pyrolyzing natural and regenerated cellulose fibers. The carbon filaments themselves were very fragile.

1881 W. B. Carpenter's U.S. patent references blow molding of cellulose nitrate (Celluloid) from sheet stock or tubular form. Steam is used to soften and expand the preform.

1881 Gutta-percha and crosslinked natural rubber (NR) established as dielectrics; gutta-percha is a natural thermoplastic mixture of plastic and crystalline isomer of polyisoprene while NR is the amorphous isomer.

1883 Nitrocellulose fibers are patented by Chardonnet; also called nitrocotton or artificial silk.

1884 Tilden (England) noted the fact that isoprene could be polymerized and seemingly had an industrial potential.

1884 Holzer (Germany) investigates the reaction of urea and formaldehyde; he isolates urea-formaldehyde condensation products.

1884 Word 'eutectic' introduced; referring to ideal melting.

1885 Cast film from nitrocellulose with the addition of camphor.

1885 Krische and Spitteler (Germany) discover the property of casein curing with formaldehyde.

1886 Baeyer describes constitution of benzene.

1887 Le Chatelier first uses differential thermal analysis (DTA) for the study of clays.

1888 Charles M. Hall (England) invents the method of aluminum manufacture by electrochemical reduction of alumina. Parallel discovery by Heroult (France). Aluminum is first available in ingots.

1889 The building of the Eiffel Tower (Paris) demonstrated that based on logical and proper engineering analysis, steel could be erected to great heights to endure long serviceable life. This was the first of the very tall structures. After the turn of the century, the first skyscrapers were built with steel frames protected by concrete, brickwork, clay tile, metal lath and plaster, and others. These were called "fireproof" buildings.

1889 George Eastman introduced transparent film and nitrocellulose support.

1890 Svante Arrhenius conducted fundamental research on rates of reaction versus temperature, expressed by Arrhenius equation.

1890 John Royle & Sons, Inc. (U.S.) produced the first screw type extruder for wire and cable rubber insulations.

1891 Tech-Art Plastics Co. (U.S.) established, first to mold natural organic plastics, and later to mold phenolics (Bakelite, 1909).

1891 Chardonnet produces the first man-made fibers from viscose rayon.

1892 Cross and Bevan developed viscose silk.

1892 Shaw Insulator Co. founded in Newark, NJ.

1892 Dr. Washington Wentworth, Sheffield (U.S.) put toothpaste in plastic squeeze tubes; previously only packaged in very expensive porcelain containers.

1892 Cellophane is a family of transparent films that is manufactured by chemically regenerating a dissolved cellulose compound into a continuous thin sheet. This compound called viscose was discovered in England; in 1912 a Swiss chemist succeeded in developing a workable film coating method.

1893 "Velox" paper invented by L. H. Baekeland.

1893 Mouren is the first to report on the preparation and identification of acrylonitrile. First commercial importance occurred at the end of the 1930's (during WW II) to produce oil-resistant rubbers. It was used as a comonomer with butadiene to produce the well known Buna-N or nitrile rubbers.

1894 Cross and Bevan produces industrial process for manufacturing cellulose acetate.

1896 X-ray named by Roentgen; the discovery of this form of radiation as to its nature was at that time unknown.

1896 J. J. Thompson discovers the electron.

1896 Alfred Nobel (1833-1896) invented dynamite, smokeless powder, blasting gelation, etc. Upon his death, established the Nobel international awards for achievements worldwide.

1897 Pauly (German) announces basic processing patents on manufacture of cuprammonium rayon.

1897 Euler made isoprene synthetically and thus, in the chemical sense, completed the synthesis of rubber.

1898 Stearn and Topham (England) starts the production of viscose rayon from wood pulp.

1898 Ehrlich introduces organo-metallic compounds.

1898 Einhorn describes polycarbonates.

1898 Haskel invented rubber-wound-core ball; typical present-day golf ball.

1898 Pechmann reports on plastic from diazomethane in ether.

1899 Krische and Spitteler (Germany) produce Galalith from casein and formaldehye; process is patented.

1899 Continuous cellulose nitrate film made by casting on a polished metal drum.

1899 Kipping begins research into organosilicon compounds.

1899 Smith publishes patent on phenol-formaldehyde composition.

1899 Lederer (Germany) improves the method discovered by Schutzenberger (France) for the preparation of cellulose acetate.

1900 German count designed, built, and flew an airship capable of speeds to 30 mph (48 km); airship included use of plastics.

1900 During the 1900's the Leominster, MA, areas concentrated in all phases of plastics manufacturing, including basic material production and tooling. It was among the world's largest. At that time, the Viscoloid Co. (later called the Doyle's Works of Du Pont) processed the greatest volume of plastic products in a single plant. What is believed to be the world's first injection molding of commercial products is by the Foster Grant Co. in Leominster.

1900 Two lead sheathed, three core, 25 kV cables, 5 km long connect generating station and overhead line to Minneapolis (U.S.). One cable had paper, the other rubber insulation.

1900 Emil Hemming, Sr. (Germany) develops cold molded plastics.

1901 Otto Rohm (Germany) awarded doctorate in Germany for his thesis on acrylate polymers.

1901 Smith discovers alkyd plastics by the reaction of glycerol and phthalic anhydride.

1902 Bernard W. Doyle formed the Viscoloid Co. in Leominster to manufacture pyroxylin plastic sheet; in 1907 hired Sam Foster as supervisor of its comb division. Company acquired by Du Pont in 1925.

1903 A. Eichengrun and T. Becker patents issued on cellulose acetate.

1903 Gautschi (France) produces the first production of aluminum foil employing the classical "pack rolling" method of reducing metal to foil thickness. He stacked a number of thin sheets of aluminum into a pack and rolled between heavy iron cylinders heated internally by hot water. This action was repeated each time with a progressively smaller gap between the cylinders until the desired foil gages were obtained.

1904 Kipping's investigation of silanes is the basis for the development of silicone.

1904 Int. Galalith-Ges. Hopf & Co. (Germany) commence the production of "Gallalith".

1904 Todtenhaupt (Germany) prepares the first casein artificial silk.

1905 G. W. Miles prepares secondary cellulose acetate and CA fibers by a new process that proved to be uneconomical at the time.

1906 George Oenslager discovers the accelerators aniline and other organic materials such as hexamethylene tetramine to speed up the rate of rubber vulcanization. Aniline, however, is toxic and after a few years was replaced by p-aminodiphenyl-aniline and diphenylguanidine.

1906 Hoffmann (Germany) carries out experiments on the polymerization of isoprene, with the aim of preparing synthetic rubber.

1906 Existence of a small but measurable dark conduction (electrical) in anthracene, as well as photoconduction, is reported. Organic semiconductor is to be revived in 1941.

1906 Chromatography so named by its inventor Tswett, who used it to analyze plant pigments which produced bands of characteristic colors.

1907 Standard Pyroxyloid Co. was founded by W. Lane and J. P. Legere to produce cellulose acetate. Slower burning than Celluloid, CA replaced Celluloid for many parts.

1907 Aniline rubber accelerators produced.

1907 Leo H. Baekeland (U.S.) develops phenol formaldehyde molding compounds.

1907 Tech-Art Plastics Co. (Loando Rubber Co.) (U.S.) molds first phenolic plastics compound.

1907 Brandenberger (Switzerland) discovers viscose film.

1907 J. von Braun at Göttingen University (Germany) discovered that self-condensation of e-aminocaproic acid led to a caprolactam polymer, which later (1930's) was polymerized to produce nylon.

1907 Eichengrun (Germany) prepares the first acetate fiber in accordance with Farbenfabriken Fr. Bayer & Co. patents.

1907 Hoffmann presented a plan to attempt rubber synthesis to the management of Farbenfabriken in Elberfeld and obtained financial backing for 10 yr.

1908 William D'Arcy discovers the first major oil well in the Middle East at Masjed Soleyman in Iran; later turns concession over to Anglo-Persian Oil Co., which becomes British Petroleum.

1908 George Eastman introduced cellulose acetate safety film.

1908 With the arrival of the developer Emil Hemming, Sr., U.S. pioneered cold molded plastics in the field of electrical insulation. Formulations included bituminous-asphaltic like plastic binders with various fillers such as asbestos and earth.

1909 Stobbe (Germany) investigates the possibility of polymerizing styrene, known since 1827 and for which a synthetic method of preparation is in existence since 1866.

1909 Leo H. Baekeland successfully reacted and produced phenolic plastics. He called the plastic "Bakelite". From 1905 to 1909 he conducted research on phenol-aldehyde reaction in his Yonkers, NY laboratory. Patent applied in 1907. In 1910 he formed the General Bakelite Co. in Perth Amboy, NJ to produce large amounts of laminating plastics for Westinghouse, GE, etc. Prior to his death in 1944, he had 119 patents pertaining to aldehyde-phenol reactions and their processing techniques.

1909 Cold molded bitumin, phenolic, and cement-asbestos introduced.

1909 Raschig starts industrial manufacture of phenol formaldehyde casting plastic in Germany.

1909 Hugh Moore founded the Dixie Cup Co. producing disposable drinking cups to meet (Kansas state health officer) Dr. Samuel J. Crumbine action to have the state of Kansas (U.S.) outlaw use of community drinking cups on trains. Action was taken to eliminate spread of diseases such as tuberculosis.

1910 Lebedor (Russia) polymerizes butadiene.

1910 American Viscous Corp. in Marcus Hook, PA, is the first in the U.S. to commercially produce man-made (plastic) rayon fiber.

1910 Condensite Co. of America formed to exploit J. A. Aylsworth's invention to produce phenolic phonograph records.

1910 Swiss brothers Henri and Camille Dreyfus initiated commercial production of acetate lacquers and film in Basle, Switzerland. Because of WW I, the U.S. War Industries Board had Dreyfus build the American Celanese plant in U.S.

1910 Hoffmann (Germany) develops methyl caoutchouc, the first commercial production of synthetic methyl isoprene rubber.

1911 Standard Tool & Die Co. was founded in Leominster by Lionel B. Kavanaugh who ranks as a pioneer moldmaker.

1911 Brandenberger (Switzerland) commercially manufactures "Cellophane" (discovered 1892).

1912 First emulsion polymerization patent applied to isoprene.

1912 Klatte synthesized vinyl chloride and vinyl acetate from acetylene.

1912 Ostromislenski patents polymerization of vinyl chloride.

1912 La Cellophane SA is the first to commercially produce Cellophane in France.

1912 I. Ostromislensky (Moscow) patents a process for poly-vinyl chloride.

1912 Patent issued to Rohm (Germany) on vulcanized polymers of esters of acrylic acid with an outgrowth of acrylic elastomers.

1912 Polyvinyl chloride was successfully polymerized by Klatte (Germany) although commercialization of PVC was not achieved until the 1930's. Regnault of France in 1838 first discovered PVC.

1912 GE Co. (U.S.) patents manufacture of alkyd plastics.

1912 Farbenfabriken Bayer (Germany) patents cellulose ethers.

1912 Klatte (Germany) creates the basis for the industrial manufacture of polyvinyl chloride and polyvinyl acetate.

1913 D. J. O'Connor's patent application is for plastics laminated sheet to replace moisture-absorbing vulcanized fiber; assigned to Westinghouse (issued 1918).

1913 Klatte (Germany) applies for a patent on the manufacture of fibers from polyvinyl chloride. The idea gains practical importance as a result of work by Hubert and Schonburg (Germany) on fiber made from post-chlorinated PVC in the year 1931.

1913 H. Faber and D. J. O'Connor (ex-Westinghouse) started Formica Products Co. to produce reinforced plastic insulators. It was based on a patent prepared by O'Connor assigned to Westinghouse resulting later in major litigation. Laminates could replace moisture-absorbing vulcanized fiber to be used in the electrically powered industrial revolution occurring at that time. Formica and Westinghouse produced laminated products supplied by Bakelite Co. Leo Baekeland's sales policy was to make customers licensees and to dictate the use to which his materials could be put; Westinghouse was permitted to make flat sheets and Formica only rings and tubes. Formica did not like the policy so it developed two other material sources: Condensate of America, Glenridge, NJ based on patents issued by J. W. Aylsworth and Karpen Brothers Co., Chicago who had hired a Canadian chemist L. V. Redman. Formica eventually became very profitable. In 1956 it became a subsidiary of the American Cyanamid Co.

1913 Commercial production in U.S. of aluminum foil started based on the 1903 French foil production technique.
1914 Klatte and Rollet files U.S. patent for peroxide acceleration of thermal polymerization of vinyl chloride.
1914 Redmanol Chemical Products Co. formed to produce phenolic furniture.
1915 The first synthetic elastomer is made at Leverkusen (Germany).
1915 Farbenfabriken Bayer and BASF (Germany) are commercially manufacturing dimethyl butadiene rubber.
1916 F. H. Banbury (U.S.) receives patent for the Banbury mixer.
1916 Terklson Machine Corp. of Boston is early builder of compression molding presses for L. Baekeland's phenolic plastic.
1916 R. Kemp applied for patent on structural reinforced plastic products; patents issued in 1921 and assigned to Westinghouse.
1916 Alkyds introduced in U.S.
1917 Albert Einstein predicts the laser theoretically; developed 1950.
1918 In a New Jersey (U.S.) refinery, isopropyl alcohol is obtained from propylene.
1918 John patents urea formaldehyde condensation plastics.
1919 Arthur Eichengrun (Germany) receives patent on powdered cellulose acetate; 1921 designed and produced an injection molding machine specifically for use with this new thermoplastic.
1919 Cellulose acetate commercially available.
1919 Sam Foster started a company in Leominster, MA; joined by his partner William Grant the next year; called the company Foster Grant Co. Advances in injection molding continued so they imported Eckert & Ziegler hand-powered injection moldings from Germany.
1919 Eichengrun (Germany) patents injection molding process for plasticized cellulose acetate.
1919 Crossley develops glass-bonded mica.
1920 Hermann Strandinger (Germany) is deeply involved in fundamental research on polymerization mechanisms which was to profoundly affect the future of plastics.
1920 Griffith reports strengths of freshly drawn undamaged glass fibers of up to 900,000 psi (6,200 MPa).
1920 Two-way electric bulb sockets molded by National Lead Co. (U.S.) for the Hemco Co. using Union Carbide phenolic plastic.
1920 Era of polymer chemistry synthesis starts at a fast rate.
1921 Eichengrun designs the modern injection molding machine.
1921 Rayon introduced commercially.
1921 R. Kemp's patent (applied 1916) concerns producing plastic products.
1922 Staudinger begins work on macromolecules.
1922 R. Kemp's patent produces an all reinforced plastic airplane.
1923 Polysulfide introduced commercially.
1923 Pollak (Austria) starts commercial production of urea plastics.
1924 Wacker (Germany) successfully accomplishes the commercial hydrolysis of polyvinyl acetate to polyvinyl alcohol.
1924 Herrman Haehnel discovers polyvinyl alcohol when adding alkali to a clear alcoholic solution of polyvinyl acetate and obtains the ivory colored PVA. First scientific reports on PVA were published in 1927.
1924 W. A. Shewhart of Bell Telephone Laboratories developed a statistical chart for the control of product variables. This is believed to be the start of statistical quality control. Later in the same decade H. F. Dodge and H. G. Romig, both of Bell Lab's, developed the area of acceptance sampling as a substitute for 100% inspection.
1924 The first commercial antioxidant is developed to inhibit natural rubber's very bad deterioration in the presence of oxygen.
1924 First commercial production in U.S. of acetate fibers is by the Celanese Corp.
1924 Casein introduced commercially.
1924 Formica patents decorative laminates.
1925 Thiazole accelerators are developed, particularly mercapto-benzthiazole (MBT), for use in natural rubber.
1925 Nitrocellulose lacquers introduced commercially.
1925 Du Pont acquires the Viscoloid Co. (Leominster, MA) and renamed it Doyle Works of Du Pont (in honor of Bernard Doyle who founded it in 1902). It added the manufacture of toiletware. This plant processed the greatest volume of plastic products ever made in a single plant, employing 2,000 people.
1925 Insulated Power Cable Engineers Assoc. founded in response to a need to improve specifications for cables.
1926 In Germany the first injection molding machines designed for plastics are produced industrially.

1926 Konrad (Germany) develops the first synthetic rubber "Buna".
1926 GE Co. introduces "Glyptal", an alkyd principally used for coatings.
1926 Analine-formaldehyde introduced in U.S.
1926 Fischer-Tropsch catalyst developed.
1926 Celluloid Corp. starts production of "Lumarith" cellulose acetate sheets, rods, and tubes.
1926 L. E. Shaw (Shaw Insulator Co., U.S.) invents transfer molding in order to provide a solution to a critical thermoset compression molding problem involving a firing pin for use by U.S. Navy. This rather giant step in molding resulted in over 150 worldwide licenses to use the process.
1926 Eckert & Ziegler (Germany) patents a horizontal injection molding 2 oz machine operating the ram injection by compressed air. Mold was held on a movable platen mounted on tie bars.
1926 Hermann and Haehnel (Germany) synthesise the first laboratory specimen of polyvinyl acetate.
1927 Term 'alkyd' was used by Kienle to describe the reaction products of polyhydric alcohols and polybasic acids.
1927 The Bakelite patents expired, stimulating the market for thermosets.
1927 Cellulose acetate introduced commercially in U.S.
1927 Celluloid Corp. reports injection studies using Eckert & Biegler machines acquired along with Eichengrun patents.
1927 W. Semon of Goodrich initiates plasticization of PVC for molding compounds.
1927 Polyacrylate introduced commercially.
1927 Camille Dreyfus of Celanese Corp. of America merges with Celluloid Corp. to form Celanese Plastics Co.
1927 Polyvinyl chloride introduced in U.S.
1927 Compression molding, very popular for processing plastics, begins to give way to injection molding. This was a landmark in the growth of the plastics industry.
1927 Cellulose returned to the scene of the plastic industry with the development of cellulose esters in the form of the acetate and butyrate produced as sheet, fibers, and molded products.
1927 GE Co. develops a phenolic laminated breaker strip for refrigerators on its famous Monitor-top model. The strip was used for thermal insulation between inner steel box lining and outer cabinet, replacing a wooden strip.
1927 IG-Ludwigshafen (Germany) patents emulsion polymerization.
1927 German, English, and U.S. developers demonstrate that quartz fibers could be used in fiber optics and reinforced plastics.
1927 Staudinger (Germany) prepares the first man-made fiber from polyoxymethylene. The fiber achieves no practical importance, but these investigations form the basis for all later research in the field of fibers.
1927 Semon discovers how to easily plasticize polyvinyl chloride.
1927 Fikentscher (Germany) introduces the term K-value to characterize the intrinsic viscosity of high polymers.
1928 W. H. Carothers starts his research on polymers and polymerization.
1928 Reid, I. G. Farben, Du Pont patents filed on interpolymerization of vinyl chloride, vinyl acetate.
1928 Urea formaldehyde introduced commercially.
1928 Vapor-phase cracking introduced commercially.
1928 Commercial production of urea formaldehyde molding compounds.
1928 Radio tube bases of phenolic were produced in automated operations.
1928 C. V. Raman and K. S. Krishman first observed the Raman effect which is sensitive to molecular motions and other conditions. Wide application was delayed until the development of the laser.
1928 Wallace H. Carothers (U.S.) started in 1928 (after leaving the Harvard University staff) to head the newly formed fundamental research laboratory of Du Pont. Here, until his death in 1937 at the age of 41, he was the first to emphasize the all important concept of functionality in polymeric reactions and the distinction between the two important classes of polymerization. By functionality he meant (and still applies today) the number of reactive groups per reacting molecule. As an example, polyfunctional molecules give rise to plastics by addition (called "A" polymerization) or condensation (called "C" polymerization).
1928 Konrad (Germany) creates Buna S, the first synthetic general purpose rubber.
1928 Rohm (Germany) successfully accomplishes the polymerization of methyl

methacrylate to glass-clear blocks; since 1933 known under the trade name "Plexiglas".

1928 Hamburger Gummiwaren Cie (Germany) starts commercial manufacture of chlorinated rubber.

1928 Start of polyvinyl chloride production in U.S.; in Germany 1931.

1928 IG-Hoechst (Germany) patents copolymerization of vinyl compounds.

1929 British Plastics Federation founded.

1929 Industrial research on styrene and polystyrene initiated in Germany.

1929 I. G. Farben (Germany) concentrates on Buna scrubber and started volume production of styrene.

1929 Urea announced; gave color to the thermosets.

1929 Eastman Kodak Co. assigned its enlarged film production to Tennessee Eastman Co.

1929 Shaw Insulator Co. produces first 24-cavity, automatic unscrewing mold (produced thermoset mechanical pencils). Pinpointing gating was started; later this type of gating was applied to injection molding molds.

1929 Coaxial telephone cable invented by Espeschied & Effel.

1929 Synthane Corp. founded world's largest laminated plastics fabricating plant.

1929 The Great Depression hits worldwide, but most plastic firms survived.

1930 Ruff & Bretschneider (Germany) begins investigating the chemistry of fluorine. One result is the synthesis of the gas tetrafluoroethylene; produces academic interest until 1938.

1930 Foster Grant Co. imports the Eckert & Ziegler hand-powered injection molding machine from Germany. In the next 3 yr Foster Grant builds 20 of these machines in Leominster.

1930 IG-Ludwigshafen (Germany) starts polystyrene and polyacrylonitrile production.

1930 Large scale production of polyvinyl acetate in Germany.

1930 The first polyethylene is produced in England during the early 1930's by researches of ICI during studies of the effects of high pressures on chemical reactions. Experiments with a mixture of ethylene and other chemicals yielded a white residue PE.

For years, nobody realized the potential of the new plastic until more thorough investigation, based on better equipment and adequate quantities of the new material, showed it to combine unusual electrical properties with toughness, flexibility at low temperatures and resistance to chemicals and water. Further development was concentrated on safe and economical methods of mass-producing PE under high pressures since of particular interest was its outstanding dielectric or electric insulation material for radar, etc.

By the mid 1940's industrial investigators worldwide began to experiment with this new plastic in such diverse fields of application as injection molding, paper coating, and the making of film, pipe, and squeeze bottles. They soon discovered that PEs could be produced with a wide range of properties for a great variety of applications; it became (and still is) the world's most widely used plastic of at least 40% by weight.

1930 First completely stable vinyl chloride polymer marketed commercially.

1930 Injection molding of polystyrene starts in Germany.

1930 Dow Chemical's (U.S.) study of styrene starts.

1930 Polysulfides introduced by Thiokol Corp. (U.S.).

1930 Glass fiber research initiated by Owens-Illinois and Corning Glass Works; supposedly when a molten glass rod was being used to apply lettering on a glass milk bottle fine fiber was blown resulting in the start of the glass wool insulation business.

1930 Plax Corp. (U.S.) started work on the first blow molded "flexible bottle" made from cellulosic plastics.

1931 IG-Ludwigshafen (Germany) starts polyethylene oxide production.

1931 Herman and Haehnel (Germany) prepare fibers from the water-soluble polyvinyl alcohol; curing with formaldehyde is successfully accomplished in Japan. The "Vinylon" fibers are insoluble in water.

1931 W. H. Carothers and co-workers develop new synthetic elastomer that results in Du Pont manufacturing it based on chloroprene which they named "Duprene". Name was later changed to "Neoprene". This name becomes accepted as the generic name for this particular group of synthetic rubbers.

1931 GE Co. formed a separate engineering and marketing department for plastics.

1931 W. H. Carothers' first patent on polyamide (nylon).

1931 Patents issued to Formica (urea formaldehyde surface on phenolic-paper core, etc.) which provides the major start for the Formica decorative laminate business.

1931 Bauer and Hill separately begin investigating esters of methacrylic acid.

1931 I. G. Farben Industrie initiated work on vinyl dispersion plastics.

1931 Tennessee Eastman Co. produces acetate yarn.

1931 Du Pont injection molding starts.

1931 HPM (U.S.) hand ram injection molding machines are produced.

1931 Rohm & Haas Co. introduces "Plexiglas" acrylic coating.

1931 Hyde begins research on organosilicone polymers.

1931 J. A. Nieuwland (Notre Dame Univ., U.S.) describes a process for obtaining resinous products from acetylene polymers.

1931 Du Pont introduces its "Freon" chlorofluorocarbon (CFC) as safer alternate to toxic refrigerants in use, such as ammonia and sulfur dioxide. With the late 1980's link between CFCs and stratosphere ozone depletion, Du Pont, as the major CFC producer, introduced a family of new refrigerants starting with "Suva" hydrochlorofluorocarbon refrigerant, etc.

1931 Canvas phenolic picker blocks and rayon buckets developed for textile machines.

1931 Toledo Scale Co.'s research project at Mellon Institute to replace heavy and expensive porcelain in its weighing scales resulted in developing urea plastics. Demand for use of urea in scales required TSC to set up a special plastics organization called Plaskon Co.

1931 Owens-Illinois designs the (glass-wool) "Dust-Stop" air filter.

1932 A. M. Howald of Toledo Synthetic Products Co. molds the first urea formaldehyde Toledo scale housing.

1932 Celluloid Corp. (U.S.) applies for a patent on a system of pre-plasticizing using an extruder screw.

1932 Hans Gastrow (Germany) patents the first heating chamber in the torpedo of injection molding machines.

1932 Buna N (acrylonitrile-butadiene) and Buna S (styrenebutadiene) developed in Germany.

1932 Neoprene is commercially produced at Du Pont's Chambers Works, Deepwater, NJ.

1932 M. W. Perrin and J. C. Swallow of ICI-England recommend work be conducted on the effect of high pressures in chemical reactions.

1932 The first commercial quantity of polychloroprene latex is produced by Du Pont.

1932 In U.S., 227 megagrams (250 tons) of polychloroprene rubber (CR) are made to insulate telephone wires, line wire, and 2 kV mining cable.

1932 PVC insulated and jacketed non-metallic 600 V cable ("Romex"); introduced as an alternate to armored cable (BX) gets large market share. Made in Rome, NY, U.S. plant of General Cable.

1932 Chadwick discovers the neutron.

1933 Carleton Ellis does original work on polyester plastics.

1933 Du Pont Viscoloid of Leominster (U.S.) purchases four Grotelite hydraulic injection molding machines.

1933 Hartford Empire Co. (later to become Emhart Mfgr. Co.), developer and manufacturer of glass machinery, envision the oncoming competition from plastics and set up a plastics experiment development station.

1933 Carbon Chemical Corp. introduces its "Vinylite" PVC colored floor tile.

1933 Eckert-Ziegler and Isoma injection molding machines imported into U.S. by several molders.

1933 Crawford devised commercial synthesis for methyl methacrylate.

1933 Ethyl cellulose introduced commercially.

1933 Norddeutsche Seekabelwerke EG patents extruded polystyrene film.

1933 Polyamides developments occur.

1933 Fawcett, Gibson, Perrin, Paton, and Williams (England) discover the high pressure polymerization of ethylene.

1933 Corning Glass Works (U.S.) starts first systematic investigations on silicones.

1933 Ciba markets "Cibanite", an aniline formaldehyde molding material.

1934 Under the direction of W. H. Carothers of Du Pont polyamide (nylon) is produced.

1934 IG-Hoechst (Germany) develops the fluoroplastics.

1934 Nature of cationic polymerization is first suggested.

1934 Production of polymethyl methacrylate starts.

1934 IG-Ludwigshafen (Germany) patents polymerization of N-vinyl carbazole.
1934 Foster Grant builds its first hydraulic injection molding machine based on an earlier German experimental concept. One machine survives and is in the National Plastics Museum (U.S.)
1934 IG-Wolfen (Germany) produces epoxy/polyamine polyadducts.
1934 IG-Rheinfelden (Germany) starts post-chlorinated polyvinyl chloride production.
1934 Tennessee Eastman commissions Pack Morin Inc. to design the first large injection molding machine, which was built (for their use) by E. W. Bliss Co.
1934 IG-Wolfen (Germany) starts production of post-chlorinated PVC fiber.
1934 H. Schlechtweg (Germany) develops the concept of nonlinear elastic materials in which strain is uniquely determined by stress; whereas in plastic materials strain is also a function of time.
1934 H. Mark (U.S.) quantitatively studies the behavior of chain polymers during plastic deformation.
1935 Polysulphide elastomers become commercially available.
1935 Henkel (Germany) forms a valuable plastic by reacting melamine with formaldehyde.
1935 First of the low (or contact) pressure curing TS polyesters from Marco Chemical Co. based on contract requirements from the U.S. Wright-Patterson AFB Materials Laboratory.
1935 Biaxial orientation process is developed in Germany.
1935 Owens-Corning Fiberglas Co. is formed by Owens-Illinois and Corning Glass Works to produce glass fibers ("Fiberglas").
1935 Ciba patents melamine formaldehyde plastics.
1935 Ethyl cellulose introduced to U.S.
1935 Ferngren & Kopitke builds first modern hot-melt blow molding machine.
1935 Staudinger proposes three phase addition polymerization process.
1935 Troester produces first extruder designed for thermoplastics.
1935 Vinyl butyral introduced commercially.
1935 Reed-Prentice (U.S.), manufacturer of machine tools, die casting machines, and portable power chain saws, designed its first plastic injection molding machine for commercial production.
1935 Carothers prepares the first spinnable polyamide.
1935 IG-Bitterfeld (Germany) patents processing of polyvinyl chloride.
1936 ABS production starts.
1936 Carleton Ellis patents unsaturated polyester plastics made by reacting glycols with maleic anhydride that can be cured to insoluble solids simply by adding a peroxide catalyst. Ellis later discovered that a more useful (quicker and easier polymerization reactions) product could be made combining the unsaturated polyester alkyd with reactive monomers such as vinyl acetate, DAP, or styrene; patent on this process applied for 1937 and granted in 1941.
1936 U.S. injection molding machine manufacturers include Di Matteo, Watson Stillman, Lester, and Reed-Prentice.
1936 Plax Corp. (U.S.) receives patent for the first plastic "flexible bottle" made from cellulosic materials.
1936 G. Slayler and J. H. Thomas patents issued on producing glass fibers (OCF).
1936 Ciba markets melamine formaldehyde molding compounds in Europe.
1936 Styrene is marketed under "Victron" by Naugatuck Chemical Co.
1936 Rohm & Haas introduces "Plexiglas" acrylic sheet molding powders.
1936 Polystyrene introduced commercially.
1936 Polyvinyl acetate introduced in U.S.
1936 Index Machinery Corp. (U.S.) introduces a clock-controlled model for processing machines.
1936 Vinyl surpasses other materials for use in phonograph records.
1936 Discovery of low density polyethylene in England.
1936 Large-scale manufacture of polystyrene in Germany.
1937 A very important use and one of the first applications for nylon was in paint brush bristles; also replacement for girls' silk stockings occurs latter.
1937 American Cyanamid starts full-scale production of melamine.
1937 Otto Bayer in Leverkusen (Germany) develops the diisocyanate polyurethane addition process. Produces the first of rigid PUR foams and thermoplastic PUR elastomers.
1937 The Society of the Plastics Industry (SPI) is incorporated in New York City to represent the interests of the fledgling industry. One hundred and thirty molders and producers attend this first annual meeting.
1937 ICI-England produces "Telcothene", blend of polyethylene and polyisobutylene used in submarine cables.

1937 Lauroyl peroxide is first offered in U.S. by Lucidol.

1937 Automatic compression molding patented and introduced commercially by Stokes Machine Co.

1937 Urea formaldehyde wood glues introduced by Aero Research Ltd. (England); now Ciba.

1937 First commercial production of TS polyester plastics.

1937 First fully automatic multi-station compression molding presses for high volume production are manufactured by New England Butt Co. in Boston.

1937 James T. Bailey, a glass consultant, joined Plax Corp. to expand development of hot-melt plastic extrusion blow molding.

1937 Cellulose propionate introduced.

1937 ICI-England patent issued on high pressure PE.

1937 Dow Chemical (U.S.) starts marketing styrenes; in 1938 produced 190,000 lb. (86,000 kg).

1937 U.S. Instrument Co., under the Shaw transfer molding patent, corrected a serious limitation in the telephone industry. Cored-out handset phones are molded, rather than compression molding internal wiring as inserts in the mold.

1937 Vinyl copolymer introduced commercially.

1937 Sparks (U.S.) discovers butyl rubber.

1937 IG-Ludwigshafen (Germany) starts polyvinyl carbazole production.

1937 IG-Schkopau (Germany) starts synthetic rubber production by the emulsion polymerization process.

1937 N. A. De Bruyne of De Havilland Aircraft Co. (England) produces reinforced plastic aircraft structural parts.

1938 Arthur W. Logozzo of GE Co. initiates chrome plating of molds.

1938 Plax Corp. purchases a fully automatic thermoforming machine from Claus B. Stauch (Germany) for production of cellulose acetate Christmas tree spires, cigarette package premiums, and ice cube trays.

1938 R. R. Dreisbach and J. J. Grebe of Dow Chemical pioneer the production of pure styrene ("Styron") and its polymerization.

1938 Roy J. Plunkett and Rack Rebok of Du Pont discover the first fluoroplastic polytetrafluoroethylene. (They succeed in polymerizing PTFE, known in Germany since 1933.) In an experiment to convert tetrafluoroethylene into a non-odorous, non-toxic, non-flammable refrigerant to replace ammonia, the TFE surprisingly polymerized overnight in a storage vessel at very low temperature. The white powder obtained resulted in PTFE.

1938 About 56% of all foil produced is aluminum; today it is in excess of 90%.

1938 Chester Carlson invented electrophotography which started the Xerox Corp.

1938 The first of several patents issued to Plax Corp. describes methods and machinery for automatically blow molding plastic products. The first, an extrusion technique but with a closed end, is based on earlier work in automatic glass blowing. Later, injection blow molding techniques are also used. All equipment is for private use.

1938 P. Schlack at I. G. Farbenindustrie (Germany) polymerizes caprolactam to high molecular weight nylon-6.

1938 Silicones introduced by Dow Corning.

1938 HPM (Hydraulic Press Mfgr.) Co. (U.S.) builds a 36 oz (1 kg) injection molding machine.

1938 Multiple injection cylinders are introduced.

1938 Cellulose acetate butyrate introduced by Union Carbide and Monsanto for use on all interlayers in safety glass.

1938 Detroit Macoid pioneers acetate extrusion for automobile trim via profile sheet rod extrusion.

1938 Colombo and Pasquetti builds twin-screw extruder for plastics.

1938 Melamine introduced commercially.

1938 Plax Corp. starts commercial blow molding of acetate and styrene.

1938 At Plax Corp. the first hot-melt extrusion blow molding machine is developed by Bailey.

1938 Schlack (Germany) succeeds in preparing polyamide fiber-forming material from e-caprolactam; this fiber under its trade name "Perlon" gains wide acceptance.

1938 Du Pont starts manufacture of nylon fiber.

1938 First of the glass fiber reinforced TS polyester plastic is produced.

1939 Patent for epoxy filed in Germany.

1939 Extraction of wood with dilute nitric acid yields a carbohydrate residue that is called cellulose.

1939 John Reilly and Ralph Wiley of Dow Chemical introduce biaxial oriented polyvinylidene chloride (PVDC) that is called "Saran". By the mid-1950's, more than 5 million rolls of Saran wrap are sold monthly to preserve meats, vegetables, etc. Saran revolutionized packaging of meats.

1939 Enrico Fermi (Italy) is the first to achieve a controlled fission reaction.

1939 Commercial production by ICI (England) of LDPE begins.

1939 Industrial Research Laboratory (U.S.) developed the first bimetallic barrels for injection molding and extrusion. The product was called "Xaloy 100".

1939 Fred M. Roddy designs a knife-type cutter that reduces plastics (granulates) into reprocessable form; became an industry standard for granulators.

1939 Gasoline pump hose of Du Pont neoprene is in general use in U.S.

1939 Bakelite Corp. became part of Union Carbide and Carbon Corp.

1939 Godha (Japan) prepares soap solution-soluble fibers from calcium alginate.

1939 First epoxy by P. Castan (Switzerland).

1939 IG-Ludwigshafen (Germany) starts production of polypyrrolidine.

1939 IG-Wolfen (Germany) starts production of fiber from polyurethane.

1939 J. H. Reilly and R. M. Wiley of Dow Chemical obtain a moldable product by polymerizing monomeric vinylidene chloride by prolonged heating in presence of 0.1% of benzoyl peroxide.

1940 PPG Co. develops for the U.S. Wright-Patterson AFB, Materials Laboratory (OH) diallylglycol carbonate (DAC-polyester) and produces it commercially under the trade name "CR-39" and "CR-38".

1940 Advances in auxiliary equipment worldwide often are the result of equipment used in other applications, such as grain handling. For example, from early experience in handling dry products in air, Sprout-Bauer (U.S.) develops a rotary valve that is used as a pneumatic airlock and feeder, including a side-entry valve used for handling plastic pellets.

1940 Germany's bioriented polystyrene used in many applications such as in electrical capacitors.

1940 U.S. Liberty ships use bearings molded from canvas-phenolic laminates.

1940 Goodrich Co. patents a nitrile rubber/PVC blend.

1940 Henry Ford's prototype plastic car of hybrid soybeans and wood fiber plastic demonstrates improved impact resistance when Ford swings an axe against the reinforced plastics car body; no damage to car.

1940 Emulsion polymerization of vinyl chloride accelerated with reducing agents and persulfates by Bacon and Morgan.

1940 Production in England of PVC.

1940 The first polyethylene prepared by Union Carbide, independent of ICI, is polymerized by high synthesis in a continuous tubular process.

1940 Production of blow molded cellulose acetate Christmas tree balls, molded by Plax Corp., is significant as they replace glass types.

1941 C. D. Shaw of Plastics Processes Inc. develops jet-molding machines.

1941 Szent-Gyorgyi develops interest in the field of organic semi-conductors.

1941 The Society of Plastics Engineers is organized in Detroit; originally called the Society of Plastics Sales Engineers.

1941 OCF, Ashton, RI plant opened for the manufacture of textile fibers (former silk mill).

1941 Shell Chemical with Devoe & Reynolds introduces epoxies in U.S.; used in surface coatings.

1941 Rubber Reserve Co. (U.S. government) initiated synthetic rubber industry of U.S.

1941 Urethane-polyester type introduced in Germany.

1941 Whinfield and Dickson invent polyethylene glycol terephthalate ("Terylene").

1941 A 36 in. (91 cm) sheet extrusion machine by Plax Corp. (U.S.) is the first to extrude plastic sheet or film with biaxial stretch. This led to the development of oriented styrene to make high-strength thin styrene sheet.

1942 Plax Corp. extrusion blow molds the first low density polyethylene bottle for spray-net and stopette bottles. Reclaimed (recycled) LDPE is used, resulting in lack of clarity and rigidity when compared to virgin LDPE.

1942 Plastic Pioneers Assoc. is established.

1942 I. T. Quarnstrom, founder of D-M-E (U.S.), standardizes and stocks mold basis and mold parts.

1942 Becton Dickinson Co. develops the thermoformed blister package.

1942 An injection blow molding technique is patented by Owens-Illinois; equipment is used for the company's private use.

1942 Continental Corp. sets up a continuous low pressure TS polyester glass fiber reinforced plastic lamination process.

1942 Society of Plastics Sales Engineers (SPSE) that started in 1941 changes its name to SPE.

1942 DME (U.S.) starts supplying standard mold bases.

1942 Dow Corning makes silicone commercially.

1942 Du Pont erects a one-million lb ($\frac{1}{2}$ million kg) plant based on the ICI licensed process.

1942 Patent issued to F. J. Stokes for automatic unscrewing of threaded closures and other threaded parts, making possible a fully automatic machine.

1942 Patent on "Redux", a thermoplastic modified phenol formaldehyde structural adhesive, is issued to Aero Research Ltd; later called Ciba-Geigy.

1942 British patent on cloth-phenolic laminates reinforced with metal granted to N. A. de Bruyne.

1942 Rein (Germany) discovers dimethyl formamide as a solvent for polyacrylonitrile and thus prepares the way for the manufacture of PAN fiber-forming substances. Almost simultaneously Du Pont (U.S.) starts a similar preparation.

1942 The first "wonder pharmaceutical drug", sulfathiazole ointment, is packaged in plastic squeeze tubes.

1943 Patent awarded to W. H. Kopitke of Fernplas Co. for an injection blow molding machine; it was actually a modified injection molding machine with specialized tooling mounted between its platens. Other similar systems are developed by Piotrowski, Moslo, and Farkus offering different advantages. The conventional injection molding machine can be used with these blow molding molds; other designs continue to exist to meet special requirements.

1943 Du Pont started pilot plant production for polytetrafluoroethylene called "Teflon"; full production started 1950.

1943 Swedlow Co. (U.S.) produces the first free blown acrylic aircraft canopy in U.S.

1943 Polyisoprene introduced to U.S.

1943 Polyurethane-polyester amide introduced to England.

1943 Arthur M. Howald of Plaskon working with personnel at Wright-Patterson AFB Materials Laboratory made the first reinforced plastic honeycomb core material (for use in sandwich structures) using large soda straws for the form.

1943 Glass fiber-TS polyester reinforced plastic, using the lost wax process sandwich core, is first conceived, developed, and designed for light airframe structures by the Wright-Patterson AFB Material Laboratory. Different parts are fabricated (1943–1944). Included was the aft fuselage of the two-place Vultee BT-15 basic trainer, complete fuselage, etc. Successful flight tests are conducted; involves 152 landings.

1943 Copper-clad laminates for use in electronics introduced.

1943 Pregwood (plastic-impregnated reinforced wood) used to construct airplane propellors.

1943 Chrysler Corp. develops the "Cycleweld" bonding process, to join aircraft parts.

1944 SPI organizes the Low Pressure Industries Division, later called Reinforced Plastics Division followed with Reinforced Plastics/Composites Division, and now called the Composite Institute (of SPI).

1944 GE Co. introduces bouncing putty (boron-containing silicone).

1944 When Baekeland died, world output of phenolic had exceeded 175,000 tons/yr.

1944 "Eagle Wing" radar antenna, located below B-29 airplane main wing, eroded and was damaged during flights through Pacific rains. Resulted in expediting development of elastomer, rubber-type, rain erosion coatings applied over reinforced plastics radomes and other surfaces.

1944 Reinforced plastic boat hulls introduced by Winner Manufacturing (U.S.)

1944 Polyethylene bottles were given to Plax Corp. salespeople as samples, launching the high volume squeeze-bottle business and helping to develop blow molding; virgin LDPE used.

1944 Improved Machinery Inc. (U.S.) entered the injection molding machinery field with a new vertical clamp, horizontal injection unit; later becomes Impco of Ingersoll-Rand.

1944 G. B. Rheinfrank, W. A. Norman, D. V. Rosato, and others report on the first flight tests for reinforced plastic aircraft fuselage, etc.

1945 Impression molding plastics with dielectric preheating introduced by Bakelite's V. E. Meharg and consultant P. D. Zotter.

1945 L. S. Meyer of Western Plastics made first production RP honeycomb by using soda straws to index corrugated sheets.

1945 Cellulose propionate introduced.

1945 Experimental car body produced under OCF sponsorship.

1946 Waldes Kohinoor Inc. (U.S.) introduces the nylon zipper.

1946 Van Dorn (U.S.) introduces hand-powered commercial injection molding machines.
1946 H. D Justi Co. (U.S.) introduces acrylic dentures.
1946 Earl S. Tupper produces polyethylene tumblers, which was the start of Tupperware Co. (U.S.)
1946 The American Society for Quality Control is formed.
1946 GE Co. starts production of silicone plastics using the Rochow process.
1946 The first National Plastics Exhibition (NPE) sponsored by SPI is held at the Grand Central Palace, New York City with 87,000 visitors.
1946 Chrysler introduces acrylic automobile taillight lenses.
1946 The utility of UV spectroscopy in the study of styrene-butadiene copolymers is demonstrated.
1946 The role of water as a co-catalyst is demonstrated.
1946 U.S. patent application for the first glass fiber spray technique (centrifugal spraying for molding).
1946 Filament winding process patented by R. E. Young.
1946 Organosols and plastisols introduced commercially.
1946 Shaw Insulator Co. molded the first polyethylene hinges; polypropylene hinges are produced later by different companies.
1946 Availability of polyethylene and lay-flat blown tubing developed by Plax Corp. opens up a large market for film packaging.
1946 Wachusett Tools & Dies Co. (U.S.) is formed to make tools and dies for plastics; it helped pioneer the use of beryllium copper for mold cavities.
1947 Irving Muskat develops the first thixotropic plastics at Marco Chemical Co.
1947 O. D. Black and D. Mackey of RCA create the first etched printed circuit.
1947 Goodrich Co. markets nitrile rubber/PVC blends under the tradename "Geon Polyblend".
1947 Vinyl silicone coupling agent for glass fibers presented in U.S. patent; improves glass-plastic bond.
1947 Roger Steele of Hexcel makes the first production of RP honeycomb using bonded stack expansion process.
1947 Copper-clad materials for commercial use developed by Synthane Co. (U.S.)
1948 Roger White and Larry Scidel of Glastic Corp. make and mold the first RP premix.
1948 Process for extruding polyethylene onto paper is developed by Du Pont. Widespread knowledge of this type of application did not come until 1953.
1948 Reifenhauser (Germany) builds first film production lines; early line output is 25 kg/hr.
1948 B. F. Goodrich Chemical Co. introduces modified acrylic elastomers ("Hycar PA" and "Hycar PA-21").
1948 Reinforced plastic injection molded toilet seats are introduced by Church Seat Co. (U.S.)
1949 Winchester Model 59 automatic shot gun incorporates a glass fiber plastic filament wound barrel.
1949 Screw plastication with automatic transfer molding developed by brothers Martin and Clyde Keaton (U.S.) using a nonreciprocating screw.
1949 Molded Resin Fiber Co. (U.S.) receives the first mass production contract in using matched metal compression hydraulic molds producing 1,000 RP trays/day.
1949 "Lupersol DDM", the first commercial methyl ethyl ketone peroxide, is introduced by Lucidol (U.S.)
1949 Crucible Steel Corp. patented "Formold"; a steel used to produce molds for compression molding.
1949 Allylic plastics introduced.
1949 Vinyl ether developments occur.
1950 Kautex Werke (Germany) introduces the first commercially available blow molding equipment. The design uses a rising mold technique with continuously extruded open end parison.
1950 E. E. Mills (U.S.) granted patent for high output continuous extrusion rotary blow molder. The design is used privately by Continental Can Co. Other wheel designs follow quickly by H. S. Ruekberg and C. C. Coats.
1950 Commercialization of ABS advances due to innovations by Borg-Warner (becomes part of GE Co.)
1950 First commercial production in U.S. of acrylic fibers by Du Pont.
1950 Paper is extrusion coated for the first time by St. Regis Paper Co. in Oswego, NY based on pioneering work by Du Pont.
1950 The invention of the hula hoop during the 1950's made of extruded polyethylene pushed extruders to their limits of capacities and created a surge in demand for PE (U.S.)

1950 Wheaton Glass Co. initiates development in injection blow molding containers smaller than 1 qt.

1950 Herman Miller introduces the polyester-glass fiber reinforced plastic "shell chair" designed by Charles Eames (U.S.)

1950 Chlorosulfonated polyethylene ("Hypalon") introduced by Du Pont.

1950 First large scale production started of "Teflon" (PTFE) by Du Pont.

1950 Epoxy plastics synthesized.

1950 Triallyl cyanurate (TAC), first basic patent by Kropa, is granted to American Cyanamid Co.; used to produce heat resistant RP molded parts.

1950 The New York Boat Show exhibits 22 glass fiber-TS polyester reinforced plastic boats.

1950 Due to the unique fatigue characteristics of RP, the development of RP helicopter and aircraft blades are emphasized by Bell Aircraft, Kaman Aircraft, Curtiss-Wright, Hamilton Standard, etc.

1950 Plax BNR injection blow molding machine first produces widemouth bottles for cold cream jars.

1950 Plax Corp. becomes part of Monsanto after a brief period with Owens-Illinois.

1950 Hoechst (Germany) manufactures polychlorotrifluoroethylene on an industrial scale.

1950 Germany starts production of unsaturated polyesters.

1950 Ziegler (Germany) and Natta (Italy) discover that ethylene can be polymerized to high molecular weight at atmospheric pressure when dissolved in a hydrocarbon and passed over a coordination catalyst.

1951 William H. Willert (U.S.) invents an inline reciprocating screw plasticizer for injection molding machines (patent issued 1956). However industry did not accept it until 1962. It revolutionized injection molding.

1951 High molecular weight PVC homopolymer introduced for better impact strength in rigid applications.

1951 Kaiser-Darrin (U.S.) introduces the first hand lay-up RP sports car body.

1951 Ferro, PPG, LOF, and Gustan-Bacon are all granted licenses by Owens-Corning Fiberglass to produce glass fibers.

1951 First chrome complex patent issued to R. K. Iier of Du Pont; basis for "Volan" glass fiber finishes.

1951 International Standards Organization establishes a technical committee on plastics (ISTO/TC61).

1951 L. Meyer and A. Hwell (U.S.) granted first pultrusion patent (for fishing rods).

1952 Du Pont commercializes oriented polyethylene terephthalate (PET) film.

1952 Owens-Corning Fiberglass goes public with 1.5M shares.

1952 RP storage tanks production expands worldwide.

1952 Translucent RP corrugated construction panels produced commercially.

1952 Demand for polyethylene increased to such a degree that PE licensing policies are broadened by court order; result of anti-trust judgements in U.S. courts against ICI and Du Pont.

1953 General Motors working with Morrison Molded Fiberglass Products Co. launched an exploratory program with its Chevrolet Corvette all RP (glass-TS polyester) body. In the first year, 300 were produced using vacuum bag molding techniques.

1953 Radiation crosslinking using gamma radiation (Cobalt 60) coverts thermoplastics to thermosets.

1953 Mobil Plastics Division of Carlyle Corp. introduces the first preimpregnated roving (glass-TS polyester).

1953 Discovery of high density polyethylene by Phillips (U.S.) and Ziegler (Germany).

1953 Polymerization of propylene and butylene by Professor Natta (Italy) using the Ziegler techniques.

1953 Phillips (U.S.), Standard Oil of Indiana (U.S.) and Ziegler (Germany) discover low pressure polymerization processes for ethylene.

1953 Natta (Italy) and Ziegler (Germany) achieve stereospecific polymerization of higher α-olefins.

1953 Staudinger receives Nobel prize for his work on macromolecules.

1953 Ziegler (Germany) made polyethylene using organo-metallic catalyst.

1954 Martin Industries' first cam-actuated Grabber automatic sprue remover is installed in an injection molding machine at Carr Fasteners (U.S.)

1954 Mobay (later called Miles Inc.) introduces polyurethane to U.S.

1954 High density polyethylene makes its appearance using the new method of stereospecific polymerization based on Ziegler-Natta process.

1954 D. V. Rosato, as a board member of the Reinforced Plastics Division of SPI, introduced the idea of expanding the Division's name to Reinforced Plastics/Composites Division in order to include RPs other than the predominant industry use of glass fiber-TS polyester. New name is approved; at that time glass-polyester represented most of the material used and today it is over 80%.

1954 Guillo Natta (Italy) worked on the polymerization of propylene by the Karl Ziegler process; resulted in a highly crystalline portion of the polymer being isolated. These polymers were assigned a stereoregular structure for which the designation "isotactic" is proposed.

1954 Eastman Chemical Products is the third LDPE manufacturer in U.S.

1954 ATT (U.S.) approved use of PE coated wires for the first transatlantic telephone cable to Europe.

1955 Early ablation studies on reentry from outer space flight tests illustrated the outstanding characteristics of glass fiber-phenolic and asbestos-phenolic moldings.

1955 Soltes and Abbot developed processes for converting both natural cellulose and rayon into fibrous carbon. Essentially the carbon fibers are produced by heat treating the precursors to temperatures on the order of 1,000°C (1,832°F) in inert atmosphere. Fiber tensile strengths are as high as 40 ksi (275 MPa).

1955 Hoechst (Germany) is first to start large-scale production of HDPE by the Ziegler process.

1955 Taylor Craft Model 20 airplane uses RP wings, engine cowlings, doors, seats, fuel tanks, instrument panels, and fuselage skins from nose to fin trailing edges.

1955 Realistic multilayer blow molding machinery and process patented by Owens-Illinois.

1955 Polyisoprene, the synthetic part of natural rubber, is polymerized using the Ziegler-Natta type stereospecific catalyst system; first commercial application started in 1959.

1955 Kautex (Germany) ships automatic blow molder to U.S.

1955 GE Co. introduces polycarbonate.

1955 Phillips Petroleum Co. discloses its new process of polymerizing ethylene under low pressure.

1956 Epoxy-glass fiber RPs are widely adopted for printed circuit boards.

1956 Commercial production begins of HDPE by Hoechst (Germany) and Phillips (U.S.)

1956 William H. Willert's patent is issued for the first reciprocating screw plasticator for injection molding machines.

1956 Kapany coins the phrase "fiber optics".

1956 Stanley J. Kaminsky develops high-speed tools for an electric hand-held hot-air gun that is the beginning of plastics welding via the Kamweld Products Co. technique.

1956 John C. Reib starts Conair Inc. with a first self-powered vacuum hooper loader and automatic coloring loader.

1956 The National Assoc. of Home Builders (NAHB), Research Foundation, Washington, DC has 5 research houses that include plastic products of all types and forms.

1956 Schnell (Germany) is successful in preparing technically processable polyesters of carbonic acid (polycarbonate); already known as early as 1898 (Einhorn, Germany).

1956 Hercules (U.S.) introduces chlorinated polyether "Penton".

1957 Disneyland's House of Tomorrow (California) opens to the public. This relatively all plastic house was created by Monsanto and designed by MIT; basic structure uses cantilever beam construction.

1957 Hoechst (Germany) is the first to manufacture polypropylene in bulk production.

1957 During the Milan Exhibition (Italy) a considerable amount of attention is drawn to an Italian all-plastic house designed by the architect Cesare Pea; consisted of prefabricated RP box structures that could be joined in a variety of ways to form different shapes and sizes of house.

1957 With the introduction of HDPE, blow molding is greatly expanded by opening up such markets as bleach, detergents, milk, and other filled bottles.

1957 Loma Industries molds the first 20 gal trash container (U.S.), using a 60 oz capacity injection molding machine.

1957 Dow Chemical commercializes thin polystyrene films (0.0008 to 0.010 in.) in U.S. as replacement for cellophane and cellulose acetate film uses.

1957 The first commercial acrylic processing aid introduced by Rohm & Hass (U.S.)

significantly aids the processing of vinyl compounds.

1957 RP luggage introduced.

1957 Hercules Inc. is the first producer of HDPE and UHMWPE in U.S. via the Ziegler process.

1957 A. Keller of the University of Bristol (England) announced a new concept of crystallinity and crystallization. Single crystal-like thin flakes of PE showed a regular rhombohedral shape and gave perfect crystal patterns in X-ray and electron deflection.

1958 Monsanto blow molds an experimental Coca-Cola bottle, forerunner of an avalanche of containers to appear in the 1970's. These bottles used Du Pont's biaxially stretched oriented injection blow molding process with acrylonitrile; unfortunately the U.S. government later outlawed use of AN (and still later it was reinstated). This process technology is later adopted with PET plastics.

1958 First commercial blow molded package for liquid aromatics (Europe).

1958 First HDPE blow molded commercial package; a 16 fl oz cylindrical bottle for Breck Shampoo with liquid detergent bottles quickly followed (U.S.).

1958 Commercial blow molding equipment displayed for the first time at the National Plastics Exhibition (Chicago). Two machines, both European, utilize the continuous extrusion process and HDPE is the plastic of choice.

1958 Willard Sutton of GE Co. makes sapphire whiskers for experimental use in metal and plastic composites.

1958 Graphite fibers commercially produced from rayon.

1958 German architect Rudolph Doernach displays at the Stuttgart Plastics Exhibition a prefabricated plastic house. It uses double curved segments consisting of plastic foam core covered with thin aluminum skins. The structure is supported at four corners only and is meant to be a small weekend country house.

1958 Piper Aircraft started investigating RP for primary structures. First plane flew in 1962.

1958 In U.S., 90% of all fishing rods are of RP.

1958 Texaco Inc. reports on the high strength and stiffness of boran fibers. Fibers are produced by chemical vapor deposition.

1959 Union Carbide begins production of carbon cloths, felts, yarns, and battings using rayon fibers as the precursor material. Carbon fibers were batch processed by heat treating the rayon in an inert atmosphere at about 900°C (1652°F), subsequently carbonizing the fibers at temperatures generally over 2.500°C (4,532°f). Tensile strengths of fibers are 48 to 130 Ksi (300 to 900 MPa).

1959 Celanese's "Celcon" acetal copolymer developed by Frank Brown and Frank Bernardinelliit.

1959 Du Pont's "Delrin" acetal homopolymer introduced.

1959 Mattel Inc. introduces the sales record-breaking plastic "Barbie Doll".

1959 B. F. Goodrich introduces to U.S. "Estane TP" polyurethane.

1960 For the first time, blow molding becomes a major topic of discussion in the U.S. at the 16th Annual Technical Conference (ANTEC) of SPE.

1960 Dow Smith Co. begins production of filament wound pressure pipe.

1960 Ethylene vinyl acetate copolymers introduced by Du Pont Co.

1960 Borg-Warner builds the "Formacar", a prototype thermoplastic car with the body underbody, and most components thermoformed from ABS. This car carried the basic styling lines of many cars on the road today.

1960 Over 55 companies, the majority European, are recognized as suppliers and manufacturers of blow molding equipment. Many of these were unknown a year earlier. By 1990, about six of the original firms exist.

1960 The Organization of Petroleum Exporting Countries (OPEC) founded by Iran, Iraq, Kuwait, Saudi Arabia, and Venezuela; membership later grows to 13 major countries.

1960 Dow Chemical Co. builds the (Leo) Windecker RP airplane. This glass fiber-epoxy plane has a monoque fuselage.

1960 The U.S. Department of Defense establishes the Plastics Technical Evaluation Center (PLASTEC), a centralized source of evaluated technical information on plastics, reinforced plastics, and adhesives.

1960 S-glass fiber developed with its improved properties compared to glass fibers, etc.

1961 Horizontal indexing system for blow molding is patented by Gussoni (Italy). This system is basically used today. Wheaton Ind. (U.S.) also is credited with developing a similar system, but did not file for patent at that time. It had acquired the rights to a Swiss process called "Novaplast" in the early 1950's which resulted in developing its own systems (only used in its plants).

1961 Plastics Institute of America (PIA) chartered.

1961 The "Glasshopper" railway tank car is fabricated from RP by Black, Sivalls & Bryson Inc. (U.S.) using glass fiber-epoxy filament wound. It is 55 ft (17 m) long by 9 ft (3 m) diameter.

1961 Gatto Machinery (U.S.) pioneers large pipe pullers used in extrusion lines.

1961 Vinylidene fluoride introduced commercially.

1961 U.S. FHA insures loans on homes equipped with ABS drain, waste, and vent pipe (DWV).

1962 Robert D. Shad, founder of Husky Injection Molding Systems Inc. (Canada), seized the opportunity for plastics to score big in the emerging vending cup market and applied his skills to designing molds that significantly increased production outputs, thereby lowering plastic cup prices. Unfortunately at that time he did not find an injection molding machine capable of keeping up with his molds. Thus, he built his own and also entered the business of manufacturing machines.

1962 Shell Chemical Co. (U.S.) begins a vast program promoting HDPE bottles for milk.

1962 Simplex (France) introduces bicycles using acetal gear changer.

1962 Du Pont introduces polyimide; provides thermal endurance of thermoplastic to 400°C (750°F).

1962 Pennwalt Co. introduces polyvinylidene.

1962 Phillips introduces styrene-butadiene block copolymer.

1962 B. F. Goodrich develops oxychlorination method for making vinyl monomer from ethylene.

1962 Polyallomers introduced by Eastman Chemical.

1962 Union Carbide produces aromatized polyether "Phenoxy".

1963 E. Leith and J. Upatnicks (Univ. of Michigan) produce the first 3-dimensional laser transmission holograms.

1963 P. T. Shurman presents to industry new ideas on double-wall blow molding.

1963 Du Pont Co. introduces ionomer.

1963 F. J. Stokes Co. introduces the "Injectoset", a 50-ton fully automatic transfer molding machine with a reciprocating screw plasticator.

1963 R. G. Angell of Union Carbide introduces a low-pressure structural-foam processing technique.

1963 F. H. Lambert develops a process for molding expandable polystyrene (EPS) foam products.

1964 Melville Dairy (U.S.) becomes the first to blow mold HDPE bottles in-house for packaging fluid milk; supplied by W. R. Grace & Co. By the 1980's virtually all plastic milk bottles are made in-house using Uniloy equipment with HDPE.

1964 First book on filament winding (D. V. Rosato) is published by Wiley; also published in Russian by USSR (1969).

1964 British designers Gibbs & Cox started a feasibility study on a 300 ft (92 m) mine sweeper of RP, which later became a reality.

1964 Holiday Inn motel units present an application for large-scale prefabrication using glass fiber-TS polyester RP units of four rooms. They are fabricated including utilities and plumbing.

1964 Formation of the ABS Council (U.S.) represents the basic material suppliers and manufacturers of ABS pipe and fittings. Specific purpose is to permit use of ABS drainage pipe with code revision.

1964 GE Co. introduces polyphenylene oxide (PPO).

1965 First CAD/CAE system is developed.

1965 Nataniel Wyeth of Du Pont Co., after a decade of development of the proper plastic and process, produces plastic beverage bottles. Patent prepared is issued 1973; stretched injection blow molding with poly-ethylene terephthalate (PET) is used.

1965 Union Carbide introduces polysulfone.

1965 U.S. walks in space with RP helmets, filament wound control gun, plastic survival kit, etc.

1965 Du Pont's "Corfam", a polyester reinforced polyurethane, goes into volume production for shoes. This $100 million venture is abandoned in 1971 (sold).

1965 Parylene introduced commercially by Union Carbide.

1965 Owens-Corning Fiberglass begins construction of RP underground gasoline tanks. OCF also introduces shipable forming package (type 30) for filament winding, pultrusion, and weaving.

1966 Metal Tube Packaging Council of North America founded; later (1970) called The Tube Council of North America since tube materials expanded to different types, particularly plastics alone or in laminated form with other materials.

1966 First Uniloy completely automatic machine for the production of HDPE extrusion blow molding milk bottles installed at the Heatherwood Dairy (U.S.)

1966 Plastic fiber optics introduced.

1966 Dome shaped medical clinic buildings built (Lafayette, IN) using polystyrene foam boards by Dow Chemical that were processed on-site using DCs "spiral generation" technique. Boards were heat-bonded in a continuous pattern. Domes were self supporting requiring no internal or external support during or after manufacture. Sections are cut out from the domes that are made into door openings, connecting halls going from one dome to another, etc. Different size domes are used.

1966 Shell Chemical introduces "Kraton", a styrenic TPE which gains wide use in pressure-sensitive adhesives and footware.

1966 Introduction of glass fiber belted bias car tire by Armstrong Rubber Co.; principal supplier to Sears.

1967 The Windecker all-RP airplane, after seven years of development, is successfully flight tested.

1967 Bob Seagren breaks world pole vault record with 17 ft, 9 in. (5.4 m) using an RP pole.

1967 Dow Chemical patented "black box" that is made commercially available. It fed proportional amounts of chopped glass fiber and plastics into an injection molding machine where the screw provided the mixing and blending.

1967 ICI (England) introduces poly-4-methylpentene-1.

1968 Owens-Illinois produces a hollow-handled PVC liquor bottle for American Distilling Co. In Europe PVC is a far more popular blow molding plastic, having been used successfully for several years for water and table wine applications. Because of U.S. government concerns, the PVC bottle is later removed from the market. The plastic liquor bottle does not return in U.S. until early 1980's, as a biaxially oriented PET container.

1968 First major book on the broad subject of environmental effects on plastics commercially published by Wiley & Sons (by D. V. Rosato and R. T. Schwartz; titled *Environmental Effects on Polymeric Materials*, Vol. I: Environments and Vol. II: Materials; 2,216 pages).

1968 Sterling Extruder introduces the "Transfermix"; extruder combines the functions of intensive mixing and extrusion.

1968 Union Carbide's low pressure process "Unipol" is developed, making possible improved polymers, such as large volume utilization of linear low density polyethylene.

1968 Boeing's SST includes use of over 6,000 lb (2,700 kg) of RP and over 6,000 lb of unreinforced plastics.

1968 Martin Ind. (U.S.) introduces its mold protector, a device that prevents damage to injection molds.

1969 Leading brassiere manufacturer replaces metal underwire with RP.

1970 In the booming history of plastics, it is difficult to find another development that captured the market as quickly as the biaxially oriented plastic bottle for carbonated beverages. By the late 1970's, just three years after the plastic bottles went into production, glass bottles almost totally left the supermarket shelves, particularly the larger sizes.

Originally two technologies, based on two glass-clear plastics, were contending for the market; Du Pont's PET and Monsanto's methacrylonitrile/styrene (AN). Though the AN bottle reached the market earlier, it was withdrawn from sale in 1977 when the FDA declined to approve its use in carbonated beverage applications.

1970 Coca-Cola test markets the world's first plastic carbonated beverage bottle, an AN bottle by Monsanto.

1970 Du Pont produces an experimental beverage bottle from biaxially oriented PET plastics. Du Pont receives patent in 1973.

1970 Du Pont introd''ces "Kevlar" aramid fibers.

1970 First (U.S.) blow molded bottles for edible oils are made of PVC.

1970 The first commercial plant using Union Carbide's "Unipol" process to produce HDPE is in Sweden.

1970 Ingersoll-Rand designs and builds for GE Co. the "Trak" injection molding system where 12 or more clamped presses continuously operate and move in a "circle" on simulated railroad tracks.

1970 Farbwerke Hoechst AG (Germany) introduces polybutylene terephthalate "Hostadur".
1971 SPI Reinforced Plastics/Composites Division changed its name to Reinforced Plastics/Composites Institute.
1971 3M Co. (U.S.) produces polyaryl sulphone "Astrel".
1971 Phillips introduces polyphenylene sulphide "Ryton".
1971 Uniroyal introduces polyaryl ether "Arylon T".
1972 Toyo Seikan (Japan) develops basic multilayer bottle from polypropylene and ethylenevinyl alcohol for food product applications.
1972 ICI (England) introduces polyethersulfone.
1972 Du Pont produces ethylene/tetrafluoroethylene copolymer "Tefzel".
1972 Bayer AG (Germany) develops polyhydantoins, known for some time as wire enamels and for cast film manufacture.
1972 Plastic Hall of Fame located in Leominster, MA, is established; in 1976 it is renamed the National Plastics Museum (NPM).
1973 Volume production of plastics surpasses that of steel worldwide; estimate plastics weight will surpass steel at the end of the 20th century.
1973 Oil shock occurs; an Arab embargo sends oil prices through the "roof" and plunges the world into a recession.
1973 All glass fiber-TS polyester RP bathrooms mass produced.
1973 Dynamit Nobel (Germany) introduces polyvinylidenefluoride "Dyflon".
1973 Du Pont receives patent for the PET biaxially oriented injection blow molding bottle technique.
1974 Monsanto receives full clearance when a patented post mold treatment is used to bind all residual monomer in the biaxially oriented acrylonitrile/styrene beverage bottle.
1974 First of reaction injection molded (RIM) fascia debuts on the Pontiac line.
1975 Cincinnati Milacron (U.S.) and Gildamister Corpoplast-Krupp (Germany) begin to offer commercial blow molding equipment for biaxially oriented PET plastics. The equipment is based on the two-step process, in which the preform and bottle are produced on separate machines in separate operations.
1975 Nitrile barrier plastics are introduced to non-food packaging.
1975 Union Carbide started in U.S. commercial production of LLDPE using its "Unipol" process.
1976 Barber-Colman (U.S.) introduces a truly integrated injection molding machine control system.
1976 First PET beverage bottles for a commercial filling application molded by Amoco for Pepsi-Cola.
1976 William P. Lear designs and builds the all-reinforced plastics Lear Fan jet.
1976 Plastic microwave cookware introduced to the consumer market.
1977 Nissei, ASB (Japan) begins to offer biaxial orientation PET blow molding equipment based on the one-step process, in which the preform and bottle are produced on the same machine.
1978 Union Carbide and Dow Chemical (independently) make significant commercial breakthroughs on LLDPE, greatly advancing the economics of blown film.
1978 The first plastic (PE) pail for latex paint is produced jointly by Hercules and Reed-Prentice.
1978 Goodyear has a two-piece man's suit and matching tie made from recycled 2-liter PET bottle. In 1990 it was donated to the new Ripley's Believe It or Not Museum in Wisconsin Dells, WI.
1979 Oil shock occurs; Iran, a major oil producer, is rocked by revolution. Price of oil soars worldwide; gas lines form in U.S., etc.
1979 ICI introduces polyetheretherketone.
1979 Using HMW-HDPE imported from South Africa, Sonoco (U.S.) test markets the "T-shirt" style plastic grocery bag; becomes very successful.
1980 Lubin and Donohue of Grumman (U.S.) publishes data on "real life testing of RP in aircraft". It shows almost no degradation in performance based on testing different parts in service for up to 20 years.
1980 Extensive use of radiation to sterilize disposable plastic medical devices inaugurates a new market for plastics.
1980 PET carbonated beverage bottles go from virtually nil in 1976 to 2.5 billion in 1980.
1980 Oil shock occurs; Iraq invades Iran, launches eight-year war. OPEC produces record 31 million barrels of oil/day; consumers demand more.
1981 Monsanto Co's introduction of "Santoprene" olefinic that is the first dynamically vulcanized TPE to be marketed, set the stage for more rapid expansion of TPE usage.

1982 Bayer AG (Germany) researchers working in Europe with the developers of compact audio disks, introduce high-purity polycarbonate for manufacture of CDs.

1982 GE Co. introduces polyetherimide.

1982 Dr. Robert Jarvik from the Univ. of Utah designs the Jarvik-7 artificial heart, made largely of plastics and principally of polyurethane.

1983 Use of microwave ovens opens a new era of plastic packaging innovations. Eastman and Goodyear are among the innovators for dual-ovenable trays.

1983 American Can introduces the first coextruded polypropylene copolymer and ethylene vinyl alcohol 28 oz bottle which is used by H. J. Heinz; thus the ketchup squeezable bottle. In 1991, Heinz converted to the more environmentally friendly PET/EVOH bottle.

1983 FCC (U.S.) regulations require the shielding of plastic-housed electronics components, which adds more development of conductive plastics for computer housings, electronic medical housings, etc.

1983 Thermoplastic elastomer (TPE) consumption in U.S. exceeds 325 million lb (148 million kg) annually, while worldwide usage is at one billion lb (0.45 billion kg).

1984 Historical first for SPE: the first Fellows of the Society are elected—E. S. Clark, R. E. Elby, K. T. Mehta, D. V. Rosato, V. V. Wenskus, and H. L. Williams.

1984 The first plastic fuel tank in a U.S. passenger car is blow molded by Bronson using Phillip's HDPE followed with Dow Chemical's sulfonation process to restrict/control gas permeability. These tanks were previously used in Europe, U.S military vehicles since the 1950's, etc.

1984 Quaker State Oil (U.S.) moved to HDPE blow molded bottles for its entire motor-oil line.

1985 Hot-filled PET with no barrier plastic is used with fruit beverage bottles commercially.

1985 Du Pont begins marketing "Alcryn" melt-processable rubber (MPR).

1986 Cincinnati Milacron redesigns its toggle type injection molding machines; cuts part production costs 40%.

1987 3D Systems (U.S.) introduces stereolithography.

1989 First worldwide book on blow molding published by Hanser (by D. V. Rosato); includes the complete and different methods used, performance materialwise, markets, and economics.

1990 Oil shock occurs; Iraq invades Kuwait and price of barrel of oil doubles; highest price in a decade.

1990 Eastman Chemical Co., as well as Goodyear Tire & Rubber Co., successfully recycle post-consumer PET bottles into monomers that are pure and can be successfully acceptable in food packaging.

1990 The combined capacity of Union Carbide's "Unipol" reactors in operation around the world is sufficient to supply 25% of the world's total demand of polyethylene.

REFERENCES

1 Rosato, D. V. et al, *Designing With Plastics and Composites: A Handbook*, Van Nostrand Reinhold, 1991.

2 Rosato, D. V. and D. V. Rosato, *Blow Molding Handbook*, Hanser, 1989.

3 Rosato, D. V., *Environmental Effects on Polymeric Materials*, Vol. 1.: Environment and Vol. 2: Materials, Wiley, 1968.

4 Rosato, D. V., Designing With Plastics, Rhode Island School of Design, Lectures 1987–1990.

5 Rosato, D. V., Product Design: Basic Processing Guide For Plastics, SPE ANTEC, pp. 1646–1650, May 1989.

6 Rosato, D. V., Advanced Designing With Plastics, Univ. of Lowell Seminars, 1986.

7 Rosato, D. V., Advanced Engineering Design—Short Course, ASME Engr. Conf., 1983.

8 Rosato, D. V., "Designing With Plastics", *MD&DI*, July 1983, pp. 26–29.

9 Rosato, D. V. and D. V. Rosato, *Plastics Processing Data Handbook*, Van Nostrand Reinhold, 1990.

10 Rosato, D. V. and D. V. Rosato, *Injection Molding Handbook*, Van Nostrand Reinhold, 1986.

11 Rosato, D. V., *Filament Winding*, Wiley, 1964.

12 Rosato, D. V., W. K. Fallo, and D. V. Rosato, *Markets For Plastics*, Van Nostrand Reinhold, 1969.

13 Rosato, D. V., "Weighing Out The Aircraft Market", *PW*, Aug./Sep. 1967.

14 Rosato, D. V. Capt., All Plastic Military Airplane Successfully Flight Tested, Wright-Patterson AF Base, Ohio, 1944.

15 Rosato, D. V., Outer Space Parabolic Reflector Energy Converters, SAMPE, June 1963.

16 Rosato, D. V., "Materials Selection" in *Encyclopedia of Polymer Science and Engr.*, Mark-Bikales-Overberger-Menges (eds.): Vol. 9, pp. 357–379, Wiley, 1987.

17 Rosato, D. V., "Thermosets" in *Encyclopedia of Polymer Science and Engr.*, Mark et al (eds.), Vol. 14, pp. 350–391, Wiley, 1988.

18 Rosato, D. V., "Polymers, Processes and Properties of Medical Plastics—Include Applications" in *Synthetic Biomedical Polymers*, Szycher-Robinson (eds.), Technomics, 1980.

19 Rosato, D. V., "Electrical Wire and Cable Plastic Coating—What's Ahead?", *Wire and Wire Products*, Mar. 1970, pp. 49–61.

20 Rosato, D. V., "Materials Selection, Polymeric Matrix Composites" in *International Encyclopedia of Composites*, Vol. 3, S. M. Lee (ed.), VCH, 1991.

21 Rosato, D. V., "Why Not Use Metal Wire In Filament Winding?", *The Iron Age*, Mar. 26, 1964.

22 Rosato, D. V., "Nose Cone Of First US Moon Vanguard Rocket Is Made In Manheim-US", *New Era-Lancaster PA Newspaper*, Nov. 30, 1957.

23 Dorgham, M. A. and D. V. Rosato, *Designing With Plastics Composites*, Underscience Enterprises, Ltd., World Trade Center Bldg., 110 Avenue Louis Casai, Case Postale 306, CH-1215, Geneva-Aeroport, Switzerland, 1986.

24 Rosato, D. V., "What To Consider in Picking An Injection Molding Machine", *Plastics Today*, Jan. 1989.

25 Rosato, D. V., Injection Molding Thermosets, SPI Reinforced Plastics/ Composites Annual Meeting Seminar, Jan. 1985.

26 Rosato, D. V., Extrusion: Technology, Markets, Economics Seminar, University of Lowell, 1987.

27 Rosato, D. V., "Choosing The Blow Molding Machines To Meet Product Demand", *Plastics Today*, Jan. 1989.

28 Rosato, D. V., Reinforced Plastics/Composites Seminar, University of Lowell, 1986.

29 Du Bois, J. H. and D. V. Rosato, "From Laminates to Composites", *PW*, Apr. 1968.

30 Rosato, D. V., "Non-Woven Fibers in Reinforced Plastics", *Ind. Engr. Chem.*, *54*, 8, 30–37 (Sep. 1962).
31 Milewski, J. M. and D. V. Rosato, The History of Reinforced Plastics, ACS Annual Conf., March 19, 1980.
32 Rosato, D. V., *Asbestos*, Van Nostrand Reinhold, 1959.
33 Lubin, G. and D. V. Rosato, Application Of Reinforced Plastics, 4th International RP Conference, British Plastics Federation, London, UK, Nov. 25–27, 1964.
34 Schwartz, R. T. and D. V. Rosato, "Structural Sandwich Construction" in *Composite Engr. Materials*, Dietz, A. G. H. (ed.), pp. 165–181, MIT Press, 1969.
35 Rosato, D. V., Testing and Statistical Quality Control, Univ. of Lowell Seminar, 1986.
36 Rosato, D. V. and J. R. Lawrence, *Plastics Industry Safety Handbook*, Cahners, 1973
37 Rosato, D. V., "25 Years of Polyethylene", *PW*, Jan. 1967.
38 Rosato, D. V. Capt., Theoretical Potential For Polyethylene, US-British Correspondence, US AF Materials Lab., Wright-Patterson Air Force Base, 1944.
39 Rosato, D. V., "Insulation News", *Wire and Wire Products*, Nov. 1970.
40 Rosato, D. V., "Wire and Wire Products—Insulation News", *Wire and Wire Products*, Dec. 1970.
41 Rosato, D. V., Design Features That Influence Performance: Detractors/Constraints, SPE-ANTEC, May 1991.
42 Rosato, D. V., "Materials Selection" in *Concise Encyclopedia of Polymer Science and Engineering*, J. I. Kroschwitz (ed.), Wiley, 1990.
43 Rosato, D. V., "Reinforced Plastics: Thermosets" in *Concise Encyclopedia of Polymer Science and Engineering*, J. I. Kroschwitz (ed.), Wiley, 1990.
44 Rosato, D. V., Product Design—Plastics Selection Guide, SPE-ANTEC, May 1990.
45 Rosato, D. V., Current and Future Trends in the Use of Plastics for Blow Molding, SME, Tech. Paper MS90–198, Jun. 1990.
46 Rosato, D. V., "Plastics and Solid Waste", *RISD*, Oct. 1989.
47 Rosato, D. V., Injection Molding Technology: Economics and Markets, SPE-ANTEC, May, 1988.
48 Rosato, D. V., Plastics Replaced Aorta Permits Living Normal Long Life, Newton-Wellesley Hospital, Mar. 1987.
49 Rosato, D. V., "Role of Additives in Plastics: Function of Processing Aids", *SPE-IMD Newsletter*, Nov. 1987.
50 Rosato, D. V., Blow Molding Expanding Technologywise and Marketingwise, SPE-ANTEC, May 1987.
51 Rosato, D. V., "History-Injection Molding Machine and Reciprocating Screw Plasticizer", *APE-IMD Newsletter*, Issue No. 15, 1987.
52 Rosato, D. V., Optimize Performance of Injection Molding Machine: Interrelate Machines/Mold/Material Performance, SPE-ANTEC, May 1986.
53 Rosato, D. V., Seminars on 21 Different Plastics Subjects from Introduction, through Design Parts, Fabrication, Quality Control and Statistical Control, Marketing via University of Lowell, Plastics World, ASME, General Motors Institute, SPE, SPI, China National Chemical Construction (Beijing), Hong Kong Production Centre, Singapore Institution, Open University of England, and Tufts Medical University, Presented Worldwide, 1974 to 1986.
54 Rosato, D. V., "Polymer Resistance to Hot Water and Steam Sterilization", *MD&DI*, July 1985.
55 Rosato, D. V., Industrial Plastics in Materials Handling, International Management Society, Oct. 1985.
56 Rosato, D. V., Plastics Industry Scenes, Plastics Monthly Editorial, *PW*, 1974–1979.
57 Rosato, D. V., "Major US Plastics Processing Plants—1979" (first issue which is updated annually), *PW*, Jan. 1979.
58 Rosato, D. V., "Plastics in Appliances", *PW*, Feb. 1979.
59 Rosato, D. V., "Materials Handling Systems", *PW*, Apr. 1979.
60 Rosato. D. V., "Extrusion Productivity", *PW*, May 1979.
61 Rosato, D. V., "Wealth of Choices: Fasteners for Plastics", June 1979.
62 Rosato, D. V., "Technology Trends in PVC Calendering", *PW*, July 1979.
63 Rosato, D. V., "Changing Economics of Plastic Buying", *PW*, Oct. 1979.
64 Rosato, D. V., "New Technology in Coextrusion Blow Molding", *PW*, Nov. 1979.
65 Rosato, D. V., "What Molders Must Do About ANSI Safety Specifications", *PW*, Apr. 1978.
66 Rosato, D. V., "Energy Conservation in Buildings Through Plastics", *PW*, Aug. 1978.
67 Rosato, D. V., "Quality Control", *PW*, Sep. 1978.

68 Rosato, D. V., "Injection Molding Machines: Cost/Performance Keep Improving", *PW*, Oct. 1978.
69 Rosato, D. V., "Process Controls", *PW*, Dec. 1978.
70 Rosato, D. V., "New Developments in Sheet Extrusion", *PW*, Jan. 1977.
71 Rosato, D. V., "Vented Barrels", *PW*, Apr. 1977.
72 Rosato, D. V., "Fatigue Testing", *PW*, May 1977.
73 Rosato, D. V., "Uniform Resin Coding", *PW*, May 1977.
74 Rosato, D. V., "Glass-Filled Resin Powders", *PW*, June 1977.
75 Rosato, D. V., "Bulk Resin Handling", *PW*, June 1977.
76 Rosato, D. V., "Plastics In Packaging", *PW*, June 1977.
77 Rosato, D. V., "The DMC-12 Car", *PW*, Sep. 1977.
78 Rosato, D. V., "Machine Replacement", *PW*, Oct. 1977.
79 Rosato, D. V., "What's New in Polymer Processing", *PW*, Oct. 1977.
80 Rosato, D. V., "Cost Reduction", *PW*, Dec. 1977.
81 Rosato, D. V., "Packaging Market: More Coverage For Plastics", *PW*, Feb. 1976.
82 Rosato, D. V., "New Developments Pave The Way For Plastics Pipe", *PW*, Apr. 1976.
83 Rosato, D. V., "Additives For Design Properties", *PW*, Jul. 1976.
84 Rosato, D. V., "Revolution In Compounding Systems", *PW*, Jul. 1976.
85 Rosato, D. V., "Extruding The Tough Ones", *PW*, Aug. 1976.
86 Rosato, D. V., "Better Parts Handling Spells Bigger Profits", *PW*, Oct. 1976.
87 Rosato, D. V., "New Roadmaps to Plastics Markets", *PW*, Oct. 1976.
88 Rosato, D. V., "Processing Methods", *PW*, Nov. 1976.
89 Rosato, D. V., "Buildings Market", *PW*, Nov. 1976.
90 Rosato, D. V., "PVC: What's Happened Since VCM", *PW*, Dec. 1976.
91 Rosato, D. V., "Plastics in Appliances", *PW*, Aug. 1975.
92 Rosato, D. V., "New Look At Extruders", *PW*, Oct. 1975.
93 Rosato, D. V., "Custom Compounding", *PW*, Nov. 1975.
94 Rosato, D. V., "Compression and Transfer Molding", *PW*, Dec. 1975.
95 Rosato, D. V., "Custom RP Molder: Budd Co.", *PW*, June 1968.
96 Rosato, D. V., "Radomes and Antennas", *PW*, April 1964.
97 Rosato, D. V., Outer Space Parabolic Reflector Energy Converters, SAMPE Symposium, Philadelphia, Jun. 1963.
98 Agarwal, B. D. and L. J. Broutman, *Analysis and Performance of Fiber Composites*, Wiley, 1990.
99 *A Glossary of Plastics Terminology in Five Languages*, Hanser, 1990.
100 Alger, M. S., *Polymer Science Dictionary*, Elsevier, 1989.
101 *ASTM Compilation of (ASTM) Standard Definitions*, ASTM 1991.
102 ASTM Index—Annual Book of ASTM Standards, ASTM Annual.
103 Avenas, J. F., *Modeling of Polymer Processing*, Hanser, 1990.
104 Aseeva, R. M. and G. E. Zaikov, *Combustion of Polymer Materials*, Hanser, 1986.
105 Bark, L. S. and N. S. Allen, *Analysis of Polymer Systems*, Applied Science Publ., London, 1982.
106 Baer, E. and A. Moet, *High Performance Polymers*, Hanser, 1990.
107 Beck, R. D., *Plastics Product Design*, Van Nostrand Reinhold, 1980.
108 Birley, A. W. et al., *Physics of Plastics*, Hanser, 1990.
109 Birzer, F., "Synergy and Competition in Electro-Erosive Sinking and Electro-Erosive Cutting", *Kunststoffe*, July 1990.
110 Brostow, W. and R. D. Corneliussen, *Failure of Plastics*, Hanser, 1986.
111 Budinski, K. G., *Engineering Materials Properties and Selection*, Prentice-Hall, 1989.
112 Canby, T. Y. and C. O'Rear, "Reshaping Our Lives—Advanced Materials", *National Geographic*, Dec. 1989.
113 Charrier, J. M., *Polymeric Materials and Processing*, Hanser, 1991.
114 Cross, N., *Engineering Design Methods*, Wiley, 1989.
115 Dealy, J. M. and K. F. Wissbrun, *Melt Rheology and Its Role in Plastics Processing*, Van Nostrand Reinhold, 1990.
116 Deming, E. W., Out of Crisis, MIT Center for Advanced Engineering Study, 1986.
117 Drug Information for the Health Care Professional, US Pharmacopeia Conventional Inc., Annual.
118 *Engineering Materials Handbook*, Vol. 1: Composite, ASM International, 1987.
119 *Engineering Materials Handbook*. Vol. 2: Engineering Plastics, ASM International, 1988.

120 Eshbach, O. W. et al., *Handbook of Engineering Fundamentals*, Wiley, 1952.
121 Finn, R. K., *Biotechnology: Fundamentals and Information*, Vol. 1 and 2, Hanser, 1988 and 1990.
122 Flory, P. J., *Statistical Mechanics of Chain Molecules*, Hanser, 1989.
123 Foston, A. L. and T. Au, *Fundamentals of Computer-Integrated Manufacturing*, Prentice-Hall, 1991.
124 French, T. E. et al., *Engineering Drawing and Graphic Technology*, McGraw, 1986.
125 Fritch, L. W., The Separate Roles of Core and Surface Orientation on Properties of ABS Injection Molded Parts, SPE-RETEC, Boston, Nov. 1990.
126 Gächter, R. and H. Müller, *Plastics Additives*, Hanser, 1990.
127 Ganic, E. N. and T. G. Hicks, *Handbook of Essential Engineering Information and Data*, McGraw, 1990.
128 Gmur, U., "Practical Aspects of Recycling of Scrap From Used Film and Sheet Products (Pol Recycling)", *Kunststoffe*, Apr. 1990.
129 Heger, F. J., *Structural Plastics Design Manual*, ASCE, 1981.
130 Hensen, F., *Plastics Extrusion Technology*, Hanser, 1988.
131 Hofmann, W., *Rubber Technology Handbook*, Hanser, 1989.
132 Hostetter, G. H., *Analytical, Numerical, and Computational Methods for Science and Engineering*, Prentice Hall, 1991.
133 Jackson, A. T., *Process Engineering in Biotechnology*, Prentice Hall, 1991.
134 Johnson, R. F., Process Validation and Good Manufacturing Practices, Univ. of Lowell Seminars, 1982–1985.
135 Kampf, G., *Characterization of Plastics by Physical Methods*, Hanser, 1986.
136 Kircher, K., *Chemical Reactions in Plastics Processing*, Hanser, 1987.
137 Krause, A. et al., *Plastics Analysis Guide*, Hanser, 1983.
138 Kroschwitz, J. I., *Concise Encyclopedia of Polymer Science and Engineering*, Wiley, 1990.
139 Ku, C. C. and R. Liepins, *Electrical Properties of Polymers*, Hanser, 1987.
140 Lee, S. M., *International Encyclopedia of Composites*, VCH, 1991.
141 Legge, N. R., *Thermoplastic Elastomers*, Hanser, 1987.
142 Lubin, G., *Handbook of Composites*, Van Nostrand Reinhold, 1982.
143 Mallick, P. K. and S. Newman, *Composite Materials Technology*, Hanser, 1990.
144 Manzione, L. T., *Applications of Computer-Aided Engineering in Injection Molding*, Hanser, 1987.
145 Margolis, J. M., *Instrumentation for Thermoplastic Processing*, Hanser, 1989.
146 Masters, G. M., *Introduction to Environmental Engineering and Science*, Prentice Hall, 1991.
147 Menges, G. and P. Plein, "Plasma Polymerization-Tailored Coats for Plastics Molder", *Kunststoffe*, Oct. 1988.
148 Michaeli, W., *Extrusion Dies*, Hanser, 1984.
149 Miller, E., *Plastics Products Design Handbook*, Part A: Components; Part B: Processes and Design, Marcel Dekker, 1981 and 1983.
150 Mitchell, J., *Polymer Analysis and Characterization*, Hanser, 1990.
151 Philips, C. L., *Feedback Control Systems*, Prentice Hall, 1991.
152 "Plastics In The 21st Century", *PW*, Sep. 1987.
153 Potter, M. C. and D. C. Wiggert, *Mechanics of Fluids*, Prentice Hall, 1991.
154 Roberts, A. D., *Natural Rubber Science and Technology*, Hanser, 1988.
155 Rubin, I., *Handbook of Plastic Materials and Technology*, Wiley, 1990.
156 Saechtling, H., *International Plastics Handbook for Technologist, Engineer, and User*, Hanser, 1987.
157 Schindler, B. M., "Made in Japan", W. Edwards Deming, *ASTM Standardization News*, Feb. 1983, p. 88.
158 Schröder, E. et al., *Polymer Characterization*, Hanser, 1990.
159 Seymour, R. B., *History of Polymer Science and Technology*, Marcel Dekker, 1982.
160 Shyapintokh, V. Y., *Photochemical Conversion and Stabilization*, Hanser, 1985.
161 Standardized Practice For Use of the International System of Units (SI): The Modernized Metric System, ASTM STD. E380–89a, 1989.
162 Stark, J., *Managing CAD/CAM*, McGraw, 1988.
163 Stevens, M. P., *Polymer Chemistry: Introduction*, Hanser, 1990.
164 Szycher, M. and W. J. Robinson, *Synthetic Biomedical Polymers*, Technomic, 1980.
165 Taniguchi, N. et al., *Energy-Beam Processing of Materials*, Hanser, 1989.
166 Tanner, R. I., *Engineering Rheology*, Hanser, 1990.

167 Tapley, B. D., *Eshbach's Handbook of Engineering Fundamentals*, Wiley, 1990.
168 Thomas, L. C., *Heat Transfer*, Prentice Hall, 1991.
169 Throne, J. L. and B. C. Wendle, *Engineering Guide for Structural Foams*, Technomic, 1976.
170 Timoshenko, S., *Strength of Materials*, Van Nostrand Reinhold, 1955.
171 Timoshenko, S. and J. M. Gere, *Elastic Stability*, McGraw, 1961.
172 Troitzsch, J. H., *International Plastics Flammability Handbook*, Hanser, 1990.
173 Tube Topics, Marketing Newsletter, Tube Council of North America, Vol. 23, No. 3, 1989.
174 Tucker, C. L., *Fundamentals of Computer Modeling for Polymer Processing*, Hanser, 1990.
175 Tummala, R. R. and E. J. Rymaszewski, *Microelectronics Packaging Handbook*, Van Nostrand Reinhold, 1989.
176 Utracki, L., *Polymer Alloys and Blends: Thermodynamics and Rheology*, Hanser, 1990.
177 Welling, M. S., *German-English Glossary of Plastics Machining Terms*, Hanser, 1979.
178 Wendle, B. C., *A Purchasing and Design Guide*, Marcel Dekker, 1985.
179 White, J. L., *Twin Screw Extrusion*, Hanser, 1990.
180 Whittington, L. R., *Whittington's Dictionary of Plastics*, Technomic, 1968.
181 Wittfoht, A. M., *Plastics Technical Dictionary*, Part 1: English-German, 1981; Part 2: German-English, 1983; Part 3: Reference Volume, 1978, Hanser.
182 Woodward, A. E., *Atlas of Polymer Morphology*, Hanser, 1989.
183 Westerfield, D. H., *Quality Control*, Prentice-Hall, 1979.
184 Trade Magazines and Publications:
Advanced Materials and Processes, ASM International, Metals Park, OH 44073
Canadian Plastics, 1450 Don Mills Rd., Don Mills, Ont., Canada M3B 2X7
Chemical and Engineering News, 733 Third Ave., New York, NY 10017
Chemical Engineering, 1221 Avenue of the Americas, New York, NY 10020
Chemical Marketing Reporter, 100 Church St., New York, NY 10007
Chemical Week, 1221 Avenue of the Americas, New York, NY 10020
Design News, 275 Washington St., Newton, MA 02158
European Plastics News, 33–39 Bowling Green Lane, London EC1R ONE, England.
European Polymer Journal, Fairwell Pk., Elmsford, NY 10523.
Journal of Commerce, 110 Wall St., New York, NY 10005
Kunststoffe, C. Hanser Verlag, Postfach 86 04 20, 8000 München 86, Germany
Machine Design, 1100 Superior Ave., Cleveland, OH 44114
Materials Engineering, 600 Summer St., Stamford, CT 06904
Medical Device and Diagnostic Industry, 2416 Wilshire Blvd., Santa Monica, CA 90403
Modern Packaging, 205 E. 42 St., New York, NY 10017
Modern Plastics, 1221 Avenue of the Americas, New York, NY 10020
Paper, Film and Foil Converter, 29 Wacker Dr., Chicago, IL 60606
Plastics Compounding, 1129 E. 17 St., Denver, CO 80218
Plastics Design and Processing, 700 Petersen Rd., Libertyville, IL 60048
Plastics Design Forum, 1129 E. 17 St., Denver, CO 80218
Plastics Engineering, 14 Fairfield Dr., Brookfield Center, CT 06805
Plastics Focus, Box 814, Amherst, MA 01004
Plastics Machinery and Equipment, 1129 E. 17 St., Denver, CO 80218
Plastics Technology, 633 Third Ave., New York, NY 10017
Plastics World, 275 Washington St., Newton, MA 02158
Rubber and Plastics News, 1 Cascade Plaza, Suite 1302, Akron, OH 44308
SAMPE Journal, 843 W Glentana, Covino, CA 91722
World Plastics and Rubber Technology, Essex House, Regent St., Cambridge CB2 3AB, England.
185 Trade Associations and Professional Groups:
Adhesives Manufacturers Assoc., 111 E. Wacker Dr., Chicago, IL 60601
American Chemical Society, 1155 16 St., NW, Washington, DC 20036
American National Standards Institute, 1430 Broadway, New York, NY 10018
American Society for Testing and Materials, 1916 Race St., Philadelphia, PA 19103
American Society of Civil Engineers, 345 E. 47 St., New York, NY 10017
American Society of Mechanical Engineers, 345 E. 47 St., New York, NY 10017
American Society of Metals, Metals Park, OH 44073
Canadian Plastics Institute, 1262 Don Mills Rd., Suite 48, Don Mills, Ont., Canada M3B 2W7
Drug, Chemical and Allied Trade Assoc., 40–42 Bell Blvd., Suite 204, Bayside, NY 11361

Factory Mutual Research Corp, 1151 Boston-Providence Tpke., Norwood, MA 02062
Industrial Designers Society of America, 1142 E. Walker Rd., Great Falls, VA 22066.
Malaysian Rubber Producers' Research Assoc., Malaysian Rubber Bureau, Washington DC
Manufacturing Chemists Assoc., 1852 Connecticut Ave., NW, Washington, DC, 20009
National Assoc. of Corrosion Engineers, Box 1499, Houston, TX 77001
National Assoc. of Plastics Fabricators, 1100 Standard Building, Cleveland, OH 44113
Polyurethane Manufacturers Assoc., 4219 S. Wolcott Ave,. Chicago, IL 60609
Rubber Manufacturers Assoc., 1901 Pennsylvania Ave., NW, Washington, DC 20006
Society of Automotive Engineers, 400 Commonwealth Dr., Warrendale, PA 15096
Society of Plastics Engineers, 14 Fairfield Dr., Brookfield, CT 06805
Society of Plastics Industry, 1025 Connecticut Ave., NW, Washington, DC 20036

186 Government Publications and Groups:
National Institute of Standards and Technology (NIST), Polymer Building, Washington, DC 20234
Naval Publications and Forms Center, 5801 Tabor Rd., Philadelphia, PA 19120
Plastics Technical Evaluation Center (PLASTEC), Picatinny Arsenal, Dover, NJ 07801
U.S. Government Publications, Available through the Dept. of Commerce, 5285 Port Royal Rd., Springfield, VA 22161
Annual Survey of Manufacturers, Bureau of the Census
Census of Manufacturers, Bureau of the Census
Directory of Plastics—Knowledgeable Government Personnel, NIST
Foreign Trade Reports, Bureau of the Census
Standard Industrial Classification Manual, Office of Management and Budget
Statistical Abstracts of the U.S., Dept. of Commerce
Synthetic Organic Chemicals, International Trade Commission
US Industrial Outlook, Dept. of Commerce
Wholesale Price Index, Bureau of Labor Statistics

A-basis The *A* mechanical property value is the value above which at least 99% of the population of values is expected to fall with a confidence of 95%. Also called A-allowable. ▷ **B-basis; S-basis; typical-basis**

abbreviation See *List of Abbreviations* on p. viii.

A-B-C-stages The various stages of cure of a catalyzed thermoset plastic are known as *A-stage*, *B-stage*, and *C-stage*. In A-stage the material is still soluble in certain liquids and is fusible. In B-stage it softens when heated and swells when in contact with certain liquids, but does not fully fuse or dissolve. Thermoset molding compounds and prepregs are examples of B-stage materials. In C-stage the plastic is fully cured; it is relatively insoluble and infusible. Basically A-stage is uncured, B-stage is partially cured, and C-stage is fully cured. ▷ **B-stage**

aberration Any error that results in image degradation. Such errors may be chromatic, spherical, astigmatic, or comatic. They can result from design, execution, or both.

abherent A release agent such as a coating or film applied to one surface to prevent or reduce its adhesion to another surface brought into intimate contact with it. Abherents applied to plastic films are usually anti-blocking agents. Those applied to molds, calender rolls, etc. are usually called release agents. They are also called abhesives. ▷ **release agent performance** and **abhesive**

abhesive 1. A material that resists adhesion. **2.** A film or coating applied to surfaces to prevent sticking, heat sealing, and so on by the presence of parting agent, mold release, or antistick material (such as fluoroplastic of low surface tension).

ablation An orderly heat and mass transfer process in which a large amount of thermal energy is expended by sacrificial loss of surface region material causing charring. The heat input from the environment is absorbed, dissipated, blocked, and generated by numerous mechanisms. The energy absorption processes take place automatically and simultaneously, serve to control the surface temperature, and greatly restrict the flow of heat into the substrate interior. As an example, the sacrificial loss of material when used as a heat shield to protect space vehicles and other vehicles during re-entry to the earth's atmosphere. The loss is due to decomposition and volatilization caused by the frictional heating in the earth's upper atmosphere. Thermal protection is provided by the material acting both as a heat sink (the loss processes being endothermic) and as a thermal insulant.

ablative plastic A material that absorbs heat (with a low material loss and char rate) through a decomposition process (pyrolysis) that takes place at or near the surface exposed to the heat. This mechanism essentially provides thermal protection (insulation) of the subsurface materials and components by sacrificing the surface layer. Ablation is an exothermic process. Typical plastics are carbon fiber-phenolic reinforced plastics that can be exposed to 1,650°C (3,000°F); also other RPs are used such as glass fiber-phenolics. There are also ceramic types (example: white silica fibers fused in an oven and coated with borosilicate glass) that are efficient up to 1,260°C (2,300°F). In these hot environments, however, the survival time of seconds exceeds that of refractory metal and ceramic; heat generated by heat friction is about 1,370°C (2,500°F). Plastic ablative materials are used in other applications such as rocket motor exhaust structures exposed to hot exhaust gases.

Relative erosion rates of various materials exposed to severe heating at 1,370°C, heating rate about 2,000 Btu/ft^2/sec, and exposure time of 10 sec are graphite with a 1.0 relative weight loss, asbestos-phenolic at 1.2, nylon-phenolic at 1.5, silicon carbide at 2.1–7.8, silicon-phenolic at 2.7, glass-phenolic at 2.7, and so on. The heating rates encountered in the reentry applications are often 100 times as high as those obtained on a kitchen range. The gas heat is sometimes three times as high as the gas range flame.

Ablation involves charring plastics. At first the plastic surface heats up and a thermal pulse progresses into the plastic. This action continues until the surface starts to decompose by charring. Then the charred surface increases in temperature and the char interface progresses into the material. Gaseous decomposition products generated at the moving interface diffuse through the char and tend to cool it. As the char thickness increases, the rate at which the interface moves decreases and the char surface temperature increases. The use of RPs under these severe conditions is related to the rate of progress of a heat pulse through the material; it is the thermal diffusivity characteristic. When examining heat absorbing capability of the various materials, the highest values tend to be with plastics. ▷ **silica**

ABL bottle An internal pressure test vessel about 460 mm (18 in.) in diameter and 610 mm (24 in.) long used to determine the quality and properties of the filament-wound material in a vessel.

abrasion 1. Loose, fine particles and any relatively hard foreign matter finding their way in between rubbing surfaces can cause abrasion. **2.** Surface loss of a material due to frictional forces.

abrasion cleaning Cleaning by abrasion removes surface contamination and increases surface roughness. Removal of surface contamination eliminates a potential existing weak boundary layer and increases roughness; both have a positive effect on adhesion. Cleaning is usually mechanical. Mechanical abrasion is carried out by several processes: dry blasting with nonmetallic grit (flint, silica, aluminum oxide, plastic, walnut shell, and so on), wet abrasive blast (slurry of aluminum oxide), hand or machine sanding, and scouring with tap water and scouring powder.

abrasion resistance Abrasion or wear resistance is the ability of a material to withstand the removal of material from its surface due to contact with another surface as the result of mechanical action of a rubbing, scraping, or erosive nature (sand and so on). Different tests are used to identify different abrasion or wear conditions. (Abrasion is only one factor in wear).

abrasion resistance index A measure of the abrasion resistance of a vulcanized elastomer/rubber relative to that of a standard vulcanized elastomer/rubber under similar conditions and expressed as:

$$\text{Abrasive Index} = \frac{S}{T} \times 100$$

where S = volume loss of a standard specimen; T = volume loss of the specimen being evaluated.

abrasive Hard, mechanically resistant material used for grinding or cutting. The greatest boon to the abrasive industry since the turn of the 20th century has been the advent of commercial plastics. Abrasive products bonded with thermoset plastics have been used to accomplish economically metal-removal operations that previously had to be done by expensive machining methods. Because of their greater resistance to thermal shock and their better impact strength, plastic-bonded products have greatly assisted the metal-working industry in developing automated, high-speed production techniques—with newer plastics and processing methods continuing to provide benefits. There are four general areas in the abrasive industry where plastics are important: (1) bonded abrasives (grinding wheels, sharpening stones), (2) coated abrasives (abrasive paper, brushes, cloth, metal and rayon screens), (3) adhesive applications (plate-mounted wheels, bushings, arbors), and (4) nonskid surfaces (stairtreads, ramps, road intersections).

All manufacturing abrasive products consist essentially of particles of an abrading material bonded together to form a wheel or abrasive bar, or adhered to a substrate to form abrasive paper, fiber pads, wire mesh, brushes, and so on. The most common abrasives are synthetic materials such as aluminum oxide, silicon carbide, boron carbide, or man-made diamond and natural products like garnet, emery, flint, or diamond. The plastics used as bonds and adhesives for the abrasive granules are usually limited to a few such as phenolic, epoxy, and principally other thermosets; this limit is imposed primarily by the properties these materials impart to a bonded abrasive tool relative to its use, processability, and material cost.

abscissas direction The horizontal direction in a diagram or curve. ▷ **stress strain curve**

absolute humidity ▷ **humidity, absolute**

absolute temperature ▷ **temperature, absolute**

absolute viscosity ▷ **viscosity, absolute**

absorbable technology This is a health technique which injects or implants drugs encapsulated in absorbable plastic under the skin, thus preventing over-medication and reducing the cost of medical treatment. It involves pharmaceutical, biotechnology, and medical devices in the use of absorbable plastics in biomedical products, particularly controlled-release drug delivery systems and implants.

As an example, hollow PVC implants appear promising as a way to deliver dopamine to the brains of Parkinson's disease patients, in work being done by Brown University and Purdue University. Such capsules could deliver drugs and biologic substances such as insulin that are needed to correct deficiencies. Research laboratories continue the search for better materials of all types of implantable devices. A new shape memory plastic developed at the National Cardiovascular Center in Japan, for example, would make it easier to patch a hole in the heart. A 4 mm, bar-shaped device can be pushed through a catheter into a vein, where it changes to a patch shape in 10 sec when hot water is added into the catheter. Result is to plug up the hole in the heart. ▷ **drug controlled release**

absorbed water Water contained within a material.

absorptance Ratio of the absorbed radiant or luminous flux to the incident flux.

absorption **1.** Penetration into the mass of the substance by another. **2.** Process whereby energy is dissipated within a specimen placed in a field of radiant energy. **3.** Capillary or cellular attraction of adhered surfaces to draw off the liquid adhesive film into the substrate. **4.** ▷ **infrared spectroscopy** **5.** ▷ **sound absorption**

absorption spectroscopy Important technique of instrumental analysis involving measurement of the absorption of radiant energy by a substance as a function of the energy incident upon it. Either absorption or emission may be examined. If the emitted energy is studied, the term resonance fluorescence is used.

absorptivity Absorbance divided by the product of concentration of the substance and the sample path length.

ABS plastic ▷ **acrylonitrile-butadiene-styrene plastic**

accelerated aging Aging in a short time by artificial means in order to obtain an indication of how a material will behave under normal conditions over a prolonged period in service. The simulated life test aging can include different conditions, such as outdoor weathering, static and dynamic loads on products, wear resistance, and so on. Test equipment and methods are described in standards prepared by organizations such as ASTM and UL.

accelerated weathering Duplicating or simulating weather conditions as much as possible by means of testing equipment; impossible to duplicate outdoor weathering since "it" does not "duplicate".

accelerator Material which, when mixed with a catalyzed plastic, will speed up the chemical reaction between the catalyst and plastic; either in polymerizing of plastic or vulcanization of elastomers with or without the use of external heat. Also called promoter.

acceptable risk Concept that has developed in connection with toxic substances, food additives, air and water pollution, related environmental concerns, and so on. It can be defined as a level of risk at which a seriously adverse result is highly unlikely to occur but one cannot prove whether or not there is a 100% safety. In these cases it means living with reasonable assurance of safety and acceptable uncertainty. Note this concept will always exist; examples include automobiles, aircraft, boats, lawnmowers, and many more—otherwise none of these products or "concerns"would be in existence. Many products and "concerns" are not perfect and can never be made perfect. Target is to approach perfection in a zero-risk society. Basically, no product is without risk; failure to recognize this factor may put excessive emphasis on achieving an important goal drawing precious resources away from certain new product development and approval. The target or goal should be to attain the proper balance between risk and benefit. ▷ **testing and reality; perfection; hazardous warning signs; responsibilities and risk retention; statistical benefits**

acceptance number Maximum allowable number of defective parts for a given acceptable quality level (AQL) and lot sample.

accordion fold Term used for two or more parallel folds which open like an accordion.

accumulator **1.** An auxiliary cylinder and piston (plunger) mounted on machines (injection, blow molding and so on). It is used to provide extremely fast molding cycles or output rates. The accumulator cylinder is filled (during the time of shot or parison deliveries) with melted plastic coming from the plasticator. The molten plastic is stored or "accumulated" in this auxiliary cylinder until the next melt is required for the shot or parison. At that time the piston in the accumulator cylinder forces the melt into the mold or die that forms the shot or parison. **2.** A device for the temporary storage or accumulation of film on an extrusion line, also called festoon. **3.** A container for storing hydraulic oil under pressure and used on certain machines or auxiliary equipment to boost oil pressure, which in turn speeds up the processing rate.

accumulator adapter The structure containing the flow passage connecting an accumulator to an injection molding machine barrel or the blow molding extruder die head (or die head manifold).

accumulator head Melt accumulator(s) vertically connected to the discharge end of an extruder and programmed for weight and thickness distribution for the extrudate or parison by means of controlling the movement up and down of the inner mandrel or outside die ring.

accumulator, injection molding ▷**injection molding, two stage unit**

accuracy Accuracy as distinguished from precision is the degree of conformity of a measured or calculated value to some recognized standard or specific value. This concept involves the systematic error of operation, which is seldom negligible. ▷**precision** and **sensor accuracy**

acetal plastic Superior properties of highly crystalline acetal in terms of strength, stiffness, and toughness makes it an important engineering thermoplastic. It is more dense than nylon but in many respects their properties are similar and they can be used for the same types of light engineering applications. In some cases a factor that may favor acetal is its relatively low water absorption. Acetal homopolymer and copolymer grades offer features to the designer that have made them prime contenders for applications based on metal, primarily die-cast metals. Properties include good fatigue life; exceptional dimensional stability, resiliency and toughness; good tensile strength and creep resistance under a wide range of temperature and humidity conditions; solvent resistance; excellent electrical properties; etc. Abrasion resistance is also generally superior to most thermoplastics. Its coefficient of friction on steel is very low. Its low dissipation factor and dielectric constant are maintained over a wide range of frequencies and up to temperatures of 121°C (250°F). Also colors are available. Acetal, also called polyacetal and polyoxymethylene (POM), is widely available as a homopolymer polymerized from formaldehyde, and as a copolymer of trioxane and other monomers.

Acetal homopolymers, modified, deliver up to seven times greater than unmodified in Izod impact tests and up to 30 times greater toughness as measured by Gardner impact tests. The general-purpose types can be used over a wide range of environmental conditions. Special UV-stabilized grades are used when requiring long-term exposure to weathering. Prolonged exposure to strong acids and bases outside the range of pH 4 to 9 is not recommended. Homopolymers have the highest fatigue endurance of any unfilled commercial thermoplastics. Under complete reversed tensile and compressive stress, and with 100% relative humidity at 22.8°C (73°F), fatigue endurance limit is 31 GPa (4,500 psi) at 10^6 cycles. Resistance to creep is excellent. Moisture, lubricants and solvents, including gasoline and gasohol, have little effect on this property, which is important in parts incorporating self-threading screws and interface fits.

Melting points of the homopolymers are higher, and they are harder, have higher resistance to fatigue, are more rigid and have higher tensile and flexural strength with generally lower elongation. Some high-molecular-weight homopolymers are extremely tough and have higher elongation than copolymers. Grades are available that are modified for improved hydrolysis resistance to 82°C (180°F), similar to copolymers.

Acetal copolymers have an excellent balance of properties and processing characteristics. Melt temperature can range from 182 to 232°C (360 to 450°F) with little effect on part strength. It is available in its translucent-natural white and in a wide range of colors and dimensionally stable, low-warpage grades. They have high tensile and flexural strength, fatigue resistance and hardness. They retain much of their toughness through a broad temperature range and are among the most creep-resistant of the crystalline TPs. Strength of copolymers is only slightly reduced after aging for one year in air at 116°C (240°F). Impact strength holds constant for the first six months, and falls off about one-third during the next six months. Aging in air at 82°C (180°F) for two years has little or no effect on properties, and immersion in water for one year at 82°C (180°F) leaves most properties virtually unchanged. Samples tested in boiling water retain nearly original tensile strength after nine months.

Good electrical properties combined with high mechanical properties and a UL electrical rating of 100°C (212°F) qualify these plastics for electrical parts requiring long time stability. Copolymers have excellent resistance to chemicals and solvents. For example, samples immersed for 12 months at room temperature in various inorganic solutions were unaffected except by strong mineral acids, sulfuric, nitric and hydrochloric. Most organic reagents tested have no effect, nor do mineral oil, motor oil or brake fluids. Resistance to strong alkalis is exceptionally good.

The copolymers remain stable in long-term, high temperature service and offer exceptional resistance to the effects of immersion in water at high temperatures. Neither type resists strong acids and the copolymer is virtually unaffected by strong bases. Both types are available in a wide range of melt-flow grades, unreinforced and reinforced grades and PTFE or silicone-filled grades. Several grades of homo or copolymer types comply with the FDA for repeated contact with food at temperatures to 120°C (248°F).

acetate **1.** A derivative of acetic acid. **2.** A generic name for cellulose acetate plastics and fibers. Where at least 92% of the hydroxyl groups are acetylated, the term triacetate can be used as the generic name for the fibers.

acetylene Industrial significance of acetylene is principally as an intermediate in the manufacture of many of the large volume monomers used in plastic such as vinyl chloride, chloroprene, acrylonitrile, vinyl acetate, and acrylic ester.

acid-acceptor Compound that acts as a stabilizer by chemically combining with the acid that may be initially present in minute quantities in a plastic, or that may be formed by the decomposition of the plastic.

acid gas Byproduct of incomplete combustion of solid waste and fossil fuels with a pH value of less than 6.5, most commonly sulfur dioxide, hydrogen chloride, and nitrogen oxides.

acid, organic ▷ **organic acid**

acid rain or acid precipitation Any form of precipitation (wet deposition) having a pH of 5.6 or less; the most deleterious components being the sulfur dioxide and oxides of nitrogen either emitted as stack gases in highly industrialized areas or resulting from volcanic activity.

acoustical board Low density, sound absorbing structural insulating board having a factory-applied finish and a fissured, felted fiber, slotted or perforated surface pattern provided to reduce sound reflection. Usually supplied for use in the form of tiles.

acoustic emission testing When flaws or cracks grow in plastic, minute amounts of elastic energy are released and propagate in the material as an acoustic wave. Sensors placed on the surface of the plastic can detect these waves, providing information about location and rate of flaw growth. These principles form the basis for the acoustic emission nondestructive test (NDT) methods such as sonic.

acoustic holography In acoustical holography, computer reconstruction provides the means for storing and integrating several holographic images. A reconstructed stored image is a three-dimensional picture that can be electronically rotated and viewed in any image plane. The image provides full characterization and detail of buried flaws.

acoustic impedance A mathematical quantity used in computation of reflection characteristics at boundaries; product of wave velocity and material density.

acrolein plastic Physical and chemical properties of acrolein plastics depend more on conditions of preparation than is normally the case with other plastics. They are colorless but become colored above 170°C (338°F) and sinter at 220°C (428°F) without melting. It is the simplest unsaturated aliphatic aldehyde. Example of properties include density of 1.32 to 1.37, refractive index is 1.529, dielectric constant is 2.84 at 156°C (310°F), and mechanical, physical and chemical resistance having a wide range of performances. Monomeric acrolein must be handled with utmost caution because of its high flammability, irritating effect on eyes and mucous membranes, and extremely pungent smell.

acronyms See *List of Abbreviations* on p. viii.

across-machine direction The perpendicular to machine direction.

acrylamide plastic This specialty plastic has limited use with principle outlets in water treatment, mining, and paper manufacture.

acrylate plastic This thermoset elastomer family of different acrylate plastics [also called acrylate rubber (ACM)] is highly resistant to oxygen and ozone, excellent flex life and permeability resistance, resistance to oil swell and deterioration, and so on. Their heat resistance is superior to that of all other commercial rubbers except silicones and fluorine containing rubbers. Water resistance is rather poor. Low temperature flex is not good and these rubbers decompose in alkaline solutions and are swelled by acids. ▷ **acrylic plastic**

acrylglass plastic Refers to acrylic plastic glazing material. Glazing of airplanes is one of the oldest applications for PMMA. It continues to increase in importance mainly because of the enormous increase of airplane traffic, increased number of smaller and larger aircraft, the latter with triple glazing of cabin windows, as well as glazing of helicopters. The volume of this plastic is small in comparison to other applications, but because of the high standards required, it is important from the technical and economical points of view. For the cockpits of fighter planes as well as for outside panes on passenger aircraft, stretched PMMA is used because of its greater toughness. For this purpose, plates and blocks 12 to 40 mm or even 60 mm or thicker are used. Since after the usual biaxial stretching of 70%, the finished thickness is about 30% of the original one, the finished sheet is between 4 to 13 or 20 mm.

For both the regular and stretched PMMA glazing, extreme high optical properties are required, such as minimum optical refraction, freedom from stress, no disturbing surface blemishes (pimples, craters, etc.), and no internal blemishes (bubbles, inclusions). Extruded PMMA will not meet these requirements. This area of application requires a great deal of precision in stretching and further processing (shaping such as thermoforming, grinding, polishing) into the final parts. ▷ **acrylic plastic** and **orientation**

acrylic A family of commercial plastics involve repeat units whose names feature the term "acryl", such as polyacrylic acid, polymethacrylic acid, poly-R acrylate, poly-R methacrylate, polymethylacrylate, polymethylmethacrylate (PMMA), polyethylmethacrylate, and cyanoacrylate plastics. PMMA is the major and most important homopolymer in the series of acrylics with a sufficient high glass transition temperature to form useful products. Repeat units of the other types are used, however, in commercially important copolymers and also in near homopolymer form in paints, adhesives, etc. Ethylacrylate repeat units form the major component in acrylate rubbers.

acrylic elastomer Under the heading acrylic elastomer (or acrylate or polyacrylate rubber or elastomer), the plastic literature has included a broad spectrum of carboxy-modified rubbers which have as a minor portion of the comonomers acrylic acid and/or its derivatives. However, in more recent usage the term acrylic elastomer is used to designate those rubbery products which contain a predominant amount of an acrylic ester, such as ethyl acrylate or butyl acrylate in the polymer chain. Fluoroacrylate elastomers are based on plastics prepared from the acrylic acid ester-dihydroperfluoro alcohols. ▷ **butadiene plastic**

acrylic fiber Acrylic fiber is defined as a manufactured fiber in which the fiber-forming substance is any long chain synthetic plastic composed of at least 85% by weight of acrylonitrile; those with less than 85% are called modacrylic fibers. ▷ **acrylonitrile**

acrylic plastic Acrylics are known for sparkling crystal clarity and surface hardness, together with superior weatherability (with optical retention) and good chemical resistance. Acrylic is supplied as monomer for coating plastics and casting sheets, rods, and tubes. It is also supplied as beads or pellets for extrusion (sheets, profiles, and so on), injection molding (automotive tail lights, lighting lenses, and so on), and other processes.

Most acrylics start with methyl methacrylate monomer (MMA). Acrylics known as polymethylmethacrylate (PMMA), also called polymethylacrylate, have grades and specifications developed by ASTM. They are light-stable and have transmission below 300 nanometers; used in medical diagnostic applications and so on. For long-term use, UV absorbers can be added to protect the acrylic from exposure to such strong UV light sources as mercury vapor lamps. Special colors have been developed for different applications. Certain transparent reds, ambers, and blues meet the three-year outdoor weatherability requirements of SAE. Acrylics have good electrical properties. Most have UL 94-HB flammability rating. ▷ **acrylglass plastic**

acrylic-styrene-acrylonitrile plastic ▷ **acrylonitrile-styrene-acrylate plastic**

acryloid plastic Early name for polymethylacrylate and other acrylates in solution for use as adhesives and coatings. Later also used for methacrylate plastics (polymers and copolymers) useful as lubricating oil viscosity modifiers.

acrylonitrile-butadiene rubber Also called nitrile rubber (NBR). It is a copolymer with 20 to 50% of acrylonitrile that was developed as a general purpose, oil-resistant rubber. Its resistance to oils, fuels, and solvents is superior to that of polychloroprene (CR). Heat aging is rather good, and abrasion resistance is high. Cost is moderate. Ozone and weathering resistance is not very good, and low temperature flexibility is quite limited in some grades. Applications include fuel and oil tubing and hose, gaskets and seals, conveyor belting, and printing rolls and pads.

acrylonitrile-butadiene-styrene plastic Family of ABSs are very tough but not brittle, hard and rigid and chemical resistant. They offer low water absorption, good dimensional stability, good electrical properties, high abrasion resistance, and some grades are easily electroplated. It is a terpolymer of the three monomers, often considered as a modified polystyrene since its properties resemble PS, except that its impact strength is much higher. A very wide variety of commercial products are available, varying not only in composition but also in morphology, due to the different procedures used in copolymer preparation.

In the past, mechanical mixtures of styrene-acrylonitrile copolymer and nitrile rubber were made, or they were obtained by co-coagulating latices of the polymers. Present products are almost entirely produced by the copolymerization of styrene and acrylonitrile in the presence of polybutadiene latex—the so-called latex grafting method. This results in considerable grafting and the products have higher impact strengths. The morphology is similar to that of high impact PS, but the dispersed rubber particles are much smaller (1 to 10 mm) and contain styrene-acrylonitrile copolymer inclusions. Other rubbers which are sometimes used are ethylene-propylene-diene monomer rubber and solution polybutadiene.

A typical ABS contains about 20% rubber, about 25% acrylonitrile, and about 55% styrene, having a T_g value of about 105°C, a tensile modulus of 2.5 GPa and an impact strength of about 4 J $(12.7 \text{ mm})^{-1}$ on an Izod test.

However, owing to the many variations possible, the properties can vary considerably (for example, "super ABS" can have a notched Izod impact strength of up to 8 J $(25 \text{ mm})^{-1}$). Also some or all of one of the comonomers may be replaced. Methylmethacrylate may replace acrylonitrile, as in MBS and MABS, with improvement in transparency, or a saturated rubber may replace the polybutadiene, as in ASA and ACS, with an improvement in oxidation resistance. ABS is mainly used as an injection molding material where good appearance and strength, together with reasonable stiffness and softening point are required.

acrylonitrile-butadiene-styrene, transparent By matching the refractive indices of the elastomer and the SAN phases, usually by incorporating methyl methacrylate, transparent products are possible. Progress in product development is achieved by further matching the properties of those of the standard ABS and also by increasing the light transmission up to 88%. Another gain is better flowability of the products. An example of an application is in transparent trays for freezers. Other applications include paper feeds for copy machines, watch crystal, transparent building blocks for toy systems, parts for medical technology, and packaging for cosmetics.

acrylonitrile-chlorinated polyethylene-styrene copolymer This ACS is a terpolymer obtained by the copolymerization of acrylonitrile and styrene in the presence of chlorinated polyethylene. Properties are similar to ABS, except that it is more resistant to embrittlement due to oxidative degradation, and has better fire resistance. It has a very high flame-retardance; ACS is classified as UL 94 V-O (1/16 in specimen). This styrenic plastic inherently resists the electrostatic deposition of dust; thus there is no need for the addition of antistatic agents to the formulation. The material's deflection temperature under load ranges from 78° to 90°C (172° to 194°F). Products made of ACS can be adhered to each other, hot stamped and painted, and find their greatest use in cabinets and housings.

acrylonitrile-ethylene/propylene-styrene copolymer AES is a terpolymer obtained by grafting styrene-acrylonitrile copolymer to ethylene-propylene or ethylene-propylene-diene monomer rubber. Similar to ABS except with better weathering resistance.

acrylonitrile-methylacrylate plastic Abbreviated [P (AN-MA)]. ▷ **acrylonitrile-styrene plastic**

acrylonitrile-methylmethacrylate plastic The use of copolymers involving about 70% of acrylonitrile and 30% of methylmethacrylate [P (AN-MMA)] repeat units is used for thick transparent products, such as glazing, which require high-impact properties and good chemical and weathering resistance.

acrylonitrile plastic This crystalline thermoplastic is most useful in copolymers. Its copolymer with butadiene is nitrile rubber. Acrylonitrile-butadiene copolymers with styrene (SAN) exist that are tougher than PS. It is also used as a synthetic fiber and as a chemical intermediate.

acrylonitrile-styrene-acrylate plastic ASA terpolymer is similar to ABS, but with a saturated acrylate rubber replacing the unsaturated polybutadiene. This blend improves its resistance to oxidative degradation. This UV-resistant material offers an excellent combination of color and property retention after outdoor exposure in both light and dark colors. There are three major markets for ASA: building and construction, leisure and recreation, and automotive.

acrylonitrile-styrene plastic This is a high nitrile plastic: styrene-acrylonitrile or other monomer acrylonitrile copolymer with a high acrylonitrile content of about 70 to 80%. Such copolymers have a very low permeability to gases (including carbon dioxide), and liquids; thus they are called barrier plastics. ANs also provide good chemical resistance. They are used in packaging, especially for bottles containing carbonated drinks. To provide higher softening points, the AN may be partially replaced by methacrylonitrile.

This was the first plastic to produce stretched two-liter Coca-Cola carbonated beverage bottles during 1958; production was by Monsanto Co. using AN plastic "Barex" (Sohia of BP Chemical International) and Du Pont's stretched injection blow molding process. Unfortunately AN, at that time, was not permitted by the FDA to be used because of possible food contamination, thus stopping production in about eight plants on the East Coast. However it was the forerunner of an avalanche of containers to appear commercially in the 1970s and continue thereafter.

acrylonitrilic This family of plastics have repeat units that feature a nitrile side group (C≡N), such as polyacrylonitrile, polymethacrylonitrile, acrylonitrile-styrene, and acrylonitrile-methylmethacrylate plastics.

activated diffusion ▷ **permeability**

activation 1. Basically it is any process whereby a substance is treated to develop adsorptive properties. **2.** The process of treating a substance, molecule, or atom by heat, radiation, or the presence of another substance so that the first mentioned substance, molecule, or atom will undergo chemical or physical change more rapidly or completely. As an example, the process of inducing radio-activity in a specimen by bombardment with neutrons or other type of radiation.

activator An additive used to promote the curing of thermoset matrix plastics and reducing cure time by increasing the effectiveness of an accelerator.

actual versus theoretical properties ▷ **data theoretical versus actual**

adaptive control ▷ **control, adaptive**

addition polymerization It has been defined by the IUPAC as polymerization, usually to form linear polymers, in which the monomers add together to form the main part of each polymer molecule without the concurrent production of other small molecules such as water. A common type of additonal polymerization is olefinic polymerization, in which the monomers are ethylene or its homologs. The term vinyl polymerization is used to denote addition polymerization of vinyl compounds. Similarly, vinyl-type polymerization refers to addition polymerization of monomers having a carbon-to-carbon bond, such as methyl methacrylate, vinylidene chloride, maleic anhydride, or tetrafluoroethylene. These addition polymerizations all involve the formation of polymers having a carbon-to-carbon single bond along the backbone.

In reality the addition-type process can occur in several ways. One way simply involves the external chemical activation of molecules that cause them to start combining with each other in a chain reaction type fashion (by the bonding of atoms directly within the reacting molecule). Another way for an addition polymerization to occur is through a rearrangement of atoms within both reacting molecules. And still a third way is for a molecule composed of a ring of atoms to open and connect with other ring type molecules being opened up under the influence of the proper catalytic activators; again with no net loss of any atoms from the polymer structure.

additive Additives are basically physically dispersed in a plastic matrix without affecting significantly the molecular structure of the plastic (polymer). Cross-linking agents, catalysts, and others normally used in thermoset systems do purposely affect their structure. Additives are normally classified according to their specific functions rather than a chemical basis. It is also convenient to classify them into groups and to subdivide them according to their specific functions, such as: *mechanical properties modifiers*: reinforcements (fibers, flakes, whiskers, etc.), interfacing agents (makes additives and plastics compatible), toughening agents, plasticizers, blowing agents, particulate fillers, etc; *processing aids*: lubricants (internal and/or external), processing stabilizers, melt flow promoters, thixotropic agents, etc; *surface properties modifiers*: adhesion promoters, slip additives, anti-block additives, anti-wear additives, antistatic agents, blowing agents, etc; *physical properties modifiers*: blowing agents, flame retardants, hollow spheres, particulate fillers, etc; *optical properties modifiers*: nucleating agents, dyes, pigments, etc; *anti-aging additives*: fungicides, anti-oxidants, UV stabilizers, etc; *reducing formulation/manufacturing costs*: particulate fillers, blowing agents, reinforcements, etc; *electrical properties modifiers*: mineral and/or metallic fillers, glass microballoons, etc; *others*: biodegradable agents, preset explosive agents, flame retardants, syntactic fillers, foam/blowing agents, etc.

Unfortunately, there is no "ideal additive" since each of the infinite number of end uses will call for a particular set of characteristics, including diverging properties such as mechanical, physical, chemical, and electrical. To be realistic, the most important requirement of any additive is that it should be effective, for the purpose for which it was designed, at an economical level. Recognize that, like a see-saw, improvements in one property can lead to deterioration in others. Furthermore, the effectiveness of compounding additives depends also on correct procedure of incorporation into the polymer matrix. However, incompatible or partial compatible are required to achieve material performance, such as in reinforced or composite materials.

The target is to set up the parameters required in a compound and when required, develop a compromise. Consideration should be given to factors such as: cost, availability, surface wetting and bonding, oil absorption, chemical resistance, and required strength. Other factors usually considered, particularly from its design requirements, are color, shape consistency, density, thermal expansion, and thermal properties.

The compatibility and diffusibility of additives in plastic compounds is normally assessed by trial and error. The theories on their behaviors do exist so that they can be used in the preliminary concepts to meet specific performance. The number of additives available and their possible combinations are enormous and their compositions are continually changing. The basic theories and knowledge of solution thermodynamics may be used to determine potential compatibility. ▷ **compounding constituents**

additive concentrate ▷ **concentrate**

adduct A chemical addition product.

adhere To cause two surfaces to be held together by adhesion.

adherent A body that is held to another body, usually by an adhesive; a detail or part prepared for bonding. ▷ **abherent**

adhesive One of the most important and most taken-for-granted applications of plastics is adhesives. Adhesive bonding with vegetable and animal by-products has been used for thousands of years. With the advent of thermoplastic and thermoset plastics over a century ago, the field of adhesives took on a new perspective. Adhesives with strengths higher than some metals have been developed. Advances in the use of plastic adhesives have made possible the adhesive bonding of structural and nonstructural parts in appliances, automobiles, electronics, bridges, aircraft, missiles, spacecraft, medical devices, and most others principally replacing welding and riveting. Many of the familiar cans purchased in the supermarket have been for decades sealed with a hot-melt adhesive, replacing soft solders. Automobiles have a rearview mirror seemingly suspended from the glass windshield; cyanocrylate adhesives are used.

Adhesive classification based on chemical compositions are: (1) synthetic plastics (thermoplastics, thermosets, and elastomers or rubbers), (2) natural plastics/resins (starches and dextrine, protein, and rubber), and (3) inorganic materials (such as silicates). There are a myriad synthetic plastics that find application as adhesives. TPs used include vinyls, cellulose esters, alkyd and acrylic esters, and many others. The TSs, those that crosslink to cure, include the epoxies, ureas, furanes, phenolics, resorcinal formaldehydes, and polyesters. Synthetic elastomers (or rubbers) are a very important source of adhesives. They are extremely versatile since many different types exist, such as SBR, nitrile, neoprene, polysulfides, and many others; most cure by solvent evaporation, and various properties can be obtained by varying the rubber and solvent system. The most widely used rubber-based adhesive is contact adhesive (also called contact cement). Its applications are diverse and there is no one application that characterizes its use. One of the most popular household adhesives is vinyl acetate, which is the familiar white glue sold in hardware stores. It is widely used for bonding wood. The most common engineering adhesive since the 1940s is epoxy. It is available in many different forms and formulations to meet many different design applications.

Mechanism of adhesion (adherence) is the phenomenon in which surfaces are held together by interfacial forces. Adhesion may be mechanical, electrostatic, molecular attraction, or solvent depending upon whether it results from interlocking action, from the attraction of electrical charges, from valence forces, or solvent action, respectively. With mechanical locking between the adhesive and the substrate, all surfaces, even polished surfaces, are basically made up of a microscopic rough surface with hills and valleys. If a surface is wet by an adhesive, the adhesive can become mechanically locked into the microtopography of the surface.

There is adhesion by molecular attraction, and more particularly with the theory of adhesive joints or bonds, and with the practical aspects of bond formation. Adhesion is sometimes called bonding, gluing, or cementing. An important aspect of this subject is the chemical nature of the adhesive. It includes the substance capable of holding materials together by surface attachment and of the adherends, i.e. the bodies being held together by the adhesive. Both the adhesive and the adherends may be high molecular weight plastics.

Many different magnitudes of bond strength can be obtained with various adhesives, but it is also important to consider the mode of loading to which an adhesive-bonded joint will be subjected. Most adhesives exhibit their maximum strength in the shear mode of load application.

Some adhesives excel in tension loading, but in all adhesive-joint designs the peel and tear modes of loading are to be avoided. Instead of distributing the load over the entire bond area, these modes of loading concentrate the stress in a very local area. The other factors to consider in analyzing the strength of an adhesive bond are the environment and the strength level required. Almost any solid can be bonded to any other solid with an adhesive as common as tape. However, the strength of the bond will be very low. Thus, in selecting an adhesive system, one must calculate the type and amount of strength required. ▷ **release agent performance**

adhesive, aerobic ▷ **aerobic adhesive**

adhesive, anaerobic ▷ **anaerobic adhesive**

adhesive assembly time The time interval between the spreading of the adhesive on the adherend and the application of pressure and/or heat to the assembly.

adhesive bonded label An adhesive may be applied during labeling or it may be preapplied to the sheet or film material and activated or exposed during the labeling. Most labels are secured by wet glue applied during labeling; some hot melt adhesives are also used for the same purpose. Preapplied adhesives are mainly pressure sensitive. Labels of this type are the most important for labeling plastic containers and other fabricated plastic parts. In addition to pressure-sensitive labels, some labels with a preapplied heat-activatable or preapplied delayed-tack adhesive are also available. Both of these are activated by heat, but the bond in the case of the former must be made immediately after the adhesive is activated; the tack is lost when the adhesive cools off. Delayed-tack types, once activated, retain the tack for long periods of time.

Pressure-sensitive adhesives adhere well to plastic surfaces, including some adhesion-difficult plastics, such as polyolefins and fluoroplastics. Also, they do not require drying after the application, unlike wet type labels. Thus, impervious label stock, such as films and metallized or laminated papers, may be used with pressure-sensitive adhesives. They are easy to apply and only a light pressure is required to secure the bond. Prior to use, adhesives are protected with a release sheet from which the labels are removed before use. Labels of irregular geometry can be die cut easily on release paper and they are much easier to handle when mounted on release paper.

Adhesives are divided by the label industry into the major categories of permanent, removable, and low temperature. A permanent adhesive is expected to secure the label firmly in place so the label will be destroyed upon removal. A removable adhesive allows clean label removal without its destruction. In some cases only temporary removability is required, such as when the label is not properly applied and requires a movement; these are called repositionable. Low temperature adhesives retain tack at refrigerator or at freezer temperatures. When used directly or indirectly on food products, FDA-approved adhesives are applied. All these labels are produced in three major steps: manufacture of label stock, label printing, and label die cutting. ▷ **release agent performance**

adhesive, cold-setting ▷ **cold-setting adhesive**

adhesive, contact ▷ **contact adhesive**

adhesive, delayed tack ▷ **adhesive bonded label**

adhesive, electromagnetic ▷ **electromagnetic adhesive**

adhesive failure Rupture of an adhesive bond such that the separation appears to be at the adhesive-adherend interface. An example of this undesirable type failure occurs when a lap shear specimen fails by leaving adhesive on one adherend and none on the corresponding area of the other adherend. Cohesive failure is when failure occurs within the adhesive, leaving adhesive on both adherends within the same contact area. When both shear areas are completely covered, it is called a 100% cohesive failure—the optimum condition.

adhesive film A plastic adhesive, with or without a carrier (usually plastic, paper, fabric, or glass), usually of the thermoset type. It is in the form of a thin, dry film of plastic used under heat and pressure as an interleaf in the production of bonded products, particularly high strength structures.

adhesive, flame treat surface ▷ **flame treating**

adhesive gap filler An adhesive subject to reduce shrinkage upon setting; it is used as a sealant.

adhesive, heat-activated ▷ **heat-activated adhesive**

adhesive, heat-sealing ▷ **heat-sealing adhesive**

adhesive, hot-melt ▷ **hot-melt adhesive**

adhesive, hot-setting ▷ **hot-setting adhesive**

adhesive, intermediate temperature setting An adhesive that sets in the temperature range from 30 to 100°C (87 to 211°F).

adhesive, isinglass A white, tasteless gelatine derived from the bladder of fishes, usually the sturgeon. It is used as an adhesive and clarifying agent.

adhesive joint ▷ **joint, adhesive** and **joining and bonding**

adhesive, lacquer type solvent ▷ **lacquer**

adhesive line The adhesive layer between two adherends. ▷ **microsphere**

adhesive, mechanical Adhesion between surfaces in which the adhesive holds the parts together by interlocking action.

adhesiveness The property defined by the adhesion stress $A = F/S$ where F is the perpendicular force to the adhesive line and S its surface area expressed in kg/cm^2 (1b/in^2).

adhesive overlap A simple adhesive joint in which the surface of one adherend extends past the leading edge of another.

adhesive penetration In adhesive operations, the amount of adhesive which seeps into the components of the joint and/or the material; it may be zero percent.

adhesive, pressure-sensitive ▷ **adhesive bonded label**

adhesive promoter A coating applied to a substrate before it is coated with an adhesive to improve the adhesion of the plastic; also called primer.

adhesive, room temperature curing ▷ **room temperature curing adhesive**

adhesive, "scotch tape" test A method of evaluating the adhesion of a lacquer, paint, and so on to a plastic substrate. Pressure-sensitive adhesive tape is applied to an area of the plastic coating, which is sometimes cross-hatched with scratched lines. Adhesion is considered to be adequate if no coating (paint, etc.) is pulled off by the tape when it is removed.

adhesive slippage The movement of adherends with respect to each other during the bonding operation.

adhesive, solvent ▷ **solvent bonding**

adhesive, specific The adhesion between two surfaces which are held together by variance forces of the same type as those which give rise to cohesion, as opposed to mechanical adhesion in which the adhesive holds the parts together by interlocking action.

adhesive spread The amount of adhesive (by weight) on the surface area of the bond line; usually expressed in kg/100 cm^2 (lb/100 ft^2).

adhesive strength Adhesive or bond strength relates to the bond between an adhesive and an adherend. It is a measure of the stress required to separate a layer of material from the base to which it is bonded. ▷ **peel strength**

adhesive, structural ▷ **structural adhesive**

adhesive tack stage The interval of time during which a deposited adhesive film exhibits stickiness or tack, or resists removal or deformation of the adhesive.

adhesive, unbonded ▷ **unbonded**

adhesive, water-soluble, emulsion and dispersion ▷ **water-soluble plastic; emulsion; dispersion**

adiabatic **1.** A process condition in which basically there is no gain or loss of heat from the environment. **2.** It describes a process or transformation in which no heat is added to or allowed to escape from the system under consideration. **3.** Even though it is not completely applicable, it is used to describe a mode of extrusion in which no external heat is added to the extruder although heat may be removed by cooling to keep the output temperature of the melt passing through the extruder constant. The heat input in such a process is developed by the screw as its mechanical energy is converted to thermal energy.

adjustable speed drive ▷ **motion control systems**

admixture The addition and homogeneous dispersion (mixture) of discrete components before cure.

adsorbate **1.** Material that has been retained by the process of adsorption. **2.** Any substance that can be adsorbed.

adsorption The adsorption of plastics plays an important role in a large number of practical applications, yet the details of the structure of the interface between the plastic and the substrate is usually not correctly understood. Plastic adsorption is important in the adhesion between solids, the applications of coating the interaction between plastic materials and solid fillers; all of these depend upon the adsorption of macromolecules on a substrate to a greater or lesser extent. Basically it is the adhesion of the molecules of gases, dissolved substances, or liquids in more or less concentrated form, to the surfaces of solids or liquids with which they are in contact. The concentration of a substance at a surface or interface of another substance.

adulterant Chemical impurities or substances that by law do not belong in food or any other regulated substance.

advanced plastics The general term advanced plastic or plastic composites, in the plastics industry, is used to indicate higher performance reinforced plastics. Thus glass fiber RPs are higher than cotton RPs, graphite fiber RPs are higher than glass RPs, and so on. The more specific definition is advanced reinforced plastics or advanced plastic composites pertaining to mechanical properties such as modulus of elasticity. ▷ **reinforced plastic, advanced**

advancing In-progress chemical reaction that results in curing the plastic.

advantages and disadvantages of plastics ▷ **plastic advantages and disadvantages**

aeration To supply air naturally or with equipment to solid waste, certain fabricating processes (such as foaming), chemical reactions, and so on.

aerobic Requiring air or oxygen, such as an aerobic adhesive.

aerobic bacteria Single-cell, microscopic organisms that need oxygen to survive, or are not destroyed by oxygen. Some aerobics are important in breaking down solid waste into simpler compounds.

aerogel Dispersion of a gas in a solid or a liquid. The reverse of an aerosol. Flexible and rigid plastic foams are examples of aerosol.

aerosol A suspension or dispersion of extremely fine solid particles or liquid particles in a gaseous medium, usually air; the particles often being in the colloidal size range. Fog and smoke are common examples of natural aerosols.

aerospace markets Traditionally, the requirements of the military have strongly influenced most of the evolution in science and technology throughout the world. Thus, aerospace technology with military and commercial aspirations is the origin of some of the strongest pressures on the technical community. The ultimate in performance in severe and unfamiliar environments is continuously sought. Costs in money and man power are, to a greater extent than in other technologies, initially secondary to performance. Aerospace applications of plastics have been very extensive since 1940. It is an endless task to keep advancing performance of materials that include all types, namely, thermoplastics, thermosets, elastomers, and reinforced plastics. Products include primary structures, transparents, coatings, adhesives, and so on. ▷ **aircraft**

aesthetic The sum total of the visual response to the beauty of an object. Elements of aesthetics may include color, shape, or particular features of the product. In packages, the texture or "feel" of the object may also be part of the appeal to desirable responses.

affinity The attraction for another substance; the tendency of atoms or compounds to react or combine with atoms or compounds of different chemical constitution.

aftercure A continuation of the process of curing after the energy has been removed. ▷ **post curing**

afterglow Glow in a material after the removal of an external source of fire exposure or after the cessation (natural or induced) of flaming of the material.

after mixer ▷ **reaction injection molding**

agglomeration **1.** A process of contact and adhesion whereby the particles of a dispersion form clusters of increasing size. **2.** Reversible or irreversible joining together of latex particles.

aggregate **1.** A hard, coarse material usually of mineral origin used with an epoxy binder (or other plastic) in plastic tools; also used in flooring or as a surface medium. **2.** Mixture of such particles as sand, gravel, crushed stone, or cinders used in cement formulations that incorporate plastics; cement plastic-aggregate mixtures used in building external walls, road building, and so on.

aging **1.** The effect of exposure of plastics to an environment for an interval of time. **2.** The process of exposing plastics to an environment for an interval of time, resulting in improvement or deterioration of properties based on type of plastic with or without additives. **3.** Regarding physical aging. ▷ **annealing 4.** ▷ **machine aging**

aging and molecular weight ▷ **molecular weight and aging**

aging, artificial The exposure of a plastic to conditions that accelerate the effects of time. Such conditions include heating, exposure to cold, flexing, application of electrical field, exposure to chemicals and UV light, and so on. Typically, the conditions chosen for such testing reflect the conditions under which the plastic product will be used. Usually, the length of time the article is exposed to these test conditions is relatively short. Properties such as dimensional stability, mechanical fatigue, chemical resistance, stress cracking resistance, creep behavior, dielectric strength, and so on are evaluated in such testing. ▷ **oven aging**

aging at elevated temperature Typically, aging at elevated temperatures involves exposing test specimens (or products) at different temperatures for different extended times. Tests are performed at room or the respective testing temperatures for whatever mechanical, physical, and electrical property is of interest. These aging tests can be used as a measure of thermal stability. ▷ **antioxidant** and **antiozonant**

aging, shelf ▷ **shelf life**

A-glass ▷ **glass fiber type**

agricultural fiber ▷ **fiber**

agricultural markets Since the introduction of plastic film in the 1930s and 1940s for greenhouse covering, fumigation, and mulching, agricultural applications of plastics have grown at an enormous rate. Many different forms of plastics (extrusions, moldings, coatings, elastomers, fibers, water-soluble plastics, and so on) are utilized in applications that include controlled release of pesticides and nutrients, soil conditioning, seed coating, gel planting, and plant protection. Also, plastics have become increasingly important because of their chemical and weather resistance, mechanical, physical, and electrical properties, as structural components of farm buildings and machinery, water transport and control, and in packaging of produce.

agricultural mulch ▷ **mulch, agricultural**

agricultural solid waste Solid waste is produced in farming. Can include animal manure and waste carcasses, plant stalks, hulls, and leaves.

air A mixture, or solution, of gases. Its composition varies with altitude and other conditions at the collection point. The composition of dry air at sea level is in percent by weight 75.53 nitrogen and 23.16 oxygen; or percent by volume 78.0 nitrogen, 20.95 oxygen, 0.93 argon, 0.033 carbon dioxide, 0.0018 neon, 0.0005 helium, and so on. ▷ **atmosphere chart** and **altitude chart**

air-assist forming ▷ **thermoforming, air-assist**

air atomization It is carried out by an air gun where a high velocity air stream breaks up the liquid plastic coating. Air atomization yields a smaller particle size than other spraying methods; the lower particle size limit is about 5 μm. It is the only method to produce a fine spray in which the diameters of all the droplets are less than 15 μm. Fine particle size allows good control of the coating thickness. The main disadvantage is considerable overspray (poor transfer efficiency) unless electrostatic assist is used. Pneumatic spraying is also inefficient from the point of view of energy utilization. Air guns not only atomize the paint, but they also shape the atomized stream. Usually a fan pattern is used because it allows better control of coverage.

air balloon ▷ **plastic air balloon**

air-bubble void Air entrapment or void within a molded, extruded, blow molded, and other products; or between the plies of reinforcements in a reinforced plastic; or within a bondline; or encapsulated area. They are usually localized, noninterconnected, and spherical in shape.

air clean ▷ **incineration fume system**

air cooling ▷ **extruder line cooling and shaping**

aircraft Since the 1940s, aeronautics technology has soared, with all types of plastics playing major roles in both pragmatic improvements and dramatic advances. Plastic's light weight and durability save on fuel while standing up to stress (creep, fatigue, etc.) and environments. In 1940, the rapid introduction of glass fiber reinforced thermoset polyester plastics (RPs) advanced the technology of composite materials. The Fig. here is an example of early developments

The 1944 Air Force airplane flight tests with glass fiber-thermoset polyester material designed and used in primary structures. The reinforced plastic sandwich structures included the wings, monoque fuselage, vertical stabilizer, etc. It was basically the first all-plastic airplane with at least all its primary and secondary structures made from reinforced plastic using hand lay-up molding process.

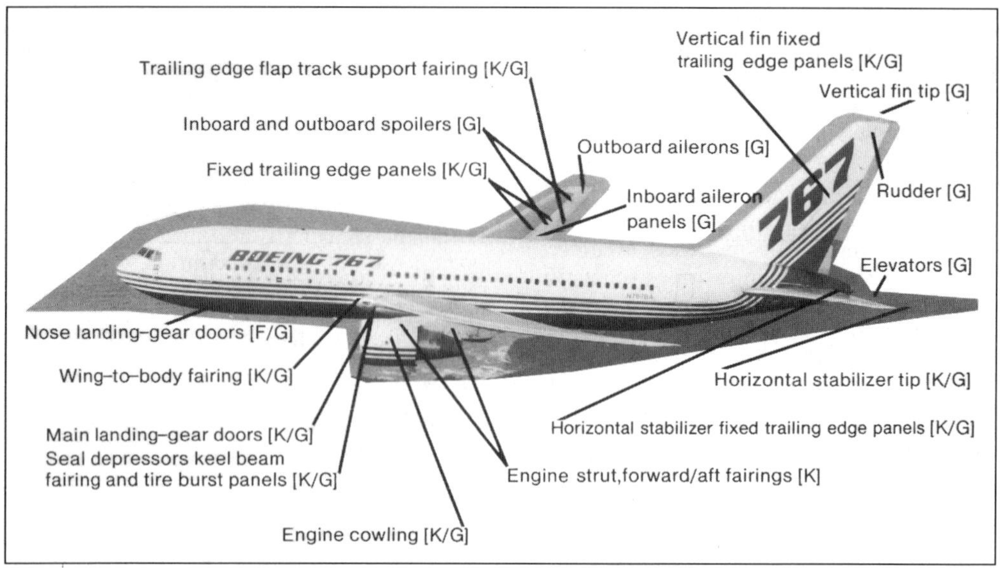

Extensive use is made of different thermoplastic and thermoset plastics, both unreinforced and reinforced, on commercial aircraft such as this Boeing 767. G = Graphite; K = Kevlar; F = Fiberglass.

in the use of reinforced plastics in primary aircraft structures. The Fig. above is more up to date on use of aircraft. ▷ **Gossamer Albatross; Solar Challenger; Windecker Eagle Airplane**

aircraft arrester ▷ **foamed ground aircraft arrester**

air-dry 1. Air containing no water vapor. 2. A condition applied to paper or pulp (also applicable to other nonwoven materials, including plastic) whereby its moisture content is in equilibrium with the atmospheric conditions to which it is exposed. According to trade custom, pulps are generally understood to be air dry when they contain 10% of moisture; for example, a pound of air-dry pulp contains 0.9 lb (0.4 kg) of oven-dry pulp and 0.1 lb (0.045 kg) of moisture.

air entrapment Air can be entrapped and form voids in the melt during processing. This can happen when plastic (pellets, flakes, etc.) is melted in a normal air environment (as in a plasticating extruder process, injection or blow molding barrel, compression mold, casting form, spray system, and so on) and the air cannot escape. Generally the melt is subject to a compression load, or even a vacuum, which causes release of air; but in some cases the air is trapped. If air entrapment is acceptable, no further action is required. However, it is usually unacceptable for reasons of performance and/or aesthetics.

Changing the initial melt temperature in either direction may solve the problem. With a barrel and screw, it is important to study the effects of temperature changes. Another approach is to increase the pressure in processes that use process controls. Particle size, melt shape, and the melt delivery system may have to be changed or better controlled. A vacuum hopper feed system may be useful. With screw plasticators, changes in screw design may be helpful. Usually, a vented barrel will solve the problem.

The presence of bubbles could be due to air alone or moisture, plastic surface agents or volatiles, plastic degradation, or the use of contaminated regrind. With molds such as those used for injection, compression, casting, or reaction injection, air or moisture in the mold cavity is usually the problem. So the first step to resolving a bubble, void, or air problem is to be sure what problem exists. A logical troubleshooting approach can be used.

Industries ASTM identifies entrapped air or air voids as generally larger than 1 mm which are not usually produced by the intentional use of an air-entrapment agent. Air entrapment concerns: (1) processing, as reviewed above; (2) plastic foam where it is deliberately entrapped to produce foam; (3) in concrete, small bubbles (about 1 mm) of air provide increase resistance to freezing or thawing damage and improved workability; bubbles are formed by the addition of small quantities of surface active chemicals.

air flotation or felting process Forming of a fibrous-felted sheet or board from an air suspension of damp or dry fibers on a batch or continuous forming machine; sometimes referred to as the dry or semidry process. ▷ **mechanical nonwoven fabric**

air flow value The volume of air per minute at standard temperature and pressure required to maintain a constant pressure differential of 125 Pa (0.5 in of water) across a flexible foam specimen about 50 × 50 × 25 mm (2 × 2 × 1 in).

air knife coating ▷ **coating air knife**

airless spraying ▷ **spraying airless**

air locks Surface depressions on a part, caused by trapped air between the mold or die surface and the plastics.

airplane ▷ **aircraft**

air ring ▷ **extruder blown film, air ring**

airship Inflatable airships have been using different type plastics in their construction. Gondolas are made of reinforced plastics. Airships with an inflated volume of 9,000 cubic yards can ascend to 6,500 feet with eight persons aboard, and cruise at 55 mph (88 km/h). The lightweight, but high-strength airship envelope is fashioned from a three-part laminate such as thermoplastic polyester fabric coated with Du Pont's neoprene and "Hypalon" elastomers.

air shot Injection molding plasticator withdrawn from the mold sprue so melt shot leaves its nozzle into the air.

air vent Small outlet, usually minute holes or grooves, to provide a path for air to flow out of a mold cavity as the plastic enters.

alchemy A medieval chemical science and speculative philosophy aiming to achieve the transmutation of the basic metals (such as lead) into gold.

alcoholysis ▷ **chemical recycling**

Alcryn Du Pont's tradename for an olefinic thermoplastic elastomer (TPE). It is one of the most "rubbery" of all TPEs. It is considered a single-phase, crosslinked ethylene interpolymer alloy that competes with thermoset rubber (TSE) parts and flexible polyvinyl chloride.

aldehyde Volatile liquids with sharp, penetrating odors that are slightly less soluble in water than are corresponding alcohols.

aldehyde polymerization It proceeds by bond opening, chain-reaction polymerization of carbonyl group of an aldehyde and results in the formation of polyalaldehydes (or acetal plastics).

algorithm A specified, step-by-step procedure for performing a task or solving a problem, sometimes in reference to a computer program. Also known as a flow chart. ▷ **genetic algorithm**

alignment of machine ▷ **machine alignment**

aliphatic hydrocarbon Saturated hydrocarbons having an open-chain structure, for example, gasoline and propane.

alkali metal and derivative The alkali metals (lithium, sodium, potassium, cesium, and francium) make up Group 1A of elements of the Periodic system. Because of their high reactivity, the alkali metals (with the exception of francium) find use in virtually every area of organic polymer synthesis, including many aspects of polymerization chemistry. ▷ **Periodic table**

alkyd The name alkyd appears to have been derived from alcohol (alk) and acid (yd). The reaction of difunctional alcohols (glycols) and difunctional acids or anhydrides gives thermoset polyesters and alkyd plastics (they are related in this class of plastics).

alkyd molding compound Compound based on unsaturated polyester plastic and formulated with relatively low amounts of crosslinking monomer and fillers, lubricants, pigments, and catalysts into a thermosetting material for use principally in compression, transfer, or injection molding.

alkyd plastic Among the important thermoset molding compounds, the alkyds' primary advantages over formaldehyde-based plastics (phenolic, etc.) are dimensional stability, superior electrical qualities, and (most important) the fact that they do not yield (condense) water during cure. Alkyds can be cured without pressure, however most are cured with pressures from contact to 10 MPa (1,450 psi) and at temperatures that depend on the peroxide and monomer used but they are generally from 93° to 177°C (200° to 350°F). Compounds are formulated with a variety of fillers and reinforcements, including clays and carbonates, glass fibers, and so on. Consequently, they are used in the electrical, automotive, and other industries. Alkyd plastics are actually an offshoot of the alkyd-coating industry introduced to the U.S. during the 1930s. Offering moderately high heat resistance, rapid cure cycle, and good mold flow, alkyds permit molding relatively complicated shapes.

The term alkyd should be used with some care. It was originally coined to designate resinous reaction products of di- and polyhydric alcohols and acids, which, when modified with

Plastic	Cost index	Yield strength index	Impact strength index
Polypropylene			
Polystyrene Impact styrene (alloy)			
ABS ABS-PVC (alloy) ABS- polycarbonate (alloy)			
Rigid PVC PVC-acrylic (alloy)			
Poly(phenylene oxide) (Noryl)			
Polycarbonate			
Polysulfone Polysulfone-ABS (alloy)			
	100 500	100 200	100 450 1250 3000

Different plastics can be combined to provide cost-performance improvements.

reactive monomers, are termed polyester plastics. When they are modified by formulating with nonvolatile monomers such as diallyl phthalate to form dry, or relatively dry, molding compounds, they are called alkyd plastics. The alkyds are actually polyesters. In the industry, the basic thermoset polyester, uncut with a monomer such as styrene, is called an alkyd. The terms alkyd, alkyd resin, alkyd plastic, and alkyd solution are used interchangeably.

allergen ▷ **antibodies and antigens plastic encapsulated**

alligator-grained surface Plastic surface embossed to resemble the grain of an alligator hide.

alligatoring A reinforced plastic or laminate surface flaw resembling the texture of an alligator's skin.

allophanate Reactive product of an isocyanate and the hydrogen atoms in a urethane.

alloprene plastic Chlorinated elastomer or rubber.

allotropy The existence of a substance, especially an element, in two or more physical states such as crystals. ▷ **graphite**

allowable property ▷ **A-basis; B-basis; S-basis; typical-basis**

allowance An intentional difference between maximum material limits of mating parts. It is the minimum clearance (positive allowance) or maximum interference (negative allowance) between such parts. ▷ **tolerance**

alloy/blend Alloys are combinations of two or more plastics which are mechanically blended; they do not depend on chemical bonds but often require special compatibilizers. Plastic alloys are usually designed to retain the best characteristics of each constituent. Most often, property improvements are in the areas such as impact strength, weather resistance, low temperature performance, and flame retardance; examples are in the Fig. above.

The terms alloy and blend are often used interchangeably but generally an alloy is a subclass of plastic blends. Most high performance blends are alloys. And alloys can be subdivided into two categories; those in which compatibilization leads to very fine dispersion, and those in which some compatibilizing agent is added to facilitate the formation of desired morphology during subsequent processing. Blending of plastics has been in existence for over a century; its growth rate has been and will continue to be nothing less than spectacular. About 4,500 alloy/blend patents are issued annually and at least 10 times as many technical treatises are published annually. ▷ **reactive polymer; miscibility**

alloy constitutional diagram Graphical representation of the compositions, temperatures, pressures, or combinations thereof at which heterogeneous equilibria of an alloy system occur; also called phase diagram or equilibrium diagram.

alloy steel A steel containing up to 10% by weight of elements such as chromium, molybdenum, nickel, and so on, usually with a low percentage of carbon. These added elements improve hardenability, wear resistance, toughness, and other properties. The low-alloy steels have up to 5% of the elements.

allyl plastic A 1940 development, the allylic plastics are among the more versatile of the thermoset plastics and possibly the least appreciated. Actually a branch of the TS polyester family, the allylics can be homopolymerized or copolymerized with alkyds. Easily molded, they can be cured at any temperature above 93°C (200°F) as homopolymers by the proper selection of peroxide, or at temperatures considerably lower by cross-linked with alkyd. Using UV-sensitive accelerators, they may be sunlight cured as alkyd copolymers. Molding processes include contact, vacuum and pressure bag, compression, and transfer molding.

The earliest allylics were formulated but found little application owing to the extreme difficulty of curing the liquid monomer. The monomer may be homopolymerized in the presence of a peroxide, but even with almost exhaustive processing it cannot be fully cured. It was eventually discovered that it was possible to cure the monomer partially and then precipitate it to form a powder of molecular weight intermediate between monomer and a fully cured polymer. This powder was termed a prepolymer and led to one of the earliest stable prepreg materials in the late 1940s. As a result of the prepolymer development, allylics are marked as either monomer or prepolymer. The processor is then free to formulate compounds with any ratio from zero to over 50% monomer, blended with appropriate peroxide, reinforcement, filler, pigment, and copolymer.

An example of a true allylic homopolymer cast from the monomer is diethylene glycol bis(allyl carbonate), which is cast and sold under the tradename CR-39 for applications such as optical sunglasses and conventional eyeglasses. CR-39 is characterized by good optical transparency and excellent hardness and scratch resistance.

Diallyl phthalate (DAP) is most widely used in combination with alkyds for applications such as polyester prepreg. The nonvolatile, stable DAP monomer confers good shelf life, excellent laminating qualities, and good surface hardness. A common example of its use is the imitation-wood-grain low pressure laminate used for furniture and wall paneling. Such prepreg contains 5 to 10% DAP.

Diallyl orthophthalate (DAOP), diallyl metaphthalate (DAMP) monomers, and prepolymers are widely used in precision compression moldings. They provide outstanding dimensional stability, low water absorption, outstanding electrical properties, and ease of molding.

alpha A prefix (α) denoting the position of a substituting atom or group in an organic compound.

alpha cellulose A very pure cellulose.

alpha loss peak In dynamic mechanical or dielectric measurement, the first peak (α) in the damping curve below the melt, in order of decreasing temperature or increasing frequency.

alpine **1.** A plant native to alpine or boreal regions that is often grown for ornaments and reinforcing plastics. **2.** Relating to competitive ski events consisting of downhill racing. **3.** Relating to the Alps in Europe. **4.** Fierce army infantry mountain fighters high in the Alpine mountains of Italy/Austria.

alternating current ▷ **electrical alternating current**

altitude chart The chart on p. 18 presents standard values for the temperature, pressure, density and molecular weight of air. It depicts idealized middle-latitude year-round mean conditions for the range of solar activity that occurs between sunspot minimum and sunspot maximum. The molecular weight of air is assumed constant from sea level to 295,276 geometric feet. Above this altitude the molecular weight decreases, mainly because of molecular disassociation and diffusive separation. ▷ **atmosphere chart**

alumina, activated A highly porous granular form of aluminum oxide that has preferential adsorptive capacity for moisture and odor contained in gases and some liquids. It is an effective desiccant and also used as a catalyst or catalyst carrier in chromatography.

alumina-silica fiber Amorphous structure, excellent resistance to all chemicals except hydrochloric acid, phosphoric acid, and concentrated alkalies. Tensile strength is 400,000 psi (2,000 MPa), modulus of elasticity 16 million psi (110 GPa), upper temperature limit in oxidizing atmosphere 800°C (1,470°F), noncombustible, low heat conductivity, and thermal shock resistance.

alumina trihydrate An inert, white crystalline mineral powder filler which provides flame retardancy, and electrical arc/track resistance to plastics. Also used as a reinforcing agent in elastomers, paper coating, fillers for cosmetics, and so on.

aluminized film ▷ **film aluminized**

aluminum Al is a metallic element of atomic number 13, Group 3A of the Periodic table. It is the third most abundant metal in the earth's crust. Does not occur free in nature. It is derived from mined bauxite which, in turn, is processed through various techniques and subsequently via electrolytic reduction. This crystalline, silver white solid has a tensile strength (annealed) of 6,800 psi (47 MPa) and cold-rolled 16,000 psi (110 MPa). Fine-powder forms of aluminum are flammable and explosive mixtures in air.

aluminum alkyl Catalyst used in the Ziegler process. ▷ **Ziegler-Natta polymerization**

aluminum foil Aluminum foil is a solid sheet of aluminum, or of an appropriate aluminum alloy, rolled very thin, varying from a minimum

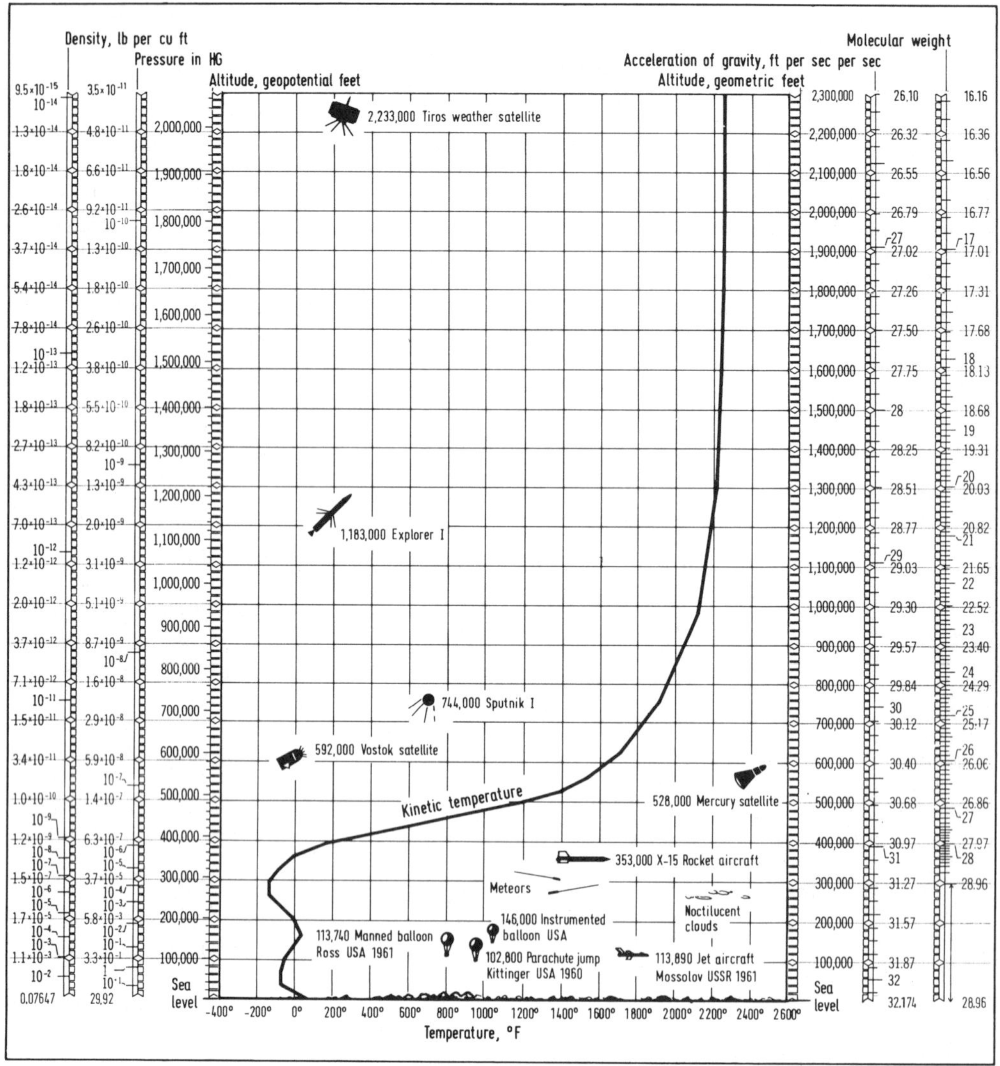

Altitude chart.

thickness of about 0.00017 in. (0.00432 mm) to a maximum of about 0.0059 in. (0.1499 mm). In the aluminum industry, thickness of 0.006 in (0.1524 mm) is sheet material. From the standpoint of packaging and other principal applications, one of the most important characteristics of aluminum foil is its permeability to water vapor and gases. Bare foil $1\frac{1}{2}$ mil (0.0015 in.) and thicker is completely impermeable; much thinner gauges laminated or coated to an appropriate plastic film form impervious composite materials, making them ideal for packaging and general insulation/barrier applications. These solid-foil semi-rigid containers account for most foil consumption.

aluminum foil, annealing As it comes from the mill, all foil is work hardened by rolling because the reduction of aluminum reroll stock to foil gauges is exclusively a cold rolling operation. Between-pass annealing process is required to restore workability. Final annealing achieves essentially the same purpose as previous intermediate anneals. This controlled heat treatment relieves the internal stresses created by work hardening; result is the alloy in a soft condition. In the annealed condition, each foil is at its optimum workability and dead-fold state, which is most advantageous for many packaging and other uses.

aluminum foil laminating adhesive A wide range of adhesives is available for use with foil, but special requirements of each application dictate selection. Requirements which affect the choice of adhesives include color, odor, toxicity, and resistance to heat, cold, and moisture.

aluminum permeability ▷ **aluminum foil**

aluminum wettability test The extent to which the residual rolling oil has been removed in the annealing process is defined as foil wettability. It is also referred to as dryness. Wettability is tested using different solutions of ethyl alcohol in distilled water, usually in increments of 10% by volume.

amber A natural plastic (resin) that has plastic formability behaviour. This fossil resin was produced in the oligocenic period by a now extinct species of pine trees. Readily accumulates static electrical charge by friction; also provides good electrical insulation.

ambient pressure ▷ **pressure, ambient**

ambient temperature ▷ **temperature, ambient**

American National Safety Institute ANSI standards (voluntary) are available that pertain to the safety requirements that exist for various plastic fabrication equipment (extruder, sprayer, and so on) and auxiliary equipment (cutter, granulator, and so on).

American Standards for Testing Materials This worldwide organization that started during the 19th century is a recognized world authority on standards for testing all types of materials, including plastics, which has thousands of testing standards.

aminolysis ▷ **chemical recycling**

amino plastic Amino family of plastics are those reaction products of amino compounds with aldehydes. The amino monomer is characteristically present as amide, for example, in urea formaldehyde plastics and melamine formaldehyde plastics. Although other aldehydes have been investigated, formaldehyde is nearly always used. It condenses with the amino compound to form methylol derivatives of the latter which, on heating, condense further to form hard, colorless, transparent plastics. When cured, or heat set, the amino resins are more properly referred to as amino plastics, also called aminoplasts.

ammonia anhydrous Colorless gas (or liquid) with sharp and intensely irritating odor, lighter than air, easily liquified, and very soluble in water, alcohol, and so on. It is the third highest volume chemical produced in the U.S. Use includes plastic formulations (manufacture of polyurethane, acrylonitrile, and others), synthetic fibers, dyeing, latex preservative, fertilizer, and rocket fuel.

amorphous plastic An amorphous thermoplastic is the type in which the molecular chains exist in random coil conformation (such as water-boiled spaghetti). There is no regularity of structure as there is with crystalline thermoplastics. The structure of an amorphous plastic is characterized by the absence of a regular three-dimensional arrangement of molecules or subunits of molecules extending over distances that are large compared to atomic dimensions; there is no long-range order. However, due to the close packing in the condensed state, certain regularity of the structure exists on a local scale, denoted as short-range order.

Use of the term often implies that the plastic is amorphous in the solid state. All thermoplastics are usually amorphous in solution or melt. An irregular conformation is adopted if the molecular structure is irregular. Thus atactic plastics, random copolymers, and thermoset plastics cannot crystallize due to molecular irregularity and hence are amorphous. Even regular plastics, which normally crystallize, may often be quenched from the melt state to the amorphous state. Amorphous plastics exhibit a strong T_g often with additional lower temperature, but weaker transitions. If non-crosslinked, they are more readily soluble than crystalline types. They are normally isotropic (unless oriented via processing methods) and homogeneous. Since they do not contain crystals to scatter light, they are also transparent.

Their structure is not static but is subject to thermally driven fluctuations. The local structure changes continuously as a function of time due to orientational and translational molecular motions. The time scale of these motions may comprise nanoseconds up to several hundred years. The structure of the amorphous state as well as its time-dependent fluctuations can be analyzed by various scattering techniques such as X-ray, neutron, electron, and polarized light. Polystyrene, acrylic, polysulfone, and polycarbonate are typical examples of amorphous plastics. ▷ **molecular arrangement structure** and **morphology**

amorphous plastic orientation The component of the overall orientation due to the amorphous regions in a plastic. There will be an amorphous component to each anisotropic property, i.e. birefringence.

amorphous plastic region A region in a crystalline plastic which has not crystallized and therefore in which the polymer chains exist in the random coil conformation; where the polymer is amorphous. Since crystallization is limited in a crystalline plastic, amorphous regions are always present, typically accounting for 10 to 70% of the material. Thus the plastic behaves as a "composite" of amorphous and crystalline polymers. Both regions contribute their characteristic properties to the overall behavior, with amorphous regions exhibiting a T_g.

amorphous plastic scatter The X-ray scattering produced by an amorphous plastic or region consists of a few diffuse halos. Although no short- or long-range order of a crystalline kind exists, a short-range order of the most probable distances between neighboring atoms does exist. This is often expressed in terms of the atomic radial distribution function, obtained from the scattering curve.

amorphous properties ▷ **morphology-amorphous properties**

amosite A fibrous, amphibole asbestos similar to crocidolite, containing a higher proportion of iron than anthophyllite. Forms fibers with a tensile strength of about 2 GPa and a tensile modulus of about 150 GPa, typically 60 to 100 nm wide and with good acid resistance. Use includes filler and/or reinforcement in plastics.

ampere ▷ **electrical ampere**

amphoteric Having a capacity of behaving either as an acid or a base.

anaerobic adhesive An adhesive that cures only in the absence of air after being confined between assembled parts.

anaerobic bacteria Single-cell, microscopic organisms that do not need oxygen to survive or not destroyed by absence of oxygen. Some anaerobics are important in breaking down solid waste into compounds. These bacteria dominate oxygen-starved landfill environments, but do not break down wastes as quickly as aerobic bacteria.

analog Information that is continuously variable, thus having infinite possible values. It is unlike digital information which is discrete and binary, having only two possible values (on/off, high/low).

analog-to-digital converter A/D or ADC is a device that converts real-world analog data, as for transducers, into binary or digital form suitable for computer processing.

analyze failure ▷ **failure analyzer**

analyzer An optical device, capable of producing plane polarized light, used for detecting the state of polarization.

anelastic deformation ▷ **viscous deformation**

anelasticity The dependence of elastic strain on both stress and time. This can result in a lag of strain behind stress. In materials subjected to cyclic stress, such as fatigue, the anelastic effect causes internal damping.

angel hair ▷ **cutting burr-free**

angle head ▷ **extruder head angle**

angstrom unit A unit of length. For practical purposes an angstrom is one hundred millionth (10^{-8}) of a centimeter. In more exact terms, it is the wavelength of the red line of cadmium (6438.4696 A). Abbreviation: A; previously Å.

anhydride A compound derived from an acid by elimination of a molecule of water. Thus carbon dioxide (CO_2) is the anhydride of carbonic acid (H_2CO_3), and so on.

anhydrous **1.** Compounds from which water was removed. **2.** Descriptive of an inorganic compound that does not contain water either on its surface or combined as water of crystallization.

aniline One of the most important of the organic bases, the parent substance for many dyes and drugs.

anion ▷ **ion**

anionic polymerization Vinyl polymerization that proceeds by the addition of certain monomers to active center bearing whole or partial negative charges. ▷ **living plastic systems**

anisotropic properties ▷ **reinforced plastic directional properties**

annealing The annealing of plastics can be defined as a heat-treatment process directed at improving performance by removal of strains and stresses set up in the material during its fabrication; also called physical aging. Based on the plastic used, it is brought up to certain temperature for a definite period of time, and then slowly cooled to room temperature. In the plastic industry, annealing is generally restricted to thermoplastics, either amorphous or crystalline. A mean result of heat treatment is to increase the density, thereby improving the plastic's heat resistance and dimensional stability when exposed to elevated temperatures. It frequently improves the impact strength and prevents crazing and cracking of excessively stressed items. The magnitude of these changes depends on the nature of the plastic, the annealing conditions, and the part's past history.

Rigid, amorphous plastics such as polystyrene and acrylic are frequently annealed for stress relief. Annealing crystalline plastics, in addition to the usual stress relief, may also bring about significant changes in the nature of their crystalline state. In turn, it is governed by the nature of the crystal structure, degree of crystallinity, size and number of spherulites and orientation. In many cases when proper temperature and pressure are maintained during processing, the induced internal stresses may be insignificant, and physical aging is not required.

Plastic blends and block copolymers typically contain other low and intermediate molecular weight additives such as plasticizers, flame retardants, and UV and thermal stabilizers. During annealing, phase and microphase separation may be enhanced and bleeding of the additives may be observed. The morphologies of blends and block copolymers can be affected by processing and quenching conditions. If their melt viscosities are not matched, compositional layering perpendicular to the direction of flow may occur. As in the case of crystalline plastics, the skin may be different both in morphology and composition. Annealing may cause more significant changes in the skin than in the interior.

annealing equipment and method It is similar to that used for preheating thermoplastic sheets, rods, tubes, and other profiles before shaping or thermoforming. Depending on the liquid or air annealing medium, different heating systems are used. The equipment for liquid baths such as water, oils, and waxes, consists of tanks or troughs that should be of suitable size. When air is used suitable systems are circulating-air or air-flow ovens.

The most desirable annealing temperatures for amorphous plastics, certain blends, and block copolymers is above their T_g where the relaxation of stress and orientation is the most rapid. However, the required temperatures may cause excessive distortion and warping. To anneal quickly, the plastic is heated to the highest temperature at which dimensional changes owing to strain release are within permissible ranges. This temperature can be determined be placing the plastic part in an air oven or liquid bath and gradually raising the temperature by intervals of 3 to 5°C until the maximum allowable change in shape or dimension occurs. This distortion temperature is dictated by thermomechanical processing history, geometry, thickness, weight, and size. Usually the annealing temperature is set about 5°C lower using careful quality control procedure.

anode The positive electrode of an electrolytic cell to which negatively charged ions travel when an electric current is passed through the cell; the electrode that supplies electrons to an external circuit.

antiblocking ▷ **film blocking**

antiblocking agent These agents are substances that prevent or reduce blocking when added to plastic compound or applied to their surface. The concentration of agent used varies from 0.1 to 1% based on the weight of the plastic. Such chemicals as stearamide, stearoguanamine, metal salts of fatty acids (calcium stearate), polyethylene, copolymers of vinyl acetate with either maleic anhydride, ethylene, or ethyl acrylate; sodium dioctylsulfosuccinate; alkylamines and alkyl quaternary ammonium compounds are effective and are usually incorporated into the plastic before extruding, molding or casting. Stearamide is widely used to prevent blocking in polyethylene. Amounts of 0.5% are usually sufficient. Other chemicals such as colloidal silica, clays, starches, silicones, guanidine stearate, and long-chain alkyl quaternary ammonium compounds may be applied to the surface either during or after extrusion, molding, or casting to reduce blocking. The concentration of antiblocking agent used varies from 0.1 to 1% based on the weight of the plastic.

antibodies and antigens plastic encapsulated Techniques are used to produce large amounts of homogeneous antibodies to order by altering normal antibody cells so they can easily be grown in the laboratory. Each cell alone produces only one specific antibody, thus such products are termed monoclonal antibodies. They are used in a wide variety of applications. They are bound to plastic supports and used to purify molecules of many types.

Also useful are the design and synthesis of specialized latex particles, such as microspheres, to which antibodies or antigens are attached. Reagents formed in this way are referred to as immunomicrospheres. They can be structured to permit identification by radioactive labeling, fluorescence, electron opacity, and magnetic and electrophoretic separation. They have been used in drug delivery systems.

anticaking agent An additive used primarily in certain finely divided compounds that tend to be hygroscopic to prevent or inhibit agglomeration and thus maintain a free-flowing condition.

antifoaming agent Antifoaming agents (antifoams, foam inhibitors) are materials used in the prevention and control of unwanted foam. A distinction can be made between defoaming agents or defoamers which are foam reducers and antifoaming agents which are foam-prevention materials; however the terms are used interchangeably. Foamed fluids are dispersions of air or other gas as the discontinuous phase in an otherwise continuous liquid phase. Usually, since air or gas makes up the larger volume portion of such a foam, the bubbles are separated only by a thin liquid film (lamella). Unwanted fluid foams are comprised of thousands of tiny uniform bubbles of mechanical or chemical origin that are generated within a liquid and that rise and accumulate at the liquid surface faster than they decay. Problems are very diverse, ranging from unaesthetic foam to foams hazardous to life and include polymerization reactions, coatings, adhesive, and so on.

Solutions of the problem may be mechanical or a chemical additive antifoaming agent. Mechanical means have the advantage of not potentially adding contaminated material. Because of the variety of plastics to be defoamed and the extreme conditions of operation, no single material has universal applications as a chemical antifoam. Agents typically contain numerous ingredients, which usually fall into one of the following categories: liquid-phase components; solid-phase components; ancillary agents such as emulsifiers, thickeners, and preservatives; or carriers such as water and solvents. Classification by chemical type is usually made.

antifouling coating Plastic coating or painting compounded with principally copper naphthenate and mercury for use on parts subjected to submersion or immersion in water, such as bottoms of ships, to protect them from attack by barnacles and other marine organisms.

antifriction compound Plastic specifically formulated to reduce or eliminate friction.

antigelling agent An additive which prevents a solution from forming a gel.

antimicrobial agent These agents are finding their way into plastic products used in building and construction to ward off what that industry refers to as "sick building syndrome" and "building-related illness" which can cause a range of ailments in humans. These side effects of indoor microbial growth become more noticeable with the construction of better-insulated, more energy-efficient homes, offices, and automobiles. Typical of such maladies is Legionnaire's disease, which was first exposed to public awareness during an outbreak of pneumonia-like sickness among attendees of a 1976 American Legion Convention at the old, original Bellevue-Stratford hotel (completely destroyed a few years later during the 1980s and a new Bellevue built) in Philadelphia. The causative agent was a bacterium isolated from the hotel's air-conditioning system.

High densities of fungi and bacteria have been found in carpets, wall coverings, hot tubs, shower heads, drains, shower curtains, refrigerator doors, and in healthcare and cosmetic products; they are believed to be the problem.

antimony oxide A white, odorless, fine powder which is used as a flame retardant as well as a pigment, catalyst, chemical intermediate, and lubricant chemical identifiied as Sb_2O_3.

antioxidant These agents are of major importance to the plastics industry because they extend the plastic's useful temperature range and service life. The variety of antioxidants available and their specific uses are extensive. An antioxidant is defined as a substance that opposes oxidation or inhibits reactions promoted by oxygen or peroxides. In the specific case for plastics, they retard atmospheric oxidation or the degradative effects of oxidation when added in small proportions. For this reason, they are also known as aging retardants. Oxidative degradation by ozone, however, is controlled by antiozonants.

Two major areas of plastic deterioration protection are of concern: during processing and product use. These protecting agents during processing and storage are often called stabilizers. In general, agents used to protect and preserve properties of fabricated products are referred to as antioxidants in elastomer technology and stabilizers in plastic technology. Agents which protect plastics from photochemical or other kinds of deterioration are often also referred to as stabilizers. An example is one which prevents hydrogen chloride elimination from polyvinyl chloride. In many applications stabilizers for the processed plastics also serve as an antioxidant in the finished product.

antiozonant The term antiozonant, in its broadest sense, denotes any additive that protects elastomers from ozone deterioration. Most frequently, the protective effect results from a reaction with ozone, in which case the term used is chemical antiozonant. Ozone is generated by electrical discharge, but a more important source is the photolysis of oxygen on sunny days. Elastomers can be protected against ozone by the addition of waxes, inert plastics, or chemically reactive antiozonants. Waxes are generally of the paraffin or microcrystalline type. Many of the chemical types contain nitrogen.

antirad ▷ **radiation-induced reaction**

antisag agent ▷ **thickening agent**

antislip agent These agents are also called slip depressants. It is usually desirable to have a certain degree of blocking between surfaces; for example, where filled plastic bags cannot be stacked because they have a tendency to slide off the piles, or where plastic fibers made into garments give excessive slippage the use of an antislip agent is used. Copolymers of ethylene and maleic anhydride, colloidal silica, finely powdered sand, mica, garnet, and other minerals effectively reduce slippage when compounded into the plastic or sprayed onto the surface. Colloidal silica solutions are used extensively for spraying surfaces; they are usually diluted with water prior to application. Agents when compounded into plastics usually are of small particle size (less than 1 μ) and the amount used is generally less than 1% by weight.

antistatic agent These additives can be applied to the surface of plastic products or incorporated in the plastic. Its function is to render the surface of the plastic less susceptible to accumulation of electrostatic charges which attract and hold fine dirt or dust on the surface of the plastic. There are two basic methods to minimize static electricity: (1) metallic devices which come into contact with the plastic and conduct the static to earth, and (2) chemical additives which give a degree of protection. The term static electricity (SE) is a misnomer, insofar as it seems to indicate a special kind of electricity. There is only one kind of electricity. SE denotes the group of phenomena associated with the accumulation of electrical charges, in contrast to the phenomena connected with rapid transport of charges which is the subject of electrodynamics. SE was discovered long before the other aspects of electricity was studied. Its simplest manifestation is the attraction that certain bodies exhibit for each other as well as for other bodies after they are brought together and then separated. It is reported that the Greek scientist Thales of Miletus, around 600 B.C., noted that when amber (a fossil polyester plastic) is rubbed with animal fur, it acquired the capacity to attract small particles such as dust. Interesting is the fact that these two kinds of materials, a plastic and a fiber, are still the most important bearers of SE today.

antistatic plastic in electronic packaging The demand for antistatic plastics in electronics applications is of major importance. The size reduction of components and the higher density packing of components on computer chips make the devices more susceptible to static damage. The electronics and computer industries have over $5 billion in static damage in their products. In many cases, the environment can be adjusted either through increased humidity, antistatic mats, or ionizing sprays to control the problem. It is during transportation and storage that static protection becomes crucially important. Components must be protected from stray electric fields, such as transients, electric motors, and discharges, that can destroy microcircuitry. One of the best ways to safeguard the components against these fields is to pack them in antistatic film bags.

apochromatic Color corrected lenses which focus the three colors, blue, green, and yellow, in the same plane.

apparent density ▷ **density, apparent**

apparent specific gravity ▷ **specific gravity, apparent**

apparent viscosity ▷ **viscosity, apparent**

appliance market A market where plastics has been exceptionally beneficial. As an example, back in the 1900s doing simple household tasks was a real chore. Washing, drying, and ironing clothes was a rigorous, two-day affair involving filling metal tubs, scrubbing; hanging to dry; cast iron flat irons heating on a stove; and other "primitive" methods based on what exists today. With new technology and plastics, laundry rooms and kitchens worldwide are operating and looking better than ever before.

application ▷ **market for plastics**

aqueous polymerization Vinyl polymerization with water as the medium and with the monomer present within its inherent solubility limit is a process generally called aqueous polymerization. It excludes, therefore, suspension polymerization and emulsion polymerization in an aqueous medium. Aqueous polymerization is of technical importance in preparing emulsifier-free latexes in which the size distribution among the dispersed particles is fairly sharp, and in preparing special plastics.

aqueous system ▷ **coating, waterborne system**

aramid fiber ▷ **aromatic polyamide fiber**

architectural folded plate form ▷ **design architectural space form**

architectural market ▷ **building and construction market**

area, circular mil A unit of area equal to $\pi/4$ (0.7854) of a square mil. The cross-sectional area of a circle in circular mils is therefore equal to the square of its diameter in mils. A circular inch is equal to one million circular mils.

areal weight ▷ **reinforced plastic weight, areal**

area under the stress-strain curve ▷ **tensile stress-strain area under the curve**

arithmetic A branch of mathematics that deals with real numbers and computations with these numbers. ▷ **mean, arithmetic**

arithmetic-logic unit ▷ **computer arithmetic-logic unit**

Arnite Akzo Chemical's tradename for high intrinsic viscosity PET that can be extrusion blow molded.

aromatic A major group of unsaturated cyclic hydrocarbons containing one or more rings, typically the 6-carbon benzene ring containing three double bonds. The vast number of plastic compounds of this important group derived chiefly from petroleum and coal tar are rather highly reactive and chemically versatile. The name is due to the strong and not unpleasant odor characteristic of most substances of this nature.

aromatic polyamide fiber Aramid is the generic name for aromatic polyamide fibers; has a long-chain synthetic polyamide in which at least 85% of the amide linkages are attached directly to two aromatic rings. Du Pont's tradename is "Kevlar"; it was the first of these high strength, high modulus, chemically and mechanically stable fibers over a wide temperature range. It is used in reinforced plastics having higher weight, greater stiffness and higher tensile strength than RPs using F- or S-glass reinforcements. Aramid fibers' specific gravity is 90.4 lb/in.^{3} (1.45 g/cm^3) and E-glass, 159.0 lb/in.^{3} (2.55 g/cm^3). There are different aramid fibers providing different properties. There are fibers with modulus up to 27×10^6 psi (1.86×10^5 MPa); E-glass at 10×10^6 psi (6.9×10^4 MPa) and S-glass at 12×10^6 psi (8.6×10^4 MPa).

Aramid fiber reinforced plastics are more electrically and thermally insulating than their glass counterparts, more damped to mechanical and sonic vibrations, and transparent to radar and sonar. These high modulus organic fibers retain the processability normally associated with conventional textiles, despite their high mechanical properties. This leads to wide versatility in the form of the reinforcement that can be obtained (yarns, rovings, woven and nonwoven fabrics, knit goods, and papers). RPs of these fibers have low creep, high impact resistance, very low notch sensitivity, and excellent creep rupture characteristics. Present cost is higher than E-glass and equivalent to some grades of S-glass on a unit-weight basis. ▷ **reinforced plastic** and **fiber nylon**

aromatic polyester ▷ **polyester, aromatic**

Arrhenius equation Refers to the rates of reaction versus temperature.

arrowhead ▷ **extruder film arrowhead**

art and science Product design is as much an art as a science. Guidelines exist regarding meeting and complying with art and science.

artificial aging ▷ **aging, artificial**

artificial intelligence AI is a continuous developing technology designed to resolve fabricating processes (injection molding, extrusion, and so on) problems much faster than conventional computer data processing. The technology mimics how the human brain works. AI takes into account the single or more important multiple problems that can occur during processing. So similar to what the best technician would do, AI instantly studies the overall situation and resets the process control.

artificial weathering ▷ **weathering, artificial**

asbestine A soft fibrous magnesium silicate. Used as a filler in plastics, elastomers, and papers.

asbestos A general name for a group of naturally occurring silicate minerals, often found in fibrous form. Useful as fillers in reinforced plastics as a reinforcement and to improve thermal properties, and so on. They provide the capability to withstand high temperature, chemical resistance, and strengths with modulus. Two classes of asbestos are found: (1) a serpentine form, chrysotile, which is by far the most widely used, and (2) an amphibole form, which is found in several different varieties with crocidolite, amosite, and anthophyllite being the best known and used. Impregnated with metal, ceramics, and plastic, asbestos fibers increase the strength and durability of all types of composites.

Long term exposure to asbestos can be hazardous. These fibers are extremely fine (microns) and inhalation of dust increases the risk of lung cancer, mesothelioma, and asbestosis, a common disease of asbestos workers. Because of the hazardous nature of asbestos fibers, suppliers and users continually search for replacements, but to date no single fiber exhibits all the characteristics of asbestos. Glass fiber is the most common replacement which, like asbestos, has a specific gravity of about 2.5 g/cm^3 and is not flammable.

asbestos roving An assemblage of carded asbestos, with or without other fibers, rubbed into a single strand without twist. ▷ **carding**

A-scan A method of data presentation on a CRT utilizing a horizontal base line that indicates distance, or time, and a vertical deflection from the base line which indicates amplitude.

aseptic liquid pouch In 1990 Du Pont Canada was the first company to receive U.S. FDA approval for a pouch system designed to extend the shelf life of low-acid and high-acid products up to a year without refrigeration. It employs a sterile filling machine, multilayer film construction incorporating barrier film, and sealing technology. The first sterile hermetic seal pouch line was installed at Kansas Food Packers Inc., Arkansas City, packaging milkshape mix, soft-serve ice cream, and other dairy products.

This pouch concept has global market potential. Du Pont chose the U.S. as its first target because FDA approval is stringent and will help to obtain approvals elsewhere. Du Pont leases the filling machines that maintain a sterile environment during the complete filling and sealing process and supply its proprietary barrier film now made in Canada. Tetra Pak Rausing SA, Switzerland, has been the world leader in aseptic packaging with its multilayer cartons.

ash **1.** Inert residue remaining after complete combustion of plastic, paper, and so on. **2.** The end product of a large-scale coal combustion as in power plants consisting principally of fly ash, bottom ash, and boiler ash. **3.** In regard to environmental waste, it is the inert residue that remains after solid waste is incinerated. Usually disposed of in landfills, some forms can be processed into building products such as gypsum. Ash or ash residue can include minerals, ceramics, metal, glass, plastic, and so on. It also can be contaminated by heavy metals.

ashing A finishing process used to produce a satin-like finish on plastic products, or to remove cold spots or teardrops from irregular surfaces which can not be reached by wet sanding. The part is applied to a loose muslin disc loaded with wet ground pumice in a rotating drum travelling at speeds of 4,000 linear feet per minute.

askarel A generic term for a group of nonflammable synthetic chlorinated hydrocarbons used as electrical insulating media. Various composition types are used. Under arcing conditions, the gases produced, while consisting predominantly of noncombustible hydrogen chloride, can include varying amounts of combustible gases depending upon the askarel type.

aspect ratio **1.** The ratio of length to diameter for plasticator screws or the barrel hole. ▷ **L/D ratio** **2.** The ratio of the major to the minor dimension of a particle. In particular, for a fiber or rod-like particle, it is the length to diameter (L/D) ratio. For an elliptical particle it is the ratio of the major to minor axis lengths. It is important in determining the effect of dispersed additive particles on the viscosity of a fluid and in turn on the performance mechanical properties of the filled solid or foamed plastic; performances change based on L/D ratio.

asperities Microscopic surface roughness.

asphalt **1.** A dark-colored solid or semisolid material which liquifies upon heating. It is often found in nature or may be obtained from the distillation of crude oil. **2.** Alternate name for bitumen.

assemble and disassemble ▷ **design snap fit**

assembly interlock system ▷ **design snap fit**

assembly/joining Different methods are used for joining or fastening and assembling plastic products (see Fig. and Tables). A wide variety of assembly and fastening techniques can be used with plastic-to-plastic and plastic-to-other

Examples of fastening methods for thermoset plastics.

Thermosets	Mechanical fasteners	Adhesives	Spin and vibration welding	Thermal welding	Ultrasonic welding	Induction welding	Remarks
Alkyds	G	G	NR	NR	NR	NR	
DAP	G	G	NR	NR	NR	NR	
Epoxies	G	E	NR	NR	NR	NR	
Melamine	F	G	NR	NR	NR	NR	Material notch sensitive
Phenolics	G	E	NR	NR	NR	NR	
Polyester	G	E	NR	NR	NR	NR	
Polyurethane	G	E	NR	NR	NR	NR	
Silicones	F	G	NR	NR	NR	NR	
Ureas	F	G	NR	NR	NR	NR	Material notch sensitive

E: Excellent, G: Good, F: Fair, P: Poor, NR: Not Recommended

Examples of fastening methods for thermoplastics.

Thermoplastics	Mechanical fasteners	Adhesives	Spin and vibration welding	Thermal welding	Ultrasonic welding	Induction welding	Remarks
ABS	G	G	G	G	G	G	Body type adhesives recommended
Acetal	E	P	G	G	G	G	Surface treatment for adhesives
Acrylic	G	G	F-G	G	G	G	Body type adhesives recommended
Nylon	G	P	G	G	G	G	
Polycarbonate	G	G	G	G	G	G	
Polyester TP	G	F	G	G	G	G	
Polyethylene	P	NR	G	G	G-P	G	Surface treatment for adhesives
Polypropylene	P	P	E	G	G-P	G	Surface treatment for adhesives
Polystyrene	F	G	E	G	E-P	G	Impact grades difficult to bond
Polysulfone	G	G	G	E	E	G	
Polyurethane TP	NR	G	NR	NR	NR	G	
PPO modified	G	G	E	G	G	G	
PVC Rigid	F	G	F	G	F	G	

E: Excellent, G: Good, F: Fair, P: Poor, NR: Not Recommended

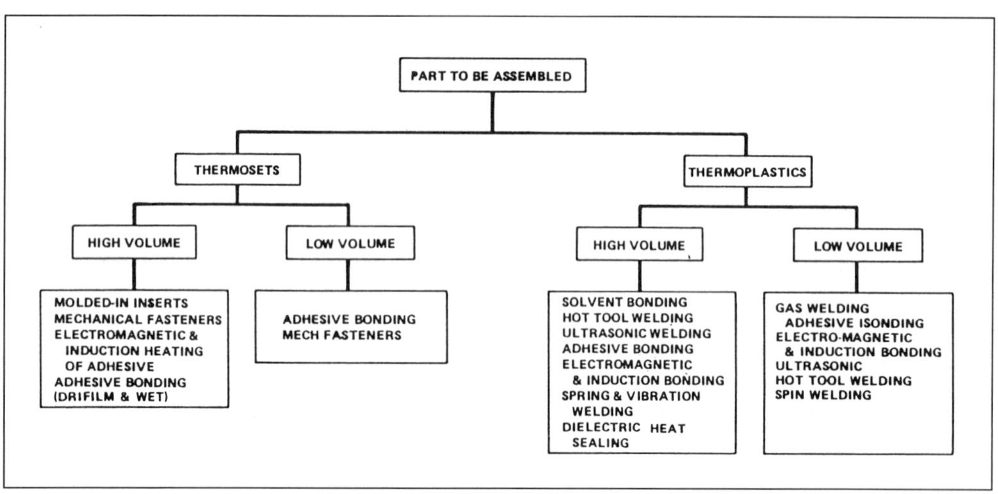

Examples of methods for part assembly.

materials. It is important to both designer and end-user that the techniques, advantages, and limitations of the various fastening methods be understood so that intelligent choices can be made among them as the application warrants. First consideration should always be given to utilizing one of the relatively simple means of mechanical fastening. Most of the existing applications use techniques of this type; the actual suitability of any of these methods depends greatly on the size, nature, and function of the part. Recognize that usually the more involved techniques are more expensive, but generally are also the ones leading to the most useful and dependable connections.

A-stage ▷ **A-B-C-stages**

asymmetric The opposite to symmetrical. Of such form or shape that no point, line, or plane exists about which opposite portions are exactly similar.

asymmetric carbon atom ▷ **carbon atom, asymmetric**

asymmetry A molecular arrangement in which a particular carbon atom is joined to four different groups.

atactic Lack of long-range repetition in plastic molecules or molecules that are more or less random, as contrasted to isotactic.

atactic plastic Plastics with molecules in which substituent groups or atoms are arranged at random above and below the backbone chain of atoms, when the latter are arranged so as to all be in the same plane. The opposite to stereospecific plastics.

atactic stereoisomerism A chain of molecules in which the position of the side chains or side atoms is more or less random.

atecticity The degree of random location that the side chains exhibit off the backbone chain of a plastic.

atmosphere 1. The pressure exerted by the air at sea level (14.696 psi) (101.325 kPa) which will support a column of mercury 760 mm high (about 30 in.) at a temperature of 0°C and standard gravity. This (atm) is a standard barometric pressure, though it varies slightly with local meteorological conditions. **2.** An environmental gas or mix of gases; an atm of nitrogen or an inert atm. **3.** The gaseous envelope that surrounds the earth and can influence performance of products made from plastics and all other materials. It is comprised of four major divisions: the troposphere (from sea level to about 10 km), the stratosphere (ozone region which extends from about 10 to 50 km), the mesosphere (from about 50 to 100 km), and the thermosphere (from about 100 to 1,000 or more). No sharp boundaries exist between layers. ▷ **atmosphere chart**

atmosphere chart The chart on p. 28 presents temperature, pressure, and density of the air at altitudes up to 100,000 geometric feet. ▷ **altitude chart**

atmosphere contamination ▷ **smog**

atmosphere controlled A gaseous environment in which the oxygen, carbon dioxide, and nitrogen are held constant at specific level; the temperature is also being controlled.

atmosphere dry deposition Deposition of materials from the atmosphere without the aid of rain or snow, e.g., particles in the range of 2.5 micron as well as pollutant gases (SO_2, NO_2).

atmosphere packaging ▷ **packaging via MAP**

atmosphere standard laboratory A laboratory atmosphere having a relative humidity of 50 ± 2% at a temperature of 23 ± 1°C (73.4 ± 1.8°F). Also: average room conditions 40% RH at a temperature of 25°C (77°F); dry room conditions 15% RH at a temperature of 30°C (86°F); and moist room conditions 75% RH at a temperature of 25°C (77°F).

atmospheric bond, chemical An attractive force between atoms strong enough to permit the combined aggregate to function as a unit. Different principal types of bonds recognized include metallic, covalent, ionic, and bridge.

atom The smallest possible unit of an element, comprised of a nucleus containing one or more protons and (except hydrogen) two or more neutrons, and one or more electrons which revolve around it. The protons are positively charged; the neutrons have no charge; the electrons are negatively charged. Atoms of the same or different elements combine to form molecules. When the atoms are of two or more different elements, these molecules are called compounds.

atom carbon, asymmetric A carbon atom to which four different atoms or groups are attached; asymmetric C-atoms give rise to optical isomerism.

atomic absorption spectroscopy AAS is one of the most sensitive analytical methods available for the determination of metallic elements in solution. The element of interest in the sample is not excited, but is merely disassociated from its chemical bonds and placed into an unexcited, un-ionized "ground" state. In this state, it is capable of absorbing characteristic radiation of the proper wavelength which is generated in a source lamp containing the sample element as the anode. The usual method of disassociation is by burning the sample in a flame of the appropriate gas or gases.

atomic number The number of protons (positively charged mass units) in the nucleus of an atom upon which its structure and properties depend. The number represents the location of an element in the Periodic Table.

atom influence on properties ▷ **chemical composition**

atomization ▷ **centrifugal atomization** and **foamed polyurethane**

attenuation 1. The diminution of vibrations or energy over time or distance. **2.** The process of making thin and slender, as applied to the formation of fiber from molten glass.

attribute statistic ▷ **statistic data collection**

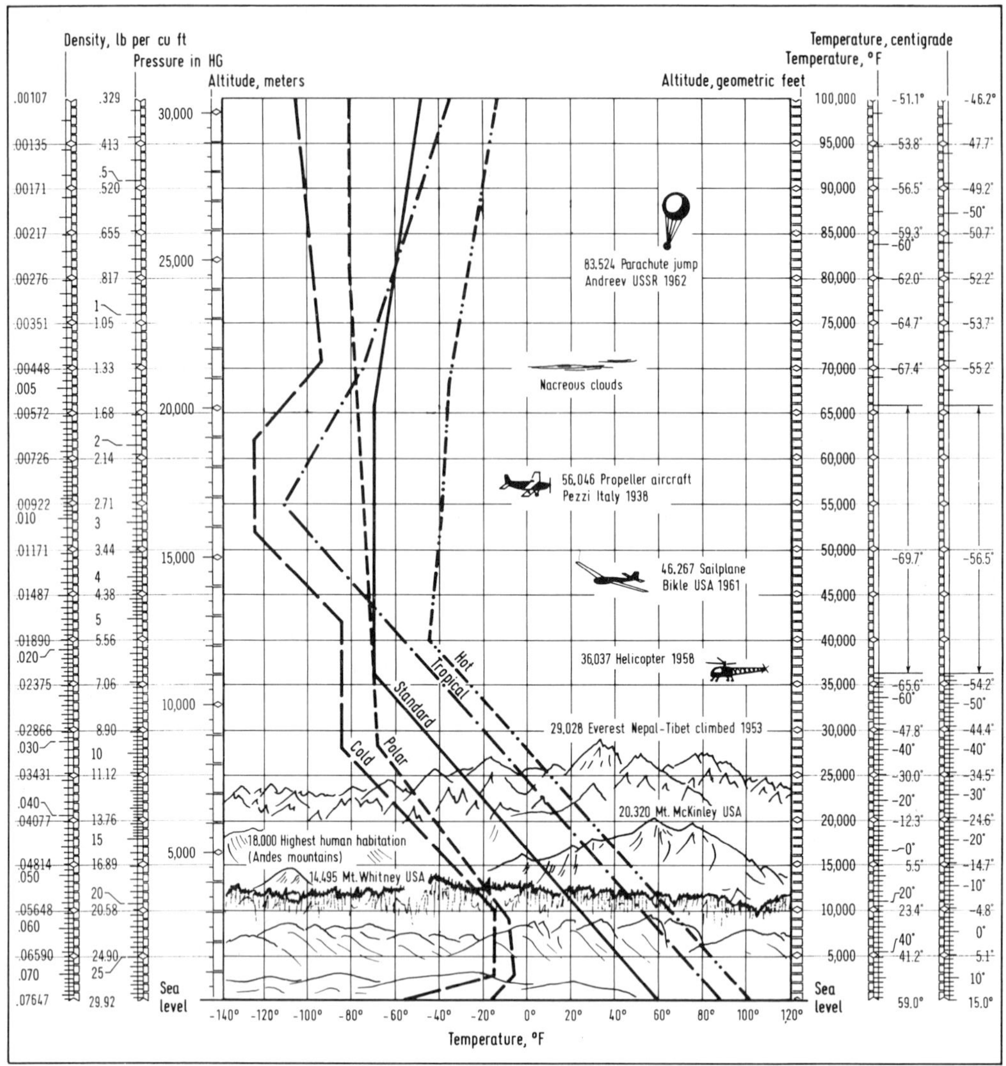

Atmosphere chart.

attrition mill A grinding machine comprised essentially of two metal plates or discs with small projections (burrs). One plate may be stationary while the other rotates, or both counter rotate. Feed, such as additives for plastic compounding, enters through a hopper above the plates, and "ground" product emerges at the bottom. To obtain very uniform ground material, different size vibrating screens are used to separate different existing sizes.

audio compact disk ▷**compact audio disk**

auger ▷**screw, auger**

autoclave **1.** Closed, strong steel vessel for conducting chemical reactions under high pressure. **2.** Vessel used for sterilization of certain plastics (and other materials), medical devices, packages, and so on. **3.** Vessel used for thermoset adhesive bonding of plastic-to-plastic, plastic-to-metal, and any material combinations. **4.** The autoclave is used to mold thermoset plastics, particularly TS reinforced plastics made up of woven and nonwoven fabrics, preforms, and so on that require curing by heat and pressure (steam, air, or air/steam) (see Figs. on p. 29 and 30). It permits molding all sizes and shapes, particularly large parts. This method of fabrication incorporates pressure bag molding. Autoclave and pressure bag molding conditions to 177°C (350°F) and 200 psi (1,379 kPa) are routinely attained. Size of autoclaves range from small ($\frac{1}{2}$ m diameter, 1 m long) to large (40 m diameter, 180 m long).

(a)

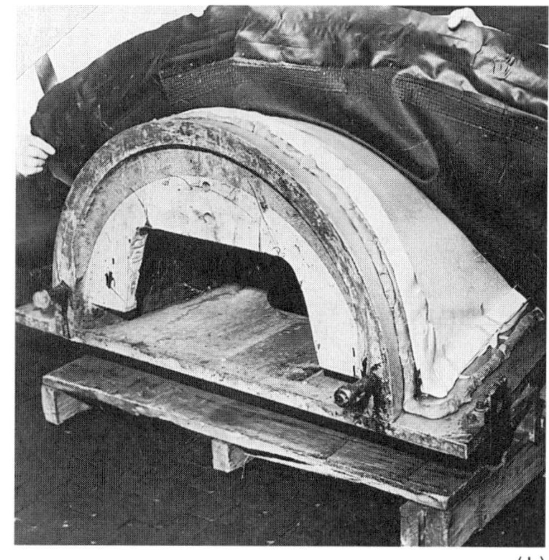

(b)

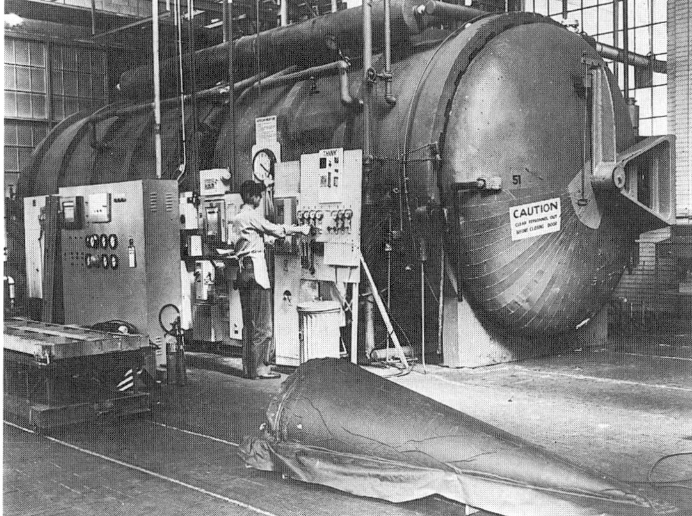

(c)

Bag molding in an autoclave producing a reinforced plastic nose cone for a rocket satelite space vehicle. (*a*) Hand layup of reinforced plastic (half of nose cone); (*b*) bagging the layup; (*c*) RP part about to enter an autoclave.

Customized autoclaves attain cure conditions that exceed 316°C (600°F) and 500 psi (3,447 kPa). The higher temperature and pressure curing autoclaves are used and required by the high melt plastics, such as polyimide plastics. If still higher pressures are required and the danger of extremely high pressures is to be avoided, a *hydroclave* can be used. It provides water pressures as high as 1,000 psi (6,900 kPa). The bag must be well sealed to prevent infiltration of high pressure air, steam, or water into the molded part. In these processes an initial vacuum may be required.

autoclave molding ▷ **autoclave**

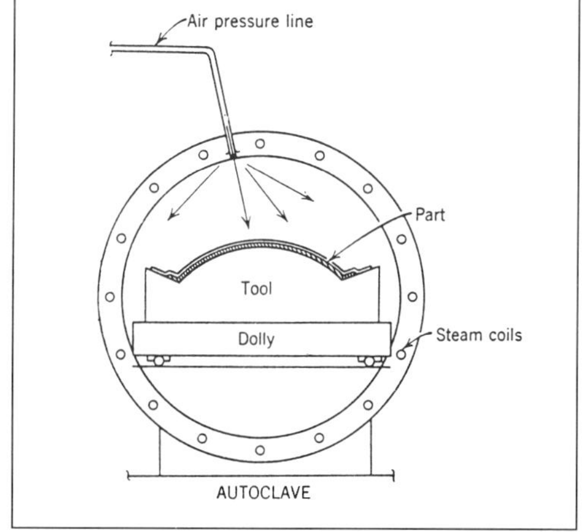

Basic schematic of bag molding in an autoclave. ▶

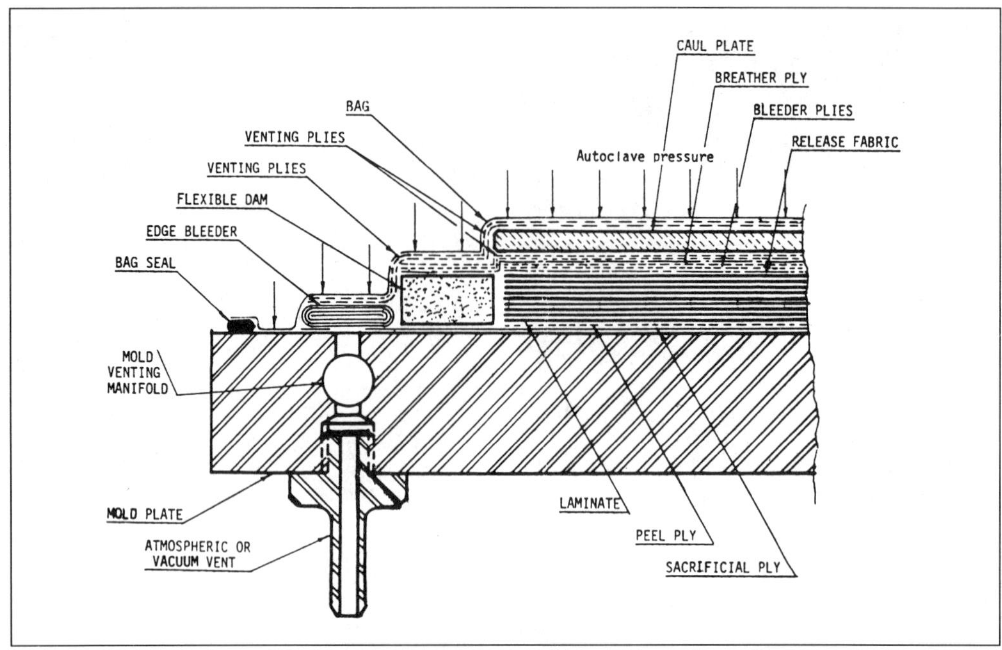

Section of reinforced plastic of autoclave molding method with a vertical bleeder. Note heavy protection against bag perforations due to increased autoclave pressures.

autoclave sterilization ▷ **sterilization, heat**

autoclave venting In autoclave mold curing of a part or assembly bonding, turning off the vacuum source and venting the vacuum bag to the atmosphere is called autoclave venting. The pressure on the part is then the difference between pressure in the autoclave and atmospheric pressure. Venting is also involved in other processes. ▷ **mold venting**

autogeneous extrusion ▷ **extruder, adiabatic**

autoignition point The minimum temperature required to initiate or cause self-sustained combustion in any substance in the absence of a spark or flame. ▷ **self-ignition temperature**

autoload ▷ **computer autoload**

automatic mold ▷ **mold classification**

automation This is the science and practice of machinery or mechanisms which are so self-controlled and automatic that manual input is not necessary during operation. Basically it is the technique of making a process automatic or self-controlling. Typically, as an industry continues to expand, automation (or more automation to control many different variables) usually becomes more important. As competition increases, costs must be reduced in order to stay ahead. At the same time, other factors are also involved such as escalating costs and low availability of labor in some parts of the country and world.

The continued development of more sophisticated processing equipment in turn allows the development of integrated processing systems. In the case of plastics processing, these developments include the use of microprocessor controls manufacturing lines, including all upstream and downstream auxiliary equipment. The controls not only handle the machine and all equipment setup and sequence of operation but provide closed-loop feedback control systems that monitor the complete process as well as make the control adjustments to maintain part quality. ▷ **communication protocol**

automation level ▷ **level of automation**

automotive market Plastics play a very important role in vital areas of transportation technology providing special design considerations, process freedom, novel opportunities, economy in transportation, and so on.

automotive plastic engine Since the 1950s different development programs have been conducted in basically advancing the use of reinforced plastics engine block assembly and determining the potential and benefits for actual automotive components, such as weight savings, lower noise, vibration and harshness levels, and reduced exhaust emissions. Different parts, such as crankcases, supports, connecting rods, and so on, have had limited production. The major development on the block is using different type RPs to meet performance-cost requirements. Areas subject to the combustion heat have metal heat shields. For decades, the use of plastics has been in racing cars, principally to reduce weight, with cost not a restriction. Since the 1950s development has been conducted on RP air compressor blades used in aircraft jet engines. The main problem concerns limiting coefficient of expansion to eliminate engine blowup. ▷ **Polimotor**

automotive risk ▷ **acceptable risk**

autothermal extrusion The same as ▷ **extruder, adiabatic**

auxiliary equipment Many different types of auxiliary equipment (AE) and supporting secondary operations (SO) can be used to maximize overall processing productivity and efficiency, and reduce fabricated product cost. Their proper selection, use, and maintenance are as important as that of the basic processing equipment (injection molder, extruder, and so on); they can cost more than the base machine. The processor determines what is needed, from upstream to downstream and secondary equipment, based on what the equipment has to accomplish, what controls are required, ease of operation and maintenance, safety devices, energy requirements, compatibility with any existing equipment, and so on. Examples of equipment are shown in the following listing (see also Figs. on p. 31 and 32):

Adhesive applicators
Bonding equipment
Cutting equipment, computerized
Cutting equipment, laser
Cutting equipment, manual
Cutting equipment, ultrasonic
Die cutting equipment
Dust-recovery equipment
Freezers/coolers
Heaters
Kitting equipment and software
Leak detectors
Mandrel extractors, hydraulic
Mandrel extractors, pneumatic
Material-handling equipment
Metal-treating equipment
Ovens
Printing/marking equipment
Process controls
Pulverizing/grinding equipment
Robotic handling equipment
Routers
Saws
Solvent-recovery equipment
Trimming equipment
Vacuum debulking and repair tables
Vacuum-storage chambers
Waterjet cutting equipment, abrasive slurry
Waterjet cutting equipment, water only
Welding equipment for thermoplastics

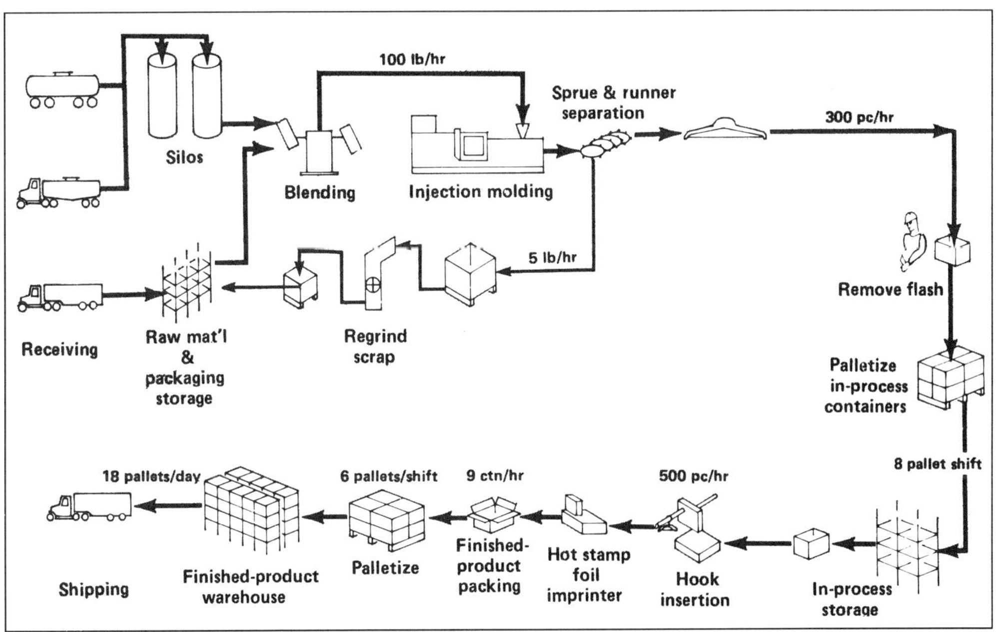

Schematic of production line starting with upstream auxiliary equipment, through injection molding, and followed with downstream equipment.

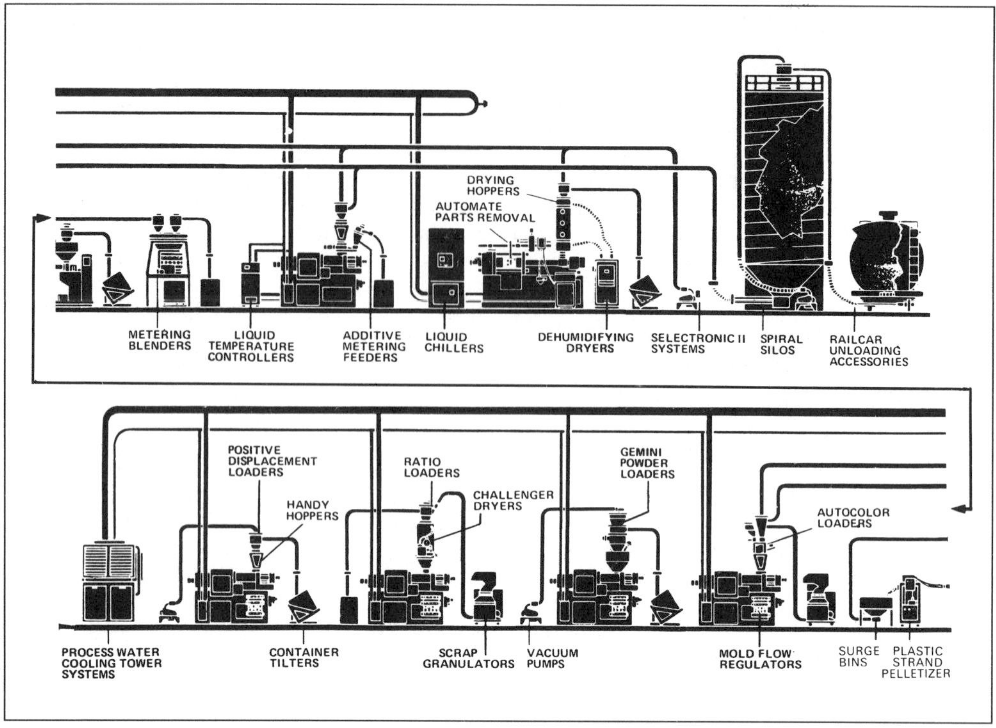

Identifying typical upstream (going from railcar) to downstream (ending with water cooling tower) auxiliary equipment.

All inline equipment has to be properly interfaced so it operates efficently. Much of the equipment used in the past did not properly interface so operations were rather inefficient compared to what could be accomplished. A set of rules have been developed that govern the communication and transfer of data between machines and auxiliary equipment called ▷ **communication protocol**

auxiliary equipment communication protocol Within a plastics processing communication protocol cell there are two basic types of auxiliary devices: (1) devices that require minimum configuration or minimum data (chillers, dryers, loaders, and so on), and (2) devices that require large amounts of configuration data or provide large amounts of process data (robots, gauging/sensors, mold/die controllers, cutters, and so on). ▷ **communication protocol**

auxiliary equipment electronic communication New generation auxiliaries that are continually produced are meaningful contributors to plant productivity via greater reliability of operation and pinpoint equipment control. As an example, fluid-chilling and temperature-control systems are major beneficiaries of the computer revolution. They become more energy efficient, reliable and cost effective with the application of microprocessor and computer-compatible controls that can communicate with primary processing equipment. They provide pinpoint control of liquid temperatures. Thus, they have become significant contributors to productivity.

average deviation ▷ **mean deviation**

average molecular weight ▷ **molecular weight, average**

Avogadro's law It basically states that equal volumes of the same or different gases under the same conditions of pressure and temperature contain the same number of molecules.

azodicarbonadide AZ is a blowing agent. ▷ **foam and blowing agent**

B

back-flow stop valve ▷ **screw tip**

backing plate ▷ **screw tip**

backlash The space between gear teeth must be made larger than the gear teeth width as measured on the pitch circle. If this were not the case, the gears could not mesh without jamming. The working clearance or difference between tooth space and tooth width is known as backlash.

backlog Accumulation of firm or definite customer orders that have not yet been processed. Backlog can be expressed in sales dollars or hours of production time.

back pressure **1.** In injection molding, it is the resistance of the plastic to flow when the mold is closed. ▷ **injection molding back pressure** **2.** With an extruder, it is the resistance of the plastic melt to forward flow.

back-pressure-relief port An opening from a mold or extrusion die for escape of excess material.

bacteria, anaerobic ▷ **anaerobic bacteria**

bacteriostat ▷ **biocide**

bad plastic ▷ **plastic bad and other myths**

Baekeland, L. H. (1863–1944) Born in Ghent, Belgium, he did early work in photographic chemistry and invented Velox paper (1893). Later he discovered in the U.S. phenol-formaldehyde plastic originally called Bakelite (1909). The reaction of phenol and formaldehyde had been investigated by Bayer in 1872, but Baekeland was first to learn how to control it to yield dependable results on a commercial scale. The Bakelite Co. was founded in 1910; it later became a division of Union Carbide Corp.

baffle **1.** In general, a device used to restrict or divert the passage of fluid through a pipe line or channel. **2.** In hydraulic systems, the device, which often consists of a disc with a small central perforation, restricts the flow of hydraulic fluid in a high pressure line. A common location for the disc is in a joint in the line. **3.** When applied to molds, the term is indicative of a plug or similar device located in a stream or water channel in the mold. It is designed to divert and restrict the flow to a desired path. Also aids in developing turbulent flow of the fluid in order to remove heat from the plastic molded part in the shortest time period. ▷ **Reynold's number**

bag drop test Film impact strength can be determined by several different methods. In the bag drop test, materials (sand, beans, golf balls, or others) are dropped from a specified height onto a smooth, hard surface. The maximum height at which the bag will sustain three successive drops without bursting serves as a measure of the film impact strength. The test, although not highly accurate, is useful because it simulates end-use requirements or conditions. Packages must be able to withstand powerful forces of shock such as those incurred by a bag full of beans or potatoes dropped from a store shelf.

Variations of this test are used for impact testing of bags under simulated end-use requirements or conditions. For example, packaging films for frozen foods are tested in a walk-in freezer by dropping bags containing 2 lb (900 g) of plastic cubes to determine the height at which the bags will not survive three drops at a given low temperature.

bag filter A large-scale, dust-collecting equipment (baghouse) composed of a large cotton or nylon bag assembled in a heavy frame or housing. The bags may be as much as 10 ft (3.05 m) high. Discharge hopper is located beneath the bag. A suction or blower system forces dust-laden air through an inlet port on one side of the frame just above the hopper space. It enters the bag where it deposits its suspended solids, while clean air is drawn through and leaves by an outlet. A motor-driven shaker mechanism agitates the bag periodically, dislodging the accumulated layer of dust which falls into the hopper. ▷ **baghouse**

bagging Applying an impermeable layer of film over an uncured reinforced plastic part and sealing the edges so that a vacuum can be drawn, such as in bag molding.

baghouse A series of bag filters. Some installations can have over 300 bags.

bag-in-box Refers to a sealed, spouted plastic bag inside a rigid outer container, generally for packaging liquid products of varying viscosities. The outer box may be made of disposable plastic, paper, or wood. They offer key space and cost efficiencies. They can also be dispensers.

bag manufacturing In a typical plastic bag making machine, the extruded blown film is drawn from the extruder or collection roll and formed into a flat tube as it passes over a forming mandrel or former. Simultaneously, heat sealing or an appropriate adhesive is applied to the edge of the web, and the seam is completed by pressure when the joint passes between a set of rollers. As the web continues, gussets are added in the tucking-former section. A cut-off converts the web into bag lengths. Bottom heat sealing or adhesive is automatically applied to the trailing edge of each bag-length tube. As it passes through the bottom station, the bottom fold and seam are made, completing the bag.

The most common bag is the automatic or self-opening style (SOS). Other styles include: flat, square, and satchel. ▷**paper and plastic bags**

bag molding Bag molding is a versatile process of manufacturing reinforced plastic parts. It is a procedure in which a combination of a reinforcement and a thermoset plastic is placed in, or over, a mold and covered with a flexible diaphragm or bag. Heat and pressure are then applied to cure the RP materials to a desired configuration. This technique has been in use since the late 1930s. There are many companies that have well-trained production personnel and aggressive RP development programs. As a result, bag molding techniques are continually being improved, and the new, extremely high-strength, high-temperature RPs are being successfully bag molded.

This process is usually recommended for prototype parts, parts with small production runs, particularly large and/or complex parts, and parts that require high strength and reliability such as aircraft primary structures, and others. The size of a part that can be made is limited only by the size of the mold and size of the curing oven or autoclave. These are the usual curing methods with the catalyzed TS plastic. Alternate curing methods include induction, dielectric, microwave, xenon flash, ultraviolet, electron beam and gamma radiation. Of the light curing systems, the UV and xenon flash radion are the most commercially developed and used. UV via outdoor sunlight has been used since the 1940s permitting practically unlimited mold and curing volume. Thin, unsymmetrically laid up and unpigmented RPs which deform excessively when thermally cured, are the more successful candidates for the light curing systems. Dielectric and microwave curing techniques have limited use and continue to be developed to meet cost-performance. Electron beam cures have been shown to be effective for thin films. Accelerated particle cures are still laboratory developments.

The general process of bag molding can be subdivided into three specific molding methods: vacuum bag, pressure bag, and autoclave bag. See each of these three reviews for more details and Figures; the Fig. shown here provides a schematic on the basic concept of bag molding. The vacuum bag and autoclave methods are the most popular methods and used to produce the vast majority of parts. Their advantages are that the tooling is relatively inexpensive and

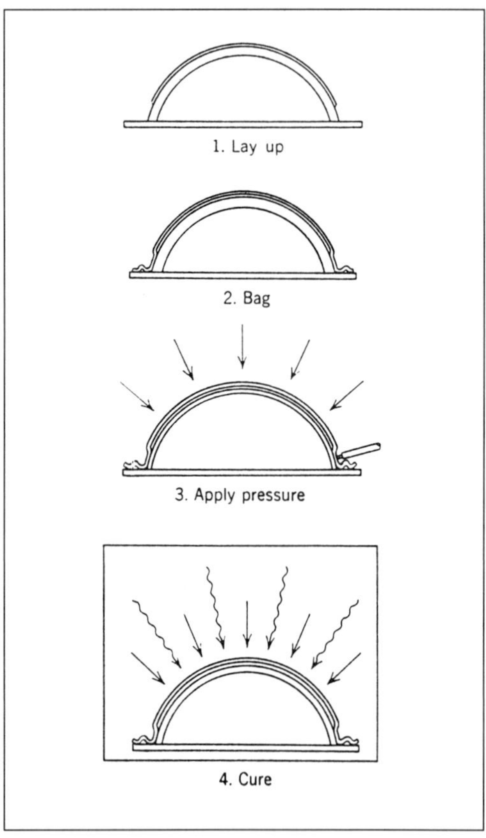

Bag molding schematic on the basic steps used during processing reinforced plastics.

that basic equipment (oven and autoclave) can be used for an unlimited variety of parts. The main disadvantage of the pressure bag method is that the tooling and equipment are integral and relatively expensive because they can only be used for the part for which they were designed. These parts are economical only for large production runs.

The general steps in the bag molding process are as follows: (1) The reinforced plastic materials, usually some form of fiber reinforcements and a thermoset plastic, are laid up in a male or female mold. Most of the RPs are glass fiber-TS polyester plastics; (2) the materials are then covered with a flexible film diaphragm (usually called a vacuum bag) and the film is sealed to the mold; (3) pressure is applied to the laid-up materials by creating a vacuum between the RPs and the diaphragm. If additional pressure is required, as in the case of autoclave molding, external air and/or steam pressure is applied to the external side of the flexible diaphragm which in turn transmits the pressure to the laid up material on the mold; (4) the RPs are then cured under pressure by the application of heat and the chemical action of the catyalist or curing agent in the plastic.

bag molding and filament winding ▷ **filament winding prepreg and bag molding**

bag molding and wet lay-up The so called wet lay-up techniques are sometimes combined with bag molding processes to enhance the properties of otherwise low stressed constructions. Because it is difficult to wet out dry fiber reinforcements with less plastic, initial volumetric fraction ratios of plastic to reinforcements are seldom less than 2:1. On a weight basis using glass fibers, the ratio is about 1:1. When contact molded, candidate structures are required to provide increased RP thicknesses to compensate for the high plastic contents. Candidates include architectural panels and enclosures, bathroom fixtures and enclosures, and RP parts in trucks and motor vehicles. There are sometimes space limitations for critical supports. Adaptations of bleed-out techniques can be used to reduce plastic contents and to enhance structural properties.

Excessively bled RPs can result in fiber washouts, ply wrinkling, gross thickness variations, and incomplete cures of thermoset plastics because of excessive losses of reactive volatiles. Such defects will degrade properties. When consolidations are properly conducted, laminates with void contents less than 2% by volume are produced.

Techniques for laying up dry reinforcements with catalyzed TS plastics are similar to the methods for contact molded hand lay-ups. The plastics for room temperature cure lay-ups are usually formulated to attain longer pot lives. Catalyzed plastics are applied by rollers, brushes, or other appropriate means, and to ensure the wet-out of reinforcements and elimination of entrapped air, the plastics are hand worked into the fibers.

When the volume fraction of plastics is less than 60% (less than 43% by weight in the RP), it is difficult to wet out the fibers. It is often necessary to force the plastic into the fibers by rolling over a thick film placed over the lay-up. Sometimes, excessive force is required which disrupts and tears up the orientation of the fibers. On those occasions, decisions are made whether to increase the plastic content, tolerate the disruptions to the fibers, or accept increased void contents.

Uniformity of distribution of plastics through reinforcements is dependent on operator skills, plastic viscosity, adequate pot life, and orientation of fibers. Difficulties encountered during fabrication of deeply contoured shapes include pooling of plastic in depressions and sagging of laid-up fibers from sloping walls. The main difference from contact molding arises from adaptations of bleed-out and bagging techniques. Lower cost glass fibers are almost exclusively used in wet laid-up RPs.

Liquid plastics for wet lay-ups (and filament wound prepregs) contain all the constituents to attain the cured state. They are formulated to attain sufficently long pot lives to complete the bag molding processes. Additives are usually fire retardants, UV barriers, and thickening agents. Most often, inert diluents are avoided. On occasion, when diluents are used to reduce viscosities, attempts are made to volatilize them prior to initiating the plastic cures. The advantages of using thickening agents in liquid plastics include: (1) enhancement of structural integrity of the cured laminate and all co-cured bonded joints, (2) retention of fibers on sloping mold surfaces during fabrication operations, (3) retention of the plastic by the fibers during the fabrication operations, and (4) control of constituent contents and cured part dimensions. Usually less than 10% by weight of thickness will achieve the desired results.

bag molding bags For vacuum bag molding, the bags (diaphragms) are used to evacuate the air from the reinforced plastic laminate and to generate the atmospheric pressure required for compaction over the mold. For autoclave molding, the bags serve to contain the compacting gases during the cure. If the pressures within the bag are not reduced from those applied to the

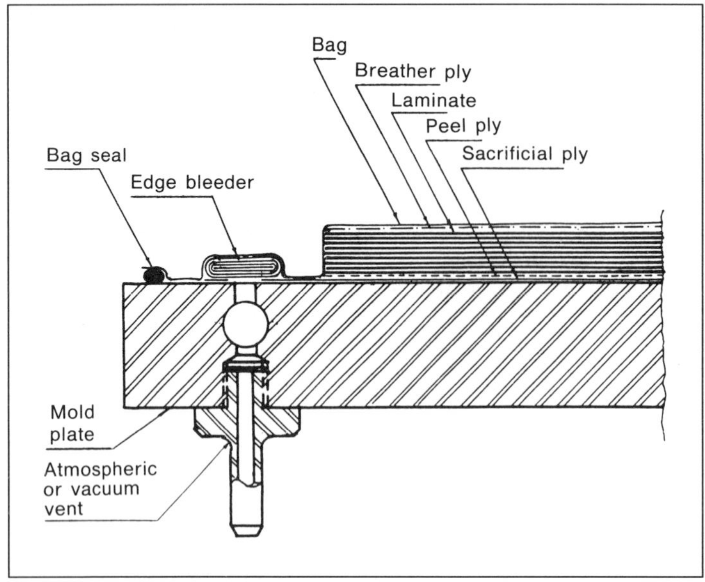

Fig. 1 Example of an edge bleed-out system used in bag molding.

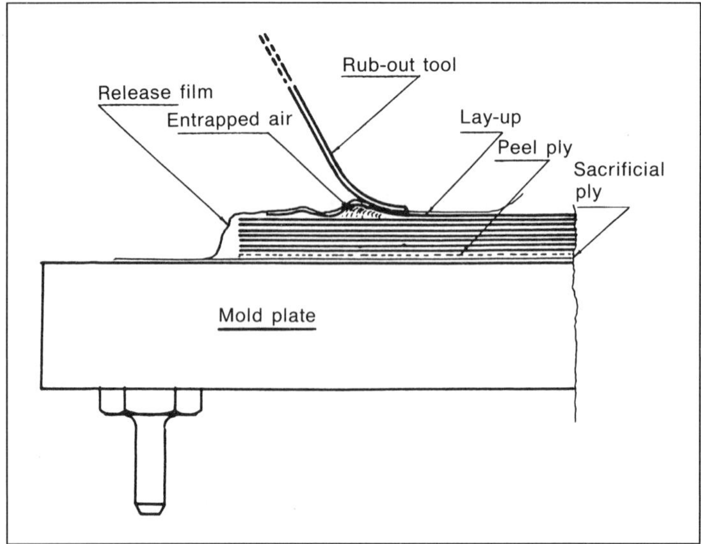

Fig. 2 Example of rub-outing of entrapped air within the bag.

bag, the membrane remains inert and there is no compaction. Bleed-out systems are devised to maintain reduced pressures within the bag's contents. As long as the pressure within the bag remains reduced, the compacting gases bear on the bag as it presses against the RP lay-up. Fig. 1 shows the lay-up assembly for bleed-out. The lay-up stacking sequence is as follows: (1) Surface of mold is prepared with the release agent; (2) sacrificial ply is laid up on the prepared surface. Usually, it is a ply of 120 glass fiber fabric with a plastic compatible with the plastic used in the main lay-up; (3) peel ply is anchored to the sacrificial ply; (4) reinforcement plies are oriented and laid up in the directions specified in the design, and rubbed out on top of the peel ply (see Fig. 2); (5) edge bleeder is positioned at least $\frac{1}{2}$ in. (1.3 cm) from the periphery of the lay-up and is joined to the ports of the venting system; (6) porous release fabric is laid up over the RP plies and is extended over the edge bleeder; (7) bag contents are evacuated and the system is checked for leaks. All leaks are sealed; (8) bagged lay-up is ready to be cured.

This system does not provide for significant plastic bleed-out and provides only a partial escape of volatiles. RPs cured using this system

Bag molding expendable materials.

Peel plies	Miltex, a heat scrubbed and set nylon fabric. Miltex 3921 is a finely woven style. Dacron release fabrics that are available from prepreg suppliers. Fiberglass fabrics. Finer woven fabrics include styles 2112, 2116, and 2120. Coarser fabrics include woven rovings for decorative architectural panels.
Release fabrics	Teflon coated 104 fiberglass scrim. Dacron release fabric.
Bleeder plies	Mochburg fabrics. Fiberglass fabrics, usually styles 2120 or 7781. Fiberglass mat, $\frac{1}{4}$ oz increments to 3 oz/ft^2. Pellon, cellulose, or polyester mats.
Breather plies	Perforated Tedlar 0.020 in. (0.05 mm) diameter perforations; 0.5–1 in. (1.3–2.5 cm) on centers. Perforated nylon, 0.020–0.030 in. (0.05–0.08 mm) hand-made perforations 0.5–1 in. (1.3–2.5 cm) on centers. Teflon coated 104 fiberglass scrim.
Manifold plies	Mochburg fabric. Fiberglass fabric, style 7781.
Bag sealer	Zinc chromate sealer tape.
Bag	Kapton, to 316°C (600°F). Silicone rubber blanket, 0.125 in. (3.2 mm) thick. Fiberglass-reinforced silicone rubber bags. Nylon, to 179°C (350°F). PVA film, to 121°C (250°F).

will usually have tapered edges from the edge of the lay-up. These are normally removed from the cured RP and sometimes are used for quality control tests. ▷ **bleeder cloth** and **vent cloth**

bag molding expendable materials The Table on this page provides an example of the preferred expendable processing materials used for bag molding.

bag molding parting film To ensure release of bleeder material from a bag molded cured part and to form a flexible diaphragm (bag) over the lay-up during cure of the TS plastic, films used include: polyvinyl alcohol, polyvinyl fluoride, cellophane, TP polyester (such as ("Mylar"), polyvinyl chloride, polyurethane, and silicone elastomer sheet. Selection of the parting film and bag film take into account the type of plastic, the curing temperature and pressure, the contour of the part, and the shrinkage characteristics of film. The upper curing temperature of PVOH, polyester, and cellophane films is 177°C (350°F) with PVC at 149°C (300°F). PVOH film has the greatest shrinkage during curing, whereas PVC stretches. Cellophane and polyester have a small amount of shrinkage. Selection should also take into account the desired surface condition of the bag side of the finished part. The pattern of the bleeder material will be imprinted on the bag's surface side of the part.

bag molding, pressure ▷ **pressure bag molding; vacuum bag molding; autoclave**

bag molding tear ply ▷ **reinforced plastic peel ply**

Bakelite A proprietary name for phenolic and other plastic materials, often used indiscriminately to describe any phenolic molding material or molding. The name is derived from that of Dr. Leo Baekeland who developed phenolic plastic in 1909.

baking finish A paint or varnish that requires a baking temperature greater than 66°C (150°F) for the development of desired properties. Such finishes are based on epoxy oil-modified alkyd, melamine, etc. Baking is usually done by infrared radiation producing high molecular weight plastic coatings that are dense and tough.

balanced construction ▷ **reinforced plastic directional properties**

balanced runner ▷ **mold runner**

balanced twist An arrangement of twisted fibers in a combination of two or more strands that does not kink or twist when the yarn produced is held in the form of an open loop.

balance tray A tray under the mold on to which the molding(s) falls during automatic cycling and which then operates to close the mold and so cause the recycling starter to operate a new cycle.

baling Compacting material into blocks to reduce the volume and simplify handling and transportation. Bales can consist of unprocessed material, sorted components such as recyclables, solid waste, etc.

ball burst test This test, pendulum impact resistance, ASTM D 3420 determines film toughness. A 5 in. square sample is struck by a hemispherically tipped pendulum and the force required to rupture the film is indicated on a scale.

ball clay A secondary clay that has good plasticity, strong bonding power, high temperature processing, high dry strength, and processes to a white or cream colored product. Used as bonding and plasticizing agent for products such as PVC floor and wall tiles.

ball mill A cylindrical or conical shell rotating about a horizontal axis, partially filled with a grinding medium such as natural flint pebbles, ceramic pellets, porcelain balls, or metallic balls. The material to be ground is added to just slightly more than fill the voids between the pellets. The shell is rotated at a speed which will cause the pellets to cascade, thus reducing the particle sizes by impact. Also called pebble mill when non-metallic grinding media are used.

balloon ▷ **plastic air balloon**

balloon effect, melt ▷ **mold cavity melt fountain flow**

balsam Canada A natural plastic from the balsam fir *Abies balsamea*. Dissolved in xylene, toluene, or benzene it is used as a mountant for permanent microscopical preparations. Its refractive index may vary from 1.530 to 1.545 and its softening point from room temperature to 100°C (212°F); these properties vary with age and solvent content. If impure, it discolors with age.

balsa wood ▷ **sandwich core material**

bamboo A grass or plant native to Southeast Asia having a rather high cellulose content which makes possible its use in speciality papers, light fixtures, fishing rods, building scaffolds, etc.

bambooing A manifestation of melt fracture in extrusion in which the extrudate consists of smooth sections interrupted by a periodic distortion of the surface, having the appearance of bamboo.

bamboo's modular structure The development of the composite system can be said to be based on the idea of utilizing the growth concept of the natural composite bamboo (which still enjoys importance as a building material in the Asian area) in a composite material for technical applications. Bamboo stalks receive their high specific strength from unidirectionally oriented cellulose fibers which are embedded in a matrix of lignin and silicic acid. A similar situation exists in wood. However, whereas the fibers in wood are usually 1 mm long, in bamboo they reach a length of up to 10 mm. This results in a long fiber composite. The hollow bamboo stalk is stabilized by evenly spaced flat, strong nodes rectangular to the longitudinal axis.

banbury Machine for compounding materials made up of a pair of contra-rotating rotors which masticate the materials to form a homogeneous batch blend. This dry ingredient batch-type mixer has an internal mixing action which produces excellent compounding for materials such as PVC. Both steam and water jacketing are provided. Small baths up to 1,000 lb (454 kg) are used. A plunger at the entrance port rides on top of the batch to furnish enough pressure for proper mixing. A hydraulically operated discharge gate is located below the mixing chamber.

band In electron diffraction, a broad intensity maximum with sharp edges.

bank In equipment such as a mill, calender, or spreader, a reservoir of material at the opening between rolls or at the spreader bar.

Barcol hardness The hardness value obtained by measuring the resistance to penetration of a spring loaded indenter steel point into the surface of the test material. The instrument, called the Barcol impressor, gives a direct reading on a 0 to 100 scale; a higher number indicates greater hardness. The hardness value is often used as a measure of the degree of cure for plastics, particularly thermoset types.

bare glass Glass fibers in the form of yarns, rovings, and fabrics from which the sizing or finish has been removed. Also, such glass before the application of sizing or finish. ▷ **glass fiber and fabric surface treatment**

Barex Sohia division of BP Chemical International's trade name for acrylonitrile plastic.

barium titanate ▷ **ferroelectric**

barometric pressure ▷ **atmosphere**

barrel Cylinder housing of the plasticating chamber of processing machines such as an extrusion, blow molding, or injection molding machine. The barrel forms the chamber within which the plastic is converted from a solid into a viscous melt. The barrel contains the plasticating screw that rotates or plunger that moves forward and backward. It can include a replaceable liner or an integrally formed special surface material. Two or more barrels can be used; referred to as twin-screw and multi-screw plasticators.

barrel burnishing The smoothing of surfaces by means of tumbling, such as in a ball mill.

barrel control thermocouple A thermocouple inserted partially into the metal wall of a barrel to sense temperature of the wall in the zone which is to be controlled.

barrel downsizing or upsizing Few installed injection molding machines run shot sizes anywhere near the full shot size capacity of the machine. Typical usage is from 20% to 60%, but in many cases less. Most machine suppliers offer several sizes for any given press tonnage. At the time of purchase, usually the target is to ensure enough is available. The problem of having too much shot capacity can render some machines unusable for certain materials and applications. The problem that develops is excessive residence time for the plastic; this applies to most of the engineering plastics. Any plastic that will degrade when held at injection temperatures for long periods usually has problems with small shots and long cycles. Result is extra cost in molding and usual reduction in part performance. Plastics that can have these problems include PC, ABS, acetal, cellulosics, and most fire retardant grades.

Where this situation exists and a change is desired, instead of replacing the entire machine, a smaller barrel and screw can be substituted. Certain equipment suppliers can provide a front-end barrel designed to smaller size. The screw is also smaller but includes an adapter to fit the unmodified drive quill. This downsizing modification also requires new, smaller heaters, a new end cap, non-return valve, and modification of the barrel shroud. An injection pressure relief valve must be installed in order to ensure excessive pressure is not developed at the discharge end.

Upsizing can also be provided in order to increase shot size. However, it will reduce the available injection pressure and can cause torque limitations on the screw. The need for upsizing is rather rare.

barrel, extruder An extruder barrel differs from injection barrels several ways. It is usually longer because L/D of 24/1 is minimum and can go to 36/1 or even longer. The injection barrel is usually 18/1 or 20/1 with an occassional 24/1. Some vented barrels are 32/1 but the trend is toward shorter. The extrusion barrel is usually designed to withstand lower melt pressures of 10,000 psi (69 MPa) maximum. This means a thinner wall and eliminates the high pressure sleeve or bell end. Extrusion barrels normally do not have an integral feed port, but are fastened to a separate water cooled feed throat casting. At the rear, there is a large diameter flange with a bolt circle to attach the barrel to the feed throat.

The extrusion barrel connects to the die adaptor at the discharge end, but the seal is made in a manner slightly different from the injection barrel and end cap. The barrel flange has a female counterbore, just like the injection barrel, but the die adapter has a counterbore instead of a pilot. The counterbore is called a breaker plate recess, for more rapid removal than in injection. This allows for ease of screen changes and die changes. The most common closures are split "C" clamp, swing gate, and bolt circle. ▷**barrel, injection**

barrel fail-safe rupture disc If barrel pressure exceeds its rated burst pressure, disc opens to relieve pressure.

barrel finishing Cleaning, smoothing, and polishing of plastic or metal parts by mechanical friction obtained by placing them in drums or barrels which rotate on their horizontal axis. An abrasive medium and water are usually added. Barrels often contain vertical dividers to make two or more compartments which can be individually loaded and unloaded.

barrel flange, front A flange at the downstream or discharge end the extruder barrel to which the die or adapting member is fastened.

barrel heater ▷**heater band**

barrel heater zone The barrel is usually divided into several zones for independent temperature control in each zone.

barrel history The original barrels were used for extruding natural rubber. They were nitrided steel or special steel alloys. They were of one-piece design with a very high chromium content. There are still foreign extrusion and injection barrels nitrided and used successfully. However, the trend continues toward bimetallic.

Industrial Research Labs developed the first bimetallic in 1939. The product was called "Xaloy 100". It was centrifugally cast, abrasion resistant, liner material inside an alloy steel outer shell. These bimetallic liners were originally used as mud pump liners in the oil fields.

This liner is available from different sources worldwide.

barrel, injection In a typical injection barrel, the feed port has an opening cut through the barrel. Internal pressure due to melt is up to 20,000 psi (138 MPa) as standard and can go up to 30,000 psi (207 MPa). This requires special considerations for the final few inches (cm) at the discharge end. Some barrels have "bell" ends to accommodate the pressure, some incorporate a high pressure sleeve and there are those that require both. The backing material is usually a medium carbon alloy steel like ANSI 4140. However, it does not give high strengths possible with such a steel because it anneals in the high temperature spinning oven followed by slow cooling. The high pressure sleeve is made of stronger heat treated ANSI 4140 material, and is shrunk over the already centrifugally cast barrel.

The injection barrel slides into a separate water cooled feed housing. The barrel is held in place by a split collar or a large nut at the rear end of the feed housing. There is also a key or machined flat to ensure against turning with the screw. On the other end, the barrel has a circular flange with a bolt circle pattern to attach the end cap or nozzel adapter. The discharge flange of the barrel has a counterbore to center the end cap. Sealing is accomplished on the vertical surface inside the pilot extending from the end cap. ▷ **barrel, extruder**

barrel inspection To ensure proper performance, different parts of the barrel can be checked, such as: (1) *Inside diameter* The very front of a barrel can be measured with inside micrometers, but this is limited, particularly deep in the bore. Inexpensive cylinder gauge, which can be put on long handles, has limited capability. There is a problem with light and the return glare off the gauge from a flashlight. There are a number of excellent boregauges available. (2) *Straightness and concentricity* Barrel straightness is difficult to determine by conventional methods. The ID and OD are not always exactly concentric. One method to measure straightness is to set the barrel on precision rollers at each end. The ID is then indicated for runout with a dial indicator. This is limited in depth. Tolerances allow deviation from a straight barrel to accumulate to a total allowable indicated runout. Another method is the use of a test bar usually about 70% of the barrel length. This is a slotted and chrome plated bar that is precision ground to about mid-range of the normal size tolerances. In theory, if the test bar slides easily through the barrel, so will the screw slide easily through the barrel. In addition, this will catch rapid changes or kinks that would otherwise be allowed under the accumulation of tolerances. A different bar size is needed to test each ID. (3) *Barrel hardness* Standard hardness testers are not able to get inside a barrel to measure hardness. One instrument most commonly used for this purpose is the Internal Mobile Hardness Tester (trademark of Page-Wilson Corp.). When testing and comparing the hardness of a bimetallic liner, it should be recognized that absolute hardness, as measured, is not necessarily in direct proportion to wear resistance. (4) *Barrel specifications* The chemistry and hardness information for various types of barrels is supplied by producers. Chemical information is for as-cast condition. The chemistry may vary widely after final machining is completed. (5) *Barrel tolerances* Each barrel manufacturer has its own set of machining tolerances, but they are in the same range.

barrel inventory In extrusion or injection molding, the amount of plastic contained in the plasticator barrel or heating chamber.

barrel jacket A jacket surrounding the outside of the barrel for circulation of a heat transfer medium.

barrel length-to-diameter ratio ▷ **L/D ratio**

barrel liner grooved A liner whose bore is provided with longitudinal grooves.

barrel liner sleeve A cylindrical housing in which the screw rotates, including replaceable liner, if used, or any integrally formed special

barrel materials Typical materials are as follows: (1) *Nitrided* These barrels are not used in U.S. extruders and rarely on injection machines. They do not wear as well as bimetallic barrels and because the case is thin, wear becomes progressive after it starts. The corrosion resistance is not as good as any of the bimetallic grades particularly when processing glass fibers and other abrasive-filled materials. ▷ **screw heat treatment** and **nitriding** (2) *Bimetallic-abrasion resistant* Standard grade of general purpose type is an iron/boron alloy. (3) *Bimetallic-corrosion resistant* The usual grades are nickel/cobalt base materials. They give much-improved chemical resistance, but sacrifice some wear resistance. (4) *Bimetallic-carbide type* The increasing use of abrasive filled compounds has required more abrasion resistance than the standard iron/boron type, namely the carbide type. It contains metallic carbides such as tungsten carbide, titanium carbide, and tantalum carbide. These finely divided carbides are suspended in a matrix of nickel, cobalt, chromium, boron, or some combination of the corrosion resistant materials. These carbide types are also more corrosion resistant than standard bimetallic barrels. Selection of a proper screw material is critical with these barrels. Some of the screw hard surfacing materials, such as "Stellite 6" (trade mark of Cabot Corp.), will pick up or gall when used in combination with some of the barrel materials. Result is very catastrophic wear.

barrel melt thermocouple It is inserted through the barrel wall and protrudes into the melt to measure the plastic melt temperature.

barrel pressure tap A hole through the barrel or die wall suitable for inserting a pressure transducer.

barrel vent A plasticizing barrel which has a vent along its length, such as halfway, through which volatile matter and air can escape. Used in conjunction with a special screw having two separate threads along its length connected by a zone where decompression of melt takes place. Two or more in-line vents are also used, particularly in compounding extruders. ▷**extruder venting** and **injection molding venting**

barrel vented safety It is common practice to plug a vented barrel and use it the same way as a solid parallel machine. It is rare but the internal pressure can exceed the strength limit of the bolts retaining the plug and in turn the plug would be released violently from the barrel. To prevent this potential hazard a number of safety precautions are taken, such as to insure retaining bolts with more than enough strength, rotate barrel downward or away from the operator, pressure gauge at the head of the extruder to provide a preliminary warning at a minimum safety pressure value followed with shot-off of machine at higher pressures (if practical or otherwise alert all in the plant), install shear pins and/or rupture disc (if not installed), ensure machine is heated adequately at the forward barrel end, etc. ▷**plasticator safety**

barrel wear ▷**screw wear**

barrel zone temperature The metal temperature of the barrel at the control point of the heating zone.

barrier Any material limiting passage through itself of solids, liquids, semi solids, gases, or forms of energy such as UV light. ▷**membrane** and **permeability**

barrier, glass coating Various processes for depositing silica vacuum coatings on plastics have been commercially used. More recently the development that is commercially viable is an optical clear, flexible, amorphous silica coating 0.5 to 0.2 microns thick. It can be deposited on PET, PE, PC, or other plastic bottles to provide an oxygen barrier comparable to metallized film.

barrier material performance Different factors influence material properties. As an example, *mechanical damage* due to impact or folding (creasing) of plastic can lead to increases in vapor permeability. *Thickness* of plastics influences barrier capabilities particularly when pinholes exist. As an example, with aluminum foil having a thickness of 0.35 mil (0.00035 in.) pinholes exist in 100% of 12 in. (3.05 dm) square sample sheets. This is reduced to 8% at a thickness of 1 mil. With foil at $1\frac{1}{2}$ mil (0.0015 in.) or more in thickness, they are pinhole-free and therefore impermeable to gases and vapors. Although plastic films are generally considered as being free of pinholes, they may be found in very thin films. Electrical conductivity can be used to indicate their existence below certain critical thickness, dependent on type material and process used to produce film. Their thickness, especially amorphous types, may alter the morphology of the film. This change in morphology can be related to the effect of the thickness. There exists nonlinear dependence of the permeability of organic vapors on the reciprocal of the thickness for PE bottles.

In general, the *density* of a plastic, as related to the free-volume content, is a good measure of the pinhole (or other factors) volume. The lower density are generally more permeable. The *molecular weight* of plastic has very little effect upon the rates of diffusion and permeation except in the very low range of MWs not normally encountered in barrier films.

Chemical modification of a plastic, including copolymerization and substitution reactions, can have a pronounced effect. In general, if the cohesive-energy density increases as a result of modification, it will decrease the value of the diffusion coefficient. However, the effect of change in the cohesive energy on the solubility coefficient depends entirely on the cohesive energy of the penetrant vapor. With *crystalline* plastics, the crystallites can be considered impermeable; thus, the higher the degree of crystallinity the lower the permeability to gases and vapors.

The permeability in an *amorphous* plastic below or not too far above its *glass transition temperature* is dependent on the degree of molecular *orientation*. It is normally reduced, as compared to higher temperatures, although small strains sometimes increase the permeability of certain plastics. The orientation of elastomers well above their T_g has relatively less effect on the overall transport property.

barrier material performance

Barrier material permeability characteristics.

Type of Polymer	Specific gravity (ASTM D 792)	Water vapor barrier	Gas barrier	Resistance to grease and oils
ABS (acrylonitrile butadiene styrene)	1.01–1.10	Fair	Good	Fair to good
Acetal-homopolymer and copolymer	1.41	Fair	Good	Good
Acrylic and modified acrylic	1.1–1.2	Fair	—	Good
Cellulosics Acetate	1.26–1.31	Fair	Fair	Good
Butyrate	1.15–1.22	Fair	Fair	Good
Propionate	1.16–1.23	Fair	Fair	Good
Ethylene vinyl alcohol copolymer	1.14–1.21	Fair	Very good	Very good
Ionomers	0.93–0.96	Good	Fair	Good
Nitrile polymers	1.12–1.17	Good	Very good	Good
Nylon	1.13–1.16	Varies	Varies	Good
Polybutylene	0.91–0.93	Good	Fair	Good
Polycarbonate	1.2	Fair	Fair	Good
Polyester (PET)	1.38–1.41	Good	Good	Good
Polyethylene				
Low density	0.910–0.925	Good	Fair	Good
Linear low density	0.900–0.940	Good	Fair	Good
Medium density	0.926–0.940	Good	Fair	Good
High density	0.941–0.065	Good	Fair	Good
Polypropylene	0.900–0.915	Very good	Fair	Good
Polystyrene				
General purpose	1.04–1.08	Fair	Fair,	Fair to good
Impact	1.03–1.10	Fair	Fair	Fair to good
SAN (styrene acrylonitrile)	1.07–1.08	Fair	Good	Fair to good
Polyvinyl chloride				
Plasticized	1.16–1.35	Varies	Good	Good
Unplasticized	1.35–1.45	Varies	Good	Good
Polyvinylidene chloride	1.60–1.70	Very good	Very good	Good
Styrene copolymer				
(SMA) Crystal	1.08–1.10	Fair	Good	Fair
Impact	1.05–1.08	Fair	Good	Fair

Crosslinking will decrease the permeability primarily due to the decrease in the diffusion coefficient. The effect of crosslinking is more pronounced for large molecular size vapors. The addition of a *plasticizer* usually increases the rates of vapor diffusion and permeation.

Barrier properties of a plastic material to *liquid penetrant* and to the corresponding *saturated vapor* should be identical if equilibrium between the two phases is maintained. However, higher permeability values are sometimes found for liquid penetrant, usually due to the conditions used in which the equilibrium is not obtained, and to the conditioning effect of the liquid, which may alter the morphology of the plastic. The effect of *mixed vapors* and *humidity* on film barrier properties depends on the behavior of each individual vapor toward the plastic. When the solvent power and/or concentration of sorbed copenetrant is small, the effect of the copenetrant on the permeability of the first vapor will be slight. As the solvent power and concentration of sorbed copenetrant increase, the effect on vapor diffusion and permeation becomes more apparent.

Composite films, including coated or laminated film barriers, are often used to reduce permeability while retaining other desirable properties of a more permeable substrate. Total protection against vapor transmission by a barrier material increases linearly with increasing thickness, but increasing the thickness of one material can be impractical and uneconomical. Thus, *coating* or *lamination* of other materials is often more effective in many products, especially when two or more materials of different functional properties are combined. The Table on p. 42 provides examples.

barrier, moisture Any material that is impervious to water or water vapor. Most effective as barriers include high polymers such as PVC, PE and EVOH.

barrier permeability coefficient ▷**coefficient of permeability**

barrier plastic A general term applied to a group of plastics that have barrier properties. They are generally characterized by gas, aroma, and flavor barrier behavior. Examples of plastic behaviors are given in the Table on this page.

barrier screw ▷**screw, barrier types**

barrier to protect the earth ▷**geomembrane liner**

barrier, vapor The barrier properties of materials (plastic, paper, foils, etc.) against various vapors and liquid that are expressed in the form of permeability constants of the materials to the penetrants. The permeation of vapors include two basic processes: the sorption and diffusion of vapors in the plastic. In the packaging industry, the resistance of wrapping materials to moisture, or their vapor barrier characteristics, is essential for the preservation of many items. In the case of food wrapping, the loss of moisture and flavor through packing materials may damage foodstuff. However, the prevention of the ingress of moisture by a barrier is essential for the storage of dry foods and other materials. The storage of foodstuffs and other items in plastic containers, both under refrigeration and elsewhere, can lead to the sorption through the package of undesirable flavors and odors from the environment. Similarly the sorption of odors and flavors from the previous contents can spoil the use of a container for other foodstuffs. With liquids and liquid mixtures in containers, the loss of the contents will decide the shelf life of the container. Also, the different rates of permeation of various components of mixtures can lead to a complete change in composition, often resulting in spoilage of the contents.

In other vapor barrier applications, the degree of resistance of plastics to water and oxygen is important for the development of corrosion resistant coatings, electrical applications, etc. The equilibrium moisture contents of various temperatures and humidities, in addition to the diffusion rates themselves, is important in these applications. For the use of vapor-phase corrosion inhibitors, the use of a proper barrier to keep in the vapor of the organic compound is very important for the long lasting effect of the inhibitor as well as the prevention of the entrance of excess moisture. Because of their low vapor permeability properties compared with many materials such as paper, and their ease of application, plastics have found wide acceptance as vapor barriers. Applications include unsupported films and molded containers.In addition, they are widely used as thin coatings on more porous materials, notably

Examples of permeability resistant capability of different plastics used in composite film constructions; X identifies permeability resistance.

Resin	Oxygen barrier	Moisture barrier	Grease resistance	Toughness	Heat sealability	Cost per cu. in.
HDPE, LDPE, EVA		X		X	X	Low
Polystyrene						Low
Ionomers		X	X	X	X	Medium
Polypropylene		X	X			Low
PVC			X			Low
ABS				X		Medium
Polyester			X	X		High
PVDC	X		X			High
Nylon	X	X	X	X		High

Examples of vapor barrier properties of commercially available plastics.

Polymer	O_2 Transmission Rate @ 25°C, 65% R.H. cc mil/100 in.^{2}/24 hrs.	Water Vapor Trans. Rate @ 40°C, 90% R.H. gm mil/100 in.^{2}/24 hrs.
Ethylene vinyl alcohol	0.05–0.18	1.4–5.4
Nitrile barrier resin	0.80	5.0
High barrier PVDC	0.15	0.1
Good barrier PVDC	0.90	0.2
Moderate barrier PVDC	5.0	0.2
Oriented PET	2.60	1.2
Oriented nylon	2.10	10.2
Low density polyethylene	420	1.0–1.5
High density polyethylene	150	0.3–0.4
Polypropylene	150	0.69
Rigid PVC	5–20	0.9–5.1
Polystyrene	350	7–10

paper. The Table above provides some vapor barrier data.

barrier via chemical modification Chemical modification of the plastic surface during or after fabrication permits controlled permeation behavior of certain parts such as diaphragms, film, and containers. An example concerned a search for better barrier materials for packaging fuels, specifically for the production of blow molded gasoline containers or tanks. Gasoline leakage through conventional HDPE tanks, even though low, was too excessive, requiring some type of barrier. Since the 1950s, it has been accomplished by having a layer of functionalized PE formed on the inside of the container wall by means of a chemical reaction. Most of this reaction is with sulphonation or fluorination. More recently, there is also oxifluorination. It is the fluorination process in which the fluorine gas is thinned with nitrogen to which several percent by volume of oxygen have been added. This combination leads to functionalization of the PE making it impermeable. This technique permits substantially reducing required fluorine and in turn gaining cost-to-performance improvements.

basket weave In this type of woven fabric reinforcement, two or more warp threads go over and under two or more filling threads in a repeat pattern. In this woven pattern, the basket weave is less stable than the plain weave but produces a flatter and stronger fabric. It is also a more pliable fabric than the plain weave and will conform more readily to simple contours. It maintains a certain degree of porosity without lack of too much firmness but not as much as the plain weave.

batch In general, a quantity of materials formed during the same process or in one continuous process. They have identical characteristics throughout the batches. Also called master batch and lot.

batch mixing The past traditional disadvantage of batch mixing compound methods, that of being labor intensive, has been largely overcome by integrating compounding machines with efficient auxilliary equipment and centralized controls. Thus, batch compounding is kept competitive with continuous process compounding for many operations. The two basic types of batch mixing machines are roll mills and internal mixers. Originated for rubber compounding, these basic designs were adapted for plastics, and continue to be refined to keep pace with plastic developments.

The usual two-roll mill has an open construction, force being applied (and energy transfered) to the material as the material is squeezed between the two rolls. A chief advantage of this type is that the process can be observed. As an example with thermoset plastics and other reactive plastics, the onset of curing can often be detected from the material's surface appearance, a feature that is also useful when investigating the compounding behavior of unfamiliar materials. The output is in sheet form, which is suitable either for granulation, for direct lamination, compression molding, etc.

Internal mixers, such as the banbury, are widely used for PVC compounds and occasionally for compounds based on other plastics. Throughput is faster than that of two-roll mills. A variety of rotor designs are available with new ones being developed to provide different capabilities for the different behaviors of materials. Internal mixers are generally controlled by monitoring melt temperature with adjustments of ram pressure during feeding and throughput rate. Power consumption can also be used to measure compounding conditions. Plastics and additives are usually preblended before they are subjected to the intensive shearing of the internal mixer. Preblending also reduces cycle time in the mixer. The usual main disadvantage of internal mixers is that the compound is discharged as a shapeless mass that requires intermediate processing before conversion to a useful form. Short length extruders or two-roll mills are used for this purpose. ▷ **computer processing batch or off-line**

batch processing 1. ▷ **batch mixing**. **2.** Collecting a lot of data and manipulating them all at once instead of little by little. This is common on mainframe computers and is also occasionally used for the databases of microcomputers.

bathtub curve ▷ **life-history curve**

batt Felted fabric materials constructed or assembled by the interlocking action of compressing fibers, without spinning, weaving, or knitting.

baud One bit per second is a baud. It is a unit of measure for the transmission speed of data over any serial link, such as a computer modem. There are standard rates such as 300, 1,200, 9,600, or 19,000 baud.

B-basis The B mechanical property value is the value above which at least 90% of the population of values is expected to fall, with a confidence of 95%. ▷ **A-basis; S-basis; typical-basis**

beading ▷ **extruder neck-in and beading**

bead molding ▷ **expandable polystyrene**

bead sealing ▷ **heat sealing**

bearing area 1. The diameter of the hole times the thickness of the material. **2.** The cross-section area of the bearing load member on the sample.

bearings ▷ **design bearing** and **silicone fluid additives**

bearings, ball type The basic ball bearing consists of four parts: the outer ring, the inner ring, the balls, and the separator (that is the ball retainer). The separator serves the purpose of always keeping the balls separated and thereby preventing them from rubbing against each other. Different type bearings are available with (1) shields to prevent dirt from entering and to retain lubricant grease, (2) shields and seals to contain lubricant for self-lubrication, and (3) snap rings and flanges that provide for simple bearing containment. Plastics are used in different parts and in the complete bearing to meet different operation and environment requirements.

bearings, journal type A bearing that supports a load in the radial direction is known as a journal bearing. It consists of two main parts: a shaft called the journal and the hollow cylinder that supports the shaft, known as the bearing. In most applications, the journal rotates while the bearing is stationary. However, there are those with the bearing rotating only and also those where both rotate. Plastics are used to meet specific performance requirements.

bearings, roller Roller bearings serve the same purpose as ball bearings, but they can support much higher loads than comparable sized ball bearings because they have line contact instead of point contact. They can be classified as: (1) cylindrical roller bearings, (2) needle roller bearings, (3) tapered roller bearings, and (4) spherical roller bearings. Plastics are used.

bearing stiffness A measure of stiffness of a material subjected to a bearing load. It is the slope in MPa (psi) unit of the straight-line portion using the stress-strain diagram obtained in a bearing strength test. Stiffness is a measure of the modulus of elasticity.

bearing strain 1. The ratio of the deformation of the bearing hole, in the direction of the applied force, to the pin diameter. **2.** The stretch or deformation strain for a sample under bearing load. ▷ **strain**

bearing strength 1. A measure of the maximum usable bearing stress that can be developed or sustained in a material. For plastics it is the stress at the point on the stress-strain diagram obtained in a bearing strength test where the slope of the curve is equal to that stress divided by a strain rate of (usually) 4%. This point can be determined by trial and error, or more readily by means of a superimposed transparent template. **2.** The bearing stress at that point on the stress strain diagram at which the tangent is equal to the bearing stress divided by n% of the bearing hole diameter. **3.** The maximum bearing stress that will not fail a reinforced plastic when applied through a cylindrical fastener surface.

bearing strength test A method of determining the behavior of materials subjected to edgewise loads such as those applied by mechanical fasteners. For plastics (ASTM D 953), a flat rectangular specimen with a bearing hole centrally located near one end is loaded gradually either in tension (Procedure A) or compression (Procedure B). Load and longitudinal deformation of the hole are measured frequently or continuously to rupture and resulting data plotted as a stress-strain diagram. For this purpose, strain is calculated by dividing change in hole diameter in the direction of loading by original hole diameter. Bearing stress is calculated by dividing load by bearing area being equal to the product of original hole diameter and specimen thickness. Test results are influenced by the edge-distance ratio, which is the ratio between distance from center of the hole to the nearest edge of the specimen in the longitudinal direction, and hole diameter.

bearing stress The applied load divided by bearing area (hole diameter times thickness). ▷ **stress**

bearing, thrust ▷ **extruder thrust bearing**

bearing yield strength Bearing strength when material exhibits a specified limiting deviation from the proportionality of bearing stress to searing strain.

beauty aid ▷ **cosmetic market**

becquerel ▷ **radionuclide decaying activity**

beeswax ▷ **wax**

bell end The enlarged portion of a pipe that resembles the socket portion of a fitting and that is intended to be used to make a joint.

belting A belt is defined as a continuous band of tough, flexible material used for transmitting power or conveying materials. The belt used in a conveyor system is composed of the cover and the reinforcement or carcass. The reinforcement is the working tension component, which is protected from the environment by the cover. The top cover is usually thicker than the bottom cover because the greatest wear is concentrated on the top or carrying side, mainly at the point of loading, where material is accelerated to belt speed. Elastomeric materials are designed to withstand wear and seal the reinforcement against water, acid, oil, and other foreign materials.

The reinforcement is usually composed of plies or layers of fabric bonded by a coat of elastomer. It may also consist of a single interwoven ply, or a single layer of cords or steel cable. An extra ply of open-weave fabric, called a breaker plate, is sometimes inserted between the top cover and the first ply of the reinforcement to give the belt added resistance against shock-loading conditions, increase the cover adhesion, and prevent tearing. Standard belt has a smooth flat surface. Specialty belts may be ribbed or cleated.

Elastomers used include natural rubber, styrene-butadiene rubber, neoprene rubber, nitrile-butadiene rubber, butyl rubber, polyvinyl chloride, ethylene-propylene rubber, and polyurethane rubber. These rubber/elastomer compositions contain many ingredients with the base elastomer content usually between 40 to 60%. The other ingredients are fine reinforcing powders (carbon black or clay), softeners to control viscosity (oils and plastics), vulcanizing agents, protective chemicals and other additives. About 10 to 25 such ingredients are blended under high pressure to yield a plastic, deformable mix. The type of elastomer/rubber compounds utilized in a belt depends on the service conditions such as type, shape, and particle size of the material, belt speed, loading conditions, and exposure.

bench mark Marks of known separation applied to a specimen and used to measure strain.

bench mark interface format ▷ **computer picture-level benchmark**

bend angle A measure of bendability. The angle through which a plastic is bent under specified loading conditions in a standard bend test.

bending, free bend The bend obtained by applying forces to the ends of a specimen without the application of force at the point of maximum bending.

bending strength An alternate name for flexural strength. Not to be confused with bendability.

bending-twisting coupling A property of certain classes of RP laminates that exhibit twisting curvatures when subjected to bending moments.

bend radius ▷ **radius of bend**

bend test A test for ductility performed by bending or folding, usually by steadily applied forces, but in some instances by blows, to a specimen having a cross section substantially uniform over a length several times as great as the largest dimension of the cross section. ▷ **flexural properties**

bent section A ridge designed into a formed part which can unfold somewhat to absorb most of the stress when the part is placed under tension.

benzene ring The six carbon atoms forming a closed circle in the benzene ring. This basic structure of benzene is the most important aromatic chemical. It is an unsaturated, resonant six-carbon ring having three double bonds. One or more of the six hydrogen atoms of benzene may be replaced by other atoms or groups.

benzoyl peroxide White, granular, crystalline solid; tasteless; faint odor of benzaldehyde; active oxygen; soluble in almost all organic solvents. It is used in dry or wet (liquid) form. Use includes polymerization catalyst with different plastics, rubber vulcanization without sulfur, embossing vinyl floor covering, etc.

beryllium copper ▷ **mold material**

beta The prefix (β) has meanings analogous to those of alpha.

beta gauge sensor ▷ **sensor, beta gauge**

beta loss peak In dynamic mechanical or dielectric measurement, the second peak in the damping curve below the melt, in order of decreasing temperature or increasing frequency, is the β loss peak.

beta particle A charged particle from a radioactive atomic nucleus either natural or synthetic. The energies of beta particles range from 0 to 4 MeV. They carry a single charge. If it is negative the particle is identical with an electron, if positive it is a positron. Beta rays cause skin burns.

bias A systematic error, in contrast to a random error.

biaxial flexure strength The maximum stress in a biaxial mode of flexure that a specimen develops at rupture. This stress will normally be the calculated maximum radial tensile stress at the centre of the convex surface. This mode of flexure is a cupping of the circular plate caused by central loading and supporting near the rim.

biaxial orientation ▷ **orientation** and **reinforced plastic, directional properties**

bicyclic An organic compound in which only two ring structures occur. They may or may not be the same type chemical ring.

bifunctional Molecule with two reaction sites for joining with adjacent molecules.

billet A roll of material that can be used in pressure forming into rods, bars, shapes, etc. ▷ **skiving**

billow forming ▷ **thermoforming**

bimetal Used as a type of thermometer in which the sensing element consists of two thin strips of metals having different expansion coefficients bonded together in a helical or spiral structure. The extent of deflection or bending induced by heat change is indicated by a pointer on a dial. Readings can range from $-185°$ to 425°C.

binary A numerical representation in computer database technology of base 2, in which each digit can have only one of two possible values of 1 or 0.

binder **1.** A bonding plastic used to hold strands or fibers together in a mat or preform prior to manufacture of a molded part. Binder content is usually $\frac{1}{2}$% by weight. **2.** A component of an adhesive composition which is primarily responsible for the adhesive forces which hold two parts together.

bingham body A substance that behaves somewhat like a Newtonian fluid in that there is a linear relation between rate of shear and shearing force, but also has a yield value.

bioabsorbable ▷ **absorbable technology**

biochemistry ▷ **chemistry, bio**

biocide There are natural and synthetic plastics that are subject to attack by biological agents. At some time during the life of these materials they may be a possible place for living organisms, a barrier to be penetrated in the search for sustenance, a substrate subject to enzymatic or chemical by-product attack, or simply a material for shelter or attachment during the life cycle of certain organisms. This may or may not manifest itself in an attack on the object, depending on the inherent properties, including the susceptibility of the plastic or its component parts to penetration or degradation. The degree of susceptibility, the anticipated end use of the material, cost, and other factors determine whether or not a chemical or other protective treatment should be applied.

Active chemical compounds used as preservatives control degradation in several ways; those which produce death are termed biocides. The more rigorous definition of a biocide as an agent which kills living organisms precludes the somewhat more common usage of the term, which implies that a biocide is an agent which kills, repels, or inhibits the growth of the biological environment in which the plastic exists. Many chemicals may inhibit the reproduction and growth of organisms without causing death. These agents may be exemplified in the two common classes of control agents known as bacteriostats and fungistats. With higher organisms (some of the mammals) the repellent qualities of a chemical agent may minimize damage adequately. These protective agents make the plastic less susceptible to biological attack and prolong the useful life of the material by preservation of its physical properties and aesthetic appearance.

Plastics such as polyolefins, polyesters, or vinyls are considered to be resistant to biological attack, for the most part particularly in relation to the plastic additives in their compounded mixture. As more general use is made of plastics, they may be subjected to different and exotic biological environments which may affect their resistance to biological attack. Plastics are seldom used alone. Other materials are added in amounts from minor to major proportions. These include plasticizers, antistats, stabilizers, etc. which may change the biological resistance of the compounded plastics.

biocompatibility Traditionally, the primary focus of the search for biomedical materials has been on finding biocompatible materials. The original definition of a biocompatible biomaterial as one that is inert toward the physiological environment has been modified to include materials having minimal interaction with the environment. It is unlikely that an absolutely inert biomaterial can be found (or will be found soon) but the physiological response to any biomaterial must be kept within acceptable bounds. ▷ **acceptable risk**

biocomputing Biocomputing refers to biological inspired approaches to creating computer software. Techniques and technologies are available. Some are proven and out in the market; others will continue to be nurtured in research laboratories. This action allows software developers to push the envelope of program complexity and size, and to allow for tractable solutions to difficult problems such as pattern recognition. The most visibly successful of these techniques are neutral networks, also known as neurocomputing, neoconnectionism, and parallel distributed processing. Other biocomputing technologies include genetic algorithms, iterated function systems, fuzzy logic, simulated annealing, fractal systems, etc. ▷ **computer, bio**

biodegradable The ability to break down or decompose rapidly under natural conditions or processes. In plastics, a quality of containing additives or organic compounds, which can be digested by microorganisms in the environment, etc. There are biodegradable plastics that are useful for applications such as sutures, surgical implants, controlled release formulations of drugs and agricultural chemicals, agricultural mulch, etc. ▷ **biocide**

biodegradable and microorganism By genetically altering microorganisms, biotechnologists have created new strains of microbes that can biodegrade hazardous waste, oil, etc. Their potential in pollution control is so great that in the future chemical companies will be able to detoxify their chemical waste by using tailor-made microbes instead of treatment plants.

There are certain plastics that can be degraded by microorganisms. It has been observed that enzymes attack noncrystalline (amorphous) regions, therefore the resistance of susceptible plastics to microbial degradation is related directly to the degree of crystallinity of the plastics. They remain relatively immune to attack as long as their molecular weight remains high. Most plastics are characteristically durable and inert in the presence of microbes.

biodegradable and waste As reviewed, biodegradable plastics exist. In fact they have existed for a century using different agents and methods to cause degradation. Actually the main target for over a century has been to produce reliable, high performance, and long-life plastics. There have been requirements in the past to produce degradables in the elimination of solid waste, cause explosives to perform when degraded (by sunlight, rain water, sunlight, etc.), medical products, etc. In regard to solid waste, starch based plastics is an example of a method used to dispose of paper and conventional plastic packaging materials in consumer waste. Potatoes, wheat, and rice are used as the raw material for the starch. This plastic compound undergoes aerobic and nonaerobic degradation and is targeted for products such as single-service food and medical products. In its present biodegradable form, the starch plastic is suitable for products which do not place high demands on physical properties.

With all the action on developing biodegradable or just degradable plastics, there is disagreement by environmentalists as to whether it is more damaging to the environment if biodegradiability is a good thing.

There are definitely applications where degradables can be used; in certain applications they are definitely required. However, in regard to waste they can cause new problems without solving the old ones, particularly if energy is important. The total energy cost of producing biodegradable plastic is considerably greater than for conventional thermoplastics (TPs represent most of the waste plastics rather than TSs). For example, a fermented product or one produced for agriculture (such as starch type) will require considerably more energy than PE, PP, or PVC. Therefore, there are situations where biodegradable plastics do not show saving advantages.

Biodegradable plastics are in direct conflict with the notion of a plastic cascade system. In practice their use would mean that no source of mixed refuse would any longer be free from biodegradable plastics. A plant recycling system would have a differentiating problem. This action could still further reduce the range of uses for which recycled material would be acceptable.

The biological decomposition of plastics releases their energy content without making it available for use. In theory at least, when considered over a long time period, the same amount of CO_2 is released as in incineration, but without providing the corresponding amount of energy in the form of electricity and useful heat.Thus, biodegradable plastics do not offer the ecological advantages of conventional plastics. Their properties are less favorable in eco-balance calculations than those of other materials. Furthermore, they cause new environmental problems, especially with regard to soil pollution. However, they will be able to fulfill certain tasks in cases where it can be shown that no risks are involved.

biological activity Basically there are three types of plastics used in a biological environment: (1) plastics used as biomaterials such as in organ replacement, bone surgery, etc., (2) plastics serving as matrices in devices that permit controlled release of an active substance over a long period of time, and (3) soluble plastics that themselves display biological activity. Use takes into acount those properties of the biological environment relevant to its interaction with plastic materials. The interactions are usually conveniently considered at different levels of organization.

On the molecular level, chemical reactions and intermolecular attractions are significant. Then there are plastics that cannot penetrate the cell membrane via diffusion. Depending on charge, charge distribution, molecular weight, hydrophobicity, conformation, and tacticity, plastics interact with cell membrane components, mainly lipids, proteins, and glycoproteins.

As far as whole organisms are concerned, as in cells, plastics meet highly compartmentalized systems, and their access to some compartments is restricted. The parenteral administration route (subcutaneous, intraperitioneal, intramuscular, and intravascular ways that are not all equivalent) is the only efficient way of administering plastics. Intravenous leads to fast distribution to all vascularized parts of an organism.

biological deposit Water-formed deposits of organisms or the product of their life processes.

biological packaging ▷**packaging biological substance**

biomedical plastic design
▷**design biomedical products**

bioplastic-biomedical Biomaterials are used to repair, restore, or replace damaged or diseased tissues. They also interface with the physiological environment. Synthetic biomaterials, such as metals, ceramics, and plastics, are often called biomaterial to differentiate them from natural biomaterials. Advances in plastic science and surgery make it possible to rebuild many parts of the human body. Plastics having a vast spectrum of properties are available; thus, some plastics have mechanical and surface properties that make them suitable as biomedical materials.

Biomedical plastics in medicine and surgery are widely used for intracorporeal, paracorporeal, and extracorporeal applications (inside, interfacing, and outside the body, respectively). Applications include: (1) implants as temporary devices (surgical dressings, sutures, etc.), simple semipermanent devices (tendons, reinforcing meshes, etc.), and complex devices simulating physiological processes (artificial kidney-blood dialysis, etc.) and (2) interfacing and outside materials, including catheters and blood bags, syringes and surgical instruments, disposables for health care delivery, etc.

Biomaterials science encompasses aspects of physical sciences, engineering, biology, and medicine. Performance in a biocompatible implant or extracorporeal device is the ultimate test of a biomaterial. In addition to performance, the evaluation determines any adverse reactions and short- and long-term effects of the physiological environment on the implant. Complex relationships exist between materials properties, design, and implantation parameters, and the biological action or response.

biostabilizer A machine that converts solid waste into compost by granulating and aeration.

birefringence The difference in the refractive indexes of two perpendicular directions in a given material such as thermoplastic. When the refractive indexes measured along three mutually perpendicular axes are identical, the plastic is classified as optically isotropic. When the plastic is stretched (molecular orientation) and the refractive index parallel to the direction of stretching is altered so that it is no longer identical to that which is perpendicular to this direction, the plastic displays birefringence.

For TP systems, the phenomenon is commonly observed by applying an anisotropic macroscopic deformation and measuring the difference between the refractive indexes along two perpendicular directions. The birefringence observed in this manner originates essentially from the anisotropy of the individual chains constituting the medium. The necessary conditions for a chain to display birefringence are that the segment or the repeat units of the chain should be optically anisotropic, they should display anisotropic polarizabilities, and the spatial configuration of the chain should be anisotropic. The first condition is fulfilled in all

TPs because of the inherent anisotropy of the structure of the repeat unit. The second condition is obtained by the presence of anisotropic microstructures or by the imposition of a microscopically anisotropic deformation on the system. The chains then exhibit different polarizabilities of all chains, leading to the total polarizability of the TP.

The techniques of birefringence, ranging from the determination of structural defects in solid plastics to more basic investigations of molecular and morphological properties, are used in a wide range of applications. ▷ **nondestructive residual strain method; optical disc; residual strain/stress; testing residual strain**

birefringence, form The contribution to the total birefringence of two phase materials, due to deformation of the electric field associated with a propagating ray of light at anisotropically shaped phase boundaries. The effect may also occur with isotropic particles in an isotropic medium if they dispersed with a preferred orientation. The magnitude of the effect depends on the refractive index difference between the two phases and the shape of the dispersed particles. In TP systems the two phases may be crystalline and amorphous regions, plastic matrix and microvoids, or plastic and filler.

biscuit ▷ **preform**

bismaleimide plastic BMIs are a type of polyimide plastic that cures by an addition rather than a condensation polymerization reaction. Result is avoiding problems with volatiles formation which is produced by a vinyl-type polymerization of a prepolymer terminated with two maleimide groups. Intermediate in temperature capability between TS polyimide and epoxy plastics.

bisphenol A A condensation product formed by reaction of two (bi) molecules of phenol with acetone (A). This polyhydric phenol is a standard plastic intermediate along with epichlorohydrin in the production of epoxy plastics.

bit The smallest piece of electronic information used by a computer. The word comes from "binary digit"; thus, a bit can be either 0 or 1.

bitumen An asphalt-like natural plastic found in asphalt, mineral waxes, and lower grades of coal. They are combustible solid to viscous and semisolid liquid. Soluble in carbon disulfide. Used in coatings, paints, sealants, roofings, hot-melt adhesives, and road coating.

bituminous material The major bituminous materials are asphalts, tars, and pitches. The generic term bitumen, as used in the U.S, relates to mixtures of hydrocarbons. In commercial practice, bitumen usually refers to semisolid or solid residue, that is, products left after distillation of various organic raw materials. Residue from petroleum and coal tars constitute by far the largest source.

black Any of several forms of finely divided carbon either pure or admixed with oils, fats, or waxes.

blackbody In radiation physics, an ideal blackbody is a theoretical object that absorbs all radiant energy falling upon it and emits it in a form of thermal radiation.

black lead ▷ **graphite**

black light Light in the near ultraviolet range of wavelengths (3,200 to 4,000 A), just shorter than visible light.

black powder Blasting powder composed of potassium nitrate, charcoal, and sulfur composite.

black rouge ▷ **iron oxide**

black speck A defect that appears in or on plastic as a small dark spot.

blank **1.** A part (such as sheet, film, preform, parison, or casting) in some intermediate stage of fabrication for forming, bending, blow molding, cupping, drawing, or hot pressing. **2.** A piece of uncured elastomer/rubber compound of suitable shape and volume to fill a mold cavity in which it is to be cured or vulcanized.

blanket **1.** Fiber or fabric plies that have been laid up in a complete RP assembly and placed on or in the mold all at one time as in bag molding. **2.** The type of bag in which the edges are sealed against the bag molding mold.

blanking ▷ **die cutting**

blast finish The process of removing flash from (usually) thermoset molded plastic parts, and/or dulling surfaces of thermoset or thermoplastics. An impinging media such as steel balls, crushed apricot pits, walnut shells, or plastic pellets is used with sufficient force to fracture the flash. When the material is not sufficiently brittle, it can be chilled to a temperature at which it is sufficiently brittle. The majority of machines are batch types comprised of wheels rotating at high speeds, fed at their centers with the media, which is thrown out at high velocity against the parts. There are also continuous machines where a speed-controlled, open wire screen conveyor belt is used.

blast furnace A vertical coke-fired furnace used for smelting metallic ores to produce iron ore.

bleed 1. To give up color when in contact with water or a solvent. **2.** Undesired movement of certain materials in a plastic, such as plasticizers in vinyl, to the surface of the finished product or into an adjacent material. Also called migradation. **3.** An escape passage at the parting line of a mold, grooves in a blow mold, or bleeder cloth in vacuum molding or resin transfer molding. It is like a vent but much deeper, thus allows plastic to escape or bleed out.

bleeder cloth A woven or nonwoven fabric layer of material (usually of glass fiber construction) used in the fabrication of reinforced plastic parts to allow the escape of excess gas and resin during cure. The bleeder cloth is removed after the curing process and is not part of the final RP part. ▷ **vent cloth**

bleed hole Hole in the mold which serves to release excess pressure (material, gases) during molding.

blend Physical mixture or compounding of two or more plastics such as PC and ABS. Such blends usually yield products with favorable properties of both components. Bleeding is essentially the same as mixing, but implies a higher degree of dispersion than simple mixing. ▷ **alloy/blend** and **reactive polymer**

blender Additive blenders or feeders are an efficient means of combining and mixing substances in order to produce products during processing. There are different types of proportioning mixes. Some are simple devices that mix different substances; others can mix up to four or at least five different substances, including pellets, granular materials, powders, and liquids. Most units can be mounted directly on a processing machine. Some of the larger blenders are floor-mounted units with pneumatic take-offs that transfer blended material directly to the processing machines (see Figs. on this and the next page).

blending extender plastic With respect to vinyl plastosols and organosols, a blending plastic is one of larger particle size and lower cost than the dispersion plastics normally used. It can be used as a partial replacement for the primary plastic. In addition to cost reduction, sometimes properties can be altered.

blind hole Hole that is not drilled entirely through.

blister 1. A raised area on the surface of a molding caused by the pressure of air or other

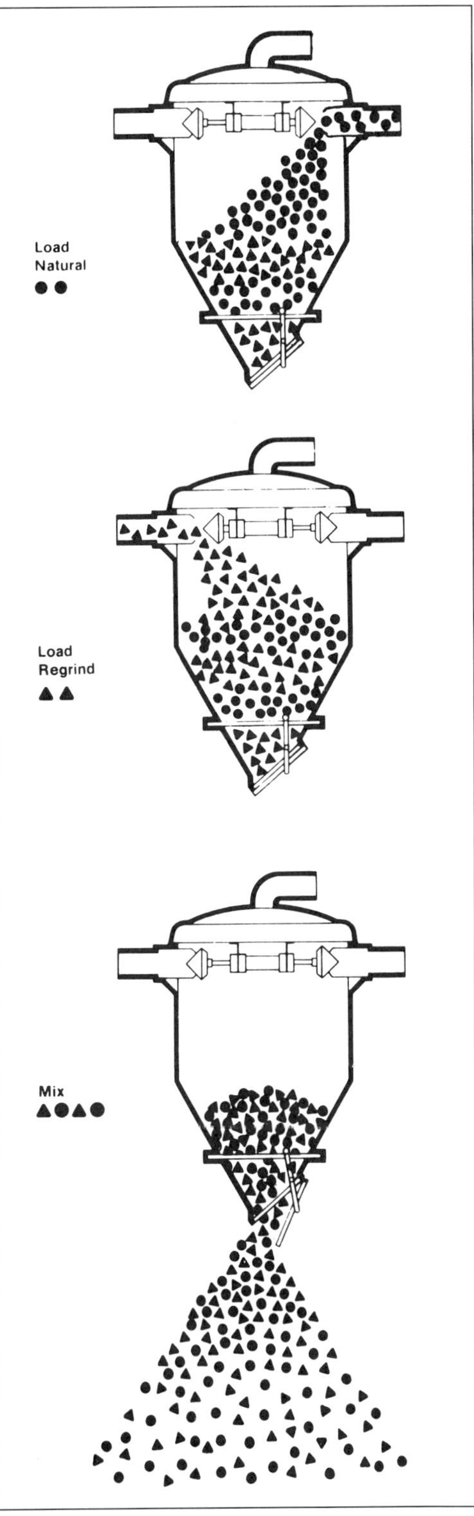

Vacuum proportioning hopper blender with blowback cycle.

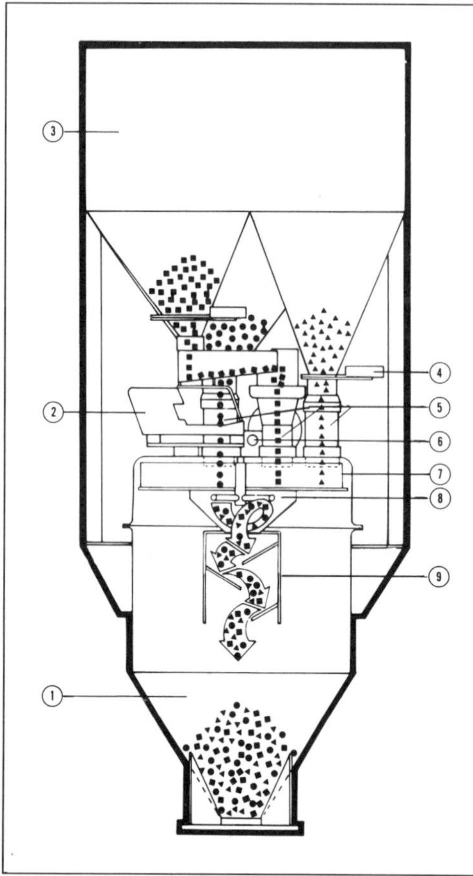

Blender components. (1) Machine supply hopper; (2) vibratory additive feeder; (3) material supply hopper; (4) slide gate; (5) material metering tubes; (6) Drive motor; (7) metering section; (8) rotating disc; (9) cascade mixing chute. ● virgin; ■ color concentrate; ▲ regrind.

gases inside it on its incompletely hardened surface; it may burst and become flattened. **2.** A thermoformed canopy or pocket roughly hemispherical in shape, for example building ceiling window, shape used in blister packaging, aircraft canopy, etc.

blister package Packages in which a thin plastic sheet is formed into the shape of a relatively small blister, then the product is placed in the blister, and the final step in a conventional processing line takes a backing material (such as plastic paper, or aluminum sheet) that is sealed to the formed sheet to enclose the product. ▷ **contour package** and **shrink package**

block 1. Undesirable cohesion of films or plastic layers of plastic. ▷ **antiblocking agent 2.** A type of plastic. ▷ **block copolymer** and **block polymer**

block copolymer A copolymer whose polymeric chain is composed of shorter homopolymeric chains which are linked together. These "blocks" can be either regularly alternating or random. Thus, an essentially linear copolymer consists of a smaller number of repeated sequences of polymeric segments having different chemical structures.

blocked curing agent A curing agent or hardener rendered unreactive, which can be reactivated as desired by physical or chemical means.

blocking film ▷ **film blocking**

blocking force The average force per unit width of blocked surface required to separate progressively two layers of plastic film from another by a rod 6.35 mm (0.025 in.) in diameter moving perpendicularly to its axes at a uniform rate of 125 mm (5 in.)/min. This force is expressed in g/cm (1b/ft) of width (ASTM D 1893).

block polymer A polymer whose molecule is made up of alternating sections of one chemical composition separated by sections of a different chemical structure or by a coupling group of low molecular weight. An example is blocks of polyvinyl chloride interspersed with blocks of polyvinyl acetate; they are made synthetically.

block polymerization The term block polymerization has been applied to both bulk polymerization (i.e., casting of a polymerizing syrup) and sequence copolymerization (i.e., block copolymerization). It is only this latter sense that is recognized by IUPAC as true copolymerization. Confusion may be avoided to some extent by the use of the prefix 'co' which implies the polymerization of more than one monomer.

blood A complex, liquid tissue of density 1.056 and pH 7.35 to 7.45. ▷ **polyvinyl pyrrolidone plastic**

bloom 1. A non-continuous surface coating on plastic products that comes from ingredients such as plasticizers, lubricants, anti-static agents, etc., which are compounded into the plastic. It is not always visible. Bloom is the result of ingredients coming out of "solution" in the plastic and migrating to the surface of the plastic. **2.** Used to describe an increase in diameter of the blow molding parison as it exits from the extruder die(s). **3.** A surface film resulting from attack by the atmosphere or from the deposition of smoke or other vapors.

blowhead Part of a forming machine serving to introduce air under pressure to blow any hollow product.

blowhole 1. A hole produced in a casting by gas which was trapped during solidification. **2.** Blow outs, pinholes, and fisheyes are holes or blisters evident in the wall surfaces of blown containers. These defects may be caused by improper blowing, sticking to the core rod, water, decomposition gases, and/or contamination.

blowing agent Compounding agent used to produce gas by chemical or thermal action, or both, in fabrication of hollow or cellular/foam products. ▷ **foam and blowing agent**

blowing film ▷ **extruder blown film** and **thermoforming twin-sheet**

blowing glass The shaping of hot glass by air pressure; started many centuries ago.

blow molding The process of forming hollow products by expanding a hot plastic (melt) against the internal surfaces of a mold. BM can be divided into three major processing categories: (1) extrusion blow molding (EBM) which uses an unsupported parison, (2) injection blow molding (IBM) which uses a preform supported by a metal core pin, and (3) stretched blow molding (SBM) for either EBM and IBM to obtain bioriented products. As shown in the Table on p. 54, almost 75% of processes are EBM, almost 25% are IBM and about 1% use other techniques such as dip blow molding (DIP), extruder drape BM, and injection neck ring BM. The different BM processes offer different advantages in producing different products based on the materials to be used, performance requirements, production quantity, and costs.

blow molding air entrapment ▷ **air entrapment**

blow molding blow cavity Forms final outside blown plastic part shape based on mold cavity shape.

blow molding blowing mandrel Part of the tooling (or mold) in a blow molding operation. It can form the opening of the container and is also a means by which air is introduced into the mold containing the parison (or preform) that ultimately is formed into a container.

blow molding blowup ratio It is the ratio of the parison (or preform) diameter to the mold cavity diameter.

blow molding clamping or press That portion of a BM machine that contains and supports the clamping platens with molds, and moves the molds in a manner required to produce and remove from the press blown parts. ▷ **clamping**

blow molding coextrusion or coinjection The use of BM multi-layer composites is a technology that provides the advantages of differing plastics that are systematically combined. The result is a composite that would be unobtainable from any single plastic. The Fig. on this page shows a coextruded part. ▷ **co-extrusion** and **coinjection**

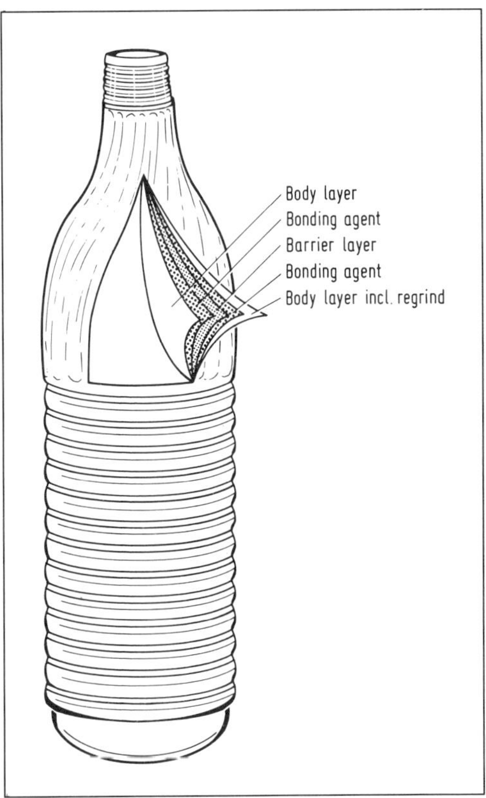

Example of a coextruded blow molded container.

blow molding cold parison Technique in which parisons (or preforms) are extruded or injection molded separately and then stored for subsequent transportation to the (second stage) BM machine for blowing.

blow molding communication protocol ▷ **communication protocol**

blow molding computer integrated ▷ **blow molding extruder programming; computer-integrated manufacturing; computer microprocessor control; computer processing control; injection molding computer-integrated**

General types of blow molding processes.

Basic process	Materials	Average production rate, parts per hour	Average container size	Approximate market penetration, percent
Continuous extrusion shuttle clamp	Polyethylene (PE), polypropylene (PP), polycarbonate (PC), polyvinyl chloride (PVC), polyethylene terephthalate glycol modified (PETG)	500–3,600	4 oz–7-$\frac{1}{2}$ gallons	50
Wheel clamp (6 to 24 clamps)	Polyethylene (PE), polyvinyl chloride (PVC), polypropylene (PP), coextrusions	2,000–5,000	32–300 oz	10
Intermittent extrusion reciprocating screw	Polyethylene (PE) and polycarbonate (PC)	500–2,500	8–128 oz	10
Accumulator head	Polyethylene (PE) and engineering plastics	50–500	5–2,000 gallons	5
Stretch blow molding	Polyvinyl chloride (PVC), polyethylene terephthalate (PET), polypropylene (PP), polyacrylonitrile (PAN)	1,200–4,000	16–48 oz	20 (including reheat)
Injection blow molding	Polyethylene (PE), polypropylene (PP), polyvinyl chloride (PVC), polyethylene tetrephthalate (PET), polycarbonate (PC), polyacrylonitrile (PAN), polystyrene (PS)	500–3,000	1–16 oz	5 (including dip molding)
Dip blow molding	Polyethylene (PE), polypropylene (PP), polyvinyl chloride (PVC), polyethylene terephthalate (PET), polyacrylonitrile (PAN), polystyrene (PS)	500–1,500	1–24 oz	(see injection blow molding)
Reheat blow molding	Polyethylene terephthalate (PET)	240–15,000 1,200–4,000 1,200–4,000	16 oz 22 liters 16–48 oz 8–48 oz	(see stretch blow molding)

blow molding cushion ▷ **cushion**

blow molding dip or displacement process Basically two pairs of dipping mandrels, equipped with neck forming tools, operate in tandem. One pair is dipped simultaneously into two separate extruder fed ports containing plastic melt. Each pair of mandrels is coated with melt. At this stage, the neck finish is formed under low pressure and a rotating potentiometer assures uniformity of the melt coating on the mandrels. Next the coated mandrels, with preformed necks, are then shuttled left to right (depending on the stage of the sequence) and descend into twin-cavity mold for blowing. Finished bottles, which show no weld or flow

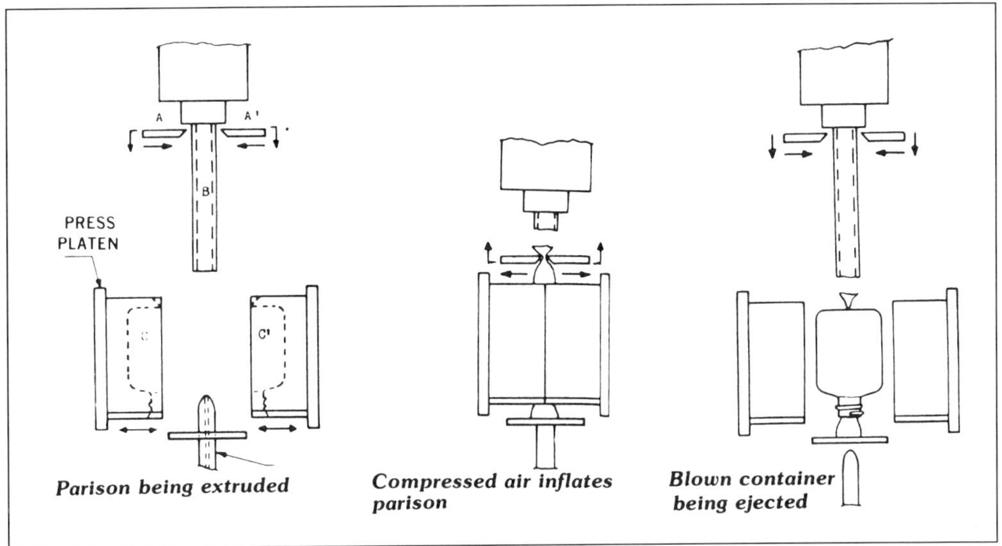

Basic extrusion blow molding process (continuous system): A = parison cutter, B = parison, C = blow mold cavity, and D = blow pin.

marks, are then deposited upright onto take-away conveyors. This process offers virtually no limit on the ratio betwen neck diameter and bottle weight.

blow molding exhaust time The length of time required to relieve the blowing air pressure in the molded part before opening the mold.

blow molding, extruder In extrusion blow molding (EBM), a parison is formed by the extruder melt output (see Figs. on this page). The parison is a tubular type of hot melt leaving the extruder die. Turning continuously, the screw feeds the melt through the die head, generally as an endless parison directly through a die. A die head can have one or more opening; so one or more parisons can be extruded. The size of the part and the amount of material to produce a part (shot size) dictate whether or not an accumulator is required. The basic nonaccumulator machine offers a continuous flow of plastic melt. With an accumulator, the flow of the parison through the die is cyclic. The connecting channels between the extruder and the accumulator, as well as the acumulator itself, are designed to prevent restrictions that might impede flow or cause the melt to hang up. Flow paths should have low resistance to melt flow to avoid placing an unnecessary load on the extruder.

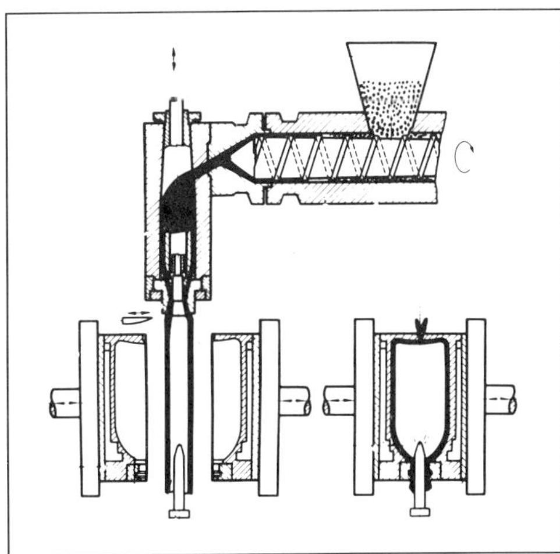

Typical phases in extrusion blow molding with an accumulator (intermittent system).

To ensure that the least heat history (residence time) is developed during processing, the design of the accumulator should provide that the first melt in is the first to leave when the ram empties the chamber; the goal is to have the chamber totally emptied at each stroke.

When the parison exits the die and reaches a preset length, a split cavity mold closes around it and pinches one end of it. Usually a blow pin is located opposite the pinched end of the "tube". Compressed air inflates the parison against the female cavity of the mold surfaces. Upon contact with the relatively cool mold surface, the blown parison cools and solidifies to the part shape. Next the mold opens, ejects the part, then repeats the cycle by again closing around the parison, shaping it, and so on.

Various techniques are used to introduce air. It can enter through the extrusion die mandrel (as with most EBM lines), through a blow pin over which the end of a parison has dropped (see Fig. on top of p. 55), or through blowing needles that pierce the parison. The wall distribution and thickness of the blown part are usually controlled by parison programming, the blow ratio, and part configuration. The Fig. shown here is an example of a part.

Hand-held 3 gal (0.01 m^3) HDPE extrusion blow molded sprayer tank.

blow molding, extruder accumulator ▷ **accumulator**

blow molding, extruder blow/fill/seal An extrusion based process where the processed container is made, then filled, and then sealed before removal from the mold.

blow molding, extruder blow pin A system of blowing whereby the blowing action is introduced into a parison through a needle(s), such as a hypodermic needle(s), usually located at the mold parting line. ▷ **mold core pin**

blow molding, extruder blow pin bottom stand Device used to support blow pin(s) stationary or moveable.

blow molding, extruder bottom blow A specific type of blow molding technique that forms hollow arteries by injecting the blowing air into the parison from the bottom of the mold; as opposed to introducing the blowing air at a container opening that is called top blow.

blow molding, extruder collapsible bottle ▷ **bottle collapsible**

blow molding, extruder continuous versus accumulator When a product is a small industrial part such as a 5-gallon gas tank, an automobile air duct, or a $7\frac{1}{2}$-gallon water container, the final selection is normally between a continuous extrusion (shuttle) or an accumulator type BM. Continuous is typically used for fabricating 2 oz to 8 g. Accumulator is typically used from $1\frac{1}{2}$ to 2,000 g. There is an overlap region, $1\frac{1}{2}$ to 8 g, in which a given part can be BM by either, thus fabricator has to determine which machine concept is most economical and best suited for BM part.

Advantages of continuous EBM generally include: excellent parison programming, excellent die tooling profiling, fast color change, faster cycle times, automatic deflashing easy to adapt and at low cost, blown part exits from BM machine in a stand-up and oriented position, and excellent for processing heat sensitive plastics such as PVC. With accumulator, advantages generally include: larger platens to blow very large parts, higher clamp tonnage, larger diameter parison drops, excellent for low melt strength plastics, and for parts with long inchoff, where considerable clamp tonnage is required.

blow molding, extruder continuous versus intermittent In regard to plastic, continuous has advantage in plastic thermal stability and melt fracture; intermittent advantages are in melt strength and swell. Equipmentwise, continuous has advantage in using less plant space; intermittent advantages are in part size and plant utilities.

blow molding, extruder cooling ▷ **blow molding, extruder parison**

blow molding, extruder core Extruder die part that controls the inside dimensions of the parison.

blow molding, extruder curtaining The vertical draping or folding caused by extruding a parison which swells; grows in diameter as it is extruded. Because of gravitational forces, the parison tends to hang directly below the die opening. As the circumference of the parison swells or grows, it tends to fold or wrinkle beneath the die.

blow molding, extruder cycle time BM cycles are shown in Figs. 1 and 2 on p. 57. To reduce cycle time a very important aspect to consider is reduction of cooling time. Cooling can take about two-thirds of the entire BM cycle. To provide good heat transfer, reducing

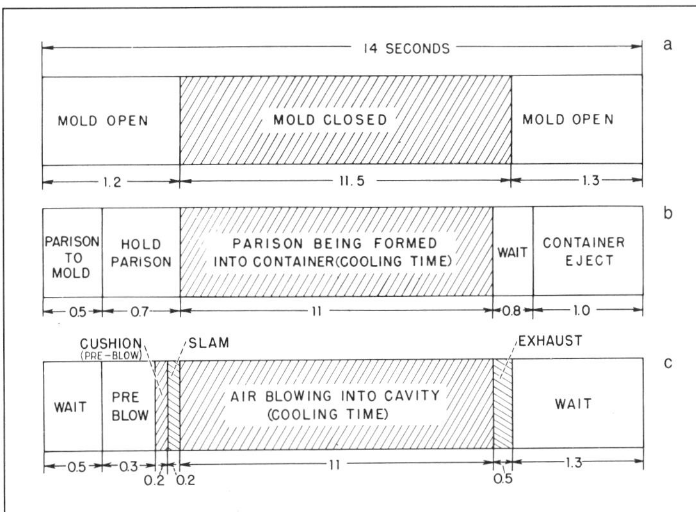

Fig. 1 Extrusion blow molding cycle. A complete cycle graph showing a typical blow molding cycle for 1 gallon container. Phases *(a)*, *(b)*, and *(c)* illustrate the breakdown of the BM cycles.

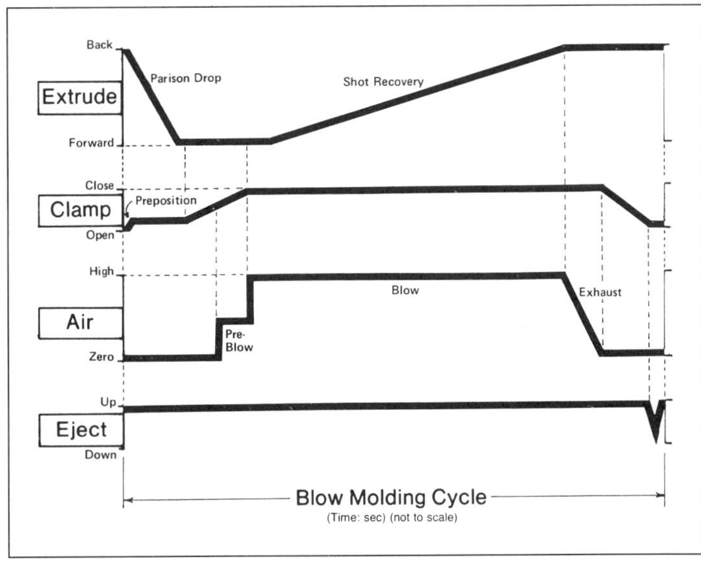

Fig. 2 Schematic of extrusion blow molding using an accumulator head.

cycle time, molds use fast heat transfer material such as aluminum, berylium copper, zinc alloys such as Kirksite, and occasionally bronze. Reduction also occurs by using CO_2, N, moist air, and other pressure blowing gases.

blow molding, extruder die ▷**die**

blow molding, extruder die ring static and flexible ▷**die ring, static and dynamic**

blow molding, extruder double wall The Fig. on this page provides an example of double wall EBM.

blow molding, extruder drape process The drape process identifies multi-dimensional EBM where flash is minimized.

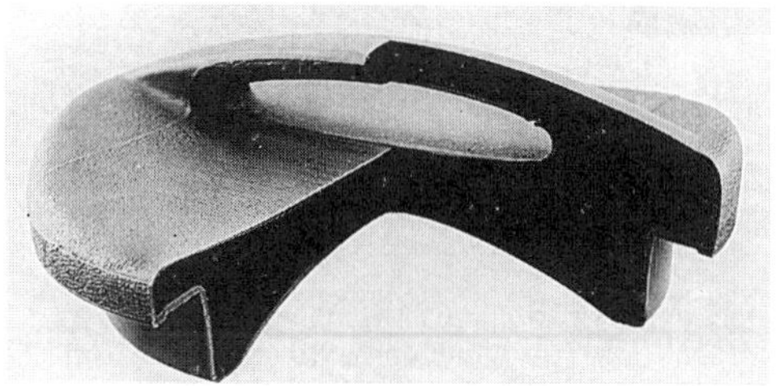

Section of HDPE extruded blow molded, double wall, integral handle of a lid container.

blow molding, extruder flat surface Many large EBM parts are designed with large flat surfaces. In some cases, when the flat surface is not joined to the other side by tack-offs, foam filling, etc., there is a tendency for the flat section to bend or flex, resulting in a less rigid feel than required (this action is called oil canning). Techniques such as crowning, arching, corrugations, ribbing, which are often used with injection molding, thermoforming, sheet metal, etc., are also used with BM to improve stiffness.

blow molding, extruder mold flood cooling ▷ **mold flood cooling**

blow molding, extruder mold multiple/combination cavities There are different multicavity molds to meet different requirements. The so-called 2-up molding is considered when part generally has a large opening at one end (however not necessary). The Fig. shows examples of BM parts.

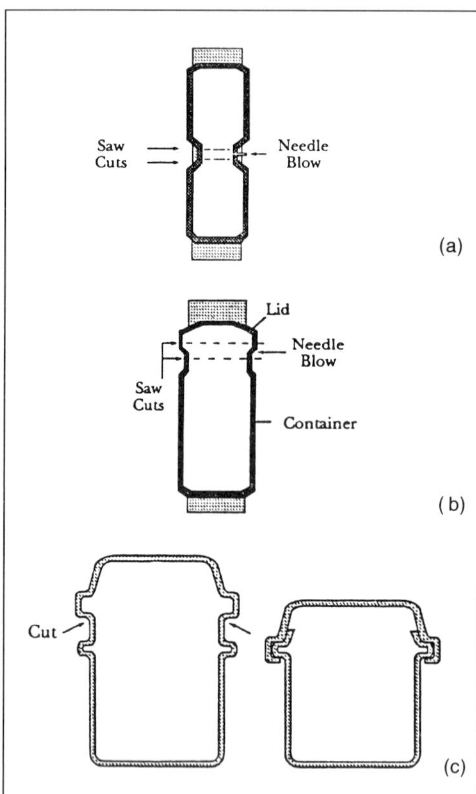

Examples of extrusion blow molding and cut to produce: *(a)* Two containers; *(b)* container with lid; and *(c)* container with snap fit lid.

blow molding, extruder parison The molten plastic tube extruded from a die is placed in the blow mold to be formed (blown) into a product.

blow molding, extruder parison blowing The air used for blowing serves to expand the parison tube against the mold cavity walls, forcing the melt to assume the shape of the mold and forcing it into the surface details, such as raised letters, surface designs, and so on. For blowing pressure guide, see Table.

Guide for air blowing pressure.

Plastic	Pressure, psi
Acetal	100–150
PMMA	50–80
PC	70–150
LDPE	20–60
HDPE	60–100
PP	75–100
PS	40–100
PVC (rigid)	75–100
ABS	50–150

The air performs three functions: it expands the parison against the mold, exerts pressure on the expanded parison to produce surface details, and aids in cooling the blown parison. During the expansion phase of the blowing process, it is desirable to use as high a volume of air as is available so that expansion of the parison against the mold walls is accomplished in a minimum time. A maximum volumetric flow rate into the cavity at a low linear velocity can be achieved by making the air inlet orifice as large as possible.

Blowing inside the neck sometimes is difficult. Small orifices may create a venturi effect, producing a partial vacuum in the tube and causing it to collapse. If the linear velocity of the incoming blow air is too high, the force of this air can actually draw the parison away from the extrusion head end of the mold, resulting in an unblown parison. The air velocity must be carefully regulated by control valves placed as close as possible to the outlet of the blow tube. Normally the gauge pressure of the air used to inflate commodity and engineering resin parisons is from 30 to possibly 300 psi (0.21–2.1 MPa). Often too high a blow pressure will "blow out" the parison. Too little pressure will yield end products lacking adequate surface details. As high a blowing pressure as possible is desirable to give both minimum blow time (resulting in higher production rates) and finished parts that reproduce the mold surface. The optimum blowing pressure generally is found by experimentation on the machine that will be used in production. The blow pin should not be so long that air is blown against the hot plastic opposite the air outlet. That action can result in freeze-off and stresses in the container at that point.

Air is a fluid, just as the parison is, and as such it has a limited ability to blow through an orifice. If the air entrance channel is too small, the required blow time will be excessive, or the pressure exerted on the parison will not be adequate to reproduce the surface details in the mold. General guidelines for determining the optimum diameter of the air-entrance orifice during blowing are: (1) up to one quart (0.95 L) use $\frac{1}{6}$ in. (1.6 mm); (2) for one quart to one gallon (0.95–3.8 L), use 0.25 in. (6.4 mm); and (3) for one to 54 gallons (3.8–205 L) use 0.5 in. (12.7 mm).

The pressure of the blowing air will cause variations in the surface detail of the molded items. Some PEs with heavy walls can be blown with air pressure as low as 30 to 40 psi. Low pressure can be used because items with heavy walls cool slowly, giving the resin more time, at a lowered viscosity, to flow into the indentations of the mold surface. Thin walls cool rapidly; so the plastic reaching the mold surface will have a high melt viscosity, and higher pressures will be required, of 50 to 100 psi (0.3–0.7 MPa). Larger items such as one-gallon containers require a higher air pressure, of 100 to 150 psi. The plastic has to expand farther and takes longer to get to the mold surface in larger items. During this time the melt heat will drop slightly, producing a more viscous mass that in itself requires more air pressure to reproduce the details of the mold.

A high volumetric air flow at a low linear velocity is desired. A high volumetric flow gives the parison a minimum time to cool before coming in contact with the mold, and provides a more uniform rate of expansion. A low linear rate of velocity is desirable to prevent a venturi effect (see above). Volumetric flow is controlled by the line pressure and the orifice diameter. Linear velocity is controlled by flow control valves close to the orifice.

The blowing time differs from the cooling time, being much shorter than the time required to cool the thickest section to prevent distortion on ejection. The blow time for an item may be computed from the Table on this page and the formula:

$$\text{Blow time, s} = \frac{\text{Mold volume, cu ft}}{\text{cu ft/s}} \times \frac{\text{Final mold psi} - 14.7\text{ psi}}{14.7\text{ psi}}$$

This is for free air; but there will be a pressure buildup as the parison is inflated, so the blow rate has to be adjusted. The value of cu ft/s is also obtained from the Table, according to the line pressure and the orifice diameter. The final mold pressure is assumed to be the line pressure for purposes of calculation. Actually, the blow air is heated by the mold, raising its pressure. Calculations ignoring this heat effect will be satisfactory when blow times are under one second (for small to medium-sized parts); but if blow times are longer, the air will have time to pick up heat, resulting in a more rapid pressure buildup and shorter than calculated blow times.

Discharge of air in cu ft/s at 14.7 psi and 70°F.

Gauge pressure, psi	Orifice diameter, in. (mm)			
	$\frac{1}{16}$ (1.6)	$\frac{1}{8}$ (3.2)	$\frac{1}{4}$ (6.4)	$\frac{1}{2}$ (12.7)
5	0.993	3.97	15.9	73.5
15	1.68	6.72	26.9	107
30	2.53	10.1	40.4	162
40	3.10	12.4	49.6	198
50	3.66	14.7	58.8	235
80	5.36	21.4	85.6	342
100	6.49	26.8	107.4	429

blow molding, extruder parison continuous
In EBM, the uninterrupted formation of an extrudate that is subsequently formed into products. The cycling of the machine is so designed that continuous extrusion can be maintained.

blow molding, extruder parison ejection rate
The rate of plastic flow through the die body in in.^{3}/s or lb/s (mm^3/s or kg/s).

blow molding, extruder parison intermittent
A parison ejected from the die head intermittently. After parison is moved into the proper position and mold closed, parison is not being extruded. Parison flow continues after blown part is removed from the mold. The accumulator die head is programmed to meet the intermittent time cycle.

blow molding, extruder parison programming The extrusion of a parison which differs in thickness profile with the length direction in order to equalize wall thickness of the blown product. This can be done with a pneumatic or hydraulic device which activates the mandrel shaft and adjusts the mandrel position during parison extrusion as reviewed in the Table and Fig. on p. 60. It can also be done by varying the extrusion output rate on accumulator type BM machins, or with certain parison preheat, two-stage systems by varying the amount of heat applied.

Electronic parison programming is an effective way to control and minimize material usage, and improve both quality and productivity. The most common method used is orifice modulation (see Fig. on p. 60). The die is fitted with a hydraulic positioner that allows position-

blow molding, extruder parison programming

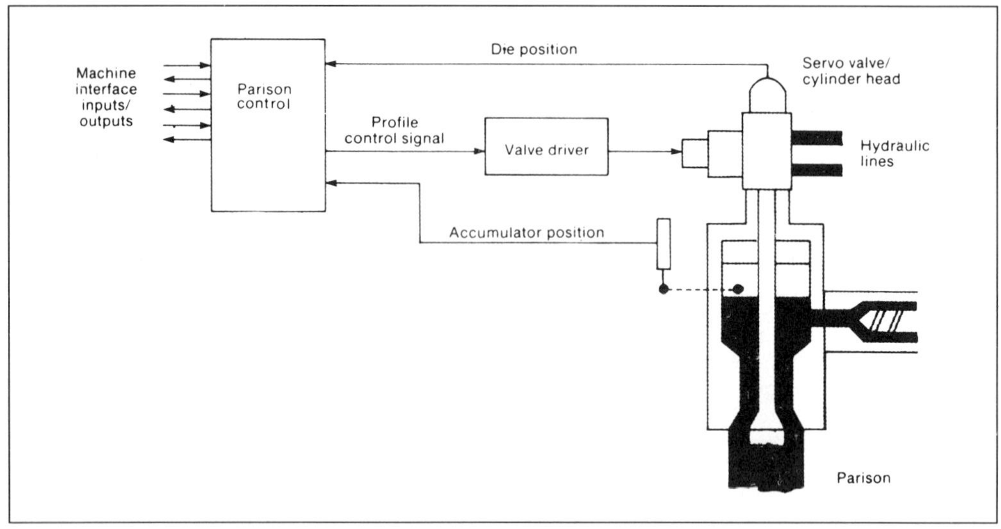

Schematic of an accumulator head with programmable process controller; controls melt characteristics (interrelates with extruder performance), rate of melt flow to form the parison, and profiling thickness as it extrudes from die.

Examples of controlling or programming extrusion blow molding dies.

Type die	Feature	Advantage/Disadvantage
Simple die	Fixed die gap	Simple; inexpensive; no adjustment facility
Die profiling	Permanently profiled; preferred in die land area	Fixed circumferential wall thickness change; time-consuming; complex
Die centering	Can be permanently shifted laterally to correct parison drop path	Compromise between required drop path and equal wall thickness
Open-loop axial die gap control	Can be axially shifted during extrusion	Equal circumferential wall thickness change possible; no feedback
Servohydraulic closed-loop axial die gap control	As above, with greater speed, accuracy, and flexibility	Equal circumferential wall thickness change possible, with feedback
Stroke-dependent die profiling	Permanently ovalized die gap	Fixed, unequal circumferential wall thickness change possible; affects entire parison length
Die/mandrel adjustable profiling	Settable adjustment of die gap profile	Settable, unequal circumferential wall thickness change possible; rapid optimization
Servohydraulic closed-loop radial die gap control	Programming ovalization and shifting of die gap	Programmable circumferential wall thickness change possible, independent of parison length

ing of the inside die diameter during parison drop. The OD and ID relationship of the tapered die orifice opening is varied in a programmed manner to increase the parison thickness.

In regard to parison control, a compromise is necessary between the desired net weight and the need to maintain a sufficient safety margin over a set of minimum specifications which include: minimum wall thickness, drop speed, drop strength, dimensional stability, and fluctuations in net weight. Most of these parameters can be directly affected by the molder's ability to control the parison wall thickness. The most common and practical way has been to adjust the gap between the die and mandrel (see Table on p. 60).

blow molding, extruder parison swell ▷ **die parison swell**

blow molding, extruder parison thickness control ▷ **blow molding, extruder parison programming**

blow molding, extruder part thickness In EBM the amount of stretching a parison is a function of the part size and configuration in relation to the parison size and orientation. This condition can be expressed as follows:

$$\text{average part thickness} = \frac{\text{parison surface area}}{\text{part surface area}} \times \text{parison thickness}$$

blow molding, extruder pinch-off The pinch-off (also called cut-off) is a very critical part of EBM, where the parison is squeezed and welded together. The Fig. on this page shows typical designs. It requires good thermal conductivity for rapid cooling and good toughness to ensure long production runs. The pinch-off must have structural soundness to withstand the plastic pressure and repeated closing cycles of the mold. It usually must push a small amount of plastic into the interior of the part to slightly thicken the weld area. It also provides a cut through the parison to provide a clean break later when flash is removed.

A gross miscalculation of pocket depth (which must be learned through experience) can cause severe problems. For example, if the pocket depth is too shallow, the flash will be squeezed with too much pressure, putting undue strain on the mold, mold pinch-off areas, and machine clamp press section. The molds will be held open, leaving a relatively thick pinch-off, which is difficult to trim properly. If the pocket is too deep, the flash will not contact the mold surface for proper cooling. In fact, between molding and automatic trimming, heat from the uncooled flash will migrate into the cool pinch-off and cause it to heat up and cause unwanted problems like sticking to the trimmer. Or, during trimming, it can stretch instead of breaking free.

blow molding, extruder pinch-off blades The part of the mold which compresses the parison to effect sealing of the parison prior to complete blowing and to permit easy removal and cooling of flash.

blow molding, extruder pinch-off land The width of pinch-off blade which affects sealing of the parison.

blow molding, extruder pinch-off relief angle The angle of the cutaway portion of the pinch-off blade measured from a line parallel to the pinch-off land.

blow molding, extruder pinch-off tail The bottom of the parison that is pinched off when the mold closes.

blow molding, extruder platform blowing Technique for BM large parts to prevent exces-

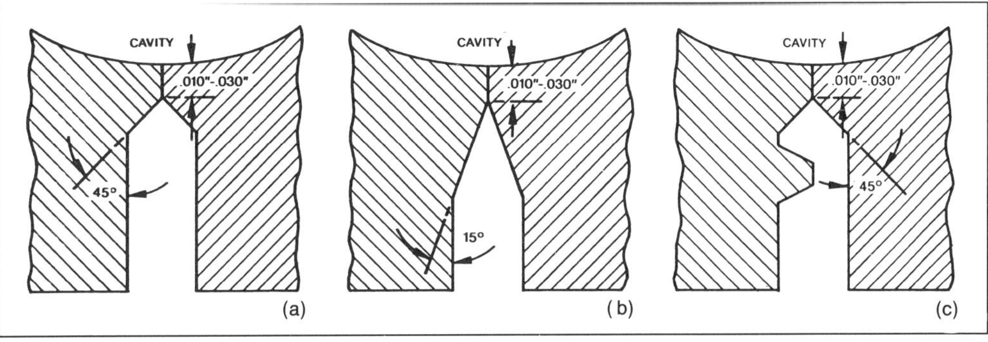

Typical pinch-off double-angle designs: *(a)* Usual type with 45° angle and a 0.010 in. (0.25 mm) land; *(b)* with large blown part relative to parison diameter, the plastic will thin down and even leave holes on the weld line, requiring 15° angles to force the melt to the inside of the blown part, thus increasing weld thickness; *(c)* this pinch-off with a dam also helps solve problems.

sive sagging of the heavy parison. The machine has a table which after rising to meet the parison at the die, descends with the parison but at a slightly lower rate than the parison extrusion rate.

blow molding, extruder pock mark Irregular indentations on the surface of a blown product caused by insufficient contact of the blown parison with the mold surface. They are usually due to low blow pressure, air gas entrapment, and/or moisture condensation on mold surface.

blow molding, extruder polyethylene low melt index Melt index and other melt flow characteristics directly influence BM capability. As an example large parts, such as plastic fuel tanks, drums, and trash cans, are BM from lower melt index, high molecular weight polyethylenes. For example, 55 g drums that used a 10 MI can now use a 2 to 6 MI. Fuel tanks are going from 10 MI to 6 MI. These lower MI of PE have been used in Europe since the 1970s. They give a tougher end product and reduce weight of parts by 5 to 10%. With their higher melt strengths, they deliver a more stable parison. Parisons up to 14 ft ($35\frac{1}{2}$ cm) are used to BM with ease products such as boats and windsurfers.

In the melt state, these PEs are much more viscous than the higher MI materials. When processed through conventional, smooth feed throat extruders with metering type screws, they build up a high melt temperature in the range of 221°C (430°F). This high stock temperature is not desirable since it increases energy consumption and cycle time, and reduces the melt strength of the plastic. Special extruders were designed and used which are able to process these high viscosity materials, in pellet or powder form, in stock temperatures of 195° to 199°C (350° to 390°F). The result is reduced energy consumption and cyclic time, and improving color changing of the head. Benefits are also gained when processing other plastics such as PP, ABS, etc.

The extruder used is typically a 20/1 L/D, or even a 24/1, and uses a noncompression screw with mixing sections. Unlike conventional, smooth feed throat screw extruders, this extruder runs at a very low screw speed thereby minimizing the shear on the plastic. The grooved feed throat optimizes the feeding of either pellet or powder form and builds a considerable pressure within the screw. This pressure is converted to energy which, along with the heated barrel and minimum shear from the screw, results in properly melting the plastic. This approach in using the plasticator with the properly designed accumulator head is very different from conventional extruders which use the compression of the screw and the shallow metering zone to melt the plastic through high shear.

blow molding, extruder pre-blow The injection of a medium, such as usual air, into a closed parison before the mold closes.

blow molding, extruder pre-pinch parison Closing off an open end of the parison before the mold pinches it together. Often used in conjunction with the pre-blow.

blow molding, extruder process to plastic interplay dilemma Basically with acceptable melt strength (viscosity), slower extrusion rate and less swell of the parison will occur. However, with poor or unacceptable melt strength there is: faster mold close, lower melt temperature and faster extrusion rate. In turn lower melt temperature will cause higher head forces resulting in thermal instability and mechanical failure of the plastic. The faster extrusion rate causes melt fracture and with raised melt temperature, thermal instability occurs. The faster extrusion rate can also cause intermittent processing that allows for part cooling, resulting in thermal instability. With less parison swell, larger tooling and smaller tooling gaps are required resulting in melt fracture and higher head pressures. The higher pressures in turn cause mechanical failure.

blow molding, extruder scrap ▷ **scrap, blow molding standard**

blow molding, extruder top blow The type of BM machine which forms hollow articles by injecting the blowing into the parison at the top of the mold. ▷ **extruder bottom blow**

blow molding, extruder two-up molding ▷ **blow molding, extruder mold multicavities**

blow molding feeder ▷ **feeder**

blow molding foamed plastic While blow molding of foamed plastics is not a common straightforward process, it has been reported that polystyrene containing CO_2 can be injection molded into parisons. They are blow molded and expanded simultaneously in the second step.

blow molding fold area Areas of excess plastic in the finished BM product can have an unwanted fold. These may be formed by the plastic melt sagging, folding, or blowing out unevenly during the blowing process.

blow molding glass, press and blow process A process of glass manufacture in which

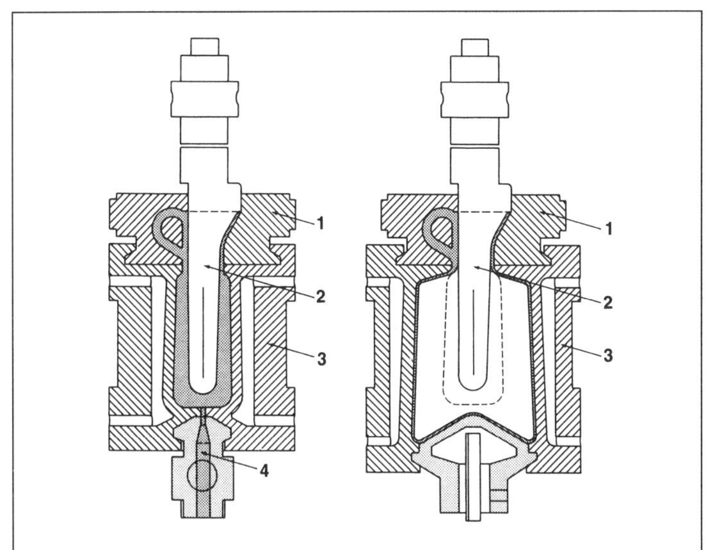

Integral carrying handle for an injection blow molded product. (1) Precision "neck" mold that includes solid handle; (2) preform core and blow pin; (3) basic water-cooled bottle female mold; (4) injection nozzle of the injection molding machine

the parison is pressed and in another step, the heated parison is blown to form the final shape.

blow molding guideline Essential BM factors for processing and operating characteristics include: plastic flow (mainly determined by basic plastic properties), parison or preform sag, parison or preform swell, molding cycle time, most favorable melt temperature, and blowing pressure. In regard to end-product, properties included are: stiffness or flexibility, resistance to environmental stress cracking (for certain plastics such as PE), resistance to attack and penetration by chemicals, appearance (especially gloss and surface defects), uniformity of wall thickness, distortion (shrinkage and warpage), parting line (where applicable in process used), weld line shape and thickness (for EBM), piece weight, discoloration, deterioration due to temperature fluctuations or UV radiation, odor and taste, and toxicity.

blow molding handle Many designers are familiar with the fact that the extrusion blown process can include a "blown" handle; typical product is the HDPE milk bottle.What many do not recognize is the fact that the injection blown process also can readily include a handle that is not blown as shown in the Fig. on this page.

This integral carrying handle was issued in the French patent, number 1,192,475 granted to the Italian company, Manifattura Ceramica Pozzi SpA. The Fig. above presents figures from this patent which show the incorporation of a traditional jug handle above the blown portion of an injection blow molded container, in this example, a pitcher. The handle is molded as part of the preform and is undisturbed when the container is blown. A direct extrapolation to stretch blow molding technology would incorporate the jug handle immediately below the neck finish of an injection molded preform. It would be necessary to mold such a preform in a split mold which suits itself to production on certain rotary type injection stretch blow equipment.

blow molding industrial versus packaging product size Any blown product that is not a bottle but includes packaging larger than 20 L (55 g) is considered by various groups as a blow molded industrial product.

blow molding, injection IBM basically has three stages, schematically shown in the Figs. on p. 64. In the first stage, hot melt is injected through an injection molding machine nozzle into a manifold and into one or more preform cavities. An exact amount of plastic is injected around a core pin(s). Hot liquid from a heat control unit is directed by hoses through mold heating channels around the preform cavity; these channels have been predesigned to provide the correct heat control on the melt within the mold cavity. The melt heat is decreased to the required amount.

The two-part mold opens, and the core pin(s) carries the hot plastic to the second stage blow mold station (counterclockwise). Upon mold closing, air is introduced via the core pin, and the plastic blows out and contacts the mold cavity surface. Controlled chilled water circulates through predesigned mold channels around the mold cavity (usually 40–50°F), and solidifies the hot plastic. The two-part blow mold opens, and the core pin carries the com-

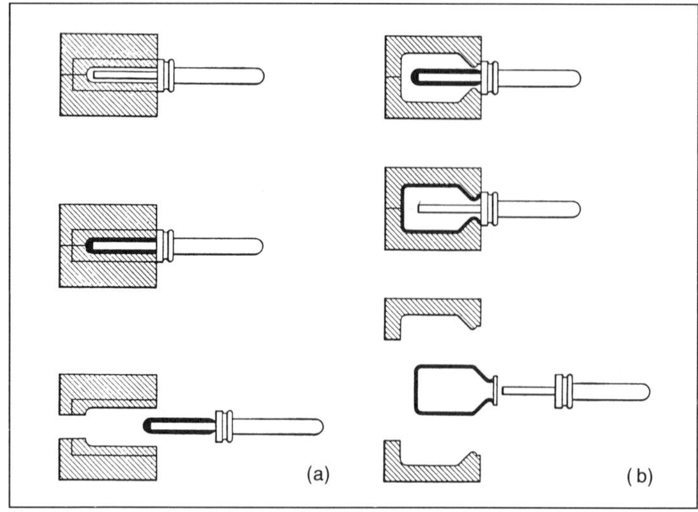

Basic injection blow molding process. (*a*) Injecting preform; (*b*) blow molding and ejection.

plete blown container to the third stage, which ejects the part. Ejection can be done by using a stripper plate and air, robots, and so forth.

IBM can have four or more stations (stages). A station can be located between the preform and blow mold stages to provide extra heat conditioning time. A station between the blow mold and ejection stages can provide additional cooling and/or provide secondary operations, such as hot stamping, labeling, and so on. A station between the ejection and preform stages can be used to detect if ejection has not occured, to add an insert to the core pin, and so forth.

The process parameters in preform production that determine the quality of the part are the injection speed, injection pressure, hold-on (packing) pressure, heat control of the preform, and melt mix. The process permits using resins that cannot be used in EBM, specifically those with no controllable melt strength such as PET, which is used in carbonated beverage bottles (stretched-blown). The information on blowing parisons, cooling, clamping, and shrinkage that was presented for EBM is also applicable to IBM.

There are several different IBM methods available, with different means of transporting the core rods from one station to another. These methods include the shuttle, two-parison rotary, axial movement, and rotary with three or more stations used in conventional IM clamping units. A variation of IBM is displace-

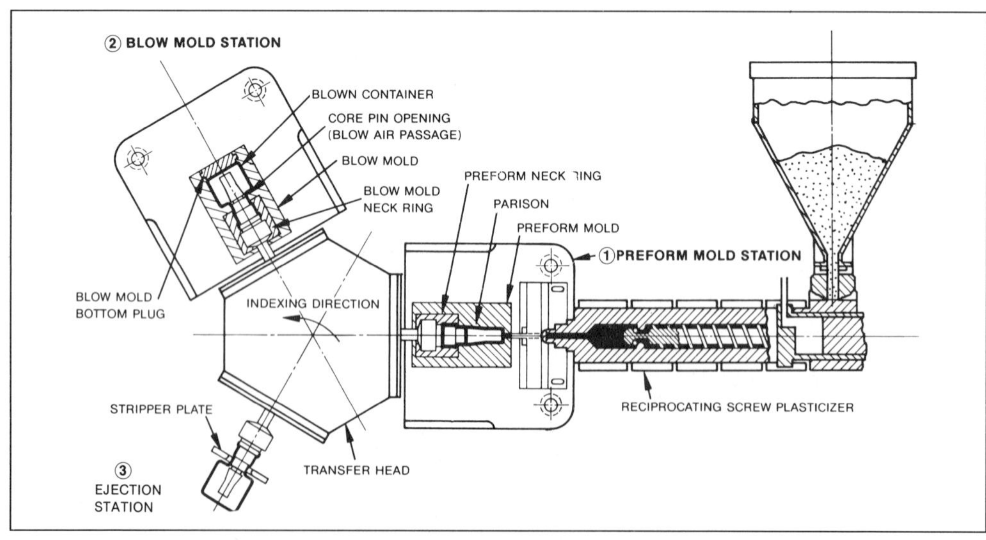

Schematic of a three-station injection blow molding machine.

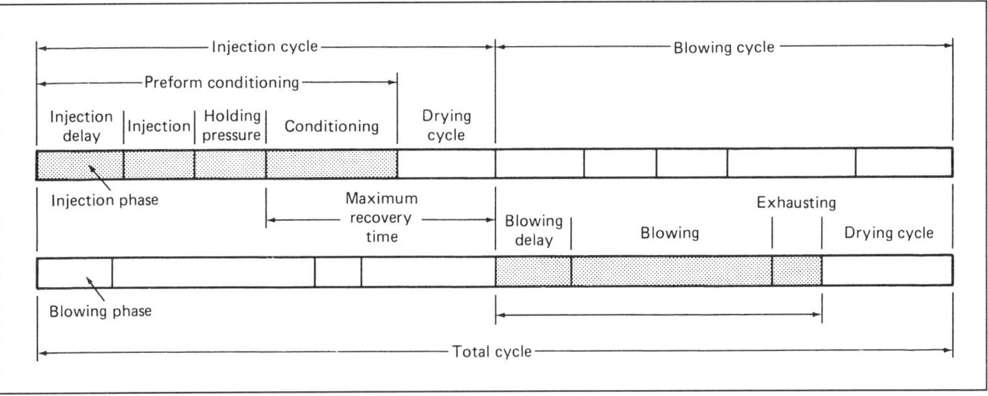

Example of injection blow molding complete cycle, starting with injection molding the preform followed by the blowing process.

ment BM or dip molding. A premeasured amount of hot melt is deposited into a cupel, the shape of a preform. A core rod is inserted into the cupel, displacing the melt and packing it into the neck finished area. It then moves to a blow station where it basically follows the procedure described above. Advantages of IBM include lower-cost machines and the fact that a nearly stress-free bottle is blown.

blow molding, injection cycle The Fig. on this page explains the various stages in the complete IBM process.

blow molding, injection ketchup bottle recycled ▷ **ketchup bottle recycled**

blow molding, injection neck ring process **1.** In IBM, these are inserts in the injection mold and the blowing mold that form the external dimensions of the finish being molded on the container. **2.** Process used to seal the plastic between the core rod and mold cavity during the IBM operation. **3.** This process permits producing an injection molded bottle finished with an extrusion molded body.

blow molding, injection preform An injection molded tube that is closed at one end, similar to a chemical laboratory test tube. The tube is hollow or formed on a rod that transfers the tube from an injection mold to a larger mold cavity where it is blown up and away from the rod to fill the cavity in the blowing operation. Air pressure is directed from the rod. It is sometimes referred to as a parison.

blow molding, injection preform rod holder core One core for each station in the IBM machine that holds the preform rods.

blow molding, injection versus extrusion With EBM, the advantages include high rates of production, low tooling costs, incorporation of blown handleware, a wide selection of machine builders, etc. Disadvantages are a usually higher scrap rate, and limited wall thickness control or plastic distribution. Trimming can be accomplished in the mold for certain type molds, or secondary trimming operations have to be included in the production lines, and so forth.

With IBM, the major advantages are that no flash or scrap occurs during processing, it gives the best of all thickness and material distribution control, critical neck finishes are molded to a high accuracy, it provides the best surface finish, low-volume quantities are economically feasible, and so on. Disadvantages are its high tooling costs, the lack (to date) of blown handleware (there is only solid handleware), its being relatively limited to relatively smaller blown parts (whereas EBM can easily blow extremely large parts), and so forth. Similar comparisons exist with biaxially orienting EBM or IBM. With respect to coextrusion, the two methods also have similar advantages and disadvantages, but mainly major advantages. With IBM, for example, PET can be processed (mono- or multilayer) and stretched into the popular 2- and 3-liter carbonated beverage bottles. The Table on p. 66 provides a cost comparison of the different BM techniques for PVC and PET.

blow molding intermittent reciprocating screw versus accumulator versus side accumulator Reciprocating advantage is basically that use can be made of multiple parisons. Accumulator head advantages are shot size and part size can be very large as well as plastic thermal stability. Side accumulator advantages

Example of manufacturing cost comparison of 16 oz blow molded bottle.

	Standard extrusion blow molding 2-parison head + fold	Stretch blow molding PVC (2) single pari-son heads + fold	Stretch blow molding PET
1.0 Machine cost incl. head, molds, ancillaries (license fee, stretch PVC and PET)	$270,000	$450,000	$850,000
2.0 Hourly machine costs			
Depre'n, 5 yr, 30 K hr, $/hr	$9.00	$14.85	$28.33
Financing cost 5 yr. 12.5%	2.80	4.65	10.20
Labor, 1 man	13.00	13.00	13.00
Energy at $0.06 per kWh	2.50	5.35	11.00
Floor space	1.50	2.00	4.00
Maintenance and consumable material	2.25	3.75	4.50
Total hourly machine costs	$ 31.05	$ 43.60	$ 71.03
3.0 Bottle specifications hourly/annual prod.			
3.1 16 oz finish wt. (454 g)			
–regular 37 g (1.3 oz)			
–stretch PVC 20 g (0.7 oz)			
–stretch PET 20 g (0.7 oz)			
Cycle time/bottles per hour	8.4 sec/1,714	7.5 sec/1,920	3.6 sec/4,000
Bottles per yr., millions	10,286	11,520	24,000
4.0 Annual costs			
4.1 16 oz (454 g)			
Resin: —37 g $0.70/lb ($1.54/ kg)	$585,200		
—20 g $0.66/lb ($1.46/ kg)		$334,950	
—20 g $0.60/lb ($1.32/ kg)			$634,360
Machine costs	186,300	261,600	426,180
Total cost p.a.	$771,500	$596,550	$1,060,540
Royalty (PET)-DuPont/year			$ 30,000
Cost per thousand	$ 75.00	$ 51.78	$ 45.44

Notes: 1. Figures are not to be considered as absolute costs, but rather reflect comparisons between various machine options.
2. All calculations are based upon 100% efficiency.
3. All bottle weights are finish weights (flash being considered as 100% reusable).

are large shot size and part size as well as multiple parisons.

blow molding machine screw wear ▷ **screw wear**

blow molding manufacturing cost ▷ **blow molding, injection versus extrusion**

blow molding market U.S. consumption of plastics, by weight, is about 65% HDPE, 22% PET, 6% PVC, 4% PP, 2% LDPE, and 1% others. Contentwise it is about 22% food, 20% beverage, 15% household chemicals, 12% toiletries and cosmetics, 8% health, 7% industrial chemicals, 5% automotive, 11% others.

blow molding melt ▷ **melt**

blow molding melting and crystallization ▷ **crystallinity and property; crystallization**

blow molding mold The mold to form hollow parts is generally made of aluminum that can have water jackets, flood cooling, cast in tubing, or drilled cooling lines. The aluminum provides faster heat transfer than steel. However, steel is also used to provide improved

Example of materials used in the construction of blow molding molds.[1]

Material	Hardness[2]	Tensile strength psi	Tensile strength MPa	Thermal conductivity Btu/in./ft² h °F
Aluminum				
A346	BHN-80	36,975	255	1,047
6061	BHN-95	39,875	275	1,165
7075	BHN-150	66,700	460	905
Beryllium copper				
23 and 165	RC-30 (BHN-285)	134,850	930	728
Steel				
0–1 and A–2	RC 52–60 (BHN-530–650)	290,000	2,000	243
P-20	R-32 (BHN-298)	145,000	1,000	257

[1] BHN = Brinell and RC = Rockwell hardness (C scale).
[2] Specific gravities (lb/cu in.): Al = 0.097, Be/Cu = 0.129–0.316, steel = 0.24–0.29.
▷ **mold materials** for more information

wear, handling, and life cycle for certain type products and operations. Isolated areas, such as threads or pinch holes, can be steel inserted in aluminum molds to extend their longevity. The Table on this page provides information on mold materials. Molds for EBM can be equipped with a method for injecting air into the parison. All molds can include air ejection system to remove blown products. ▷ **mold** and **mold materials**

blow molding multilayer Two or more layers that are processed by coextrusion, coinjection or laminating can be used to blow mold products. The laminated construction is usually by thermoforming.

blow molding neck The part of a container where the shoulder cross-section area decreases to form the finish.

blow molding neck bead A protruding circle on a container at the point where the neck meets the finish, the diameter of which usually equals the outside diameter of the closure.

blow molding neck, false A neck construction which is additional to the neck finish of a container and which is only intended to facilitate the BM operation. Afterwards the false neck part is removed from the container.

blow molding orientation ▷ **blow molding stretched**

blow molding outgassing ▷ **outgassing**

blow molding parison ▷ **blow molding, extruder parison**

blow molding preform ▷ **blow molding, injection preform**

blow molding pressure Air pressure used to expand the parison or preform within a blow mold. Air is the usual media; others used to reduce cycle time include CO_2, moist air, N_2, etc.

blow molding process control ▷ **process control**

blow molding process control statistically ▷ **statistical process control**

blow molding product design rules Basic rules to follow when possible are to use generous radius, slant, and taper product. ▷ **design blow molded panel concept** and **design parameters**

blow molding programmable controllers safety circuit ▷ **programmer controllers safety circuit**

blow molding purging ▷ **purging**

blow molding safety ▷ **processing with safety; programmable controllers safety; safety and machine; safety interlock**

blow molding scrap ▷ **scrap blow molding standard**

blow molding screw ▷ **screw**

blow molding screw length to diameter ratio ▷ **L/D ratio**

blow molding shrinkage The shrink behavior of different resins and the part geometry must be considered. Generally, shrinkage is the difference between the dimension of the mold at room temperature of 22°C (72°F) and the dimensions of the cold blown part, usually checked twenty-four hours after production. The elapsed time is necessary to allow the part to shrink. Trial and error determines what time period is required to ensure complete shrinkage. The coefficients of expansion and different shrinkage behaviors depend on whether the plastic materials are crystalline or amorphous.

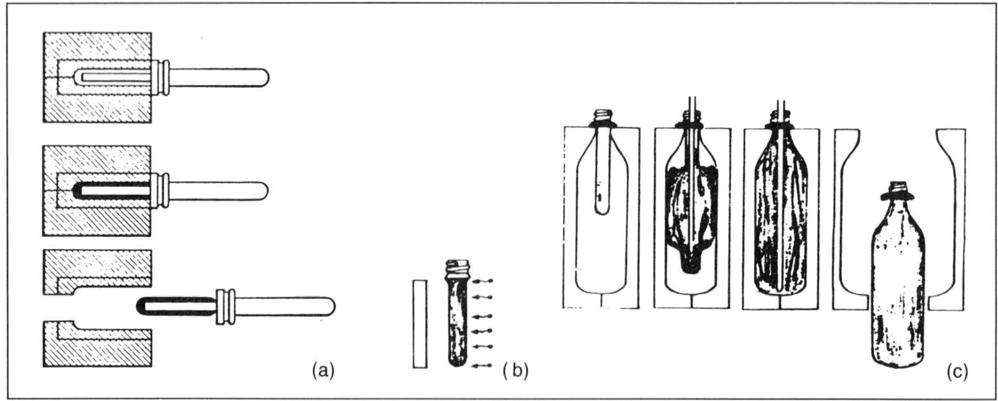

Schematic of stretch injection blow molding. (*a*) Inject preform; (*b*) reheat preform; (*c*) stretch blow molding and ejection.

Lengthwise shrinkage tends to be slightly greater than transverse shrinkage. Most horizontal shrinkage occurs in the wall thickness rather than a body dimension. With PE, higher shrinkage occurs with the higher-density polymers and thicker walls. Lengthwise shrinkage is due to the greater crystallinity of the more linear types of plastics. Transverse shrinkage is due to slower cooling rates, which result in more orderly crystalline growth. ▷ **shrinkage**

blow molding stretched High speed extrusion BM and injection BM are taken an extra step in stretching or orienting. The Fig. on this page shows stretched IBM; with EBM the stretching action is similar to this, as it occurs during compressed air inflation. In EBM, the parison, which is mechanically held at both ends, is stretched rather than just blown. Stretching can include the use of an expanding rod within the IBM preform or an external gripper with EBM.

By biaxially stretching the extrudate before it is chilled, significant improvements can be obtained in the finished containers. This technique allows the use of lower-material-grade resins or thinner wall thicknesses with no decrease in strength; both approaches reduce material costs. Stretched BM gives many resins (mono- or bioriented) improved physical and barrier properties (see Tables on this page). This process allows wall thicknesses to be more accurately controlled and also allows weights to be reduced.

Draw ratios used to achieve the best properties in PET bottles (typical 2- and 3-litre carbonated beverage bottles) are 3.8 in the hoop and 2.8 in the axial direction, and will yield a bottle with a hoop tensile strength of about 29,000 psi (200 MPa) and an axial tensile of 15,000 psi (104 MPa).

Stretch blow is extensively used with PET, PVC, ABS, PS, AN, PP, and acetal, although most TPs can be used. The amorphous types, with a wide range of thermoplasticity, are easier to process than the crystalline types such as PP. If

Volume shrinkage of stretch blow molded bottles.[1]

Type of bottle	%
Extrusion blow molded PVC	—
Impact-modified PVC (high orientation)	4.2
Impact-modified PVC (medium orientation)	2.4
Impact-modified PVC (low orientation)	1.6
Non-impact-modified PVC (high orientation)	1.9
Non-impact-modified PVC (medium orientation)	1.2
Non-impact-modified PVC (low orientation)	0.9
PET	1.2

[1] Seven days at 80°F.

Gas barrier transmission comparisons for a 24 oz container weighing 40 g.[1]

Type of bottle	Rate, square meters per day	
	Oxygen, CC	Water vapor, G
PET (oriented)	10.2	1.10
Extrusion blow molded PVC	16.4	2.01
Stretch blow molded PVC (impact-modified)	11.9	1.8
Stretch blow molded PVC (non-impact-modified)	8.8	1.3

[1] At 100°F.

PP crystallizes too rapidly, the bottle is virtually destroyed during the stretching. New grades of PP called "clarified" have virtually zero crystallinity and overcome this problem.

There are in-line (1-step) and two-stage (2-step) processes as outlined in Figs. 1–3 on this and the next page. In-line processing is done on a single machine whereas two-stage require either an extrusion or an injection line to produce the solid parisons or preforms. With either type of process, a specific reheat blow machine is used to produce the bottle. With in-line systems, the hot-firm plastic preform or parison passes through the conditioning stations that bring it down from the "melt" heat to the proper orientation heat (see Table on next page). A rather tight heat profile is maintained in the axial direction. Advantages of this approach are that the heat history is minimized (crucial for heat-sensitive resins), and the preform or parison can be programmed for optimum material distribution.

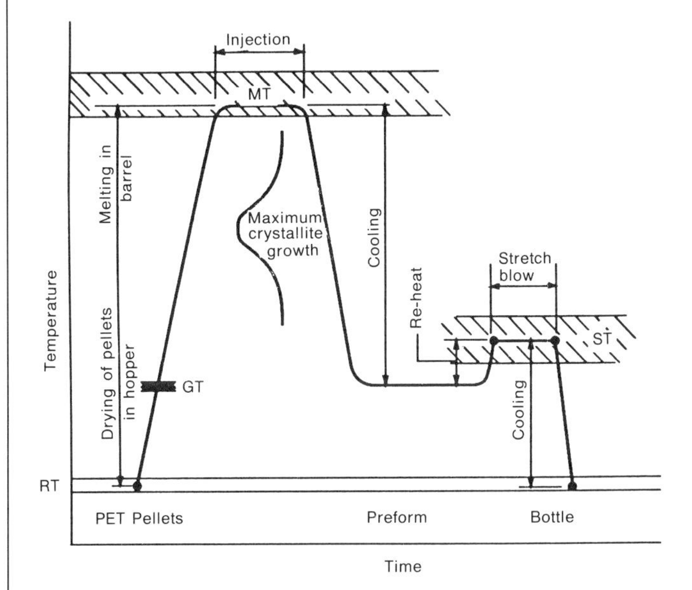

Fig. 1 In-line injection stretch blow molding of PET. RT = room temperature; GT = glass transition temperature, T_g; MT = melt temperature, T_m; ST = stretch temperature, T_s.

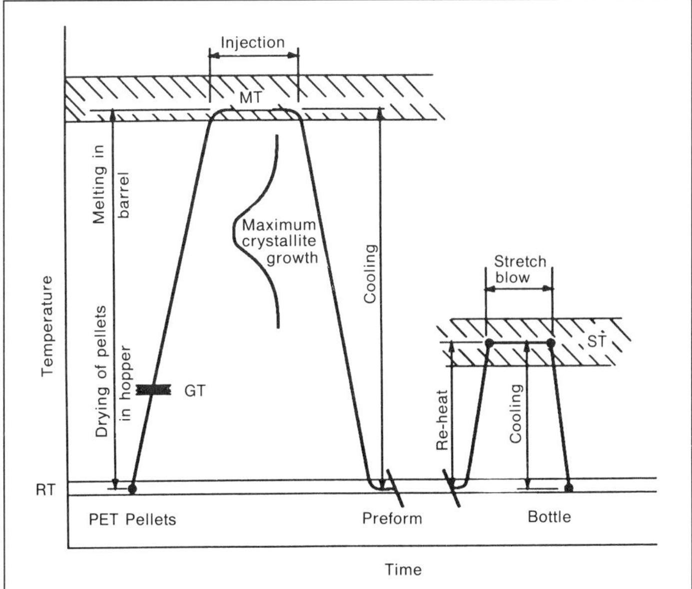

Fig. 2 Two-stage injection stretch blow molding of PET. RT = room temperature; GT = glass transition temperature, T_g; MT = melt temperature, T_m; ST = stretch temperature, T_s.

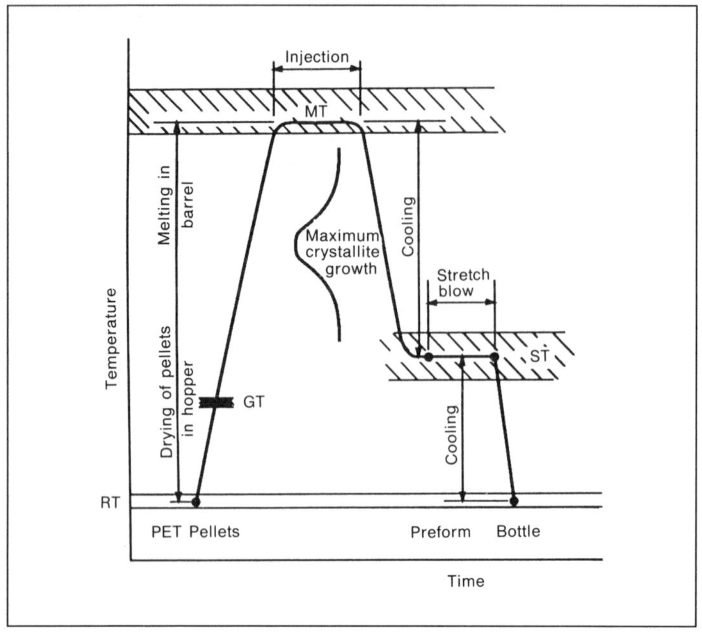

Fig. 3 Alternative in-line injection stretch blow molding of PET.
RT = room temperature; GT = glass transition temperature, T_g; MT = melt temperature, T_m; ST = stretch temperature, T_s.

With the two-stage process, cooled preforms or parisons are conveyed through an oven (usually using quartz lamps) that reheats them to the proper orientation heat profile. Advantages include minimization of scrap (for EBM, there being no scrap with IBM using either the in-line or the two-stage process), higher output rates, and the capability to stockpile preforms or profiles and improve thread finishes (EBM). In-line stretch IBM, which offers more flexibility from a material view, does not give the degree of parison programming available in EBM-stretched. An extruded parison can be heat-stabilized, and then the parison is held externally and pulled to give an axial orientation while the bottle is blown radially.

Another technique stretches and preblows the parison before completing the blowing operation. In both of these operations, scrap is produced at the bottle neck and at its base. The processes completely orient the whole bottle, including the threaded end; this neck orientation does not occur with stretch IBM. With EBM, threads are post-mold-finished.

Extrusion processes also can use programmed parisons and two sets of molds. The first mold is used to blow and heat-condition the preform—actually to cool it to the orientation heat. The second mold uses an internal rod to stretch and blow the bottle. With two-stage EBM, the preforms or parisons are usually open-ended. They are reheated, and then stretched by pulling one end while the other end is clamped in the blow mold. Minimum scrap can be produced, and the compression-molded threads provide a good neck finish. This system utilizes a conventional extrusion line and a reheat blow machine whose oven contains quartz lamps to provide the proper heat. When used to heat the preform for parison, they rotate in a heat-profile-controlled oven to provide uniform heat circumferentially. ▷ **orientation**

blow molding stripping The idea of stripping blow molded containers started with the

Stretch blow molding characteristics.

Plastic	Melt temperature		Stretch orientation temperature		Maximum stretch ratio
	°F	°C	°F	°C	
PET	490	250	190–240	88–116	16/1
PVC	390	199	210–240	99–116	7/1
PAN	410	210	220–260	104–127	9/1
PP	334	168	250–280	121–136	6/1

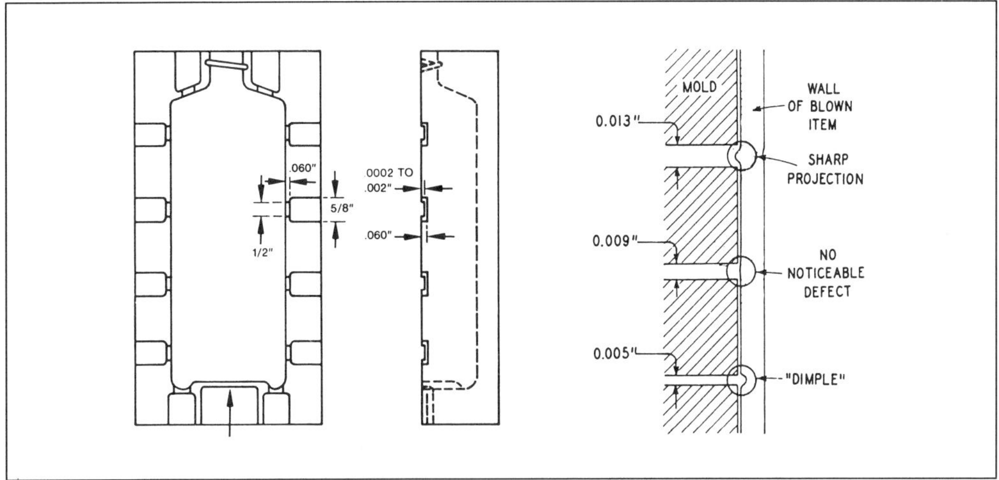

Example of venting a mold for blow molding.

smaller containers and extended to the larger sizes of 55 g, or larger. With transparent plastic, with or without graduations marked, they are used in single and double (coextrude) extruded blow molded products.

blow molding tail flash The lower portion of flash on an extruded blow molded part.

blow molding, thermoforming ▷**thermoforming, clam shell**

blow molding tolerance-shrinkage The shrinkage behavior of different plastics and the part geometry must be considered. Generally shrinkage is the difference between the dimension of the mold at room temperature (72°F) and the dimensions of the cold blown part, usually checked 24 hours after production. The elapsed time is necessary to allow the part to shrink. Trial and error determines what time period is required to ensure complete shrinkage. Coefficients of expansion and the different shrinkage behaviors depend on whether plastic materials are crystalline or amorphous.

Lengthwise shrinkage tends to be slightly greater than transverse shrinkage. Most of the horizontal shrinkage occurs in the wall thickness rather than a body dimension. With PE, higher shrinkage occurs with the higher-density polymers and thicker walls. Lengthwise shrinkage is due to the greater crystallinity of the more linear type plastics. Transverse shrinkage is due to slower cooling rates, which result in more orderly crystalline growth. Part shrinkage depends on many factors, such as plastic density, melt heat, mold heat, part thickness, pressure of blown air, and control or capability of blow molding production line. ▷**tolerance**

blow molding, two stage Two-stage, also called two-step, system. ▷**blow molding stretched**

blow molding venting Well designed molds are vented, as entrapped air in the mold prevents good contact between the parison and mold cavity surface. When air entrapment occurs, basically the surface of the blown part is rough and pitted in appearance. A rough surface can be undesirable because it can interfere with the quality of decoration and can detract from the over-all appearance. Examples of mold venting are illustrated in the Fig. on this page.

The air between parison (preform) and mold must be expelled as completely as possible during blowing so that the molded part receives the correct shape and can cool down by contact with the mold walls. To insure minimum cooling time, it is important that the mold be adequately vented. Entrapped air or air which is not removed rapidly enough from the mold can hold the plastic away from the mold wall and thus prevent or delay efficient cooling.

blow molding versus injection molding A very significant difference exists between BM and IM. BM usually only requires 25 to 150 psi (0.17 to 1.03 MPa) pressures, with possibilities for certain plastics of up to 200 to 300 psi (1.38 to 2.07 MPa). For IM, the pressure is usually 2,000 to 20,000 psi (13.8 to 137.8 MPa), and in some cases up to 30,000 psi (207 MPa). The lower pressures generally result in lower internal stresses in the solidified plastics and a more proportional stress distribution. The result is improved resistance to all types of strain (tensile, impact, bending, environmental, etc.).

As the final mold equipment for BM consists of female molds only, it is possible simply by changing the machine parts or melt conditions to vary the wall thickness and the weight of the finished part. If the exact thickness required in the finished product cannot be accurately calculated in advance, this flexibility is a great advantage from the standpoint of both time and cost. With BM, it is possible to produce walls that are almost paper-thin. Such thicknesses cannot be achieved by conventional IM, but, with certain limitations, can be produced by thermoforming. Both BM and IM can be successfully used for very thick walls. The final choice of process for a specific wall section is strongly influenced by such factors as tolerances, reentrant curved shapes, and cost.

BM can be used with plastics such as PE that have a much higher molecular weight than is permissible in IM. For this reason, items can be blown that utilize the higher permeability, oxidation resistance, UV resistance, and so on, of the high-MW plastics. This feature is very important in providing resistance to environmental stress cracking. This extra resistance is necessary for plastic bottles used in contact with the many industrial chemicals that promote stress cracking.

With BM, the tight tolerances achievable with IM are not obtainable. However, in order to produce reentrant curved or irregularly shaped IM products, different parts can be molded and in turn assembled (snap-fit, solvent-bonded, ultrasonically bonded, etc.). In BM of a complete irregular/complex product, even though IM tolerances cannot be equaled, the cost of the container is usually less. No secondary operations such as assembly (adhesives, etc.) are required. Other advantages also are achieved, such as significantly reducing (if not eliminating) leaks, reducing total production time, and so forth.

blow molding, void ▷ **air entrapment**

blow molding,volume adjustment ▷ **volume adjustment, blown container**

blow molding wall thickness control ▷ **sensor**

blow molding zero defect ▷ **zero defect**

blown bottle terminology The Figure on the next page provides terminology and position identification.

blown film ▷ **extruder blown film**

blown tubing ▷ **extruder tube**

blow rate The speed at which the air enters and expands the parison (or preform) during blow molding.

blow time The length of time the blow medium is contained in the mold(s). ▷ **blow molding, extruder cycle time** and **blow molding, injection cycle**

blowup ratio ▷ **blow molding, blowup ratio**

blueing A mold blemish in the form of a blue oxide film which occurs on the polished surface of a mold as a result of the use of abnormally high mold temperature.

blueing agent Used to remove yellow light. ▷ **optical brightener**

blueing off The checking of the accuracy of mold cutoff surfaces by putting a thin coating of Prussian blue on one half and checking the blue transfer to the other half.

blush **1.** Precipitation of water vapor in the form of colloidal droplets on the surface of a varnish, lacquer, or plastic film caused by lowering of the temperature immediately above the coated surface due to solvent evaporation. This results in greying of the dried film; can be avoided by use of less volatile solvent or slower drying solvent in the coating. The term blushing is also used. **2.** The terms blushing, chalking, or crazing are used when plastics turn white in areas that are highly stressed such as the mold gate.

boat **1.** A tungsten container used to hold aluminum during vacuum metalizing. **2.** Different types and size marine vehicles.

body **1.** A part having a unique physical property. ▷ **blackbody** **2.** A non-specific term approximately synonymous with consistency or viscosity; usually descriptive of a liquid. **3.** In biochemistry, an agglutinous substance present in the blood or tissues.

bogus A descriptive term applied to papers and paperboards manufactured principally from old papers or inferior or low-grade stock in imitation of grades using a higher quality of raw material.

boiling ▷ **latent heat**

boiling point The temperature of a liquid at which its vapor pressure is equal to or very slightly greater than the atmospheric pressure of the surrounding environment. For water at sea level, with 14.7 psi (100 kPa) atmospheric pressure, it is 100°C (212°F). ▷ **atmosphere**

boiling pressure At a specific temperature, the pressure at which a liquid and its vapor are in equilibrium.

bolster ▷ **mold chase**

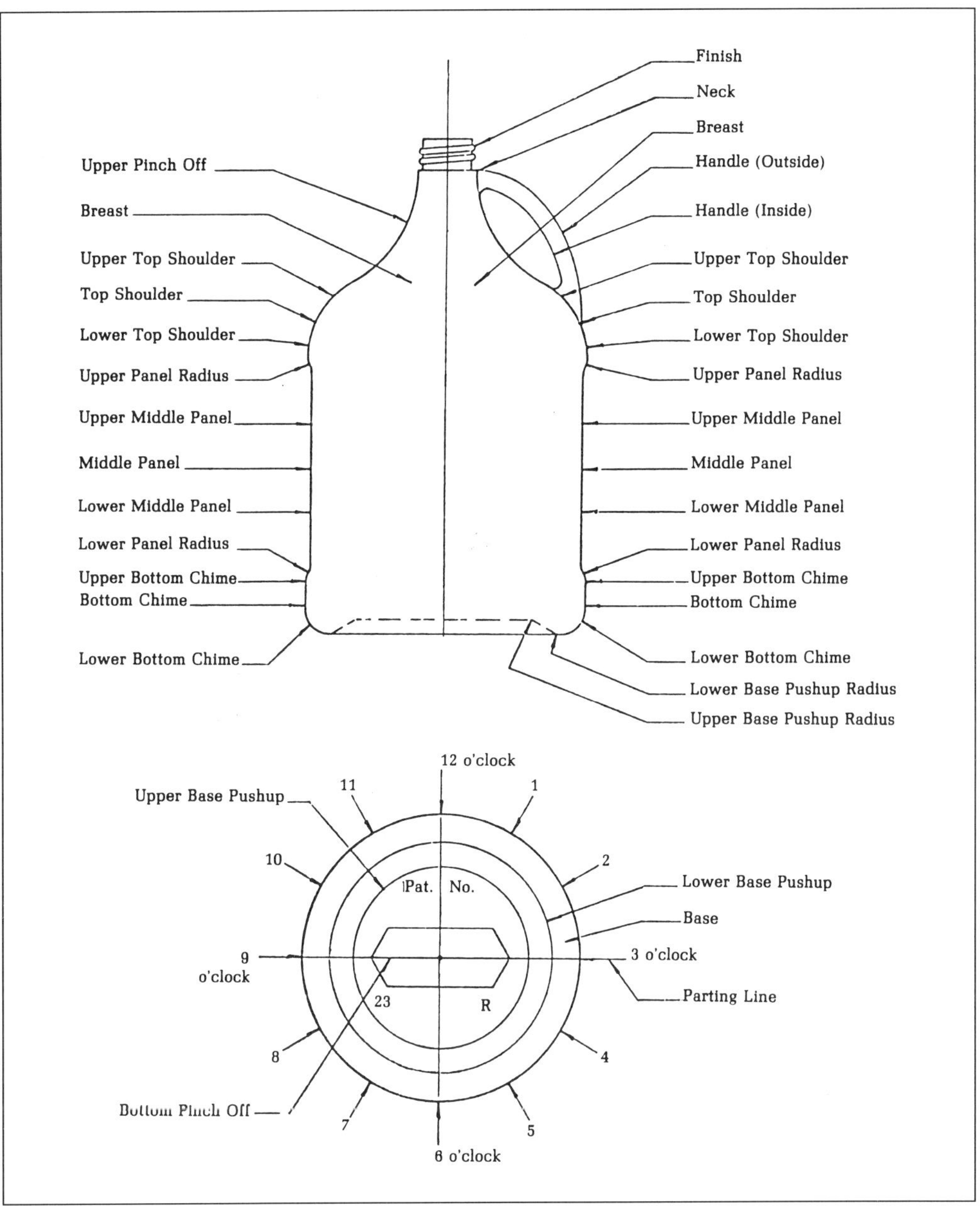

Bottle terminology and position identification. Note: 12 o'clock position is at top as specified above, 90° from parting line and in position so any Patent No., Mold No., Manufacturer's No. can be easily read.

bolt preload ▷ **design bolt preload**

Boltzmann, Ludwig Born in Vienna, Ludwig Boltzmann (1844–1906) was interested primarily in physical chemistry and thermodynamics. His work has importance for chemistry and plastics because of his development of the kinetic theory of gases and rules governing their viscosity and diffusion. The mathematical expression of his most important generalization is known as Boltzmann's Law and Principle, still regarded as one of the cornerstones of physical science.

Boltzmann superposition principle This principle provides a basis for the description of all linear viscoelastic phenomena. Unfortunately, no such theory is available to serve as a basis for the interpretation of nonlinear phenomena, i.e., to describe flows in which neither the strain nor the strain rate is small. As a result, there is no general valid formula for calculating values for one material function on the basis of experimental data for another. ▷ **viscoelasticity**

Considerable effort has been made in improving an understanding of non-linear behavior and some useful concepts have been developed. While a universal theory of nonlinear viscoelastic behavior still is nonexistent, limited success can be claimed in the development of theories useful for particular types of deformation. One approach to the formation of a nonlinear constitutive equation, via John M. Dealy, is an intuitive one making use of empirical equations for quantities such as the rates of creation and loss of entanglements. It should be noted that empirical model building in the area of nonlinear viscoelasticity is not at all analogous to the devising of equations for fitting relationships between scalar quantities. Substantial complications arise from two aspects of the problem. These are the involvement of tensor-valued quantities (stress and strain) and the fact that the response of the material to a stress or strain imposed at time depends not just on these quantities but also on strains or stresses imposed at previous times.

Because of these complicating factors, it is a significant challenge simply to establish an acceptable form for a nonlinear constitutive equation. Certain general hypotheses have proven useful in this regard. The use of such general criteria to formulate empirical constitutive equations is called the continuum mechanics approach to nonlinear viscoelasticity. Once the general form has been established, the selection of the specific nature of the equation is guided by a study of experimental results.

The alternative approach to the development of nonlinear models is to start from a model for molecular behavior and use statistical mechanics to derive a constitutive equation. This approach is mathematically very complex, and as a result, many simplifying assumptions are necessary in order to make it possible to obtain an equation that allows the stress to be calculated from strain history. These assumptions result in limitations on the applicability of the final constitutive equation.

bombardment Impingment upon an atomic nucleus of accelerated particles such as neutrons or deuterons for the purpose of inducing fusion or of creating unstable nuclei which become radioactive.

bomb effect ▷ **plasticator safety**

bond breaker A release material placed in a joint to prevent undesired adhesion of the sealant to the substrate or the back-up material.

bonded abrasive ▷ **abrasive**

bonded fabric ▷ **fabric bonded**

bonding ▷ **adhesion** and **joining and bonding**

bonding, fusion ▷ **fusion bonding**

bonding, hot plate ▷ **hot plate bonding**

bonding, induction ▷ **induction bonding**

bonding, secondary ▷ **secondary bonding**

bonding, solvent ▷ **solvent bonding**

bonding, thermocompression ▷ **thermocompression bonding**

bonding, ultrasonic ▷ **ultrasonic bonding and sealing**

bond strength The unit load applied in tension, compression, flexural, peel, impact, cleavage, or shear, required to break an adhesive assembly with failure occurring in or near the plane of the bond. Also called adherence.

bone ash An ash composed principally of tribasic phosphate but containing minor amounts of magnesium phosphate, calcium carbonate, and calcium fluoride. They are noncombustible. Obtained from calcining bones; synthetic product also produced. Use includes cleaning and polishing, coating molds, etc.

bone china Ceramic tableware of high quality in which a small percentage of bone ash is incorporated. Made chiefly in England.

bone surgery ▷ **biological activity**

"book" opening press ▷ **press platen "book" opening**

booster Uses a large volume of low-pressure liquid to produce a low volume at high pressure. Also called intensifier.

booster ram A hydraulic ram used as an auxiliary to the main ram of a molding press.

boral A composite material consisting of boron carbide crystals in aluminum with a cladding of commercially pure aluminum. Use includes reactor shields, neutron curtains, etc.

borate glass A glass in which the essential glass former is boron oxide instead of silica.

bore **1.** The inside of a barrel. **2.** To enlarge a hole with a boring tool, as in a lathe or boring mill. Distinguished from drill.

boron Elemental boron is polymeric, being either amorphous and reactive, or crystalline, melting at about 2,300°C (4,172°F), almost as hard as diamond and very inert, depending on the method of its preparation.

boron compound They find numerous applications in the field of polymer chemistry. The largest area of application in this field for inorganic and organic compounds of boron is as catalysts for polymerization.

boron fiber Boron filaments are produced by chemical vapor deposition from a gaseous mixture of hydrogen (H_2) and boron trichloride (BCl_3) on primarily an electrically heated tungsten substrate of 0.5 mil (12.5 μm) diameter. The final filament diameter is either 4 mil (100 μm), 5.6 mil (140 μm), or 8 mil (200 μm), in descending order of production quantities; however, both larger and smaller diameters have been produced in experimental quantities.

Performancewise, they have exceptionally high tensile strength of 350,000 to 500,000 psi (2.4 to 3.5 GPa) and modulus of elasticity of 45 million psi (310 GPa) with a relatively low density of 2.6 cm^{-3}. Upper temperature limit in an oxidizing atmosphere is 250°C (480°F). It is very useful as a reinforcing fiber in high performance reinforced plastics, principally in aerospace applications due to its high cost; matrix is usually an expensive high performance epoxy plastic. This was the first of high strength, high modulus fibers to be produced; U.S. Airforce Materials Laboratory, Dayton, OH was very influential in its development during the early 1950s. They are used as individual short and long fibers in nonwoven fabrics and particularly in woven fabrics. Boron RPs have been used in some sporting goods equipment such as tennis rackets, fishing rods, golf clubs, etc. ▷ **silicon carbide fiber** and **chemical vapor deposition**

bosses and edges Bosses are projections that provide for attachment and support of related components; they may be hollow or solid. Solid bosses are sometimes called studs. It is often possible to design intricate systems of structurally interdependent bosses and ribs that provide dimensional stability, while providing for attachment of related components, maintaining proper wall thickness ratios, and reducing material usage as well as molding cycle time.

The unsupported edges of a part may be stiffened or strengthened by turning the edge or changing the plane of the wall. These methods may be employed to provide edge rigidity and reduce or eliminate warpage, especially when minimum wall thicknesses are used. The radius at both external and internal plane intersections should be as generous as possible to improve the flow of the processing plastic and minimize stress concentration when the article is under a load.

Boston round ▷ **container, Boston round**

bottle base radius The radius at the base of a bottle which connects the body (or wall) of the container with the bottom bearing surface of the bottle. It varies in size, depending on the design and geometry of the bottle.

bottle bill Proposed legislation or laws requiring a returnable deposit on certain containers and a redemption system, to discourage disposal of containers and encourage recycling. Also called deposit laws.

bottle coating with glass ▷ **barrier, glass coating**

bottle, collapsible There are bellows-style collapsible containers such as bottles that are foldable. As shown in the Fig. on p. 76, technology of foldable containers in contrast to that of the usual "passive" bottles provides advantages and conveniences such as reduced storage, transportation, disposal space, prolonged product freshness by reducing oxidation and loss of carbon dioxide, and provides continuous surface access to foods like mayonnaise and jams.

The bellows of collapsible containers overlap and fold to retain their folded condition without external assistance, thus providing a self-latching feature. This latching is the result of bringing together under pressure two adjacent conical sections of unequal proportions and different angulations to the bottle axis. On a more technical analytical level the latching is created by the swing action of one conical section around a fixed pivot point, from an outer to an inner, resting position. The two symmetrically opposed pivot points and rotating segments keep a near constant diameter as they travel along the bottle axis. This action explains the bowing action of the smaller, conical section as it approaches the overcentering point.

bottle manufacturing ▷ **blow molding**

bottle refill ▷ **Coke PET bottle refilled**

bottle sealing plane The plane on the inside of a bottle cap along the sealing surface.

bottle sorter ▷ **optical bottle sorter**

bottle standard reference material Environmental agencies, as well as others studying pollution in the nation's waterways, need materials containing an accurate composition of various compounds as a check to verify the reliability of laboratory instruments and methods. The

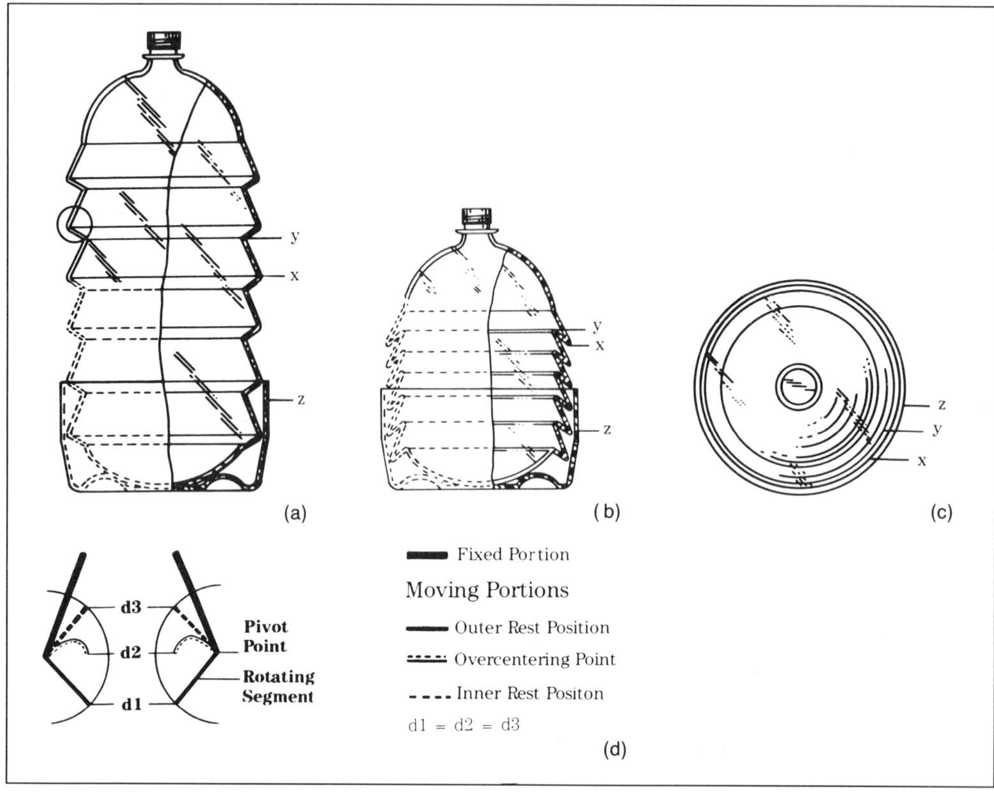

The theory and operation of the patented collapsible bottle; (*a*) an uncollapsed bottle, (*b*) a collapsed bottle, (*c*) a top view of the bottle, and (*d*) the bottle definitions. The initial collapsing of such a bottle should occur no later than three to ten hours after manufacture—the sooner the better. Additional pressure is needed for this first-time collapse in order to create permanent fold rings. The subsequent collapsing and expansion of such bottles before filling them can be performed at the recommended ambient temperature of 20°C (68°F) or higher. In most disposable applications these bottles would undergo three changes of volume: (1) an initial collapsing of the container before shipment and storage; (2) expansion of the container at its destination, before or during filling; and (3) finally collapsing the bottle for disposal.

National Institute of Standards and Technology (NIST) has developed a bottle standard reference material (SRM) for this purpose. It contains marine sediment with a wide range of pollutant compounds of interest to environmental scientists. The sediment material, which has certified values of 11 polycyclic aromatic hydrocarbons (PAHs), was collected from the Chesapeake Bay area near Baltimore harbor. It is in a dry powdered form which can be reconstituted into wet form so that the compounds can be extracted by solvents from organic analysis.

bottle terminology ▷ **blown bottle terminology**

bottle weight controller A closed loop control system that adjusts extruder or injection blow molding operations in response to a high speed bottle weigher on the output conveyor.

Bouguer's law The absorbance of a homogeneous sample is directly proportional to the thickness of the sample in the optical path. Also known as Lambert's law.

bouncing putty ▷ **putty, bouncing**

bowed roll One of the oldest types of film spreader roller is the bowed roller. It consists of a flexible center shaft, a series of bearings placed along the shaft, a flexible metal inner covering, and a smooth-surfaced, one-piece elastomeric outer sleeve. The bowed roller removes wrinkles by creating an ever-increasing skew or angle on the roller rotation, providing a shift in web direction from the roll's center outwards toward the ends.

The major benefit of the bowed roller is that the roller "crown" or skew can be adjusted while the line is running to shift the orientation of the web as it passes over the roller. However, the bowed roller design can alter the natural flow of the web, creating uneven tension across the face of the roller, resulting in possible drag in the processing line. This can cause the web to stretch and distort, especially with thin-gauge films.

Another potential limitation is that the bowed roller needs careful maintenance. Due to the continual flexing or skewing of the roller surface, and the increased tension and abrasion exerted by the web on the center of the roller, the roller covering wears more frequently. Since these rollers are often power-driven, there are many parts that require maintenance. Bowed rollers cannot be installed on every processing line because they cannot be positioned in tight spaces. Bowed rollers require a specific amount of space to provide optimum performance, which depends on the application and roll design. ▷ **extruder web guide**

box beam ▷ **design optimized; design shape**

Boyer-Beaman rule A statement of the relationship between the glass transition temperature (T_g) and the melting temperature (T_m) of a plastic. The ratio of T_g/T_m (with T expressed in degrees Kelvin) usually lies between 0.5 and 0.7.

Boyle's law The volume of a sample of gas varies inversely with the pressure if the temperture remains constant; true for an imaginary perfect or ideal gas. This law is satisfactory for practical calculations except when pressures are high or temperatures are approaching the liquefaction point. Van der Waal's equation is a refinement to take care of the inherent inaccuracy of Boyle's law.

Brabender plasti-corder flow An instrument (rheometer) which continuously measures the torque exerted in shearing a thermoplastic or thermoset material or compounded specimen over a wide range of shear rates and temperatures, including those conditions anticipated in actual manufacturing. It records torque, time, and temperature on a graph called a plastogram, from which much information can be obtained with regard to processability of the material. It shows the effects of additives and fillers, measures and records lubricity, plasticity, scorch, cure, shear, and heat stability and plastic consistency. It measures and records the meter-grams of torque against the "working" or mixing time. Result is a flow curve that is a measure of the compound's "flow life" (processability). The device is made up of a heated mixing head containing a pair of sigma-shaped roller blades which are driven by a dynamometer run at a controlled speed.

The material is fed into the mixing head, which is heated externally usually to either 120°C (248°F), 150°C (302°F), or 165°C (329°F). The measuring head rotors encounter an immediate resistance torque which causes the dynamometer to rotate in the opposite direction. The reaction torque acts upon the indicator scale through a lever system of analytical balanced precision, simultaneously recording on a strip chart. The Brabender plastograph is made in Germany. A similar instrument is made in the U.S. under the registered trade mark Brabender plasti-corder.

brackish water Water that is lower in salinity than normal sea water and higher in salinity than freshwater, ranging from 0.5 to 30 parts salt per 1,000 parts water located between sea water and fresh water. ▷ **desalination**

braiding Weaving of fibers into a tubular shape instead of a flat fabric. Used in reinforced plastic products such as antenna poles, golf club shafts, fishing rods, cherry picker high-rise booms, etc.

branching The growth of a new polymer chain from an active site on an established chain, in a direction different from that of the original chain. ▷ **polymerization; polymer, branched; polyethylene, branched plastic**

brass An alloy of copper and zinc, used in molds, dies, etc.

breaker extension The elongation necessary to cause rupture of the test specimen; the tensile strain at the moment of rupture.

breaker plate ▷ **extruder screen pack**

breaker ply ▷ **belting**

breaking factor The breaking load divided by the original width of the test specimen, expressed in lb/in. (kg/mm).

breaking length A measure of the breaking strength of reinforcing yarn. The length of a specimen the weight of which is equal to the breaking load.

breaking strength ▷ **fracture strength or stress**

breakout ▷ **fiber breakout**

breathable film A film which is at least slightly permeable to gases due to the presence of open cells throughout its mass or to imperfection.

breather ▷ **bleeder cloth** and **vent cloth**

breathing **1.** The opening and closing of a mold to allow gases to escape early in the molding cycle. Also called degassing, bumping, and dwell pause. ▷ **vacuum press** **2.** When referring to plastic sheeting, breathing indicates permeability to air.

brick refractory A highly heat-resistant and nonconductive material used for furnace linings as in glass and steel industries' processing ovens and other applications where temperatures above 1,600°C (2910°F) are involved.

bridge fold ▷ **web fold**

bridging **1.** Plastic at the bottom of a hopper is overheated and solidifies so that plastic does not flow into the processing machine. ▷ **screw bridging** **2.** In pultrusion shrinkage causes inside radius bridging. **3.** Condition in which fibers do not move into or conform to radii and corners during molding, resulting in voids and dimensional control problems.

brightener ▷ **optical brightener**

brine **1.** Any solution of sodium chloride and water usually containing other salts. **2.** Water having more than approximately 30,000 mg/liter of dissolved matter.

Brinell hardness An indentation hardness test using calibrated machines to force a hard ball under specified conditions, into the surface of the material under test and to measure the diameter of the resulting impression after removal of the load. ▷ **hardness**

Brinell hardness number Abbreviated HB, it relates to the applied load and to the surface area of the permanent impression made by a ball indenter computed from the equation:

$$\mathrm{HB} = \frac{2P}{\pi D(D - \sqrt{D^2 - d^2})}$$

where: P = applied load, kgf; D = diameter of the ball, mm; d = mean diameter of the impression, mm.

HB of nearly all materials is influenced by the magnitude of the indenting load, the diameter of the ball indenter, and the elastic characteristics of the ball. In general, a ball 10 mm in diameter of suitable composition should be used with applied loads 3,000, 1,500, or 500 dgf, depending upon the hardness of the material being tested. Although Brinell hardness numbers may vary with the test load used with the 10 mm ball, when smaller balls are used on thin specimens, test results will generally be in agreement with a 10 mm ball test when the ratio of the test load to the square of the ball diameter is held constant.

bristle **1.** A generic term for a short stiff, coarse fiber. **2.** Specific and restricted term for the hair of the hog.

British thermal unit Btu is the energy needed to raise the temperature of 1 lb of water 0.6°C (1°F) at sea level. As an example, one pound of solid waste usually contains 4,500 to 5,000 btu. Plastic waste contains greater btus than other materials of waste. Regarding energy to produce materials ▷ **energy consumption, different materials**

brittle Material easily broken, damaged, disrupted, cracked, and/or snapped.

brittle erosion behavior ▷ **erosion brittle behavior**

brittle failure A complete fracture of the material in a direction perpendicular to the direction of loading without obvious, uniform cold drawing.

brittle fracture ▷ **fracture, brittle**

brittle lacquer technique It is used to provide experimental quantitative stress-strain measurement data. A brittle coating is sprayed on a part. Then, as the part is loaded in proportion to loads that would be encountered in service, cracks begin to appear in the coating. The extent of cracks is noted for each increment of load. The coating is "calibrated" by spraying it on a simple beam and observing the strain at which cracks appear. This nondestructive test method can be used to aid in placing strain gauges for further measurements. ▷ **photoelasticity**

brittleness The lack of toughness. Plastics which are brittle frequently have lower impact strength and higher stiffness properties. Major exception are reinforced plastics. ▷ **extruder film brittleness**

brittleness temperature That temperature statistically calculated where 50% of the specimens would probably fail 95% of the time when a stated minimum number are tested by the method. The 50% failure temperature may be determined by calculation, or by plotting the data on the probability graph paper.

brittleness temperature and glass transition temperature The brittleness temperature is related to the T_g. Generally, thermoplastics below T_g are brittle; thermosets are not.

brittle point The highest temperature at which a plastic or elastomer fractures in a prescribed impact test procedure.

broach 1. To finish the inside of a hole to a shape usually other than round. 2. A tool with serrated edges pushed or pulled through a hole to enlarge it to a required shape.

broadgood Fiber woven to fabric up to usually 1,270 mm (50 in.) wide. It may or may not be impregnated with plastic and is usually furnished in rolls of 25 to 140 kg (50 to 300 lb).

bronze An alloy of copper and tin, unless otherwise specified i.e., an aluminum bronze is an alloy of copper and aluminum ▷ **mold material**

bronze pigment Simulated bronze or gold colored pigments made by staining aluminum flakes with yellow or brown colorants.

bronzing 1. A term sometimes used for bleeding. 2. It usually refers to the appearance of an iridescent metallic luster caused by a film of dry pigment on a glossy surface.

Brookfield ▷ **viscometer**

Brownian movement The continuous zigzag motion of particles in a colloidal suspension, such as elastomer latex particles. The motion is caused by impact of molecules of the liquid on the colloidal particles.

B-scan A means of data presentation which provides a cross-sectional view of the test piece.

B-stage Many thermoset molding compounds and laminating fabrics are processed while in the B-stage ▷ **A-B-C-stage**. The materials manufacturer partially cures (advances) the plastics in the materials according to order specifications. The procesor, upon receipt of the material, stores the plastic at the appropriate temperature until ready to use it. Some B-stage materials are stored at room temperature, but most must be refrigerated. B-stage materials have specified shelf life to permit ease of processing based on temperature and time in storage; temperature-time in shipment is usually important to record.

With some TS systems, the chemical reaction cannot be stopped at the B-stage once it is started. Many systems that require an elevated temperature cure can be B-staged, most room temperature curing systems cannot. In general, the more advanced the material, the greater the pressure requirement. But, the greater the pressure, the denser and stronger the part. B-staging, however, is not always feasible. The designer and processor must know when to specify B-stage and how far to advance the plastic. Some highly advanced compounds have limited flow and can only be used for shallow parts.

Bu Informal abbreviation for butyl.

bubble A spherical, internal void, globule of air or other gas trapped within a plastic.

bubble forming ▷ **thermoforming, bubble forming**

bubble pack Plastic cushioning material used in packaging, usually laminated thermoplastic film which incorporates air bubble pockets.

bubbler ▷ **mold bubbler**

bubble test A form of leak test of gas containing enclosures in which a leak is indicated by the formation of a bubble at the site of a leak.

buckling 1. Crimping of the fibers in a reinforced plastic, often occuring in glass reinforced thermosets due to plastic shrinkage during cure. 2. In RP, a failure mode usually characterized by fiber deflection rather than breaking because of compressive action. 3. A mode of failure generally characterized by an unstable lateral material deflection due to compressive action on the structural element involved. 4. With buckling failure pressure, the external gauge pressure at which buckling occurs. Buckling is characterized by a sharp discontinuity in the pressure-volume change graph and subsequent fracture in the test specimen appearing as an axially oriented crack. Buckling is an elastic instability type failure and is normally associated with thin-walled pipe.

budgeting ▷ **profit planning and budgeting**

buffer A material or device placed in a container to position and protect the contents from the forces of impact, usually made of a cushioning, corrugated, or compressible material.

buffer action The resistance of a solution to change pH.

buffer, spectrochemical ▷ **spectrochemical buffer**

buffing The smoothing of a surface by means of a rotating flexible wheel to the surface of which fine, abrasive particles are applied in liquid suspension, paste, or grease stick form.

building and construction markets Plastics have a wide range of applications; about 20% of all plastics consumed enter this market. Packaging is in first place at 30%, by weight. Plastics are durable, aesthetic, easy to install and cost effective. Plastics will continue to be used in different applications, such as those shown in the Fig. on p. 80.

building sick syndrome ▷ **antimicrobial agent**

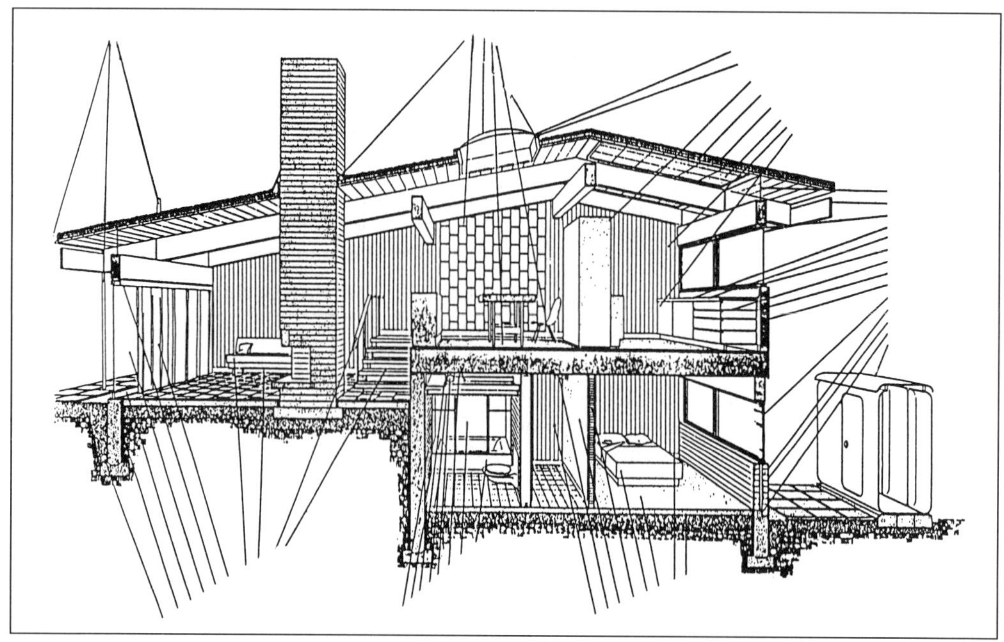

The house that plastics built. All lines point to plastic parts.

bulk density ▷ **density, bulk**

bulk factor 1. Ratio of the volume of loose molding powder (or other plastic materials) to the volume of the same weight of plastic after being fabricated; the ratio of the density of the solid plastic object to the apparent density of the material in loose form, prepreg, etc. **2.** Ratio of the volume of waste before and after compaction.

bulk modulus ▷ **modulus bulk**

bulk molding compound BMC is a thermosetting plastic mixed with strand glass reinforcements that are usually $\frac{1}{4}$ to $\frac{1}{2}$ in. in length, fillers, and other additives into a viscous compound for compression or injection molding. Its preparation is with a sigma blade mixer. The compound is delivered to the processor in the form of a ball, a slab, or an extruded log. For compression molding, BMC is put into the cavity of the mold, with or without preheating. When injection molded, a stuffer ram feeder is used to move the BMC into the plasticator.

bulk polymerization Polymerization in bulk, that is, from undiluted low molecular weight starting materials is the simplest and oldest method for the synthesis of macromolecules. This mass polymerization is important not only for preparations and kinetic studies in the laboratory but also in industrial production. In comparison with other methods of polymerization, it has the following advantages: (1) the equipment or apparatus required is relatively simple, (2) the reaction is relatively rapid and the yield good, (3) plastics of high purity are formed directly from the reaction, and (4) the plastics are obtained in a form immediately processable. The technique of polymerization in bulk is applicable to both addition and condensation polymerizations. Fundamental differences exist, however, in the reaction mechanisms of the two processes. Polycondensation in bulk, the principal use of which is in the preparation of linear polyesters and polyamides, however, is not considered to be a true bulk polymerization.

Basically the polymerization process involves only monomer and polymerization initiator or catalyst; it is carried out in the absence of solvent or other dispersion medium. The minimum of polymerization additives are present, so the purest plastic is targeted to be formed. Many step-growth polymerizations, such as polyester and polyamides, are conducted in bulk, usually as melt polymerizations. In chain polymerization, especially in vinyl polymerization, the main disadvantage for large scale plastic production is the difficulty of dissipating the heat of polymerization especially at high conversion when the viscosity is high and stirring is difficult. Therefore, bulk polymerization is frequently taken only to about 50% conversion or is conducted in two stages. In the first stage there is about 20% conversion, followed by a second stage in which the heat is dissipated by having a large surface area to the polymerization reactor. With bulk polymerization directly in a mold, it is called monomer casting. ▷ **reactor polymerization**

bulk specific gravity ▷ **specific gravity, bulk**

bullet proof glass ▷ **safety glass**

bumping ▷ **breathing**

burlap A coarse, loose woven fabric made from jute or similar fiber. Used in low cost, low performance laminated reinforced plastics.

burning ▷ **flammability** and **fire**

burning rate A term describing the tendency of plastic articles to burn at given temperatures. Certain plastics burn readily at comparatively low temperatures. Other will melt or disintegrate without actually burning, or will burn only if exposed to direct flame. The latter types are often refered to as self-extinguishing.

burnish To smooth or polish by a rolling or sliding tool under pressure.

burn line A dark streak of material in a product (such as blow molded container) resulting from decomposed material dislodged from the plasticator (extruder, injection molder, etc.) and incorporated in the material being processed.

burn mark An area of degraded or oxidized plastic in a molding that could be due to insufficient cavity venting or improper melting of plastics. It can show evidence of thermal decomposition through some discoloration, distortion, or destruction of the surface of the plastics, similar to the action with a burn line.

burn, mass Incineration of solid waste without previous processing, such as removing recyclable components.

bursting strength **1.** The ability of a material to resist rupture by pressure such as internal hydrostatic or gas dynamic pressure. **2.** The force required to rupture a fabric, under specified conditions.

bus A cable used to transmit data from one part of a computer to another or between components of the system.

bushing **1.** In extrusion, the outer ring of any type of a circular tubing or pipe die which forms the outer surface of the tube or pipe. **2.** A special, extra heavy, load-carrying short cylinder inserted in bolt or pin holes. **3.** A removable sleeve or liner for a bearing. **4.** A guide for a tool in a jig or fixture. **5.** An electrically heated alloy container encased in insulating material. Used for melting and feeding glass in the forming of individual fibers of filaments. **6.** ▷ **mold leader pin and bushing**

business card, electronic reader/writer Integrated-circuit business card that has an electronic chip sandwiched between thin layers usually of either PVC or ABS. It is the size of a business card. Introduced (1990) by Citizen of Japan, it has the capacity to hold 3 kilobytes of information (more than 3,000 bytes or series of bits), 40 times more than conventional magnetic cards. As a result, the cards can keep a complete record of transactions, which could be useful in insurance, banking, health care, organisations where they provide the user with a complete and up-to-date record of all transactions.

business failure ▷ **failure, business**

butadiene A gas insoluble in water but soluble in alcohol and ether, obtained from the cracking of petroleum, from coal tar benzene, or from acetylene produced from coke or lime. It is widely used in the formation of copolymers with styrene, acrylonitrile, vinyl chloride, and other monomeric substances, and imparts flexibility to the resultant moldings.

butadiene-acrylonitrile copolymer ▷ **nitrile rubber**

butadiene rubber ▷ **polybutadiene rubber**

butadiene-styrene thermoplastic ▷ **styrene-butadiene thermoplastic**

butt, fusion ▷ **hot plate welding**

butt joint ▷ **joint, butt**

butt wrap Tape wrapped around an object in an edge-to-edge condition, such as in filament winding, etc.

butyl diglycol carbonate Colorless liquid of low volatility, widely used as a plasticizer that is compatible with many plastics.

butylene plastic Plastics based on materials made by the polymerization of butene or the copolymerization of butene with one or more unsaturated compounds, the butene being the greatest amount by weight.

butyl epoxy stearate A plasticizer for PVC, imparting low temperature flexibility.

butyl rubber ▷ **polyisobutylene, butyl rubber**

butyl thermoplastic The two types of rubber in this category are both based on crude oil.

One is polyisobutylene with an occasional isoprene unit inserted in the plastic chain to improve vulcanization characteristics. The other butyl is the same, except that chlorine is added at about 1.2% by weight, resulting in greater vulcanization flexibility and cure compatibility with the other general purpose rubbers. They have outstanding impermeability to gases and excellent oxidation and ozone resistance. The chemical inertness is further reflected in lack of molecular weight breakdown during processing, thus permitting the use of hot mixing processes for plastic/filler interaction. Flexing, tear and abrasion resistance approach those of NR and moderate tensile strength of 2,000 psi (13.8 MPa) of unreinforced compounds that can be made at competitive costs. However, butyls lack the toughness and durability of some general purpose rubbers.

butyl stearate A mold lubricant and also a plasticizer compatible with natural and synthetic rubbers, chlorinated rubber, ethyl cellulose, etc. In PS production, it is added to the emulsion polymerization system to impart good flow properties to the plastic.

butyraldehyde An aldehyde that can be used in place of formaldehyde in the production of plastics. It reacts with polyvinyl alcohol to form polyvinyl butyrate.

butyrate The salt of butyric acid.

butyrate plastic A common name for cellulose acetate butyrate (CAB).

butyrolactone A hygroscopic, colorless liquid obtained by the dehydrogenation of 1,4-butyrolactone. It is a solvent for epoxy, cellulosics, and vinyl copolymer plastics.

buy-back system An operation in which a manufacturer or waste processor buys recyclable materials from the public. Usually associated with collection centers where the public can bring recyclables.

buy or lease ▷**capital equipment investment**

by mechanical treatment Without causing a significant change in size.

byte A unit of storage made up of a string of bits, or binary digits. A byte is usually the size of one character of information, a letter, or a number for example (equivalent to one character or 8 bits). ▷**computer random access memory**

by thermal treatment Without causing recrystallization.

C

cable insulation ▷ **extruder wire and cable**

cadmium 1. In plastics, CD can be an ingredient of pigments. **2.** A heavy metal element that accumulates in and harms the environment; proper methods for its disposal are required.

cage mill A device which consists of two rotating structures similar to water wheels, one fitted inside the other. They are provided with horizontal cross-bars or breaker plates. The assembly is covered with a close fitting housing. The two wheels or cages rotate at high speed in opposite directions on a horizontal axis. The material to be reduced in size is fed into the smaller cage from a hopper. It is ejected at speeds up to 12,000 ft/m (61 m/s) and is fragmented by contact with the bars. As the pieces are thrown back and forth within the cages they are reduced further by mutual impact. Some types have only one cage and others have more than two.

calcite The most common form of natural calcium carbonate ($CaCO_3$); used as a filler for plastics.

calcium carbonate Also referred to as ground limestone, marble dust, chalk, whiting, and calcite filler extender. Each shares the common mineral form of calcite and is used as a filler and extender. $CaCO_3$ is 98% pure with silica, iron, aluminum and/or magnesium. It occurs in nature as aragonite, oyster shell, calcite, chalk, limestone, marble, etc. It is a nuisance particulate dust if not properly contained and handled.

calcium oxide A white powder with affinity for water, with which it combines to form calcium hydroxide. It has been used to remove traces of water in vinyl plastisols.

calcium silicate A naturally occurring mineral found in metamorphic rocks, used as a reinforcing filler in polyester molding compounds, low density polyethylene, and so on. $CaSiO_3$ provides smooth molded surfaces and low water absorption.

calcium sulfide Yellow to light-gray powder with the odor of hydrogen sulfide in moist air and irritating to skin. CaS use includes luminous paint, lubricant additive, and flotation agent.

calculus Calculus is the mathematical tool used to analyze changes in physical quantities (comprising differential and integral calculations). It was developed in the 17th century to study four major classes of scientific and mathematical problems of the time, namely, (1) find the tangent to a curve at a point, (2) find the length of a curve, the area of a region, and the volume of a solid, (3) find the maximum and minimum value of a quantity, such as the distance of a planet from the sun, and (4) given a formula for the distance traveled by a body in any specified amount of time, find the velocity and acceleration of the body at any instant. These problems were resolved by the greatest minds of the 17th century, culminating in the crowning achievements of Gottfried Wilhelm (Germany, 1646–1727) and Isaac Newton (England, 1642–1727).

calender Machine performing the operation of calendering.

calender bowl deflection The distortion suffered by calender rolls resulting from the pressure of the plastic (or elastomer) running between them. If not corrected the deflection produces a sheet (or film) thicker in the middle than at the edges.

calender coating One special application of the calender is the coating of paper, textile, or plastic. For one-sided coating a calender with three rolls is usually sufficient, although four rolls are frequently used for extremely thin coatings ▷ **calendering**. Double-sided coating can either be done simultaneously on both sides of a fabric on a four-roll calender or sequentially by two three-roll calenders. Roll configurations are shown in the Fig. on p. 84; the most popular configuration is the inverted L. However, these and other configurations are used to meet different product requirements.

calendering The calendering process is used to produce plastic films and sheets. It melts the plastic and then passes the pastelike melt through nips of a series of precision heated and

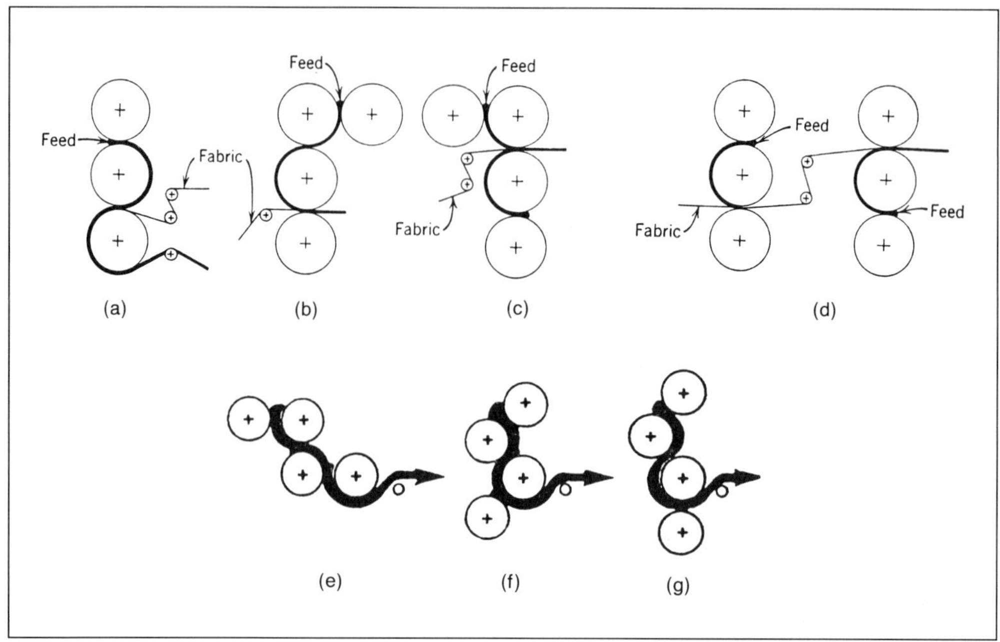

Calender coating parallel rolls schematics provide examples of different arrangements: (*a*) One-sided coating with vertical three-roll; (*b*) one-sided coating with inverted L four-roll; (*c*) double-sided coating with inverted L four-roll; (*d*) double-sided coating with two three-roll; (*e*) one-sided coating with Z configuration four-roll; (*f*) one-sided coating with S configuration four-roll, and (*g*) one-sided coating with modified S four-roll.

rotating speed-controlled rolls into webs of specific thickness and width as shown in the Fig. on p. 85. The extremely flat surface parallel rolls have either the same or slightly different speeds; web may be polished or embossed, and may be either rigid or flexible. Although this basic plastic forming operation occurs in the calender itself, additional downstream equipment has to be used for the production of thermoplastic film or sheet. In the mixer (either the usual Banbury or screw mixer) the raw material that is usually in powdered form is blended upstream of the calender with the desired additives, such as plasticizers or fillers. From the upstream blending and *plasticizing* of the mix, the pastelike melt passes through the multiple roll mill that can have two to at least six rolls (usually they are four-roll).

Very vital to this operation is the removal of any metal, including microscopic metallic particles; they would destroy the precision (and very expensive) surfaces of the calender rolls and downstream cooling rolls. All kinds of precautions are taken to remove any contaminants starting with the incoming raw materials, fillers, and additives going through screens and metal detectors. The compound is usually fed through an extruder with a screen. Metal detectors tend to be used along the flow line of the plastic just prior to reaching the nip rolls, including detectors under the belt that conveys the final melt that may be in a "rope" form 5–10 cm (2–4 in.) in diameter.

After the actual forming process through the multiple rolls of the calender, the film or sheet is cooled by passing through precision temperature and surfaced cooling rolls and/or a cooling tower. Thickness gauges are usually located within this cooling section of the production line that provides a feed back and can automatically correct for thickness adjustments. Gauge controls can also be incorporated in the neckdown section where the hot plastic leaves the calender rolls and transfers to the cooling rolls. After cooling, the material is trimmed at the edges and wound. Trim, that may account for up to 5% of the width depending on the line's operating efficiency, is usually immediately directed back through a granulator and blended with the virgin mix.

This sequence is typical for a calender train (line); however, many variations are possible depending on the end product required. For example, auxiliary equipment can be included such as annealing, quench-tank, decorating, slitting and heat sealing bags, orienting (uniaxial or biaxial stretching), floor tile cutter, and so on.

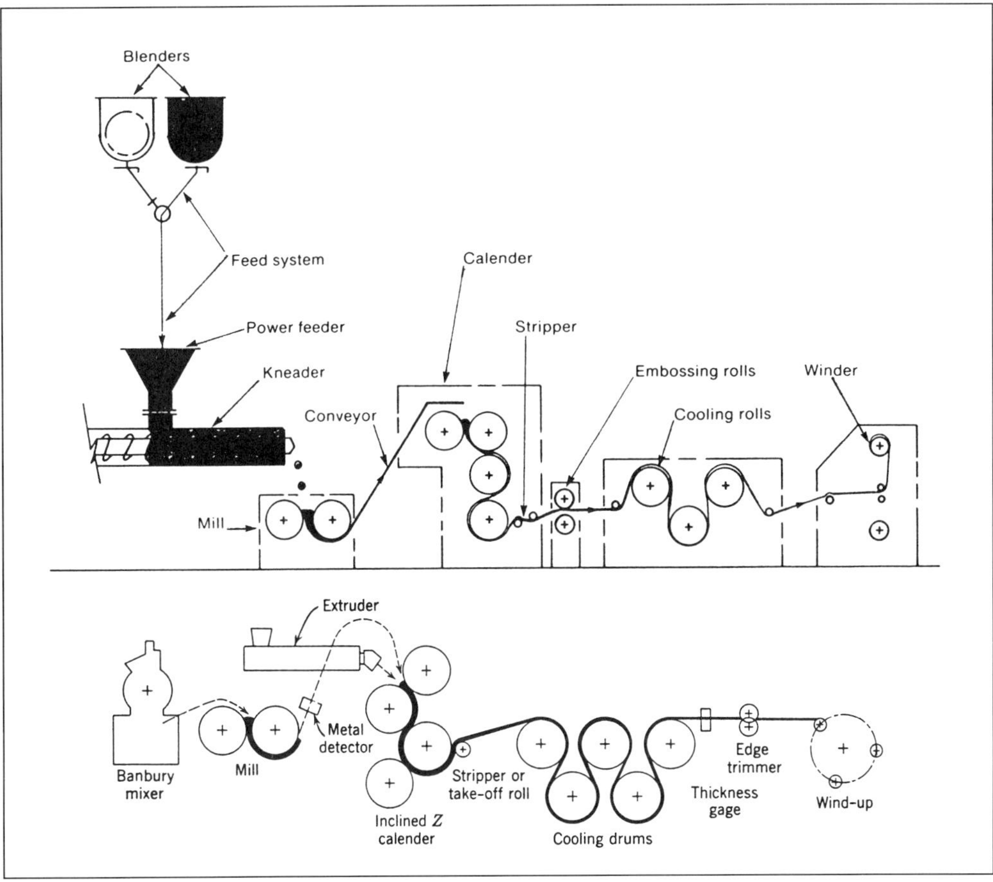

Calendering schematic lines.

Although calendering was developed over a century ago for the processing of natural rubber, it is now used principally with thermoplastic rigid or plasticized polyvinyl chloride (at least 80% of the market), polyethylene, and so on. A major product produced is rubber/elastomer tire-fabric coating. Calendering is a highly developed art. A scientific understanding of the process did not occur until recently because of the complexity in combining melt behavior and interfacing with the mechanics of the operation. This type of action has resulted in making calenders more productive by increasing their speed, producing films with smaller thickness tolerances and more uniformity, and handling thicker sheets with tight tolerances and uniformity.

calendering advantages over extrusion Usually calendered sheeting is less glossy than extruded material. It may be preferable for some applications where high tensile properties and unusual close gauge control are required. Embossing can also be obtained on calenders. Extrusion of colored films or sheets requires that the extruder be cleaned and purged when changing colors. A calender requires a minimum of cleaning between color changes. Calendering is definitely used for long production runs to be economically profitable; applications include window shade stock, electrical tape, PVC tile, PE coated fabric, and so on. The accompanying Table on p. 86 provides general manufacturing comparison of calendering with combination extruder-calender, extrusion blown film, extruder with flexible lip die, plastisol-cast, and melt roll.

calendering coating, frictional Friction calendering is a process whereby an elastomeric compound is forced into the interstices of woven or cord fabrics while passing through the rolls of the calender.

calendering control Automatic web-thickness profile control, well known since the 1940s in extrusion, is used in calendering plastics such as PVC. As an example, a row of many (64 to 76) individually temperature controlled air nozzles across the sheet creates zones in which the

Comparing manufacturing methods of PVC film and sheet.

	Calender	Extruder-calender	Blown film	Flex lip extruder	Plastisol cast	Melt roll
Lines installed, USA	155	2	90	40	60	5
Relative resin cost	Lowest	Low	Higher	Higher	Highest	Low
Machine cost, $ million	1–3	1–2.5	0.3–0.6	0.3–0.6	0.3–0.7	0.3–1.3
Rate and range, lb/hr	800–8000	500–1500	600 ($4\frac{1}{2}$ in.)	750 ($4\frac{1}{2}$ in.)	750	100–1000
Product gauge range, in.	0.002–0.050	0.002–0.005	0.001–0.003	0.001–0.125	0.001–0.012	0.0015–0.020
Sheet accuracy, %	3(1–5)	3(1–5)	10	10	7	5(2–10)
Time to heat, hr	6	5	3	3	$\frac{1}{2}$	3
Time for "on stream"	2–5 min	10 min	2 hr	5 hr	10 min	2–5 min
Gauge adjust time	Sec	Sec	5–30 min	5–30 min	Sec	1 min
Auto gauging capability	Yes	Yes	No	No	No	No
Color or product change time	5–30 min	10–40 min	30–60 min	30–60 min	15 min	30–60 min
Wind-up speed ypm, average (max)	80(150)	60(80)	15(20)	15(30)	20(40)	20(30)
Limitations	High capital cost, heat time	Lower rate, versatility problem	Poor accuracy, long on stream time, low rate, degradation, reduced versatility		Fumes, inefficiency, high energy cost, resin cost, release paper cost	Reduced rate and range, soft materials only, slow manual gauge change
Applications and advantages	Versatility, high rate, accuracy, ease & adjust, ease at re-process	Accuracy, gauge adjust, reduced cost	Low investment, multi-plant capability utilization, thin gauge (0.003 in. and under) and heavy gauge (0.050–0.125 in.)		Grain retention (pattern cast in), soft hand and drape	Good on wall covering, thin material, coated fabric, accuracy, reduced investment

web can be selectively cooled to adjust thickness profile. Low-mass heating elements provide a control response of maximum 15 sec. Control zones need not be evenly spaced. They can be concentrated at sheet edges, for example, and can be as narrow as 1.5 in. (3.8 cm). Reduced cross-web thickness variation by 40% can occur, resulting in increased usable production by more than 20%, and reducing scrap by over 90%.

calendering foam ▷ **foamed sheet stock**

calendering grain The name given to the difference in properties lengthwise (machine direction) and crosswise (transverse direction) in the calendered film or sheet. Properties in these two directions differ; as an example, higher tensile strength occurs in machine direction.

calender-in-train The operation of two calenders as a single unit, generally where the first calender coats one side of a material (plastic, fabric, and so on) which is led immediately to the second calender where the other side is coated.

calibrate **1.** To determine the indication or output of a measuring device with respect to that of a standard. **2.** To determine a characteristic of a measuring instrument or tool and mark it at one or more places corresponding to exact values of an established standard scale, such as capacity or weight.

calibration die ▷ **extruder line cooling and shaping** and **die, dry sleeve calibration**

caliper Measuring devices, such as micrometers and venier calipers, having a graduated scale for exact measurements.

calorie The amount of heat needed to raise 1 g of water 1°C at 1 atm. The abbreviation for calorie is capital C or when identifying kilogram calories use kcal.

calorimeter An instrument capable of making absolute measurements of energy deposition (or absorbed dose) in a material by measuring its change in temperature and imparting a knowledge of the characteristics of its material of construction, such as ▷ **differential scanning calorimeter**

camber Deviation from edge straightness; usually the maximum deviation of an edge from a straight line of given length.

camelback Tread-type rubber compound extruded in a variety of thicknesses and widths for use in tire retreading. The standard section is in the shape of a regular trapezium, but variations are made to suit particular types of tire and different makes of molding equipment. The name is derived from the shape of the section which resembles the hump of a camel; the width of the top of the section or the shoulder width is still occasionally termed the hump width. The use of the name camelback has principally replaced "tread rubber", which in certain contexts can be ambiguous.

camera-ready Copy which is ready for photography, etc.

Campus database This computer-aided material preselection program provides uniform standards of testing methods in comparing different plastic materials from different material suppliers. This database concept was started by four German material manufacturers who used a uniform software system, namely BASF, Bayer, Hoechst, and Hulls. It is given in the form of diskettes in German, English, French, Italian, or Spanish. Each diskette contains the uniform test and evaluation program, as well as the range of the respective material producers. Other material suppliers include their data; includes European producers and operations with worldwide participation and use developing. European material suppliers include Dow Chemical, GE, Ciba-Geigy, Exxon, etc. (source from KU-A-KFC, Geb. B207, D-5090, Leverkusen, Germany).

Canadian flow test A method of determining the rheology or flow properties of thermoplastics. It is referred to as the CIL flow test, developed by Canadian Industries Ltd. In this test, the amount of the molten plastic that is forced through a specified size orifice per unit of time when a specified, variable force is applied gives a relative indication of the melt flow properties of plastics.

candela ▷ **luminous flux**

canopy **1.** An ornamental rooflike structure that includes transparent and/or translucent plastic enclosures in shapes such as blisters, corrugations, and ribbing. **2.** The transparent plastic enclosure over an airplane cockpit. **3.** A cloth covering suspended over a bed; usually of woven plastic fibers. **4.** The lifting or supporting surface of a parachute; usually made of woven nylon fibers and nylon major support cords.

canopy, rain forest On display during the Paris Europlastic, June 11–16, 1991, was the "raft of the skies" by Atochem, a unique large domed structure for scientists studying in the canopy that simulates a tropical rain forest. Transparent large plastic panels are supported by geometric reinforced plastics in large window frames.

cantenane A compound with interlocking rings which are not chemically bonded but which cannot be separated without breaking at least one valence bond. The model would resemble the links of a chain.

cantilever beam ▷ **flexural testing**

cantilever snap fit ▷ **design snap fit**

cantilever spring ▷ **design spring**

capacitance ▷ **electrical capacitance**

capacity differential Difference between the hourly production cost based on expected volume and the hourly cost based on practical capacity volume.

capacity overhead rate Manufacturing overhead hourly rate based on the practical capacity volume of an operation.

capacity utilization The degree to which facilities are used. Usually measured in terms of a percentage of total capacity.

capillarity The attraction between molecules, similar to surface tension, which results in the rise of a liquid in small tubes or fibers (as could occur in filled compounds, reinforced plastics etc.).

capillarity drying ▷ **drying, capillarity**

capillary attraction The force of adhesion or bonding between a solid and a liquid in capillarity.

capillary rheometer ▷ **rheometer capillary**

capillary viscometer ▷ **viscometer capillary**

capital equipment investment When a manufacturing operation is to purchase new equipment, the task at hand may not be as simple as it appears even with cash in the bank. The financial manager needs a variety of qualitative and quantitative skills to determine if cash will be used. A loan or lease can be used.

A successful business usually makes use of a goal-oriented financial structure to meet its overall objectives. The company should ensure that all operations, including equipment purchase, are helping to achieve the objectives which result in meeting the forecasted profit level. In the past the person in a plastic processing plant that handled its finances usually had a very limited role. This person with financial responsibility, who could be the financial or accounting manager, had a rather easy job compared to what has to be done today. People kept accurate financial records, prepared reports on the company's status and performance, managed cash so that the bills could be paid on time and obtained funds when they ran short of cash.

With a business becoming larger, more complex and/or more competitive, the financial managers transcended their important traditional role of raising external funds. They became involved in the problems and decisions related to the management of the company's assets. It included allocation of funds to differeing projects, such as large sums of money for capital equipment. In this context, the financial person needs a much broader outlook of the company's operation and, most important, a much stronger grasp of the nature and scope of the finance function.

New developments, particularly those related to the production of equipment, can have a sharp impact on the need for working capital. If new equipment is purchased that processes materials at a faster rate, permanent inventory will go up. So if cash is used to purchase equipment, additional cash will be required to purchase more plastics, possibly also more material handling equipment, storage facilities, and even more warehouse space for storing finished products. This example is a rather straightforward situation that can easily provide the answer to the method of buying. However the cash flow situation can be drastically changed when other developments occur.

Rapid changes in technology can make your product obsolete or nonprofitable to use new equipment. Diversification into different product lines or into new markets could require better use of existing funds. Financial decision-making is concerned with these type situations, as well as many more, so cash-on-the-barrelhead for new equipment may not be the best approach.

When considering capital equipment investment, which can range from a few thousands to billions of dollars, there are the financial alternatives of cash purchase, bank, or institutional loan and leasing. Determining "true" cost of each investment is based on developing the proper comparisons. If the comparison is based on total cost, then the usual way to go is cash. If cash is not available, the loan is a consideration. Even with a simplified analysis there are benefits gained through leasing. They will vary from company to company. Those with low tax rates or investment tax credit adsorption limitations could find leasing more attractive. Leasing should be viewed as an alternative source of financing when there is a need to leave bank credits open for anticipated working capital. It is an arrangement that provides a firm with the use and control over equipment without receiving title to it.

There are different issues related to leasing equipment that include the following important considerations: (1) *Cost* Usually it is more costly to lease than borrow. In some cases the expertise of leasing allows economics that reduce the cost of leasing below loans. (2) *Cash outlay* With certain transactions leasing eliminates the need for a down payment. There are other situations where the user is able to borrow 100% of the asset cost. (3) *Borrowing capacity* In most cases leasing increases the firm's borrowing capacity since the lender is less conscious of leases than debts. (4) *Freeing funds* Leasing may be a way to gain additional assets but it does not necessarily free funds for more profitable investments, and (5) *Obsolescence* There is no shifting the risk of obsolescence from the lessee to the lessor. In most cases the risk is considered and charged in the lease contract. Because leases can be written for periods considerably shorter than the equipment's normal depreciation, the lessee can recover costs more quickly and can be back in the market for better performing equipment after the short time period.

Leasing offers a hedge on inflation. In favor of leasing are different non-economic factors. It conserves working capital and lines of credit without normally restricting a company's borrowing capacity. The red tape associated with capital appropriations is eliminated in some plants. Money paid in the future will have a decreased value when compared with today's dollar. With leasing it is possible to make future lease payments with deflated dollars. Balanced sheets are improved since true leasing is accepted as off-balance sheet financing. Lease payments can include delivery payment, installation costs, service/maintenance insurance, and sales taxes that can be substantial. Leasing can provide longer terms than available with conventional loans, so amortization of equipment cost can be spread over a longer period. There is no down payment or compensating balance required other than possibly a security deposit in the form of advanced rentals.

Thus, take advantage of the different sorts of financing available to maximize profits and growth potentials.

capping film ▷ **extruder film capping**

caprolactam A cyclic amide type compound, containing six carbon atoms. When the ring is opened, caprolactam is polymerizable into a nylon plastic known as type-6 nylon or polycaprolactam plastic.

capstan ▷ **extruder capstan**

captive molder ▷ **molder, captive**

cap torque ▷ **torque, cap**

carbanion ion Negatively charged organic compound (ion).

carbide A binary solid compound of carbon and another element. The most familiar carbides are those of calcium, tungsten, silicon, boron, and iron (cementite). They are made into cemented carbides, refractory carbides, etc. Uses include compound filler, abrasive compound, etc.

carbon Basically carbon is the element that provides the backbone for all organic plastics. Graphite is a crystalline form of carbon. Diamond is the densest crystalline form of carbon. Diamond, one of the hardest of materials, and graphite, one of nature's softest, are naturally occurring elemental forms that have important specialized industrial uses. The third form of elemental carbon, amorphous carbon, has a much broader functional base and is used in large quantities in the field of plastic technology. The term amorphous carbon is commonly used in reference to a wide range of natural and artificial carbon such as coal, active carbon, and carbon black; however the term amorphous as applied to carbon black gives a false impression of its true nature as revealed by X-ray analysis. Plastic filler carbon black, a product of incomplete combustion of oil or natural gas, has a carbon content of 82 to 99+%, by weight.

carbonaceous matter The component of a fuel, including solid wastes, that consists of pure carbon or compounds, usually associated with the residue of incineration.

carbon, activated Activated carbon is a family of carbonaceous substances manufactured by processes that develop adsorptive properties.

carbonated beverage bottle ▷ **blow molding** and **Coke PET bottles refilled**

carbon atom ▷ **atom, carbon**

carbon black Carbon black is generally accepted as the generic name for the family of finely divided carbon pigments produced by thermal decomposition of hydrocarbons. Originally the name was limited to carbon pigments made by the impingement process, but is now used to cover all types. Its classification by type is usually based on process differences, namely furnace, impingement, thermal, lampblack, and acetylene. Usage in plastics can be divided into basic categories such as colorant, stabilizer, filler, electrical conductor, and weather-resistant applications.

carbon-carbon composite A composite of carbon fiber in a carbon matrix.

carbon dioxide CO_2 is a nonpoisonous and colorless gas produced during incineration, decomposition of solid wastes, automobile fuel combustion etc.

carbon disulfide Clear, colorless, or faintly yellow liquid; almost odorless when pure; poisonous; toxic; flammable. It is a reaction of natural gas or petroleum fractions with air and other reactions. Use includes production of viscose rayon and cellophane.

carbon fiber A reinforcement fiber (for reinforced plastics) known for its light weight, high strength, high stiffness, and other properties. The technology for producing fibers since the early 1950s (Wright-Patterson Air Force Base, Ohio, etc.) generally centers on the thermal decomposition of various organic precursors. Precursors investigated include rayon, polyacrylonitrile (PAN), pitch, polyester, nylon, polyvinyl alcohol, polyvinyl chloride, polyphenylene, and phenolic plastics. Of these, polyacrylonitrile (PAN), pitch, and rayon have been found to offer the greatest potential in terms of carbon yield and cost.

Carbon fibers are produced by pyrolysis of the organic precursor fiber in an inert atmosphere at temperatures above 980°C (1,800°F). The material may also be graphitized by heat treating above 1,650°C (3,000°F). During the pyrolysis process, molecules containing oxygen, hydrogen, and nitrogen are driven from the precursor fiber, leaving continuous chains of carbon. PAN-based fibers in the form of filament, tape, and tow are by far the dominant reinforcement for advanced reinforced plastics (or plastic composites). ▷ **graphite fiber; chemical vapor deposition; oxidation**

carbon fiber and graphite fiber characteristics ▷ **graphite fiber and carbon fiber characteristics**

carbonium ion Positively charged organic compound (ion).

carbonization The process of pyrolyzation in an inert atmosphere at temperatures ranging from 800 to 1,600°C (1,470 to 2,910°F) and higher, but usually at about 1,315°C (2,400°F). In this ablative action, all noncarbon elements are removed. Range of temperature is influenced by precursor requirements, processing system of the individual manufacturer, and final properties desired. Basically, carbonization is the charring from the loss of side components, leaving only the carbon from the precursor plastic.

carbon monoxide Carbon monoxide (CO) is a poisonous, colorless, and odorless gas produced during incomplete combustion or microbial decomposition of solid wastes in oxygen-limited atmospheres.

carboxymethylcellulose plastic CMC is water-soluble. Used similar to ▷ **methylcellulose plastic**

carburizing A surface hardening process primarily intended to resist wear or abrasion and produced on a low carbon steel used in different plastic fabricating primary and secondary equipment, including molds and dies. To prepare a low carbon steel for heat treatment it is packed in a box with carbonizing material, such as wood charcoal, and heated to about 1,093°C (2,000°F) for several hours, then allowed to cool slowly.

carcass ▷ **belting**

carcinogen Any substance that can cause or contribute to cancer.

carded package, blister The conventional blister package consists of a thermoformed plastic blister and pre-printed card backing which are heat-sealed together, securing products inside.

carding The process of untangling and partially straightening fibers by passing them between two closely spaced surfaces which are moving at different speeds, and at least one of which is covered with sharp points. Process converts a tangled mass of fibers to a filmy web. Use includes proving reinforcement for plastics. ▷ **mechanical nonwoven fabric**

Carothers, Wallace H. (1896–1937) Born in Iowa. Many of his accomplishments occurred after joining the research staff of Du Pont in 1928 where he undertook the development of polychloroprene (later called neoprene). His crowning achievement was the synthesis of nylon.

carousal clamp ▷ **rotary press**

carpet coating ▷ **powdered coating**

carrier **1.** A neutral material such as diatomaceous earth used to support a catalyst in a large scale reactor system. **2.** A gas used in chromatography to convey the volatilized mixture to be analyzed. **3.** An atomic tracer carrier. **4.** ▷ **binder**

carton Different constructions are used to produce cartons to meet different requirements; includes the use of different plastics (single material and laminations), paper, etc. As an example there are aluminum foil folding cartons (foil alone and laminated or coated with plastics and other materials). They can have the foil lining on the inside, center, or outside of the wall carton; also have foil on both sides. Cartons may be of conventional or sift-and-leak proof designs. Printing is done by any method, prior to cutting and creasing, or other forming and bonding operations. Folding cartons offer important protective and display characteristics unique in packaging, and have some of the advantages of both the flexible and the rigid container. Before use, when it is folded flat, the folding carton offers the storage economy of the flexible bag. When it is filled, it offers much of the protection of the set-up box.

cascade **1.** Coined term used to describe a large number of compounds derived from a common source. **2.** A series of operational units or stages so arranged to perform specific functions such as: (a) heat produced in the first unit serves as the heat for the second unit, and so on, or (b) mechanically filtering fillers, such as calcium carbonate and short fibers, through a woven mesh screen (usually wire screen) to separate particle sizes; different size screens are used starting with the largest openings and stepping down to smaller size screens.

case hardening A process which imparts a hard surface to a material (certain steels, certain plastics, etc.) while the interior remains soft and tough. Surface hardens to a relatively shallow depth. It is usually accomplished by heating; with steel, for example, it is out of contact with air while packed in carbonaceous material followed by cooling-heating-quenching.

casein This family of plastics was important in the early years of the plastics industry as a sizing and coating adhesive; as a binder for finely divided materials; as a dispersant, emulsifier, and protective colloid; and as an adhesive for wood, paper, etc. but is of less importance today. It is a protein material precipitated from skimmed milk by the action of either rennet or dilute acid. Rennet casein finds its main application in the manufacture of plastics. Acid casein is a raw material used in a number of industries including the manufacture of adhesives.

cashew plastic A thermoset produced from the phenolic fraction of cashew nut shell oil.

cash flow ▷ **capital equipment investment**

casing A term coined by AT&T Bell Laboratories as an abbreviation for the process of crosslinking by activated species of inert gases, developed to impart printability and adhesive receptivity to plastics such as fluoroplastics and polyethylene. In this process, the products are exposed to a flow of activated inert gases in a glow tube, which forms a shell of highly crosslinked molecules on the product surfaces. This chemically converted surface provides the cohesion strength so printing links and adhesives bond firmly to the product.

cast film ▷ **extruder film**

casting The choice of casting material, type of mold, and methods of fabrication vary with the application. The terms casting, embedding, potting, molding, impregnation, and encapsulation are often used interchangeably. Casting differs from many of the other processes (injection molding, extrusion, etc.) in that it generally does not involve pressure or vacuum, although certain materials and complex parts may require pressure or vacuum casting. Generally plastics that are free-flowing and have low surface tensions with low viscosities are used for castings of intricate shapes and fine detail in design. Low-viscosity plastics are also more suitable for producing bubble-free castings. High-viscosity systems usually produce castings with better physical properties than do low-viscosity plastics; however, handling of high-viscosity is usually more difficult. Most plastics suitable for castings are two-component systems. A specified amount of hardener or accelerator is added to the plastic. This is then mixed either mechanically or by hand. This compound is poured into a mold, which is usually coated with a mold release agent, air is removed when necessary, and the plastic is allowed to set (harden).

Setting takes place at either room temperature or elevated temperatures. During the chemical reaction there is usually the liberation of heat. The quantity of heat evolved is independent of the casted shape. The rate of heat dissipation, though, is important and leads to differing approaches in casting thin or heavy sections. In thin sections, where a large area in relation to the total volume of the plastic is exposed, the heat of the exothermic reaction is dissipated rapidly and the temperature of casting is not very high. Thus, thin sections can be cast at room temperature with no danger of cracking. When the loss of heat is excessive, application of heat may be necessary to properly accomplish the cure.

Air bubbles are present in any casting operation; therefore methods for their removal must always be a consideration. Air is present in both the plastic and the hardener; also introduced when the two are mixed and poured into the mold. The number of air bubbles that form depends on the viscosity and surface tension of the plastic-hardener system, the solubility of air in the system, and the characteristics of the mold surface. Although fillers extend the plastic and lower bulk cost, they tend to retain mixed-in air. Many air removal problems can be avoided by proper design of the mold. Elimination of sharp corners and provisions of an adequate number of sprues to facilitate movement of air helps considerably to minimize the amount of air in the casting. Plastic and hardener should be deaerated when possible. Use of high speed mixers and vortexing should be avoided.

Basically some thermoplastics and thermosets begin as liquids that can be cast and polymerized into solids. In the process, various ornamental or utilitarian objects can be embedded in the plastic. By definition, casting applies to the formation of an object by pouring a fluid monomer-polymer solution into an open mold where it completes its polymerization (see Fig). Casting can also lead to the formation of film or sheet, made by pouring the liquid plastic onto a moving belt or by precipitation in a chemical bath. The term film casting is also used for the process of producing extruder film. ▷ **vacuum casting**

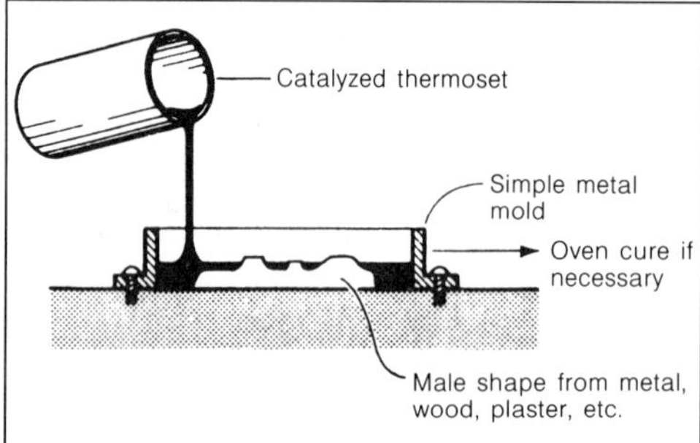

Casting of thermoset plastic.

casting acrylic sheeting Since the 1930s cast acrylic sheeting has been made by polymerization of methyl methacrylate in a cell assembled from two glass plates and a flexible gasket. Heating for a few hours until polymerization is complete gives sheets with very excellent optical properties. Sheeting is also made by continuous casting (sometimes called extrusion casting); a monomer-plastic-catalyst mixture is fed onto a stainless steel belt on which polymerization is completed. Continuous casting is not as optically clear as cast sheeting; parallelism and flatness of surfaces, as well as optically uniform density, is not nearly as uniform. All products are used to meet different product requirements such as glazing and thermoforming.

casting, air entrapment ▷ **air entrapment**

casting alloy ▷ **die casting alloy and mold material**

casting area The moldable area of a thermoplastic in in.^{2} (cm^2) for a given thickness and under a given set of molding conditions. Casting area is a measure of melt flow under actual molding conditions where flow is unrestricted by cavity boundaries.

casting, centrifugal ▷ **centrifugal casting**

casting, dip ▷ **dip casting**

casting, film ▷ **film casting**

casting, foam ▷ **foamed casting**

casting, investment ▷ **investment casting**

casting, metal cored ▷ **soluble core molding**

casting, monomer ▷ **bulk polymerization**

casting, rotational ▷ **rotational molding**

casting, shell mold type This is a process where the mold is made by coating wood, plaster of Paris, cast metals, nonferrous alloys (aluminum copper, zinc alloy, etc.), or sand with usually a thermoset plastic. Type of mold support material, when required, depends on factors that range from production rate to cost limitations.

casting solid Refers to casting of plastics.

casting, solvent ▷ **solvent casting**

casting syrup Identifies casting of plastics. Also called potting syrups when used for encapsulating parts such as electrical components.

casting, vacuum ▷ **vacuum casting**

cast iron Generic term for a group of metals that basically are alloys of carbon and silicon with iron. Relative to steel, they are high in carbon (0.5 to 4.2%, by weight) and silicon (0.2 to 3.5%). They are used in all types of plastic processing equipment, including molds and dies.

catalysis A substance that changes the rate of a chemical reaction without itself undergoing permanent change in composition or becoming a part of the molecular structure of a product. It markedly speeds up the cure of a compound when added in minor quantity, compared to the amounts of primary reactants. There rarely exists a single polymerization process in which certain accelerating regulating and modifying ingredients are not used with great advantage even though they might be present only in very small quantities. In the early years of producing plastics, when there did not yet exist a well founded understanding of the mechanism of polymerization processes, the action of these ingredients and additives so much resembled the phenomenon of normal catalysis that the name catalyst was used for them. With the development in the theory of polymerization reactions, it became evident that in most cases the role of these materials during the formation of macromolecules does not fall in the domain of the classical definitions of the words catalysis or catalyst. However, since the misnomer is now well established and such correct expressions as initiator, transfer agent, terminator or telomer, crosslinking agent, accelerator, curing agent, hardener, inhibitor, or promoter are frequently used interchangeably with the general term catalyst.

catalysis, auto- An autocatalysis is a catalytic reaction induced by a product of the same reaction. This action occurs in some types of thermal decomposition.

catalysis coordination ▷ **Ziegler-Natta catalyst**

catalyst converter ▷ **incineration fume system**

catalyst, enzyme ▷ **enzyme catalyst**

catalyst, negative An agent (inhibitor, retarder) which reduces the speed of a reaction.

catalyst, physical A physical catalyst is a radiant energy capable of promoting or modifying a chemical reaction.

catalyst, stereospecific ▷ **stereospecific catalyst**

catalyst, Z-N ▷ **Ziegler-Natta catalyst**

catastrophic failure Failures of a mechanical and unpredictable nature. ▷ **acceptable risk**

catenary ▷ **roving**

catheter Balloon angioplasty catheters, which in the past used latex and PVC for the balloon portion, are also using PET plastic. The catheters are used to dilate constrictions of blood vessels by inflating a balloon a few millimeters in diameter within the blood vessel. This technology provides patients with an alternative to surgical by-pass procedures. Generally in the past, latex balloons were typically specified because expansion was easily controlled. Problems with compressing the latex balloons could make them inflate unevenly. PVC can be used, but may not be strong enough when inflated. PET film balloons tend to have a low profile when collapsed and have the necessary strength even at thinner thicknesses such as 0.0013 in. (0.0033 cm).

cathode The negative electrode of an electrolytic cell to which positively charged ions migrate when current is passed as in electroplating baths. In a primary cell (battery), the cathode is the positive electrode.

cathode ray tube CRTs are the most widely used visual display; essentially a TV screen. Also called a visual display tube (VDT).

cathode sputtering ▷ **sputtered coating**

cation An ion having a positive charge. Cations in a liquid subjected to electric potential collect at the negative pole or cathode. ▷ **ion**

cationic polymerization Broadly speaking, a cationic polymerization is one in which the active end of the growing plastic molecule is a positive ion. The ion may be the carbonium ion, in which case the process is frequently referred to as a carbonium ion polymerization, or the ixonium ion.

cationic reagent One of several surface-active substances in which the active constituent is the positive ion. Used to flocculate and collect minerals that are not flocculated by oleic acid or soaps.

catsup bottle The popular biaxial stretched coextruded blow molded PP/EVOH barrier/PP squeezable plastic catsup bottle was converted to recyclable PET with barrier plastic in 1991. Heinz, which pioneered and introduced the lightweight, shatter-proof and easy-to-use plastic squeeze bottle in 1983, made the change for environmental reasons (see Fig).

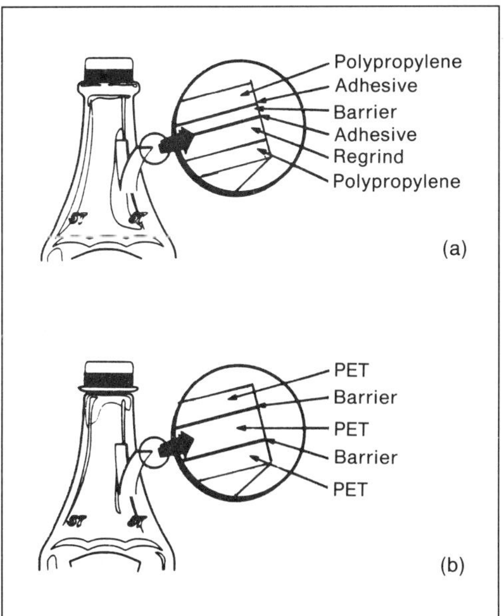

Catsup bottle cutaway schematics of (*a*) the original PP technology and (*b*) the recyclable PET technology.

Cauchy-Riemann differential equation Equations have been developed that concern flow behavior of materials. They have been applied to studying the plastic melt flow during processing. Two-dimensional patterns in different positions and locations during processing of plastics can be produced. As an example, they can be related to shrinkage of plastic melt in a mold cavity during injection molding.

caulking compound A soft plastic consisting of pigment and vehicle used for sealing joints in buildings, boats, and other structures where normal structural movement may occur. Compounds retain their plasticity for an extended period of application depending on the type of plastic used; there are those that can last for centuries. They are available in forms suitable for application by gun and knife, and in extruded preformed shapes.

caul plate Smooth metal plates (usually of aluminum), free of surface defects, that are the same size and shape as a high pressure laminate or reinforced plastic. They are used to contact the multiple lay-up of plastic laminated surface, caul between each laminate, during the curing process in order to transmit press pressure and temperature. Result is to provide smooth surfaces on the cured laminates. They are used extensively to produce thermoset decorative and functional high pressure laminates. Also called caul stock.

Caul stock is usually produced by laminating 0.0005 in. (0.0013 cm) gauge aluminum foil to either kraft or coated litho paper and applying a release coating to the foil surfaces. The aluminum foil is laminated to the paper web by means of roll to roll wet bond laminator using a heat resistant water base adhesive. The release agent is applied by use of a smooth coating roll or gravure cylinder. The caul stock lamination may be made of bright foil surface out or the matte foil surface out, depending on the high pressure plastic laminate finish desired. ▷ **molding high pressure**

cauoatchouc A natural rubber from the *Hevea brasiliensis* tree (originally only existing in the South American Amazon basin). Charles de la Condamine described this material to the French Academy (1736); the word being of Indian origin and derived from "cahutchu".

cavitation The formation and collapse, within a liquid, of cavities or bubbles that contain vapor or gas or both. In order to erode a solid surface by cavitation, it is necessary for the cavitation bubbles to collapse on or close to the surface. In general, cavitation originates from a decrease in static pressure in the liquid. It is distinguished in this way from boiling, which originates from an increase in liquid temperature.

cavitation cloud A collection of a large number of cavitation bubbles. The bubbles in a cloud are small, typically less than 1 mm (0.04 in.) in cross section. A surface that is being eroded by cavitation is usually obscured by a cavitation cloud.

cavitation erosion It is the progressive loss of original material, particularly steel, from a solid surface due to continued exposure to cavitation. With increasing ship speeds, the development of high speed hydraulic equipment and the variety of modern fluid flow applications to which materials are being subjected, the problem of cavitation erosion becomes increasingly important. Erosion may occur in either internal flow systems such as piping, pumps and turbines or in external flow systems such as ships' propellers. The phenomenon of cavitation was identified as early as 1873 by Osborne Reynolds. By the turn of the century it had been called "cavitation" by R. E. Froude, Director of the British Admiralty Ship Model Testing Laboratories.

Cavitation occurs in a rapidly moving fluid because of a decrease in pressure in the fluid below its vapor pressure and the presence of nucleating sources such as minute foreign particles or definitive gas bubbles. As a result, a vapor bubble is formed and continues to grow until it reaches a region of pressure higher than its vapor pressure, when it will collapse. When these bubbles collapse near a boundary, high intensity shock waves are produced which radiate to the boundary and result in mechanical damage to the material. The force of the shock wave radiating from the collapsing bubble or of the impinging jet may be sufficient to cause "plastic" flow or fatigue failure of a material after a number of cycles, depending on the properties of the material, hydrodynamic conditions and foil design parameters.

The behavior of materials in cavitating fluids results in erosion mechanism, including mechanical erosion and electrochemical corrosion. The straightforward way to fight cavitation is to use hardened materials, chromium, chrome-nickel compounds and/or plastics. Other cures are to reduce the vapor pressure with additives, reducing turbulence, changing the liquid temperature or adding air to set as a cushion for the collapsing bubbles.

cavitation erosion test A procedure whereby the surface of a solid is subjected to cavitation attack under specified, or measurable, or at least repeatable conditions. Such tests can be divided into two major classes depending on whether flow cavitation or vibratory cavitation is generated. ▷ **ultrasonic cavitation test device**

cavity ▷ **mold cavity**

cell 1. A single cavity formed by gaseous displacement in a plastic material that forms cellular or foamed plastics. Each single small cavity is surrounded completely or partially by walls. ▷ **foamed closed cell** and **foamed open cell 2.** In solid waste disposal, the holes into which waste is dumped, compacted, and covered with layers of dirt on a daily basis.

cell collapse A defect in foamed plastic characterized by slumping and cratered surfaces, and collapse of internal cells resembling stacked leaflets when viewed in cross section under a microscope. The condition is caused by excessively rapid permeation of the blowing gas through cell walls, or by weakening of the cell walls by plasticization.

cellophane Cellophane or regenerated cellulose is the name given to a thin transparent film consisting of a base sheet of cellulose, regenerated from viscous, containing variable amounts of water and softener, and coated on one or both sides to render it moistureproof and capable of being sealed with heat or solvent. With variations of base sheet thickness, type, and amount of softener, color, plastic treatment, and type and amount of coating, over a hundred different varieties of cellophane have been produced. This versatility enables the film to satisfy the requirements of a wide range of applications, most of which are in the packaging markets. They also have good electrical properties.

The raw materials required, as for nylon viscose, are wood pulp, sodium hydroxide solution, and carbon disulfide. The regenerated transparent cellulose plastic is made by mixing cellulose xanthate with a dilute sodium hydroxide solution to form a viscose. Regeneration is carried out by extruding the viscose, in sheet form, into an acid bath to create cellophane.

cellular A material containing cells or small voids usually identified as a foamed material.

cellular concrete A lightweight product consisting usually of portland cement, cement-silica, cement-pozzolan, lime-pozzolan, or lime-silica pastes containing blends of these ingredients and having a homogeneous void or cell structure, attained with gas-forming chemicals or foaming agents. Autoclave curing is usually used. Different binder ingredients are used to provide different properties; includes use of plastics to provide color and service (particularly weather) resistance.

cellular elastomer A cured elastomeric material containing cells or small voids that can provide different degrees of flexible to rigid foamed plastics.

cellular glass thermal insulation Insulation composed of glass processed by fusion to form a homogeneous rigid mass of closed cells.

cellular material A generic term for materials containing many cells, either open or closed or both, dispersed throughout the mass to form a foam structure.

cellular plastic ▷ **foamed plastic**

cellular striation A layer of cells within a cellular plastic that differs from the characteristic cell structure of the foamed material.

celluloid ▷ **cellulose nitrate plastic**

cellulose The term cellulose in the strict scientific sense applies only to natural pure plant cell material consisting of macromolecules of at least several hundred to several thousand anhydroglucose units. This natural high polymeric carbohydrate is found in most plants; the main constituent of dried woods, jute, flax, hemp, ramie, etc. Cotton is almost pure cellulose. ▷ **fiber rayon**

cellulose I The crystalline modification of cellulose that normally occurs in nature.

cellulose II The crystalline modification of cellulose that is found in mercerized cellulose, in regenerated cellulose, and in cellulose produced by the hydrolysis of various cellulose derivatives.

cellulose III A crystalline modification of cellulose produced by treatment, under certain conditions, with ammonia or sometimes amines. The method of removing the reagent determines the modification produced.

cellulose IV A crystalline modification of cellulose produced by heat treatment of cellulose II.

cellulose acetate butyrate plastic CAB is an ester of cellulose made by the action of a mixture of acetic and butyric acids, and their anhydrides on purified cellulose. It is used in the manufacture of thermoplastics which are similar in general properties to cellulose acetate plastics but are tougher and have better moisture resistance and dimensional stability.

cellulose acetate fiber Acetyl derivative of cellulose; triacetate designation can be used when not less than 92% of the cellulose groups are acetylated.

cellulose acetate phthalate plastic A mixed ester of cellulose containing both acetate and phthalate groups.

cellulose acetate plastic CA has been made in the U.S. since 1913, although the manufacturing process was not perfected until 1930. It replaced cellulose nitrate as photographic film owing to its low burning rate. It is also important as a textile fiber commonly used in coat linings. Properly plasticized with up to 40% plasticizer to permit ease of processability and toughness, CA has been used in such diverse molded applications as appliance and tool handles, telephone handsets, and containers. Injection molding of this thermoplastic is typically at a temperature of 193°C (380°F) and barrel pressures ranging from 5,000 to 8,000 psi (34.5 to 55.1 MPa). It is important that the mold be heated to about 66°C (150°F) to avoid defective parts.

CA is manufactured from the same cellulose feedstock as cellulose nitrate. The raw cellulose is dried, then reacted with glacial acetic acid, acetic anhydride, and sulphuric acid catalyst. After hydrolysis to reach a controlled level of chain degradation, the plastic is precipitated from the chemical solution, washed, and dried. The molecule closely resembles cellulose nitrate except for the presence of the acetate group.

cellulose acetate propionate plastic Usually called cellulose propionate. ▷**cellulose propionate**

cellulose, alpha A very pure cellulose prepared by special chemical treatment. The major components are wood and paper pulp. Use includes as a filler in different plastics.

cellulose derivative A substance derived from cellulose by substitution of one or more of the hydroxyl groups with some other radical. Most derivatives are ethers or esters.

cellulose ester plastic A derivative of cellulose in which the free hydroxyl groups attached to the cellulose chain have been replaced wholly or in part by acidic groups such as nitrate, acetate, or stearate groups. Esterification is effected by the use of a mixture of an acid with its anhydride in the presence of a catalyst, such as sulfuric acid.

cellulose ether Derivatives of cellulose in which one or more of the hydroxyl hydrogens have been replaced by alkyl groups.

cellulose ethyl plastic ▷**ethyl cellulose plastic**

cellulose lacquer A liquid coating material containing as the basic film-forming ingredients cellulose esters or ethers and plasticizers with or without plastics.

cellulose nitrate plastic The first of the commercial synthetic plastics (1868), CN has an interesting history of use as molded parts (combs, stiff shirt collars, shirt fronts, nurse's caps, ladies' corset stiffeners, curtain in the first automobiles, dolls, etc.), photographic films, and projectile propellants. When properly formulated with stabilizers, it is characterized by toughness, dimensional stability, and low water absorption. Its characteristic high flammability caused people to be burned due to smoking and other fire sources, so by the end of the 19th century many molded parts were no longer made from CN. However, a major market that originally started and is even more abundant involves using it with nitroglycerine, of mixed-base gun powder and small rocket propellant, and other similar products.

A relatively brittle thermoplastic, CN is usually blended with plasticizers to afford useful properties so that useful products could be made such as ping-pong balls and fountain-pen barrels. Other than mixed-base powder, the major present applications are films and coatings.

The molecule of CN is one of the most complicated among thermoplastics. It is composed of six-sided rings having carbon in each position except one, which is occupied by an oxygen atom. Attached from this ring are carbon, hydrogen, and oxygen atoms. Alternating with the ring in the molecular chain are oxygen atoms. However, manufacture of CN is basically a simple process consisting of treating cellulose fibers with hot nitric acid, then washing and drying the fibers. The raw cellulose may be cotton linters (the original source), wood pulp, or paper or cotton waste.

Celluloid plastic is a type of CN. The CN is manufactured to contain 10.8 to 11.1% of nitrogen. The latter figure is the nitrogen content of the dinitrate.

cellulose plastic Plastics based on cellulose compounds such as esters (cellulose acetate) and ethers (ethyl cellulose).

cellulose propionate plastic An ester of cellulose made by the action of propionic acid and its hydride on purified cellulose. Similar to cellulose acetate butyrate, but requires less plasticizer and is more compatible with more plasticizers. CP uses include molding products such as toothbrush handles, cosmetic containers, face shields, and fuel filters.

cellulose, regenerated plastic ▷**cellophane** and **rayon**

cellulose sponge A sponge of regenerated cellulose; highly absorbent, soft, and resilient when wet. It will not scratch, can be sterilized by boiling water, and is not affected by ordinary cleaning compounds.

cellulose triacetate plastic A cellulose plastic in which the cellulose is almost completely esterified by acetic acid. It is not soluble in acetone. Use includes base for magnetic tapes, textile fibers, and as a protective coating that is resistant to most solvents.

cellulosic fiberboard A generic term for a homogeneous panel made from lignocellulosic fibers (usually wood or cane) characterized by an integral bond produced by inter-felting of the fibers. Other materials may have been added to improve certain properties.

cellulosic plastics They represent a family of plastics such as cellulose acetate butyrate, cellulose acetate phthalate, cellulosic acetate, cellulose acetate propionate, cellulose ester, cellulose ethyl, cellulose nitrate, cellulose propionate, cellulose triacetate, etc.

Celsius The designation of the degree on the International Practical Temperature Scale and used for the name of the scale (Celsius temperature scale). Prior to 1948, called centigrade. The degree C is related to the K (kelvin) and is used in place of K for expressing C temperature (t) defined by the equation $t = T - T_0$, where T is thermodynamic temperature and $T_0 =$ 273.15 K by definition. ▷ **temperature; centigrade; Fahrenheit; Kelvin**

cement A term broadly applied to a number of adhesives as well as a bonding element.

cementation With metals, it is a process in which steel or iron products are coated with another metal by immersing them in a powder of the second metal and heating to a temperature below the melting point of any of the metals involved. In the plastic industry, it can be associated with fluidized bed coating; applies a coating to metal, plastic and other materials.

cement-coated Surface coated by tumbling or immersion metal parts, such as nails, in plastic or shellac to produce limited temporary bond between driven nail and surrounding wood, not removed during driving. Thus, reduces rusting during storage of nails and while in service.

cement construction A process in which the outsole is attached to the upper by cementing instead of sewing or by other methods. Also known as the compo process, after Compo Industries, Inc., which introduced this method commercially into the U.S. shoe industry about 1930.

cement, contact Mixture of elastomeric rubber and organic solvents that cure upon evaporation of the solvent. A coating is applied to both bonding surfaces. The surfaces are then joined by adhesive bonding when an aggressive tack develops within several minutes.

cementing ▷ **solvent bonding**

cement, organic Any of various types of rubber or elastomer cements, silicone adhesives, etc.

cement portland ▷ **portland cement**

centering The operation on lens elements wherein the element is optically lined up with the axis of rotation and the edges ground concentric with the optical axis.

centerline The axis around which character elements are located for letters, numerals, symbols, diagrams, etc.

center gate ▷ **mold gate**

center of gravity A fixed point in a material body through which the resultant force of gravitational attraction acts; point through which the resultant of gravitational forces of attraction of the body on other bodies emanates.

centigrade The designation (obsolete) of the degree on the International Temperature Scale prior to 1948. ▷ **Celsius**

centipose A unit of viscosity, conveniently and approximately defined as the viscosity of water at room temperature; viscosity is at 1 cp. The usual viscosity unit used is in pascalsecond (Pa.s) where 1 cp = 0.001 Pa.s.

centrifugal atomization coating Plastic or paint centrifugal atomizers consist of a rotating disk or bell. The plastic spray flows to the periphery of the rotor and disintegrates as it leaves the rotor's edge. The atomization is generally poor and the paint direction is difficult to maintain, but the process is very efficient mechanically. In order to improve the atomization, the rotor speed must be increased to very high levels, which is mechanically difficult, thus electrostatic assist is used. If not for ESA technique, centrifugal atomization coating would not be used as widely as it is today.

centrifugal casting A method of forming plastic in which the dry or liquid plastic is placed in a rotatable container (see Fig. on p. 98). It is heated to a molten condition by the transfer of heat through the walls of the container, and rotated (single axis) such that the centrifugal force induced will force the molten plastic to conform to the configuration of the

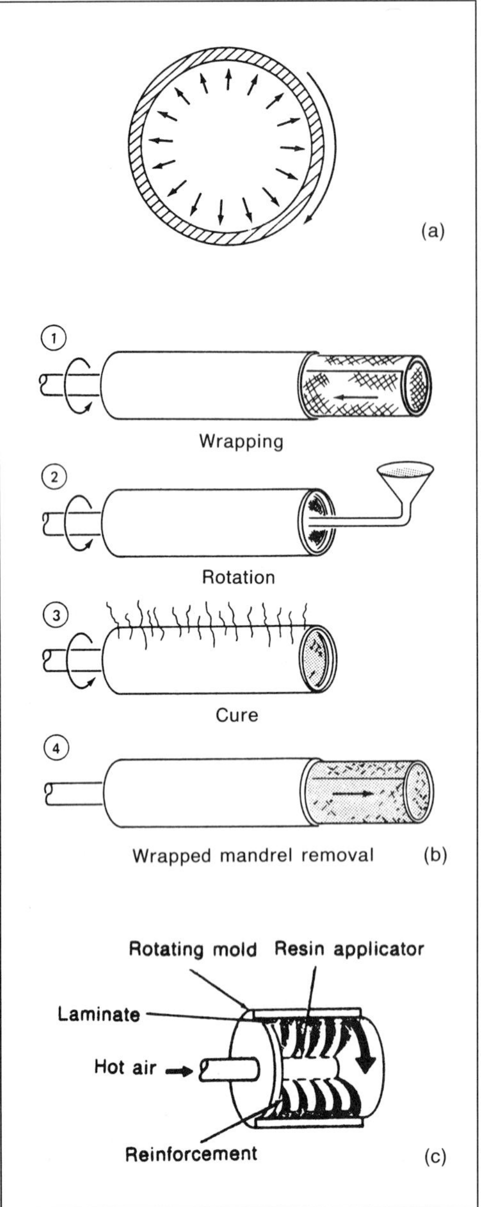

Centrifugal casting or molding schematics using fiber reinforcements with plastics. (*a*) Example of centrifugal force that occurs during rotation; (*b*) wrapped mandrel removal; (*c*) example where heat can be directed from center tube.

interior surface of the container. Use includes fabricating tanks, large diameter pipe with or without fiber reinforcement, etc. This method differs from rotational molding in that roto-molding involves rotating the mold slowly around two axes simultaneously. Also called centrifugal molding.

centrifugal impact mixer A device used for mixing free-flowing dry blends, comprising a conical hopper in which are rotated at high speeds a rotor disc and a peripheral impactor. The plastic is fed to the center of the rotor, which throws it against the impactor blades, which in turn throw the plastic against fixed impactors at the extremities of the cone. From there, the plastic flows downward to a discharge orifice.

centrifugal molding ▷ **centrifugal casting**

centrifugal or rotational coating ▷ **coating, centrifugal or rotational**

centrifugation, equilibrium A method for determining the distribution of molecular weights by spinning a solution of the specimen at a speed such that the molecules are not removed from the solvent but are held at a point where the centrifugal force tending to remove them is balanced by the dispersive forces caused by the thermal agitation.

centrifuge Centrifugation is a separation technique based on the application of centrifugal force to a mixture or suspension of materials of closely similar densities. The smaller the difference in density, the greater the force required (10,000 rpm or more) to impart a force up to 17,000 times gravity.

ceramic A product manufactured by the action of heat on earthy raw materials in which silicon with its oxide and complex compounds known as silicates occupy a predominant position. Ceramic materials contain metallic and nonmetallic elements.

ceramic fiber Reinforced plastics include the use of alumina/silica fibers. Ceramic fibers possess unique wear and corrosion resistance, and high temperature stability. They consist of approximately 50% alumina and 50% silica (by weight), with traces of other inorganic materials. The fibers are made by atomizing a molten ceramic stream using high pressure air or spinning wheels; also use chemical vapor deposition, melt drawing, and special extrusion processes. (Although glass fibers are also ceramic material, they are not generally categorized as ceramic fiber. They are called glass fibers.)

The fibers produced are discontinuous, with diameters ranging from 1 to 10 μm, and a distribution of fiber lengths that average between 15 μm and 1 in. (2.54 cm). Particulate matter, or shot, is also produced in the process and can be removed with further processing. Because of their whisker-like nature, sufficient dispersion of the individual ceramic fibers is critical to providing satisfactory plastic reinforcement.

When the fibers are blended into liquid plastic systems, relatively high shear forces are needed to disentangle the fibers. These forces can be achieved by basically two ways: (1) using high shear mixing (3,000 rpm) with a low viscosity plastic or compound, or (2) using medium shear mixing with a sigma blade or similar mixer for a high viscosity plastic or compound.

When the fibers are blended into powder plastic systems, fibers should first be disentangled by using high speed choppers for 5 to 10 sec. After the powder is added, the entire mixture should be combined using a high speed chopper-mixer for 10 to 15 sec. The short shear times are designed to coat each fiber with plastic without reentangling the fibers.

ceramic matrix composite CMCs are materials consisting of a ceramic or carbon fiber surrounded by a ceramic matrix, usually silicon carbide (SiC). They include so-called advanced composite materials. The CMC technology developed offers a range of properties. They are primarily developed to perform at temperatures that are beyond the capabilities of high performance metals. To be serious candidates for structural applications, CMCs have to be tougher than monolithic ceramics in resisting rapid crack propagation. Moreover, if they are going to be used successfully in extremely high temperatures, CMCs must surpass coated carbon/carbon composites in resisting attack by aggressive and corrosive environments.

As a rule of thumb, CMCs are categorized according to their failure mode and processibility. Continuous fiber ceramic composites (CFCC) tend to fail catastrophically because their mechanical behavior is fiber dominated, whereas whisker and particulate reinforced CMCs, which are controlled by the properties of the matrix, fail catastrophically due to the matrix. The latter are relatively easy to process, while CFCCs often require special consolidation techniques.

Whisker reinforcements are single crystal materials with ultrahigh strength that are used to enhance the toughness, strength, and hardness of ceramics (also with plastics). CMCs reinforced with whiskers, consequently, are ideal for wear resistant applications such as with alumina for high speed cutting tools. Another potential application, and a large volume one, is turbochargers in automotive engines.

ceramic precursor, plastic The usually extremely high softening temperature of ceramics precludes their being shaped into fibers, films, moldings, or other complex shapes through melt processing common to organic plastics. The use of preceramic plastics (ceramic precursors), which are processed as ordinary plastics to the desired shape and then pyrolyzed to ceramics, overcomes the high temperature shaping problem. ▷ **injection molding ceramic**

ceramics A general term applied to the art or technique of producing products by a ceramic process.

certified reference material CRM is a reference material, the composition or properties of which are certified by a recognized standardizing agency or group. ▷ **testing certification**

C-glass A glass fiber with soda-lime-borosilicate composition that is used in reinforced plastics for its chemical stability in corrosive environments.

chain, folded Chain folded is the conformation of a flexible polymer molecule when present in a crystal. The molecule exists and reenters the same crystal, frequently generating folds.

chain length distribution The length of the stretched linear macromolecule. It is usually expressed by the number of identical links, that is, the degree of polymerization (DP). ▷ **polymer chemistry terminology**

chain polymerization Polymerization processes are of two basic types: stepwise (or step reaction) and chain reaction. The kinetics of the two types of reaction are entirely different; the properties of the plastics they produce differ with respect to molecular weight distribution and usually, although not inevitably, differ in kind. Chain reactions are as follows: (1) plastic of high MV is formed at all stages even during the first fraction of a second reaction, (2) the polymer molecules formed do not react with one another to produce material of higher MW, and (3) the "active centers" responsible for the reaction are free radicals or ions; in the former case, a kinetic chain is brought to an end by mutual reaction between two of the intermediates, and in the latter case, by a reaction involving two ions of opposite charge. The vast majority of chain reaction polymerizations are those generally known as addition polymerizations involving the conversion of vinyl-type monomers.

chain scission The breaking of a molecular bond causing the loss of a side group or shortening of the overall chain.

chain stiffening A polymer strengthening mechanism significantly different from linear, branched, or crosslinked polymer systems is chain stiffening. The chain stiffening polymer has a monomer that is physically large and unsymmetrical. The ability of a chain to flex is impaired. A typical example is polystyrene.

chainstitch ▷ **thread, chainstitch**

chain transfer Refers to the termination of a growing polymer chain and the start of a new one. The process is mediated by a chain transfer agent, which may be the monomer, initiator, solvent, polymer, or some species that has been added deliberately to affect chain transfer. Because CT occurs in all radical polymerization, it must be taken into account in any quantitative consideration of these reactions. CT always decreases the molecular weight of the product and may decrease the rate. It is used to regulate and limit MW in a polymer reaction. CTs are also used for telomerization, the production of very low MW polymers (telomers). ▷ **telomer**

chain transfer agent A molecule from which an atom, such as hydrogen, may be readily abstracted by a free radical.

chalk A natural calcium carbonate composed of the calcareous remains of minute marine organisms, decomposed by acids and heat. It is odorless and tasteless.

chalking Dry, chalk-like appearance or powdery residue deposit on the surface of a plastic or paint that occurs with certain materials particularly when exposed to outdoors. Chalking usually results from decomposition of the binder, due principally to the action of UV rays. In addition there can be migration of ingredient, or both degradation and migration.

chalking resistance Usually a pigmented coating on plastic to resist degradation and migration.

challenge ▷ **design analysis; design technology**

chamfer **1.** To bevel a sharp external edge. **2.** The broken edge of the jaw serrations.

chamfer angle The angle of the chamfer measured from the normal to the axis of the part generally specified in conjunction with either a length or a diameter.

chance failure phase ▷ **life-history curve**

change can mixer A planetary type mixer comprising several paddle blades mounted on a vertical shaft rotating in one direction while the can or container rotates in the opposite direction. The paddle shaft usually is mounted on a hinged structure so that it can be swung out of the can, permitting the can to be removed and replaced easily. This type mixer is employed for relatively small batches of 3 to 125 gallons (0.013 to 0.55 m^3) of fluid dispersions and dry materials. Also called pony mixer.

channel black **1.** A type of carbon black made by impingement of a natural gas flame against a metal plate, from which the deposit is scraped at intervals. **2.** High color channel black (HCC) is a type of channel carbon black of particle size about 10 mm and of the highest tinting power.

Chapter 11 US permits legal protection from creditors under Chapter 11 of the US Federal Bankruptcy Act.

char Formation of carbonaceous material by pyrolysis (ablation) or incomplete combustion.

character alignment The vertical or horizontal position of characters with respect to a given reference line.

characteristic A property of items in a sample or population which, when measured, counted, or otherwise observed, helps to distinguish between the items.

charge Precise, weighted amount of material placed in an open mold. Also determined by volumetric measurement which is usually not as accurate.

charge couple device CCD is an electronic scanning device used in image systems.

charged area development CAD is a process in electrostatic copying where the photoconductive element is charged with a charge of the opposite sign (as that of the toner). A light source is used to discharge all areas on the photo-conductor that are not to receive the toner to form the image.

charge-transfer polymerization Initiated by means of charge-transfer interactions involving monomers as one or both components of an electron donor-acceptor system. The terms charge-transfer initiation and charge-transfer propagation distinguish polymerizations involving charge-transfer phenomena in the initiation process from those involving charge-transfer complexes in the propagation process. Thermally and photochemically induced charge-transfer polymerizations involve novel types of initiation. Another class of polymerization that involves charge-transfer interactions is spontaneously initiated or free-radical initiated 1:1 alternating radical copolymerization of an electron donor monomer with an electron acceptor monomer. Charge-transfer interactions have also been widely observed in conventional ionic and free-radical polymerizations. Charge transfer or partial electron transfer to form charge-transfer complexes and complete one-electron transfer to generate ion radicals should be distinguished from each other in their quantum chemical meaning and in discussing chemical reactions. The term charge-transfer is frequently used to include complete one-electron transfer.

charging The process of establishing an electrostatic surface charge of uniform density on an electrical insulating medium.

Charpy impact test A test for shock loading in which a centrally notched sample bar is held or supported at both ends and broken by striking (impact) the back face in the same plane as the notch; unnotched specimens also used.

charring ▷ **char**

chase ▷ **mold chase**

check ring ▷ **screw tip**

cheese A supply of glass fiber wound into a cylindrical mass.

chelate Five or six membered ring formation based on intermolecular attraction of H, O, or N atoms.

chelating agent Basically a sequestering or complexing agent that, in aqueous solution, renders a metallic ion inactive through the formation of an inner ring structure with the ion. Term was derived from the Greek word "chele", meaning claw. Thus, a chelating agent is a substance whose molecules are capable of seizing and holding metallic ions in a "clawlike" grip.

chemical Chemical reaction or solvent effect, causing failure or deterioration of plastics.

chemical analysis Chemical analysis in its broadest sense refers to the determination of chemical structure and chemically active species. It involves both direct measurements and use of specific compounds to achieve selective reactions of a component of the substance being analyzed; to produce a readily measurable species; or to determine a reactive end product. Detection may involve simple visual or optical observations, recording of an electrical or thermal response, or use of sophisticated spectroscopic or other complex automated instrumentation with computerized controls and data handling capabilities.

The chemical characterization of plastics (polymers) is not basically different from the analysis of organic compounds of low molecular weight. However, the absence of functional groups of sufficient reactivity, the general low solubility and chemical inertness, and the complexity of most polymeric systems require modifications of the usual procedures so that the component or functional group being determined can be brought into intimate contact with the reagent. Depending on the analysis being performed, contact with the reagent is brought about by degradation or ashing, by extraction of the polymer, or by solution techniques.

chemical assay A chemical measurement of the quantity of one or more components of material.

chemical blowing agent ▷ **foam and blowing agent**

chemical changes They can occur during processing, such as: (1) polymerization and crosslinking, which increases viscosity, (2) depolymerization or damaging of molecules, which reduces viscosity, (3) complete changes in the chemical structure, which may cause color changes, and (4) already degraded plastics may catalyze further degradation.

chemical characterization of plastics ▷ **molecular structure; molecular size; molecular weight distribution; sonic testing; designing with model, plastic-chemical structure**

chemical composition and properties of plastics The chemical structure and nature of plastics have a significant relationship not only to the properties of the plastic but to the ways in which it can be processed, designed, or otherwise translated into a finished product. The chemical composition is basically organic polymers that are very large molecules composed of chains of carbon atoms

```
  |   |   |   |   |   |   |   |   |   |
—C—C—C—C—C—C—C—C—C—C—
  |   |   |   |   |   |   |   |   |   |
```

generally connected to hydrogen atoms (H), and often also to oxygen (O), nitrogen (N), chlorine (Cl), fluorine (F), and sulfur (S). The first polymers were synthesized by nature (natural rubber, cellulose and starch in trees and plants, proteins in plant and animal life, etc.) and since the mid-1800s utilized in the laboratory that modified them chemically to meet emerging industrial needs. More recently, modern industrial organic chemists have learned to synthesize a much greater variety of new polymers (plastics), controlling and varying their structures to balance processability and properties (see Table on p. 102) in tens of thousands of different products.

During the first half of the 20th century, raw materials were most often coal tar chemicals, salt, water, and air. Since the late 1930s, petroleum chemistry has offered the easiest and most economical starting point for the manufacture of most polymers. If petroleum supplies become too scarce or expensive, industrial organic chemists could make all of our commercial polymers from coal and from completely

Examples of the general relationships between chemical composition and plastic properties.

General features of chemical composition	Effects on polymer properties
	Processability
Reactivity	Pot life, polymerization, and cure
Bond strength	Thermal stability
Similarity of atoms, groups, polarity, and H-bonding	Solubility
Volatile impurities	Bubbles and toxicity
	Mechanical properties
Volatile impurities	Low rigidity, strength, and dimensional stability
Surface energy	Friction
	Acoustic properties
Atomic weights	Sound absorption
	Thermal properties
Atomic constants	Specific heat
Bond strength	Thermal stability
Specific elements	Flame resistance
	Electrical properties
Polarity of bonds	Dielectric constant
Polar and ionic impurities	Conduction
Conjugated unsaturation	Conduction
	Optical properties
Polarity of bonds	Refractive index, spectroscopic absorption
Conjugated unsaturation	Color, ultraviolet light sensitivity
	Chemical properties
Similarity of atoms, groups, polarity, and H-bonding	Solubility and permeability
Bond strength	Reactivity and stability
Surface energy	Adhesion
Specific elements and functional groups	Toxicity
	Price
Elements and groups	Cost of synthesis
Atomic weights	Specific gravity

renewable materials such as wood and plant life.

While polymers thus form the structural backbone of plastics, they are rarely used in pure form. In almost all plastics, other useful ingredients are added to modify and optimize the properties for each desired process and application. Additives most often included are stabilizers, fillers and reinforcements, and colorants; processing aids, plasticizers, flame retardants, blowing agents, crosslinking agents, and more specialized additives are also used. All these additives affect both processability and product performance.

A molecule of regular structure may fold back and forth upon itself to form a submicroscopic crystallite, and these tiny crystals may further group radially into microscopic circular structures called spherulites; this crystallization process can greatly speed the product fabricating cycle, and the resulting structures can greatly harden and strengthen the final product.

chemical coupling agent ▷ **glass fiber and fabric surface treatment**

chemical etching The exposure of certain plastic surfaces to a solution of reactive chemical compounds. This treatment causes a chemical surface change, such as oxidation, thereby improving surface wettability (increasing its critical surface tension). It may also remove some material, introducing a micro-roughness to the surface. Chemical etching requires immersion of the part into a bath for a period of time, then rinsing and drying. The process is more expensive than most other surface treatments, such as flame treatment, and therefore it is used only when other methods are not sufficiently effective. Fluoroplastics are often etched chemically because they do not respond to other treatments, ABS parts may be chemically etched for metallic plating, etc. Etching solutions are oxidizing chemicals, such as sulfuric and chromic acids, or metallic sodium in naphthalene and tetrahydrofuran solution. Such solutions are highly corrosive; thus, require special handling and disposal procedures.

chemical foamed plastic A plastic of cellular structure in which the cells are formed by a blowing agent or by the reaction of constituents. ▷ **foamed plastic**

chemical milling A controlled etching process that depends on the etching action of an acid or alkali, depending on the type plastic, that uniformly attacks all exposed areas of the work piece. A mask or protective coating is used on those surfaces which are not to be etched. Also called *chemical etching*, *chemical blanking* or *chemical machining*.

chemical modeling ▷ **computer-aided molecular graphics**

chemical modification of plastic ▷ **barrier via chemical modification**

chemical origin of life ▷ **life, origin**

chemical polymer In chemistry, a polymer is described by drawing its physical structure of atoms. As an example, polyethylene is described as:

$$\left[\begin{array}{cc} H & H \\ -C & C- \\ H & H \end{array}\right]_n$$

where H = hydrogen atom, C = carbon atom, n = molecular weight (number of repeating units), [ ] = monomer symbol, — = electron bond. The bonds on the carbon atoms indicate that molecules can form bonds with like molecules to form a polymer (plastic) chain. Many polymers can be made from the same carbon atom backbone, as is shown with PE. To accomplish this change may involve complex processing equipment, but from the chemistry standpoint, it simply involves substituting another element or chemical compound for one or more of the hydrogen atoms. As an example, take the PE monomer that is drawn above and substitute a chlorine atom for one hydrogen; result is polyvinyl chloride.

Polymer molecules are distinguished from other chemical compositions primarily by their tremendous size, and most of their properties result from this unusual size. Also many of the properties and applications of plastics are greatly influenced by the individual atoms and functional groups within the polymer molecule as summarized in the Table on p. 102 under ▷ **chemical composition and properties of plastics.**

chemical processing pump ▷ **design chemical processing pump**

chemical properties Material characteristics that relate to the structure of a material and its formation from the elements. These properties are usually measured in a chemical laboratory, and they cannot be determined by visual observation. It is usually necessary to change or destroy a material to measure a chemical property.

chemical reaction, electro ▷ **electrochemical reaction**

chemical reaction engineering ▷ **reactor technology**

chemical reactor, extruder type ▷ **extruder reactive processing**

chemical reactor technology ▷ **reactor technology**

chemical reclamation With chemical reclamation, plastics are decomposed by physiochemical processes that take them back to their basic building blocks. Gaseous or liquid hydrocarbon compounds can thereby be reclaimed. Processes that are being used include hydration of plastics wastes, hydrolysis (alcoholysis, glycolysis), and pyrolysis.

chemical recycling Material recycling can conflict with energy recycling. Chemical recycling is beginning to assume an intermediate position between material recycling and burning. This technique seeks to break down the polymer molecules in various ways into low-molecular substances that can be used to manufacture plastics again. Thus, chemical recycling is recommended when mixtures of plastics cannot be physically separated or plasticated. The pyrolysis and hydration of plastics, to give mineral-oil-like substances, have received intensive study and been tested on the pilot scale. They are uneconomic thus far, and not yet practiced industrially.

A specific type of chemical decomposition—hydrolysis, alcoholysis, or aminolysis, depending on the decomposition reagent used, occurs with a rather small group of plastics which, in addition to carbon atoms, have ester, amide, urethane, carbonate or acetal structures in the polymer chains. Under quite mild reaction conditions these structures can be broken down selectively into their starting monomers by reversal of the polymerisation reaction. A favored area of activity is the variant-rich polyurethane sector which calls for the return of chemical recycling from both the chemical and practical standpoints.

Polyurethanes (PUR) are easily decomposed thermally because they are relatively unstable, but the decomposition products are inhomogeneous and cannot be reused readily. Selective scission of PUR chains can be achieved by reaction with water; the starting polyol, carbon dioxide, and the amine corresponding to the starting isocyanate are formed:

$$\sim R'—NH—CO \mid O—R—O \mid CO—NH—R'—NH—CO \mid O—R\sim$$

$$HO \mid H \qquad H \mid OH \qquad HO \mid H$$

$$\downarrow$$

$$\sim R'—NH_2 + CO_2 + HO—R—OH + CO_2 + H_2N—R'—NH_2 + \\ + CO_2 + HO—R\sim$$

An increase in the reaction rate is achieved by operating under pressure and at high temperatures. A series of studies has been published, principally in the form of patent specifications, where the depolymerization reaction occurs either discontinuously, or continuously in an extruder.

chemical resistance Part of the wide acceptance of plastics is due to their relative chemical compatibility, particularly with moisture as compared to other materials. Plastics are largely immune to the electrochemical corrosion to which metals are susceptible. Consequently, they can frequently be used profitably to contain water and corrosive chemicals that would attack metals. Some plastics have outstanding chemical resistance, with minimal change in appearance, dimensions, mechanical properties, and weight over a period of time. Test conditions include the length of exposure, concentration, temperature, and internal stress. The final classification as chemical resistant depends on the application.

There are plastics that can absorb, react chemically, plasticize, dissolve, or be stress cracked by chemical environments. Chemical change is stimulated by heat and concentration. If the chemical exposure is limited or infrequent, the service life of the plastic part may be long, but some change in properties can occur. Fabrication, compounding, and application can affect chemical resistance. The following guidelines should be considered when choosing a plastic: (1) solubility is reduced and resistance enhanced by increasing molecular weight, (2) susceptibility to oxidation increases with saturation, (3) solubility is favored by chemical similarity of solute and solvent, and (4) solubility of a plastic is reduced by chain branching and crosslinking.

Many plastics can be used in specialized chemical resistant applications. With few exceptions such as fluoroplastics, most plastics are attacked by one or more chemicals. But, though vulnerable to some chemicals, a specific plastic can be highly resistant to several others. By careful material selection, lightweight, unbreakable plastics can be used to replace glass and stainless steel as chemical containers. In many instances, reinforced plastics have replaced stainless steel as industrial ducting used to carry away chemical vapors. The chemical resistances of some plastics are given in the following Table on pp. 106 and 107.

chemical spray process ▷ **silver spray plating**

chemical structure modeling ▷ **designing with model, plastic-chemical structure**

chemical synonym datacase A chemical source for identification that includes codes, formulas, tradenames, common names, and official names for chemicals.

chemical tests For many problems, spectroscopic techniques serve to identify unknown plastics rapidly. However, depending on the information sought and the availability of equipment, simple chemical tests may serve as well or better than elaborate instrumental procedures. For example, the way in which a material burns, solubility or elemental analysis, origin, or price may serve to identify or to allow a choice to be made between one of several possible materials.

chemical treatment A method of making inert plastic to render them receptive to inks, adhesives, paints, etc. Techniques include chemical etching, flame treatment, abrading surface, etc.

chemical vapor deposition CVD is a process in which desired reinforcement material is deposited from vapor phase onto a continuous core; boron on tungsten, and silicon carbide on carbon monofilament substrates are examples. In the CVD process, a solid is formed by the decomposition or reduction of one or more gaseous molecules on a heated substrate. Fine-grained materials may be formed at one third or less of the melting point of the material for simple crystal structures and somewhat higher for more complex crystal structures. The crystallite size also depends on the rate of deposition and the surface mobility. Typically, a filament is run through a chamber where the filament is resistance heated, and suitable gases decompose on the heated substrate. Although the linear deposition rate is quite high by plating process standards, the contact time required to deposit the necessary coating thickness is in tens of seconds or more. Hence, for any appreciable production rate, many reactors must run in parallel. This process results in filament output that is rather expensive.

chemisorption Adsorption, especially when reversible, by means of chemical forces in contrast with physical forces.

chemistry The great development of the theory of organic chemistry or more particularly of our understanding of the mechanism of the reactions of carbon compounds, which has occurred since the early part of this century, has wrought a vast change outlook over the whole of the science. At one time organic chemistry appeared as a vast body of facts, often apparently unconnected, but the more recent developments in theory (that continually occur) have changed all this so that organic chemistry is a much more ordered body of knowledge in which a logical pattern can be clearly seen. It has undergone continuous modification improving its value and importance permitting an endless growth of new plastics with improved performances.

chemistry, analytical Analytical chemistry is the subdivision of chemistry concerned with identification of materials (qualitative analysis) and with determination of the percentage composition of mixtures or the constituents of a pure compound (quantitative analysis). The gravimetric and volumetric (or wet) methods such as precipitation, titration and solvent extraction are still used for routine work; newer titration methods are available. Among these are infrared, ultraviolet, and X-ray spectroscopy; also chromatography of various types. Optical and electron microscopy, mass spectrometry (MS), microanalysis, nuclear magnetic resonance (NMR), and others fall within the area of analytical chemistry.

chemistry, bio Biochemistry was originally a subdivision of chemistry but now is an independent science. It includes all aspects of chemistry that apply to living organisms that can influence the behavior of certain plastics.

chemistry, cryo- Cryochemistry is that branch of chemistry devoted to the study of reactions occurring at extremely low temperatures of −200°C (−328°F) and lower.

chemistry, electro ▷ **electrochemistry**

chemistry, inorganic ▷ **inorganic chemistry**

chemistry, photo ▷ **photochemistry**

chemistry, polymer ▷ **polymer chemistry terminology; chemical composition and properties of plastics; chemical polymer; polymer**

chemometric ▷ **computer chemometric**

chicle A natural thermoplastic, gum-like material obtained from the latex of the sapodilla tree native to Mexico and Central America. Softens at 32.3°C, insoluble in water, soluble in most organic solvents, and its major use is as a chewing gum after adding sugar and specific flavoring.

chill **1.** To cool a mold by circulating water through it (see Fig. on p. 108). **2.** To cool a mold, die, plasticator barrel, etc. with an air blast; for molds also by immersing it in water. **3.** An object, usually metal, imbedded in a portion of the mold to accelerate the local rate of heat removal from the material being processed. **4.** To refine a graphite structure or cause formation of primary carbides.

chiller A self-contained (individual or central) system comprised of a refrigeration unit and a coolant circulation mechanism consisting of a reservoir and a pump. Chillers maintain the optimum balance in plastic processing by constantly recirculating chilled cooling fluids to injection molds, extruder baths, etc. For cooling below the freezing point, antifreeze such as ethylene glycol is included in the water. A central water chiller is a refrigeration unit that produces and delivers chilled water at −1 to 21°C (30 to 70°F) to several molding machines via a central pipe system. Most central chillers range from 30 to 200 tons cooling capacity (one ton = 12,000 btu/h). The basic components of these units include chiller barrels, condensers, thermal expansion valves, and compressors. Condensers can be air cooled (self-contained outdoor types are a split system with a remote condenser and an indoor chiller). Most applications have cooling tower requirements which favor water cooled condensing. They also have a lower initial cost than air cooled units and avoid the need for extensive refrigerant head pressure controls required by air cooled units for year round operation.

Central chiller compressors are either semi-hermetic or open drive designs. Semi types are only partially accessible and share the same housing with the motor, the windings of which are cooled by refrigerant gas. Open drive compressors are coupled to an external motor located outside the refrigerant circuit, and either directly connected to the motor (direct drive) or driven at reduced speeds by belts and sheaves (belt drive). The open drive units are field rebuildable. In general, there is a price premium for open types in smaller sizes, but in larger sizes of 100 tons and up, the open types are cost competitive. Most semi-hermetic and large open drive chillers have multiple independent refrigerant circuits which ensure availability of partial chilling capacity if one circuit fails.

chill film ▷ **extruder film**

chill roll ▷ **extruder chill roll**

chime In packaging, the rim of a container, such as a drum, barrel, or can.

china clay A natural clay with good whiteness, used as a filler in such materials as PVC electrical compounds.

chip **1.** Common term for a computer integrated circuit device, fabricated on a small piece of silicon. **2.** In semiconductor wafers, region where material has been removed from the surface or

Resistance of plastics against chemicals. ▷ **chemical resistance**

		Resistance against[1]																
		Aromatic solvents		Aliphatic solvents		Chlorinated solvents		Weak bases and salts		Strong bases		Strong acids		Strong oxidants		Esters and ketones		24 h water absorption
Plastic at °C	Abbreviation	25	90	25	90	25	90	25	90	25	90	25	90	25	90	25	90	Change % by weight
Acetals		1–4	2–4	1	2	1–2	4	1–3	2–5	1–5	2–5	5	5	5	5	1	2–3	0.22–0.25
Acrylics		5	5	2	3	5	5	1	3	2	5	4	4–5	5	5	5	5	0.2–0.4
Acrylonitrile-butadiene-styrene	ABS	4	5	2	3–5	3–5	5	1	2–4	1	2–4	1–4	5	1–5	5	3–5	5	0.1–0.4
Aramids (aromatic polyamide)		1	1	1	1	1	1	2	3	4	5	3	4	2	5	1	2	0.6
Block copolymers, crystallizable		2	4	2	4	4	5	1	1	1	1	1	3	1	4	1	3	< 0.01
Cellulose acetates	CA	2	3	2	3	3	4	2	3	3	5	3	5	3	5	5	5	2–7
Cellulose acetate butyrates	CAB	4	5	1	3	3	4	2	4	3	5	3	5	3	5	5	5	0.9–2.0
Cellulose acetate propionates	CAP	4	5	1	3	3	4	1	2	3	5	3	5	3	5	5	5	1.3–2.8
Diallyl phthalates, filled	DAP	1–2	2–4	2	3	2	4	2	3	2	4	1–2	2–3	2	4	3–4	4–5	0.2–0.7
Epoxies		1	2	1	2	1–2	3–4	1	1–2	1	2	2–3	3–4	4	4–5	2	3–4	0.01–0.10
Ethylene-vinyl acetates	EVA	5	5	5	5	5	5	1	2	1	5	1	5	1	5	2	5	0.05–0.13
Ethylene-tetrafluoroethylene copolymers	ETFE	1	1	1	1	1	1	1	1	1	1	1	1	1	1	1	1	< 0.03
Fluorinated ethylene-propylenes	FEP	1	1	1	1	1	1	1	1	1	1	1	1	1	1	1	1	< 0.01
Perfluoroalkoxies	PFA	1	1	1	1	1	1	1	1	1	1	1	1	1	1	1	1	< 0.03
Polychlorotrifluoroethylenes	PCTFE	1	1	1	1	3	4	1	1	1	1	1	1	1	1	1	1	0.01–0.10
Polytetrafluoroethylenes	PTFE	1	1	1	1	1	1	1	1	1	1	1	1	1	1	1	1	0
Furans		1	1	1	1	1	1	2	2	2	2	1	1	5	5	1	1	0.01–0.20
Ionomers		2	4	1	4	4	4	1	4	1	4	2	4	1	5	1	4	0.1–1.4
Melamines, filled		1	1	1	1	1	1	2	3	2	3	2	3	2	3	1	2	0.01–1.30

Nitriles (high barrier alloys of ABS or SAN)		1	4	1	2–4	1–4	2–5	1	2–4	1	2–4	2–5	5	3–5	5	1–5	5	0.2–0.5
Nylons		1	1	1	1	1	2	1	2	2	3	5	5	5	5	1	1	0.2–1.9
Phenolics, filled		1	1	1	1	1	1	2	3	3	5	1	1	4	5	2	2	0.1–2.0
Polyamide-imides		1	1	1	1	2	3	1	1	3	4	2	3	2	3	1	1	0.22–0.28
Polyarylsulfones	PAS	4	5	2	3	4	5	1	2	2	2	1	1	2	4	3	4	1.2–1.8
Polybutylenes	PB	3	5	1	5	4	5	1	2	1	3	1	3	1	4	1	3	< 0.01–0.3
Polycarbonates	PC	5	5	1	1	5	5	1	5	5	5	1	1	1	1	5	5	0.15–0.35
Polyesters, thermoplastic		2	5	1	3–5	3	5	1	3–4	2	5	3	4–5	2	3–5	2	3–4	0.06–0.09
Polyesters, thermoset, glass-fiber-filled		1–3	3–5	2	3	2	4	2	3	3	5	2	3	2	4	3–4	4–5	0.01–2.50
Polyethylenes																		
LDPE–HDPE		4	5	4	5	4	5	1	1	1	1	1–2	1–2	1–3	3–5	2	3	0.00–0.01
UHMWPE[2]		3	4	3	4	3	4	1	1	1	1	1	1	1	1	3	4	< 0.01
Polyimides		1	1	1	1	1	1	2	3	4	5	3	4	2	5	1	1	0.3–0.4
Poly(phenylene oxide)s, (modified)	PPO	4	5	2	3	4	5	1	1	1	1	1	2	1	2	2	3	0.06–0.07
Poly(phenylene sulfide)s	PPS	1	2	1	1	1	2	1	1	1	1	1	1	1	2	1	1	< 0.05
Poly(phenyl sulfone)s		4	4	1	1	5	5	1	1	1	1	1	1	1	1	3	4	0.5
Polypropylenes	PP	2	4	2	4	2–3	4–5	1	1	1	1	1	2–3	2–3	4–5	2	4	0.01–0.03
Polystyrenes	PS	4	5	4	5	5	5	1	5	1	5	4	5	4	5	4	5	0.03–0.60
Polysulfones		4	4	1	1	5	5	1	1	1	1	1	1	1	1	3	4	0.2–0.3
Polyurethanes	PUF	3	4	2	3	4	5	2–3	3–4	2–3	3–4	2–3	3–4	4	4	4	5	0.02–1.50
Poly(vinyl chloride)s	PVC	4	5	1	5	5	5	1	5	1	5	1	5	2	5	4	5	0.04–1.00
Poly(vinyl chloride)s, chlorinated	CPVC	4	4	1	2	5	5	1	2	1	2	1	2	2	3	4	5	0.04–0.45
Poly(vinylidene fluoride)s	PVDF	1	1	1	1	1	1	1	1	1	2	1	2	1	2	3	5	0.04
Silicones		4	4	2	3	4	5	1	2	4	5	3	4	4	5	2	4	0.1–0.2
Styrene-acrylonitriles	SAN	4	5	3	4	3	5	1	3	1	3	1	3	3	4	4	5	0.20–0.35
Ureas, filled		1	3	1	3	1	3	2	3	2	3	4	5	2	3	1	2	0.4–0.8
Vinyl esters, glass-fiber-filled		1	3	1–2	2–4	1–2	4	1	3	1	3	1	2	2	3	3–4	4–5	0.01–2.50

[1] On a descending scale from 1 to 7.
[2] Ultrahigh molecular weight polyethylene.

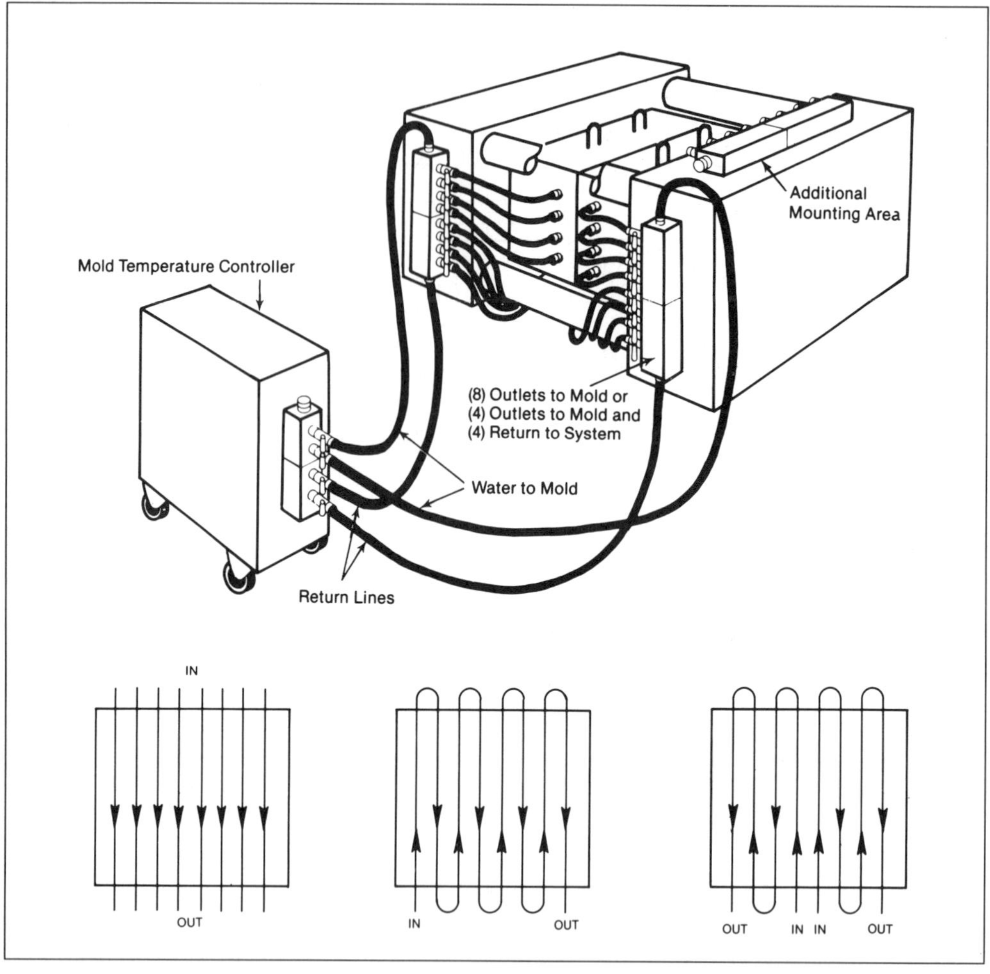

Example of chilling/cooling mold with circulating water with different cooling patterns of water lines in the mold to provide or adjust for required heat transfer media from the plastic melt in the cavity.

edge of the wafer. **3.** Area along an edge or corner where the material has broken off. **4.** Crushed angular rock fragment of a size smaller than a few centimeters. **5.** An imperfection due to breakage of a small fragment out of an otherwise regular surface. **6.** ▷ **pultrusion chip**

chlorinated hydrocarbon An organic compound having chlorine atoms in its chemical structure. Trichloroethylene, methyl chloroform, and methylene chloride are chlorinated hydrocarbon solvents; polyvinyl chloride is a plastic.

chlorinated polyether CP is a corrosion and chemical resistant thermoplastic whose primary use has been in the manufacture of products and equipment for the chemical and processing industries; also pumps and water meters, pump gears, bearing surfaces, etc. Its heat insulating characteristics, dimensional stability, and outdoor exposure resistance is also excellent. The plastic is obtained from pentaerythritol by preparing a chlorinated oxetane and polymerizing it to a polyether by means of opening the ring structure.

chlorinated polyethylene elastomer The moderate random chlorination of polyethylene suppresses crystallinity and yields CPE, a rubber-like material that can be crosslinked with organic peroxides. Also called CM. The chlorine (Cl) content is in the range of 36 to 42%, compared to 56.8% for PVC. Such rubber has good heat, oil, and ozone resistance. It is also used as a plasticizer for PVC.

chlorinated polyethylene plastic Thermoplastic CPEs are amorphous or crystalline providing a wide range of properties.

They go from soft and elastomeric to hard. Substitution of chlorine (Cl) atoms for some hydrogen (H) atoms in the polyethylene chain affects crystallinity (to improve fire and oil resistance, etc.). These plastics have inherent oxygen, ozone, and weather resistance, resistance to chemical extraction and plasticizer volatility; exceptional high tear strength and heat/aging, excellent oil and chemical resistance, etc.

chlorinated polyvinyl chloride CPVC is a plastic produced by the post-chlorination of PVC. Adding more chlorine raises the glass transition of CPVC at 115 to 135°C (239 to 275°F) and the resultant heat deflection under load from that of PVC at 70°C (158°F) to a level of 82 to 102°C (180 to 219°F), depending on formation. CPVC has improved resistance to combustion and smoke generation, with higher tensile strength and modulus while maintaining all the good properties that rigid PVC possesses. Traditional uses are hot and cold water distribution piping and fittings and industrial chemical liquid handling pipe, fittings, valves, and other different applications.

chlorinated solvent A group, different from the hydrocarbons. They will dissolve oil and fat, not ordinarily dissolved by aromatics. Common chlorinated solvents are carbon tetrachloride, methylene chloride, ethylene dichloride, and trichloro-ethylene.

chlorine Highest volume chemical produced in the U.S. Nonmetallic halogen element of atomic number 17, group 7A of the Periodic Table. It is dense, greenish-yellow, diatomic gas, noncombustible but supports combustion (oxidizing agent), pungent, has a very irritating odor, and hence can be hazardous if not properly handled. Liquid is clear. Used to produce PVC and many other plastics.

chlorobutyl rubber ▷ **polyisobutylene, butyl rubber**

chlorofluorocarbon CFCs are a family of inert, nontoxic, nonflammable, and easily produced liquified chemicals principally used in refrigeration, air conditioning, packaging, and insulation or as solvents and aerosol propellants. The plastics industry has been phasing out CFCs, once widely used in producing foam products. CFC's chlorine components reportedly destroy ozone in the upper atmosphere. A targeted world complete phase-out of CFCs by the turn of the century was among the amendments to the Montreal protocol approved unanimously by 93 nations at a June 1989 meeting in London. Participating nations also agreed to use hydrochlorofluorocarbons (HCFCs) only where other alternatives are not feasible. A phase-out for HCFCs is planned for no later than 2040. The alternative HCFCs are 98% less ozone depleting than CFCs.

Many things taken for granted today (a safe and varied food supply, comfortable and energy-efficient homes, cars and workplaces) would not be possible without CFCs. Despite these benefits, what we now know about the role of CFCs in depleting stratospheric ozone makes it clear that CFC emissions must be eliminated. The plastics industry worldwide has taken action. Results as of 1989 in the U.S.: (1) Fully halogenated CFCs were eliminated in polystyrene foam food packaging and containers. Substitute blowing agents now used are either no threat to the ozone or are a 95% improvement over fully halogenated CFCs. (2) Foam cups now are 100% CFC-free. Less than 10% of foam cups and only 35% of foam food containers are made with CFCs. (3) Use of CFCs in extruded polystyrene insulation has been cut by 50%, with the goal by major producers to eliminate all CFCs at this time. (4) The goal to eliminate all CFCs in flexible polyurethane foam is set for 1994. Conversion to substitutes has already been occurring. (5) Packaging is the first segment of the polyurethane industry expected to phase out CFCs. Use already has been cut significantly. ▷ **ozone** and **propellant**

chlorofluorocarbon plastic Plastics made with monomers composed of chlorine, fluorine, and carbon only.

chlorofluorohydrocarbon plastic Plastics made from monomers composed of chlorine, fluorine, hydrogen, and carbon only.

chloroprene plastic ▷ **neoprene**

chlorosulfonated polyethylene elastomer CSPE (or CSM) corresponds to the moderate random chlorination chlorine (Cl) and the incorporation of infrequent chlorosulfonic groups (SO_2Cl) as preferred crosslinking sites. It has excellent weather resistance even in light colors; good resistance to ozone, heat, chemicals, and solvents; good electrical properties; low gas permeability for a rubber; and good adhesion to substrates. Use includes hoses, roll covers, tank liners, wire and cable covers, footware, and building products.

chlorosulfonated polyethylene plastic CSM (or CSPE) is a thermoset elastomer that has excellent combinations of properties that include total resistance to ozone; excellent resistance to abrasion, weather, heat, flame, oxidizing chemical, crack growth, and dielectric properties; low moisture absorption; resistance to oil similar to neoprene; and low temperature flexibility is fair at −40°C (−40°F). Can be made into a wide range of colors because carbon black is not required for reinforcement (as usually required in high performance elastomers).

chlorotrifluoroethylene ▷ **polychlorotrifluorethylene**

choked neck ▷ **container, choked neck**

choker bar ▷ **die, restrictor bar**

chopped glass strands In contrast to continuous glass filaments, chopped glass strands are cut to lengths of 5 to 35 cm after leaving the spinneret by means of a steam or compressed air jet during its manufacture. Continuous filaments are also chopped (cut) and used as reinforcements in plastics.

chopper Chopper guns, long cutters, roving cutters cut glass fibers into strands and shorter fibers to be used as reinforcements in plastics (preform, spray, etc.).

chromatic aberration In resinography, a defect in a lens or lens system resulting in differential focal lengths for radiation of different wavelengths. The dispersive power of a single positive lens focuses light from the blue end of the spectrum at a shorter distance than from the red end. An image produced by such a lens shows color fringes around the border of the image.

chromatography A technique for separating a sample material into constituent components and then measuring or identifying the compounds by other methods. The components to be separated are distributed between two mutually immiscible phases. The heart of any chromatography is the stationary phase, which is sometimes a solid (such as clay, gel, or paper) but is most commonly a liquid. The stationary phase is attached to a support, a solid inert material. The sample, often in vapor form or dissolved in a solvent, is moved across or through the stationary phase. It is pushed along by a liquid or gas which is the mobile phase. As the mobile phase moves through the stationary phase, the sample components undergo a large number of exchanges (partitions). The differences in the chemical and physical properties of the components are used to bring about the separation and control the rate of movement which is referred to as migration of components. When a sample component emerges from the end of the equipment, it is said to have been eluted. Separation is obtained when one component is retarded sufficiently to prevent overlap with the peak of an adjacent neighbor. ▷ **gas chromatography; gel chromatography; ion chromatography; liquid chromatography; thermal analysis**

chromium Hard, brittle, semi-gray metal. Cr is very important and extensively used in the metal working industry, alloying, and plating element on plastics. Important as a metal substrate/plating for corrosion resistance; protective coating for molds, dies, tool cavities, etc. It is only available and mined in the former U.S.S.R., South Africa, Zimbabwe, Philippines, Turkey, and Cuba.

chromium plating An electrolytic process that deposits a hard film of chromium metal principally onto working surfaces of other metals where resistance to corrosion, abrasion, and/or erosion is needed. Other uses include plating plastics that include aesthetic advantages.

chronology See *Plastics Chronology* on p. xxxvii.

chronotherapeutic In the medical community it is the timing of treatments to take advantage of biological cycles. Medical body implant formulations are used in materials such as certain plastics to distribute the medication in controlled biological rhythms; release of the drug is controlled rather than by using pills.

chrysotile ▷ **asbestos**

cine-radiography The production of a series of radiographs that can be viewed rapidly in sequence, thus creating an illusion of continuity.

circuit **1.** One complete traverse of the fiber feed mechanism of a filament winding machine. **2.** Electrical circuit pattern.

circuit board ▷ **printed circuit**

circular bend Simultaneous, multidirectional deformation of a fabric in which one face of a flat specimen becomes concave and the other becomes convex.

civilization and materials Materials have always been closely associated with human progress. This is because the human species makes things such as clothing, homes, vehicles, electronic devices, etc. All these products, of course, have to be made of the appropriate materials, with the required properties, in the specified shapes, and often with a desired appearance. Over time (many centuries, going back to the cave people), improvements in materials have occurred and it has been possible to make more sophisticated products. Plastics have definitely made a major contribution to the progress of civilization and materials.

civil justice ▷ **forensic science and plastic**

clad Surface sheathed.

cladding Applying a plastic coating on different materials such as plastics, metals, aluminum, etc. Purpose is to improve specific properties of the base material. Properties obtained, such as abrasive and corrosion resistance, color, and so on, depend on the plastic used and methods of processing.

clamping Different fabricating methods use devices or systems that provide pressure to molds or dies such as injection molding, blow molding, compression molding, reaction injection molding, etc. The clamping unit is that portion of an injection molding machine in which the mold is mounted. It provides the motion and force to open and close the mold and to hold the mold closed during plastic injection. When the mold is closed in a horizontal direction, the clamp is referred to as a horizontal clamp. When closed in a vertical direction, the clamp is referred to as a vertical clamp. This unit can also provide other features necessary for the effective functioning of the complete molding operation. In blow molding, clamping units provide a great variety of movement and action, particularly in large BM machines. Controls, such as proportional valves in hydraulic clamping systems, permit machine operation to run more smoothly and more exactly to allow a wide variety of action in the mold attached to the platens. Accurate control of the closing speed is essential: the delayed closure action in the final phase of mold closing determines pinch-off weld formation and the reproducibility of this delayed closure phase ensures the uniformity of extruded BM parts.

clamping area The largest rated molding area the machine can hold closed under full molding pressure.

clamping capacity ▷ **injection molding clamping tonnage and mold size**

clamping, close low pressure A provision in the machine to lower the clamp closing force during the clamp closing cycle. The lower clamp forces minimize the danger of mold damage caused by parts caught between the mold faces. Provisions are also made for parting mold faces at a timed interval in case of an obstruction.

clamping, close preposition, ejector mechanism A provision in the machine circuit to allow the clamp to fully open and then close to a predetermined position. It is generally used to allow the mold ejector (knockout) mechanism to retract so that inserts can be placed in the mold.

clamping, close slow down A provision in the machine designed to slow down the moving platen for an adjustable distance before the mold faces come in contact.

clamping, close stroke interruption A complete stop of the clamp closing stroke to allow an auxiliary operation(s) before completion of the closing stroke.

clamping daylight The distance, in the open position, between the moving and the fixed platens of a press. In the case of a multiplaten press, daylight is the distance between adjacent platens. Daylight provides space for mold insertion and removal of the molded part from the mold that is attached to the platens. As shown in the Fig., basically there is a maximum and minimum open distance; when in the closed position, platens have a maximum and minimum shut distance.

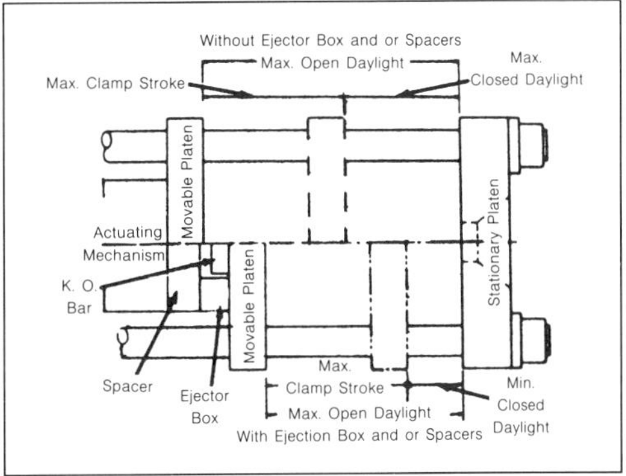

Schematic of a clamping daylight divided in half to show maximum and minimum positions of platens.

clamping, daylight closed maximum That distance between the stationary platen and the moving platen when the actuating mechanism is fully extended without ejector box and/or spacers.

clamping, daylight closed minimum That distance between the stationary platen and the moving platen when the actuating mechanism is fully extended with standard ejector box and/or spacers.

clamping, daylight closed or minimum mold thickness The distance between the stationary platen and the moving platen when the actuating mechanism is fully extended with or without ejector box and/or spacers. Minimum mold thickness will vary, depending upon the size and kind of ejector boxes and/or spacers used.

clamping, daylight open maximum The maximum distance that can be obtained between the stationary platen and the moving platen when the actuating mechanism is fully retracted without the ejector box and/or spacers.

clamping, ejector ▷ **mold ejection** and **clamping close preposition**

clamping, electric A press in which the molding forces are created by electrical drive systems instead of the usual hydraulic systems.

clamping force (pressure) The pressure that is applied via platens to the mold to keep it closed. It opposes the melt fluid pressure of the compressed plastic material within the mold cavity(s) and applicable cold setting runner(s) system; or in other systems such as blow molding, the pressure exerted on the mold halves during the formation of the plastic blown product. Usually this force is expressed in tons.

clamping force full A clamping unit actuated by a mechanism (hydraulic and/or electrical system) is connected directly to the moving platen. This pressure is used to open and close the mold, and to provide the clamping force to hold the mold closed during injection of the plastic melt.

clamping force measured Different methods are used to measure clamping force such as (1) pressure transducer between platens (the usual), (2) sum of the tie bar forces, (3) force in a toggle mechanical system, and (4) determined from the oil pressure in hydraulic systems and/or electrical power that use electrical drive systems. Measurements in the tie bars offer the advantage of monitoring the forces in the individual tie bars. Thus, uneven loads or even overloading of individual tie bars caused by unbalanced or worn molds (and other problems) can be identified quickly to avoid major problems. The advantages of force measurement in tie bars have been known and used for many decades worldwide. Various measurement systems have been in use to meet different requirements: (1) strain sensors mounted with straps on bars, (2) force measuring rings/washers under the tie bar nuts, and (3) strain sensors in a central bore in the tie bar which work with piezoelectric, capacitive, inductive, or resistance measuring systems. Mounted strain sensors have limitations because they could be subjected to rough conditions during the press operations. Rings can be expensive and cause false readings. These systems can be used, with care, but the usual advantage is with measurements in the tie bars.

clamping, hydraulic Consists basically of a high speed, variable hydraulic pump, valving, a fast acting cylinder, and a high pressure cylinder. Cylinders can be single (see Fig) or combination units such as replacing the single large cylinder with basically four energy saving short-stroke cylinders mounted on the ends of the tie bars, either on the moving or stationary platen.

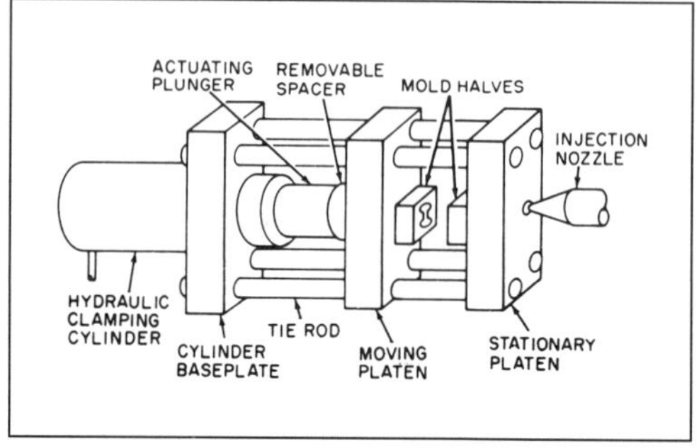

Hydraulic clamp schematic.

clamping hydraulic leak control ▷ **injection molding hydraulic leak control**

clamping hydraulic maintenance ▷ **hydraulic fluid maintenance procedures**

clamping hydroelectric Identifies a system that uses a combination of hydraulic and electrical systems to take advantage of reduced floor space, reduced energy consumption, faster operation, etc.

clamping hydromechanical A press in which the molding forces are created partly by a mechanical system (such as a toggle) and partly by a hydraulic system.

clamping mold slow breakaway A provision designed to provide slow platen movement for an adjustable distance during the initial opening of the mold.

clamping opening force The maximum force that a machine will exert to initiate the opening of the mold.

clamping open slow down A provision designed to slow down the moving platen for an adjustable distance before it reaches its maximum open position. This sequence is often employed to reduce the effect of knockout impact when mechanical KOs are used. Sometimes referred to as ejector or clamp open cushion.

clamping open stroke interruption A complete stop of the clamp opening stroke to allow an auxiliary operation(s) before completion of the opening stroke.

clamping platen The mounting plates of a press to which the entire mold assembly is fastened via bolts, mechanical devices, snap fits, and/or others.

clamping platen, floating The floating platen is the moveable platen(s) between the stationary platen and normal actuated/moveable platen, resulting in two (or more) daylight openings where two (or more) molds can be used. This multiple platen concept has been used since the beginning of this century in laminating, compression molding, injection molding, etc.

clamping platen, moving That member of the clamping unit which is moved toward a stationary member. The moving section of the mold is bolted to this moving platen. This member usually includes the ejector (knockout) holes and mold mounting pattern of bolts or "T" slots. A standard pattern is recommended by SPI.

clamping platen speed The closing and opening speed of platen movement in in./s (cm/s).

clamping platen, stationary The fixed member on which the stationary section of the mold is fastened (bolted, etc.). This member usually includes a mold mounting pattern of bolt holes or "T" slots; standard pattern recommended by SPI. This stationary platen usually includes provisions for locating the mold on the plate (injection, transfer, etc. machines) and aligning the sprue bushing of the mold with the nozzle of the melting unit. Normally, this platen does not move during the molding operation.

clamping preclose Closing the mold to some point near the closed position before final closing. Permits bumping, improved parison pinch areas (blow molding), safety measure.

clamping pressure ▷ **clamping force (pressure)**

clamping, rotary ▷ **rotary press**

clamping, shuttle A clamp system in which molds (usually two, but can be more) are moved so that one mold is in position to receive material (injection, blow molding, compression, etc.) and then moves permitting other mold to receive material with this cycle repeating. The effect is a reduced molding cycle.

clamping stroke, maximum The maximum distance which the opening and closing mechanism can traverse a platen. This may usually be adjusted to shorter travel to meet mold or molding requirements.

clamping tie rod Those members of the clamping unit which join and align the stationary platen with the clamping force system and which serve as the tension members of the clamp when it is holding the mold closed. These two, three, but usually four tie bars provide structural rigidity to the clamping mechanism. The moveable platen rides on the tie bars. During mold clamp-up, the tie bars resist the strain created by the unit's pressure/force action that is clamping the moveable platen against the stationary mold. Also called strain rods.

clamping tie rod distance The distance between tie rods is a measure that determines the maximum width of a mold that can be mounted, either horizontally or vertically, or both. There are systems where a tie rod is retractable so that molds can be used that would cover the complete platen surfaces, less tie rods.

clamping, toggle A mechanism which exerts pressure developed by the application of force on a knee joint; used as a method of closing presses and applying pressure at the same time. The toggle mechanism increases the working applied force. It is directly connected to the moving platen (see Fig. on p. 114). A hydraulic and/or electrical system provides the initial force.

clamping tonnage and mold size Machines are rated in tonnage and maximum mold dimensions. ▷ **molding pressure required**

clamshell molding ▷ **thermoforming, clamshell**

clarifier An additive that increases the transparency of a material.

clarity, medical device packaging ▷ **medical device packaging, clarity**

classified by UL ▷ **Underwriters' Laboratory classified product**

classifying plastic ▷ **plastic classification ASTM D 4000**

clay filler Natural occurring sediments rich in hydrated silicates of aluminum, predominating in particles of colloidal or near colloidal size (china clay, kaolin, etc.). Used extensively in thermoset and thermoplastic materials to reduce cost, change melt viscosity, and/or others.

cleaning ▷ **ultrasonic cleaning**

clearance A controlled distance by which one part of a unit is kept separated from another part by a specified distance (tolerance).

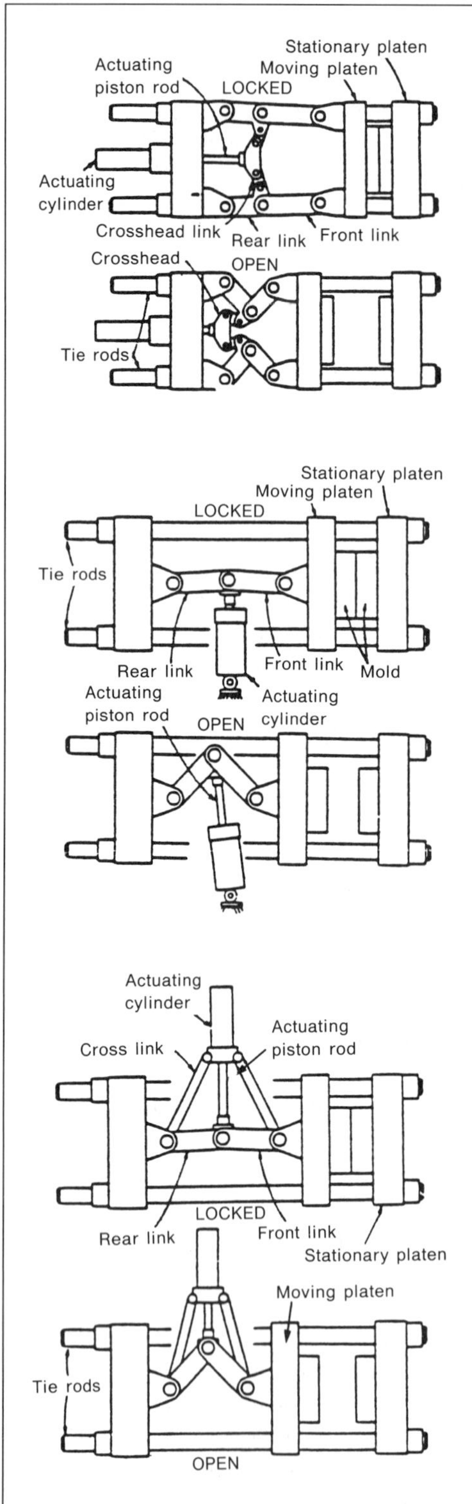

Examples of different toggle mechanical clamp systems.

clearance fit A limit of size so prescribed that a clearance always results when mating parts are assembled.

cleavage Breakage of covalent chemical bonds.

clogging For geotextiles, the condition where soil particles move into and are retained in the openings of a fabric, thereby reducing hydraulic conductivity.

close cell ▷ **foamed closed cell**

closure **1.** Any structure or device which is designated to close off the opening of a container and prevent loss of its contents. **2.** In filament winding, the complete coverage of mandrel with one layer (two plies) of fiber. When the last tape circuit that completes mandrel coverage is laid down adjacent to the first without gaps or overlaps, the wind pattern is said to have closed. **3.** In grouting, closure refers to achieving the desired reduction in grout take by splitting the hole spacing. If closure is being achieved, there will be a progressive decrease in grout take as primary, secondary, tertiary, and quaterary holes are grouted. **4.** A closure or joint designed so that a sealing action is obtained by compressing elastomeric components. Also called a compression joint.

closure error The algebraic sum of pitch errors of a predetermined number of functional patterns. Also called runout and cumulative pitch error.

closure strip An asphalt or rubber compounded preformed filler strip having the same shape and pitch as the asbestos-cement corrugated product and used to close openings in the corrugated sheets at window beads, eaves, lower edge of siding, and similar places.

cloth ▷ **woven fabric** and **nonwoven fabric**

cloud point In condensation polymerization, the temperature at which the first turbidity appears, caused by water separation when a reaction mixture occurs.

coagulant A substance which (1) initiates the formation of relatively large particles in a finely divided suspension, or (2) assists in gel formation; result is accelerated settling of the particles or their deposition on a substrate.

coagulation Physical or chemical change inducing transition from a fluid to a semi-solid or gel-like state.

coalesce To combine into one body or to grow together.

coated fabric Desirable properties of a fabric can be supplemented by coating it with a plastic. The fabric provides tensile, tear, and elongation control; reduces porosity; protects the fabric from chemical and physical environment; and can provide decorative effects. Fibers include cotton, rayon, polyester, polypropylene, nylon, and glass. The properties of the substrate are determined by the fiber properties and fabric construction. In the U.S., about 70% coated is woven, 20% nonwoven, and 10% knitted.

In woven and knitted fabrics, the yarns almost always need to be sized or lubricated. However, prior to coating they are removed; also may require finishes. The plastic portion of the coating material provides many of the required properties. Coating materials include polyvinyl chloride, polyurethane, and elastomers. Processing is governed by the properties of the substrate and the plastic; viscosity of plastics must permit flow around the yarn or fiber surface. In calendering or extrusion, the compound is fluidized by pressure and heat; casting, viscosity is reduced by solution or dispersion.

Wall covering, upholstery, and apparel are examples of decorative coated fabrics. Inks are applied with one or more gravure printers to correct color or add patterns. Relief patterns are obtained by applying heat and pressure with embossing rolls. The outermost layer has a slip finish, a hard, thin layer which confers a final gloss adjustment, imparts the right feel to the product, and protects the ink coat from abrasion.

coating Plastics are applied as coatings for functional, protective, decorative, and many other reasons. Most coating methods can be used for a wide range of base materials and coating compositions; however, the best selection is based on product requirements. Some coating systems can be grouped together such as powder methods that include electrostatic, spray coating, flame coating, and fluidized bed coating. There are special coating methods, such as in-mold coating used in compression, transfer, injection, reaction injection, resin transfer, and so on. See the following coating methods:

air knife
antifouling
calender
cast
centrifugal
curtain
decorating
dip
electrocoating
electrodeposition
electron beam
electrophoretic deposition
electroplating
electrostatic spray
emulsion
Engel
engraved roll
extruder
film
flame spray
flocking
flood
flow
fluidized
gravure
Heisler
in-mold
intumescent
ion-beam
kiss-roll
knife
offset
paint
plasma polymerization
powder
printing
radiation
reverse-roll
roller
rotational
silver spray
sinter
solution
spray
spread
sputtered
vacuum

▷ **metallizing plastic; encapsulation; microencapsulation coating; polyester, water-soluble plastic**

coating, air knife A knife coating technique especially suitable for thin coatings on plastics, metals, paper, etc. and as an adhesive film, wherein a high-pressure jet of air is forced through orifices in the knife under controlled conditions resulting in the required coating thickness. ▷ **extruder film** and **extruder sheet roll deflection**

coating bottle with glass Coating plastic bottle with glass. ▷ **barrier, glass coating**

coating, centrifugal or rotational Coating methods whereby powder is placed or metered into the inside of a rotating object and fused (solidified). As an example, linings can be applied to drums or pipes in this manner. The external surface of pipe and similar objects can be coated by feeding powder from a feed roll or vibrator-type feeder while the preheated part is being rotated. Flat sheets or plates can also be coated on a continuous conveyer with this type of feeding equipment, possibly using a chill roll-nip roll to smooth the coating.

coating, conformal ▷ **encapsulation**

coating metal fiber ▷ **metallic fiber**

coating, neck-in ▷ **extruder coating, neck-in**

coating, recreational surface ▷ **recreational surface**

coating reinforced concrete rod ▷ **concrete reinforced composite**

coating, waterborne system Vehicles or solutions in which at least 80% of the liquid is water are classified as aqueous systems. There are three categories: those in which the binder is soluble in water, those in which it is colloidally dispersed, and those in which it is emulsified to form a latex. Water-soluble binders are low molecular weight plastics (5,000–10,000). Colloidal-dispersion plastics have 10,000–50,000, and emulsion plastics have 10^6 or more. The emulsion types have the best film properties and resistance to water. The water-soluble binders are the poorest in these respects, and the colloidally dispersed plastics are intermediate. ▷ **organosol** and **nonaqueous dispersions**

coating weight The weight of coating per unit area. In the U.S. usually per ream, i.e., 500 sheets 24 in. × 36 in. or 3,000 ft^2 (61 cm × 91 cm or 279 m^2), but sometimes only 1,000 ft^2 (93 m^2).

cocatalyst Chemicals which themselves are rather weak catalysts, but which greatly increase the activity of a given catalyst; also called promoters.

co-curing The act of curing a reinforced plastic (composite) and simultaneously bonding it to some other prepared surface, or curing together an inner and outer tube of similar or dissimilar fiber-plastic combinations after each has been wound or wrapped separately. ▷ **secondary bonding**

coefficient of cornering The ratio of cornering force to the vertical load.

coefficient of cubical expansion ▷ **coefficient of linear thermal expansion**

coefficient of elasticity The reciprocal of Young's modulus in a tension test. ▷ **compliance** and **modulus of elasticity**

coefficient of expansion The fractional change in length or volume of a material for a unit change in temperature. ▷ **coefficient of linear thermal expansion** and **coefficient of thermal expansion**

coefficient of friction Resistance to sliding or rolling of surfaces of solid bodies (products) in contact with each other is stated as k = F/W in which F is the force required to move one surface over another and W is the weight pressing the surfaces together. ▷ **friction**

coefficient of gas permeability The volume of a gas flowing normal to two parallel surfaces at a unit distance apart (thickness), under steady-state conditions, through a unit area under a unit pressure differential at a stated test temperature. An accepted unit is 1 cm^3 (at standard conditions)/s · cm^2 · cm Hg/cm of thickness at the stated temperature of the test (generally 23°C).

coefficient of linear thermal expansion The change in unit of length (or volume) accompanying a unit change of temperature. The Table shows examples of CLTE for plastics and other materials. The Figure on p. 117 provides contraction at low temperature. CLTE change can be related to shrinkage. As an example, once a mold has been filled and the plastic

Coefficients of linear thermal expansion (CLTE) for plastics and other materials.[1]

Material	in./in./°F × 10^{-5}	(cm/cm/°C × 10^{-5})
Fused quartz	0.02	(0.036)
Liquid crystal-GR	0.3	(0.54)
TS polyester-GR	0.3	(0.54)
Phenolic-GR	0.4	(0.72)
Silicone-GR	0.4	(0.72)
Pine wood	0.4	(0.72)
Glass	0.4	(0.72)
DAP-GR	0.5	(0.9)
Epoxy-GR	0.6	(1.08)
Nylon-GR	0.6	(1.08)
Steel	0.6	(1.08)
Concrete	0.8	(1.44)
Copper	0.9	(1.62)
Bronze	1.0	(1.8)
Brass	1.0	(1.8)
PPO-GR	1.2	(2.2)
Aluminum	1.2	(2.2)
PC-GR	1.3	(2.3)
TP polyester	1.3	(2.3)
Polyimide	1.3	(2.3)
Magnesium	1.4	(2.5)
ABS-GR	1.6	(2.9)
Zinc	1.7	(3.1)
PS/HI	1.8	(3.2)
PP-GR	1.8	(3.2)
PPS-GR	2.0	(3.6)
Acetal-GR	2.2	(4.0)
Zinc	2.2	(4.0)
PVC/rigid	2.7	(4.9)
Acrylic	2.8	(5.0)
TS polyester	3.0	(5.4)
Polysulfone	3.0	(5.4)
Epoxy	3.0	(5.4)
Polycarbonate	3.6	(6.5)
Phenolic	3.8	(6.8)
ABS	4.0	(7.2)
Nylon	4.5	(8.1)
Acetal	4.8	(8.6)
Polypropylene	4.8	(8.6)
TP polyurethane	5.6	(10.1)
Polyethylene/LD	5.6	(10.1)
Fluorocarbon	5.6	(10.1)
Epoxy	6.0	(10.8)
Polyethylene/HD	6.1	(11.0)
TPX	6.5	(11.7)
TP Polyester	6.9	(12.4)

[1] These are only typical values to account for many different grades, molding conditions, producer shapes, wall thicknesses, and other variants. The plastics presented are basically unfilled or reinforced. GR refers to glass-fiber-reinforced compounds that usually have 10 to 40 percent, by weight, reinforcement. Other reinforcements, particularly graphite, and different fillers can result in significantly different CLTES.
CLTES on specific plastics or compounds are available from material suppliers. Then apply those data or your derived data to the design.

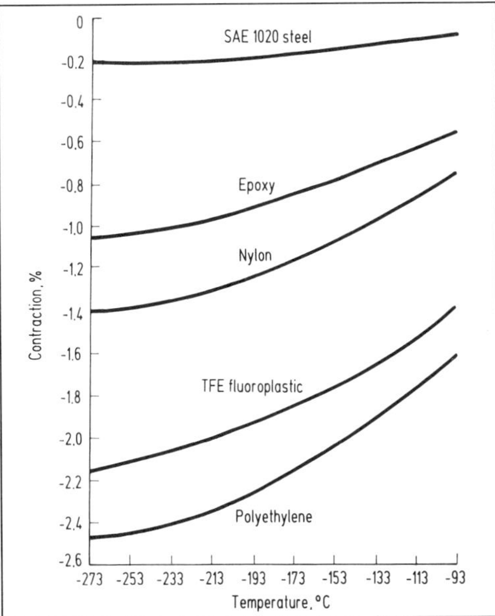

An example at low temperatures of thermal contraction in unfilled plastic and steel. With filled, particularly certain reinforced thermoset plastics, dimensional change can be significantly reduced or even be zero. When subjected to increased heat, certain graphite filled compounds will shrink rather than expand (as expected).

proceeds to cool, decreasing thermal vibration produces decreasing free volume. The practical result is mold shrinkage, which must be compensated for by foresight in mold design. Since the ends of plastic molecules have the greatest mobility, they play a major role in free volume and therefore in shrinkage. Increasing molecular weight decreases the concentration of end groups, and therefore the shrinkage during curing.

If the plastic part is free to expand and contract, then its thermal expansion property is usually of little significance. However, if it is attached to another material having a lower CLTE, then movement of the part will be restricted. Temperature change will then result in the development of thermal stresses in the part. The magnitude of the stresses will depend on the temperature change, method of attachment and relative expansion and modulus characteristics of the two materials at the exposed heat.

Expansion or contraction can be controlled in the plastic by orientation, cross-linking, adding fillers or reinforcements, etc. With certain additives the CLTE value could be zero or near zero. As an example, with graphite filler during a temperature rise, the plastic contracts rather than expands. As shown in the Table, reinforced plastics with glass fiber reinforcements can be used to match those of metal and other materials. In fact, TSs are compounded to have very little or no change.

In a TS, the ease or difficulty of thermal expansion is dictated for the most part by the degree of cross-linking, as well as the overall stiffness of the units between cross-links. Less flexible units are also more resistant to thermal expansion. Influences such as secondary bonds have much less effect on the thermal expansion of TSs.

Any cross-linking has a substantial effect on TPs. With the amorphous type, expansion is reduced. In a crystalline TP, however, the decreased expansion due to cross-linking may be partially offset by loss of crystallinity.

coefficient of optical stress Stress-optical coefficient (SOC) is the constant of proportionality between the stress in a material and the birefringence resulting from the molecular orientation produced, as expressed in the stress-optical law.

coefficient of permeability The permeability coefficient of a barrier material to a vapor is defined as the cubic centimeters of vapor at STP (standard temperature and pressure) permeating through a barrier material of unit area (cm^2) and unit thickness (cm) under a partial pressure difference of one cm Hg per unit time (s), regardless of the mechanics used, thus CP is (ml at STP) (cm)/(cm^2) (s) (cm Hg). Since permeability coefficients in these units have values for most plastics in the range of 10^{-7} to 10^{-12}, many larger number units have been used in practical application studies. The most common of these is in units of g · mil/m^2 · 24 h · atm. The various units may readily be converted from one to another. In the case of permeability to liquids or vapors, the vapor pressure at ambient temperature is often omitted; however, the vapor pressure is necessary to convert the values to the proper units as listed above.

Since permeability coefficients are often highly temperature dependent, values should be quoted at a given temperature. With organic vapors, and often with water vapor, the permeability coefficients are dependent on the vapor pressures themselves, and it is necessary to specify the exact conditions of measurement. In general, the permeability coefficient at a given temperature may be: (1) almost constant for all vapors and independent of pressure (capillary flow or pinhole), (2) a constant for a particular vapor and independent of pressure (the ideal activated diffusion process), and (3) a coefficient which varies with vapor pressure (nonideal activated diffusion process).

coefficient of scatter The rate of increase of reflectance with thickness (weight per unit area) at infinitesimal thickness of material over an ideally black box.

coefficient of static The ratio of the force resisting initial motion of the surface.

coefficient of thermal conductivity The amount of heat that passes through a unit cube of material in a given time when difference in temperature of two faces is one degree; identified as the K factor. ▷**thermal conductivity**

coefficient of thermal expansion ▷**coefficient of linear thermal expansion**

coefficient of viscosity ▷**viscosity coefficient**

coercive field ▷**electrical coercive field**

Examples of common commercial coextruded composite structures.

Applications	Properties	Combination of Layers					
		1 Inside	2	3 Middle	4	5	6 Outside
Detergents Cosmetics Motor oil	Surface gloss	HDPE	—	—	—	—	LDPE
	Clear-stripe	HDPE LDPE Stripe	—	—	—	—	—
Insecticides Pesticides Chemicals	Resistant to aggressive substances	PA	—	Bonding agent	—	—	PE Filler Regrind Color
Milk	UV-protection	HDPE White	—	HDPE Black	—	—	HDPE White
Cosmetics Hand lotions Hair cosmetics Pharmaceuticals Toothpaste Skin oils Medicine Infusions	Squeezable Printable Scratch-resistant Aroma-barrier O_2 barrier	HDPE LDPE PP Regrind Color	—	Bonding agent	—	—	PA EVAL
Food Soy sauce Ketchup Beverages Milk Liquor Handleware	Short shelf life; hot fill	PP	—	Bonding agent	—	—	PA EVAL
	Transparent Hot fill Gas barrier Rigid	PC	—	EVAL PET	—	—	PC
Food Ketchup Baby food Mayonnaise Edible oil Salad dressing Spaghetti sauce Fruit juice Soup concentrate	Squeezable Transparent (5) Translucent (6) Long shelf life Hot fill Gas barrier Moisture barrier	PP	Bonding agent	EVAL PET	Bonding agent	(Regrind)	PP
Sterilized milk Carbonated drinks Liquor Tea Coffee Peanut butter Handleware	Rigid Returnable Gas barrier (N_2, O_2, CO_2) Moisture barrier Transparent	PC PP	Bonding agent	EVAL PET PETG PAN PVDC	Bonding agent	(Regrind)	PC

coextrusion Coextrusion provides composite multiple layers—usually using one or more extruders with melts going through one die—that are bonded together. This technique permits using melt heat to bond the various plastics (see Tables here and opposite) or using the center layer as an adhesive. Coextrusion is an economical competitor to conventional laminating processes by virtue of reduced materials handling costs, raw materials costs, and machine-time cost. Pinholing is also reduced with coextrusion, even when it uses one extruder and divides the melt into at least a two-layer structure. Other gains include elimination or reduction of delamination and air entrapment. A number of techniques are available; basically three exist, namely feedblock, multiple manifold, and a combination of these two (see Table below).

Examples of compatibility between plastics for coextrusion.[1]

	LDPE	HDPE	PP	Ionomer	Nylon	EVA
LDPE	3	3	2	3	1	3
HDPE	3	3	2	3	1	3
PP	2	2	3	2	1	3
Ionomer	3	3	2	3	3	3
Nylon	1	1	1	3	3	1
EVA	3	3	3	3	1	3

Code: (1) Layers easy to separate.
(2) Layers can be separated with moderate effort.
(3) Layers difficult to separate.

With the feedblock die, different melts are combined just upstream of the die, prior to entering the die via a special adapter. Laminar flow keeps the layers from mixing together so that the layup exits as an integral construction from the die.

A multiple manifold die involves the combination of melts within the die. Each inlet port leads to a separate manifold for the individual layers involved. The layers are combined at or close to the final land of the die, and they exist as an integral construction through a single lip. Although the multi-manifold die can be more costly than the feedblock type, it has the advantage of more precise control of individual layer thickness.

A third approach combines the feedblock and multi-manifold types, and provides further processing alternatives as the complexities of coextrusion increase. This approach has been used successfully in barrier sheet coextrusions where requirements preclude other alternatives. The feedblock is placed on the manifold or manifolds, permitting the combination of materials of similar flow characteristics in the feedblock while feeding dissimilar materials directly into the die.

coextrusion tie-layer When nonbonding layers are desired in a coextruded composite structure, a plastic tie-layer can be used. Choosing an adhesive layer is by no means a simple operation; there are many different types,

Comparison of feedblock and multiple manifold coextrusion dies.

Characteristic	Feedblock	Multi-manifold
Basic difference	Melt streams brought together outside die body (between extruder and die) and flow through the die as a composite.	Each melt stream has a separate manifold; each polymer spreads independent of others; they meet at die pre-land to die exit.
Cost	Lower.	Higher.
Operation	Simplest.	—
Number of layers	Not restricted; seven- and eight-layer systems are commercial.	Generally restricted to three or four layers.
Complexity	Simpler construction; no adjustments basically.	More complex.
Control flow	Contains adjustable matching inserts, no restrictor bar.	Has restrictor bar or flow dividers in each polymer channel; but with blown film dies, control is by individual extruder speed or gear boxes.
Layer uniformity	Individual layer thickness correction of ± 10 percent.	Restrictors and manifold can meet ± 5 percent.
Thin skins	Better on dies > 40 in.	Better on dies < 40 in.
Viscosity range	Usually limited to 2/1 or 3/1 viscosity range of materials.	Range usually much greater than 3/1.
Degradable core material	Usually better.	—
Heat sensitivity	More.	Less.
Bonding	Potentially better; layers are in contact longer in die.	—

with specific capabilities, with EVAs forming the bulk. Selection of a material is based on its providing good adhesion and surviving the process. For example, high melt strength in a blown film improves bubble stability. At temperatures above 238°C (460°F), EVAs could suffer from gel formation and decomposition. High melt strength also can help in cast extrusion and thermoforming processes, and the melt draw is important in coextrusion of cast film/sheet or a coating. Good melt draw is required to run higher takeup speeds and/or thinner adhesive layers without causing flow-distribution or edge-weave problems. Effects such as "neck-in" and "edge bead" are also minimized by choosing adhesives with a good draw.

Various processing conditions can require the tie plastic to fall into a particular melt index (MI) classification. MI is inversely related to molecular weight (MW); a high-MW adhesive will have a low MI. Most adhesives are available in a range of MIs to meet different requirements. The melt stability or flow is easily influenced by regrind. It is important that the regrind be compatible with the adhesive.

cohesion The propensity of a single substance to adhere to itself; the internal attraction of molecular particles toward each other; the force holding a single substance together.

cohesive failure ▷ **adhesive failure**

cohesive strength Intrinsic strength of an adhesive.

coiling ▷ **extruder take-off profile coiling**

coining Coining, also called injection stamping and more often injection-compression molding, is a variant of injection molding (see Fig. below). The essential difference lies in the manner in which the thermal contraction of the molding during cooling (shrinkage) is compensated. With conventional injection molding, the reduction in material volume in the cavity due to thermal contraction is compensated by forcing in more plastic melt during the pressure holding phase. By contrast with injection-compression molding, the melt is injected into a cavity that has a relatively short shot in a compression type mold (male plug fits into a female mold) rather than the usual flat surface

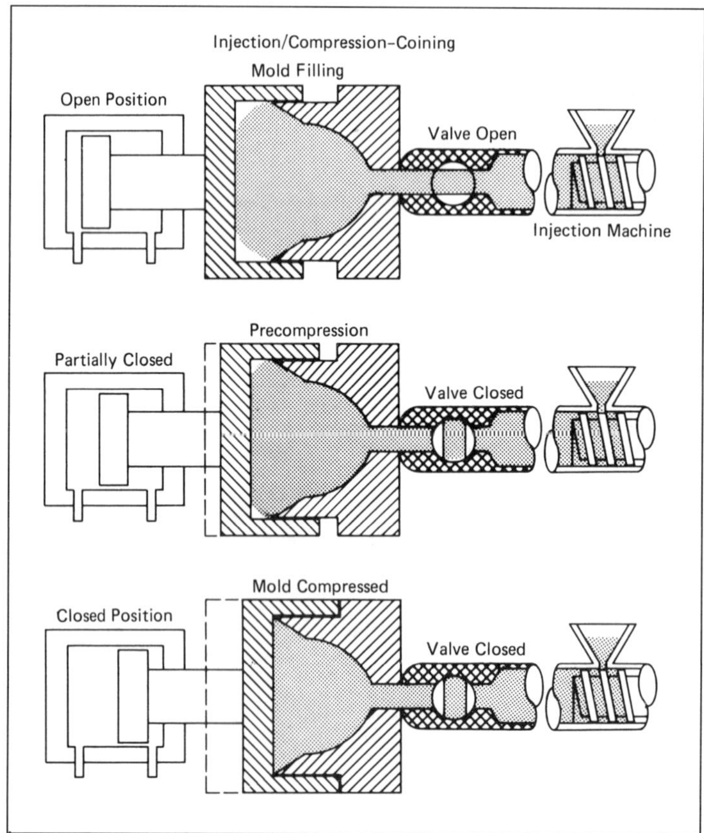

Schematic of the coining process, which combines injection molding and compression molding.

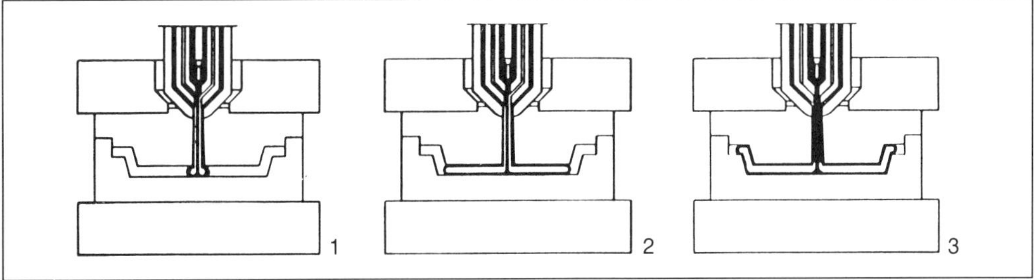

Coinjection three-channel system that simultaneously injects two different plastic melts. Courtesy of Battenfeld.

matching mold halves for injection molding. The melt injected into the cavity is literally stress-free; it works without a holding pressure phase and the transport of plastic melt which accompanies this action avoids stresses in the part, particularly in the gate area(s). The ICM process for thermoplastics has been used for different size parts, particularly for thick-walled parts with tight dimensional requirements, such as optical lenses. When melt enters the mold, it is not completely closed. Thus, the short shot melt literally flows unrestricted in the cavity and is basically stress-free. After injection is completed, the mold is closed, with pressure on the melt very uniform.

coining hinge It is possible to create hinges in some of the tougher engineering thermoplastics by coining techniques; also called cold-working. A molded or extruded part is placed in a fixture between two coining (shaped) bars. Pressure is applied to the bars, with or without heat, the part is compressed to the desired thickness elongating the plastic. Coining is effective only when the material is elongated beyond the tensile yield point. ▷ **hinge**

coinjected neck ▷ **blow molding coinjected neck**

coinjection Coinjection, like coextrusion, basically means that two or more different plastics are formed into a composite or laminated structure. These plastics could be the same except for some different property such as color. When different plastics are used, they must be compatible in that they provide proper adhesion (or use a tie-layer), melt at about the same temperature, etc. Two or more injection units are required, with each material having its own injection unit, operating simultaneously or in sequence. The plastics can be injected into specially designed molds that operate alone, or used in rotary, shuttle, etc. mold systems. The term coinjection can denote different products, such as sandwich construction, double-shot injection, multiple-shot injection, structural foam construction, two-color molding, inmolding, etc. The Fig. above is an example of three channel coinjection.

coinjection tie-layer ▷ **coextrusion tie-layer**

coin test ▷ **reinforced plastic tapping test**

coke **1.** Carbonaceous residue resulting from the pyrolysis of pitch. **2.** Abbreviation for Coca-Cola.

Coke PET bottles refilled Coca-Cola Co., Atlanta, launched 1.5 L refillable Coke bottles during 1990 in Germany. The introduction defined the shift of the European market to include refill as well as disposable bottles. Refill PET bottles were first introduced in 1989 in the Netherlands by Coca-Cola as well as Pepsi-Cola International.

coking Refinery recycling in high temperature; batch process (coker) units favored in refining heavy feedstock.

cold cure foam ▷ **foamed cold cure**

cold drawing Stretching process used to improve properties, such as tensile strength and modulus, of thermoplastic film, sheet, or filament by orientation of molecules. Also called cold stretching.

cold flow The distortion (via creep, strain relaxation, melt flow, etc.) that takes place in materials under continuous or noncontinuous load at temperatures within the working range of the material without a phase or chemical change.

cold forging ▷ **forging** and **cold forming**

cold forming A process of changing the shape of primarily a thermoplastic sheet or billet in the solid phase through plastic (permanent) deformation with the use of pressure dies (see Fig. on p. 122). The term implies that the deformation occurs with the material at room temperature. Its use, however, has been ex-

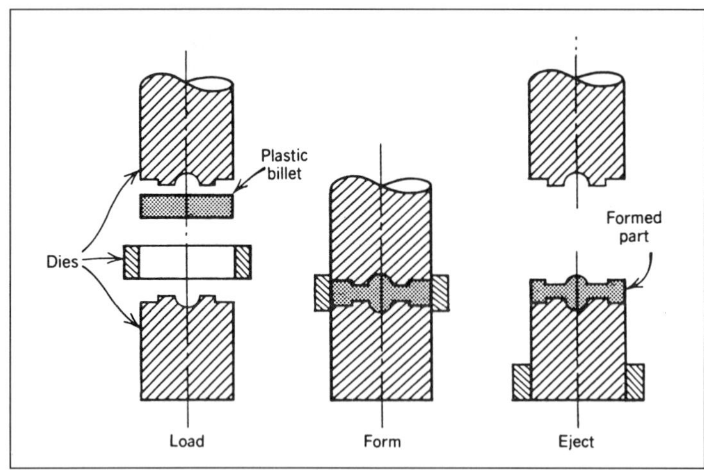

Cold forming process.

panded to include forming at higher temperature or warm forming, but much below the plastic melt temperature and lower than those used in thermoforming. Within this process there are special methods, such as solid phase pressure forming (SPPF), that use cold and warm forming as well as thermoforming.

Cold forming plastic techniques are basically the same as those used for metal forming. In fact, most metal forming techniques such as stamping, extrusion, forging, drawing, coining, rolling, etc. are used on plastics, usually thermoplastics. Thermosets such as those in the B-stage can be used. The main differences between metal and plastic forming are the time dependence of deformation and springback, or recovery, in thermoplastics. Not all TPs are cold formable, mainly because of their brittleness. Heat generation in work pieces during forming, owing to "plastic" working, can be significant, especially in forging. The resultant temperature rise can affect final properties. In contrast to metals and melt processed TPs, a cold formed TP part exhibits molecular orientation along principal strain directions. Mechanical properties, such as tensile strength and modulus, are enhanced in the direction of orientation, but reduced in the other direction. All cold formed materials exhibit some strain recovery or springback (reversion toward initial undeformed geometry). In TPs, this process depends on temperature, deformation history, and time (as opposed to time-independent elastic springback in metals). For any given forming temperature, holding the part in the deformed state for a given period (hold or dwell time) to allow for stress relaxation reduces the degree and rate of springback.

cold heading A process for forming plastic rods into rivets by uniformly loading the shaft end or projection in compression while holding and containing the shaft trunk. All thermoplastics can be cold headed, with acetal and nylon particularly suited and used.

cold parison ▷ **blow molding, two stage**

cold press molding A molding process in which inexpensive plastic male and female molds can be used with room temperature curing plastics to produce accurate parts. It includes molding material compounds into preforms (pills, billets, logs, etc.) which hold their shape and form during preheating and/or loading into the mold. Some plastics are warmed to facilitate preforming.

cold rubber, synthetic rubber ▷ **polybutadiene-styrene thermoplastic**

cold runner ▷ **mold runner**

cold setting adhesive A plastic adhesive capable of hardening at normal temperature; an adhesive that sets at temperatures below 20°C (68°F).

cold shot ▷ **extruder cold shot**

cold slug ▷ **mold cold slug**

cold stamping Process in which heated plastic sheet is stamped (formed) into relatively complex shapes in matching dies using stamping presses.

cold stretch A pulling operation with little or no heat, such as on extruded filaments which are oriented to increase tensile properties.

cold worked hinge ▷ **coining hinge**

cold working Any form of mechanical deformation processing carried out on a plastic below its crystallization temperature.

collapsible bottle ▷ **bottle, collapsible**

collapsible core ▷ **mold, collapsible core**

collapsible squeeze tube ▷ **tube, collapsible squeeze type**

collapsing frame ▷ **extruder blown film**

collet **1.** A rigid, lateral container for the mold-forming material. **2.** A dam or a restriction box. **3.** The drive wheel that pulls glass fibers from its bushing during manufacture; a forming tube is placed on the collet and a package of strand is wound up on the tube. **4.** A metal band, ferrule, collar, or flange, often used to hold a tool or work piece.

collimated Relative to rendering parallelism; applies to filament arrangement, light source, etc.

collimator In resinography, a device for controlling a beam of radiation such that its rays are as nearly parallel as possible.

colloidal A state of suspension in a liquid medium in which extremely small plastic particles are suspended and dispersed but not dissolved.

colloidal mill A device for preparing emulsions and reducing particle size, consisting of a high speed motor and a fixed or counter-rotating element in close proximity to the rotor. The fluid is conveyed continuously from a hopper to the space between the shearing elements, then discharged into a receiver.

colloidal solution ▷ **solution, colloidal**

color and light ▷ **light and measurement**

colorant They are substances capable of imparting color to a material, such as plastic, paper, etc. Colorants are generally divided into dyes and pigments. They may either be naturally present in a material, admixed with it mechanically, or applied in a solution. A valid distinction between dyes and pigments is almost impossible to draw. Some have established it on the basis of solubility or on physical form and method of application. As the term is used in industry, black and white dyes and pigments are also considered to be colorants. Like all color, each has many different shades. Included as colorants are heavy metals (lead, cadmium, mercury, etc.) that pose no harm to the consumer when used, but present a problem in waste disposal. They can constitute a toxic residue following incineration if they are not properly handled and disposed of. Safer alternates are being used based on environmental requirements.

color concentrate A measured amount of dye or pigment incorporated into a predetermined amount of plastic; the plastic concentrate contains a specified high loading of color. The pigmented or colored plastic is then mixed into larger quantities of plastic material to be used for processing (injection, extrusion, etc.). This mixture is added to the bulk of plastic in measured quantity in order to produce a precise, predetermined color of finished products. Concentrates provide a dust-free method of handling colors.

color-fast The ability to resist change in color, particularly in outdoor UV light.

colorimeter An instrument for matching colors with results about the same as those of visual inspection, but more consistent. Basically the sample is Illuminated by light from three primary color filters, and scanned by an electronic detecting system. It is sometimes used in conjuction with a spectrophotometer, which is used for close control of color in production. ▷ **spectrophotometer**

colorless dye Synonym for optical brightener.

color matching ▷ **Kubelka-Munk theory**

color migration The movement of dyes or pigments through or out of a material.

color pellet sorter Color sorting system detects and separates off-color or contaminated pelletized or granular materials from acceptable materials. The system can separate light from dark, dark from light, transparent from opaque materials, or by color difference. The system detects and automatically rejects particles as small as 0.5 mm. The operating principle of the system is based on light reflectance of materials of different brightness or color. There are two or three photo-electric eye sensors, a highly polished background plate, a signal amplifier/transmitter, a series of electromagnetically actuated air valve ejectors, and an oscilloscope for tuning the system to the acceptable brightness or color range.

Materials are fed from chutes onto a conveyor belt. The sensors and background plate are electronically tuned to produce a reflectance range corresponding to the brightness range of the acceptable materials. When off-color material passes in front of the sensors, the amount of light reflection changes, which results in a change in the magnitude of the electric signal going to the amplifier. This error signal is amplified and used to actuate the air valve ejectors. These valves open in a millisecond. Sorters can accommodate throughputs up to 1,000 lb/h (450 kg/h) that are monochromatic (having two electric eye sensors) and 220 lb/h (100 kg/h) that are bichromatic (having three electric eye sensors) (Satake Engineering Co., Ltd. of Tokyo).

color pigment dispersion Ground coloring materials in a thick liquid which is compatible with the plastic system in which it will be used. When added to the plastic, the pigment dispersions give it color.

color selection Color selection for a plastic product may be important for reasons other than aesthetics. It is a well known fact that the surface temperature of an object exposed to sunlight is dependent on its color. If the product is for exterior use, then the selection of color may be critical from this stand-point. For example, with products such as chairs, golf cart bodies, etc., everyday use involves considerable contact with a person's body. For these type products, it is essential that the surface temperature build-up be held to a level which "feels comfortable to the touch"; thus color is put to another use.

color shade A term descriptive of a lightness difference between surface colors whose other attributes are essentially the same. Shade is derived from shadow and so should be applied only to change toward darker color; in practice reference is made to lighter as well as darker shades.

color stability versus processing Generally the most significant signal and control factor contributing to color shift is melt temperature. Other processing parameters or control factors having a lesser degree of significance on both the mean and variance are cycle time or rate of melt flow, and melt pressure.

column crush A measure of the resistance of a plastic container to deformation under a vertical load, applied along the container's vertical axis.

combination mold ▷ **mold combination**

combustibles Any substance that will burn, regardless of its autoignition temperature or whether it is a solid, liquid, or gas (solid wastes, including paper, plastics, wood, and certain food wastes).

combustion An exothermic oxidation reaction which may occur with any organic compound as well as with certain elements. As an example, controlled burning of solid wastes for disposal or, in an oxygen-starved process via pyrolysis, to produce combustible solid and gas fuels that can be burned to generate energy. ▷ **flammability**

combustion modular unit An incineration device of low capacity. Small waste-to-energy systems can be created from several such units or modules.

combustion, spontaneously ▷ **pyrophoric material**

comma, decimal marker ▷ **number marker**

commingled plastic **1.** Plastics not sorted by type in the waste stream. **2.** A material made by melting unsorted plastics together.

commingled yarn A hybrid yarn made with two types of materials intermingled in a single yarn; for example, thermoplastic filaments intermingled with carbon filaments to form a single yarn.

comminute To reduce size of particles by grinding or even pulverizing.

commodity plastic and engineering plastic By using different modifiers, additives, fillers, and reinforcements with the various plastics, more than 15,000 compounds are commercially available. They are classified as commodity plastics (90% by weight) and engineering plastics. Commodities such as PE, PP, PS, and PVC account for two-thirds of plastics sales. Engineering plastics are characterized by better heat resistance, higher impact strength, high stiffness, and/or many other "improved" properties, and thus bring a higher price than commodity resins. Among the more significant engineering plastics are PA, PC, PS, PEEK, ABS, and so on. Some commodity plastics contain certain reinforcements, and/or are alloyed with other resins, that put them into the engineering categories. Many thermosets generally are classified as engineering plastics. Perhaps the major distinction between them is cost.

communication protocol A set of rules governing communication or transfer of data between computer hardware and/or software. When related to plastic processing equipment, communication includes reference to exchange of process controls, meeting standards, following production schedules, etc. that permits the interchanging of action such as molding machines with auxiliary equipment.

communication protocol interface The information that is required to monitor and configure a manufacturing operation is distributed among various units of auxiliary equipment. This information is transferred to the central control. Communication interfaces and communication protocols have been developed to allow this information to be exchanged. Successful communication requires a durable interface and a versatile protocol. A communication interface must be both mechanically and electrically durable. Mechanical durability is achieved by use of suitable attachment hardware and cable strain relief. Electrical durability is achieved by use of suitable transceiver circuitry. Circuitry meeting the requirements of ANSI RS-485 is ideal for both half and full duplex protocols. It is designed for use where more than one device may "talk" at one time. Less durable circuitry, such as RS-232 and RS-422, may fail if more than one device "talks".

communition A mechanical shredding or pulverizing process of solid waste or waste water.

comoforming, cold molded ▷ **thermoforming, comoforming cold molded**

comonomer A monomer which is mixed with a different monomer for a polymerization reaction, the result of which is a copolymer.

compact audio disk Manufactured with high purity polycarbonate plastic; introduced by Bayer AG, Germany.

compacting, roll Roll compacting is the progressive compacting of materials by the use of a rolling mill. Synonymous with powder rolling (see Fig. below).

compaction **1.** Compressing waste, often in collection vehicles, to reduce volume 50 to 80%. **2.** In reinforced plastics and composites, the application of a temporary vacuum bag and vacuum to remove trapped air and compact the lay-up.

compatibility The ability of two or more substances combined with each other to form a homogeneous composition of useful plastic properties. For example, the suitability of a sizing or finish for use with certain general plastic types, and nonreactivity or negligible reactivity between materials in contact. ▷ **microphase structure**

compatibilizer agent The advent of compatibilizing agents was a major milestone in alloy/blend development and important to making useful blends of dissimilar plastics. If natural compatibility is absent, one plastic can be chemically modified, such as by grafting, to improve reactivity with the second plastic (polymer), or a third agent can be added to do the blending. Since they typically require small amounts, this makes it possible to mix polymers that resist compounding (including recycled plastics). They help bridge the interface of polymers that want to separate. Two-component and multi-component mixtures are used. The most common agents are block or graft copolymers and polymer cosolvents. These are either synthesized and added to a polymer mixture or generated during compounding by controlled reactive processing. The first method requires sophisticated chemistry and extensive research; price of the interfacial agent is high, but the amount required is very small, typically 1 to 2%. The second method involves chemical engineering, with closed-loop control. These agents may have an increased role in recycling as processors investigate the reclamation commingled plastics.

competition For over a century plastics have successfully competed with other materials providing cost-performance advantages. This action will continue and expand as is evident by new plastics and applications on the horizon. To help plastics expand, there has been and will continue to exist plastics-to-plastics competition to meet all kinds of requirements (including high and safe performance in all kinds of environments).

complete information management This explanation is sometimes used in conjunction with ▷ **computer integrated manufacturing** or CIM.

complex agent A compound that will combine with metallic ions to form complex ions.

complex dielectric constant The vectorial sum of dielectric constant and the loss factor.

complex modulus The ratio of stress to strain in which each is a vector that may be

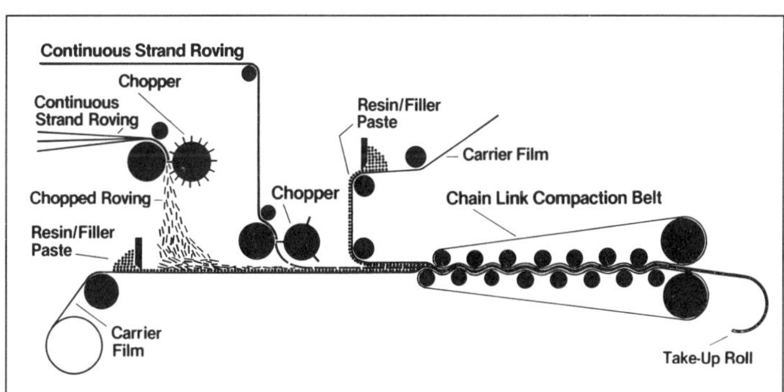

Example in the use of a compaction roll belt system at the end of a sheet molding compounding line producing a directional SMC.

represented by a complex number. May be measured in tension or flexure, compression, or shear.

complex shape Molded parts with undercuts, i.e., articles which cannot be released in the direction of mold opening, require molds with more than one parting line. For such articles, various methods have been developed such as molds with side cores, wedges, rotating cores, and loose cores or inserts. The choice of method, or a combination of these methods, is controlled by the shape of the article and the properties of the plastic (flexibility, rigidity, shrinkage, etc.) but also by the standards of quality to be met by the molded part. For articles with external screw thread, for instance, either side cores or rotating cores can be included in the mold. However, with side cores, the mold parting line is visible.

complex Young's modulus The vertical sum of Young's modulus and the loss modulus. Analogous to the complex dielectric constant.

compliance 1. Tensile compliance is the reciprocal of Young's modulus. ▷**modulus 2.** Shear compliance is the reciprocal of shear modulus. **3.** The term is also used in the evaluation of stiffness and deflection.

composite A composite is a combination of two or more materials with properties that the component materials do not have by themselves. Nature made the first composite in living things. Wood is a composite of cellulose fibers held together with a glue or matrix of soft lignin. In engineering materials, composites are formed by coatings, internal additives, and so on. A metal composite is clad metals. There are steel reinforced concrete composites.

A very important composite is the reinforced plastic (RP); basically a combination of a reinforcing material (usually in fiber form) and plastic. The most common and abundantly used (about 80% by weight of all high strength plastic composites) is glass fiber-thermoset polyester plastic. Glass fibers are very strong but if notched they fracture readily. By encapsulating these fibers in a plastic matrix, they are protected from fracture-damage; the plastic transfers applied loads to the glass fibers so that their stiffness and strength can be utilized. Higher performance RPs use fibers such as aramid, carbon, graphite, and boron.

Composites, specifically the plastic RPs, as a class of engineering materials provide almost unlimited potential for high strength, stiffness, corrosion resistance, processability, and so on over other materials. They will probably be the "steels" of the future. ▷**data theoretical versus actual properties**

Basically composites are considered to be combinations of materials differing in composition or form on a micro scale, and the constituents retain their identities in the composite (reinforced plastic), that is they do not dissolve or otherwise merge completely into each other although they act in concert. Normally the components can be physically identified and lead to an interface between components. The behavior and properties of this interface also generally control the properties of the composite (RP).

This definition is obviously imprecise, and it includes some materials often considered not to be composites. Furthermore, some combinations may be thought of as composite structures rather than composite materials; the dividing line is not "sharp", and the difference of opinion can easily exist particularly in different industry disciplines such as building and construction, electronics, and so on. Composites may be classified in a number of different ways, but the following generally is accepted:

(1) fibrous-plastic matrix
(2) fibrous-ceramic matrix
(3) fibrous-metal matrix
(4) laminar-layers of unreinforced plastics, etc.
(5) laminar-layers of reinforced plastics
(6) laminar-layers of glass-plastics (safety glass)
(7) laminar-layers of different metals and/or nonmetals
(8) particulate-plastic matrix
(9) particulate-metal matrix
(10) particulate-ceramic matrix
(11) skeletal-plastic matrix
(12) flake-plastic matrix
(13) flake-ceramic matrix
(14) steel rod-concrete matrix
(15) carbon fiber-carbon matrix
(16) metal fiber-metal matrix
(17) metal fiber-plastic matrix
(18) ceramic fiber-metal matrix
(19) ceramic fiber-plastic matrix
(20) whisker-plastic matrix
(21) whisker-metal matrix
(22) aggregate-cement matrix (concrete)
(23) wood-plastic matrix (compreg)
(24) microsphere glass-plastic matrix (syntactic)
(25) asbestos fiber-concrete matrix
(26) glass ceramic-amorphous glass matrix
(27) concrete-plastic matrix
(28) metal strip-metal strip matrix (thermoset)
(29) amorphous plastic-crystalline plastic matrix
(30) aluminum film-plastic film matrix
(31) amorphous plastic-crystalline plastic matrix
(32) ceramic fiber-matrix ceramic (CMC)

(33) carbon-carbon matrix
(34) potassium nitrate-charcoal-sulfur (blasting powder)
(35) cellulose fiber-lignin/silicic matrix (bamboo stalk)
(36) plastic-plastic (coextruded, coinjection, laminated)
(37) flexible reinforced plastics
(38) and many more different composites made up of distinct parts which contribute, either proportionately or synergistically, to the properties of the combinations.

The skeletal and flake are usually grouped together; they can also be included under particulate composites. Thus, there are plastic composites, metal composites, ceramic composites, glass composites, wood composites, and so on. Result is that the term composite encompasses many different combinations of materials, practically endless, with basically plastic being one type. Consequently, the term reinforced plastics is more meaningful within the plastic industry and tends to be used more often worldwide. (For the record, D. V. Rosato in 1954, as a Board member of the Reinforced Plastics Division of the SPI, was successful at introducing and later expanding the name of the Division to Reinforced Plastics/Composite Division. Thus, plastic composites would be applicable to all types of composite that incorporated plastics. A few decades later it became the Composite Division). ▷ **reinforced plastic** for details on RPs.

composite, advanced ▷ **advanced reinforced plastic**

composite and bamboo ▷ **bamboo's modular structure**

composite, boral ▷ **boral**

composite carbon-carbon matrix ▷ **carbon-carbon composite**

composite ceramic fiber-ceramic matrix ▷ **ceramic matrix composite**

composite, cermet A composite material or article comprised of a ceramic and a metal alloy, interdistributed in any of various geometrical forms but intimately bonded together.

composite curved bar, delamination analysis One of the major causes of stiffness and strength degradations in laminated plastic composite structures is the delaminations between composite layers. In most engineering applications, laminated composite structures have certain curvatures and, therefore, are subject to potential delamination problems during service (cyclic bending loads).

One of the most appealing geometries of a test coupon for studying the plastic composite delamination phenomenon is the semicircular curve bar shape (C-shape). When such a test specimen is subjected to end forces, the peak radial stress and the peak shear stress induced in the curved bar will be identical in magnitudes but are out of phase in the tangential direction by $\pi/2$. Namely, the peak radial stress is located at the midspan point of the semicircular curved bar, but the peak shear stresses occur at both ends of the semicircular curved bar. The radial distance of both the peak radial stresses and the peak shear stresses are exactly the same.

The above nature of the semicircular curved bar offers an excellent situation for studying the initiation and subsequent propagation of delamination zones (open-mode or shear-mode) under cyclic loadings and for studying the fatigue behavior (degradation of stiffness and strength) of multilayered composites. The classical anisotropic elasticity theory was used to construct a "multilayer" composite semicircular curved bar subjected to end forces and end moments. The radial location and intensity of open-mode delamination stress are calculated and compared with the results obtained from the anisotropic continuum theory and from the finite element method. The multilayer theory provides more accurate predictions of the location and the intensity of the open-mode delamination stress than those calculated from the anisotropic continuum theory. The multilayer theory developed can be applied to predict the open-mode delamination stress concentrations in horse-shoe-shaped composite test specimens. (NASA TM-4139, N90-12669 by W. L. Ko and R. H. Jackson).

composite film ▷ **coextrusion** and **lamination**

composite, flammability ▷ **flammability, composite**

composite future ▷ **reinforced plastic future**

composite, hybrid ▷ **hybrid**

composite metal matrix Compared to monolithic metals, MMCs (metal matrix composites) show a great promise in performance advantages. Advanced aircraft propulsion systems seem impossible to develop without them. But proving technical confidence in the materials has been an expensive, slow process. R&D into combining fiber reinforcements with metals started in the early 1940s using continuous fiber and particle/whisker reinforced metallic composites. Results have shown that MMCs could surpass any metals in terms of high modulus, temperature resistance, strength, hardness, dimensional stability, damping, etc. They are very expensive raw materialwise and processwise. Certain MMCs are used in special applications:

boron fiber/aluminum support struts in space shuttles, structural support elements, and microwave carrying masts on high-gain antennas.

composite, moisture and electrical resistance In unidirectional composites, the normalized change in electrical resistance is measured and found to vary with the square of the moisture content. For multi-dimensional composites, a different method is used. A modified, four-terminal method minimizes resistance of the contacts, which, in turn, eliminates error. Resistance measured across the thickness of multidimensional samples is linearly proportional to the moisture content.

composite mold ▷ **mold**

composite plastic-concrete ▷ **concrete-plastic**

composite processing method ▷ **reinforced plastic processes**

composite reinforced concrete ▷ **concrete reinforced**

composite skin ▷ **skin, synthetic**

composite silicon carbide ▷ **silicon carbide fiber**

composite variation, reliability factor ▷ **material variation, reliability factor**

composite wood ▷ **wood-plastic impregnated**

composition The elemental and chemical components that make up a material and their relative proportions.

composition board Refers to a product which was originally made by reducing wood to small particles and re-forming these particles into a rigid panel. The particles are bound together in the panel by an adhesive action, which is developed from the natural adhesive action of the wood substance or through addition of various adhesive binders. These binders range from low cost naturally occurring products, such as starch, to highly sophisticated plastics products, such as those made from phenol and formaldehyde. Although wood is the most commonly used raw material, composition boards are also made from other vegetable materials, such as sugar-cane, bagasse, straw, flax, etc. whenever these materials are available at a price competitive with wood or residue wood.

compost Organic materials, such as food, sewage sludge, and yard wastes, mixed with soil in which aerobic bacteria have broken down the waste to an intermediate humus-like state. The end product is often used as a soil conditioner. Decomposition is accelerated by adding ammonia bicarbonate. Waste piles are turned over frequently to increase aeration. High piles maintain a high temperature in the pile to destroy pathogenic organisms. With proper decomposition action, waste's volume is reduced from 20 to 60% of original volume. Although U.S. has composed sludge for years, only recently (late 1980s) has the treatment become popular for managing municipal solid waste (MSW). Managing organic MSW through composing has been prevalent in Europe (particularly Germany) since the early 1900s.

composting council The Solid Waste Composting Council (of SPI) is made up of a number of plastic producing companies, consumers, composting companies, and others involved in solid waste incorporating plastics. SWCC was formed to provide quality, waste-derived compost to the marketplace, to promote wide public and regulatory acceptance of the product, and to ensure development of viable end markets. Compost processes and product specifications are defined to ensure national and international market acceptance and regulatory consistency. The council works with state and federal officials in developing consistent regulatory standards. It is projected that composting can treat at least 40% by volume of the solid waste problem.

compound Since the first plastics were produced commercially (1868–cellulosics), there has been and will continue to be a growing demand for specialty plastics. Higher standards are turning material suppliers' and compounders' attention increasingly toward specialized and even tailor-made compounds or alloys. This approach has been very beneficial to the plastic industry (performancewise and costwise). Compounding, alloying, blending, and so on, will always be in the forefront since they are a natural occurrence with all types of plastics. As an example, the terpolymer ABS can provide different properties based on the mix. The classical objective of alloying and blending is to find two or more plastics (scientifically or initially in most cases from the practical approach) whose mixtures having property improvement beyond a purely additive effect resulting in a synergistic effect. An example of this synergistic effect that has become a classic in the industry is combining PVC and ABS.

Compounding, in its simplest definition, is the combining of a base plastic with colors, modifiers, additives, reinforcements, fillers, and/or other plastics to make the base plastic perform better, cost less, process more easily, look more attractive, or otherwise improve its characteristics (see Table on p. 129). In other words, through the

Additives and reinforcements used as compound constituents.

Filler or reinforcement	Properties improved													
	Chemical resistance	Heat resistance	Electrical insulation	Impact strength	Tensile strength	Dimensional stability	Stiffness	Hardness	Lubricity	Electrical conductivity	Thermal conductivity	Moisture resistance	Processability	Recommended for use in[1]
Alumina, tabular	●	●	●	●		●	●					●	●	S/P
Aluminum powder										●	●			S
Aramid	●	●	●	●	●	●	●	●	●				●	S/P
Bronze							●	●		●	●			S
Calcium carbonate	●	●	●	●		●	●	●					●	S/P
Carbon black		●					●			●	●		●	S/P
Carbon fiber										●	●			S
Cellulose				●		●	●	●						S/P
Alpha cellulose			●			●						●		S
Coal, powdered	●											●		S
Cotton			●	●	●	●	●	●						S
Fibrous glass	●	●	●	●	●	●	●	●				●		S/P
Graphite	●				●	●	●	●	●	●	●			S/P
Jute				●			●							S
Kaolin	●	●	●			●	●	●	●			●	●	S/P
Mica	●	●	●			●	●	●	●			●		S/P
Molybdenum disulfide							●	●	●			●	●	P
Nylon	●	●	●	●	●	●	●	●	●				●	S/P
Orlon	●	●	●	●	●	●	●	●				●	●	S/P
Rayon			●	●	●	●	●	●						S
Silica, amorphous			●									●	●	S/P
Sisal fibers	●			●		●	●	●				●		S/P
Fluorocarbon						●	●	●	●					S/P
Talc	●	●	●			●	●	●	●			●	●	S/P
Wood flour			●			●								S

[1] P = thermoplastic; S = thermoset.

science/art of compounding, plastics can be changed to meet any one (or more) of literally hundreds of different price/performance parameters dictated by the requirements of the supplier, processor, or end user. Under this broad definition, even the smallest processor who feeds a color concentrate into the hopper of a machine or who mixes two different grades of plastics together is performing a compounding function. However, the structure of the compounding industry as it is recognized does have a very definite shape and form. Basically, there are three major elements in the compounding industry: plastic suppliers, independent compounders, and processors/end users. Compounding materials are referred to simply as "compounds", although this term should not be taken to imply formation of a chemical compound. Compounded materials for use in molding are called molding compounds or molding powders, the latter even in the form of granules. ▷ **statistical benefits**

compounding constituents Common compound constituents are listed in the Table above and in the following listing:

Polymer or resin intermediate	Filler or reinforcement
Reclaimed polymer or compound	Plasticizer
	Plasticizer extender
Crosslinking agent	Viscosity depressant
Accelerator	Stiffener
Activator	Blowing agent
Thermal stabilizer	Foam promoter
Antioxidant	Slip agent
Antiozonant	Antiblocking agent
Ultraviolet absorber	Fire retardant
Colorant	Antistatic agent
Impact modifier or toughening agent	Antifogging agent
	Fungicide or bacteriostat
Lubricant	
Processing aid	Reodorant

compound intermediate This means that the compound is in itself not useful or of little primary importance, but is used as a stepping stone for preparation of something else.

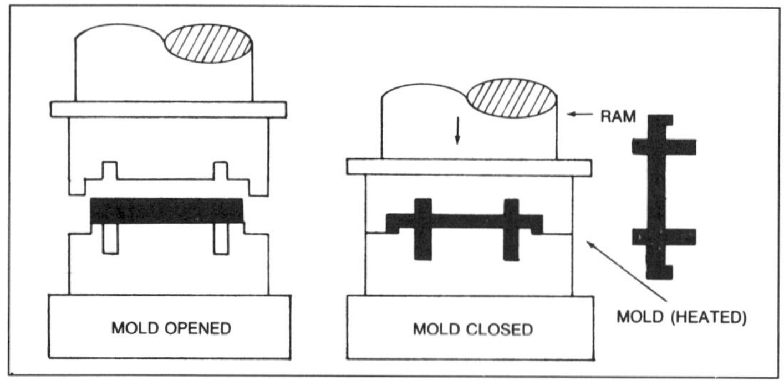

Schematic of compression molding.

compreg A contraction of compressed plastic impregnated wood usually referring to wood assembly of veneer layers and other wood-plastic impregnated combinations. Originated during the 1920s as a hardwood impregnated with a phenolic plastic under heat and pressure. Plastic treated compressed wood (via presses, autoclaves, etc.) produced wood with reduced swelling and shrink characteristics and increased density and strength properties.

compregnate To impregnate and simultaneously or subsequently compress, as in the production of compregs, aluminum castings, etc.

compressibility The ability of a material to be compressed, such as the extent to which a gasket material is compressed by a specified load in the short-time compressibility and recovery test. Compressibility (%) is calculated by dividing difference between original thickness under preload and thickness under major load by original thickness under preload and multiplying by 100. It is usually reported in conjunction with recovery and does not indicate behavior of a material under prolonged load.

compression-injection molding ▷ **coining**

compression molding A technique principally for thermoset plastic molding in which the molding compound (generally preheated) is placed in the heated open mold cavity (see Fig. above), mold is closed under pressure, causing the material to flow and completely fill the cavity, pressure being held until the TS material has cured. Some TSs, such as certain polyesters, require only lower pressures of down to 50 psi (345 kPa) or even just contact (zero) pressure. CM has been a very common method of molding TSs since 1909. ▷ **thermoset molding**

compression molding, air entrapment ▷ **air entrapment**

compression molding, balance tray ▷ **balance tray**

compression molding, breathing ▷ **breathing**

compression molding, bulk ratio ▷ **bulk factor**

compression molding, clamping ▷ **clamping**

compression molding, flash ▷ **mold flash**

compression molding, fusible core A technique similar to that used and identified as ▷ **injection molding, fusible core**

compression molding, in-mold coating, decorating, and labeling ▷ **in-mold coating, decorating, and labeling**

compression molding, loading tray A device in the form of a specially designed tray which is used to load the charge of material or metal inserts simultaneously into each cavity of a multicavity mold by the withdrawal of a sliding bottom from the tray (see first Fig. on p. 131). Also called charging tray.

compression molding mold An example of different molds used is shown in the second Fig. on p. 131; for information on molds ▷ **mold, compression**

compression molding, outgassing ▷ **outgassing**

compression molding, plastic material well Space provided in a compression mold to handle the bulk factor of the material being loaded.

compression molding polytetrafluoroethylene ▷ **skiving**

compression molding, postcuring ▷ **postcuring**

compression molding, preforming material ▷ **preforming**

compression molding, preheating material ▷ **preheating**

compression molding pressure The unit pressure applied to the molding material in the

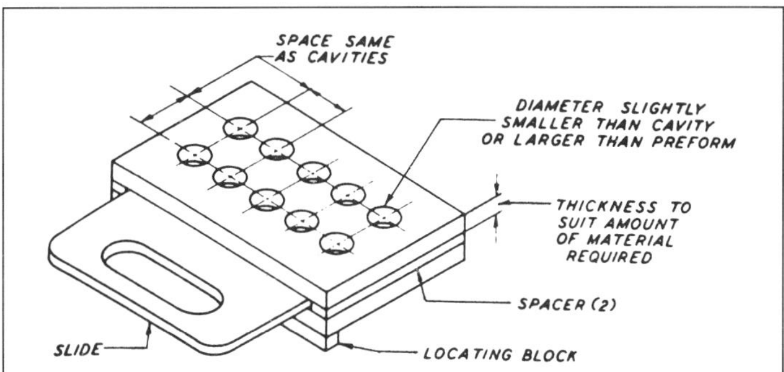

Schematic of a compression molding loading tray.

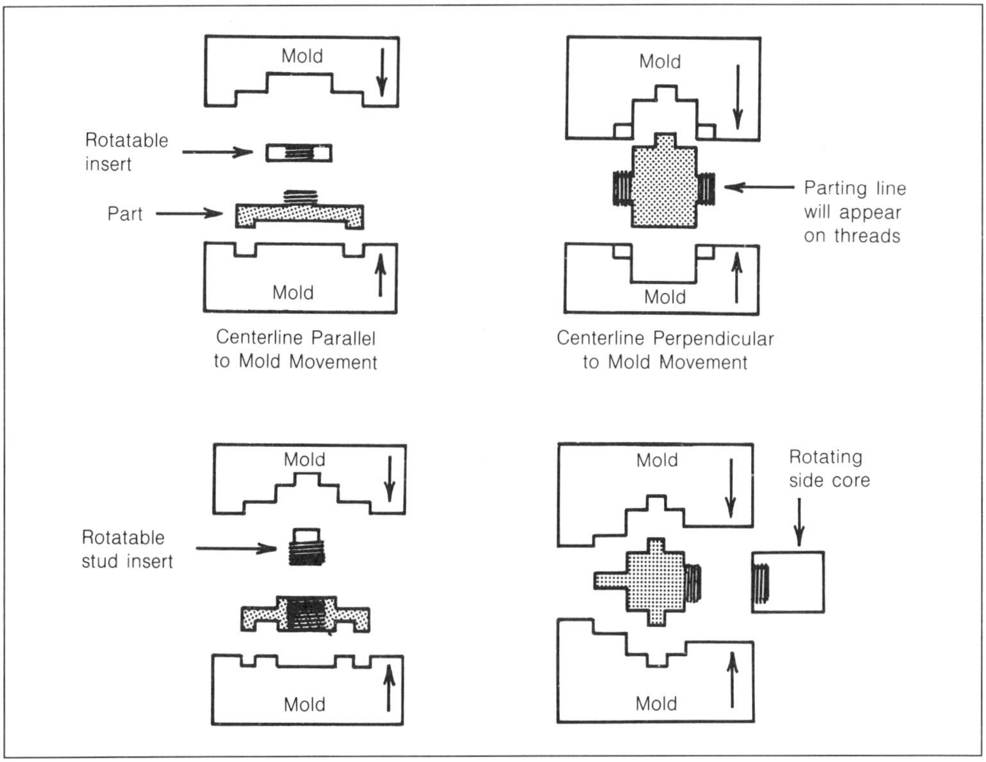

Example of a mold used in compression molding, forming threads in various positions.

mold cavity. It includes all areas under pressure during the complete closing of the mold; involves direct compression area (cavity projected area taken at right angles to the direction of the applied pressure) and depth of cavity in the mold. The Table on p. 132 provides a guide for molding pressure. ▷ **molding pressure required**

compression molding, screw preplasticizer Screw preplasticator is used next to the compression mold. It preheats materials, particularly bulky materials such as BMCs and with an automatic loading tray, directs specific shot size to cavities. Fig. 1 on p. 132 shows the complete CM machine using a three-screw preheater; Fig. 2 shows the three screws retracted from their barrels (for inspection, cleaning, etc.); and Fig. 3 shows preheated compound exiting the preplasticizer with a guillotine knife located above the exit and preset to automatically cut the required amount of material. These screws do not require any special designs, as required for injection, extrusion, etc. plasticators.

compression molding, thermoset plastic ▷ **thermoplastic**

compression molding, venting Molds re-

Compression molding pressure guide.

Depth of molding (in.)	Pressure table Pressure psi of projected land area			
	Conventional phenolic		Low-pressure phenolic	
	Preheated by high frequency	Not preheated	Preheated by high frequency	Not preheated
$0-\frac{3}{4}$	1000–2000	3000	350	1000
$\frac{3}{4}-1\frac{1}{2}$	1250–2500	3700	450	1250
2	1500–3000	4400	550	1500
3	1750–3500	5100	650	1750
4	2000–4000	5800	750	2000
5	2250–4500	[1]	850	[2]
6	2500–5000	[1]	950	[2]
7	2750–5500	[1]	1050	[2]
8	3000–6000	[1]	1150	[2]
9	3250–6500	[1]	1250	[2]
10	3500–7000	[1]	1350	[2]
12	4000–8000	[1]	1450	[2]
14	4500–9000	[1]	1550	[2]
16	5000–10000	[1]	1650	[2]

[1] Add 700 psi for each additional inch of depth; but beyond 4 in. in depth it is desirable (and beyond 12 in. essential) to preheat.
[2] Add 250 psi for each additional inch of depth; but beyond 4 in. in depth it is desirable (and beyond 12 in. essential) to preheat.

Fig. 1 Compression molding machine with preplasticizer.

Fig. 2 Three screws of preplasticizer retracted.

Fig. 3 Preheated compound exiting the preplasticator.

quire a means by which air and any potential volatiles are evacuated from the cavities. Bumping can be used, but the usual technique incorporates openings, generally located at the mold parting line. Their size depends on the plastic compound's viscosity, but they are usually 0.25 in. wide × 0.001 to 0.003 in. deep, located where the cavity will be filled last. The vent-opening location also depends on the heating pattern of the mold, particularly if the heat flow pattern was not logically planned. CAD

Comparison guide for compression and transfer molding.

Characteristic	Compression	Transfer
Loading the mold	1. Powder or preforms. 2. Mold open at time of loading. 3. Material positioned for optimum flow.	1. Mold closed at time of loading. 2. RF heated preforms placed in plunger well.
Material temperature before molding	1. Cold powder or preforms. 2. RF heated preforms to 220–280°F.	RF heated preforms to 220–280°F.
Molding temperature	1. One step closures—350–450°F. 2. Others—290–390°F.	290–360°F.
Pressure via clamp	1. 2,000–10,000 psi (3,000 optimum on part). 2. Add 700 psi for each inch of part depth.	1. Plunger ram—6,000–10,000 psi. 2. Clamping ram—minimum tonnage should be 75% of load applied by plunger ram on mold.
Pressure in cavity	Equal to clamp pressure.	Very low to maximum of 1,000 psi.
Breathing the mold	Frequently used to eliminate gas and reduce cure time.	1. Neither practical nor necessary. 2. Accomplished by proper venting.
Cure time (time pressure is being applied on mold)	30–300 s—will vary with mass of material, thickness of part, and preheating.	45–90 s—will vary with part geometry.
Size of pieces moldable	Limited only by press capacity.	About 1 lb maximum.
Use of inserts	Limited—inserts apt to be lifted out of position or deformed by closing.	Unlimited—complicated. Inserts readily accommodated.
Tolerances on finished products	1. Fair to good—depends on mold construction and direction of molding. 2. Flash—poorest, positive—best, semi-positive—intermediate.	Good—close tolerances easier to hold.
Shrinkage	Least.	1. Greater than compression. 2. Shrinkage across line of flow is less than with line of flow.

programs are available to provide the proper heating pattern. With excessive heat in one section of the mold, the viscosity of the compound could be low enough to require a vent opening in that area. Knockout pins often provide a means for venting, and they may require recessed sections, such as "flats" ground on the OD, that will allow venting. ▷**mold, compression**

compression molding versus transfer molding Comparison is provided in the Table above.

compression molding, void ▷**air entrapment**

compression plane strain A method of loading the central area of a sheet specimen by compressing it between the faces of two molds or dies with rectangular cross sections. Thus, the area of the specimen being stressed is constant, so that the true, not nominal, stress is the most readily calculated. Also, unlike uniaxial compression, the friction between molds/dies and sample remains constant with increasing strain. It may be necessary to correct for edge effects.

compression press uses vacuum, not hydraulics Compression molding press used particularly for low pressure molding reinforced plastics uses vacuum pump power. In comparison to the usual hydraulic press system, it consumes less energy (such as 20%) and reduces operating cost (such as 50%). It operates without oil. Press can provide in-mold pressures of up to 145 psi (1 MPa). Closing and opening are achieved with a single piston powered by a light weight vacuum cylinder on top of the press.

During closing, air is evacuated from the lower cylinder chamber below the piston head, and atmospheric pressure in the upper chamber provides up to 2.2 T (2200 kg) of closing and opening force per cylinder. The sequence is reversed during opening of the mold. Cycle times can be 1 to 8 s, depending on the size of vacuum pump used to drive the piston (and to evacuate the mold cavity).

With multiple such as four vacuum cylinders, press can operate with molds weighting up to 10 T (10 000 kg). Further pressure for forming is supplied by evacuating air from the mold itself, creating an *autoclave* effect. Because the mold cavity is often substantially smaller than the entire mold, pressures in excess of 14.5 psi (0.1 MPa) can be achieved. The autoclave effect also eliminates part surface defects caused by air inclusions that can be a problem in compression molding. (Press patent applied by Stauch GmbH, Hilden, Germany.)

compression properties The majority of tests to evaluate characteristics of plastics are performed in tension and/or flexure; hence, compressive stress-strain behavior is not well described for many plastics. Generally, behavior in compression per ASTM D 695 is different from that in tension, but the stress-strain response in compression is usually close enough to that of tension so that differences can be neglected. Compression modulus is not always reported since defining a stress at a strain is equivalent to reporting a secant modulus. However, if a compression modulus is reported, it is generally an initial modulus. ▷ **modulus, tension**

compression ratio in screw ▷ **screw, compression ratio**

compression set A permanent deformation resulting from compression stress or load.

compression strain ▷ **strain**

compression strength The maximum load (or crushing load) sustained by the specimen divided by the original cross section area of the specimen. ▷ **strength**

compression strength induced Strength achieved by introducing compressive stresses into the surface of a nonductable material; such as surface hardening via heat.

compression stress The normal stress caused by forces directed toward the plane on which they act. ▷ **stress**

compression test A method of determining behavior of a material subjected to a uniaxial compressive load. A specimen is compressed axially at controlled speed until it fails. Frequent or continuous measurements of load and deformation are made, compressive stress and strain calculated, and a stress-strain diagram constructed. From the stress-strain diagram can be determined elastic limit, modulus of elasticity, proportional limit, yield point, yield strength and, for some materials, compressive strength. ▷ **stress-strain**

compression-transfer molding ▷ **transfer molding**

compressive modulus The ratio of compressive stress to compressive strain below the proportional limit. Theoretically equal to Young's modulus determined from tensile tests.

computer Computers permeate all areas of the plastic industry and science and engineering, as they do most areas of business, entertainment, and so on. Computer technology is implied or directly involved in many modern designs, synthesis, characterization, manufacturing/processing, and testing of plastics. Computers have their place, but most important is the person(s) involved with proper knowledge in using the hardware and software in order to be efficient. They are another tool and guideline for the user, such as the designer. ▷ **plastic, computer and design** and **microprocessor control**

computer accessibility In industry, the drawings and other information produced by computers (CAD, CAM, CAE, CAM, and so on) are valuable and critically important to design, manufacturing, and marketing. They should not be generally accessible. Most systems will require a password in order to log-on. This is not generally true of low-cost systems, but a password can easily be added. Networks almost invariably work with a password system, and since most systems are networked in industry, two passwords may be necessary; one to log-on and the other to access particular files.

computer acoustic holography In acoustic holography, computer reconstruction provides the means for storing and integrating several holographic images. A reconstructed stored image is a three-dimensional picture that can be electronically rotated and viewed in any image plane. The image provides full characterization and detail of buried flaws.

computer-aided Describes any task accomplished with the help of a computer; implies faster than it would be without the computer; including CA model making. ▷ **modeling stereolithography**

computer-aided design The profitability and success of a plastic product are fixed largely at the design stage. This provides the basic data for manufacturing; some 80% of the cost responsibility for a part rests with the design department. Faults generated during part design can be eliminated later only with difficulty and potential big cost increases. The use of computers as design aids (the computer-aided design approach: CAD) is well established. Cost of hardware and software for small and medium-sized operations is justifiable on the basis that, by means of test simulation on the computer, it is possible to obtain information previously obtained only by tests on prototypes; this reduces the expense of experimental effort. Basically CAD is the process of solving design problems with the aid of computers. This includes computer generation and modification of graphic images on a video display, printing these images as hard copy on a printer or plotter, analysis of design data, electronic storage with retrieval of design information. Many CAD systems perform these functions in an integrated fashion, which can increase the designer's productivity manyfold.

Recognize that the computer does not change the nature of the design process and that it is simply a tool to improve efficiency and productivity. It is appropriate to review the designer and the CAD system as a design team: the designer provides knowledge, creativity and control, the computer assists with accurate, easily modifiable graphics and the capacity to perform complex design analysis at great speeds and to store and recall design information. Occasionally, the computer can augment or replace many of the designer's other tools, but it is important to remember that it does not change the fundamental role of the designer.

Powerful computer software programs have been written based on the method of finite element analysis (FEA). As an example, by the use of FEA approximations to desired geometries, boundary conditions, loads, and material characteristics can be handled in a single matrix-oriented computer model, and solutions obtained. These are strongly recommended when calculations of the effects of complicated geometry, combined with the variable potential behaviour of plastics, cannot be made to sufficient accuracy with the more conventional procedures of mechanics and strength of materials, particularly on a time basis.

Using a CAD system is very different from writing programs for computer graphics. You lose control over the process that lets you produce anything that you desire. However, you are provided with a ready-made program (actually a set of programs) that will do far more for you than you would ever have time to write a program on your own, assuming you knew how. Although CAD systems are much more powerful than traditional instrument drawing, particularly where the replication and manipulation of already recorded (by CAD) drawings are concerned, they have several distinct disadvantages when compared to traditional graphics, such as: (1) They are more expensive by a ratio of at least 10 to 100. (2) The training period prior to productive work is much longer on a CAD system (the first few times). (3) CAD expertise has a low portability rate. What you learn on one CAD system usually will only have a general applicability on another. This means that the drafter or designer will have to do more training with most new CAD systems, although it will be much quicker after the first time. So, when possible, plan ahead on hardware and software for the future that will easily integrate. (4) Because a CAD system is a set of computer programs, there is a limit to the number of things it can do. However, as CAD becomes more sophisticated, the limitations become less important and the things that it does better, such as shape manipulation, become critical in the comparison. (5) CAD has two contrary influences on creativity in design. It involves the creation of extensive files of drawings of objects that tend to become standard and modular because of their ease of use. This tends to reduce the creativity of the design (or designer). However, on the plus side, the ease of editing and the power of shape manipulation encourages the designer to do things that were too tedious or too difficult to do before.

Regardless of these so called disadvantages, CAD takes over designing all types of industrial

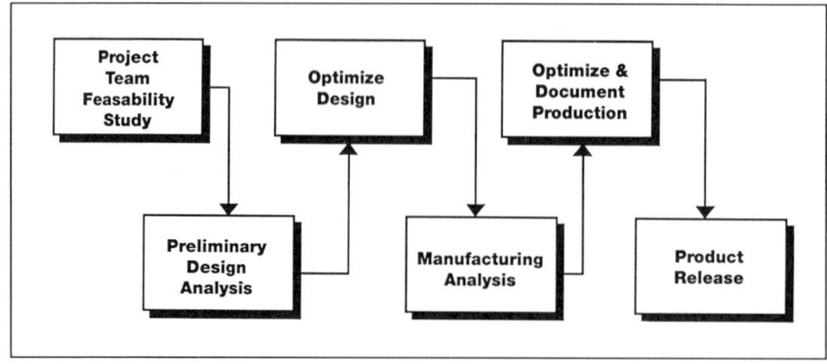

Product design flow pattern.

drawings from traditional methods of graphics/designs because the increased productivity (timewise, qualitywise, and so on) of CAD outweighs expenditure and other disadvantages. CAD acts like a magnifying glass. It makes good designers better, and exaggerates the inferiority of a bad design.

computer-aided design/computer-aided manufacturing A combination of computer-aided design and manufacturing functions. In practical terms, it means that design information generated on a computer-aided design (CAD) system is readily usable by a computer-aided manufacturing (CAM) system (see Fig. above).

computer-aided design drafting As reviewed in computer-aided design, the computer assists generation of working drawings and other documents. When just referring to graphics the phrase computer-aided design drafting (CADD) is used.

computer-aided drafting ▷ **computer-aided design drafting**

computer-aided engineering CAE is not a synonym for computer-aided design/computer-aided manufacturing (CAD/CAM), but a step up from CAD, specifically including engineering design analysis, system modeling, simulated structure analysis, finite element analysis, and so on. The goal of CAE technology is to improve product quality and lower product development time/cost by analyzing production equipment (molds/dies, decorating, and so on) feasibility to define suitable processing conditions before the equipment is produced and/or purchased for use on the production floor. A successful CAE application requires an analyst who not only understands the product requirements and processes, but also possesses advanced knowledge of modeling and numerical techniques. The Fig. below is an example of CAE as it applies to an injection molded product. ▷ **mold cavity melt flow analysis**

computer-aided equipment maintenance program The past tools available to a maintenance person would not allow them to diagnose the behaviour of the machine(s) and other equipment in the production line. Accordingly, shop maintenance generally occurred when something failed, resulting in downtime that could have been prevented by planned maintenance. The monitoring capabilities of the computer-integrated manufacturing (CIM) program provide maintenance personnel with sophisticated tools that allow them to look into the behavior of the process to a depth not previously possible. With this insight, mainte-

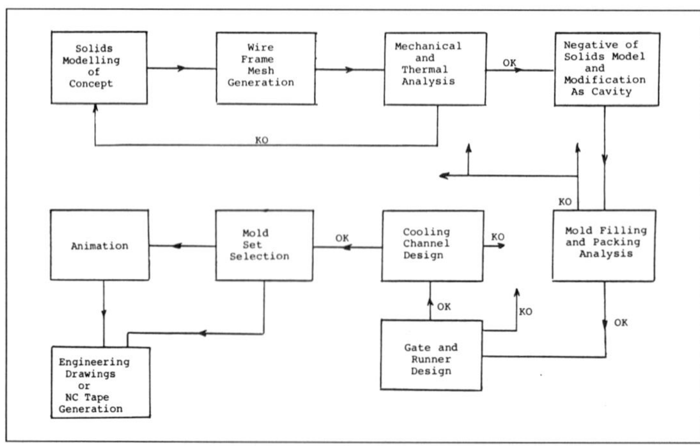

Computer-aided engineering applied to plastic part and mold design. OK = proceed; KO = knock out; return to designated starting point.

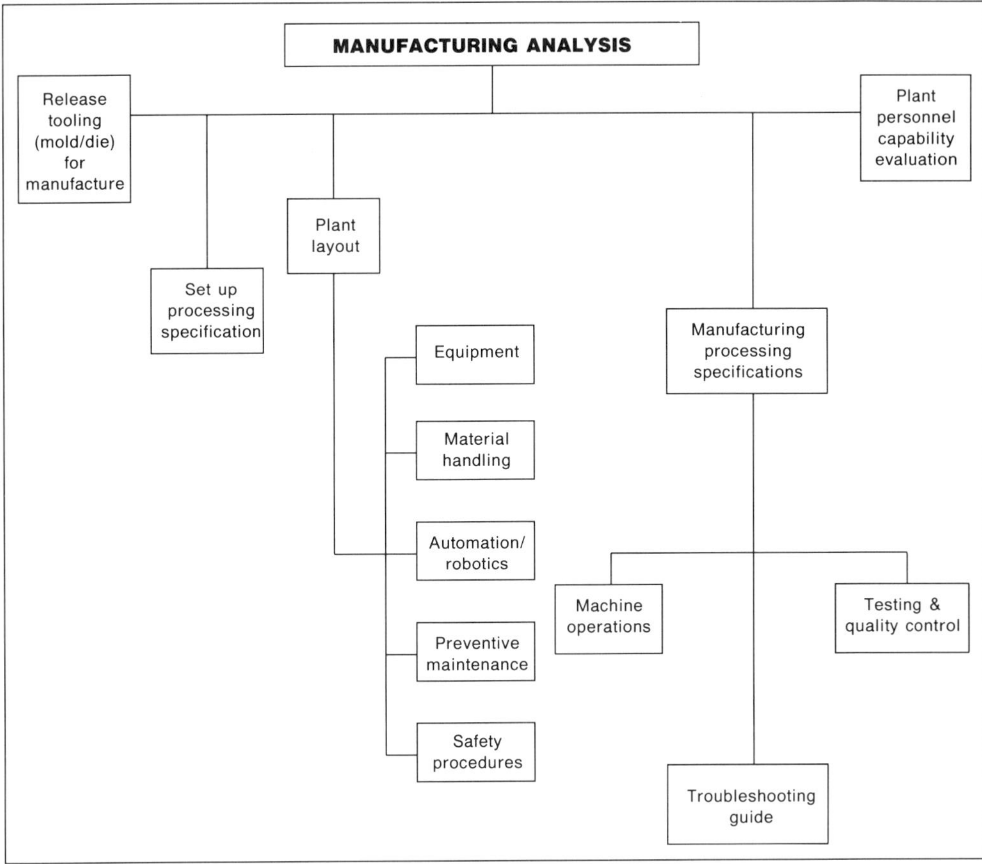

Manufacturing analysis.

nance managers can review daily (or less) the operation of all machines and auxilliary equipment in a matter of seconds to minutes, depending on how the computer is programmed. Downtime will be considerably reduced, if not eliminated, and surprises almost totally eliminated.

computer-aided manufacturing Computer-aided manufacturing describes a system that can take a computer-aided designed product, devise the essential production steps and electronically communicate this information to manufacturing equipment (see Fig. above). This type of action reduces lead time, and leads to more efficient material use, greater accuracy, improved inventory functions, and so on.

computer-aided molecular graphic Traditionally, chemists have used the well-known Kendrew and Corey, Pauling, and Koltun (CPK) wire and stick models to visualize the structure of molecules. It was extremely time consuming to build such models, and with the advent of computer-aided molecular graphics (CAMG) systems, research utilizing these models has been very useful. The field of molecular graphics as applied to polymer science has been developed since the 1970s. Development in CAMG has been expanding in the areas of hardware, software, and the techniques in using these programs. ▷ **designing with model**

computer-aided process planning With this CAPP system the computer supports all steps of manufacturing planning, such as choosing the best and/or available machine for the job, programming delivery of raw materials, molds/dies, and so on.

computer-aided testing In the CAT system, the computer is actively involved in testing that takes place in all stages of product development from design to producing the product; includes factors such as quality control, statistical analysis, and so on. An advantage to CAT is that sensors measuring the characteristics of the prototype or the finished product can exercise the product model to improve its accuracy, or to identify design modifications. In this way testing integrates design and fabrication into an ongoing self-correcting development process.

computer-aided tomography A diagnostic technique using X-ray photographs in which the shadows of structures before and behind the section under scrutiny do not show by other methods.

computer analog-to-digital converters An analog signal must be digitized before it can be read and understood by the computer. This step is accomplished by an A/D converter (also abbreviated ADC) whose sole job is to assign a set of binary digits that is indicative of the analog signal's intensity. At theoretical zero or baseline, the registers are filled with 0s. When the signal intensity increases, the values in the registers increase accordingly. An example is the difference between an 8-bit and a 12-bit A/D converter in the number of registers which contain the associated number. At theoretical zero the 8-bit unit has 8 zeros whereas the 12-bit unit has 12.

computer and statistics Computers make statistics a more flexible tool and help prevent "cookbooks" (the blind application of the same standard techniques no matter what problem exists). Basically, a statistical perspective can be a simple route to substantially increase productivity, quality and profit. Statistics is concerned with design of efficient experiments and with transformation of data into information, or in other words, with asking good questions and getting good answers. For most people, "statistics" conjures up endless tables of uninteresting numbers. But modern statistics has very practical applications and, thanks to computers, is no dreary science of number-crunching drudgery.

Statistical methods should be applied to decision-making at all stages of production – from incoming materials to outgoing products. For example, statistics can help with forecasting, a problem managers face every day: should raw materials be reordered; should marketing and advertising techniques be changed? The data used to make these decisions represent random variation – white noise – as well as real changes, such as drops in sales or increases in production. ▷ **Quality control** is an area where that management strategy can be applied easily. In the past, quality control simply meant throwing out bad products, and management regarded it as a trade-off with productivity. That meant quality control was being exercised too late. Quality control should mean learning about the variability of all aspects of production, including maintenance, purchasing, marketing, and design.

computer arithmetic-logic unit The ALU performs the arithmetic and logic operations on data presented to it. Data are processed in the form of binary words, each word containing a specified number of binary bits. Arithmetic operations include addition and subtraction. Logic operations involve shifting all bits of a word to the left or right.

computer assembly-language program Next in the hierarachy of programming languages is assembly language. Each machine instruction is represented by a set of mnemonics. The instruction "add" in assembly language replaces the machine binary code of 10000110. Assembly-language programs are easier to write yet are comparable in execution and efficiency to machine-language programs. A program known as an assembler translates symbolic assembly-language instructions into machine-language programs. When resident in the main memory, a program written in assembly-language can be written, translated into object instruction, and executed on a single computer. Assemblers are machine-dependent so that instructions defined for one type of computer cannot be executed by another type of computer.

computer-assisted design and drafting CADD is used in different industries by industrial designers, design engineers (plastics, etc.), architects, and so on. Since the 1970s, they have found that the ability to design on a computer screen has enhanced both the quality and efficiency of their work. However, much of the efficiency and accuracy of CADD is lost in conventional plotting and diazo printing of hard copy documents. Using conventional methods, it can require a week to plot a project (transfer it to hard copy) and still another week to produce it in blueprint form via the diazo printing process. Also, standard electrostatic plotters, with resolution capabilities of 400 dots per inch, produce less-than-sharp images. An example of obtaining significant improvements in all the different aspects to improve quality and time period of obtaining drawings is Du Pont's "Camex" image and laser photo plotter systems. It works with tapes or disks and the stored drawing data are converted into dot patterns with a resolution of one thousand dots per inch. Result is color-coded, high resolution documents in quantity and full size "as built" documents/drawings.

computer-assisted makeup CAM, also called composition and makeup, refers to video devices for graphic arts production.

computer-assisted manufacturing
▷ **computer integrated manufacturing**

computer autoload When the computer is turned on it will immediately find instructions telling it to load and run a given program, such as starting up production on a certain day and time. This means the user does not have to type in any starting instructions.

computer automated laboratory through production A microprocessor is a single integrated circuit capable of providing centralized control and data manipulation for a number of attached devices. Its heart is a tiny computer. Add a set of programmed instructions (a Read-Only Memory) and some form of input and output for communication with the outside world, and a fully functional microcomputer is created. The few electronic components which make up the microcomputer may replace hundreds of discrete components which would do the same control and computational tasks. In an automated system, dedicated microprocessors and software operate interactively with interim data from a prescribed series of analytical measurements. Throughout these interactive operations the instrument automatically and iteratively adjusts key parameters as the series of measurements continues.

computer automatic storage and retrieval system An AS/RS is an automated warehouse or storage room. The computer-operated equipment finds products, delivers them where needed, and also keeps track of inventory. All this action is in real time.

computer batch or off-line process
▷ **computer processing batch or off-line**

computer, bio A biocomputer is a computer in which the silicon in the microchips has been replaced by a synthetic protein or polypeptide coated with a silver compound. This combination behaves as a metallic semiconductor. They can improve storage capability and operating efficiency of silicon chips substantially. The materials used have been polysine on a glass substrate coated with an acrylate plastic and treated with silver nitrate. ▷ **biocomputing**

computer central processing unit The combination of CU (computer unit and ALU arithmetic-logic unit) is known as the central processing unit (CPU). Critical parameters in evaluating CPU operation are the minimum time required to execute specific instructions and the number of bits in a computer word. These parameters determine the rates at which data can be acquired and processed.

computer chemometric The application of computer data/analysis techniques to the classification, assimilation, and interpretation of chemical information. Its major purpose is to correlate data in such a way that trends or patterns are indicated.

computer command center CCC is basically a data collection device facilitating two-way communication with all monitoring terminals. This central computer supports the machine network, to which all data collection systems are connected, and the remote data display network, to which production monitors are connected, facilitating dissemination of information throughout the plant. It usually is a high-speed unit, equipped with optically isolated network controllers and heavy duty disk drives, since on the order of 2.5 megabytes of data can be collected in 24 hrs from as many as 20 or more operations or plants.

computer component control unit The control unit is responsible for coordinating the operation of the entire computer system. It generates and manages the operation of the computer by organizing and controlling the transfer of information between units and properly sequencing and executing the instruction of program processed by the computer. The control unit manages the control signals necessary to synchronize the flow of data on all the buses with the operation of the functional units. It also obtains, decodes, and executes successive instructions (a program) stored in the memory unit.

computer controlled dielectric monitoring
▷ **thermoset curing, dielectric monitoring**

computer controlled flexible manufacturing system A plastic processing system in which a group of machines usually are controlled by a system of conveyors and part handling (or transport) devices so that a variety of similar but different products can be manufactured automatically.

computer cost modeling, technically The adoption of any technology for producing manufactured products is characterized by a wide range of processing, materials, and economic consequences. Although considerable talent can be brought to bear on the processing and engineering aspects, economic questions remain. Cost problems are particularly acute when the technology that will be employed is not fully understood, as much of cost analysis is based on historical, past experience, and individual accounting practices.

Historically, technologies have been introduced on the shop floor incrementally, with their economic consequences measured directly. Although incorporating technical changes in the plant to test their viability may have been appropriate in the past, it is economically infeasible to explore today's wide range of alternatives in this fashion. Technical cost modeling (TCM) has been developed as a method for analyzing the economics of alternative manufacturing processes without the prohibitive economic burden of trial-and-error innovation and process optimization.

TCM is an extension of conventional process modeling, with particular emphasis on capturing the cost implications of process variables and economic parameters. By coordinating cost estimates with processing knowledge, critical assumptions (processing rate, energy used, materials consumed, etc.) can be made to interact in a consistent, logical, and accurate framework of economic analysis, producing cost estimates under a wide range of conditions.

For example, TCM can be used to determine the plastic process that is best for production without extensive expenditures of capital and time. Not only can TCM be used to establish direct comparisons between processes, but it can also determine the ultimate performance of a particular process, as well as identifying the limiting process steps and/or parameters.

computer cybernetic ▷ **cybernetic**

computer, design ▷ **design and computer**

computer digital-to-analog converter An analog output can be produced from a digital input through the use of a summing operational amplifier circuit. The operational amplifier sums the input currents and converts them to a scaled output voltage. Converters with 4 to 16 bits are common. D/A converters are used to operate any device that requires an analog input signal and that is interfaced to a digital source such as a computer.

computer direct memory access With a DMA controller, a peripheral device can autonomously have read/write access to the microprocessor's main memory without having to interact with the central processor. A high degree of efficiency is achieved with respect to the simultaneous utilization of the instrument and the microprocessor. This type of controller is appropriate when a large amount of data must be exchanged between the CPU and the peripheral devices or a great deal of processing is expected from the microprocessor.

Basically DMA is a method of transferring data very quickly between a peripheral such as a printer or CRT and memory without using the CPU to read or write the data. A special DMA controller, not available in all computer systems, is used to supervise such functions. DAF, or direct-access files, are terms sometimes used for RAF (random-access files) or RAM (random-access memory).

computer drawing There are choices of mode and function to be made in computer programs. Some of the choices of mode are positioning, grid choice, zoom, and line quality. In positioning, a digitizing tablet may be sensitive to differences of 0.01 in. or less. Most people's hand-eye coordination is less than this, and very few raster-scan monitors have such a fine resolution. A CAD program provides a grid constraint called "snap-lock" or "nearest pen". In this system the drafter will work with a grid set at a chosen spacing and the computer will "snap" the drawn point to the nearest grid point if the drawn point is within a set distance or "gravity field" of that point.

Regarding grid choice, although a drafter will typically use a square grid for a snap-lock device, an isometric grid may also be used. This is very useful for producing isometric sketches.

With zoom, as with a camera, the zoom function produces a magnification of a given part of a drawing. This part is usually identified by using a window. Zoom also helps solve the problem of the limited accuracy of hand-eye coordination by enlarging the details of a drawing.

Line quality is where there are several variations of lines that are usually available: line thickness, line type (solid, dashed, centerline, etc.), and color.

computer editing Editing consists of two types of activities. One type is that of using the erase, or delete, function to remove unwanted features from the drawing. The other is that of using other functions to modify the drawing, such as drawing, labeling, and transformation. Thus, the edit function usually means erasing, because that is what it does that is unique. Note that erasing will involve the same type of feature specification function in its submenu that is found in drawing and labeling. To be able to erase a line or a circle, you must be able to specify it.

computer genetic algorithm ▷ **genetic algorithm**

computer graphic CG involves the application of the capabilities of a computer to the analysis and synthesis of engineering problems; also the communication of solutions in a graphic format.

computer hardware The basic hardware configuration of every electronic digital computer comprises five standard hardware components which are connected by the internal signal pathways that make up the bus. These units are the arithmetic-logic unit (ALU), the control unit, the input and output units (collectively denoted as I/O), and the memory. The heart of a computer is the central processing unit, which is made up of the control unit and the arithmetic-logic unit. Regarding hardware selection, ▷ **computer software**

computer high-level language The high-level languages are convenient and user-oriented. They include Basic, Cobol, Fortran, Algol, and Pascal. These languages are either algebraic or English in nature. Each line of the source program generates many lines of object code. High-level language programs are machine-independent so a source-code program can run on different computers provided a translator program (to translate the code into machine language) is available for each brand of computer.

Structural programming is a technique often used with high-level languages. Algorithms are systematically formulated utilizing a top-down approach in which individual tasks at each level of complexity are broken down into a series of commands called subroutines. These subroutines can be written and tested as separate units. Structural programs consist of a hierarchy of interacting subroutines. Commands are flexible and easily understood by the operator.

computer image-processor An important aspect of the machine vision system, image-processing, is performed by a computerized unit called "vision engine". Many of these units have been designed for specific types of analysis, for example, gauging or pattern recognition. Many applications are highly data-intensive and, with certain types of image-capturing devices, could require a high order of computing power. Many of the applications-specialized processors use special techniques to simplify the analysis problem and reduce the data processing load. For any given application, therefore, it is important to match the characteristics of the vision engine to the specific needs of the job.

Machine vision systems can be classified as: configurable, task-specific, or custom (dedicated). Configurable systems are basically non-specialized systems that can be adapted for a specific application. They can be converted to other uses if the original application terminates.

The task-specific equipment performs a single function, such as measuring dimensions, as one of different examples. While they can accommodate a variety of objects, measurement is all they can do. Some of the task-specific systems, however, use configurable vision engines. In these installations it is the peripheral equipment-camera mounting arrangement, lighting, part fixturing, and/or material handling devices that makes the system task-specific. As with the generically configurable systems, the vision engines in the task-specific types can be used in other applications consistent with their performance envelope.

Customized, dedicated systems are analogous to fixed automation; the system becomes obsolete when the application disappears. Only the individual components might be reused.

computer in-line (or integrated) system When the computer becomes an integral, dedicated part of the packaged instrument, the configuration is known as in-line or integrated system. The computer supervises instrument operation by prompting the analyst for input parameters, by monitoring and actively controlling the instrument operation, and by processing the data and outputting it in predetermined formats. In these systems electrical and mechanical components are replaced by instructional statements (programs) that are stored in ROM (read-only memory). These programs are placed in the computer by the manufacturer and cannot be altered by the analyst. However, ROM chips can be replaced and the system upgraded. This permits changes in instrument control and data manipulation without the necessity of extensive and costly hardware modifications.

In-line computer systems are used with chromatographs (gas and liquid) and spectrophotometers where precise control of instrument parameters and the ability to perform repetitive analysis are required. Instrument accuracy is ensured by automatic instrument calibration coupled with built-in diagnostic testing. Communication between the instrument and other computer systems provides capabilities for the storage of large amounts of data, analysis of intermediate results, and coordination between different instruments.

computer input/output unit I/O units provide the computer with the external links which enable information to enter and leave the computer system. I/O units interface directly with the arithmetic-logic unit or the main memory. External sources of data include keyboards, remote terminals or memory devices, card readers, optical scanners, sensors, and instruments. Output units transfer data from the ALU (arithmetic-logic unit) or internal memory to external devices such as printers, plotters, external memory devices, visual display devices such as light-emitting diodes and video terminals, and control devices such as switches and stepper motors.

The efficiency of the I/O units is largely determined by which of two techniques are used: programmed I/O or direct memory access. In programmed I/O the arithmetic-logic unit sequentially executes instructions whose function is to transfer data between an I/O unit and memory. During this time other execution is inhibited. With direct memory access the memory controller autonomously transfers data between the I/O unit(s) and memory while the arithmetic-logic unit continues to process other instructions.

computer-instrument interface, software control Interactions between the central processor and peripheral devices are controlled in one of three ways: scanning (programmed I/O), interrupt, and direct memory access.

computer-integrated manufacturing CIM is a computer or system of computers that coordinates different (all) stages of manufacturing, which will enable the manufacturer to custom design products efficiently and economically. CIM begins with the integration of all equipment into a computer network. All equipment and processes that have an effect on productivity or quality control will be monitored and controlled by a central computer. This CIM addresses different functional aspects of plant operation that have a major impact on productivity and quality, such as process control, quality control, response on all systems, equipment maintenance and communication, production control, tooling, real-time process decisions, and so on.

computer integrating (counter), converter Integrating converters average the analog input over a fixed period of time and count out the average as a digital value. The size of the count is proportional to the magnitude of the analog input signal. The conversion time is directly proportional to the magnitude of the input signal, a limiting factor in most applications involving computer interfacing.

computer interface An interface system is used to connect a variety of I/O units and memory devices to programmable and nonprogrammable instruments, computers, and peripherals as needed when building an instrumentation system.

computer interrupt, central processor unit An interrupt mechanism is used when either the response time for the processor to service the peripheral device is critical or when too much processing time would be consumed by scanning. A special control lead is run over the control bus between the device(s) and the central processor unit. When this lead is activated, the CPU immediately interrupts its current task and begins to service the request. The CPU must first identify the interrupting peripheral. Then it determines the nature of the service request via the status register, and finally fulfills the request. This type of operation requires more complex hardware and software. Since the CPU is affected only when an interrupt occurs, this approach is more efficient when there are infrequent requests for services. Several tasks can be handled simultaneously (multitasking ability). Operations can be scheduled for definite time periods.

computer intraline Several microcomputers distributed within a single instrument constitute subsystems that have the capability to change the nature of the measurement system. These subsystems replace both hard-wired circuits and more general microcomputers. This improves the cost-performance characteristics of the entire system because maintenance costs are decreased. The analysis is more complete and reliable because the analyst is prompted to enter and check all variables. The accuracy of results is improved because the instrument is calibrated periodically. Built-in diagnostic tests check the functions of the instrument components. The precision of the results is improved through signal processing.

computerized database, plastics There are many materials, especially plastic materials (literally over 15,000 compounds), so just to review what is available in a relatively small grouping of a specific type(s) as well as the proliferation of constantly new types could be considered mind boggling. With a logical approach (designwise, engineeringwise, productionwise, etc.), it can become practical. However for certain individuals or organizations, manually it would probably be impossible to keep up to date even for the "veteran". As a result, manual searching that will do the job usually at lower cost can become a phenomenal and expensive task. On-line, computerized databases cut through this information overload by organizing materials (properties, processing, availability, updated cost, storage, etc.) into a manageable format. These programs not only significantly reduce acquisition time but also add options, such as update on what is new and those no longer available, etc.

computerized heat-transfer extruder roll analysis ▷ **extruder web heat-transfer roll adjustment**

computerized laboratory Laboratory (plastic, chemical, polymer, mechanical, etc.) instrumentation and procedures continually undergo dramatic changes. The thrust of the technical articles and the manufacturer's products are all oriented, wherever possible, to computer-assisted laboratory instrumentation and automation. Even the balance, the most basic analytical instrument, as well as temperature readings are coupled to a computer. People no longer have to record data by hand. In the computer-assisted laboratory the combination of the microcomputer and microprocessor relieves people of many manual manipulations involved in the procedure and simultaneously presents the results of the analysis both as hard copy (from a printer) and on screen (from the CRT). The trend is to expedite and improve the productivity of the laboratory and, at the same time, to minimize experimental errors and the amount of calculation required. To understand the role of a computer in a specific instrumental method, the interactions among the instrument, the computer, and the analyst or user must be considered. And as usual, a person has the prime responsibility to set-up requirements to be met and insure that complete and reliable results are obtained.

computer local area network LAN is a combination of computer hardware and software that enables stand-alone computers to transfer common data electronically.

computer machine interface unit MIU is a piece of computer hardware placed on or near a machine to collect and represent data from various sensors and/or other microprocessor-based devices.

computer machine-language program Computers execute binary-coded instructions stored in the primary memory. Machine-language programs are sequences of these binary instructions which take the form—operation/address. The operation is a function to be performed by the computer; the address is the location of the data to be manipulated. Writing machine-language programs is a tedious, time-consuming task which should be avoided whenever possible. Programs written in higher-level languages must eventually be converted into machine-language instructions, referred to as object programs.

computer mainframe A large computer with a minimum word size of 32 bits.

computer management information system MIS is a set of software applications generic to most business operations outside the manufacturing floor, including accounting, inventory control, quoting, job costing, overhead, return on investment, etc.

computer materials requirement planning MRP specifically identifies software used for materials planning but often a misnomer used to describe the entire set of business operations software or management requirement planning.

computer memory All information required by CPU (computer processing unit) is stored in a memory. Memory stores two basic classes of information, namely data and instructions. Each instruction represents a specific operation to be performed by the computer. Instructions are retrieved individually from memory and placed into specific registers in the CPU where they are interpreted (decoded) and executed by the computer. A sequence of instructions which performs a special task is called a program. Instructions also operate data. When required, data are moved from memory into the ALU (arithmetic-logic unit). Results from operations performed in that unit may again be stored in memory. Performance considerations of memory are volatility, capacity, and access time or speed. Volatile memory loses its information when the power is removed; this includes most semiconductor or solid-state memories. Memory capacity is commonly expressed as the number of data storage locations within a computer.

computer menu ▷ **computer software menu**

computer microprocessor control Reduced to a common denominator, the usual requirements for processing are better quality with reduced material consumption. Correspondingly, a control system is expected to provide exact acquisition of the significant process parameters, minimum response times, and high reproducibility. All important process data should be stored via an interface in a master computer or PC (personal computer). This type of system allows one to react promptly to quality changes, or even an increasing number of rejects. Constant maintenance of production documentation is important, not least because of the manufacturer's liability for the product. Further requirements are for relief of the operating staff and communication with other systems. Microprocessor control in processing technology is ideal for all these tasks and much more. This applies equally to the acquisition of all influencing variables, such as materials throughout, temperatures and pressures, as to communication through standardized interfaces. ▷ **temperature controller**

Apart from the control functions in continual production, a microprocessor control aids rapid production start-up with the usual heating program and shutdown with a cooling program. The preselected entry for heating and production start-up (exact day, hour, and minute) ensures the exact starting point. If during computer-aided start-up the machine does not start, the production temperature must be automatically cut down, thus preventing overheating the plastic and avoiding risks to people and machine. ▷ **microprocessor control**

For optimum results the microprocessor control synchronizes, as an example in an extruder, the dc motors. Once the speed ratio between the drive motors for the extruder, dosing mechanism, and take-off has been specified, this action will apply to future start-ups and for run-up to production conditions. Also being monitored are the torque of the main drive motor, the melt pressure, the axial force, etc. By limiting these parameters to a threshold value, the machine automatically shuts down in an emergency.

Any fault is indicated by a display in clear text. A special store, the alarm memory, enables the last number of faults (such as the usual 40, but also more) to be retained. Production evaluation is thus possible without paperwork or documentation for immediate action. The alarm signals are recorded with date and time, and are stored even when the unit is switched off. An important safety factor is the redundant data of the most important functions. This makes it possible for the machine to idle at low speed if the control fails. Torque monitoring and cut-off are also effective in this example. ROM (read-only menu) cassettes are used for data storage. They can store the record of many machines (15 and above). The index of each cassette can be read separately. This prevents unintentional overwriting. The advantage of these cassettes is that they operate without moving parts, and are therefore highly reliable.

computer millions of instructions per second MIPS is the speed at which a computer is capable of executing commands.

computer minicomputer A class of computer in which the basic element of the central processing unit is constructed of a number of discrete components and integrated circuits rather than being comprised of a single integrated circuit, as in the microprocessor.

computer modeling There are currently three predominant methods of building three dimensional (3-D) models of products and storing them in data bases. Each of these methods has advantages and limitations with associated costs. ▷ **modeling wire frame; modeling surface; modeling solid**

computer modem Derived from **MO**dular/**DEM**odulator, signifying an acoustic-coupling device permitting two computers to communicate over telephone lines. Its function is to convert analog form, required for phone lines which need "voice-like" signals, which are in turn demodulated into digital data again by a modem at the receiving end.

computer optical data storage ODS is the technology for storage, processing, and retrieval of vast quantities of data. In various formats, it is suitable for applications where mass replication of predetermined data is required, long-term (over 10 years) archiving, recording of legally nonalterable records, and where infinite erasability and rerecording are required. Because optical storage provides very high data density (up to 1 gigabyte per second on a 130 mm disk), removability from the drive, random access, and low cost per bit, it will be used to supplement and replace magnetic and micrographic storage devices.

This advance in data storage is possible by using a modulated laser beam as the recording head. A continuous laser beam functions as the playback probe. Information storage occurs in a recording layer on the surface of a support or substrate. During playback or reading, differences in the optical properties of the disk, which correspond to the encoded information, modulate the reflected read beam to produce a signal that corresponds to the input data. In replicated, ROM or read-only memory systems such as audio disks, information in the form of surface pits is manufactured in place. Modulation of the read beam is achieved by optical interference resulting from the depth of the pits. The surface of the disk is uniformly highly reflective. In the example of a user-recordable disk, the recording process changes the optical properties of the recording layer. These changes may be physical or chemical, but in all practical systems they must be completely made in nanoseconds and must be immediately detectable; they must not require a subsequent developing step. This type of recording, usually called DRAW (direct read-after-write), is necessary if data recorded are to be immediately verified. ▷ **holography**

computer overview It is practical for engineers (and others) to have a full complement of computer tools to take a design from the original idea through analysis, modeling, dimensioning, documentation, NC programming, and a wide variety of other design-related activities.

computer password ▷ **computer accessibility**

computer, personal ▷ **personal computer**

computer person, control happy ▷ **microprocessor control**

computer picture-level benchmark PLB is a program for running graphics and display performance tests on a vendor's hardware. It measures the length of time needed to execute a series of transformations for a specific picture, or a set of 2-D, 3-D, and/or bitmap data suited for a particular application. Geometry is defined in a data format called BIF (benchmark interface format). PLB program is available from the Standards and

Technical Service Department of the National Computer Graphics Association (NCGA). Sim Graphics Engineering Corp. (96 Monterey Rd., South Pasadena, CA 91030) developed the software for PLB.

computer, plastic and design ▷ **plastic, computer and design**

computer plastic flow analysis ▷ **design mold** and **design die**

computer plastic research transformation Scientists are creating membranes of block copolymers with pores so microscopic they could separate blood cells from plasma. The ability to accomplish this feat came as a result of a field of mathematics involving "minimal surfaces" or special shapes that take the least surface area under various kinds of constraints. This theory was developed during the 1850s by German mathematicians. Dr. Erwin Thomas, a professor in materials science and engineering at MIT, learned about the theory from two mathematicians at the University of Massachusetts-Amherst. Thomas' interest in the work grew from his research with block copolymers, a relatively new group of materials that could enhance microcircuits, membranes, and other miniature devices. His breakthrough came when a computer-generated pattern of a theoretical surface matched a photograph of the dividing surface in one of his real-life polymers. This development opened up defining materials with equations.

computer plotter A device that displays data output from a computer in graphical form.

computer printer The final output of a computer is usually generated on paper or by a plotter. There are three main types of printers: the daisy-wheel, the dot-matrix, and the laser printer. In the daisy-wheel printer a hammer hits the end of a particular spoke (which has a raised character on its end) onto a ribbon, which is between the paper and the spoke, thus imprinting a character. Dot-matrix printers use patterns of tiny dots in a matrix array to form each individual character. The quality of the printing depends largely on the number of pins in the print head array. The pins hit a ribbon, thus transferring the pattern to the paper. Laser printers work with computer input to determine which characters are to be printed. The actual printing process is similar to that of a copy machine. High-quality graphics can be printed along with text.

computer processing batch or off-line The batch (or off-line) mode of processing uses computer systems which incorporate mainframe central processing units. Data are collected from the instrument and stored on an external input medium, such as magnetic tape, punched cards, or a floppy disk. Then, along with a user-written program, the operator (user) schedules everything for input to the computer as a single package. Computer programs are written in an analyst-oriented language such as Fortran or Basic. This type of processing tends to optimize the use of the central processing unit because it allows all data and software to be available concurrently when needed. The output from a run is stored on a peripheral device for subsequent printing or display. Batch processing is useful for complex calculations or for manipulation of large amounts of data. Since there is no direct communication in a batch environment between the computer and the instrument or between the computer and the operator, this configuration tends to be unresponsive to the immediate needs of instrumentation or analysis. Orders are processed in the order submitted.

computer processing control Computer-controlled process automation can be applied to any process engineering problem, including typical tasks in plastics processing (injection molding, extrusion, adaptive control in haul-off auxiliary equipment, etc.). Automation can be installed if the process is easy to survey and can be described by experimental data. Clear physical relationships can seldom be set up in plastics processing because the flow processes are coupled with thermal and mechanical models. A valid description is usually only achieved by experiments (such as trial and error runs). The important process parameters are changed one after another to the limits of the working point ▷ **molding area diagram**. The results are summarized by mathematical formulas in the form of linear, logarithmic, and power functions. If a physical formula can be assumed, such as Arrhenius function, it can be included.

Many devices are available for process control, such as sensors, actuators, or computers. These devices can be connected with automation apparatus and integrated into a procedure. Automation improves efficiency and product quality, and reduces costs. Early analog systems have been replaced by digital automatic controls. The applications range from front-end computers which serve a single control circuit to process guidance systems that coordinate a complete operation. Digital systems for the past decades have been offering the advantage of flexible parameterization and connection of devices over the exchange of digital data. The process and its control system can only function with the help of appropriate instrumentation for the exchange of data.

computer processing control, statistically A statistical process control (SPC) system begins with the premise that the specifications for a product can be defined in terms of the product's (customer's) requirements, or that a product is or has been produced that will satisfy those needs. An SPC manufacturing process is highly automated, with a series of communications loops between process and computers. Generally the computer communicates with a series of process controllers which operate in individual data loops. The computer sends set points (built on which performance characteristics the product must have) to the process controller, which constantly feeds back to the computer to signal whether or not these set of points are in fact being maintained.

The systems are programmed to act when key variables affecting product quality deviate too far from desired levels. Before SPC, almost everything was done manually. Now it is practically all computer-driven, tracking, monitoring, and controlling the entire process.

computer program ▷ **software** and **algorithm**

computer programmable PCs are "changeable" computers, usually employing up to 16-bit word length, used to control machines and processes. A PC uses digital electronics and has a programmable memory, a set number of I/O, and a specific programming language. The PC can, in fact, be a full-blown microcomputer or minicomputer. Basically it is a control system often used to operate machinery in place of the standard electromechanical relays. The controls are programmed rather than permanently wired as in standard control methods. ▷ **computer microprocessor controller** and **microprocessor control**

computer random-access memory RAM is data that can be put into or retrieved from memory in any order. It can be dynamic or static and is usually volatile. The dynamic or volatile memory in a microprocessor used to hold and access information, such as a program, in a computer is prompted by the user. The amount of RAM available for data or program storage is expressed in kilobytes (thousands of bytes; kb) or megabytes (millions of bytes; Mb).

computer read only memory ROM is an area of a computer memory in which operating instructions and other programs reside permanently. The user can activate, but not alter, programs in this area.

computer real time or on-line In real-time systems the computer is connected directly to one or more instruments through an electronic interface. Data from one experiment can be fed directly into the computer system where they are processed and made available immediately to the operator. The analyst interacts with both the computer and the instrument to obtain and process data, control instrument operation, and retrieve results. Further processing of data can be requested. In this mode the computer responds instantaneously to data acquired from the instrument and thus can be used to control or modify the conditions of the experiment. All the data generated can be stored for future reference.

Basically, real time is information that represents a condition or set of conditions as they exist at the time. The computer and the instrument form a symbiotic relationship which provides a dynamic approach to experimentation and analysis. Methods that require the rapid execution of complex mathematical transformation functions, such as infrared spectroscopy and Fourier transform nuclear resonance, would be rather limited without on-line computers.

computer scanning Scanning is carried out by the central processor, which periodically surveys a device (or each of several devices) to determine if action or service is required. A status register is maintained by each instrument to indicate its needs for service and the specific nature of the request. This is the register which is interrogated by the microprocessor during interface operations. A positive response causes the processor to prompt the instrument for the specific nature of the request, which the processor then satisfies. If no service is required, the processor either scans another device or returns to rescan the first device at a later time. Scanning techniques are simple to implement both in hardware and software. However, they place a moderate amount of overhead on the central processor and should be used only when processor time is available or when a large number of positive service requests are expected.

computer software Selection of hardware should be one of the last steps in the purchase of any computer system. The software (also called program) provides instructions for the hardware, and without the software, the most impressive hardware specifications are meaningless. One would first choose the software, and then select the computer that is compatible with the software. Data acquisition and control applications require computers to respond to events in the real world. These external events intrinsically set the parameters of the response required of the computer and are independent of the computer's optimal mode of operation. These applications make some unique demands on a computer system, particularly when the system is operating near maximum capacity.

The user communicates with the digital computer through a sequence of instructions (program) written in a computer language. Programs are referred to as software in contrast to the hardware or physical components of the computer. All computations done by the computer must be predefined by a series of logical steps (logarithms). The lowest level of programming is in binary code and is machine-oriented. Higher-level languages are machine-independent.

computer software menu The menu is a software device that makes the user of the program aware of the structure of the program and what its component parts can do for the user. Thus, the menu is a list of choices in a program that were included in the program (software). For instance, a computer loaded with a production program can ask the user if the person wants to know about inventory, production levels, or any other facet of production among the preprogrammed selections. There is also a "menu-driven" program that prompts the user by presenting questions such as: what do you want to do next, look at, and/or change next. Options would be listed. The program will not continue until a reply(s) is entered. Another example is with a CAD program that would entail deciding whether or not user will be printing out a drawing, digitizing a paper or vellum drawing, or doing a new drawing. User may also be required to make choices on drawings that involve factors such as editing, labeling and other text transformations, and dimensioning.

computer storage disk and tape The disk device is the primary device used in personal computers (PC) and mainframe computers for reading, writing, and storing programs and data. Disk drives store data magnetically. They are quickly accessed, and old data can be overwritten when no longer needed. The disk is read by an electromagnetic head. In PC systems, hard disks have data capacity of 10 to 100 Mb. Floppy disks (or diskettes) are designed to be moved in and out of their drives but have less storage space (0.36 to 1.4 Mb). They are primary means of moving information from one station to another, and most vendors supply their software in this form. Magnetic tapes, either cassettes or larger reel-to-reel tapes, are used for long-term storage on many mainframe systems. Access time may be very long, and for this reason, fixed disks are prefered for day-to-day use and tapes are reserved for archiving purposes.

computer successive-approximation converter A successive-approximation converter uses a series of logical guesses (approximations) to determine the digital equivalent of the analog input. It offers high resolution and fast conversion times which are independent of the magnitude of the analog input signal. The converter requires N^{th} (so many) approximation for an N-bit conversion.

computer support planning ▷**just-in-time**

computer "thinks" Engineers of the future could have computerized assistants that really understand their projects. R&D projects, past and present, have the ability to create a computer system that would understand how its human boss likes to approach design problems and the language used to talk about them, would remember past projects, and even anticipate the user's need for data. Purpose would be to speed the product delivery process, from initial concept, through development and design, to production.

computer time sharing system A software system that permits multiple users on a computer at the same time. While the computer actually does only one thing at a time, it is fast enough to service several users with only slight, imperceptible delays.

computer tolerance analysis Computer programs developed since the 1980s continually have made it possible to aid in modeling the complex interactions of the many processing factors that include plastic properties and behavior, geometry of the part, toolmaking quality applied in building the mold or die, and, very importantly the processing conditions and fluctuations inherent in the equipment. It is not reasonable to expect an engineer, using manual methods, to calculate these complex interactions, even when only modest part complexity exists, without omissions or errors. Computerized process simulation is a practical approach to monitor the influence of design alternatives on processability of the part, and to select processing conditions that ensure the required part quality. Also provides information when parts cannot meet standards tolerancewise. ▷**tolerance; shrinkage; limit dimensioning; designing without sink and shrinkage**

computer voltage-to-frequency converter Voltage-to-frequency converters transform an analog signal to a train of digital pulses at a rate that is proportional to the input voltage. The train is then counted over a fixed time interval to create a digital value. Voltage-to-frequency conversion offers excellent resolution and minimizes noise when data are transmitted over some distance but requires a conversion time of about 0.4 s. Speed is traded for the ability to represent accurately low-level input signals.

computer warmware In the computer business people are identified as warmware.

computer wetware In the computer business the human brain is identified as wetware.

computing, bio ▷ **biocomputing**

concave surface Surface curved inward, such as the inner surface of a food bowl.

concavity A hollowed portion or place in an article.

concentrate A measured amount of additive (dye, foaming agent, flame retardant, fiber reinforcement, etc.) is incorporated into a predetermined small amount of plastic. This concentrate can then be mixed into larger quantities of plastic to achieve a desired mix and required property for the processed part.

concentricity **1.** The ratio, expressed in percent, of the minimum wall thickness to the maximum wall thickness. **2.** For a container, the shape in which various cross sections have a common center.

concrete A conglomerate composite of gravel, pebbles, sand, crushed stone, blast-furnace slag, or cinders, termed the aggregate. They are embedded in a matrix of either mortar or cement, usually standard portland cement in U.S.

concrete, cellular ▷ **cellular concrete**

concrete-plastic These composites have been used since at least 1943 to improve the mechanical properties and durability of concrete products based usually, but not exclusively, on portland cement. Basically modification of cement or concrete products is done by various techniques that include: (1) plastic impregnated concrete using a liquid monomer that is polymerized in situ, (2) monomer or plastic latex in the mix of cement aggregate and water usually called polymer portland cement concrete, and (3) water-soluble plastic in a cement-water mix to give rheology eliminating macroscopic defects owing to poor particle packing and entrapped air. Increased comprehensive strength (tensile, flexural, modulus, etc.), reduced water permeability and absorption, increased abrasion resistance, color retention in mixes, and resistance to aggressive environments such as rain water, freeze-thaw cycles, or seawater, result. Different plastics are used, including thermoset polyester, acrylic, phenolic, and polyethylene. Mixes of cement-plastics produce non-shrink characteristics; filling cracks eliminates shrinkage voids.

concrete reinforced Composite reinforced concrete and ferro concrete contain steel rods in various forms to significantly increase performances (strength, etc.) over unreinforced concrete. In areas near the (saltwater) ocean or big bodies of water, steel is protected from corrosion by a cover of plastic, usually polyethylene or polypropylene.

concrete, reinforced oriented composite Steel rods can be prestretched during solidification of the concrete to provide increased performance over unstretched steel reinforced concrete. ▷ **orientation**

condensation A polymerization reaction in which simple byproducts, for example water, are formed.

condensation agent Chemical compound which, besides its catalytic action, furnishes a complement of material necessary for the achievement of the polycondensation of a plastic.

condensation plastic A plastic formed by polycondensation, such as alkyd, phenolaldehyde, and urea formaldehyde plastics.

condensation polymerization It is defined by IUPAC as polymerization by a repeated condensation process, i.e., with elimination of simple molecules. The products of condensation polymerization reactions are termed condensation polymers (plastics). If a plastic is formed, the process is called polycondensation. Just as esters and amides are products of simple condensation reactions of monofunctional reactants, so polyesters and polyamides are the products of condensation polymerization of difunctional acids with difunctional alcohols or amines. Water is frequently the small molecule split off during condensation; other common by-products of polymerizations based on plastic used are ammonia, hydrogen chloride, carbon dioxide, sodium bromide, nitrogen, methanol, etc. ▷ **polymerization reaction**

conditioning The subjection of a material to a stipulated treatment so that it will respond in a uniform way to subsequent testing or processing. The term is frequently used to refer to the treatment given specimens before testing. (Standard ASTM test methods that include requirements for conditioning are indexed in the index of ASTM Standards.)

conductive plastic ▷ **plastic conductivity**

conductivity Transfer of thermal or electrical energy along a potential gradient. It is the reciprocal of volume resistivity—electrical and thermal conductance of a unit cube of any material (conductivity per unit volume). ▷ **dielectric heating; plastic conductivity; thermal conductivity; electrically conductive**

conduit **1.** A pipe for conveying fluid. **2.** A

tubular raceway for carrying electrical wires, cables, or other conductors.

cone calorimeter test ▷ **fire, tests, cone and lift**

confidence interval The range of values of a population parameter computed so that the statement "the population parameter lies in this interval" will be true on the average, in a stated proportion of the times such statements are made.

confidence level The probability that the true value lies within a stated range (the confidence interval).

confidence limit The limits on either side of the mean value of a group of observations which will, in a stated fraction or percent of the cases, include the expected value. Thus the 95% confidence limits are the values between which the population mean will be situated in 95 out of 100 cases.

configuration **1.** Related chemical structures produced by the cleavage and reforming of covalent bonds; arrangement of polymers along a plastic molecule chain. **2.** The structural makeup of a chemical compound, especially with reference to the spatial relationship of the constituent atoms.

conformal **1.** Leaving the size of an angle between corresponding curves unchanged. **2.** Representing small areas in their true shape.

conformal coating ▷ **encapsulation**

conformation The morphological disposition of a molecule in its environment, for example, the coiling of a macromolecular chain in a poor solvent and the uncoiling in a good solvent.

conical dry blender A device consisting of two hollow cones joined at their bases by a short cylindrical section, mounted on a horizontal shaft passing through the sides of the cylinder section. Material is charged and discharged at openings in the apexes of the cones. Mixing is accomplished by cascading, rolling, and tumbling actions as the cones rotate.

conjugated In chemistry, referring to the regular alternation of single and double bonds between atoms of a molecule.

conjugate planes Two plånes of an optical system such that one is the image of the other.

connector ▷ **fastener** and **electrical connector**

conservation of energy ▷ **energy conservation**

consistency A property of a material determined by the complete flow force relation.

consolidation A processing step that compresses fiber and matrix to reduce voids and achieve a desired density.

constant amplitude loading In fatigue loading, a loading in which all of the peak loads are equal and all of the valley loads are equal.

constantin A copper-nickel alloy, wires of which are used in conjunction with wires of a different metal (usually iron) in thermocouples for measuring temperatures.

constant rate test machine ▷ **tensile test machine test rates**

constituent In general an element of a larger grouping. As an example in reinforced plastics, the constituents are the fibers and the plastic matrix.

construction and building ▷ **building and construction**

consumption of energy ▷ **energy consumption**

consumption of plastics ▷ **plastic consumption**

contact adhesive An adhesive that is apparently dry to the touch and that will adhere to itself simultaneously upon contact. An adhesive that, when applied to both adherends and allowed to dry, develops a bond when the adherends are brought together without sustained pressure.

contact angle The angle (θ) formed by a droplet in contact with a solid surface, measured from within the droplet. Applicable in determining degree of adhesively bonding or laminating based on wettability of the surface. An advancing contact angle is formed when the droplet (usually water) advances onto a fresh surface. A receding contact angle is formed when the droplet is withdrawn from a portion of the surface with which it has been in contact. A contact angle of zero implies complete wetting of the solid by the liquid, a value of $\theta = 180°$ (rarely, if ever, encountered) would correspond to absolute non-wetting, and intermediate values correspond to various degrees of incomplete wetting.

The contact angle θ is related to the interfacial tensions of the solid-vapour γ_{SV}, and liquid-vapor γ_{LV} interfaces through the following expressions:

$$\cos\theta \frac{\gamma_{LV} - \gamma_{SL}}{\gamma_{LV}} \text{ (units in degree)}$$

contact lens Contact lenses range from hard to soft. Conventional hard lenses contain no less than 95% PMMA. They are designed and fit in such a manner that the tear fluid supplies the oxygen required by the cornea. Hard and semirigid lenses permeable to oxygen are produced; most often made from copolymers of siloxanes and methacrylates. Flexible, oxygen-permeable silicone lenses are also available. Soft contact lenses are prepared from polymers that absorb large quantities of water to become hydrogels; the aqueous phase of the hydrogels is oxygen-permeable.

The difference between these contact lenses is the manner in which they fit in the eye. Hard contact lenses and hydrophobic flexible lenses require a relatively thick tear film between their surfaces and the cornea; this is of optical and physiological importance. Soft hydrogel lenses adhere closely to the cornea with only a tear film of capillary thickness between the lens and the cornea.

Different processing methods are used to produce lenses. Starting from a plastic or a semifinished lens, most hard contact and silicone-acrylate lenses are made by standard methods of machining and polishing; CAB and PMMA are also injection molded. Soft contacts are prepared by several methods such as centrifugal casting of hydrogel contact lenses. A monomer solution containing a mixture of a cross-linking agent, modifiers, and an initiator is polymerized in a mold rotating about its central axis. The result is swollen materials, which are equilibrated in physiological saline solution. A more widely used method is a standard machining operation similar to that used for hard lenses.

Direct casting of finished contact lenses (so-called dry-state) has been used for various plastics. The monomer mix containing appropriate initiators is placed in disposable plastic molds and cured by either thermal or ultraviolet initiated polymerization. Minor finishing steps, such as edge buffing, may be used. Direct casting followed by hydration is an economical route to finished hydrogel lenses.

Rigid lenses represent 10 to 15% of the contact lens market and are used by 85% of people who have astigmatism. All contact lenses not made of PMMA are regulated by the FDA. In the U.S., new contact lenses must be approved by the FDA. The FDA also has jurisdiction over lens-care products.

contact molding A process for molding reinforced plastics in which the reinforcement and plastic are placed on a mold. Cure is either at room temperature using a catalyst-promoter system or by heating in an oven, without additional pressure or very little. Also called open molding or contact pressure molding.

contact plastic A synthetic thermoset plastic characterized by cure at relatively low pressure. The usual components are an unsaturated, high molecular weight monomer, such as allyl ester, or a mixture of styrene or other vinyl monomer with an unsaturated polyester or alkyd. Cure requires heat and a catalyst as well as contact pressure. The curing does not result in any byproduct such as water (as with condensation plastics). These type thermoset polyester plastics were developed in 1942 to meet military aircraft reinforced plastic requirements.

contact pressure The force per unit area of physical contact between two contacts. This term is frequently but improperly used when contact force is meant. The area of physical contact is usually difficult to determine and quite different from the apparent area of contact.

contact pressure molding ▷ **molding pressure, contact**

contact pressure plastic Liquid plastics that thicken (polymerize) upon heating and require little or no pressure.

container A receptacle that contains material, such as a milk bottle. They range from simple to very complex shapes.

container blown, volume adjustment ▷ **volume adjustment blown container**

container, Boston round A particular shape of the container; cross section as well as shoulders are round.

container, chime ▷ **chime**

container, choked neck Narrowed or constricted opening in the neck of a container.

container code system The Plastic Bottle Institute of SPI established (1988) a nationally recognized voluntary material identification system to assist separators of plastic bottles and create a higher value for recycled material. Bottles are coded by the most widely used plastics as shown in the Fig. on p. 151. The code is located on the bottom of the bottle or container.

container collapse Contraction of the walls of a container upon cooling after manufacture (such as in blow molding, etc.) leading to a permanent deformation of the container.

container, collapsible or foldable ▷ **bottle, collapsible**

container, column crush ▷ **column crush**

container, head space The space between the fill level of a container and the sealing plane.

Code		Material
1	PETE	Polyethylene terephthalate (PET)
2	HDPE	High-density polyethylene
3	V	Vinyl/polyvinyl chloride (PVC)
4	LDPE	Low-density polyethylene
5	PP	Polypropylene
6	PS	Polystyrene
7	Other	All other resins and layered multimaterial

Examples of container code system for plastic bottles. The stand alone bottle code is different from standard industry identification to avoid confusion with registered trademarks.

container, heel The part of a container between the bottom bearing surface and the side wall.

container, heel radius The degree of curvature at the extreme bottom end of a container extending upward from the bearing surface. Also called base radius.

container, hot fill ▷ **packaging, hot fill**

container, neck-down A phrase used to describe a tapering, downward and inward, of a container body.

container, oblong A particular shape. A container which has a rectangular cross section perpendicular to the major axis.

container, off center Any condition where the finish opening is not centered over the bottom of the container. Also, the condition where the mandrel is not concentric with the ring of the blowing head.

container, oil canning ▷ **oil canning**

container, recessed panel A container designed with a label panel in which the area for labeling is indented or recessed.

container, refillable Designed to be refilled as long as the container is not cracked, chipped, or uncleanable.

container, returnable In states with a deposit law, both refillable and nonrefillable containers are returnable containers.

container, rocker A bottle with bottom deformed so it does not stand solid (rocks).

container, round square Particular shape of a container which has sides of equal width with well-rounded corners and shoulders.

container, sealing surface The surface of the finish of the container on which the closure forms the seal.

container, top load The amount of weight bearing on the top of a container. The term is sometimes used to indicate the maximum load the container will bear without becoming distorted.

container, wall thickness determination Different devices are used, including mechanical measurements/calipers, optical sensors, and different radiation sensors such as infrared.

contaminant A material that makes a primary material impure and usually reduces or affects one or more properties when recycled. ▷ **recyclable plastic and scrap; recycling clean; railcar hopper contamination**

continuous phase In a solution or mixture, the major component is called the continuous or external phase and the minor component is called the dispersed or internal phase. The latter may or may not be uniformly dispersed in the continuous phase.

continuum mechanics ▷ **Boltzmann superposition principle**

contour package Packages in which a thin plastic sheet is formed over the product and simultaneously sealed to a paperboard or plastic backing. The product serves as a mold. Also called skin package. ▷ **blister package** and **shrink wrapping**

contract law ▷ **product liability law**

contract processor ▷ **processor, contract**

control In any process or experiment, the reference base with which the results are compared. The control represents known or target requirements of facts and/or figures. The use of a control is vital to provide interpretation of the final product. ▷ **process control** and **motion control systems**

control, adaptive A method by which input from sensors automatically and continuously adjusts to provide near optimum process control.

control, automatic Maintaining desired process conditions by means of sensing devices which function either electromechanically (such as thermostat) or electronically (feedback).

control, close-loop A device that will recognize a fault in a process and automatically correct it.

control, computer ▷ **computer component control unit**

control, electronic logic Permits complex timing and sequencing functions in different processing equipment to be programmed and controlled.

control, front-end ▷ **control, open-loop**

control happy ▷ **microprocessor control**

controlled atmosphere ▷ **atmosphere, controlled**

controlled release, delivery system ▷ **microencapsulation coating**

controller Device that manages functions and/or sequences. ▷ **programmable controller**

controller, automatic reset Technique used in modern controllers (compared with older proportional controllers) which permits accurate control of temperature at set point from full heating to full cooling even in the presence of lag time from remote locations.

controller, multizone Microprocessor that monitors (temperature, etc.) signals from several sensors to achieve more reliable and efficient performance, either independently or coordinated.

control, microprocessor ▷ **microprocessor control**

control, open-loop A device that will recognize a fault but not correct it; corrective action is taken manually by a person or the machine can be set to stop operating. Also called front-end control.

convection Basically energy transfer by moving or flowing gas or liquid. Natural convection results from differences in density caused by temperature differences. Thus warm air is less dense than cool air; the warm air rises relative to the cool air, and vice versa. Forced convection involves motion caused by pumps, blowers, and/or other mechanical devices. ▷ **heating plastic**

conversion, English-metric-English factors See *Conversion Tables* on p. xxiii.

converter A term used primarily in the packaging industry. They buy plastic film or sheeting in the form of roll stock and convert it to useful forms by slitting, die cutting, heat sealing into bags, etc. for resale to packaging firms.

conveyor Usually a mechanical device to transport material, products, and tools from one point to another, often continuously. The most important of these auxiliary equipment types are as follows: chain, belt, screw, and pipeline; nonmechanical are gravity roller, bucket, and pneumatic.

convexity That portion or place on an object which protrudes as a roughly spherical shape.

convex surface Surface curved outward, such as the surface of a sphere.

coolant It is any liquid or gas having the property of absorbing heat from its environment and transferring it efficiently away from its source. Coolants are used in different processes such as those using molds. One of the most effective and low cost coolants is water. Coolants operating below freezing incorporate an antifreeze such as ethylene glycol. ▷ **chiller** and **Reynold's number**

cooling and shaping extrudate ▷ **extruder line cooling and shaping**

cooling channel ▷ **mold cooling channel**

cooling fixture A fixure of wood or metal used to maintain the shape or dimensional accuracy of a molded part after it is removed from the mold. Permits reducing cycle time by removing a part from the mold before it is completely cooled.

cooperage The manufacture of barrels, formerly only of wood (decades ago) but now including plastics such as reinforced thermosets and blow molded thermoplastics.

coordinated laminate A reference coordinate system used to describe the properties of a reinforced plastic generally in the direction of principal axis.

coordinate measuring machine CCM makes multiple measurements on parts with contours and irregular surfaces or shapes in a fraction of time required for conventional manual gauges. They are used in-line and off-line production for inspection or quality control. Usually a computer controls and records the 3-D measurements with a probe that can have a contact or noncontact measuring sensor (optical, IR, etc.).

copal A group of fossil plastics still used to some extent in varnishes and lacquers. Insoluble in oils and water. Most important types are Congo, kauri, and manila.

copolyester elastomer These COPES were developed to replace rubber and thermoplastic elastomers (TPEs) and some high performance engineering TPs. As an example, they are generally tougher than PURs. In general they are easier and more forgiving in processing.

copolymer A compound resulting from the chemical reaction of two chemically different monomers with each other that results in long change molecules.

copolymer alternating A copolymer in which each repeating unit is joined to another repeating unit in the polymer chain (–A–B–A–B–).

copolymer halogenated ▷ **halogenation**

copolymerization The building up of linear or non-linear macromolecules (copolymers) in which many monomers, possessing molecules having one or more double bonds, have been located in every macromolecule of different size which constitutes the copolymerizate, following alternations which may be regular or not. ▷ **polymerization; block copolymer; graft copolymer**

copper Excellent conductor of electricity and heat. More resistant to atmospheric corrosion than iron. Cu use includes electroplating coating on plastics, catalysts, antifouling plastic paints, alloys (beryllium copper) used in molds to provide relatively fast heat transfer, and as whiskers used in thermal and electrical reinforced plastics.

copper-clad laminate Laminated plastic surface with copper foil, used for preparing electrical printed circuits.

coral Skeletons of the coral polyps found in the warmer oceans and consisting mainly of calcium carbonate colored with ferric oxide. Use includes plastic encapsulation for ornaments and jewelry.

cordage Includes all types of threads, twine, and rope produced by twisting fibers together.

core **1.** Male element in a mold or die that produces a hole or recess in a product. **2.** Part of a complex mold that molds undercut products. Cores are usually withdrawn to one side before the main sections of the mold open (usually called side cores). **3.** A channel in a mold for circulation of a heat-transfer medium. **4.** A device on which prepreg is wound. **5.** The central member of a sandwich (core) construction to which the faces of the sandwich are attached. Core materials include foamed plastics, honeycombs (plastic film or fiber construction; glass, carbon, aramid, etc. fiber; aluminum foil, etc.), balsa wood, solid sheets (plastic, wood, aluminum, metal, etc.) and different shapes such as fluted cores. **6.** In blow molding, that part of the extruder die that controls the inside dimension of the parison. **7.** The central member of a plywood assembly. **8.** Core is used in wrapping film, fabric, etc.

core pin ▷ **mold core pin**

core pulling sequence ▷ **mold core pulling sequence**

Corey, Pauling, and Koltun mode ▷ **computer-aided molecular graphic**

Corfam Du Pont's tradename for a tough, leatherlike, nonwoven sheet of polyurethane polymer fibers deposited in a random manner and held together with a binder of polyester plastic to obtain uniform strength in all directions. It contains many pores, permitting "breathing". Used as a substitute for shoe leather, packings and seals for chemical pumps, etc.

coring **1.** The removal of excess material from the cross section of a molded part to attain a more uniform wall thickness. **2.** The method of sizing and shaping a blown bottle opening by appropriate tools. **3.** A variable composition between the center and outside of a unit of structure.

cork A form of cellulose comprising the light outer bark of the tree known as *Quercus suber*. It grows naturally in Europe and Northern Africa, and has been cultivated in Southwestern U.S. Its special properties are extreme lightness, relatively impervious to water, resilient structure, and low rate of heat transfer. Use includes bottle stoppers, insulation, wallboard, sound deadening insertions, gaskets, and core in sandwich constructions that include reinforced and/or reinforced plastic skins.

corona ▷ **electrical corona**

co-rotating screw ▷ **extruder, screw multiple type**

corotational molding ▷ **rotational molding**

corrosion Basically corrosion is the deterioration and removal by chemical attack of common metals. Basically this action does not occur on plastics. However, when a broad term is applied to many different environmental conditions (rather than a true corrosive situation), plastics can be affected. Corrosion actually represents the electrochemical degradation of metal or its alloys due to reaction with their environment, which is accelerated by the presence of moisture, acids, and/or bases. Corrosion products often take the form of metallic oxides. This is actually beneficial in the case of aluminum and stainless steel, for the oxide forms a strong adherent coating which effectively prevents further degradation.

corrosion fatigue Synergistic effect of fatigue and aggressive environment acting simultaneously, which leads to a degradation in fatigue behavior.

corrosion inhibitor Any material used by the steel industry to inhibit corrosion. This includes the use of plastic coatings.

corrosion resistant coating ▷ **barrier material performance**

corrugated Different materials wrapped in parallel ridges and furrows for rigidity; materials include paper and cardboard, plastic, aluminum, steel, etc.

cosmetic market The cosmetic industry has made use of plastic technology, in particular paints, coatings, and containers. Plastics used in formulations of cosmetics must meet stringent safety requirements (FDA, etc.) because, like pharmaceuticals and food, they are in intimate contact with the consumer. The range of plastics used is rather wide; many different types are used to meet many different requirements.

A ruling by the FDA in 1973 requires the cosmetic industry to include the ingredients on the label of a cosmetic sold in the retail market. The CTFA (the industry representative before FDA) published a compendium containing the designations for most cosmetic ingredients. These names are acceptable to the FDA. The purpose of this compendium is to warn users who might have allergies. The names chosen do not, however, reflect the chemistry in all ingredients. They are designed to fit easily on a package or label.

cost As shown by the Figures and the Table on this and the next page, cost involves: (1) materials, (2) purchasing method, (3) processing method, and (4) manufacturing costs. It is a misconception that plastics are "cheap"; there are low-cost types but also more expensive types when compared to other materials and performance requirements. To put plastics in its proper cost perspective, it is usually best to compare material cost based on volume, rather than weight. The real cost advantage of plastics is based on low cost processing.

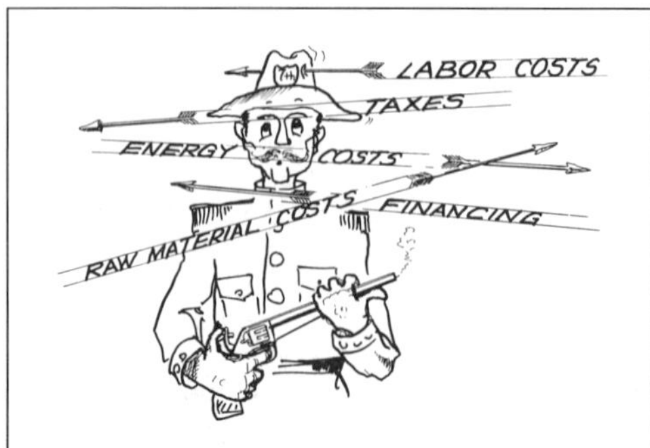

Examples of manufacturing costs.

Cost comparison of plastic products and different processes (cost factor × material cost = purchase cost of product).

Process	Cost factor	
	Overall	Average
Blow molding	$1\frac{1}{16}$ to 4	$1\frac{1}{8}$ to 2
Calendering	$1\frac{1}{2}$ to 5	$2\frac{1}{2}$ to $3\frac{1}{2}$
Casting	$1\frac{1}{2}$ to 3	2 to 3
Centrifugal casting	$1\frac{1}{2}$ to 4	2 to 4
Coating	$1\frac{1}{2}$ to 5	2 to 4
Cold pressure molding	$1\frac{1}{2}$ to 5	2 to 4
Compression molding	$1\frac{3}{8}$ to 10	$1\frac{1}{2}$ to 4
Encapsulation	2 to 8	3 to 4
Extrusion forming	$1\frac{1}{16}$ to 5	$1\frac{1}{8}$ to 2
Filament winding	5 to 10	6 to 8
Injection molding	$1\frac{1}{8}$ to 3	$1\frac{3}{16}$ to 2
Laminating	2 to 5	3 to 4
Match-die molding	2 to 5	3 to 4
Pultrusion	2 to 4	2 to $3\frac{1}{2}$
Rotational molding	$1\frac{1}{4}$ to 5	$1\frac{1}{2}$ to 3
Slush molding	$1\frac{1}{2}$ to 4	2 to 3
Thermoforming	2 to 10	3 to 5
Transfer molding	$1\frac{1}{2}$ to 5	$1\frac{3}{4}$ to 3
Wet lay-up	$1\frac{1}{2}$ to 6	2 to 4

cost and molecular weight The MW of a commercial plastic may have a number of significant effects on price. Most often, high molecular weight are more expensive to produce and process. In general, they require the use of more highly purified monomer, which is costly to produce. In many addition polymerization reactions, HMW requires lower polymerization temperature, often involving costly refrigeration and longer polymerization time. In conventional molten bulk condensation polymerization reactions, HMW plastics require longer polymerization time, higher temperatures, etc. Also, HMWs of high viscosity require more power and time during compounding and processing.

Occasionally it is low molecular weight plastic which is more costly to produce. This may happen for a variety of reasons. For example, in coordination polymerization of olefins, it is often very easy to reach extremely HMWs, and much more difficult to stop at controlled LMW required temperatures, which create higher vinyl chloride monomer pressures, etc. Many of the

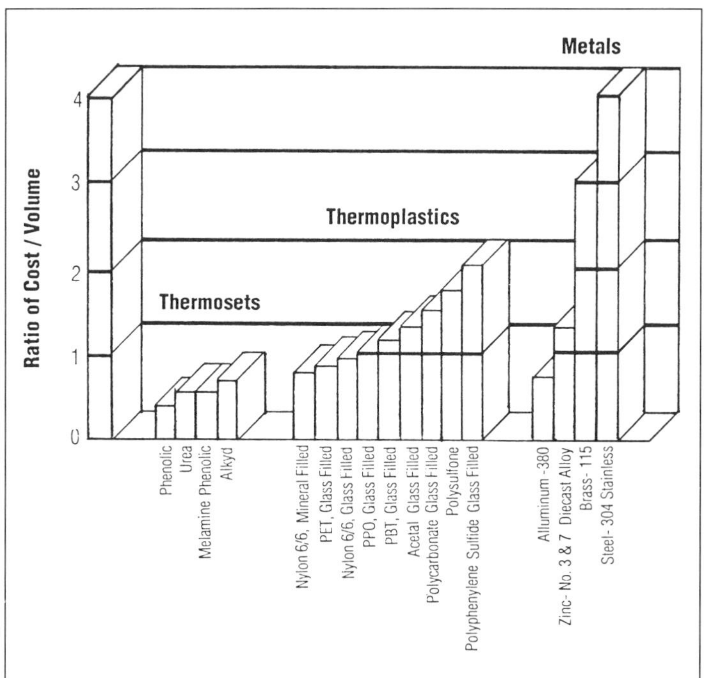

General cost comparison based on volume for the general classification of materials.

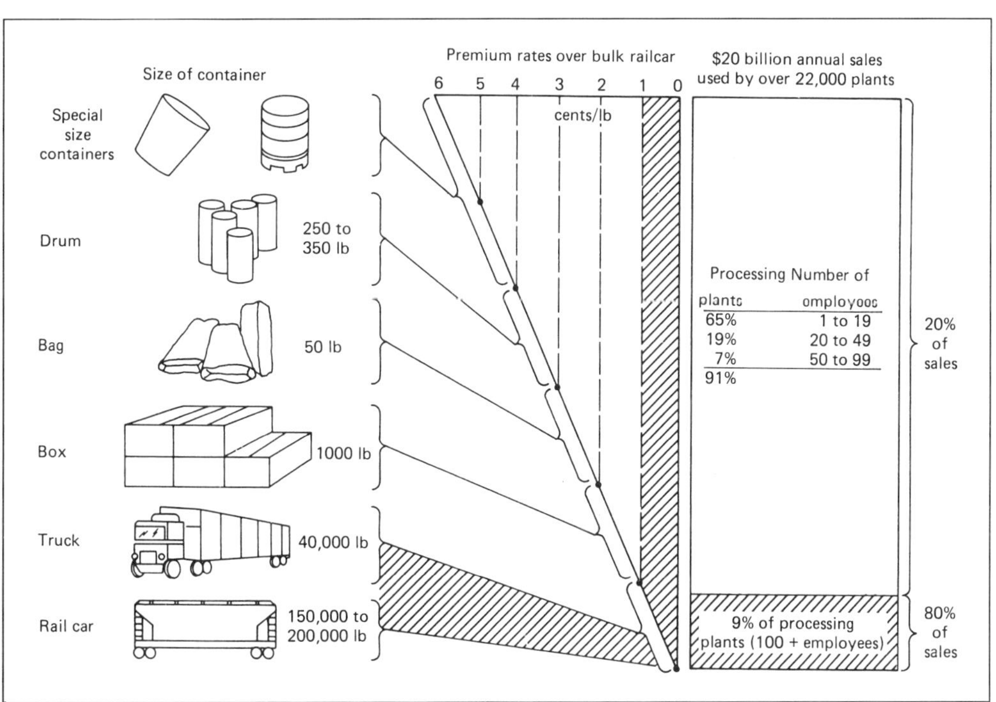

Example of material cost based on method of purchasing, as well as plastic dollar purchases by plant size.

B-stage thermosets and liquid plastics are so reactive that they have at best a limited shelf life during room temperature storage, and thus require careful control during production and stabilization during storage, etc. For these reasons LMWs may sometimes be more expensive to produce than conventional MW plastics.

When a specific MW distribution is required, this may also involve additional manufacturing costs. In particular, the production of very narrow MW monodispersed systems can be accomplished either through specialized polymerization techniques or through highly selective fractionation after polymerization. Both of these methods can be very expensive. In most cases it would appear that the best balance of properties is obtained at a rather broad MWD, so that the cost of producing such NMW monodispersed systems may be quite impractical. In polyethylenes, however, MWD is most conveniently controlled by degree of longchain branching.

cost comparison The application of unit costs as a basis for comparisons between alternative manufacturing solutions is inappropriate for flexible automated manufacturing for the following reasons: (1) Unit costs can only be related to a particular point in time. A manufacturing investment, however, remains in effect for a period of time (a year through many years) so it requires a computational procedure related to a certain period. (2) Unit costs as manufacturing costs already contain residual production overheads. These are normally determined by a fixed percentage, and therefore do not reflect relevant differences between alternative investments. (3) Unit costs have to be determined and totalled for all, or at least for the representative products, and are thus work-intensive. ▷ **computer cost modelling, technically**

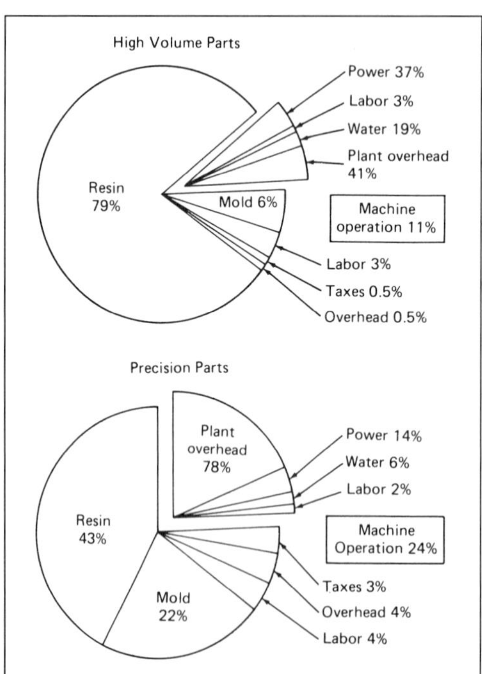

Share of cost to injection molding high volume products and precision products.

cost comparison, process-material See the Figure below.

cost contribution The portion of the net sale dollar left after all variable costs have been deducted.

cost conversion The cost of direct labor and overhead required to make the finished product.

cost, crude oil versus polyethylene See the Figure on p. 157.

cost fixed Those costs that will not vary markedly within the normal range of operations.

cost, freight car retention ▷ **demurrage**

cost, injection molding ▷ **injection molding product cost** and **zero defect**

cost modeling ▷ **computer cost modeling, technically** and **cost comparison**

cost of investment ▷ **capital equipment investment**

cost rate Labor or machine-hour rates that have been marked up to the selling price level.

cost replacement differential The difference between the hourly production cost based on historical accounting depreciation and the hourly cost based on depreciation computed using the replacement cost of equipment.

cost variable Those costs that fluctuate with changes in volume of production.

cost variation They may be due to: improper performance requirements, improper design of part, improper selection of plastic, improper selection of hardware, improper operation of the complete line (Fallo approach), and improper setup for testing/quality control/troubleshooting (assuming some method of examination is being used).

cotton Staple fibers, surrounding the seeds of various species of Gossypium. Cotton is the major textile fiber and an important source of cellulose which constitutes 88 to 96% of the fiber. Uses includes plastic reinforcement and fillers.

coulomb ▷ **electrical quantity**

Cost of crude oil versus polyethylene.

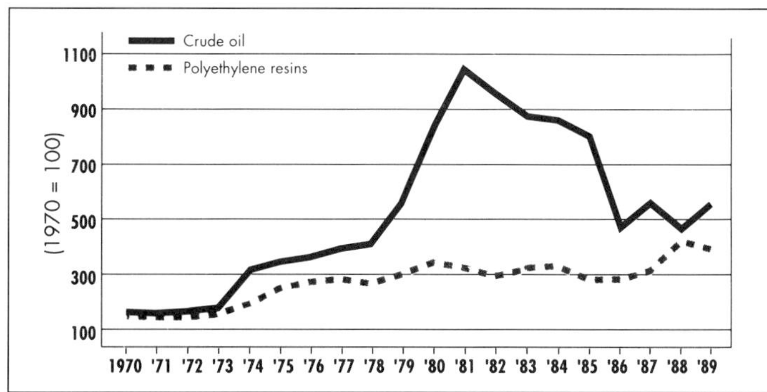

count **1.** In fabric, the number of warp and filling yarns per in. (cm) in woven cloth. **2.** In yarn, the size based on relation of length and weight. Basic unit is 10.

counterfeit money ▷ **plastic money**

counter pressure molding ▷ **foamed injection molding, gas counter pressure**

counter rotating screw ▷ **extruder, screw multiple type**

countersink An internal chamfer.

coupling agent Any chemical substance designed to react with both the filler or reinforcement and plastic such as in compounds and particularly in reinforced plastics. Result is stronger bond at their interface. With RP, most commonly used are organotrialkoxysilanes and organic acid-chromium chloride coordination complexes. They are applied to the reinforcement phase from aqueous or organic solution, from the gas phase, or added to the matrix as an integral blend. ▷ **glass fiber and fabric surface treatment**

coupon Usually a specimen for a specific test, as a tensile coupon.

cowoven fabric A reinforcement fabric woven with two different types of fibers in individual yarns; for example, thermoplastic fibers woven side by side with glass fibers.

CR-39 PPG Industries Inc.'s tradename for allyl carbonate (diethyleneglycol), an optical or transparent plastic.

crack An actual separation of fabricated plastic, visible on opposite surfaces of the product, and extending through the thickness. It represents a fracture. ▷ **microcracking** and **crazing**

crack damage tolerance ▷ **damage tolerance**

crack growth Rate of propagation of a crack through the material due to a static or dynamic applied load. ▷ **fatigue crack**

crack growth resistance A measure of resistance to growth of a crack under repeated bend flexing, particularly for elastomers. Two tests are used. In the Di Mattia Flexing Machine Test, crack growth resistance may be expressed as the number of cycles needed to reach a specified crack length, average rate (in./kc) of crack growth over the entire test period, or rate of cracking (in./kc) during a specified portion of the test. In the Ross Flexing Machine Test, crack growth resistance is usually expressed as the number of cycles needed for each 100% increase in crack length up to 500%. Crack growth resistance does not necessarily indicate ability of a material subjected to bend flexing to resist initial formation of a crack.

crack, hairline ▷ **hairline crack**

cracking A refining process involving decomposition and molecular recombination of organic compounds, especially hydrocarbons obtained by means of heat, to form molecules suitable for monomers, using petrochemicals, gas, etc.

crack initiation or propagation ▷ **fatigue**

cradle-to-grave A study of a material from its manufacture and use through disposal. The time period also is called life-cycle analysis.

cratering Depressions on coated plastic surfaces which are caused by excessive lubricant. Cratering results when paint thins excessively and later ruptures, leaving pin holes and other voids. Use of fewer thinners in the coating can reduce or eliminate the problem as can less lubricant.

crazing Crazing in certain plastics is the presence of numerous tiny internal and surface cracks aligned in the same direction and often arranged in more or less parallel planes. Crazing is most noticeable in clear parts. When the part is held in one position these cracks may

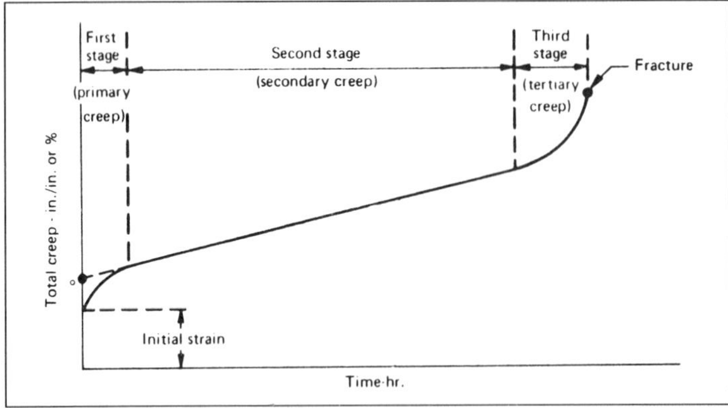

Basic concept for evaluating creep-test data.

not be visible, but they become so as the part is rotated so that incident light strikes each of the tiny planner cracks. Crazing may be brought about by mechanical factors (stress) or by environmental factors (such as contact with certain chemicals). The size of the cracks may vary. If they are very tiny, for example, the crazing may appear as a blush mark on the part. These cracks may be absent at the time of fabrication only to appear at some later date if the part is subjected to stress or to contact with certain chemicals. A crazed part may suffer some loss in strength but it will support a considerable load before failure. Films and coatings can sometimes be observed to craze when they are flexed, stretched, or bent to an unusual degree. Crazing in all products can be averted completely or kept to a permissible amount by a careful process control during fabrication to eliminate unwanted internal stresses.

Molecular orientation is the most significant source of residual internal stress. It is caused by forcing hot, fluid plastic under high pressure through mold or die restrictions (with improper process control) and then freezing the stress pattern into place during cooling. Internal cracks can be eliminated with proper processing techniques being used. ▷ **environmental stress cracking; stress crack; stress whitening**

creativity ▷ **design analysis; design technology**

creel A spool, along with its supporting structure, that holds the required number of roving balls or supply packages in a desired position for unwinding for the next step, that is, weaving, braiding, filament winding, etc.

creep Basically it is the dimensional change in a material under physical load over time beyond instantaneous elastic deformation. If it continues to increase without any increase in load (or stress), the material is said to be experiencing creep or cold flow as shown in the Fig. above. Primary creep is that portion of the creep which is recoverable in time after the load is released. Secondary creep is that portion which is non-recoverable.

creep behaviour, guidelines Examples of factors to consider when reviewing creep properties or behaviors follow: (1) predictions can be made on creep behavior based on creep and relaxation data. (2) There is generally a less pronounced curvature when creep and relaxation data are plotted log-log. This facilitates extrapolation and is commonly practiced, particularly with creep modulus and creep rupture data. (3) Increasing the load on a part increases the creep rate. (4) Increasing the level of reinforcement in a composite increases its resistance to creep. (5) Particulate fillers provide better creep resistance than unfilled resins but are less effective than fibrous reinforcements. (6) Glass fiber reinforced amorphous TPs composites generally have greater creep resistance than glass fiber reinforced crystalline TPs composites containing the same amount of glass fiber. (7) Carbon fiber reinforcement is more effective in resisting creep than glass fiber reinforcement. (8) The effect of a flame-retardant additive on flexural modulus provides an indication of its effect on long time creep. (9) Many plastic products during the past century worldwide have been successfully designed for long time creep performance based on information and different type test data available at that time; much more exists now and will do in the future.

creep isometric and isochronous graphs Creep curves are a common method of displaying the interdependence of stress-strain-time. However, there are also other methods which may be useful in particular applications; namely *isometric* and *isochronous* graphs. The isometric graph is obtained by taking a constant strain section through the creep curves and replotting as stress vs. time. It is an indication of the relaxation of stress in the material when the strain is kept constant. These data are often used as a good approximation of stress relaxation in a plastic. In addition, if the vertical axis (stress) is divided by the strain, then one obtains a graph of modulus against time. The graph provides a good illustration of the time dependent variation of modulus.

The isochronous graph may be obtained by taking a constant time section through the creep curves and plotting stress vs. strain. It can also be obtained experimentally by performing a series of brief or quick creep and recovery tests on a plastic. A stress is applied to a plastic test-piece and the strain is recorded after a time period, typically 100 seconds. The stress is then removed and the plastic allowed to recover, normally for a period factor of 4 (4 × 100 sec). A larger stress is then applied to the same specimen and after recording the strain at the 100 sec time period, this stress is removed and the material allowed to recover. This procedure is repeated until sufficient points have been obtained for the isochronous graph to be plotted.

creep loading, intermittent behavior The creep behavior of plastics is usually reported at the level of the applied stress being constant. However, in service the material may be subjected to a complex pattern of loading and unloading cycles. In these cases it is useful to develop intermittent loading data.

creep loading, long time behavior With high performance plastics dynamic loads such as creep, fatigue, impact and related issues are important considerations in many designs (ASTM D 4092). These material behaviors are influenced by many factors. They include, in particular, temperature, time, previous stress history as well as ambient conditions. In order that these influencing factors can be examined separately from one another, test methods are used which permit a separation of the individual factors.

If a plastic product fails in the performance of its normal long time function, it is usually caused by one of two factors: excessive deformation or fracture. For plastics it will more often than not be excessive creep deformation which is the limiting factor. However, fracture, if it occurs, can have more catastrophic results. Therefore it is essential that designers recognize the factors which are likely to initiate fracture so that steps can be taken to avoid them.

creep modulus, apparent The concept of apparent modulus is a convenient method for expressing creep because it takes into account initial strain for an applied stress plus the deformation or strain that occurs with time. Thus, apparent creep modulus

$$E_A = \frac{\text{stress}}{\text{initial strain} + \text{creep}}$$

Because parts tend to deform in time at a decreasing rate, the acceptable strain based on service life of the part must be determined; the shorter the duration of load, the higher the apparent modulus and the higher the allowable stress. ▷ **modulus**

creep rate Rate of creep is the slope of the creep-time curve at a given time; deflection with time under a given static load.

creep recovery The time-dependent decrease in strain in a solid, following the removal of the load (force). ▷ **recovery, initial**

creep relaxation A transient stress-strain condition in which the strain increases concurrently with the decay of stress.

creep rupture strength The stress that will cause fracture in a creep test at a given time, in a specified constant environment. This is also called stress-rupture strength.

creep strain, initial The strain produced in a specimen by given loading conditions before creep occurs. ▷ **strain**

creep strength The stress that causes a given creep in a creep test at a given time in a specified constant environment. ▷ **stress**

criminal justice and plastics ▷ **forensic science and plastic**

crimp **1.** The waviness of a fiber. It determines the capacity of fibers to cohere under light pressure. Measured either by the number of crimps or waves per unit length, or the percent increase in extent of the fiber on removal of the crimp. **2.** Corrugations on a part to lock them in place.

crocidolite An amphilbole asbestos of chemical structure (blue asbestos), occasionally used as a filler in plastics, such as vinyl floor tiles. Unlike the commoner chrysotile asbestos, the fibers are lath-like and the molecules consist of ladder-like silica chains lying parallel to each other, being joined together by metal ions. Fiber diameter is about 100 nm and bundle length about 20 mm. Mechanical properties are similar to chrysotile asbestos; tensile strength is 3.5 GPa and tensile modulus is 175 GPa. Stiffness is higher and resistance to acids is much better. The toxic hazard associated with asbestos requires careful handling and use. ▷ **asbestos**

crocking Removal of a dye or pigment from the surface of a paint or textile by rubbing or attrition.

cross breaking strength An alternative name for flexural strength.

crosshead **1.** In extrusion, it is a device generally employed in wire coating which is attached to the discharge end of the extruder cylinder, designed to facilitate extruding plastic at any angle. Normally, this is a 90° angle to the longitudinal axis of the screw. **2.** Crossheads are also used in other processes, such as coinjection, sandwich construction, etc.

cross laminate A laminate in which some of the layers of material are oriented about right angles to the remaining layers with respect to the strongest direction in tension. Also called bidirectional. ▷**reinforced plastic, directional properties**

crosslinked plastic ▷**molecular crosslinked** and **radiation-induced reaction**

crosslinked polyethylene plastic The usual polyethylenes are thermoplastics, however when crosslinked (chemically or by irradiation) the PE becomes a thermoset identified as XLPE. It provides improved properties such as strength, stiffness, wear resistance, etc. ▷**initiator** and **extruder wire coating, crosslinkable PE with peroxide**

crosslinking With thermosets and certain thermoplastics, the setting up of chemical links between the molecular chains occurs. When extensive, as in most TSs, crosslinking makes an infusible super molecule of all the chains. In rubber, it is just enough to join all molecules into a network. If during the polymerization reaction one would expect the individual chains to form chemical bonds to each other, one would expect the resultant structure to be very strong and rigid. This, in fact, is what happens in most TSs. The phenomenon of crosslinking involves primary bonds between polymer chains as shown in the Fig. below. The plastic formed usually cannot be remelted because the bonds are too strong. Interactions between polymer chains, such as branching and crosslinking, do not occur to the same extent in different polymers. The greater the degree of crosslinking, the greater the rigidity of the material, the less it is soluble, and the less it responds to remelting. Most TSs can withstand temperatures as high as 204°C (400°F); linear polymers with their less complicated structure seldom can be used in temperatures in excess of 121°C (250°F). ▷**molecular crosslinked polymer**

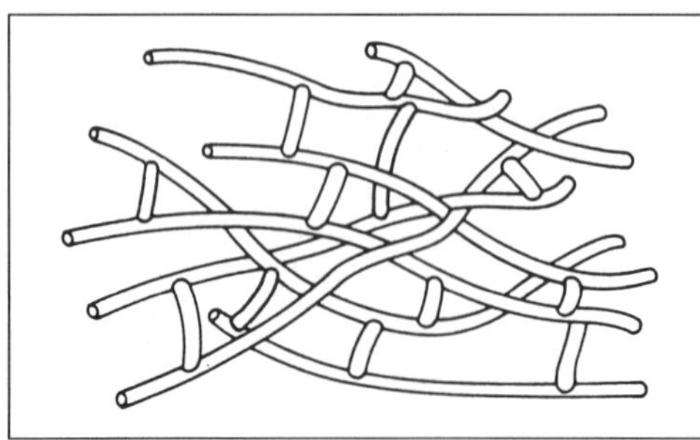

Crosslinked three-dimensional network structure schematic.

crosslinking, chemistry ▷**polymer chemistry terminology**

crosslinking density ▷**density, crosslinked**

crosslinking with radiation The interaction of electromagnetic radiation with plastics can lead to the formation of three-dimensional network structures, which generally improve the overall physical and chemical properties of the original substrate polymer. Network structures form under a wide variety of radiation conditions (ionizing or nonionizing radiation, photochemical or thermal chemical cure systems). In general, crosslinking and the related technologies involve four main variables: the type of radiation and its source, the nature of the polymer structure to be irradiated and its response characteristics, mechanisms or theories of reaction, and chemical, physical and mechanical properties of network formation. The most common radiation source for commercial crosslinking of organic materials is cobalt 60, low and high energy electron accelerators, light energy (ultraviolet-visible), infrared sources of energy, and plasma or glow-discharge energy sources (microwave or radio-frequency range).

crosswise direction **1.** Refers to the cutting of specimens and to application of load. **2.** For rods and tubes, it is any direction perpendicular to the long axis. **3.** For other shapes or materials that are stronger in one direction than in the other, it is the direction that is weaker. **4.** ▷**machine and transverse directions** **5.** For materials that are equally strong in both directions, it is an arbitrarily designated direction at right angles to the lengthwise direction.

crowfoot ▷**four-harness satin**

crucible A cone-shaped container having a curved base and made of a refractory material; used for laboratory calcination and combustibles, such as very high melt plastics and reinforced plastics.

crude oil ▷**petroleum** and **cost, crude oil versus polyethylene**

cryogenic **1.** Producing very low temperature. **2.** Study of behavior of material at temperatures below −200°C (−328°F). **3.** The use of liquified gases.

Cyrogenic low temperatures.

	°C	°F	K
Room temperature	25–27	77–81	298–300
Liquid oxygen (O_2) temperature	−183.1	−297.4	90.1
Liquid fluorine (F_2) temperature	−187.0	−304.6	86.0
Liquid nitrogen (N_2) temperature	−195.8	−320.8	77.3
Liquid hydrogen (H_2) temperature	−252.9	−423.4	20.4
Liquid helium (He) temperature	−268.9	−452.0	4.2
Absolute zero	−273.16	−459.69	0

cryogenic properties The field of cryogenics is normally considered the production and effect of very low temperatures on various materials, including plastics. Environmental temperatures frequently encountered in cryogenics are shown in the Table above (for the cryogenic liquids, temperature represents the boiling points at 1 atm.).

In regard to material performances, embrittlement is a conspicuous shortcoming of some metals, particularly of carbon steel. However, most other ordinary structural metals such as aluminum, copper, nickel, and most of their alloys do not exhibit low-temperature brittleness. This also applies to authentic stainless steel. Generally plastics have shown relatively good properties at low temperatures, although thermal shock is a critical problem with certain plastics, particularly with reinforced plastics. Fluoroplastics have shown superior resistance to embrittlement and polyester films are useful in specialized problems with liquid hydrogen. In general, most materials are about twice as strong at cryogenic temperatures as at room temperature.

In general, as temperature decreases there are increases in strengths (tensile, compression, flexural, bearing, tensile fatigue, tensile-compressive fatigue), modulus, total thermal contraction, and strength-to-weight. There is variable change in impact strength, adhesive shear strength, and coefficient of thermal conductivity. Decreases occur in ductility, elongation, coefficient of expansion, and specific heat. There are exceptions to this summation.

cryogenic service Usually refers to temperatures when below −100°C (173 K).

Cryovac W. R. Grace & Co. tradename for a light, shrink film, transparent packaging material based on polyvinylidene chloride. Used especially for meats and other perishables.

crystal The normal form of the solid state of materials. Crystals have characteristic shapes and cleavage planes due to arrangement of their atoms, ions, or molecules which comprise a definite pattern called lattice.

crystalline plastic They have their molecules arranged in a very regular repeating lattice structure, so precise that every atom of the polymer molecule must recur at very specific points in the repeat structure. While no material is completely crystalline (typically less than 80%), very regular polymers can be mostly crystalline with only small amorphous areas remaining between the crystallites. Technically it is more accurate to refer to these plastics as semicrystalline but in general the industry refers to them as crystalline. Typical highly crystalline types are HDPE, PP, acetal, polyester (TP), and nylon. Less regular types include LDPE or PVC.

Basically the individual molecules tend to pack into a neat orderly crystalline arrangement of high density, sharp melting point, and low solubility. Their stability at low temperatures and energy levels is demonstrated by the heat of fusion or enthalpy which is liberated during the formation of the crystal, and which must be supplied in order to melt and disperse the molecules out of the crystal. At higher temperatures and energy levels, however, vibrations and Brownian motions of the molecules tend to drive them apart, destroying the crystals and dispersing them into a highly random and disordered state containing many degrees of freedom. The balance between these two factors determines the melting point of each particular plastic. ▷**molecular arrangement structure** and **morphology**

crystalline plastic relaxation A relaxation with its accompanying transition associated with the crystalline regions. The most important relaxation or the primary relaxation is melting. Sometimes there is additional action of a crystal-crystal relaxation and transitions are observed as with polyisoprene and polytetrafluoroethylene. Certain secondary transitions are also sometimes observed, such as premelting and even lower transitions. These may be identified with particular molecular processes, especially where considerable morphological information is available. Such is the case with polyethylene.

crystalline region ▷**amorphous plastic region**

crystallinity and property When molecules

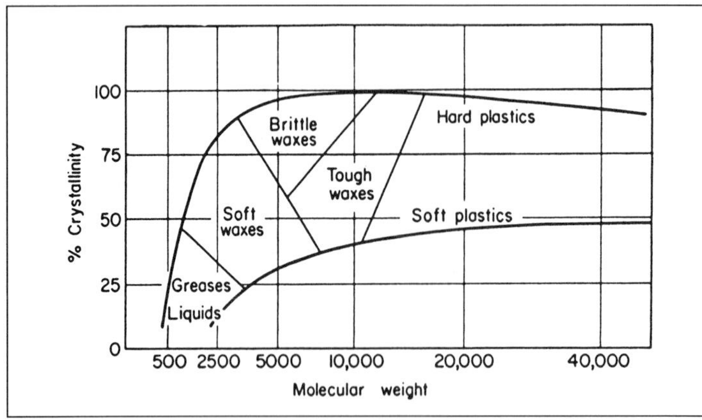

Effect of crystallinity and molecular weight upon the physical properties of polyethylene.

crystallize, this high degree of organization becomes a major factor in overall structure. In particular, the forces holding the polymer molecule into the crystalline lattice greatly restrict its mobility and thus affect most of its properties. Thus most properties depend upon the percent of crystallinity (see Fig. above) and the size of the crystals present. ▷ **amorphous plastic; morphology, amorphous and crystalline characteristics; engineering materials, the solid state**

crystallinity and orientation Intermolecular order refers to the geometic arrangement of adjacent polymer molecules in the solid mass. Orientation of the crystalline axis with reference to some fixed direction often refers to the direction of deformation (machine direction).

crystallite The name given to the crystals present in a crystalline polymer, which, in contrast to nonpolymer crystals, are so small as to be observable only with an electron microscope. Typical sizes are 10^{-5} to 10^{-6} cm. Usually they are of lamellar habit (lamellae) which aggregate such that each crystallite is closely joined to each other; they are linearly organized as in parallel fiber construction. ▷ **polariscope**

crystallization The formation of crystallites or groups of molecules in an orderly structure within the plastic as the plastic is cooled from its amorphous melt state to a temperature below its crystallization temperature. ▷ **injection molding, melting and crystallization**

crystallization first-order transition A change of state associated with crystallization, melting, or a change in crystal structure of a polymer.

crystallization secondary Slow crystallization process that occurs after the main solidification process is complete. Often associated with impure molecules.

crystallography The study of the crystal formation of solids, including X-ray determination of lattice structures, crystal habit, and shape, form, and defects of crystals. When applied to metals, this science is called metallography.

crystal polystyrene This styrenic material is an amorphous homopolymer that offers stiffness, dimensional stability, good optical properties, and electrical insulation capabilities. It is produced by polymerization of styrene monomer usually by mass continuous manufacture. The styrene-butadiene styrene block copolymers with a polybutadiene content of up to 30% are referred to as crystal clear, impact resistant PS. They are different from standard impact resistant PS.

crystal-pulling Method of growing single crystals by slowly pulling a "seed" crystal away from a molten pool.

crystal structure The ordered, repeating arrangement of atoms or molecules in a material.

C-scan The back-and-forth scanning of a specimen with ultrasonics. A nondestructive testing technique for finding voids, delaminations, defects in fiber distribution, etc.

C-stage ▷ **A-B-C-stages**

cull ▷ **transfer molding, cull**

cullet In ancient glass manufacturing, chunks of glass of varying sizes and colors furnished to artisans for shaping and finishing. Today, the term refers to fragments of scrap glass from production operations which are collected and recycled to the furnace for remelting. In the plastics industry, plastic scrap in production is collected and recycled to the melt processing machines.

cupola A vertical furnace similar to a blast furnace used for melting iron and other metals for casting.

cure To change the physical properties of a material by chemical reaction, which may be condensation, polymerization, or vulcanization. It is usually accomplished by the action of heat and catalysts, alone or in combination with or without pressure. This reaction is usually associated with thermosets where an irreversible change occurs. The term cure is also used (even though it is not correct) when melting thermoplastics during injection molding, extrusion, etc. As an example it is stated that the cure cycle during injection molding is a certain time period for, say, polystyrene, but there is no catalytic reaction or basically any chemical change per the correct meaning of curing. It is used with thermoplastics as a carryover from the beginning of the century when thermosets were principally used in injection molds and the term was correctly applied.

cure degree The degree of cure is the extent to which curing (or hardening) of a thermoset plastic has progressed.

cure dielectrically ▷ **dielectric curing**

cure monitoring electrically ▷ **electrical cure monitoring**

cure, step Step cure is a cure that starts at lower temperature and is gradually brought up to the cure temperature. This allows gasses to escape before solidification of the plastic, such as in the curing of phenolics.

cure stress ▷ **stress, cure**

curie The official unit of radio-activity where Ci is defined as exactly 3.70×10^{10} disintegrations per second. This decay rate is nearly equivalent to that exhibited by one g of radium in equilibrium with its disintegration products. A millicurie (mCi) is 0.001 curie; a microcurie (μCi) is one millionth curie.

curie point The temperature at which ferromagnetic materials can no longer be magnetized by outside forces.

curing agent A catalytic or reactive agent that brings about polymerization causing crosslinking. ▷ **hardener**

curing agent, latent A latent curing agent produces long-time stability at room temperature but rapid cure at elevated temperatures.

curing kick over Shop jargon describing the curing of a thermoset plastic to the solid state. Also called set-up.

curing temperature Temperature at which a cast, molded, extruded, reinforced plastic, adhesive, etc. is subjected to curing.

curing time The period of time during which a part is subjected to heat and/or pressure to cure the plastic. It is the interval of time between the instant of cessation of relative movement between the moving parts of a mold and the instant that curing condition(s) is released. Further cure may take place after removal from the conditions of heat and/or pressure. Also called molding time.

curling A condition in which the blow molding parison curls upward and outward, sticking to the outer face of the die ring. Balancing the temperatures of the die and mandrel will usually relieve this problem.

current density ▷ **density, current**

current good manufacturing practice ▷ **good manufacturing practice**

curtain coating A method of coating which may be used with low viscosity plastics or solutions, suspensions, or emulsions of plastics in which the substrate to be coated is passed through and perpendicular to a free flowing liquid "curtain", or "waterfall". Equipment used include an extruder and special machines such as pumping through a slotted die. The flow rate of the falling liquid and the linear speed of the substrate passing under the curtain are coordinated in accordance with thickness of coating desired. Usually to obtain the best coating performance (bonding to substrate, wear resistance, etc.) the plastic melt is at the critical high temperature and pressure. This action requires very closely monitored operating conditions.

curvature A condition in which the blow molding parison is not straight, but somewhat bending and shifting to one side, leading to a deviation from the vertical direction of extrusion. Centering of ring and mandrel can often relieve this defect.

cushion **1.** In cxtrusion blow molding this is the slowing down of the molds just prior to their coming together. **2.** Injection molding cushioning involves packing the mold cavity. ▷ **mold cavity packing**

cushioning material A material, such as plastic foam, to isolate or reduce the effect of externally applied shock or vibration forces, or both.

custom molder ▷ **molder, custom**

custom product Customized products have been tailored to a particular customer's specifications.

cut **1.** Number of 100 yd lengths per pound (wool, glass, graphite, etc.). **2.** A length of woven fabric about 60 yd in graygoods.

cut, fly A fly cutting operation is where a cutter(s) is rotated around one center point, such as on an extruded plastic pipe line. ▷ **extruder take-off cutter**

cut, kerf A kerf cut is the width of a cut made by a saw blade, torch, water jet, laser beam, etc.

cut layer With laminated plastics, a condition of the surface of machined or ground rods and tubes as well as sanded sheets in which cut edges of the surface layer or lower laminations are revealed.

cutter Cutters are often the preferred method of cutting extruded plastic products. They produce clean, accurate cuts. The best cuts come from quickly slicing material rather than chopping, which can distort the plastic and result in uneven cuts. The criteria in selecting a knife for a particular cut are attack angle, force required, and cut time. Attack angle describes the angle between a blade's cutting edge and its axis. A high attack angle means good slicing action; a zero attack angle means a chopping action.

Force required varies with the size, density, hardness, and composition of the plastic. Higher forces may require a thicker knife, which in turn increases force requirements to compensate for wedging (force required to work the thick blade down through the product). In general the thinnest knife is used to do the job without breaking or deflecting. Cut time describes how long it takes for the knife to pass through the product. This number is usually related to the inverse of cutting time.

cutter, guillotine ▷ **guillotine**

cutting and deburring The removal of burrs, sharp edges, or fins by mechanical, chemical, or electrochemical means.

cutting burr-free Some products such as those for medical applications (tubing, punched sheets, etc.) require an absolutely clean cut without burrs, dust, or so-called "angel hair". Lubricating the knife with water, alcohol, or mineral oil can often help to provide a smooth, clean cut. Also knives coated with PTFE or of highly polished chrome are used to reduce friction, resulting in clean cuts.

cutting die ▷ **die cutting**

cutting, electro-erosive ▷ **electro-erosive cutting**

cutting flexible tubing Small diameter tubing made of slippery, flexible plastics (such as silicone, PTFE, latex, etc.) is best cut with a razor blade.

cutting fluid A liquid applied to a cutting tool to assist in the machining operation by washing away chips or serving as a lubricant (also coolant). Commonly used fluids are water, oil, water emulsion of detergent, etc. Fluid used depends on the requirement of specific plastic used.

cutting large diameter, thin-walled tubing It is generally difficult to produce clean cuts on thin-walled, large tubes. Because the tubing collapses when impacted by the conventional knife system, the cut tends to be wavy or angular. Successful cuts can be made with a special shaped knife such as one with a point in the middle. The point enters the tubing first, minimizing its tendency to collapse. Then a contoured blade slices the tubing in both directions from the point. Tailor the curvature of the knife blade and the location of the point to each application.

cutting modern tool steel ▷ **electro-erosive cutting** and **machining and cutting**

cutting plastic ▷ **machining and cutting**

cutting reinforced plastic RP provides one of the more difficult challenges to knife and cutter bushing design. Generally requires the need to take two steps: (1) use a knife edge hardened with a material such as tungsten carbide and (2) custom design the bushing and knife as a unit for each type and shape of material to be cut. Actual cutter used depends on type fiber or fabric to be cut.

cutting template ▷ **template**

cutting, water jet ▷ **water jet cutting**

cyanate plastic Thermoset plastics that are derived from bisphenols or polyphenols, and are available as monomers, oligomers, blends, and solutions. Also known as cyanate esters, cyanic esters, and triazine plastics.

cyanoacrylate plastic CNA is a strong contact adhesive; polymerizes with water moisture acting as a catalyst.

cybernetic Creative use of machinery, systems, explored in search for solutions to urgent problems. Technically the term cybernetics is the "human use of human beings" that would "render unto people the things that are people's and unto the automatic control the things which are the controller's." Emphasis is on the systematic and intelligent application of cybernetics; the study of control and communication in man and machine. The ultimate in control is the computer; however, to date no computer accomplishes the job of a "thinking" machine. The advent of the real "thinking" machine is coming; perhaps before the 21st century.

cycle 1. The complete, repeating sequence of operations in a process or part of a process. As an example in molding, the cycle time is the period, or elapsed time, between a certain point in one molding cycle and the same point in the next. ▷ **injection molding** 2. Different testing cycle procedures are used such as stress to the number of cycles in fatigue (S–N diagram).

cycle ratio The ratio of cycles endured under load.

cyclic load ▷ **fatigue**

cycling material ▷ **material cycle**

cyclone A dust collecting device consisting of a cylindrical chamber with the lower portion tapered to fit into a cone-shaped receptacle placed below it. The dust-laden air enters through a vertical slot-like section in the upper wall of the chamber at the rate of at least 100 ft/s (30.5 m/s). Since the particles enter at a tangent, they whirl in a circular or cyclonic path within the chamber. The centrifugal force exerted on the particles is proportional to their weight and to the square of their velocity. The particles slide along the walls of the chamber and gradually circulate down into the conical receptor while the clean air escapes through a central pipe at the bottom. The dust accumulates in the cone and is discharged at intervals or continuously. The larger the particles, the more efficient the removal. Particles as small as 20 microns can be removed, some systems to 10 microns.

cyclyd A coined term referring to the cyclic alkyd coatings used in air-drying maintenance paints and baking metal primers.

cylinder 1. In plasticators such as extruders, injection molding, etc., the cylinder (or barrel) contains the screw(s). ▷ **barrel** 2. Any of various rotating members used in different processing lines such as a three-roll sheet stand, compounding rotary cylinder, rotary offset printing press, etc.

D

Dacron Du Pont's tradename for TP polyester fiber made from polyethylene terephthalate. Available as filament, yarn, tow, and fiber fill.

daisy-wheel printer ▷ **computer printer**

dam Boundary support or ridge used to prevent excessive edge bleeding or plastic runout of a reinforced plastic and to prevent crowning of bag molding during cure.

damage tolerance **1.** A design measure of crack growth rate. Cracks in damage-tolerant designed structures are not permitted to grow to critical size during expected service life. **2.** A measure of the ability of products to retain load-carrying capability after exposure to sudden loads such as impact-drop.

damping Basically diminishing the intensity of vibrations. The dynamic mechanical behavior of plastics is of great interest and importance for many reasons. The dynamic modulus, or the modulus measured by any other technique, is one of the most basic of all mechanical properties; its importance is well known in any structural application. The role of mechanical damping, however, is not so well known. Damping is often the most sensitive indicator of all kinds of molecular motions which are going on in a material, even in the solid state. Aside from the scientific interest in understanding the molecular motions which can occur, these motions are of great practical importance in determining the mechanical behavior of plastics. For this reason, the absolute value of the damping and the temperature and frequency at which damping peaks occur are of considerable interest.

High damping is sometimes an advantage and sometimes a disadvantage. For instance, high damping in a car tire tends to give better friction to the road surface, but at the same time, it causes heat build-up, which causes a tire to degrade more rapidly. Damping reduces vibrations (mechanical and acoustical) and prevents resonance vibrations from building up to dangerous amplitudes. However, high damping is generally an indication of reduced dimensional stability, which can be very undesirable in structures carrying loads for long time periods. Many other mechanical properties are intimately related to damping; these include fatigue life, toughness and impact, wear and coefficient of friction. ▷ **torsional pendulum**

damping, critical In dynamic mechanical measurement, that damping required for the borderline condition between oscillatory and nonoscillatory behavior is its critical value.

damping factor Alternative name for tangent of the loss angle.

damping gamma loss peak In dynamic mechanical measurement, the third peak in the damping curve below the melt, in order of decreasing temperature or increasing frequency.

damping index In dynamic mechanical behavior, a measure of the damping, being defined as the number of oscillations between two arbitrarily fixed boundary conditions, e.g. amplitudes in a series of waves. It is principally used in torsional analysis.

damping, mechanical Mechanical damping gives the amount of energy dissipated as heat during the deformation of a material that is subjected to an oscillatory load or displacement. Perfectly elastic materials have no mechanical damping. Damping terms may be calculated by many methods, which include use of the logarithmic decrement, the area of hysteresis loops, etc. ▷ **dynamic mechanical measurement** and **resonant forced**

damping, specific capacity The specific damping capacity is a measure of the damping of a material when its dynamic mechanical behavior is considered. Defined as the ratio of the energy dissipated per cycle of the alternating stress field to the maximum energy stored (or the elastic energy).

damping vibration ▷ **dash pot**

dancer roll A roller used as a tension sensing device in the extrusion-coating of wire; provides an evenly controlled rate of wire movement through the die to obtain uniform plastic coating.

Danner process A mechanical process for continuous drawing material, such as glass cane or tubing, from a rotating mandrel.

dart drop test There are several types of falling dart (impact) tests: ASTM D 1709 for film, D 2444 for thermoplastic pipe, and D 3029 for rigid plastic parts. In each of these tests, a weight is dropped from a tower on to a specimen. The weight, known as a tub or falling dart, is usually cylindrical with a rounded nose that contacts the specimen. Steel balls can also be used. The weight can either hit the specimen directly, or for some versions of D 3029, hit a metal impactor resting on the specimen. Specimens can be supported or clamped to a metal ring, depending on test procedure used. The amount of weight and the drop height are varied until half (or more in special tests) of the specimens break.

dash pot A device used in hydraulic systems for damping down vibration. It consists of a piston attached to the part to be damped and fitted into a vessel containing fluid or air. It absorbs shocks by reducing the rate of change in the momentum of moving parts of machinery.

databank A collection of information held in a computer's memory whose data is handled by a database.

database Different from databank, this is a set of computer software programs that make it easy to handle data in different ways. It is an electronic filling system, allowing users to put in any information, cross-reference it, alter, delete and add to it, and retrieve it in forms specified by the user. The database handles the data in the databank. Another term for database is data management. A distinction sometimes exists: spelling together as "database" refers to highly organized data and separated as "data base" refers to data without regard to organization. The usual is database.

database management system DBMS is a computer system with management and administrative capabilities for control of record storage, selection, updating, formatting, and reporting from a database.

database referral A database directory, or an index to contents of database and/or manually searchable files.

data collection ▷ **statistical data collection**

data file A collection of related data elements stored together in the computer system (sometimes called databank). The entire file may be used in various operations (file copy, merge, concatenate, delete, etc.) or the individual elements may be operated upon (record, read, write, alter, etc.).

data, theoretical versus actual properties Through the laws of physics, chemistry, and mechanics, theoretical values can be determined for different materials. These are compared to actual values in the Table on p. 168. With steel, aluminum, and glass the theoretical and actual experimental values are practically the same, whereas for polyethylene, polypropylene, nylon, and other plastics they are far apart, and have the important potential of reaching values that are far superior to those of the other materials.

When polyethylene was first produced in the early 1940s, physicists in England, the U.S., and Germany predicted a tremendous potential for it. At that time the properties of PEs were much lower than those presently available. Out of that original general-purpose PE have been developed such specific PEs as LDPE, HDPE, and UHMW PE.

datum They are a basis for calculating or measuring; have a dual nature of being both a theoretical perfect element of part geometry and when a part is actually produced.

daylight opening ▷ **clamping, daylight**

deaerate To remove air from a plastic in order to obtain its maximum performance (such as strength, aesthetic, permeability resistance, and/or others). Examples include during injection molding. Deaeration is an important step in the production of vinyl plastisols, accomplished by subjecting the fluid to a high vacuum with or without agitation, to remove air which would cause objectionable bubbles or blisters in finished parts.

debond **1.** A deliberate separation or delamination of a bonded joint or interface, usually for repair or rework purposes. **2.** An unbonded or nonadhered region, such as in reinforced plastic where a separation at the fiber-matrix interface is due to strain incompatibility. **3.** the term can refer to accidental damage.

debossed An indented or depressed design or lettering that is molded into an article so as to be below the main outside surface of that part.

debug To find and eliminate problems.

debugging ▷ **life-history curve**

debulking **1.** Process in which air is squeezed out of prepreg reinforced plastic in order to promote fiber-matrix adhesion and improve properties. **2.** Compacting of a thick laminate under moderate heat and pressure and/or vacuum to remove most of the air, to ensure seating on the tool, and to prevent wrinkles.

decal An abbreviation for decalcomania. It is a printed design on a temporary carrier such as

Comparison of the theoretically possible and actual experimental values for modulus of elasticity and tensile strength of various materials.[1]

Type of material	Modulus of elasticity			Tensile strength		
		Experimental			Experimental	
	Theoretical, N/mm² (kpsi)	Fiber, N/mm² (kpsi)	Normal polymer, N/mm² (kpsi)	Theoretical, N/mm² (kpsi)	Fiber, N/mm² (kpsi)	Normal polymer, N/mm² (kpsi)
Polyethylene	3000,000 (43,500)	100,000 (33%) (14,500)	1,000 (0.33%) (145)	27,000 (3,900)	1,500 (5.5%) (218)	30 (0.1%) (4.4)
Polypropylene	50,000 (7,250)	20,000 (40%) (2,900)	1,600 (3.2%) (232)	16,000 (2,300)	1,300 (8.1%) (189)	38 (0.24%) (5.5)
Polyamide 66	160,000 (23,200)	5,000 (3%) (725)	2,000 (1.3%) (290)	27,000 (3,900)	1,700 (6.3%) (246)	50 (0.18%) (7.2)
Glass	80,000 (11,600)	80,000 (100%) (11,600)	70,000 (87.5%) (10,100)	11,000 (1,600)	4,000 (36%) (580)	55 (0.5%) (8.0)
Steel	210,000 (30,400)	210,000 (100%) (30,400)	210,000 (100%) (30,400)	21,000 (3,050)	4,000 (19%) (580)	1,400 (6.67%) (203)
Aluminum	76,000 (11,000)	76,000 (100%) (11,000)	76,000 (100%) (11,000)	7,600 (1,100)	800 (10.5%) (116)	600 (7.89%) (87)

[1] For the experimental values the percentage of the theoretically calculated values is given in parenthesis as (47).

plastic film, paper, or aluminum, which is used for decorating many materials, including plastics. The imprint is adhered to the plastic surface by means of pressure-sensitive adhesive, solvent welding, or heat and pressure.

decal transfer Hot transfer decorating or printing. A decal is prepared in a way similar to a transfer foil, except that a complete multicolor design is printed on the foil and transferred as a unit. Hot transfer decals may be screen printed and are subject to the general limitations of screen printing (limited tonal effects and primarily fine line printing) but also have the advantages of screen printing, such as good opacity and low cost in preparing screens and setup. Transfers can also be gravure printed, which can reproduce photographic effects as well as line drawings. Transfers of this type have a much higher print quality, but the first cost is higher and relatively large runs are required to make it economically feasible. Decal transfers are widely used to decorate plastic bottles, compacts, and other molded products. Standard hot stamping equipment is used, and a special registration feed system may be required. ▷ **sublimable dye transfer**

decibel The term dB is used to identify 10 times the common logarithm of the ratio of two like quantities proportional to power and energy (electric and acoustic). Thus one dB corresponds to a power ratio of $10^{0.1}$ and ndB corresponds to a power ratio of $(10^{0.1})^n$. It is a unit for expressing the relative intensity of sounds on a scale from zero for the average perceptible sound to about 130 dB for the average pain level.

decimal system The decimal system of units was conceived in the 16th century when there was a great confusion and jumble of units of weights and measures. It was not until 1790, however, that the French National Assembly requested the French Academy of Sciences to work out a system of units suitable for adoption by the entire world. This system, based on the metre (▷ **meter**) as a unit of length and the gram as a unit of mass, was adopted as a practical measure to benefit industry and commerce. Physicists soon realized its advantages and it was adopted also in scientific and technical circles. The importance of the regulation of weights and measures was recognized in Article 1, Section 8, when the U.S. Constitution was written, but the metric system was not legalized in the U.S. until 1866. In 1893, the international metre (meter) and kilogram became the fundamental standards of length and mass in the U.S., both for metric and customary weights and measure. ▷ **SI** and **number marker**

deck The platen of a compression molding press.

deckle rod 1. ▷ **die deckle rod** 2. In papermaking, the width of the web sheet as it comes off the wire of a paper machine.

decolorizing agent Any material that removes color by a physical or chemical reaction. Also refers to bleaches involving a chemical reaction for removing color.

decomposition Usually identified as the process by which bacteria and fungi break down and stabilize waste products. Decomposition may occur as a result of (1) reaction at room temperature, (2) heating in air, (3) electrolysis (inorganic compound), (4) bacteria or enzyme action (fermentation), (5) radiation (photodecomposition) as degradable plastics exposed to sunlight, and (6) heating in the absence of air (pyrolysis or thermal decomposition). Fundamentally it is a type of chemical change. In simple decomposition, one substance breaks down into two substances, e.g., water yields hydrogen and oxygen. In double decomposition, two compounds break down and recombine to form two different compounds, i.e., $2HCl + CaCO_3 - CaCl_2 + H_2CO_3$. In some cases heat is absorbed and in others it is released.

decomposition temperature For applications having moderate thermal requirements, thermal decomposition may not be an important consideration. It is largely determined by the elements and bonding within the molecular structures, as well as the characteristics of additives, fillers, and/or reinforcements that may be in the compounds (see Table).

Temperature decomposition (T_d) ranges for various plastics.

Type of material	T_d, °F
PP	610–750
PC	645–825
PVC	390–570
PS	570–750
PMMA	355–535
ABS	480–750
PA	570–750
PET	535–610
Fluoropolymer	930–1020

Note: Adding certain fillers/reinforcements can raise decomposition temperatures.

decontamination A technical term in radiochemistry for the removal of traces of radioactivity in equipment, in areas, or from personnel.

decorating-finishing-printing The finishing of plastics includes different methods of adding decoration, printing, or functional surface effects to the part. Plastics are unique in that color and decorative effects can be added prior to, during, and/or after processing. Plastics of two or more colors are easily processed together such as coextrusion and coinjection. Integral coloring includes use of color concentrates, liquid additives, and color mixing in tumble barrels. Although the older established methods of painting are still widely used, they are continually being improved by newer and more versatile methods to give the user an almost unlimited choice of decorating designs and effects. The decision as to what method is to be used is governed by a number of factors, such as the size and shape of the part, the number of parts to be decorated, and the variations in color that are required. Although there are numerous methods listed here, the most common are direct screen, pad, and hot stamping. Methods of decorating include:

Airless spraying	Letterpress
Chrome plating	Lithographic resist
Coextrusion	Offset
Coinjection	Pad transfer
Decal	Painting
Dry print	Printing
Dye application	Roller coating
Electroplating	Roll leaf
Embossing	Rubber plate
Fill and wipe	Screen
Flexographic	Spanishing
Flocking	Spray and wipe
Foil	Spray paint
Gravure	Sublimable dye transfer
Hot stamping	Thermographic transfer
Hot transfer	Vacuum metalizing
In-lay	Valley printing
In-mold	

decorating, preparation problems With surface decoration, an important requirement is that the surface be clean and prepared in the right manner for the method of decorating. Some of the common causes of failure are contamination from processing lubricants, dust, natural skin greasiness and excess surface plasticizers, surface moisture and humidity conditions, and strain frozen into the processed part. Each plastic (material type with their different additives/filters/reinforcements) must be considered separately when selecting coatings, thinners, decals, foils, etc. Some plastics are prone to solvent attack, particularly certain thermoplastics. Frequently it is necessary to preheat, flameheat, or chemically treat a plastic surface before it can be painted or decorated. This is true of polyolefins. Static electricity on surfaces tends to cause major problems. Airborne impurities become attracted to and settle on the plastic surface. Wiping or rubbing with a cloth usually only increases the charge and aggravates the problem. There is equipment to remove the static charge. Decorating any material should be carried out in clean, controlled room conditions.

decorating second surface A method of decorating a transparent part from the back or reverse side. The decoration is visible through the part, but is not exposed.

decorating, spray and wipe ▷ **spray paint, spray and wipe**

decorating surface preparation For bond preparation, methods used include sandblast, plasma etch, water wash, solvent etch, chemical etch, etc. Flash removal includes tumbling, wheelabrator, hand filing, grinding, machining, etc.

decorative sheet A laminated plastics sheet used for decorative purposes in which the color and/or surface pattern is an integral part of the sheet. ▷ **high pressure laminate**

deep well Location of temperature sensor as close as possible to plastic as mechanical considerations will allow.

defect In processed plastics different kinds of structural irregularities or defects can occur. They can be caused by the molecular structure of the polymer chain; type additives, fillers, or reinforcement used; and processing conditions.

definite proportions law The combination of elements in simple ratios of 1:1, 2:1, 2:3, 3:4, etc.

definition It is important to define words or terms in order to ensure that proper communication exists. At times there can be more than one definition in order to meet different requirements as set up by different organizations, industries, etc. This book includes many multiple definitions, such as sandwich, trouble-shooting flaw, and Rosato.

definition of plastic ▷ **plastic**

deflashing Any technique or method which removes excess, unwanted material from a processed plastic, usually thermoset moldings. Specifically, the excess is removed from those places on the part where parting lines are formed. Methods of removal are tumbling, pressure blasting, and wheelabrating.

deflashing, airless blast Removing unwanted material by bombarding it with tiny nonabrading pellets which break off flash by impact. This technique can be used to improve or produce polished surfaces. ▷ **blast finish**

deflashing at low temperature Various low temperature methods are used depending on material as well as size and shape of part. Dry ice or liquid nitrogen are used in some type of air-moving system. Dry ice pellets are usually sprayed at 200 to 225 psi (1.4 to 1.6 MPa).

deflection **1.** Deformation or displacement from the part's original contour or shape. **2.** The linear distance that a test specimen bends at the center from no load to stated load when loaded as a beam.

deflection, residual ▷ **residual deflection**

deflection temperature under load DTUL is the temperature at which a specimen will deflect a given distance, such as 0.25 mm (0.010 in.), at a given load, such as 0.45 to 1.82 mm (66 to 264 psi), under prescribed conditions of test per ASTM D 648. It should not be interpreted as the safe temperature for satisfactory continuous operation. This latter temperature is usually somewhat lower, the limit depending upon the specimen temperature, magnitude and nature of mechanical stress, and the design of the part. DTUL can be used as a guide with proper interpretation. Formerly, DTUL was called heat distortion temperature.

deflection temperature under load versus crystallinity High degree of crystallinity, as in HDPE, PP, and nylon, has little or no effect upon the rigidity of the glassy amorphous state at low temperatures and only minor effect upon the phenomenon of the glass transition. But it introduces so much stiffening into the flexible amorphous state that it becomes quite tough and rigid. They also extend this tough rigid state out to much higher temperatures, and thus greatly broaden the range of useful rigid properties, until true crystalline melting occurs quite sharply to a fluid liquid state.

deflocculation Dispersion of colloidal particles within a liquid suspension.

defoaming agent ▷ **antifoaming agent**

deformation Basically the change in the form of dimensions of a product. It can be divided into two types: flow and elasticity. Flow is the irreversible deformation: when the stress is removed, the material does not revert to its original configuration. This means that work is converted to heat. Elasticity is reversible deformation: the deformed body recovers its original shape, and the applied work is recoverable. Viscoelastic materials, such as plastics, show both flow and elasticity. A good example is bouncing (silly) putty which bounces like a rubber ball when dropped, but slowly flows when allowed to stand.

deformation, elastic ▷ **elastic deformation**

deformation, elongation ▷ **elongation**

deformation, immediate set It is determined by measurement immediately after the removal of the load causing the deformation. ▷ **mold deformation** regarding other deformations.

deformation under load The dimensional change of a material under load for a specified time following the instantaneous elastic deformation caused by the initial application of the load. ▷ **cold flow; creep; viscous deformation; elasticity; deflection temperature under load**

deformation, viscous ▷ **viscous deformation**

deformer ▷ **antifoaming agent**

degassing ▷ **breathing**

degating Separating the molded part, automatically or manually, from an injection molded solid runner system.

degradable 1. Basically capable of being broken down into natural elements or simpler compounds under normal environmental conditions. ▷ **biocide; biodegradable; photodegradable; photo-oxidation 2.** EPA's 1990 report *Methods to Manage and Control Plastic Waste* concluded that degradable plastics will not alleviate the landfill-capacity crunch. The report says that while benefits of degradables may exist, more information on degradation rates and by-products is necessary before appropriate applications for the materials can be identified. Greenpeace-U.S. had similar conclusions on their studies. **3.** Recognize that for over a century, plastics have been developed to provide longer life with improved performance. However, degradables have their place.

degradable versus recycling ▷ **recycling versus degradable**

degradating plastic with moisture ▷ **drying**

degradation A deleterious change in the chemical structure, physical properties, and/or appearance of a plastic. ▷ **radiation-induced reaction**

degreasifying ▷ **solvent cleaning**

degree of polymerization DP may be defined as the average number of base units per molecule if the molecules are composed of regularly repeating units, or as the average number of monomeric units (mers) per molecule. These definitions are not necessarily equivalent. It should also be noted that, except in the case of plastics, they are homogeneous with respect to molecular weight: the definition is not precise unless the type of averaging is specified. The length in monomeric units of the average polymer chain at time t in a polymerization reaction (dimension of unity) follows: $DP = M_t/M_0$ where M_t = molecular weight at time t and M_0 = molecular weight of one monomeric unit.

degree of saturation DS is the ratio of the weight of water vapor associated with a pound of dry air to the weight of water vapor associated with a pound of dry air saturated at the same temperature.

dehumidifier Equipment to remove moisture from plastic pellets and powders.

dehydration Removal of water from a material either through ordinary drying or heating, or by absorption, chemical reaction, condensation of water vapor, centrifugal force, or hydraulic pressure.

dehydrogenation The removal of hydrogen from a compound by chemical means.

delamination 1. The separation of layers in plastic film or sheet laminates through failure of the heat sealing, adhesive, etc., includes coextrusion and coinjection structures. **2.** The separation or splitting of fiber-matrix in reinforced plastics or loss of bond between RP laminated plies.

deliquescent Capable of attracting moisture from the air.

delivery system ▷ **drug controlled release**

Delrin Du Pont's trade name for a type of TP acetal plastic.

Di Mattia flexing machine test ▷ **crack growth resistance**

Deming, W. Edwards An advocate and teacher in the use of statistical methods to improve quality in industrial manufacturing since the 1930s.

demulsification The process of destroying or "breaking" an unwanted emulsion.

demurrage A fee imposed on shippers of plastics, chemicals, etc. by the railroads for freight cars at loading docks for more than a given period of time, usually 24 h.

dendritic plastic Since the start of the century, a substantial number of synthetic plastics have evolved, replacing natural materials in many ways. Most notable are those involving highly branched (dentritic) precursors that lead to three-dimensional gels and networks. These systems are broadly recognized as thermosets.

denier A unit of weight expressing the size or coarseness but particularly the fineness of a relatively continuous fiber or yarn. The weight in grams of 9,000 meters is one denier (or 1/9 tex). The lower the denier, the finer the yarn. Sheer women's hosiery usually runs 10 to 15 denier. ▷ **yarn construction number**

densification process Consolidation of a loose or bulky material. ▷ **preform**

densifier To compact (reduce volume) of material such as film scrape that is processed.

densimeter Instrument used to measure the light transmittal properties of film.

density The ratio of mass to volume of a material. Density is important as a basic molecular property that affects almost every essential physical property. It can be determined in g/cm^3 (kg/m^3) (lb/in.^{3}) by weighing a sample at 23°C (73.4°F) first in air and then submerged in an inert (chemically inactive) liquid of known density such as gas-free distilled water. This is called the hydrostatic method (ASTM D 792). This method may be used for standard plastic density determination. However, to find the density of a finished part or of pellets if the available sample is too small, the density-gradient method is more useful (ASTM D 1505). Density-gradient columns are tall glass tubes containing a liquid with a density slowly decreasing from bottom to top. Small pieces of film, molded items, small cubes, etc. can be put into one of these columns and allowed to sink to the level where the liquid has the same density as the sample. Since the density of the liquid at any given point is known, one can tell the density in g/cm^3 of the specimen.

density, air at altitude ▷ **atmosphere chart** and **altitude chart**

density and specific gravity Per ASTM D 792, the relationship of density (D) to specific gravity (sp gr) or vice versa at 23°C (73.4°F) temperature is given the following equation where D is in g/cm^3: D = sp gr × 0.9975; ▷ **specific gravity** for its definition. Note that water retains its maximum density of 0.999 973 g/cm^3 at 3.98°C. The density of water in terms of milliliters and cubic centimeters is strictly only interchangeable at 3.98°C. At 20°C the density of water is 0.998 20 g/cm^3. For water, the temperature t in °C of maximum density at different pressures p in atmospheres is given by the following equation:

$$t = 3.98 - 0.0225(\mathrm{p} - 1)$$

where one atmosphere = 101 325 Pa.

density apparent The weight per unit volume of a material including voids inherent in the material as tested. Also used is the term bulk density that is commonly used for materials such as molding powder (ASTM D 883).

density, bulk ▷ **density apparent**

density, crosslinked The fraction of polymer chain units, normally the repeat units, that are crosslinked. If there is N such units (since each crosslink links two such units) the fraction number of crosslinks will be $N/2$. ▷ **network parameter**

density, current In an electroplating bath or solution, the electric current per unit area of the product or specific surface of a product being plated. Expressed in amperes per cm^2 or more usually A/cm^2.

density, filament linear expression ▷ **tex**

density, gross Density of the unprocessed plastic, such as a molding compound.

density, linear With yarn number, mass per unit length expressed as g/cm or equivalent.

density of plastic The weight per unit volume of material at 23°C (73.4°F) expressed as D23c, g/cm^3 (kg/m^3) per ASTM D 1505.

density, optical ▷ **optical density**

density, reduced The reduction in the weight of plastics such as the ratio of foam plastic bulk density to unfoamed plastic (processed-solid) bulk density.

density, true Mass bulk density divided by true (pore or void free) density.

dental market It can be said that dentistry has led the health-science field in taking advantage of the rapidly expanding types of plastics. However, the volume of dental plastics is insignificant, due to strict requirements. The search for useful preventive and restorative dental materials has brought epoxy and amine-peroxide initiator systems, specially developed for rapid cures. Similar cures of polyesters and acrylics, activated chemically at ambient temperatures, have found diverse uses as cements in orthopedic and neurosurgical applications. The largest volume is consumed in the construction and repair of prosthetic devices such as denture base, repair and relining materials, and plastic teeth. Other uses include operative dentistry (restore, cavity liners, etc.), protective sealants, elastomers for impressions of oral structures, mouth protectors, patterns for metal inlays, oral implants, etc.

depletable resource Nonreplaceable resources.

depolymerization The reverse of a plastic to its monomer, or to a polymer of lower molecular weight. Such reversion occurs in some plastics when exposed to very high temperatures.

deposition The process of applying a material to a base by means of vacuum, electrical, chemical, screening, or vapor methods, often with the assistance of a temperature and pressure container.

deposit law ▷ **bottle bill**

depth In the case of a beam, the dimension parallel to the direction in which the load is applied; in a container, it is the internal depth.

depth dose The variation of absorbed dose with distance from the incident surface of a material exposed to radiation. Depth-dose profiles give information about the distribution of absorbed energy in a specific material.

derivative The basic mathematical tool for studying rates of change.

desalination Desalting concerns any of several processes for removing dissolved mineral salts from ocean water, brackish water, or other brines. Most important, with plastics included as prime materials of construction, are solar distillation systems, electrodialysis, reverse osmosis, and flash distillation that appear "today" to be the most effective method so far developed for sea-water or brackish water desalination, accounting for about 90% of world production capacity (Middle East, etc.).

desiccant A hygroscopic material, such as activated alumina, calcium chloride, silica gel, or zinc chloride, which can be used for drying purposes because of its affinity for water. It absorbs water vapor from the air. A desiccant is the heart of a dehumidifying hopper dryer system.

desiccator A tightly closed vessel containing a desiccant. Used for drying plastics, storing molds or dies, etc.

design The term "design" has many connotations. Essentially it is the process of devising a product that fulfills as completely as possible the total requirements of the end user and, at the same time, satisfies the needs of the producer in terms of marketing and cost-effectiveness (return on investment). The efficient use of available materials and production processes, including the all-important tooling aspects, should be the goal of every design effort. Product design is as much an art as a science. Guidelines exist regarding meeting or complying with art and science. Basically design is the mechanism whereby a requirement is converted to a meaningful plan. The Fig. on p. 174 shows a design flow diagram.

design allowable A limiting value for a material property that can be used to design a structural or mechanical system to a specific level of success. Statistics can help define material allowable property strengths, usually referring to stress or strain. ▷ **A-basis; B-basis; S-basis; typical-basis**

design analysis The reputation of plastics has been harmed a great deal by the fact that in many cases designers and engineers have, after deciding tentatively to try to introduce plastics, lavishly copied the metal part which it is suppose to replace. Too much emphasis can not be laid upon the general principle that if plastics are to be used with the maximum advantage and with the minimum risk of failure, it is essential to cast aside all preconceived ideas of design in metals and treat the plastics (see Fig. on p. 175) on their own merit (such as with metal, glass, wood, etc.).

design analysis, pragmatic approach Plastics and reinforced plastics have some mechanical characteristics that differ significantly from those of possibly more familiar metals to a designer. Traditional design analyses are being used that relate to metals.

Under these circumstances it is both tempting and common practice for designers to treat plastics and reinforced plastics as though they were traditional materials and to apply familiar design methods with what seem appropriate materials constants. It must be admitted that this pragmatic approach does often yield acceptable results. However, it should also be recognized that the mechanical characteristics of plastics are different from those of metals, and the validity of this pragmatic approach is often fortuitous and usually uncertain. It would be more acceptable for the design analysis to be based on methods developed specifically for the plastics, but this action will require the designer

design analysis, pragmatic approach

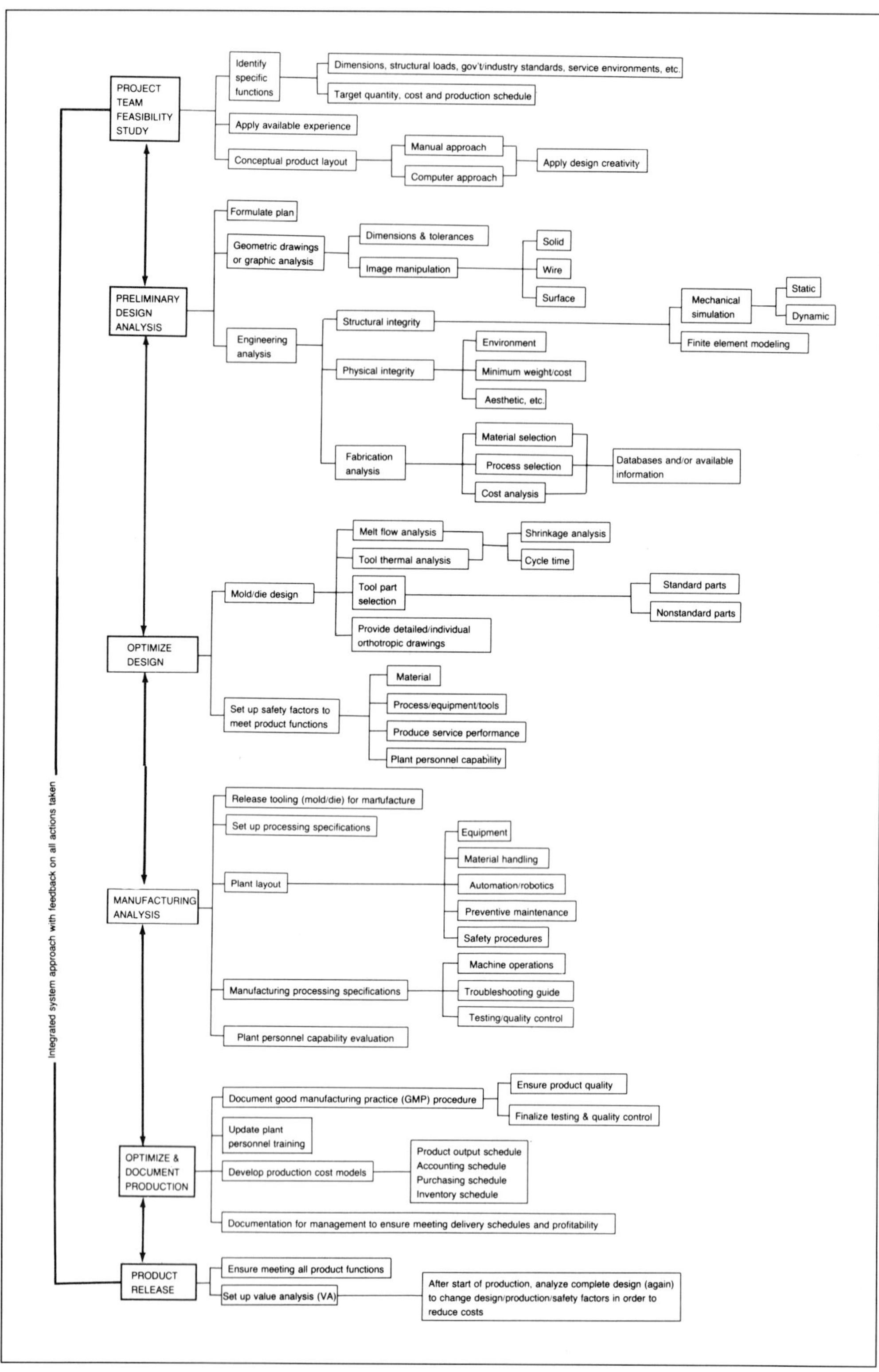

Design flow diagram to produce products.

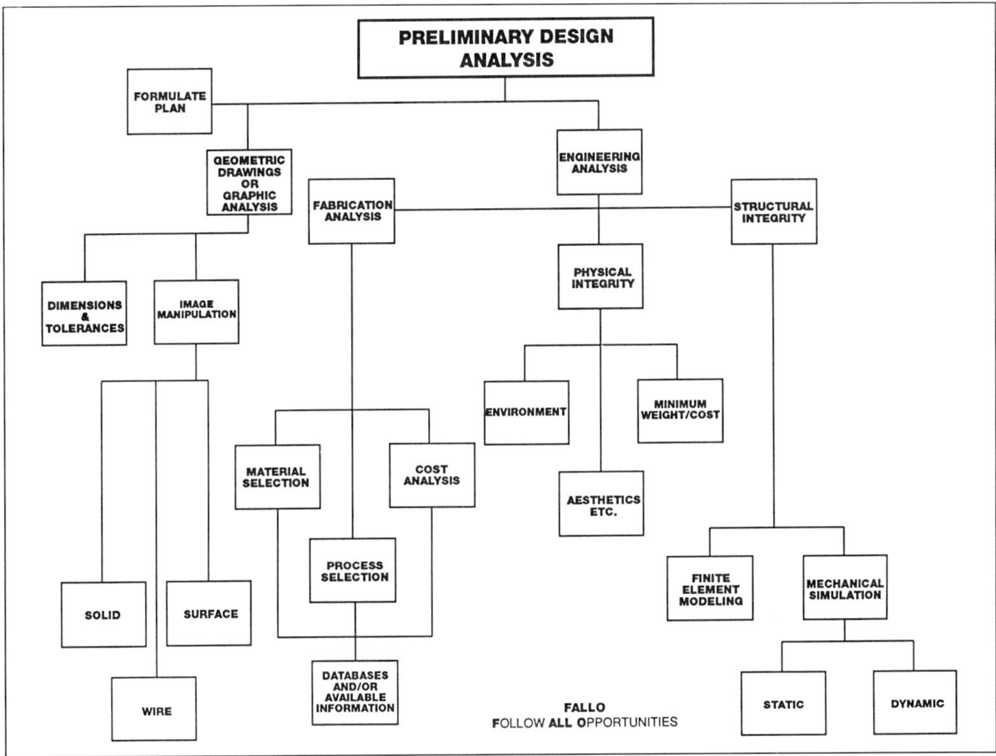

Preliminary design analysis.

of metals to accept new ideas. Obviously, this acceptance becomes easier to the degree that the new methods are presented as far as possible in the form of limitations or modifications to the existing methods discussed in this book. ▷ **zero defect**

design architectural space frame Plastics are ideal materials for use in outer space since they are lightweight, strong, and easily formed. Since the room in a missile nose cone or space vehicle is necessarily limited, expandable architectural forms for space are applicable. These are basically: (1) variable geometry with rigid components, (2) elastic recovery systems, (3) inflatable balloon, (4) airmatt, (5) rigidized membrane, and (6) expandable honeycomb. The technique of variable geometry with rigid components is a very old and familiar method of packaging. Hinging and telescoping mechanisms are utilized to deploy structures. Solar panels or sensors are examples of structures using this form of expansion.

design and cost ▷ **computer cost modeling, technically**

design bearing Self-lubricating molded plastic bearings can be used in place of plain metal bearings in bushings, flange, and thrust configurations; some are used as replacements for gauge and needle bearings. But plastic behaves differently from metal, and successful application requires awareness of differences.

design biomedical product To choose a plastic, the scientist or clinician must specify which physical properties are required (as with other products). Design parameters are based on a thorough understanding of the physiological functions and conditions under which the device must operate. Considerations include mechanical properties, purity, fabrication, stability, and tolerance.

design blow molding, two-up ▷ **blow molding, extruder mold multiple/combination cavities**

design die The function of a die is to accept the available melt from an extruder and deliver it to takeoff equipment as a shaped profile (film, sheet, pipe, filament, etc.) with minimum deviation in cross-sectional dimensions and a uniform output by weight, at the fastest possible rate. A well-designed die should permit color and compatible resin changes quickly with little off-grade material. It will distribute the melt in

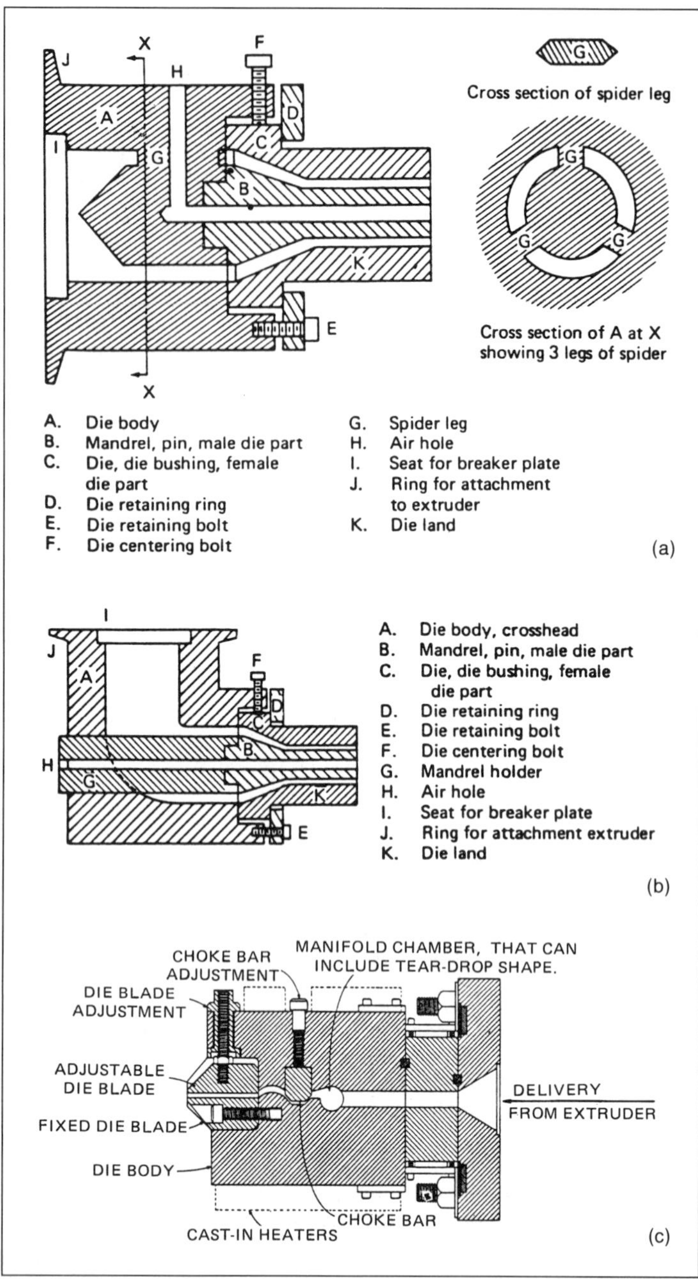

Examples of dies with nomenclature. (*a*) Pipe or tubing die for in-line extrusion; (*b*) pipe or tubing die for crosshead extrusion; (*c*) sheet extrusion die.

the die flow channels so that it exists with a uniform density and velocity (see Fig. above).

The flow rate is influenced by all the variables that can exist in preparing the melt during extrusion—namely, die heat and pressure with time in the die. Unfortunately, in spite of all the sophisticated polymer flow analysis and the rather mechanical computer-aided design capabilities, it is very difficult to design a die. An empirical approach must be used, as it is quite difficult to determine the optimum flow channel geometry from engineering calculations. It is important to employ rheological flow properties and other melt behavior via the applicable CAD programs for the type of die required. The most important ingredient is experience, which, for the novice, is properly recorded in a computer program. Nevertheless, die design has remained more of an art than any other aspect of process design. Design experience can work only if the operator of the processing line has developed the important ability to debug.

A well-built die with adjustments—temperature changes, restricter/choker bars, valves and other devices—may be used with a particular group of materials. Usually a die is designed for a specific resin meeting its particular rheological behaviors. To simplify the processsing operation, the die design should consider certain factors, if possible. The goals are to have the extrudate (product) of a uniform wall thickness (otherwise the heat transfer problem is magnified); to minimize the use of hollow sections; to minimize narrow or small channels; and to use generous radii on all corners, such as a minimum of 0.5 mm (0.02 in.). An "impossible" or difficult process can still be designed, but it requires extensive experience (both practical and theoretical), with trial-and-error runs, to make it practical.

design die, basics of flow The non-Newtonian behavior of a plastic makes its flow through a die somewhat complicated. One characteristic of plastic is that when a melt is extruded from the die, there is some swelling (see Figs. on this page). After exiting the die, it is usually stretched or drawn down to a size equal to or smaller than the die opening. The dimensions are then reduced proportionally so that in an an ideal resin the drawn-down section is the

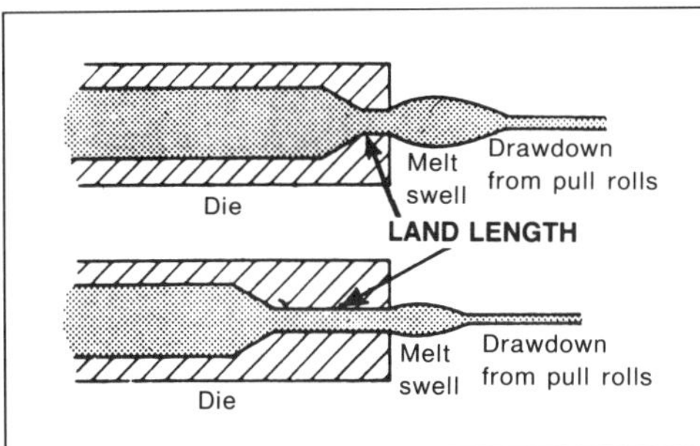

The effect of land length on swell.

same as the original section, but smaller proportionally in each dimension. Because of the melt-elasticity effects of the material, it does not draw down in a simple proportional manner; thus, the drawdown process is a source of errors in the profile. Errors are significantly reduced in a circular extrudate, such as wire coating. These errors must be corrected by modifying the die and takeoff equipment.

There are substantial influences on a material created by the flow orientation of the molecules, so there are different properties in the flow direction and perpendicular to the flow. These differences have a significant effect on the performance of the part.

Another important characteristic of melts is that they are affected by the orifice shape (see Fig. below and Figs. on pp. 178 and 179.). The effect it produces is related to the melt condition and the die design (land length, etc.), but a slow cooling rate can have a significant influence, especially with thick parts. Cooling is more

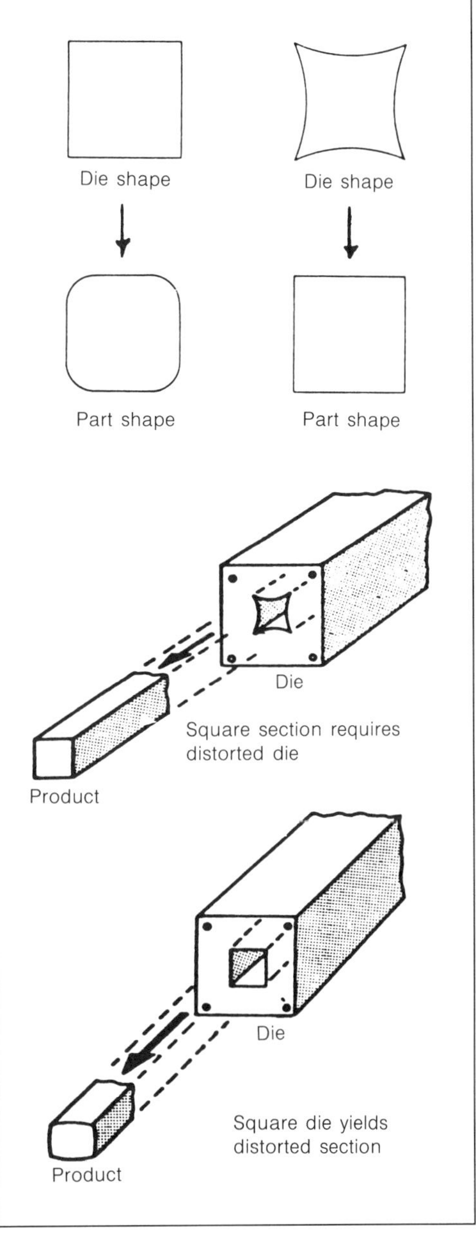

The effect of die orifice shape on the extrudate.

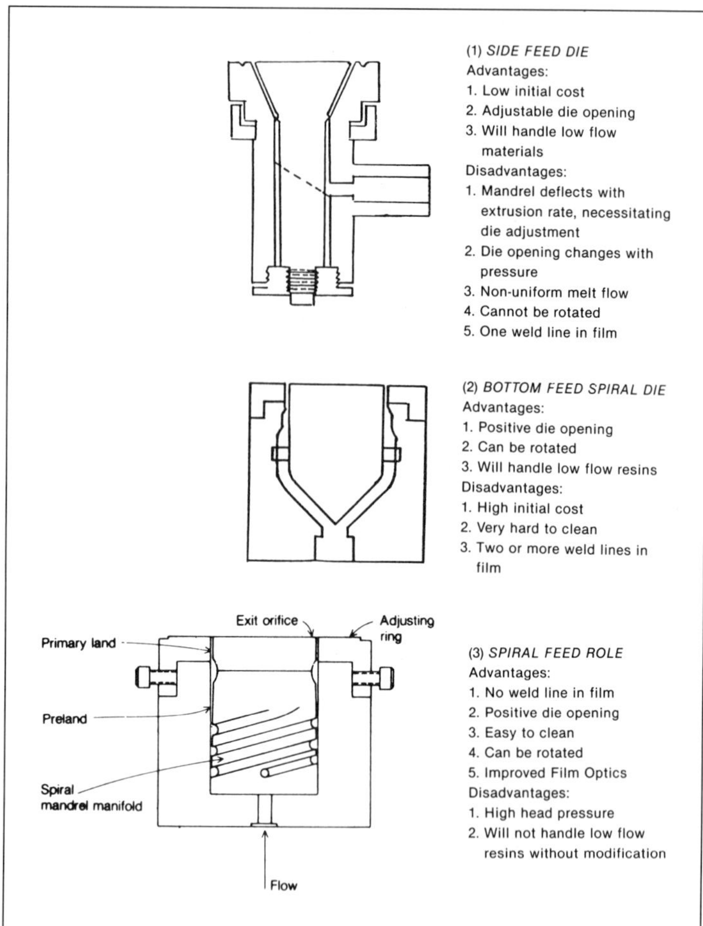

(1) SIDE FEED DIE
Advantages:
1. Low initial cost
2. Adjustable die opening
3. Will handle low flow materials
Disadvantages:
1. Mandrel deflects with extrusion rate, necessitating die adjustment
2. Die opening changes with pressure
3. Non-uniform melt flow
4. Cannot be rotated
5. One weld line in film
(2) BOTTOM FEED SPIRAL DIE
Advantages:
1. Positive die opening
2. Can be rotated
3. Will handle low flow resins
Disadvantages:
1. High initial cost
2. Very hard to clean
3. Two or more weld lines in film
Exit orifice
Adjusting ring
Primary land
Preland
Spiral mandrel manifold
Flow
(3) SPIRAL FEED ROLE
Advantages:
1. No weld line in film
2. Positive die opening
3. Easy to clean
4. Can be rotated
5. Improved Film Optics
Disadvantages:
1. High head pressure
2. Will not handle low flow resins without modification

Blown film dies, with the spiral groove method used as the best method to distribute melt flow evenly; distribution can be improved by lengthening the spirals and/or increasing the number of distribution points.

rapid at the corners; in fact, a hot center section could cause a part to "blow" outward or include visible or invisible vacuum bubbles. The popular coat-hanger die, used for flat sheet and similar products, illustrates an important principle in die design. The melt at the edges of the sheet must travel farther through the die than the melt that goes through the center of the sheet. Thus, a diagonal melt channel with a triangular dam in the center is used to restrict the direct flow to some degree. The principle of built-in restrictions is used to adjust the flow in many dies. With blow molding dies and profile dies, the openings require special attention to provide the proper product shape. See Fig. in ▷ **die deckle rod**

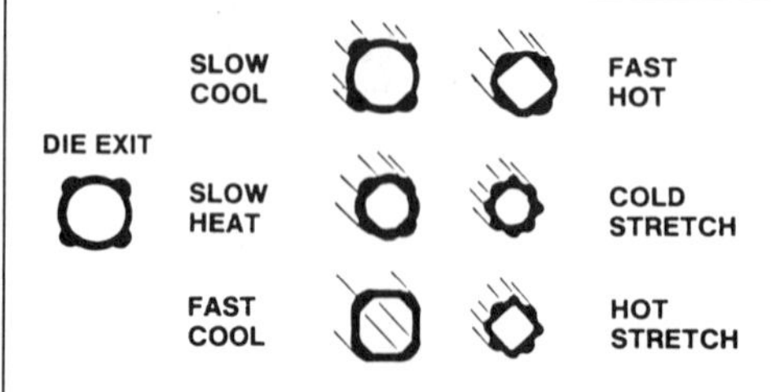

Examples of how temperature, pressure, and takeoff speed (time) variations can potentially influence the shape of an extrudate.

design engineer ▷ **engineering design**

design ethics ▷ **ethics**

design factor of safety ▷ **design safety factor**

design failure analysis ▷ **failure analysis** and **fault tree analysis**

design failure theory In many cases, a product fails when the matrial begins to yield "plastically". In a few cases, one may tolerate a small dimensional change and permit a static load that exceeds the yield strength. Actual fracture at the ultimate strength of the material

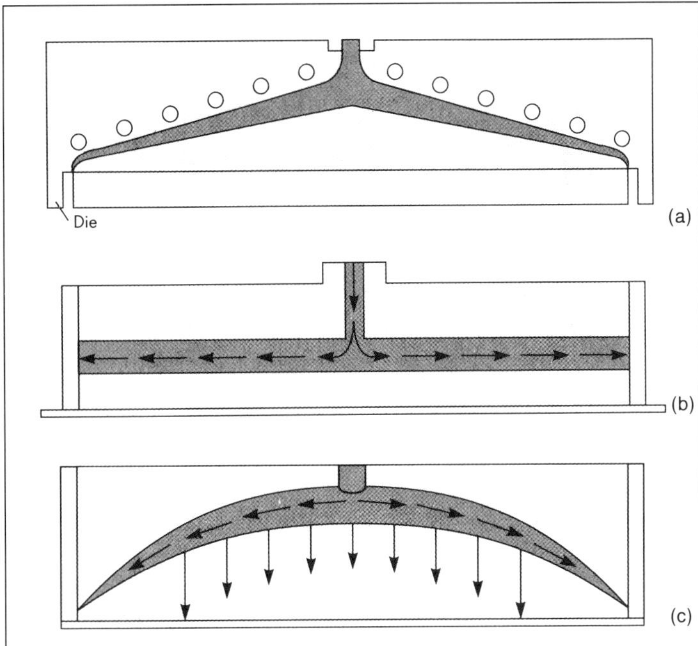

Examples of melt distribution with die geometry. Each die has limitations for certain type melts: (*a*) fishbone die has a reduction in its land restriction that makes it basically difficult with most melts for producing a uniform melt distribution; (*b*) T-type die with high viscosity melts does not produce a uniform distribution; however, with high temperature coating, low viscosity melts, distribution is acceptable; and (*c*) coathanger die provides a uniform distribution; it is used commonly, even though it is more expensive.

would then constitute failure. The criterion for failure may be based on normal or shear stress in either case. Fatigue failure is the most common mode of failure. Other modes of failure include excessive elastic deflection or buckling. The actual failure mechanism may be quite complicated; each failure theory is only an attempt to explain the failure mechanism for a given class of materials. In each case, a safety factor is employed. However, with proper part design, these failures are eliminated or can be permitted since part performance is met.

design fashion Fashion is almost automatically considered to be synonymous with "Paris, Rome, and New York". For a long time France and high culture were inseparably linked concepts. Times have changed and designers are no longer afraid to assert their individualities, demonstrated by the fashion shows at the Rhode Island School of Design. Overall design with graphics has to be daring, innovative, and pioneering, although criteria such as comfort, quality, and conformity with strict bodily requirements also have to be met. It is here that creative spirit comes into its own, using these concepts as a basis to seek to revamp and adapt clothing, jewelry, and accessories to constant changes in outlook.

design for perfection ▷ **perfection**

design graphics It covers the principles of engineering drawings, computer graphics, descriptive geometry, and problem solving. The overall study of graphics involves three aspects: terminology, skills, and theory. ▷ **computer drawing**

design, industrial ▷ **industrial design**

designing with acceptable risk ▷ **acceptable risk**

designing with adhesive ▷ **adhesive**

designing with finite element analysis ▷ **finite element analysis**

designing with model ▷ **modeling wire frame; modeling surface; modeling solid**

designing with model analytically An analytical model of a designed part is a compromise, attempting to idealize the system of loading and the load-relationship as well as the design geometry and materials used. Result is a reasonably simple solution to produce the part.

designing with model mathematically The purpose of modeling, in general, is two-fold: (1) to obtain a "physically correct" functional form for a state or process as an aid in the interpolation and extrapolation of properties, and (2) to provide the potential for new insight into the state or process modeled.

designing with model nonlinear viscoelasticity ▷ **Boltzmann superposition principle**

designing with model, plastic-chemical structure Modeling of a "glassy" or vitreous state of polymers is particularly important, because the peculiar condition called glass is not very well understood and/or applied. This condition is often and easily realized with polymers, and polymeric glasses are technologically very significant. Connected with the quest for structure and properties of the glassy state is the need to understand the ranges of temperature, stress (or pressure), and time (or frequency) where the conventional states, most importantly liquid, undergo the glass transition or glass formation and become glassy.

designing with model, plastic tailor-made Model polymers (plastics), also referred to as tailor-made macromolecules, were originally defined as polymer species in which the linear structure of the molecules and their average size are defined unambiguously. Also where the fluctuations in molecular weight and in composition are very low. A broader definition now exists with the more complex molecular structures as well as their more specific properties and applications. They include branched macromolecules, block copolymers, graft copolymers, and polymeric networks with elastically effective chains of known average length. There exists accurate control of molecular structures for these polymers. Specific methods have been designed for the preparation of model polymers, allowing proper control of the parameters governing chain growth. These methods, sometimes called macromolecular engineering, have been developed to synthesize structurally controlled polymers. ▷ **modeling stereolithography** and **computer-aided molecular graphic**

designing with model, processes A model is used to describe a process using mathematical equations. The mathematical formulation enables the model to be used for a variety of purposes, including design, control, and exploration of process control to study effects of changes in process variables.

designing without sink and shrink Designers, engineers, processors, and others can use graphics tools to help them predict what types of sink, shrink (see Fig.) and resulting warp to expect as a result of actual plastic processing. They can predict where the sink marks occur, what volume of material will be affected by sink, etc. New software continually is being developed to improve the accuracy of these predictions. These defects usually do not affect the part performance, but can detract significantly from its appearance, causing a depression or haze across the surface of the plastic.

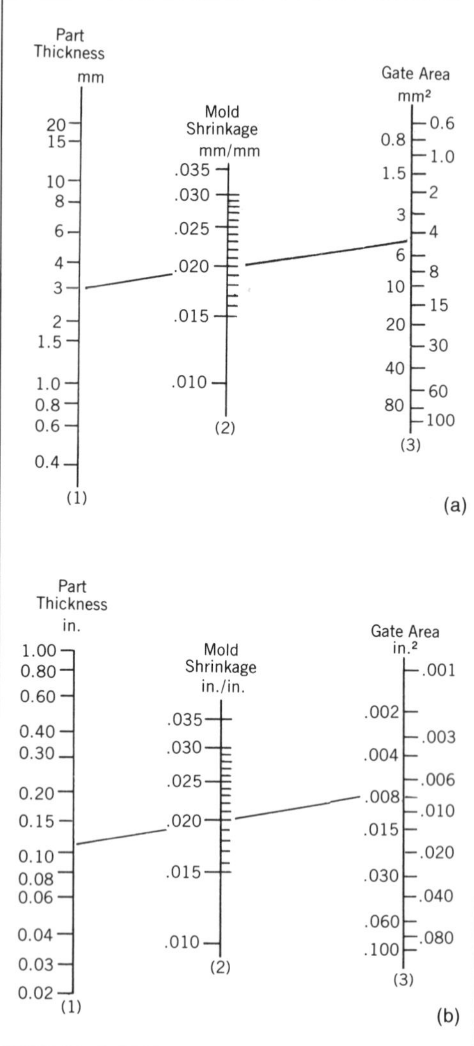

Simplified example in determining shrinkage of an injection molded plastic. Each plastic has its own mold shrinkage characteristic which is related to specific molding conditions. Examples: A straight line connecting a part thickness of 3 mm (0.12 in.) on Line 1 to a gate area of 4.5 mm² (0.0072 sq.in.) (Gate: 1.5 mm/0.06 in.) thick × 3 mm wide (0.12 in.) on Line 3 intersects Line 2 at 0.020 mm/mm (0.020 in./in.), the estimated mold shrinkage at a mold temperature of 93°C (200°F). (*a*) Nomograph in SI units; (*b*) nomograph in English units.

designing with pseudo-elastic method Viscoelastic behavior of plastics shows that their deformations are dependent on such factors as the time under load and temperature ▷ **viscoelasticity**. Therefore, when structural (load bearing) plastic products are to be designed, it must be remembered that the standard equations that are available for designing springs, beams, plates, and cylinders, and so on have all been derived under the assumptions that (1) the strains are small, (2) the modulus is constant, (3) the strains are independent of the loading rate or history and are immediately reversible, (4) the material is isotropic, and (5) the material behaves in the same way in tension and compression.

Since these assumptions are not always justifiable when applied to plastics, the classic equations cannot be used indiscriminately. Each case must be considered on its merits, with account being taken of such factors as the mode of deformation, the service temperature, the fabrication method, the environment, and others. In particular, it should be noted that the traditional equations are derived using the relationship that stress equals modulus times strain, where the modulus is a constant. Except for reinforced thermosets and certain engineering plastics, many plastics do not generally have a constant modulus. Several approaches have been used for the nonconstant situation, some of which are quite accurate. The drawback is that these method can be quite complex, involving numerical techniques that are not attractive to designers. However, one method has been widely accepted, the so-called pseudo-elastic design method.

In this method appropriate values of such time-dependent properties as the modulus are selected and substituted into the standard equations. It has been found that this approach is sufficiently accurate in most cases if the value chosen for the modulus takes into account the projected service life of the product and the limiting strain of the plastic, assuming that the limiting strain for the material is known. Unfortunately, this is not just a straightforward value applicable to all plastics or even to one plastic in all its applications. This value is often arbitrarily chosen, although several methods have been suggested for arriving at a suitable value. One is to plot a secant modulus that is 0.85 of the initial tangent modulus and note the strain at which this intersects the stress-strain characteristic. However, for many plastics, particularly the crystalline TPs, this method is too restrictive, so in most practical situations the limiting strain is decided in consultation between the designer and the plastic material's manufacturer. Once the limiting strain is known, design methods based on its creep curves become rather straightforward.

designing with trial and error ▷ **computer-aided design; computerized laboratory**

designing workplace ▷ **ergonomic**

design mold A mold, specifically for injection molding, is a controllable complex device that must be an efficient heat exchanger. The Fig. below and the Figs. on pp. 182 and 183 provide schematics on different mold constructions.

If not properly designed, handled, and maintained, it will not be an efficient operating device. Hot melt, under pressure, moves rapidly through the mold. Water or some other medium circulates in the mold to remove (for TPs) or add (for TSs) heat. Air is released from cavities to eliminate melt burning or voids in the part. All kinds of actions operate, including sliders and unscrewing devices. Parts like knockout pins as well as air are ejected at the proper time. These basic operations in turn require all kinds of interactions, including such parameters as fill-time, hold pressure, and other variables.

Each of the plastics used has special distinctive properties. Some are abrasive or corrosive; others require very tight heat control and

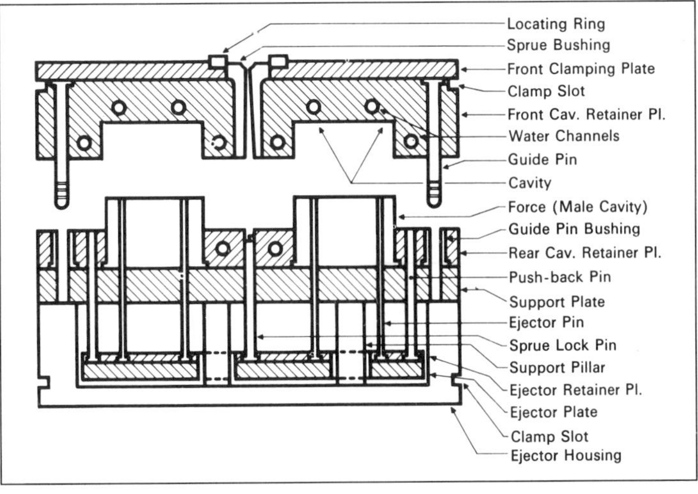

A two-part standard mold.

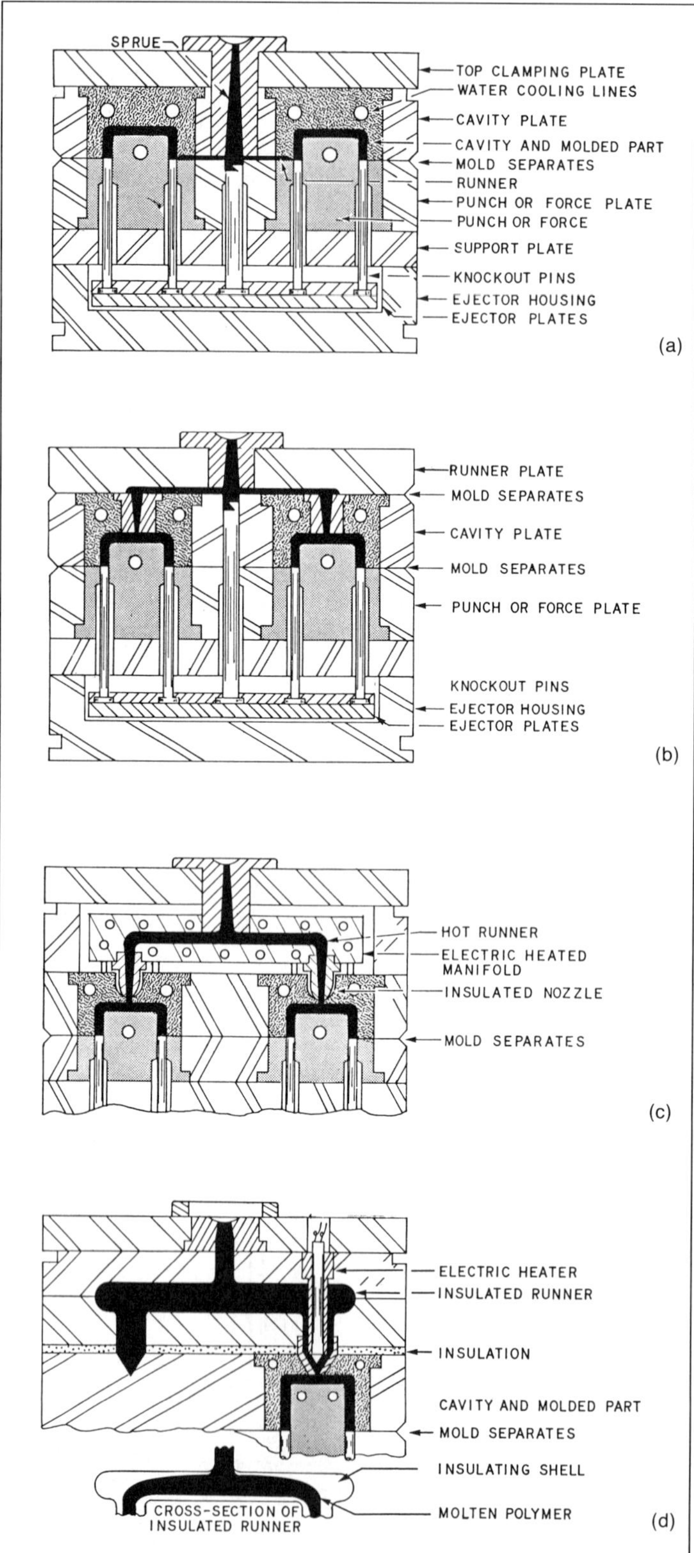

Types of injection molds: (*a*) Two-plate injection mold; (*b*) three-plate injection mold; (*c*) hot runner mold; (*d*) insulated runner injection mold.

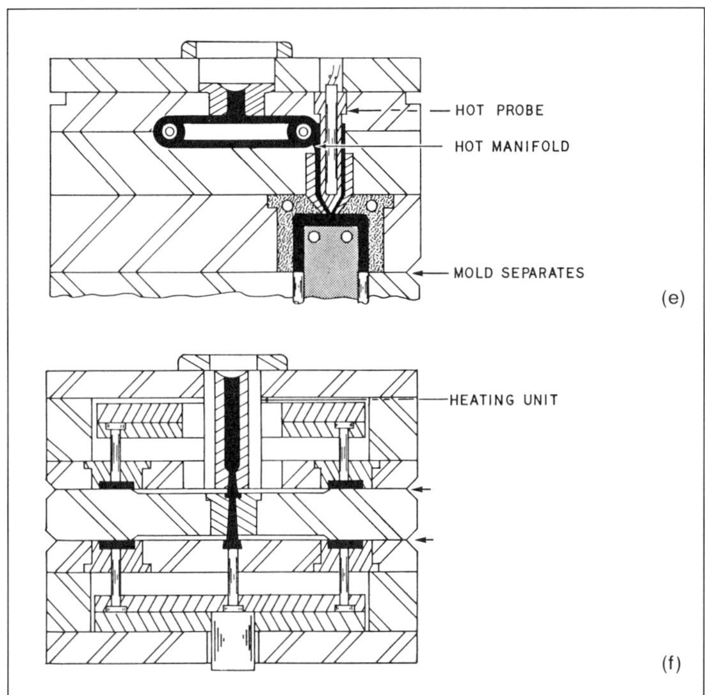

Types of injection molds (*continued*): (*e*) hot manifold injection mold; (*f*) stacked injection mold.

pressure. Settings that work for one resin probably will not work for another, or a machine change to a duplicate will probably require different settings. Shrinkage requires special attention. Crystalline resins shrink more than amorphous ones. Differential shrinkage can cause warpage. With tight part tolerances it is necessary to leave more, rather than less, steel in the mold so that corrections requiring metal "cutting" can correlate processing with tolerances.

CAD and CAE programs are available that can aid in mold design and in setting up the complete process. These programs are concerned with melt flow to-part solidification and the meeting of performance requirements. Many different factors are incorporated, including heat transfer, thermal conductivity, thermal expansion, the coefficients of friction, machine and mold operating setup, and so on.

design mold, basics of flow There are variables during molding that influence part performance. The information presented here shows how melt flow variables behave to influence products' properties. A flow analysis can be made to aid designers and moldmakers in obtaining a good mold. Of paramount importance is controlling the fill pattern of the molding so that parts can be produced reliably and economically. A good fill pattern for a molding is one that is usually unidirectional in nature, thus giving rise to a unidirectional and consistent molecular orientation in the molded product. This approach helps avoid warpage problems caused by a differential orientation, an effect best demonstrated by the warpage that occurs in thin center-gated disks. In this case all the radials are oriented parallel to the flow direction, with the circumferences transverse to the flow direction. The difference in the amounts of shrinkage manifests itself in terms of warpage of the disk.

In order to achieve a controlled fill pattern, the mold designer must select the number and location of gates that result in the desired pattern. Flow analysis can help by allowing the designer to try multiple options for gate locations and evaluate the impact on the molding process. This analysis often can be conducted with the product designer to achieve the best balance of gate locations for cosmetic impact and molding considerations. The Figs. on p. 184 show various flow patterns, orientation patterns, and property performances.

In the practical world of mold design, there are many instances where design trade-offs must be made in order to achieve a successful overall design. While naturally balanced runner systems are certainly desirable, they may lead to problems in mold cooling or increased cost due to excessive runner-to-part weights. Additionally, there are many cases such as parts requiring

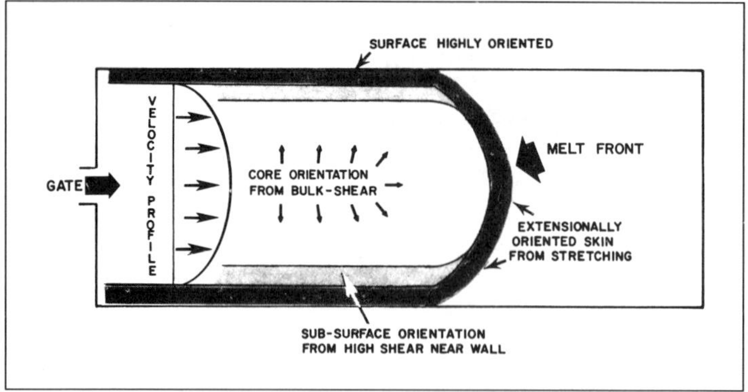

Cavity melt flow looking at a part's thickness.

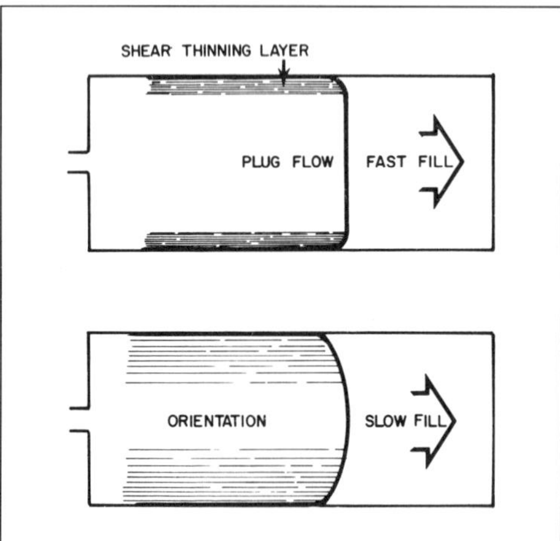

The effects of different fill rates.

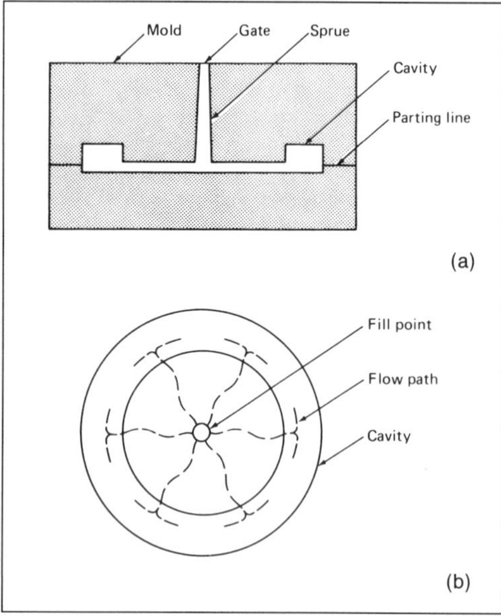

Plastic melt does not flow uniformly through the diaphragm of plate mold (*a*) in the compensating phase, but spreads in a branching pattern (*b*).

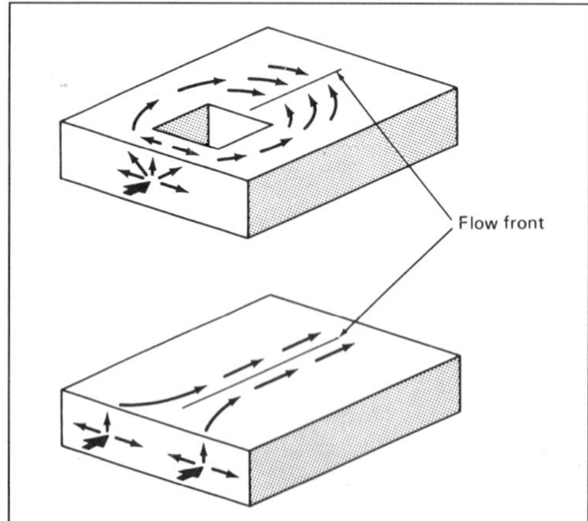

Flow paths are determined by part shape and gate location. Flow fronts that meet head on will weld together, forming a weld line. Parallel fronts tend to blend, however, producing a less distinct weld line but a stronger bond.

multiple gates or family molds in which balanced runners cannot be used. Flow analysis tools allow successful designs of runners to balance for pressure, temperature, or a combination of both. ▷ **mold cavity melt flow analysis**

design optimized With plastics and reinforced plastics, to a greater extent than other materials, an opportunity exists to optimize design by focusing on material composition and orientation, as well as on structural member geometry (see Figs. on pp. 185 and 186). There is also an important interrelationship between shape, material selection (including reinforced plastics, elastomers, foams, etc.), consolidation of parts, manufacturing selection and others that provide low cost-to-performance products. For

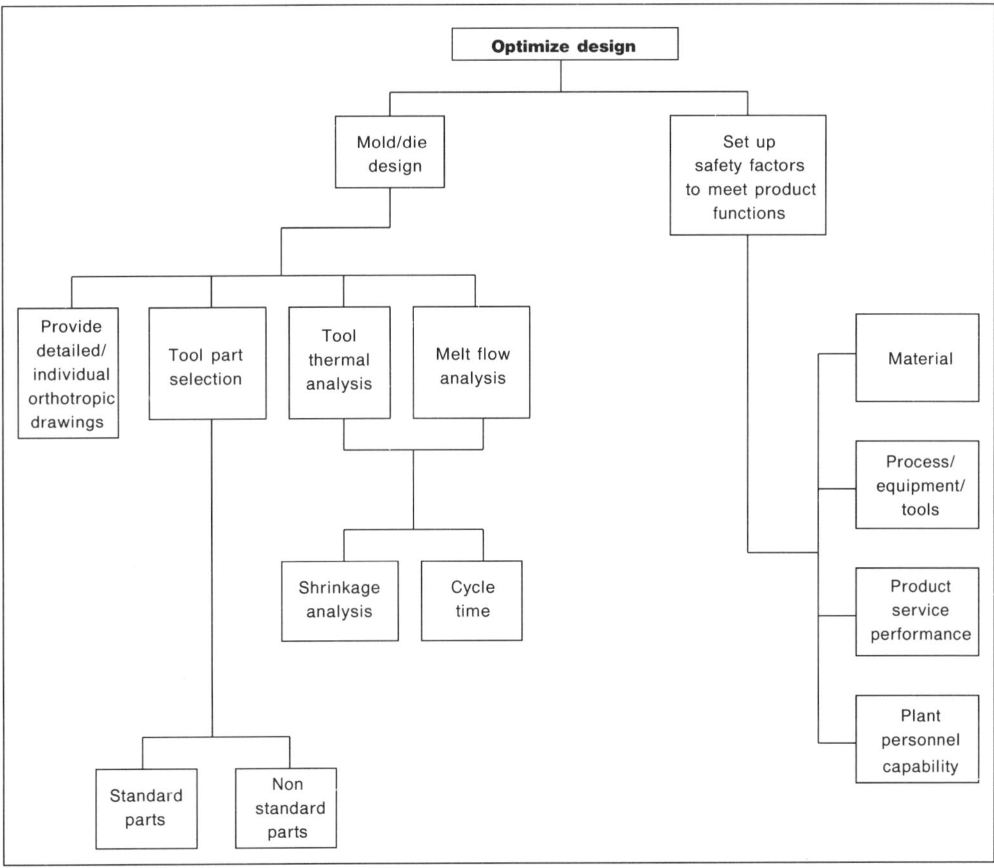

Optimize design.

the many applications that only require minimum mechanical performance, shape with processing techniques can help overcome limitations with commodity (lower cost) plastics, such as low stiffness. When extremely high performance is required, RP and other engineering plastics are available.

design reinforced plastic ▷**reinforced plastic micromechanical analysis**

design risk ▷**acceptable risk**

design safety factor A factor of safety (FS) or safety factor (SF) is used to provide for the uncertainties associated with any design. In addition to the basic uncertainties of graphic design, a designer may also have to consider additional factors: (1) *Variations in material properties* Because no two plastic (or steel, for that matter) melts are exactly alike—some may have inclusions and so on—the strength properties given in materials tables are usually average values. If the value stated is a manufacturer's value, it probably is the minimum value, which can significantly reduce or eliminate its uncertainty. (2) *Effect of size in stating material strength properties* Property tables, unless otherwise stated for plastics, metals, and so on, list strength values based on a specified size, yet larger components generally fail at a lower stress than a similar smaller component made of the same material. (3) *Type of loading* A simple static load is relatively easy to recognize, but there are cases that fail between impact and suddenly applied loads. One thus takes into account infrequently applied fatigue loading mixed with some shock loads, as for example cams, links, or feeding devices. (4) *Effect of processes* The fabricating operations for plastics, steel, glass, and so forth may, and usually do, introduce stress concentrations and residual stresses. (5) *Overall concern for human safety* All design must consider safety of the user who may be near or in contact with the product. Unexpected overloads or other situations may cause breakage and considerable bodily harm.

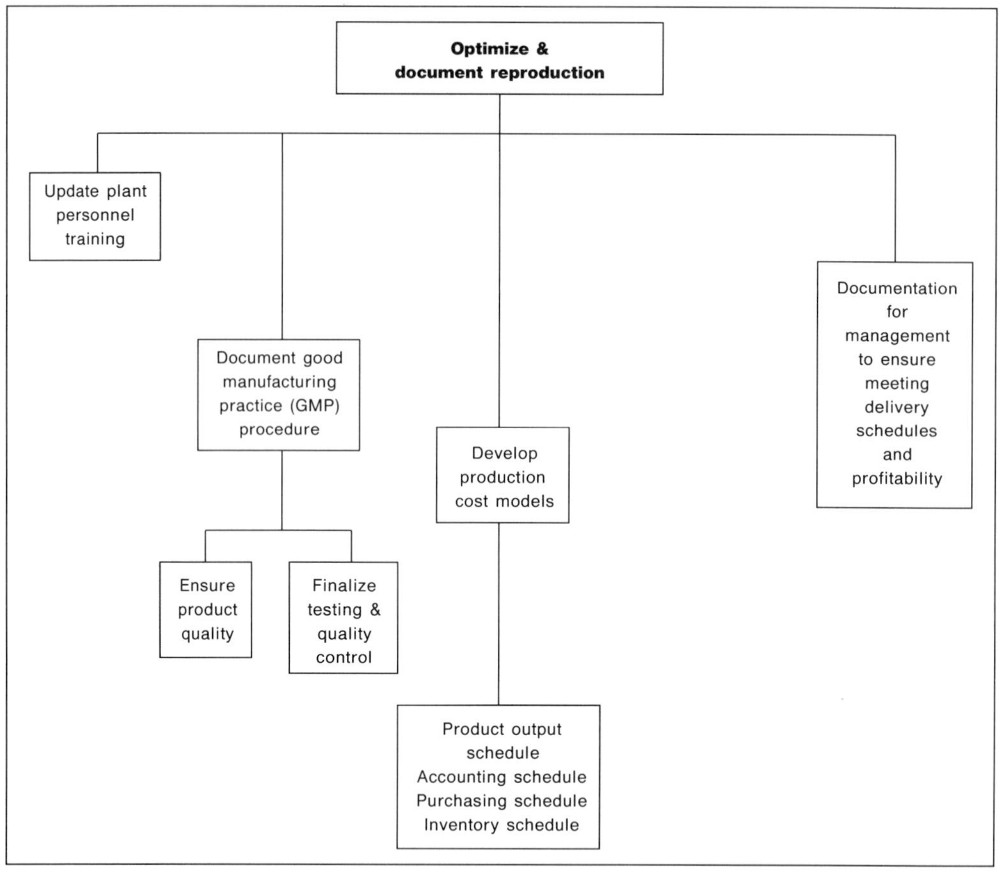

Optimize and document reproduction.

In order to take uncertainties into account in design, there is the safety factor of the so-called "factor of ignorance." Many designers do use the SF, but improper use of it may result in needless waste or the cost of extra material, or even physical or operational failure. Thus, one must define the use of SF. ▷ **uncertainties** and **perfection**

design screw (for processing plastic) The virtue of keeping things simple is well known (▷ **kiss** approach), but screw designs for different plasticizing machines (injection molding, extrusion, blow molding, etc.) offer dozens of different options. They include complex, but controllable types. ▷ **screw** for description of the screw.

With practically all machines, only the cylinder temperature is directly controlled. The actual heat of the melt, within the screw and as it is ejected from the nozzle, can vary considerably, depending on the efficiency of the screw design and the method of operation. The factors affecting melt heat include the time the plastic remains in the cylinder; the internal surface heating area of the cylinder and the screw, per volume of material being heated; the thermal conductivity of the cylinder, screw, and plastic; the heat differential between the cylinder and the melt; and the amount of melt turbulence in the cylinder. In designing the screw, some balance must be maintained between the need to provide adequate time for heat exposure and to maximize output most economically.

In general, heat-transfer problems have led screw designers to concentrate on making screws more efficient as heat-transfer devices. As a result, the internal design and performance of screws will vary considerably to accommodate the different plastics used. Most machines are single, constant-pitch, metering-type screws to handle the majority of plastics.

When it is impossible for a processor to choose the most suitable screw for a particular job, recognize that screw designs are ordinarily compromise solutions for a variety of possible processing problems. When selecting a general purpose screw, it should be kept in mind that the more shallow the screw flights, the smaller the plastic volume conveyed to the tip of the screw, limiting output. Heating the melt (to increase output) more than necessary increases cooling time and therefore the cost of processing. Deep draw screws will provide higher output, but may not heat and plasticize the melt adequately. Recognize that there are screws to meet specific requirements, providing the requirements for the screw to melt the plastic are known and correctly applied to the design to obtain the best melt.

design shape Formability into almost any conceivable shape is one of plastics' design advantages, so it is important for designers to understand what can be done. Shape, which can be almost infinitely varied in the early design stages, is capable for a given weight of materials to provide a whole spectrum of strength properties, especially in the most desirable areas of stiffness and bending resistance.

design shell structure Shell structures that use plastics can be either singly or doubly curved via different methods. Example of the singly curved shell is the barrel vault supported on rigid end diaphragms. The barrel can have various types of cross sections (circular, parabolic, elliptical, etc). The cross section can even be corrugated to prevent local buckling of the skin.

design snap fit For high-volume production, snap-fit designs provide economic, rapid assembly. In many products, such as inexpensive housewares or hand-held appliances, they are designed for one assembly only, with no nondestructive means for disassembling them. Where servicing them is anticipated, provision is made for the release of the assembly with a tool. Other designs, such as those used in the battery compartment covers for calculators and radios, are designed for easy release and reassembly many hundreds of times.

There is always some part of a snap fit that must flex like a spring, usually past a designed-in interference, and quickly return, or at least nearly return, to its unflexed position, to create the assembly of two or more parts. The key to successful design is to provide sufficient holding power, without exceeding the elastic limits of the plastic. The Fig. below shows a typical design. Using the beam equations, calculate the maximum stress during assembly. If it stays below the yield point of the plastic, the flexing finger will return to its original position. However, for certain designs there will not be enough holding power because of the low forces or small deflections.

It has been found that with many plastics the calculated flexing stress can far exceed the yield point stress, if the assembly occurs too rapidly. In other words, the flexing finger will just momentarily pass through its condition of

Shape of cross section ▶ / Type of design ▼		A Rectangle	B Trapezoid	C Ring segment	D Irregular cross section
(Permissible) deflection	1 Cross section constant over the length	$y = 0.67 \cdot \frac{\epsilon \cdot l^2}{h}$	$y = \frac{a+b_{(1)}}{2a+b} \cdot \frac{\epsilon \cdot l^2}{h}$	$y = C_{(2)} \frac{\epsilon \cdot l^2}{r_2}$	$y = \frac{1}{3} \cdot \frac{\epsilon \cdot l^2}{c_{(3)}}$
	2 All dimensions in direction y, e. g. h or Δr, decrease to one-half.	$y = 1.09 \cdot \frac{\epsilon \cdot l^2}{h}$	$y = 1.64 \frac{a+b_{(1)}}{2a+b} \cdot \frac{\epsilon \cdot l^2}{h}$	$y = 1.64 \cdot C_{(2)} \frac{\epsilon \cdot l^2}{r_2}$	$y = 0.55 \cdot \frac{\epsilon \cdot l^2}{c_{(3)}}$
	3 All dimensions in direction z, e. g. b and a, decrease to one-quarter	$y = 0.86 \cdot \frac{\epsilon \cdot l^2}{h}$	$y = 1.28 \frac{a+b_{(1)}}{2a+b} \cdot \frac{\epsilon \cdot l^2}{h}$	$y = 1.28 \cdot C_{(2)} \frac{\epsilon \cdot l^2}{r_2}$	$y = 0.43 \cdot \frac{\epsilon \cdot l^2}{c_{(3)}}$
Deflection force	1, 2, 3	$P = \overbrace{\frac{bh^2}{6}}^{Z} \cdot \frac{E_s \epsilon}{1}$	$P = \overbrace{\frac{h^2}{12} \cdot \frac{a^2+4ab_{(1)}+b^2}{2a+b}}^{Z} \cdot \frac{E_s \epsilon}{1}$	$P = Z_{(4)} \cdot \frac{E_s \epsilon}{1}$	$P = Z_{(4)} \cdot \frac{E_s \epsilon}{1}$

Equation for designing geometrically complex cross sections of snap fits (courtesy of Miles Inc.).

maximum deflection or strain, and the material will not respond as if the yield stress had been greatly exceeded. A common way to evaluate snap fits is to calculate their strain rather than their stress. Then compare this value with the allowable dynamic strain limit for the particular plastic. In designing the finger it is important to avoid having sharp corners or structural discontinuities that can cause stress risers. A tapered finger provides a more uniform stress distribution, which makes it advisable where possible.

A snap fit can be rectangular or of a geometrically more complex cross-section, as shown in the Fig. on p. 187. The design approach for the finger is that either its thickness, *h*, or width, *b*, tapers from the root to the hook. Thus, the load-bearing cross-section at any location relates more to the local load. The result is that the maximum strain on the plastic can be reduced and less material will be needed. With this design approach, the vulnerable cross-section is always at the root. ▷ **blow molding, extruder mold multiple/combination cavities**

design specification Good product design includes good specifications. ▷ **specification or standard**

design, statistical ▷ **statistical benefits**

design technology Design technology is the prediction of performance in its broadest sense, including all the characteristics and properties of a material that are essential to the process of material selection. To the designer or product engineer, a strict definition of a design property is one that permits calculating of part dimensions from a stress analysis, e.g., the use of Young's modulus to calculate the thickness of a beam. Such properties obviously are the most desirable upon which to base material selections. However, even with metals, there are many stresses that cannot be analyzed. Hence, we are forced to rely on properties that correlate with performance. In plastics, these correlative properties, together with those that can be used in design equations, generally are called engineering properties. They encompass a variety of stress situations over and above the basic static strength and rigidity, such as impact, fatigue, high and low temperature capability, flammability, chemical resistance, and arc resistance.

design theory and strength of materials There is no fine line separating the "theory of elasticity" from the methods of "strength of materials". The value of one approach over the other depends on the particular application. In most engineering problems, both methods assume homogeneous, isotropic, linearly elastic material. Both methods require that equilibrium of force be satisfied. To determine a 3-D stress distribution using the theory of elasticity, six stress-strain equations and six strain displacement equations can be used in addition to three equilibrium equations (see Ref. No. 170 and 171 on p. lxv). The unknowns, six stress components and three displacements, may be found for given loading and boundary conditions. If the problem is formulated in such a way that the displacements are not explicitly included, it is necessary to establish compatibility of strains, that is, one must show the material to be continuous in the stressed as well as the unstressed state.

An alternative problem formulation assumes a state of stress that satisfies equilibrium of forces and corresponds to the loading and boundary conditions. Compatibility of strains is not necessarily satisfied. This method, the strength of materials approach, solves problems that would be very unwieldy by elasticity methods. Because the stress distribution is assumed beforehand, it is apparent that this approach would be meaningless if one were required to find the stress concentration due to a hole in a tension member or for any problem where one would have no rational basis for assuming a certain stress distribution.

Where the theory of elasticity results in a tractable formulation, the solution is accurate to the degree described in the loading and boundary conditions. Also to the degree to which the material approaches the ideal assumed homogeneous, isotropic solid. These conditions being met to a reasonable degree, one would expect the elasticity solution to be superior to the strength of materials. On the other hand, an assumed stress distribution may accurately portray the system due to factors such as local yielding and, in such cases, the strength of materials method may be favorable. ▷ **material and engineering**

desizing The process of eliminating sizing, usually starch, from greige goods (gray goods) before applying special finishes or bleaches for yarns such as glass and cotton fibers. Also involves removing lubricant size following the weaving of a cloth.

desorption A process in which an absorbed material is released from another material. Desorption is the reverse of absorption, adsorption, or both. It may be accomplished by heating, pressure reduction, pressure from another more strongly absorbed substance, or a combination of these means.

destaticization Treating plastic materials to minimize their accumulation of static electricity, and consequently, the amount of dust picked up by the plastic because of such charges.

detector ▷ **ultrasonic**

detergent Any substance that reduces the surface tension of water, specifically surface-activated agents which concentrate at oil-water interfaces, exerts emulsifying action and thus aids in removing soils.

deterioration A permanent change in the physical properties of a plastic evidenced by impairment of its properties.

detonation The extremely rapid, self-propagating decomposition of an explosive accompanied by a high pressure-temperature wave that moves at from 1,000 to 9.000 m/s. May be initiated by mechanical impact, friction, or heat. Detonation is a characteristic of high explosives which vary considerably in their sensitivity to shock. Use includes forming high molecular weight plastics that are not capable of being processed easily and many plastic parts that are large in size.

deviation Variation from a specified dimension or design requirement, usually defining upper and lower limits.

devitrification The formation of crystals (seeds) in a glass melt, usually occurring when the melt is too cold. These crystals can appear as defects in glass fibers.

devolatilization, basics In devolatilization, one or more volatile components are extracted from the polymer. It can be either in the solid state or in the molten state. Two types of actions occur: (1) the volatile components diffuse to the polymer-vapor interface, and (2) the volatile components evaporate at the interface and are carried away. Thus, the first part of the process is diffusional mass transport and the second part a convective mass transport. If the diffusional mass flow rate is less than the convective mass flow rate, the process is diffusion-controlled. In polymer-volatile systems, the diffusion constants are generally very low and, therefore, in many polymer devolatilization processes, the process is diffusion-controlled. ▷ **reactor volatility**

The important relationship in diffusional mass transport is Fick's law. It states that in a one-dimensional diffusion, the positive mass flux of component "A" is related to a negative concentration ingredient. This law is valid for constant densities and for relatively low concentrations of component "A" in component "B". The term binary mixture is used to describe a two-component mixture. A binary diffusivity constant of one component is a binary mixture. The diffusional mass transport is driven by a concentration gradient, as described by Fick's law. This is very similar to Fourier's law, which relates heat transport to a temperature gradient. It is also very similar to Newton's law which relates momentum transport to a velocity gradient. Because of the similarities in diffusional mass transport, heat transport, and momentum transport, many problems in diffusion are described with equations of the same form as used in heat transfer problems or momentum transfer problems. Also several of the dimensionless numbers that are used in heat transfer problems are also used in diffusional mass transfer problems.

devolatilization process Since the contaminants in most cases are volatile relative to their polymer, they are removed from the condensed phase (polymer) by evaporation into a contiguous gas phase. Such separation processes are commonly referred to as devolatilization (DV). The plastic to be devolatilized may be in the form of a melt or particulate solid. Separation is effected by applying a vacuum or by using inert substances, such as purging with nitrogen gas or steam. Devolatilization is an important unit operation in the processing of plastics into products without contaminants.

devulcanization Technically a misnomer since vulcanization is irreversible (thermoset action). The term is used to describe the softening of a vulcanizate caused by heat and chemical additives during reclaiming (recycling).

dew/frost-point hygrometer An instrument that measures the surface temperature at which ambient water vapor condenses.

dew point DP is the temperature to which water vapor must be reduced to obtain saturation vapor pressure, that is, 100% relative humidity. As air is cooled, the amount of water vapor that it can hold decreases. If air is cooled sufficiently, the actual water vapor pressure becomes equal to the saturation water vapor pressure. Any further cooling normally results in moisture condensation.

Basically, DP is the temperature at which the water will condensate or separate from the air. Air, as we naturally see it and breathe it, has a percentage of water. This is what the weather reporter calls humidity. Mother Nature removes this water from the air at night when the temperature drops around 7.2°C (45°F). This is the water we see in the morning on our driveways, grass, car, etc. This means that the DP of that air was about 45°F.

D-glass A high boron content glass made especially for reinforced plastics or laminates requiring a precisely controlled dielectric constant. ▷ **glass fiber types**

diadic polyamide plastic Polyamide plastic produced by the condensation of a diamine and a dicarboxylic acid.

diallyl compound ▷ **allyl plastic**

diallyl isophthalate plastic ▷ **diallyl phthalate plastic** and **allyl plastic**

diallyl phthalate plastic Diallyl phthalate (DAP) and diallyl isophthalate (DAIP) are the principal thermosets in the allyl family; DAP is predominantly used. They are used for preimpregnated glass cloth and paper which in turn go through a heat, time, pressure cycle to produce parts. Molding compounds are reinforced with fibers to improve mechanical and physical properties. Glass fibers impart mechanical performance, acrylic fibers provide improved electrical performance, polyester fibers improve impact resistance, and other fibers, as well as fillers, can impart different performances.

In some applications DAPs are competitive with TS polyester compounds. They can offer longer shelf life (BMC, etc.), less shrinkage during curing, somewhat better chemical or electrical properties and higher heat resistance. In general the allyls are more expensive and, therefore, find few uses in consumer products. They can be molded at lower pressures and in faster molding cycles. With the triallyl cyanurate formulation, temperatures range as high as 500°F (use in high speed radomes, etc.). Major advantages of all allyls over TS polyesters are freedom from styrene odor, low toxicity, low evaporation losses during fabricating evacuation cycles, no subsequent oozing or bleed-out and long term retention of electrical-insulating performances.

DAPs' major use is in electrical connectors used in communications, computer and aerospace systems. Their high thermal resistance permits their use in vaporphase soldering. Other uses include arc-track-resistant switchgear and TV components, circuit boards, etc. ▷ **allyl plastic; unsaturated polyester plastic; polyester thermoset plastic**

dialysis When a semipermeable membrane (includes plastics such as nylon, fluoroplastic, etc.) is used to stabilize the concentration gradient between a solution on one side and pure solvent on the other, the minimum requirements for simple dialysis have been met. The kinetic movement of the solute molecules will tend to drive them through the membrane in the direction of lower concentration. On the other hand, as a result of osmosis (osmotic-pressure difference), the net movement of the solvent molecules will be in the opposite direction.

diamagnetic susceptibility A relative measure of the degree to which a molecule or atom is repelled by a magnetic field.

diametral clearance ▷ **screw diametral clearance**

diamond ▷ **carbon**

diaper ▷ **disposable diaper**

diaphragm ▷ **bag molding parting film**

diaphragm gate ▷ **mold gate**

diaphragm pressure forming ▷ **bag molding**

diatomaceous earth This diatomite is a siliceous white powder used as a filler in plastics. This earth material can increase properties such as plastics hardness, heat resistance, dielectric strength, etc. It is an excellent filter; provides special filtration action with the brewing of beer.

diatomic Containing two atoms.

dibasic Acids having two displaceable hydrogen atoms per molecule.

dice cut Material for processing in the shape of cubes of about 2 to 3 mm in size.

dicing The process of cutting with production auxiliary equipment plastic strands or sheets for further processing, includes RP thermoset prepreg materials.

die A die is identified as a device, usually of steel, having a specific shape or design geometry which it imparts to plastics using different methods of processing, such as extrusion, impact stamping, casting, cutting etc. The terms die, mold, and tool are virtually synonymous in the sense that they have a female or negative cavity through or into which a molten plastic moves usually under heat and pressure. However, it principally refers to an extruder die in the plastic processing industry. ▷ **design die** for schematics and terminology used with dies. In the following definitions of the different aspects of "dies", they are principally concerned with extrusion, unless otherwise stated. Also ▷ **extruder**

die adaptor That part of an extruder which holds the die block. It moves the melt from the plasticator (extruder) to the die.

die adjustment Means moving the die relative to the die pin.

die and pin set or shaping A matching bushing and pin dimension to form the extrudate.

die blade Deformable member(s) attached to an extruder die body which determine the slot opening and which are adjusted to produce uniform thickness across the film or sheet produced.

die body The main structure of the die head excluding the bushing and pin.

die bolt heater Expands die bolt usually on sheet extrusion line to control transverse thickness. Provides a very important process control procedure.

die bushing An adjustable bushing (outside ring forming wall) at the bottom of the die body which determines the final orifice outer diameter or surface and shape.

die bushing adjustment Means of moving the die bushing relative to the die pin.

die casting Usually identifies the shaping of metal products by forcing a molten metal or alloy under high pressure into a female or negative cavity by means of a hydraulic ram. Also is applied to shaping of plastic parts.

die casting alloy Alloys with melting points sufficiently low so they can be cast into reusable dies; commonly zinc based or aluminum based alloys. ▷ **mold material**

die classification via operation ▷ **mold classification via operation;** it also applies to dies.

die coathanger The Fig. below shows that the shape of die opening is the shape of a "clothes hanger" that produces sheet. It shows the principle of built-in restrictions to adjust the melt flow across the die opening; also applicable in other dies.

die convergent A die in which the internal channels leading to the orifice are converging; only applicable to dies for hollow bodies.

die cutting Cutting shapes from sheet stock by sharply striking it with a shaped knife-edge, known as steel rule die. This hard metal knife edge cuts against a softer support matting backup plate. Clicking, dinking, and blanking are other names for die cutting of this type.

die deckle rod A rod or plate attached to each end of an extruded film or coating die which is used to reduce and/or adjust the width of the die opening. As shown in the Fig. on p. 192, they can be inserted or clamped to the opening face of the die. ▷ **melt distribution, die**

die design ▷ **design die**

die divergent A die for hollow products in which the internal channels leading to the die orifice are diverging.

die diverter valve A valve used to divert melt from one extruder die passage to another; applicable in dies for coextrusion, blow molding, etc.

die, dry sleeve calibration The dry sleeve calibration system for precision extrusion profiles is a well designed streamline die (with no dead spots or eddy flow patterns), a series of vacuum calipers (similar to a sizing sleeve in a cooling vacuum tank) to supply specifically metered vacuum and cooling water to the calipers, air cooling and radiant heating stands to keep the profile straight, a puller meeting the required pulling force, and a reliable cutoff saw and stacking system.

die entrance angle Maximum angle at which the melt enters the land area of the extruder die, measured from the center line of the mandrel.

die fan tail An extrusion die of divergent form.

die finish ▷ **surface finish** and **polish**

die flat A die with its slit opening used in an extrusion film line. Also called a slot die.

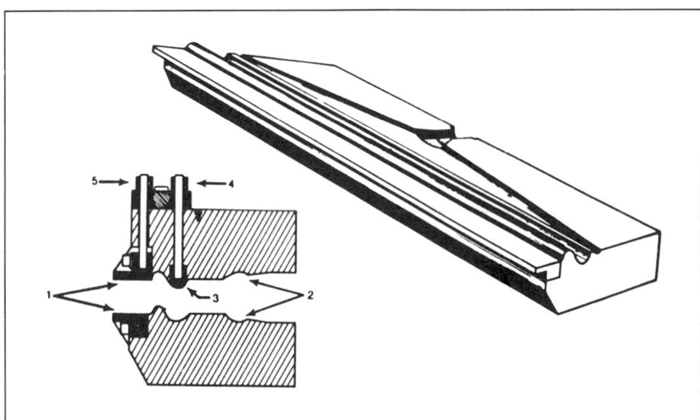

Example of a coat hanger die, showing lower half and cross section. (1) Die lips; (2) manifold; (3) choke bar; (4) choke bar adjustment screw; (5) die lip adjustment screw.

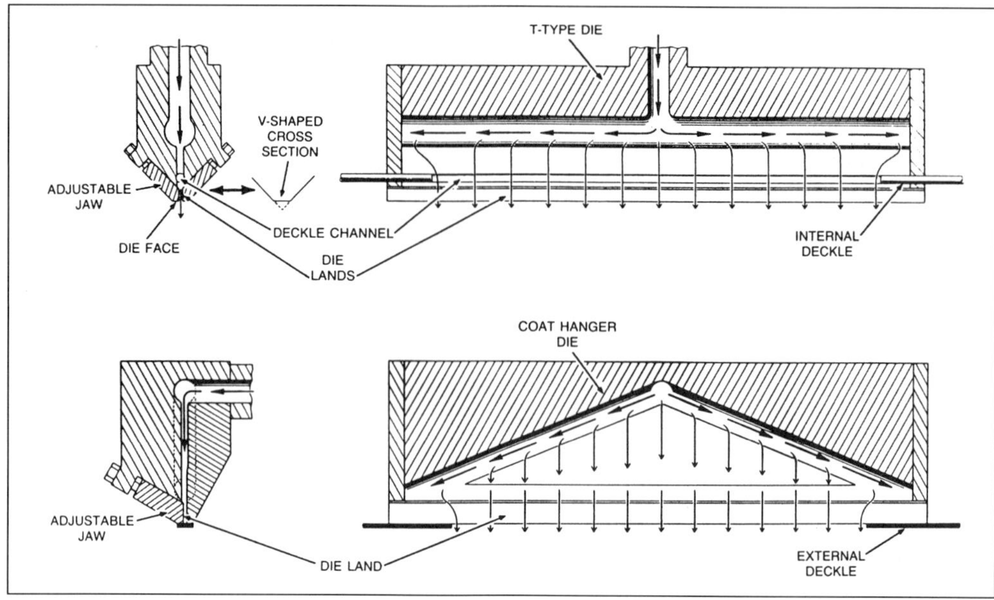

Deckle rods inserted in the T-type die and external deckle plates attached to the coat hanger die.

die flow instability ▷ **melt flow** and **design die, basics of flow**

die gap The distance between the metal faces forming the die opening (orifice).

die grooving Long, narrow grooves or depressions in a surface, parallel to its length. Usually caused by die fouling or by a spot of plastic buildup on the die surface, effectively changing the shape of the cross section.

die head The entire structure used to form the extruder die.

die head adjustable A die head whose orifice opening is adjustable.

die head mandrel The center section of the die head about which the melt flows. The mandrel supports the die pin.

die head mandrel diverter A die head in which the melt is fed into the side of the die head and diverted around the mandrel by flow guides.

die head mandrel moving A die head whose mandrel or die pin can be moved vertically so as to vary the orifice opening.

die head manifold A structure containing the flow passage that carries the melt to multiple head.

die head programmed A die head with provisions for variation of orifice opening at specific points during melt extrusion so as to program the extrudate such as in a blow molding parison. As the parison drops, its thickness will vary based on program setting.

die heater-adapter That part of an extrusion die around which heating medium is located.

die land A parallel section of the pin and bushing just before the exit of the die head; in the direction of the melt flow. It is vital to shaping the extrudate shape and its dimensional control.

dielectric 1. A dielectric material is an insulator or a nonconductor of electricity; the ability of a material to resist the flow of an electrical current. **2.** In radio-frequency (RF) preheating, dielectric refers to the material that is being heated prior to processing, such as in compression molding of TS materials.

dielectric absorption An accumulation of electrical charges within the body of an imperfect dielectric material when it is placed in an electrical field.

dielectric analysis DEA measures qualitatively or quantitatively a variety of changes in plastic properties induced by exposure to a periodic electrical field and quickly translates those measurements into meaningful results. It performs both thermal and rheological analysis. Through these analyses, it can determine flow, degree and rate of cure, molecular relaxation, thermal transition, and dielectric properties of TP and TS plastics, elastomers, reinforced plastics, adhesives, and coatings in their various forms such as solids, liquids, pastes, and films.

dielectric beta loss peak ▷ **beta loss peak**

dielectric constant Normally the relative dielectric constant; for practical purposes it is the ratio of the capacitance of an assembly of two electrodes separated by a plastic insulating material to its capacitance when the electrodes are separated by air (ASTM D 150).

dielectric constant complex The vectorial sum of the dielectric constant and the loss factor.

dielectric constant, relative Ratio of change in density arising from an electric field with and without the material present.

dielectric curing The curing of a TS plastic by the passage of an electric charge (produced from a high-frequency generator) through the plastic. ▷ **thermoset curing, dielectric monitoring**

dielectric heating The heating of plastics by dielectric loss in a high-frequency electrostatic field. The material is exposed between electrodes and is heated quickly and uniformly by absorption of energy from the HF electrical field. The plastic to be heated forms the dielectric of a condenser to which is applied a high-frequency (20 to 80 mc) voltage. Process is used for sealing or welding films, preheating TS molding compounds, etc.

dielectric loss A loss of energy evidenced by the rise in heat of a dielectric placed in an alternating electric field. It is usually observed as a frequency-dependent conductivity.

dielectric loss factor The product of the dielectric constant and the tangent of the dielectric-loss angle for a material. Also called the dielectric-loss index.

dielectric loss tangent The difference between 90° and the dielectric-phase angle. Also called the dielectric-phase difference.

dielectric, Maxwell-Wagner effect ▷ **Maxwell-Wagner effect**

dielectric phase angle The angular difference in phase between the sinusoidal alternating potential difference applied to a dielectric and the component of the resulting alternating current (ac) having the same period as the potential difference.

dielectric piezoelectric material ▷ **piezoelectric material**

dielectric power factor The cosine of the dielectric-phase angle (or sine of the dielectric-loss angle).

dielectric properties When a polar plastic is placed in an electric field, the polar groups in the plastic will tend to orient in that field. If the plastic is very flexible, or at least if the polar groups are flexible as connected in a chain structure, they will orient easily and quickly.

dielectric relaxation Dielectric-relaxation spectroscopy is the study of the frequency dependence of the electrical permittivity or dielectric constant.

dielectric spectroscopy ▷ **dielectrometry**

dielectric strength This is a measure of the electrical breakdown voltage resistance of a plastic under an applied voltage stress. In the ASTM D 149, voltage is increased at a uniform rate to electrodes attached to each side of a flat plastic specimen. At breakdown, the specimen is no longer able to hold back the increasing voltage, which results in an electrical surge through the specimen. The dielectric strength is reported as the volts per mil (0.001 in.) of thickness of the sample, determined at the highest voltage prior to failure. Sixty cycles per second are assumed, since that is the standard alternating current (U.S.). Different frequencies give different results. Thickness changes the value; thin insulation will stand more volts per mil than thick insulation. Temperature preconditioning of the material also affects dielectric strength.

dielectric welding ▷ **dielectric heating**

dielectrometry Use of electrical techniques to measure the changes in dielectric loss factor (dissipation) and in capacitance during cure of the TS plastic in a laminate. Also called dielectric spectroscopy.

die line Vertical mark on the extrudate when osbtruction(s) exist in the die such as spider supports, damaged die, or contamination on the cavity that are in the melt flow path. ▷ **die spider line**

dic lip heater Heater embedded in the die lip used to control lip temperature and friction characteristics on sheet extrusion line to aid in controlling transverse thickness.

die maintenance and care The die is an expensive and delicate portion of any extrusion line. Great care should be taken in the disassembly and cleaning of components. Disassembly should be attempted only when the die has had sufficient time to heat-soak or at the end of a run. Experience has shown a temperature of 232°C (450°F) to be adequate for cleaning up most nondegradable resins. For degradables, cleanup should begin immediately after shutdown to prevent corrosive action on the flow surfaces. While the heat is left on, all die bolts should be broken loose. The heat should then be turned off, and all electrical and thermocouple connections removed—carefully; then while it is still hot, the equipment is disassembled and thoroughly cleaned with "soft" brass and copper tools.

If the extruded materials tend to cling to the flow surfaces, it is usually best to purge the die prior to cleanup, with a purging compound. During assembly, the die bolts should be just snugged tight until the die heat is in the normal operating range. Once this heat is reached and a sufficient heat soak has been allowed (which could take at least 15–30 min.), all bolts should be tightened to the manufacturer's recommended sequence and torque levels. If the die is stored disassembled, care should be taken in its handling to prevent damage to individual components and to flow surfaces, which can include storage in a vacuum sealed container. After cleaning die parts, it is common practice to treat them with a rust inhibitor. Careful storage of die parts prevents loss and mechanical damage. Some dies are the property of the customer who buys the extruded product, and the manufacturer using the die is responsible for its use and care.

die materials of construction Usually flat film and sheet dies are constructed of medium carbon alloy steels. Die flow surfaces are chrome-plated to provide corrosion resistance. The exterior of the die is usually flash chrome-plated to prevent rusting. Where chemical attack can be a severe problem (with PVC, etc.), various grades of stainless steel are used.

Profile, pipe, blown film, and wire coating dies generally are constructed of hot rolled steel for low pressure melt applications. When high pressure dies are required, 4140 steel is utilized. Chrome plating generally is also applied to the flow surfaces, particularly with EVA. Stainless steel is used for any die subject to corrosion. ▷**mold material**

die melt flow ▷**design die, basics of flow**

die melt swell ▷**design die, basics of flow**

diene plastic Family of plastics based on unsaturated hydrocarbons or diolefins having two double bonds. When the double bonds are separated by only a single bond, the diene is called a conjugated diene. In an unconjugated diene the double bonds are separated by at least two single bonds.

die netting Dies can be designed to produce different flow patterns, such as tubular to flat netting types. For a circular output, a counter-rotating mandrel and orifice have semicircular-shaped slits through which the melt flow emerges. If one part is held stationary, then a rhomboid or elongated pattern is formed; if both parts rotate, then a true rhombic mesh is formed. When the slits overlap, a crossing point is formed where the emerging threads are "welded." For flat netting, the slide is in opposite directions.

die orifice The opening in the extruder die formed by the orifice bushing (ring) and mandrel.

die orifice bushing The outer part of the die in an extruder head.

die oscillating ▷**extruder blown film, gauge distortion**

die parison ▷**parison**

die parison swell In blow molding, it is expressed as the ratio of the cross sectional area of the parison to the cross sectional area of the die opening. The parison enlarges as it emerges from the die. ▷**design die, basics of flow**

die parting line 1. In blow molding, it can represent the line on the molded part caused by the parting line of the mold; more accurate to call it the "mold parting line, blow molded part". ▷**mold parting line 2.** A lengthwise flash or depression on the surface of a pultruded RP part. The line occurs where separate pieces of the die join together to form the cavity.

die pin The removable extension of the die mandrel forming the inside wall of the final orifice.

die pin and bushing blank The maximum pin size and minimum die bushing size supplied unfinished.

die plates In blow molds (as in injection molds), the mold halves which are attached to the clamping platens.

die polishing ▷**mold polishing**

die pressure The hydraulic pressure of the stock (melt) measured in the die cavity.

die profile An extrusion die for the production of continuous shapes (film, sheet, tube, and pipe are not called profiles by the plastic industry).

die restrictor bar An extension into the flow channel of an extrusion sheet die at its widest point to produce a balanced melt flow and equal pressure across the die. Also called choker bar.

die ring The outside forming wall in an extrusion die that determines the final orifice OD and extrudate shape.

die ring, static and dynamic To better control the extrudate wall thicknesses, particularly in blow molded parisons to reduce product weight without loss of product performance, static and/or dynamic die rings are available. A static ring is a thin wall die made from a highly flexible steel and surrounded by adjusting bolts. These adjusting bolts, when properly positioned, flex the die and thus ovalize and shape the parison as it is extruded. It is called a static ring, since once it is adjusted, it remains in that position during processing unless further adjustments are required. A conventional die would require removal, machining, and remounting of the die. The dynamic die ring (radial wall programming) are also flexible but are continuously flexed via two hydraulic cylinders as the parison is extruded. Typically, the cylinders mounted 180° apart (opposite each other) are controlled by servo valves, an electronic programmer, and a closed loop system. They act like the vertical parison programmer except the change in wall thickness can be circumferentially, etc.

die rotary ▷ **extruder blown film, gauge distribution**

die spider A die head in which the melt flows over a torpedo and around spiders supporting the torpedo and mandrel.

die spider line Vertical lines which appear on extrudate that uses spider designed die, caused by improper welding of melt flow fronts formed by spider legs in the die. ▷ **die line**

die swell ▷ **design die, basics of flow**

diethylene glycol bis (allyl carbonate) plastic ▷ **allyl plastic**

die, t-type The T-die is a term used to denote a center-fed slot extrusion die for film which, in combination with the die adapter, resembles an inverted "T", as shown in the Fig. of ▷ **die deckle rod.**

differential curve **1.** In thermal analysis a curve resulting from the differential method of thermal analysis when the difference in temperature between a specimen and a neutral body is plotted against the temperature of the latter. **2.** In dilatometry a curve produced by plotting against the temperature the difference in changes of length or volume between a body of known expansivity and a body (specimen) of unknown expansivity.

differential gravimetric analysis DGA is a variation of differential thermal analysis in which additional information is obtained by determining the rate of change in weight during the heating process.

differential scanning calorimeter Differential scanning calorimetry (DSC) directly measures the heat flow to a sample as a function of temperature. A sample of the material weighing 5 to 10 g (18–36 oz.) is placed on a sample pan and heated in a time- and temperature-controlled manner. The temperature usually is increased linearly at a predetermined rate. The DSC method is used to determine specific heats, glass transition temperatures, melting points, and melting profiles, percent crystallinity, degree of cure, purity, thermal properties of heat-seal packaging and hot-melt adhesives, effectiveness of plasticizers, effects of additives and fillers and thermal history.

DSC is also used to determine the percentage of crystallization. A significant consideration in using polyolefins is their susceptibility to crystallization. The molder needs to know how rapidly material crystallizes as it is cooled. A comparison of materials from different lots will indicate whether they will crystallize in the same manner under the same molding conditions. (Polyolefins are provided in both nucleated and nonnucleated grades. A nucleating agent is added to a material to increase the material's rate of crystallization, a factor bearing on the performance of parts molded from that material.)

DSC is a very useful technique for monitoring the level of antioxidant in, for example, polyolefins such as polypropylene. One of the materials most susceptible to oxidation, polypropylene experiences some brittleness and cracking, with the amount depending partly on the end use of the molded part. Antioxidants are added to extend the service life and project the material during the molding operation, but they are sacrifically oxidized to protect the polymer during molding. Once the antioxidants have been depleted, the material is again vulnerable to oxidation. The end user of the part needs the antioxidant protection, however, and will not be well served if the antioxidant is used up during the molding operation. Therefore, the molder needs to ensure that sufficient antioxidant is in the raw material before processing and that enough antioxidant remains in the material after molding to meet the customer's needs.

differential thermal analysis DTA is a method of precisely measuring the temperature and rate of temperature change as heat is added to or abstracted from a sample of material that is in a controlled constant environment. The method determines whether the sample is a pure material (neat) or a mix and yields information about its composition and thermal properties.

differential thermocouple Two thermocouples placed in series opposition.

diffraction **1.** A modification which radiation undergoes, as in passing by the edge of opaque bodies or through narrow slits, in which the rays appear to be deflected. **2.** Coherent scattering of X-radiation by the atoms of a crystal which necessarily results in beams in characteristic directions. Sometimes called reflection. **3.** The scattering of electrons, by any crystalline material, through discrete angles depending only on the lattice spacings of the material and the velocity of the electrons.

diffraction pattern, Fresnel ▷ **Fresnel**

diffraction, X-ray ▷ **X-ray diffraction**

diffusate ▷ **dialysis**

diffusion The movement of a material, such as a gas or liquid, in the body of a plastic. If the gas or the liquid is absorbed on one side and given off on the other side, the phenomenon is called permeability. Diffusion and permeability are not due to holes or pores in the plastic but are caused and controlled by chemical mechanisms.

diffusion couple An assembly of two materials in such intimate contact that each diffuses into the other.

diffusion, Fick's law ▷ **devolatilization**

diffusion, molecular A process of spontaneous intermixing of different substances, attributable to molecular motion and tending to produce uniformity of concentration.

diffusion, water vapor ▷ **water vapor diffusion**

diffusivity, thermal ▷ **thermal diffusivity**

difunctional Dual functions.

digestion Decomposition of processed organic wastes into methane and carbon dioxide under oxygen-starved conditions.

digit One of 10 arabic numbers (0 to 9).

digital Information in discrete numerical values, as opposed to analog information, which represents a relative position on a continuous scale of values. Also refers to information in binary form.

digital controller Microprocessor controller that converts signals from a pressure or temperature sensor to an output signal to a power unit to hold device at the set point value.

digital speed controller Feeds a signal from an encoder to a microprocessor which can control speed to accuracy as close as 0.01%. Can employ phase lock loop technique which allows different RPMs on the same line to be slaved together for perfect synchronization.

digitized Converted into computer-readable form wherein all information units (letters, numbers, symbols, graphs, picture elements) are represented by on-off sequences of electronic impulses.

digit, significant Any digit that is necessary to define a value or quantity.

diisocyanate An organic compound containing two reactive isocyanate groups.

dilatancy A rheological flow characteristic evidenced by an increase in viscosity with increasing rates of shear. It is the opposite of pseudoplasticity. ▷ **non-Newtonian flow**

dilatometer These instruments are used to measure the thermal expansion or contraction of solids and liquids (ASTM E 7). They are also used to study polymerization reactions; it can measure the contraction in volume of unsaturated compounds. Basically a dilatometer is a pyncometer equipped with instruments to study density as a function of temperature or time.

diluent **1.** An ingredient used to reduce the concentration of an active material to achieve a desirable and beneficial effect, such as in thinning paints and reducing viscosity of TS plastics. **2.** Materials such as certain additives to reduce cost of plastics. **3.** a substance which dilutes another substance, such as an organsol; the diluent of a volatile liquid such as naphtha lowers the viscosity without solvating and is evaporated during processing. **4.** An inert powdered substance added to an elastomer or plastic to increase its volume. **5.** The term diluent is also used in place of the term plasticizer.

diluent, reactive As used in epoxy formulations, a compound containing one or more epoxy groups that functions mainly to reduce the viscosity of the mixture.

dilute solution When a solution contains a relatively small amount of solute.

dilute solution viscosity ▷ **viscosity, dilute solution**

dimension A geometric element in a design (product), such as length or angle, or the magnitude of such a quantity.

dimensional change ▷ **tolerance**

dimensional properties They are not listed in property handbooks, and they are not even a legitimate category by most standards. However, the available size, shape, finish, and tolerances on materials are often the most important selection factors. Thus one establishes a category (or obtains guides) of properties relating to the shape of a material and its surface characteristics. Surface roughness is a dimensional property. It is measurable and important for any application.

dimensional stability Dimensional stability of a part is its ability to maintain its original dimensions in use. In practice, the concern is with problems arising from dimensional instability. This instability to varying degrees is common to all materials (plastics, metals, woods, etc.). Instabilities or changes can occur to conditions such as: temperature, time-dependent strain recovery, additives such as plasticizers, moisture, etc.

dimensioning and tolerancing, geometric GD&T is a system of symbols and internationally accepted notation that greatly increases the expressive power of the drafting language (ANSI Y 14.5M). A datum is one component of the GT&D language that allows dimensional networks to be established in ways that make functional sense. Datums help to clearly express relationships between key elements of a part: to guide how a part should be aligned in manufacturing and how it must be set up at inspection, how it will be assembled, etc.

dimensioning limit Limit dimensioning is a system of dimensioning where only the maximum and minimum dimensions are shown. Thus, the tolerance is the difference between these two dimensions.

dimensionless quantities The values of so-called dimensionless quantities, for example refractive index and relative permeability, are expressed by pure numbers.

dimension, reference A reference dimension is a dimension without tolerance used for information purposes only.

dimer A substance (comprising of molecules) formed from two molecules of a monomer. ▷ **mer**

dimple ▷ **sink mark**

diol Dyhydric alcohol; alcohol containing two hydroxyl radicals.

dioxin A class of organic compounds found in gas released when carbon compounds in refuse are not burned completely. Certain variations in these classes are considered toxic. ▷ **polyvinyl chloride plastic and the environment**

dip casting The process of submerging a hot mold into a plastic. After cooling, the cast product is removed from the mold.

dip coating Applying a plastic coating by dipping the article to be coated into a tank of melted plastic or plastisol, then chilling the adhering melt.

dip forming A process similar to dip coating, except that the fused, cured or dried deposit is stripped from the dipping mandrel. Most frequently used for making vinyl plastisol products, the process comprises dipping a preheated form shaped to the desired inside dimensions of the finished product, which gels in a layer of desired thickness against the form surface. The coated plastic is then withdrawn, heated to fuse the layer, cooled, and the deposit stripped off.

diphenyl oxide plastic TS plastic based on diphenyl oxide and possessing excellent handling properties and heat resistance.

dip molding **1.** Another term used for dip forming. **2.** In injection blow molding, a special technique where the blow pin dips into plastic melt rather than receiving a preform via conventional injection molding.

dipole moment Product of electronic charge and charge separation distance.

direct current, electrical ▷ **electrical, direct current**

direct gate ▷ **mold gate**

directional fabric ▷ **fabric**

directional properties ▷ **reinforced plastic, directional properties**

direction of twist ▷ **twisting fiber**

direct memory access computer ▷ **computer, direct memory access**

disadvantages of plastics ▷ **plastic, advantages and disadvantages**

disbond An area within the bonded interface between two adherends in which an adhesion failure or separation has occurred. Also, colloquially, an area of separation between two laminae in the finished laminate (in this case the term delamination is preferred).

disc Common types of computer memory storage devices, which can be considered a cross between a phonograph record and a cassette tape. Information is contained in the magnetic coating of the disc. Data are "written" and "read" by a disc drive, a sort of record player which also records. A DOS is a "disk operating system", meaning a system with disc memory. A variety of floppy and hard discs are used, which can hold various amounts of data. As an example, polycarbonate laser-read memory discs are only 120 mm in diameter and 1.2 mm thick. These discs offer enormous advantages with respect to storage capacity compared to the various forms of magnetic media available today. ▷**computer storage, disc and tape**

disc and cone agitator Mixing devices comprising discs or cones rotating at speeds of 1,200 to 3,600 rpm or higher, which displace fluid contacting their surfaces by centrifugal force. They are used in preparing pastes and dispersions.

disc, fail-safe rupture ▷**barrel fail-safe rupture disc**

disc feeder Horizontal, flat, or grooved discs installed at the bottom of hoppers feeding extruders to control the feed rate by varying the speed of rotation of the disc, or by varying the clearance between the disc and the scraper, which removes material from it.

disc flow test ▷**flow test, TS disc type**

disc mixing A disc instead of a conventional screw has been the basis of a number of continuous mixing extruder designs. For compounding, the disc machines can be flat, but may be wedge-shaped discs for different applications. Series combinations of the disc units increase the machine's mixing or dispersion capability; parallel combinations increase its throughput. In operation, plastic is fed into the first unit, and if appropriate, additives can be metered into intermediate units. The material being compounded can be recirculated between the input and output ports for further dispersion.

discoloration Any change from the original color, often caused by overheating, light exposure, irradiation, chemical attack, blocked vents, and stagnant material during processing.

disc reinforcement ▷**reinforcement, disc**

discrete 1. In information services, constitutes a separate entity; it is individually distinct. **2.** In plastic chemical structure, elements that are distinct or not connected.

disc safety ▷**plasticator safety**

disease ▷**disposable reduce disease**

dished Showing a symmetrical distortion or warp of a flat or curved section of a plastic part, so that, as normally viewed, it appears concave or more concave than intended.

disinfectant A substance used on inanimate (plastic, etc.) products which destroys harmful microorganisms or inhibits their activity.

dislocation Any variation from perfect order and symmetry in a crystalline lattice.

Disneyland house ▷**plastic house**

dispersant In an organsol, a liquid component which has a solvation action on the plastic, so as to aid in dispersing and suspending it. Prevents coalescing.

dispersing agent Materials added to a suspending medium to promote and maintain the separation of discrete, fine particles of solids or liquids. They are used in the grinding of pigments and for dispersing water-insoluble dyes.

dispersion 1. Finely divided liquids or particles (powders) of a plastic held in suspension in another material. **2.** Difference in index of refraction; red light versus blue light. **3.** The phenomenon of varying speed of transmission of waves, depending on their frequency.

dispersion coating A process of applying a (flexible barrier) material, suspended or dispersed in a vehicle, to a surface in such a way that a continuous, coalesced, adherent layer results when the vehicle liquid (usually water) is evaporated.

dispersion staining The color effects produced when a transparent object, immersed in a liquid having a refractive index near that of the object, is viewed under the microscope by a transmitted light and precise-aperture control.

dispersion types Types of plastic dispersions are emulsions (liquids in liquids), suspensions (solids in liquids), foams (gases in liquids), and aerosols (liquids in gases). Also fillers and pigments in molding compounds, plastisols, and organosols.

dispersion, vinyl ▷**vinyl dispersion**

displacement rate ▷**mold, displacement rate**

display The graphic representation of data on an output device.

disposable diapers Accounts for 1 to 2% of waste, by volume, in the U.S.

disposable material Products intended to be used only once. Can include materials such as food service utensils, medical devices, containers, towels, etc.

disposable reduce disease Use of disposable foodservice items (plates, utensils, etc.) can help reduce the incidence of disease.

disposal Refers to various types of waste, such as solid waste.

disposal and reuse ▷**waste, granulating**

disproportionation Termination by chain

transfer between macroradicals to produce a saturated and an unsaturated polymer molecule.

dissipation factor ▷ **electrical dissipation factor**

dissipation of energy ▷ **energy dissipation**

dissociation **1.** As applied to heterogeneous equilibria, the transformation of one phase into two or more new phases, all of different composition. **2.** In leak testing, the breakdown of a substance into two or more constituents.

distance between tie rods ▷ **clamping, tie rods**

distillation A separation process in which a liquid is converted to a vapor and the vapor then condensed to a liquid. The latter is referred to as a distillate, while the liquid material being vaporized is the charge or distilland. The usual purpose of distillation is purification or separation of components in a mix.

distortion **1.** The product of a different shape from that required, generally apparent immediately after processing. However this warp situation can occur after processing, particularly if internal stress relaxation occurs. **2.** In a reinforced plastic, the displacement of the fibers relative to their planned location due to motion during lay-up and/or cure. **3.** In fabric, the displacement of fill fiber from the 90° angle (right angle) relative to the warp fiber. **4.** Regarding optics, an aberration of lens systems where axial and marginal magnifications are unequal.

distortion temperature ▷ **deflection temperature under load**

divalent and trivalent Valence of 2 or 3.

divergent die ▷ **die, divergent**

diverter valve ▷ **die, diverter valve**

doctor blade, bar, or knife A straight piece of material used to spread plastic at a regulated, controlled rate. Used in application of a thin film of plastic for use in hot-melt adhesives, adhesive film, prepreg preparations, coating substrates (plastic film, aluminum foil, etc.), etc. As an example, the device is used to regulate the amount of liquid plastic on the rollers of a spreader. Also called paste metering blade.

doctor roll A roll which operates at a different speed or in the opposite direction as compared to the primary roll of a coating machine, thus regulating the uniformity and thickness of material on the roll before it is applied to a substrate.

doily ▷ **filament winding doily**

dolly A low platform or structure mounted on wheels or casters, designed primarily for moving bulky loads for short distances.

dolomite A double carbonate of lime and magnesia having the formula $CaCO_3 \cdot MgCO_3$. Uses include as a plastic filler.

domain A morphological term used in noncrystalline systems, such as block copolymers, in which the chemically different sections of the chain separate, generating two or more amorphous phases.

dome **1.** Showing a symmetrical distortion of a flat or curved section of a plastic part, so that as normally viewed, it appears convex, or more convex than intended. **2.** ▷ **filament winding dome**

dopant **1.** A chemical element incorporated in trace amounts in a semiconductor crystal to establish its conductivity type and resistivity. **2.** A material added to a plastic to change a physical property.

dope **1.** Sizing formulation consisting of solutions of nitrocellulose, cellulose acetate, or other cellulosic plastics applied to crepe yard goods to set the twist and assist creping; to leather and form a high-gloss finish. **2.** A combustible, such as wood pulp, starch, sulfur, etc. used in "straight" dynamites. **3.** A trace impurity introduced into ultrapure crystals to obtain desired physical properties, especially electrical propererties.

doppler effect ▷ **electronic doppler effect**

dosimeter ▷ **radiation dosimeter**

dosing A measured quantity of material added during a process, such as injection molding.

dot In printing, the individual element of ▷ **halftone photography**

dot-matrix printer ▷ **computer printer**

double bond A type of molecular structure in which a pair of valence bonds joins a pair of carbon or other atoms, or a covalent linkage in which atoms share two pairs of electrons.

double cavity mold ▷ **mold cavity**

double-cavity processing ▷ **coextrusion** and **coinjection**

double crimp fabric ▷ **fabric double crimp**

doubler **1.** In filament winding, a local area with extra reinforcement, wound integrally with the part, or wound separately and fastened to the part. **2.** Localized area of extra material (plastic ribs, reinforcements, etc.) usually to provide stiffness or strength for fastening or the abrupt load transfers.

double refraction ▷ **optical properties** and **birefringence**

double-screw extruder ▷ **extruder, twin-screw**

double-shot molding **1.** The technique of molding parts in two colors or two materials in a single mold or set of molds. This process is accomplished by injecting the material into a closed mold, transferring half of the mold to mate with another mold half of different cavity shape, and injecting the second material around the first material. **2.** Another approach, usually called coinjection, is to inject a partial shot of solid plastic melt, inject another material which forces the first material to the mold surface, and then complete the fill with the first material or a new (third) material. The core of this sandwich construction can be recycled scrap, foamed plastic, etc. For this method and the previous reviewed method separate injectors (plasticators) are required for each different plastic.

dough A term used for a reinforced plastic compound of dough-like consistency in a B-stage cured stage. ▷ **bulk molding compound**

dough blender A simple screw-type extruder that can prepare dough (BMC) material. Its output is cut into what is called "logs".

downstream The plastic discharge end of the fabricating equipment, such as the take-off equipment in an extrusion line. ▷ **upstream**

downstream control ▷ **extruder control downstream**

downtime Refers to equipment that cannot operate when it should be operating. Reason for this downtime could be shortage of plastic (not available, etc.), electrical power problems, operators not available, etc. However, in the plastic industry, it usually refers to the equipment being inoperable.

draft The degree of taper of a side wall or the angle of clearance designed to facilitate removal of parts from a mold.

draft, back The back draft is an area of interference in an otherwise smooth-drafted encasement; an obstruction in the taper which would interfere with the withdrawal of the part from a mold.

drafting ▷ **computer-aided design drafting**

drafting serif A drafting compensation in artwork to prevent fillets.

drag reduction In a plastic, it is the phenomenon whereby extremely dilute solutions of high molecular weight plastics exhibit frictional resistance to flow much lower than the pure solvent. The principal interest is to relate this condition to the fluid mechanics effect of turbulence and turbulent flow. These areas are so complex that progress has been slow, and the understanding of the flow details in plastic solutions is limited. Known is that polymers of molecular weight above 100,000, of a generally linear structure and soluble in the liquid of interest, reduce turbulent friction by up to 70 to 80%. Many plastics fall into this category.

drape The ability of a fabric, plastic film, sheet molding compound, prepreg, etc. to conform to a contoured surface.

drape forming ▷ **thermoforming, drape assist frame**

draw In plastic working, as in metal working, to gradually reduce the diameter of a material (or other shape) by pulling it through perforations of successively diminishing size in a series of rollers or plates. They may be cold-drawn (without preheat) or hot-drawn (heated to softening point).

drawdown **1.** In extrusion, the process of pulling the extrudate away from the die at a linear speed higher than that at which the melt exits, thus reducing the cross section dimensions of the extrudate. **2.** In blow molding, the decrease in parison diameter and wall thickness due to gravity.

draw down ratio ▷ **extruder draw down ratio**

drawing graphics ▷ **computer drawing** and **design graphics**

drawing process Mechanically stretching thermoplastic film, sheet, rod, filament, etc. to reduce its cross sectional area. Usually employed as it leaves the extrusion die. Stretching results in molecular orientation, which improves certain properties. ▷ **orientation**

drawn fiber Fiber with a certain amount of orientation imparted by the drawing process by which it is formed, such as stretching up to three times in order to have many fibers meet performance requirements.

draw ratio A measure of the degree of stretching during the orientation of plastic material expressed as a ratio of the cross sectional area of the undrawn material to that of the drawn material.

drier agent A substance used to accelerate the drying of plastic coatings, paints, varnishes, printing inks, etc. by catalyzing the oxidation of the plastics, drying oils, etc.

drift velocity Net velocity of electrons in an electric field.

drooling nozzle ▷ **injection molding nozzle**

drop weight test Impact resistance tests where weights are dropped on the specimen from varying heights. ▷ **dart drop test**

drug application Pharmaceutical industry has aimed at adjusting concentrations of drugs in the body for therapeutic need and at increasing the duration of drug action at the target site. Using plastics, better dosage forms have been developed. Plastics used include TP polyesters, cellulosics, hydrogels, etc.

drug controlled release-delivery system Descriptive of a compound manufactured in such a way that its effect will be kept uniform over an extended time period. This delivery system not only provides more effective release control, but also reduces the waste involved in using unnecessarily high concentrations. This principle has been applied successfully to pharmaceuticals-drugs, fertilizers, pesticides, flavors, and fragrances. Release mechanisms extensively use plastics blended and/or coated with the controlled compound. There are chemically controlled release systems and diffusional delivery systems. Diffusional drugs include nonbiodegradable plastic, degradable plastic, transdermal plastic (delivery into the body's circulatory system), liposomal plastic, oral plastic encapsulation, and osmotic pump systems. ▷ **absorbable plastic; antibodies; biodegradable; implant; microencapsulation coating**

drug handbook Drug information handbooks cover actions, reactions, and interactions, and can provide guidance and understanding to plastic uses, blends, etc. Useful in the control release systems.

drum coloring ▷ **dry coloring**

drum tumbler Equipment used to mix plastic pellets with color concentrates, recycled plastics, etc. The materials are charged into cylindrical drums which are tumbled end-over-end or rotated about an inclined axis for a sufficient time to thoroughly blend the components.

dry air ▷ **air, dry**

dry blasting ▷ **abrasion cleaning**

dry blend Refers to a molding compound, containing all necessary ingredients mixed in a way that produces a dry-free-flowing, particulate material. This term is commonly used with PVC molding compounds and TS molding compounds.

dry-bulb temperature ▷ **temperature, dry-bulb**

dry coating ▷ **powder coating** and **coating**

dry coloring Method commonly used by fabricators for coloring plastic by tumble blending uncolored particles of the plastic with selected dyes, pigments, etc.

dry deposition ▷ **atmosphere dry deposition**

dryer Numerous types of equipment are used to remove moisture or water from plastic material or substances (additives, etc.) during processing. There are a great variety of choices available for drying such as belt, centrifugal, convection, conveyor, flash, fluid-bed, freeze, pan, rotary drum, rotary tray, vacuum, screw, tunnel, vibrator, etc. types (See Fig. below and Fig. on p. 202). Within

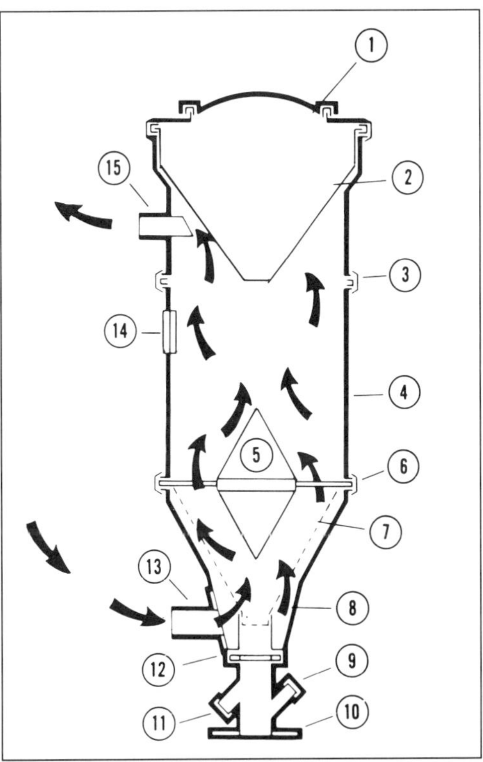

Example of a drying hopper (plenum drying hopper). (1) Manual load plate with removable cover; (2) air trap cone; (3) upper swing clamp with gasket; (4) tank section; (5) diverter cone; (6) lower swing clamp; (7) perforated air diffuser cone; (8) lower outer cone; (9) purge inlet; (10) square mounting plate; (11) drain outlet; (12) slide gate; (13) delivery air from dryer; (14) sight glass; (15) return air to dryer.

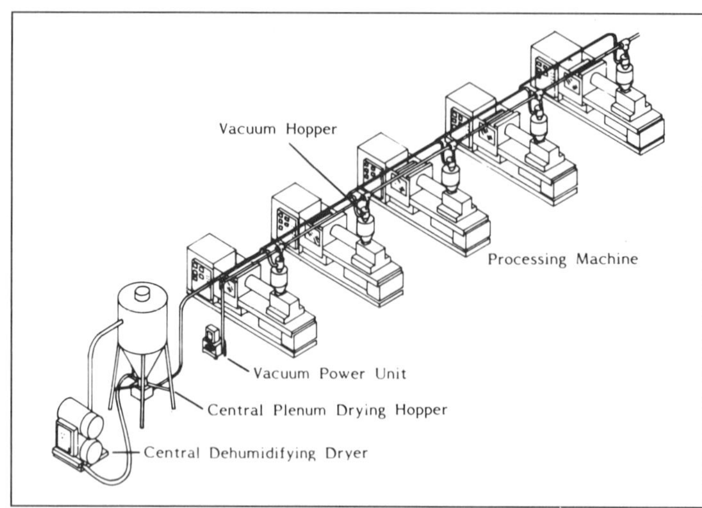

Example of a central dehumidifying dryer with central plenum hopper system.

each choice there are different systems (types). These dryers provide different capabilities, such as drying hygroscopic materials.

dry-heat sterilization ▷ **sterilization**

drying, capillarity The outer surface of a porous solid has pore entrances of various sizes. As surface liquid is evaporated during constant-rate drying, a liquid meniscus forms across each pore entrance, and capillary forces are set up by interfacial tension between the liquid and solid. These forces draw liquid from the interior to the outer surface.

drying, constant-rate During constant-rate drying, vaporization proceeds as from a liquid surface of constant composition and vapor pressure; material structure has no influence. Drying proceeds by diffusion of vapor from the wet surface through a gas film into the environment.

drying, critical moisture content The critical moisture content, i.e., the average material moisture content at the end of the constant-rate drying period, is a function of material properties, the constant-drying rate, and particle size.

drying, diffusion ▷ **diffusion**

drying, equilibrium moisture content ▷ **moisture content equilibrium**

drying equipment for solvent removal The past U.S. Clean Air Act and its numerous amendments to aid in producing "clean air" have mandated a significant reduction in the amount of volatile organic compounts (VOC) that may be emitted into the air. Most hydrocarbon solvents used to apply inks, coatings, adhesives, etc. to substrates (plastics, aluminum, etc.) are usually classified as VOCs.

drying, falling-rate The principal mass-transfer mechanisms controlling falling-rate drying are liquid diffusion in continuous, homogeneous materials; capillarity in porous and fine granular materials; gravity flow in granular materials; vapor diffusion in porous and granular materials; flow caused by shrinkage-induced pressure gradients; and flow of liquid and vapor when a material is heated on one side and vapor escapes from the other side.

drying hygroscopic plastic ▷ **hygroscopic plastic**

drying, mechanical Mechanical heat convection hot air dryers can be adequate for some plastics; is not satisfactory for hygroscopic plastic.

drying mechanism Although it is sometimes possible to select a suitable drying method simply by evaluating variables such as humidities and temperatures when removing unbound moisture, many plastic drying processes involve removal of bound moisture retained in capillaries among fine particles or moisture actually dissolved in the plastic. A knowledge of internal liquid and vapor mass-transfer mechanisms applies. These mechanisms are best identified by measuring drying-rate behavior under controlled conditions. A change in material-handling method or any operating variable, such as heating rate, may affect mass transfer.

drying monomer and polymer Drying is a unit operation in which a volatile liquid is separated from a solid or semisolid material by vaporization. The drying of monomers involves the removal of moisture or other volatiles from fluids. When drying gases, condensable vapors are separated from noncondensable gases by cooling to below the dew points of the condensable fractions, vapor adsorption on solid desiccants, absorption in desiccant liquids, or gas compression and cooling. Polymer drying is an important industrial operation employed to isolate the saleable product from the reaction process. Before melting and fabricating, many polymers must be dried again because they are slightly hygroscopic and susceptible to degradation if melted in the presence of moisture. Drying is usually necessary following the three common polymerization processes: solution, suspension, and emulsion.

drying oil An oil that possesses to a marked degree the property of readily taking up oxygen from the air and changing to a relatively hard, tough, elastic substance when exposed in a thin film to air.

drying, oven The condition of a material that has been heated under prescribed conditions of temperature and humidity until there is no further significant changes in its mass.

drying plastic All plastics, to some degree, are influenced by the amount of moisture or water they contain prior to processing. With minimal amounts in many plastics, mechanical, physical, electrical, and aesthetic properties may not be affected, or may be of no consequence. However, there are certain plastics that, when compounded with certain additives, could have devastating results ▷**hygroscopic plastic drying mechanism**. Interesting is the fact that a major problem that has continually influenced degradation of plastics being processed is moisture. Even those which are not generally affected by moisture can only tolerate a certain amount. (Day-night moisture contamination can be a source of problems if not adequately eliminated; otherwise it has a cumulative effect.)

drying process As illustrated in the first Fig. below, at ambient temperature and 50% relativehumidity, the vapor pressure of water outside a plastic pellet is greater than that within. Moisture migrates into the pellet, thus increasing its moisture content until a state of equilibrium exists inside and outside the pellet.

However, inside a drying hopper with controlled environment, conditions are very different as shown in the second Fig. below. As an example at a temperature of 177°C (350°F) and −40°C (−40°F) dewpoint, the vapor pressure of water inside the pellet is much greater than

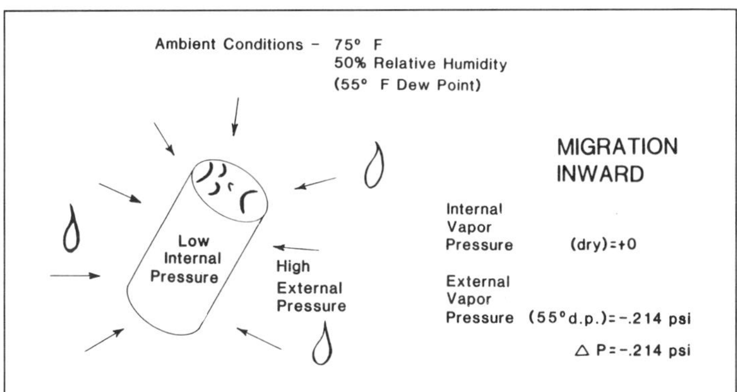

Mechanics of moisture absorption in plastics.

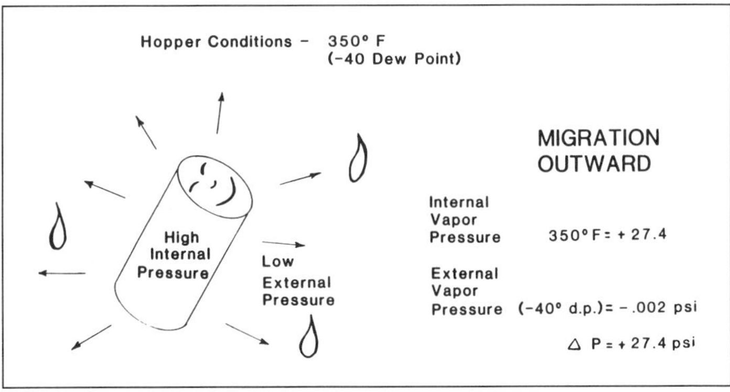

Mechanics of moisture migrating out of plastics

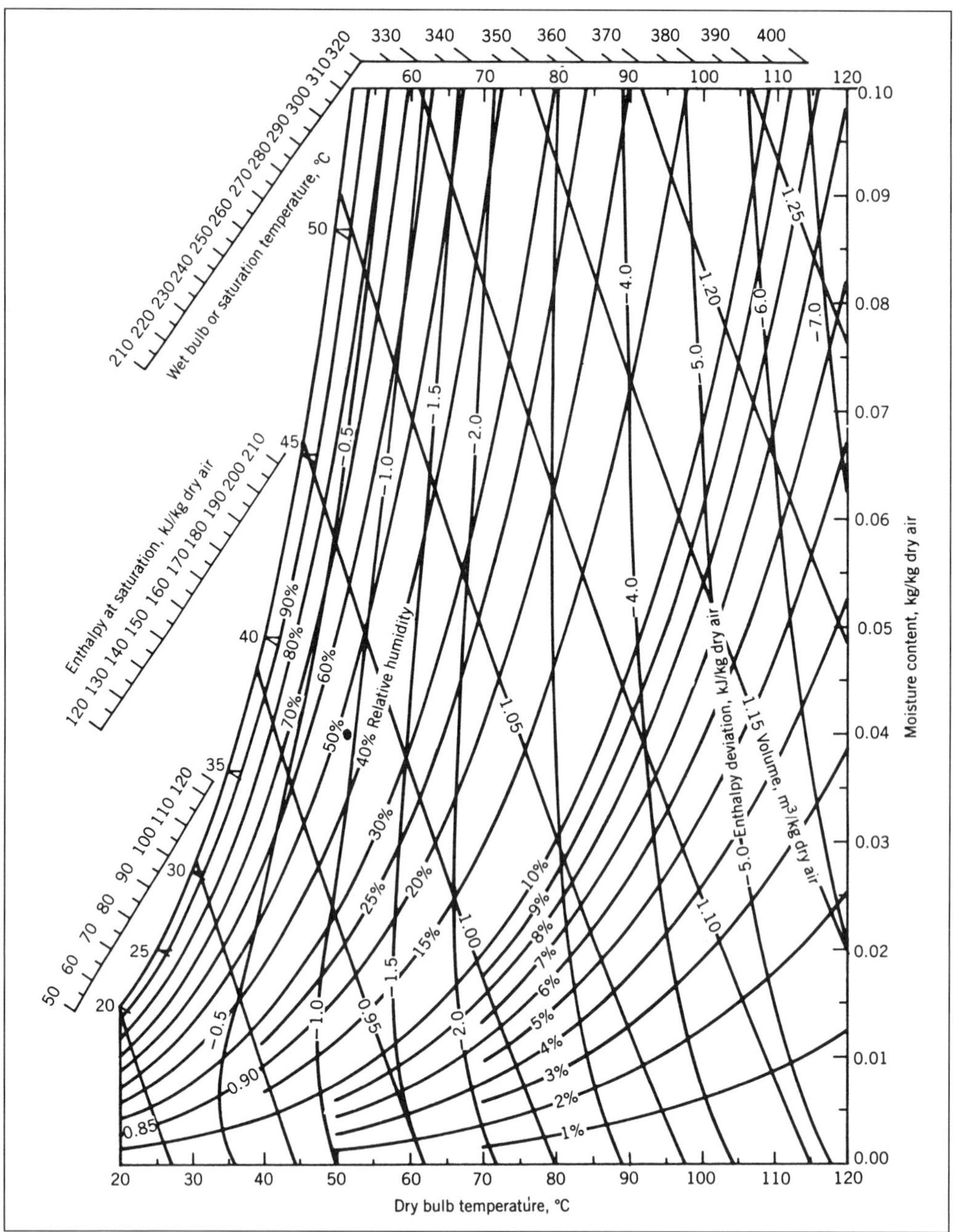

Psychrometric chart, air-water vapor at 101.3 kPa (1 atm).

that of the surrounding air, so that moisture migrates out of the pellet and into the surrounding airstream, where it is carried away to the desiccant bed of the dryer.

drying, psychrometry Before drying can begin, a wet material must be heated to such a temperature that the vapor pressure of the liquid content exceeds the partial pressure of the corresponding vapor in the surrounding atmosphere. The effect of the atmosphere vapor content of a dryer rate and material temperature is conveniently studied by construction of a psychrometric chart (see Fig. above). It plots moisture content, dry bulb temperature, wet bulb or saturation temperature, and enthalpy at saturation. ▷ **psychrometer** and **temperature, wet-bulb**

drying, pulse combustor Researchers at Sandia National Laboratories (Albuquerque, NM) patented a new pulse combustor that is designated for use in industrial drying and other chemical processes. The low pressure, valve-free combustor offers improved efficiency compared with conventional heating devices. Until recently, water heaters, space heaters, and forced-air furnaces have been the major uses for pulse combustion. Now it has expanded industrially. Described as an acoustically enhanced drying system, it can be added to conventional drying equipment.

drying shrinkage Shrinkage related to drying is the change in contraction of a body during the drying process, expressed as linear percent of the original length or volume percent of the original volume.

drying time The period of time during which a material or part is allowed to dry with or without the application of heat and/or pressure, or both.

dry laminate ▷ **reinforced plastic starved area**

dry lay-up Construction of a reinforced plastic laminate by the layering of preimpregnated reinforcement (B-stage) in a female mold or on a male mold. Curing of the RP lay-up is by bag or autoclave molding.

dry offset printing-coating ▷ **offset printing-coating**

dry powder coating ▷ **flood coating** and **coating**

dry printing ▷ **hot stamping**

dry process, nonwoven fabric ▷ **mechanical nonwoven fabric**

dry sleeve calibration ▷ **die dry sleeve calibration**

dry spinning ▷ **fiber spinning**

dry spot **1.** Area of incomplete plastic surface film on substrate. **2.** In fabric coating, an area of incomplete surface plastic coating. **3.** In laminated safety glass, an area over which the plastic interlayer and the glass have not become bonded.

dry strength The strength of a material determined immediately after drying under specified conditions or after a period of conditioning in the standard laboratory atmosphere.

dry winding ▷ **filament winding**

DSD "Duales System Deutschland" recycling plan for Germany. ▷ **recycling packaging via DSD**

dual-ovenable tray ▷ **packaging dual-ovenable tray**

ductile erosion behavior Erosion behavior having characteristic metal properties that can be associated with ductile fracture of the exposed solid surface. Considerable "plastic" deformation precedes or accompanies material loss from the surface which occurs by gouging or tearing, or eventual embrittlement through work hardening that leads to crack formation. This type erosion is sometimes associated with plastic materials. ▷ **rain erosion** and **cavitation erosion**

ductile fatigue ▷ **fatigue, ductile**

ductile fracture ▷ **fracture, ductile** and **metal fracture**

ductility of plastic The ability of a material to deform "plastically" without fracture; being measured by elongation or reduction of its cross sectional area of the material. Relates to a measure of strain that accompanies fracture. Bendability, crushability, elongation, results of cup draw, flattening, kinking, repeated bending, and twisting are considered some indication of ductility. It is also the ability of a material to be stretched, pulled, or rolled into shapes without destroying its integrity. The different plastics provide a wide range of ductility, from very little (or zero) to extreme amounts, such as with thermoplastic elastomers. It is usually expressed as a percent elongation in a 2 in. (5.1 cm) tensile gauge length test specimen. With a value of 5% or greater, the plastic is usually considered ductile; under 5% it is brittle.

ductility transition temperature Temperature that separates the regime of brittle fracture from the higher temperature range of ductile fracture.

dullness A lack of surface gloss or shine.

dumping **1.** Waste material can be dumped. **2.** It can refer to material imports being delivered (dumped) into a country at a low price in order to sell at a depressed price, targeted to use over-abundance in the warehouse or to enter a market.

durable goods Products with a relatively long useful service life without significant deterioration, if any at all.

durometer An instrument for measuring hardness, that is, the resistance to the penetration (without puncturing) of the indentor into the surface of a material.

durometer hardness An arbitrary numerical value which measures the resistance to indentation of the blunt indentor point of the durometer (ASTM D 2240). Higher number indicates a

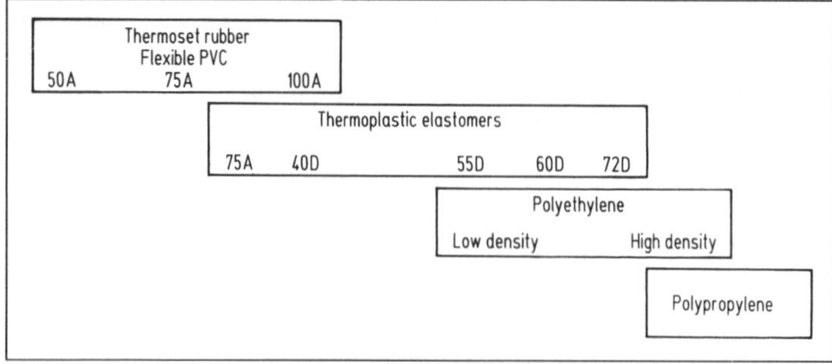

Durometer scale relationships and hardness ranges for different materials; letter designations refer to Shore hardness tests.

greater indentation hardness (see Fig. above). ▷ **hardness**

dust An imprecise term referring to particulates capable of temporary suspension in air or other gases. ▷ **dust, industrial**

dust collector ▷ **bag filter** and **filter**

dust, industrial Finely divided solid particles may have: (1) damaging effects on personnel by inhalation or skin infection, (2) constitute a fire hazard, (3) damage the plastic products being fabricated, and (4) damage processing equipment. There are air suspensions of particles 10 microns or less in diameter; through sizes up to 50 microns that can be present. Such dust includes metallic particles, additives-fillers (mica, talc, silica, calcium carbonate, graphite, glass, etc.), and organic materials (chemicals, coal, etc.).

dusting agent A powdery solid used as an adherent or release agent; used to keep film from adhering, part release from a mold, etc.

dust, marble ▷ **calcium carbonate**

dwell 1. A pause in the application of pressure or temperature to a mold, made just prior to complete closure. Allows escape (or "breathing") of gas and/or moisture from the molding material. **2.** In filament winding, the time that the traverse mechanism is stationary while the mandrel continues to rotate to the appropriate point for the traverse to begin a new pass. **3.** In autoclave cure cycle, an intermediate step in which the matrix (of reinforced plastics) is held at a temperature below the cure point for a specific period of time to produce a desired degree of staging (processing). Used primarily to control plastic melt flow.

dye Dyes, or dyestuffs, are soluble colorants and generally either form a chemical bond with the substrate or become closely associated with it by a physical process. They are characterized by good transparency, high tinctorial strength, and low specific gravity. Examples of important families of dyes are the azo, anthraquinone, vat, sulfur, and reactive dyes. Synthetic or natural organic chemicals are soluble in most common solvents; there are water-insoluble types.

dye, aniline Any of a large class of synthetic dyes made from intermediates based upon or made from aniline. Most are somewhat toxic and irrating to eyes, skin, and mucous membranes.

dye color removal ▷ **stripping**

dye, direct A water soluble dye taken up directly by fibers from an aqueous solution containing an electrolyte, presumably due to selective adsorption. Usually applied to cellulosic fibers.

dye, dispersed A dye that may be in any of three clearly defined chemical classes; nitroarylamine, azo, and anthraquinone. Almost all contain amino or substituted amino groups but not solubilizing sulfonic acid groups. They are water-insoluble, suspension in water and are absorbed by the fiber. Their use is primarily for cellulose acetate, nylon, polyester, etc. fibers and TP materials.

dye, sensitizing The inclusion of dye-stuffs into a photoconductive coating to alter its spectral response.

dye, sublimable ▷ **sublimable dye transfer**

dying assistant Any material added to a dye bath to promote or control dying in plastic parts and fibers.

dynamic A branch of mechanics that deals with forces and their relation primarily to motion and also to the equilibrium of bodies. Variation and contrast in force exist, including their intensity.

dynamic accuracy ▷ **sensor, dynamic**

dynamic die ring ▷ **die ring static and dynamic**

dynamic fatigue Fatigue that occurs under a load which is varying, usually periodically and often sinusoidally. The lower the loading stress, the more loading cycles that are needed for failure, or, as it is called, fatigue life. As the applied stress, or rather its amplitude when it is sinusoidally varying, is lowered further, a value is reached (the fatigue limit) below which the material does not fail even after a finite number of cycles. The most common mode of deformation is flexure and the input function (although usually sinusoidal), may be a square wave. Another variable is the frequency, while the loading may be through the stress or strain. Thus, there are many different modes of deformation that a sample may experience. As the temperature is increased, the time to failure decreases. Under the same conditions of temperature and frequency, when the plastic shows high loss of mechanical energy, high temperature rises in the material can occur. If above the T_g, the plastic becomes more permanently deformed and thermal failure occurs.

dynamic flow A flow in which the external influence causing the flow varies with time.

dynamic load measurement An important objective of dynamic testing of materials, in addition to determining the number of cycles to failure, is to establish the cause and pattern of failure. Normally in such tests the stress and strain are measured and an elastic modulus derived from these values. However, this can be only the initial step in the direction of developing a complete description of the failure pattern. ▷ **photoelasticity** and **stress-strain measurements**

dynamic mechanical analysis The DMA measures the viscoelastic properties (modulus and damping) of a material as functions of time and temperature. The material is deformed under a periodic resonant stress at a low rate of strain. Microprocessor data-reduction techniques provide graphical and tabular outputs of these properties as functions of time or temperature. The values determined, the modulus and damping data, aid in establishing realistic structural design criteria; the speed of analysis provides high throughput and low labor cost; precise temperature control can be used to simulate processing conditions; the breadth of material types ranges from rubbery to very high stiffness; and the data obtained correlate both structure-property and property-processing characteristics.

The DMA instrument can be calibrated to provide quantitative accuracy and precision in the range of $\pm 5\%$ coefficient of variation. To achieve this level of accuracy, the analyst considers several factors in the mathematical treatment of data: instrument compliance (i.e., the measurement system is not infinitely stiff), length compensation (to counteract end-effects at the clamps), Poisson's ratio (the ratio of lateral to axial strains for mixed shear/flexure deformation or interconversion, G' to E'), and shear distortion (for shear deformation in a flexural mode). Also called dynamic mechanical spectroscopy (DMS).

dynamic mechanical behavior Dynamic mechanical tests measure the response or deformation of a material to periodic or varying forces. Generally the applied force and the resulting deformation both vary sinuosoidally with time. From such tests it is possible to obtain sumultaneously an elastic modulus and a mechanical damping. The mechanical damping gives the amount of energy dissipated as heat during the deformation of the material.

dynamic mechanical beta loss peak ▷ **beta loss peak**

dynamic, mechanical damping ▷ **damping, mechanical**

dynamic mechanical measurement A technique in which either the modulus and/or damping of a material under oscillatory load or displacement is measured as a function of temperature, frequency, or time, or their combinations. ▷ **hysteresis measurement gives dynamic characteristics; resonant forced and vibration technique; nonresonant forced and vibration technique**

dynamic mechanical relaxation Relaxation in which a specimen is subject to a periodic (usually sinusoidal) variation of the applied stress (or strain). The strain (or stress) response is monitored either as a function of the frequency at constant temperature or as a function of temperature at a constant frequency. From the data, the frequency (or temperature) dependence of the moduli (especially the shear moduli) may be obtained. The results are usually displayed as the dynamic mechanical spectrum (an anelastic spectrum) and provide data of multiple transitions in both crystalline and amorphous plastics. Techniques used include the torsion pendulum, vibrating reed, and sonic modulus systems.

dynamic mechanical spectroscopy ▷ **dynamic mechanical analysis**

dynamic mechanical spectrum Data of the storage or loss moduli against temperature or frequency plastic (viscoelastic material). Plots are usually made of log modulus or log frequency because of the wide range of values developed.

dynamic mechanical vibration This forced

vibration method is a technique for the determination of the dynamic mechanical properties of a plastic in which the specimen is firmly attached at one end to a force transducer and at the other to a strain gauge. A sinusoidal tensile or shear displacement is applied by a powerful vibrator. The complex modulus is given by the force and elongation with the length and cross sectional area of the sample. The phase angle difference between the force and displacement signals may be recorded electronically. Frequency ranges from 0.1 to 10^3 Hz may be studied for materials with moduli in the range of 0.1 MPa to 10 GPa. The method is especially useful for high loss materials for which other materials may not be suitable, such as torsion pendulum.

dynamic modulus The ratio of stress-to-strain under cyclic conditions calculated from data obtained from either free or forced vibration tests in shear, compression, or tension. It is an alternative name for complex modulus.

dynamic modulus, effective An indication of vibration absorption characteristics of elastomers or rubbers. A measure of dynamic stiffness deformed beyond the straight-line portion of the load-deflection diagram in the Yerzley mechanical oscillograph test. It is calculated as follows:

$$K_c = 210\ If^2$$

$$K_s = 105\ If^2$$

where K_c = effective dynamic modulus in compression, psi; K_s = effective dynamic modulus in shear, psi; I = moment of inertia of beam and weights, slug ft^2; f = frequency, cps.

dynamic osometry ▷ **osmosis, dynamic**

dynamic rheometer ▷ **rheometer, dynamic**

dynamic viscosity **1.** Alternative name for coefficient of viscosity; used to distinguish from the kinematic viscosity. **2.** It also denotes a frequency-dependent quantity in which shear stress and shear rate have a sinusoidal time dependence. **3.** The dynamic viscosity is one gram per cm per s = one dyne-second per cm^2 and is called one poise (symbol P). The SI unit is one newton-second per m^2 and is equivalent to 10 P. Frequently centipoise (symbol cP) is used ($1\ cP = 10^{-2}\ P$). ▷ **Poise**

dynamic vulcanization A process in which the elastomer phase is cured during mixing of the plastic, rather than just mechanical blending of plastics.

dynamometer ▷ **fatigue dynamometer**

Dynatub test In this test, the impact energy is delivered in much the same way as the falling weight test.

A tub is dropped from some height onto a specimen. However in the Dynatup test the same amount of impact energy is delivered to each sample, and this energy is high enough to ensure that each sample breaks. Data from each impact is recorded (stored in a computer). From this information the crack-initiation energy, crack-propagation energy and the total energy absorbed by the material during impact can be calculated and plotted. Of the impact tests, Dynatup is considered the most complete. However, it is a very expensive test (compared to the others) and is more difficult to adapt to nonambient test temperatures.

E

earth **1.** Any siliceous or clay-like compound or mixture (diatomaceous earth, etc.). **2.** A natural metallic oxide sometimes used as a pigment (red and yellow iron oxide, etc.). **3.** A series of chemically related metals that are difficult to separate from their oxides or other combined forms, specifically rare earths and alkaline earths.

earthenware A glazed or unglazed nonvitreous ceramic whiteware.

earth protection ▷**geomembrane liner**

ebonite A hard material made by sulfur vulcanization of rubber in which the hardness is substantially obtained by the action of the sulfur.

eccentricity The ratio of the difference between maximum and minimum dimensions on a part, such as wall thickness. It is expressed as a percentage to the maximum.

ecology The study of the interactions between plant and animal organisms and their environment; the latter is conceived to include everything that is not an intrinsic part of the organism and thus includes both living and non-living components.

ecology and plastic ▷**environment, life, plastic, ecology**

economic and product quality There tends to be a positive correlation between the quality of the fabricated products (goods) offered by a company with fulfillment of explicit requirements or implicit customer expectations and its profit margin. Studies indicate that the return on investment (ROI) as a yardstick for a company's profit depends not only on market share but above all on product quality. Hence, the notion "quality first . . . profit is its logical consequence". Generally the customer is only in a position to assess a few of the quality features at the instant of purchase; so purchase is and remains a matter of trust. An endeavor to improve the market share calls for strengthening this trust. Above all, customer loyalty, as defined by the proportion of customers who will buy the same make of product again, largely depends on the customer's experiences with products of that make. Clearly there is a close connection between quality and cost-effective production.

economic control of equipment In view of continuous rising costs, the main consideration in investing capital must be the ratio of earnings to costs. Production aids can make a considerable contribution towards reducing costs. The most important are those required for feeding the raw material, deflashing, granulating and recycling scrap, demolding, stacking, packing, automatic machining and bonding, and decorating. Basically the only item that does not rise in cost is the fabricating machines performances, such as injection molding, extrusion, blow molding, etc. There are always new machines that will cost less to melt the plastics. An important consideration is to evaluate how much energy a machine (including auxiliary equipment) requires for its operation. Energy efficiency for some relatively new machines, but particularly many older machines, is poor and most will need replacement, particularly when overall capabilities are reviewed.

economic-design-recycling balance ▷**recyclable plastic and scrap**

economic efficiency and profitability Investment decisions in private enterprise must fundamentally rest on a determination of the profitability of the planned actions as reviewed in the Fig. below. This basic requirement has to

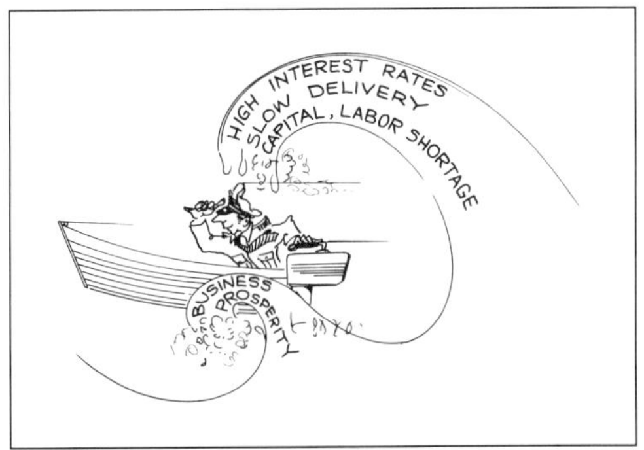

Simplification in viewing economic efficiency and profitability.

be fulfilled during planning stage of a capital investment. The concepts of economic efficiency and profitability are in essence synonymous. Economic efficiency proper is the relationship between the output and the costs, with both these factors expressed in money terms.

Profitability is the relationship between the profit obtained and the capital invested. When the output is specified, the most economical solution is thus also the most profitable. Specification of a particular output in manufacturing as a rule takes the form of a demand for a particular yield from a workpiece or product range, fixed in a quantity framework. In detailed profitability studies, of course, additional attention should be paid to optimistic and pessimistic quantity framework. With such risk analysis, the probability character of sales forecast can be better taken into account.

economic evaluation The abundance of petrochemicals represents a scientific and engineering achievement, as well as an economic success. Each step along the way required a compromise between the economic interests of the producers and the consumers. The price of petrochemicals had to be high enough to induce producers to accept the risks involved in building the necessary plants, but low enough to induce consumers, who have other choices, to buy the products. Economic evaluations are based on the following basic principles: (1) proposed investment normally provides more benefits, but requires more investment, (2) economic decisions are based on future cash flows, (3) accounting charges that do not reflect an actual flow of cash should be ignored such as depreciation; only actual cash flow should be counted, (4) if possible the project should be divided into steps and each step analyzed separately with final review incorporating proper overall analysis, and (5) an economic evaluation covers only the economic aspects of a problem.

economic evaluation method Discounted cash flow is one of the best ways to perform economic evaluations because it expresses a project's attractiveness as an equivalent interest rate, and permits direct comparison to the cost of money. Discounted cash flow also recognizes the time value of money.

economic evaluation reliability This action can yield a wide range of results. The mathematics of discounting are rigorous. The problem is that all the cash flows in the analysis are projections and therefore uncertain. The plant might cost more, take longer to build, and cost more to operate than expected. Operating problems or slower sales growth might delay reaching design capacity. Selling price might fall faster than expected. Recessions might cause less than expected capacity utilization during a number of years. Reliable economic evaluations require realistic projections of these cash flows.

economic indicator A measure that expresses the direction of the business economy.

edge support ▷**bosses and edges**

educational information There is a continuing source of information on all aspects of plastics such as types, methods of processing, chemical structure, rheology, testing and quality controls, designing with plastics and reinforced plastics, engineering data, environmental service, thermodynamics, statistical analysis, computer analysis, and many more. Sources include books, universities, technical and nontechnical society and association conferences, seminars, material suppliers, equipment suppliers, and others. All this action is international in scope. There is always more desired and "more" is always becoming available. Unfortunately there are those that complain nothing (or very little) is available since they are in a world of their own; sometimes information does not fall into one's lap (or perhaps time or energy does not permit one to properly obtain the good and useful information). Remember that for over a century millions of new beneficial developments were brought about by people with the available information of that time. It is very unreasonable to state information is not available; there is always room for more development.

effluent Any gas or liquid emerging from a pipe or similar outlet; usually refers to waste products from plants and buildings as stacked gases and liquid mix; also exhaust from energy power machines (automobiles, busses, trucks, etc.)

E-glass fiber A family of glasses with calcium aluminoborosilicate composition and a maximum alkali content of 2.0%. A general-purpose fiber that is most often used in reinforced plastics. It is suitable for electrical laminates because of its high electrical resistivity; also called electrical grade fiber. All E-glass accounts for over 80%, by weight, of RP material consumed. It is similar to Pyrex glass in its composition. These glass fiber types are drawn during their manufacture so that their properties are very different from those of bulk glass. They are very sensitive to surface abrasion, which greatly reduces their strength, so they are treated with a lubricating size before being gathered into strands. Virgin fibers have a tensile strength of about 3.7 GPa, a modulus of elasticity of about 76 GPa, and a density of 2.54 g/cm^3. Refractive index is 1.548. Among the more common glasses, the strength is only exceeded by S-glass, and resistance of E-glass reinforced plastics to hydrolysis is particularly good.

eight-harness satin weave This type of fabric weave has a seven-by-one weave pattern in which a filling thread floats over seven warp threads and under one. Like the crowfoot weave, it looks different on one side than the other. This weave is more pliable than any of the others and is especially adaptable to forming around compound curves, such as domed shapes. Since this weave will allow comparatively high fabric counts, it contributes maximum strength to RP in all directions.

ejection pressure **1.** The pressure of the ejection screw against the plastic melt at the force acting on the ejection piston during injection molding. **2.** Pressure applied to an ejection mechanism in the injection molding machine required to knockout the part(s) from a mold cavity(s).

ejector mechanism or systems ▷ **mold ejection** and **clamping, close preposition, ejector mechanism**

Ektar Eastman Performance Plastic's trade name for its copolyester elastomer.

elastic deformation Any portion of the total deformation of a body that occurs immediately when loaded (stress) is applied and disappears immediately when the load is removed. Also called viscous deformation.

elastic fracture ▷ **melt fracture**

elastic hysteresis ▷ **hysteresis, elastic**

elasticity **1.** With plastic parts, it is the mechanical property of a material by virtue of which it tends to recover its original size and shape after deformation. If the strain is proportional to the applied stress, the material is said to exhibit Hooke's law or ideal elasticity that follows the modulus of elasticity. **2.** Elasticity behaviour also pertains to melt flow or melt elasticity. ▷ **viscoelasticity**

elasticity, coefficient of ▷ **coefficient of elasticity**

elasticity, viscous ▷ **viscous elasticity**

elastic limit ▷ **stress, elastic limit**

elastic liquid A liquid, which unlike a purely viscous liquid, exhibits elastic effects as well as viscous flow. These may be either stress relaxation effects, where the stress does not become instantaneously isotropic or zero as soon as the liquid is held in a fixed shape, or they may be elastic recovery effects, where the shape does not remain constant as soon as the stress is made isotropic or zero. Many plastic fluids (melts and solutions) show such elastic effects.

elastic memory The ability of a thermoplastic to return to its original shape when exposed to heat beyond its heat distortion point. As an example, a flat sheet that has been thermoformed to a new shape reverts to a flat sheet if sufficiently heated.

elasticity, modulus ▷ **modulus**

elasticoviscous fluid Alternative name for viscoelastic fluid. Sometimes the term is used to refer only to those viscoelastic fluids in which the viscous flow effects predominate and only minor elastic effects are present.

elastic-plastic transition The change from recoverable elastic behavior to non-recoverable plastic strain, which occurs on stressing a material beyond the yield point.

elastic recovery That fraction of a given deformation which behaves elastically, thus

$$\text{elastic recovery} = \frac{\text{elastic extension}}{\text{total extension}}.$$

With a perfectly elastic material, it has an elastic recovery of = 1. A perfectly "plastic" material has an elastic recovery = 0. These dimensions are expressed as percent recovery for a given percent elongation.

elastic reservoir molding ▷ **foamed reservoir molding**

elastic solid A material which can exist in a unique equilibrium shape at zero stress and in which, when held at any other shape by stressing, a nonisotropic equilibrium shape exists. If both these conditions are attained instantaneously on changing the stress, then the material is perfect (or ideally) elastic. If either of these conditions takes a finite time to be attained, then the material is non-ideally elastic or viscoelastic. In contrast, a liquid can have any equilibrium shape.

elastic stability It concerns buckling of parts due to compressive load.

elastic strain ▷ **strain**

elastic-thermal behavior ▷ **thermoelastic effect**

elastic turbulence Another name for melt fracture.

elastodynamic extruder ▷ **extruder, elastic melt**

elastomer An elastomer may be defined as a natural or synthetic material that exhibits the rubberlike properties of high extensibility and flexibility. Although the term *rubber* originally meant the TS elastomeric material obtained from the para rubber tree (*Hevea braziliensis*), it now identifies any thermoset elastomer (TSE) or thermoplastic elastomeric (TPE) material. Such synthetics as neoprene, nitrile, styrene butadiene, and butadiene are now grouped with natural rubber. The terms "rubber" and "elastomer" are used interchangeably.

These TSEs and TPEs serve engineering's need in fields dealing with shock absorption, noise and vibration control, sealing, corrosion protection, abrasion and friction resistance, electrical and thermal insulation, waterproofing, and all types of load-bearing products.

They are differentiated on the basis of how long such a material if deformed requires to return to its approximately original size after the deforming force is removed, and by its extent of recovery. The standard ASTM D 1566 defines an elastomer as a macromolecular material that is capable at room termperature of recovering substantially in shape and size after the removal of a deforming load. This standard has details on the rates of conducting tests as they relate to quick and forcible deformations. Basically, an elastomer must be capable of retracting within one minute to less than 1.5 times its original length after being stretched at room temperature to twice that length and being held for one minute prior to release. (Consult the standard for the actual definition, the test conditions, and so on.)

The ASTM D 2000 and SAE J 200 standards designate rubber or elastomeric materials according to their performance in thermal and oil immersion tests (see Table below). Thermal tests define the types based on their maximum service temperatures, ranging from 21 to 135°C (70 to 275°F) for rubber and 71 to 274°C (160 to 525°F) for elastomers, using letters A through J. The class designations are based on the maximum volume of swelling upon immersion in the prescribed ASTM #3 oil test and use the letters A through K to designate the 10 classes of their volume swell behaviour. These type and class designations are then written together.

▷ **thermoplastic elastomer; vulcanized elastomer; reactive system elastomer; polyisoprene rubber; polybutadiene rubber; polychloroprene rubber; polyisobutylene butyl rubber; styrenebutadiene elastomer; acrylonitrile-butadiene rubber; ethylene-propylene rubber; chlorinated polyethylene elastomer; chlorosulfonated polyethylene elastomer; ethylene-vinylacetate copolymer plastic; ethylene-acrylate copolymer rubber; fluoroelastomer or fluorine rubber; silicone elastomer; epichlorohydrin rubber; polysulfide rubber; propyleneoxide rubber; polynorbornene rubber; polyorganophosphazene plastic**

Examples of popularly used elastomers per ASTM D 2000 and SAE J 200.

Type ↓ ↓ class	Typical
AA	Natural rubber, styrene butadiene, butyl, ethylene propylene, polybutadiene, polyisoprene
AK	Polysulfide
BA	Ethylene propylene, styrene butadiene (high temperature), butyl
BC	Chloroprene, chlorinated polyethylene
BE	Chloroprene, chlorinated polyethylene
BF	Nitrile
BG	Nitrile, urethane
BK	Polysulfide, nitrile
CA	Ethylene propylene
CE	Chlorosulfonated polyethylene, chlorinated polyethylene
CH	Nitrile, epichlorohydrin
	Ethylene/acrylic
DA	Ethylene propylene
DE	Chlorinated polyethylene, chlorosulfonated polyethylene
DF	Polyacrylate (butyl-acrylate type)
DH	Polyacrylate
FC	Silicone (high strength)
FE	Silicone
FK	Fluorinated silicone
GE	Silicone
HK	Fluorinated rubbers

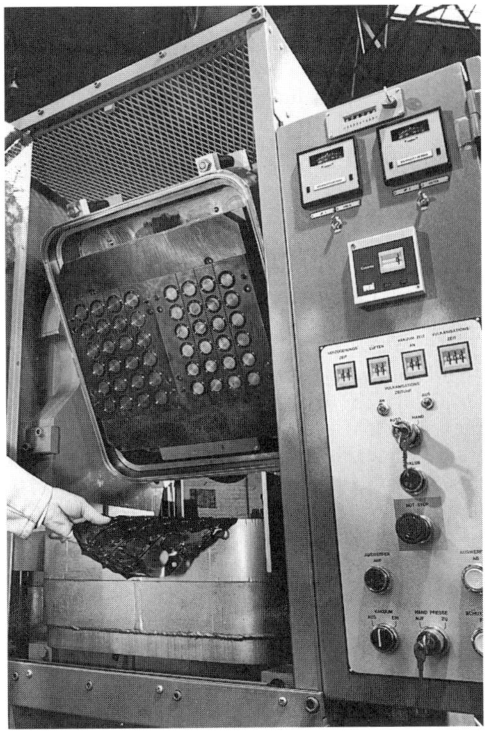

Compression-molding press producing small TSE O-rings.

elastomeric alloy This class of TPEs consists of mixtures using two or more polymers that have received proprietary treatment to give them properties significantly superior to those of simple blends of the same constituents. The two basic types are TP vulcanizates (TPVs) and melt-processible rubbers (MPRs). TPVs are essentially a fine dispersion of highly vulcanized rubber in a continuous phase of a polyolefin. Its crosslinking gives them high tensile strength (1,100–3,900 psi), high elongation (375–600%), resistance to compression and tension set, oil resistance, resistance to flex fatigue and maximum service temperature of 275°F. Specific gravity of TPVs is 0.9–1.0; MPRs is 1.2–1.3.

elastomeric shape factor For an elastomeric slab loaded in compression, the ratio of the loaded area to the force-free area.

elastomeric surface ▷ **recreational surface**

elastomeric tooling A tooling system that used the thermal expansion of elastomer (rubber) materials to form, as an example, reinforced plastic parts during cure.

elastomer processing Many different molding processes, such as compression, injection, casting, reaction injection, etc., can be used to manufacture elastomeric products. Compression is the major process used. The Fig. opposite shows a BIP Company rubber compression molding press with 120 ton clamping force, "book" opening or tilting platen, and vacuum chamber to enclose mold (removes gases, etc. during TSE curing of small O-rings).

elastoplastic A substance which exhibits a greater or lesser degree of resiliency and will return to, or close to, its original size and shape if deformed to some extent below its elastic limit, as opposed to a brittle substance.

electric Plastics are used extensively in electrical applications mainly because they are excellent electrical insulators. The most significant dielectric properties are dielectric strength, dissipation factor, dielectric constant, and resistivity (see Fig. below). These properties are affected by many factors including time, temperature, moisture content, etc. Furthermore, these factors can interact in a complex manner. Test instruments

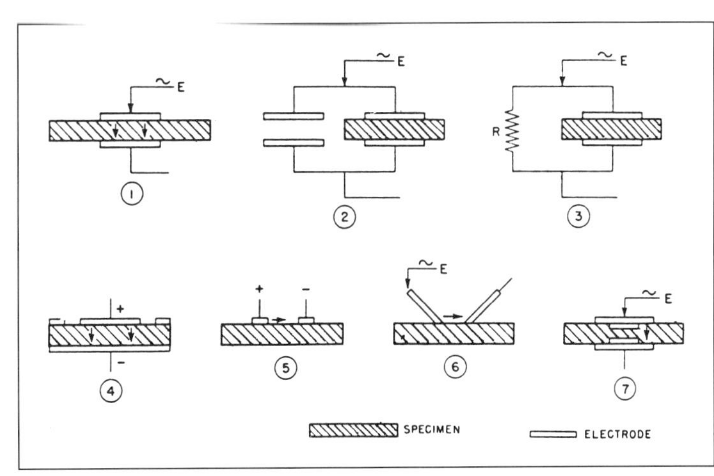

Schematics of different electrical tests. (*1*) Dielectric strength; (*2*) dielectric constant; (*3*) dissipation factor; (*4*) volume resistivity; (*5*) surface resistivity; (*6*) arc resistance; (*7*) corona resistance.

used for automatic measurement provide the capability for using changes in dielectric properties as a meter to monitor plastics processing. Also, electrical tests can be conducted that relate to mechanical properties.

electrical, alternating current AC is an electric current that reverses its direction at regularly recurring intervals as opposed to direct current.

electrical ampere The ampere is that constant current which, if maintained in two straight parallel conductors of infinite length, of negligible circular cross section, and placed one meter apart in vacuum, would produce between these conductors a force equal to 2×10^{-7} newton per meter of length.

electrical arc resistance The ability of a material to withstand the discharge across its surface of a specified, at first and then continuous, high-voltage, low-current arc. Materials may fail through the eventual formation of a conducting path across their surface, and must then be judged for arc resistance, by their probable ability to withstand some lesser amount of arcing. It is reported as the time in seconds that an arc may play across the surface without rendering it conductive; measured by ASTM D 495, failure is dependent on temperature, frequency, and conditioning.

electrical arc tracking A phenomenon which occurs on the surface of an insulator when an arc is set up near that surface, under a low voltage and a medium intersity, such as 10 to 20 amperes.

electrical breakdown voltage The voltage (dielectric strength) to breakdown is measured by applying increasing voltage across a sample until physical breakdown of the plastic results in catastrophic decrease in resistance.

electrical cable armor A solid or braided metal jacket for imparting maximum abrasion resistance to the completed cable. Braided armor is sometimes used in lieu of solid armor for improved flexibility.

electrical capacitance The property of a system of conductors and dielectrics that permits the storage of electricity when potential difference exists between the conductors. Its value is expressed as the ratio of quantity of electricity to a potential difference. A capacitance value is always positive.

electrical circuit board ▷**printed circuit** and **injection molding circuit board**

electrical coercive field Electric field required to remove residual polarization.

electrical conductance The siemens (S) is the electric conductance of a conductor in which a current of one ampere is produced by an electric potential difference of one volt (A/V).

electrical conductor 1. A wire, or combination of wires not insulated from each other, suitable for carrying electricity. **2.** Plastics that have electrical transparent conductors.

electrical connector Connectors perform the simplest role, but an absolutely vital one. Its design is constantly obliged to change because of all the ever-changing technology around it. Originally, in the beginning of this century, thermoset plastics were the dominant material. But thermoplastics started gaining acceptance during the 1960s to become the most often used plastic at first nylons and polycarbonates, then PBTs). Other engineering and commodity plastics were used such as polysulfones, PPSs, polyacrylates, polyketones, PET, different alloys, and more recently LCPs Markets exist for higher temperature stability and higher dimensional stability. Printed wiring boards (PWBs) become crowded. Surface-mount technology is crowding more devices on the board, often on both sides. The connectors are always faced with handling more increased I/O counts, and with resisting high temperatures of the various soldering reflow techniques. Connectors run up to 18 inches long (46 cm) and offer 1,600 pin positions.

electrical corona An electrical discharge effect which causes ionization of oxygen and the formation of ozone. It is particularly evident near high-tension wires and in spark-ignited automotive engines. The ozone formed can have drastic oxidizing effect on plastic wire insulation, cable covers, and hose connections unless oxidation-resistant plastics, such as nylon, neoprene, etc., are used.

electrical corona discharge The flow of electrical energy from a conductor to the surrounding air or gas. The phenomenon occurs when the voltage is high enough (5,000 or more volts) to cause partial ionization of the surrounding gas. The discharge is characterized by a pale violet glow, a hissing noise, and the odor of ozone.

electrical corona discharge treatment A method for rendering inert plastics, such as polyolefins, more receptive to inks, adhesives, or decorative coatings by subjecting their surfaces to a corona discharge. A typical method of treating films is to pass the film over a grounded metal cylinder above which is located a sharp-edged high-voltage electrode spaced so as to leave a small gap. The corona discharge oxidizes the film by means of the formation of polar groups on reactive sites, making the surface receptive to coatings.

electrical corona resistance The time that insulation will withstand a specific level of field-intensified ionization that does not result in the immediate complete breakdown of the insulation.

electrical corona shield Plastic (electromagnetic interference type), metal, etc. covering placed around exposed high-voltage components to prevent electrical discharge.

electrical coulomb ▷ **coulomb**

electrical coulometer An electrolytic cell arranged to measure the quantity of electricity by the chemical action produced in accordance with Faraday's law.

electrical cover In wire coating, a coating whose primary purpose is to "weather-proof" or to prevent casual grounding (such as contact with a wet tree branch), or to otherwise protect a conductor.

electrical cure monitoring Use of electrical techniques to detect changes in the electrical properties and/or mobility of the plastic molecules during cure. An example is measuring of thermoset plastic cure. ▷ **dielectrometry**

electrical current density ▷ **current density**

electric dielectric material ▷ **dielectric**

electrical direct current DC is an electrical current flowing in one direction only and substantially constant in value. When electrical voltage is applied to a material, current flows. If the voltage is steady (direct), the current is defined by Ohm's law: $A = V/\Omega$ where A = current, V = voltage, and Ω = resistance. Such a simple relationship rarely holds in practical situations. Voltage is never absolutely steady and usually varies in ac cyclic fashion (alternating current) with a repetition rate of 0.1 to 10^{11} Hz (cycles per second) or more. The dc resistance depends on the dimensions of the material and a number of factors such as ambient conditions, heat induced by the current flow, and the characteristics of the material.

electrical dissipation factor When an alternating voltage is applied to a "perfect" dielectric, current will flow so that it is 90° out of phase with the voltage. Since no insulating material is perfect, the current actually leads the voltage by something less than 90°. The dissipation factor is the tangent of the small angle of 90° minus the actual angle at which the current leads the voltage (ASTM D 150). Since the dissipation factor is also equivalent to the ratio of current dissipated into heat to the current transmitted, the smaller values of the dissipation factor correspond to a better dielectric material. Temperature, frequency, and contaminants like moisture affect the dissipation factor.

electrical dry cell A primary battery that can be encased in plastic having a zinc anode, a carbon or graphite cathode surrounded by manganese dioxide, and a paste containing ammonium chloride as electrolyte. Such batteries are not reversible and therefore have a limited operating life.

electrical eddy current A current caused to flow in a conductor by the time or space variation, or both, of an applied magnetic field.

electrical eddy current testing A nondestructive testing method in which eddy current flow is induced in the test object. Changes in the flow by variations in the specimen are reflected into a nearby coil or coils for subsequent analysis by suitable instrumentation and techniques.

electrical-electronic market Among the most important functions of plastics is their application in its fifth largest market, electronics. Many new and important developments in the field of electricity and electronics would not have been possible without the many and continuing developments in the field of plastics. Their wide use is based primarily on their excellence as insulating materials. Although insulation requirements vary widely, there exist one or more plastics which will meet nearly every electrical insulation requirement.

electrical erosion breakdown In an electrical conductor insulation, erosion breakdown is caused by chemical attack of corrosive chemicals, such as ozone and nitric acid, which are formed by corona discharge from a high voltage cable.

electrical, Faraday ▷ **Faraday**

electrical galvanic cell A cell containing two dissimilar metals and an electrolyte.

electrical glass fiber ▷ **E-glass fiber**

electrical inductance The henry (H) is the inductance of a closed circuit in which an electromotive force of one volt is produced when the electric current in the circuit varies uniformly at a rate of one ampere per second (Wb/a).

electrical induction The process by which an electrical conductor becomes electrified when near a charged body or by which the electromotive force is produced in a circuit by varying the magnetic field linked with the circuit.

electrical interference ▷ **electromagnetic interference**

electrical jacket A tough sheath to protect an insulated wire or cable, or to permanently group two or more insulated wires or cables.

electrical loss angle The anti-tangent of the electrical dissipation factor. ▷ **dielectric loss angle**

electrical loss angle, tangent The dissipation factor of an electrical condenser of which the insulating material forms the dielectric when the electrodes of such a condenser are subjected to an alternating emf. ▷ **dielectric loss factor**

electrically conductive plastic **1.** There are plastics with certain chemical structures (conjugated π-electron backbones) that display unusual electronic conductive properties such as low energy optical transitions, low ionization potentials, and high electron affinities. The result is a class of plastics that can be oxidized or reduced more easily and more reversibly than conventional plastics. Charge-transfers agents (dopants) effect this oxidation or reduction and in doing so convert an insulating plastic to a conducting plastic with near metallic conductivity in many cases. **2.** Typically, metallic conductive fillers and/or reinforcements such as carbonaceous powders, aluminum or steel powders, etc., are used with plastics to make them conductive. Different constructions have been produced since the 1940s with reinforced plastics such as the use of metallic coated glass fibers, aluminum or steel wire filaments with other fibers, etc. There are conductive RPs using high aspect ratio fillers producing a combination of desired conductivity of metal with the processing ease and economy of plastic.

electrical moisture content test ▷ **reinforced plastic moisture content test electrically**

electrical motion control systems ▷ **motion control systems**

electrical nondestructive test With electrical nondestructive testing, the dielectric constant and dissipation factor (or loss tangent) can be used as nondestructive methods for determining variability in a reinforced plastic. For a given thickness and composition, changes in degree of cure of thermosets can be assessed by dielectric constant and dissipation factor measurements, the values for these parameters decreasing as the plastic is cured. Similarly, moisture content can be within ±1%.

electrical orientation ▷ **orientation, electrical properties**

electrical ozone ▷ **antiozonant agent**

electrical peak voltage For ac meters, the voltage that will discharge across the air gap or across a defect. The peak voltage is the RMS voltage multiplied by 1.414.

electrical permeability, magnetic ▷ **permeability, magnetic**

electrical permittivity A factor giving the influence of an extensive, isotropic dielectric medium on the forces of attraction or repulsion between two electrified bodies. It is the product of the "relative permittivity" and the "permittivity of free space (vacuum)".

electrical power The watts (W) is the power which gives rise to the production of energy at the rate of one joule per second (J/S).

electrical power factor At the very high frequencies used in radio work the leakage of power through even the best of insulating materials can be very serious. Power factor is given as a direct percentage measurement of this power loss in the material. It will usually differ according to frequency. Measurements are usually made at million-cycle frequencies. PF is the cosine of the phase angle; ratio of the dielectric constant ε to the absolute value of the complex constant ε*. It is related to the dissipation factor D as follows:

$$\mathrm{PF} = \frac{D}{\sqrt{(1+D^2)}} = \frac{\varepsilon''/\varepsilon'}{\sqrt{1+\frac{\varepsilon_2''}{\varepsilon'}}} = \frac{\varepsilon'}{|e^*|}$$

electrical power loss The power, per unit volume, that is transformed into heat through hysteresis. It is the product of energy loss and frequency.

electrical properties Uncompounded and compounded plastics are used in many electrical applications since most are electrical insulators or dielectics and exhibit high resistivity (low conductance). In other cases they may have primarily a structural function but also an electrical function. The electrical properties are understood and taken into account for many different applications. The electrical behavior of insulating materials is influenced by temperature, time, moisture and other contaminants, geometric relationships, mechanical stress and electrodes, and frequency and magnitude of the applied voltage. These factors interact in a complex fashion.

To determine their useful electrical properties for engineering purposes, it is necessary to duplicate conditions of service as closely as possible. Simple rather than complex and lengthy tests are usually justified and should be determined as a function of variables such as temperature and time. Time is an important variable in voltage degradation and moisture exposure.

electrical properties and orientation ▷ **orientation and electrical properties**

electrical quantity The coulomb (C) is the quantity of electricity transported in one second by a current of one ampere (A · s).

electrical resistance The ohm(Ω) is the electric resistance between two points of a conductor when a constant difference of potential of one volt, applied between these two points, produces in this conductor a current of one ampere, this conductor not being the source of any electromotive force (V/A). Materials are classified broadly by resistivity as shown in the Table and Fig. The classes are conductors when hot or wet, or when they contain carbon or SiC powder.

Materials resistivity classification.

Resistivity, Ω · cm[1]	Class
$0-10^3$	Conductor
10^3-10^7	Partial conductor or semiconductor[2]
10^5-10^{18} and higher	Insulator

[1] Unit resistance between two opposite faces of a 10 mm cube.
[2] Solid-state materials, eg, silicon.

electrical resistance, plastic Plastics in general display high electrical resistance and very little conduction of an electrical current. The small conductivity observed is more than likely attributed to electrolytic motion of ionic impurities in the polymer. Thus a decrease in volume resistivity is generally the result of both (1) ionic impurities and (2) mobility. Ionic impurities are somewhat difficult to determine but are generally recognized as coming from incomplete polymerization and subsequent buffering/washing of the resinous product. Mobility is more easily determined; for example, by plotting the modulus vs. temperature (Clash-Berg ASTM D 1043), the effect of the addition of a plasticizer can also be related to changes in thermal characteristics of the compound—conductivity, linear expansion, processing temperature profile, and flexibility at low temperatures.

electrical resistance temperature detector ▷ **temperature electrical resistance detector**

electrical RMS voltage ▷ **root-mean-square voltage**

electrical static charge ▷ **electrostatic charge**

electrical strength or dielectric strength That property of an insulating material which enables it to withstand electric stress; the highest electric stress which an insulating material can withstand for a specified time without the occurrence of electrical breakdown by any path through its bulk.

electrical surface conductance The direct current conductance between two electrodes in

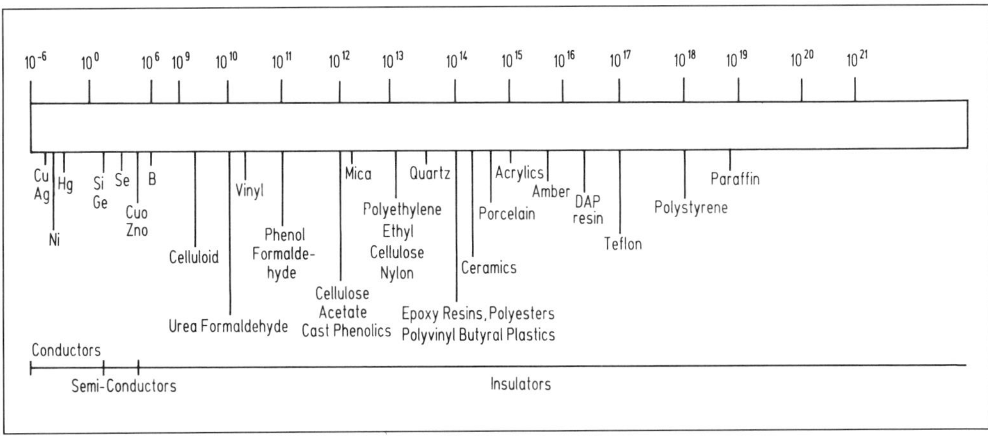

Volume resistivity spectrum.

contact with a specimen of solid insulating material when the current is passing only through a thin film of moisture on the surface of the specimen.

electrical surface resistivity The ratio of the potential gradient parallel to the current along its surface to the current per unit width of surface, usually expressed in ohms (Ω). Surface resistivity is numerically equal to the surface resistance between opposite sides of a square of any size when the current flow is uniform (ASTM D 257).

electrical tracking A phenomenon wherein a high voltage source current creates a leakage or fault path across the surface of an insulating material by slowly but steadily forming a carbonized path.

electrical transparent conductor Available are transparent conductive films for electronic components. They were developed for use in electroluminescent lamps (ELLs), membrane touch panels, EMI/RFI shielding, plastic liquid crystal displays (LCDs), groundplanes, and heating elements. The visual transparent and electrically conductive films are offered with abrasion resistant hardcoats (clear and non-glare), high adhesion properties for inks and phosphors, and low shrink heat-stabilized PET substrates (or other plastics). With PET, the film can be comprised of a single layer of Indium tin oxide deposited on a flexible (PET) film substrate. Coating manufacture includes using DC magnetron sputtering, e-beam evaporation, or a combination of both. Applications include solar control window films, photoreceptor groundplanes of copy machines and laser printers, transparent barrier coatings for the packaging industry, and anticounterfeiting pigment for high value currency and documents.

electrical volt The volt (V, a unit of electrical potential difference and electromotive force) is the difference of electric potential between two points of a conductor carrying a constant current of one ampere, when the power dissipated between these points is equal to one watt (W/A). For voltage variations, the concept of capacitance is introduced: C = Q/V; where C = capacitance, Q = charge, and V = voltage. An insulating material (dielectric) can be represented by a combination of resistance and capacitance in several ways (see Fig.) The more complex and realistic relationship (Fig. *a*) can be simplified to the equivalent circuits shown in Figs. *b* and *c*. If the voltage is suddenly applied to the series circuit, a current that is limited by resistance flows to charge the capacitance. With voltage built up across the capacitance, the current decreases. With a good dielectric, the resistance is low. In the parallel schematic however, with the higher resistance, the better the dielectric and the less current bypassed or leaked.

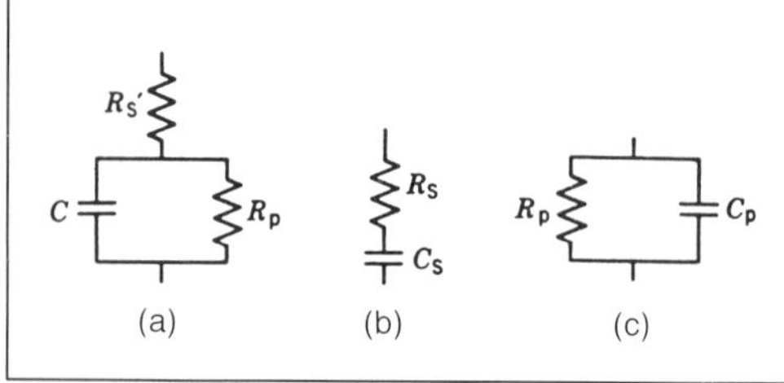

Examples of voltage variations where C = capacitance, R = resistance, and subscripts p and s refer to parallel and series, respectively. (*a*) Schematic representation of an insulating material (dielectric); (*b*) equivalent series circuit; (*c*) equivalent parallel circuit.

When an alternating voltage is applied to a perfect dielectric, a current flows that is displaced in time in such a way that it is 90° out of phase with the voltage. Since no insulating material is perfect, the voltage leads the current with time. In considering the influence of alternating voltage on plastic insulation, it is important to realize that not all of the conductance observed must derive from the migration of charge carriers in the material. An insulating material may contain charge or, under the influence of electrical stress, develop additional bound charges of various types that are displaced to a limited extent by the action of the electric field.

electrical voltage-to-frequency converters ▷ **computer voltage-to-frequency converter**

electrical volume resistivity This is a measure of the resistance of electrical dc current through the thickness of a specimen. Generally it is expressed as ohm·cm which is a unit of resistance between two opposite faces of a one centimeter cube. Materials with resistivities above 10^8 ohm·cm are considered insulators, while those with values of 10^3 to 10^8 ohm·cm are partial conductors.

electrical watt The unit of active power. One watt is energy, work, or quantity of heat expended at a rate of one joule per second.

electrical watt density The watts per unit area emitted from radiant heaters.

electrical wire resistant strain gauge ▷ **stress-strain measurements**

electric discharge machining ▷ **machining electric discharge**

electricity The word electricity, coined in the eighteenth century, was derived from the Greek word for amber, *elektron*.

electric polarization material ▷ **ferroelectric**

electrification time The time during which a steady direct potential is applied to electrical insulating materials before the current is measured.

electrochemical cell An electrochemical system consisting of an anode and a cathode in metallic contact and immersed in an electrolyte.

electrochemical reaction Many chemical reactions can be classified as oxidation-reduction reactions (so called redox reactions) and can be considered to be the result of two reactions, one oxidation and the other reduction. An element is said to have undergone oxidation if it loses electrons or if its oxidation state has increased, that is, it has attained a more positive charge. An element is said to have undergone reduction if it gains electrons or if its oxidation state has been reduced; that is, it has attained a more negative charge. Atoms of elements in their elemental state have a zero charge.

electrochemistry The branch of science and technology which deals with transformations between chemical and electrical energy.

electrocoating A process of applying plastic primer paint to products in which the metal piece to be coated becomes the anode in a tank of water-based paint. Products include appliances, automobile parts, etc. The electrodeposition coating deposited on the metal can be uniform regardless of complex shapes. Large-scale use is on automobile bodies. In this process, electrically charged waterborne, film-forming organic macroions are attracted by an electrode of opposite polarity where they are deposited. Well-known plastic paints with excellent properties include epoxies, polyesters, and many others. Their film-forming properties are usually associated with the chemical nature of the plastic and a molecular weight range of 2,000 to 20,000.

electrode The energized or grounded conductor portion of electrical test equipment which is placed near or in contact with the material or equipment being tested.

electrodeposition coating The precipitation of a material at an electrode as the result of the passage of an electric current through a solution or suspension of the material, for example, elastomer/rubber from latex, plastic paint films on metal, etc. The electrode is in the shape of the desired product. An important advantage of this process is that very complex products can be coated with rather exact thickness control. It offers very high corrosion protection on metals, low cost, and compliance with environmental regulations. It is used for the coating of articles of various sizes including steel building trusses, car bodies, furniture, appliances, toys, and nuts and bolts. The success of this process is due to the use of water-dispersible, electrodepositable macroions as film formers. The process is also called electrocoating, electropainting, and e/coat.

Low viscosity of the paint bath, about equal to that of water, facilitates agitation and pumping and allows fast entry and drainage of workpieces. Freshly deposited coats are composed of 97% nonvolatile substances and therefore allow immediate gentle handling; there is no tendency to sag or wash off during cure. A second coat, usually a color coat, of waterborne or solvent-borne spray paint can be applied directly over the uncured electrocoat. Approximately 95% of the applied paint is utilized because the liquid paint, which adheres or fills cavities of freshly coated pieces, is rinsed back into the coating tank. Overall savings, accounting for materials, labor, capital investment, energy, etc., are about 20 to 50% when compared with spray, electrostatic spray, or dip-coat painting.

electro-erosive cutting and sinking They represent a prominent place among processes for manufacturing plastics processing tools (molds and dies) as well as cutting and stamping tools. With cutting and sinking technologies, the tool steel that is used has a considerable effect on the performance of the tools and the quantity of the parts that are manufactured with them. Their most important process parameters are current, ignition and working voltage, and duration of impulse and pause. These parameters can be varied and have a direct effect on the quality features of the machined workpiece.

electroformed mold ▷ **mold material, electroformed**

electroforming The production or reproduction of articles by electrodeposition upon a mandrel or mold that is subsequently separated from the pattern. The pattern material can be wax or a flexible material. These molded parts are usually employed at low or moderate molding pressures.

electrokinetic recycling Use of an electric arc to break down plastic waste into useful industrial gases.

electroless plating The deposition and formation of a continuous metallic film on a nonconductive plastic surface without the use of an electric current. It is the controlled reduction of a solution of a metal ion by a dissolved reducing agent at a catalytic interface to give a coherent film. Most electroless plating phenomena have analogues to classical electroplating. The simplest electroplating baths consist of a solution of a soluble metal salt. Electrons are supplied to the conductive metal surface, where electron transfer to and reduction of the dissolved metal ions occur. These simple baths are usually not satisfactory. Additives are required to control conductivity, pH, crystal metal structure, throwing power, etc. Electroless copper was introduced during the 1950s. There are now also electroless platings with nickel, chromium and silver, but most are with copper in its many varieties. Their formulated baths differ in deposition rate, ease of treatment, stability, bath life, copper color, and ductility, operating temperature, and component concentration. Most have been developed for specific processes; all deposit nearly pure copper metal.

Plating on plastics consists of the following steps: etching, etch neutralization, catalyst application, catalyst activation, and plating. Most commercial applications, except RFI shielding, use the initial deposit as a base for subsequent electrolytic plating. The initial copper or nickel layer is coated with successful layers of electrolytic copper, nickel, and chromium. The exact types and thicknesses of metal used are determined by the end use of the part, such as automotive exterior, decorative, plumbing, etc. The plating depends on a precise series of chemical to clean, roughen, and catalyze the surface before plating. These steps are very critical for formation of an adherent, continuous electroless coating, and for optimum durability in service. There are automatic processing lines that allow low cost production of plated parts even though equipment and solution control costs can be high. Rejects are usually less than 5% of production. Defective parts can be stripped and replated, or reground and remolded.

electroluminescence Luminescence resulting from electrical excitation.

electrolysis Production of chemical changes of the electrolyte by the passage of current through an electrochemical cell.

electrolyte A substance that will provide ionic conductivity when dissolved in water or when in contact with it. Such compounds may be either solid or liquid types, including acids, bases, or salts, or other media such as ionized gases.

electromagnet A soft iron core surrounded by a coil of wire that temporarily becomes a magnet when an electric current flows through the wire.

electromagnetic adhesive Method for joining thermoplastics in which a metallic preform is placed in the joint area to convert electromagnetic energy into electric heat for fusion bonding.

electromagnetic field Magnetic forces developed by the passage of an electric current through a conductor core; usually wrapped around an iron or similar metal or alloy.

electromagnetic-induction welding This type of welding uses a radio frequency (rf) magnetic field to excite fine, magnetically sensitive particles, either metallic or ceramic. The particles can be imbedded in a preform, filament ribbon, adhesive, coextruded film, in a molding compound, etc. The most common is to include an extra part, such as a preform containing the magnetically active particles. The preform is placed at the joint interface and exposed to an electromagnetic field. Electromagnetically induced heat is conducted from the particles through the preform and to the part joint as the parts are pressed together.

electromagnetic interference EMI in the radio-frequency (rf) range consists of undesirable rf signals superimposed on a wanted signal. These signals may originate from a device intended to transmit or from a device not intended to transmit, but with components that are transmitters in the rf range. The latter group is used in commercial equipment (U.S.) and this creates problems with rf receiving devices. The method for measuring the EMI of a device is given in Appendix C of FCC Methods of Measurement of Radio Noise Emissions for Computing Devices, available from the FCC Office of Science and Technology, Washington, D.C. This regulation also applies for devices not intended for communication. Many electronic devices that inherently, but not intentionally, transmit a rf signal are enclosed in housing made of plastic. Unfilled types offer very little attenuation of rf energy. Thus, plastic using appropriate fillers and/or metal or aluminum plate or foil are used, permitting compliance to FCC regulations and protection of rf sensitive components such as hospital electronic patient controller, computer hardware, etc. The result is no accumulation of electrostatic charge in a nonconductor.

electromagnetic interference, conductive plastic Conductive plastics are grouped by the Electronic Industries Association (EIA standard 541) into two basic classifications that describe the type and degree of protection they render. Starting at the low conductivity end, these are electrostatic dissipative (ESD), and electromagnetic and radio-frequency interference (EMI/RFI) shielding. These generic classifications are defined numerically in terms of surface resistivity or volume resistivity for EMI/RFI applications. The numerical values are expressed as powers of 10; the units are ohms/square. The lower the value, the higher the conductivity and the better the static-dissipative and shielding properties. EMI/RFI compounds are defined as having surface resistivities of less than 10^5 ohms/square. For less conductive, range is 10^5 to 10^{12} ohms/square. Above 10^{12} the compound is considered insulative, though antistatic performance can be obtained with the conductive effects of chemical additives and sprays. Performance standards, however, are not based on these material properties, but on functional tests.

For ESD, the tests measure how long it takes for a specified voltage to dissipate from the surface of the material into the air. Different performance specifications exist from organizations that are Federal, military, etc. The tougher standard is from the National Fire Protection Association requiring a 0.5 second decay but at 50% humidity. EMI/RFI shielding compounds are rated by other types of tests. They measure the ability of the conductive material to block (attenuate), by a combination of reflection and absorbence both rf waves and magnetic fields. The results, called shielding effectiveness, are expressed in decibel (dB) units, For most applications, 20 to 40 dB is adequate; for critical service or high energy exposure at least 50 dB is required.

electromagnetic interference shielding effectiveness Shielding effectiveness (SE) is defined as the ratio of the incident field strength to the transmitted field strength, as illustrated in the Fig. above.

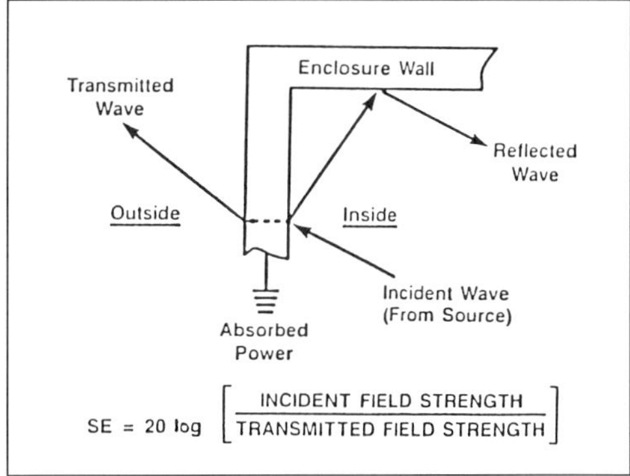

EMI shielding mechanism schematic; shielding effectiveness (SE).

electromagnetic phenomena ▷ **dielectric heating**

electromagnetic radiation ▷ **infrared spectrometry** and **neutron scattering**

electromagnetic spectrum As shown in the Fig. below, it includes different wavelength regions. They are energy propagated by an electromagnetic field.

electromagnetic testing Nondestructive test methods for materials, including magnetic materials, that use electromagnetic energy having frequencies less than those of visible light to yield information regarding the quality of testing materials. ▷ **nondestructive testing**

electromagnetic welding ▷ **electromagnetic-induction welding**

electron A fundamental particle of matter that can exist either as a constituent of an atom or in a free state. It has a negative charge. The number of electrons in an atom of any element

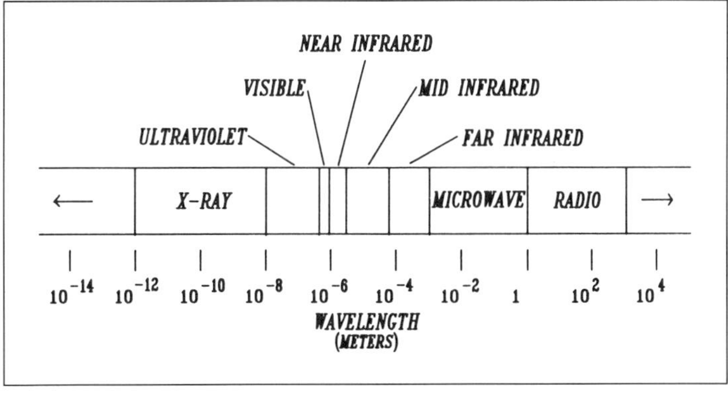

The electromagnetic spectrum.

is the same as the number of protons in the nucleus, i.e., the atomic number ▷ **Periodic Table**. Electrons can be removed from the atoms of metals and some other elements by means of heat, light, electric energy, and bombardment with high energy particles such as radiation and ionization.

electron beam A stream of electrons in an electron optical system.

electron beam polymerization EB polymerization is much slower than plasma polymerization. Monomeric materials that have been irradiated to produce plastic films include silicones, butadiene, styrene, methyl methacrylate, divinyl-benzene, and epoxy. However, the lack of selectivity of this energy source results in contamination. Film properties can be tailored somewhat by varying the acceleration voltage. ▷ **vacuum coating**

electron beam welding A welding process wherein coalescence is produced by the heat obtained from a concentrated beam composed primarily of high velocity electrons impinging upon the surfaces to be bonded.

electron diffraction The phenomenon or the technique of producing diffraction patterns through the incidence of electrons upon matter.

electron gun A device for producing and accelerating a beam of electrons.

electronic Relating to or utilizing devices constructed or working by the methods or principles of electronics.

electronic chip Traditional chips are totally encapsulated with a plastic that is almost always epoxy plastic. The glob-top microprocessing chips have only a single drop of epoxy applied to their tops.

electronic doppler effect A shift toward longer electronic wave lengths for waves reaching an observer when the source of the waves is moving away from the observer or instrument (radar device, etc.).

electronic dot generation EDG is a method of producing halftones electronically on scanners and prepress systems.

electronic heating ▷ **dielectric heating**

electronic logic control ▷ **control, electronic logic**

electronic microminiaturization The technique of packaging a microminiature part or assembly composed of elements radically different in shape and form factor. Electronic parts are replaced by active and passive elements through use of fabrication processes such as screening, vapor deposition, diffusion, etc.

electronic packaging ▷ **packaging electronic logic** and **antistatic in electronic packaging**

electronic printing Any technology that reproduces pages without the use of traditional ink, water, and chemistry. Most often they are electrostatic or electrophotographic.

electronics A branch of physics that deals with emission, behaviour, and effects of electrons and with electronic devices.

electronic sewing machine ▷ **dielectric heat sealing**

electronic treating A method of oxidizing a plastic, such as a polyethylene film, to render it printable by passing the film between electrodes and subjecting it to high voltage corona discharge. Also provides other advantages such as permitting adhesive bonding, etc.

electron image A representation of an object formed by a beam of electrons focused by an electron optical system.

electron optical system A combination of parts capable of producting and controlling a beam of electrons to produce an image of an object.

electron spin resonance A form of spectroscopy similar to nuclear magnetic resonance, except that the material studied is an unpaired electron, not a magnetic nucleus.

electrophoresis Migration of suspended or colloidal particles in a liquid such as rubber latex due to effect of potential differences across immersed electrodes. It is one of a group of phenomena referred to generally as electrokinetic phenomena, which include electroosmosis and streaming potential as well as electrophoresis. These conditions rest upon the relationship between an electric potential and the flow of one substance (having a net charge) through another; that is, two different materials in relative motion tend to generate an electric potential or, conversely, an externally applied electric potential will tend to produce relative motion in a system of two different materials. The term ionophoresis is sometimes used for the migration of low molecular weight substances in an electric field, especially when the migration takes place in a stabilized medium, such as gel.

electrophoretic deposition The process of depositing material on a workpiece by immersing in a liquid suspension of the coating plastic material. It is similar to electroplating in which the workpiece forms one electrode of a pair immersed in the bath. Upon application of a direct current to the electrodes, particles of the suspended material migrate to the workpiece due to the movement of particles under the influence of the impressed direct current voltage. Plastics used include PVC, PVDC, PE, PTFE, etc.

electroplating The deposition of a metal coating (such as chromium, nickel, copper, silver, etc.) on a product by passing an electric current through an aqueous solution of a salt containing ions of the element being deposited. The material being plated (plastic or metal) constitutes the cathode. The anode is often composed of the metal being deposited; ideally it dissolves as the process proceeds. The anode must be an electrical conductor; it cannot dissolve during the plating. Plastics generally are not conductive, so they are made conductive by pretreating with a base conductive coating, or the plastic includes a conductive filler. Electroplating requires an understanding of both the molding processes and the plating. Stresses in molding can have immediate or in service delamination of the coating due to stress relieving. In regard to chrome plating, the important aspects relate to current efficiency, the degree to which the process deposits a bright metallic film. It determines the film thickness and physical properties of the deposition. It is generally evaluated by current density and film thickness.

Another aspect related to current density is the coating appearance. Areas designed with a deep vertical wall are subject to insufficient coverage, usually distinguished by a brown cast. Another problem resulting in poor appearance is the problem of burning in the chrome tank, the result of excessive and overly rapid application. ▷**vacuum metallizing** and **sputtered coating**

electrospray mass spectrometry ESMS is where a plastic solution is sprayed through a fine jet to give a supersonic molecular beam. In this way it is possible to produce isolated and charged molecules which may be analyzed according to their mass.

electrostatic assist While electrostatic forces may cause the disintegration of a fluid stream, this method is not used alone. It is extremely useful, however, as an assist with spray methods, especially with centrifugal spraying. An electrostatic force improves the disintegration of the electrically charged paint stream, but most important, it directs the charged paint particles to the oppositely charged target, usually at ground potential. This increases transfer efficiency. The plastic surfaces are made conductive by a light spray of conductive salt sufficient to maintain the required charge on the part to be painted.

electrostatic charge A charge, often negative, induced or transferred onto a surface. Static electrical charging by contact electrification (triboelectrification) is a property of interest in commercial applications. A triboelectric series may be established that roughly follows the dielectric constants of the plastics.

electrostatic copying ▷**charged area development**

electrostatic discharge detector ESD detection device provides visual identification that an ESD event has occurred on a printed circuit board or an electronic sub-assembly. The plastic enclosed unit is designed to be mounted to ESD-sensitive circuit boards and assemblies during their manufacture. It can also be attached to tote boxes, shipping containers, and personnel. If the detector is "zapped" by an ESD during manufacturing or shipping, a small display changes color to indicate potential damage. Once triggered, the detector switches to a latched condition and remains locked until cleared by a resetting device that is an integral part of the detection system.

electrostatic dissipative ▷**electromagnetic interference**

electrostatics The science of forces and fields of electric charges in a state of rest.

electrostatic spray coating Coating thicknesses are in the range of 3 to 30 mils (0.08 to 0.8 mm), depending on the service performance required of the part. In this process, a dry coating plastic powder is withdrawn from a reservoir in an air stream and electrostatically charged in the high voltage corona field of a spray gun. The charged particles are attached to the grounded product (metal or surface conductive plastic) to be coated and adhere to it by electrostatic attraction. The coated substrate is then placed in an oven and the coating is fused to form a continuous film. If the powder is sprayed on a preheated product, the powder melts and fuses directly on the hot surface; further heating to fuse or cure the coating may be required depending on the type of coating powder and the substrate material. When the powder builds to a certain thickness, usually about 8 mils (0.2 mm), a dielectric barrier is created and more powder is rejected. The part must be heated before additional coating can be applied.

element An element is a pure substance that cannot be broken down by chemical means to a simpler substance. Elements are listed in the ▷**Periodic Table**. It is important in engineering materials to recognize the names and symbols for the more useful elements. This table lists elements by atomic number. The element hydrogen was assigned an atomic number of 1, and all the others derive their atomic number from a comparison of the "size" of the atoms to the element hydrogen. The atomic number is really the number of protons in the nucleus of an atom. Atoms are far more complicated, but present knowledge characterizes atoms as being composed of protons (positively charged particles), neutrons (neutral particles), and electrons which orbit the nucleus (or core of an atom). For simplicity, atoms are often characterized as a "sun" (nucleus), surrounded by orbiting planets (electrons). Electrons have mass, but their "orbits" are not well defined rings. There are many intricacies involved in analyzing the nuclear atom. Its structure is unimportant in most work in ordinary metallurgy, but can have some application in deducing bonding tendencies between atoms.

Many elements are used as engineering materials in their pure elemental state. Many metals fall into this category: copper, gold, platinum, etc. However, a larger percentage of engineering materials utilize the elements in combined forms in alloys, compounds, and mixtures ▷**alloy/blend; compound; mixture**. Many solids are compounds formed by chemical reactions such as plastics. The smallest part of a compound that still retains the properties of that compound is the molecule. Usually molecules contain various atoms with definite ratios of one atom or another.

An element is one of the 109 presently known kinds of substances that comprise all matter at and above sea level. All the atoms of a given element are identical in nuclear charge and number of electrons and protons, but they may differ in mass, i.e., hydrogen has mass numbers of 1, 2, and 3 called hydrogen, deuterium, and tritium, respectively. The atomic number of an element indicates its position in the Periodic Table and represents the number of atoms present, which is the same as the number of electrons.

element strongly negative They are called nonmetallic and have a tendency to acquire electrons.

element strongly positive They are termed metallic and have a tendency to give up electrons.

Ellis model A model describing the flow behavior of a non-Newtonian fluid. The model predicts Newtonian behavior when the viscosity is at zero shear rate.

Elmendorf tear test A very common test to assess the tear resistance of a film material, in which a specimen containing an edge slit is clamped with one movable clamp attached to a pendulum (which is sometimes a sector of a wheel). On release of the pendulum from its raised position, it tears the specimen and the force (energy) expended in this tear action is recorded by a pointer reading on a scale on the dial of the pendulum. This rapid rate of shear is measured in grams per mil of film thickness (1 mil = 25.4 microns) per ASTM D 1922.

elongation The elongation or extensibility of a material is the amount of increase in length resulting from, as an example, the tension to break a specimen. It is expressed usually as a percentage of the original length. Elongation, tensile strength, and other tensile properties are determined simultaneously. Elongation is also identified as the strain or stretch of a material. ▷**extensibility**

elongation between gauges Changes in length produced between fixed gauge points on the specimen by a load.

elongation, creep ▷**creep**

elongation, fatigue ▷**fatigue test**

elongation, maximum The elongation at the time of fracture, including both elastic and plastic deformation of the tensile specimen. It is also called ultimate elongation or break elongation.

elongation, melt flow ▷**melt flow elongation**

elongation, uniform The elongation determined when the maximum load is reached. Applies to materials whose cross section decreases uniformly along the gauge length up to maximum load.

elongation, ultimate Ultimate elongation corresponds to force at rupture. Also called elongation at rupture. ▷**tensile testing machine test rates**

embedding The terms embedding, casting, potting, molding, impregnation, and encapsulation are often used interchangeably. Generally, embedding implies complete encasement in some uniform external shape; most of the package consists of the embedment material. However, encapsulation is a coating and the part is normally dipped in a high viscosity or thixotropic plastic material to obtain a thin coating usually 0.25 to 12.7 mm thick. The primary protection is provided by a seal, which often imparts mechanical strength. The casting, mold, and assembly are designed to provide minimum internal stress as the plastic shrinks during curing. Potting is similar except that the shell (or container) is not separated from the finished part. Molding is a technique of embedment in which the part is encased in a plastic that flows into the mold under pressure. Impregnation is a specialized method of embedding used mainly for coils and transformers in which liquid plastic is forced into interstices of the component.

Embedment is a useful technique for the protection or decorating of a device or assembly. Components and circuits may be embedded in various types of plastics (liquids, granular, or powdered solids). Applications range from electrical insulation and protective packaging to mechanical devices. The major use is for electrical and electronic devices; provides protection from oxygen, moisture, temperature, electrical flashover, current leakage, salt spray, radiation, solvents, chemicals, microorganisms, mechanical shock, vibration, etc. Embedding materials include epoxies, silicones, polyurethanes, polyesters, polysulfides, and allylic plastics. These plastics incorporate many different fillers, extenders, flexibilizers or plasticizers, foams (epoxy, syntactic, polyurethane, expandable polystyrene, etc.), decorative embedments, and others to meet different performance requirements applicationwise and servicewise.

Characteristics during the embedding that can influence part performance are the stresses that develop between the components and the plastic during cure. Differentials between thermal expansion coefficients are a source of design and fabricating problems. Measures can be taken to eliminate the problem, such as use of flexible plastic systems, controlling plastic viscosity to permit ease of mixing and pouring, curing heat control, etc. The embedment of large components has the risk of runaway exotherms. Excessive stresses and even cracking throughout the casting may result from temperature variations causing localized shrinkage. High temperatures caused by exotherm may volatilize the curing agents and modifiers, causing bubble entrapment.

embossing Technique creates permanent depressions of a specific pattern or texture on thermoplastic films or sheeting. Heat and pressure are applied simultaneously to the material. In pressure embossing, a raised metal surface is forced into the warm plastic which is then cooled to retain the engraving. Vacuum embossing is used where textures deeper than the thickness of the plastic are desired. It is done by preheating the plastic and then drawing it by vacuum against a mold or engraved design containing holes for suction (similar to thermo forming). The plastic is cooled and the shape is retained. This process may be carried out by batch process or continuous roll process inline with extruders and calenders or offline in an unwind, emboss, and rewind operation.

embrittlement Hardening of a plastic or a metal (especially steel) results in loss of strength and impairment of other physical properties. In metals, the primary cause is exposure to hydrogen, though other causes such as corrosion also are involved. With certain plastics, such as ABS, embrittlement is due to formation of a vitreous matrix as well as to environmental oxidation of the butadiene particles in the matrix.

emissivity The ratio of the total heat radiating power of a surface to that of a black body of the same area and of the same temperature.

emission spectroscopy Study of the composition of substances and identification of elements by observation of the wavelengths of radiation they emit as they return to a normal state after excitation by an external energy source. When atoms or molecules are excited by energy input from an arc, or flame, they respond in a characteristic manner; their identity and composition are signaled by the wavelengths of incident light they emit. The spectra of elements are in the form of lines of distinctive color. The number of these lines present in an emission spectrum depends on the number and position of the outermost electrons and the degree of excitation of the atoms.

emission standard ▷ **finishing system, reduce solvent**

emittance The ratio of the radiant flux emitted by a specimen to that emitted by a blackbody at the same temperature and under the same conditions.

empirical formula ▷ **formula, chemical**

emulsifier A substance that modifies the surface tension of colloidal droplets, keeping them from coalescing, and keeping them suspended.

emulsifying agent A substance that increases the stability of an emulsion.

emulsifying agent, latex A surface-active substance used to facilitate the dispersion of an immiscible liquid compounding material in another liquid and to stabilize the emulsion thereby produced.

emulsion A suspension of globules or fine droplets of one liquid in another. Can also include the suspension of solids such as plastics and waxes in liquids. Technically, it is a stable dispersion of one liquid in another, generally by means of an emulsifying agent which has affinity for both continuous and discontinuous phases. There is strong evidence that the emulsifying agent, discontinuous phase, and continuous phase together can produce another phase which serves as an enveloping (encapsulating) protective phase around the discontinuous phase.

emulsion polymerization This is a technique in which additional polymerizations are carried out in a water medium containing an emulsifier (a soap) and a water-soluble initiator. It is used because emulsion polymerization is much more rapid than bulk or solution polymerization at the same temperatures and produces plastics with molecular weights much greater than those obtained at the same rate in bulk polymerization. The reaction in the emulsion type takes place within a small hollow sphere composed of a film of soap molecules, called miscelle. Monomer diffuses into these miscelles and control of the soap concentration, overall reaction-mass recipe, and reaction conditions provide additional controls over the reaction.

Polymerization techniques can have significant effect on the number, size, and characteristics of the plastic molecules formed and will thus have a significant effect on the properties of the plastic. Thus, batches of a plastic such as polystyrene, which can be made by any of four polymerization techniques, will differ depending on which type of polymerization method was used to make the material. ▷ **polymerization** and **reactor technology**

encapsulation The terms encapsulation, casting, embedding, potting, conformal, molding, impregnation and embedding are often used interchangeably. Basically encapsulating is enclosing a part (such as an electronic component, decorative article, etc.) in a closed envelope of plastic, by immersing the object in a casting plastic and allowing the plastic to polymerize or, if hot, to cool. ▷ **microencapsulation, coating**

end **1.** A strand of roving consisting of a given number of filaments gathered together. **2.** The group of filaments is considered an end, or strand, before twisting, and a yarn after twist has been applied. **3.** An individual warp yarn thread, thread, fiber, or roving.

end count An exact number of ends supplied on a ball or roving.

endothermic A process or change that takes place with absorption of heat and requires high temperature for initiation and maintenance as with using heat to melt plastics and then remove heat; as opposed to exothermic. ▷ **ablative plastic** and **exotherm**

endothermic analysis ▷ **thermal analysis**

endurance limit A measure of load-carrying ability of a material subjected to infinitely repeated loading or cycling. A special limiting value of fatigue strength for some materials. The maximum alternating stress amplitude that can be sustained by a material subjected to a specified mean stress for an infinite number of cycles without failure. It is obtained from the S-N Diagram in the fatigue test and is equal to the constant stress corresponding to that portion (if any) of the curve which is parallel or asymptotic to the "N" axis. Endurance limit has no real meaning for a material that does not exhibit the type of S-N curve described above. Actually the term is often used as an alternate for fatigue strength for such materials, but number of cycles actually tested should be specified. ▷ **fatigue endurance limit; fatigue S-N diagram**

endurance strength ▷ **strength, fatigue**

energy The joule (J) is the work done when the point of application of a force of one newton (N) is displaced a distance of one meter in the direction of the force (N·m).

energy absorption A term that is both general and specific. Generally, it refers to the energy absorbed by any material subjected to loading. Specifically it is a measure of toughness or impact strength of a material; the energy needed to fracture a specimen in an impact test. It is the difference in kinetic energy of the striker before and after impact, expressed as total energy (ft-lb or in.-lb) for metals and ceramics, and energy per inch of notch for plastic and electrical insulating materials. A higher energy absorption indicates a greater toughness. For notched specimens, energy absorption is an indication of the effect of internal multiaxial stress distribution on fracture behavior of the material. It is merely a qualitative index and cannot be used directly in design. Notch behavior of most metals can be deduced from results of the tension test, but notch behavior of ferritic steels is not predictable. Transition temperature, derived from a series of energy absorption measurements, is commonly specified for such materials. Energy absorption is quite sensitive to variations in materials and in test conditions, especially temperature, striking speed and energy, and specimen size and shape. Only results for identical specimens and notches may safely be compared.

energy conservation Energy conservation in the plastic industry can be considered from several view points (going from producing plastic material, processing into products, and products performance in service). In practically all evaluations, utilization of plastics saves or re-

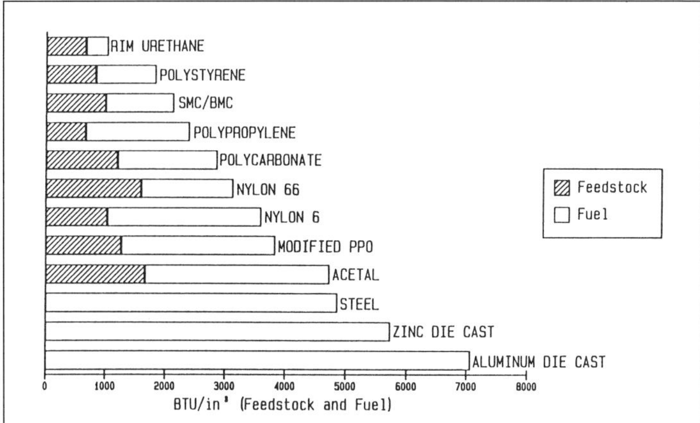

Structural part energy consumption of different materials.

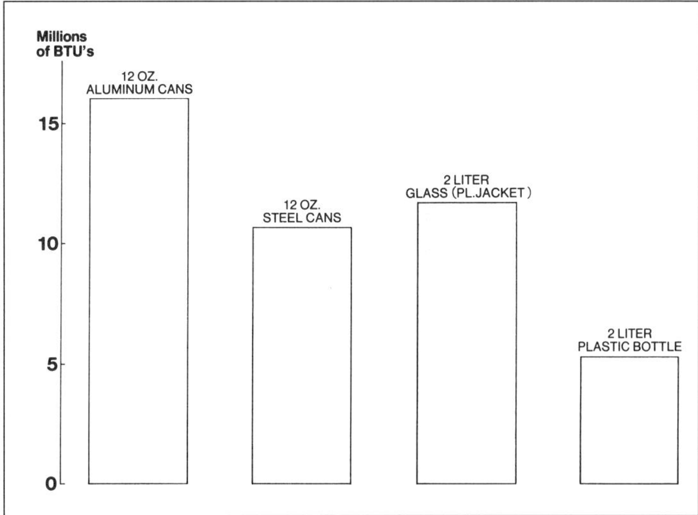

Total energy required to deliver 1,000 litres of beverage.

duces energy requirements. In automobiles, aircraft, and other means of transportation the increasing use of plastics reduces weight and fuel consumption (a well-known example is replacement in aircraft of the small whiskey glass bottles by plastic bottles). Using plastics in U.S. construction instead of nonplastic alternatives saved 467×10^{12} btu in 1988; amount of energy equivalent to 79,000,000 barrels of oil (SPI report 1992). ▷**foundry plastic**

energy consumption and pollution Opponents of plastics point to the fact that they are made from petroleum, a non-renewable resource. However, most of the plastics familiar to American consumers are manufactured from ethylene. During the distillation of petroleum, the ethylene fraction comes off as a byproduct which used to be burned for its energy value in refinery processes. Today, this waste gas is the building block for many plastics.

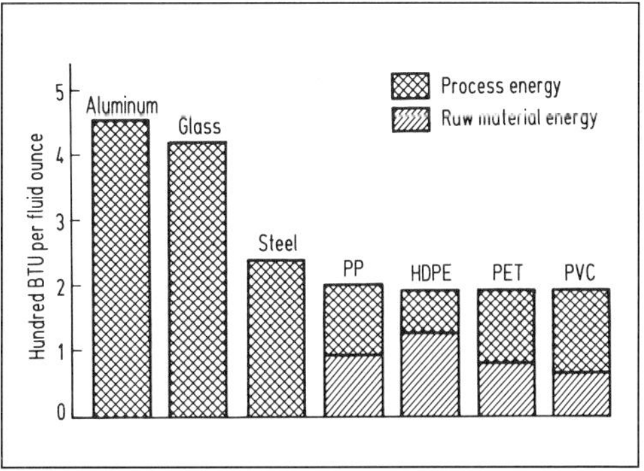

Total energy required to produce equivalent of 24 oz container.

The plastics industry consumes roughly two percent of total annual petroleum consumption by the U.S. See Figs. here and Table on p. 228.

energy consumption, different materials

Examples of energy consumption of packaging materials.

Btus/lb	Paper	Glass	Steel	Aluminum	Plastic
Btus required to make originally	20,000	8,700	22,800	120,000	35,950
Btus required to recycle into new container	11,500	6,525	15,960	19,100	1,000
Btus recovered by burning	8,500	0	0	0	17,875

This use is more than offset by the savings that plastics create. A study conducted for the British Plastics Federation determined that:

- Plastics in the average motorist's car cuts fuel consumption by nearly 5% and contributes to improved safety performance.
- Plastics packaging has helped reduce food spoilage in the industrialized world to around 2%. Developing countries have a spoilage rate of between 30 to 50%.
- Plastics neither rot nor rust and applications continue to increase. Witness the increased use of plastic lumber.
- Best of all—plastics can be recycled.

In a cradle to grave analysis, conducted by Franklin Associates, that compared plastic bottles to aluminum and glass for the delivery of 1,000 gallons of soft drink, the study found that plastic out-performed glass and aluminum in all categories. The study compared the materials on the basis of energy consumption, air emissions, waterborne wastes and solid wastes produced. ▷ **recycling, energy consumption** and **oil and gas**

energy consumption, different materials In comparison with other materials, plastics have the lowest specific energy requirement for their manufacture (also lowest recycling energy consumption). The Table below shows values for the energy requirement of finished (packaging and utensils) products of various materials. These guideline values have plastics emerging with the advantage. These values cannot be used to calculate ecological balances for individual products. For each product the requirements differ from one material to another as a result of design variations, so that different quantities of raw materials are needed in each product. ▷ **British thermal unit** and **recycling, energy consumption**

energy due to friction A major problem faced by engineers and most industries through the years has been how to prevent loss of useful energy due to friction. It is estimated that of all energy produced throughout the world, as much as one-third to one-half is wasted because of friction. ▷ **friction** and **bearings, ball type**

energy in solid waste ▷ **British thermal unit**

energy, kinetic ▷ **kinetic energy dissipated**

energy loss The energy per unit volume that is lost in each deformation loading cycle. Energy loss is in the hysteresis loop area, calculated with reference to the coordinate scales.

energy, plastic work ▷ **plastic work**

energy thermal reclamation Plastics are suitable for thermal reclamation (recycling) because their energy content or heat value is mostly higher than that of coal. Often it is of the order of heating oil. For this reason it is rational to

Estimated guideline values for estimating the specific energy requirements of different materials used for packaging and utensils.

Materials	Energy requirement E MJ/kg	Recovered heat to be subtracted H MJ/kg	Net requirement $E-H$ (theoretical) MJ/kg	Net requirement $E-H$ (theoretical) MJ/l	Requirement relative to PE (approx.)	Specific energy requirement per functional unit MJ/l of material
Polyethylene (PE)	70–85	43	27–42	35	1.0	35
Polystyrene (PS)	80–90	40	40–50	47	1.0	47
Polyvinylchloride (PVC)	57–61	18	39–43	45	0.8	36
Paper	60–75	18	45–57	31	3.3	102
Glass	10	–	10	25	5–8	125–200
Iron/steel	20–25	–	20–25	172	0.3	52
Aluminum	115–140	–	115–140	344	0.3	103
Tin-plate	30	–	30	235	0.6	140

reuse plastic wastes that are not suitable for material or chemical reclamation thermally. Especially in waste incineration plants, energy is obtained in the form of community heat and electrical power. Most plastics can be incinerated without problems and with a low (controllable and confining) emission of pollutants. Only for halogenated plastics such as PVC, special available care and systems can be used to permit incineration. ▷ **incineration fume system**

Engel coating process This process is used for coating starting with a cold mold filled with plastic powder, for example polyethylene. The mold is closed, usually with a heat insulating cover. The mold is placed in an oven operating from 260° to 400°C (500° to 750°F). The higher temperatures are normally preferred. (According to the patent, the mold is not rotated.) The plastic close to the inner mold wall melts and fuses into a continuous layer. The thickness of the fused layer is determined by oven temperature, heating time, and to some extent, the density and melt index of the plastic.

The hot mold is removed from the oven, the cover detached, and the unmelted, excess powder is dumped out. The mold is returned to the oven without its insulating cover for a period of time necessary to remove bubbles and smooth the inner surface of the molded part. The mold is removed from the oven and cooled either by immersion in water or by spray. The completed part is removed from the mold.

engine ▷ **automotive plastic engine**

engineer The modern engineer is a problem solver thrust into society's challenges, and called upon to bridge theory and application, and science and technology, meeting the world's needs without despoiling the environment. The engineer is expected to evaluate the problem, with all the implied scientific abstractions, and subsequently generate a technically feasible and economically sound solution. (Of course, the engineer has other functions and services.)

engineering and materials ▷ **materials and engineering** and **design theory and strength of material**

engineering approach and practical approach With the practical approach, most plastic products are required only to withstand static mechanical loads (that is, no dynamic loads). Thus, conventional short-term static tests generally suffice. The engineering approach recognizes that many plastic products have been used since its inception to take long-term static and/or dynamic loads based on varying environmental conditions such as temperature; thus consider creep, fatigue, stress, and other data. The engineering design is based on plastic's behavior, such as its viscoelastic properties.

engineering design The area of engineering which involves the application of graphic principles and practices to the solution of engineering problems. It is the systematic process by which a solution to a problem is created. A definition that contains the necessary ideas and speaks broadly of design follows: Engineering design is an iterative, decision-making activity whereby scientific and technological information is used to produce a product or system, which is different, in some degree, from what the designer knows to have been done before and which is meant to meet new needs.

engineering design risk ▷ **acceptable risk**

engineering drawing A detailed set of instructions that tells the user how to make a part to the shape, size, and dimensions specified. ▷ **allowance; tolerance; limit clearance fit; computer drawing**

engineering judgement ▷ **design analysis**

engineering material Overall industrywise, a metal, plastic, or other material used in fabrication of machinery and its components, structural shapes, tools, instruments, tanks, piping, etc. They are characterized by strength, dimensional stability, hardness, machinability, nonflammability, and resistance to corrosion, most acids, solvents, and heat.

engineering materials, the solid state Engineering materials are depicted as solids formed from various elements ▷ **element** and **molecule**. A solid can be a pure element such as gold, a compound such as sand of silicon and oxygen (SiO_2), or a combination of molecules such as plastics. Solids are formed when definite bonds exist between component atoms or molecules. In the liquid or gaseous state, atoms or molecules are not bonded to each other. The bonds that hold atoms or molecules together can be very specific and orderly or they can be less defined. Solids of the former type have a crystalline structure; those that do not have a repetitive three-dimensional pattern of molecules (atoms) are said to be amorphous.

engineering plastic ▷ **commodity plastic and engineering plastic**

engineering problems ▷ **theory and strength of materials**

engineering problem solving ▷ **statistical method**

engine, technology Engine technology phrase identifies and provides means for the varied technologies to work together. For example, the computer and communication protocol that allows them to exchange information among each other.

English to metric conversion See *Conversion Tables* on pp. xxiii ff.

engraved-roll coating This coating method is also called gravure coating. The amount of coating applied to the web (film) is metered by the depth of the overall engraved pattern in a print roll. This process is frequently modified by interposing a resilient offset roll between the engraved roll and the web.

engraving pantographically ▷ **pantographic engraving**

enthalpimetric analysis EPA (thermal analysis) includes the titrimetric and calorimetric modes. It utilizes the temperature change in a system while a titrant is gradually added or measures the thermal energy released during a controlled reaction of the specimen.

enthalpy The quantity of heat, equal to the sum of the internal energy of a system plus the product of the pressure-volume work done on the system such as the action during heat processing of plastics. As a thermodynamic function, it is defined by the equation $H = U + PV$, where H is the enthalpy, U is the internal energy, P is the pressure, and V is the volume of the system. ▷ **thermoelastic effect** and **design mold**

entrapped air ▷ **air entrapment**

entropy A measure of the unavailable energy in a thermodynamic system, commonly expressed in terms of its exchanges on an arbitrary scale, the entropy of water at 0°C (32°F) being zero. The increase in entropy of a body is equal to the amount of heat absorbed divided by the absolute temperature of the body. ▷ **thermodynamic property**

envelope material The envelope is a special type of flat bag, usually sealed on three sides, with a fold over flap on the open side. Variations include open end, gusseted sides, reusable closures, and special features with die-cut windows and integral cushioning. Materials used include the usual Kraft paper, manila paper, and plastics. Plastic types are PE, PP, PMMA, CA, PA, etc. Popular cushioning material is spun bonded polyethylene ("Tyvek").

envenomation The process by which the surface of a plastic close to or in contact with another surface is deteriorated. Softening, discoloration, mottling, crazing, or other effects may occur (ASTM D 883).

environment The aggregate of all conditions that externally influence the performance of an item. Conditions include contamination, temperature, humidity, radiation, magnetic and electric fields, shock and vibration. ▷ **waste**

environmental assessment A written analysis, usually by a private consulting firm, prepared under the National Environmental Policy Act to determine if an action would affect the environment, requiring a more detailed statement on environment impact.

environmental consideration for bearing ▷ **bearings, ball type**

environmental earth protection ▷ **geomembrane liner**

environmental impact statement A document describing positive and negative effects of an action, required of federal agencies for projects or legislative proposals that would significantly affect the environment.

environmental risk ▷ **acceptable risk**

environmental stress cracking ESC is the susceptibility of a thermoplastic part to crack or craze formation under the influence of certain chemicals, aging, weather, and/or stress. An ESC test is the bent-strip type (ASTM D 1693). It is conducted on molded specimens $\frac{1}{8}$ in. (3.2 mm) thick, $1\frac{1}{2}$ in. (38.1 mm) long, and $\frac{1}{2}$ in. (12.7 mm). The specimens are first heated in boiling water to relax frozen-in stresses. A surface cut of specified length and depth is then made on the sample parallel to the long axis with a mounted razor blade. The specimens are then stressed by bending them 180°, lining them up in a rack, and placing them in a test tube containing the reagent. To accelerate the effect of the cracking agent, the test tube is placed in a bath kept at a temperature of 50°C (122°F). At short intervals, the specimens are inspected for visual cracks perpendicular to the cuts. At each inspection the number of failures are recorded. A sample under the test is considered to have failed when half of the specimens show cracks perpendicular to the cuts. ▷ **stress whitening**

environment and color ▷ **colorant**

environment and ocean From ships to submarines to mining at sea bottom, certain plastics can survive sea environments that are considered more hostile than those on earth or in space. In regard to surface vehicles many

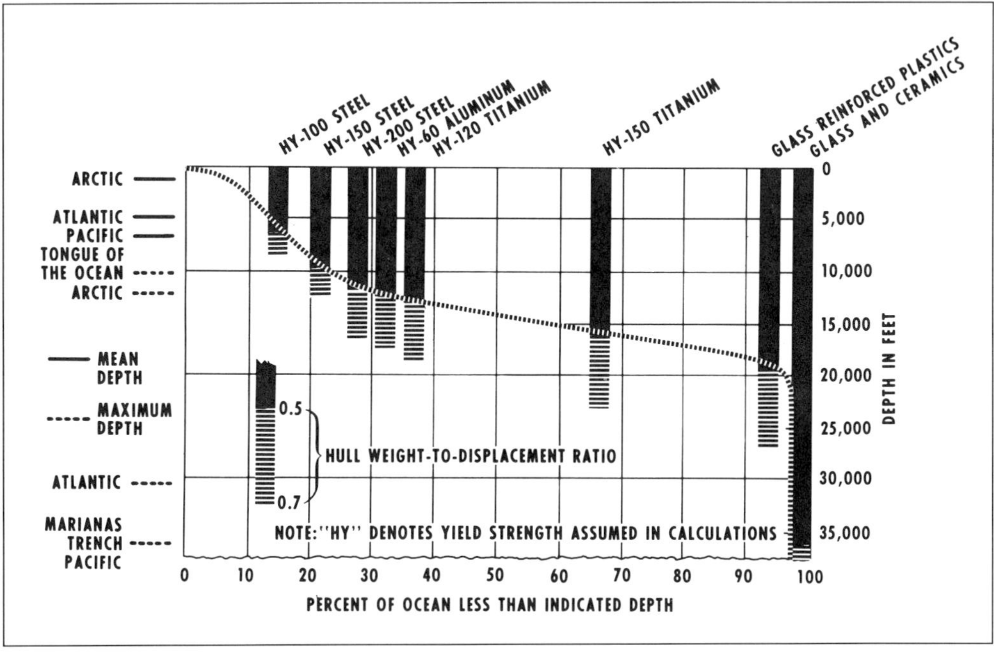

Design approach in analyzing use of different materials in an underwater structure.

different plastics have been used successfully in fresh and sea water (see Fig. above).

environment and public opinion The strength of public opinion is a very strong "weapon" and unfortunately can fit the old phrase: Do not give me the facts, my mind is made up. This was the case when McDonald's decided in November 1990 to drop its ubiquitous polystyrene foamed clamshell hot food container; it made a last minute switch only days before it was to have announced nationwide recycling of foam. What happened was unbelievable but public opinion had to win. McDonald's had just commissioned an independent scientist to study all the environmental charges against PS. The findings: PS is the bost possible packaging material from an environmental and economic perspective. McDonald's consistently had been a leader in developing plastics recycling and plastics re-use programs. No matter what positive steps McDonald's took, however, it was still a victim of senseless attacks by environmental groups. A few days prior to its announcement on the clamshell, a group called the Earth Action Network broke the windows and scattered supplies at a McDonald's restaurant in San Francisco as an environmental protest. In Massachusetts, sixth and seventh graders were given flyers at a school-sponsored event encouraging them to stage plastic-burning news conferences in front of fast-food restaurants.

The environmental groups' actions had almost taken on a McCarthy-like tone in their use of nasty public opinions and relations tactics and "refusal to acknowledge facts". To ordinary citizens it appeared that McDonald's had finally seen the light. The new container would insulate as well, open and close as easily, and be as resistant to grease. What counted in the minds of most people was that the clamshells attack the ozone layer (neither CFCs nor HCFCs were used in making them), resist degradation (this was irrelevant in landfills), and flood the waste stream (they were a fraction of a percent by weight). Many of these environmentalists truly believed they were right. Somehow in their minds the substitution of nonrecyclable paper goods for actively recycled plastic made sense. They also ignored the fact that paper requires more energy to produce than plastic, and that paper products are bulkier, resulting in even more nondegradable waste going into dumps.

Low-key logic is not going to win these type battles. Consumer products companies like McDonald's, Procter & Gamble, and others will take whatever steps are required to keep their products on the shelves, no matter who wins the intellectual argument. Perhaps, though, the McDonald's switch is more than a public-relations ploy. The company said that it was serious about composting and that its action was the first in a long-term strategy of redesigning both containers and the systems for disposing of them. Thus, the appropriate plastics industry response was to come up with similar forward-looking programs, including alternatives to recycling. But surely this is no reason to abandon recycling. ▷ **recycling** and **environment, life, plastic, ecology**

environment and space ▷ **space and environment**

environment and waste ▷ **waste and environment**

environment and water ways ▷ **bottled standard reference material**

environment, life, plastic, ecology Without the consumption of energy and materials and without generating waste products, human life does not exist. Nature, too, knows no such form of life. Life results from a process involving the formation of non-equilibrium structures, which is driven by a flow of energy from a source (sun) to a sink (earth). In this process waste products, such as helium that is formed in the sun, also appear. On the earth, too, there are waste products that are no longer needed by nature, or which she puts into "temporary storage"; examples are deposits of CO_2 in the form of calcareous rocks, chalks, and dolomites, organic matter in the form of peat, coal, oil, natural gas, and inorganic matter in the form of sediments and mineral deposits.

Natural life forms are sometimes destructive; cormorants kill the trees in which they nest within a few years; gannets destroy the chance for life on rocks on which they breed; in both cases the cause is the excrement left by birds. The growth and decay of population in many species (grasshoppers, etc.) shows wild fluctuations, with irregular steep rises and falls, caused by the animals destroying their means of subsistance by excessive multiplication. Such catastrophes are an integral part of ecological regualatory mechanisms, which are by no means gentle in the way they work. However, the human race has continually been engaged in destroying ecological control mechanisms, and thereby its own life support system. It is not possible to have an environmentally gentle industry. However, we need to find a lifestyle and a manufacturing style which allows the ecological mechanisms to remain effective.

There is an increasingly committed level of public discussion about the protection of the environment and of nature. Regrettably, however, the need to simplify complex situations often results in these being reduced to short descriptions that are easy to convey, and this can lead to wrong conclusions lacking in objectivity. The usual discussions on problems of waste are of low priority in worldwide terms, although by no means unimportant. World problems include in order of urgency: (1) protect nature and living species for the functioning of earth's ecosystem; (2) climate of CO_2, ozone, rain forest; (3) soil versus poisoning, buildings, erosion; (4) energy of fossil fuel depletion, climate, nuclear waste storage; (5) drinking water and marine pollution; (6) acid rain; (7) raw materials shortage; and (8) wastes. Although the problem of wastes must be solved, an objective appraisal shows that this aim is merely a cosmetic one unless it is accompanied by radical measures for the protection of nature and the other items listed above. Of course other so-called high priority items have to include world hunger and wars. Regarding plastics and waste ▷ **waste, plastic; energy; oil consumption; recycled plastic; thermal insulation; water purification; corrosion; pollution; polyester thermoplastic and the environment; polyvinyl chloride plastic and environment**

Enviropet packaging This package trade name from Continental Can Co. is for the Heinz catsup squeeze bottles that are easy to recycle. It is a biaxial stretched coinjection blow molding using a 5-layer construction (PE/barrier/PET/barrier/PET).

enzyme Enzyme polymers are the catalysts of the living cell and because microorganisms are able to synthesize thousands of complex organic molecules, they represent an enormous catalytic potential to the industrial chemist. A remarkable aspect of enzymes is their enormous catalytic power; they can enhance reaction rates by a factor of from 10^8 to 10^{20}. Also they can function in dilute aqueous solution under moderate conditions of temperature and pH.

epichlorohydrin rubber ECHR (or CO) is the basic epoxidizing plastic intermediate in the production of epoxy plastics; use includes seals, gaskets, and wire covering. It contains an epoxy group and is highly reactive with polyhydric phenols such as bisphenol A. Suitable to −40°C (−40°F), high T_g, good flame resistance, etc. Owing to continually rising specifications with regard to the resistance of fuels, ozone, weathering, and permeation by liquids, there has been a dramatic increase in the use of this rubber (CO, ECO) blend, especially for hoses. Because of the low permeability of CO and ECO, these materials have largely replaced NBR in blends used for fuel hoses.

epitaxy The oriented growth of a crystalline substance on a substratum of the same or different crystalline substance.

epoxy molding compound Compounds are mineral filled epoxy powders which can be molded in compression or transfer molding presses.

epoxy plastic The family of epoxy thermoset resins (EPs) includes epichlorohydrin with bisphenol-A. These most widely used epoxies range from low-viscosity liquids to high-molecular-weight solids. The novolacs are another important class that offer higher thermal properties and improved chemical resistance. The cycloaliphatic types also are important, for applications requiring high resistance to arc tracking and weathering.

Epoxies are more expensive than other equivalent plastics, such as the TS polyesters, but they outperform these materials because of their improved performance. Their general properties include toughness, having less shrinkage during curing, good weatherability, low moisture absorption, curing without the evolution of by-products, good wetting and adhesion to a wide variety of surfaces, good mechanical properties and thermal capabilities, excellent fatigue resistance, outstanding electrical properties from low to high temperatures, exceptional water resistance, practically complete resistance to fungus, general corrosion resistance, and other such characteristics.

The variety of combinations available in epoxies and reinforcements provides wide latitude in the properties of fabricated parts. Some fiber-reinforced and composite materials can withstand service temperatures even above 260°C (500°F) for brief periods. Their excellent electrical and mechanical performance qualifies them for use in many electro-structural parts.

The EPs are used in all the methods of processing plastics. Filled and liquid systems are used for potting and encapsulating electronic and other components, producing excellent adhesion. The casting cycle can be significantly accelerated by using liquid or reaction-injection molding. Another important use for epoxies is in coatings, both as liquids and powders. Such finishes have excellent flexibility, impact and abrasion resistance, are decorative and corrosion resistant, and so on. They adhere to most substrates of plastic, steel, aluminum, and other materials. And they are exceptional adhesives to bond similar or different materials of plastic, steel, aluminum, wood, or glass.

equation A formal statement of the equality or equivalence of mathematical or logical expressions.

equation, cross A cross equation is an empirical equation for the shear rate dependence of the apparent viscosity of a plastic fluid.

equator ▷ **filament winding**

equilibrium centrifugation ▷ **molecular weight distribution resinography**

equilibrium diagram ▷ **alloy constitutional diagram**

equipment ▷ **auxiliary equipment; machine; fabricating processes**

equipment customized Equipment designed and manufactured to meet certain specific requirements.

equipment-economic control ▷ **economic control of equipment**

equipment financing ▷ **capital equipment investment** and **financing equipment**

equipment lubrication ▷ **lubrication for processing equipment**

ergonomic Literally, the science of work. Ergonomic is the key to designing a better workplace; situations where tools, task, and user come together with a minimum of stress.

erosion ▷ **cavitation erosion; rain erosion; corrosion; spalling**

erosion, brittle behavior Erosion behavior having characteristic properties that can be associated with brittle fracture of the exposed surface, particularly with metals. Little or no plastic flow occurs, but cracks form that eventually intersect to create erosion fragments. In solid impingement an easily observable aspect of erosion helps to distinguish brittle from ductile behavior. This is a manner in which volume removal varies with the angle of attack. With brittle erosion the maximum volume removal occurs at an angle near 90°, in contrast to about 25° for ductile erosion behavior.

erosion-electrical breakdown ▷ **electrical erosion breakdown**

error The substitution of one character for another.

error of the first kind The rejection of a statistical hypothesis when it is true.

error of the second kind The acceptance of a statistical hypothesis when it is false.

ester Reaction products of alcohols or phenols with acids in a process known as esterification. Transesterification is the term employed for the conversion of one ester into another by interchange of the ester alkyl group and the alkyl group of an appropriate alcohol.

ester gum A plastic (also called resin) made from rosin or rosin acids and a polyhydric alcohol, such as glycerin or pentaerythritol.

estimation In statistical analysis, a procedure for making a statistical inference about the numerical values of one or more unknown population parameters from the observed values in a sample.

etching Controlled preferential attack on a surface of material. ▷ **chemical etching**

ethenic plastic The term ethenic comes from the fact that this family of plastics has the basic monomer structure of (as an example) ethylene, a carbon-to-carbon double bond ($H_2C = CH_2$). A series of plastics with greatly different characteristics can be obtained by altering a monomer structure by removing a hydrogen atom and substituting another functional atom or group of atoms (substitute group). Thus, a family of ethenic plastics is formed.

ether-oxide plastic The common name of a number of industrially important plastics specifically include the words ether or oxide, which reflects the presence of an ether or oxygen linkage (-O-) in the backbone of the repeat unit. Plastics include acetal, polyethyleneoxide, polypropyleneoxide, polyphenyleneoxide, and polyphenyleneether.

ethics Although there is no substitute for individual action based on a firm philosophical and ethical foundation, designers, processors, etc. have developed guidelines for professional conduct based on the experience of many of them who have had to wrestle with troublesome ethical questions and situations previously. These guidelines can be found in the published codes of ethics for designers and engineers of a number of industry and technical societies.

ethyl cellulose plastic A plastic based on polymers of ethylene or copolymers of ethylene with other monomers, the ethylene being in greatest amount by mass. EC is characterized by toughness over a wide temperature range, dimensional stability, and freedom from odor. Its use includes helmets, gears, slides, flashlight housings, and particularly tool handles. ▷ **cellulose, ethyl**

ethylene A colorless, flammable gas derived by cracking of petroleum and natural gas feedstocks. This monomer is polymerized into many different and important olefin polymers (plastics) such as the different types of polyethylene, polypropylene, etc. The demand for polyethylene worldwide moves in concert with economic activity. Demand cycles are more pronounced for LDPE, LLDPE, and HDPE. The decline in global ethylene demand reflects the 1975, 1982, 1985, and 1990 recessions, cycles that have become the "fingerprints" of the industry.

ethylene acid copolymer plastic EAA is the copolymerization of ethylene with acrylic or methacrylic acid to produce an ethylene copolymer containing carboxyl groups distributed along the backbone and side chains of the molecule. These carboxyl groups reduce polymer crystallinity, which improves optics, lowers the temperature required to heat seal, and adds functionality to provide adhesion to polar substrates. By varying the comonomer content and molecular weight, a range of products can be tailored to produce films, extrusion coatings, adhesives, and alkali-dispersible grades of plastics. ▷ **polyethylene plastic**

ethylene-acrylate copolymer rubber EARS are copolymers of ethylene (E) and methylacrylate containing carboxylic side groups (COOH) as cure sites; provide high resistance to ozone; better energy absorbers than butyl rubbers. There are also different rubber copolymers of ethylene acrylates identified as EEA or EMA which have relatively small amounts of ethylacrylate or methylacrylate, a way of reducing the crystallinity and introducing polarity, which increases flexibility, environmental stress-cracking resistance, compatibility with fillers and other plastics. Alloys of polyethylacrylate and polymethylacrylate.

ethylene acrylic plastic This family of rubbers, Du Pont's Vamac being perhaps best known, are moderately priced, heat and fluid resistant, and surpassed only by the expensive specialty types such as the fluorocarbons and fluorosilicones. A special feature of the ethylene/acrylics (EAMs) is their nearly constant damping characteristic over a broad range of temperatures, frequencies, and amplitudes. They have good resistance to hot oils and hydrocarbon- or glycol-based proprietary lubricants as well as to transmission and power-steering fluids. EAMs are not recommended, however, for use with esters, ketones, or high-pressure steam.

ethylene-carboxylic acid copolymer plastic EAA or EMAA has relatively small amounts of acrylic acid (AA) or methylacrylic acid (MAA) repeat units that feature carboxyl groups (COOH). Particularly noted for their outstanding adhesion. Tackiness, as well as a tendency to corrode metals and to crosslink, require special precautions in processing. They are modified to form such materials as ionomers, polyacrylic acid, and polymethylacrylic.

ethylene-chlorotrifluoroethylene plastic ECTFE is a predominantly 1:1 alternating copolymer of ethylene and chlorotrifluorethylene, forming linear chains with repeating unit. It has a melting point of 240°C (464°F) and a density of 1.68. The material has useful properties from cryogenic temperatures to 166°C (330°C). Its strength, wear resistance, and creep resistance are significantly greater than those for PTFE, FEP, and PFA. ECTFE is resistant to most corrosive chemicals and organic solvents at room and elevated temperatures. Dielectric constant (2.6) is low and stable over a wide temperature and frequency range. It resists ignition and flame propagation. Upon exposure to flame it decomposes to a carbonaceous char. About 70% of the production of this melt processable copolymer goes into insulation and coating of cables and lines. It is also used in the form of powder coatings and sheet linings in chemical plant construction (about 30%).

ethylene-ethyl acrylate plastic EEA is one of the copolymers of LDPE such as ethylene-methacrylate (EMA) and ethylene-vinyl acetate (EVA). EEA is similar in structure to EMA. Its superior heat resistance, flex-resistance, and low temperature flexibility make it a desirable choice for electrical cable compounds. As a film, it is not as transparent as EVA.

ethylene glycol Clear, colorless, syrupy liquid, hygroscopic, soluble in water and alcohol material. Used as coolant and antifreeze. Most popular use is in automobile radiators. ▷**glycol**

ethylene-methacrylate plastic EMA copolymers are similar to EVAs, but exhibit a greater thermal stability in extrusion and produce a softer film. Thus, EMAs are found in medical packaging, disposable gloves, upholstery wraps, and cable compounding.

ethylene plastics A plastic based on polymers of ethylene or copolymers of ethylene with other monomers, the ethylene being in the greatest amount by mass. Usually called polyethylene. ▷**polyethylene**

ethylene-propylene copolymer plastic [P(E-P)] is a very small proportion of polypropylene (PP) type repeat units that can be used to lower the crystallinity of linear polyethylene. When large amounts of comonomer are used, two commercially important copolymers result: polyallomers and EP rubbers.

ethylene propylene plastic Like the butyls, there are basically two types of ethylene propylene. One is a fully saturated chemically inert copolymer of ethylene and propylene (EPR). The other, called EPDM, has the ethylene and the propylene, plus diene monomer. EPDM is chemically reactive and capable of sulfur vulcanization. The copolymer, EPR, is cured with a peroxide catalyst.

The physical properties of EPR and EPDM are not as good as those obtainable with NR. Nevertheless, their property retention is better than that of NR on exposure to heat, oxidation, or ozone. Their bonding is somewhat more difficult, however, especially with EPR. They have a broad resistance to chemicals, but not to oils and other hydrocarbons. Their electrical properties are good.

ethylene-propylene rubber EPRs are unsaturated, have excellent ozone and weathering resistance and good heat aging. These are EP copolymers, referred to as EPR unsaturated. By incorporating the monomer diene D, allows conventional vulcanization and corresponds to EPDM rubbers; also sometimes referred to as EPT rubbers (terpolymers). EPR's limitations relate to low resistance to oils and fuels, poor adhesion to many substrates or reinforcements, and generally low compatibility with other rubbers.

ethylene-tetrafluoroethylene plastic ETFE is a predominantly 1:1 alternating copolymer of ethylene and tetrafluoroethylene forming linear chains that have repeating units. It is a tough material with high impact resistance and useful mechanical properties from cryogenic temperatures to 180°C (356°F). Chemical resistance, electrical properties, and weathering resistance are similar to those of ECTFE and approach those of fully fluorinated plastics. ETFE melts and decomposes upon exposure to flame.

ETFE translucent thermoplastic combines mechanical toughness with very good chemical and dielectric properties, weather resistance, continuous service temperature from about 190° to 155°C, and flame retardancy, and has a low density and better radiation resistance than PFTE. ▷**fluoroplastic**

ethylene-vinylacetate copolymer plastic A wide range of EVAs are available that correspond to vinylacetate contents up to 50%. Use includes films, as well as flexible molded or extruded products. When compared to PE, stiffness is reduced, and increases occur in water vapor permeability, oil and grease resistance, and cling (blocking) tendency.

ethylene-vinyl acetate plastic Ethylene-vinyl acetates (EVA) copolymers are in the polyolefin family of thermoplastics. They are used in all processes, particularly for extrusion, injection molding, and blow molding. They are used either alone or are coextruded or coinjected and used in compounds to provide unique properties. They approach elastomeric materials in their softness and flexibility.

EVA parts have good clarity and gloss, stress-crack resistance, barrier properties, low-temperature toughness, adhesion, resistance to UV radiation, little or no odor, and retain their flexibility at low temperatures. Their main limitation is their comparatively low resistance to heat and solvents. Chlorinated hydrocarbons, straight-chain paraffinic solvents, and benzene all attack EVAS' resins. However, alcohols, glycols, and weak organic acids do no damage. EVAS are used principally in specialty parts, competing with PVC and rubber. FDA approval exists for their use in direct contact with food. Some EVA products include medical tubing, tubing for beverage vending, milk-packaging and beer-dispensing equipment, appliance bumpers, blow-molded bellows for seals, gaskets, and toys, and in hot-melt adhesives.

ethylene-vinylalcohol copolymer plastic EVOHS find applications as barrier layers or as interlayers (tie layers) between poorly compatible materials. ▷ **polyvinyl alcohol**

ethylene-vinyl alcohol plastic By combining the processability of ethylene plastics with the barrier properties obtained from vinyl alcohol plastics, ethylene-vinyl alcohol copolymers offer not only excellent processabiltiy, but also superior barriers to gases, odors, fragrances, solvents, etc. These plastics are abbreviated EVOH. (EVAL is not used since it is the trade name for the EVAL company, producer of EVOH). It is these characteristics that have allowed plastic containers using EVOH barrier layers to replace many glass and metal containers for packaging food. They have a very high resistance to oils and organic solvents, rather high mechanical strength, elasticity, surface hardness, abrasion resistance, highly antistatic, and weatherability. EVOH is the most thermally stable of all the high-barrier plastics. This stability allows it to be reground and reused. Due to the presence of hydroxyl groups in their molecular structures, EVOHS are hydrophilic and will absorb moisture. As moisture is absorbed, the gas-barrier properties are affected. However, through the use of multilayer technology (coextrusion, coinjection, laminating) to encapsulate the EVOH plastic layer with high moisture-barrier plastics such as polyolefins, the moisture content of the EVOH is controlled, eliminating the problem.

ethylene-vinyl alcohol plastic recycled ▷ **ethylene-vinyl alcohol plastic**

ethyl terminated imidothioether plastic ETI have been prepared from the reaction of N-(3-ethynylphenyl) maleimide and aromatic dimercaptans. Blends of ETIS and ethynyl terminated arylene ether (ETAE) oligomers of various molecular weights were also prepared. The physical and mechanical properties of the cured blends followed a trend depending upon crosslink density. In general, the blends exhibited excellent processability and the cured blends showed good fracture toughness, solvent resistance, adhesive and composite properties. This invention was made by employees of the U.S. Government and its assignees and may be manufactured and used by or for the Government for government purposes without payment or any royalties therein or therof. Linear polyimidothioethers, also referred to in the literature as polyimidosulfides, are commonly synthesized by the reaction of aromatic or aliphatic dimercaptans with aromatic or aliphatic bismaleimides.

High molecular weight aromatic polyimidothioethers can form tough flexible films with good tensile properties and can be compression molded. They are generally soluble in the N,N-dimethylformamide, N,N-dimethylacetamide, dimethylsulfoxide, N-methylpyrrolidinone, hexafluoroacetone and *m*-cresol. Uncrosslinked polyimidothioethers are susceptible to solvent attack, especially in a stressed condition and upon exposure undergo solvent induced stress crazing and cracking.

The ethynyl terminated imidothioethers of this invention constitute new composition of matter. The properties of cured ETIS are similar to cured bismaleimides of similar structure.

Euler equation A special case of the general equation of motion; it applies to flow systems in which the viscous effects are negligible.

European communication for auxiliary equipment ▷ **communication protocol**

European Community The radical changes that have occurred in the European Single Market (1993) and the opening up of the borders to Eastern Europe affect all companies both large and small (and of course other situations change for the good of Europe and the world). The European Community (EC) over the rest of this century will develop more rapidly than previously expected. December 31, 1992 is the target date for the present 12 nations of EC to eliminate all tariffs and other barriers to the movement of people, goods, and services, and adopt common standards and regulations for health and safety in products, the workplace and the environment.

eutectic A mixture of two or more substances which solidifies as a whole when cooled from the liquid state, without changing composition. It is the composition within any system of two or more crystalline phases that melts completely at the minimum temperature. Also, the temperature at which such a composition melts (usually metals such as zinc-aluminum). They have been used during plastic processing rather extensively since the early 1940s; using bag molding, compression molding, injection molding, etc. After parts are molded where the eutectic was "enclosed" in the plastic melt, the part is heated to the eutectic melting point and permitted to flow out of its enclosure via drilled holes in the solidified plastic or by some other methods. ▷ **injection molding fusible core**

eutectic arrest In a cooling curve (or heating curve) an approximately isothermal segment, corresponding to the time interval during which the heat of transformation from the liquid phase of two or more conjugate solid phases is being evolved (or conversely).

eutectic composition The composition with the minimum melting temperature; at the interaction of two or more liquid solubility curves.

eutectic deformation The composition within a system of two or more components which, on heating under specified conditions, develops sufficient liquid to cause deformation at the minimum temperature.

eutectic, divorced A structure where the components of a eutectic appear to be entirely separate.

eutectic temperature Melting temperature of an alloy with a eutectic composition. Temperature (T_e) is at the interaction of two liquid solubility curves.

EVAL Company ▷ **ethylene-vinyl alcohol plastic**

exfoliation ▷ **vermiculite**

exotherm The temperature versus time curve of a chemical reaction or a phase change giving off heat, particularly the polymerization of thermoset plastics. Maximum temperature occurs at peak exotherm. Some room temperature curing polyesters (TS) and epoxies will exotherm severely if processed incorrectly. For example, if too much MEKP (catalyst) is added to a polyester that contains cobolt naphthenate (promoter), the mix can get hot enough to smoke and even catch fire. Exotherm can be a help or hindrance, depending on the application. Wet polyester layups can be processed at room temperature, using only exothermic heat to achieve cure. This is particularly advantageous when the layup is too large for available oven space. While exotherm can be an advantage to the laminator, it can be a detriment to processors involved in casting and potting. Only a few thermosets, such as silicone rubbers (RTVs), certain polyurethanes, and epoxy-polyamides, can be cast in large volumes without or with very little exotherming. Some TS mixes that require applied heat to initiate the curing action will also show an exothermic rise in temperature. During the compression molding of a phenolic laminate, the temperature of the laminate will rise sharply when it reaches 104° to 116°C (220° to 240°F). At the conclusion of the exothermic cycle, the temperature will return to normal. Note that endothermic refers to the absorption of heat in a chemical reaction.

exotherm curve A graph of temperature plotted against time during the curing cycle. Peak exotherm is the point of highest temperature of a plastic during cure.

exothermic analysis ▷ **thermal analysis**

exothermic heat Heat given off during a polymerization reaction by the chemical ingredients as they react and the plastic cures.

exothermic reaction A reaction in which the evolution of heat occurs.

expandable honeycomb core Layers of flat sheets or films (RP, aluminum, etc.) that have strips of adhesives applied. After curing in a flat press, the sheets are mechanically expanded to form sandwich cores.

expandable plastic ▷ **foamed plastic**

expandable polystyrene EPS molding illustrates the use of blowing agents. Resin beads containing a blowing agent are supplied to the molder in solid form. Each about 0.1 to 0.3 mm in diameter, these beads or spheres contain a small amount of a hydrocarbon liquid, usually pentane, that is used as the blowing agent. The process involves two major steps (see Fig. on p. 238). The first consists of a preexpansion of the virgin beads by heat (steam, hot air, radiant heat, or hot water). Steam is the most-used medium, as it is the most practical and most economical to produce densities of 0.75 to 10 lb/ft^3 (12 to 160 kg/m^3).

The next step conveys these beads, usually through a transport tube by air, to the mold cavity(s). The final expansion occurs in the mold, usually with steam heat, either by having live steam go through perforations in the mold itself or by means of steam probes that are withdrawn as the beads are expanding. During expansion the beads melt together, adhering to each other and forming a relatively smooth skin, filling the cavity or cavities. The pressures used are usually below 50 psi (0.35 MPa), allow-

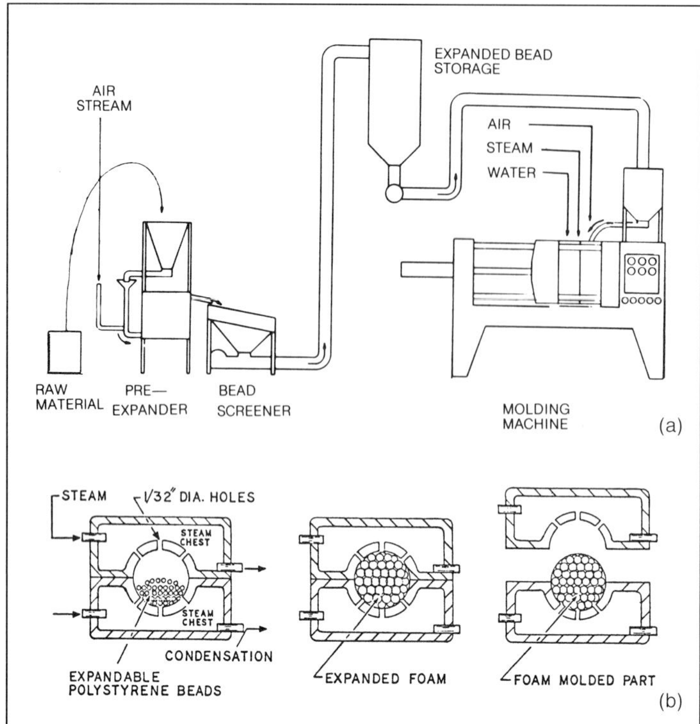

(*a*) Schematic of the expandable polystyrene foam molding process to produce expanded foam; (*b*) action in the mold during expansion of the expanded foam. Left diagram shows volume size of EPS raw material in relation to volume of cavity.

ing the use of relatively low-cost aluminum tooling. With small parts, multiple cavities can be used. After the heat cycles the cooling cycle starts. Because the EPS is an excellent thermal insulator, it takes a relatively long time to remove its heat prior to demolding, or the part will distort. Cooling is usually done by directing a water spray on the mold. To facilitate removal, particularly for complex shapes, mold-release agents are used.

An outstanding property of EPS is its extremely low density (when compared to other processes), which—by alteration of the preforming treatment—can be varied according to the end use. Other types of plastics are employed to produce expandable plastic foam EPF, including PE, PP, PMMA, and ethylene-styrene copolymers. They can use the same equipment, with only slight modifications. These plastics have different properties from those of PS and open up new markets; they provide improved sound insulation, resistance to additional heat deformation, better recovery of shapes in moldings, and so on. ▷ **polystyrene foam**

expandable polystyrene bead mold Mold is made of cast or fabricated aluminum. Since most molds are shell cavities and cores are mounted to a steam chest, the casting method is more appropriate for shaped molds.

expandable sheet stock ▷ **foamed sheet stock**

expander roll A type of spreader roller used in film production is the expander roll. It originally consisted of metal or wooden slats with internal elastic bands connected to angled end plates. The connection of the bands to pitched end plates caused the bands to expand as the roller rotated, pulling apart the slats to provide a spreading action. There are several variations of this roller, including some with internal mechanical mechanisms. The next generation eliminated the wooden or metal slats with more substantial elastic cords; however, they are still attached to the pitched end plates. With these expander rollers, the substrate enters at a point where the cords are relaxed and then exits at the point of maximum cord expansion to achieve web spreading. The amount of spreading action can be adjusted by changing the angle of the roller's end plates. The direct elastic cord and substrate contact provide better coefficient of friction and are less abrasive than the metal or wooden slats.

However, while these rollers offer adjustable spreading action, they eventually lose their effectiveness because the rubber cords do not fully recover to their original state after continual stretching. Another limitation is that at high web (film) speeds, air enters between the elastic bands and is trapped under the web. This causes the web to float over the roller surface, negating its function. The individual cords can also cause web marking.

One of the later generation of rollers operates on the same principle, but features a stretchable one-piece rubber sleeve supported by a series of disc brushes. As the roll rotates, the entire roller sleeve, as opposed to individual cords, expands and contracts to provide spreading action. The amount of spreading is controlled by two factors: the wrap or angle at which the web enters onto the roller, and the angular displacement of end caps. Notable advancements in this expandable-sleeve roller include a smooth, continuous surface, which does not produce marking or allow air to enter under the web. However, the stretching of the rubber still causes the roller to wear over time. ▷**extruder web guide**

expansion coefficient ▷**coefficient of expansion**

experience and science No true scientist will claim that existing knowledge is complete and no sincere craftsman (with experience) will pose as a final authority. The combination of these two worlds of experience and science is required to be productive and advance the state of the art in all industries or endeavors, including plastics and space travel.

explosive limit The minimum or maximum concentration of a substance in air that will propagate an explosion.

export-import U.S. plastics trade The U.S. Department of Commerce provides periodic dollar values on U.S. exports and imports, including plastic materials and fabricated plastic products.

export trading company A proposal to create this company for plastic parts, processing equipment, or materials under the auspices of the SPI-Machinery Division was approved in May 1990. An SPI-sponsored export trading company would permit to specific export activities a sharing of price information and other marketing strategies forbidden by U.S. anti-trust laws. The proposal will take effect when approved by the SPI Board of Directors, the U.S. Commerce Dept., and the U.S. Justice Dept..

extended pigment Organic pigments diluted with an extender, for example alumina trihydrate, blanc fixe, or calcium carbonate. ▷**pigment**

extender A substance added to a plastic composition to reduce the amount of plastic required per unit volume without significantly lessening properties. Additives are usually low-cost materials to dilute or extend high-cost plastics. Generally they have adhesive action. ▷**plasticizer extender**

extensibility The ability of a material to extend or elongate upon application of sufficient force, expressed as a percent of the original length. ▷**elongation**

extensional-bending coupling A property of certain classes of RPs, such as laminates, that exhibit bending curvatures when subjected to extensional loading.

extensional-shear coupling A property of certain classes of RPs, such as laminates, that exhibit shear strains when subjected to extensional loading.

extensometer A device (mechanical, electrical, optical, etc.) for determining elongation of a specimen as it is strained due to mechanical stress.

extraction ▷**molecular weight extraction**

extrudate The product of the extrusion process; plastic that exits an extruder such as film, pipe, etc.

extruded-bead sealing A method of welding or sealing continuous lengths of thermoplastic sheeting or thicker sections by extruding a bead of the same material between two sections and immediately pressing the sections together. The heat in the extruded bead is sufficient to cause it to weld to the adjacent surfaces.

extruded hinge ▷**hinge**

extruded log ▷**bulk molding compound**

extruded particleboard A particleboard manufactured by forcing a mass of particles (such as wood) coated with an extraneous binding agent (such as phenolic plastics) through a heated die with the applied pressure parallel to the faces and in the direction of extruding.

extruded shape A hollow or solid extruded section, long in relation to its cross sectional dimensions, whose cross section is other than that of wire, rod, bar, or tube.

extruded tube An extruded hollow section, long in relation to its cross sectional dimensions, which is symmetrical and either round, square, rectangular, hexagonal, octagonal, or elliptical with sharp or rounded corners, and has uniform wall thickness except as affected by corner radii.

extruded wire An extruded solid section long in relation to its cross sectional dimensions, having a symmetrical cross section that is square or rectangular with sharp or rounded corners or edges, or is round, hexagonal, or octagonal, and whose diameter, width, or greatest distance between parallel faces is less than 3/8 in. (9.52 mm).

extruder The extruder, which offers the advantages of a completely versatile processing technique, is unsurpassed in economic importance by any other process. This continuously operating process, with its relatively low cost of operation, is predominant in the manufacture of shapes such as films, sheets, tapes, filaments, pipes, rods, in-line postforming, and others. The basic processing concept is similar to that of injection molding (IM) in that material passes from a hopper into a cylinder in which it is melted and dragged forward by the movement of a screw. The screw compresses, melts, and homogenizes the material. When the melt reaches the end of the cylinder, it usually is forced through a screen pack prior to entering a die that gives the desired shape with no break in continuity (see Fig. below).

A major difference between extrusion and IM is that the extruder processes plastics at a lower pressure and operates continuously. Its pressure usually ranges from 1.4 to 10.4 MPa (200 to 1,500 psi) and could go to 34.5 or 69 MPa (5,000 or possibly 10,000 psi). In IM, pressures go from 14 to 210 MPa (2,000 to 30,000 psi). However, the most important difference is that the IM melt is not continuous; it experiences repeatable abrupt changes when the melt is forced into a mold cavity. With these significant differences, it is actually easier to theorize about extrusion and to process plastics through extruders, as many more controls are required in IM.

extruder-adapter ▷ **die adapter**

extruder, adiabatic A method of extrusion in which, after the extrusion apparatus has been heated sufficiently by conventional means to plastify (melt) the material, the extrusion process can be continued with the sole source of heat being the conversion of the drive energy, through viscous resistance of the plastic mass in the extruder. Also called autothermal extrusion and autogeneous extrusion.

extruder air entrapment ▷ **air entrapment**

extruder barrel or cylinder ▷ **barrel**

extruder barrier screw ▷ **screw, barrier**

extruder base or stand The metal structure on which are mounted the basic extruder components such as barrel, thrust housing, gear pump, etc.

extruder blow molding ▷ **blow molding, extruder**

extruder, blown film More plastics go through blown film lines than other extrusion lines. The process can vary in direction (up, down, or horizontal) and in the method of flattening the film prior to wind-up (see Fig. on p. 241). Developments in these lines relate to the extruder, dies, takeoff systems, and automation components. The development of new high-speed extruders with a grooved feed zone and barrier screws makes it possible to increase output while providing processing flexibility—which, particularly in coextrusion, renders changes of screws unnecessary. Blown film dies have been developed with the goals of low pressure consumption, good self-cleaning, material changes, and ease of maintenance. The automation of blown film plants to reduce film thickness tolerances involves the increased use of linear weight control systems (upstream and downstream), as well as greater opportunities to influence profile thickness via suitable control elements on the die and cooling systems.

Regarding the film direction, horizontal operation entails no overhead installation and a low building height, but requires a larger floor space with probable adverse effects of gravity

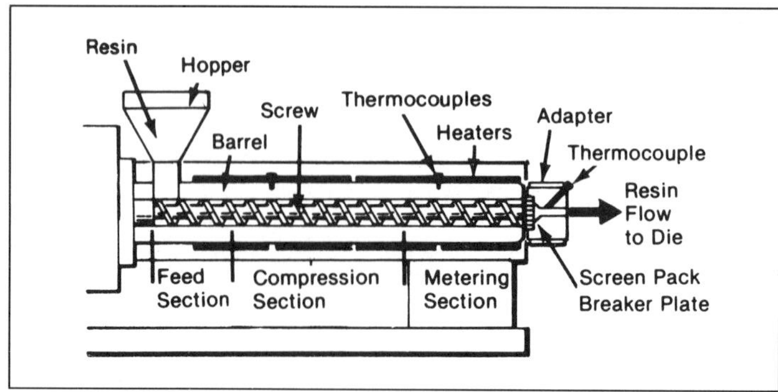

Cross section schematic of a single screw extruder.

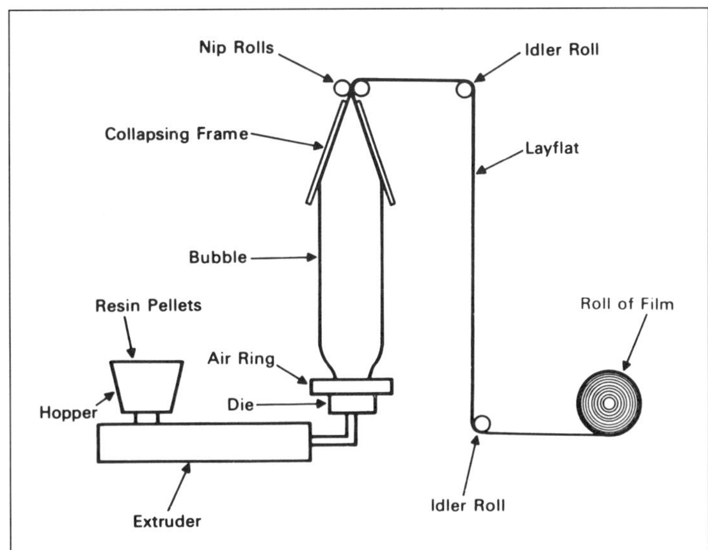

Schematic of a basic, vertical-up, extrusion blown film line.

and uneven cooling. Vertical-down operation has the advantage of start-up without flooding of the annular die gap by exiting hot melt. However, vertical-up operation is the usual method, provided sufficient melt strength exists for an upward start-up, and so on. Special die blow heads are designed, with (usually) a multiple threaded helical mandrel discharging into an expansion space. The tubular melt assumes its final shape in a "smoothing-out" zone, which in all heads is a cylindrical land in a parallel position between the mandrel and the orifice. Its length is about 10 to 15 times the annular gap width (the lower value applies to thin film and the higher to thick film). The gap width is generally 0.5 to 2.0 mm.

extruder blown film air ring A circular manifold used to distribute an even flow of air onto a hollow tubular film (bubble) passing through the center of the ring as it exits the die. The air cools the film uniformly to aid in producing an even film thickness and speeding up the production line.

extruder blown film bag manufacturing ▷ **bag manufacturing**

extruder blown film blocking ▷ **film blocking**

extruder blown film blow up ratio Blow up ratio is the ratio of the final diameter (before gusseting, if any) to the original die diameter opening. It usually ranges from $1\frac{1}{2}$ to $4\frac{1}{2}$; depends on type material, type die, speed of line, etc.

extruder blown film "frost" line With certain plastics, such as polyethylene, a line or ring-shaped zone located at about the point where the film initially reaches its final diameter. This zone is characterized by a "frosty" appearance to the film caused by the film temperature falling below the softening range of the plastic. The frost line is not always visible so, for practical purposes, it is defined where the final diameter is reached. When visible, the line should be level. Its height above the die is an important factor. The higher it is, the more critical gauge control becomes. The frost line is essential for controlling molecular orientation of the melt in the machine and transverse directions, thus influences some physical properties such as tear, tensile, and impact strengths.

The frost line can be raised or lowered by means of extruder output or take-off speed. However, the preferable way of adjusting the height of the frost line is by means of the volume of cooling air blown against the bubble. When the screw speed (and resin output) goes up, the distance between the die and the frost line is increased. When more cooling air is blown against the bubble, the frost line drops; a decrease in cooling air causes it to rise.

Raising the frost line gives the film more time to solidify, resulting in a smoother surface and higher clarity and gloss. However, too high a frost line may cause the film to block (stick) when rolled up.

A too high frost line may result in the film sticking to the nip rolls. This becomes less of a problem if the nip rolls are high above the extruder and if water of about 27°C (80°F) is circulated through the driven stainless steel nip roll.

The frost line must always be as level as possible. The primary cause for a rising or dropping of the frost line in spots may be improper adjustment of the die opening. This may cause variations in film thickness, non-uniform film cooling and a non-level frost line. A non-level frost line may also be caused by uneven cooling around the air ring.

extruder blown film gauge distortion Gauge thickness can be extremely nonuniform due to melt flow behavior on exiting the die and/or distortions of the collapsing frame. To provide uniformity, rotating dies or oscillating film hauloffs are used. Each of these systems have different technical approaches. As an example, rotations could be oscillating 180° or rotating platform 360° with action in different positions (horizontal, vertical, etc.). The different systems available meet different requirements such as web width, cooling system effect, degree of tacky or stiff material, line speed, and/or gauge thickness, particularly with thin-gauge versus width of web.

extruder blown film internal cooler IBC provides additional cooling advantages for the film traveling from the die to the nip rolls; further improving total cooling with the air ring. Its success depends on factors such as providing a smooth, controlled exchange of internal air and to maintain tight tolerances with respect to bubble geometry.

extruder blown film nip rolls A pair of rolls situated at the top (or bottom) of the tower which close the blown film envelope, seal air inside of it, and regulate the rate at which the film is pulled from the extrusion die. One roll is usually covered with a resilient material, the other being bare metal with internal cooling means.

extruder blown film oscillating or rotary die ▷ **extruder blown film gauge distortion**

extruder blown film selection of machine The output rate of extruders is largely dependent upon the type of screw used, L/D ratios, horsepower available, the screw speed (rpm), the type of barrel cooling used, and the back pressure of the melt in the barrel. The following summarize these parameters and their influence on output rate: (1) *Screw type* The trend of the industry has been to long metering section screws (8 to 10 turns are standard). This type of screw offers better shearing of the melt and a better film quality. (2) *L/D Ratio* An L/D ratio must be selected which will allow a proper "dwelltime" (residence time) of the melt in the barrel. 24:1 L/D and larger are standard. Note there is a possible upper limit to the L/D above 30:1 where the screw becomes too weak to support the applied torque. (3) *Horsepower* The trend has been to increase the drive horsepower along with the L/D ratio to up the output rate. A general rule of thumb is that 6 lbs per hour output can be expected per applied horsepower. (4) *Screw Speed* Speeds continue to increase to obtain the maximum output of acceptable film. (5) *Liquid Cooling* Becomes more important for the larger extruders. Cooling requirements increase as longer screws and higher speeds are used. The frictional heat which is developed lowers power costs but must be controlled effectively. (6) *Pressures* Pressures for blown film extrusion should range in the neighborhood of 3,000 to 4,000 psig when good die design and streamlined melt flow are used. Note: an extruder barrel is usually rated for 10,000 psig maximum pressure. However, one should not exceed 5,000 psig for reasons of safety.

extruder blown film stretching-orienting The blow up ratio determines degree of circumferential orientation and the pull rate of the bubble determines longitudinal orientation. With the proper orientation blow up ratio and temperature profile, increased film performance develops. ▷ **orientation** and **extruder film orientation**

extruder blown film tower Apparatus for handling film between the extruder die and take-up equipment. The blown film tube (bubble) passes through the tower where it is cooled and the size and gauge are regulated. At the top, or near the end, the sides converge, collapsing the bubble prior to winding.

extruder blown film wrinkles Wrinkles are problems which have always plagued extruders. They can occur intermittently and are annoying and costly. Badly wrinkled film rolls must be scrapped. Wrinkling on the windup roll may be caused by conditions such as frost line too high and/or die ring out of adjustment. Bias is a condition where the two halves of the tube circumference are unequal. This causes excessive friction at the guide rolls or forming tent or unbalanced pull at the nip roll, resulting in ruffle-like wrinkles across the center of the lay-flat width of the wound roll. Film may be too cold when it reaches the nip rolls and its stiffness may cause crimping at the nip. Use of higher density plastic will increase the stiffness and its susceptibility to wrinkles. The guide rolls may not be properly aligned with the nip rolls. The use of spreader or expander rolls is often helpful in removing wrinkles caused by uneven or too high web tension. Surging of the extrudate and air currents in the shop are detriments.

Methods are used to compensate or take positive corrective action when the source of the problem is determined.

extruder breaker plate ▷**extruder screen pack**

extruder capstan Mechanical tension control machine used to ensure even rate of movement such as required in a wire or cable extrusion coating line.

extruder cast or chill film ▷**extruder film**

extruder chemical reactor ▷**extruder reactive processing**

extruder chill roll A cored roll, usually temperature controlled with circulating water, which cools the web before winding. For chill roll (cast) film, the surface of the roll is highly polished. In extrusion coating, either a polished or a matte surface may be used depending on the surface desired on the finished coating.

extruder cleaning Cleaning the extruder and die is a costly operation and is to be avoided if possible. It is hard work for the operator and no product is produced. Cleaning should be planned. It is usually required after running black resin. Planning can provide a schedule for maintenance of cooling and take-off equipment. Cleaning of the hot extruder often starts by adding to the hopper a material called a flushing, cleaning, or purging compound. It aids in removing deposits from the screw and barrel. Before using some compounds, it is necessary to remove the die and breaker plates as they don't really melt and flow like a plastic. If the die is not removed, excessive pressures could develop with damage to the equipment. High screw speeds may be used to scrub the barrel. Once the compound comes through clean, the screw is pumped dry and screw rotation is stopped.

extruder coating Plastic coatings are applied in different forms and shapes on many different products, such as wire, cable, profiles (plastics, wood, aluminum, etc.), films/foils (plastics, aluminum, steel, paper, etc), rope and so on. Certain coatings only require snug fits, whereas others require excellent adhesion, usually necessitating cleaning, priming, and/or heating substrates. An example of typical surface coverage using polyethylene coating plastic is given in the Table. With $3\frac{1}{2}$ in. extruders, coating widths range from 600 to 1,200 mm; with $4\frac{1}{2}$ in. from 900 to 2,500 mm; with 6 in. from 1,000 to 4,000 mm; and with 8 in. from 3,000 to 5,000 mm (see the Fig. below). ▷**film coating**

Example of a surface coverage of PE coating plastic with average density of 0.92 g/cm³.

Thickness (mm)	One m² of substrate requires (g)	0.45 kg PE covers (m)
0.001	5.8	175
0.002	11.6	85
0.004	23.2	42.5
0.008	46.4	21

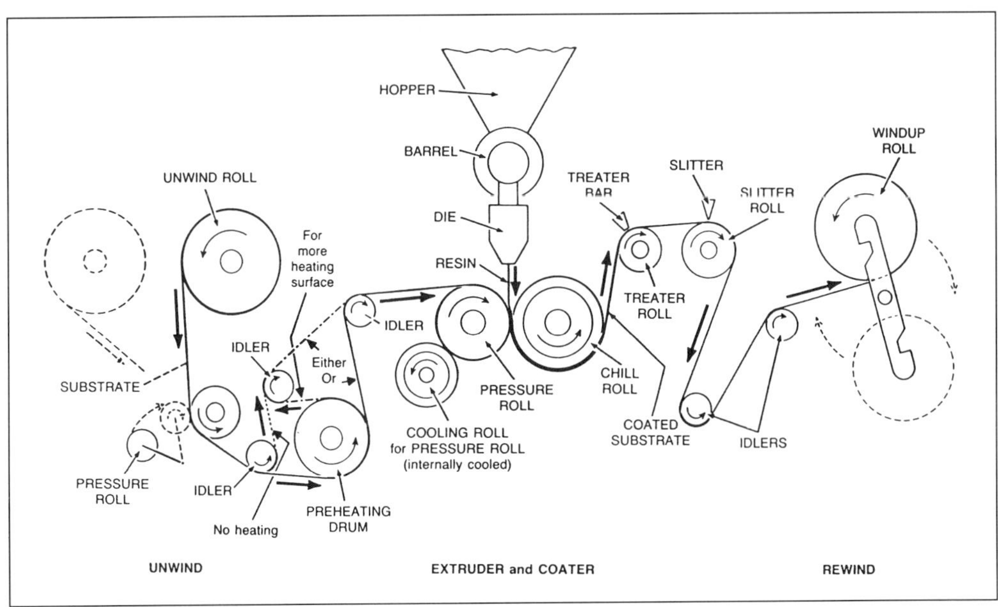

Schematic of an extruder coating line.

extruder coating air gap The distance from the die opening to the nip formed by the pressure roll and the chill roll.

extruder coating film/foil Extrusion coatings, using many different plastics, are applied to film, foil, or sheet substrates of plastic, wood, aluminum, steel, paper, cardboard, and so on. Basically a "curtain" of very hot melt is extruded downward from a slit die (similar to flat film slit dies). Preheating and/or cleaning operations may be required. Hot melt contacts the substrate, which is supported by a large, highly polished chill roll with a small rubber or metal nip roll. The nip roll applies the required pressure to ensure proper air-free adhesion. As the melt is usually at its maximum heat and pressure, "delicate" operation is required in the equipment and the surrounding area. Changes in air currents and moisture can cause immediate down time; tighter controls may not be necessary if all that is required is not to open a "door"—particularly a large garage door.

extruder coating neck-in and beading ▷ **extruder neck-in and beading**

extruder coating preheat roll A heated roll installed between the pressure roll and unwind roll whose pressure is to heat the substrate before it is coated.

extruder coating wire Wire coating is performed by extruding plastic around a wire. This may be accomplished by feeding the wire directly through a hole in the center of the feed screw, or, by far the more popular method, by using a crosshead die (see Fig. in ▷ **design die**), through which the wire is fed. Hot melt is extruded over a preheated wire to improve adhesion and reduce shrinkage stresses. Before the wire enters the die, preheating is done by an electric current, radiant heaters, and so on; thick wires or cables can be heated by a gas flame or hot gas. Wire travels at rates up to at least 1,300 m/min (4,000 ft/min). Regardless of the speed, the rate of movement has to be held extremely uniform (or "perfect"). In order to achieve uniformity, all peripheral (expensive) equipment is carefully controlled and monitored, from the wire input drum to the output windup drum.

There are two basic types of dies used, called high and low pressure coaters. With high pressure, the melt meets and coats the wire between the die lips prior to exiting the die. The result is good contact of plastic to wire, tight control of the plastic OD, and the ability to handle plastics that require tight melt control, particularly with operation at "peak" heats and pressures. In the low pressure type, the melt makes contact with the wire after they both exit the die. Plastic hugs the wire, with formation of a loose jacket that facilitates removal of plastic insulation. If spiders are used to support the central mandrel, they are usually thin and streamlined to minimize disruption of the velocity. Adjustment of the wall thickness distribution and concentricity via die centering bolts can be manual or automatic. Automatic control can be achieved with in-line wall thickness measurement probes, and so forth. With high pressure dies, a vacuum can be used in the die just before the wire goes through its snug central support, to obtain an air-free and better bond. With a low pressure die, low air pressure is applied through the center of the mandrel tube to prevent collapse of the melt tubing on exiting (eliminating melt adherence on the front of the die, which requries down time and cleanup) and to aid in maintaining the plastic ID.

Cooling of the thermoplastic coated wire usually occurs as soon as it leaves the die through water cooling troughs, which may have cascading heated sections. The troughs are usually 20 to 100 ft long. With thermoset plastics or elastomers and natural rubber, the required higher heat of melt solidification is added via hot gas systems, vulcanization cures, and so forth. ▷ **extruder, wire and cable**

extruder coextrusion ▷ **coextrusion**

extruder cold shot Starting up an extruder on a blow molding machine requires that temperature equilibrium be achieved sufficient to melt the plastic at a rapid enough rate to form a parison from which to blow the container. Before this is achieved, during start-up several incomplete parisons will be formed while cycling the machine during heat-up of the machine. These imperfect and unusable parisons are called "cold shots".

extruder communication protocol ▷ **communication protocol**

extruder compound mixing The basic functions of a compounding extruder are to melt the polymer and evenly disperse and distribute additives or fillers to obtain the specifications of the end product. Large-scale compounding is done on either single or twin screw extruders. Single screws are used for basic operations where little variation in material formulation and viscosity is expected. Twin screw compounders offer better conveyance characteristics.

extruder computer integrated ▷ **computer processing control; computer integrated manufacturing; computer microprocessor control**

extruder control downstream Downstream product controls can be interconnected with process controllers so that any variation in the product is immediately reflected as a corrective change. A decision is derived from the feedback signal about the kind and extent of adjustment that should be made to a control variable; in other words, the system has to be matched to the process.

extruder cut-off ▷ **extruder take-off cutter to shipping**

extruder cylinder ▷ **barrel**

extruder die ▷ **design die** and **die**

extruder die head pressure Range of melt pressure in different die heads are as follows: sheet, pipe, and cast film at 500 to 1,500 psi (3.5 to 6.9 MPa); monofilament at 1,000 to 3,000 psi (6.9 to 20.7 MPa); wire coating at 1,500 to 8,000 psi (10.3 to 55.1 MPa); and layflat film at 2,000 to 6,000 psi (13.8 to 41.3 MPa).

extruder die maintenance ▷ **die maintenance and care**

extruder die melt ▷ **design die**

extruder die melt swell ▷ **design die** and **design die, basics of flow**

extruder die netting ▷ **die netting**

extruder displacement rate ▷ **injection molding displacement rate** that can provide guidelines.

extruder draw down rate Sometimes called melt extensibility, it is defined as the maximum take-off rate, without breaking of film, sheet, pipe, profile, etc. through a given die opening at constant temperature and output.

extruder draw down ratio A measure of the degree of stretching during the orientation of a fiber, filament, etc. expressed as the ratio of the cross sectional area of the undrawn material (or die opening) to that of the drawn material, or the thickness of the die opening to the final thickness of the extruded part.

extruder draw resonance A phenomenon occurring with plastics such as PE, PP, and PS in which the extrudate is drawn into a quenching bath at a certain critical speed which creates a cyclic pulsation in the cross sectional area of the extrudate. The pulsation increases with increased drawing speed until it eventually breaks at the interface of the cooling medium and air.

extruder drive The entire electrical and mechanical system used to supply mechanical energy to the input shaft of the gear reducer. This includes motor, constant or infinitely variable speed system, flexible coupling, etc. ▷ **extruder motor and gear reducer**

extruder drive power calculation Calculating DC drive power can be accomplished even if the extruder panel only provides screw speed and motor current. From the relationship power (watts) = (current) (voltage) and the conversion hp = kilowatts divided by 746. The most difficult reading to obtain is the drive armature voltage, but this is proportional to speed, and may be accurately estimated from motor name plate data as

$$\text{(arm voltage)} = \text{screw speed} \times \frac{\text{(max. armature voltage)}}{\text{maximum screw speed}}$$

Make sure to check the calibration of your screw speed and current readouts!

$$\text{hp} = \frac{\text{amps}}{746} \times \frac{\text{speed}}{\text{max. speed}} \times \text{max. voltage}$$

extruder, elastic melt A type of extruder in which the material is fed into a fix gap between a stationary and a rotating plate, is melted by frictional heat and flows in a spiral path towards the center of rotation, from which it is discharged through a die. Only rubbery plastics with certain elastic properties are suitable for the process. Also called elastodynamic extruder.

extruder energy consumption Like the output capacity, the energy efficiency of an extruder is dependent on the torque available on the screw, screw RPM, heat control, and material being processed. Unfortunately, costly energy losses can occur, ranging from 3 to 20% and due to various factors, with the major loss occurring in the drive system. The power for screw rotation is supplied by a variable speed motor drive system, and is transmitted through a gear reduction unit, a coupling, and a thrust bearing. Gear reducers impart the final speed and torque to the screw. Most gear reducers use double-reaction helical or herringbone gears for their ruggedness and to hold noise levels within acceptable limits. Worm and pinion gear combinations have been used on smaller extruders. The efficiency of the power transmission gear with the worm is a maximum of 85%, that of the helical gear reaches 95%, and the herringbone 97%.

extruder feeder ▷ **feeder**

extruder festoon ▷ **festoon**

extruder fiber formation Plastic fiber extrusion or fiber formation is the overall process of "fiber spinning". Typical lines use spinneret dies (with multiple holes) and orienting devices to develop molecular orientation with its associated improved fiber/filament performance.

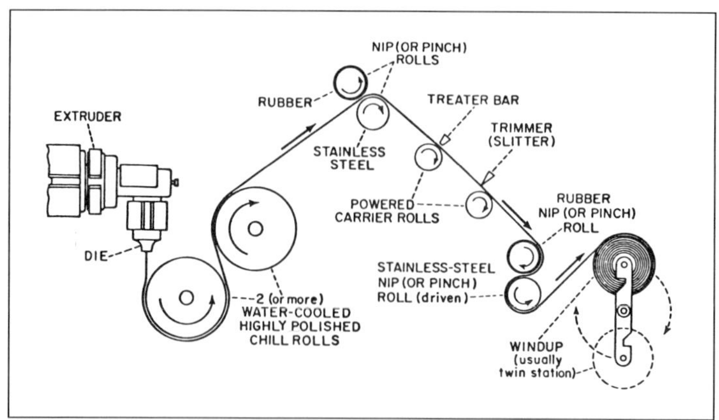

Schematic of flat-film extrusion line using chill rolls.

extruder film In addition to extruded blown film, there is extruded flat film. Flat film is extruded directly by using cooling rools, quench water bath, or both. The cooling roller system is also called chill roll or cast film. Flat films processed through slit dies are cooled principally by using chilled rolls. Many different resins are used, with thicknesses ranging from 15 to 200 μm (see Fig. above). Alternatively, certain plastics go directly into a water tank, but that creates many technical difficulties in production. Thus, the chill roll process is preferred; and film up to 3 m in width will have output rates of at least 120 m/min.

In this process, the melt film contacts (as quickly as possible, vertically or at an angle) the first water-cooled highly polished (to 1 μm) chrome-plated roll. An air knife can be used; its placement parallel to the die makes it possible to press the film smoothly onto the first cooling roll by means of a cold air stream. Lubricant plate-out on the cooling rolls is avoided by operation with contact rolls. At haul-off rates of up to 60 m/min, reel change is carried out by hand. At higher rates, automatic changeover equipment is required.

Advantages of the chill roll process (vs. blown film) include: preparing almost transparent film from crystalline resins (the frost line forms about 50 mm above the contact line with the chill roll); no risk of blocking; a simple crease-free wind-up; continuous film thickness control; high output; relatively small space requirement; and the fact that pretreatment for printing can be applied simultaneously to both sides of the film. Disadvantages are: the limitation on maximum width of about 3 m (blown film layflat is at least up to 12 m); loss through edge trimming; and basically only uniaxial orientation. ▷ **extruder film quench-tank**

extruder film arrowhead Lines meeting at a rounded angle. They point in the direction of extrusion.

extruder film blocking ▷ **film blocking**

extruder film bowed rolls ▷ **bowed rolls**

extruder film brittleness Film brittleness is the tendency of a plastic, such as polyethylene bags, to split along a fold, crease, or gusset or across the bag face when rapidly stressed. This property depends mainly upon plastic density and molecular orientation. Films made of lower density are less brittle than films of higher density plastics. Film made of plastic of lower melt index is also slightly less brittle than higher MI. A narrow molecular weight distribution has favorable influence. Since film brittleness also depends on the structural orientation, it may be quite different in the machine direction versus the transverse direction. Flat film, especially when extruded at a high take-off speed, is oriented more in the machine direction. Most blown film is also oriented more in the machine direction, although to a lesser degree than flat film.

extruder film brittleness temperature test The temperature at which a plastic becomes sufficiently brittle to break when subjected to a sudden blow (ASTM D 746).

extruder film capping The Fig. shown under ▷ **extruder coating** is an example of capping or laminating a substrate (paper, aluminum foil, plastic, fabric, etc.).

extruder film clarity Most film producers desire a product with high clarity and a minimum of haze or frostiness. Clarity is imperative in the packaging field where transparency of the package enhances the sales appeal of wrapped articles. However, film clarity can vary considerably with extrusion processing conditions; different optical properties can be achieved.

extruder film cooling roll versus quench-tank In chill roll or cast film extrusion, the heat extruded through the die slot is cooled by the surface of two or more water-cooled chill or casting rolls. This offers substantial improvements in optical properties, transparency with freedom from haze and gloss, potentially increased output, and production of stiffer films. A major problem that could be encountered in cast-film is "puckering". Puckers are film nonuniformities usually developing on the first chill roll. They run in rows in the machine direction and look like small pockets or bags. They impair the film's appearance and printability.

extruder film draw down rate ▷ **drawdown**

extruder film fisheye ▷ **fisheye**

extruder film gauging ▷ **extruder web**

extruder film haze Slight haziness is a characteristic of certain plastics, such as polyethylene. Surface roughness diffuses light passing through the film and contributes to its haziness. Surface roughness is a function of the extrusion conditions and the fundamental structure of the plastic. The partly crystalline, partly amorphous structure of the plastic also contributes to the haziness. The crystalline areas have a larger index of refraction than the surrounding amorphous material, which accounts for the somewhat milky appearance.

extruder film haze test Tests are available such as a standard pivotable-sphere hazemeter in accordance with ASTM D 1003. The method determines the light transmitting properties and, from these, the wide-angle light-scattering properties of film. The percentage of light diffused by the specimen, as measured by means of a photocell inside the pivotable spherical photometer, is recorded.

extruder film impact strength The impact strength of film (its resistance to shock impact) should not be confused with film tear strength. Higher density plastics generally decrease this property. ▷ **impact strength; tear strength; bag drop test; dart drop test; ball burst test**

extruder film orientation Films can be produced in a wide combination of orientation patterns by controlled stretching and heat-setting techniques ▷ **orientation**. Films are stretched to obtain the desired physical properties, which are normally increased tensile strength and modulus or heat-shrinkability. Properties may vary in different directions depending on the stretch patterns such as single axial or biaxial (also called bioriented). Flat-die extruded films can be stretched in the machine (long) axis by means of differentially heat controlled driven rolls and in the transverse (short) axis by means of a tenter frame (a take-off of the fabric tenter frame) using clamps or hooks to hold the film in the transverse stretch (see the Fig. below and on top of p. 248). The sequence of the operation is not critical in most cases. Heat setting under restraint, to stabilize the orientation, is a vital part of the process. ▷ **orientation** regarding the process conditions and the properties of oriented films.

extruder film oxidized gels and color specks Imperfections which are yellow-brown to black in color. These appear as flakes, chunks of material, or as gels with discolored centers. ▷ **gel**

extruder film pinpoint gels Small, round imperfections which look as if the film had been pricked with a pin. They are usually uniformly dispersed and numerous enough to cause a grainy appearance in the film. These defects are usually confined to plastics of 0.931 g/cm^3 and above as well as those containing certain additives. They are undesirable in thermoforming, hermetic sealing, etc.

extruder film quench-tank In quench-tank film extrusion, the film is cooled in a water bath (see second Fig. on p. 248). From under the polished guide shoe or roller in the bath, the cooled film is pulled out by a pair of nip (or pinch) rolls. The thick edge or "bead" is trimmed, and the film is wound on a windup roll.

extruder film take-off equipment The draw-

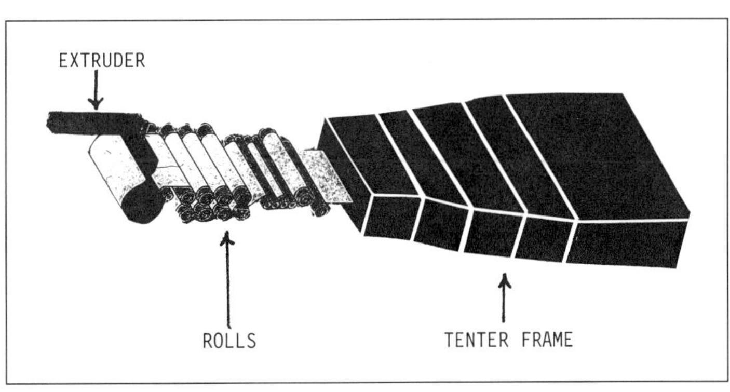

Schematic of an example for a complete biaxial film orienting processing line. The extruded film travels around (machine direction stretching) heated rolls and through the (transverse direction stretching) heated tenter frame.

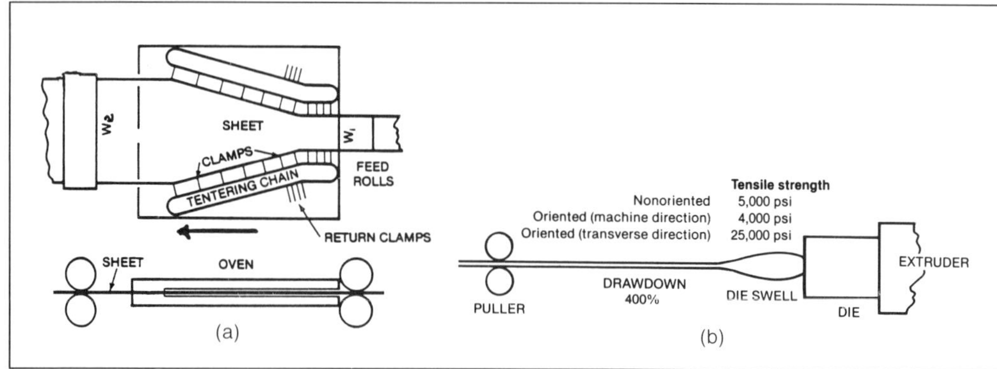

Use of tenter frame to biorient film or sheet. In (*a*), the feeder-roll speed to puller-roll speed ratio is 1:4 (the ratio of width W_2 to width W_1). Part (*b*) is a schematic of the drawdown phenomenon with die swell to produce orientation in the longitudinal (machine) direction.

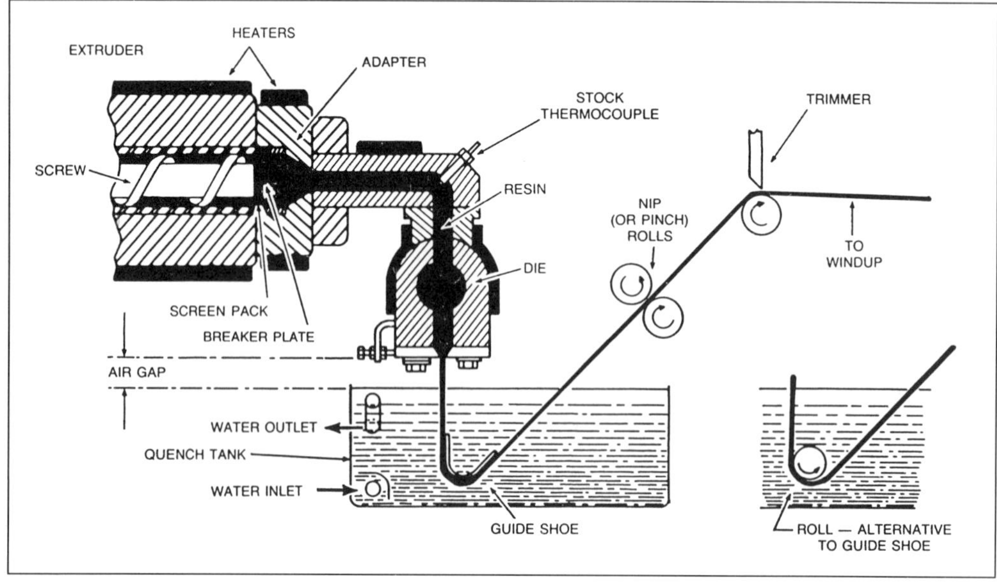

Schematic of quench-tank system for flat-film extrusion line.

down rate and gauge of the film is controlled by the speed of the take-off equipment. Take-off speeds in flat-film extrusion are usually higher than in blown-film extrusion. Higher speeds require better plastic properties and usually result in thinner film. ▷ **extruder take-off**

extruder film tear strength ▷ **tear** and **Elmendorf tear test**

extruder film winder or rewinder An example of a winder is shown in the Fig. on p. 249.

extruder foamed plastic ▷ **foamed sheet stock** and **foamed extruded film**

extruder forming ▷ **postforming**

extruder front end or discharge end The end toward the die and in the downstream direction.

extruder gear pump ▷ **gear pump**

extruder gravimetric feeding-blending Its use is well established. The key advantage of gravimetric or loss-in-weight technology lies in its ability to meter material with pinpoint accuracy despite variations in bulk density. They are usually more expensive than their volumetric counterparts, but for applications where precise feeding or blending is critical, the advantages can be significant. They basically consist of the feeder (including discharge device), scale, and

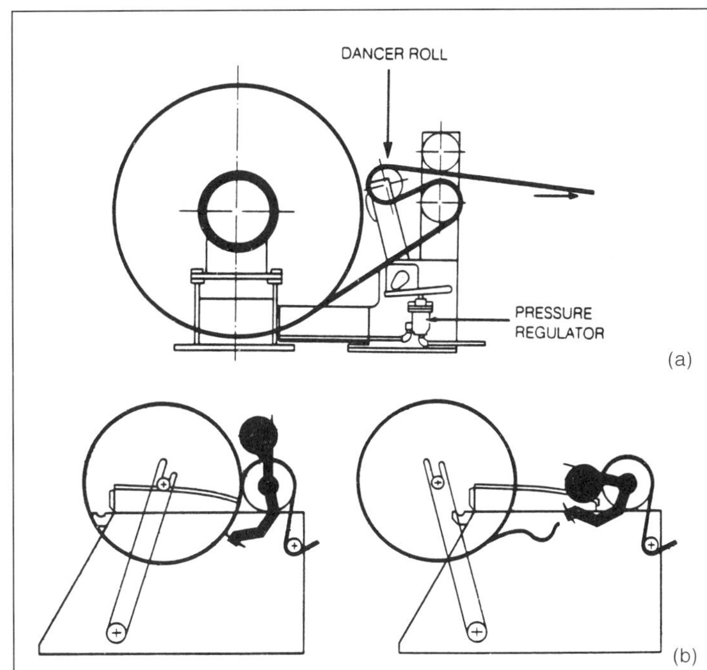

(*a*) Schematic of an example in film winding where the film is always at constant tension and fast change-over occurs from a fully wound spool to the start of a new spool with no interruption in the film speed output from the extruder; (*b*) reel-change systems.

control unit. A separate feeder system is used for blending each plastic. These feeders can either be tied into the hauloff to control weight per length, or screw speed to control (weight/time), or both, depending on the process and whether the end product is sold according to weight or length. There are both batch and continuous type weighing units.

extruder grooved feed The characteristics of an extruder change dramatically when grooves are machined in the internal barrel surface in the feed section of the extruder, particularly for certain types of plastics. The advantage is that friction between solid plastic particles and the barrel surface is considerably higher than that of a smooth bore barrel. The higher friction results in a larger friction force at the barrel surface acting on the plastic. Since the frictional force at the barrel is the driving force at the barrel and the driving force for the solids conveying process, the extruder output is usually higher and the process stability improved. The rules for screw designs are very different for grooved versus smooth barrel extruders.

extruder head The end section in which the melt exits.

extruder head angle An extruder head positioned at an angle (45°, 90°, etc.) with the axis of the extruder screw, rather than having the head in the usual position of being inline with the screw. Used in wire coating, etc.

extruder heat profile The temperatures required along a barrel, adapter, and die depend largely on the specific extrusion operation being conducted, plastic used (see Table below), and available process controls. Heat to soften the plastic is supplied in two ways: by external heating of the barrel (sometimes also via the screw) and by internal frictional forces brought

Examples of melt temperature in an extruder.

Plastic	Temperature, °C
Cellulose acetate	160–205
Cellulose acetate butyrate	160–205
Cellulose propionate	160–205
Ethylcellulose	190–230
FEP fluorocarbon	380–400
Ionomer	230–290
Nylon-6	250–270
Polycarbonate	290–300
Polyethylene, low-density	230–260
Poly(ethylene terephthalate)	285
Poly(methyl methacrylate)	180–210
Polypropylene	270–300
Polystyrene	240
Polyurethane elastomer	165–220
Poly(vinyl chloride)	
Rigid	160–165
Nonrigid	190–205
Copolyester	200–250
Chlorotrifluoroethylene copolymers	260–320
Vinylidene chloride—vinyl chloride copolymers	175–190

about on the plastic due to the action of the screw ▷**screw melt** and **melt flow**. The amount of such frictional heat supplied is appreciable. In many extrusion operations it represents most of the total heat supplied to the plastic. Electricity, steam, or hot oil can be used. Electric resistance heating is generally preferred because it is the most convenient, responds rapidly, is easiest to adjust, requires a minimum of maintenance, and is generally the least expensive in terms of initial investments.

Accurate control of the barrel temperatures is essential because the viscosity of plastics can change with temperature fluctuations. The hopper is usually water-cooled to prevent the plastic from melting prematurely and bridging or sticking to the hopper throat before reaching the screw. With electric resistance heaters, there are usually 2 to 8 independently heated zones, the temperature of each zone regulated by a proportioning or a stepless temperature controller.

extruder, hollow cores For basic concept that is applicable to extrusion. ▷**injection molding, gas**

extruder, hydrodynamic Similar to an elastic melt extruder. ▷**extruder, elastic melt**

extruder instabilities or variabilities In extrusion, as in all other processes, an extensive theoretical analysis has been applied to facilitate understanding and maximize the manufacturing operation. However, the "real world" must be understood and appreciated as well. The operator has to work within the many limitations of the materials and equipment (the basic extruder and all auxiliary upstream and downstream equipment). The interplay and interchange of process controls can help to eliminate problems and/or aid operation with the variables that exist. The greatest degree of instability is due to improper screw design (or using the wrong screw). Proper instrumentation, particularly barrel heat is important to diagnosis of the problem(s). For uniform/stable extrusion, it is important to periodically check the drive system, the take-up device, and other equipment, and compare it to its original performance. If variations are excessive, all kinds of problems will develop. An elaborate process control system can help, but it is best to improve stability in all facets of the extrusion line. Examples of instabilities and problem areas include: (1) nonuniform plastics flow in the hopper; (2) troublesome bridging, with excessive barrel heat that melts the solidified plastic in the hopper and feed section and stops plastic flow; (3) variations in (a) barrel heat, (b) screw heat, (c) screw speed, (d) screw power drive, (e) die heat, (f) die head pressure, and the (g) take-up device; (4) insufficient melting and/or mixing capacity; (5) insufficient pressure generating capacity, (6) wear and/or damage of the screw and /or the barrel; (7) melt fracture/sharkskin; and so on.

Finally one must check the proper alignment of the extruder and the downstream equipment. Proper alignment and isolation of the vibrators is a must for high-quality and high-speed output.

extruder, isothermal An extrusion process where the melt stock remains constant for a good portion of the extruder screw channel. This type of operation is most common for small diameter extruders.

extruder, laminating A laminating process where a plastic is extruded between two layers of a substrate. ▷**laminate**

extruder length to diameter ▷**L/D ratio**

extruder line cooling and shaping After heating the plastic and shaping it in the die, some type of cooling action takes place in order to keep its shape. Water and/or air are used as may be indicated by the shape and plastic. The simplest method is to draw the extrudate directly into a long water bath, keeping it submerged so that the water can provide direct cooling. Sizing plates and/or tubes having the shape of the finished extrusion are often used to hold the plastic as it passes through the water. Depending on the shape, other means may be used such as rollers, adjustable fingers or blocks of material to direct its movement, etc. The water bath temperature may vary from cold to boiling hot, depending on material and shape. The bath tank may be hotter near the entrance and cooler when it leaves the bath.

Air cooling follows much of the same basic approach as water cooling, except that streams of air are blown against the extrudate. Sizing plates, fingers, rollers, etc. are also used to hold and/or guide the plastic (see Fig. on p. 251).

Another method used to make hollow sections, such as tubes, pipes, etc., is the vacuum box. In this system the extrudate is directed through a box (tank) partly filled with water. At the entrance end there would be a sizing unit (rings, plates, tubes, etc.). When the lid of the box is closed, a vacuum is induced inside the box. The air inside the section can now push walls of the plastic out against the sizing device and thus hold the section firmly while it is cooled and set. The water acts as a lubricating agent between the plastic and sizing device.

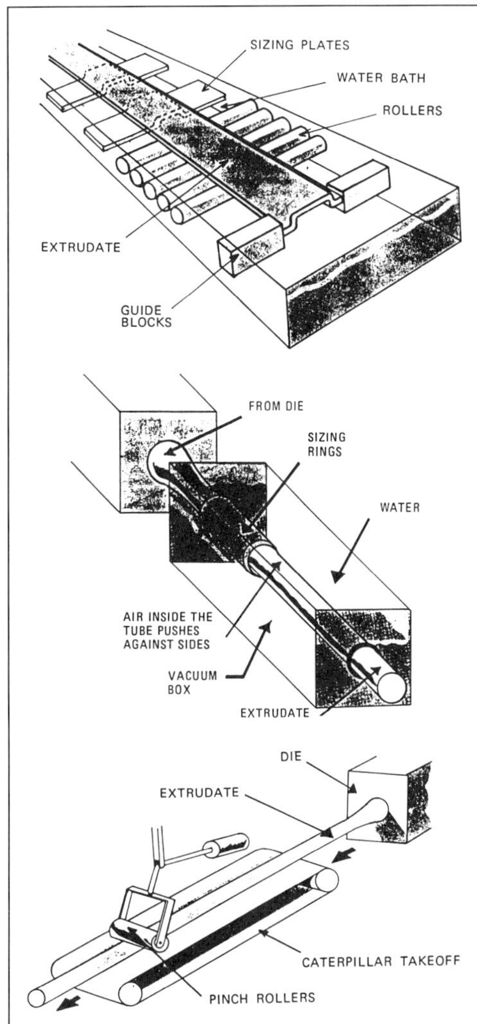

Schematics of cooling and retaining shapes of extrudate from an extruder.

extruder line microprocessor control ▷ **microprocessor control**

extruder line processing interrelations Each line has interrelating operations as well as specific line operations to simplify processing.

extruder machine setup record ▷ **injection molding machine setup record** that can be used as a guide to extrusion.

extruder, maintenance ▷ **die maintenance and care** and **extruder screw pulling**

extruder mark Mark or line formed accidentally in an extruder on an extrudate.

extruder melt flow defects ▷ **melt flow defects**

extruder melt flow orientation Different techniques are used to control molecular orientation of plastics during processing. ▷ **orientation** for details. Special processing techniques are also used, such as the Scortec process. The live-feed method uses multiple pistons installed around the periphery of a pipe die cavity to direct the melt's flow. By sequencing the piston strokes, the process makes the melt front rotate as it cools. The resulting shear orients both the plastic molecules and the glass fibers (when used) around the pipe circumference and prevents axial die lines. This method can increase the hoop strength of reinforced polypropylene pipe by 65%, eliminating spider line weakness, voids, etc. ▷ **injection molding push-pull** and **Scorim**

extruder melt flow properties The correct design of the metering section of the extruder is strongly dependent on the melt flow properties of the plastic and the amount of pressure to be generated in the metering section ▷ **screw metering section**. The important flow property to consider is the melt viscosity. The melt viscosity is dependent on the shear rate. Such materials are said to be non-Newtonian. The viscosity of a plastic melt reduces with increasing shear rate; this is called pseudoplastic or shear thinning behavior. The dependence of the viscosity on shear rate is often described by a power law approximation, indicating a power law dependence between viscosity and shear rate. ▷ **design die**

extruder melt fracture ▷ **melt fracture**

extruder melting and crystallization ▷ **injection molding melting and crystallization**

extruder motor and gear reducer The power to turn a screw comes from the extruder drive system with an often very large motor. Power requirements are usually 5 to 10 lb/h/motor HP. Thus, an extruder processing 100 lb/h (45 kg/h) output requires 10 to 20 HP motor. The speed of electric motors is usually much too fast, such as 1,700 RPM, for direct connection to the screw. Common screw speeds range from 20 to 200 RPM. For this reason, a large gear reducer is used between the motor and screw. Reduction can also be sheaves with pulleys and belts connecting the motor and gear reducer.

extruder, multilayer Process of combining (laminating) two or more layers of different and/or similar plastic films and /or sheets. Other materials such as aluminum foil, decorative paper, and plywood can be incorporated. This inline process takes extruded film and/or sheet from their respective dies and laminates them through squeeze rolls or other techniques. ▷**coextrusion**

extruder multiple screw ▷**extruder screw multiple type**

extruder neck-in and beading With coating (as well as other flat film or sheet processes), upon exiting the die the hot film will shrink across the width. This shrinkage, or "neck-in", is the amount of shrinkage from the die face to the coating width. With neck-in there is also "beading", which is a thickening at both edges of the film. The neck-in and beading influence the performance of a coating (as well as a film/sheet), including wrinkling, sagging, coating breaks near the bead, induced unwanted stresses, and so on. The quality of coated edges is unpredictable and may require more than the usual trimming widths. The amount of neck-in and beading varies for different plastics (one should get manufacturers' inputs on minimum amounts, etc). The processing conditions definitely influence these undesirable effects. (Certain die designs practically eliminate edge bead, but the designs are specific for given plastics). One should determine the minimum neck-in and bead size based on processing conditions, and use those observations as control parameters. Sensors of neck-in and beads can be used in automatic process control. ▷**neck-in**

extruder operating requirements Features to consider in matching the extruder to the product performance requirements should include the following: screw design, extruder diameter, L/D ratio, screw rpm range and changeability, available torque and horsepower, gearbox and thrust ratings, distribution of barrel zones, type of barrel cooling, need for venting, need for screw cooling, screw and barrel hard-surfacing, and control instrumentation.

extruder operation Machine operation takes place in three stages. The first stage covers the running of a machine and its peripheral equipment. The next involves setting processing conditions to a prescribed number of parameters for a specific material, with a specific die, and in a specific line. The final stage is devoted to problem solving and fine-tuning of the operation, which will lead to meeting product performance requirements at the lowest cost of operation. A successful operation requires close attention to many details, such as the quality and flow of feed material, a heat profile adequate to melt but not degrade the material, and a startup and shutdown that will not degrade the plastic. Processors must become familiar with a troubleshooting guide.

Care should be taken to prevent conditions that promote surface condensation of moisture on the resin and moisture absorption by the pigments in color concentrates. Processors must avoid contamination from other plastics, dust, paper clips, and so on, and take special care in cleaning feed hoppers, hopper dryers, blenders, scrap granulators, and other material handling equipment. Plastic silos, containers, and hoppers should be kept covered to prevent contamination. Also certain established procedures for startup should be followed to prevent contamination, overheating, and excessive pressures (see Table below).

extruder, orientation ▷**orientation; extruder blown film stretching-orientating; extruder film orientation; extruder, pipe and profile orientation; extruder, sheet orientation; blow molding stretched**

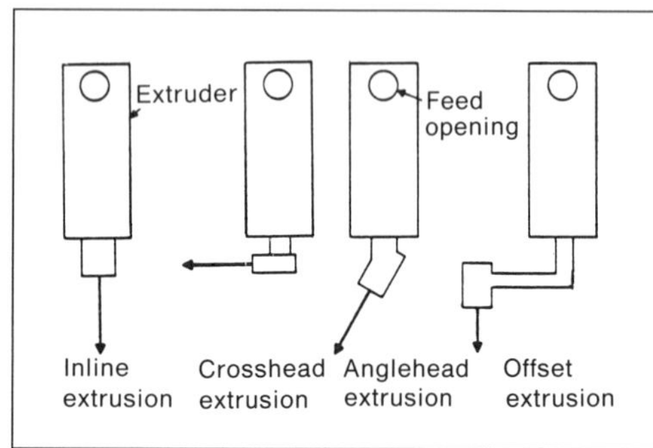

Extrusion output directions.

Example of extrusion operations for different products in low density polyethylene; all temperatures are °C.

Product	HP	Barrel temperature		Die temperature	Pressure, psi	Material temperature
		Rear	Front			
Pipe	40	150	160	165	1500	165
Tubular film	40	150	160	165	1500	165
Flat film	40	200	240	250	1000	250
Coating	100	250	315	325	1000	320
Wire coating	50	220	240	240	3000	240
Contours	20	175	200	205	1500	200

Means of increasing output and improving product quality.

Machine conditions	To increase output	To improve end product quality
Barrel pressure through valving (back pressure)	Decrease	Increase
Screen pack (Screen mesh or number of screens)	Decrease	Increase
Screw temperature	Increase	Decrease
Screw speed	Increase	

extruder output direction The Fig. opposite shows examples of different directions for melt exiting a die to meet different production line requirements. The "inline" is principally used since it is preferred; melt remains in one direction.

extruder output quality The Table summarizes machine conditions by which extruder output can be increased or end product quality can be improved. These conditions are true for all types of extrusion. There is, however, an optimum range for each of these conditions beyond which the output can no longer be significantly increased and some essential properties may begin to decline.

extruder output rate The weight of plastic discharged from the extruder per unit time based on continuous operation, usually expressed in lb/h or kg/h. As shown in the Fig. below, basically with improvements in plastic behaviors and machined performances the cost of melt output goes down with time.

extruder output recovery rate The volume of melt discharged from the screw per unit time in in^3/s (cm^3/s) when the screw runs on an on-off cycle.

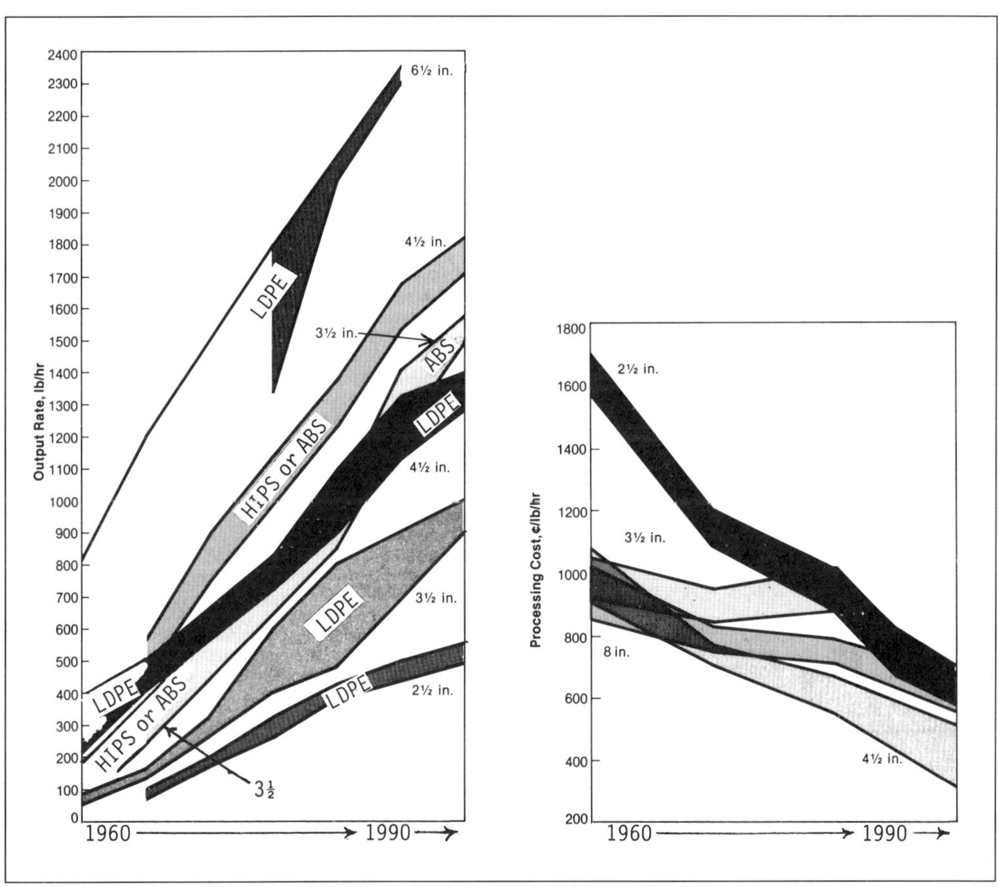

These curves represent historical and projected growth rates for the most commonly used extruders for output rates and processing costs.

extruder output variation Flow variation can be estimated by measuring the pressure variations using the following equation:

$$\Delta Q(\%) = \Delta P(\%) n$$

where n is the power law index of the resin being extruded. Understanding this equation helps one to realize the importance of maintaining a uniform head pressure, if constant flow rate is important.

extruder output versus screw diameter The Fig. shown here is an example of how to match extruder size to the output required, log-log scale is used.

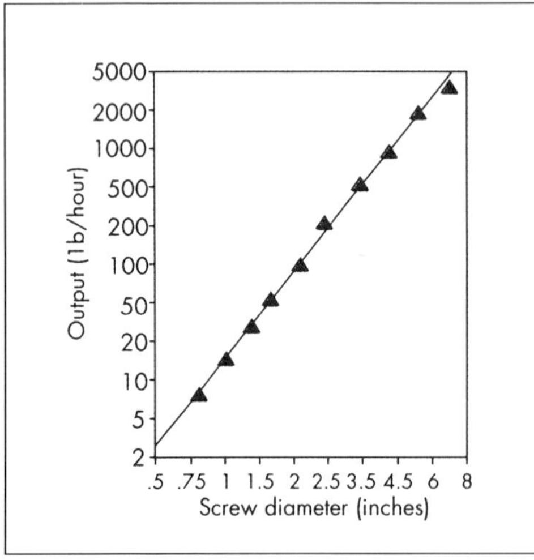

Example of extruder output versus screw diameter.

extruder paste The "paste extrusion" process is unique for PTFE plastics. The plastic is blended with 15 to 20% of a lubricant which may be any one of many organic liquids such as naphtha, odorless kerosene, or white oil. The blend appears much like the powder alone. It is readily compressed and extruded to form thin insulation on wire, thin-walled tubing, ribbon, and other shapes. These operations are usually carried out at temperatures between room temperature and 100°C (212°F). The procedures are semicontinuous, with the extrudate going from the extruder through a drying operation for removal of the lubricant and then through a sintering operation. Interruption occurs when a new charge of lubricated powder (usually preformed) enters into the cylinder of the extruder.

extruder, pipe A typical pipe line consists of a single or a twin screw extruder, a die, equipment for inside and outside calibration, a cooling tank, a wall thickness measuring device, marking equipment, haul-off and automatic cutting and pallet equipment, or a windup unit for self-supporting pipe coils or lengths that are coiled on a drum (see Fig. below). Single screw extruders are generally used when processing PVC compound in granule form; twins handle powders of PVC. The adjustment and control of back pressure are very critical. PVC pipe is a big and very competitive market, so quality and profitability have been the most important requirements for years. Improving the equipment is almost of secondary importance because the equipment for good-quality products is already available.

extruder, pipe and profile orientation To improve properties of pipe and profiles during processing the required temperature downstream can be incorporated, usually requiring a caterpiller (puller) between cooling tanks (see Fig. on p. 255).

extruder, planetary screw A multiple screw device in which a number of satellite screws, generally six, are arranged around one longer and larger diameter screw. The portion of central screw extending beyond the satellite screws serves as the final pumping action as in a single screw extruder. The planetary screws provide the discharge of volatiles toward its hopper end when processing powders such as dry-blended PVC.

extruder plasticating capability For the extruder to deliver a high quality melt to the end of the screw, the plasticating or melting process has to be completed a considerable distance before the end of the screw. In the melting zone the solid bed of plastic is usually pushed against

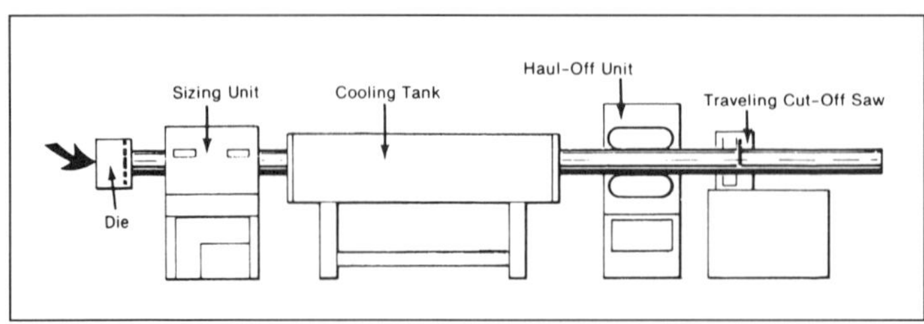

Schematic of downstream equipment used in pipe and profile extrusion.

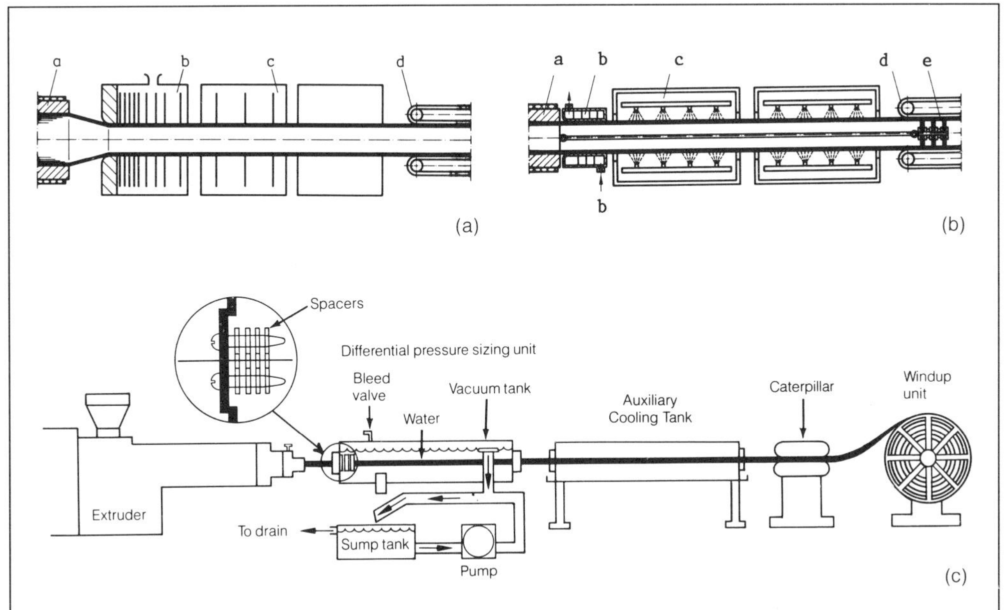

Example of calibration systems for pipe/tube extrusion line that can produce unoriented or oriented products. (*a*) *Vacuum tank* calibration of rigid pipe used with water baths: (a) pipe die, (b) vacuum with discs, (c) heated zone water baths and (d) caterpillar take-off puller; (*b*) *pressure* calibration of rigid pipe using plug insert with water spray cooling: (a) pipe die, (b) pressure calibration, (c) water spray cooling, (d) drag lugs on conveyor belt and (e) caterpillar take-off puller; (*c*) *differential pressure* sizing for flexible tubing.

the trailing edge of the flight with a thin melt film between the solid bed and the barrel. From an analysis of the melting process, it can be determined that melting is improved by using; small flight clearances, large helix angle, narrow flight width, barrier or multiple flights, and internal screw heating. Limitations exist due to plastic melt behavior, particularly those that are heat sensitive. ▷ **plasticating**

extruder plastic handling Care should be taken to prevent conditions that promote surface condensation of moisture on the plastic and moisture absorption by any existing pigments in color concentrates. As explained throughout this book, surface condensation can be avoided by proper storage of the plastic and by keeping it in an area at least as warm as the operating temperature for at least 24 h prior to its use. If moisture absorption by a color concentrate is suspected, heating for 8 to 24 h in a 120 to 150°C (250 to 300°F) oven should permit sufficient drying. With hygroscopic resins, special precautions and drying are required. A hopper dryer's heat can be used to improve melt performance and extruder output capacity (see Fig. on top of p. 256). When the dryer preheat is insufficient, heat can be applied in the screw's solids conveying zone and/or the barrel feed throat (assuming the capability exists).

A typical heat profile that is adequate at low screw speed may be inadequate when speeds are increased, because of the greater rate of material flow through the extruder. (In fact, the heat profile may even be inadequate at low speed.) The output may not increase at a linear rate with increasing speed unless the heat profile increases (see second Fig. on p. 256). With a proper heat profile, a linear relationship between speed and output can be maintained through a wider operating range. However, too high a heat at low screw speed is likely to cause melting all the way back to the barrel throat, causing resin bridging and degradation.

Different techniques are used to improve feeding from the hopper—a ram stuffer, a tapered (larger) screw in the throat section, a grooved feed section, starved feeding, and so on. All have advantages and disadvantages, based on the capabilities of the machines and of the resin being processed. What may help with one machine in the plant may be useless in another machine using the same resin. Use of a barrel feed with an intensively water-cooled grooved feed section basically avoids early melting. The grooves impart better solids conveying for resins with a low coefficient of friction such as UHMWPE and other resins where additives make them extremely slippery. The grooves

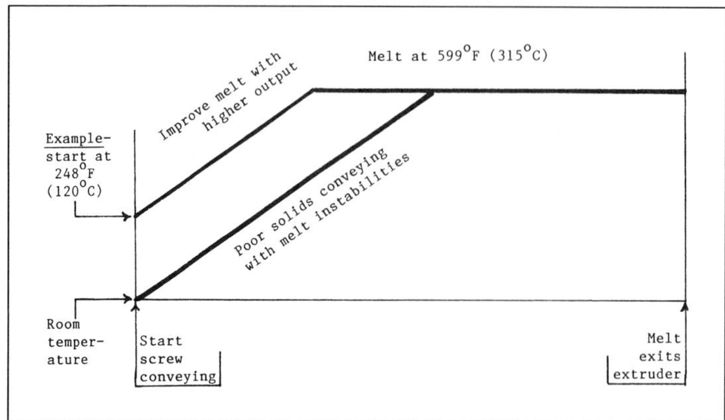

Technique for improving plastic and/or machine performance by preheating "solids" entering the extruder's feed throat.

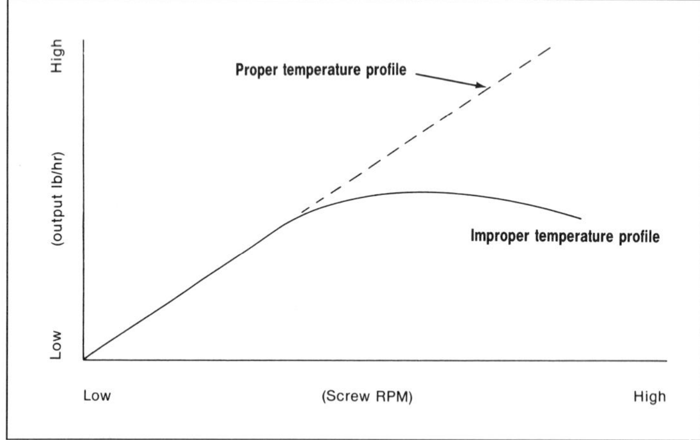

Illustration showing that a higher temperature input for plastics entering the barrel throat will increase the extruder output capacity with an increase in RPM.

usually have right-angle profile and axial arrangements, although helical grooves are used for certain materials. Optimum sizing and dimensioning of the feed section and the correct control of cooling are necessary, as well as proper design of the feed screw, to achieve a high-output revolution with a low-friction load.

extruder postforming inline ▷ **postforming**

extruder pressure valve system Pressure valves provide good control and can take away this function from die and screen-pack arrangement (particularly in extrusion coating). Various types of valves are used internally and externally. The internal valve is a movable screw which can be adjusted forward or backward to increase or decrease pressure. Moving the screw varies the size of the opening between the end of the screw and the breaker plate and adapter. External pressure valves make use of some type of pin arrangement which varies the size of the opening at the extruder adapter, thereby varying pressure.

extruder process control Controlling extrusion processes takes two types of systems, one on the extruder and another on the finished extruded product. In turn, these controls have to be interfaced. Extruder controls include heats, pressures, hopper feed rate, screw RPM, back pressures, etc.), and product controls include wall thicknesses, rate of travel, width indicators, weight, etc.). Extensive efforts are continually being made to achieve the maximum in speed and precision. For products with specific requirements, typically the best approach has always been to control the weight per unit area or the length of output that is directly related to a constant melt throughput, by weight. As reviewed in this chapter (and others), many machine controls and designs are required, such as feed rate of loading, screw design, and so on. In regard to products such as film, thickness gauges were once very popular for adjusting takeoff speeds. However, better control is achieved now with weight control systems. Depending on the given weights per unit length or area and the speed of the line, the

Window profile extrusion line (courtesy of Battenfeld).

melt throughput rates of the extruder are pre-calculated accurately enough to ensure, via a melt throughput control system, that the weight can be kept constant within a tolerance range of at least ±0.5%.

extruder process control statistically ▷**statistical process control**

extruder processing high molecular weight plastics ▷**blow molding, extruder polyethylene low melt index**

extruder profile As with pipe, the profile market is largely dominated by PVC and is highly competitive. Automation at the processor's level continually reaches advanced performance. High performance lines operate over 2 m/min. The Fig. under ▷**extruder, pipe** provides an example applicable to a profile line. The Fig. above shows a high performance window profile extrusion line with a gravimetric dosing integrated in the Battenfeld BEC control system. As changes have been made in PVC compounding to optimize processing, there has been a considerable change in the type of impact modifier used. The use of acrylic, with butyl acrylate, has almost replaced modification with EVA. When modification is carried out with acrylate, the elastomer phase is embedded in the form of beads in a continuous PVC matrix. During processing it is retained to the decomposition range. This wide processing latitude has at least made it easier to achieve the present high outputs in profile extrusion. It also has provided low shrinkage, high heat distortion, and good weather resistance. ▷**die dry sleeve calibration** and **extruder line cooling and shaping**

extruder profile coating system The Fig. below is an example of a profile being coated as the profile moves through the crosshead die. Basic approach is similar to the much more popular system of extrusion wire coating.

extruder profile output dimensional tolerances Typical tolerances for profiles are given in the Table on p. 258.

extruder profile structure, hollow core with gas Gas air, nitrogen, etc. can be used similar to the plug assist with internal air pressure system used to extrude pipe immediately upon extrudate leaving the die. ▷**injection molding, gas**

extruder programmable controllers safety circuit ▷**programmable controllers safety circuit**

extruder purging ▷**purging**

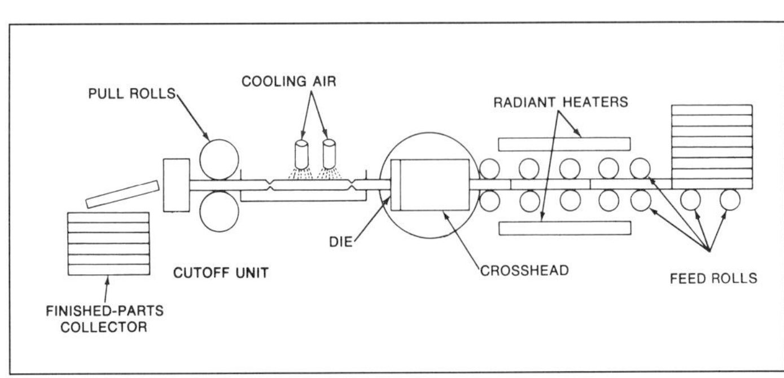

Schematic of non-continuous profiles being automatically coated with plastics.

Recommended dimensional tolerances for plastic profile extrusions.

Dimension	Rigid vinyl (PVC)	Polystyrene	ABS
Wall thickness	±8%	±8%	±8%
Angles	±2°	±2°	±3°
Profile dimensions, ±mm (in)			
0–3 (0–$\frac{1}{8}$)	0.18 mm (0.007 in)	0.18 mm (0.007 in)	0.25 mm (0.010 in)
3–13 ($\frac{1}{8}$–$\frac{1}{2}$)	0.25 mm (0.010 in)	0.30 mm (0.012 in)	0.50 mm (0.020 in)
13–25 ($\frac{1}{2}$–1)	0.38 mm (0.015 in)	0.43 mm (0.017 in)	0.63 mm (0.025 in)
25–38 (1–1$\frac{1}{2}$)	0.50 mm (0.020 in)	0.63 mm (0.025 in)	0.68 mm (0.027 in)
38–50 (1$\frac{1}{2}$–2)	0.63 mm (0.025 in)	0.75 mm (0.030 in)	0.90 mm (0.035 in)
50–75 (2–3)	0.75 mm (0.030 in)	0.90 mm (0.035 in)	0.94 mm (0.037 in)
75–100 (3–4)	1.10 mm (0.045 in)	1.30 mm (0.050 in)	1.30 mm (0.050 in)
100–125 (4–5)	1.50 mm (0.060 in)	1.70 mm (0.065 in)	1.70 mm (0.065 in)
125–180 (5–7)	1.90 mm (0.075 in)	2.40 mm (0.093 in)	2.40 mm (0.093 in)
180–250 (7–10)	2.40 mm (0.093 in)	3.00 mm (0.125 in)	3.00 mm (0.125 in)
Dimension	**Polypropylene**	**Flexible vinyl (PVC)**	**Polyethylene**
Wall thickness	±8%	±10%	±10%
Angles	±3°	±5°	±5°
Profile dimensions, ±mm (in)			
0–3 (0–$\frac{1}{8}$)	0.25 mm (0.010 in)	0.25 mm (0.010 in)	0.30 mm (0.012 in)
3–13 ($\frac{1}{8}$–$\frac{1}{2}$)	0.38 mm (0.015 in)	0.38 mm (0.015 in)	0.63 mm (0.025 in)
13–25 ($\frac{1}{2}$–1)	0.50 mm (0.020 in)	0.50 mm (0.020 in)	0.75 mm (0.030 in)
25–38 (1–1$\frac{1}{2}$)	0.68 mm (0.027 in)	0.75 mm (0.030 in)	0.90 mm (0.035 in)
38–50 (1$\frac{1}{2}$–2)	0.90 mm (0.035 in)	0.90 mm (0.035 in)	1.00 mm (0.040 in)
59–75 (2–3)	0.94 mm (0.037 in)	1.00 mm (0.040 in)	1.10 mm (0.045 in)
75–100 (3–4)	1.30 mm (0.050 in)	1.70 mm (0.065 in)	1.70 mm (0.065 in)
100–125 (4–5)	1.70 mm (0.065 in)	2.40 mm (0.093 in)	2.40 mm (0.093 in)
125–180 (5–7)	2.40 mm (0.093 in)	3.00 mm (0.125 in)	3.00 mm (0.125 in)
180–250 (7–10)	3.00 mm (0.125 in)	3.80 mm (0.150 in)	3.80 mm (0.150 in)

extruder ram system An extruder in which the plastic is moved through the barrel and die by means of a ram or plunger rather than the usual screw. Ram extrusion (also ram injection molding) dates back to at least 1872 processing cellulose nitrate. The screw method took over all plasticating processes early in this century since it provides a better method of melting, etc. However, the ram method is still used particularly for plastic melts that are not feasible in screws such as PFTE and heat sensitive plastics such as PVC. ▷ **molding; billet; extruder wire and cable; skiving**

extruder reactive processing Reactive extrusion (REX) is a terminology similar to reaction injection molding (RIM) where the plastic is not fed into the extruder. Rather the monomers (prepolymers) are fed and in turn the extruder develops the chemical reaction to produce the plastic (polymer) prior to leaving the plasticator and traveling through the die. REX is also called reactive processing or reactive compounding. The extruder is especially suitable as a polymer reactor instead of only as a processing aid. Operating on the principle of drag flow, it is capable of pumping and mixing viscoelastic materials while generating high pressures and maintaining high temperatures. A particular advantage of the extruder in this context is the absence of solvent as the reaction medium. No solvent stripping or recovery process is required, and product contamination by solvent or solvent impurities is avoided.

Because of their versatility, most REXs are twin-screw extruders that possess a segmented barrel, each segment of which can be individually cooled and heated externally (see Fig. on p. 259). In addition to external heating, a melt may be shear heated by the resistance of viscous material to the conveying motion of the screw; these processes provide energy for chemical reaction. The screws often have specialized sections or configurations such as high shear mixing sections. REX provides a combination of several chemical process operations into one machine with accompanying high space-time yields of

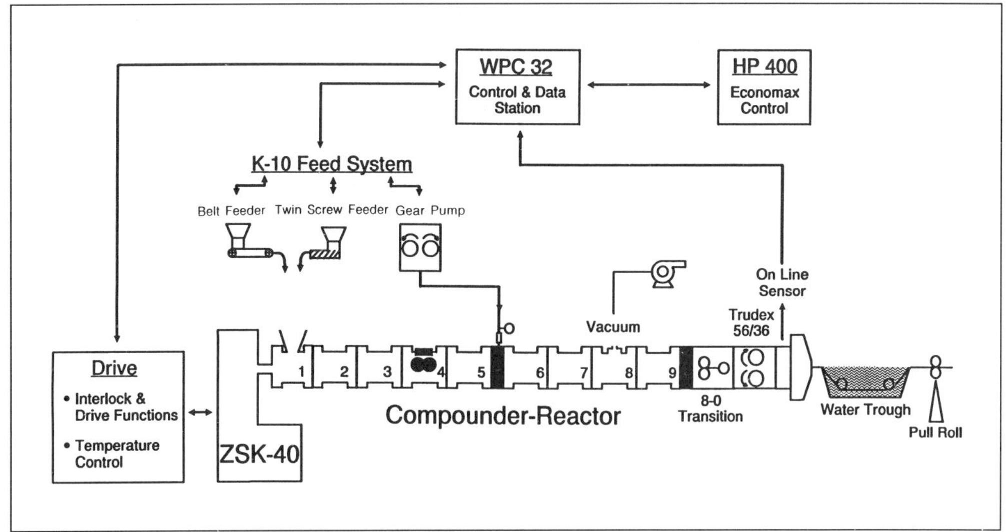

Process flow diagram illustrates the reactive process and multivariate control system; Werner & Pfleiderer Corp. laboratory reactor is equipped with co-rotating, closely intermeshing, self-wiping screws.

product. It provides the ability for short or long runs. ▷ **reactive processing**

extruder rear end The end toward the feed or upstream.

extruder, reciprocating ram Two ram extruders are used to produce a continuous extrudate through a die that is fed melt from both rams. The die block aided with open-shut devices (valves, etc.) alternately receives melt from each ram unit so that there is a continuous extrudate. ▷ **extruder ram system**

extruder reduction gear A gear device (gear reducer) used to reduce speed between the drive motor and the extruder screw. Supplementary speed reduction means may also be used, such as belts and sheaves.

extruder rheometer ▷ **rheometer, extrusion**

extruder safety ▷ **safety; processing rules to remember and forget; programmable controller safety; safety and machines; safety interlock; barrel fail-safe rupture disc**

extruder salt bath process ▷ **salt bath**

extruder screen pack Melt from the screw usually is forced through a breaker plate with a screen pack. Extra heat develops when melt goes through the screens, so some heat-sensitive materials cannot use a screen pack. The function of a screen pack initially is to reduce rotary motion of the melt, remove large unmelted particles, and remove other contaminants. This situation can be related to improper screw design, contaminated feedstock, poor control of regrind, and so on. Sometimes screen packs are used to control the operating pressure of extruders. However, there are advantages in processing with matched and controlled back pressure, operating within the required melt pressure, as this can facilitate mixing, effectively balancing out melt heat.

In operation, the screen pack is backed up by a breaker plate that has a number of passages, usually many round holes ranging from $\frac{1}{8}$ to $\frac{3}{16}$ in. in diameter. One side of the plate is recessed to accommodate round discs of wire screen cloth, which make up the screen pack (see Table).

Screens used before the breaker plate to filter out contaminants in the melt.[1]

Contaminant	Metal fibers	Wire mesh		Sintered powder
		Square weave	Dutch twill[2]	
Gel captured	5	1	2	3
Contaminant capacity	6	2	3	3
Permeability	4	4	1	2

[1] Range is from poorest (1) to best (6). Multiple screens usually are used; example screen pack has 20-mesh against breaker plate, followed by 40-, 60-, and 100-mesh (coarsest mesh has lowest mesh number).
[2] Woven in parallel diagonal lines.

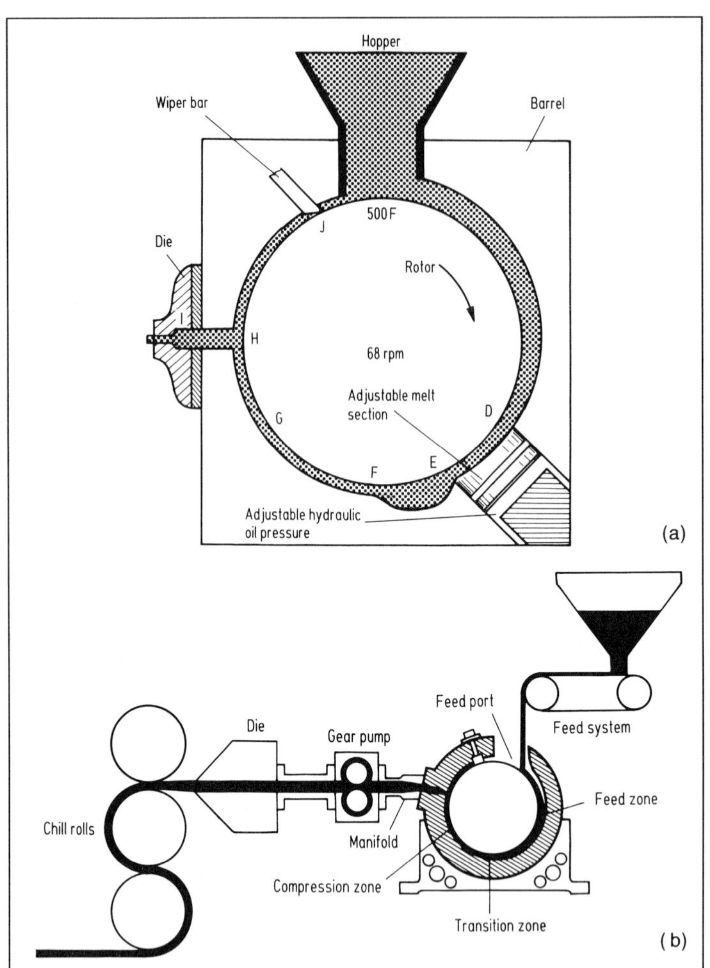

Schematic of a screwless extruder; (*a*) cross section of the rotor extruder. Schematic shows material moving from hopper A to hot rotor surface B. Feed section goes from B to C, transition/compression section C to D, melt section D to E, vent section from exhaust port E to F, transition/compression section F to G, melt section G to H, die opening section H to I and adjustable wiper bar J. (*b*) sheet line.

Pressure controls should be used on both sides of the breaker plate to ensure that the pressure on the melt stays within the required limits. Based on the processing requirements, manual to highly sophisticated screen changers are used. With limited runs or infrequent changes, manual systems are used. The packs are usually mounted outside the extruder between the head clamp and the die and can be changed via mechanical or hydraulic devices. Continuous screen changes also are used. The more sophisticated the system, the higher its costs.

extruder screw design ▷ **design screw**

extruder screwless In a conventional extruder, the shear between the screw flights and the barrel is higher than the shear between the screw root and the barrel. This higher shear does not occur in a rotary extruder, because there is no screw. Instead a shear is created by a smooth rotor spinning in an eccentrically bored barrel. Different designs of this isothermal rotor extruder are designed or targeted to reduce processing energy consumption, reduce and provide more uniform shear to improve properties, reduce residence time, etc. The Fig. above provides general information on the InstaMelt Systems, Inc. (Midland, TX) screwless extruder.

extruder, screw multiple type As contrasted to conventional single screw extruders, these machines involve the use of two or four screws (conical or constant depth). Types include machines with intermeshing counter-rotating screws, intermeshing co-rotating screws, and nonintermeshing counter-rotating screws. ▷ **extruder, twin screw**

extruder, screw planetary type ▷ **extruder, planetary screw**

extruder screw pulling Removal of the screw is the next step in the cleaning process. This is often called "pulling the screw", but

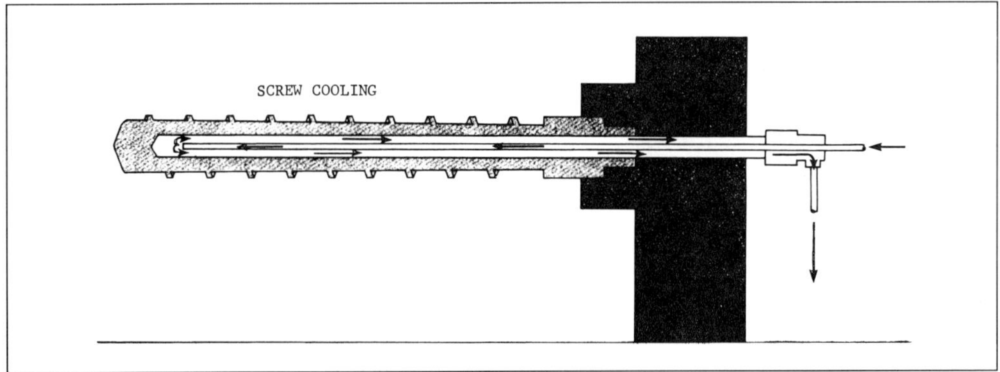

Schematic of a screw with internal heat or cooling system.

removal actually starts by using a "screw pusher". It is inserted through the hollow drive shaft at the rear to push on the shank of the screw. With the die and breaker plate removed the screw is pushed out of the barrel far enough so that it can be pulled the rest of the way out. The pusher may be a brass rod used as a ram to pound on the screw. More often, the pusher is a threaded shaft which is attached to the rear of the extruder. The screw is "jacked" out of the barrel using the extruder drive for power. The shaft is kept from turning and a threaded nut attached to the drive forces the shaft forward pushing the screw in front of it. Sometimes there is a tight fitting key in a keyway of the screw. When the key is passed, the screw can be moved with less force.

The screw is conveniently cleaned while it sticks out of the barrel. The process is easy if the purging compound did a good job. Excess compound is brushed off with a power-driven wire brush or may be removed with a wiremesh cloth using the two-handed action of polishing shoes. The screw should be cleaned to bare metal, and chrome-plated screws should attain a high-gloss shine. The barrel is cleaned while hot with a brush of the type used for cleaning a furnace. Wire mesh cloth may be wrapped around it for scrubbing action or a rag for a final wipe-down. The barrel should be free of carbon and should shine. Solvents will aid in the removal of some resins from the screw and barrel. Resin suppliers' recommendations should be followed. With many resins, solvents will be of no help.

extruder, screw single type The single screw extruder basically consists of a screw, barrel, drive mechanism, plastic feed arrangement, and controls. The constantly turning screw augers the resin through the heated barrel where it is heated to proper temperature and blended into a homogenous melt. Before the melt can leave the barrel, it usually must pass through a breaker plate and screen pack. This unit builds up back pressure in the barrel, filters out contaminants, and tends to convert turbulent melt flow into more laminar flow. The melt is then extruded through the die into the desired shape.

extruder screw wear ▷ **screw wear**

extruder, screw with internal heat control At times, an internal heat control is used in a screw as shown in the Fig. above. It provides an improved method for controlling melt temperature during processing when required by certain plastics.

extruder, sheet Sheet is usually defined as being thicker than film, or thicker than 1 to 4 mm ($\approx$0.003–0.010 in.). Sheet thickness can be at least 2 mm (0.5 in.), and widths can be up to 30 m (10 ft). Basically, hot melt from a slit die is directed to a combination of an air knife with two cooling rolls, or, a more popular choice, to a three-cooling-roll stand (see Fig. on p. 262), which cools, calibrates, and produces a smooth sheet. To aid the chill rolls, end sections of the die are operated at a higher heat than the center. Cooling rolls require this type of heat control from their ends to the center. The operation (as well as design) of a slit die, particularly for wide sheets, requires extensive experience. Its rather high melt pressure can deform the die. ▷ **sheet train**

extruder, sheet curling and warping To eliminate or reduce these processing problems, examine one or a combination of causes such as an unbalance of roll temperatures versus stock temperature and extruder output rate, improper design or adjustment, insufficient cooling in sheet train, hot spots on chrome rolls, and/or high stock temperature. ▷ **extruder web heat transfer roll adjustment**

extruder, sheet draw down rate ▷ **drawdown**

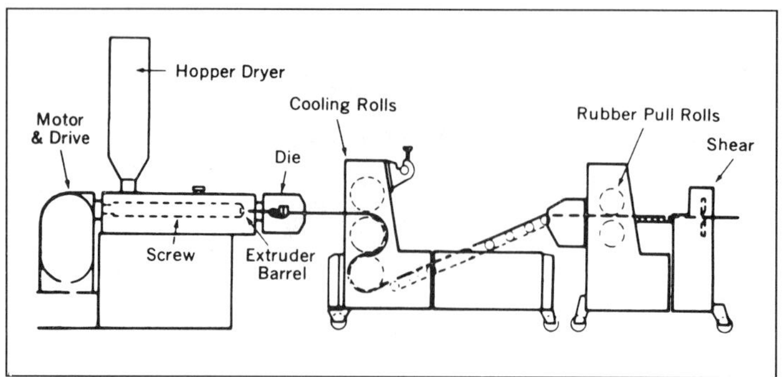

Schematic of a sheet line using a three-cooling-roll stand.

extruder, sheet orientation Unwanted orientations, principally in the machine (pull) direction could be caused by one or a combination of causes such as too large a die-lip opening, low stock temperature, excessive sheet tension from pull rolls, polished rolls to cold, too great a distance from die lip to roll nip, and/or excessive bead (at nip) build-up. However, usually orientation is desired and specifically provided during processing. ▷ **extruder film orientation** and **orientation**

extruder, sheet roll deflection When producing light gauge sheet on a three-roll stack surface imperfections due to non-uniform roll contact can begin to occur with sheet 0.020 in. (5 mm) or thinner, particularly if the operators are not skilled or if the equipment used has small rolls which deflect easily. To minimize the problem and produce thinner gauge consider the following: (1) specify on new equipment large enough roll diameter, (2) have one or both rolls crowned so that under loading they will straighten out in the nip area, (3) consider a silicone rubber roll instead of a steel roll, (4) use an air knife to "wet" the sheet to the center roll: very effective where a first class double polished finish is not required, (5) cross the rolls slightly so that under load deflection the resulting nip gap is uniform, and (6) run with minimum nip loading—this can be done by carefully selecting screw design and/or adding a melt pump to minimize machine direction surging and to very carefully adjust the die to ensure as uniform transverse direction thickness as possible.

extruder shutdown Usually, shutdown is quite simple. The flow of material from the hopper to the feed throat is stopped, but the screw rotation is continued until nothing more comes from the die. Then the screw is stopped. This is called "pumping the screw dry." At the same time feed is stopped, the electricity to the barrel and die heaters may be turned off. Full cooling may be used on the barrel. The purpose of this is to cool the barrel and to provide for the coldest possible plastic to remain in the die, minimizing degradation of the plastic.

When very high barrel temperatures are used, the previously described shutdown procedure may not be good enough. It may be necessary to continue passing plastic through the extruder while bringing the barrel temperature down. Simply pumping the barrel dry would allow the plastic remaining to be oxidized and crosslinked by air at the very high temperature. "Burning" of the plastic in the extruder may cause gel formation and die lines. Then a complete cleanout of the equipment may be needed. Shutdown may involve changing by purging. There may be a preferred material to have in the extruder for reheating and startup.

extruder size The normal inside diameter of an extruder barrel or outside diameter of screw.

extruder sizing Three sizing methods are used to produce profiles, pipe, tubes, etc., namely vacuum, water-sizing tank, or dry vacuum calibration. They maintain the dimensional stability of the extrudate depending upon the plastic and type of extrusion.

extruder sizing plate ▷ **extruder line cooling and shaping**

extruder slot Slot extrusion is a method of extruding films or sheet in which the molten thermoplastic is forced through a straight slot.

extruder solid-state Solid-state extrusion (SSE) is a means for the deformation and evaluation of uniaxial molecular chain orientation and extension for a wide range of semicrystalline and amorphous thermoplastics. Via SSE investigation, HDPE can be drawn into fibers with some of the highest specific tensile moduli and strengths. A two-step drawing process was developed for the preparation of polyoxyethylene, polypropylene, and polyethylene fibers. The polymer is first drawn up to the natural draw ratio at a fast rate and subsequently slowly superdrawn at a temperature that depends on the crystalline dispersion temperature; ordered structures can be produced.

A highly oriented extrudate can be obtained by extruding through a capillary rheometer with a conical die at temperatures close to the melting point. Initial work led to the development of transparent and fibrous linear polyethylene extrudates. These were obtained by extruding HDPE from the molten state (132–136°C) above a critical shear rate in a capillary rheometer and through a conical die. This procedure was subsequently modified by processing HDPE exclusively in the solid state where the polymer is semicrystalline before extrusion through the die. This modification produced continuous transparent fibers with moduli in the range of 30 to 70 GPa ($4.35 \times 10^6 + 0 - 10 \times 10^6$ psi) for linear polyethylene. ▷ **orientation**

extruder startup Startup of an extrusion operation differs with the type of product to be produced, but there are some common aspects. Also process differs if a clean empty machine is used or one which contains plastic and is reheated. It is necessary to wait until the barrel and die are at the correct operating heat before starting based on the plastic being used. It is common practice to purge some plastic through the extruder before "stringing up" the extrudate. Purge may simply be permitted to fall on the floor. Since melt is very hot and sticky, prevent contact with skin and clothing. Startup is at the rate the operator can handle; it may be very slow compared to operating speed. It involves pulling the extrudate and "threading it" in, around, and through cooling assembly and other downstream equipment (decorators, cutters, pullers, etc). Once a reasonable part is being made, take-off speed can be increased. All speed-controlled equipment has to be done simultaneously either manually or preferably by computer process control. Follow with checking dimensions (or what is required). Change conditions to meet requirements (speed, temperatures, etc.).

This heating procedure produces a flowable melt at the die and extruder rear rather than leaving solid plugs. Plugs would allow gas from decomposition to build up pressure. Then, when pressure becomes high enough, or when the plug becomes loose from heating, the plug would blow from the die followed by molten, decomposed plastic. If the plug is melted first, pressure cannot develop behind it. Gas may form but it can escape as bubbles without serious pressure buildup.

A precautionary measure is not to stand in front of the extruder, particularly during startup, for any thermal upset can cause an unexpected high velocity discharge at the die at any time. Also do not look into the hopper at startup or during problem times. Once plastic comes out of die and is clean, problems generally are not expected.

extruder starved feeder When too much material is trying to go through the extruder, a feed system at the hopper reduces input. Cause could be using an improper screw for the plastic, improper cleaning of barrel and screw, etc.

extruder surging A pronounced fluctuation in output over a short period of time without deliberate change in operating conditions. Melt exiting the die could be very erratic causing changes in dimensions and other properties in the extrudate.

extruder take off Downstream of the die different types of take off equipment are used to meet different requirements. They include sizing fixtures, cooling tanks, coiling equipment, line speed controls (mechanical or sonic), tension control (capstans, etc.), extrudate pull devices (pinch rolls, caterpillar/pair of opposite moving belts, etc.), cutters inline, collecting equipment (troughs, tanks, stackers, etc.), etc.

extruder take off cutter to shipping At the end of a line, it must be reduced to its most useful form such as spooled in long lengths or coiled, sawed to long or short lengths, sheared, punched, trimmed, buffed, polished, die cut, etc. A machine with flying blades may chop it into very short lengths, or a traveling saw may be used. Close tolerance "on-demand" cutter to large scale traveling saws include rotary cutting with flywheel cutting and cut-off saws (blades, guillotines, etc.). For cutters and other downstream equipment, different styles exist in each type suited for specific applications.

extruder take off slitting film The conversion of a given width of plastic film (or sheet) to several widths or slits is by some type of cutter, usually flat blade knives or razors, or circular knives. Slitting can be inline or offline. A few of the approaches to slitting are shown in the Fig. on p. 264.

extruder throat The section of the extruder holding the feed hopper, frequently water cooled, through which plastic is introduced into the extruder by the feed opening.

extruder thrust The total axial force exerted by the screw on the thrust bearing. For practical purposes equal to the extrusion pressure times the cross section of the barrel bore.

extruder thrust bearing The bearing used to absorb the thrust force exerted by the screw.

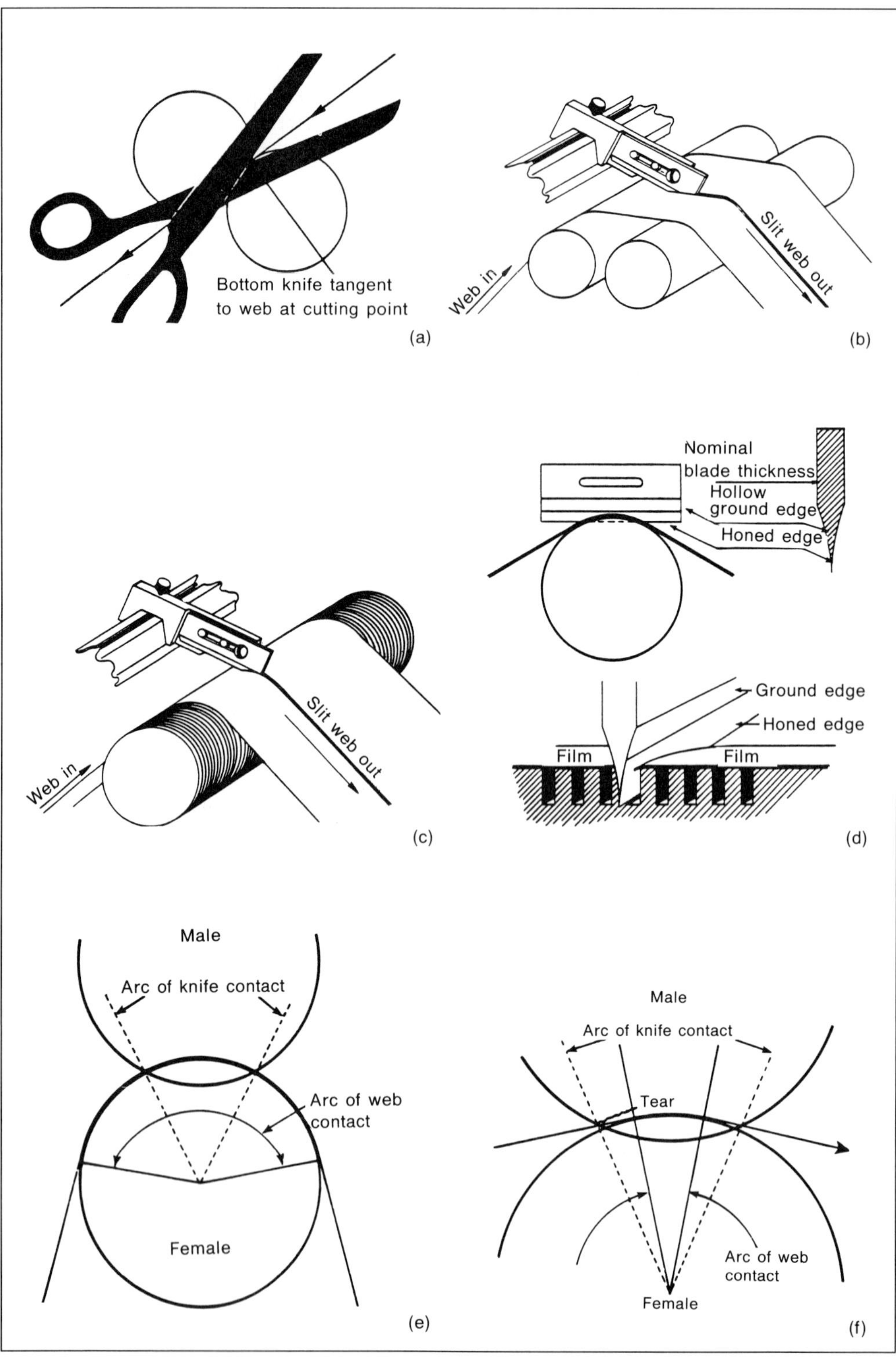

Examples of slitting extruded film: (*a*) shear slitting principle; (*b*) razor blade slitting in air; (*c*) razor blade slitting in grooved roll; (*d*) grooved roll, magnified section; (*e*) arc of contact between male knife and female knife; (*f*) detail of contact arc.

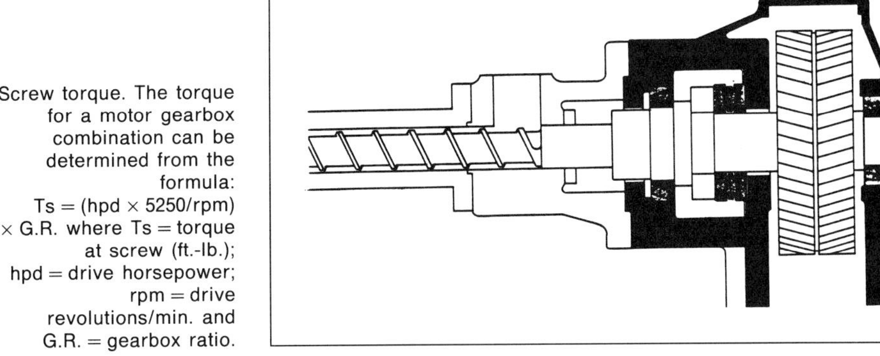

Screw torque. The torque for a motor gearbox combination can be determined from the formula: Ts = (hpd × 5250/rpm) × G.R. where Ts = torque at screw (ft.-lb.); hpd = drive horsepower; rpm = drive revolutions/min. and G.R. = gearbox ratio.

extruder thrust bearing rate Predicted life (hours) of the thrust bearing. This is listed as a B-10 life rating usually rated at a screw speed of 100 rpm and a discharge pressure of 10,000 psi (per Bearing Manufacturers Assoc.). The B-10 life is the expected life of 90% of the thrust bearings manufactured, having met certain specifications. For most bearings the B-10 life is increased by a factor of 8 to 10 if the thrust load is reduced by 50%. Also B-10 is directly proportional to screw rpm.

extruder torque See Fig. above. ▷ **torque**

extruder train A train used in extrusion of products such as pipe, profile, tape, etc. which denotes the entire equipment assembly used to fabricate products from the extruder to the end of the line. ▷ **sheet train**

extruder tube blown Blown thin film tubing is produced by extruding a tube, applying a slight internal air pressure to expand it while still molten, and then subsequently cooling it to set. The tube is then flattened through guides and wound up flat on rolls.

extruder, twin screw Two screws, side by side placed in a barrel. The screw profile is designed to meet different operations along the screw length; feeding, melting, mixing, venting, die pressurization, etc. The type of screw element used to perform each unit operation is based on a fundamental understanding of the working principles of the different types of screws.

Both co- and counter-rotating intermeshing machines have certain general screw geometries in common. Conveying screws are used to transport material, characterized by pitch and conveying direction (forward or reverse). Screw pitch is used to control the residence time distribution and degree-of-fill. Conveying screws can have single, double, or triple flights.

Nonintermeshing counter-rotating extruders vary the screw channel depth to effect changes in volume rather than by varying screw pitch or the number of screw flights. Thus, residence time and degree-of-fill are controlled by selection of screw channel depth.

Reverse pitch screw elements are used to create back pressure. Degree-of-fill increases to 100% upstream of the reverse pitch screw; the preceding forward conveying screws must overcome this resistance. The resulting pressure drop is used for creating a melt seal. Reverse pitch screws have the significant impact of increasing residence time distribution and shear input.

Kneading elements are used for melting, mixing, dispersing, and homogenizing. The kneading elements are comprised of individual kneading discs of various widths, which are offset from each other. The kneading discs can be staggered for forward conveying, reverse conveying, or zero conveying and may have one, two, or three lobes. The level of shear input and type of mixing action are controlled by selecting a disc width, offset angle, number of kneading discs, and direction of conveying.

Various other types of screw geometries utilize interrupted or cut screw flights. The working principle is the same as for kneading elements; conveying efficiency is reduced to the benefit of backflow for mixing. The degree to which the screw flight is interrupted directly influences the degree of mixing.

extruder, twin screw color change Cleaning time between color changes can usually be sped up, without time-consuming screw pulling, when soap is sprayed into the feed hopper together with the purged plastic. Dry color pigments coat the screw flights in the solid conveying section. Soap water wets the pigments; foam and steam are generated in the barrel, removing the loose pigments. After

Film gauging.

Equipment	Web control capability	Product application	Cost ratio
Open-loop microprocessor software Low-resolution sensor Slow-response nuclear source	5% to 10% thickness tolerance improvement; 10% to 15% startup time reduction.	Shrink and stretch wrap, ag film and sheet, industrial liners, disposable thermoform sheet, construction film, heavy-duty sacks.	15–25
Closed-loop microprocessor, software based on extrusion program Nominal target control High-resolution sensor Predictive control Fast response nuclear source Self-diagnostics	7% to 12% thickness tolerance improvement; 15% to 20% startup time reduction. Streak detection; 2% to 3% throughput increase.	Appliance liners, diaper backing, clear film, glazing sheet, HDPE deli paper.	25–35
Target-management software program Predictive control High-resolution sensor Fast-response nuclear source Self-diagnostics Automatic throughput control	10% to 25% thickness tolerance improvement; 20% to 25% startup time reduction. Streak detection; 5% to 7% throughput increase	Downgaged films, blister pack sheet, two-color coextruded sheet, medical thermoform sheet, coextruded snack and cereal liner.	30–45
Automatic profiling software program Automatic profile die Target-management software Predictive control sensor High-resolution sensor Fast-response nuclear source Automatic throughput control Triple CRT resolution Self-diagnostics 100% spare part inventory	40% to 60% thickness tolerance improvement; 50% to 75% startup time reduction. Streak detection; 10% to 15% throughput increase. Detects short term process variations.	Engineering film and sheet, optical grade polycarbonate sheet, barrier coextrusions, polyester capacitance films, die-cut sheet, photographic films, extrusion coating, biaxially-oriented PP film.	40–100

melting is accomplished, the hydraulic wiping in the intermeshing extruder screws will take care of the final clean out. The clean-out process is finished, when the soapy foam in the feed opening turns colorless.

extruder, two-stage screws ▷ **screw, two-stage**

extruder venting During extrusion, as in injection molding, melts must be freed of gaseous components (monomers, moisture, plasticizers, additives, air, etc.), so a vented screw is used. ▷ **injection molding venting** for the action that occurs in the screw. It is especially difficult to completely remove air from some powdered materials unless the melt is exposed to vacuum venting (a vacuum is connected to the vent's exhaust). The standard machines operate on the principle of melt degassing. The degassing is assisted by a rise in the vapor pressure of volatile constituents, which results from the high melt heat. Only the free surface layer is degassed; the remainder of the plastic can release its volatile content only through diffusion. Diffusion in the nonvented screw is always time-dependent, and long residence times are not possible for melt moving through an extruder. Thus a vented extruder is used. ▷ **screw, two-stage**

Most single screw vented extruders have two stages; a few have two vents and three stages. The first stages of the transition and metering sections are often shorter than the sections of a single-stage conventional screw. The melt discharges at zero back pressure into the second stage, under vacuum instead of pressure. The first stage extrudate must not be hot enough to become overheated in the second stage. Also, the first stage must not deliver more output per screw revolution at discharge pressure than the second stage can pump through the die under the maximum normal operating pressure, such

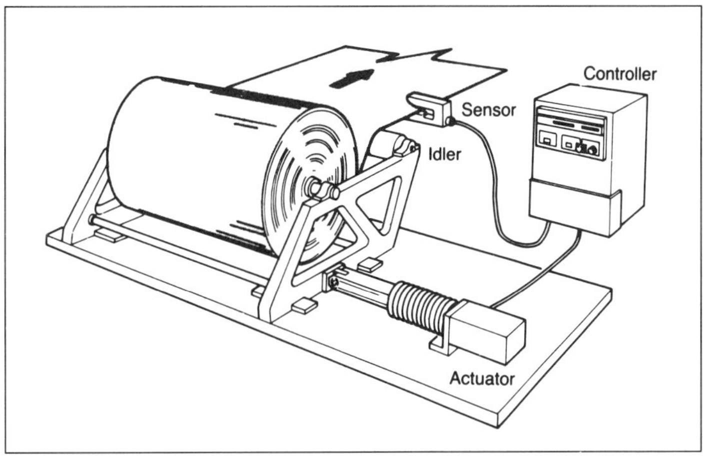

Web unwind guiding.

as might occur just prior to a screen pack change. Usually this requirement means that the second stage metering section must be at least 50% deeper than the first stage.

In practice, the best metering section depth ratio (pump ratio) is about 1.8:1. The best ratio depends on factors such as screw design, downstream equipment, feedstock performance, and operating conditions. With a high compression ratio or metering depth ratio that is a little too low, melt flow through the vent is likely. If this ratio is moderately high, gradual degradation of the output occurs. If the screw channel in the vent area is not filled properly, the self-cleaning action is diminished, and the risk of plateout increased. In any case, sticking or smearing of the melt must be avoided, or degradation will accelerate. ▷ **barrel vented safety**

extruder, vertical position An extruder arranged so that the barrel is in the vertical position (rather than the usual horizontal) and the extrudate moves downward. Provides products with special capabilities for operations such as wire coating.

extruder, void or air in extrudate ▷ **air entrapment**

extruder wear ▷ **screw wear**

extruder web A web defines a film or sheet. The film becomes a sheet when thickness is 0.010 in. (4 mm) or more. However, in certain industries, particularly packaging, the difference is 0.003 in. (1 mm).

extruder web gauging The Table opposite provides a guide to type of gauging film from basic to total line control.

extruder web guide control Controlled alignment is essential in providing a quality roll and in reducing scrap. Improved alignment can be achieved by using the most appropriate of available web-guiding techniques. As materials are unwound and fed into a process or machine, they must be properly aligned in order to operate efficiently, such as thermoforming. Unwind guiding is the technique that senses the web as it enters the machine (see Fig. above). The sensor, mounted on the machine frame, is placed so its center is located at the desired position of the web. The actuator moves the roll stand laterally across the machine to bring the edge of the web onto the center of the sensor. The controller or amplifier directs the movement of the actuator. An idler roll must be mounted as part of the unwind stand to maintain a fixed path through the sensor as the unwind roll decreases in diameter. The sensor must be mounted between the idler roll on the back stand and the first idler roll on the machine. If the sensor is mounted after the first machine idler roll, the lateral drag induced by the web transversing the idler roll will cause continual overcorrection or hunting.

Roll steering guiding is the method that is normally used in mid-process for minor corrections as a web passes through several processes within a machine (see Fig. on p. 268). The steering rolls pivot, detecting the web to the left or right as necessary to hold the web in the center of the sensor. The sensor is mounted to the machined frame with its center position aligned with the desired web-edge position. This sensor must be mounted after the web leaves the steering roll and before the next idler on the machine frame. Any rolls located between the sensor and steering rolls will create lateral drag on the web and cause hunting.

Windup roll-stand guiding is the reverse of unwind guiding (see Fig. on p. 268). In windup-stand guiding, the web position is sensed by a sensor mounted as part of the movable windup

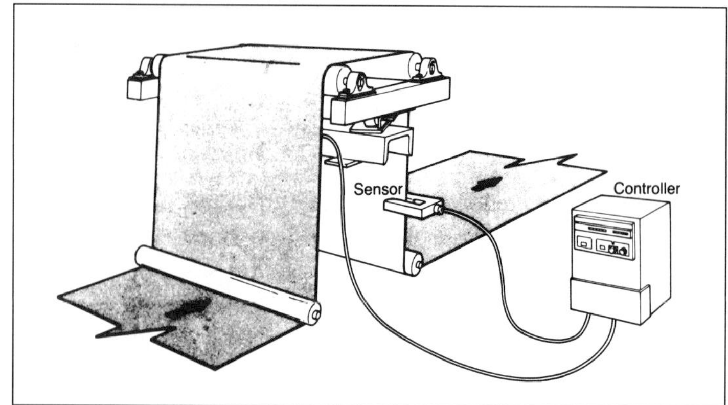

Roll steering guiding.

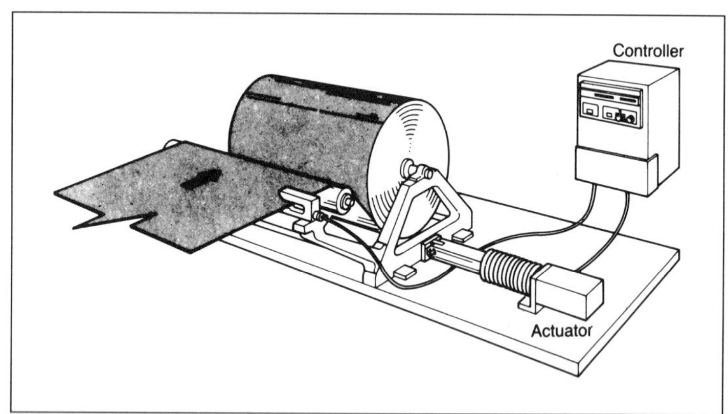

Windup roll-stand guiding.

roll stand. It must be positioned before the last roll on the machine. As the web position moves within the sensor, the controller signals the actuator to move the windup roll into the web edge. ▷ **bowed roll; expander roll; motion control system**

extruder web heat transfer roll adjustment With web converting technology sophistication, precise and predictable heat transfer becomes increasingly important because cast films, multi-layered laminates, coextrusions, the curing and finishing of coatings, and the heating and cooling of high speed webs all depend on the precise performance of heat transfer rolls. Its performance depends on numerous process variables, from line speed and web thickness to web temperature and the amount of wẹb wrap.

Most of the process variables cannot be changed. Therefore, a heat transfer roll can be designed to adapt to the specific requirements of the process. At stake is the quality of the product and sometimes the capital investment in the process line. To predict roll performance when there are so many process variables, use is made of a computerized heat transfer analysis program. An example is a program's computer modeling that divides the roll and web into a finite number of axial and circumferential elements. The number of elements selected depends on the size of the system and heat transfer process.

Within each element, temperatures throughout the web-and-roll system are calculated radially, from inside the roll to the outer surface of the web. In turn elements are in layers that accurately calculate temperatures for the internal part of the roll, including the heat transfer fluid, the shell, the roll surface, the air-boundary layer between the roll and web, and several points in the web itself. It can also evaluate the change in temperature occurring during travel between roll stations. Input is made to the computer on web material properties, geometry, and process conditions. The heat transfer analysis program creates a matrix of simultaneous equations that are repeatedly solved. They converge on the periodic, steady-state energy balance of the web-and-roll system.

extruder web tension control There are various tension control techniques available. The proper selection involves decisions on how to

Web gauging methods.

Gauging method	Material limitations	Applications limitations	Type of extrusion
Roller-contact	None	Requires rigid material	All
Air	None	Requires reasonably flat surface	Sheet, profile
Magnetic-reluctance	Nonmagnetic materials with thin walls	Position control important	Sheet, tube
Sonic	Material with good sound transmission	Material with good sound transmission	Pipe, sheet
Optical	None	For dimensional control	All
Laser-intercept	None	For dimensional control	All
Laser-interferometry	May be transparent in infrared	For dimensional control	Thin tube, sheet
Capacitance	Materials with higher dielectric constant	For thickness control	Sheet, tube
Proximity	Materials with higher dielectric constant	Requires nonconductive materials	All
Beta-ray	None	Requires relatively smooth surface	Thin sheet

produce the tension, how to sense the tension, and how to control the tension. There are many applications that are unique and cannot use the standard approach. The tension system selection process depends primarily on the data sensitive to the application. For instance, if the material has very low tension requirements and if exact control is required, then perhaps, using a magnetic particle brake with an electrical transducer roll with appropriate electronic control is best. However, if the material is in large diameter rolls and can be unwound at slow speeds, then a roll follower system can be used effectively. It would be a tremendous project to correlate all design and application parameters and variables for a given tension control system. There are manual adjustment systems like the canvas drag brake, various pony brakes, and pneumatically operated brakes. The most expensive would be the regenerative drive systems. The transducer rolls and dancer roll systems would be a close second. These systems are usually required in high web speed applications where accurate tension control of expensive and/or sensitive material is paramount. Where this sophistication is not required, other less equally effective devices can be used.

By definition the unwind stand tension system must maintain constant tension control as the roll of material changes in diameter. The simplest and least expensive method of automatic constant tension control is to use the roll follower diameter sensing systems. There are also systems that permit a decrease in tension level as the material is wound. With web surfaces that cannot be touched (surface fragile, embossed, tacky, etc.) roll monitoring cannot be done mechanically. The ultrasonic detector system is an example of a noncontact diameter detection of sensitive materials.

extruder web thickness gauging The Table above provides examples of applications and limitations of gauging methods. ▷ **sensor**

extruder web thickness sensor The role of the sensor is usually fundamental to the function of a process-control system. The computer uses the information on product thickness obtained by the sensor to calculate the required compensating adjustment such as screw speed and line speed. To meet the wide variety of extruded products (film, sheet, pipe, profile, etc.) with their wide variety of materials, shapes, and sizes, a broad range of sensors are available and used. ▷ **sensor**

extruder web wrinkle free For any web substrate to achieve optimum packaging, printing, coating, laminating, metallizing, etc., it must be free of wrinkles. Processors running thinner, more delicate substrates at faster line speeds significantly increase the potential for creasing and wrinkling. To achieve smooth, taut webs, a wide variety of wrinkle-removing rollers, known as spreader or stretcher rollers, is available. As their name implies, spreader rollers are designed to pull and stretch a substrate during production to remove costly wrinkles.

Wrinkles can develop in a web for a number of reasons, but one thing is certain, the longer the web has to go, and the more processes it must go through, the greater the opportunity for wrinkles. Creases may also develop if the web has large wrap angles, if web tension varies along the processing line, if web gauge is incon-

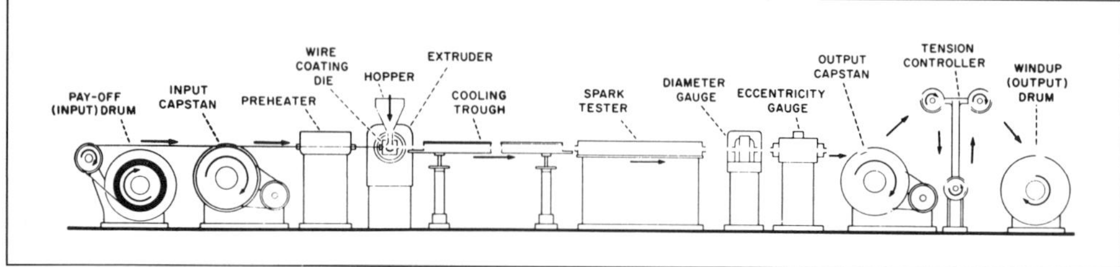

Example of wire coating line.

sistent, if the web is exposed to static electricity or improperly aligned rollers, and if the web is tacky due to semi-dry coatings (as in the production of adhesive-backed products such as tape).

The optimum location of a spreader roller varies, depending on the cause of the wrinkles. On coaters, laminators, and printing presses, stretcher rollers most often are placed in the first idler position off the unwind, the idler position before the first print unit or coating or adhesive applicator, and in the last idler roller position prior to rewinding. Spreader rollers are also utilized on extrusion lines to smooth webs prior to corona treating, winding, slitting, etc. There are five basic families of rollers: bowed rolls, expander stretcher rolls, grooved metal rollers, grooved rubber rollers, and angle-grooved soft-rubber idler rolls. Many variations exist within each family. While there is no universal spreader roller, some processors utilize a number of different types of rollers on a single line. The reason for this action is because the degree of wrinkles and each roller's stretching capability and limitations differ.

extruder, wire and cable The Fig. above shows a wire coating line using typical upstream and downstream equipment with the crosshead wire coating die. Information on processing is given in ▷**extruder coating wire.** For most wire coating lines the screw plasticating system is used. An exception is when processing a very low melt flow plastic such as PTFE. It does not easily melt, particularly in the production of heavy wall PTFE wire coatings. Coating is accomplished using the ram system ▷**extruder ram system** and **billet.** As an example, the system can coat stranded wire with a jacket 3/32 in. (0.4 mm) thick or more directly from powdered PTFE feed, and coat up to eight wires at the same time. Also used for heavy coatings is the ram processing of PTFE paste. With the multiple-strand ram extrusion die, output can be increased with cost reduction.

extruder wire coating, crosslinkable PE with peroxide There are various systems used by the wire and cable industry to cure peroxide-based XLPE compounds. They include steam cure, nitrogen cure, and pressurized liquid continuous vulcanization systems. All these methods involve heat to cause the peroxide to decompose into a reactive radical and initiate the cure cycle.

extruder wire coating, radiation crosslink without peroxide Radiation crosslinking is performed by passing the wire or cable through a beam of electron radiation. Usually, the full dosage is not applied in a single pass because of the rapid temperature increase that accompanies electron beam exposure. To solve this problem, the wire or cable is usually festooned on a series of pulleys and passed through the beam several times until the desired dosage is reached. Radiation curing is commonly used in the production of appliance wire and control cable. These type applications are most suitable because of their relatively thin insulating layers, which allow penetration of low power electron beams. The materials used for this procedure are similar to those used in peroxide curing, except that the peroxide has been eliminated and, in some cases, a crosslinked accelerator has been added. The quality and physical properties of radiation crosslinked materials are virtually identical to those produced by peroxide curing.

extruder zero defects ▷**zero defect**

extrusion A process in which heated or unheated plastic is forced through a shaping orifice (a die) in one continuous formed shape, as in film, sheet, pipe, profile, coating, etc. These different shapes are reviewed in this book under ▷**extruder**

extrusion mark A mark or line formed accidentally in an extruder on an extrudate.

exudation Migration of constituents (additives, plasticizers, solvents, etc.) from the interior to the surface of a plastic part. Sometimes referred to as bleed out.

eyebolt holes Eyebolt holes are used to lift and move molds, dies, etc. They should be used in molds and dies where balanced lifting is possible. Holes should be tapped on surfaces perpendicular to the slots. The forged steel eyebolts have a safe load-carrying capacity based on diameter as follows: $\frac{1}{2}$ in. (0.13 mm) of 2,600 lb (1,180 kg), 3/4 in. (0.2 mm) of 6,000 lb (2,722 kg), and 1 in. (0.25 mm).

eyepiece The lens system used in an optical instrument for magnification of the image formed by the obective.

eyepiece parfocal Eyepieces with common focal planes so that they are interchangeable without focusing.

fabric ▷ **fabric woven** and **fabric nonwoven**

fabricating The manufacture of plastic products directly or indirectly. The direct fabricating or manufacture of plastic products via a process (injection molding, extrusion, casting, etc.). Indirect includes taking the processed plastics through secondary operations (machining, punching, painting, heat sealing, fastening, etc.). Also called fabrication.

fabricating and people ▷ **people**

fabricating planning ▷ **perfection**

fabricating plant inspection ▷ **Underwriters' Laboratory factory inspection**

fabricating processes Many different processes are used to fabricate or manufacture plastic products. The type of process to be used depends on a variety of factors including product shape and size, type plastic to be used, quantity to be produced, quality and accuracy (tolerances) required, design load performance, cost limitation, time schedule, etc. The major processes are: extrusion (consuming about 36% by weight of all plastics), injection molding (32%), blow molding (10%), calender (6%), coating (5%), compression molding (3%), and others (6%). Each of these processes provide different methods to produce different products. As an example, extrusion, with its many methods, produces film, sheet, pipe, profile, wire coating, etc. Some of the processes overlap since different segments of the industry use them. Also terms such as molding, embedding, casting, potting, impregnation, and encapsulation sometimes overlap and/or are used interchangeably. However, they each have their specific definitions.

Fabricating processes include the following: ▷ **autoclave molding; bag molding; blow molding; bulk molding compound; calendering; casting; centrifugal casting; centrifugal molding; coating; contact molding; coextrusion; coining; coinjection; cold press molding; compression molding; contact pressure; counter pressure molding; dip molding; double-shot molding; electrostatic spray coating; encapsulation; expandable polystyrene; filament placement process; filament winding; flocculation; fluidized bed coating; foam and processing method; foam reservoir molding; forming; forging; fusible core; gas counter pressure molding; gas injection molding; hand layup molding; high pressure molding; injection molding; inverse lamination; isotactic molding/pressing; jet molding; lagging molding; laminate; lamination; liquid injection molding; lost wax molding; low pressure molding; matched die molding; one-shot molding; open molding; orientation; plunger molding; powder coating; powder molding process; preform molding; prepolymer molding; pressure bag molding; pulp molding; pultrusion; ram extrusion and injection molding; reaction injection molding; reactive processing; reinforced plastic; resin transfer molding; rock-and-roll processing; rolling; rotary molding; rotational molding; salt bath; screw plunger transfer molding; Scorim; shell molding; sintering; skiving; slot extrusion; slush molding; sheet molding compound; soluble core molding; solvent casting; solvent molding; spinning; spraying reinforced plastic; sprayup molding; squeeze molding; structural foam; tape placement wrapped molding; thermal expansion molding; thermoforming; transfer molding; trickle impregnation; two-color molding; vacuum bag molding; wet layup molding; vinyl dispersion; wood-plastic impregnated**

fabricating processing guides The Tables on pp. 273–275 provide general guides.

fabrication residence time ▷ **residence time**

fabric bias Fabric consisting of warp and fill fibers at an angle to the length of the fabric.

fabric bonded A web of fibers held together by an adhesive medium which does not form a continuous film.

fabric count The number (counted units) of warp yarns (ends) and filling yarns (picks) per inch.

fabric cowoven ▷ **cowoven fabric**

fabric crimp Cloth woven with about equal corrugations in both warp and fill.

fabric designations ▷ **glass fabric designations**

fabric elastic Fabric made from an elastomer either alone or in combination with other textile

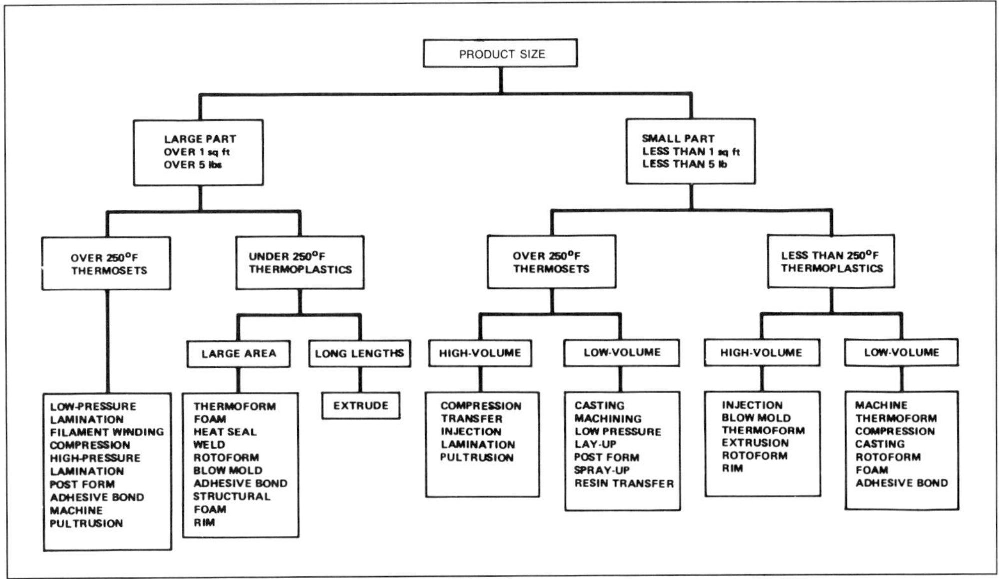

Guide to product size.

materials. At room temperature it will stretch under tension and will return quickly and forcibly to its original dimensions and shape when tension is removed. It may be manufactured by weaving, braiding, knitting, etc.

fabric fill face That side of a woven fabric on which the greatest number of yarns are perpendicular to the selvage.

fabric, flash-spun ▷ **flash-spun nonwoven fabric**

fabric, fluted core ▷ **fluted core**

fabric gout Foreign matter, usually lint or waste, woven in a fabric by accident.

fabric, greige ▷ **greige goods**

fabric, hand The softness of a piece of fabric, as determined by the touch (individual judgement).

fabric handling characteristics ▷ **glass fabric RP weave pattern**

fabric impregnated A fabric in which the interstices between the yarns are completely filled with the impregnating compound throughout the thickness of the material, as distinguished from sized or coated materials, where these interstices are not completely filled.

fabric, melt-blown ▷ **melt-blown nonwoven fabric**

fabric nebs Little lumps of tangled fibers or small thickened places, found in fabric or yarn.

fabric nested ▷ **reinforced plastic nesting**

fabric nonwoven Fibrous sheets made without the conventional spinning, weaving, or knitting. They include "mechanical" bonded fabrics, "flashspun" fabrics, "melt-blown" fabrics, and "spun-bonded" fabrics. The interlocking of fibers is achieved by mechanical work, chemical action, moisture, solvents, nonconventional spinning, and/or heat. They may consist of one or more types of fibers.

fabric prepreg batch Prepreg containing fabric from one fabric batch and impregnated with one batch of plastic in one continuous operation. ▷ **prepreg**

fabric, spun-bonded ▷ **spun-bonded nonwoven fabric**

fabric, three-dimensional ▷ **three-dimensional fabric**

fabric, twill weave This fabric interlaces one or more warp yarns over and under two or more filling yarns in a regular pattern. This produces either a straight or a broken diagonal line in the fabric, which, consequently, has greater pliability and better drapability than both plain weave and basket weave.

fabric warp face That side of a woven fabric on which the greatest number of yarns are parallel to the selvage.

fabric woven A material mechanically constructed of interlaced yarns, fibers, or filaments; usually a planar structure. Randomly integrated

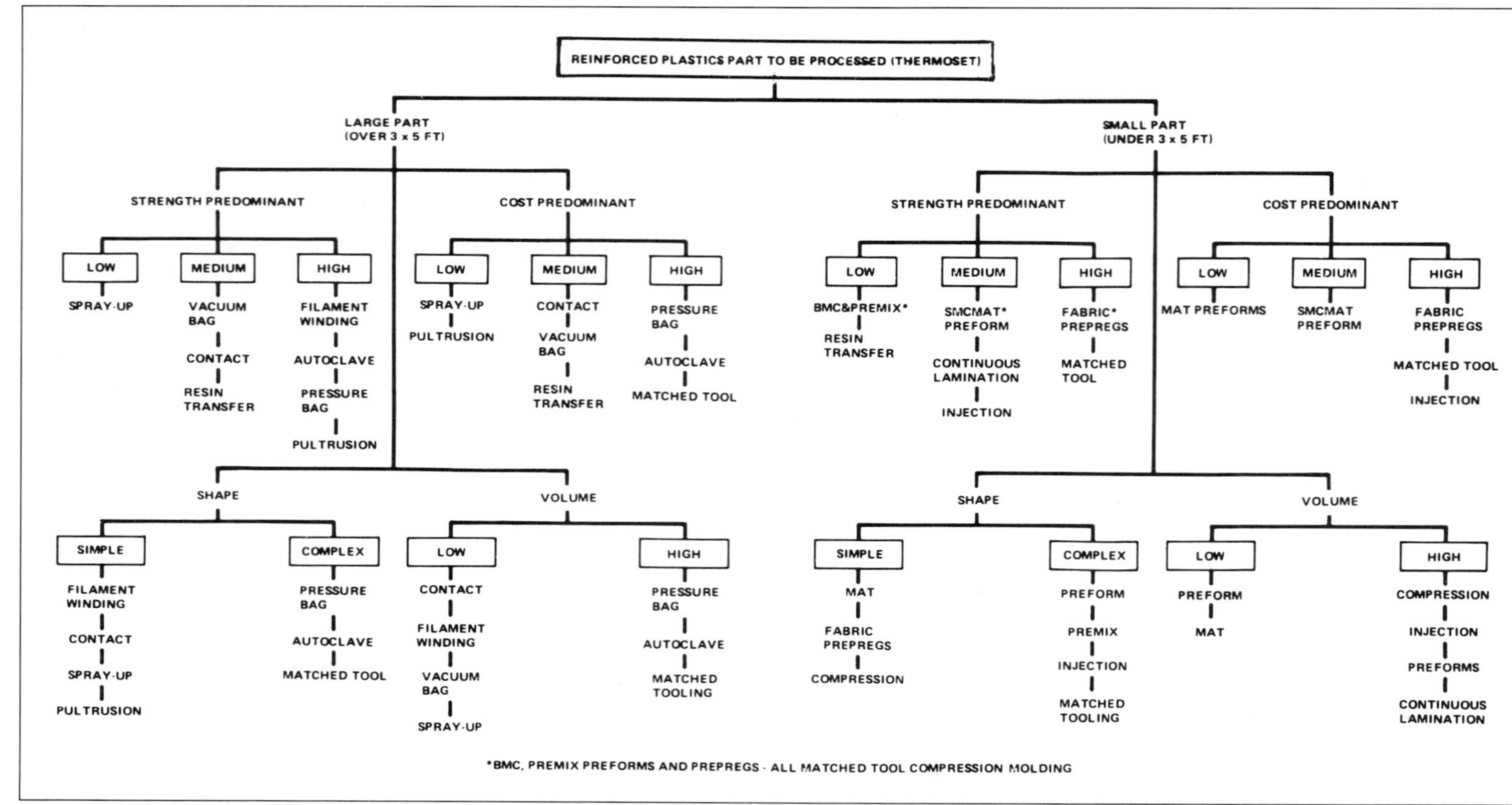

Guide to reinforced plastic processing.

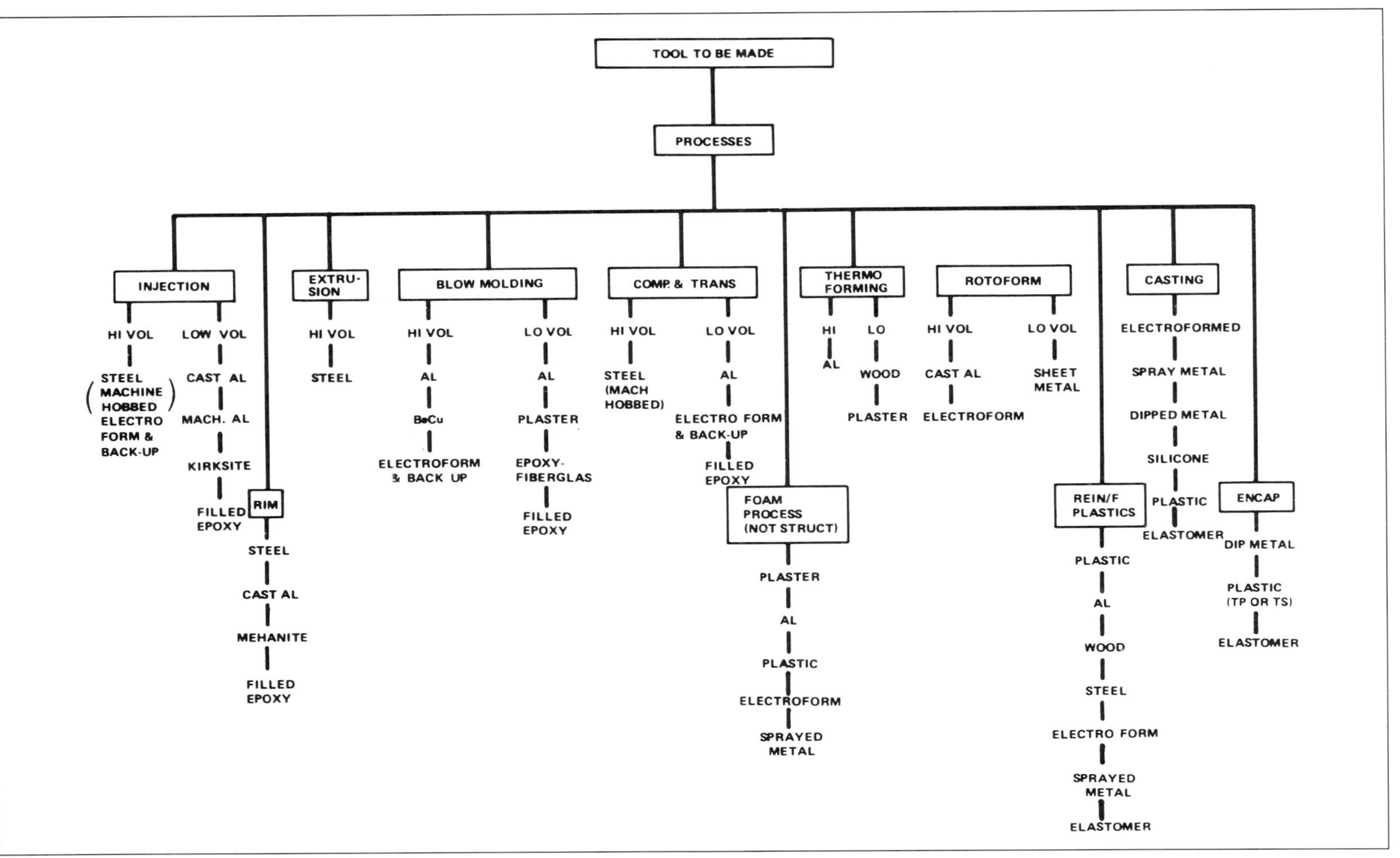

Guide to tool (mold, die) selection.

nonwovens are sometimes included in this classification. The properties and contribution to product performance of (reinforced plastic) fabric are dependent on the fabric construction, that is fabric count, warp yarn, and filling yarn construction and weave pattern.

Fabric count consists of the number of warp yarns ("ends") per inch (centimeter) of fabric width and the number of filling yarns ("picks") per inch (centimeter) in the lengthwise direction. The warp yarn ("end") is the yarn lying in the lengthwise (machine) direction of the fabric, whereas the filling yarn ("pick") is the yarn lying in the crosswise direction of the fabric (i.e., at right angles to the warp yarn). Therefore, fabric weight, thickness, and breaking strength are proportional to the number and types of yarn used in weaving.

There are a variety of weave patterns that can be used to interlace the warp and filling yarns so as to form a stable fabric. The weave pattern controls the handling characteristics of a fabric and (to some degree) the properties of the product using it as reinforcement. Some applications require that all fabric-construction variables be specifically designed into the fabric so that the desired performance criteria can be met.

Fabrics woven with heavy warp yarns and fine filling yarns in either the crowfoot or long-shaft satin weave patterns are called unidirectional fabrics. These fabrics are characterized by a high strength contribution to reinforced plastics in the heavy yarn direction. Fiber yarns are also woven into tapes, contoured fabrics, fluted-core fabrics, and three-dimensional fabrics. Tapes may contain woven feathered edge; the filling yarns protrude beyond the exterior warp yarns. Contoured fabrics, woven on specially designed looms, provide a geometrical shape matching the shape of the RP part to be made. Fluted-core comprise two parallel layers of fabric tied together by stringers of woven fabric such that the cross sectional configuration is triangular or rectangular. Three-dimensional fabrics are not, in the true sense, 3-D; rather they are planar fabrics woven with yarns in three distinct directions within the fabric plane. Thus, yarns are interwoven in machine direction, at plus 45° from the machine direction, and minus 45° from the machine direction.

Fabric styles and nomenclature used most in the plastic industry are: plain, unidirectional, harness satin, 4-harness (crowfoot), 8-harness satin, basket, twill, braided, scrim, plied, braiding, mat, etc. ▷ **reinforced plastic, directional properties**

facing material ▷ **sandwich construction**

fact and fiction ▷ **plastic bad and other myths**

factor ▷ **statistical factor**

factor of ignorance This term is sometimes used instead of safety factor.

factor of safety ▷ **design safety factor**

factory inspection ▷ **Underwriters' Laboratory factory inspection**

fadeometer An apparatus for determining the resistance of plastics and other materials to fading. This apparatus accelerates the fading by subjecting the product to high intensity UV rays of about the same wavelength as those found in sunlight.

Fahrenheit The designation of the degree and the temperature scale used in public life and some U.S. engineering circles. Related to International Practical Temperature by means of the equation when converting from °C or:

$$°F = 9/5°C + 32.$$

To change °F to °C use equation:

$$°C = 5/9°F(°F - 32).$$

The temperature of boiling water, at sea level or 760 mm H_g, is 212°F (100°C). Freezing point of water is 32°F (0°C). ▷ **Centigrade; Celsius; Kelvin**

failure analysis The systematic examination of the nature product service termination, the synthesis of the cause, and positive recommendations for future improvements. ▷ **rupture** and **life-history curve**

failure, catastrophic ▷ **catastrophic failure**

failure, plastic products ▷ **plastic advantages and disadvantages**

failure theory ▷ **design failure theory**

failure, thermal ▷ **thermal aging, relative thermal index**

fairing ▷ **structural fairing**

falling weight test ▷ **dart drop test** and **Gardner impact test**

FALLO approach FALLO is the abbreviation of Follow **ALL O**pportunities and refers to the Fig. on p. 277. This block diagram basically summarizes what should be considered to ensure a good return on investment to produce all types and shapes of products for all types of plastic fabricating processes. This Figure pertains to any fabricating process (extrusion, injection, blow, etc.). As the diagram shows, many important steps are involved that must come together properly in order to produce

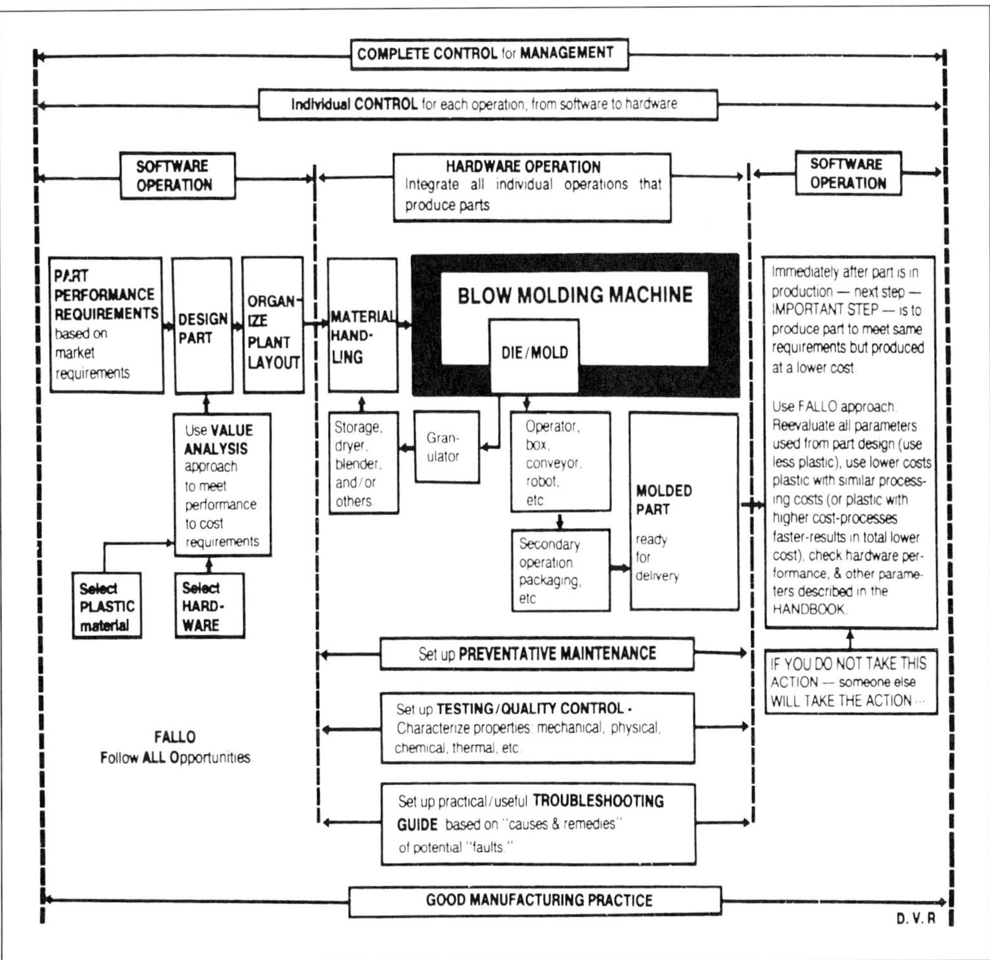

The FALLO approach.

parts consistently meeting performance requirements at the lowest cost. The Fig. on top of p. 278 represents an illogical plan.

fallout ▷ **radiation**

family mold ▷ **mold, family**

fan gate ▷ **mold gate, fan**

Farad ▷ **electrical capacitance**

Faraday The quality of electricity that can deposit (or desolve) one gram-equivalent weight of a substance during electrolysis (about 96,500 coulombs).

fastener Fasteners involve many different assembly and joining methods. There are basically permanent types (rivits, weldments, stakings, etc.) and detachable types (screws, snap fits, etc.). Constructions are of plastic and/or other materials.

fastener accreditation program Hoping to reduce principally imports of counterfeit and substandard screws, bolts, washers, and other fasteners, the American Society of Mechanical Engineers has a Fastener Accreditation Program (FAP). To receive FAP, suppliers must document their quality control programs and submit to on-site inspections by ASME teams.

fastener, locking ▷ **snap fit** and **vacuum lock fastener**

fast food waste ▷ **waste myths**

fatigue Fatigue is the phenomenon of having materials under cyclic loads at levels of stress below their static yield strength. Fatigue data are used so the designer can predict the performance of a material under cyclic loads. The fatigue test, analogous to static long-term creep tests, provides information on the failure of

Confusion approach in a "mythical" processing plant; illogical plan.

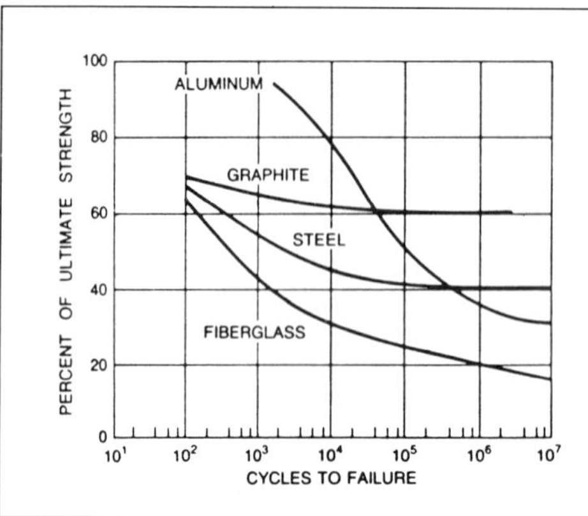

Example of fatigue properties of graphite and glass fiber thermoset polyester reinforced plastics, steel, and aluminum.

materials under repeated stresses. This fatigue behavior is by no means a new problem—the term was applied to the failure of a wooden mast by hoisting too many sails too often in the pre-Christian era.

As plastics replaced metals and other materials in many critical structural applications, fatigue tests became even more important, since the maximum oscillatory load that a material can sustain is a part of its tensile strength. Thus, the more conventional short-term tests give little indication about the lifetime of an object subjected to vibrations or repeated deformations. Fatigue tests are especially important for the designer of plastics and reinforced plastics that are used in load-bearing structures that will be subjected to varying loads (see Fig.).

fatigue crack Basically, under a repeated applied cyclic load, fatigue cracks begin somewhere in the specimen and extend during the cycling. Eventually the crack will expand to such an extent that the remaining material can no longer support the stress, at which point the part will fail suddenly. However, failure for different service conditions may be defined differently than just as the separation of two parts. ASTM D 671 defines failure as occurring also when the elastic modulus has decreased to 70% of its original value. Fatigue crack can also be identified as the number of cycles both to initiate and propagate a defect to some critical length, thus:

$$N_t = N_i + N_p$$

where N_t = total fatigue life, N_i = number of cycles to initiate a crack, and N_p = number of cycles to propagate a crack to a critical length necessary for failure. ▷ **crack growth resistance**

fatigue crack propagation Plastic components may contain material defects, such as porosity and inclusions, and may also suffer damage as a result of fabrication and service. These defects may not cause immediate fracture under intended design stress, but these cracks may grow slowly to critical dimensions under the influence of cyclic loading. For this reason, the kinetics of fatigue crack propagation (FCP) must be adequately identified. FCP data for amorphous, crystalline, and multiphase plastics are available in the literature.

fatigue ductility The ability of a material to deform "plastically" before fracturing, determined from a constant strain amplitude, low cycle fatigue test. Usually expressed in percent in direct analog with elongation and reduction of area ductility measures. ▷ **ductility of plastic**

fatigue ductility exponent The slope of a log-log plot of the plastic strain range and the fatigue life.

fatigue, dynamic ▷ **dynamic fatigue**

fatigue dynamometer An elastic calibration device for use in verifying the indicated loads applied by a fatigue testing machine. It permits the accurate determination of the magnitude of the average strain, in a region of uniform transverse cross section, when the dynamometer is subject to a tensile or compressive force along its longitudinal axis. ▷ **microdynamometer**

fatigue endurance limit To develop S-N curves (▷ **fatigue S-N diagram**) like those in the Fig. below, the fatigue specimen is loaded until, for example, the maximum stress in the sample is 275 MPa (40 ksi). At this stress level it may fail in only 10 cycles. These data are recorded and the stress level is then reduced to 206 MPa (30 ksi). This specimen may not break until after 1,000 stress cycles at this rather low stress level.

This procedure is repeated until a stress level is determined below which failure does not occur. In this example of a relatively high fatigue performance material that develops a flat portion of the S-N curve, this stress level is found to be 158 MPa (23 ksi). A test duration of 10 million (10^7) stress cycles is usually considered infinite life. This type of testing is expensive, principally because it involves a large number of samples and much statistical evaluation. The end result, determining the fatigue endurance limit of a material, is an extremely important design property. This property should be used in determining the allowable stresses in products, rather than just the short-term yield strength, any time a part will see cyclic loading in service.

Cyclic loading significantly reduces the amount of allowable stress a material can withstand. If data are not available on the endurance limit of a material being considered for use, a percentage of its tensile strength can be used. This percentage varies with the different material systems. For engineering plastics the endurance limit could be about 50 percent of its tensile strength, as with metals. Taking this 50 percent approach requires the designer to become familiar with fatigue-testing results on plastics and other materials, so that the proper evaluation can be applied. However, to design correctly requires obtaining reliable S-N curves with the required endurance limit. Plastics are subject to fatigue, with a wide range of performance, and efforts should be made to arrive at endurance limit information if a fail-safe design is desired.

fatigue fretting Fretting fatigue takes place when two mating parts, which are in close contact, rub against each other because of vibrations or repeating loads. The rubbing is usually confined to local areas and contributes to the deterioration of the contact surfaces.

fatigue hysteretic heating Since plastics are viscoelastic, there is the potential for having a large amount of internal friction generated within the plastics during mechanical deformation, as in fatigue. This action involves the accumulation of hysteretic energy generated during each loading cycle. Examples of products that behave in this manner include coil or leaf springs and shoe soles.

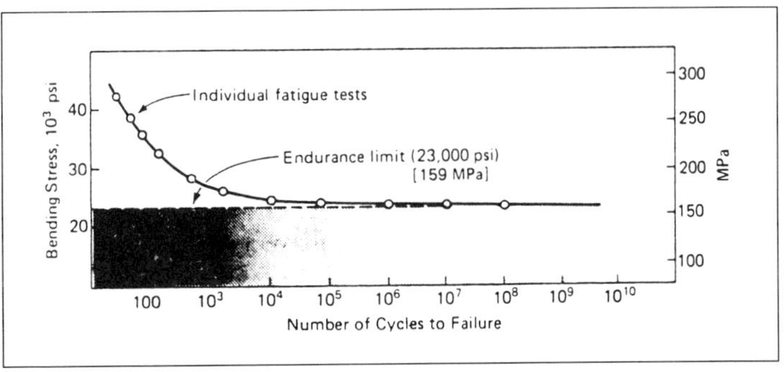

The use of an S-N curve to establish a fatigue endurance limit strength. The curve asymptotically approaches a parallel to the abscissa, thus indicating the endurance limit as the value that will not produce failure. Below this limit the material is much less susceptible to fatigue failure.

Because this energy is dissipated mainly in the form of heat, the material experiences an associated temperature increase. When heating takes place the dynamic modulus decreases, which results in a greater degree of heat generation under conditions of constant stress. The greater the loss modulus of the material, the greater the amount of heat generated that can be dissipated. Plastics for fatigue applications can therefore have low losses. If the plastic's surface area is insufficient to permit the heat to be dissipated, the specimen will become hot enough to soften and melt. The possibility of adversely affecting its mechanical properties by heat generation during cyclic loading must therefore always be considered. The heat generated during cyclic loading can be calculated from the loss modulus or loss tangent of the plastics.

The rate dependence of fatigue strength demands careful consideration of the potential for heat buildup in both the fatigue test and in service. Generally, since the buildup is a function of the viscous component of the material, the materials that tend toward viscous behavior will also display a sensitivity to cyclic load frequency. Thus, thermoplastics, particularly the crystalline polymers like polyethylene that are above their glass-transition temperatures, are expected to be more sensitive to the cyclic load rate, and highly cross-linked plastics or glass-reinforced plastics are less sensitive to the frequency of load. ▷ **hysteresis**

fatigue life The number of loading cycles of a specified character that a given specimen sustains before failure of a specified nature occurs.

fatigue life for p% survival An estimate of the fatigue life that p% of the population would attain or exceed under a given loading (ASTM E 1150). The observed value of the median fatigue life estimates the fatigue life for 50% survival. Fatigue life for p% survival values, where p is any number, such as 95, 90, etc., may also be estimated from the individual fatigue life values.

fatigue limit ▷ **fatigue endurance limit**

fatigue notch factor Also called strength reduction ratio. A measure of the actual effect of a notch or other stress concentrator on fatigue strength of a material. The ratio of measured fatigue strength of a material free of known stress concentrators to that of a material with known stress concentrators, assuming specimens are otherwise comparable and test conditions identical. The empirical fatigue notch factor is usually lower than the theoretical stress concentration factor because of stress relief that occurs in conjunction with local plastic deformation. For a given material, a higher fatigue notch factor indicates the likelihood of a lower fatigue strength or endurance limit. ▷ **notch factor**

fatigue ratio The ratio of fatigue strength or endurance limit to tensile strength. For many materials it is constant enough so that fatigue strength can be estimated from tensile strength, provided that stress concentration conditions in test and service are comparable. Mean stress and alternating stress must be stated.

fatigue, reinforced plastic ▷ **reinforced plastic, fatigue**

fatigue S-N diagram A plot of stress (S) against the number of cycles (N) to failure in fatigue testing. A log scale is normally used for N. For S, a linear scale is often used but sometimes a log scale is used. The S-N curve plotted represents the number of alternating stress cycles a material can sustain without failure at various maximum stresses. Condition of testing can involve different conditions (standard room temperature/humidity, high and/or low temperatures, corrosive atmosphere, etc.)

fatigue, static Static fatigue is also called creep fracture or stress rupture. It is the fracture that occurs after long-term loading under a steady load, as opposed to the fast fracture that occurs under the more usual direct loading type of fracture, where the load is continuously increased until fracture. This type of fracture is highly time dependent, greater times needing lower stresses to produce fracture. Also as temperature increases, fracture occurs more quickly. Since even direct loading must take place over a certain time interval (although much shorter) there must also be a static fatigue component in operation here. Both brittle and ductile fracture may be observed, the former being more likely at higher stresses. In brittle static fatigue, progressive stress crazing is frequently observed.

fatigue strain Fatigue tests are conducted to evaluate the fatigue response of plastics under constant strain amplitude test conditions involving fully reversed tension-compression loading conditions. During the course of such testing, the height of the hysteresis loops may either increase or decrease, reflecting conditions of cyclic strain hardening and softening, respectively. Both changes in material properties have been identified for different materials (metals, plastics, etc.).

fatigue strength Also called endurance strength, it is the maximum, completely reversed

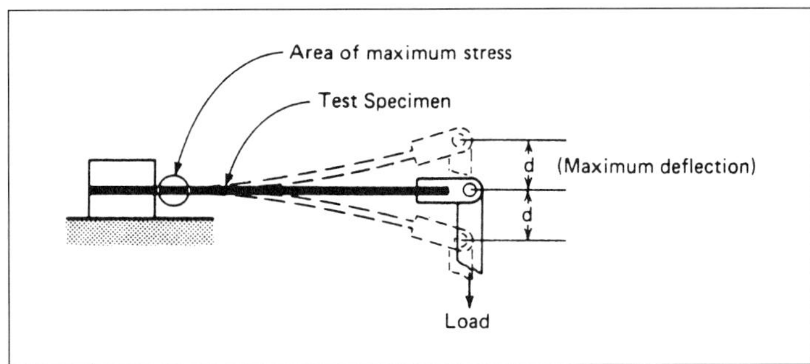

Example of cantilever bending (flexural) fatigue test setup.

stress under which a material will fail after it has experienced the stress for a specific number of cycles. It is obtained from a fatigue S-N curve.

fatigue strength versus tensile strength The fatigue strength of most TPs is about 20 to 30% of the ultimate tensile strength determined in the short-term test but much higher for thermoset RPs. It decreases with increases in temperature and stress-cycle frequency and with the presence of stress concentration peaks, as in notched components.

fatigue stress ▷ **fatigue strength** and **stress**

fatigue test In testing, a specimen is subjected to the periodic varying of stresses by means of a mechanically operated device. The stresses applied generally alternate between equal positive and negative values or from zero to the maximum positive or negative values. For practical purposes, in testing plastics a certain minimum stress, instead of zero, is often used. The test can be performed in alternating bending (called flexural fatigue testing; see Fig. above), and also as tensile, compression, or torsion testing, or as an alternating tensile-compression test.

Fatigue data are normally presented as a plot of the stress (S) versus the number of cycles (N) that cause failure at that stress; the data plotted defined as an S-N curve. Test results are illustrated graphically in the form of curves. Examples of fatigue curves for unreinforced and reinforced plastics are shown in the Fig. below. The values for stress amplitude and the number of load cycles to failure are plotted on a diagram with logarithmically divided abscissa and English or metrically divided ordinates.

The fatigue behavior of a material is normally measured in either a flexural or a tensile mode. Specimens may be cracked or notched prior to testing, to localize fatigue damage and permit measuring the crack-propagation rate. In constant-deflection amplitude testing a specimen is repeatedly bent to a specific outer fiber strain level. The number of cycles to failure is then recorded. In constant flexural load amplitude testing a bending load is repeatedly applied to the specimen. This load causes a specified outer-fiber stress level. The number of cycles to failure is then recorded.

Both modes of fatigue testing can be related to the performance of real structures, one to

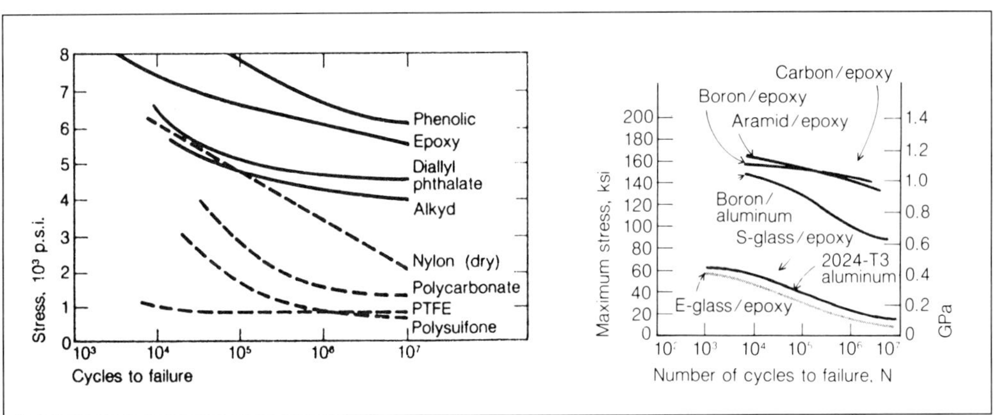

Examples of room temperature fatigue characteristics for certain TPs, TSs, and RPs. The stresses are from cantilever bending under constant load, zero mean stress, and a frequency of 1,800 cycles/min.

those that are flexed repeatedly to a constant deflection and the other to those that are repeatedly flexed with a constant load. In constant-elongation amplitude testing, a specimen is repeatedly stretched to a specified tensile strain or elongation level.

fatty acid An organic acid obtained by the hydrolysis (saponification) of natural fats and oils, e.g., stearic and palmitic acids. These acids are monobasic, may or may not have some double bonds, and contain 16 or more carbon atoms.

fault tree analysis FTA is the procedure where engineers or designers analyze the individual components of a product and show how failure(s) would affect its function. ▷ **process flow diagram, basics** and **zero defect**

feather edge ▷ **fin**

feature An individual characteristic of a part, such as thread, hole, taper, etc.

feedback armature Technique used to adjust drive speeds by measuring and controlling electric motor armature voltage. Good for many less exacting speed systems.

feedback control ▷ **process control**

feed bushing ▷ **mold bushing, feed**

feeder An auxiliary or accessory piece of equipment which provides controlled flow of materials (from powders to pellets) to or from processing operations. Major types are gravimetric, volumetric, and vibrator types. ▷ **hopper**

feeder, crammer To provide consistent flow of materials into processes that use a hopper or material loading mechanism. The crammer (mechanical ramming device) can help with high bulk feed material, etc. (see Fig.).

feeder, helical screw Devices for conveying and metering dry materials, comprising a tube containing a screw, fed from a supply hopper.

feeder, starved ▷ **extruder starved feeder**

feeder, vibratory Devices for conveying dry materials from storage hoppers to processing machines, comprising a tray vibrated by mechanical or electrical pulses. The frequency and/or amplitude of the vibrations control the rate of flow.

feed, gravity The movement of materials from one place to another (in a hopper, container-to-container, etc.) by force of gravity. See Fig. and ▷ **extruder gravimetric feeding-blending**

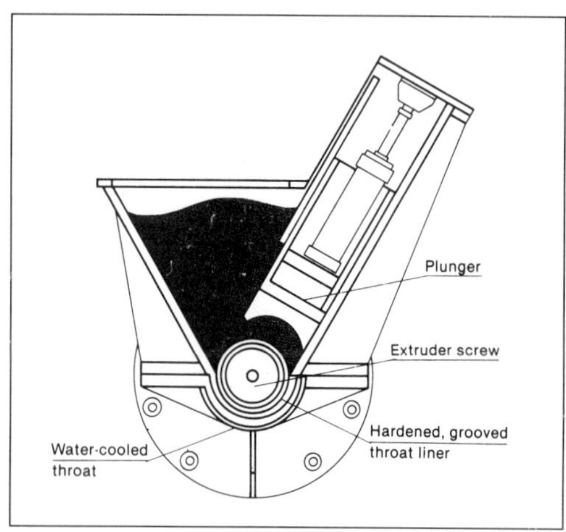

Ram stuffer crammer provides positive feed schematic used in certain extruders.

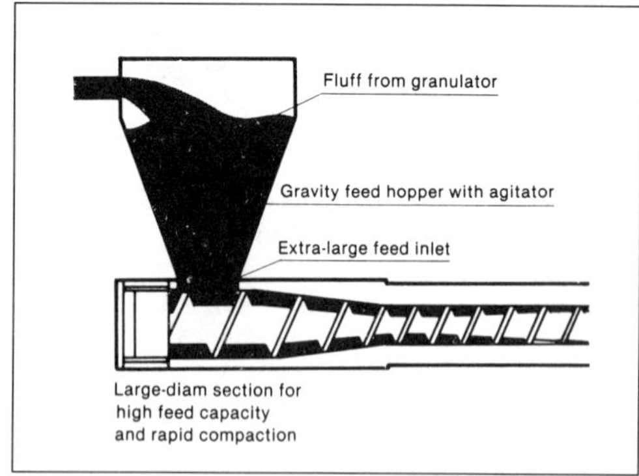

Example of a gravity feeder with dual diameter screw for certain extruders to accelerate gravity feeding.

feed hopper A funnel mounted directly on equipment, such as a plasticator barrel over the screw feed section, to hold a reserve of material.

feed opening A hole through the feed section, such as a plasticator barrel, for introduction of feed material.

feed sections of screw ▷ **screw**

feed side opening An opening which feeds the material at an angle into the side of a processing machine (barrel, etc.) rather than the usual direction from the top.

feedstock Plastic materials are generally derived from crude oil or natural gas through a series of chemical processes such as thermal or catalytic cracking. Of the total oil and gas production worldwide, about $1\frac{1}{2}$ to 2% produce plastics. These feeds are described as petrochemicals; chemicals derived are hydrocarbon-based. Specific feedstocks needed to make plastics are methane, ethylene, benzene, acetylene, naphthalene, toluene, and xylene. Other feedstocks are used, such as coal, vegetation, etc. ▷ **petrochemical; oil and gas; coking; energy consumption and pollution**

feed, tangential opening In a plasticator screw melt system, an opening having one surface tangent to the downward moving periphery of the screw.

feed throat The section in a machine supporting the feed hopper through which material is introduced to the melting action, such as in extruders, blow molders, etc.

feed vertical opening An opening on a vertical centerline; can be circular, square, or rectangular. Shape can influence rate and uniformity of material flow through the opening.

feed volumetric An enclose device that meters a specific volume of materials. Bulk handling particle size and moisture content usually influence uniformity of metering capability. ▷ **feed, gravity** and **feeder, vibratory**

feldspar ▷ **china clay**

felt The term felt is used to describe (nonwoven) fabrics, matts, and batts prepared from staple fibers without spinning, weaving, or knitting; made up of fibers interlocked by mechanical, plastic, chemical, moisture, and/or heat action. In the beginning of this century a felt identified only a wool composite. It expanded so that various fibers (natural and synthetic) including inorganic fibers (glass, carbon, etc.) are all called felts. Use includes reinforcing plastics. ▷ **air filtration** and **wet felting**

female cavity ▷ **mold cavity**

ferris wheel clamp ▷ **rotary press**

ferrite A compound (multiple oxide) of ferric oxide with another oxide such as sodium ferrite ($NaFeO_2$). Those with trivalent iron are usually magnetic. Oxides are used as plastic fillers.

ferroelectric A crystalline material such as barium titanate, monobasic potassium phosphate, or potassium-sodium tartrate (rochelle salts) that, over certain limited temperatures, have a natural or inherent deformation (polarization) of electrical fields or electrons associated with atoms or groups in the crystal lattice. Used in plastic embedded capacitors, transducers, computer technology, etc.

festoon A device for the temporary accumulation or storage of material (film, wire, tape, etc.) in different fabricating processing lines (extrusion, calendering, thermoforming, impregnating substrates, etc.). As an example, it is a downstream section in an extrusion line where the film is looped between two (or more) sets of rolls to accumulate an inventory of film to facilitate the changing of wound rolls of film. During normal running, the two sets are close together. When the film roll is being changed, the distance between the rolls increases to accumulate film until the winder returns to full operation.

festooning oven An oven used to dry, cure, or fuse plastic-coated fabrics with uniform heating. The substrate is carried on a series of rotating shafts with long loops or "festoons" between the shafts.

fiber A term basically used to refer to filamentary materials. Often, fiber is used synonymously with filament, monofilament, whisker, and yarn. It is any material in a form such that it has a minimum length to average maximum transverse dimension of 10 to 1, a maximum cross sectional area of 7.85×10^{-5} in.^{2} (5.06×10^{-2} mm^2) in diameter (corresponding to a circular cross section of 0.010 in. /0.254 mm), and a maximum transverse dimension of 0.010 in. (0.254 mm). Fibers can be continuous or specific short lengths (discontinuous), normally not less than 1/8 in. (3.2 mm). There are also milled fibers (glass, etc.) ▷ **glass fiber designations, composition** and **reinforcement**. The plastics industry uses natural and man-made (organic and inorganic synthetics) fibers as additives and reinforcements providing many different performance improvements that range from lowering material cost to producing the strongest materials in the world. The synthetics are predominantly produced by fiber spinning processes (wet, dry, melt, or jet). Types used include: acrylic, acetate, alumina silica, aluminum, aramid, boron, carbon (PAN, pitch, and rayon bases), cotton, glass, graphite, nylon, olefin (PE), polyester (PET), quartz, rayon, saran, spandex, silicon carbide, steel, vinyon, wood, etc. ▷ **glass fiber and fabric surface treatment**

fiber acetate ▷ **acetate**

fiber acrylic ▷ **acrylic fiber**

fiber and twisting ▷ **twisting fiber**

fiber aramid ▷ **fiber nylon**

fiber biconstituent A hybrid or composite fiber comprising a dispersion of fibrils of one synthetic plastic within and parallel to the axis of another; also a fiber made up of plastic and a metal or alloy filaments.

fiber birefringence The algebraic difference of the index of refraction of the fiber for plane polarized light vibrating parallel to the longitudinal axis of the fiber and the index of refraction for light vibrating perpendicular to the long axis.

fiber breakout Fiber separation or break on surface plies at drilled or machine edges.

fiber bridging ▷ **pultrusion, fiber bridging**

fiber cellulose ▷ **fiber rayon**

fiber ceramic ▷ **ceramic fiber**

fiber combing A lining up of fibers.

fiber content The amount of fiber present in reinforced plastics usually expressed as a percentage volume fraction or weight fraction. Since fibers as well as plastics have different densities, it is usually more beneficial to use volume.

fiber count 1. The number of filling yarns per inch (mm) of woven fabric. **2.** In braided rope, the number of strands rotating in one direction in one cycle length divided by the cycle length ▷ **yarn construction number. 3.** The number of fibers per unit width of ply present in a specified section of a reinforced plastic.

fiber density ▷ **density, linear**

fiber diameter The measurement (expressed in hundred thousandth in. or mm) of the diameter of individual filaments.

fiber direction ▷ **reinforced plastic directional properties**

fiber dry Dry fiber is a condition in which fibers are not fully encapsulated by plastic, such as during pultrusion, fabric impregnation, etc.

fiber dry spinning ▷ **fiber spinning**

fiber entanglement ▷ **ceramic fiber**

fiber extrusion Extrusion of fibers is the overall process of "fiber spinning".

fiber fan In fiber forming, such as glass fiber, the fan-shape that is made by the filaments between the bushing and the fiber collection "shoe".

fiberfill Virgin man-made fibers especially engineered as to linear density, cut length, and crimp for use as a textile material (ASTM D 123 and 13).

fiberfill molding A term sometimes used for an injection molding process employing pellets containing short fiber with plastic (molding compound). The more popular term is reinforced plastics injection molding.

fiber fineness A relative measure of size, diameter, linear density, or mass per unit length expressed in a variety of units. For all fibers, the fiber number is in tex units. ▷ **tex**

fiber finish and sizing ▷ **finish** and **sizing**

fiber flax ▷ **flax**

fiber flexural rigidity A measure of rigidity of individual strands or fibers; the force couple required to bend a specimen to unit radius of curvature.

fiber flexural stress ▷ **flexural strength; flexural test, short beam shear**

fiber fly Fibers which fly out into the atmosphere during carding, drawing, spinning, or other textile processes.

fiber formation ▷ **fiber spinning**

fiber fuzz 1. Untangled fiber ends that protrude from the surface of a yarn or fabric. **2.** Accumulation of short, broken filaments after passing glass strands, yarns, or rovings over a contact point. Often weighted and used as an inverse measure of abrasion resistance.

fiber gear protection A driven plastic gear of a material of somewhat lower strength than the driven gear (such as cast iron); for example designed RP of glass fiber-TS polyester or an engineered plastics such as nylon. It is intended to fail under overload. Thus, it protects the driven cast iron master gear from destructive stress.

fiber glass ▷ **glass fiber**

fiber "Glasshopper" ▷ **rail car hopper**

fiber glass, reinforcement Fibers added to enhance the overall performance of a plastic matrix. ▷ **reinforced plastic**

fiber grasshopper A stiff bunch of parallel fiber strands in a fibrous mat.

fiber, grez system ▷ **grex system**

fiber, hard The non-elastic yarn wound around an elastic core in covered elastic yarns.

fiber hemp ▷ **hemp**

fiber, high silica ▷ **silica fiber**

fiber, hollow ▷ **hollow fiber**

fiber hydrodynamic specific surface The specific surface of a fibrous material as measured by the filtration resistance of a compacted pad formed from a fiber suspension under specific conditions.

fiber, jute A bast fiber obtained from the stems of several species of the plant *Corchorus* found mainly in India and Pakistan. Used as a filler for plastic molding compounds, and as a reinforcement for TS polyester plastics.

fiber knot tenacity ▷ **yarn tenacity**

fiber length When applied to a pulp, this applies to the mean fiber length; both the experimental details and the calculations must be specified.

fiber linter Short fibers that adhere to the cotton seed after ginning. Used in rayon manufacture as fillers for plastics and as a base for manufacture of cellulosic plastics.

fiber loaded Pertains to roving or mat.

fiber loop tenacity The tenacity or strength value obtained by pulling two loops, such as two links in a chain, against each other to demonstrate the susceptibility of a fibrous material to cutting or crushing; loop strength.

fiber loss on ignition Weight loss, usually expressed as a percent of the total, after burning off an organic sizing from glass fibers, or an organic plastic from a glass fiber laminate.

fiber, man-made A class name for various genera of fibers (including filaments) produced from fiber-forming substances including plastics synthesized by "man" from simple chemical compounds, modified or transformed natural plastics, or glasses. ▷ **fiber**

fiber melt spinning ▷ **fiber spinning**

fiber metal ▷ **metal fiber**

fiber, milled Glass fibers that have been hammer milled through a screen, resulting in a distribution of filament lengths below the nominal screen size.

fiber modacrylic Composed of less than 85% but at least 35% by weight of acrylonitrile except when it is a rubber.

fiber modulus ▷ **textile modulus**

fiber, mohair The fiber from the fleece of the Angora goat.

fiber, nonwoven sheet ▷ **fabric nonwoven; mechanical nonwoven fabric**

fiber, nylon Generic name for a fiber composed of polamide plastic in which less than 85% of the amide groups are attached directly to two aromatic rings. If there are more than 85% of such links, the fiber is an aramid.

fiber, nytril A manufactured fiber containing at least 85% of a long chain plastic of vinylidene dinitrile where the vinylidene dinitrile content is no less than every other unit in the polymer chain.

fiber olefin Composed of at least 85% by weight of ethylene, propylene, or other olefin, except when amorphous as rubber; principally polypropylene.

fiber, optical A fiber of glass through which light can be transmitted and from which the escape of light is prevented or minimized.

fiber optics Fiber optics may be defined as the guidance of electromagnetic radiation along transparent dielectric glass fibers. More specifically, the guidance usually involves the mechanism known as total internal reflection. If the fibers are of dimensions comparable to the wavelength of light, the fiber will act as a wave guide to conduct the radiation in discrete modes. Fibers with plastic coating are used. A fine-drawn silica (glass) fiber or filament of exceptionally high purity and specific optical properties (refractive index) that transmits laser light impulses almost instantaneously with high fidelity is used. ▷ **holography** and **plastic optical fiber**

fiber optic strain gauge By employing a network of fiber-optic strain gauges, buildings, bridges, aircraft, trains, etc. are able to monitor structural loading in real time. The system senses and determines the magnitude and location of structural damage. Combining these fiber-optic sensing mechanisms with powerful software packages also enables the making of intelligent decisions about possible structural overload conditions. At the heart of these capabilities lies a fiber-optic sensing system that operates much like a conventional electric strain gauge. The system, however, offers significant advantages over conventional strain gauges: electromagnetic interference does not affect it because it is not electrical, and it can be embedded during fabrication of plastics. ▷ **strain gauge**

fiber optic thermoset curing sensor ▷ **reinforced plastic, thermoset cure monitoring**

fiber orientation During processing of particularly plastic fibers, many can be stretched to significantly increase their tensile strength and modulus by taking advantage of molecular orientation at their respective temperature requirements. As an example a procedure is used to move fibers over heat controlled rolls with the downstream rolls progressively rotating faster. Based on plastic being stretched, they can increase $1\frac{1}{2}$ to 4 times. ▷ **orientation** and **extruder solid-state**

fiber orientation fabric Fiber orientation in a nonwoven or a mat laminate where the majority of fibers are in the same direction, resulting in a higher strength in that direction. ▷ **reinforced plastic directional properties**

fiber pattern visibility Visible fibers on the surface of laminates or moldings; the thread size or weave of cloth. Techniques such as using gel coatings, scrim cloth, etc. eliminate this situation.

fiber PE ▷ **solution spinning process**

fiber pick **1.** An individual filling yarn running the width of a woven fabric at right angles to the warp (fill, woof, weft). **2.** To experience tack. **3.** To transfer unevenly from an adhesive applicator mechanism due to high surface tack. **4.** To offset onto opposing surfaces. **5.** The relative integral strength of a cellulosic substrate relating to its ability to resist fiber distention when applied to a tacky surface and removed.

fiber polyester This thermoplastic fiber is composed of at least 85% by weight of an ester of a dihydric alcohol and terephthalic acid.

fiber, quartz ▷ **quartz fiber**

fiber ramie A natural fiber obtained from the stems of the plant *boehmeria nivea* of the hemp family. High wet strength, absorbent but dries quickly, can be spun or woven, wears well, tensile strength four times that of flax, and elasticity of 50% greater than flax. Use includes reinforcement of filler for plastics.

fiber rayon The generic term for fibers, staples, and continuous yarns composed of regenerated cellulose, but also frequently used to describe fibers obtained from cellulose acetate or cellulose triacetate. Rayon fibers are similar in chemical structure to natural cellulose fibers (cotton) except that the synthetic fiber contains shorter units. Most rayon is made by the viscous process. Basically, all methods for producing these fibers or filaments depend upon solubilizing relatively short fibered forms of cellulose, then reshaping the cellulose into long-fibered products by extrusion through the small holes of a spinnert, immediately followed by converting the fiber again into solid cellulose.

Rayon, the first man-made fiber, came into being at the end of the 19th century, and was called artificial silk. In 1924 the name rayon was adopted officially by the National Retail Dry Goods Assoc. Use includes as a filler and reinforcement for plastics. ▷ **regenerated fiber** and **viscous process**

fiber-reinforced plastic A general term (FRP) for a plastic that is reinforced with cloth, mat, strands, or any other fiber form; usually the FRP is only identified as RP (reinforced plastic).

fiber reinforcement, three-dimensional ▷ **reinforcement; three-dimensional fabric**

fiber saran Composed of at least 80% by weight of vinylidene chloride units.

fiber saturation point Upper limit of moisture adsorption onto fibers; the limit of volume expansion by moisture absorption.

fiber show Strands or bundles of fibers that are not covered by plastic because they are at or above the surface of a reinforced plastic.

fiber shrinkage, solvent induced When plastic fibers are exposed to solvents, melting points and glass transition temperature are depressed, resulting in shrinkage. Solvent-induced shrinkage and solvent interaction with fibers can occur during processing and use in plastics.

fiber shrinkage, thermal induced At elevated temperatures, thermoplastic fibers contract; near the melting point they assume longitudinal dimensions close to those before drawing (orienting). The thermal shrinkage is the result of the contraction of extended-chain tie molecules that assume random coil configurations or crystallized in chain-folded crystals. This behavior is important in the fabrication of RPs where temperatures can be sufficiently high to cause shrinkage, leading to losses in strength and modulus. Exposure of fibers to elevated temperatures also activates latent heat asymmetric stresses introduced by various crimping processes, i.e., a relatively straight fiber or yarn develops crimp upon heating.

fiber silica ▷ **silica fiber**

fiber, silicon carbide ▷ **silicon carbide fiber**

fiber single-strand strength The breaking strength of a single strand of yarn, monofilament, or cord, not knotted or looped but running straight between the clamps of the testing machine.

fiber sisal A leaf fiber from the plant *agave sisalana* consisting of stiff strands 50 to 100 cm in length, which can be creamy white in color. It is a cellulose fiber containing about 6% lignin. Use includes as a filler and reinforcement in plastics.

fiber skein A continuous filament, strand, yarn, or roving wound up to some measurable length and usually used to measure various physical properties.

fiber sliver A number of staple or continuous-filament fibers aligned in a continuous strand without twist. Pronounced "slyver".

fiber spandex A polyurethane plastic in fiber form (generic name), strictly one containing a thermoplastic PUR elastomer with at least 85% polyurethane content. Compared to other major elastomeric fibers, including natural rubber, spandex has higher tensile strength and modulus, as well as superior resistance to oxidation and fire.

fiber spinning Man-made fiber manufacture is based on three common methods of fiber formation or spinning. The term spinning should be used more properly for that textile manufacturing operation where staple fibers are formed into continuous textile yarns by several consecutive attenuating and twisting steps. A yarn so formed from natural or man-made staple fibers is referred to as a spun yarn. In the context of man-made fiber manufacture, spinning refers to the overall process of plastic extrusion and fiber formation. The three common methods are melt spinning, dry spinning, and wet spinning. Other techniques are flash spinning, jet spinning, reaction spinning, and split-fiber process. ▷ **spinneret**

fiber spinning process Thermoplastic fibers are made by forcing the plastic through a multiple orifice spinneret. These contain as many as 50 to 110 holes, each less than 0.2 mm in diameter. In melt spinning, the plastic is heated to low viscosity. The slender, emerging fibers cool quickly in a current of air which causes a degree of solidification of the plastic before they travel over take-up rolls and on to bobbins. This method is used for the commercial production of nylon, polyethylene, terephthalate, polypropylene, and polyvinylidene chloride fibers.

Rayon is made by a dry spinning operation. It is dissolved in acetone to produce a thick solution that is extruded through the spinneret. The acetone evaporates (collected and reused) to permit the fibers to dry before going over the take-up rolls and onto the bobbins. In both the melt and dry spinning methods, the fibers travel at about 15 m/s (3,000 ft/m).

The slower process is the wet spinning. It is used when the fibers, such as cellulose, must react with a bath to complete the polymerization reaction after they leave the spinneret. From the water bath fibers go over take-up rolls and on to the bobbins.

fiber spinning row nucleation The mechanism by which stress-induced crystallization is initiated, usually during fiber spinning or hot drawing.

fiber spiral In glass fiber forming, the device that is used to traverse the strand back and forth across the forming tube.

fiber spraying ▷ **flocking**

fiber spun ▷ **spun bonded**

fiber staple Short fibers as opposed to continuous filaments. All natural fibers, apart from silk, are staple fibers with lengths varying from 2 to 4 cm in cotton, 7 to 15 cm in wool, and several hundred cm in jute and hemp. Man-made fibers are produced as continuous fibers; in plastics they are used in continuous form and also frequently chopped to form usable staples.

fiber strain in flexural ▷ **strain, flexure of fiber**

fiber strength, knot ▷ **yarn knot tenacity**

fiber tenacity The tensile stress expressed as force per unit linear density of the unstrained specimen. ▷ **tenacity**

fiber tenacity, effective The tensile stress at a specified extension, calculated on the basis of the linear density of the strained specimen, that is, the linear density at the specified extension; for example, grams-force/tex, or grams-force/denier.

fiber tensile critical stress longitudinally The longitudinal stress necessary to cause internal slippage and separation of a spun yarn. This is the stress necessary to overcome the inter-fiber friction developed as a result of twist. The result $= P\mu S$, where P = pressure normal to the fiber surface (psi or kPa), μ = coefficient of friction between fiber surface, and S = specified surface of the fiber.

fiber tensile stress, mass Force per unit mass per unit length; grams/denier, etc. Used the same way as force per unit area.

fiber textile Fibers of filaments that can be processed into yarn or made into a fabric by interlacing in a variety of methods, including weaving, knitting, and braiding.

fiber throwing A textile term referring to the act of imparting twist to a yarn, especially while plying and twisting together a number of yarns; a throwster.

fiber torsional rigidity The resistance of a fiber to twisting. The couple needed to put a fiber in unit twist, i.e., unit deflection between the ends of a fiber of unit length. Units are in $g \cdot cm^2 \, sec^{-2}$ or dyne-cm.

fiber tow An untwisted bundle of continuous filaments, usually referring to man-made fibers, such as glass, carbon, graphite, aramid, etc. Designation is by a number followed by "K" indicating multiplication by 1,000, thus, 140 K has 140,000 filaments. These multiple filament strands are suitable for conversion into staple fibers or slivers, or for direct spinning into yarn.

fiber tracer ▷ **tracer**

fiber vinal Generic name for a manufactured fiber in which the fiber-forming substance is any long chain plastic composed of at least 50% by weight of vinyl alcohol units and in which the total of the vinyl alcohol units and any one or more of the various acetal units is at least 85% by weight of the fiber. It has good chemical resistance, low affinity for water, etc.

fiber vinyon Generic name for a manufactured fiber in which the fiber-forming substance is any long chain plastic composed of at least 85% by weight of vinyl chloride units.

fiber, virgin An individual fiber (filament) that has not been in contact with any other fiber or any other hard material (plastic, etc.). ▷ **virgin plastic**

fiber vulcanized Cellulosic material that has been partially gelatinized by action of a chemical (usually zinc chloride), then heavily compressed or rolled to required thickness, leached free from the gelatinizing agent, and dried. Use includes in electrical insulation and in packaging.

fiber wadding A loose cohering mass of fiber in sheet or lap form.

fiber warp ▷ **warp**

fiber wash Splaying out of woven or nonwoven fibers from the general reinforcement direction during certain RP processes (compression, resin transfer, reaction injection, and other molding processes). Fibers are carried along with bleeding plastic during cure to form flash.

fibrid A generic name for fibers made of synthetic plastics.

fibril A single crystal in the form of a fiber.

fibrillar A fiber-like aggregation of molecules.

fibrillation **1.** Production of fiber from film. **2.** The phenomenon wherein filament or fiber shows evidence of basic fibrous structure or fibrillar crystalline nature, by a longitudinal opening up of the filament under rapid, excessive tensile or shearing stresses. Separate fibrils can then often be seen in the main filament trunk. The whitening of polyethylene when unduly strained at room temperature is a manifestation of fibrillation.

Fick's law of diffusion ▷ **devolatilization, basics**

figure **1.** A numerical figure is an arithmetic value expressed by one or more digits. **2.** A diagram or pattern.

filament The smallest unit of a fibrous material. The basic units formed during drawing or spinning, which are gathered into strands of fiber for use as reinforcements. Normally, filaments are not used individually. They are usually of extreme length and very small in diameter (less than 25 μm (1 mil)). They are used in tows, yarns, rovings, etc.

filamentary reinforced plastic An RP composed of laminae in which continuous filaments are in nonwoven, parallel, uniaxial arrays. Individual uniaxial laminae can be combined into specifically oriented, multiaxial laminates.

filament, continuous An individual small diameter reinforcement that is relatively flexible and indefinite in length.

filament number The linear density of a filament expressed in suitable units such as tex, denier, millitex, etc.

filament placement process A continuous process for fabricating reinforced plastic shapes with complex contours and/or cutouts by means of a device that lays preimpregnated fibers (in tow form) onto a nonuniform mandrel or tool. It differs from filament winding: there is no limit on fiber angles; compaction takes place online via heat, pressure, or both; and fibers can be added and dropped as necessary. The process produces more complex shapes and permits a faster putdown rate than filament winding.

filament shoe A device for gathering the numerous filaments into a strand in glass fiber forming.

filament weight ratio In a reinforced plastic material, the ratio of filament weight to total weight of the RP.

filament winding In filament winding (FW), continuous filaments are wound onto a mandrel after passing through a plastic bath, unless preimpregnated (prepreg) filaments or tapes are used, which eliminates the plastic bath. The shape of the mandrel is the internal shape of the finished part. The configuration of the winding depends upon the relative speed of rotation of the mandrel and the rate of travel of the reinforcement-dispensing mechanism. The three most common types are helical winding, in which the filaments are at a significant angle with the axis of the mandrel (see Fig. on top of p. 289); circumferential winding, in which the filaments are wound like thread on a spool; and polar winding, in which the filaments are nearly parallel to the axis of the mandrel, passing over its ends on each pass (see Fig. on bottom of p. 289).

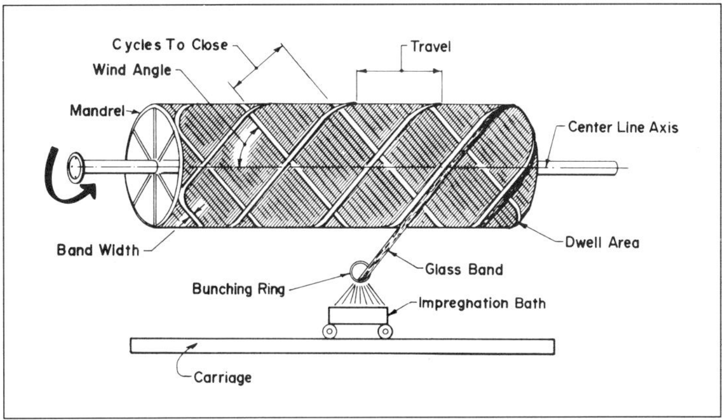

Schematic of filament winding using a helical winding pattern.

Different configurations can be employed on successive passes and the orientation of the filaments be tailored to the stresses set up in the part. For example, with pipe, continuous helical winding can be employed on a segmental mandrel, an extruded mandrel, or on release film placed on a stationary mandrel. Other filament winders include braiding machines, loop wrappers, small to large storage tank machines, rectangular box-frame machines, and many different special fiber-placement machines with several degrees of freedom for intricate shapes. As filaments are continuous and tightly packed, they permit a high filament-to-plastic ratio. This capability often results in products having the highest strength-to-weight ratio obtainable in any structures (see Fig. below).

Even though most FW uses glass filaments, all types of filaments can be used. Precautions must be observed if superior properties are to be achieved. Glass fibers are strong, but as glass

CLASSICAL HELICAL WINDER

CIRCUMFERENTIAL WINDER

POLAR WINDER

CONTINUOUS HELICAL WINDER

Schematic representation of basic methods and types of filament placement.

This filament winding machine produced gigantic FW tanks; designed and built in 1966 by the Rucker Co. for Aerojet-General to wind 32 ton NASA all-plastic rocket motor case. The machine is 22 ft. (56 m) high, 60 ft. (152 m) wide, 125 ft. (318 m) long, and had a 100 ton metal mandrel. Total weight of steel constructed machine was 200 tons. Its 150,000 gal (568 m^3) tank measured 21 ft. (53 m) long by 156 ft. (396 m) in diameter, contained about 156 million miles (251 million km) of glass fiber, used 8 tons textile creel containing 60 spools of glass fiber moving up to $4\frac{1}{4}$ mph (7.24 km/h), and took three weeks to produce each epoxy RP case, in the Todd Shipyard in Los Angeles. People are standing below the FW case.

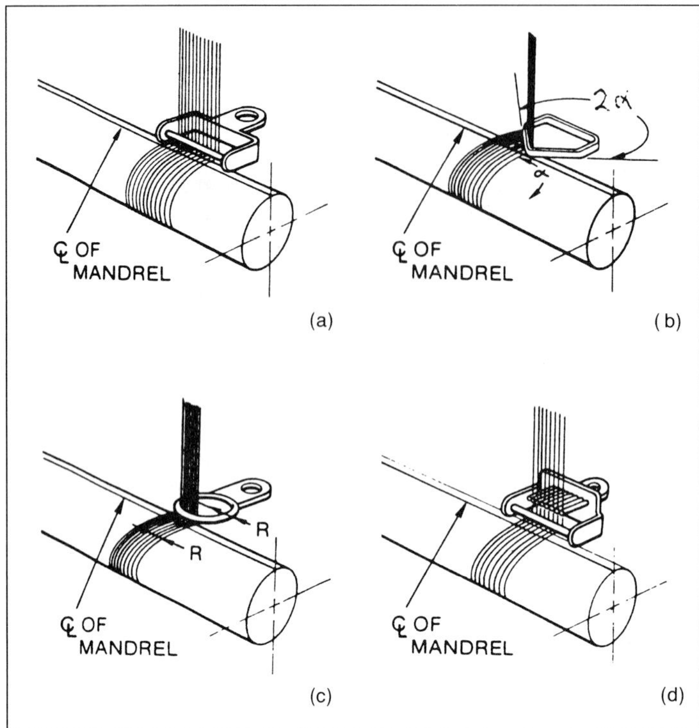

Examples of filament winding band formations: (*a*) band forming with straight bar; (*b*) band forming using bent bar with straight arms; (*c*) band forming with ring or curved bar; (*d*) band forming with comb.

they are subject to a severe loss in strength with surface abrasion. They must be carefully handled and processed to avoid such deterioration. In a lay-up for FW, as well as others, plastic abrasion-resistant fibers or (usually) film can be included. This construction permits parts to operate in severe load environments, such as under vibration, twisting, and so on, and eliminates or at least significantly reduces glass-to-glass abrasion where a high fiber-to-resin ratio exists. Other types of fibers should be studied to determine whether fiber damage can occur when the part is in service. Certain fibers, with or without resins, might be brittle, and other problems could develop. The designer of the part should have knowledge of the potential problems. If problems do develop, steps can be taken during processing to overcome them. If unwanted porosity occurs, for instance, linears (gel coatings, elastomeric materials, etc.) can be included during FW.

filament winding angle The winding angle is the angular measure in degrees between the direction parallel to the filaments and an established reference. It is usually referenced to the centerline through the polar bosses, that is, the axis of rotation.

filament winding angle wrap Tape laying fabric that is wrapped on a starter dam mandrel at an angle to the centerline.

filament winding axial winding The winding with the filament parallel to, or at a small angle to, the axis (0° helix angle). ▷ **filament winding polar winding**

filament winding, balanced design A winding pattern so designed that the stresses in all filaments are equal.

filament winding, balanced-in-plane contour A head contour in which the filaments are oriented within a plane and the radii of curvature are adjusted to balance the stresses along the filaments with the pressure loading.

filament winding band density The quantity of fiber reinforcement per inch (mm) of band width, expressed as strands (or filaments) per inch (mm).

filament winding band formation Examples are shown in the Fig. above.

filament winding band thickness The thickness of the reinforcement as it is applied to the mandrel.

filament winding band width The width of the reinforcement as it is applied to the mandrel.

filament winding barrier coat ▷ **barrier**

filament winding biaxial winding The helical band is laid in sequence, side by side, with no cross over of the fibers.

filament winding bladder An elastomeric (barrier) lining for the containment of hydroproof and hydroburst pressurization medium in FW structures.

filament winding bleedout The excess liquid plastic that migrates to the surface of a winding. ▷ **bleed**

filament winding circuit One complete traverse of the fiber feed mechanism of a winding machine; one complete traverse of a winding band from one arbitrary point along the winding path to another point on a plane through the starting point and perpendicular to the axis.

filament winding circumferential A winding with the filaments essentially perpendicular to the axis (90° or level of winding).

filament winding displacement angle The advancement distance of the winding ribbon on the equator after one complete circuit.

filament winding doily The planar reinforcement applied to a local area between windings to provide extra strength in an area where a cutout is to be made, i.e. port openings in a container. Usually placed at the knuckle joints of cylinder to dome.

filament winding dome The portion of a cylindrical container that forms the spherical or elliptical shell ends of the container.

filament winding doubler ▷ **doubler**

filament winding dry Dry winding is a term used to describe FW using preimpregnated reinforcement (rovings, etc.), as differentiated from wet winding in which unimpregnated reinforcement is pulled through a plastic bath just before being wound onto a mandrel.

filament winding dwell time ▷ **dwell**

filament winding equator The line in a pressure vessel described by the junction of the cylindrical portion and the end dome. Also called tangent line or point.

filament winding forming cake ▷ **forming cake**

filament winding gap The space between successive windings in which windings are usually intended to lay next to each other; separations between fibers within a filament winding band; the distance between adjacent plies in a layup of unidirectional tape materials.

filament winding geodesic-isotensoid contour Pressure vessel with a dome contour in which the filaments are placed on geodesic paths so that filaments exhibit uniform tensions throughout their length under pressure loading. Basically results in the strongest structure to weight that can be manufactured with any material, including steel.

filament winding helical winding A winding in which a filament band advances along a helical path, not necessarily at a constant angle, except in the case of a cylinder.

filament winding knuckle area The area of transition between sections of different geometry in a FW part, for example, where the skirt joins the cylinder of the pressure vessel. Also called Y-joint.

filament winding lap winding ▷ **lap**

filament winding lattice pattern A pattern with a fixed arrangement of open voids.

filament winding liner The continuous, usually flexible coating on the inside surface used to protect the RP from chemical attack, abrasive action, prevent leakage under stress, etc. ▷ **barrier**

filament winding longos Low-angle helical or longitudinal windings.

filament winding mandrel Mandrel design is comparatively simple for open end structures such as cylinders or conical shapes. Either cored or solid steel or aluminum serves satisfactorily. When end closures are integrally wound, as in pressure vessels, careful consideration must be given to mandrel design and selection of a suitable material. A proper design will minimize fiber damage during part removal as well as dimensional intolerances and excessive residual stresses. The mandrel must resist sagging due to its weight and applied winding tension. It must retain sufficient strength during cure at elevated temperatures and be easy to remove after cure. Construction concepts include the following: (1) *Segmented collapsible metal* These are costly and are not warranted for less than 25 parts. The suggested diameter range is 3–5 ft (0.91–1.52 m). Removal can be complicated with small polar openings. (2) *Low melting alloys* These are high in density and tend to creep under moderate winding tension. They are limited to small vessels in the order of 1 ft (0.3 m) in diameter by 1 ft (0.3 m) in length. (3) *Eutectic salts* These are better suited than the alloys and are applicable up to 2 ft (0.6 m) in diameter. With care, they can be slush molded, and they are easy to remove. (4) *Soluble plasters* These have a long plastic stage and can be wiped to contour. They are easily washed out.

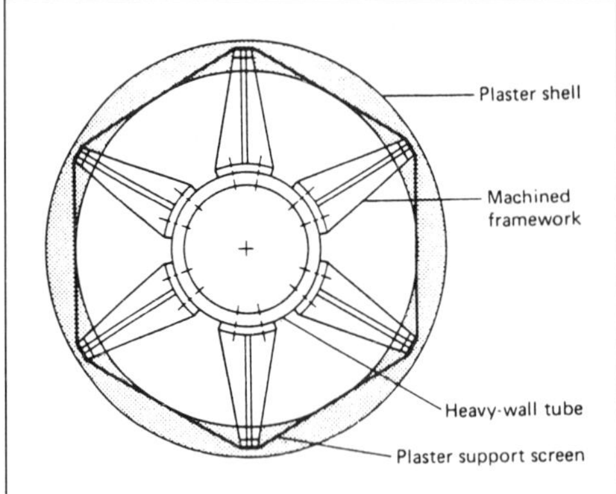

Framework for a wash-out plaster mandrel.

The Fig. above is a schematic of the support structure for a wash-out plaster mandrel. (5) *Frangible or break-out plasters* These are used best with large diameters. Internal support is required, and break-out is difficult and can cause damage. Chains can be imbedded to facilitate removal. (6) *Sand—PVA* This material is an excellent choice for diameters up to 5 ft (1.5 m) and for limited quantities. It dissolves readily in hot water, but requires careful molding control. Low compressive strength is a limitation. (7) *Inflatables* These are not suitable where it is necessary to resist torque loads. One technique for improving the torque resistance is to fill the mandrel with a material such as sand and to apply a vacuum. Another use for inflatables is to transfer the uncured winding to a closed mold and to cure with pressurization through the mandrel.

The properties of several mandrel materials are given in the Table below.

filament winding multicircuit winding A FW that requires more than one circuit before the band repeats by laying adjacent to the first band.

filament winding netting analysis The analysis of FW structures that assumes that the stresses induced in the structure are carried entirely by the filaments, and the strength of the plastic is neglected. It is also assumed that the filaments possess no bending or shearing stiffness, and carry only the axial tensile loads.

filament winding overtravel The additional carriage or eye travel beyond the ends of the part mandrel that is necessary to provide laydown of the fiber on the mandrel.

filament winding pattern The total number of individual circuits required for a winding path to begin repeating by laying down immediately adjacent to the initial circuit; a regular recurring pattern of the filament path after a certain number of mandrel revolutions, leading eventually to the complete coverage of the mandrel.

filament winding planar helix A planar helix winding is a winding in which the filament path on each dome lies on a plane that intersects the dome, while a helical path over the cylindrical section is connected to the dome paths.

filament winding planar winding A type of FW in which the filament path lies on a plane that intersects the winding surface.

filament winding polar winding A winding in which the filament path passes tangent to the

Mandrel materials.

Material	Kerr DMM[1]	Hydrocal B-11[2]	Brak-away[3]	Paraplast 36[3]	Sand/PVA
Type	Wash-out plaster	Frangible plaster	Frangible plaster	Soluble salt	Wash-out
Compressive strength, psi (MPa)	700 (4.8)	3800 (26.2)	375 (2.6)	14,000 (96.5)	500 (3.5)
Specific gravity	1.25	1.36	0.8	2.08	
Moisture pick-up % at 75% RH % at 70% RH	 0.07	 0.45 86.5			
Maximum use temperature, °C (°F)	204+ (400+)	204+ (400+)	204+ (400+)	177 (350)	177 (350)
Set time, minutes	20–25	45–55	10–15		
Set expansion, in./in.	0.043	0.0004	0.0015		

[1] Kerr Mfg Co
[2] US Gypsum
[3] Rezolin, Inc

polar opening at one end of the chamber and tangent to the opposite side of the polar opening at the other end. A one-circuit pattern is inherent in the system.

filament winding polepiece The supporting part of the mandrel used in FW, usually on one of the axes of rotation.

filament winding prepreg and bag molding On occasions, it is economical or structurally desirable to wind multi-layered prepregs. These are windings taken from the mandrel for subsequent bag molding. Mandrels are first overwrapped with compliant plastic films which later serve as backings for the prepregs. The FW prepreg must contain the complete sequence of angle plies required for the lay-up. When the fibers are collimated, fiber volume content fractions of 60 to 65% are attained.

After the winding is staged, the excess of built-up windings adjacent to the poles is trimmed away. The backing, together with the wound prepreg, is cut parallel to the mandrel axis. It is then lifted off the mandrel and placed on the molding surface. It is seldom desirable to lay up the prepreg on a reversed curved surface. If a male form is used, the backing should be against the mold surface. If a female form is used, the resinous surface should be laid into the cavity. If the prepreg is adequately advanced, the backing may be removed after the lay-up is completed in a cavity or an auxiliary backing is positioned for laying up the prepreg on a male form. Otherwise, the backing must remain in place until the composite is cured.

filament winding prepreg solvent system Sometimes, inert solvents must maintain plastics in a sufficiently fluid state to wet the reinforcements during FW prepregs. When such systems are used, additional equipment is required. Besides a device to meter the amount of plastic to remain on the fibers, other equipment is required to volatilize the solvents and stage the prepregs. Adaptions of drying tunnels and staging towers are used. Multi-layered prepregs can then be wound without appreciable solvent content to nucleate voids.

filament winding random pattern A winding with no fixed pattern. If a large number of circuits is required for the pattern, a random pattern is approached. A winding in which the filaments do not lie in an even pattern.

filament winding reverse helical As the fiber delivery arm traverses one circuit, a continuous helix is laid down, reversing direction at the polar ends, in contrast to biaxial, compact, or sequential winding. The fibers cross each other at definite equators, the number depending on the helix. The minimum region of crossover is three.

filament winding single circuit The filament path makes a complete traverse of the chamber, after which the following traverse lies immediately adjacent to the previous one.

filament winding skirt The extension of a container or motorcase from the tangency plane, used for interstage connections, usually wound or laid up as an integral part of the container.

filament winding slip angle The angle at which a tensioned fiber will slide off a FW dome. If the difference between the wind angle and the geodesic angle is less than the slip angle, the fiber will not slip off the dome. Slip angles for different fiber-plastic systems vary and must be determined experimentally.

filament winding solvent plastic system ▷ **filament winding wet** and **filament winding prepreg and bag molding**

filament winding stress In a FW part, usually a pressure vessel, the stress calculated using the load and the cross sectional area of the reinforcement only.

filament winding tangent line ▷ **filament winding equator**

filament winding tape wrap ▷ **lagging molding**

filament winding tension In FW or tape wrapping, the amount of tension on the reinforcement as it makes contact with the mandrel.

filament winding wet The process of FW in which strands are impregnated with liquid plastic before and during winding onto the mandrel.

filament yarn continuous Yarn that is formed by twisting two or more continuous filaments into a single continuous strand.

filing Manual filing is sometimes used to bevel, smooth, deburr, and fit the edges of plastic parts. The process is limited to parts that can not be tumbled easily.

fill **1.** Reinforcing yarn (orienting) from selvage to selvage at right angles to the warp in a woven fabric. **2.** In injection molding, packing of a cavity or cavities to provide complete parts.

fill-and-wipe Parts are with depressed designs; after application of paint, surplus is wiped off leaving the paint remaining only in the depressed areas. Also refers to spray-and-wipe and wipe-in.

filler Usually a relatively inert substance added to plastic compound to reduce cost and/

Examples of fillers and reinforcements.

Filler or Reinforcement	Properties Improved													
	Chemical resistance	Heat resistance	Electrical insulation	Impact strength	Tensile strength	Dimensional stability	Stiffness	Hardness	Lubricity	Electrical conductivity	Thermal conductivity	Moisture resistance	Processability	Recommended for use in [1]
Alumina, tabular	●	●	●	●		●	●					●	●	S/P
Aluminum powder										●	●			S
Aramid	●	●	●	●	●	●	●	●	●				●	S/P
Bronze							●	●		●	●			S
Calcium carbonate	●	●	●	●		●	●	●					●	S/P
Carbon black		●				●	●			●	●		●	S/P
Carbon fiber										●	●			S
Cellulose				●		●	●	●						S/P
Alpha cellulose			●			●						●		S
Coal, powdered	●											●		S
Cotton			●	●	●	●	●	●						S
Fibrous glass	●	●	●	●	●	●	●	●				●		S/P
Graphite	●				●	●	●	●	●	●	●			S/P
Jute				●			●							S
Kaolin	●	●	●			●	●	●	●			●	●	S/P
Mica	●	●	●			●	●	●	●			●		S/P
Molybdenum disulfide							●	●	●			●	●	P
Nylon	●	●	●	●	●	●	●	●					●	S/P
Orlon	●	●	●	●	●	●	●	●				●	●	S/P
Rayon			●	●	●	●	●	●						S
Silica, amorphous			●									●	●	S/P
Sisal fibers	●			●		●	●	●				●		S/P
Fluorocarbon						●	●	●	●					S/P
Talc	●	●	●			●	●	●	●			●	●	S/P
Wood flour			●			●								S

[1] P = thermoplastic, S = thermoset.

or to improve physical properties, particularly hardness, stiffness, and impact strength (see Table above). A filler differs from a reinforcement in that it is small and it does not markedly improve the tensile strength. The most commonly used general purpose fillers are clays, silicates, talcs, carbonates, and wood flour. Some fillers also act as pigments (carbon black, chalk, and titanium dioxide). Graphite, molybdenum disulfide, and PTFE are used as fillers to impart lubricity. Magnetic properties can be obtained by using magnetic mineral fillers such as barium sulfate. Other metallic fillers such as lead or its oxides are used to increase specific gravity; powdered aluminum imparts higher thermal and electrical conductivity, as do other powdered metals such as copper, lead, and bronze. Graphite powder can be used to cause the plastic to shrink when heated: rather than the expected expansion. ▷ **additive** and **reinforcement**

filler specks Visible specks of a filler used, such as wood flour, which stand out in color contrast against a background of a plastic binder.

fillet **1.** A rounded filling of the internal angle between two surfaces specified by a radius. **2.** A rounded filling (plastic or adhesive) that fills the corner or angle where two adherends are joined.

filling yarn ▷ **yarn, filling**

fill point The level to which a container must be filled to furnish a designated quantity of the contents.

fill-sanding plastic A general purpose polyester (TS) used to soak and fill reinforcing material in the initial lay-up of a surfacing application; usually contains wax.

film Films are formed by melt extrusion using flat or circular dies, by calendering, by solvent casting, by chemical conversion, or by skiving. The resulting films may be uniaxially or biaxially oriented or rolled to modify their properties. Films are distinguished from sheets in the plastics and packaging industries by their thickness. A web under 10 mils (0.0254 cm) thick is usually called film, however under 4 mils (0.01 cm) is also used. Material over these dimensions are called sheets. The 4 mil value tends to be more applicable to the manufacture of plastic films.

Films are primarily used for packaging with compositions designed for specific end uses. They can be made permeable or impermeable to moisture and other gases, heat sealable, heat shrinkable, heat formable (vacuum), heat resistant, insoluble or soluble, transparent, opaque to UV light, weatherable, flammable, fire resistant, conductive or nonconductive to electricity, bondable, postformable after lamination, and are available in a wide range of colors, etc. To further enhance their performance, films can be coated, sprayed, etc. ▷ **skiving**

film adhesive ▷ **adhesive film**

film, aluminum ▷ **aluminum foil**

film and tape Films are shaped plastics that are comparatively thin in relation to their breadth and width. Tape is the term used for relatively narrow films, such as from 1/16 to 4 in. (0.025 to 1.6 cm) in width.

film bead ▷ **extruder film quench-tank**

film blocking An adhesion between touching layers of plastic, such as that which may develop under pressure during storage or use. The extent of blocking depends upon temperature, pressure, humidity, physical properties of the plastic itself and processing conditions. If the plastic has a low softening point or if it picks up moisture readily, it will have a greater tendency to block than a plastic which has a high softening point and does not pick up moisture. The physical properties of the plastic itself upon which blocking depends are as follows: (1) smooth surfaces adhere more readily than rough, (2) adhesion will depend on the amorphous or crystalline character of the plastic with amorphous having a greater tendency to block, (3) if one surface is readily wet by the other, the tendency to block is increased, (4) if the melting point is low, there will be an increased tendency to block, (5) if a surface shows flow under pressure, the tendency to block may be severe, (6) blocking is promoted by the tendency of the film to pick up water vapor, and (7) film and sheet that develop static electricity readily adhere to each other.

The inability to slide one film layer is usually the result of poor slip or a high coefficient of friction, such as with polyethylene film. It may also be caused by the attraction of two very smooth, glossy film surfaces to one another. Blocking is a function of some inherent plastic property in addition to processing conditions. There is a relationship between slipping and antiblocking properties, though good slip does not necessarily correlate with resistance of a film to blocking. Additives are also used to overcome both poor slip and blocking. Use of too much tension at the windup by the film extruder greatly increases blocking tendencies. This can be further aggravated by insufficient cooling of the film so that the film is still warm, particularly at fast speeds. Thus, blocking may be substantially reduced by low tension windup, slower windup rates, increasing the distance between the die and nip rolls, using a minimum nip roll pressure in blown film extrusion, and extruding hot flat film into a comparatively cool water bath in flat film extrusion.

Surface blocking is more of a problem in blown film than in flat film extrusion. The inflated bubble travels at high speed and, cooled only with air, is squeezed together and wound only a few seconds from leaving the hot die lands. Blocking may occur on the inside of the tube, on its outside, or in extreme cases, both inside and outside. Thicker films are easier to separate than thinner ones because of a better transmission of the shear forces applied (during bag opening). Generally, lower melt index PE requires less antiblocking additive than higher melt index plastics. The influence of higher density is even more beneficial. An excess of film surface treatment used for good printing ink adhesion frequently causes blocking. Such treatment alters the surface chemically (which is essential for ink adhesion) and warms the film. The treatment drives off slip agents from the surface treated side and thus, enhances blocking. To reduce these adverse influences (including the above processing comments), overtreatment must be avoided. ▷ **antiblocking agent; antistatic agent; antislip agent; lubricant; dusting agent; slip additive**

film blowing ▷ **extruder, blown film** and **thermoforming, clam shell**

film brittleness ▷ **extruder film brittleness**

film casting **1.** The process of making unsupported film or sheet by casting a fluid plastic compound on a temporary carrier, usually an endless belt or roll (drum), followed by solidification and removal of the film from the carrier. Liquid plastic on a substrate is stabilized by evaporation of solvent, by fusing after deposition, or by allowing a melt to cool. Cast films are usually made from solutions or dispersions. **2.** The term film casting has been used also for the process of extruding a molten plastic through a slot die onto chill rolls.

film coating Films are coated to extend the utility of the base film by enhancing previously existing film properties or adding new and unique properties. Coatings may impart heat sealability, impermeability (to moisture, water vapor, or other gases), energy barrier (to UV light or heat), modify the optical or electrical properties, or alter the coefficient of friction and the tendency toward blocking. Coatings are differentiated from laminations of two or more free formed films (polyester film to aluminuum foil, etc.) in that the coating "film" is ordinarily formed in the coating process and is relatively thinner than the base film. The coating process involves the application (by solution, emulsion, or extrusion coating) of a plastic onto the base film with subsequent formation of a film. Coatings are generally 0.05 to 0.2 mil (0.13 to 0.5 cm) thick. In lamination most films are at least 0.25 mil (0.6 cm) thick, more commonly 0.5 to 2 mil (1.3 to 5 cm) thick.

The lamination coating of polyethylene is a special case because thick layers of PE are applied (0.25 to 2 mil) and the resulting physical properties are affected by the thick PE film. Generally this method would be classified as a lamination. The PE film is actually formed in the coating step and is not preformed. This process is therefore considered to be a special case and is called a lamination coating.

film core The film core is a vortex of productivity in the extremely competitive film market where extrusion, casting, coating, laminating, and winding equipment is wider and faster for maximized productivity and profitability. Several criteria should be considered when selecting a film core: dimensional consistency, strength options, outer surface options, structural appearance, and supplier's capabilities. Evaluating cores with these criteria will ensure that the one chosen has the greatest value. Because most film lines are fully or partially automated, it is essential that the core's length and inner diameter specifications be consistent. If cores with varying dimensions are used on automated equipment, unnecessary downtime and costly material waste can result.

film, electronic treatment ▷ **electronic treatment**

film formation Film coatings can involve chemical reaction, polymerization, or crosslinking; some merely involve coalescence of plastic particles. The various mechanisms involved in the formation of plastic coatings are as follows: (1) coating formed by chemical reaction, polymerization, or crosslinking (epoxy, polyester (TS), phenolic varnishes, polyurethanes, silicones, etc.), (2) dispersions of a plastic in a vehicle; after removal of the vehicle by evaporation or bake, the plastic coalesces to form a film (plastisols, organosols, water based or latex paints, fluorocarbons, etc.), (3) plastic dissolved in solvent; solvent evaporates, leaving a plastic film (vinyl lacquers, acrylic lacquers, alkyds, shellac, chlorinated rubbers, cellulose lacquers, etc.), (4) pigments in an oil that polymerizes in the presence of oxygen and drying agents (alkyd enamels, varnishes, oil paints/linseed base, etc.), (5) coatings formed by dipping in hot melt of plastic (polyethylene waxes, asphalt, etc.), and (6) coatings formed by coating with a plastic powder and melting the powder to form a coating (many thermoplastics).

film impact strength A material's ability to withstand shock loading as measured by the work done in fracturing a specimen such as with the Izod impact test. ▷ **extruder film impact strength**

film orientation ▷ **orientation**

film processing Virtually every thermoplastic material can be used in film form. Most TP films are prepared by conventional extrusion techniques based on calendering, solvent casting, blown film, or tenter film systems. In the selection of a film for a particular application, the properties of the TPs must be considered in view of the applications. Thermal properties, molecular characteristics, and crystallinity of the plastic affect processing and film properties. Additives influence extrusion and orientation processes and improve film properties. Manufacturing processes include extrusion (coextrusion, casting, uniaxial orientation, and biaxial orientation), solvent solution casting (coagulation and evaporation), rolling, and calendering. Finishing operations include coating and embossing.

film recycling ▷ **recycling film and sheet** and **densifier**

film, shrink ▷ **shrink film**

film skiving ▷ **skiving**

film slitting ▷ **extruder takeoff slitting film**

film tear strength ▷ **Elmendorf tear test**

film toughness ▷ **ball burst test** and **toughness**

film tower ▷ **extruder blown film**

film wrinkle ▷ **extruder web wrinkle free**

filter media Almost any water-soluble porous material having a reasonable degree of rigidity can serve as a filter. Sand is used in simple large-scale water filtration (such as in processing equipment, water equipment, water cooling systems); the voids between the grains provide porosity. For handling and conveying plastic raw materials (pellets, flakes, powder, liquid) and removal of fines, there are cotton duck, woven wire cloths, nylon cloths, and glass cloth. Other filters used to meet different requirements use diatomaceous earth, plastic membranes, etc. ▷ **bag filter**

filtration The operation of separating suspended solids from a liquid (or gas) by forcing the mixture through a porous barrier ▷ **filter media.** Filtration equipment is usually classified by the following types: gravity, pressure, vacuum or suction, edge, clarification, and bag filters (dust collectors).

fin Feather edge protrusion from the surface or excess material left on a molded part at those places where the molds or dies mated. Also, the web or flash remaining in holes or openings in a molded part, which must be removed in finishing operations.

financial ▷ **cost; economics; management**

financing equipment ▷ **capital equipment investment**

fines The portion of a powder, pellet, etc. composed of particles which are smaller than a specified size, usually under 200 mesh screen.

fining Removal of gas bubbles from molten glass.

finish 1. With fibers, a mixture of materials for treating glass or other fibers. It contains a coupling agent to improve the bond of plastic to the fiber, and usually includes a lubricant to prevent abrasion. It is also a binder to promote strand integrity. With graphite or other filaments, it may perform any or all of the above functions. ▷ **glass fiber-fabric surface finish** and **silane coupling agent 2.** In molded containers, the opening area of the container which is shaped for a closure device, usually threaded. **3.** To complete the secondary work on a molded part so that it is ready for use. Operations such as filing, deflashing, buffing, drilling, tapping, decorating, flash removal, polishing, and degating are examples of finishing operations.

finish, surface ▷ **glass fiber and fabric surface treatment**

finish system, reduce solvent Finishing systems that replace conventional solvents with carbon dioxide are used to reduce volatile organic compound (VOC) levels in order to meet emission standards. ▷ **Unicarb**

finite element analysis The opportunity for creative design by viewing many imaginative variations would be blunted if each variation introduced a new set of doubts as to its ability to withstand whatever stress might be applied. From this point of view the development of computer graphics has to be accompanied by an analysis technique capable of determining stress levels, regardless of the shape of the part. This need is met by finite element analysis.

Finite element analysis (FEA) is a computer-based technique for determining the stresses and deflections in a structure. Essentially, this method divides a structure into small elements with defined stress and deflection characteristics. The method is based on manipulating arrays of large matrix equations that can be realistically solved only by computer. Most often, FEA is performed with commercial programs. In many cases these programs require that the user know only how to properly prepare the program input. ▷ **computer-aided design**

FEA is applicable in several types of analyses. The most common one is static analysis to solve for deflections, strains, and stresses in a structure that is under a constant set of applied loads. In FEA a material is generally assumed to be linear elastic, but nonlinear behavior such as plastic deformation, creep, and large deflections also are analyzed. The designer must be aware that as the degree of anisotropy increases the number of constants or moduli required to describe the material increases.

Uncertainty about a material's properties, along with a questionable applicability of the simple analysis techniques generally used, provides justification for extensive end-use testing of plastic parts before approving them in a particular application. However, it should be noted that as the use of more FEA methods becomes common in plastic design, the ability of FEAs to handle anisotropic materials will demand greater understanding of the anisotropic nature of plastics.

FEA does not replace testing; rather, the two are complementary in nature. Testing supplies only one basic answer about a design—either pass or fail. It does not quantify results, because it is not possible to know from testing alone how close to the point of passing or failing a design actually exists. FEA does, however, provide information with which to quantify performance.

fire Destructive burning; as manifested by any or all of the following: light, flame, heat, and/or smoke (ASTM E 176). ▷ **Underwriters' Laboratory fire resistance index**

fire burning rate ▷ **burning rate**

fire endurance A measure of the elapsed time during which a material or assemblage continues to exhibit fire resistance.

fire exposure The heat flux of a fire, with or without direct flame impingement, to which a material, product, building element, or assembly is exposed.

fire hazard The potential for harm associated with fire.

fire hazard standard An obsolete term, replaced by the term fire risk assessment standard.

fire performance test A procedure that measures a response of a material product or assembly to heat or flame under controlled fire conditions.

fire point The lowest temperature at which a solid or liquid evolves vapors fast enough to support continuous combustion. It is usually close to the flash point.

fire protection coating ▷ **intumescent coating**

fire resistance The property of a material or product to withstand fire or give protection from it.

fire resistance classification A standard rating of fire resistance and protective characteristics of a building construction or assembly (ASTM C 11).

fire resistance index, UL ▷ **Underwriters' Laboratory fire resistance index**

fire resistive Having fire resistance.

fire retardance The resistance to combustion of a material when tested under specified conditions. Different regulations, such as those of the Federal Aviation Administration, Department of Transportation, and local building codes, mandate that the designs of certain products comply with specific flammability test requirements. Flame-retardancy requirements generally include limits on flame spread, burning time, dripping, and smoke emission. A multitude of flammability tests have been developed, with more than 100 known just in the U.S. The most common ASTM tests are given in the Table above.

Flammability tests.

Property	Test	Type
Ignitability	ASTM D 1929	Setchkin apparatus
	ASTM D 635	Bunsen burner
	UL 94	Bunsen burner
Flame spread	ASTM E 162	Radiant-panel test
	ASTM E 84	Steiner tunnel test
Smoke	ASTM E 662	NBS smoke chamber
	ASTM D 2843	XP-2 smoke chamber
	ASTM E 84	Steiner tunnel test
Oxygen content	ASTM D 2863	Glass column

By far the most stringent and most widely accepted test is UL 94, concerning electrical devices. This test, which involves burning a specimen in a vertical position, is the one used for most flame-retardant plastics. In this test the best rating is UL 94 V-0, which identifies a flame with a duration of 0 to 5 s, an afterglow of 0 to 25 s, and the presence of no flaming drips to ignite a sample of dry, absorbent cotton located below the specimen. The ratings go from V-0, V-1, V-2, and V-5 to HB, based on specific specimen thicknesses.

The flame spread and dripping tendencies of test materials are also characterized in ASTM standard D 635. In this a horizontal test specimen provides the results of the average time of burning (ATB) and average extent of burning (AEB). In both the UL and ASTM tests, the presence of glass fibers and other reinforcements or fillers improves flammability ratings and significantly inhibits dripping.

A more quantitative measure of a material's resistance to burning can be determined from ASTM D 2863. This standard measures the minimum concentration of oxygen in an oxygen–nitrogen mixture that will support candlelike burning for three minutes or longer. The results are reported as a Limiting Oxygen Index (LOI). Composites with LOIs above 28 percent are usually listed as UL 94 V-0. Obviously, the higher the LOI value (that is, the more oxygen needed), the lower the combustibility. Since air contains about 21 percent oxygen, any rating below 21 will probably support combustion in a normal, open environment.

Smoke emission is measured in an air column above a burning specimen in a National Institute of Standards & Technology (previously the National Bureau of Standards) smoke chamber. In the NIST test a specified area of plastic is exposed to heat under flaming conditions, with smoke measurements being reported as "specific optical density." This dimensionless value represents the optical density measured over a unit of path length within a chamber of unit volume that is produced from a test specimen of unit surface area. The optical density measurement (D_{max}) is based on the amount of attenuation of a light beam by smoke accumulating within the closed chamber during flaming combustion. As a reference, the D_{max} for red oak is 76.

Smoke generated during combustion consists of suspended soot particles that form between the pyrolysis zone and the flame's front. These particles are molecules of highly condensed ring structures that are most readily formed by aromatic polymers such as SAN, SMA, and polyphenylene ether. The polymers having aliphatic carbon backbones, such as polypropylene and nylon, tend to generate less smoke, but in the FR compounds this effect is offset by an increase in smoke caused by halogenated flame-retardant additives. Plastics with a higher thermal stability, such as PC, PSF, PES, PEEK, and PPS, produce the least smoke of the available UL 94 V-0 TPS.

There are seemingly endless programs to better understand fire tests and continually develop more realistic fire tests. Ohio State University has one with specific heat limits. The NIST has a cone calorimeter for heat release that is more sophisticated than the OSU one. And the National Institute of Building Science has an evolutionary version of the NIST smoke and toxicity test.

The outcome of fires involving plastics in buildings and transportation vehicles and the odds of survival for the occupants can be predicted by a personal computer program called Hazard I, developed by the Center for Fire Research, which is a part of the NIST, in Gaithersburg, MD. Based on a user-constructed scenario, Hazard I draws on its modules and databases to quantify such key fire variables as flame spread, oxygen depletion, and smoke and toxic-gas generation as fire spreads through imaginary premises. Any combination of furniture, furnishings, and building products, with their related plastics and ignition conditions, can be specified. Besides showing the types and amounts of combustion by-products, this program also figures the amount of time available for escape and, based on behavior models, predicts the likely number of fatilities among the occupants and their probable cause of death.

Hazard I has obvious applications for writing fire-code standards and could be useful for establishing liability in fires involving fatalities. It can also be used by compounders to predict the performance of developing FR plastics and to compare plastics. This software package is available from the National Fire Protection Association, Batterymarch Park, Quincy, MA, 02269.

fire retardant A descriptive term which implies that the described product, under accepted methods of test, will significantly: (1) reduce the rate of flame spread on the surface of a material to which it has been applied, (2) resist ignition when exposed to high temperatures, or (3) insulate a substrate to which it has been applied and prolong the time required to reach its ignition, melting, or structural-weakening temperature.

fire retardant barrier A layer of material which, when secured to a combustible material or otherwise interposed between the material and a potential fire source, delays ignition and combustion of the material when the barrier is exposed to fire. ▷ **intumescent coating**

fire retardant chemical A chemical which, when added to combustible material, delays ignition and combustion of the resulting material when exposed to fire.

fire retardant coating ▷ **intumescent coating**

fire risk The probability that a fire will occur, and the potential for harm to life and damage to property resulting from its occurrence.

fire risk assessment standard A standardized method for assessing fire risk of a material, product, or assembly in a specific environment or application; formerly called fire hazard standard (ASTM E 176).

fire test protocol ▷ **protocol fire test**

fire tests, cone and lift Underwriters' Laboratory uses several tests to obtain fire performance data. The response of a material to fire involves a variety of parameters including heat-release rate, smoke-density rate, time to ignition, and lateral flame spread. As an example, there are the "cone calorimeter" and "LIFT" small scale flammability tests. The CCT heat and visible-smoke release rate is named for the electrical heater rod that is wound into the shape of a truncated cone. Rate of heat release is the primary measurement obtained. It is now recognized as probably the most important fire performance measurement, since almost all of the other processes involved in fire development are driven by heat-release rate. The LIFT apparatus, similar to CCT, is used for two procedures: measuring ignition and lateral flame spread.

fire tunnel test ▷ **tunnel fire test**

firing The sintering process used to agglomerate ceramic powders into a monolithic solid; sometimes includes plastic binder for special shapes.

firing expansion The increase in the dimensions of a material or product during thermal treatment.

Fischer–Tropsch process, synthetic fuel About 1935 two German scientists, Hans Fischer and Otto Tropscher, discovered a commercially viable process for converting coal to gasoline. In this process a mixture of carbon monoxide and hydrogen called "synthesis gas" is produced from coal and made to react with an iron catalyst. Through a series of reactions, a type of crude oil is produced. This process was more expensive than drilling and refining oil. The search for new and better catalysts, as well as other techniques such as reducing capital investment, is on-going to make the conversion competitive. South Africa, which is very rich in coal but relatively poor in oil, has been getting most of its gasoline (and other by-products, including plastics) from the F–T process. It put the chemical reactors right on top of coal mines. U.S. coal reserves are "tremendous" with oil reserves also significant; there is enough coal to last over three centuries based on energy consumption continuing to expand at the rate it has been expanding. And, of course, new developments will occur that will make coal and other feedstocks more efficient. ▷ **steel resource in U.S. limited**

fishbone **1.** A striation that does not reach entirely across the fracture surface. **2.** ▷ **process flow diagram, basics** and **zero defect**

fish eye A small, globular mass that has not completely blended into the surrounding material; particularly evident in a transparent or translucent material. They vary in size, from barely visible to as large as 1/16 in. ($1\frac{1}{2}$ mm) or more in diameter, and are usually unevenly dispersed.

fish paper Electrical-insulation grade of vulcanized fiber in thin cross section.

fishscaling A defect appearing as small half-moon shaped fractures somewhat resembling the scales of fish.

fission The splitting of an atomic nucleus induced by bombardment with neutrons from an external source and propagated by the neutrons so released.

fissure Surface defects consisting of narrow openings or cracks.

fit ▷ **press fit** and **snap fit**

fixed-feed grinding The process of feeding a material to a grinding wheel at a given rate or in specific increments.

fixing agent **1.** A mechanical substance (albumin) capable of holding pigments permanently upon textile fibers. **2.** Certain gums and starches which hold dyes and other substances mechanically upon textile fibers long enough to be processed. **3.** A substance which aids fixation of mordants upon textiles by uniting chemically with them and holding them on the fiber until the dyes can react with them.

fixture Means of holding a part during a machining or other operation.

flake **1.** Used to denote the dry, unplasticized base of plastics. **2.** A small wood particle, resembling a small piece of veneer, of predetermined thickness. **3.** ▷ **glass flake**

flake powder Flat or scale-like additive particles whose thickness is small compared with the other dimensions.

flaking ▷ **scaling**

flaky ▷ **finish flaky**

flaky finish Appearance of crazing, checking, or flaking with or without separation of finish film. ▷ **scaling**

flame A hot, usually luminous zone of gas, of particulate matter in gaseous suspension, or both, that is undergoing combustion.

flame annealing Annealing in which the heat is applied directly by flame.

flame fusion Procedure for growing single crystals within a high temperature flame.

flame hardening A surface hardening process in which only the surface layer of a suitable workpiece is heated by a flame to above the upper transformation temperature and immediately quenched; usually with metals. ▷ **screw heat treatment**

flame resistance Ability of a material to extinguish flame once the source of heat is removed. ▷ **self-extinguishing plastic**

flame retardant Not a defined term as an adjective. Use only as a modifier with defined compound terms; flame-retardant chemical, flame-retardant coating, etc. ▷ **polystyrene plastic, flame retardant**

flame-retardant chemical A chemical which, when added to a combustible material, delays ignition and reduces flame spread of the resulting material when exposed to flame impingement.

flame-retardant coating A surface covering on a combustible material which delays ignition and reduces flame spread when exposed to flame impingement. ▷ **intumescent coating**

flame retarded plastic A plastic which is compounded with certain chemicals to reduce or eliminate its tendency to burn. As an example, polyethylene and similar plastics, chemicals such as antimony trioxide and chlorinated paraffins are useful. However, there are plastics that basically do not or have the tendency not to burn (fluorinated types, etc.)

flame spray coating It consists of blowing a powder through a flame which partially melts the powder and fuses it as it hits the substrate. The surface is preheated with the flame usually to about 204°C (400°F) with polyethylene. Only a few square feet (m^2) are coated at a time so temperature can be controlled. The flame is then adjusted and the powder passed through the flame and melted on the substrate surface. The powder is then shut off and the surface post-heated with the flame. Flame spraying is useful for coating items with surface areas too large for heating in an oven. Disadvantages are the problems associated with an open flame and the need for skilled operators to apply the coating. ▷**coating**

flame spread index FSI is number or classification indicating a comparative measure derived from observations made during the progress of the boundary of a zone of flame under defined test conditions (ASTM E 84). ▷**tunnel fire test**

flame treating A method of rendering inert thermoplastic parts receptive to inks, lacquers, paints, adhesives, etc. in which the part (polyolefin, etc. container, bag, etc.) is bathed or exposed to an open flame. Flame treatment oxidizes the surface and makes it more easily wettable. The plastic surface is contacted for a period of less than one second with the oxidizing portion of the flame. The gas is burned using 10 to 15% excess air over the stoichiometric ratio in order to obtain an oxidizing flame with a temperature of 1,100 to 2,800°C (2,012 to 5,072°F). Often the print is also flame treated to dry the ink and to further improve its adhesion. This treatment is especially useful in treating irregular, complex shapes.

flammability Basically those characteristics of a material that pertain to its relative ease of ignition and relative ability to sustain combustion. There are different industry standards and specifications to meet the many different and diversified fire conditions. Ignition tests determine the ease with which a material ignites. Burning tests determine the burning rate and the ability to self-extinguish on removal of the ignition source. The oxygen index test accurately determines relative flammability. Heat-contribution tests determine relative contribution to the temperature rise of combustion gases. A popular burning test related to electrical devices is the Underwriters' Laboratory flammability UL-94 test.

Smoke evolution is important in determining combustion characteristics and can be greatly affected by the addition of fire-retardant materials. Smoke development usually increases as the rate of flame propagation is decreased. Products of degradation are measured in a variety of ways, including collection, analysis, and toxicity testing of gases and pyrolyzates. Conventional spectroscopic and chromatographic methods are used for the identification of combustion degradation components. Thermal methods such as TGA are used to measure char yields and to develop weight-loss profiles.

When plastics are used, their behavior in fire must be considered, as is true of other materials where the fire potential exists. Ease of ignition, rate of flame spread, rate of heat release, smoke release, toxicity of products of combustion and other factors must be taken into account. Some plastics, as well as other materials, burn readily, others with difficulty and still others do not support their own combustion (see Table on p. 302). Behavior in fire depends upon the nature and scale of the fire, as well as the surrounding conditions. Fire is a highly complex, variable phenomenon and the behavior of plastics in a fire is equally complex and variable.

In early decades of this century it was thought that the matter of fire hazard was a simple enough one; does the material burn or does it not? Wood burns; steel does not. Although these statements about wood and steel are certainly true, they are almost irrelevant to the relative fire risk of the two materials. Compare the cases of fire in two different buildings; one framed of heavy timbers or certain plastic arches, and the other of steel framing. The steel frame, particularly light steel framing, will collapse after relatively few minutes of exposure to fire, while it may require a fire of long duration to bring down the timber/plastic framing. Fire reaches 1,370°C (2,500°F) and steel basically only takes up to about 538°C (1,000°F), thus it collapses like a "pretzel". Wood, like certain plastics, can take the heat and takes a rather long time to self destruct, leaving time for people to escape danger. The problem of fire hazard turns out to be a complicated one.

Fire tests of plastics, like fire tests generally, are frequently highly specific and the results are specific to the tests. The results of one type of test do not often correlate directly with another, and may bear little relationship to actual fires. Some tests are intended mainly for screening purposes during research and development; others, such as the large-scale tests, more nearly approximate actual fires. Consequently, such often used terms as self-extinguishing, nonburning, flame spread and toxicity must be under-

Flammability characteristic of different materials related to heat values.[1]

					Potential heat		
	Thickness		Density		Weight basis		Volume basis
Material	in.	mm	lb./ft.^{3}	g/cm^3	Btu/lb.	cal/g	Btu/ft.^{3}
Woods							
Douglas fir, untreated	0.75	19	38.0	0.609	8,400	4,670	319×10^3
Douglas fir (retardant treatment "A")	0.75	19	37.2	0.596	8,290	4,600	308.0
Douglas fir (retardant treatment "B")	0.75	19	47.2	0.756	7,860	4,370	371.0
Douglas fir (retardant treatment "C")	0.75	19	38.8	0.622	7,050	3,920	274.0
Maple, soft, untreated	1.0	25	39.5	0.633	7,940	4,410	314.0
Hardboard, untreated	0.25	6.3	59.8	0.958	8,530	4,740	510.0
Plastics							
Polystyrene, wall tile	0.075	1.9	65.4	1.05	17,420	9,680	1,140.0
Rigid polyvinyl chloride, retardant treated	0.147	3.73	86.0	1.38	9,290	5,160	799.0
Phenolic laminate	0.063	1.6	76.4	1.22	7,740	4,300	592.0
Polycarbonate resin	0.25	6.3	78.7	1.26	13,330	7,406	1,050.0
Insulation							
Glass fiber, semirigid, no vapor barrier	1.0	25	3.0	0.048	3,040	1,690	9.1
Rock wool batting, paper enclosure	3.0	76	2.4	0.038	1,050	583	2.5
Roof insulation board	1.0	25	10.4	0.167	3,380	1,880	35.1
Cork (reconstituted cork sheet)	0.25	6.3	14.8	0.238	11,110	6,172	164.0
Cellulose mineral board	2.0	5.1	47.8	0.766	2,250	1,250	108.0
Concrete							
Cinder aggregate			93.0	1.49	3,080	1,710	286.0
Slag aggregate			110.1	1.764	80	44	8.9
Shale aggregate			80.5	0.0206	10	5.5	0.5
Calcareous gravel aggregate			133.1	2.132	−250	−77	−33.1
Siliceous gravel aggregate			166.8	2.672	−40	−22	−6.7
Miscellaneous							
Paint "E" (dried paint film)	0.05	1.3			3,640	2,020	
Asphalt shingles (fire retardant)	0.25	0.64	70.7	1.13	8,320	4,620	588.0
Building paper (asphalt impregnated)	0.042	1.1	42.8	0.686	13,620	7,567	583.0
Building paper (rosin sized)	0.018	0.46	23.6	0.378	7,650	4,250	181.0
Linoleum tile	1/8	3.2	86.0	1.38	7,760	4,310	667.0
Brick, red, face	2.25	57	139.1	2.228	20	11.1	2.2
Charcoal, coconut					13,870	7,706	

[1] All weights and percentages refer to original air-dry weight.

stood in the context of the specific tests with which they are used.

Some materials may burn quite slowly, but may propagate a flame very rapidly over their surfaces. Thin wood paneling will burn readily, yet a heavy timber post will sustain a fire on its surface until charred and thereafter will smoulder at a remarkably slow rate of burning. Bituminous materials may spread a fire by softening and running down a wall. Steel does not burn, but as reviewed, it is catastrophically weakened by the elevated temperatures of a fire. PVC does not burn, but softens at relatively low temperatures and emits irritating fumes of hydrogen chloride. Other plastics may not burn readily but may emit copious amounts of smoke. Some flammable plastics, such as polyurethane, may be made flame retardant by incorporating additives such as antimony oxide. There are also plastics that basically do not burn (silicone, fluorine, etc.).

The principles of good design for fire safety are as applicable to plastics as they are to other materials. The specific design must be carefully considered, the properties of the materials taken into account, and engineering judgement applied. When evaluating the fire risk that exists with plastic products, it is always best to perform appropriate tests on the end item. However, it is often helpful to select plastic materials for specific applications by evaluating the flammability of candidate plastics in laboratory tests. The flammability tests that are often used for material specification fall into the categories of small-scale and large-scale tests. Of course, as with evaluating any properties, prior knowledge or obtaining reliable data that applies to the fire or other requirements is an ideal situation to exist. ▷ **underwriters' Laboratory flammability UL-94 test**

flammable material Any solid, liquid, vapor, or gas that will ignite easily and burn rapidly. There are several types: (1) dust or fine powders, and (2) films, fibers, and fabrics of low ignition point. They can ignite spontaneously at low temperature, or internal heat is built up by macrobial or other degradation activity.

flare 1. The spreading of filaments at the cut end of a strand or the spreading of strand ends at the cut end of a cord. **2.** Extraneous light in the dark area.

flash ▷ **mold flash**

flash gate ▷ **mold gate, flash type**

flash ignition temperature ▷ **ignition temperature**

flash mold ▷ **mold, semipositive**

flashover 1. The electrical discharge or arc occurring between electrodes and over or around, but not through, the equipment being tested. **2.** A disruptive electrical discharge at the surface of electrical insulation or in the surrounding medium, which may or may not cause permanent damage to the insulation.

flash point 1. The temperature at which a substance gives off vapor sufficient to form an ignitable mixture with the air near the surface of the material or within a test vessel at 1.0 atmosphere (101.3 kPa) (760 mm Hg). For the purpose of the official shipping regulations, the flash point is determined by the Tagliabue open cut (TOC) method per ASTM E 176. **2.** The lowest temperature at which vapors above a volatile combustible substance ignite in air when exposed to a flame (ASTM E 1316).

flash-spun nonwoven fabric The production of spun-bonded webs by flash spinning is a radical departure from the conventional melt spinning methods to produce nonwoven fabrics. In flash-spinning a 10 to 15% solution of, for example, high density polyethylene in trichlorofluoromethane or methylene chloride, the material is heated to 200°C (392°F) and pressurized to 4,500 kPa (650 psi) or more. The pressurized vessel is connected to a spinneret containing a single hole. When the pressurized solution is permitted to expand rapidly through the single hole, the low boiling solvent is instantaneously flashed off, leaving a three-dimensional film-fibril nonwoven network referred to as a plexifilament. The film thickness is 4 μm or less; 3-D effect results from the cross-linking interconnection of the subdenier fibers. Thus a multitude of individual but interconnected fibers are created from a single-hole spinneret. Flash spinning is a complex and rather difficult method of manufacturing spun-bonded fabrics because of the need to spin heated pressurized solutions under precise conditions. The result, however, is a unique structure producing unique properties.

flat 1. A surface that is free of gloss. **2.** A surface that is flat.

flat glass Architectural (and window) glass product.

flattening agent A substance ground into minute particles of irregular shape and used in paints and varnishes to disperse incident light rays so that a dull or "flat" effect is produced. They are heavy metal soaps, silica, and diatomaceous earth.

flaw ▷ **troubleshooting, flaw**

flaw characterized ▷ **nondestructive testing**

flax Natural fiber obtained from the inner bark of the flax plant. It is used as plastic filler and reinforcement, apparel fabric (linens), thread, rope, cigarette paper, duplicating paper, etc. Fibers are 20 in. (51 cm) long. They are stronger and more durable than cotton.

flexibility That property of a material by virtue of which it may be flexed or bowed repeatedly without undergoing rupture.

flexibilizer An additive that makes a finished plastic more flexible or tough. More often called plasticizer.

flexible Easily hand-folded, flexed, twisted, and bent.

flexible bag molding ▷ **bag molding**

flexible membrane liner ▷ **geomembrane**

flexible mold ▷ **mold material, flexible**

flexible packaging Superior flavor retention and longer shelf life are the principal advantages of plastics alone or in combination with other plastics, with or without aluminum foil, paper, fabric, etc. They can be made impervious to light, air, water, and most other gases and liquids. They make retortable pouches practical for cooked foods, and provide advantages in many other packages.

flexible polyvinyl chloride ▷ **polyvinyl chloride plastic**

flexible reinforced plastic ▷ **reinforced plastic, flexible**

flexion The condition of decreasing the angle between two body segments; opposite of extension.

flex life **1.** The number of cycles required to produce a specified state of failure in a specimen that is flexed in a prescribed method. **2.** The time of heat-aging that an insulating material can withstand before failure when bent around a specific radius (used to evaluate thermal endurance).

flex life test A laboratory method used to determine the life of a product when subjected to dynamic bending stresses.

flexographic printing Developed mainly as a method suitable for printing on plastics. It is basically a letterpress process, since it prints from the raised image, but it employs a hard metal plate instead of a soft and rubbery plate. For a comparison of different printing methods ▷ **printing**. Printing ink is transferred from the inked relief surface to the product by applying some pressure. High quality printing is possible. The process is economical because of the simplicity of press design and the ability to set up and preregister off the press with a saving of press time when compared to other methods. Thus, in addition to long runs, it is particularly economic in short runs. Flexography printing is primarily useful for printing line designs, but halftone reproductions in lower line/inch range are utilized for some applications. Film speeds up to 600 ft/min (3 m/s) are used.

Various solventborne links are used. They are based on alcohol-soluble plastics and are formulated to contain about 30% or more solids. Such inks can be dried at a high speed. The viscosity is very low; about 70 centipoise. These inks have good resistance to water, but poor alcohol resistance; may require topcoating if used on a package containing alcohol. UV-curable or catalytic cured coatings may be used as topcoatings. Pigments and dyes are used as colorants. Dye-based colorants have a very high strength, give clean and bright colors, but have poor light resistance and may fade in sunlight in a few hours. Dye-based inks have good coverage, up to 400,000 in.^{2}/lb compared to the pigment-based inks of about 150,000 in.^{2}/lb. Waterborne inks are also used. Certain acidic plastics are soluble in aqueous alkaline solutions and can be used as a base for such inks. Aqueous emulsions can also be used as ink base.

Flexomer Union Carbide's tradename for a modified polyethylene thermoplastic elastomer. It is the result of in-reactor process with applications in compounding as an alternative to rubber vulcanizates used in blending TPOs and other rubber-modified plastics.

flexometer A machine that subjects a test specimen to a cyclic deformation which may be in compression, tension, or shear, or in any combination thereof, including bending motion.

flexural modulus Flexural modulus of elasticity is the ratio of stress to strain for a given material within its proportional limit under bending load conditions. ▷ **flexural properties** and **modulus**

flexural properties Like tensile testing, flexural stress-strain testing according to ASTM D 790, determines the load necessary to generate a given level of strain on a specimen, typically using a three-point loading (see Fig. below). The sample is characteristically 0.125 × 0.5 × 5 in. (0.25 × 0.5 × 5 in. for foamed material).

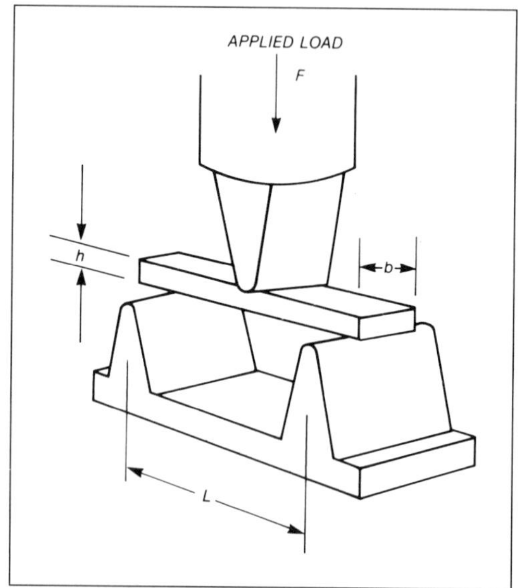

Schematic of the typical three-point flexural test specimen on a bending fixture. There are other loadings used (based on type material being tested), such as a four-point loading where the applied load is through two, rather than this one point.

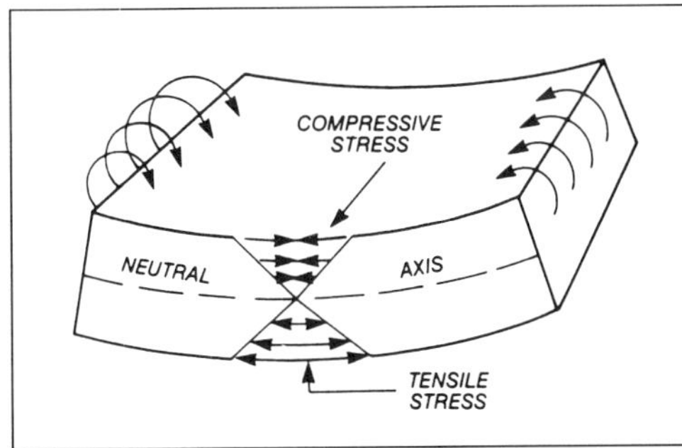

Example of how a flexural test specimen is subjected to compressive and tensile stresses.

The bar is supported across a 2 in. span (or 4 inches for structural foam) with a load applied at its center. Testing is performed at a constant rate of cross-head movement, typically 0.05 in./min. for solids and 0.1 in./min. for foamed samples.

Simple beam equations are used to determine the stresses on specimens at different levels of cross-head displacement. Using traditional beam formulas and section properties, the following relationships can be derived where Y is the deflection at the load point.

Bending stress

$$\sigma = \frac{3FL}{2bh^2}$$

Bending or flexural modulus

$$E = \frac{FL^3}{4bh^3Y}$$

Using these relationships, the flexural strength, also called the modulus of rupture, and the flexural modulus of elasticity can be determined. The flexural modulus reported is usually the initial modulus from the load-deflection curve. (The flexural data can be useful in product designs that involve such factors as bending loads.)

Significantly, a flexural specimen is not in a state of uniform stress. When a simply supported specimen is loaded, the side of the material opposite the loading undergoes the greatest tensile loading. The side of the material being loaded experiences compressive stress (see Fig. above). These stresses decrease linearly toward the center of the sample. Theoretically the center is a plane, called the neutral axis, that experiences no stress.

The stress-strain behavior of plastics in flexure generally follows from the behavior observed in tension and compression for either unreinforced or reinforced plastics. The flexural modulus of elasticity is nominally the average between the tension and compression moduli, where they differ. The flexural yield point is generally that which is observed in tension, but this is not easily discerned, because the strain gradient in the flexural (RP) sample essentially eliminates any abrupt change in the flexural stress-strain relationship when the extreme "fibers" start to yield.

flexural rigidity A measure of rigidity of a plate (D) in in./lb (cm/kg), thus:

$$D = \frac{Eh^3}{12(1-v)}$$

where E = Young's modulus; h = thickness of plate; v = Poisson's ratio.

flexural strength A measure of the ability of a material to withstand rupture when subjected to bend loading; the ultimate strength of a material in the flexural test ▷ **flexural properties.** The flexural strength for most plastics under standard ASTM bending tests is typically somewhat higher than their ultimate tensile strength, but flexural strength itself may be either higher or lower than compressive strength. Since most plastics exhibit some yielding or nonlinearity in their tensile stress-strain curve, there is a shift from triangular stress distribution toward rectangular distribution when the part is subject to flexure (see Fig. on top of p. 306). This behavior is similar to that assumed for plastic design in steel and for ultimate design strength in concrete. Thus, the modulus of rupture reflects in part nonlinearities in stress distribution caused by plastification or viscoelastic nonlinearities in the cross-section. Shifts in the neutral axis resulting from differences in the yield strain, and postyield behavior in tension and compression can also affect the correlation between the modulus of rupture and the uniaxial strength results.

Even plastics with fairly linear stress-strain curves to failure—for example, short-fiber reinforced TSs—usually display moduli of rupture values that are higher than the tensile strength obtained in uniaxial tests; wood behaves much like this. Qualitatively, this can be explained from statistically considering flaws and fractures and the fracture energy available in flexural samples under a constant rate of deflection as compared to tensile samples under the same load conditions. These differences become less as the thickness of the bending specimen increases, as would be expected by examining statistical considerations.

flexural testing Other methods of flexural testing (other than the usual three-point test) include the cantilever beam method (see second

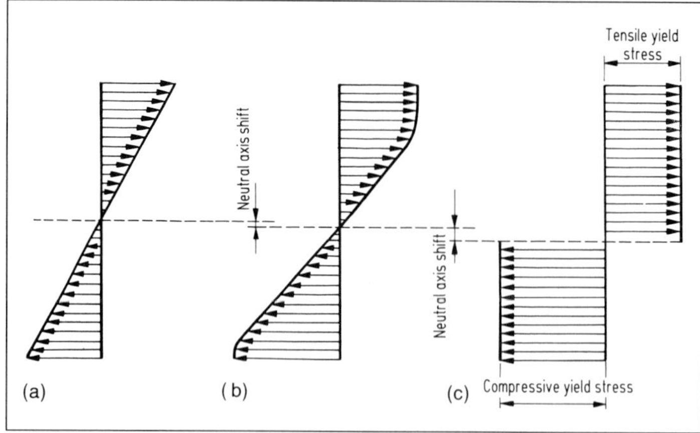

Examples of the elastic and plastic flexural behavior of unreinforced and reinforced plastics. (*a*) No yield linear stress; (*b*) extreme fibers yield; (*c*) full plastification of cross section.

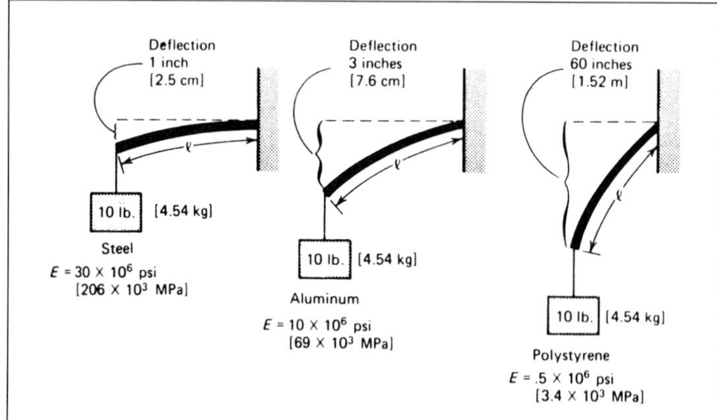

Examples of cantilever test specimens, all having the same length and cross sections. Compares the effect of modulus of elasticity on elastic deflection for different materials.

Fig. above). It is used in creep and fatigue testing and for conducting tests in different environments.

flexural test, short beam shear SBS is a three-point flexural test of a specimen having a low test span-to-thickness ratio (such as 4:1), with result that failure is primarily in shear. It is particularly applicable in testing reinforced plastics or plastic compounds with high additive contents.

flexure cold bend test A test for measuring the flexibility of a material at low temperatures. The specimen is bent to a predetermined radius while maintained at the stipulated temperature.

flexure fiber stress When a beam of homogeneous, elastic material is tested in flexure as a simple beam supported at two points and loaded at the midpoint, the maximum stress in the outer fiber occurs at mid-span.

flexure plate pivot A type of pivot or hinge in which the motion occurs through the bending of a thin elastic plate.

flexure stress-strain ▷ **stress-strain**

flight of screw ▷ **screw**

flint Natural rock of very fine grained silica, used as a plastic filler.

flint glass **1.** Lead-containing glass. **2.** Term used by industry for colorless glass.

flitter ▷ **glitter**

float **1.** Component of a boom that provides buoyancy. **2.** In woven fabric, the portion of a warp or filling yarn that extends unbound over two or more filling or warp yarns. **3.** A defect in which a warp or filling yarn extends unbounded over the ends with which it should be interlaced.

floating chase ▷ **mold chase, floating**

floating platen ▷ **clamping platen, floating**

floc A loose, open-structured mass produced in a suspension by the aggregation of minute particles.

flocculate To aggregate into larger particles, to increase in size to the point where precipitation occurs. Flocculants are usually formed in a gas or liquid suspension, and those formed in a liquid can generally be broken up by gentle shaking or stirring.

flocculation A process of bringing together small particles to form larger particles, often highly porous in nature. The initial fine particles are usually thought of as being too small to be seen with the naked eye; they settle or are filterable only slowly. The process produces a large particle, a floc, that can be distinguished by the unaided eye, that can be rapidly filtered, and that will settle rapidly. In flocculation the final structure of the floc is usually a loose, three-dimensional network, resulting from the bridging of macromolecular flocculants between particles. In the past materials such as alum and ferric salts were only used to induce and bring about flocculation in the purification and treatment of water. More recently either synthetic or natural plastics are used to rapidly expand the scale of flocculants in a wide variety of industrial applications. Typical plastics are polyelectrolytes such as carboxyl-containing polyacrylamide or polyethylenimine.

flock A material obtained by reducing textile fibers (cotton, glass, etc.) and wood to fragments as by cutting, tearing, or grinding. Results are minute particles used as fillers in plastics. Various degrees of comminution exist, usually ranging from $\frac{1}{2}$ to 6 mm in length.

flocking or floc spraying A method of coating by spraying finely dispersed powders or fibers. With the usual hot-flocking techniques, materials are dispersed in air and sprayed or blown onto a preheated substrate, where they melt and form a coating. In a variation of this process, small parts are preheated and dropped into a bed of powder or fibers kept in a mobile state of vibration. In this method, the parts are completely coated with an unfused layer on the surface.

flood coating The simplest of the dry powder coating techniques. It is best for coating regularly-shaped objects where minor variations in coating thickness are not objectionable. The non-fluidized bed is a form of flood coating. Hollow objects can be coated by filling the preheated part with powder and dumping out the excess.

flood cooling ▷ **mold flood cooling**

flooring material Flooring materials in which plastics are used can be divided into three types. The first type includes smooth-surfaced, resilient coverings such as vinyl linoleum, vinyl-asbestos tile, solid vinyl tile (based on PVC and ply-vinyl chloride-vinyl acetate), vinyl sheet goods, asphalt tile, rubber tile, and cork tile. The second type is composed of seamless, monolithic, and troweled floor coverings that include different plastics, such as epoxy, phenolic, etc. The third type is prefinished impregnated hardwood usually using acrylics.

floppy disk A memory disk made of flexible plastic film. This magnetic disk is capable of storing up to several million bytes of data per disk. It holds less information than a hard disk, but unlike the hard type, it can be physically transferred from one disk drive to another. ▷ **computer storage disk and tape**

flour Organic fillers, such as wood flour and shell flours. The wood type is finely ground commonly made from soft woods. Shell type is usually from peanut and rice hulls. They are used as fillers, extenders, and reinforcements in plastics.

flow 1. A qualitative description of the fluidity of a plastic material during processing such as in molds, through dies, coatings, etc. **2.** The potential gradual distortion of a material; also called creep.

flow cavitation ▷ **cavitation**

flow channel The portion of a flow net binded by two adjacent flow lines.

flow chart or diagram A chart or line drawing used to indicate successive steps in developing a process, marketing effort, materials input-output matrix, waste developments, and other relevant data. ▷ **algorithm; process flow diagram, basics; design plastic future; plastic properties**.

flow coating Process of coating a product by causing the slip to flow over its surface and allowing it to drain.

flow, cold ▷ **cold flow**

flow defects ▷ **melt flow defects**

flow, dynamic ▷ **dynamic flow**

flow, Ellis model ▷ **Ellis model**

flow, laminar ▷ **laminar flow**

flow life ▷ **Brabender test**

flow line A mark on a molded or extruded part made by the meeting of two flow fronts during fabrication. Also called striae, weld mark, or weld line. ▷ **weld line**

flow, liquid ▷ **Reynold's number**

flow mark Distinctive wavy surface appearance on a part caused by improper injection of

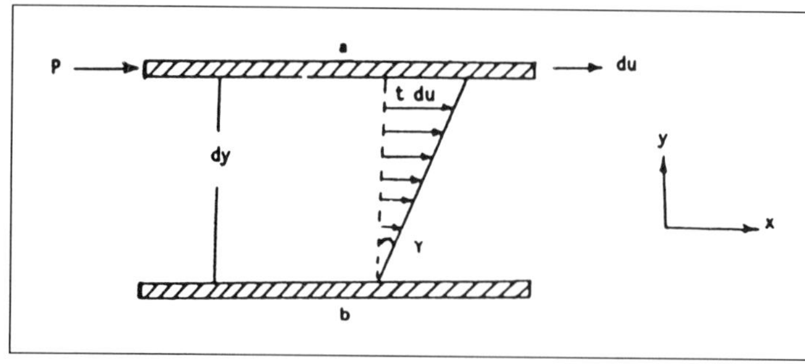

Basic flow model with laminar shearing motion occurs between two parallel plates where one plate is subjected to a force.

the plastic melt into a mold, through a die, etc. ▷ **splay mark**

flow, melt ▷ **melt flow**

flow, melt index test ▷ **melt index**

flowmeter An instrument for measuring the rate of flow of a fluid through a pipe or duct system. The instrument is calibrated to give volume or mass rate of flow.

flow model Many mathematical modes exist for describing the flow behavior of non-Newtonian fluids. Their starting point is the basic isothermal Newtonian concept with modifications to fit the physical situation. The usual has a fluid located between two parallel plates where one plate moves (a) and the other is stationary (b) separated by a distance (*dy*). As shown in the Fig. above, the application of force (*P*) to plate (a) results in a constant velocity (*du*) when compared to plate (b). With laminar flow and steady state, thus:

$$\text{shear stress } T_{yx} = \frac{P}{A}$$

where A = surface area of plate (a), y = orientation of the surface, and x = direction of stress. In time, t, a fluid particle will move the distance ($t\,du$), thus flow deformation

$$V = \frac{du}{dy}\,t,$$

where V = strain. The rate of deformation becomes

$$\frac{dV}{dt} = \frac{du}{dt},$$

where $t\,du/dy$ = rate of shear or velocity gradient.

According to the Newtonian fluids law, shear stress is directly proportional to the rate of shear in laminar flow, thus:

$$\tau_{yx} = \mu\frac{du}{dy},$$

where μ = Newtonian viscosity coefficient. This becomes the basic flow equation for Newtonian fluid and the starting point for non-Newtonian flow modes. For laminar flow on non-Newtonian fluids, different models are derived that mathematically provide flow behavior, such as the Power law model, Prandtl Eyring model, and Sisko model. Comprehensive details of the development of these models have been published, with new ones becoming available.

flow modeling The technique of producing leatherlike materials by placing a die-cut plastic blank (usually solid or expanded vinyl or vinyl coated substrate) in a mold cavity. Usually silicone rubber molds are used. Melting of plastic is accomplished by applying power through a high-frequency radio frequency generator. Result is the plastic flows in the plain or texture cavity producing the desired texture, etc.

flow plasticity ▷ **plasticity**

flow, Poiseuille Poiseuille flow is an alternate name for pressure flow in general, but often refers to axial streamline flow in a circular cross section pipe for which Poiseuille law holds for Newtonian fluids. ▷ **pressure flow**

flow, pressure ▷ **pressure flow**

flow properties ▷ **melt index; viscosity, pseudoplastic; rheology; flow model**

flow test, Canadian A method of determining the rheology or flow properties of thermoplastics; developed by the Canadian Industries Ltd. and referred to as the CIL flow test. In this test, the amount of molten plastic that is forced through a specified size orifice per unit of time when a specified, variable force is applied gives a relative indication of the flow properties of various plastics.

flow test, thermoplastic ▷ **melt flow test**

flow test, thermoset This is a very simple test in which a measured quantity of room temperature, loose compound is compressed between two heated die plates at a specific pressure and temperature. The resultant molded disc is measured in thickness to determine flow.

The thicker the disc, the stiffer the flow. This test is called Disc Flow I. In the Disc Flow II, as in the DF I, a measured quantity of compound is compressed between heated die plates and the resultant molded disc is compared in diameter with a target having five concentric rings. The larger the disc, the softer the flow.

As with a cup closing test also used for TS plastics, the two disc flow tests are best suited for measuring the flow of compounds that will be compression molded. These three tests are easy to perform and are often used to check the flow of compounds on the production line. They are useful in spotting possible color or other contamination during production.

flow through capillary tube ▷ **Hagan–Poiseuille law**

flow, viscous ▷ **viscous flow**

fluidity The coefficient of flowability; reciprocal of viscosity.

fluidization A technique in which a finely divided solid is made to behave like a fluid by suspension in a moving gas (air, etc.) or liquid.

fluidized bed coating A two-chambered container (one on top of the other) separated by a porous medium that retains plastic powder in the top container but allows free passage of gas (usually compressed air) through the powder. The porous flat plate can range from sintered metal, to steel plate with many minute holes, to simple acoustic ceiling tile. Air is forced from the bottom chamber through the porous medium into the powder (see Fig.). The rising gas separates and suspends the powder, causing it to increase in volume to many times the height of the powder at rest until a steady state is reached. Then, the pressure drop of the rising gas will no longer support the weight of the powder. At this point, the gas being vented through the top of the bed forms an equilibrium with the gas being supplied. The top container has its top side opened. Even though the gas-powder mix is uniform, most systems also use a mechanism to vibrate the bed; this improves distribution especially in shallow beds and assists powder flow during the dipping of parts to ensure uniform coating.

The powder is dry and free of agglomeration, so that the gas can completely surround individual particles. Thus the gas-suspended powder acts very much like a liquid; hence the term "fluidized bed". Powdered particles range in size from less than 20 micron to about 200 microns. Those larger than 200 microns are difficult to suspend. Particles smaller than 20 microns may create excessive dusting and release of particles from the top of the bed. Powders may also contain fluidizing aids to keep the powder free-flowing.

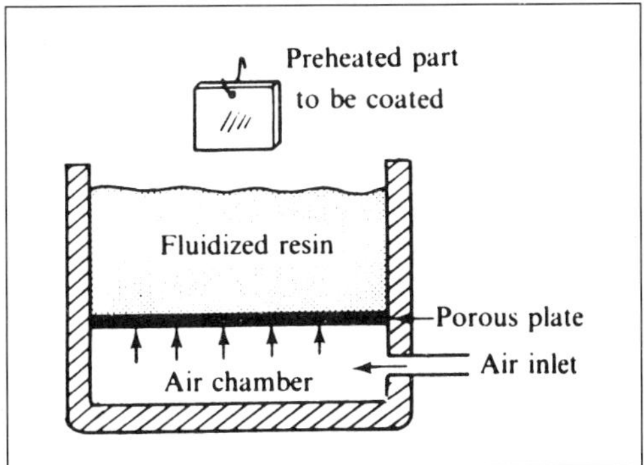

Schematic of fluidized bed coating system where part will be dipped into the powdered fluid.

The part to be coated (usually metal) is heated to a temperature above the melt temperature of the powder and is then immersed into the fluidized bed. As the powder contacts the hot substrate, the particles adhere, melt, and flow together to form a continuously conforming coating. The part is removed from the bed when the desired coating thickness is obtained, or when its maximum thickness is reached (dependent on heat transfer characteristic of powder and heat retention in the substrate). With thermoplastics, the coating cools and solidifies. The thermoset plastic usually requires after removal from the bed additional time at elevated temperature to complete the cure. Many TPs can be used particularly if they have low melting points. Higher melting plastics must have a sufficiently low melt viscosity so that the particles can flow and fuse together to form a coating with good integrity. Most common TPs are nylon, PVC, PMMA, PE, PP, PUR, silicone, EVA, PS, etc. TSs are limited largely to epoxy, polyester, and epoxy/polyester hybrids. TSs such as phenolics or DAPs give off by-products during cure. These volatiles can create voids in the coating, damaging its integrity and function. ▷ **coating**

fluorescence A type of luminescence in which an atom or molecule emits visible radiation in passing from a higher to a lower electronic state. The term is restricted to a phenomenon in which the time interval between absorption and emission of energy is extremely short (10^{-8} to 10^{-3} sec). This distinguishes fluorescence from phosphorescence, in which the time interval may extend to several days.

fluorescence, resonance ▷ **absorption spectroscopy**

fluorescent light exhibits ▷ **fluorescence**

fluorescent pigment By absorbing unwanted wave lengths of light and converting them into light of desired wavelengths, these pigment additive colors seem to possess an actual glow of their own.

fluorescent processing aid ▷ **spectrometer, X-ray fluorescence**

fluorescent radiation ▷ **Stoke's law**

fluorescent screen A sheet of material which emits visible light when exposed to invisible radiation.

fluorescent whitening agent FWA is a dye or pigment that absorbs near ultra-violet radiant flux and re-emits the power as visible light (violet-blue), thereby causing a whiter appearance when added to a yellowish-white material.

fluorinated ethylene propylene plastic FEP plastics are hard, tough thermoplastics; its formal name is polytetrafluoroethylene-co-hexafluoropropene. This fluorocarbon is a copolymer of polytetrafluoroethylene and hexafluoropropylene, possessing most of the PTFE properties and having a melt viscosity low enough to permit conventional thermoplastic processing.

fluorination The process of chemically reacting a material with fluorine-containing compound to produce a desired product. As an example, it can improve the gas barrier of PE to nonpolar solvents. A barrier is created by the chemical reaction of the fluorine and the PE, which form a thin (20 to 40 mm) fluorocarbon layer on the surface. Two systems can be used to apply the treatment depending on the results desired. With the "in-process" system, such as that used during blow molding PE gasoline tanks, fluorine is used as a part of the parison expanding gas in the blowing operation (result is no gasoline leakage when tank is used). The barrier layer is created only on the inside. In a "post-treatment" system, bottles and other parts are placed in an enclosed chamber filled with fluorine gas. This method forms barrier layers on both the inside and outside surfaces. ▷ **barrier via chemical modification**

fluorine One of the most reactive elements occurring in nature. It is so aggressive that, up to 1930, research into its behavior was held up for a long time because workers could not readily find any material to contain it.

fluorocarbon plastic These plastics (also called fluoroplastic) are based on polymers made with monomers composed of fluorine and carbon only. This family of plastics include: polytetrafluoroethylene (PTFE), polychlorotrifluoroethylene (PCTFE), polyvinylidene fluoride (PVDF), fluorinated ethylene propylene (FEP), perfluoro alkoxy (PFA), etc. They are characterized by good thermal and chemical resistance, nonadhesiveness, low electrical dissipation factor, and low dielectric constant. They are available in a variety of forms, such as molding materials, extrusion materials, dispersions, film, or tape. ▷ **fluoroplastic**

fluorocarbon plastic prefix When the monomer is essentially tetrafluoroethylene, the prefix TFE is sometimes used to designate these plastics. It is preferable to use the accepted abbreviation PTFE. TFE should not be used by itself to mean PTFE. When the plastics are copolymers of TFE and hexafluoropropylene, the plastics may be designated with the prefix FEP. Other prefixes are adopted to designate other fluorocarbon plastics (ASTM D 883).

fluorochemical Organic compounds, not necessarily hydrocarbons, in which a large percentage of the hydrogen directly attached to carbon has been replaced by fluorine.

fluoroelastomer or fluorine rubber Of all types of elastomers, those containing fluorine have the highest resistance to heat deformation and chemical attack. By far the most important are the FPM rubbers, which are mainly made from vinylidene fluoride, TFE, and hydropentafluoropropylene or perfluoromethyl vinyl ether. There are also alternating copolymers made from propylene TFE (TFE/P), from polyfluoroalkoxyphosphazene, and from fluorosilicone elastomer (FMQ or FSIE) that have been used.

fluoroethylene plastic ▷ **polyvinyl fluoride plastic**

fluorohydrocarbon plastic Plastics based on polymers made with monomers composed of fluorine, hydrogen, and carbon only.

fluoroplastic These plastics contain the monomer of fluorine. They are paraffinic hydrocarbons in which all or part of the hydrogen atoms have been replaced with fluorine atoms and may also include chlorine atoms in their structure. This family of plastics includes: ethylene-tetrafluoroethylene (ETFE), polychlorotrifluoroethylene (PCTFE), ethylene-chlorotrifluoroethylene (ECTFE), polyvinylidene fluoride (PVDF), polyvinyl fluoride (PVF), perfluoromethylvinylether (PFMV), etc. Their common characteristics are outstanding chemical inertness, resistance to temperatures from −220°C (−425°F) to as high as 260°C (500°F), low

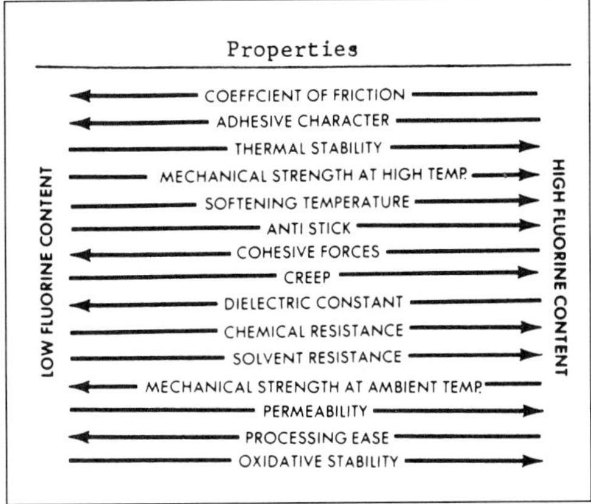

Fluoroplastics' general properties; arrows show increasing values of properties.

coefficient of friction, good electric properties, low permeability, practical zero moisture absorption, and good resistance to weathering and ozone. The Fig. above provides examples of fluoroplastics' and fluorocarbon plastics' general properties.

fluororubber Alternative name for fluoroelastomers.

fluorosilicone elastomer FVMQ is a silicone elastomer based on polytrifluoropropylmethylsiloxane with a small amount of vinylmethyl units for ease of peroxide vulcanization. The vulcanizates have a much improved solvent resistance, especially to fuels and other hydrocarbons, compared with other silicone rubbers, while retaining the rather extreme low temperature flexibility and the excellent high temperature resistance of silicones and fluoroplastics. Uses include seals and O-rings for fuel pumps, aerospace applications, and underground use. ▷ **silicone elastomer**

fluorotriazine elastomer A rubbery copolymer consisting of s-triazine rings linked through perfluoroalkylene groups, thus a perfluororalkylenetrizine elastomer. These plastics have outstanding thermo-oxidative stability but reduced with the use of curing agents and fillers; hydrolytic stability is not good.

flute Helical and, sometimes, vertical deformation rolled onto shank.

fluted core An integrally woven (usually fabric) reinforcement material consisting of ribs between two skins in a unitized sandwich construction. It incorporates a plastic matrix that results in RP ribs.

flux 1. A plastic composition additive incorporated during processing to improve flow. For example, coumarone-indene plastics are used as flux during the milling of vinyl plastics. **2.** A term indicating a state of fluidity. **3.** A number of particles flowing through a given area per unit time.

flux density ▷ **magnetic induction**

fly ash Soot and ash generated during combustion of powdered coal with forced draft and often carried off with flue gases. Can be recovered and reprocessed into products such as gypsum, absorbent for oil spills (silicone coated), plastic filler, etc.

fly cut ▷ **cut, fly**

foam A dispersion of gas in a solid (or liquid). The gas globules may be of any size, from colloidal to microscopic. Foams made by mechanical incorporation of air using plastics is the technique widely used in the food industry. Chemical mixing and other methods are used. ▷ **foamed plastic**

foam and blowing agent For the production of foamed or cellular plastics, depending on the basic material and process, different blowing agents (also called foaming agents) are used to produce gas and thus generate cells or gas pockets in the plastics. They can produce rigid to flexible types and may be divided into two broad groups: physical blowing agents (PBAs) and chemical blowing agents (CBAs). PBAs are represented by both compressed gases and volatile liquids. The compressed gases most often used are nitrogen and carbon dioxide. These gases are injected into a plastic melt under pressure (higher than the melt pressure) and form a cellular structure when the melt is released to atmospheric pressure or low pressure as in a mold cavity with a short shot, etc. The volatile liquids are usually aliphatic hydrocarbons which may be halogenated and include materials such as hexane, methylene chloride, and chlorofluorocarbons that are being phased out ▷ **chlorofluorocarbon**. The liquids act as a gas source by vaporizing during processing. Regardless of their physical form, they rely solely on pressure for controlling gas development in a foaming process.

CBAs, generally solid materials, are of two types: inorganic and organic. Inorganics include sodium bicarbonate, by far the most popular, and carbonates such as zinc or sodium. These materials have low gas yields and do not yield as uniform a cell structure as organic CBAs. Organics are mainly solid materials designed to evolve gas within a defined temperature range, usually referred to as the decomposition temperature range. This is their most important characteristic and allows control over gas development through both pressure and temperature. This increased control results in a finer and more uniform cell structure as well as better surface quality in the foamed plastic. There are over a dozen different types available that decompose at temperatures from 104°C (220°F) to at least 371°C (700°F). Many of these CBAS can be made to decompose below their decomposition temperature through the use of activators.

Typical activators include compounds such as zinc oxide, various vinyl heat stabilizers and lubricants, acids, bases, and peroxides. The reduction in decomposition temperature achieved is dependent upon the particular activator used, its concentration, and the particle size of the blowing agent.

In addition to selecting the proper CBA to meet temperature requirements, other factors to be considered that relate to the plastic and process used include: types of gases evolved, solid decomposition residues, degree of self nucleation, discoloring/staining characteristics, and FDA approval. CBAs could affect certain plastics going through certain processes; they could become yellow, and their life span could be shortened. CBAs should possess the following desirable qualities: (1) long-term storage stability, (2) gas release over a controlled time and temperature range, (3) low toxicity, odor, and color of both the blowing agent and its decomposition products, (4) no deleterious effects on the stability and processing characteristics of the plastic, (5) produce cells of uniform size, (6) produce a stable foam; gas is not lost from the cell causing it to collapse, and (7) acceptable cost-performance relation and availability.

Examples of blowing agents for certain plastics are: (1) physical blowing agents that evaporate at the processing temperature, (2) hydrocarbons such as pentane for the production of expandable polystyrene, (3) chemical blowing agents which split off, for example, nitrogen at the temperature of processing; these are used in the foaming of PE and PVC, and (4) blowing agents which, through the reaction of the raw material components, release a gas (usually carbon dioxide): PUR soft foam is produced in this manner.

By far, most foams are thermoplastics; however, thermosets are also foamed with CBAs but problems exist with certain plastics. A popular TS foam is polyester. This plastic is an unsaturated polyester dissolved in styrene. In this system, thermal decomposition of the blowing agent cannot be applied because the heat of polymerization is not high enough to induce decomposition. Chemical reactions, however, simultaneously produce gas and free radicals. Such reactions typically involve oxidation and reduction of a hydrazine derivative and a peroxide; they are catalyzed by metals, which can be used repeatedly.

Virtually all plastic foams are blown with inert gas; chemical blowing agents release inert gases including hydrocarbons. Certain hydrocarbons, chlorinated hydrocarbons and chlorofluorocarbons are flammable and pose a fire hazard during fabrication and have to be handled properly.

foam and processing method Practically all fabricating processes are used to produce foamed plastics. Different plastics with different blowing agents are used. The major technique used involves the expansion of the plastic by a blowing agent. Cells are initiated and grow to produce the final foam. As gas is produced, an equilibrium is established between material in the gas phase and the material dissolved in the solid state. The gas dissolved in the solid state migrates from the solution into the gas phase. The cells formed initially are under higher than ambient pressure because they must counteract the effects of surface tension. Because the pressure due to surface tension depends on the reciprocal of the cell radius, the pressure within the cell is reduced as the cell grows. Thus, small cells tend to disappear and large cells tend to increase in size because the gas migrates through the substrate (plastic) or the cell walls break.

After forming cells, the foam has to be stable; the gas must not diffuse out of the cell too quickly, thereby causing collapse or excessive shrinkage. The stability of the foam depends on the solubility and diffusivity of the gas in the matrix. The wide variety of processes used provides many methods of cell initiation, cell growth, and cell stabilization. A convenient method of classifying these methods is based on the cell growth and stabilization processes.

The growth of the cell depends on the pressure difference between the inside and surrounding medium of the cell. Such pressure differences may be generated by lowering the external pressure (decompression) or by increasing the internal pressure in the cells (pressure generation). Other methods of generating the cellular structure are by dispersing gas (or solid) in the fluid state and stabilizing this foamed state, or by sintering plastic particles together in a structure that contains a gas phase. Foamable compositions in which the pressure is increased within the cells with respect to the surroundings have generally been called expandable types. Both PBAs and CBAs are used. There is no single name for the group produced by the decomposition processes; principal processes used are extrusion, injection molding, and compression molding. Both PBAs and CBAs are also used.

The processes of major importance based on production output are: (1) extrusion (using PUR, PS, PE, PVC, CA, etc.), (2) expandable (PS, PE, PVC, PUR, phenolic, epoxy, PF, EP, SI, etc.), (3) spray (PUR, EP, UP, etc.), (4) froth (PUR, PVC, UF, EP, etc.), (5) compression (PE, PVC, UP, etc.), (6) sintering (PS, PE, PTFE), and (7) leaching (PE, PVC, CA). The processes used are identified by different names, with some overlapping. They include: bead molding, calender foaming, expandable plastic foam, expandable PS, expandable sheet stock, expandable PVC, extruded foam, injection molded foam (low, high and counter-pressure types), mechanical foaming, reaction injection molding, reticulated foam, spray foam, steam foam molding, structural foam, syntatic foam, and the following all starting with the word "foamed" (as an example foamed blow molding), thus blow molding, casting, extruded film, frothing, gas counter pressure, injection molding, liquid, reservoir molding, rubber, PE, PS, PUR, PVC, preform, sandwich structure, sheet stock, silicone, spray, steam molding, in-place, pouring, short shot molding, and mechanical.

foamed air flow rise The air flow parallel to foam rise is the air flow value obtained when the air enters and leaves the mounted specimen parallel to the foam rise.

foamed blow molding ▷ **blow molding foamed plastic**

foamed casting A simple nonmechanical version of reaction injection molding or liquid injection molding. Liquid components of the plastic with suitable additives are mixed and poured into an open mold. Polymerization and foaming take place in the mold cavity, which could include a matching mold cavity to enclose the foaming action. Heated molds are generally used and/or ovencured.

foamed cell collapse ▷ **cell collapse**

foamed classification ▷ **foam and blowing agent; foam and processing method; foamed plastic**

foamed closed cell Individual cells are noninterconnecting. The cells are basically without access to the surrounding air or fluids; cells are not communicating.

foamed cold-cure Used to produce high-resiliency flexible foams.

foamed collapsed Inadvertent densification of foam or cellular plastic during fabrication resulting from the breakdown of cell structure.

foamed cream time Length of time between pouring mixed foam (usually PUR) and when the material turns creamy or the beginning of foaming. ▷ **foamed rise time**

foamed extruded film Foamed film uses extruders; also see foamed sheet stock. The Table on p. 314 provides a troubleshooting guide.

foamed flame resistance coating ▷ **intumescence coating**

foamed frothing This process is similar to the process used for making dessert topping (lemon meringue, etc.). A gas is dispersed in a fluid which has surface properties to produce a foam of transient stability. The foam is then permanently stabilized by chemical reaction. The fluid may be a homogeneous material, a solution of a heterogeneous material. ▷ **foamed polyurethane**

foamed ground aircraft arrester A bed system of closed cell, rigid phenolic foam sheets that can be arrayed in an airport overrun or safety area of an airport runway. This safety approach is designed to slow and stop airliners that overrun runways. Foam is designed to crush under the aircraft's landing gear, creating sufficient drag to stop the plane safely.

foamed inhibitor ▷ **antifoaming agent**

foamed injection molding, gas counter pressure In this method, a sealed mold is pressurized to 400 to 500 psi (2.8 to 3.5 MPa) with an inert gas, enough pressure to suppress foaming as the plastic mix enters the mold cavity. After the measured shot is injected, mold pressure is released allowing the instantaneous foaming to form the core between the already formed solid skins. Action of mold is a take-off used in coining. There are also other techniques, such as gas injection molding, used to develop similar foamed structures. After plastic in contact with the mold solidifies, gas pressure is released to permit the remaining melt mix to foam and form the part's foamed core.

foamed injection molding high pressure High pressure, expandable-mold, so-called structural foam molding is a take-off of conventional injection molding. The heated melt mix (with blow agent) is injected into the mold creating a cavity pressure higher than the blowing agent gas pressure but usually much higher

Foam film guide.

Problem	Probable cause(s)	Correction
Random poor cell structure	Low melt pressure.	Increase screw speed. Reduce die-lip temperature. Decrease gauge of screen packs. Use resin of lower melt index. Reduce die gap.
	Hangup in die.	Reduce land length. Clean die.
	Stagnant low-pressure areas in head.	Increase screw speed.
	Irregular cells in spider area or opposite die-ring feed.	Use bottom-fed spiral die. Increase head pressure.
Poor skin formation	Too much blowing agent.	Reduce blowing-agent level.
	Linear skin speed too low.	Increase screw speed.
	Loss of melt pressure in die land.	Reduce land length. Increase *L*/*D* ratio. Increase screw speed.
	Die-block temperature too low.	Increase temperature.
Pinholes in film or bubble burst on surface	Too much blowing agent.	Reduce blowing-agent level.
	Die temperature too high.	Reduce die temperature.
	Resin melt index too high.	Decrease resin melt index. Reduce processing temperature.
	Blowing agent decomposing too soon.	Reduce processing temperature. Increase screw speed. Reduce blowing-agent level.
	Poor flow within polymer skin.	Improve flow in head and die.
Cells collapsing	Resin melt index too high.	Decrease melt index. Reduce processing temperature.
	Cooling too fast.	Reduce cooling rate.

to ensure no loss in pressure during injection. Pressure for certain machines could be from 5,000 to 20,000 psi (34.5 to 138 MPa). The mold is entirely filled so that the pressure prevents any foaming from occurring while the skin portion starts solidifying against the mold surfaces. As soon as the skin surface hardens to a desired thickness, the cavity mold pressure is reduced to allow the remaining melt to foam between the skins. Depending on type of equipment and size as well as configuration of the part, these two provisions are made either by withdrawing cores or by special press motions that partially open the mold halves (such as the compression molds used in coining to provide two-dimensional action; three-dimensional mold actions have been used). Degree of foam density, wall thickness, and surface finish depends on foam mixture (constituents and amounts) and machine controls with mold action.

foamed injection molding low pressure Low pressure or short shot conventional foam processing methods are the most commonly used (compared to other IM methods) because they are easy and simple and best suited for economical production particularly of large, complex, three-dimensional parts. In this process a controlled melt mixture (plastic and blowing agent) is injected into a mold cavity creating a low cavity pressure usually from 200 to 500 psi (1.4 to 3.5 MPa). This mixture can be injected directly from the barrel of a conventional injection molding machine (with limited modifications) or, as shown in the Fig. on p. 315, via an accumulator. The mixture only partially fills the mold (short shot), and the gas bubbles, having been at higher pressure, expand immediately and fill the cavity. As the cells collapse against the mold surface, a relatively solid skin of melt is formed over the rigid foam core.

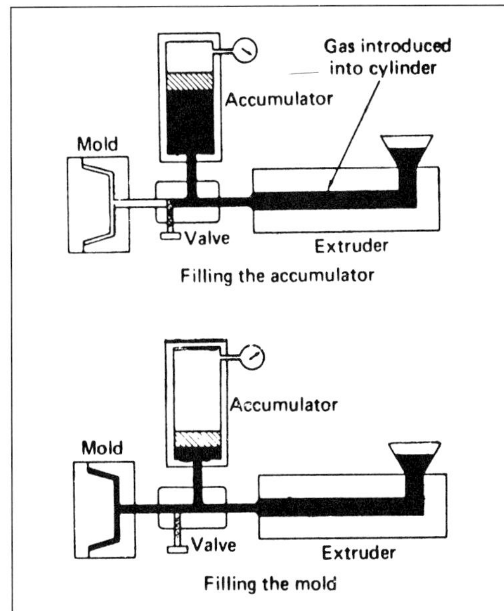

Low pressure foam injection molding using a continuously melting extruder that supplies melt mixture to an accumulator, which in turn instantaneously delivers the required shot size to the mold through one or more nozzles.

Skin thickness is controlled by amount of melt injected, mold temperature, type and amount of blowing agent, temperature and pressure of the melt, and capability of the molding machine, particularly speed of injection.

foamed injection molding low pressure, coinjected This technique involves the usual separate injection of two compatible plastics ▷ **coinjection**. A solid plastic is injected to form the solid, smooth skin against the mold cavity surfaces. Simultaneously a second material, a measured short shot containing a blowing agent, is injected to form the foamed core. This approach can also take a relatively full core shot and have the mold open (as in coining) after the skin solidifies, having the melted core expand with mold opening action.

foamed injection molding low pressure surface finish In low pressure SF molding (not using coinjection or coining techniques), the molding cavity volume is always larger than the volume of the plastic in the unfoamed state. The low pressure allows microbubbles to nucleate and grow. Foam expansion occurs during filling and growing bubbles are carried to the mold surface, resulting in unacceptable surface irregularities and imperfections called splay or swirl pattern. It is both visual and tactile: surface roughness can be as much as 1,000 microinch (0.000025 m). Parts that require smooth, finished surfaces require secondary operations, usually sanding, filling, and painting. There are techniques to improve surface appearance during fabrication. Principal process variables are melt and mold temperature, injection rate, and nature or type as well as concentration of blowing agent. Cyclic heating and cooling of the mold surface, direct injection of blowing agent into the melt as it is being injected into the mold, and other methods are used.

foamed-in-place or in-situ In reference to the deposition of foams when the foaming machine must be brought to the work that is in place as opposed to bringing the work to the foaming machine. Also foam mixed in a container and poured into a mold or into a cavity brick work, where it rises to fill the cavity.

foamed latex ▷ **latex**

foamed liquid ▷ **foamed polyurethane** and **foam and blowing agent**

foamed metal A foamed or cellular metallic structure, usually aluminum or zinc alloys, made by incorporating titanium or zirconium hydride in the base metal. Hydrogen evolves during heat processing. Principally used in absorption of shock impact without elastic rebound. Fiber reinforced light-metal composite foams can be used in structural applications such as in furniture or automobiles; during early 1940s used on aircraft wing leading edges for de-icing.

foamed mold material ▷ **mold material**

foamed open-cell Individual cells that are generally interconnected; basically pores are accessible to surrounding air or fluids. This construction is called reticulated or web-like.

foamed orientation Plastic foams are produced by expanding tiny gas bubbles in a semimolten plastic, stretching the interfacial walls between the gas bubbles, and thus orienting them in a single-step multiaxial stretch. At the corner where three bubbles intersect, the interfacial walls between them may be subjected to some type of three-dimensional orientation, particularly when incorporating short fibers in the mix.

foamed, peanut ▷ **peanut foam packaging material**

foamed plastic Thermoplastics or thermoset plastics with an apparent density which is significantly decreased by the presence of numerous cells disposed throughout its mass usually

Rigid foamed plastic properties.

Property	ASTM test	Cellulose acetate	Epoxy	Phenolic	Polystyrene		
					Expanded plank		
Density, kg/m^3		96–128	32–48	32–64	16	32	80
Mechanical properties							
Compressive strength, kPa at 10%	D 1621	862	138–172	138–620	90–124	207–276	586–896
Tensile strength, kPa	D 1623	1,172		138–379	145–193	310–379	1,020–1,186
Flexural strength, kPa	D 790	1,014		172–448	193–241	379–517	
Shear strength, kPa	C 273	965		103–207		241	
Compression modulus, MPa	D 1621	38–90	3.9			3.4–14	
Flexural modulus, MPa	D 790	38				9.0–26	
Shear modulus, MPa	C 273			2.8–4.8		7.6–11.0	
Thermal properties							
Thermal conductivity, W/(m–K)	C 177	0.045–0.046	0.016–0.022	0.029–0.032	0.037	0.035	0.035
Coefficient of linear expansion, 10^{-5}/°C	D 696		1.5	0.9	5.4–7.2	5.4–7.2	
Maximum service temperature, °C		177	205–260	132	74–80	74–80	74–80
Specific heat, kJ/(kg · K)	C 351						
Electrical properties							
Dielectric constant	D 1673	1.12			<1.05	1.02	1-02
Dissipation factor		20			<0.0004	0.0007	0.0007
Moisture resistance							
Water absorption, vol %	C 272	4.5		13–51	1–4	1–4	1–4
Moisture vapor transmission, g/(m · s · GPa)	E 96		58		<120	35–120	23–35

by an expanding gas foam blowing agent. This gas phase is usually distributed in voids or pockets called cells; they can be foamed open-cell or the usual foamed closed-cell. The open-cell or reticulated foams are made by removing the cell membrane from conventional closed-cell foam leaving a 3-D skeletal structure which consists of the interconnected framing edges of the individual cell faces. These strutlike members are formed during the course of the foaming reaction, where adjacent cell sides meet, and are generally appreciably thicker than the thin membranes attached to them. The removal of the membranes can be accomplished by a variety of methods, all of which are dependent upon the cells being interconnected by an opening in at least one of the membranes connected to its neighbors; thus open-cell foam. The single most important class of reticulated foams is polyurethanes.

The term foamed plastics is used interchangeably with cellular plastics. Also called expandable plastics, structural foams. They can range from very flexible to very rigid. Classifications of foams are generally made with reference to the properties of type plastic, such as, expandable polystyrene, foamed polyurethane, foamed polyvinyl chloride, etc.; by processing method, such as, foamed-in-place, frothing, pour-in-place, foamed reservoir molding, expandable plastic foam, etc.; by construction of product, such as, sandwich structure, structural foam, thermal insulation, sponge, sealant, etc. There are also foamed plastics that are not gas generated during processing, such as syntactic foams.

foamed plastic market Practically all markets use foamed plastics. Consumption by weight percentagewise are; insulation 18%, cushioning

Polystyrene						Polyurethane				
Extruded plank		Extruded sheet		PVC		Polyether		Isocyanurate: Bun	Isocyanurate: Laminate	Urea-formaldehyde
35	53	96	160	32	64	32–48	64–128	32	32	13–19
310	862	290	469	345	1,035	138–344	482–1,896	210	117–206	34
517		2,070–3,450	4,137–6,900	551	1,207	138–482	620–2,000	250	248–290	
1,138				586	1,620	413–689	1,380–2,400			
241				241	793	138–207	413–896	180	117	
10.3				13.1	35	2.0–4.1	10.3–31			
41				10.3	36	5.5–6.2	5.5–10.3			
10.3				6.2	21	1.2–1.4	3.4–10.3		1.7	
0.030		0.035	0.035	0.023		0.016–0.025	0.022–0.030	0.054	0.019	0.026–0.030
6.3	6.3					5.4–7.2	7.2	7.2		
74		77–80	80			93–121	121–149	149	149	
1.1						ca 0.9	ca 0.9	ca 0.9		
1.19–1.20	<1.05	1.02	1.27	1.28			1.05	1.1	1.4	
0.028–0.031	<0.0004	0.0007	0.00011	0.00014				13	18	
0.02	0.05									
35		86	56	15		35–230	50–120		230	1,610–2,000

12%, packaging 12%, construction 10%, transportation 10%, consumer 8%, furniture 6%, flooring 6%, bedding 4%, appliance 2%, and others 12%.

foamed plastic material Practically all plastics (TPs and TSs) can be foamed but only a few are principally used; by percentage weightwise polyurethane 45% (flexible 27% and rigid 18%), polystyrene 24%, polyvinyl chloride 13%, and others 18%.

foamed plastic mechanically A material having a structure produced by physically or mechanically incorporating gases in the plastic rather than the usual blowing agents.

foamed plastic properties Low to high weight density foams are produced, ranging from at least 10 to 300 kg/m^3 (0.6 to 19 lb/ft^3) with some going up to at least 600 kg/m^3 (37 lb/ft^3). With the different plastics, processes, and densities used, a wide range of properties are available (see Table above and on pp. 318–319). Properties are influenced by composition, structural integrity of cell, structural relationship of part (skin thickness, sandwich foram, coinjection, coextrusion, etc.). Cell size is generally characterized by measurements of the cell diameter and as a measurement of average cell volume. Mechanical, physical, optical, thermal, and other properties depend on cell size. The geometry or shape of cells is controlled mainly by the final foam density and the external forces exerted on the foam prior to stabilization. In the presence of external forces, the cells may be elongated or flattened. Cell shape and orientation can influence many properties.

Flexible foamed plastic properties.

Property	ASTM test	Expanded natural rubber		Expanded SBR	Latex foam rubber		Polyethylene	
							Extruded plank	Extruded sheet
Density, kg/m^3		56	320	72	80	130	35	43
Cell structure		closed	closed	closed	open	open	closed	closed
Compression strength 25% deflection, kPa	D 3574, D 3575							48
Tensile strength, kPa	D 3574		206	551	103		138	41
Tensile elongation, %	D 3574				310		60	276
Rebound resilience, %	D 3574				73			50
Tear strength, (N/m) × 10^2	D 3574						10.5	26
Maximum service temperature, °C		70	70	70			82	82
Thermal conductivity, W/(m · K)	C177	0.036	0.043	0.030		0.050	0.053	0.040–0.049

With close-cells, the gas phase in the cells can contain blowing agents (so-called captive), air, or other gases generated by the plastic during foaming. The cell-gas composition can influence properties, such as thermal and electrical conductivity. Close-cells perform better than other thermal insulation when exposed to moisture, particularly when subjected to a combination of thermal and moisture gradients. Environmental performance of any type foam structure is governed almost entirely by the type plastic and mix.

Foams by themselves are poor materials for reducing sound transmission. They are, however, effective in absorbing sound waves of certain frequencies, particularly open-cells.

foamed plastic recycled Like all plastics, foams can be recycled. ▷ **recyclable** and **packaging loose, fill plastic**

foamed Poisson ratio, negative ▷ **Poisson ratio, negative**

foamed polyethylene, expandable ▷ **expandable polyethylene**

foamed polyethylene ionization The process of foaming PE by exposing it to ionizing radiation which evolves hydrogen from the PE, causing it to foam.

foamed polystyrene ▷ **expandable polystyrene**

foamed polyurethane Liquid (pour-in-place), froth (modified pour-in-place), and spray foaming techniques are examples of the different methods used with PUR foaming (see Fig. opposite). When the liquid ingredients are mixed, gases are produced which cause the mass to expand at the same time it stiffens and hardens. The reaction is complete in a few minutes. As an example in a sandwich structure, the liquid mix is poured between the cover sheets and foams between them, bonding directly to the sheets without an adhesive. (EPS requires an adhesive on the sheets if bond is required.) As foamed-in-place materials expand, they can exert appreciable pressure so that the sandwich sheets have to be held in a rigid frame to prevent bulging until the reaction is completed. To overcome this pressure, the liquid mix may be allowed to form a froth of almost its ultimate volume prior to pouring. Result is little or no pressure and a rigid foam is produced. Basically, flexible PUR foam, such as what is used in upholstery, is made by continuous deposition on a belt. Subsequently it is cut into blocks or sheets of desired shape and size. Other foam materials may be handled in somewhat similar ways, and may be prefoamed or foamed-in-place.

The component-forming blowing gas in PUR soft, flexible foam formulation is water, which forms carbondioxide with isocyanates. The heat and the evolution of temperature resulting from this gas-generating reaction, however, necessitate additionally the use of other blowing agents (such as dichloromethane) which are used at the

	Polypropylene		Polyurethane				Silicone	
Cross-linked sheet	Modified	Sheet	Standard cushioning	High resilience type	Poly(vinyl chloride)		Liquid	Sheet
26–28	64–96	10	24	40	56	112	272	160
closed	closed		open	open	closed	closed	open	open
	206	4.8	5.7	4.6				
	344		118	103	10.3	24	36 at 20%	
276–480	1380	138–275	205	160			227	310
	75		40	62				
			4.4	2.4				
79–93	135	121					350	260
0.036–0.040	0.039	0.039			0.035	0.040	0.078	0.086

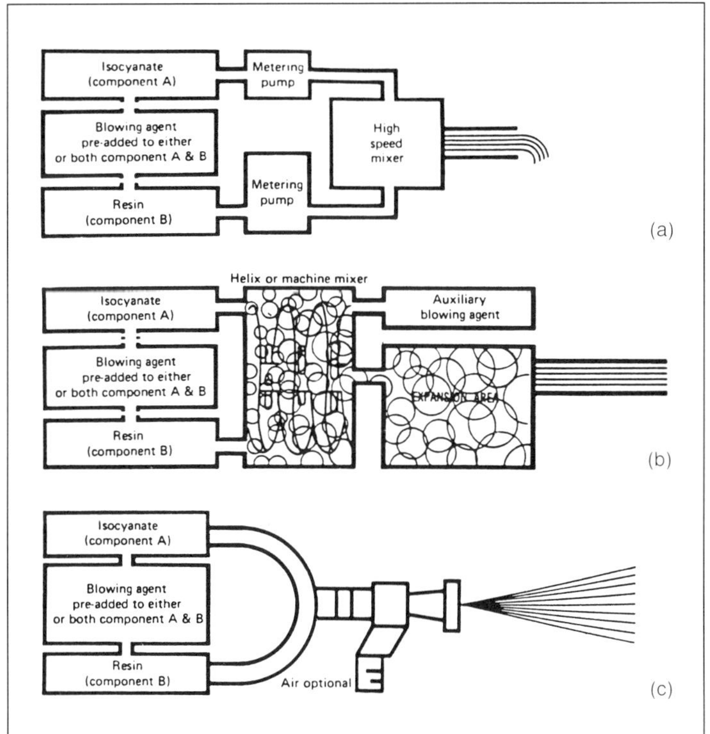

Schematics of different methods used for producing polyurethane foams. (*a*) Liquid process; (*b*) froth process; (*c*) spray method.

same time as coolants in the production of low density foam of less than 20 kg/m^3. Flexible PUR foams have open cells and are used in the furniture, automotive, packaging, insulation, mechanical (sealants, sponges, etc.), and other industries.

A rigid, foamed crosslinked PUR, usually with closed cells, is formed by the reaction of a diisocyanate (sometimes containing components of a higher functionality) and often MDI (methane diisocyanate) or polymeric MDI with a polyester or more usually with a polyether polyol. Foaming may result from the incorporation of water, which reacts with isocyanate groups to form carbon dioxide, but usually is the result of using other blowing agents sometimes in combination with water. They become rigid, compared to flexible foams, by being more heavily crosslinked. This is accomplished by the use of polyols, usually polyoxypropylene glycols of low molecular weight (about 500) which are highly branched by mixing of higher functionality comonomers (such as sorbitol or pentaerythritol). Prepolymer processes and quasi-prepolymer processes are used with TDI (toluene diisocyanate) to reduce the toxic hazard of this material. One-shot processes are used with MDI and polymer MDI with polyethers; normally a tertiary amine and/or organotin catalyst system is used, together with a silicone surfactant as with flexible foams. Catalysts are usually also used to give the right balance of reaction rates so that the gas bubbles are trapped in the liquid plastic melt as the viscosity increases due to polymerization and crosslinking. A surfactant, usually a silicone-polyether block copolymer, is also often present to control cell morphology. The major application for these foams is for thermal insulation as it has exceptional low thermal conductivity.

A variation of the polyurethane foam-in-place method is foam frothing. The liquid PUR chemical mixture is dispensed in a partially expanded froth state. Frothing is achieved by using a mixture of blowing agents in the basic mix to give a two-step blowing action. The first expands the mix into a froth and cools, delaying the second (and final) expansion for about a half minute. ▷ **polyurethane**

foamed polyurethane cream time ▷ **foamed rise time**

foamed polyurethane mixing head The mechanism in which polyol and isocyanate streams are combined by impingement mixing, such as is used in reaction injection molding.

foamed polyurethane molding one-shot A system in which the isocyanate, polyol, catalyst, and other additives are mixed together directly and a foam is produced immediately; as distinguished from prepolymer.

foamed polyurethane molding prepolymer The formation of a polymer from a precursor polymer by chain extension and/or crosslinking reactions. The term is especially used for the formation of PURs, a two-stage process. In the first stage a polyester or polyol is reacted with a diisocyanate to form an isocyanate-terminated prepolymer. It is chain extended and/or crosslinked in the second stage. This latter is by reaction with a diol, amine, water, or further isocyanate groups for PUR elastomer formation, or with water, catalysts, and other ingredients for polyether based flexible PUR foam. The liquid prepolymer is supplied to fabricators (the first stage mix) with a second premixed blend of additional polyol, catalyst, blowing agent, and so forth. When the two components are subsequently mixed, foaming occurs.

The polymer process was originally the main one used because of the low reactivity of polyether polyols. However, with the discovery of more active catalyst systems, the one-shot process became possible and more important. Rigid PUR foams, especially those using TDI, are also produced by the prepolymer process. A disadvantage, apart from having an extra processing step, is that the isocyanate-terminated prepolymers often have a limited stability, due to reaction with atmospheric water. Also the prepolymers may have high viscosities, thus making mixing difficult in the second stage.

foamed polyurethane reticulated Very low-density PUR foams characterized by a three-dimensional skeletal structure of strands with few or no membranes between the strands. They contain up to 97% or more of void space. Conversion is usually made by treating an open-cell foam with a dilute aqueous sodium hydroxide solution under controlled conditions so that the thin membranes are dissolved, leaving the strands substantially unaffected. Ultrasonic vibrating is sometimes used to assist the solution process. Uses include air filters and cleaners, acoustical panels, etc.

foamed polyvinyl chloride Although vinyl foams can be produced by many methods, including mechanical frothing, decompression techniques, and leaching out of soluble additives, the most widely used procedure is chemical blowing. From 1 to 2%, by weight, of a blowing agent such as azobisformamide is incorporated in PVC compound or dispersion, remaining inert until it is decomposed by processing heat to release gas. Such compounds are processed by conventional methods such as calendering, extrusion, injection molding, compression molding, slush casting, and rotational molding. In a majority of these processes either rigid or flexible foams can be made depending upon the amount and type of plasticizer used. Vinyl foams are widely used in clothing, flooring, footware, furniture, packaging, etc.

foamed pouring A method of foam processing where the complete foam mix is poured into an open mold. Usually molded into a large bun but also other shapes are formed.

foamed, pour-in-place ▷ **foamed-in place**

foamed preform Preformed material such as polystyrene is commonly extruded in the form of large "logs" several feet across and in densities usually ranging from one or two lb/ft^3 (16 or 32 kg/m^3) for building insulation. These are cut into boards, planks, and blocks for installation in buildings. The closed-cell foams with the low vapor permeability of PS provide integral vapor barriers; used in basements, roof slabs, insulating plaster base, etc.

foamed reservoir molding This process, also known as elastic reservoir molding, consists of making basically a sandwich of plastic-impregnated open-celled flexible polyurethane foam between the face layers of fibrous reinforcements. When this plastic composite is placed in a heated mold and squeezed, the foam is compressed, forcing the plastic and air outward and into the reinforcement. The elastic foam exerts sufficient pressure to force the plastic impregnated reinforcement into contact with the mold surface (see Fig).

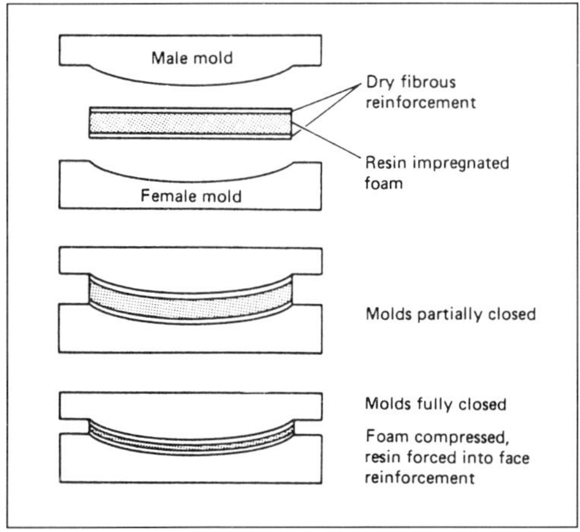

Schematic for the foamed reservoir molding process.

foamed reticulated ▷ **foamed polyurethane reticulated**

foamed rise time In plastic foam molding, particularly with PUR, the time between the pouring of the PUR mix and the completion of foaming. ▷ **foamed cream time**

foamed rubber Made from a liquid starting material. There are two types: (1) latex foam rubber is produced by mechanically whipping air into a rubber latex, gelling the latex, and vulcanizing it and (2) foamed polyurethane rubber is produced from liquid monomer mix. ▷ **foamed polyurethane**

foamed rubber microcellular A cellular or foamed rubber with small cells produced by molding a mixture of a rubber with a blowing agent and high impact polystyrene plastic. Expansion occurs only after removal from the mold.

foamed sandwich structure ▷ **sandwich construction**

foamed security system A novel polyurethane foam-based system to secure valuable articles in vehicles, etc. This Instant ARMY (Instantaneous Anti-Rubbery Mass Foam-Yielding System) when activated will deliver a mass of rapidly expanding PUR foam to engulf the valuables being carried (armored cars, etc.). Basically a ▷ **foamed polyurethane molding prepolymer** is used. The expanding foam (foam mass is 150 times the liquid volumes) jams the doors of a security vehicle as well as its contents within 8 sec. Design is by automatic equipment specialist (joint venture by two Italian companies, Pa.je.t Srl and Apco Italia Snc.). During the early 1940s some low flying airplanes had PUR prepolymer p.s. mixes that activated when the pilot was in trouble, could not parachute because of low altitude, and thus "foamed-in-place". On impact semiflexible foam was "targeted" to protect the pilot from the impact.

foamed self-skinning Foam that produces tough outer surface skin over a foamed core upon curing. Also called integral skin foam.

foamed sheet stock Usually refers to expandable sheet stock produced by calendering in which a decomposable blowing agent is milled into a plasticized polyvinyl chloride below the decomposition temperature of the blowing agent. Subsequent heating causes the decomposition and expansion of the blowing agent. Cooling of the expanded plastic is necessary for stabilization of the expanded state. Use includes thermoforming egg cartons, meat trays, fast-food containers, etc.

foamed silicone Processes include use of fluid silicone plastic made by mixing with a catalyst and blowing agent, pouring the mixture into molds, and curing at room temperature for about 10 hrs; at elevated temperatures much less time is required. Silicone foam sponge is made by mixing unvulcanized silicone rubber with a blowing agent and heating at vulcanization temperature.

foamed spray Very fast reacting polyurethane or epoxy foams are fed in liquid streams to the spray gun and sprayed on the surface. On contact, the liquid starts to foam. Other plastic foams are used such as thermoset polyester quick acting mixes.

foamed steam molding ▷ **expandable polystyrene**

foamed, structural So-called structural foam (SF) is also called integral skin foaming or reaction injection molding (RIM) and can overlap in performance as well as use with the significantly larger market of the more conventional foamed plastics (previously reviewed). Up until the 1980s in the U.S., the RIM and SF processes were kept separate. Combining them in the market place was to aid in market penetration. During the 1930s to 1960s, liquid injection molding (LIM) was the popular name for what later became RIM and SF.

SF is characterized as plastic structures with nearly uniform density foam cores and integral near-solid skins. Definition of SF by the SF industry is a plastic product with integral skins, a cellular core, and enough strength-to-weight ratio to be classified as structural. When these foams are used in load-bearing applications, the foam bulk density is typically 50 to 90% of the plastic's unfoamed bulk density. Most SF products (90%) are made from different thermoplastics, principally PS, PE, PVC, and ABS. Polyurethane is the primary thermoset. Unfilled and unreinforced plastics represent about 70% of products. The principal method of processing (75%) is modified low pressure injection molding. Extrusion and RIM account for about 10% each. See the various processes listed under ▷ **foamed injection molding**

foamed, syntactic ▷ **syntactic foam**

foamed unicellular ▷ **foamed closed cell**

foamed vinyl ▷ **foamed polyvinyl chloride**

focus A point at which rays originating from a point in the object converge or from which they diverge, or appear to diverge, under the influence of a lens or diffracting system.

fog 1. A loose term applied to visible aerosols in which the dispersed phase is liquid. Formation by condensation is usually applied. **2.** In meteorology, a dispersion of water or ice. **3.** A general or local density in a developed photographic image that is not associated with image-forming exposure and is caused by chemical action or stray radiation.

foil A very thin sheet of material that usually identifies aluminum foil, but also includes other materials (plastic, paper, etc.).

foil decorating Molding aluminum, plastic, paper and/or textile foils printed with compatible inks directly into a plastic part (injection molded, blow molded, laminated, etc.) so that the decorative foil is visible below the surface of the part as integral decoration.

foil, hot stamping ▷ **hot stamping**

fold, dead A dead fold does not spontaneously unfold.

folded plate structure ▷ **design architectural space frame**

fold, web ▷ **web fold**

Follow ALL Opportunities ▷ **FALLO approach**

food additive ▷ **acceptable risk**

Food and Drug Administration enforcement policy FDA, the U.S.'s foremost line of consumer protection, is a scientifically based law enforcement agency. The enforcement function of the FDA is twofold: to safeguard the public health, and to ensure honesty and fair-dealing between the regulated industry and consumers. Action by FDA includes: (1) encourages and expects compliance with the laws and regulations it enforces, (2) constantly conducts surveillance and investigations over the industry it regulates, to continuously assess compliance and discover noncompliance, (3) protects the public by relying on any and all of its varied enforcement tools, both administrative and jucicial, according to the seriousness of the violation, (4) does not tolerate fraud, intentional violations, or gross negligence, and promptly seeks prosecution to punish and deter whenever appropriate, (5) uses fair and scientifically sound law enforcement and regulatory work to assure efficiency in its enforcement activities and maintain the public trust and confidence, (6) cooperates with, and enlists the cooperation of, other federal, state and local agencies, and foreign governments and international organizations, to extend the scope and increase the effectiveness of its consumer protection programs, and (7) continuously evaluates and updates its law enforcement programs and needs.

food-in-tube ▷ **tube, collapsible**

food solid waste ▷ **solid waste food**

footcandle ▷ **illumination, footcandle**

force 1. The male half of a mold (injection, etc.) which enters the cavity and exerts pressure on the plastic causing it to flow during processing. **2.** Either half of a compression mold (top force and bottom force) but most often the half which forms the inside of the molded part. **3.** A physical influence exerted by one body on another which produces acceleration of bodies that are free to move and deformation of bodies that are not free to move (compare to ▷ **strength**). ▷ **Newton 4.** Force per SI standard is the Newton rather than kilogram-force when used to form derived units which include force, for example, energy ($N \cdot m = J$) and power ($N \cdot m/s = W$). ▷ **load** and **weight**

foreign matter Undesirable particles that may exist in a material, additive, etc. such as dust, dirt, sand, etc.

forensic science and plastic Forensic science is the collective term for a hybrid applied science embracing any of the natural, engineering, or medical sciences that may be called upon for assistance in the administration of criminal or civil justice. Utilization of plastics as items of tract evidence is an example of plastic usage. Plastics are usually of interest for one of the following reasons: (1) trace evidence; may be crushed to powder, melted, left behind, or carried away, burned, or broken, (2) failures; plastics like other materials can fail and such failures are most often studied with regard to civil cases involving liability litigation, although they occasionally have bearing on a criminal case, (3) burned plastics; most cases are civil, the flammability of various plastics or fabrics and their suitability for a particular use, and (4) fibers; a frequent problem is identification and comparison of fibers transferred from an item of clothing, carpet, or vehicle to a suspect, victim, or crime scene.

forepressure ▷ **pump forepressure**

forging A production method whereby usually heated stock material (steel, plastic, etc.) is shaped to a desired form by compression forces (impression molding) or by sharp hammer-like blows. Virtually all ductile materials may be forged and in some cases preheating is not required. When the material is forged below the melt temperature, it is cold forged; with plastics it is generally called cold forming or solid-phase pressure forming. When worked above the melt temperature, it is said to be hot forged.

formaldehyde A colorless gas (HCHO) usually employed as a solution in water. It has a suffocating, pungent odor. This gas is derived from the oxidation of methanol or low-boiling petroleum gases such as methane, ethane, propane, or butane. The major use (about 55%) is as 30 to 55% aqueous solutions for the production of phenol-formaldehyde (phenolic), urea-formaldehyde (urea), and melamine-formaldehyde (melamine) plastics. Smaller amounts are used for the production of polyoxymethylene, hexamethylenetetramine, and pentaerithrytol. Sometimes plastics or other derivatives of formaldehyde are used as a source of formaldehyde in polymerization or curing reactions. These include paraformaldehyde (prepared by the distillation of aqueous formaldehyde solutions), trioxane (a cyclic trimer prepared by heating a strong 60% solution with 2% sulphuric acid), and hexamethylenetetramine (prepared by reaction of formaldehyde with ammonia).

form birefringence ▷ **birefringence, form**

form, fill, and seal ▷ **thermoforming form, fill, and seal**

form, fill, and seal with zipper on-line ▷ **thermoforming form, fill, and seal with zipper on-line**

Formica Original Formica Corp. tradename for high pressure laminated sheets of melamine (surface) and phenolic plastics used in decorative applications, etc.

forming Formed or shaped plastics provide a great variety of marketable products, in a wide size range. Different techniques are used, with thermoforming being the most productive and the most diversified. Other techniques are basically similar to thermoforming but usually use less heat than it requires and are more limited as to the type of plastic used; these processes include cold forming, stamping or compression forming, flow molding, rubber pad molding, diaphragm forming, coining, forging, and so on. Formed parts are used in many different applications and production lines (form, fill and seal, etc.). Food, electronic devices, medical products, and other parts use continuous thermoforming operations at the end of high-speed production lines to reduce the handling of products, provide hermetically sealed contents, reduce costs, and so forth.

Certain thermoplastics, when formed, require handling normally not available with conventional thermoforming machines; so other processes of formation have evolved. Most of these methods tend to reduce the amount of heat required or even eliminate it entirely. One popular technique is high pressure forming, which is like conventional compression molding. The techniques that are used modify conventional metal working tools. They can be classified as: (1) cold forming (performed at room temperature with unheated tools), (2) solid-phase forming (plastic is heated below the melting point and formed), and (3) compression molding of reinforced/composite sheets (heat is used). Other methods so used are classified as forging (which includes closed-die forming, open-die forming, cold pressing, etc.), stamping, rubber pad or diaphragm forming, fluid forming, coining, spinning, explosive forming, and so on.

Cold forming and solid-phase forming include the use of ABS/PC, PC, conventional PP, and HMWHDPE. By using solid-phase forming, processors can make more efficient use of ultrahigh molecular weight, high density plastics that are difficult or impossible to process by other methods. Forming by these techniques can usually use existing metalworking equipment with minor modifications. Tooling is inexpensive, and production rates can be high. Flash, trim, or weld lines can be eliminated by using some of these processes. ▷ **thermoforming** and **postforming**

forming cake In filament winding, the collection (package) of glass fiber strands on a mandrel during the forming or winding operation.

forming cold ▷ **cold forming**

forming, dip ▷ **dip forming**

forming, electro ▷ **electroforming**

forming, extruder in-line system ▷ **postforming**

forming scrapless Various techniques are used to form different products such as containers having different shapes that completely or practically eliminate the usual "excessive" scrap that develops during conventional thermoforming. Examples are shown in the Figs. below and opposite.

forming shape mandrel A shaped support post typically used to form and size necks or threads in products.

forming slip ▷ **slip forming**

forming, solid-phase pressure SPPF or solid-state stamping basically uses a male metal plug mold that matches a female metal cavity mold and can be used only with crystalline-type resins. Below their glass transition temperatures (T_g) amorphous-type resins are generally too stiff to be rapidly formed into stable products. Crystalline types can be permanently deformed at temperatures between their T_g and melting point. Molecular orientation, the mechanism that allows this to occur, relates to the draw ratio. Draw ratios can vary from 5:1 for PET and nylon to 10:1 for low molecular weight PP. The major advantage of solid-state forming is that parts can be produced in very fast cycle times, usually 10 to 20 s. The surface finish of these parts is rather smooth, as the fibers do not surface.

forming, stamping ▷ **stamping**

forming superplastic ▷ **superplastic forming**

forming temperature range The sheet temperature range in which any particular thermoplastic can be formed where the sheet is

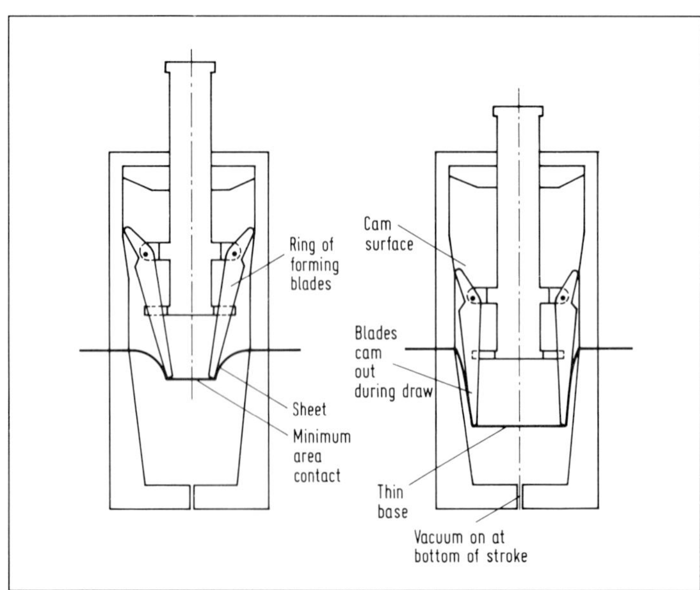

Rampart's multilayer barrier containers are made by virtually scrapless solid-phase forming process starting from a shaped billet.

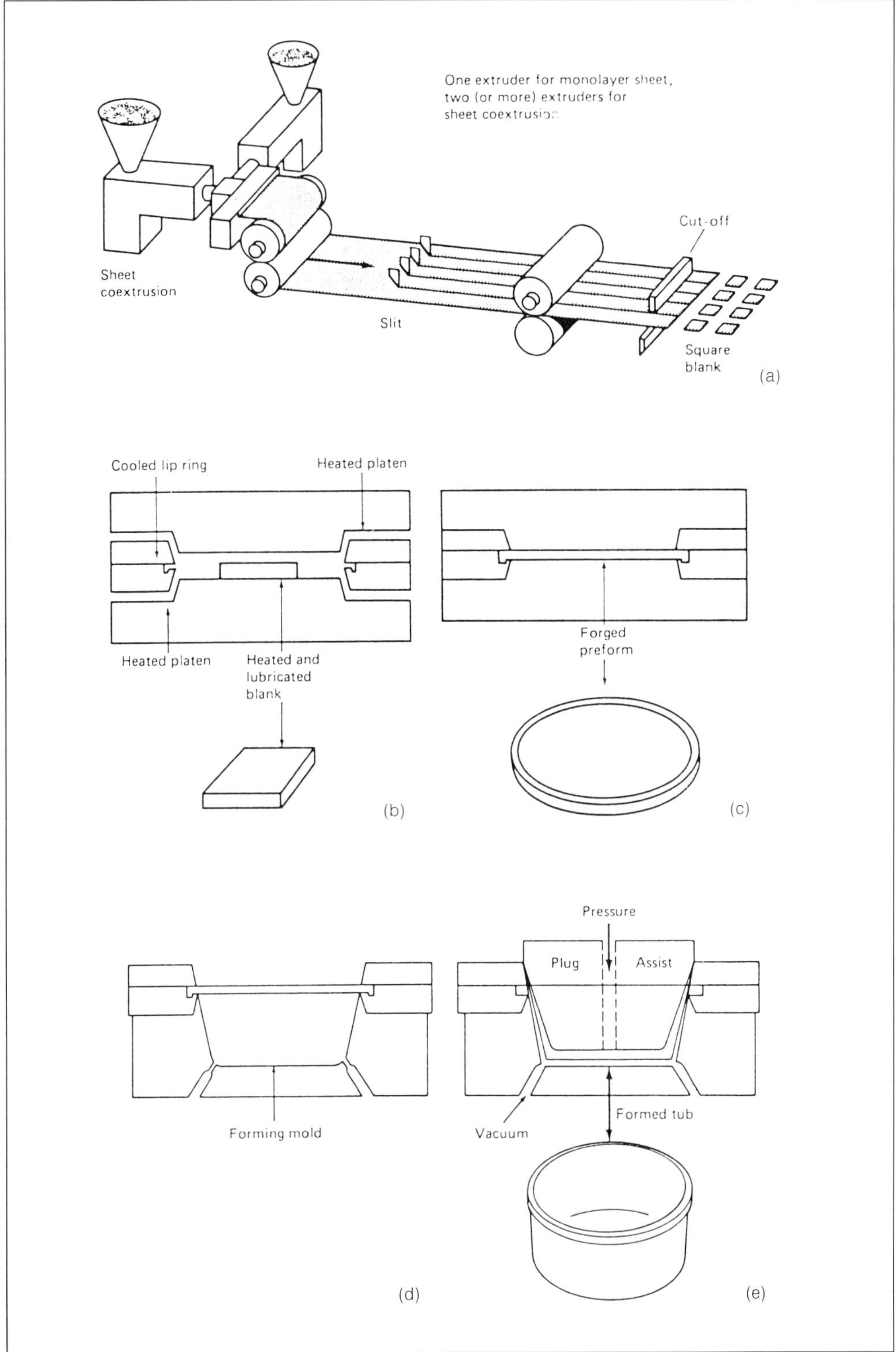

Dow Chemical's solid-phase forming (SPF) process: (*a*) co-extruder; (*b*) start of process; (*c*) pressed closed; (*d*) transfer; (*e*) pressure form.

stretchable but not molten. ▷ **thermoforming temperature control**

formula 1. A group of numerical symbols associated to express briefly a single concept. 2. A combination of signs in a logical calculus approach. 3. A symbolic expression of the chemical composition of a substance; a written representation using symbols, as an example, of a chemical entity or relationship.

formula product A list of ingredients and their amounts or percentages (by weight or volume) required in a product.

formulation Selection of components of a product formula or mixture to provide optimum specific properties for the end use desired; to be more specific, determining the proper proportion of ingredients in a mixture, blend, compound, etc.

foundry plastic The foundry industry uses several procedures for casting metal parts; permanent mold casting, centrifugal casting, and sand casting. Permanent molds are made of metal, graphite, or a ceramic. In sand casting, molds and cores are used. Cores are required for hollow castings and must be removed after the metal has solidified. Cores are used in both sand and permanent molds. Binders are used to strengthen the cores, which are the most fragile part of a mold assembly. Plastic-based binders are used because of their versatility and performance, as well as resulting in significant labor and energy savings with higher productivity. In practice, these binders are mixed with sand (usually 1 to 2 parts binder added to 100 parts of sand), the mixes are compressed into the desired shape of the mold or core. They are hardened or cured by chemical and/or thermal/heat reactions.

Various types of fabrication processes are used to produce molds and cores from sand and plastic binders. In the no-bake and the cold-box processes, the binder is cured at room temperature, while in shell-molding, hot-box, and oven-baked processes, heat cures are applied. Selection of the process and type of binder depends upon the size and number of cores or molds required, production rates, and available equipment. The usual binders are phenolic, furan, and TS polyester plastics. In addition, various blends, such as phenolic-furan combinations, are also used. Certain types of the phenolic and polyester plastics used with polymeric isocyanates are applied as two-component (polyurethane-forming plastic) binder systems. Phenolics are the most widely used.

fountain flow melt ▷ **mold cavity melt fountain flow**

fourdrinier The machine most widely used for papermaking; used with plastic fibers to produce nonwoven manufactured "plastic" papers or fabrics. ▷ **mechanical nonwoven fabric**

four-harness satin A fabric weave, also called crowfoot satin because of the weaving pattern. When laid out on cloth design paper, resembles the imprint of a crow's foot. In this type of weave there is a three-by-one interlacing. That is, a filling thread floats over the three warp threads and then under one. The two sides of the fabric have different appearances. Fabrics with this weave are more pliable than either plain or basket weaves, and are easier to form around curves such as complex reinforced plastic parts.

Fourier's law ▷ **devolatilization, basics**

Fourier transition ▷ **spectroscopic Fourier transform**

fractionation ▷ **molecular fractionation**

fracture Refers to the separation of a body. Defined both as rupture of the surface without complete separation of the material and as complete separation of a body because of external or internal forces. Some plastics can show similar failure at very much longer times under stresses substantially lower than those necessary to bring about short-time rupture. The occurrence of this extended time-scale phenomenon is often accelerated by the presence of an applicable environment, which may or may not cause chemical degradation of the plastic. There may also be reason to regard these failures as analogous in some ways to similar failures in metals, usually referred to as stress-corrosion cracking, season cracking, or fatigue cracking. The analogies are not exactly parallel, however, and although certain similarities between behavior patterns exist, so do many obvious differences. ▷ **stress cracking and crazing** and **Griffith theory**

fracture, brittle Fracture without plastic (behavior) deformation, hence with little energy absorption that follows the Griffith theory.

fracture, ductile Fracture ductility is the true plastic strain of fracture. It is accompanied by plastic deformation and, therefore, by energy absorption.

fracture, elastic ▷ **melt fracture**

fracture mechanics The fracture mechanics theory developed for metals is also adaptable for use with plastics. The basic concepts remain the same, but since metals and plastics are different they require different techniques to describe their fatigue-failure behaviors. Some of the comments made about crack and fracture influences on fatigue performance relate to the theory of fracture mechanics. The fracture mechanics theory method, along with readily measured material properties, component geometry, and loading information, can be used to design against fatigue failure. The fracture mechanics model also gives insight into materials' development by showing how their resistance to crack propagation depends on both molecular and structural factors.

Service failures in plastics can be caused by fatigue. When time is the critical factor, this type of failure is called static fatigue or creep rupture. If mechanical load reversal or the number of cycles controls failure, the term employed is cyclic fatigue. Interaction between the material and an environment capable of damaging it can lead to stress cracking in the static case and fatigue in the cycle one. An additional failure mode is thermal degradation, in which the temperature increases within the sample from hysteretic energy dissipation. ▷ **fracture plane stress**

fracture, metal ▷ **metal fracture**

fracture, nonductile It has negligible plastic deformation and a minimum of energy adsorption; brittle fracture.

fracture, plane stress In fracture mechanics, a model for crack growth in which there is a state of plane stress in the yielded zone ahead of the crack tip, such that the tensile stress parallel to the crack front is zero. This is most likely to apply in thin specimens and when the yielded zone is at least as large as the specimen thickness.

fracture strength or stress The normal stress at the beginning of fracture. Calculated from the load at the beginning of fracture during a tension test and the original cross sectional area of the specimen (this is usually taken as the fracture strength). To obtain the true strength, the load at separation should be divided by the cross sectional area at the time of separation.

fracture toughness A measure of the damage tolerance of a material containing initial flaws or cracks. Used in critical structural design and analysis such as aircraft, bridge, amusement park fast moving devices, etc.

free fall dart test ▷ **dart drop test**

free-radical polymerization They proceed by a complex mechanism of initiation, propagation, and termination of which the propagation and termination steps are typically very fast. Heat removal is complicated by the rapidly increasing solution viscosity. The increasing viscosity also lowers the diffusivity of plastic chain segments, but has less effect on the diffusivity of the monomers. This leads to a common phenomenon in bulk polymerization known as the Trommsdorff or gel effect. Polystyrene and polymethyl methacrylate are usually manufactured by this technique. Polyvinyl chloride is usually using this system with chemical initiators at moderate temperatures, that is below 100°C (212°F). Polyethylene and ethylene-rich copolymers are sometimes formed in a free-radical bulk process using the older high pressure technology.

freeze The term freeze is associated with the melting to solidify a plastic, such as during injection molding. As soon as the hot melt makes contact with the mold cavity wall (whose temperature is either cooler for thermoplastics or hotter for thermosets) it immediately "freezes". It is the development initially of plastic solidification, thus forming the product in the cavity but not completely solidified. After the complete cooling (freezing) cycle for TPs or heating (freezing) of TSs, the mold opens with completely cooled TPs or cured TSs. The term relates to any melt that solidifies. ▷ **injection molding nozzle freeze**

freeze-dried color Pigments dispersed in a vehicle that solidify at room temperature or when chilled. They are usually commercialized in flake or chip form. ▷ **colorant**

freezing ▷ **latent heat**

freezing index The number of degree-days between the highest and lowest points on the cumulative degree-days-time curve for one freezing season. The index for air temperature at 4.5 ft (1.4 m) above the ground is commonly designated as the air freezing index, while that determined below a surface is known as the surface freezing index.

freezing point The temperature at which the liquid and solid states of a substance are in equilibrium at a given pressure (usually atmospheric). For pure substances it is identical with the melting point of the solid form. ▷ **melting point**

freight car retention cost ▷ **demurrage**

French mold ▷ **mold, French**

Freon II Du Pont's tradename for trichlorofluoromethane.

frequency The number of cycles per unit of time.

Fresnel diffraction pattern Pattern that occurs when the radiation intensity at any point is the result of disturbances coming directly to that point from all parts of the exposed wavefront. The plane at which the diffraction pattern is observed is at a relatively small distance from the diffracting element, as in contact printing.

Fresnel lens, circular A sheet of transparent material into which concentric grooves have been formed in such a pattern that light will be focused as with a lens.

Fresnel lens, linear A sheet of transparent material into which parallel grooves have been formed in such a pattern that light will be focused as by cylindrical lens.

Fresnel reflection The process by which radiant flux is reflected from an optically smooth interface between two dielectric media. The reflectance depends on the angle of incidence, the ratio of refractive indexes of the two media, and the state of polarization of the incident beam relative to the normal to the interface.

frettage A surface damage wear action caused by small movements between mating surfaces, as in a press fit. The constant oscillation removes any film that may have formed, which acts as an abrasive and causes more serious damage. Also known as fretting erosion or false brinelling. ▷ **wear**

fretting, fatigue ▷ **fatigue fretting**

friction The opposing force that develops when two surfaces move relative to each other. Basically, there are two frictional properties exhibited by any surface: static friction and kinetic friction. ▷ **antifriction**

frictional energy ▷ **energy due to friction**

frictional heat, screw plasticator Heat generated within the stock as a result of mechanical working that occurs between the screw rotation and the stationary barrel.

friction, coefficient of ▷ **coefficient of friction** and **kinetic coefficient of friction**

friction welding A method of welding thermoplastics whereby the heat necessary to soften the components is provided by friction using such techniques as spin welding or vibration welding.

frit **1.** A ground glass used in making glazes and enamels, also for making so-called frit seals. **2.** Finely powdered glass may be called a frit. The term is also used for finely ground inorganic minerals, mixed with fluxes and coloring agents which turn into a glass or enamel on heating. **3.** Frit use also includes additives for plastics.

frog skin Surface of plastics processed, usually molded, may have what can be called a pimply finish and interfere with the part's performance. Also called frog skin or frizzle surface.

frost line ▷ **extruder blown film "frost" line**

frothing ▷ **foamed frothing**

frozen-in stress ▷ **stress frozen-in** and **orientation**

frozen strain ▷ **residual strain**

fuel, synthetic ▷ **Fischer–Tropsch process, synthetic fuel** in regard to using fuel to produce plastics.

fuller's earth A porous colloidal aluminum silicate (clay) which has high natural adsorptive power, noncombustible, and gray to yellow color. Use includes elastomer plastic filler.

full hydraulic clamp ▷ **clamping hydraulic**

fume cleanup ▷ **incineration fume system**

function Mathematically, the term function denotes the dependence of one quantity on another, as an example, the area "A" of a circle depends on its radius "r" by the equation $A = \pi r^2$; it is said that "A" is a function of "r".

functionality The ability of a compound to form covalent bonds. Compounds may be monofunctional, difunctional, trifunctional, and polyfunctional; i.e., one, two, three, and many functional groups participating in a reaction, respectively.

functional layer In coextrusion, coinjection, laminated structure, and different layup systems, functional layers provide specific improvements in product performance. Functionl examples include physical and mechanical properties, higher temperature performance, improved appearance, chemical resistance, barriers (to resist permeation of oxygen, water, and/or other gases or liquids), etc.

fundamentals of design ▷ **design**

fungistats ▷ **biocide**

fungus resistance The resistance of a material to attack by fungi in conditions promoting their growth.

furan plastic FUN is a generic term for a thermoset resinous product that contains a heterocyclic unsaturated furan ring in its molecular structures. Pentosans from corn cobs and rice hulls are the main sources for the key ingredient, furfural. Commercially, the furfural alcohol polymer is the most important. All furan resins are dark in color and have a reddish-black appearance; when catalyzed to cure they become black.

Their biggest use in the corrosion-resistance field is in the manufacture of chemical-resistant cements and equipment. For instance, furan cements have been used for years to bond acid-proof brick. The surfaces of the brick may be saturated with alkaline substances and mineral or organic acids as well as many solvents, alone or in combination. Cements can be used in areas where it would be impossible to use other construction materials. They offer corrosion protection to concrete and steel structures, which lengthens their life. As pump base cements, furans can be used in chemical-processing plants, metal-finishing plants, petroleum refineries, fertilizer plants, and pulp and paper mills. The floors and walls of such structures as processing tanks, continuous-strip pickle lines, processing towers, collecting sumps, neutralizing tanks, pits, manholes, and tank cappings can be protected with furan cements. FUNs have also found wide use in the manufacture of grinding wheels and foundry molds. A typical furan-based composite possesses good heat and chemical resistance, excellent surface hardness, and is inherently nonflammable. However, its use in the form of fiber-reinforced plastics is still comparatively uncommon.

furnace An enclosed chamber or structure lined with firebrick or similar refractor and containing a heat source of coal, coke, gas, or electric elements.

furnace black A type of carbon blacks (additives) produced by burning natural gas or oil with a supply of air much lower than that required for complete combustion. Used extensively in rubber and plastic compounds. The high abrasion furnace black (HAF) is one of the most widely used types of carbon black of particle size about 30 nm giving medium to high reinforcement with processability improving and modulus increasing in compounds with increasing structure. High structure black (HAF-HS) is a standard choice for tire treads and other grades are useful for belt, mechanical extruded products, etc.

furnace gradient A furnace within which a known temperature gradient is maintained between the two ends. Sometimes known as a Rosenhain furnace.

furniture finish ▷ **finishing system, reduce solvent**

furniture market Plastics are used in different applications (see Table below) to provide different benefits based on material used that include high gloss, bright colors, decorate to simulate wood, wear resistance, etc.

fusible core ▷ **injection molding fusible core; soluble core molding; eutectic**

fusion **1.** In vinyl dispersions, the heating of a dispersion to produce a homogeneous mixture. **2.** The process of melting, usually the result of interaction of two or more materials. **3.** An endothermic nuclear reaction yielding large amounts of energy in which the nuclei of light atoms unite or fuse to form helium.

fusion bonding ▷ **hot-plate welding**

fusion Kling test A method for determining the relative degree of fusion of flexible vinyl sheets, coated fabrics, and thin sections of cast or molded parts, by immersing the folded specimen in a solvent and noting the time in which disintegration commences. Typical solvent systems use MEK, ethyl acetate, and carbon tetrachloride. The preferred system is one that will initiate degradation within 5 to 10 min on a fully fused specimen.

fuzz ▷ **fiber fuzz**

Examples of plastic applications in furniture (continued on next page).

Resin	Methods of fabrication	Applications
Acrylics	Forming; injection molding; machining	See-through furniture; lamps
ABS	Rotational and expansion casting; injection molding	Chair and sofa frames; cast chair shells; decorations; modern furniture
Alkyds	Spray or brush coating	Combined with other varnish or enamel resins
Cellulosics	Spray or brush coating	Lacquer coatings
Epoxies	Casting; lamination; compression molding	Imitation marble tabletops; decorative parts and trim; bonding adhesive; coating; molds
Polyamides	Injection molding	Drawer guides, bearings, wheels; fiber reinforcement

Examples of plastic applications in furniture (continued).

Resin	Methods of fabrication	Applications
Phenolics	Compression molding; lamination	Bonding agent for plywood; molded decorative panels
Polyesters	Casting; compression molding; reinforced-plastics molding; coating; machining	Tabletops and bases; imitation slate and marble; decorative fronts, trim, and panels; molded chairs; modern furniture
Polyethylene	Rotational molding; blow molding; injection molding	Molded chairs; drawer guides; institutional seating; door tracks
Polypropylene	Injection molding; extrusion; blow molding	Molded institutional chairs; shelving; decorative trim
Polystyrene	Injection molding; structural foam molding; extrusion	Wood-grain-patterned chair parts; panels; trim; mirror frames; drum tables; pedestals; other decorative and structural parts
Polyurethane		
rigid	Casting; expansion molding; RIM	Chair frames and shells; sofa frames; decorative trim and components; decorative and structural parts
flexible	Foam molding by slabstock extrusion or injection	Upholstery cushioning; modern furniture
coating	Spray or spread coating	Coating of upholstery fabrics
Poly(vinyl acetate)	Spray or brush coating	Coating; adhesive
PVC	Lamination; rotational casting; extrusion; injection molding; calendering; spread coating	Veneers and wood-grain-patterned film for lamination; other decroative and structural parts
Amino	Compression molding; laminating	Urea adhesives for plywood, particle board; melamine laminates for decorative tabletops

G

galling The type of wear caused by adhesion between two contacting materials that are welded together and then sheared by the relative motion between the sliding parts. Also called scuffing, scoring, or sizing.

galvanization The process of coating steel with zinc to give galvanic protection.

galvanizing Coating of a ferrous metal by passing it through a bath of molten zinc or by electro-deposition of zinc.

gamma A prefix denoting the position of a group of atoms or a radical in the main group of a compound.

gamma irradiation ▷ **sterilization, radiation**

gamma ray Electromagnetic radiation of extremely short wavelength and intensely high energy. Use includes radiation crosslinking polyethylene and other plastics, testing via X-ray, thickness sensors, etc.

gap ▷ **filament winding gap**

garbage ▷ **waste**

garbage in, garbage out GIGO is a phrase meaning that putting in invalid data produce invalid results. Today, several microprocessor-based controls for machinery will display GIGO when inappropriate data are entered by an operator.

Gardner impact test A falling dart impact test utilizing the kinetic energy of a free-falling projectile to assess the impact resistance of a plastic. A flat or contoured test specimen is rigidly clamped to a supporting metal ring and a metal dart of known weight is dropped onto the specimen from a known height. The end of the dart which impacts the specimen (the tub) is hemispherical, with a known diameter. This test is a variation of the falling-dart method; test specimens are supported by a metal ring but are not rigidly clamped in place. Also, the hemispherical tub is separate from the falling weight. The tub rests on the test specimen, serving as an anvil for the falling weight during impact.

To determine the impact resistance of a material, 20 to 26 identical specimens are each subjected to a single impact of known energy. This energy is varied incrementally by changing dart weight and drop height. Specimen failure is defined as a visible crack on the underside of the specimen. Typical units of energy are joules (J) or foot-pounds (ft-lb).

gas One of three states of aggregation of matter, having neither independent shape nor volume and tending to expand indefinitely. ▷ **oil and gas**

gas analysis, residual ▷ **residual gas analysis**

gas, black ▷ **carbon black**

gas chromatography GC separates, characterizes, and quantifies the vaporized components of samples using both conventional and pyrolysis techniques. This procedure is used for identification of plastics and elastomers by GC finger-printing, compositional analysis of copolymers and blends, and determination of residual monomers and highly evaporative agents. GC can be used to identify a polymer or the products of a degradative process, to monitor purity of monomers, to follow reaction rates and polymerizations, and to determine residual monomers. The term "gas chromatography" indicates that the moving phase is a gas. Gas–solid chromatography refers to the use of an active solid absorbent as the column packing. Gas–liquid partition chromatography refers to the use of a liquid distributed over the surface of a solid support as the column packing. ▷ **chromatography**

gas counter pressure molding ▷ **foamed injection molding, gas counter pressure**

gas injection molding ▷ **injection molding, gas**

gasket A shaped section or flat sheet of unreinforced or reinforced compounded plastic fitted between two matching faces to make a fluid or gas tight joint. ▷ **compressibility** and **creep behaviour, guidelines**

gasket versus moisture and EMI Many electronic black boxes require special gaskets on bulkhead mounting surfaces to seal out hostile environments, shield against electromagnetic interference (EMI), and establish solid electrical grounds for all components. With the boxes made of aluminum, it has become common practice to use filled elastomers as gaskets; they contain fine silver or silver-plated particles.

This approach works well except in situations where the filled elastometer fails to provide a complete seal against moisture. When even small amounts of moisture penetrate the seal, a galvanic cell forms, and corrosion of the aluminum surfaces results. To deal with this problem, a gasket is used which consists of a Monel mesh impregnated with a soft silicone gel. It shields against EMI and provides a good grounding path while inhibiting the entry of moisture. Little or no corrosion occurs even after very lengthy exposure to harsh environments. Monel as a mesh contains 70% nickel and 30% copper; it is widely used in non-sealing EMI gaskets.

gasoline tank permeability The usual plastic automobile fuel tank is a HDPE (HMW-HDPE, etc.) blow molded container that is chemically treated on the inside to meet performance requirements ▷ **barrier via chemical modification** and **sulfonation**. Since the 1960s, in addition to developments with these monolayer tanks, work to meet essentially emission-free tank test conditions [no more than 2 g of hydrocarbons in a 24 hr period under standard SHED (Sealed Housing for Evaporative Determination)] has continued in the use of multilayer construction using EVOH, nylon etc. as the barrier material on the inside. Cost performance of these coextruded constructions (such as HDPE, tie layers, nylon) that are thermoformed are now also available in limited quantities. In 1992 about 25% of all auto fuel tanks in North America were *blow molded* plastics compared to 70% in Europe and 5% in Japan.

gas permeability, coefficient of ▷ **coefficient of gas permeability**

gas-phase polymerization An ideal process for polymerization of polyolefins was introduced in the late 1960s. It entailed gaseous monomer and catalyst going into a continuous reactor, followed by removal of dry, free-flowing plastic powder ready to be pelletized and sold. Common to this technology are polymerization kinetics, heat transfer, mass transfer, and dynamics of powder mixing and transport. While previous processes required a reactor design that accommodated the first three, in a gas-phase reactor, powder dynamics must also be considered. With better than 98% reliability, a single catalyst particle produces a single powder particle. The catalyst is activated by contact with a cocatalyst. The monomer migrates and is adsorbed on the catalytic surface in the correct orientation (especially for propylene). The addition reaction is highly exothermic, 3.83 MJ/kg (917 kcal/kg) for ethylene, and this heat must be transferred from the heterogeneous solid catalyst to a gas stream, a boiling liquid monomer, or other cooler solid particles which rapidly remove the heat from the reactor. Failure to transfer this heat in a rapid, controlled fashion produces a fused, agglomerated mass accompanied by uncontrollably rising temperatures.

The management of heat transfer has been resolved in several ways. In a vertical stirred bed of particles, the gas is recirculated through an external heat exchanger and cooled (ethylene process) or partially condensed (propylene process). In a horizontal stirred bed, the flow of powder from one end to the other approaches plug flow, with cooling in each zone by sprays of condensed propylene. As an example, the Unipol process (Union Carbide) for HDPE or LDPE uses a fluidized-bed reactor. Use of the process has grown because of its simplicity and favorable economics. Its success depends on the use of highly active and selective catalysts.

gas pocket A pocket of gas or air entrapped in a plastic material.

gassing ▷ **breathing**

gas transmission rate GTR is the volume of a gas flowing normal to two parallel surfaces, at steady-state conditions, through unit area, under unit pressure differential, and the conditions of test (temperature, specimen thickness). An accepted unit of 1 GTR is 1 cm^3 (at standard conditions)/24 · h · m^2 · atm. The test specimen thickness and test temperature must also be stated.

gas welding ▷ **hot gas welding**

gate, mold ▷ **mold gate**

gauge A gauge (or gage) is an instrument for measuring and indicating such process variables as pressure, thickness, width, vacuum, etc. The many types of gauges are activated by mechanical, ultrasonic, electronic, magnetic, and/or pneumatic sensors. Some operate on the principle of automatic control (in-line). In materials technology, this term is often synonymous with thickness of film, sheet, etc. ▷ **sensor**

gauging film ▷ **extruder web gauging** and **sensor**

gauss The unit of magnetic induction in the cgs electromagnetic system. The gauss is equal to 1 maxwell per square cm or 10^{-4} tesla.

Gaussian distribution ▷ **statistical normal curve**

gaylord Plastic storage container that holds 1,000 lb (454 kg) of material.

gear extruder ▷**extuder, screw multiple type**

gear, fiber type ▷**fiber gear**

gear pump Gear pumps, also called melt or metering pumps, have been standard equipment for decades in textile fiber production and in postreactor polymer finishing. In the 1980s they established themselves in all kinds of extrusion lines. They consist of a pump, a drive for the pump, and pump controls, located between the screen pack (or screw) and the die. Two counter-rotating gears will transport a melt from the pump inlet (extruder output) to the pump discharge outlet (die) (see Fig. below). Gear rotation creates a suction that draws the metal into a gap between one tooth and the next. This continuous action, from tooth to tooth, develops surface drag that resists flow; so some inlet pressure is required to fill the cavity.

The inlet pressure requirements vary with material viscosity, pump speed, and mixing requirements. These pressures are usually less than 1,000 psi but cannot go below certain specified pressures such as 300 psi. An extruder specifically designed for use with a pump only has to "mix," with no need to operate at high pressures to move the melt. It only has to generate the low pump inlet pressure; thus it can deliver melt at a lower than usual heat, requiring less energy and often yielding a higher output rate. The positive displacement gear device pumps the melt at a constant rate. It delivers the melt to the die with a very high metering accuracy and efficiency. Pressure differentials as high as 4,000 psi between the pump inlet and discharge are common.

The pump's volumetric efficiency is 85 to 98%. Some melt is deliberately routed across the pump to provide lubrication, and some slips past the gears. An incomplete fill on the inlet side will show up as a fast change in output and pressure at the exit. The extended loss of inlet pressure can damage the pump by allowing it to run dry. Overpressurization at the inlet, caused by the extruder's sudden surge, will at least change the melt conditions and in extreme cases can be dangerous to both equipment and operator. However, closed loop pressure controls are available for the inlet and exit, which eliminate the problem. To prevent overfeeding the overpressure, the screw metering section should have a larger than normal barrel clearance.

Melt pumps are most appropriate when the screw and die characteristics combine to give a relatively poor pumping performance by the total system. This can happen when die pressures are low but more often occurs when they are extremely high (5,000–8,000 psi), or when the melt viscosity is extremely low. When pumps are used to increase the production rate by reducing the extruder head pressure without a corresponding increase in the screw speed, the extrudate solids content often is increased. The result is an inferior product. This problem often necessitates additional filtration, which serves only to increase pressure and may counteract many of the benefits expected from the pump, as well as increasing the financial investment even further.

Depending on the screw design, the extruder often creates pulses, causing the production rate to fluctuate. Some products usually cannot tolerate even minor fluctuations, and a pump often can assist in removing these minor product nonuniformities. In general, a pump can provide output uniformity of $\pm 0.5\%$ or better. Products include films (down to 0.75 mil thickness), precision medical tubing, HIPS with 3,500 lb/h output, fiber-optic sheathing, fibers, PET magnetic tape, PE cable jacketing (weight/ft

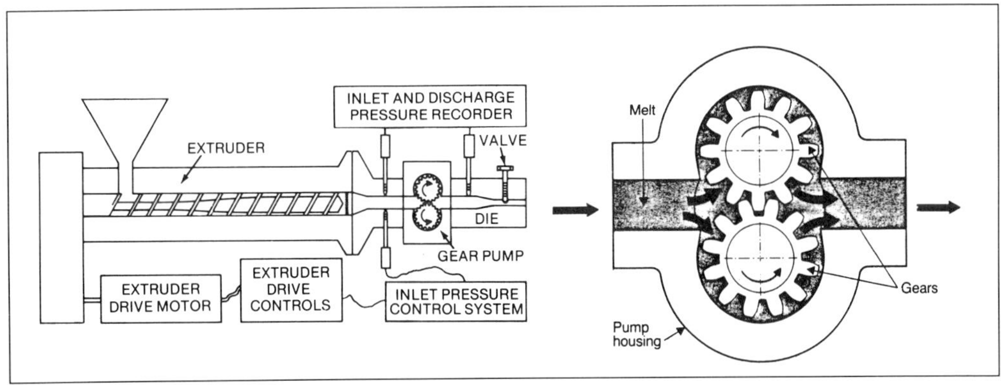

Schematics of gear pump used in an extruder processing line.

variation reduced from 14 to 2.7%), and so on.

Pumps are very helpful to sheet extruders who also do in-house thermoforming, as they often run up to 50% regrind mixes. This normally variable-particle-size mix promotes surging and up to 2% gauge variation. Pumps practically eliminate the problem and make cross-web gauge adjustments much easier. Pumps are recommended in: (1) most two-stage vented barrels where output has been a problem, such as ABS sheet; (2) extremely critical-tolerance extrusions, such as CATV cable, where slight cyclic variations can cause severe electrical problems; (3) coextrusion, where precise metering of layers is necessary and low pressure differentials in the pump provide fairly linear outputs; and (4) twin screw extruders, where pumps permit long wear life of bearings and other components, thus helping to reduce their high operating costs.

Besides improving gauge uniformity, a pump can contribute to product quality by reducing the resin's heat history. This heat reduction can help blown film extruders, particularly those running high viscosity melts such as LLDPE and heat-sensitive melts such as PVC. Heat drops of at least 20 to 30°F will occur. In PS foam sheet extrusion, a cooling of 10 to 15°F occurs in the second extruder as well as a 60% reduction in gauge variation by relief of back pressure. One must be aware that all melts require a minimum heat and back pressure for effective processing.

Pumps cannot develop pressure without imparting some energy or heat. The melt heat increase depends on melt viscosity and the pressure differential between the inlet and the outlet (or ΔP). The rise can be 5°F at low viscosity and low ΔP, and up to 30°F when both these factors are higher. By lowering the melt heat in the extruder, there is practically no heat increase in the pump when ΔP is low. The result is a more stable process and a higher output rate. This approach can produce precision profiles with a 50% closer tolerance and boost output rate 40%. Better control of PVC melt heat could increase the output up to 100%. In one case, the output of totally unstabilized, clear PVC meat wrap blown film went from 600 to over 1,000 lb/h with the use of the gear pump.

With pump use, potential energy savings amount to 10 to 20%. Pumps are 50 to 75% energy-efficient, whereas single screw extruders are about 5 to 20% efficient.

Although they can eliminate or significantly improve many processing problems, gear pumps cannot be considered a panacea. However, they are worth examining and could boost productivity and profits very significantly. Their major gains tend to be principally in (1) melt stability, (2) temperature reduction in the melt, and (3) increased throughput with tighter tolerances for dimensions and weights.

gear reducer ▷ **extruder motor and gear reducer**

geer oven An oven used in the accelerated aging of materials.

gel A gel is a cross-linked plastic network swollen in a liquid medium. Its properties depend strongly on the interaction of these two components. The liquid prevents the plastic network from collapsing into a compact mass, and the network retains the liquid. There are (1) a semisolid system consisting of a network of solid aggregates, in which liquid is held, and (2) the initial jelly-like solid phase which develops during the formation of a plastic from a liquid. Both types of gel have very low strengths and do not flow like a liquid. They are soft and flexible, and will rupture under their own weight unless supported externally.

Gels are important intermediates in the manufacture of plastics such as plastics, rubbers, films, adhesives, and membranes. They are used as an absorbent in disposable diapers, for water purification, and in chromatography and electrophoresis, where molecules are separated according to the speed with which they pass through or are expelled by the pores. Gels are widely used as implants in plastic surgery and for artificial and soft contact lenses.

gelatin **1.** Formation of a gel. **2.** In vinyl dispersions, formation of gel in the early stages of fusion. **3.** Gelations can be derived from collagen, the primary protein component of animal connective tissues, such as bone, skin, and tendon.

gelation The point in a plastic cure when the plastic viscosity has increased to a point such that it barely moves when probed with a sharp instrument; formation of infinitely large plastic networks in the reaction mixture. ▷ **plastisol**

gel chromatography GC assesses the composition and characteristics of a plastic or compound by separating its components on the basis of molecular size (molecular weight). Since the weights of the organic molecules in a material vary from a few million to a few thousand, polymers, oligomers, monomers, or additives (antislip, antistats, plasticizers, and many others), each component can be readily separated by size. The process requires that the sample be in a liquid form. Besides liquid

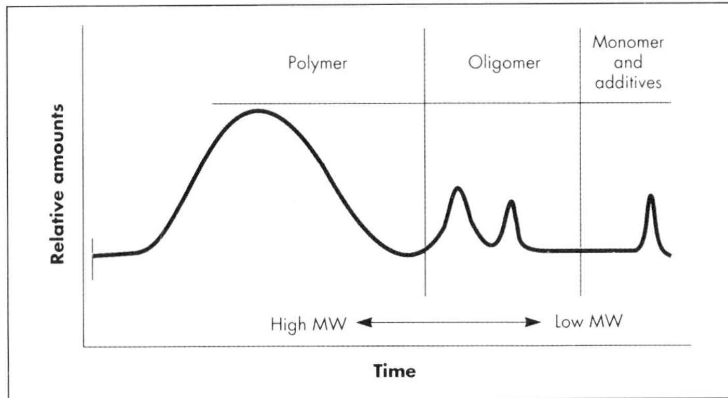

GC characterizes plastic by molecular weight distribution.

plastics, any organic solid material that can be dissolved can be analyzed. This includes virtually all thermoplastics and the unreacted components in B-stage thermoset plastics (prepregs, RPs) and crosslinkable compounds (polyesters, epoxies, phenolics, XLPE, etc.), and others.

Basically, GC processing involves pumping the liquified sample at a controlled rate though a filter medium made with a precise range of pore sizes. As the test progresses, the various components emerge at different times, in the order of their molecular weight (MW); the larger molecules come earlier because they penetrate less deeply into the pores of the filter. From the eluted stream develops a strip chart (or other output) showing a peak for each different MW material present (see Fig. above). The MW graph provides a "finger print" of the compound and can be used to check against graphs of acceptable batches of the same material.

Beyond the content comparison check, GC data offers valuable insights into the processability and performance of a compound, not obtainable from standard tests. One of the most useful is an analysis of the molecular weight distribution (MWD) of the plastic(s). ▷ **molecular weight distribution; thermal analysis; chromatography**

gel coating A quick-setting plastic used in fabricating processes to provide an improved surface for reinforced plastics. It is the first plastic applied to the mold after the mold release agent. The gel coat becomes an integral part of the finished RP. It produces a decorative, high protective, glossy, colored surface which requires little or no subsequent finishing. Techniques of application include: (1) *Paint on* Uncontrolled thickness–unadvisable, non-production method. (2) *Cup gun* Pre-catalyzed, air-atomized; throw away mixing cup; inexpensive, low-production method; gravity feed, pre-mixed. (3) *Pressure pot* Catalyst and gel coat under pressure; mixed at nozzle; air-atomized, and (4) *Airless sprayer* Similar (or the same as) spray-up equipment.

Quality control procedures include: (1) Preweigh gel coat and catalyst. (2) Mold should be a different color from the gel coat being sprayed so that uniform and complete coverage can be easily seen. (3) Use wet film gauge (should be, at minimum, 18($\pm$2) mils), and (4) check for proper catalyst levels.

gelling additive ▷ **thickening agent**

gel permeation chromatography GPC is used to provide the molecular weight distribution of a polymer by a fractionation technique. In the final forming operation, the behaviour of the plastic depends on whether the range of species is wide or narrow and whether or not the distribution is skewed. GPC (size exclusion) separates molecules in solution by size. The effective size of a molecule in solution is related closely to the molecular weight.

The separation is accomplished by injecting the sample solution into a continuously flowing stream of solvent that passes through highly porous, rigid gel particles, closely packed together. The pore sizes of the gel particles cover a wide range. As the solution passes through the gel particles, molecules with small effective sizes will penetrate more pores than will molecules with larger effective sizes, and therefore, will take longer to emerge and to be detected.

gel point The point at which a thermosetting system attains an infinite value of its average molecular weight. As shown in the Fig. on p. 336 its viscosity exhibits pseudoelastic properties. This stage may be observed from the inflection point on a viscosity-time plot.

gel polymerization effect ▷ **free-radical polymerization**

gel, silica ▷ **silica, synthetic**

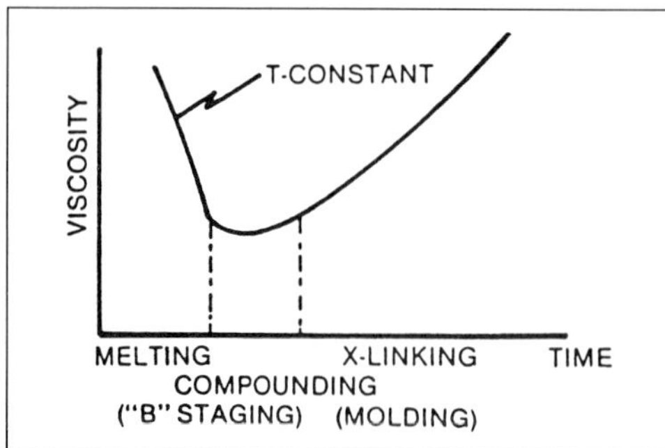

Viscosity change during curing of a thermoset; the B-stage represents the start of the heating cycle, which reduces viscosity, followed by a chemical crosslinking reaction, and solidification of the plastic.

gel test Thermoset curing behavior can be described in terms of the SPI Gel Test that is usually used with TS polyesters. A quantity of plastic is catalyzed and placed in a test tube. A thermocouple probe is immersed in the plastic and the assembly is then suspended in a constant temperature water bath maintained at 82°C (180°F). The time-temperature curve that develops is known as the exotherm curve. The temperature that rises rapidly as polymerization accelerates is a result of the "gel effect".This test permits comparing the influence of different amounts and kinds of catalysts, inhibitors, and accelerators.

gel time The period of time from the initial mixing of the reactants of a liquid material composition to the point in time when gelation occurs, as defined by a specific test method. ▷ **prepreg gel time**

general purpose GPs are sometimes used to denote types of plastics and molding compounds suitable for a wide range of applications.

generic algorithm GAs are a class of machine-learning techniques that gain their name from a similarity to certain processes that occur in the interactions of natural, biological genes. Thus, a GA is a method of finding a good answer to a problem, based on feedback received from its repeated attempts at a solution. The judge of GA's attempts is called an objective function. GAs do not know how to drive a problem's solution, but they do know, from the objective function, how close they are to a better solution.

Each attempt a GA makes towards a solution is called a gene: a sequence of information that can somehow be interpreted in the problem space to yield a possible solution. A GA gene is analogous to a biological gene in that both are representations of alternative solutions to a problem. In the biological world, the problem is evolutionary survival, and a particular gene represents one possible solution to survival within a competitive environment. In the digital world, the stated problem will vary from one application program to another, as well as the objective function. The coding of a GA's gene will also depend on the problem being addressed.

geodesic The shortest distance between two points on a surface.

geodesic isotensoid Constant stress level such as in a reinforced plastic contoured shape in any given filament at all points in its path. ▷ **filament winding geodesic-isotensoid contour**

geodesic ovaloid A contour for reinforced plastic end domes, that is, the fibers forming a geodesic line; the shortest distance between two points on a surface of revolution. The forces exerted by the filaments are proportional to meet hoop and meridional stresses at any point.

geogrid ▷ **geotextile**

Geolast Monsanto's tradename for an olefinic thermoplastic elastomer. This specialized TPE alloy uses nitrile rubber vulcanizates crosslinked with olefinics during processing.

geomembrane liner They can be categorized as: (1) solid waste containment; hazardous landfill, landfill capping, and sanitary landfill, (2) liquid containment; canal, chemical/brine pond, earthen dam, fish farm, river/coastal bank, waste-water, and recreation, (3) mining; heap leach pads and tailing ponds, and (4) specialities; floating reservoir caps, secondary containment, tunnel, and vapor barrier. The need to place protective barriers between man's sometimes destructive activities and earth has existed since the start of people. The market for these membranes during 1990 (U.S.) was at least 230 million lb (145 million kg) of 20 to 120 mil thick flexible membrane liners (FMLs). They have been used in various forms since the 1950s. Plastics used include medium to very low density PE, PVC, and chlorosulfonated PE (CSPE). Favored as a water barrier is PVC; in 30 mil thick sheets it provides a million times more permeation-resistance than 3 ft of clay as canal, dam, and lake liner. CSPE is important in reservoir caps due to its good weatherability. Both have helped to conserve water. In the 1980s, the growing volume and toxicity of solid and hazardous waste drew attention to medium density PE's ability to resist chemical attack. It was recognized that landfills entombed by liners above and below would best prevent leacate from polluting ground-water, the major source of drinking water throughout the world. ▷ **geotextile**

geometric dimensioning ▷ **dimensioning and tolerancing, geometric**

geometric metamerism ▷ **light metamerism**

geometry A branch of mathematics that deals with the measurement, properties, and relationships of points, lines, angles, surfaces, and solids.

Geon B. F. Goodrich's tradename for a group of polyvinyl chloride plastics, available as general purpose, rigid, flexible, insulation, compounded, latex, paste, polyblends, soluble types, etc.

geonet ▷ **geotextile**

geoscience Science dealing with the earth.

geosynthetic Use of synthetic materials, such as plastics, with the earth. ▷ **geotextile**

geotextile Geotextiles, as well as geonets, geogrids, and geomembranes, represent a major market for plastics. They appear in all manner of civil works, from roads to canals, from landfills to landscaping. In many cases they have been substituted for traditional materials, for example geonets for drainage gravel and geomembranes for clay. They often prove more durable, more easily worked, and more cost-effective than nature's products.

Using fabric to augment and enhance man-made structures is a concept that has been around for a while. Roman builders laid down mats to hold cobblestones. Jute sacks for sandbags were another early geotextile application. Today, many homeowners use geotextiles; they put a polyester sheet beneath sandboxes to permit drainage of water and prevent growth of weeds.

The primary plastics in geosynthetics are filament extruded polyester, nylon, polypropylene, and high density polyethylene. Then fabrics are made in both woven and nonwoven varieties. The former are characterized by high-tensile, high-modulus, and low-elongation traits; the latter, by high-permeability and high-elongation. Geogrids are relatively rigid lattice-like fabrics that are especially useful in reinforcement work. Geomembranes chiefly provide impermeable barriers. The choice of material depends on the application and chemical compatibility. Most of the products are designed to resist degradation from one or more sources, such as microorganisms, ultraviolet light, moisture, chemicals, and pressure.

Reinforcement and repair of roadways are major uses of geotextiles. For example, sheets of geotextiles can separate a stone base from the subgrade, improving a roadway's load-carrying capability. And in resurfacing badly cracked asphalt roads, geotextiles act as a moisture barrier to prevent surface cracking.

G-fiber ▷ **glass fiber types**

Gibbs indophenol test A test for detecting the presence of phenols in finished plastics.

Gibbs process One of the processes for making alkyd plastics.

gilsonite A black substance, resembling asphalt, used as an ingredient in the manufacture of cold molding compounds, paints, etc.

glass Glass has an unusual role in the technical world. It contains the most abundant elements of the earth (sand); it has a long history. Although basically a ceramic product, glass is also an amorphous inorganic plastic. Glass is always used in its elastic range (below glass transition temperature, T_g). Young's elastic modulus of all the silicate-based glasses is dictated by the Si-O bond and has values of 70,000 MPa (10×10^6 psi). If a major part of the SiO_2 is replaced by B_2O_3, the elastic modulus drops to 50,000 MPa. The strength of glass can be very high because it cannot undergo shear loads. However, its tensile behavior is severely affected by flaws or surface imperfections. The subtle effects of surface imperfections may be illustrated by measuring the strength of a freshly drawn (pristine) glass fiber without surface finish. It is possible to get values as high as 5,000 to 10,000 MPa (0.7 to 1.4×10^6 psi). However, if this type glass is touched by one's hand, by another fiber, or allowed to be in moisture-containing air a few hours, the strength drops drastically to less than 500 MPa. ▷ **glass fiber types** and **quartz fiber**

glass blowing The shaping of hot glass by air pressure. ▷ **blow molding**

glass-ceramic A polycrystalline silicate plastic, produced by the controlled crystallization of a largely amorphous glass, often embedded in a minor proportion of a residual amorphous glass composite. They combine the resistance to high temperatures of crystalline silicates with isotropic mechanical properties due to the fineness of the crystalline dispersion.

glass cloth Woven glass fiber material.

glass devitrified Glass with controlled crystallization.

glass fabric designations The wide variety of glass fiber yarns that can be produced made it necessary to have an exact system for yarn identification. Its nomenclature is based on both alphabetical and numerical designations. The first letter of the alphabetical designation identifies the glass fiber composition, the second letter specifies the filament type (C = continuous, S = staple, and T = texturized), and the third (and fourth) letter identifies the filament diameter.

The first series of numbers in the numerical designations represents 1/100th of the basic strand yield, whereas the second series (which resembles a fraction) specifies the number of single strands twisted together (the "numerator") and the number of the twisted yarns plied together (the "denominator"). The total number of basic strands in a plied yarn is determined by multiplying these two digits (zero being multiplied as 1), whereas its yield is obtained by dividing the basic strand yield by the total number of strands in the yarn. A third number combined with either an "S" or "Z" termination will sometimes be included as part of the numerical designations. This specifies the final number of turns per inch and the direction of twisting in the yarn.

For example, a yarn designated as ECG 150 4/2 3.8S contains E-glass continuous filament of G diameter with a basic strand yield of 15,000 yd/lb (33 Tex). Four basic strands of ECG 150 1/0 are twisted together ("Z" twist) to form ECG 150 4/04.0Z. Plying two of these strands together (using the "S" twist to create balance) results in ECG 150 4/23.8S yarn. Thus, this yarn contains 8 (4 × 2) basic 150 strands with a bare glass yield of 1,875 (15,000 ÷ 8) yd/bl (264 Tex). ▷ **glass fiber designations, composition; glass fiber types; twist direction of yarn; tex; yarn construction number**

glass fiber A fiber melt, spun from various types of glass, that has cooled to a rigid condition without crystallizing. A continuous filament is a glass fiber of great or indefinite length; a staple fiber is a glass fiber of relatively short length, generally less than 17 in. (430 mm) but also extremely short lengths (such as milled glass fibers). The length is dependent on the forming or spinning process used. The shorter fibers relate to type of auxiliary cutting equipment. Glass fibers are typically hard and relatively brittle, and have a conchoidal fracture. ▷ **spinnert** and **yarn construction number**

glass fiber and fabric surface treatment Continuous glass fiber strands intended for weaving are treated at the bushing with a starch-oil binder. A typical starch-oil binder consists of partially or fully dextrinized starch or amylose, hydrogenated vegetable oil, cationic wetting agent, emulsifying agent, and water. Small amounts of a film former (e.g., gelatin or polyvinyl alcohol), a small amount of fungicide (to prevent fungus growth), and a trace of disinfectant (e.g., pine oil) may also be added.

These binders protect the fibers from damage by lubrication during their formation and such subsequent textile operations as twisting, plying, and weaving. Fabrics from looms containing the original yarn binders applied at the bushing are usually not compatible with thermoset plastics; thus, they are used primarily in combination with thermoplastic resins and elastomer coatings as well as with various varnishes for flexible electrical insulation materials.

When used in conjunction with thermosetting plastic, the starch-oil binder acts as a barrier between the glass surface and the resin boundary. The hydrophilic character of the binder allows moisture to penetrate the glass-resin interface, which leads to degradation of composite properties in wet and humid environments. Therefore, the binder must be removed prior to combination with other materials. This is accomplished by exposing the fabric to carefully controlled time-temperature cycles, which allows efficient and complete removal of all organic matter. Unfortunately, fabrics in this heat-cleaned state manifest the weakness of incomplete interfacial bonding between the glass surface and the resin, which is especially important with respect to resistance to degradation in wet or humid environments. However, this weakness can be overcome by treating the fabric with such chemical sizing coupling agents as methacrylic chromic chloride complex, organosilanes, etc. ▷ **silane**

These coupling agents function by reacting at one end of the molecule with the hydroxyl groups on the glass surface and at the other end with the plastic. In this way, a chemical bridge is formed between the glass surface and the plastic matrix, thus imparting to the composite an improved resistance to moisture attack and degradation. Chemical functionality of the coupling agent determines the resistance to other environments (e.g., chemical and thermal).

glass fiber designations, composition The compositions of different glass fibers used with plastics are given in the first Table on p. 339 (by % weight).

glass fiber designations, diameter Stranded filament diameters are listed and defined in the second Table on p. 339.

glass fiber finish A material applied to the surface of glass fiber to improve the bond between the glass and plastic. ▷ **glass fiber and fabric surface treatment** and **coupling agent**

Glass fiber composition, by % weight.

Components	Grade of glass			
	A (High alkali)	C (Chemical)	E (Electrical)	S (High strength)
Silicon oxide	72.0	64.6	54.3	64.2
Aluminum oxide	0.6	4.1	15.2	24.8
Ferrous oxide	—	—	—	0.21
Calcium oxide	10.0	13.2	17.2	0.01
Magnesium oxide	2.5	3.3	4.7	10.27
Sodium oxide	14.2	7.7	0.6	0.27
Potassium oxide	—	1.7	—	—
Boron oxide	—	4.7	8.0	0.01
Barium oxide	—	0.9	—	0.2
Miscellaneous	0.7			

Glass fiber diameters.

Filament designation	Filament diameter	
	in. × 10^{-4}	μm
B	1.5	3.8
C	1.8	4.5
D	2.1	5
DE	2.5	6
E	2.9	7
G	3.6	9
H	4.2	10
K	5.1	13

glass fiber heat cleaned A condition in which glass or other fiber is exposed to elevated temperatures to remove preliminary sizings or binders not compatible with the plastic to be reinforced. ▷ **glass fiber and fabric surface treatment**

glass fiber history For over 3500 years, mankind has been aware of the fact that molten glass could be drawn into fine lengths (which were originally used for both making and decorating ornamental glass objects). Late in the 19th century, it was theorized that glass drawn into very fine fibers would be suitable for use in various textile applications. Although experimental glass fibers blended with silk fibers were woven into novel dresses and gowns in France and the U.S., commercial glass fiber did not become a reality until 1939 with the formation of Owens-Corning Fiberglass Corporation (an outgrowth of research efforts by Owens-Illinois and Corning Glass Works). About 25% of fiber glass is used in the reinforced plastics industry; the balance is in glass fiber insulation products.

glass fiber milled Continuous glass fiber strands are hammer milled into very short fiber lengths, generally 1/64 to 1/4 in. (0.40 to 6.35 mm). The actual lengths are determined by the diameter of the screen openings through which the fibers pass during milling. They are used as inert fillers for a variety of thermoplastic and thermoset plastics.

glass fiber production Both continuous and stable fibers are made by the same manufacturing process up until fiber drawing as shown in the Fig. on p. 340. Temperature of glass melt and actual production method vary depending on glass composition; generally about 1,260°C (2,300°F) with melts extruding though platinum multi-opening bushing.

glass fiber texturizing Glass fiber yarns (single or plied) can be subjected to a jet of air impinging on their surface, which causes random but controlled breakage of surface filaments and a general fluffing of the yarn surface. This is referred to as texturizing or bulking of the yarn. Although the mechanical damage to the surface weakens the yarn, its bulkiness allows greater plastic absorption. The presence of these fibers in woven fabrics is advantageous when low glass-to-plastic ratios and maximum fiber contributions are desired.

glass fiber types Glass fibers used in plastics are made up of different compositions ▷ **glass fiber designations, composition**. The *E-glass* constitutes the majority of textile fibers in production. It exhibits excellent electrical insulation properties. The *A-glass* provides good chemical resistance. For special applications in which neither A-glass nor E-glass fibers are suitable, compositions have been tailored to meet the desired performance characteristics. Where extremely good chemical resistance is desired, *C-glass* (sodium borosilicate) fibers can be used. For applications requiring high tensile strength (such as in structural reinforced plastics for the aircraft/aerospace industry, *S-glass* (magnesium aluminosilicate) fibers have been produced. The tensile strength (in single-fiber form) of S-

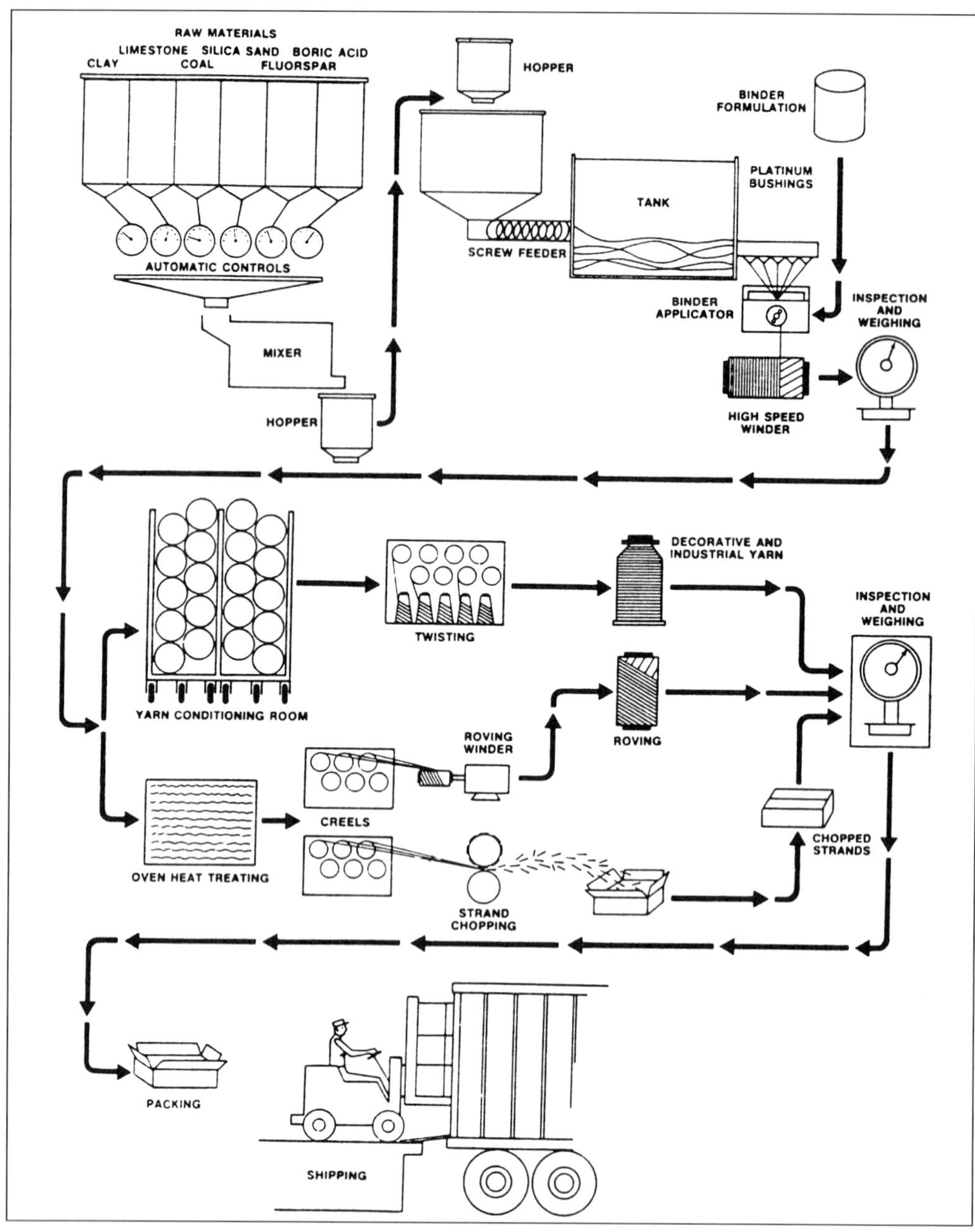

Example of a direct-melt glass fiber manufacturing process.

glass is approximately 40% higher than that of E-glass, thus resulting in higher-strength reinforced plastics. Furthermore, at elevated temperatures, S-glass will return significantly higher tensile strengths than E-glass. The S-glass fibers are available in high-performance grade and in moderate-cost/performance grade (S2-glass).

Several specialty glass compositions have been developed to take advantage of specific properties. The *M-glass* yields fibers having a high modulus of elasticity (16.4×10^6 psi = 113 GPa). Unfortunately, the presence of beryllia (beryllium oxide) in the glass prevented its commercialization.

The low-dielectric *D-glass* composition was developed for high-performance electronic applications. Its low dielectric constant relative to that of E-glass would be advantageous in such applications as radomes. The *L-glass* (lead glass) composition has the advantage of radiation protection; hence, it is suitable for use in x-ray technologists' gowns and as a tracer yarn in composites where nondestructive x-ray examination can verify fiber alignment. *AR-glass* (for alkaline-resistant glass) was developed for reinforcing cements and concretes.

The general overall industry glass fiber reinforcement available form can be listed in the following groups: (1) chopped strand mat: low cost general purpose reinforcements consisting of 2 in. (5 cm) long randomly distributed and bonded (about 2% plastic such as PS), (2) chopped strands: fibers range from $\frac{1}{2}$ to 2 in., (3) hammer milled: specially sized; use includes dispersion in casting plastics to prevent cracking, (4) needled mat: two in. chopped strands held together mechanically by needling on to a backing material, (5) overlay mat: a tissue of staple fibers lightly bonded to ensure wetting out plastic surfacing to provide a smooth surface, (6) reinforcement cord: loosely twisted cord made up of rovings used to provide edge reinforcements, such as ribbing, (7) roving: continuous strands wound parallel with no appreciable twist, (8) surfacing mat: a tissue of stable fibers well bonded which wets-out rapidly with plastics to provide plastic-rich surfaces, (9) woven cloth: woven continuous cloth used to provide high and directional strengths, (10) woven roving fabric: heavy fabrics from continuous filament in roving form that drape well, are quickly impregnated, and are intermediate in cost between mats and cloth fabrics, (11) woven tape: various thicknesses woven from continuous filament yarns, and (12) yarn: continuous filament yarn of various counts for weaving, braiding, and winding.

glass filament A form of glass that has been drawn to a small diameter and extreme length.

glass filament bushing The unit (platenum) through which molten glass is drawn in making glass filament.

glass flake Thin, irregular shaped flakes of glass used as a reinforcement with plastics.

glass former An oxide which forms a glass easily; also an oxide which contributes to the network of silica glass when added to it.

Glasshopper ▷ **railcar hopper**

glassine A thin, transparent, and very flexible paper obtained by excessive beating of wood pulp. It may contain an admixture such as urea-formaldehyde plastic to improve strength.

glass mat A thin mat of glass fibers with or without a plastic binder. ▷ **glass fiber types**

glass mirror art ▷ **silver spray plating**

glass, percent by volume ▷ **muffle furnace; reinforced plastic**

glass-plastic laminate ▷ **safety glass**

glass-rubber transition Alternate name for glass-transition temperature.

glass, safety ▷ **safety glass**

glass scrim ▷ **scrim**

glass switchable A window-size (or other size) glass changes from transparent to translucent with the flick of a switch. A thin film coated with liquid crystal droplets in a crystalline form makes this possible. The film is laminated with polyvinyl butyral (PVB) interlayers between panels of heat-strengthened flat glass. When voltage is applied, the liquid crystals along the curved inner surfaces of each droplet align to transmit light. The panel looks like a normal window. When voltage is off, the liquid crystals realign randomly, scattering light and turning the panel translucent. In the translucent or frosted mode, light passes through the glass, but because the molecules are not aligned, the glass appears milky.

glass tempered ▷ **tempered glass**

glass-transition Glass-transition is the reversible change in an amorphous polymer or in amorphous regions of a partially crystalline polymer from a viscous or rubbery condition to a hard and relatively brittle one. The transition generally occurs over a relatively narrow temperature region and is similar to the solidification of a liquid to a glass state; it is not a phase transition. Not only do hardness and brittleness undergo rapid changes in this temperature region but other properties, such as thermal expansion and specific heat, also change rapidly, which directly affect its rheological flow characteristics. This phenomenon has been called second order transition, rubber transition and rubbery transition.

glass-transition temperature The glass-transition temperature (T_g) is the point below which plastic behaves as glass does—it is very strong and rigid, but brittle. Above this temperature it is neither as strong or rigid as glass, but neither is it brittle. At T_g the plastic's volume or length increases (see Fig. on p. 342). The amorphous TPs have a more definite T_g.

The T_g is unique to amorphous TPs. It occurs at a relatively specific temperature that depends on pressure and specific volume and is lower than the melting point. Designers should know that above T_g the mechanical properties are reduced. Most noticeable is a reduction in

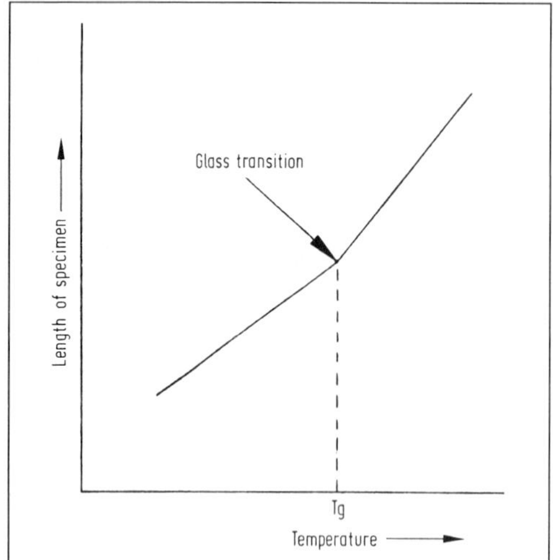

Example of effect of glass-transition temperature on the length (or volume) of thermoplastics.

stiffness by a factor that may be as high as 1,000. Therefore, the operating temperature of an amorphous TP is usually limited to below its T_g. Amorphous TPs generally have several transitions.

The glass-transition temperature is usually reported as a single value. However, the glass transition occurs over a temperature range and is kinetic in nature. Although many techniques are available, the measurement of T_g is more complex than is commonly appreciated. Some of the common techniques are dsc; calorimetry; dynamic mechanical methods including torsional braid, torsional pendulum, and Rheovibron; and spectroscopic techniques including NMR, infrared, and x-ray diffraction.

The glass transition temperature can be determined readily only by observing the temperature at which a significant change takes place in a specific electric, mechanical, or other physical property. Moreover, the observed temperature can vary significantly, depending on the specific property chosen for observation and on details of the experimental technique (for example, the rate of heating, or frequency). Therefore, the observed T_g should be considered to be only an estimate. The most reliable estimates are normally obtained from the loss peak observed in dynamic mechanical tests or from dilatometric data (ASTM D 20).

glass transition temperature and crystalline melting point Mechanical and physical properties are strongly dependent on temperature. A dramatic shift in properties is observed for linear amorphous polymers and copolymers at the glass-transition temperature T_g. At or above the crystalline melting point T_m, polymer chains exhibit extensive translational movement or flow. The melting of semicrystalline polymers as measured by a variety of techniques occurs over a temperature range, the upper point of which is taken as T_m; this is a function of a number of properties, including molecular weight, MWD, percent crystallinity, and dimensions of the polymer crystallites and others. The most common methods used to measure T_m are dsc, dta, and hot-stage optical microscopy; NMR, x-ray, and infrared techniques are less satisfactory.

glassy state The state of a plastic in which cooperative chain motions are "frozen", so that only limited local motions, such as side group rotations, are possible. Material behaves largely elastically since stress causes only limited bond angle deformations and stretching. Thus, it is hard, rigid, and often brittle with a modulus of about 10^8 to 10^{10} Pa. Such behavior is found in amorphous plastics at about 20°C or more below the T_g. Deformation is usually about 1%, so the plastic is subject to brittle fracture with a potential low impact strength. However, there can be limited plastic deformation. ▷ **orientation and crystallization**

glaze A mixture similar to porcelain enamel applied to different substrates.

glitter A group of special decorative materials consisting of flakes large enough so that each separate flake produces a plainly visible sparkle or reflection. They are incorporated directly into the plastic during compounding.

gloss The shine or luster of the surface of a material; the degree to which a surface simulates a perfect mirror in its capacity to reflect incident light. It may be characterized by the ratio between the light flux scatter within a specified solid angle of the geometrical reflection direction (the specular direction) and the incident flux, for one or more angles. Usually an angle of 45 or 60 is used.

glossmeter A device for measuring the gloss of a plastics specimen.

gloss test In a glossmeter, a bright light is reflected off a specimen at an angle and the luminance, or brightness, of the reflected beam is measured by a photodetector. Most commonly, a 60° angle is used. Shinier materials can be measured at 20°, and matte surfaces at 85°. The glossmeter is calibrated by using a black glass standard with a gloss value of 100; plastics have lower values (ASTM D 523 for rigid plastics).

ASTM D 2457 provides a method for measuring the gloss of films, which provide special problems in maintaining a flat plane to measure reflectance. The specimen is held flat against a plate in the sample holder by vacuum. In addition to the 60° and 20° regimes, a 45° regime is used for intermediate- and low-gloss films.

glue Over a century ago, glues started with an impure form of a gelatine obtained by the action of heat and water on animal tissue such as bones and hides. Generally, glues absorb cold water and dissolve in hot water. Among many types available today are fish glue, vegetable glue, casein glue, and particularly plastic glues. Plastic glues are usually adhesives.

gluing ▷ **adhesive**

gluten A tough, rubbery substance of grey-brown color used in the production of adhesives and amino-acid production.

glyceride An ester of glycerol and fatty acids in which one or more of the -OH groups of the glycerol have been replaced by acid radicals.

glycerol A clear, colorless, syrupy liquid obtained from saponification of fats in the soap industry, and used as the basis of one of the groups of plasticizers.

glycerol ester Products of the esterification of glycerol with acids. They are used as plasticizers in the production of certain plastic compounds.

glycerol mono-lactate triacetate A liquid plasticizer compatible in all proportions with cellulose acetate where it imparts flexibility without tackiness. It increases gasoline resistance and, in cellulose acetate powders, gives sharp and flexible moldings.

glycol A term for dihydric alcohols, which are similar to glycerol used in many plastic materials. When an alcohol contains two hydroxyl (OH) groups, it is known as a glycol. For example, when a second hydroxyl group is introduced into ethyl alcohol, the resulting product is known as ethylene glycol. The additional hydroxyl group greatly increases the ability of compounds to take up and hold moisture from the atmosphere, raises their boiling points about 100°C, and decreases correspondingly to their evaporation rates. They are also useful in lowering the freezing point of water (used in chillers, autos, etc.) and they have excellent solvent properties.

glycolysis Partial breakdown in the presence of glycol of reaction or condensation type plastics into monomer, which may in turn be repolymerized.

gold Chemically nonreactive, attacked by chlorine and cyanide solutions in the presence of oxygen. Use includes plating mold cavities when processing with certain plastics and/or to obtain surface finishes on processed plastics.

gold leaf stamping ▷ **hot stamping**

gondola **1.** It hangs from an airship or air-balloon; includes use of different plastics including reinforced plastics primary structure. **2.** A freight car with sides and ends but without a top covering.

goniometer An instrument devised for measuring the angle through which a specimen is rotated.

good manufacturing practice Quality, or the lack of it, is important with the business community. Many meaningful, well intended quality improvement programs start out strong and enthusiastic, only to stumble just a few weeks after the starting date. Basically, first identify goals and tasks to be performed on products (▷ **design**), equip your organization, and staff it to meet all requirements. Production procedures have to be set up so that a target of zero defects can be met. This action is called Good Manufacturing Practices (GMP) or Current Good Manufacturing Practices (CGMP), in other words keep GMP current.

Even though GMP and CGMP have specifically been set up by FDA government regulations to control products such as drugs, medical devices, and foods, they can be used by all manufacturers, including designers to ensure that products will meet performance requirements. The objective is to provide greater quality assurance than the mere testing of a few samples. There needs to be assurance that the samples tested are truly indicative of every remaining single unit in the batch. Such confidence is only achievable through operational assurance against contamination, mix-ups, and presence of defects.

In order to obtain confidence in the quality of finished products, one must first have assurance that every component is acceptable for use in the manufacturing process. While the supplier (resins, components, etc.) may not be directly responsible for compliance to CGMP, contracts for purchase should have certain product liability risks with intent to produce zero defect parts. ▷ **process control; statistical process control; testing; testing inadequacies; process validation; quality control**

good manufacturing practice and design controls The FDA's GMP regulation, that has been in use for decades in manufacturing medical devices, is to include design controls. DCs make sense in the medical and other businesses in that it is always better to design quality up front than to solve problems after products are brought to market ▷ **FALLO approach**. FDA data shows that 44% of all medical device quality-related problems resulting in recalls between FY 1983 and FY 1989 were related to poor or inadequate design.

Gossamer Albatross airplane An historic feat occurred June 12, 1979 when the Californian Bryan Allen became the first to fly 23 miles (38 km) across the English Channel by using only his muscles to power the practically all-plastic craft. It took 2 hr. 54 min., moving at an average height of about 30 ft. (9.2 m) from Cape Gris Nez, France, to Folkestone, England. Dr. Paul Mac Cready, a California scientist, designed the craft and collected a $200,000 prize from the British industrialist Henry Kremer (to encourage human-powered flight that goes back to da Vinci's dreams). This project was undertaken by Du Pont which used lightweight, durable engineering plastics that produced a 70 lb (32 kg) craft with a 96 ft. (29 m) wingspan. *Mylar* polyester film covered the wings and also enclosed the pilot's compartment (see Fig. below). Cords of *Kevlar* aramid fibers connected the controls and also braced interior structures. *Delrin* acetal was used in the pulleys. The craft was powered by a single rear positioned propellor connected by a bicycle-like pedalling device operated by the seated pilot. Allen, a bicycle racer, provided the required 0.25 hp.

Gossamer Albatross airplane.

Previously (August 23, 1977), the Gossamer Condor made aviation history, when Allen pedaled it over a 1.35 mile (21 km), figure-eight course in $7\frac{1}{2}$ min. to win the $50,000 Kremer prize. Power input was only 0.33 hp.

Gough-Joule effect When rubber (elastomer) is stretched adiabatically (without heat entering or leaving the system), heat is evolved. The effect was originally discovered by Gough in 1805 and rediscovered by Joule in 1859. ▷ **Wiegand pendulum**

government regulatory agencies ▷ **regulatory agencies**

grading Size distribution of fillers and reinforcements.

graft copolymer Basically a chain of one type of polymer (plastic) to which side chains of a different type are attached or grafted, such as polymerizing butadiene and styrene monomer at the same time. As an example, a polymer which consists of a polymer chain (poly-A) to which are attached one or, usually, more polymer chains of another polymer (poly-B). Block copolymers may be considered as graft copolymers in which the B chains are attached to the ends of the A chains. The copolymers are generally formed by forming active sites on Poly-A in the presence of monomer B, which are capable of initiating polymerization of monomer B. However, unlike block copolymers, it is usually difficult to attach the poly-B chains in a regular manner or to control their growth to chains of equal length. Thus, the resultant copolymer is rather heterogeneous in structure. Also, frequently homopolymerization of monomer B also occurs and the homopolymer is difficult to separate from the copolymer. Grafting sites may be produced by generating free radicals on Poly-A by transfer grafting, activation grafting, or by chemical grafting. Alternately, ionic grafting sites may be introduced giving anionic or cationic grafting. The grafted monomer can provide advantages such as increased dyeability in fibers by having a polar grafted monomer such as acrylic acid or improved membranes such as cellulose graft copolymers (for desalination). These are examples of surface grafting.

grafting **1.** A deposition technique whereby organic plastics can be bonded to a wide variety of other materials, both organic and inorganic in the form of films, fibers, particles, and other shapes. **2.** Grafting of two dissimilar materials often involves a third plastic whose functions is to improve the compatibility of the two principal components. The "compatibilizer" material is a grafted copolymer consisting of one of the principal components and similar to the other component. The mechanism is similar to that of soap improving the solubility of a greasy substance in water. The soap contains components that are compatible with both the grease and water. **3.** ▷ **radiation-induced reaction**

grafting efficiency In graft copolymerization, the ratio of the amount of a monomer grafted onto a polymer to the total amount of monomer polymerized as both grafts and homopolymer.

graft polymer A polymer (plastic) comprising molecules in which the main backbone chain of atoms has attached to it at various points side chains containing different atoms or groups from those in the main chain. The main chain may be a copolymer or may be derived from a single monomer.

grain **1.** The smallest unit of weight in the avoirdupois system; 1 grain = 0.0648 gram, 1 ounce = 437.5 grains. **2.** Crystalline particles of metals. **3.** Wood grain on plastics; application is by hand, roller coating, printing, etc. **4.** Any cereal plant, such as wheat, corn, barley, etc.

granular polymerization ▷ **suspension polymerization**

granular powder Particles having about equidimensional nonspherical shapes.

granular structure Nonuniform appearance of finished plastic material due to retention of, or incomplete fusion of, particles of composition, either within the mass or on the surface.

granulating In practically all processing plants, it is necessary to reclaim reprocessable thermoplastic scrap, flash, rejected parts and so on. If possible, the goal is to eliminate "scrap" because it has already cost money and time to go through the process; granulating just adds more money and time. Different types of granulators are available from many different suppliers, and selection of a granulator depends on such factors as the type of plastic used, the type of reinforcement, product thickness and shape (see Fig.), and so on. With granulation (metal-to-metal cutting action) usually metal contamination is included in the output that could only be microscopic. There are some serious units in which subsystem granulators incrementally reduce the size from a large one to the required small size.

An easy "cutting" unit is required, to granulate with minimum friction, as too much heat will destroy the plastic ▷ **residence time**. General-purpose types have definite limitations. As stressed throughout this book, blending with virgin material definitely influences, and can significantly change, melt processing conditions and the performance of the end product. Recycled material is denser and usually has a variable-size regrind that could affect the product's properties, as shown in the Fig. on p. 346.

granulator Machine used to reclaim scrap, waste, and rejected parts by reducing the particle size so that it can be reprocessed. Also called grinders and recyclers. ▷ **recycling film and sheet**

granule Small ceramic or natural colored mineral pellets or grains used as fillers in plastics.

graphical database A data file that pictorially represents the material in the file such as chemical structure, plastic compound mix, product design, production line set up, etc.

graphic art Plastics play various roles in the graphic arts, both as media of artistic expression and in printing. Techniques of the graphic arts are also applied to plastics for functional or aesthetic purposes. ▷ **design graphics** and **decorating**

graphic association The National Computer Graphic Assoc. (NCGA) is the administrator for the computer picture-level benchmark (PLB) project. ▷ **computer picture-level benchmark**

graphic design ▷ **designing with graphics; computer-aided design drafting; computer picture-level benchmark**

graphic molecular structure ▷ **computer-aided molecular graphics**

graphite A crystalline allotropic form of carbon.

graphite fiber They have been made from a number of precursors; they are principally produced from polyacrylonitrile (PAN), pitch, and rayon. They derive their enormous strength and

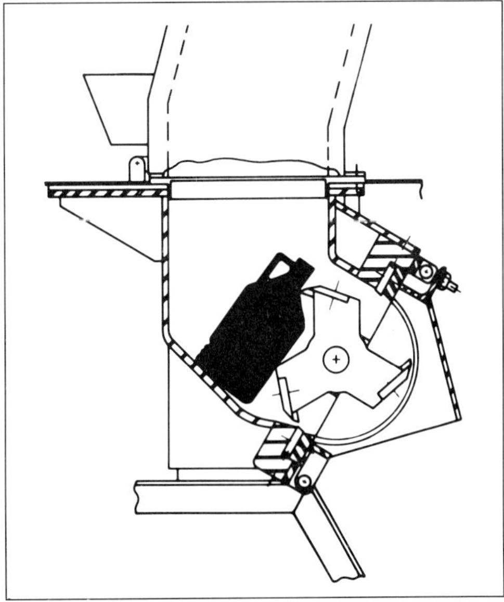

Different types of granulators are available, including those used to properly granulate blow molded bottles.

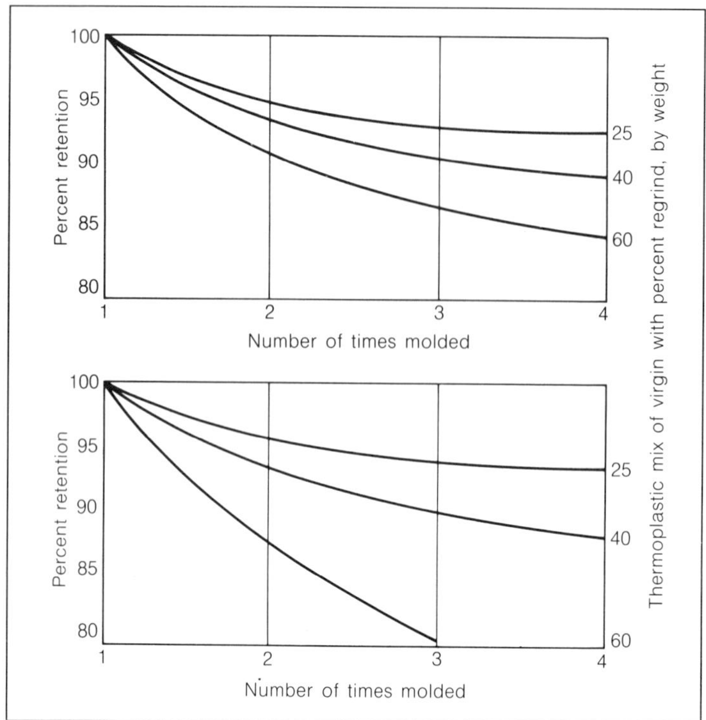

Examples of potential effects of regrind on performance of injection molded thermoplastic mixed with virgin plastics. *Top*: tensile strength. *Bottom*: impact strength.

modulus from the alignment of covalently bonded basal planes of carbon atoms along the axis of the fiber. The fibers are made by an oxidation, carbonization, and graphitization process which produces the graphite structure. ▷ **carbon fiber; reinforcement; oxidation**

graphite fiber and carbon fiber characteristics The terms are often used interchangeably, though they do differ. The basic differences lie in the temperature at which the fibers are made and heat treated, in the amount of elemental carbon produced, and mechanical properties. Carbon fibers typically are carbonized in the region of 1,315°C (2,400°F) and assay at 93 to 95% carbon. The graphite fibers are graphitized at 1,900 to 2,480°C (3,450 to 4,500°F) and assay at more than 99% elemental carbon. Regarding properties ▷ **reinforcement**

graphite lubricant A crystalline form of carbon, having a sheet-like plastic structure and consisting of layers of fused benzene rings at a separation of 3 to 4 A. The intermolecular forces between layers are low, thus they readily slide past each other providing the lubricating property. It has extensive electron delocalization resulting in high electrical conductivity. It is useful as a conducting and lubricating filler in plastics.

graphite mesophase An intermediate phase in the formation of carbon from a pitch precursor. This is a liquid crystal phase in the form of microspheres. After prolonged heating above 400°C (750°F), they coalesce, solidify, and form regions of extended order. Heating to above 1,900°C (3,450°F) leads to the formation of the graphite structure.

graphite, pyrolytic A dense, nonporous graphite stronger and more resistant to heat and corrosion than ordinary graphite; exhibits tensile strengths 5 to 10 times higher than commercial graphite and maintains its strength above 3,000°C.

graphitization The process of polymerization in an inert atmosphere at temperatures in excess of 1,925°C (3,500°F), usually as high as 2,480°C (4,500°F), and sometimes as high as 5,400°C (9,750°F), converting carbon to its crystalline allotropic form. Temperature depends on precursor and properties desired.

grave-from-cradle ▷ **cradle-to-grave**

gravimetric analysis ▷ **differential gravimetric analysis**

gravimetric feeding-blending ▷ **extruder gravimetric feeding-blending**

gravity acceleration Gravitational pull or acceleration due to gravity is 32.16 ft/s/s (9.8 m/s/s). ▷ **altitude chart**

gravure printing Depositing ink on plastic film, sheeting, or products from depressions of a specific depth, pattern, and spacing, which have been either mechanically or chemically engraved into a printing cylinder. It is capable of applying finely detailed prints in one or more colors on continuous film or sheet rolls at high speeds by direct or reverse printing. ▷ **rotogravure; sheet-feed gravure; offset gravure**

gravure printing narrow web With shorter press runs and just-in-time (JIT) concept, there are narrow-web gravure presses that will reduce job-changeover time and material waste. The movement towards narrow web, which typically refers to web widths up to 80 cm (32 in.), started in Europe and had been adopted in the U.S., etc.

gray ▷ **radiation absorbed dose**

gray goods ▷ **greige goods**

Greek alphabet See Table below for symbols.

The Greek alphabet.

alpha	α	A	nu	ν	N
beta	β	B	xi	ξ	Ξ
gamma	γ	Γ	omicron	o	O
delta	δ	Δ	pi	π	Π
epsilon	ε	E	rho	ρ	P
zeta	ζ	Z	sigma	σ	Σ
eta	η	H	tau	τ	T
theta	θ	Θ	upsilon	υ	Υ
iota	ι	I	phi	ϕ	Φ
kappa	κ	K	chi	χ	X
lambda	λ	Λ	psi	ψ	Ψ
mu	μ	M	omega	ω	Ω

green dot Means that solid-waste materials plastics, etc. can be recycled. ▷ **recycling packaging via DSD**

greenhouse effect Gradual rise in average global temperature due to absorption of IR radiation principally because of the increasing amount of carbon dioxide in the air, which retards dissipation of heat from the earth's surface.

green strength ▷ **tensile green strength**

greige goods Any fabric before finishing as well as any yarn or fiber bleaching or dyeing. Also called grey goods.

grex system A universal yarn numbering system in which the yarn number is equal numerically to the weight in grams of 10,000 meters. The lower the grex number, the finer the yarn. ▷ **yarn construction number**

Griffith theory This theory expresses the strength of a material in terms of crack length and fracture surface energy. Brittle fracture is based on the idea that the presence of cracks determines the brittle strength and crack propagation occurs. It results in fracture rate of decrease in elastically stored energy that at least equals the rate of formation of fracture surface energy due to the creation of new surfaces. It follows from the Griffith criterion that the breaking strength of a plate under uniaxial tension perpendicular to the fracture is:

$$\sigma_B = (2E_\gamma/\pi c)^{1/2}$$

for plane stress and

$$\sigma_B = [2E_\gamma/\pi c(1-\nu^2)]^{1/2}$$

for plane strain

where E = Young's modulus; γ = specific surface energy; c = one-half of the crack length; ν = Poisson's ratio.

grinding Removal of material usually by means of rotating rigid wheels containing abrasives.

grinding, centerless A technique for machining parts (such as plastic rods) having a circular cross-section, consisting of grinding the rod which is fed without mounting it on centers. Grinding is accomplished by working the material between wheels, which rotate at different speeds, the faster wheel being the abrasive wheel which does the cutting. Variations of the basic concept can be used to grind internal surfaces.

grinding media Balls ranging in diameter from $\frac{1}{4}$ to 2 in. (1 to 8 mm) but can be smaller to larger depending on application and type ball mill used. They are made of porcelain, flint, bronze-alumina, alloy steels, and/or different plastics (soft to hard, such as polyethylene to phenolic). They perform an efficient size reduction action, surface polishing action, and/or removal of flash from different type plastic products.

grinding-type plastic A vinyl plastic which requires grinding to effect dispersion in plastisols or organosols.

grit blast A surface treatment of a mold in which steel grit or sand materials are blown on the walls of the cavity to produce a roughened surface such as in a blow mold. For certain blow molding plastics, air escape from the mold is easily accomplished. Special appearances can be obtained on molded parts using different processes (injection, compression, blow, etc.). ▷ **abrasion cleaning**

grocery bag Polyethylene plastic grocery sacks, or "T-shirt" bags as they are known in the packaging trade, are stronger than paper bags, take up 30% less storage space, provide water and puncture resistance, etc. They are also recycleable.

grooved feed ▷ **extruder grooved feed**

grooved metal roller A type of film spreader or stretcher roller is the grooved metal idler roll which is frequently also used for tracking as well. A variation of this roller consists of PTFE tape wrapped on a smooth metal roll to create a grooved surface. The grooved metal roller (see Fig. below) has opposing, etched spiral grooves, which start at the roll's center and spiral toward the ends. As the roll turns, air flow, which follows the direction of the grooves along the metal surface, is generated. Since the groove pattern proceeds from the center of the roller out, the air travels in the same path, forcing web wrinkles out towards the ends of the roll.

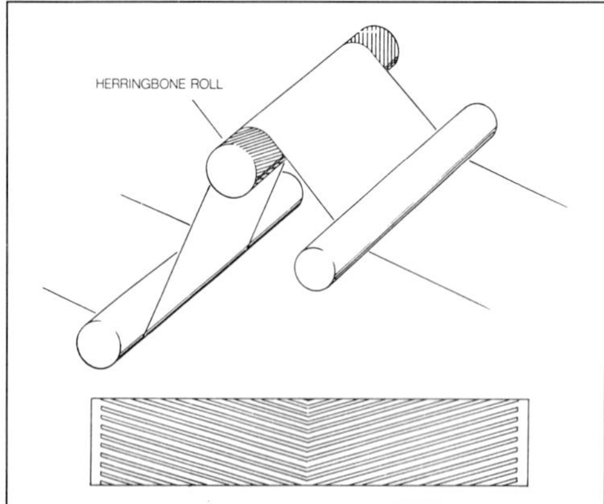

Grooved metal roller using herringbone pattern. This idler roll will assist in reducing the apparent wrinkles coming from an irregular web.

The major advantages of this roll are that it is free-turning and existing idler rolls can be easily modified for this application. However, as web processing line speeds have increased, this roller has been losing effectiveness. Because the roll has a smooth surface, it has a low coefficient of friction. Subsequently, as line speeds increase, so does the air flow, causing the web to slide over without making complete contact with the roll. If the roller does not make contact with the web, it does not rotate. So its ability to remove wrinkles is insignificant.

The surface of this type roller also has other limitations for certain applications. For films, metallized, printed, and coated materials, the roller's hard surface can produce undesirable marks on the substrate as its passes the grooves. ▷ **extruder web wrinkle free**

grooved rubber roller The same basic principle of the grooved metal roll has been applied to hard rubber rollers to improve performance of grooved rollers. With a hard rubber surface, the depth of the grooves can be increased for greater air flow and consequently increased spreading action. Rubber also has a higher coefficient of friction, so line speeds can be increased without the web completely floating over it. However, these rollers are still limited by line speeds. Although the web maintains contact at higher speeds than the metal roller, if speeds get too high, the roller has the same restrictions as the metal idler rollers. ▷ **extruder web wrinkle free**

gross density ▷ **density, gross**

guide pin ▷ **mold guide pin**

guillotine A cutter that uses a wide-blade operating in an up-down chopping motion used in different plastic fabricating operations, particularly for extruder take-off cutting operations. Its straight downward chop can distort some types of tubing and semi-soft products, and the blade could interrupt the extrudate travel long enough to disturb upstream equipment. However, it is still a satisfactory cutting method for some slow-speed elastomer extrusion lines. ▷ **machining**

gum An amorphous substance or mixture which, at ordinary temperatures, is either a very viscous liquid or a solid which softens gradually on heating, and which either swells in water or is soluble in it. Natural gums, obtained from the cell walls of plants, are carbohydrates or carbohydrate derivatives of intermediate molecular weight.

gunk A premixed charge of premix molding which contains all of the ingredients for molding, usually chopped glass fiber roving, plastic, pigment, filler, and catalyst. ▷ **premix molding compound** and **bulk molding compound**

gusset **1.** Inward fold in blown plastic film which reduces the width of the tube when collapsed. **2.** A piece used to give added size or strength in a particular location of a part. ▷ **rib**

gutta-percha Tree producing material that is a tough natural plastic substance from the latex of several Malaysian trees (*genera payena* and *palaquium*) of the *sapodilla* family that resembles natural rubber but contains more plastic.

gypsum A natural hydrated calcium sulphate used in the production of plaster-of-Paris.

H

habit The characteristic mode of growth or occurrence of a crystal; characteristic assemblage of forms (free faces) at crystallization leading to a usual appearance.

Hagen-Poiseuille law Many methods that are commonly used to measure viscosity make use of the flow through capillary tube that includes the H-P law. ▷ **rheometer, capillary on-line**

hairline crack Small fissures in plastic products (such as coatings) often caused by uneven cooling or curing during processing. ▷ **reinforced plastic hairline craze**

halftone photography It is done through the grid pattern of a halftone screen. The original halftone screen consisted of a grid of straight lines or bars on two sheets of optically flat glass cemented together at right angles. The lines were of the same width as the spaces. Screens with 60 to 100 lines per inch are used for printing pictures in newspapers, 120 to 150 in magazines and commercial printing, and 150 to 250 for high quality process color printing. The lines per inch correspond to the screen ruling of the halftones produced by the screen. Glass screen photography requires precision equipment with experienced expert craftsmen. It has become practically obsolete, and all halftones now are produced by contact screens or electronic dot generation.

halocarbon plastic Plastics based on material made by the polymerization of monomers composed only of carbon and a halogen or halogens.

halogen These are groups of elements headed by fluorine in the vertical Periodic Table; namely fluorine, chlorine, bromine, iodine, etc. (listed in order of their activity with fluorine being the most active). The word means "salt forming".

halogenation Incorporation of one of the halogen elements, usually chlorine or bromine, into a chemical compound.

hammer mill A crushing or shielding device consisting of four or more rectangular metal hammers or sledges mounted on a rotating shaft, the hammers being free to swing on pins. As the shaft rotates, the hammers impact the material introduced from above, crushing and/or bouncing it against a stationary breaker plate. The resultant material is carried downward. Like a plastic granulator, it has a porous grid (holes of desired size in a steel plate); those that are too large do not pass through and return to the hammer action to be made smaller. Since the 1950s, this type mill has been used to produce thermoset (usually polyester, but also phenolics, DAP, etc.) plastic molding compounds from B-stage prepreg sheet materials. The action in this mill is not sufficient to overheat the B-stage material. Its major use includes crushing or shredding coal, limestone, and other mineral aggregates, as well as wood, to produce fillers for plastic compounds. ▷ **fiber, milled**

hand lay-up molding A reinforced plastic fabrication method in which reinforcement layers are placed in a mold by hand, then cured to the formed shape.

This is the oldest, and in many ways the simplest and most versatile, process; but it is slow and very labor-intensive. It consists essentially of the hand tailoring and placing of layers of (usually glass fiber) mat, fabric, or both on a one-piece mold and simultaneously saturating the layers with a liquid TS resin (usually polyester). The assemblage is then cured with or without heat, commonly without pressure. Alternatively, preimpregnated B-staged, partially cured dry material (such as SMC) may be used, but in this case heat is applied with the probability of applying low pressure.

Fabrication begins with a pattern from which a mold is made. The mold may be of any low-cost material, including wood, hard plaster or hydrostone, concrete, a metal such as aluminum or steel, and glass fiber reinforced polyester or epoxy. If only a few parts are to be made, a single mold will suffice; otherwise multiple molds may be required. If the volume is large enough and speed is important, heating elements such as lines for steam or other fluids, or electrical heat units, may be incorporated. Automated equipment also may be installed (see first Fig. on p. 350). The mold may be male

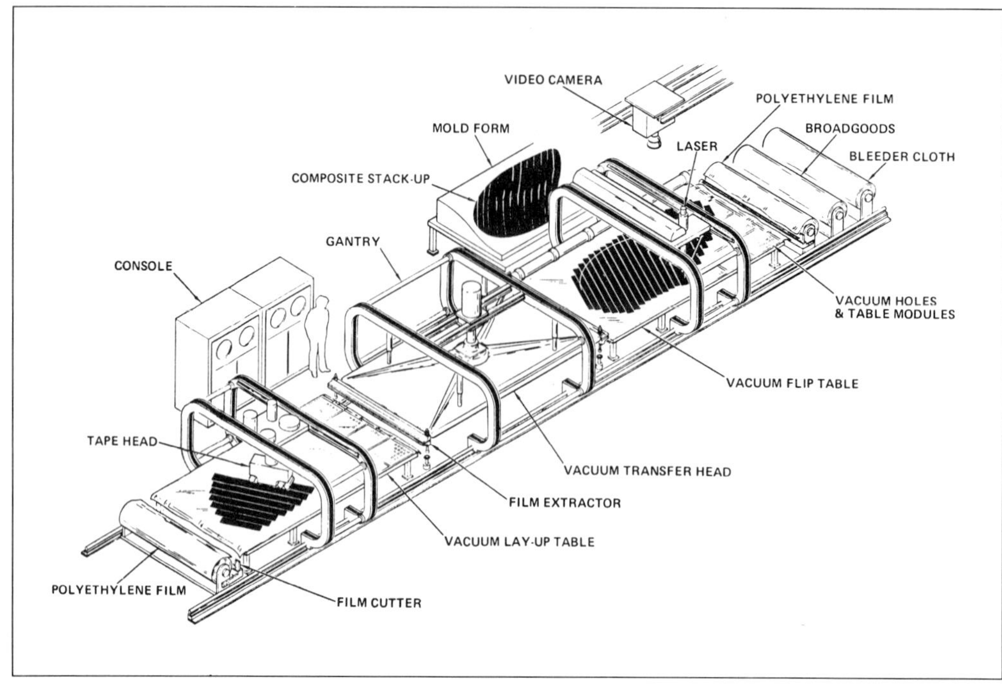

Schematic of automated-integrated reinforced plastics lay-up process that uses thermoset plastic preimpregnated reinforced sheets.

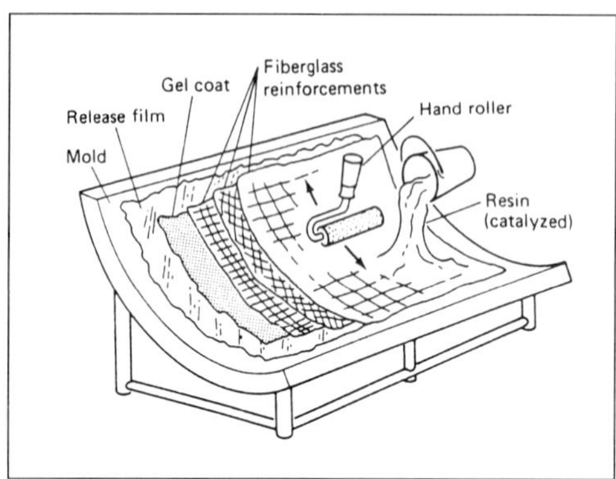

Hand-lay process.

(plug) or female (cavity), depending upon which side of the formed part is to have the accurate configuration (the other side will be rough).

Prior to the actual lay-up the mold must be sealed if it is porous, such as wood, and coated with a mold release agent to prevent sticking of the molded part. Waxes, silicones, thin films, and other agents are used. Lay-up consists of tailoring the sheet materials to fit, and placing them in layers on the mold, saturating the layers by brush, spray, or any other suitable means, and working them with a serrated roller to consolidate the layers, reducing or eliminating voids and porosity (see Fig.).

Frequently, to provide resistance to weathering, erosion, or chemical attack, a resin-rich surface coat (gel coat) is added.This surface layer is applied first and then allowed to stiffen into a tough layer (not cured) before additional layers are applied. It usually is reinforced with a surface veil using C-glass (rather than the usual E-glass) if chemical resistance is required, or a synthetic fiber veil may be used for resistance to weather, particularly sunlight. The resin may be a special formulation that includes TP to improve the surface appearance. Subsequent layers of mat, fabric, or combinations are then applied.

Inserts, strengthening ribs (of wood, metal, or glass fiber shapes), and other devices can be incorporated. They are placed in the lay-up. ▷ **aircraft**

handle ▷ **blow molding handle**

handling life The out-of-refrigeration time during which a material retains its handleability. ▷ **pot life**

hand mold ▷ **mold classification**

hard A nontechnical word used with a variety of meanings unless related to a test. ▷ **hardness**

hardboard A generic term for a panel manufactured primarily from inter-felted lignocellulosic fibers (usually wood), consolidated under heat and pressure in a hot press to a density of 31 lb/ft^3 (specific gravity 0.50) or greater, and to which other materials (particularly plastics) may have been added during fabrication to improve certain properties.

hard copy Permanent, printed data from a computer, as contrasted with information stored "invisibly" in memory or displayed temporarily on a CRT screen. Also called paper copy.

hard disc A storage memory disc device made of a rigid material such as aluminum; it is normally more durable and tends to have far greater storage capacity than a floppy disk. Unlike a floppy disc, generally it cannot be removed from the disc drive unit. ▷ **disc**

hardener 1. A substance or mixture added to a plastic composition to promote or control the curing action by taking part in it; as opposed to a catalyst. **2.** A substance added to control the degree of the hardness of a cured film.

hardening, case ▷ **case hardening**

hardness Hardness of plastics, which may be defined as the resistance to local deformation, is a complex property related to such mechanical properties of a material as modulus, strength, elasticity, and plasticity. This relationship to mechanical properties usually is not straightforward, but there is a tendency for high modulus and strength to correlate with higher degree of hardness within classes of materials. Hardness therefore has no simple, unambiguous definition; it can be measured and expressed only by careful standardized tests. Hardness testing is used mainly as a simple, rapid, nondestructive test for control in production, as an indication of cure of some thermoset plastics, and as a measure of mechanical properties affected by changes in chemical composition, microstructure, and aging. The wide range of hardness makes it impractical to produce a tester that would discriminate over the range from very soft to very hard plastics.

Hardness is usually characterized by a combination of three measurable parameters: (1) scratch resistance, (2) abrasion or mar resistance, and (3) indentation under load. To measure scratch resistance or hardness, a specimen is moved laterally under a loaded diamond point. The hardness value is expressed as the load divided by the width of the scratch. In other tests, especially in the paint industry, the surface is scratched with lead pencils of different hardnesses. The hardness of the surface is defined by the pencil hardness that first causes a visible scratch. Other tests include a sand-blast spray evaluation.

Abrasion resistance is usually measured by the material's loss in weight or the change in optical transmission and reflectance after a sample has been exposed to an abrasive surface. This is usually done under load, for a predetermined number of cycles or a time period specified by ASTM methods.

Tests for indention under load are performed basically like the ASTM tests used to measure the hardness of other materials, such as metals and ceramics (see Figs. on pp. 352 and 353). There are at least four popular hardness scales in use. Shore A and Shore D are for soft to relatively hard plastics and elastomers. Barcol is used from the mid-range of Shore D to above it. Rockwell M is used for very hard plastics. The Fig. on this page shows the relative ranges covered by these durometers. ▷ **Barcol hardness, Knoop hardness; Mohs hardness; Rockwell hardness; Shore hardness; Brinell hardness; scleroscope hardness; Vickers hardness; Vicat hardness; durometer hardness**

hardware The actual, physical parts of a mechanical device (molding machine, cutting tool,

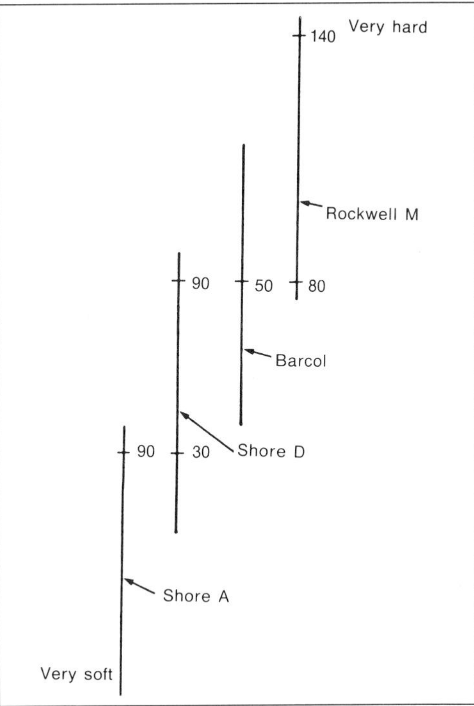

Guide regarding range of hardness common to plastics.

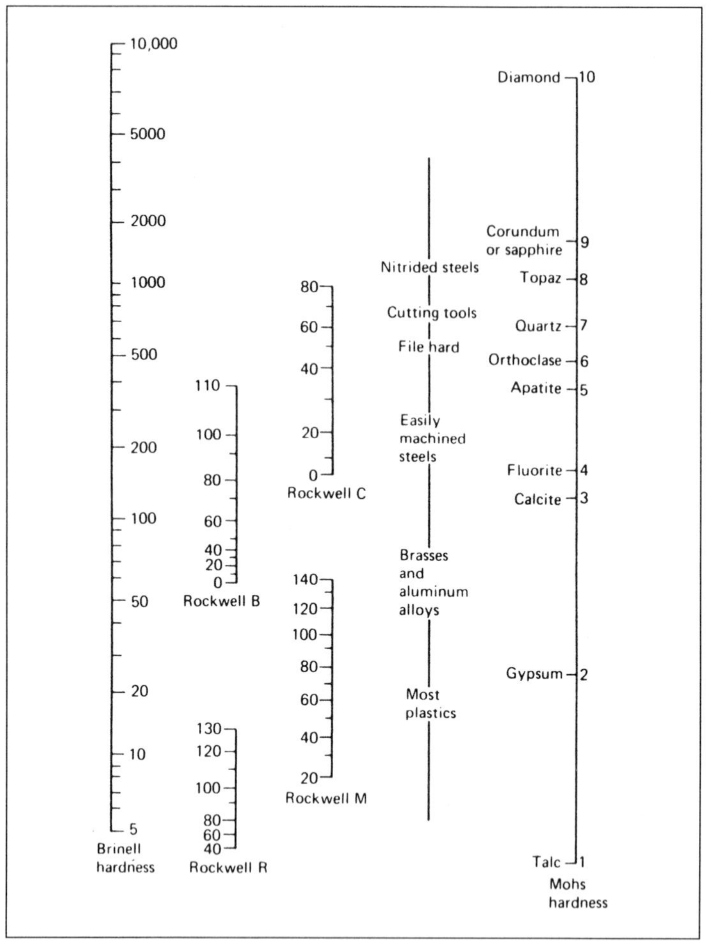

An approximate comparison of different hardness scales.

etc.) and electronic control system (computer equipment, specifically housings containing circuitry, monitors, disk drives, sensors, etc.). ▷ **software**

hardwood The wood from trees regardless of whether it is actually hard or soft.

harness satin weave A fabric with a weaving pattern producing a satin appearance, such as eight-harness satin and four-harness satin.

Hastelloy Cabot Corp. tradename for a series of high-strength, nickel-base, corrosion resistant alloys. Use includes surface hardening of plasticating screws and interior of barrels.

hawser twist ▷ **twist, hawser**

hazard ▷ **acceptable risk** and **Underwriters' Laboratory listing service**

hazard, fire ▷ **fire hazard**

hazardous equipment ▷ **safety and equipment**

hazardous material Any material or substance which in normal use can be damaging to the health and well-being of a person.

hazardous material transportation ▷ **label**

hazardous warning signs It is a rare day when a hazardous warning of one sort or another is not issued. If they are as hazardous as implied, it is nothing short of a miracle that the human race has survived as long as it has. So now comes the notice that the use of toothpicks is a hazard, particularly if swallowed. Well, so are splinters and needles.

The warning is well intended, of course, but also demonstrates the extremes to which the hazard warning frenzy can go. Let us face the fact that anything we do is hazardous (driving, walking, eating, sex, working in any environment, reading, breathing, pumping gasoline, sewage, fires, etc). There is definite need for legitimate, realistic hazards (including war and famine). There should however, be a rational

Test	Indenter	Shape of Indentation: Side View	Shape of Indentation: Top View	Load	Formula for Hardness Number
Brinell	10 mm sphere of steel or tungsten carbide	D, d	d	P	$\text{BHN} = \frac{2P}{\pi D[D - \sqrt{D^2 - d^2}]}$
Vickers	Diamond pyramid	136°	d_1, d_1	P	$\text{VHN} = 1.72P/d_1^2$
Knoop microhardness	Diamond pyramid	t; $l/b = 7.11$; $b/t = 4.00$	b, l	P	$\text{KHN} = 14.2P/l^2$
Rockwell					
A	Diamond cone	120°, t		60 kg	$R_A =$ } 100-500t
C				150 kg	$R_C =$
D				100 kg	$R_D =$
B	$\frac{1}{16}$ in. diameter steel sphere	t		100 kg	$R_B =$ } 130-500t
F				60 kg	$R_F =$
G				150 kg	$R_G =$
E	$\frac{1}{8}$ in. diameter steel sphere			100 kg	$R_E =$

Examples of hardness tests.

assessment of risks and benefits. To avoid falling into a "trap", search out the most reliable source of information and look for the rationale, the data on which the sources statements are based. Accept nothing as "gospel". There is always room to eliminate hazards the quickest and most proper way. In the real world, nothing is perfect and is never likely to be. We must learn and practice the art of compromise to achieve the greatest benefit for the most acceptable risk, rather than rejecting everything containing any risk. ▷ **acceptable risk** and **perfection**

hazardous waste containment ▷ **geomembrane liner**

hazards, Department of Agriculture This U.S. organization (USDA) controls items used in producing foods and that come in contact with foods as they are produced. All articles produced for use in this area require approvals and certifications.

hazards, Environmental Protection Agency The U.S. organization EPA has a broad authority over emissions to the environments of land, air, and water. The requirements are massive and should be carefully studied to assure compliance. Proper testing and record keeping are essential. Duplicate records are suggested in case of fire or loss of originals.

hazards, Federal Register 29 cfr 1910.1200 Known as the Right-to-Know law, this law covers employees' right to know about the chemical hazards to which they are exposed in the manufacturing sector. This law applies to fabricators and requires the employer to provide training and Material Safety Data Sheets (MSDS) on all hazardous materials with which employees may come in contact. The nature of a specific processing operation, the amount of other secondary operations provided, and other operations within the facility will dictate the extent to which training must be provided and reports made to the government.

hazards, Food and Drug Administration The U.S. organization FDA controls and approves those items contained in or relating to human consumption. Whenever a product is to be used in conjunction with consumable items the ingredients in that item must meet FDA specifications. Proper records of these certifications are essential and a method of tracking the flow of the materials they cover through a plant into the end product is required.

hazards, Occupational Safety and Health Act This act was one of the first attempts to provide safety guidelines relating to workplaces. Many specific standards have been established by OSHA regarding electrical safety, hazard guarding, color coding, etc. Both state and federal agencies exist and can be contacted for detailed information regarding safety needs. Training courses are available in occupational safety practice and administration.

hazards, state health communication standards Many states have adopted standards known as right-to-know laws. These laws differ from the federal standards in that they specifically address the community's right to know about the hazards in a local workplace.

hazards, Superfund Amendments and Reauthorization Act of 1986 This SARA law builds upon the EPA Chemical Preparedness Program (CEPP) and various state and local programs aimed at helping communities to better meet their responsibilities in regard to potential chemical emergencies. This law affects all manufacturing facilities. The most prominent section of the law known as SARA Title III,the Emergency Planning and Community Right-to-Know Act of 1986 requires: (1) emergency planning, (2) emergency notification, (3) community right-to-know reporting requirements, and (4) toxic chemical release reporting emissions inventory.

haze Indefinite cloudy appearance within or on the surface of a plastic, not describable by the terms chalking or bloom ▷ **extruder film haze**

haze test Although haze is sometimes thought of as the opposite of gloss, which would probably be absorption of an incident beam, the test method actually measures absorption, transmittance, and deflection of a direct beam by a translucent material. A specimen is placed in the path of a narrow beam of bright light so that some of the light passes through the specimen and some continues unimpeded. Both parts of the beam pass into a sphere equipped with a photodetector which allows the operator to determine two quantities: the total strength of the light beam and the amount of light scattered by more than 2.5 degrees from the original beam. Gloss can be measured for any material, while haze is appropriate only for translucent or transparent materials. Haze is caused by the scattering of light within a material, and can be affected by molecular structure, degree of crystallinity, or impurities at the surface or interior of the plastic (ASTM D 1003).

head-to-head On a polymer chain, a type of configuration in which the functional groups are on adjacent carbon atoms.

head-to-tail On a polymer chain a type of configuration in which the functional groups on adjacent polymers are as far apart as possible.

health care and laws ▷ **hazards Food and Drug Administration**

heat A form of energy associated with and proportional to molecular motion. It can be transferred from one body to another by radiation, conduction, or convection: sensible heat is accompanied by a change in temperature but latent heat is not. ▷ **latent heat**

heat-activated adhesive A dry adhesive that is rendered tacky or fluid by application of heat, or heat and pressure, to the assembly.

heat, adiabatic ▷ **adiabatic heat**

heat aging ▷ **aging at elevated temperature**

heat and photosensitive Thermochromic and photochromic compounds show changes in color and in light absorption, transmission, or reflection depending on the time and temperature history to which they have been subjected.

heat buildup The rise in temperature in a part resulting from the dissipation of applied strain energy as heat due to hysteresis effect or from applied mold cure heat.

heat capacity The heat capacity, or specific heat, is the amount of energy required to raise the temperature of a unit mass of a material one de gree. It can be measured at constant pressure or volume; at constant pressure, it is larger than at constant volume because additional energy is required to bring about the volume change against external pressure. The specific heat of amorphous plastics increases with temperature in an approximately linear fashion below and above T_g; a step-like change occurs near the T_g. No step occurs with crystalline type. For plastics it is usually reported during constant pressure heating. Plastics differ from traditional engineering materials since specific heat is temperature sensitive.

heat cleaned fiber and fabric ▷ **glass fiber and fabric surface treatment**

heat coating protection ▷ **intumescent coating**

heat control ▷ **process control** and **processing**

heat convertible plastic A thermoset plastic convertible by heat to an infusible and insoluble mass.

heat deflection ▷ **deflection temperature under load**

heat dielectrically ▷ **dielectric heating**

heat distortion point The temperature at which a standard test bar deflects a specific amount under a stated load. ▷ **deflection temperature under load**

heat due to fatigue ▷ **fatigue hysteresis**

heated-tool welding ▷ **hot plate welding**

heat electromagnetic energy ▷ **electromagnetic heating**

heat emissivity ▷ **emissivity**

heat endurance The time of heat aging that a material can withstand before failing a specific physical test.

heater band Basically an electrical resistance or induction heater in the form of a cuff encircles the barrel (cylinder), nozzle, etc. and provides heat. Many different types and shapes are used to meet different processing equipment requirements.

heater cartridge Cylindrical-bodied, electrical heater for providing heat in injection, compression, etc. molds; injection nozzles; runnerless mold system; hot stamp dies; sealing system; etc.

heat exchanger A vessel or unit in which an outgoing liquor or vapor transfers a large part of its heat to an incoming cool liquid. In the case of vapors, the latent heat of condensation is thus utilized to heat the entering liquid. The shell-and-tube type is widely used in which the hot liquid or vapor is contained in the shell while the cool liquid passes through the tubes. Tubes are usually arranged in coils for maximum contact with heat source.

heat flux The energy incident on a surface element per unit time (W/in^2) (Btu/ft^2·h).

heat forming ▷ **forming** and **thermoforming**

heat gun Electrically heated guns for softening, curing, drying, preheating, and welding plastics, coatings, and compounds; shrinking of heat shrinkable plastic tubing and plastic films; etc.

heat history ▷ **residence time**

heating chamber or cylinder In processing machines, that part in which the cold plastic feed is reduced to a hot melt.

heating, induction Heating by electrical induction.

heating, microwave Microwave ovens similar to those used in rapid heating of foods have been used for preheating molding powders, nylon overlap curing, vacuum bag curing, autoclave curing, etc. When a dielectric plastic is placed in a microwave field, the dipolar molecules will tend to align their dipole moment along the field intensity vector. When the field intensity vector varies sinusoidally with time, the direction of the vector will reverse every half cycle. This will cause a realignment of the polar molecules. The internal friction that has to be overcome involves loss of energy from the electromagnetic wave. This results in the conversion of a portion of the electromagnetic energy into thermal energy. Thus, the heat generation is proportional to the number of reversals of the electric field vector (the frequency). The amount of displacement that occurs during each reversal is determined by the electric field strength. Just as with RF heating, the heat generation is also a function of the electric field strength.

Microwave heating is closely related to dielectric heating, the main difference being the higher frequencies of microwave ranging from 1,000 to 100,000 megahertz. This is about two to three orders of magnitude higher than the frequency spectrum of dielectric energy. The wavelength of microwave energy is defined as being in the range of the spectrum between 1 m and 1 mm. This corresponds to a frequency range of 300 MHz (3E8 Hz) to 300 GHz (3E11 Hz). The frequencies that can be used in the U.S. are controlled by FCC. For industrial applications, the two most important microwave frequencies are 915 MHz and 2,450 MHz. The lower frequency is generally used for high-powered systems (over 200 kW) where the power factor of the material is reasonably high. The higher frequency is used for low-power systems (less than 100 kW) where the material has a relatively low power factor. Consumer microwave ovens operate at 2,450 MHz. ▷ **electromagnetic spectrum**

heating overshoot circuit Used in temperature controllers to inhibit temperature overshoot on warm-up.

heating, viscous ▷ **viscous heating**

heating zone, barrel ▷ **barrel zone temperature**

heat, latent ▷ **latent heat**

heat mark ▷ **sink mark**

heat of adsorption The heat evolved during adsorption.

heat of fusion Energy required to melt a solid (per gram, or per mole).

heat of hydration Energy released as heat during the chemical (hydration) reaction, such as curing a thermoset plastic reaction when water solidifies portland cement.

heat pipe A heat pipe is a means of heat transfer that is capable of transmitting thermal energy at near isothermal conditions and at near sonic velocity. The heat pipe consists of a tubular structure closed at both ends and containing a working fluid. For heat to be transferred from one end of the structure to the other, the working liquid is vaporized; the vapors travel to and condense at the opposite end, and the condensate returns to the working liquid at the other end of the pipe. The heat transfer ability of saturated vapor is many times greater than that of solid metallic material.

Heat pipes can be used either to remove or to add heat. The smaller heat pipes, which can be used to operate against gravity, are equipped with thick homogenous wicks and have higher thermal resistance, so that the heat transfer will not be quite as fast as in the case of gravity-positioned pipes. Even with the higher thermal resistance, these heat pipes still have a very high heat-transfer rate in comparison with solid metals. Also called thermal pin and mold heat transfer device. ▷ **mold heat transfer device**

heat resistance The property or ability of plastics and other materials to resist the deteriorating effects of elevated temperatures.

heat resistant coating ▷ **intumescent coating**

heat resistant plastic Usually defined as materials that retain mechanical properties for thousands of hours at 230°C (446°F), hundreds of hours at 300°C (572°F), minutes at 540°C (1,004°F), or seconds up to 760°C (1,400°F). These temperatures may be encountered during fabrication and/or use of the product. ▷ **ablative plastic**

The chemical factors that influence heat resistance include primary bond strength, secondary or van der Waals bonding forces, hydrogen bonding, resonance stabilization, mechanism of bond cleavage, molecular symmetry (structure regularity), rigid intrachain structure, crosslinking, and branching. The physical factors include molecular weight and molecular weight distribution, close packing (crystallinity), molecular (dipolar) interactions, and purity. The primary bond strength is the single most important factor contributing to the heat resistance.

The characteristics that contribute to thermal stability also make it more difficult to process; they have poor solubility and high melt viscosity.

heat resistant plastic determination Heat resistance is determined by thermogravimetric analysis (TGA), isothermogravimetric analysis (ITGA), differential scanning calorimeter (DSC), dynamic mechanical analysis (rheovibron or torsional-braid analyzer), thermal mechanical analysis (expansion, penetration). and dielectrometer. Heating rate, sample form, atmosphere, frequency, load, and thermal history affect the test results.

heat reversible ▷ **Peltier coefficent**

heat sealing A method of joining certain plastics, such as films, by simultaneous application of heat and pressure to areas in contact. Heat may be supplied conductively (hot plate welding) or dielectrical heating.

heat-sealing adhesive A thermoplastic adhesive that is melted between the adherend surfaces by heat application to one or both of the surfaces.

heat shield ▷ **ablation**

heat shrinkable tubing Tubing that will reduce in diameter to a predetermined size by the application of heat.

heat sink A material or device for the absorption or transfer of heat away from a critical element or part. Different liquids, bulk graphite, etc, are used as a heat sink. ▷ **heat pipe** and **mold heat transfer device**

heat softening point The heat softening point (such as the Vicat softening temperature per ASTM), not to be confused with the melting point, is the temperature at which the material or part becomes too soft to withstand stress and keep its shape. It is the temperature at which a flat-ended needle of 1 mm cross section under a load of 1kg penetrates 1 mm into a plastic, such as polyethylene film. In the Vicat test, temperature of the specimen is increased at a uniform rate.

heat, specific ▷ **specific heat**

heat stability The resistance to change in color or other properties as a result of heat encountered in either processing or product use. Such resistance may be enhanced by the incorporation of a heat stabilizer.

heat sterilization ▷ **sterilization, heat**

heat test Developed in 1990 by SPI to evaluate performance of parts at elevated temperatures as a supplement to heat distortion rating tests. The basis of the test involves heating in increments of 25°C (77°F) until a strength retention level of 50% or better is achieved.

There is no true measure, only guidelines, of how a plastic will perform at temperature. However, the Underwriters' Laboratories (UL) thermal index rating is a popular guide. A heated product is allowed to cool and if it retains its shape, a rating is assigned. Tests show that a product can take heat for a certain amount of time and, after it cools, it can take a certain amount of stress and pressure.

heat transfer Transmission of thermal energy from one location to another by means of a temperature gradient existing between two locations. It may take place by conduction, convection, and/or radiation.

heat transfer, extruder roll ▷ **extruder web heat transfer roll adjustment**

heat transfer label A label applied to a container by transferring the label, preprinted on a substrate, to the container surface.

heat transfer printing Multicolor effects are readily achieved with this process, since printing is done separately on film, and then transferred to the part. The recess should be shallow and sufficient clearance is required for the heated die. ▷ **decal**

heat treating Term used for annealing, hardening, tempering, and other heat processes. ▷ **screw heat treatment**

heat treatment Proper heat treatment of certain materials (plastics, metals, etc.) can be extremely beneficial in improving their properties, such as fatigue. Residual stresses may be introduced which, if properly used during fabrication, have beneficial effects. ▷ **orientation**

heavy metal Elements with high atomic weights, such as arsenic, cadmium, chromium, lead, mercury, tin, and zinc. Low concentrations of these metals can harm organisms. In plastic wastes, heavy metals such as lead and cadmium can be found in heat stabilizers and pigments.

heel, container ▷ **container, heel**

Heisler coating process This plastic coating process consists of the following steps: (1) the mold is preheated to 165° to 245°C (325° to 475°F), (2) the hot mold is partially filled with plastic, such as polyethylene powder, (3) molds with one closed end are filled in the upright position and then rotated about the long axis at a slight angle from the horizontal; molds with both ends open are filled with an excess of plastic and seesawed, (4) the plastic close to the inner mold wall melts and fuses into a continuous layer, (5) the excess powder is dumped from the mold, (6) if thicker walls are desired, steps (1) to (5) are repeated several times to build up the required thickness, (7) the mold is reheated to smooth the inner walls of the fused part, and (8) the mold is cooled by either quenching in or spraying with water.

helical winding ▷ **filament winding**

helix angle ▷ **screw**

hemp As soft, white fiber obtained from the stems of the plant *cannabis satura*. It can be used as a filler or reinforcement for plastics.

henry ▷ **electrical inductance**

Hertz Hz is a unit of frequency equal to one cycle per second (cps).

heterocyclic compound Compounds containing molecules whose atoms are arranged in a ring, the ring containing two or more elements.

heterogeneous Materials consisting of dissimilar constituents separately identifiable. They have regions of unlike properties separated by internal boundaries. Note that not all nonhomogeneous materials are necessarily heterogeneous.

heterogeneous nucleation In the crystallization of plastics, the growth of crystals on vessel surfaces, dust, or added nucleating agents.

heteropolymerization A special case of additive copolymerization which involves the combination of two dissimilar unsaturated organic monomers.

Hevea rubber Natural rubber comes from the *Hevea Braziliensis* tree.

hexa An abbreviated form of hexamethylenetetramine, a source of reactive methylene for curing novolac plastic.

high density polyethylene plastic ▷ **polyethylene, high density plastic**

high frequency heating ▷ **dielectric heating**

high impact polystyrene plastic ▷ **polystyrene, high impact plastic**

high molecular weight high density polyethylene plastic ▷ **polyethylene, high molecular weight high density plastic**

high polymer ▷ **polymer, high**

high pressure laminate ▷ **molding pressure, high**

high pressure molding ▷ **molding pressure, high**

high pressure structural foam molding ▷ **foamed, structural**

hindrance ▷ **steric hindrance** and **nonstaining antioxidant**

hinge, mechanical There are different methods of producing mechanical hinges such as molding holes at the parting lines or drilling holes where projections exist at the parting line and in turn pins are inserted. There are also snap fit types.

hinge, integral The following techniques are used to fabricate thermoplastic hinges: molded-in (during injection or blow molding), cold worked, extruded, and coining. These so-called "living" hinges take advantage of molecular orientation to provide the bending action in the plastic hinge ▷ **orientation**. An integral hinge can be molded by conventional processing techniques, providing certain factors are observed. The desirable molecular orientation runs transverse to the hinge axis. This can best be achieved by a fast flow through the hinge section, using high melt temperatures. Since these requirements are also consistent with good molding practice, optimum production rates can be maintained. The main concern in integral-hinge molding is to avoid conditions that can lead to delaminating in the hinge section. These include filling the mold too slowly, having too low a melt temperature, having a nonuniform flow front through the hinge section, suffering material contamination as from pigment agglomerates, and running excessively high mold temperatures near the hinge area.

An integral hinge can also be produced by postmold flexing. In this process the hinge section is molded, then subjected to stresses beyond the yield point immediately after molding, by closing the hinge. This creates a necking down effect. Stretching the oriented polymer molecules on the outer surface of the hinge radius provides the remarkable flex strength of the thinned-down hinge section. Flexing the molded hinge must be done while it is still hot, through an angle sufficient to stress its outer surface. This postmolding step provides a maximum and uniform orientation in the hinge area but a minimum of applied stresses. The thinness of the hinge area requires that pigments be well dispersed so that agglomerates will not provide focal points of weakness in the hinge structure.

Where parts are heavy or complex, it may be impractical to force the necessary quantity of plastic through the hinge sections. In such cases integral hinges can be obtained by cold working. Thinner hinges are usually made by using a flexible backing like stiff rubber. The deformation of this type of backing produces the hinge contour by stretching the softened plastic and generally results in thinner cross-sections.

Forming the hinge cross-section by using an extruder die results in a hinge with poor flex life. Because hinges are formed in the direction of the polymer flow, they cannot be sufficiently oriented when flexed. However, if an extruded hinge is formed by the take-off mechanism while the polypropylene still retains internal heat, the hinge will have properties approaching those of cold working.

It is also possible to create hinges in some of the tougher engineering thermoplastics by coining techniques. In this technique a molded or extruded part is placed in a fixture between two coining bars. Pressure is then applied to the bars and the part is compressed to the desired thickness, elongating the plastic. Coining is effective only when the material is elongated beyond its tensile yield point. The process is usually used for such materials as acetal and nylon, which cannot normally be molded in a sufficiently thin section for a strong, durable hinge.

histogram ▷ **statistical normal curve**

hobbing ▷ **mold hobbing**

hog A machine for reducing particle size or grinding scrap, similar to a granulator but more heavily constructed, equipped with more cutting knives, and using forced air to direct material through a perforated screen.

hold-down groove ▷ **mold hold-down groove**

holder block ▷ **mold chase**

hole edge distance ratio The distance from the center of a hole (such as in a bearing) to the edge in the direction of the principal stress, divided by the diameter of the hole.

hollow core extrusion ▷ **extruder profile structure, hollow core with gas**

hollow gas injection molding ▷ **injection molding, gas**

hollow fiber Hollow fibers spun from plastics are of interest in the textile industry to produce high bulk, low density fabrics. Other fiber configurations such as trilobal cross section are being used for high bulk textiles. The spinning technology developed for hollow textile fibers, particularly in the manufacture of spinnerets, has been very useful in the development of hollow fiber membranes. They have been made by three conventional synthetic fiber spinning methods: (1) wet spinning (spinning from a plastic solution into a liquid coagulant), (2) dry spinning (spinning from a solution of a plastic in a volatile solvent into an evaporative column), and (3) melt spinning. In all cases the tubular cross section was formed by extruding the molten plastic or plastic solution through an annular die or spinneret. Spinneret design and precision of manufacture are critical features of successful hollow fiber spinning. ▷ **osmosis reverse; desalination; membrane**

hollow needle blowing ▷ **blow molding, extruder blow pin**

hollow shape ▷ **blow molding; injection molding, gas; thermoforming twin sheet; spin welding**

hollow sphere ▷ **sphere, hollow**

holography Production of unique 3-D image on photographic film by means of an interference pattern created by a laser beam that is split by a mirror-like device. ▷ **computer** and **nondestructive holography test**

holography, acoustic ▷ **acoustic holography**

holography nondestructive test ▷ **nondestructive holography test**

homogeneity A material that exhibits the same properties throughout (3-dimensional) is said to be homogeneous. Homogeneity is an ideal state that is not achieved by real materials such as plastics, metals, etc. However, there are materials where the variation is so small that calculations for stress and deflection assume that a material is homogeneous throughout. There are materials that are not homogeneous, such as reinforced plastic filament wound structures.

homogeneous This term, in its strictest sense, describes the chemical constitution of an element or compound. A compound is homogeneous since it is composed of one or only one group of atoms represented by a formula.

homogeneous nucleation In the crystallization of plastics, the primary nucleated species generated by the plastic molecules.

homogenizing Eliminating all concentration gradients in each phase, usually by an elevated temperature heat treatment.

homologous Belonging to or consisting of a series of organic compounds differentiated by the number of methylene groups (CH_2).

homologous temperature ▷ **temperature, homologous**

homopolymer The result of the polymerization of a single monomer, a homopolymer consists of a single type or repeating unit. This (high) polymer consists of molecules containing (neglecting the ends, branch junctions, and other minor irregularities) either a single type of unit or two or more chemically different types in regular sequence.

homopolymer, halogenated ▷ **halogenation**

homopolymerization The IUPAC considers that in homopolymerization the number of molecular species contributing to the polymer structure is the minimum number required for the types of reactants employed. In ordinary addition polymerization this minimum number is one; in most condensation polymerization it is two.

honeycomb reinforced plastic core Plastic impregnated woven or nonwoven fiber fabric material manufactured in usually hexagonal cells that serves as a core in sandwich constructions. Honeycombs may also be made from plastic film or sheet, aluminum, steel, etc. (see Fig. below). ▷ **sandwich core material**

Hooke's law It is implicit in the definition of the modulus of elasticity; it relates to elasticity. Directly stated it says that stress is proportional to strain up to the proportional limit of the material. Thus, when a load is applied to any

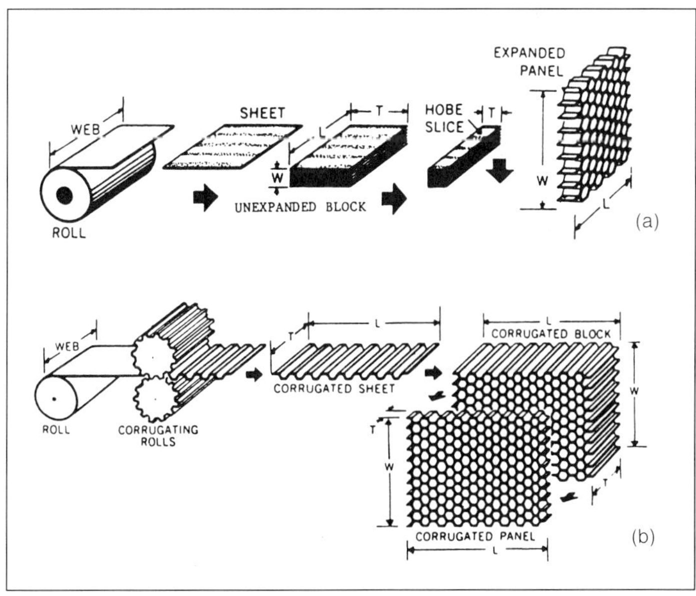

Methods of producing honeycomb core; most is produced by the expansion method. (*a*) Expansion process: In this process all adhesive bonds are made simultaneously while the corrugation method is essentially a one-layer-at-a-time operation. (*b*) Corrugation process: Materials which can be converted using this process include metals, plastics, plastic-reinforced glass, and paper. Some high-temperature resistant metal foil honeycombs are welded at the nodes rather than being adhesively bonded.

elastic material so that the material is deformed, strained, or stretched, then the resulting stress is proportional to the strain. Stress is measured in units of force per unit area; strain is the extent of the deformation. In general, Hooke's law applies only to a certain stress called the yield strength. In this elastic region, where the stress is proportional to strain, the proportionality constant, called modulus of elasticity or Young's modulus, is

$$E = \sigma/\varepsilon$$

where E = modulus of elasticity (MPa or psi), σ = stress (MPa or psi), and ε = strain (mm/mm or in./in.). Hooke's law was first recorded in 1678 by Robert Hooke. ▷ **stress-strain curve or diagram strength, yield; tensile strength**

hoop stress The circumferential or tensile stress in the wall of a pipe or cylindrical form subjected to internal or external pressure.

hopper Plastic feed reservoir into which plastic material is loaded and from which it is directed to a processing system, sometimes through a metering device (see Fig.). ▷ **feeder** and **railcar hopper**

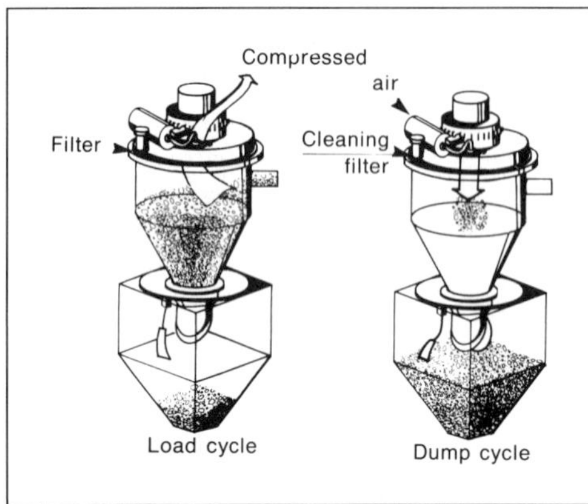

Example of a hopper loader.

hopper blender Mixes multiple materials such as virgin plastic, regrind, additive, filler, and/or reinforcement. Materials to be blended are metered in ratio to a mixing chamber and then discharged into the feed throat of the processing machine.

hopper capacity The capacity in kg or lb that can be obtained in a hopper based on the bulk density of the material it will process.

hopper car ▷ **railcar hopper**

hopper dryer A combination feeding and drying device. Usually hot, dry air flows upward through the hopper containing the feed material.

hopper loader A curved pipe through which plastic to be processed is pneumatically or mechanically (screw drive) conveyed from shipping drums to machine hoppers. ▷ **auxiliary equipment**

hopper magnet A safety device used in the bottom of a hopper to protect against damage to the process (such as screws, mold, die, rolls, etc.) caused by pieces of ferrous metal occasionally found in material, particularly regrind. It should be used even if special equipment was used to remove the foreign matter prior to entering the hopper.

horticultural and agricultural market Since the 1940s, farmers (and others) have been using plastic materials in significant and increasing amounts to grow more and better plants faster, in less space, and at lower cost. The plastics range from the ground to the building and equipment. Applications include: (1) growing enclosures (greenhouses, row covers, hotbeds, cold frames, etc.), (2) crop culture (mulching and fumigation), (3) water conservation (collection, conveyance, storage, etc.), (4) semipermanent structures (animal shelters, silage containers, equipment shelters, containers, piping, etc.), and others.

hotbench test A method of determining gelation properties of plastisols, employing a temperature gradient plate on which a film is cast.

hot elongation The elongation or extensibility of a heated thermoplastic sheet. This extensibility varies widely with the material and is also greatly affected by sheet temperature, speed of stretching, and method of stretching (by differential air pressure or mechanical means).

hot fill ▷ **packaging hot fill**

hot flocking coating ▷ **flocking or floc spraying**

hot forging ▷ **forging**

hot-gas welding A technique for joining thermoplastics (usually sheet) in which the materials are softened by a jet of hot air from a welding torch and joined together at the softening points. Generally when required, a thin rod of the same material is used to fill and consolidate the gap. ▷ **welding**

hot isotactic pressing ▷ **isotactic molding/pressing**

hot leaf stamping ▷ **hot stamping** and **stamping**

hot melt 1. Thermoplastic compounds which are normally solid at room temperatures but become sufficiently fluid when heated to be

Materials for hot plate welding.

Material	% weld strength 100	90	80	70	60
Acrylonitrile butadiene styrene			x		
Acetal		x			
Acrylic			x		
Acetate			x		
Butyrate			x		
Propionate			x		
Ethylene vinyl acetate			x		
Nylons		x			
Polycarbonate				x	
Low-density polyethylene	x				
Ultrahigh-molecular-weight polyethylene		x			
High-density polyethylene	x				
Polypropylene	x				
Polysulfone					x
General-purpose styrene			x		
High-impact styrene		x			
Flexible vinyl		x			
Rigid vinyl		x			
Thermoplastic rubber		x			

pourable or spreadable; they are used as adhesives and coatings. **2.** ▷ **melt**

hot melt adhesive An adhesive that is applied in a molten state and forms a bond after cooling to a solid state. ▷ **hot melt.** This type of adhesive performs by temperature changes rather than adhesives that achieve the solid state through evaporation of solvents or chemical cure; including absorption or evaporation of water (moisture in the air, etc.). ▷ **adhesive** and **reinforcement, metal**

hot melt gun Self-contained systems that dispense hot melt adhesives on demand.

hot plate welding Also called fusion bonding, heat sealing, and butt fusion. Process takes two mating thermoplastic parts and changes the mating surfaces to a liquid state by induced heat. While in the molten state, they are rapidly pressed together to form a homogeneous bond. Examples of weld strengths achievable are shown in the Table above. Most thermoplastics, including some dissimilar materials such as PE and PP, acrylic to ABS, and rigid to plasticized PVC, can be welded by this process. As with most other methods of joining TPs, the percentage, content, and type of filler used in a material can affect weld strength. Also processing method can influence bond; injection moldable grades of nylon generally obtain higher weld strengths.

hot quenching An imprecise term (alone) used to cover a variety of quenching procedures in which a quenching medium is maintained at a prescribed temperature and time period.

hot runner ▷ **mold, runner**

hot setting adhesive An adhesive that requires a temperature at or above 100°C (212°F) to set.

hot stamping Also called dry printing, roll leaf stamping, gold leaf stamping, and stamping print. This one-step decorating technique involves the transfer of a carrier film onto the surface of a plastic substrate by applying heat and pressure. It is carried out by bringing a heated die (flat, round, etc.) in contact with the product to be decorated while interposing a stamping foil between them. The die may be engraved in order to transfer the mirror image of the engraved pattern. The Fig. shows a rotating roll-on system. A flat die may be used to transfer the foil only to the high points of a molded plastic part. This dry, one-step process normally does not require any pretreatment, solvents, or drying and the rate of will range at least from 60 to 4,500 parts an hour. With the use of roll-on equipment to eliminate air entrapment potential problems, marks up to 12 × 24 in. ($30\frac{1}{2}$ × 61 cm) in solid color can be obtained around a 360° arc (90° for reciprocating equipment). Special "bottom-up" equipment can handle lengths up to 62 in. (158 cm). The process is essentially limited to flat parts or those with simple curves. Special equipment with silicone dies is used on mild compound curves.

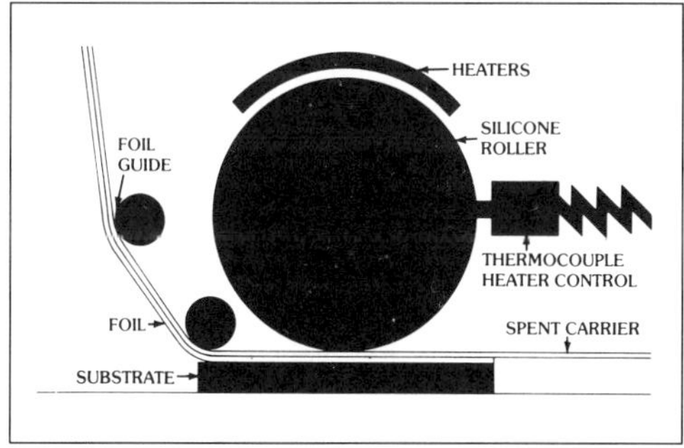

Schematic of hot stamping using a roll-on machine.

Heat and pressure affect the foil transfer. Once the finish layer is applied, the foil becomes a permanent part of the substrate, enhancing the value of the product being decorated. In addition to visual appeal, it can also enhance the physical properties of the substrate by adding extra resistance to scuffs, abrasion, sun fade, moisture, chemicals, etc. Its strength properties can be included in the design of a product, such as a blow molded bottle, where less foil is required.

The foil is actually a series of coatings applied to a polyester carrier 0.0005 to 0.003 in. (0.0001 to 0.0008 mm) thick. A simple foil construction would include a release coat followed by various color or decorative coats and finished by one or more bonding coats. The release coat allows all subsequent coatings to shear cleanly from the carrier film at a specified application temperature. The next coating then becomes the top surface or decorative finish. This coating also serves as a protective layer that adds to the physical properties of the substrate being decorated. The final coat, the bonding agent, must be chemically compatible with the substrate in order to achieve a permanent bond. Most foil constructions are more complex. A highly abrasion-resistant wood grain or exterior chrome requires as many as 10 to 12 separate coatings. These additional coatings are added to achieve textured patterns and higher gloss, tones and grains, as well as added physical properties. ▷ **sublimable dye transfer** and **thermographic transfer decorating**

hot strength The resistance of a heated thermoplastic material to being stretched or formed to the mold shape.

hot transfer decorating There are several methods that fit into this category. ▷ **hot stamping; decal transfer; sublimable dye transfer**

hot wire cutter Electrically heated wires are used in different plastic processes such as cutting the parison in blow molding (between the die and mold), and splitting certain types of plastic foam blocks into smaller pieces. Heated wires slowly melt through the blocks as they are fed into the wires by gravity or conveyor belt.

hot wire welding Electrical hot (resistant) wire is used to provide local heat to thermoplastics in order to produce fusion of the areas being joined. Pressure is usually applied to ensure complete bonding action. ▷ **welding**

hot working Any form of mechanical deformation processing (bending, shaping, forming) a product at temperatures above its recrystallization point but below its melting point.

house, plastic ▷ **plastic house**

hue A particular color, as distinct from other colors; a quality that distinguishes colors in the visible portion of the spectrum; the first of three dimensions of color that are hue, lightness, and saturation. ▷ **saturation**

human implantation An important continuing breakthrough in surgery implanted devices has been the use of plastics in the human body. Strong, tough, non-allergenic plastics are finding increased use as replacements for defective blood vessels and other damaged parts of the body including providing desirable cosmetics.

human tissue burn tolerance In the testing of thermal protective clothing, the amount of thermal energy which causes a second degree burn in human tissues.

humectant ▷ **moisture, humectant agent**

humidify To increase, by any process, the quantity of water vapor within a given space.

humidistat A regulatory device, activated by changes in humidity, used for automatic control of relative humidity.

humidity The condition of the atmosphere in respect to water vapor content. ▷ **psychrometer**

humidity, absolute The weight of water vapor present in a unit volume of air, for example, grain/ft^3 or grain/m^3. When the amount of water vapor is reported in terms of weight per unit weight of dry air (grains/lb of dry air), it is not the absolute humidity. It designates humidity ratio, specific humidity, or moisture content.

humidity, blush ▷ **blush**

humidity indicator An instrument or device that displays the approximate humidity condition within a package. As an example, cobalt salt (cobaltous chloride) changes color as the humidity of the environment changes. It is pink when hydrated (moisture present) and greenish-blue when anhydrous (no moisture present).

humidity ratio In a mixture of water vapor and air, the mass of water vapor per unit mass of dry air.

humidity, relative The ratio of the actual pressure of existing water vapor to the maximum posssible (saturation) pressure of water vapor in the atmosphere at the same temperature, expressed as a percentage.

humidity, specific In a mixture of water vapor and air, the mass of water vapor per unit of moist air.

humification A process by which organic matter decomposes.

Hyatt, John Wesley Hyatt (1837–1920) is generally credited as being the father of the plastic industry with his first commercially productive plastic. In 1869, he and his brother patented a mixture of cellulose nitrate and camphor which could be molded and hardened. Its tradename was "celluloid".

hybrid **1.** A reinforced plastic consisting of laminae of two or more different materials, such as plastic matrix with fiber reinforcement. **2.** A combination of two or more different fibers, such as carbon and glass or carbon and aramid, in a structure of tapes, fabrics, etc. (see Fig.). **3.** ▷ **commingled yarn; fiber biconstituent; yarn, combination**

These tennis racket frames use hybrid reinforced plastics that provide better performance during competition; RP construction is graphite/glass fiber-epoxy plastic.

hydrate Compounds containing water that is combined in a definite proportion are called hydrates. The water present is water of hydration, also called water of crystallization.

hydrated lime A dry powder obtained by treating quicklime with water enough to satisfy its chemical affinity for water under the conditions of its hydration. It consists essentially of calcium hydroxide ($Ca(OH)_2$), or $Ca(OH)_2$ and magnesium oxide ($Mg(OH)_2$) or $Mg(OH)_2$, etc.

hydrated silica ▷ **silica, synthetic**

hydration To cause, to take-up, or combine with water or the elements of water; results in a hydrate.

hydration, heat of ▷ **heat of hydration**

hydraulic **1.** Descriptive of a machine or operation in which a liquid is used to exert or transfer pressure such as a hydraulic press. The liquid can be water or oil. **2.** Description of a material that hardens on addition of water, such as hydraulic cement.

hydraulic clamp ▷ **clamping, hydraulic**

hydraulic fluid A liquid or mixture of liquids designed to transfer pressure (power) from one point to another in a system on the basis of Pascal's law where pressure on a confined liquid is transmitted equally in all directions throughout the liquid. ▷ **pressure flow**

hydraulic fluid influenced by heat The pressure of excessive heat in the operation of machine tool hydraulic systems (injection molding machine, etc.) can have a broad based negative effect on the machine operation of the entire system. Heat can and does affect five major areas of machine tool hydraulics which in turn affects plastic product cost or performance and production rates: (1) hydraulic fluid life, (2) energy loss, (3) erratic operation of components, (4) formation and removal of sludge and varnish, and (5) operating conditions that cause overheating. The overheating causes leakage of check valves, leakage of relief valves in the pump, etc.

hydraulic fluid maintenance procedures Select the viscosity and type of hydraulic fluid recommended by the component and hydraulic equipment manufacturer, include fluids which are not necessarily petroleum based. Be sure that fluid is clean to the degree required by the component or equipment manufacturer. On certain machines with servo systems, the filtration requirements are generally 10 micrometers (microns) absolute or less. This means that when adding fresh hydraulic fluid in any quantity, the fluid must be filtered by some auxiliary means to the degree recommended for the equipment. This same procedure for extra clean or ultrafine filtration follows for systems with electrically modulated hydraulic valves. The same filtration applies for fluid being transferred from holding tanks, lubrication charts, and partially opened barrels of fluids.

Temperature control can be a very effective way of increasing fluid life. The operating temperature is generally held from 100 to 120°C (212 to 248°F) for best results if at all possible. Heat exchangers should be periodically cleaned to make sure they are functioning properly. Check fluid condition for both foreign particle contamination and chemical condition every 90 to 120 days. On systems requiring ultraclean filtration, checks should be made every 60 days or less. Periodic inspection and test of hydraulic fluid on a regular schedule are vital parts of any effective fluid conservation program.

hydraulic fluid storage and handling Hydraulic fluid can be contaminated before it is even added to a hydraulic processing system, causing problems from the start. Improper stor-

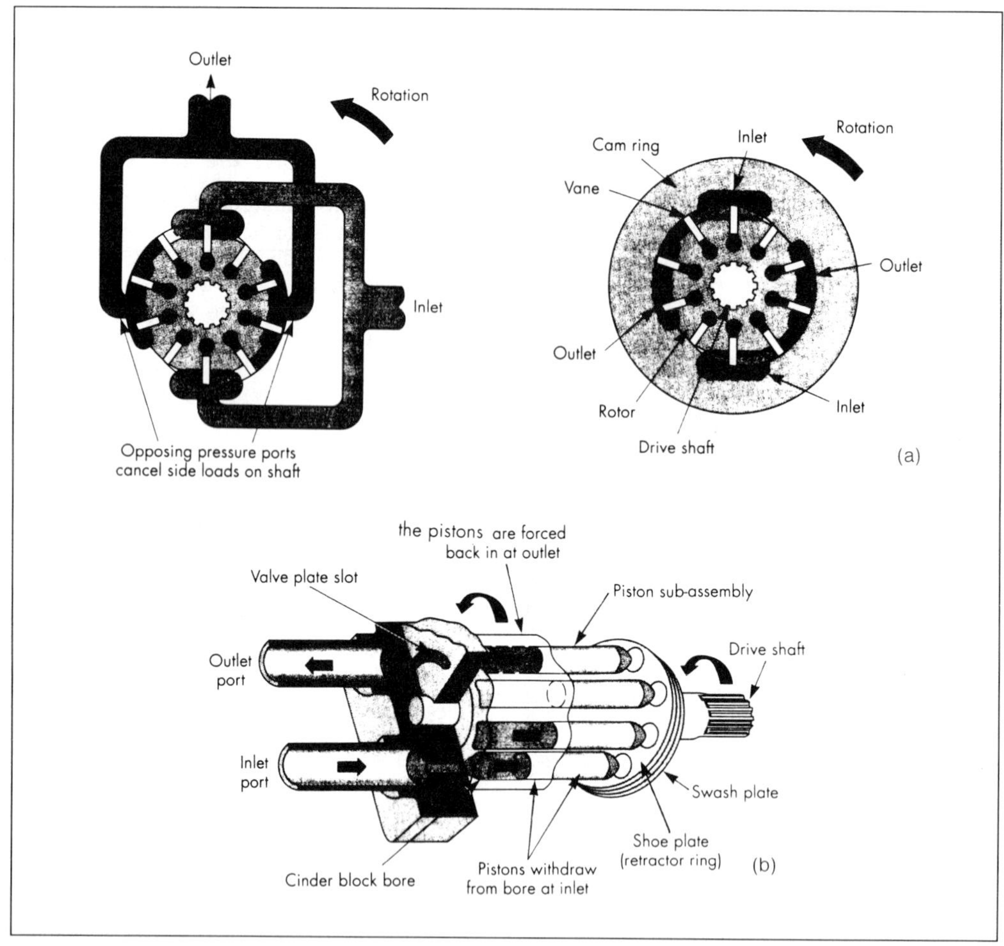

Schematic examples of hydraulic pumps: (*a*) Fixed-volume balanced vane pump; (*b*) axial piston variable-volume pump.

age of fresh fluid either outside or inside the plant, where the contaminants can collect on the exterior of drums, can result in harmful dirt and other contaminants being introduced. Use the proper and fluid suppliers' recommended methods of storage to eliminate moisture and other contaminants from developing.

hydraulic gradient The loss of hydraulic head per unit distance of flow.

hydraulic knockout ▷ **mold ejection**

hydraulic leakage control There are many reasons for controlling and/or eliminating hydraulic leaks. The most obvious is to reduce consumption and waste. The reduction in the actual cost alone can result in substantial savings in fluid used. Actually, the greatest single need for reducing leakage is to reduce the generation of hazardous waste.

hydraulic line pressure Line pressure (injection molding machines) is a design compromise between the highest pressure which can be efficiently generated and used, as well as the highest pressure which can be safely and surely contained with a minimum likelihood of systems leaks. It is generally agreed that the 2,000 to 3,000 psi level is most desirable.

hydraulic press A press in which the molding force is created by the pressure exerted by a fluid.

hydraulic pump, injection molding machine There are basically fixed and variable pumps (see Fig. above) with no single type that is perfect for every class and size of injection molding machine. Fixed pumps can be single units or can be staged in multiple pump configurations for powering large clamp tonnage machines. Big machines theoretically could use multiple variable volume pumps, but such systems could be rather expensive. Fixed volume balanced vane pumps are quite popular and generally operate at 2,000 to 3,000 psi (13.8 to 20.7 MPa) with 90% volumetric efficiencies.

In vane pumps a slotted rotor is spinned to the driveshaft and turns inside of the cam ring. Vanes are located in the rotor vane slots and follow the inner surface of the cam ring as the rotor turns. Centrifugal force and outlet pressure under the vanes hold them out against the cam ring and are enclosed by inlet and outlet support plates. The varying, continuous pressure under the vane area reduces wear and usually assures a high level of pump efficiency.

Vane-type fixed-volume pumps are not the only types. For bigger tonnage machines (above 800T) use is made of multiple groupings of fixed-displacement internal gear pumps. They can be matched and sized to a variable-volume type range of outputs. Also, they are rugged and forgiving so that they are often used in rigorous industrial equipment such as earth-moving machinery.

Oil output based on machine cycle status requirements is the key feature of variable-volume pumps making them very popular. The cylinder block is turned by the drive shaft. Pistons fitted to bores in the cylinder are connected through piston shoes and a retracting ring so that the shoes bear against an angled swash plate. As the block turns, the piston shoes follow the swash plate, causing the pistons to reciprocate. Displacement is also determined by the size and number of pistons and piston stroke length. It is a function of the swash plate angle.

The swash plate is installed in a movable yoke for variable displacement. Pivoting the yoke changes the swash plate angle to increase or decrease the piston stroke. The yoke can be positioned manually, with a servo control, a pressure-compensation control, or other means. There are variable-displacement pumps that provide at least 96% volumetric efficiency. Most can operate over 3,000 psi (20.7 MPa). There are also radial-piston variable-volume pumps for self-contained presses.

Generally fixed-volume pumps are easier to maintain and variable-volume pumps provide more energy efficiency. However, there are pumps that can match each other's benefits.

hydrocarbon plastic Plastics based on material made from the polymerization of monomers composed of carbon and hydrogen only.

hydrocellulose plastic Water-insoluble products of the hydrolysis of cellulose with acids. They are molecularly heterogeneous in the sense that they are composed of molecules varying in degree of polymerization.

hydrochloric acid An acid emitted as a gas during combustion, one of the most significant components of acid gas found in flue gas, etc.

hydrochlorofluorocarbon plastic ▷ **chlorofluorocarbon plastic**

hydroclave molding ▷ **autoclave**

hydrodynamic specific surface The specific surface of a fibrous material as measured by the filtration resistance of a compacted pad formed from a fiber suspension under specified conditions. Relates to plastic penetration during processing reinforced plastics.

hydroelectric system injection molding ▷ **clamping hydroelectric**

hydrogel Hydrogels or water-containing gels are plastics characterized by hydrophilicity and insolubility in water. In water they will swell to an equilibrium volume, but preserve their shape. Synthetic hydrogels are used in prosthetic materials, soft lenses, and membranes for controlled drug release because of their compatibility with living tissues. Natural hydrogels are used in pulp and paper production, artificial silk, cellulose membranes, and biomedical applications. ▷ **silica, synthetic**

hydrogen The lightest element, with an atomic weight of about one.

hydrogenated nitrile rubber ▷ **nitrile rubber, hydrogenated**

hydrogenation Hydrogenation of plastics, mainly polymers and copolymers of dienes, has been accomplished with a variety of catalysts and a wide range of conditions. Destructive hydrogenation of natural and synthetic polymers at high temperatures has been helpful in determining the structures of polymers. Nondestructive hydrogeneration of polymers at moderate conditions has provided a variety of products which cover the range in properties to vulcanizable rubbery materials. One of the main benefits resulting from hydrogenating is the increase in stability; for example, polybutadiene, of which about 90% of the original double bonds has been saturated, shows good resistance to ozone.

hydrogen embrittlement Hydrogen-induced cracking or severe loss of ductility caused by the presence of hydrogen in materials, particularly metals.

hydrogen sulfide H_2S is a poisonous gas produced by decomposing organic matter that contains sulfur and by the breakdown of sulfates in such matter. Characteristic odor of rotten eggs is present.

hydrolysis Chemical decomposition of a substance involving the addition of water. ▷ **chemical recycling**

hydrolytic adsorption The adsorption of a weakly ionized acid or base formed by the hydrolysis of some type of salt in aqueous solution.

hydrolytic stability The ability to withstand the environmental effects of high humidity.

hydromechanical press ▷ **clamping, hydromechanical**

hydrophilic Having an affinity for water; wettable by water; tending to absorb water; as opposed to oleophilic.

hydrophobic Capable of repelling water; poorly wetted by water; having little affinity for water; tending to repel water. Property is characteristic of many plastics and finely divided powders like carbon black and magnesium carbonate. If in any liquid, it is called lyophobic.

hydrosol A term that identifies a suspension of PVC plastic or nylon in water. ▷ **latex**

hydrostatic design stress The recommended maximum hoop stress that can be applied continuously with a high degree of certainty that failure of the pipe will not occur.

hydrostatic pressure **1.** Refers to pressure applied by means of a fluid and is not limited to water; use oil, etc. **2.** A state of stress in which all the principal stresses are equal, and there is no shear stress.

hydrostatic test A test of the ability of a part to withstand internal hydrostatic pressure.

hydrothermal crystallization Procedure for growing single crystals within a heated aqueous solution.

hydrotropy The increase in solubility of a substance which is only slightly soluble in an aqueous system by the addition of a third substance. This third substance is called a hydrotropic agent.

hydroxy A group of OH compounds (methyl alcohol, methanol, or carbinoll). Alcohol is characterized by the general formula ROH where R represents an alkyl group.

hydroxyethylene cellulose plastic Any of several cellulose ethers in which some of the hydroxyl groups have been substituted with hydroxyethyl groups. Except for very low degrees of substitution, it is water soluble.

hydroxyethylmethacrylate plastic HEMA is water-soluble, but when it is polymerized in the presence of ethylene glycol dimethacrylate (EGDMA), which acts as a crosslinking agent, a network plastic is formed. The network plastic is no longer soluble in water, but can be swollen to an extent controlled by the degree of crosslinking to form hydrogels. The soft hydrogel possesses the combination of properties (including good oxygen permeability) required to produce soft contact lenses.

hydroxyl group A chemical group consisting of one hydrogen atom bonded to one oxygen atom (OH).

hydroxyl number The number of milligrams of potassium hydroxide (KOH) equivalent to the hydroxyl content of 1 g of sample.

hydroxyl value A measure of hydroxyl (univalent OH) groups in an organic material. In plasticizers, the hydroxyl value includes OH groups present in any free unesterified alcohol as well as those of the plasticizer molecule itself. In some plasticizers, large hydroxyl values are indicative of the possibility of the plasticizer becoming incompatible on aging.

hygrometer Any instrument for measuring the humidity of the atmosphere.

hygroscopic plastic Basically, attracting, absorbing, and retaining atmospheric moisture. Thermoplastics such as polyurethanes, nylons, polycarbonates, acrylics, ABS, etc. are categorized as hygroscopic. They absorb moisture, which has to be removed before they can be processed into acceptable finished parts. Drying these plastics should not be taken casually. Simple tray dryers or mechanical convection hot air dryers, while adequate for some plastics, simply are not capable of removing water to the degree necessary for proper processing of hygroscopic plastics. With improper drying, splays, nozzle drool between injection molding shots, foamy melt, bubbles in parts, sinks, and/or lower mechanical properties are examples of the results of high water content during processing operations. With extrusion, include gels, trails of gas bubbles, arrowheads, wavefronts, surging, lack of size control, poor appearance, etc.

The most effective and efficient drying system for hygroscopic plastics is one that incorporates an air-dehumidifying system in the material storage/handling network, which can consistently and adequately provide moisture-free air in order to dry the "wet" plastic. While all systems are designed to accomplish the same end, the approaches to regeneration of the desiccant beds vary widely. Years of experience with these systems have shown that breakdowns are not usually the fault of the equipment, but are due to the user's lack of attention to preventative maintenance details as outlined by the equipment manufacturers.

hygroscopic water content The water content of an air-dried material. ▷ **moisture content equilibrium**

hygrothermal effect Change in properties due to moisture absorption and temperature change.

Hypalon Du Pont's tradename for chlorosulfonated polyethylene elastomer.

hypervelocity impact ▷ **impact strength**

hypothesis A supposition or conjecture put forward to account for certain facts, and used as a basis for further investigation by which it may be proved or disproved.

hysteresis Incomplete recovery of strain during unloading cycle due to energy consumption. This energy is converted from mechanical to frictional energy (heat).

hysteresis diagram In fatigue, the stress-strain path during the cycle.

hysteresis, elastic The difference between resilience of a material at a specified stress and deformation energy recovered from the material unloaded from the same stress, the loading and unloading occurring at a constant and specified rate.

hysteresis loop In dynamic mechanical measurement, the closed curve representing successive stress-strain status of the material during cyclic deformation; it is the cyclic noncoincidence of the elastic loading curves (see Fig.) under cyclic loading. The area of the resulting

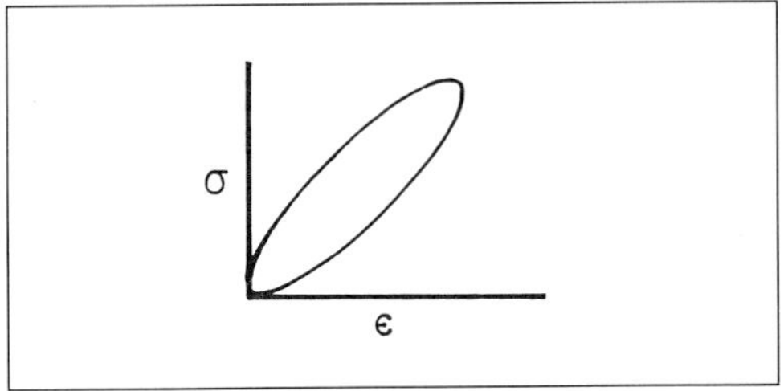

Hysteresis loop; stress versus strain.

elliptical hysteresis loop is equal to the heat that is generated in the system. These loops may be centered around the origin of coordinates or, more frequently, displaced to various levels of strain or stress; in this case, the shape of the loop becomes variously asymmetrical, but this effect is frequently disregarded. ▷ **tensile hysteresis**

hysteresis loss The loss of mechanical energy due to hysteresis.

hysteresis measurement gives dynamic characteristic An objective of dynamic testing, in addition to the determination of the number of cycles to break, is to establish causes and patterns of failure. Normally in such tests, stress and strain (extension) are measured and the elastic modulus is derived from these values. However, this can only be an initial step in the direction of a complete description of the failure pattern.

hysteresis, mechanical The energy absorbed in a complete cycle of loading and unloading, including any stress cycle regardless of the mean stress or range of stress.

hysteretic heating ▷ **fatigue hysteretic heating**

I

-ide Compounds ending with the suffix-ide (sodium chloride, sodium sulfide, calcium chloride, etc.) contain only two elements.

identification of plastic ▷ **plastic** and **recyclable plastic identified**

ignition The initiation of combustion.

ignition loss **1.** The difference in weight before and after burning. **2.** The burning off of binder or size, as with glass fiber.

ignition point ▷ **autoignition point** and **spontaneous ignition**

ignition temperature The lowest temperature at which sustained combustion of a material can be initiated under specific conditions. ▷ **fire tests, cone and lift**

ignorance factor ▷ **factor of ignorance**

illuminance The lux (lx) is the illuminance produced by a luminous flux of one lumen uniformly distributed over one square meter ($1\ lx/m^2$).

illumination, footcandle The unit of illumination when foot is the unit of length. It is the illumination on a surface, $1\ ft^2$ ($6\frac{1}{2}\ cm^2$) in area, on which is uniformly distributed a flux of 1 lm. It equals $1\ lm/ft^2$ or $10.8\ lm/m^2$.

image **1.** Any single geometric form appearing in a layout. **2.** The optical counterpart of an object produced by means of an image-producing device.

image quality indicator ▷ **quality indicator, image**

imide A nitrogen-containing acid having two double bonds, used to produce a family of temperature resistant plastics such as polyimide polyetherimide, and polyamide-imide.

immiscible With respect to two or more substances of the same phase or state of matter that cannot be blended; incapable of attaining homogeneity. It usually applies to liquids such as oil and water. The term may also refer to powder (and other solid materials) that differ widely in some physical property such as specific gravity.

immunomicrosphere ▷ **antibodies and antigens plastic encapsulated**

impact angle An angle that could be either the angle of attack or the angle of incidence. Because of this ambiguity, this term should be specifically defined when used, or preferably used only in contexts where the ambiguity does not matter.

impact bar A test specimen of specified dimensions, utilized to determine the relative resistance of a plastic to fracture by shock.

impact energy absorption This quantity is measured in terms of the work required to break a standard specimen reported in joule (ft-lb). Also refers to impact resistance and impact strength. ▷ **energy absorption**

impact failure weight That missile weight, estimated statistically, at which 50% of the specimens would fail in the specified test.

impact, falling dart ▷ **Gardner impact test**

impaction A forcible contact of particles of matter, a term often used synonymously with impingement.

impact loading **1.** In hardness testing, a phenomenon in which a momentary overload is inadvertently applied to the indenter by the inertia of parts of the tester subjected to large accelerations. **2.** Whenever a part is loaded very rapidly, it can be said that the part is subjected to impact loading. Any part which is moving has kinetic energy. When this motion is stopped due to collision, energy must be dissipated. The ability of a plastic part to absorb energy is determined by factors such as its shape, size, thickness, type of material, method of processing, environmental conditions, etc. Although impact strength of plastics is widely reported, the property usually is of no particular design value. However, they are very important because they can be used to compare relative response of materials. It can pick up discriminatory response to notch sensitivity. A better measure is impact tensile values, but unfortunately these data are generally not reported.

impact loading strain rates The Fig. on p. 369 compares strain rates versus deformation for materials tested under different conditions.

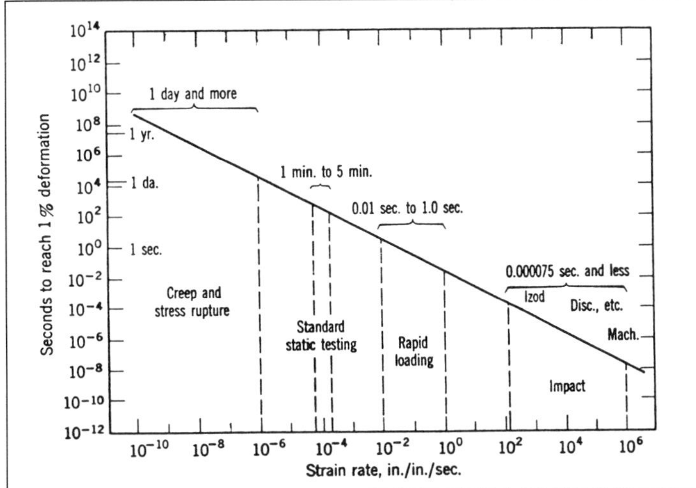

Comparison of rapid loading strain rates using different methods of testing.

impact modifier A general term for any additive, usually an elastomer or a different type plastic, incorporated in a plastic compound to improve impact resistance.

impactor A sampling device that employs the principle of impaction (impingement). The cascade impactor refers to a specific instrument which employs several impactions in series to collect successively smaller sizes of particles.

impact polystyrene An alternative name for high impact polystyrene (HIPS).

impact press Generates high velocity to die cut, punch, pierce, blank, stamp, and form a wide variety of materials including reinforced plastics, films, elastomers, metallic foils, gasketing materials, metals, etc. Tool travel can be adjusted to provide for "kiss cutting" laminated materials.

impact resistance Relative susceptibility of material to fracture by shock force; such as indicated by the energy expended by a standard pendulum-type impact machine in breaking a standard specimen in one blow.

impact shock A stress transmitted to a material (plastic, elastomer, adhesive, etc.) which results from sudden impact, jarring or vibration.

impact strength The property of a material to resist physical breakdown when subjected to a rapidly increasing applied force. It is expresssed as the impact energy obtained from a particular impact test; as the energy absorbed by the object during fracture at a very high testing rate. Energy can be expressed as in several forms: as the energy per unit cross sectional area fractured, the energy per unit volume, the energy per unit width of part (or length of notch in a notched test specimen), or the most popular of energy per width of specimen. Impact measurements are made by recording the energy loss of a weighted pendulum which strikes a specimen in the form of a bar or recording the fracture rate when a weight is allowed to fall on a specimen. The bar (notched and unnotched) test is the most used method.

The value of impact strength increases with increasing temperature, especially in the region of the glass transition temperature (T_g). Plastics with high impact strength below T_g have important secondary transitions. Orientation increases impact strength in the direction of orientation, but decreases it in the perpendicular direction. Since impact loading is multiaxial and specimens break at the weakest direction, uniaxial orientation frequently lowers impact strength. Generally, crystallization decreases impact strength, especially if large spherulites are formed. Strength may be considerably increased, especially in brittle plastics, by the addition of rubbery plastics as toughening agents. ▷ **tensile stress-strain area under the curve** and **tensile testing machine test rates**

impact test Different impact tests are performed to meet different performance requirements. Each test has its own advantages and disadvantages or limitations. The most common tests conducted on plastics are the Izod and Charpy tests. ▷ **Izod impact test; Charpy impact test; tensile impact test; dart drop test; Gardner impact test; Dynatub test; bag drop test; ball burst test; impact test instrumented.** Basically, impact tests are destructive tests in which the material is subjected to one or more impacts of specified magnitude and energy absorption or a proportionate value is determined. The drop ball impact test and the repeated blow impact test utilize a series of impacts that increase in severity until failure occurs. The most common impact tests utilize a single impact sufficient to produce failures. These are three common types of single-blow impact tests, depending on direction of load application and manner in which the cylindrical or rectangular specimen is held. In the Charpy impact test, the specimen is supported as a simple beam and load is transverse. In the Izod impact test, the specimen is supported as a cantilever beam and load is transverse. In the tension impact test, the specimen is supported at one end and the load is axial and tensile. In each case the blow is delivered by a pendulum striker. The test may be conducted at various specified levels of velocity (linear velocity of strike at impact) and energy (energy of striker at impact). The impact tests can be very controversial if the results are not carefully (and properly) interpreted for proper and, most important, for a specific application. Like most test, incorrect interpretation or application can occur if data are not properly evaluated and applied.

impact test, film ▷ **extruder film impact strength**

impact test instrumented Instrumented tests can be done with either a pendulum or a drop weight impact machine. The tester must be equipped with an instrumented striker. The instrumented striker sends a signal to a computer data acquisition system, which calculates the load, deformation, and energy absorbed by the specimen during impact. By breaking down the impact event into its components, load and deflection, instrumented tests provide designers with a guide to see what service conditions a material can endure, how the part will fail (ductile versus brittle), and the margin of safety between incipient damage and total failure.

There are standard test specimens for instrumented testing, but actual parts can also be tested; when possible, part testing is the way to go. In that mode, instrumented testing can more closely simulate actual service conditions than any other impact test. Although instrumented tests reveal a lot more information about a material's behavior, they can require sophisticated interpretation (ASTM D 3767).

impact test, reverse This is the term used when the usual impact test is conducted in which a material is struck by a pendulum or falling object, and the reverse side is inspected for damage.

impact, tub A falling weight (tub) impact test developed specifically for pipe and fittings. There are several variables that can be selected (ASTM D 2444).

impalpable ▷ **powder**

imperfection Any defect or blemish in or on material that detracts from its appearance or lowers its utility. In grading rules, a class of limitation on manufacturing practice.

impingement mixing Intermixing of two liquid chemical streams upon high velocity injection into a small chamber in the mixing head.

implanted medical devices ▷ **absorbable technology; bioplastic-biomedical; human implantation; lens implanted; microencapsulation, coating**

impreg Wood impregnated with usually thermoset plastics that is cured-in-place to reduce material swelling and shrinking of the wood on exposure to varying environmental conditions. Depending on type of plastic used, can improve different properties, such as wear resistance, toughness, strength, etc; also can provide different decorative appearances.

impregnate **1.** In reinforced plastics, to saturate the reinforcement with a plastic. **2.** Process of plastic impregnation of nonplastics, such as aluminum, steel, copper, etc., using heat with vacuum and/or pressure to saturate the substrate, followed with curing. Thermoset plastic is usually used. Improves performance of substrate, particularly making them impervious to liquids and gases (air, etc.).

impregnated fabric A woven or nonwoven fabric, as well as other fiber forms (rope, tape, etc.). impregnated with a plastic. When using the usual solvent-thermoset plastic (polyester, phenolic, etc.), solvent recovery systems are recommended. ▷ **prepreg**

impregnation The process of thoroughly soaking, filling of voids and interstices of a material such as fabric, wood, and paper with a plastic. Generally, the porous materials serve as reinforcements for the plastic binder or matrix after cure. The process is usually carried out in an impregnator such as heated liquid saturation bath that includes a vacuum and/or pressure applicator. Amount of impregnation is controlled by solids content of plastic mix, speed of material going through the liquid impregnator, and pressure control (such as doctor blade or roll).

impression **1.** The imprint or dent made in a specimen by the indenter of a hardness-measuring device. **2.** The reproduction of the surface contours of a specimen formed in a plastic material after the application of pressure, heat, or both. **3.** ▷ **mold cavity impression 4.** ▷ **forging** regarding impression molding.

impulse sealing A heat sealing technique in which a pulse of intense thermal energy is applied to the sealing area for a very short time, followed immediately by cooling. It is usually accomplished by using a radio frequency (RF) heated metal bar that is cored for water cooling or is of such a mass that it cools rapidly at ambient temperatures.

impurity The presence of one substance in another, often in such low concentration that it cannot be measured quantatively by ordinary analytical methods. ▷ **purification**

inches per rack In warp knitting, IPR is the length of fabric in one rack measured on the machine under operating take-up tension.

inching ▷ **mold inching**

incidence angle The angle between a ray impinging on a surface at a point and perpendicular to the surface at that point. In the description of a beam, the angle of incidence of the ray at the centre of the beam.

incineration Basically controlled burning of solid, liquid, or gas wastes to break them into gas byproducts and ash. Plastics are a safe component in municipal waste incineration. In modern waste-to-energy facility equipped with available high-tech pollution control devices, all wastes can be safely incinerated and their energy value recovered. Because plastics are practically all petroleum and natural gas derivatives, they burn at a higher temperature than other wastes and help to make the combustion process more complete. A more complete burn is a cleaner burn. Incineration plays an important role behind reduction and recycling in the EPAs four-tiered hierarchy for disposal of municipal solid waste, It can safely reduce waste volume by 90 to 98% in the U.S. and worldwide garbage by converting that waste into useful energy.

incineration and energy ▷ **energy thermal reclamation** and **British thermal unit**

incineration fume system Unlike dealing with particulate-laden emissions (a relatively simple process employing existing equipment with low operating costs) meeting EPA's fume-cleanup standards requires more sophisticated systems that generally involve large capital investments and substantial operating costs. Therefore, the choice of a fume-incineration system might significantly affect a company's profitability. There are four basic types of fume-incineration systems, all of which use thermal oxidizers to destroy volatile organic compounds (VOCs) by converting hydrocarbon-laden fumes to water vapor and carbon dioxide. While each type effectively destroys VOCs, the systems have varying operating costs and are based on different oxidation theories. They are: (1) *Common afterburner* This system heats fumes to incineration temperatures to destroy VOCs and maintains those temperatures for the time specified by regulation. While the afterburner is relatively inexpensive to buy and install, it typically consumes 2,000% more fuel than other systems. As a result, this system is typically suitable for low-throughput applications that process contaminated air at rates of 500 ft/min ($2\frac{1}{2}$ m/s). (2) *Catalytic converter* Hydrocarbon-laden fumes are pushed by a fan through a preheat section, where the temperature of the fumes is raised to 371°C (700°F). The fumes then pass through another section that contains the catalyst, which is able to thermally oxidize hydrocarbons at 700°F. This system is more efficent than an afterburner. It works well on "clean" hydrocarbon fumes but performs poorly with fumes contaminated with particles, plastics, heavy metals, or silicones commonly found in heating and drying processes. Catalytic converters are best suited for clean-link processes that do not employ silicones. (3) *Recuperative thermal oxidizer* This system is economical to operate, as some of the heat generated during incineration can be recycled as building heat, for generating steam, or returned to the incineration system. Factors such as equipment size, heat transfer coefficents, and stress limit the system's efficiency. Reusing the excess heat requires additional investments to buy and maintain heat-transfer equipment. This system is suitable for processes that incinerate fumes with a high solvent content. (4) *Regenerative thermal oxidation* In this system, oxidized gases from the combustion chamber pass through a porous heat-transfer section, where the fumes are preheated by conduction of the stored heat to within 5% of oxidation temperature. This system is simple and reliable, requiring little or no additional fuel, even when hydrocarbon levels approach zero. It is recommended for large processes with low solvent concentration, because the high rate of primary-heat recovery reduces fuel costs.

incinerator Trash threatens to bury "us", so "they" report. Landfills are filling up. Proposed large incinerators often face the "not in my backyard" type of opposition (however, there are lots of available lands so why pick on someone's backyard...to save money?). Here is one of many possibilities. A small incinerator and energy recovery plant is about the size of a 42 gallon (4.9 m^3) barrel of oil. It consumes such waste as diapers, garbage, bones, magazines, bacon fat, tires, wood, paper, plastics, etc., all without smoke or flyash. Fuel enters through the center tube, air through the concentric tube around the fuel tube. A small baffle extends the smoke path to enhance heat transfer to the water jacket around the fire box. Flue temperatures higher than 927°C (1,700°F) are obtained in the range necessary for a clean burn. Ash analysis shows no unburned carbon material and nothing that would require disposal in a controlled landfill.

inclusion A physical and mechanical discontinuity occurring within a material or part, usually consisting of solid, incapsulated foreign material. Inclusions are often capable of transmitting some structural stresses and energy fields, but to a noticeably different degree than from the parent material. ▷ **void**

increment In sampling, a portion of material removed from a lot of a single operation.

indentation hardness Hardness evaluated from measurements of area or indentation depth caused by pressing a specified indentation into the surface of a material with a specified force.

index of refraction ▷ **refractive index**

indicia Any markings such as symbols, lettering, small pictures, etc. applied to a plastic product.

induction bonding The use of high-frequency electromagnetic fields to excite the molecules of metallic inserts placed in the plastics or in the interfaces, thus fusing the plastics. The inserts remain in the joint.

induction hardening A surface hardening process in which only the surface of a suitable ferrous workpiece is heated by electrical induction to above the upper transformation temperature and immediately quenched. ▷ **screw heat treatment**

induction heating A method of heating electrically conductive materials, usually metallic parts, by placing the part or material in a high-frequency electomagnetic field generated by passing an alternating electric current through a primary coil. The alternating field induces electromotive forces in the work which generates heat. Plastics, generally being poor conductors, cannot be heated directly by induction heating but the process is used indirectly in welding of plastics and in heating of extruder barrels.

induction, magnetic Flux density in a magnetic field.

induction welding A method of welding thermoplastics by placing a conductive metal insert on the surface of two sections to be joined, applying pressure to hold the sections together, heating the metallic insert by means of a high frequency generator until the surrounding plastic is softened and welded together, then cooling the welded joint.

industrial design The industrial designer (ID) is an essential part of (all) industry that relates to research, engineering, production, and marketing activities. IDs must exercise the creative imagination which sets them apart from being a mere modifier of what the competition offers. They must exercise it in cooperation with others that keep them abreast of new materials, products, etc. There is a difference between IDs and other professions whose functions are sometimes confused with those of the ID. The true artist, for instance, produces a personal interpretation of what one feels and creates (by definition) the final object alone. The ID does not; they help to provide the directions by which others create the final product. Since the ID is usually a significant part of the team which creates the products of industry, they must differ in their approach or they would be an engineer. Thus, what distinguishes the target of engineering design from those of other design activities is the extent to which technological factors must contribute to their achievement.

industrial waste Wastes generated in industrial operations or manufacturing. Categorized as scrap, which can be recycled at a profit, or solid wastes which cannot be recycled or reclaimed but can be incinerated at a profit.

inelastic deformation The portion of deformation under stress that is not annulled by removal of stress.

inert Not participating in any fashion in chemical reactions.

Inert additive A material such as a filler, added to a plastic compound, which may alter the properties of the finished part but which does not react chemically with any other constituents of the composition.

infinite thickness Term applied to a layer of material so thick that increasing its thickness does not change its reflectance or other optical properties.

inflation A rise in the general price level, usually expresssd as a percentage rate.

information/data center A specific organization committed to handling a set of material under a formalized information/data storage and retrieval system. If stored material is reviewed by experts in the field, the activity is called an information (or data) analysis center.

information system A mechanism for acquiring, filing, storing, and retrieving an organized body of knowledge, together with the access mechanisms and other user assists. Also called information storage, retrieval system.

infrared IR pertains to that part of the electromagnetic spectrum betwen the visible light range and the radar range. Radiant heat is in this range, and IR heaters are frequently used in the thermoforming, curing, etc. of plastics. The energy transferred to the plastic is converted into vibrational and rotational enegy of the molecules. The desired heating up to the desired temperature takes place in the interior of the plastic, whereas electrical resistance heating first heats the surface and moves gradually towards the interior. The IR region of the electromagnetic spectrum starts immediately at the limit of visible light at a wavelength of about 0.78 μm, and ends at about 400 μm (see Fig. below). The technologically usable part lies between 0.8 mm to about 6 μm going from near-IR through mid-IR to far-IR.

infrared heating A heating process used in plastic processing, employing lamps (see Table) or heating elements which emit invisible radiation. ▷ **infrared**

infrared polymerization index The IRPI number represents the degree of cure of phenolic plastics, defined as the ratio of absorbances of absorbance peaks at 12.2 and 9.8 microns (μ). The background absorbance at each wavelength is subtracted from the peak absorbance, and the index is obtained by dividing the difference at 12.2 μ by the difference at 9.8 μ.

infrared sensing device One of a wide class of instruments used to display or record, or both, information related to the thermal radiation received from any object surfaces viewed by the instrument. Instruments vary in complexity from spot radiometers to 2-dimensional real-time imaging systems. ▷ **sensor**

Effective radiating temperatures and energy efficiencies for different types of IR sources.

Type	Temperature °C	Efficiency
Long-wavelength ceramic lamp	512	0.46
Medium-wavelength fused quartz lamp	905	0.66
Medium-wavelength quartz glass lamp	930	0.72
Short-wavelength quartz glass lamp	2200	0.90

infrared spectroscopy Infrared spectroscopy or spectrometry records spectral absorptions in the infrared region using pyrolysis, transmission, and surface-reflectance techniques, exposing the sample to light in the infrared range and recording the absorption pattern yield in a "fingerprint" of the material. Infrared spectroscopy is used for identification of plastics and elastomers, polymer blends, additives, surface coatings, thickness, and chemical alteration of surfaces. This is one of the most common analytical techniques used with plastics. The easy operation and the availability of this type of equipment have contributed to its popularity. Although the infrared spectrum characterizes the entire molecule, certain groups of atoms give rise to absorption bands at or near the same frequency, regardless of the rest of the molecule's structure. The persistence of these characteristic absorption bands permits identification of specific atomic groupings within the molecular structure of a sample.

The IR region of the electromagnetic spectrum includes radiation at wavelengths between

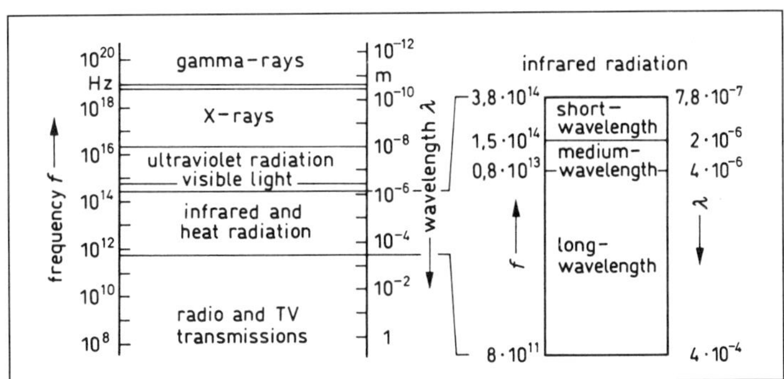

Frequency and wavelength regions of IR radiation and their relationship to electromagnetic vibrations in general.

0.7 and 500 μm, in wave numbers, between 14,000 and 20 cm^{-1}. Molecules have specific frequencies which are directly associated with their rotational and vibrational motions. IR absorptions result from changes in the vibrational and rotational state of a molecular bond. Coupling with electromagnetic radiation occurs if the vibrating molecule produces an oscillating dipole movement that can interact with the electric field of the radiation.

For qualitative analysis, one of the best features of an IR spectrum is that absorption or the lack of absorption in specific frequency regions can be correlated with specific stretching and bending motions and, in some cases, with the relationship of these groups to the rest of the molecule. Thus, when interpreting the spectrum, it is possible that certain functional groups are present in the material and certain others are absent.

infusible Not capable of melting when heated, as are all cured thermoset plastics.

ingot A large casting that is subsequently rolled or forged.

inhibition and retardation Inhibitors prevent the formation of measurable amounts of plastic under conditions that otherwise would permit such polymerization. Retarders reduce the rate at which the polymer is formed.These effects may occur as a result of a reaction between the chain-initiating species and the inhibitor or retarder. Thus, in a catalytically initiated polymerization, the inhibitor destroys the catalyst. If all the catalyst is destroyed, one observes inhibition; if part of it is destroyed, the rate of subsequent polymerizations is proportionally reduced and retardation has occurred. These phenomena occur in Ziegler-Natta type and ionic polymerizations.

inhibitor A substance that retards a chemical reaction. Also used in certain types of monomers and plastics to prolong life.

initial modulus ▷ **modulus, initial**

initiator Source of free radicals, often peroxides or azo compounds. They are used in free-radical polymerizations, for curing thermoset plastics, and as crosslinking agents for elastomers and crosslinked polyethylene.

injection blow molding ▷ **blow molding, injection**

injection-compression molding ▷ **coining**

injection molding The injection molding (IM) process is greatly preferred by designers because the manufacture of parts of complex shape and three-dimensions can be more accurately controlled and predicted with IM than with other processes. As its method of operation is much more complex than others, IM require a thorough understanding. The Figs. below show schematics of the load profile and the molding cycle that highlight the way in which the melt is plasticized (softened) and forced into the mold, the clamping system for opening and closing the mold under pressure, the type of mold used, and the machine controls.

Plastic moves from the hopper onto the feeding portion of the reciprocating extruder

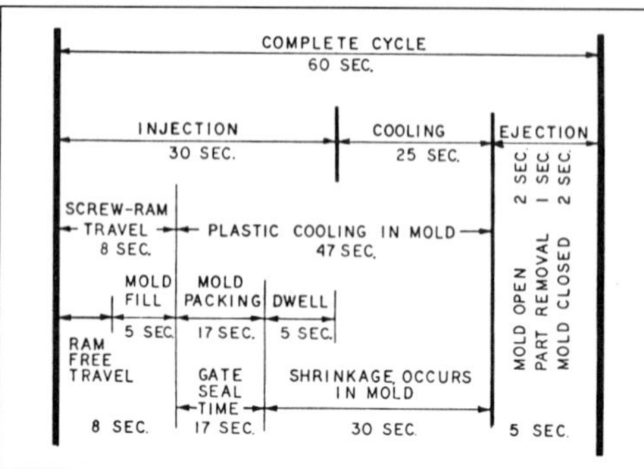

Example of an injection molding cycle processing thermoplastic.

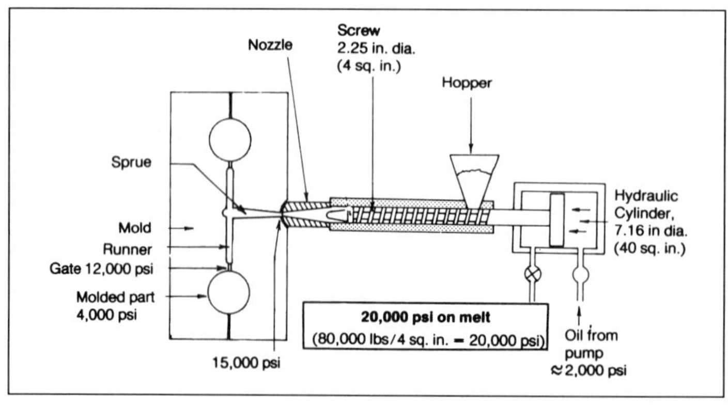

Schematic of pressure loading on plastic melt during injection molding.

screw. The flights of the rotating screw cause the material to move through a heated extruder barrel where it softens (is made fluid) so that it can be fed into the shot chamber (front of screw). This motion generates pressure (usually 50–300 psi), which causes the screw to retract. When the preset limit switch is reached (or a position transducer on newer machines), the shot size is met and the screw stops rotating; and at a preset time the screw acts as a ram to push the melt into the mold. Injection takes place at high pressure (up to 30,000 psi melt pressure in the nozzle). Adequate clamping pressure must be used to eliminate mold openig (flushing). The melt pressure within the mold cavity ranges from 1–15 tons/sq. in., and is dependent on the plastic's rheology/flow behavior.

Even though most of the literature on processing specifically identifies or refers to thermoplastics (TPs), some thermosets (TSs) are used (TS polyesters, phenolics, epoxy, etc.) TPs reach maximum heat prior to entering "cool" mold cavities, whereas TSs reach maximum temperature in "hot" molds. ▷ **injection molding thermoplastic or thermoset**

injection molding, air entrapment ▷ **air entrapment**

injection molding automated The use of flexibly automated injection molding controls and systems definitely depends on the tasks the machine has to perform and the production sequences required. Automation is one possibility for putting in-house "aims" into practice and/or for meeting market-dictated demands such as: (1) production costs reduction, (2) short job processing time, (3) low expenditure on setting-up, (4) greatest possible preparedness for meeting delivery, (5) large product range, and (6) improved delivery consistency.

In order to utilize the advantages of flexibly automated IM cells, a considerably higher capital investment is necessary than with other choices of systems, which are less automated and flexible. This increases the investment risk, with the question as to the profitability of such systems becoming more urgent. The following are examples of the productivity-increasing effects: (1) an increase in the annual utilization time, (2) the increase in annual production volume, (3) the reduction of demolding time, and (4) a shortening of transit time, if additional activities can be carried out within the programmed cycle time.

The profitability of a flexibly automated IM plant is influenced by: (1) rising capital cost, (2) reducing personnel costs due to fewer personnel required, and (3) changes in energy-costs and the mold-cost structure. With this action new goals can be met through plant flexibility, such as : (1) improved delivery consistency, (2) greatest possible preparedness for meeting deliveries, (3) large range of products, and (4) short job processing time. There is also the quality-related effects that result in improved quality assurance and reduced number of rejects. Work environment changes occur in (1) psychological and physical stresses on staff, (2) qualification requirements from staff, (3) social welfare of staff employed on IM machine, and (4) the accident risk situation. An evaluation of the utilization efficiency serves for assessing the criteria that cannot be quantified in monetary terms. An established utilization efficiency value can be taken as decision-aid, which in conjunction with the investment calculation will allow a better selection of alternatives under consideration.

injection molding auxilliary equipment ▷ **auxiliary equipment**

injection molding back pressure Indicates resistance to the backward movement of the screw during preparation for a subsequent melt shot. This pressure is exerted by the plastic on the screw while it is being fed into the shot chamber (forward end of the barrel, in front of the screw). During rotation of the screw and the material under pressure, thorough mixing of the plastic is achieved, and some temperature increase also results. In dealing with heat-sensitive and shear-rate-insensitive plastics, care must be taken to keep this value within prescribed limits. The action reviewed concerns a conventional screw where back pressure is used to improve the melting characteristics of an otherwise marginally performing screw for the plastic being processed.

With a two-stage screw, the first stage is hydraulically isolated from the second stage screw by the unfilled devolatization zone. Consequently, back pressure cannot be used to affect melting. Applying back pressure affects the second stage only, and serves to increase the reverse pressure flow component. This will necessitate a longer filled length of the second stage to produce adequate conveying, and thus the length of unfilled channel will be reduced and devolatilization impaired. In an extreme case, back filling can progress to the vent port and vent bleed will occur. The only practical advantage lies in the additional mixing it induces in the second stage. However, the additional length of a two-stage screw is almost always ssufficient to ensure adequate mixing without application of back pressure.

injection molding barrel ▷ **barrel**

injection molding capacity volume The maximum (theoretical) calculated swept volume (or trapped volume in a plunger unit) in in.^{3} (cm^3) which can be displayed by a single stroke of the injection screw (being used as a plunger) or plunger, assuming no leakage and excluding the use of a rotating screw to displace additional volume (referred to as intrusion molding when screw continues to rotate as it injects into the cavity(s)). The capacity is also expressed by weight in oz, lb, or kg. However, the more precise method is by volume since plastic densities differ. When specifying by weight, either the plastic one specifies is used or the general industry type is used, namely general purpose polystyrene (GPPS). During molding the usual shot size used is about 80% of the capacity available. The lower the percentage, the greater the potential of a residence time problem, particularly with heat sensitive plasics.

injection molding capacity, (volume) thermoset Due to the lack of a non-return valve on thermoset plastic screws, the swept volume cannot be used to convert to true shot size since some material flows back over the screw during injection. The amount of back flow is dependent on variables in both the machine and molding material.

injection molding ceramic In order for powder ceramic compounds to be processed through IM machines, they must be specially prepared. This involves the addition of a binder. These binders usually consist of plastic blends of various compositions. The binder is a temporary aid which makes it possible to carry out the IM process. Before the IM parts are fired to produce the final ceramic part, the binder must be removed as fully as possible since otherwise the parts could explode, swell (expand), or break. Drying or volatilization (debindering) is a rather complex operation in the entire production process. Exact adherence to temperature-time curve specified according to the particular material and size, shape and wall thickness of the preform is very important for the quality of the fired part.

Thermoset binders are less suitable than thermoplastic binders because of their greater thermal stability at temperature and the resulting complications for the debindering process. In each case, the amount of plastic which is later to be decomposed should be kept as low as possible. IM of any powdered parts makes high demands on the wear resistance of different machine components, particularly on screws, non-return valves, cylinders, and molds. Efforts in powder and binder manufacture are directed towards minimizing machine wear and improving end product quality. Although a reduction in particle size brings improvments in the material and IM, it also increases the difficulty of removing the binder gently by drying. Thus, tradeoffs exist. Regardless of these, ceramics have advantages such as: complicated parts (with thread, undercuts, etc.) can be made, high strength of the preforms permit automatic productioin, constant shrinkage behavior in the sintering process can be accurately controlled, and owning to the good slip properties of the binders, the IMs are very highly and uniformly compacted. ▷ **injection molding metal powder**

injection molding circuit board Injection molded substrates for printed wiring boards have the potential of providing cost savings over standard epoxy/glass plastic substrates. The 3-dimensional features such as spacers, stand-offs, soldering sites, and holes for through-hole connections can be molded-in rather than added.

injection molding clamping operation and mechanism ▷ **clamping**

injection molding clamping tonnage (force) The maximum force holding the mold closed between the press platens. Tonnage required during molding is dependent basically on the pressure the plastic melt requires in the mold cavity times the projected area of melt. The total area at the mold parting line is based on the area of the part(s) which is projected onto a plane at right angles to the direction of the mold cavity. It includes runners, sprues, vents, or culls in the mold that solidify during molding.

injection molding, coinage ▷ **coining**

injection molding, coinjection ▷ **coinjection**

injection molding communication protocol ▷ **communication protocol**

injection molding computer integrated The ultimate result of computer integrated injection molding (CIIM) in software packages is to translate the results of computer simulation of the molding of a specific part into machine settings for specific microprocessor-controlled machines. (see Fig. on p. 377). CIIM automates the entry of a large number of set points in microprocessor-controlled machines and maximizes their efficiency.

injection molding core pulling sequence ▷ **mold core pulling sequence**

injection molding crystallinity effect ▷ **crystallinity and orientation**

injection molding cycle ▷ **cycle**

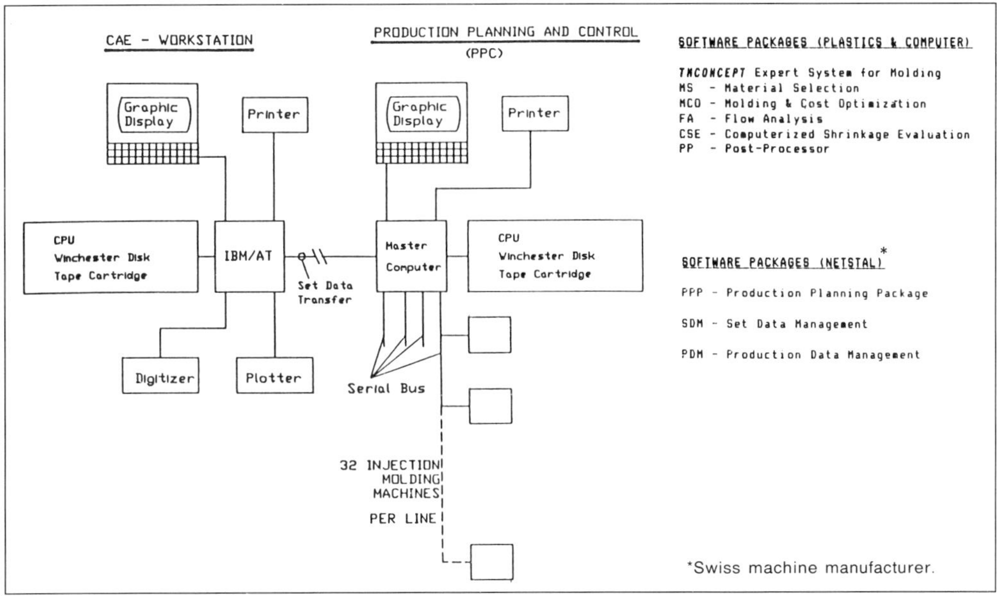

Overview of computer integrated injection molding (CIIM).

injection molding daylight opening ▷ **clamping daylight**

injection molding displacement rate Machine builder's displacement rate is basically the rate of flow of melt from the screw into the mold during the injection portion of the molding cycle in in.^{3}/s (cm^3/s). The actual amount is usually slightly less due to factors that reduce flow rate, such as thickness and length of cavity, absence or amount of mold venting, plastic viscosity, melt and mold temperature distribution, and gate size(s). Lack of adequate venting could be the second (to gate size) common cause of reducing displacement rate. Actual rate is determined by first taking a full shot, determining precise time (s) for the shot, and weighing the shot. Convert weight to volume by dividing shot weight (g) by the plastic's specific gravity x 16.36. This volume (in.^{3}) of melt shot divided by the time period (s) results in a displacement rate for the plastics used in a specific machine based on the machine control settings.

injection molding, electrical drive In addition to the usual hydraulically operated IM machines, there are also electrical direct servo powered lines in the injection end, clamping end, or both. ▷ **clamping electrical**

injection molder feeder ▷ **feeder**

injection molding foam ▷ **foamed injection molding**

injection molding fusible core The use of fusible metal core technology (FMCT) as well as soluble core technology (SCT) to IM parts with cavities that could not be formed or released otherwise has been known in the plastics industry since as least the 1940s, but not frequently used (since it was more of a mystery in the past). More recently, fusible cores and soluble cores have been used. As an example, there are automobile engine intake manifolds molded of glass fiber reinforced nylon that have shown to be economical and technologically interesting as an application. Utilization of the fusible core to mold the complex, curved part produced the high quality, smooth interior surface sought. The air resistance coefficient of a 90° bend was reduced by more than 50% in going from a rough diecast to a smooth plastic surface of the hollow inner spaces of the curved manifold. The diecast aluminum parts required extensive postmachining assembly operations: the RP provided the design freedom required to consolidate several manifold components into one, greatly reducing assembly and finishing costs.

The basic fusible core technique makes it possible to produce simple to very complex hollow structural products (take-off of cored metal casting). It involves using a fusible core inside the plastic shape or structure. The core permits forming of the desired plastic shape, to date usually RP.

Core material is a type that will not collapse or change shape during a pressure-temperature-time processing cycle. Shape is not usually the problem since the core material is restricted. The core material used depends on actual processing requirements, paticularly temperature. It can range from a wax, thermoplastic, and to different ratios of zinc-aluminum eutectic mixtures (alloys) to special fusible eutectic alloys. Core material has to melt below the temperature of the plastic. These shaped cores are usually inserted in a mold cavity where it is retained by the mold (such as used with a mold core puller) or by "spiders" (as used in certain metal core supports for extrusion dies). After processing, the core material is removed by heating it to its melt temperature. Release is via an existing opening or a hole is drilled through the plastic to the core.

This technique is used in different processes, such as injection molding, compression molding, reaction injection molding, and various RP methods. ▷ **eutectic** and **soluble core molding**

injection molding, gas Parts can be molded by gas injection using injection molding machines. This process is most effective and economical when used for large parts. It offers a way to mold parts with only 10 to 50% of the clamp tonnage that would be necessary in conventional IM.

The technique—practiced in several variations, with some patented—involves the injection of an inert gas, usually nitrogen, into the melt as it enters the mold. This is not structural foam, as no foam core is produced; instead the gas forms a series of interconnecting hollow channels in the thicker sections of the part. The gas pressure is maintained through the cooling cycle. In effect, the gas packs the plastic into the mold without a second-stage high-pressure packing in the cycle as used in IM, which requires high tonnage to mold large parts.

Molded-in stresses are miminal. The thick but hollow sections provide rigidity and do not create sink or warpage problems. The cycle time is reduced because the thick sections are hollow. As the gas is not mixed with the melt, there is no surface splay, which is typical of low-pressure structural foam molding. The finished part exhibits an excellent surface finish with minimum distortion. The nitrogen gas pressure tank usually at about 4,300 psi (30MPa). Gas injection is being used with commodity and engineering plastics.

injection molding gas counter pressure ▷ **foamed injection molding gas counter pressure**

injection molding, granulated plastic ▷ **granulating**

injection molding high pressure foam ▷ **foamed injection molding high pressure**

injection molding history IM machines for processing plastics, derived from metal diecasting presses, started worldwide with the U.S. patent issued in 1872 to John W. Hyatt, a printer (who in 1868 issued the first patent in U.S. for a plastic, cellulose nitrate called celluloid). Many patents and new concepts have emerged worldwide, such as the reciprocating screw plasticator that has been used since the 1960s; however it was conceived in 1951 by William H. Willert.

injection molding, hydraulic clamp ▷ **clamping, hydraulic**

injection molding, hydroelectric clamp ▷ **clamping, hydroelectric**

injection molding, injection rate adjustable The ability to adjust the injection rate in stepless control between the maximum and minimum rate.

injection molding, injection rate maximum The maximum calculated rate of displacement expressed in volume per second (in.^{3}/s or cm^3/s) computed at maximum injection pressure.

injection molding, injection rate minimum The minimum calculated rate of displacement expressed in volume per second (in.^{3}/s or cm^3/s) computed at maximum injection pressure.

injection molding, in-mold coating, decorating, and labeling ▷ **in-mold coating, decorating and labeling**

injection molding intensification ratio The ratio of the injection pressure to the pressure of the hydraulic fluid (line pressure). It is numerically equal to the area of the hydraulic cylinder which actuates the screw or plunger divided by the area of the screw or plunger itself.

injection molding, intrusion For the molding of heavy sections or when the shooting capacity of the machine is not adequate, intrusion molding is used where the screw turns continously, filling the cavity directly. When the cavity is filled, a cushion is extruded in front of the plunger (screw), which then comes forward to supply the needed injection pressure.

injection molding, jet method Jet molding is a processing technique characterized by the fact that most of the heat is applied to the plastic as it passes through the nozzle, rather than in a heating cylinder, as is done in conventional IM. ▷ **injection molding offset method**

injection molding, jetting The turbulent flow of plastic from an under-sized gate or thin section into a thicker mold cavity, as opposed to the usual desired laminar flow of plastic progressing radially from a gate to the extremities of the cavity. Melt spurts without wetting the walls near the gate into the large unrestricted area of the cavity at high injection speeds. Results include ripples on surface, nonuniform density, unwanted stresses, etc. Corrective action usually requires reducing injection rate; enlarge gate or relocate it away from the open area.

injection molding, liquid Liquid injection molding (LIM) has been used much longer than reaction injection molding (RIM), but the processes are practically similar. The advantages it offers in the automated low pressure processing of (usually) thermoset resins—fast cycles, low labor costs, low capital investment, energy saving, and space saving—may make LIM competitive to potting, encapsulating, compression transfer, and injection molding, particularly when insert molding is required.

Different resins can be used, such as polyester, silicones, polyurethanes, nylon, and acrylic. A major application for LIM with silicones is encapsulation of electrical and electronic devices.

LIM employs two or more pumps to move the components of the liquid system (such as catalyst and resin) to a mixing head before they are forced into a heated mold cavity. In some systems, screws or static mixers are used. Only a single pump is required for a one-part resin, but usually two (or more)-part systems are used. Equipment is available to process all types of resin systems, with unsophisticated or sophisticated control systems. A very critical control involves precision mixing. If voids or gaseous by-products develop, vacuum is used in the mold.

injection molding, lost core method ▷ **injection molding fusible core**

injection molding low pressure foam ▷ **foamed injection molding low pressure**

injection molding machine hydraulic leak control ▷ **hydraulic leakage control**

injection molding machine, hydraulic pump ▷ **hydraulic pump**

injection molding machine setup record The Table on pp. 380 and 381 is a guide for injection (and extrusion) machine settings. Specific information on all machine settings and plastic properties initially is acquired by using the plastic supplier's data sheet on a particular material to be used.

injection molding machine size selection Important parameters to consider in selecting injection molding machines are projected area vs. clamping force, part weight vs. machine injection capacity, mold size vs. platen size, mold thickness vs. closed daylight, part depth vs. open daylight, part depth vs. clamp stroke, cycle time, screw recovery vs. cycle time.

injection molding machine specification The Fig. on p. 382 is a guide in specifying an IM machine.

injection molding melt extractor Usually refers to a type of injection machine torpedo but could refer to any type of device which is placed in a plasticating system for the purpose of separating melt from partially molten pellets and material. It thus ensures a fully plasticated discharge of melt from the plasticating system.

injection molding melt flow ▷ **mold cavity melt flow; mold cavity melt fountain flow; injection molding with rotation; orientation**

injection molding melt flow defects ▷ **melt flow defects**

injection molding melt fracture ▷ **melt fracture**

injection molding, melting and crystallization When the injection molder melts crystalline plastic, one finds that higher molecular weight requires higher melting temperatures and longer times, which may increase the molding cycle. Then, once the melt has filled the mold, one must cool it until it crystallizes before opening the mold and beginning another cycle. Here one finds that lower molecular weight provides the molecular mobility needed for plastic molecules to fit into the growing crystal lattice structure and thus hasten crystallization and shorten the molding cycle (see Table). Of these two conflicting factors, fast crystallization during mold cooling is usually the more critical, so low molecular weight favours faster molding cycles.

Example of molecular weight and crystallization of polyethylene terephthalate (PET).[1]

Molecular weight[2] (number average)	Halftime of crystallization minutes
11,200	3.5
13,600	9.0
14,000	15.0
15,200	17.5
15,800	18.5

[1] At 118°C, starting with an amorphous sample.
[2] Obtained from osmotic pressure data.

injection molding melt temperature There are different approaches to determining melt

Injection molding and extrusion machine settings guide.

Resin data[1]	Specific gravity, g/cm^3	Density, lb/ft^2	Specific volume, $in.^3/lb$	Specific volume, cm^3/g	Extrusion temperature, °F	Injection temperature, °F	Linear mold shrinkage, in./in.	Specific heat, btu/lb/°F	Water absorption % in 24 hours	Maximum water content allowable for molding
ABS-extrusion	1.02	64.0	27.0	0.980	435		0.005	0.34	0.25	
ABS-injection	1.05	65.0	26.0	0.952		500	0.005	0.40	0.40	0.20
Acetal-injection	1.41	88.0	19.7	0.709		390	0.020	0.35	0.25	
Acrylic-extrusion	1.19	74.3	23.3	0.839	375		0.004	0.35	0.30	
Acrylic-injection	1.16	72.0	24.1	0.868		450	0.005	0.35	0.20	0.08
CAB	1.20	74.6	23.1	0.833	380	440	0.004	0.35	1.50	0.15
Cellulose acetate-extrusion	1.28	80.2	21.6	0.781	380		0.005	0.40	2.50	
Cellulose acetate-injection	1.26	79.0	21.9	0.794		450	0.005	0.36	2.40	0.20
Cellulose proprionate-extrusion	1.22	76.1	22.7	0.821	380		0.004	0.40	1.70	
Cellulose proprionate-injection	1.22	75.5	22.9	0.828		425	0.004	0.40	2.00	0.25
CTFE	2.11	134.0	13.1	0.473		550	0.008	0.22	0.01	
FEP	2.11	134.0	12.9	0.465	600	600	0.010	0.28	<0.01	
Ionomer-extrusion	0.95	59.6	29.0	1.050	500		0.007	0.54	0.07	

Ionomer-injection	0.95	59.1	29.2	1.060		420	0.007	0.54	0.20	
Nylon 6	1.13	70.5	24.5	0.886	520	550	0.013	0.40	1.60	0.15
Nylon 6/6	1.14	71.2	24.3	0.878	510	510	0.015	0.40	1.50	0.15
Nylon 6/10	1.08	67.4	25.6	0.927		450	0.011	0.40	0.40	0.15
Nylon 6/12	1.07	66.8	25.9	0.935	475	500	0.011	0.40	0.40	0.20
Nylon 11	1.04	64.9	26.6	0.962	460	450	0.005	0.47	0.30	0.10
Nylon 12	1.02	63.7	27.1	0.980	450	445	0.003		0.25	0.10
Phenylene oxide based	1.08	67.5	25.6	0.926	480	525	0.006	0.32	0.07	
Polyallomer	0.90	56.2	30.7	1.110	405	405	0.015	0.50	0.01	
Polyarylene ether	1.06	66.2	30.7	0.940	460	535	0.006		0.10	
Polycarbonate	1.20	74.9	23.1	0.832	550	575	0.006	0.30	0.20	0.02
Polyester PBT	1.34	83.6	20.7	0.746		460	0.020		0.08	0.04
Polyester PET	1.31	8.18	21.1	0.746	480	490	0.002	0.40	0.10	0.005
HD polyethylene-extrusion	0.96	59.9	28.8	1.040	410		0.025	0.55	<0.01	
HD polyethylene-injection	0.95	59.3	29.1	1.050		480	0.025	0.55	<0.01	

[1] These are strictly typical, average values for a resin class. Consult your resin supplier for values and more accurate information.

INJECTION MOLDING MACHINE — SPECIFICATION FORM

Sheet 1 of 2
Date Prepared: ______
Supersedes Issue Dated: ______

Manufacturer: ______
Address: ______
Machine Model No.: ______

CLAMPING UNIT			Measurement U.S.	Measurement Metric
Type Horizontal "H", Vertical "V"				
Full Hydraulic Clamp "FH", Toggle Clamp — Hydraulic Actuated "HT" Toggle Clamp — Mechanical Actuated "MT", Other (Explain)				
Clamping Force (Tons)				
Clamp Opening Force (Tons)				
Clamp Stroke Max. (in., mm.)				
Open Daylight Max. (in., mm.)				
Closed Daylight Max. (in., mm.)				
Closed Daylight Min. (in., mm.)				
Platen Dimensions	Horizontal (in., mm.)			
	Vertical (in., mm.)			
Platen Bolting Pattern (SPI Specification — Other)				
Distance Between Tie Rods or Beams	Horizontal (in., mm.)			
	Vertical (in., mm.)			
Tie Rod Diameter or Beam Equivalent Diameter (in., mm.)				
Mold Size:				
Max. Horizontally	Horizontal (in., mm.)			
	Vertical (in., mm.)			
Max. Vertically	Horizontal (in., mm.)			
	Vertical (in., mm.)			
Max. Thickness — Toggle Clamp (in., mm.)		(Hydraulic Clamp Variable with Stroke and Daylight)		
Min. Thickness — Toggle Clamp (in., mm.)		(Hydraulic Clamp — with Ejector Box and/or spacers)		
Ejector Knockout				
Mechanical "M", Hydraulic "H"				
Force (Tons)				
Stroke (in., mm.)				
Pattern (SPI specifications — other)				
Mold Thickness Adjustment				
Toggle Clamp — Single Point Die Height Adjustment Standard "S", Optional "O", None "N"				
Toggle Clamp — Multiple Point Die Height Adjustment Standard "S", None "N"				
Hydraulic Clamp — "HC"				

INJECTION MOLDING MACHINE — SPECIFICATION FORM

Sheet 2 of 2
Date Prepared: ______
Supersedes Issue Dated: ______

Manufacturer: ______
Address: ______
Machine Model No.: ______

INJECTION PLASTICIZING (PLASTICATING) UNIT		Measurement U.S.	Measurement Metric
Type — Plunger Unit "P", Two-Stage Plunger "2P" Two-Stage Screw "2S", Reciprocating Screw "RS"			
Injection Capacity — Calculated (cu. in., cu. cm.)			
Injection Capacity — Calculated G.P. Polystyrene (oz., gm.)			
Plasticizing (Plasticating) Capacity — Cont. G.P. Polystyrene (lb./hr., kg./hr.)			
Recovery Rate — G.P. Polystyrene SPI Test Procedure	cu. in./sec., cu. cm/sec.		
Effective 1-1-68 at 50 per cent injection capacity	oz./sec., gm./sec.		
Injection Pressure — Max. (psi, kg./sq. cm.)			
Injection Rate Adjustable (Yes or No)			
Injection Rate — Max. at Max. Pressure (cu. in./sec., cu. cm./sec.)			
Injection Rate — Min. at Max. Pressure (cu. in./sec., cu. cm./sec.)			
Injection Stroke — Min. (in., mm.)			
Injection Plunger or Reciprocating Screw Diameter (in., mm.)			
Screw Diameter — 2-Stage Screw (in., mm.)			
Barrel L/D Ratio			
Screw Speed Range (RPM)			
Screw Drive — Hydraulic "H", Electric "E"			
Torque (in.-lbs., mm.-kg.) Calculated 100 per cent efficiency of input torque			
HYDRAULIC SPECIFICATIONS			
Pump Capacity — Total (gpm)			
Oil Reservoir Capacity (gal.)			
ELECTRICAL SPECIFICATIONS			
Number of Electric Motors			
Total Rated HP			
Total Heating Wattage (kw)			
Number of Heat Control Zones			
Number of Rheostats			
Number of Pyrometers			
MACHINE DIMENSIONS — OVERALL			
Length (in., mm.)			
Width (in., mm.)			
Height (in., mm.)			
Weight (lbs., kg.)			

Injection molding machine specification form.

temperature, each with advantages and disadvantages (limitations); a few are to be reviewed. The simplest technique is the insertion of a thermocouple (T/C) probe into the melt collected from an air shot (separating the barrel nozzle from the mold and shooting a shot into the air). The temperature range can be found by measuring at different locations within a single shot. However, the targets of measurements are random and operator dependent. Another method utilizes a T/C situated between the nozzle and the screw, flush mounted in the inner barrel surface. It has the advantage of being a continuous reading which is not operator dependent. Unfortunately, only a limited portion of the shot can be sampled.

Incorporating a fiber optic/IR melt temperature sensor system has the advantage of a fast response time compared to a T/C and is nonintrusive. However, the focal point of the IR measurement as well as the absorption characteristics are temperature dependent, rendering the interpretation of the signal potential difficult. Also melt temperature is measured with a T/C fixed at the screw tip and facing downstream. The signal is relayed to the data acquisition system through a slipping arrangement in a cored screw. Although this system is quite suitable in following melt temperatures, it is subject to viscous errors because sensors are facing downstream. ▷ **Boyer-Beaman rule**

injection molding metal powder Metal injection molding (MIM) has the ability to produce parts with injection molded finish and geometry (threads, side core features, etc.) not obtainable with precision zinc die casting and sintering without second operations. The choices in metal powders are quite broad, including stainless steel and a variety of iron and nonferrous alloys. MIM provides superior physical and mechanical properties when compared to wrought metals. ▷ **injection molding ceramic; Thixomolding**

injection molding methods IM encompasses different or alternate methods of processing plastics with the so-called conventional injection molding reciprocating screw method (▷ **injection molding**) that processes over 90% of all plastics going through IM machines. The other methods include: coinjection, foam, soluble core, plunger, multiple, gas, jet, offset, liquid, reaction, ceramic, metal powder, push-pull, multi-live feed, etc.

injection molding mold The tool to form a product using the IM process. ▷ **mold**

injection molding mold cavity melt flow ▷ **mold cavity melt flow analysis**

injection molding molding area diagram ▷ **molding area diagram**

injection molding mold venting ▷ **mold venting**

injection molding multi-live feed The "Scorim" process is a molding method to improve strength and stiffness of parts by eliminating weld lines and controlling orientation of fibers. A conventional IM machine uses a special head that splits the melt flow into the mold into two streams (see Fig. on p. 384). During the holding stage, two hydraulic cylinders alternately actuate pistons above and below the head, compressing the material in the mold in one direction and then the other. This action aligns the fibers, removes weld lines, and induces orientation in liquid crystal polymers (LCPs). Used with thermoplastic and thermoset plastics. Process is similar to the push-pull method. ▷ **injection molding push-pull**

injection molding multiple clamping With conventional IM most machines only use one mold in one clamping system (using two platens). To increase output for certain products, there are stacked molds and multiple clamping systems. The stacked system uses one floating platen between the two regular platens; molds are located on both sides of the floating platen. Multiple systems have more than one floating platen and handle more "stacked" molds. The stacked mold system is also referred to as multiple clamping. ▷ **clamping**

injection molding multiple screw ▷ **extruder, screw multiple type**

injection molding nozzle The orifice-containing plug at the end of the injection cylinder or melt transfer chamber which contacts the mold sprue bushing and directs the plastic melt into the mold. The nozzle is shaped to form a seal under pressure against the bushing. Its front end may be either flat or (usually) spherical in shape providing a leakproof connection with the bushing. The hollow cored metal nose nozzle screws into the plasticating cylinder. Its orifice is tapered to maintain the desired flow of plastic. Sometimes a check valve is included to prevent backflow, or an on-off valve to interrupt the flow at any desired point in the molding cycle.

injection molding nozzle drooling Leakage from the nozzle or around the nozzle area during injection step into the mold drools, an undesirable situation that can be corrected. Problem may be due to plastic getting trapped between the nozzle tip and the mold bushing.

injection molding nozzle extended An ex-

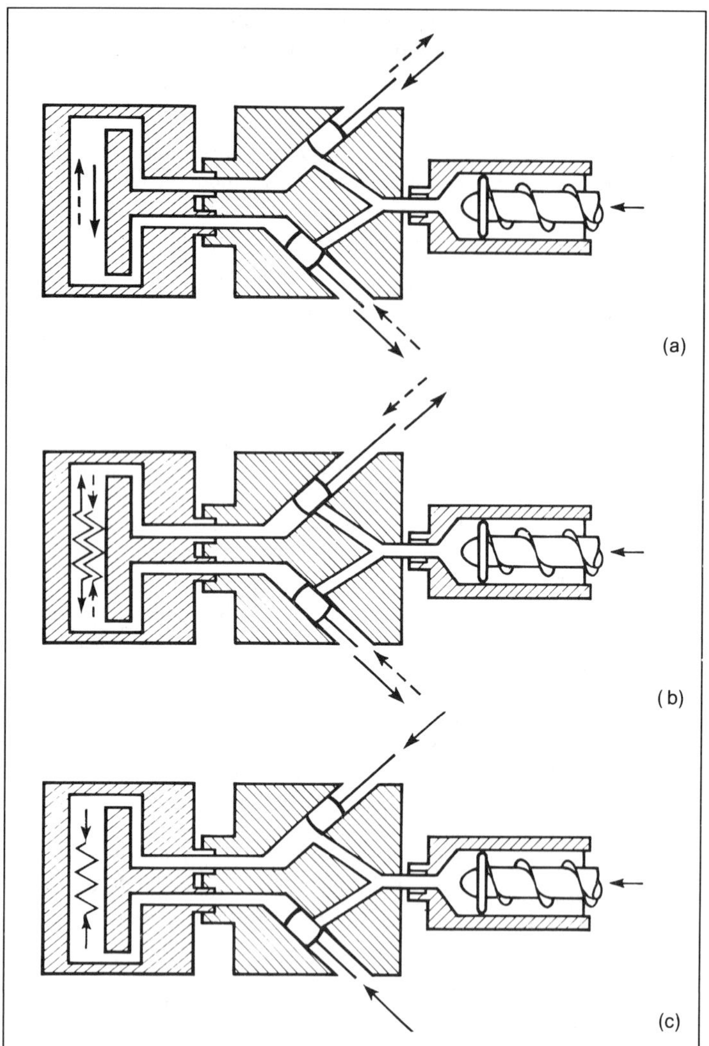

Schematic of the multi-live feed "SCORIM" molding process. (*a*) Two packing pistons oscillate 180° out of phase; (*b*) two packing pistons oscillate in phase; (*c*) two packing pistons compress melt with equal constant pressure.

tension of the nozzle which penetrates into the mold and shortens or eliminates the need for a sprue bushing.

injection molding nozzle freeze-off Freeze-off is the solidification of melt in the nozzle orifice (opening) preventing the transfer of melt from the plasticator to the mold. Solutions to the problem include: removing contaminated material from the nozzle, raising gate mold temperature if controller is used, increasing manifold temperature, increasing melt temperature, reducing cycle time, opening nozzle orifice, etc.

injection molding nozzle gate A nozzle whose tip is part of mold cavity, thus feeding material directly into the cavity, eliminating the need for sprue and runner system. The nozzle becomes the mold gate.

injection molding nozzle retraction stroke The maximum stroke of the mechanism (usually a hydraulic cylinder) used to separate the injection unit from the bushing of the mold for cleaning and/or purging purposes.

injection molding nozzle shut-off A nozzle which incorporates some type of valve which prevents leakage from the nozzle. ▷ **screw tip**

injection molding nozzle temperature control To provide improved melt flow control with certain machines (such as using rather long nozzles) and plastics (such as heat sensitive types), heat control of the nozzle is used.

injection molding offset method A specialized adaptation of IM which permits use of incompletely cured thermoset plastics by heating only a small charge at one time, heating the charge just enough to make the plastic melt, using very high pressures for injection, utilizing the heat of compression and friction heat developed during injection, and finally adding additional heat only as the plastic passes through the nozzle. ▷ **injection molding jet method**

injection molding operator's sequences ▷ **operation, manual; operation, semi-automatic; operation, automatic**

injection molding, orientation ▷ **orientation and injection molding melt flow** and **injection molding with rotation**

injection molding, outgassing ▷ **outgassing**

injection molding, packing mold ▷ **mold cavity packing**

injection molding parting line control ▷ **mold parting line control**

injection molding plasticating Refers to the melting of the plastics in the injection barrel prior to injection in the mold. ▷ **plasticate** and **screw melt**

injection molding plasticating performance test The SPI Injection Molding Division guideline bulletin on plasticating performance recommends a performance test procedure for screw IM machines. The purpose of this test is to define a uniform comparative method of rating the plasticizing (plasticating) rate of a screw IM machine. This method is not intended to provide an absolute rating of the capacity of the device in any given situation or material, but rather provides a means of comparing the performance of one machine with another under certain specified situations and materials.

injection molding plastication versus shot size Machine selection of screw size usually only includes maximum shot size, but also important is the plasticating ability. It is usually incorrect to assume that the screw's plasticating ability remains the same regardless of the shot size being used. As an example, when the screw reciprocates in preparing the melt, that may be 25% or 90% of shot capacity, thus it loses a portion of the screw feed section that influences the plasticating ability.

injection molding plasticizing capacity The amount of plastic that can be melted, homogenized, and heated to processing temperature in the barrel per unit of time (lb/h or kg/h). If the plasticizing capacity is too low in relation to shot size required, the chances are that the injected plastic will not yet be completely molten, whereas too high a capacity may result in thermal degradation of the plastic due to excessively long barrel dwell times.

injection molding plasticizing, continuous With a screw unit, maximum capacity is generally expressed in weight/hour as calculated from the recovery rate for thermoplastics. The interplay of many machine design and material variables, particularly screw design and back pressure conditions, has made it impractical to establish any standards for plasticizing capacity and recovery rate for thermoset IM machines.

injection molding plate dispersion plug Two perforated plates, held together with a connecting rod, that are placed in the nozzle to aid in dispersing a colorant in a plastic as it flows through the orifices in the plates.

injection molding, plunger In the plunger machine (not a screw type), the material is fed into the heating barrel (see Fig. on top of p. 386). The plunger or ram forces the material through the cylinder where it is heated by conduction of heat from the barrel wall. As the material is forced forward, it passes over a spreader or torpedo within the barrel which causes mixing. The plunger continues to force the material through the nozzle and into the mold. Different designs or versions are used with this basic concept of the plunger IM machine including combinations with screw types.

Since the introduction of IM plastics (1872) until the 1960s, it was practically the only method used. With the development of the screw type IM machines during the 1960s, the plunger method practically became extinct worldwide. It is now used in special cases such as processing unmeltable thermoplastics in screw machines and its main use with special thermoset bulk molding compounds (BMC) producing certain size or shape parts. However, BMCs are also used in screw machines. ▷ **plunger molding**

injection molding plunger prepack Prepacking, also called stuffing, is a method which can be used to increase volumetric output per shot of the injector plunger unit by prepacking or stuffing additional reinforced plastic material into the heating barrel by means of multiple strokes of the injector plunger (applies only to plunger unit type IM machines).

injection molding plunger preposition The position of the injection plunger by either limit switches or pressure switches, so that total travel during injection is reduced. The primary purpose is to reduce overall time by eliminating unnecessary plunger travel time during injection.

injection molding, postcuring ▷ **postcuring**

injection molding pressure Pressure applied to the injection screw (or plunger) to force the

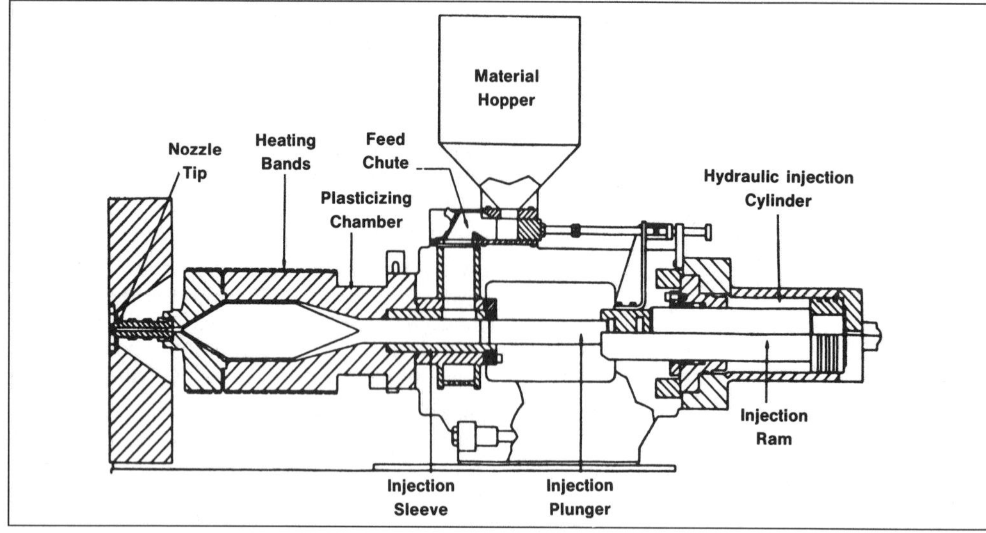

Schematic of a plunger injection molding machine.

melt from the barrel into the mold, measured in psi or MPa. ▷**molding pressure required**

injection molding process control Proper injection of plastic into the mold is influenced by several conditions (see Fig. below). Any one condition (or combinations) can affect cycle time and part quality. The obvious factors to consider are the temperature of the plastic and thus its viscosity. Injection pressure and speed are the two most commonly changed parameters when molders try to improve cycle time and part quality. However, there are other conditons that also affect the process: gate size, mold temperature, part wall thickness, length of melt flow, type of material (amorphous versus crystalline), presence or absence of mold venting, injection speed and displacement rate, hold pressure, etc. The top Fig. opposite is an example of the variables that can develop. Usual problem in setting up process control involves one or only a few conditions. The relation of machine settings versus performances is shown in the Fig. on p. 388. ▷**process control** and **mold process control**

injection molding process control, compensation approach Conventional process control systems are designed for closed loop control

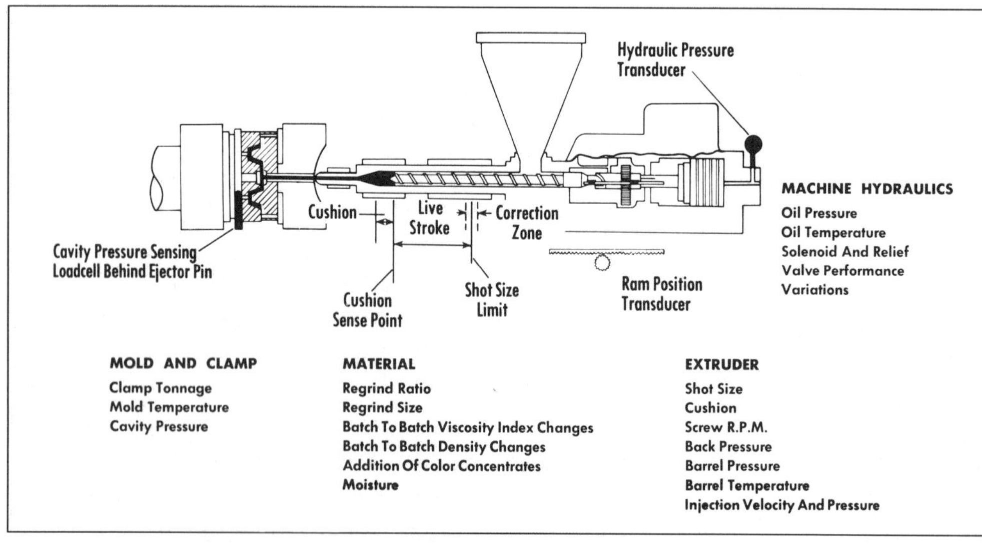

Examples of factors that influence injection molding.

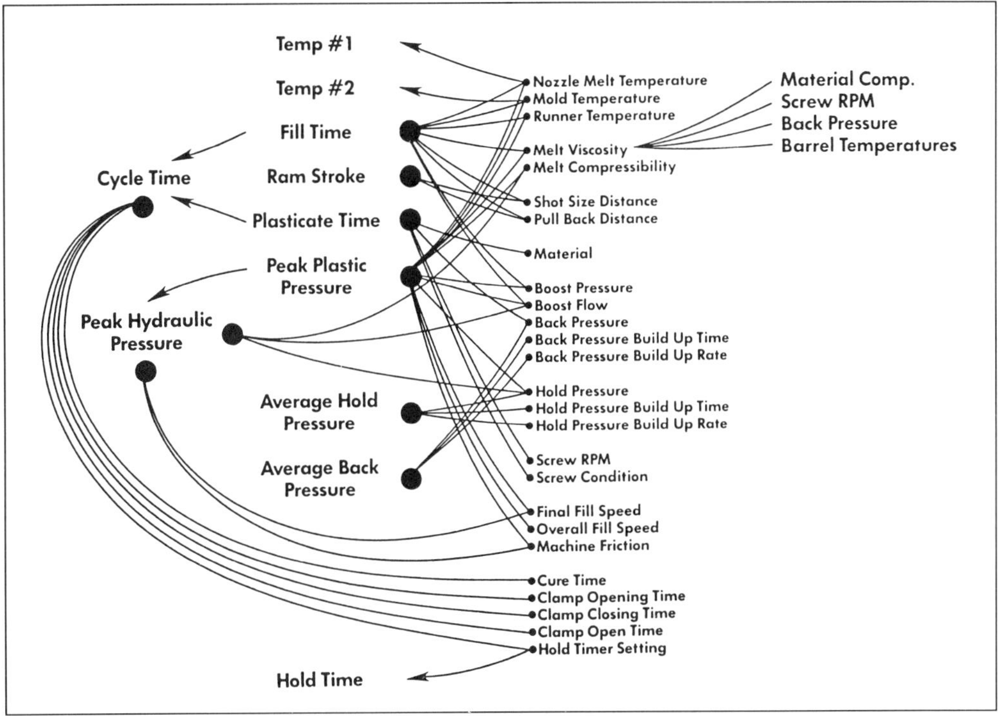

Examples of process control factors that can influence cycle time and part performance of injection molded products.

of IM parameters such as injection velocity holding pressure, cushion, and recovery stroke. However, there are processing parameters such as melt temperature and mold temperature which affect the consistency of the molded part to an even greater extent. These are generally left out of the conventional process control concepts. There is a method which compensates for variations in melt and mold temperature by adjusting the holding pressure profile in real time. Compared with conventional closed loop process control, this method, called pvT (pressure, volume, temperature by Battenfeld) holding pressure optimization, results in reduced weight savings, parts with lower internal stress, higher dimensional stability, and significantly less waste in start-up. Essentially, pvT holding pressure optimization is superimposed on a system that already supports closed loop, process control. Therefore, the degree of control provided is above and beyond that of a system which many would already call fine tuned.

The various phases which a shot of a plastic undergoes during IM using pvT holding pressure optimization are represented schematically by the teardrop shaped diagram (see Fig. below).

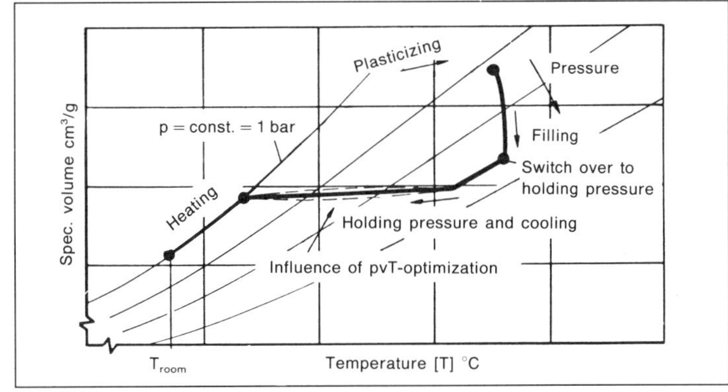

Method to compensate for variations in melt and mold temperature by adjusting the holding pressure profile in real time, called pvT from Battenfeld.

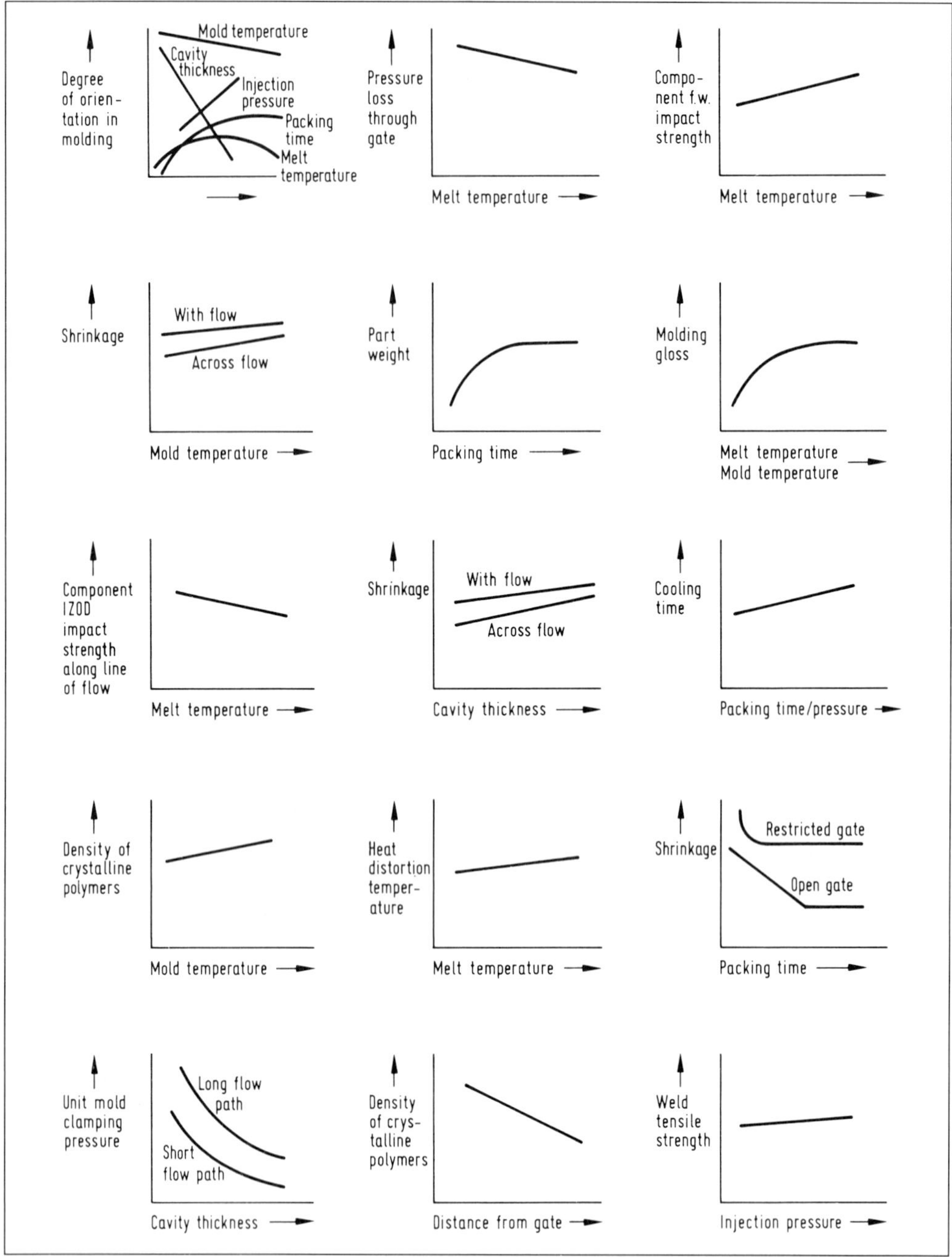

Examples of how injection molding machine settings can affect properties of plastics.

The pvT optimization routine is concerned with the quantities p (pressure), v (specific volume), and T (temperature), as well as the profile of the mean temperature in the mold determined by a cooling calculation. In the diagram, pressure values are represented by diagonal isobar lines. One bar, the uppermost diagonal line, is atmospheric pressure, and the lines below indicate sucessively higher pressures. Specific volume may be defined as volume of plastic per unit of weight, for example, in.^{3} (cm^3) per ounce (kg). Specific volume is the inverse of density. The objective of the pvT holding pressure optimization is to reduce the molded part to the same temperature at atmospheric pressure after cooling. This assures that the specific volume (and therefore the density and part weight) will be consistent.

injection molding process control statistically ▷ **statistical process control**

injection molding processing parting line control This technique controls the process by using the movement between the two halves as the plastic is injected into the mold as the feedback variable. This movement across the mold parting line is used to initiate the transfer from injection to holding pressure; it therefore performs as a transfer point controller (TPC). TPC has been around for some time and is a common component of most process control packages for IM. Four strategies are included in the usual commercial transfer point packages; parting line adds a fifth. Parting line has a major advantage in that its sensor is simply added to the outside of the mold. This technique results in little or no machining cost. This system provides for an add-on to older machines without full control packages. While this concept may sound simple, it requires numerous developments in sensors, amplifier stability, and special signal processing. TPC developments have been conducted by Eastman Kodak Co., Manufacturing Research & Engineering Organization.

injection molding processing temperature The Fig. on this page is an example of the thermal load profile for thermoset plastics during IM. Processing temperatures for various plastics are given in the Table below.

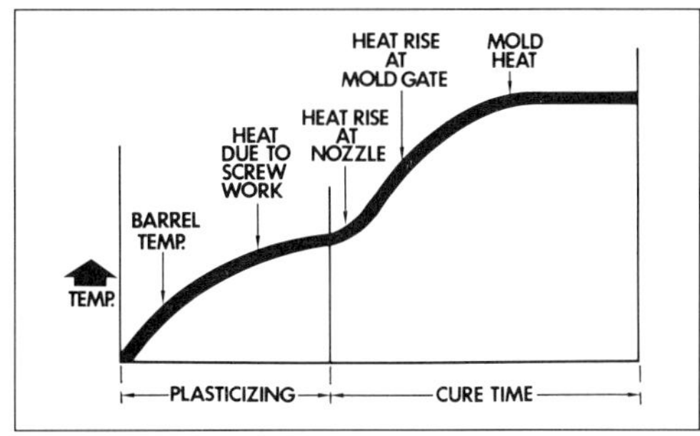

IM thermal profile for a thermoset plastic; for thermoplastic the curve is similar from the start to the heat rise at the gate, thereafter it descends during its cooling period.

injection molding, processing versus properties The Table on p. 390 is an example of the effect of varying IM processing conditions on the final properties of a dry blended styrene-maleic anhydride copolymer at 260°C (500°F).

injection molding product cost The first Fig. on p. 390 shows share of cost for high volume parts and precision parts that are IM.

injection molding programmable controller safety circuit ▷ **programmable controller safety**

injection molding purging ▷ **purging**

injection molding push-pull This method ("Scorim" process) offers to reduce anisotropy in fiber reinforced plastics and to strengthen knit lines in reinforced and liquid crystal polymers (LCPs). The mold cavity is filled from two

Example of IM processing temperature used with heat resistant, engineering thermoplastics, whereas typical commodity plastics use about 400° to 550°F (204° to 288°C).

Polymer	Type	T_g, °F	Processing temperature, °F
Polyetherether-ketone (PEEK)	Semicrystalline	290	650
Polyphenylene sulfide (PPS)	Semicrystalline	185	630
Polyarylene ketone	Semicrystalline	400	700–780
Polyarylene sulfide	Amorphous	410	625–650
Polyetherimide (PEI)	Amorphous	Varies	Varies
		450	575–650
		545	650–700
Polyarylether	Amorphous	476	650
Polyethersulfone (PES)	Amorphous	510	575
Polyamide-imide (PAI)	Amorphous	470	650
Polyimide	Pseudo-thermoplastic	480	680
		482	660
		536	660
		536	660

Example of comparing IM *processing versus properties.*

	Control	Check value	Gate size	Back pressure	Screw speed	Fill time
Check valve	Ring	Ball	Ring	Ring	Ring	Ring
Gate size, in.	0.13 × 0.25	0.13 × 0.25	0.062 × 0.063	0.13 × 0.25	0.13 × 0.25	0.13 × 0.25
Back pressure, psi	0	0	0	125	0	0
Screw speed, RPM	73	73	73	73	52	73
Fill time, s	1	1	1	1	1	4
Notched Izod impact strength, ft/lb/in.	3.2	2.6	1.9	1.5	4.0	3.9
Flexural strength, 10^3 psi	17	17	17	17	19	18
Flexural modulus, 10^6 psi	0.98	0.98	0.98	0.98	1.00	0.98

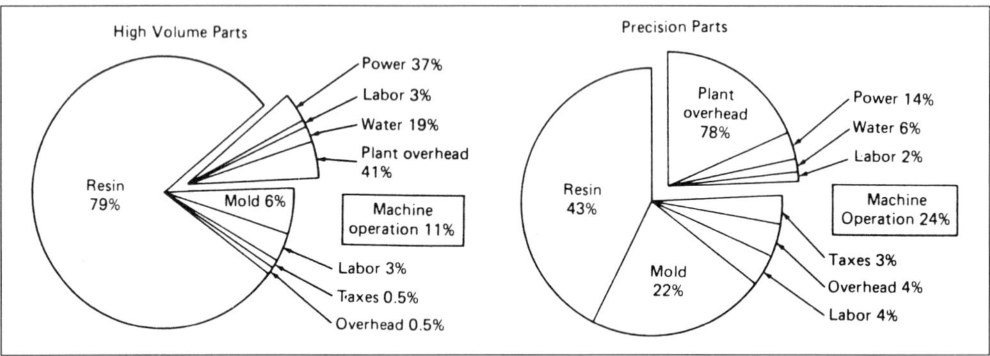

Share of cost to IM high volume and precision parts.

different directions. It requires two injection units, suitable microprocessor controls, and a mold with two sets of melt channels and gates into the cavity (see Fig. below). During the injection cycle, the two units take turns in injecting plastic (push-pull) in a series of alternating strokes until freeze-off. The process takes advantage of the fact that fibers and self-reinforcing plastics like LCPs orient with flow and shear stress. By repeatedly switching the flow direction during molding filling, push-pull creates a series of layers from skin to core having different orientations. This controllability makes it possible to optimize part properties. This process is similar to the multi-live feed method. ▷ **injection molding multi-live feed**

injection molding, quick mold change ▷ **quick mold change**

injection molding ram ▷ **injection molding, plunger**

injection molding, reactive processing IM practically always uses a plastic, not a monomer (prepolymer) that would react in the mold cavity(s). However, reactive molding in conventional machines is used that is similar to the reaction injection molding (RIM). ▷ **reactive processing**

injection molding, reciprocating A combination plasticating and injection unit in which an extrusion device with a reciprocating screw is used to plasticate the plastic. The injection of material into a mold can take place by direct extrusion into the mold, by reciprocating the screw as an injection plunger, or by a combination of these two. When the screw serves as an injection plunger, this unit acts as a holding,

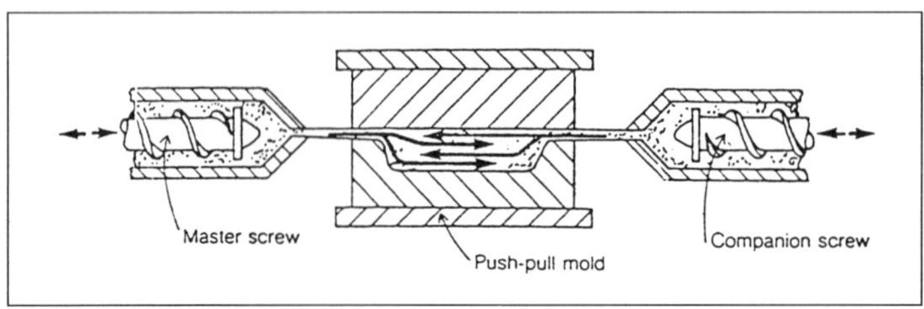

Schematic of the principle of push-pull injection molding.

measuring, and injection chamber, or the conventional IM machine.

injection molding reinforced plastic Thermoplastic and thermoset plastic with reinforcements, such as short fiber or milled glass fibers, provide products with certain improved properties when compared to their counterpart unreinforced plastics. ▷ **reinforced plastic**

injection molding rotating spreader A type of injection torpedo (for injection molding plunger unit) which consists of a finned torpedo that is rotated by a shaft extending through a tubular cross section injection ram behind it.

injection molding rotometer Water flow meter can be installed in water line. Flow is through a vertical transparent tube marked with a scale. A ball-shaped float (or other device) is inside the tube; it moves up or down based on the water flow rate. There are also air flow meters to control air flow (around the mold, and other processes). Water flow is used to control temperature of water cooled molds, hydraulic oil, or both.

injection molding, runnerless ▷ **mold, runnerless injection molding**

injection molding safety ▷ **safety; safety and processing; safety and machines; safety interlock; barrel fail-safe rupture disk; programmable controller safety**

injection molding sandwich structure ▷ **coinjection; foamed, structural; sandwich structure**

injection molding screw decompression The aim of decompression (also called screw decompression or suck back) is to decompress the plastic melt when the plasticator (injection unit) after the injection pressure stroke completes the mold filling. In turn the screw is pulled back towards the hopper causing decompression or suck back, eliminating drooling of the melt from the nozzle.

injection molding screw design ▷ **screw**

injection molding, screw length-to-diameter ratio ▷ **L/D ratio**

injection molding, screw pulling The screw can be removed from a barrel manually, which can be difficult and a time-consuming task, or it can be pushed out of the barrel automatically (hydraulically, etc.), eliminating the need for special extraction devices and reducing chances of screw damage. ▷ **extruder screw pulling**

injection molding screw tip ▷ **screw tip**

injection molding shot capacity ▷ **injection molding capacity volume**

injection molding, shrinkage and tolerance Certain IM parts can be molded to extremely close tolerances of less than a thousandth of an inch, or down to 0.0 percent, particularly when TPs are filled with additives or TS compounds are used. To practically eliminate shrink and provide a very smooth surface, one should use a small amount of chemical blowing agent ($<0.5\%$, by weight) and a regular packing procedure. For conventional molding, tolerances can be met of $\pm 5\%$ for a part 0.020 in. thick, $\pm 1\%$ for 0.050 in., $\pm 0.5\%$ for 1.000 in., $\pm 0.25\%$ for 5.000 in., and so on. Thermosets generally are more suitable than TPs for meeting the tightest tolerances.

Economical production requires that tolerances not be specified tighter than necessary. However, after a production target is met, one should mold "tighter" if possible for greater profit. The Table on p. 392 reviews factors affecting tolerances. Many plastics change dimensions after molding, principally because molecular orientations/molecules are not relaxed. To ease or eliminate the problem one can change the processing cycle so that the plastic is "stress-relieved", even though that may extend the cycle time, and/or heat-treat per the resin supplier's suggestions.

injection molding, soluble core ▷ **injection molding fusible core**

injection molding sprue break After injection and screw decompression (suck back), the nozzle may be moved back from the mold sprue bushing to give a small gap during the period when the mold is opened. This process is called sprue break.

injection molding stages The injection machine basically goes through the following stages: (1) *Plasticizing* Heating and melting of the plastics, and venting of the melt; (2) *Injection* Injection under pressure of the melt into the mold, while closed. Solidification of the polymer begins during this injection first at the cavity walls; (3) *After-filling* Maintaining the injected material under pressure for some time to prevent backflow of polymer, and to compensate for the decrease in volume due to solidification; (4) *Cooling* Cooling the molded article until it is sufficiently rigid to be ejected; (5) *Mold Release* Opening the mold, ejection of the molding, and closing of the mold again, ready for the next cycle.

injection molding structural foam ▷ **foamed, structural**

Parameters that influence part tolerance.

Part design	Part configuration (size/shape). Relate shape to flow of melt in mold to meet performance requirements that should at least include tolerances.
Material	Chemical structure, molecular weight, amount and type of fillers/additives, heat history, storage, handling.
Mold design	Number of cavities, layout and size of cavities/runners/gates/cooling lines/ side actions/knockout pins/etc. Relate layout to maximize proper performance of melt and cooling flow patterns to meet part performance requirements; preengineer design to minimize wear and deformation of mold (use proper steels); lay out cooling lines to meet temperature to time cooling rate of plastics (particularly crystalline types).
Machine capability	Accuracy and repeatability of temperature/time/velocity/pressure controls of injection unit, accuracy and repeatability of clamping force, flatness and parallelism of platens, even distribution of clamping on all tie rods, repeatability of controlling pressure and temperature of oil, oil temperature variation minimized, no oil contamination (by the time you see oil contamination damage to the hydraulic system could have already occurred), machine properly leveled.
Molding cycle	Set up the complete molding cycle to repeatedly meet performance requirements at the lowest cost by interrelating material/machine/mold controls.

injection molding, tandem machines When a large enough machine is not available and/or limited production exists, two IM machines can be set up to operate in tandem (see Figs. below).

injection molding thermoplastic or thermoset With thermoplastics the mold is kept at a low temperature below the solidification point of the plastic, causing the injected melt to "freeze", thus forming the part. After cooling, the mold opens and the part is ejected. From 85 to 90% of all plastics IM are thermoplastic.

When processing thermosets, the melt is kept below the temperature where it would cause solidification due to its exothermic reaction until it enters the cavity. In turn the cavity temperature is kept at a high temperature to cause the melt to solidify. ▷ **thermoplastic** and **thermoset**

View of two IM machines operating in tandem.

View of large mold located in tandem machines.

injection molding, thermoset machine The basic difference between an IM machine processing thermoplastic or thermoset is in the barrel, screw, and nozzle. TS barrels generally use water jackets for temperature control to provide required temperature control of melt. Screws are shorter (in the range of 13/1 and 16/1 L/D), compression ratio is usually one, and do not have a non-return valve at the tip. Nozzles may or may not be temperature controlled, depending on size and other design details. ▷ **screw, thermoset type**

injection molding thickness adjustment To compensate for shrinkage of a part during cooling (or curing), an opening or recess in the cavity wall with an adjustable plug (usually round) can be used if part can tolerate its surface finish. As melt shrinks and is still molten, the plug pushes melt into the cavity. This is one of many techniques used. ▷ **coining**

injection molding, tie-bar growth One problem that most controls do not consider involves the effect of heat on tie-bars, which can directly influence mold performance, particularly at start-up. If the heat differs from top and bottom bars, it is necessary to insulate the mold from the platens. The insularor pad used also confines heat more to the mold, producing savings in heat and/or better heat control.

injection molding, toggle clamp ▷ **clamping, toggle**

injection molding, tolerance ▷ **injection molding, shrinkage and tolerance**

injection molding troubleshooting guide An example of a guide is shown in the Table on pp. 394 and 395.

injection molding, two-color This is sometimes called double-shot molding. It uses an IM machine for making two-color molded parts by means of successive molding operations. This is accomplished by first molding the basic case or shell and then, using this as an insert, with the next shot around or in the original molded part (see Fig. below). These steps can be accomplished using two separate machines or have two injection units (with the different plastics) delivering melts in sequence into a shuttle or rotary mold held between platens.

injection molding, two-stage screw ▷ **injection molding venting**

injection molding, two-stage unit There are different many machines but they all basically provide the same action and conveyance of melt to mold parts. The two-stage plasticator/injection unit utilizes two separate stages to perform its function (see Fig. on top of p. 396). The first, or plasticating stage, is devoted to the melting and mixing of the melt by utilizing a long, rotating screw. This screw does not require a reciprocating action since it only conveys melt forward where, by means of a diverter valve, it is transferred into the injection or holding cylinder. When a sufficient quantity of melt has been plasticated and transferred, the diverter valve shifts to create a flow path from the injection cylinder to the mold. The second stage (injection stage) now begins. The melt is forced out of the injection cylinder by a hydraulic driven piston or plunger. After injection is completed, the diverter valve again shifts to connect the flow path from the rotating screw to the injection cylinder to transfer more melt for the next shot.

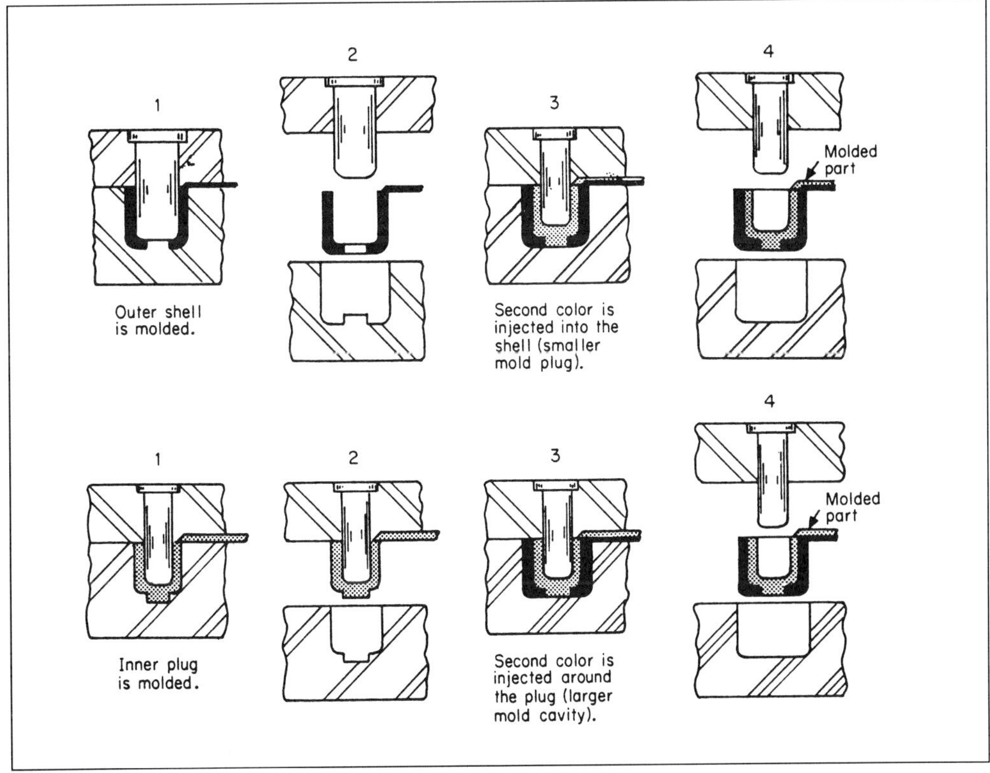

Examples of two-color injection molding.

Injection molding troubleshooting guide.

Suggested remedies	Problems: Drooling at nozzle	Short shot	Screw does not return	Sink marks	Burning	Surface blemishes	Flashing	Dull surface	Laminations	Part sticks in mold	Runner breaks	Parts distort	Discoloration of Sprue	Flow lines	Brittle parts	Wavy surfaces	Worm tracks on part	Melt temperature too high	Streaks on part	Voids in part
Increase injection pressure		●													●	●				
Decrease injection pressure							●					●								
Increase stock temperature		●				●		●	●			●		●	●	●	●		●	
Decrease stock temperature					●		●			●			●			●		●	●	●
Increase holding pressure and time				●												●				●
Decrease holding pressure and time							●			●	●	●			●			●		
Increase nozzle temperature		●		●		●			●								●			●
Clear nozzle		●																		
Clear shutoff valve	●	●																		
Increase screw r.p.m.			●			●		●	●						●		●			
Decrease screw r.p.m.																		●	●	
Tighten nozzle or shutoff valve													●						●	
Inject with rotating screw		●				●		●	●			●		●	●					
Increase clamping pressure							●													
Start injection later	●																			
Decrease injection speed				●	●	●	●	●	●	●		●	●		●	●	●		●	●
Increase injection speed		●												●		●				

Increase back pressure		●				●		●	●			●		●	●		●		●	
Decrease back pressure			●	●														●		
Enlarge nozzle orifice		●		●	●			●	●				●	●		●	●			
Increase mold temperature		●				●		●	●	●		●	●	●	●					●
Decrease mold temperature				●		●	●	●		●	●	●			●	●		●		●
Polish mold and break corners						●		●		●										
Rework mold							●			●										
Polish sprue, runners and gates						●					●									
Increase size of gates		●		●	●	●		●	●				●	●	●		●			●
Provide vents in mold		●			●									●						
Enlarge cold slug well						●								●		●		●		
Use dry material			●			●		●	●					●	●		●		●	
Use uncontaminated material								●	●											
Fill hopper or remove obstruction			●																	
Increase feed		●		●										●		●				●
Use mold release										●										
Adjust nozzle pressure	●																			
Check radius of nozzle, & of sprue bushing		●									●	●								
Reduce nozzle temp., break sprue later	●																			
Reduce temperature-rear zone[1]			●																	
Balance mold filling; rework runners				●																
Provide air for ejection										●										
Lengthen cooling and mold-open time											●	●				●			●	
Shorten cooling and mold-open time																		●		

[1] Exception: Increase temperature for nylon.

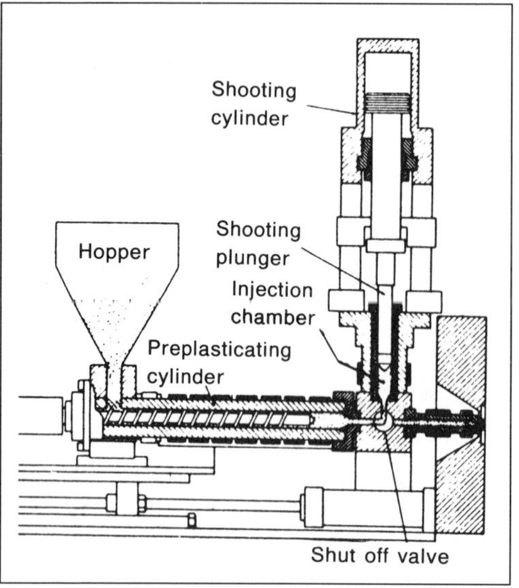

Two-stage screw injection molding machine.

injection molding unit pivot A pivoting injection unit permits removal of the screw from the front of the barrel rather than removal from the rear or disassembly of the complete screw and barrel from the machine. The pivoting action is either done manually or automatically (hydraulics, etc.).

injection molding, vacuum 1. Literally putting a mold in a vacuum box; actually developing a vacuum around the mold cavity (via seals). Thus vacuum can remove air and gas by-products that develop when melting certain plastics or elastomers. **2.** The reinforced plastics vacuum method is a molding process using a male and female mold (compression type) in which reinforcements are placed in the mold. A vacuum is applied, and a liquid plastic is injected into the cavity to saturate the reinforcement.

injection molding venting Moisture retention in and on plastics has always been a problem for all processors. Surface moisture or moisture absorbed within the plastic can cause splay, an unsightly surface defect of the molded part, and reduce mechanical properties. The increased use of hygroscopic plastics also requires care and the assurance of proper drying of material via the usual technique, using dryers and/or vented barrels such as the two-stage shown in the Fig. below. There are advantages of using vented barrels as opposed to the more familiar dryers such as: elimination of predrying, rapid startup and color or material changes, energy efficiency, removal of all volatiles, less space required, greater use of regrind, reduced mold venting, etc. ▷ **venting**

injection molding volume diagram
▷ **molding volume diagram**

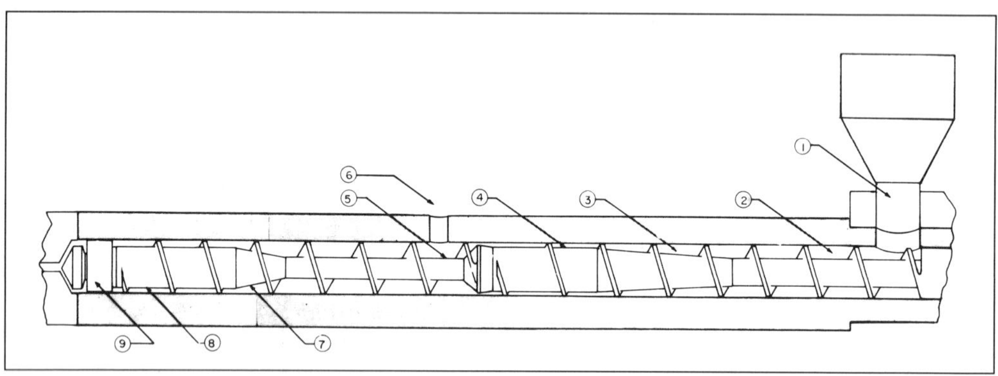

Basic operation of a vented barrel. (1) Wet material enters from a conventional hopper. (2) The pellets are conveyed forward by the screw feed section, and are heated by the barrel and by some frictional heating. Some surface moisture is removed here. (3) The compression or transition section does most of the melting. (4) The first metering section accomplishes final melting and even flows to the vent section. (5) Resin is pumped from the first metering section to a deep vent or devolatilizing section. This vent section is capable of moving quantities well in excess of the material delivered to it by the first metering section. For this reason, the flights in the vent section run partially filled and at zero pressure. It is here that volatile materials such as water vapor, and other nondesirable materials, escape from the melted plastic. The vapor pressure of water at 500°F is 666 psi. These steam pockets escape the melt, and travel spirally around the partially filled channel untill they escape out the vent hole in the barrel. (6) Water vapor and other volatiles escape from the vent. (7) The resin is again compressed and pressure is built in the second transition section. (8) The second metering section evens the flow and maintains pressure so that the screw will be retracted by the pressure in front of the non-return valve. (9) A low resistance, sliding ring, non-return valve works in the same manner as it does with a nonvented screw.

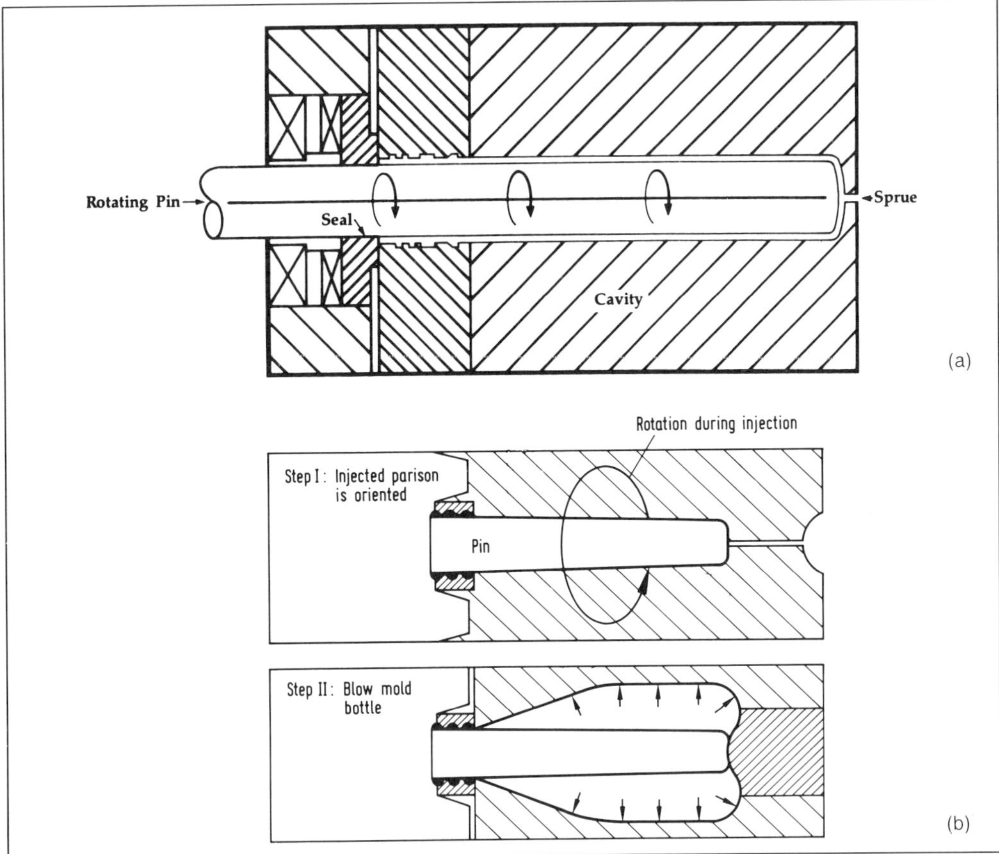

Schematic of injection molding with rotation: (*a*) example of pin rotating and (*b*) example of cavity rotating.

injection molding weld line ▷ **weld line**

injection molding with rotation When reviewing the stretching technique which is very popular in blow molding, an important potential on its use is by the Dow Chemical USA technique called molding with rotation (MWR). MWR uses basically existing injection molding equipment but special mold design modifications are required. A simplified schematic is shown in the Fig. above. Either the cavity or pin (core) rotates. Thus, orientation of the melt occurs during injection molding of the oriented preform. The mold opens and oriented melt is quickly transferred to a blow mold. ▷ **blow molding stretched** and **orientation**

injection molding, zero defects ▷ **zero defect**

ink ▷ **printing ink** and **printing**

ink, aniline A fast-drying ink used on polyethylene, cellophane, etc.

inlay and overlay They can be applied to plastic moldings during or after molding. ▷ **decal**

inlay printing ▷ **valley printing**

in-line pouch with zipper ▷ **thermoforming, form, fill, and seal with zipper on-line**

in-line processing ▷ **processing in-line**

in-mold coating, decorating, and labeling Various methods have been developed in order to eliminate an operation that otherwise must be carried out separately. In-mold labeling challenges pressure-sensitive and heat-transfer labeling.

innocuous Cannot injure or harm; harmless.

innovate Just as the computer is a superior control and filing device, it is also a management tool. Even today, the more sophisticated captive and custom molders rely on their multicolor CRT screens and daily computer-generated management reports to check the pulse of their business. The leaders of the industry are so busy today that they could not possibly work any harder. They have to work smarter. Thus they will increasingly rely on the computer to provide them with the information they need to intelligently settle the disposition of manpower, machines, and materials. They will let the product designers worry about part design, the plant engineers and machinery builders be concerned about science, the production people see about molding the part, etc.—while they run the business.

Today, these people are seen as innovators. They are busy further automating their plants, in some cases integrating molding with the entire manufacturing operation. They are looking for ways to improve molding quality by controlling temperature and humidity in their buildings and saving energy by using the heat that escapes from the molding process.

inorganic Being or composed of matter other than hydrocarbons and their derivatives, or matter that is not of plant or animal origin, such as earthy or mineral matter. ▷**material origin**

inorganic chemistry A major branch of chemistry that is generally considered to embrace all substances except hydrocarbons and their derivatives, or all substances that are not compounds of carbon oxides and carbon disulfides.

inorganic plastic ▷**plastic, inorganic**

input/output data ▷**computer input/output unit** and **standard industrial classification**

insert An integral part of a plastic molding consisting of metal, plastic, or other material which may be molded into position or may be pressed into the molding after the molding is fabricated. If metal inserts are to be molded, their shape should have no sharp edges since the effect of the edges would be similar to that of the notch. A knurled insert should have sharp points smoothed, again to avoid the notch effect. ▷**residual stress** and **ultrasonic insertion**

insert anchorage Part of the insert that is molded inside of the plastic and held fast by the shrinkage of the plastic.

inserted pin A pin which keeps an inserted part (insert) inside the mold, by screwing or by friction; removed when withdrawing the object from the mold.

insert, eyelet type Insert having a section which protrudes from the material and is used for spinning over in assembly.

insert joggle A term sometimes used for matching inserts for exact positioning of a multipiece mold.

insert molding Process by which components, such as terminals, pins, studs, and fasteners, may be molded into a part. Also called molded-insert.

insert, open hole An insert having a hole drilled completely through it.

in-situ In the natural or original position. ▷**foamed in-situ**

insoluble Substances that dissolve in water to only a very small extent.

inspection Process of measuring, examining, testing, gauging, and/or using other procedures to ascertain the quality or state, detect errors or defects, or otherwise appraise materials, products, services, systems, or environments to pre-established standard. ▷**barrel inspection** and **screw inspection**

inspection visual ▷**visual inspection**

instability ▷**stability**

instrumentation system Used for the plant and laboratory operations. As an example, plastic material systems can be evaluated for rheological behavior using a number of steady shear and dynamic oscillatory instruments. Plastic solutions and melts as well as rigid solids may be evaluated.

insulated capacity ▷**permittivity, relative**

insulated runner ▷**mold runner, insulated**

insulation, photoconductive plastic ▷**photoconductive plastic**

insulation resistance, electrical The electrical resistance between two conductors or systems of conductors separated by insulating material; the electrical resistance of an insulating material to a direct voltage. ▷**electrical resistance**

insulator **1.** A material of such low electrical conductivity that the flow of current through it can usually be neglected; the insulator has significant electronic resistivity. **2.** A material of low thermal conductivity, such as that used to insulate structural buildings, cryogenic containers, etc. ▷**Tyvek**

insurance ▷**management**

integral hinge ▷**hinge, integral**

integral skin ▷**foamed, self-skinning**

integrated circuit IC is a general term for semiconductor chip devices. These one-piece components contain the equivalent of thousands of circuits etched in micro-miniaturized form on the surface of the chip. ▷**business card electronic reader/writer**

intelligence, artificial ▷**artificial intelligence**

intensifier ▷**booster**

intensive mixer Mixers for dry-blending plastics such as PVC with plasticizers and other additives, comprising a propeller-like impeller rotating at high speed in the bottom of a stationary container, continously recirculating the materials between closely spaced stationary and rotating pins.

interface 1. The boundary between the individual, physically distinguishable constituents of a material. The junction or surface between fillers and plastics in molding compounds. With fibers, the contact area between the fibers and the sizing or finish. In a laminate, the contact area between the reinforcement and the laminating plastic. **2.** The means of information exchange. ▷**communication protocol 3.** The boundary between two systems across which information is transmitted, using a link such as a bus. **4.** Interface is also used to indicate a human working with a computer, or a computer with a peripheral.

Interfacial polymerization A polymerization reaction that occurs at the interfacial boundary of two solutions. A simple example is the making of nylon thread from a beaker containing a lower layer of a solution of sebacyl chloride in carbon tetrachloride an upper layer of hexamethylene diamine in aqueous solution. A pair of tweezers is gently lowered through the top layer, closed on the interfacial layer of plastic, then drawn upward to pull with it a continuous strand of nylon.

interfacial tension The contractile force of an interface between two phases. ▷**surface tension**

interference In testing, an effect due to the presence of a constituent or characteristic that influences the measurement of another constituent or characteristic.

interference fit It is one having limits of size so described that an interference always results when mating parts are assembled. As an example, a joint or mating of two parts in which the male part has an external dimension larger than the internal dimension of the mating female part, thus the fit creates a stress that can cause self destruction.

interior design The interior of a home (office, etc.) has become to symbolize lifestyle and has taken on its own personality with different plastics very involved.

interlaminar shear ▷**shear, interlaminar**

interlaminar shear strength ▷**shear** and **shear strength**

interlayer An intermediate sheet in a laminated construction.

interlock assembly ▷**design snap fit**

intermediate Chemical ingredients used in the formation of plastics, polymers, or other finished compounds.

intermittent parison ▷**blow molding extruder parison**

intermolecular bonding ▷**molecular bonding**

internal bubble cooling ▷**extruder blown film**

internal gas pressure ▷**injection molding, gas**

internal mixer Mixing machines using the principal of cylindrical containers in which the materials are deformed by rotating blades or rotors. The containers and rotors are cored so that they can be heated or cooled to control temperature of a batch. These mixers are extensively used in the compounding of a plastic and rubber materials. They have the advantage of keeping dust and fume hazards to a minimum.

International standard of units ▷**SI**

interpenetrating network IPNs is a branch of blend technology; it combines two polymers into a stable interpenetrating polymer network. There are all types of blends prepared throughout the plastic industry such as synergistic types. IPN is a related system of strengthening plastics which has been used since the 1980s. In true IPNs, each polymer is crosslinked to itself, but not to the other, and the two polymer networks interpenetrate each other; these are thermoset (TS) plastics. In semi-IPNs, only one of the polymers is crosslinked; the other is linear and by itself would be a thermoplastic. Semi-IPNs lend themselves to thermoplastic (TP) processing. The rigidity of IPN structures increases mechanical and other properties such as chemical resistance. A polyurethane and isocyanate system is an example of a full IPN. A semi-IPN can be made by polymerizing a rubbery thermoplastic like polysulfone within a crosslinked epoxy. This concept can even be used with a single polymer system; crosslinked nylon can be penetrated by linear nylon. These types can usually be fabricated by conventional injection molding. TS/TP and TP/PS networks usually require processing by TS process such as compression molding.

Methods of preparing IPNs include the simplest approach of sequential preparation. A crosslinked polymer is produced, then swelled in a second monomer and crosslinker, and crosslink/polymerize in-situ. The result is a suspension-type TS plastic or a true IPN. Another method of preparing true IPNs is simultaneous synthesis. Here the two components are polymerized more or less simultaneously but by different routes, such as addition polymerization for one and condensation polymerization for the other, so there is no interference. And there are many variations. Latex IPNs may have a core shell structure, with two different networks on the same latex particle, or two latex materials may be bonded together, with two crosslinked networks. These IPN strengthening techniques produce new engineering plastics with properties not currently available.

interphase The boundary region between a bulk plastic (polymer) and an adherend in which the plastic has a high degree of orientation to the adherend on a molecular basis. It plays a major role in the load transfer process such as between the fiber and the laminate matrix plastic, the bulk of an adhesive and its adherend, etc.

interpolymer A particular type of copolymer in which the two monomer units are as intimately distributed in the polymer molecule that the substance is essentially homogeneous in chemical composition. It is sometimes called a true copolymer.

interpretation The determination of whether indications are relevant or nonrelevant.

interstice Unoccupied space between atoms or ions.

intracorporeal material Also called implant material.

intrinsic Belonging to the essential nature of a thing.

intrinsic viscosity ▷ **viscosity, intrinsic**

introfaction The change in fluidity and wetting properties of an impregnating material, produced by the addition of an introfier.

introfier A chemical that converts a colloidal solution into a molecular type.

intrusion molding ▷ **injection molding, intrusion**

intuitive design ▷ **plastic, computer, and design**

intumescence The foaming and swelling of a plastic when exposed to high surface temperatures or flames. It has particular reference to intumescent coatings and ablative materials.

intumescent coating Coating (plastic type) formulated with an intumescent action to protect an object from intense heat of flames by decomposing into a foam barrier.

invention The chief requirement of an invention is that (1) it be unobvious to a person having ordinary skill in the art to which the claim pertains and (2) knowing everything that has gone before is not applicable. ▷ **patent**

inventory In a screw plasticator such as in injection molding or extrusion machines, the amount of plastic contained in the heating barrel (cylinder).

inverse lamination The ICI Rigid-Faced Urethane Laminate Process, "inverse lamination", starts as laydown paper (flexible facing) and receives urethane chemicals from a mixing head (see Fig. on p. 401). The adjustable laydown gap permits thinner or thicker foam, or faster or slower formulation. Foam forms on the flexible facing as it moves around a heated platen. The inverted foam bonds to the rigid facing moving from right to left. The three-part laminate cures under the floating platens as it moves toward the trimming and cut-off section.

investment capital ▷ **capital equipment investment**

investment casting A cost-effective method for producing complex metal or ceramic castings, sometimes called the lost wax process that is used to produce reinforced plastic parts. To improve strengths, such as with aluminum castings, silicone carbide fibers are used with the wax replicate of the intended shape to form a porous ceramic shell model. ▷ **soluble core molding**

in vitro Medical or scientific term that literally means "in glass"; outside the living body and in an artificial environment. Such as a laboratory test tube.

in vivo Medical or scientific term that refers to "in the living body" or exists in a living body.

iodine value Also called the iodine number, it is the number of grams of iodine that 100 grams of an unsaturated compound will absorb in a given time under arbitrary conditions. It is used to indicate the residual unsaturation in

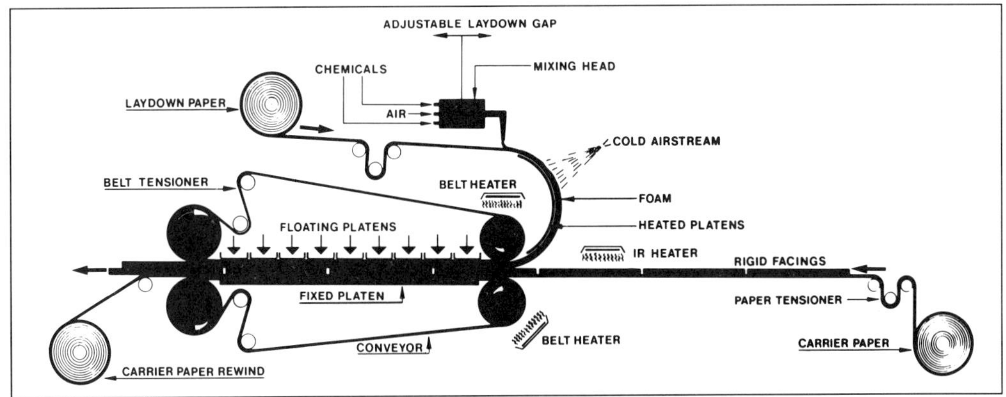

Inverse lamination.

epoxy plasticizers; a low value implies a high degree of saturation.

ion An atom or group of atoms that carries a positive or negative electric charge as a result of having lost or gained one or more electrons. When an electron is gained the ion is negatively charged and is called an anion. A positively charged ion is called a cation.

ion-beam polymerization Ion beams can be used in a manner similar to electron beams to polymerize gaseous organic monomers. ▷ **vacuum coating**

ion beam surface modification With highly reproducible ion beam, a surface modification process makes biomaterial silicone elastomer hydrophilic, anti-thrombogenic, and wettable by ink. This occurs without changing its bulk properties. Thus, application of the low-friction plastic does not require fluorosilicone oil. It also provides a smooth rather than a wrinkled surface morphology, facilitating resistance to cells, especially platelets. Process was developed by Spire Corp., Bedford, MA.

ion chromatography IC utilizes the principles of ion exchange to separate mixtures of ionizable materials and, in most instances, a conductivity detector to sense the components resolved. In practice, a liquid sample is introduced at the head of an appropriate separator column into a stream of ionic eluant which then carries the mixture through the column and toward a detector. The rate of travel of each sample component through the system depends upon its particular affinity for the column packing under the conditions of analysis. If migration rates are sufficiently different, each elutes from the column as a discrete band, ready for measurement.

The time at which a component exits the column is a clue to its identity, whereas the size of the peak is related to concentration. The heart of the IC system is the separator column(s). Usually, this is a tube packed with an ion exchange plastic designed to separate either anions or cations. The plastic is generally a material with known charge and exchange capacity, tailored to meet specific application requirements.

ion exchange plastic Small granular or bead-like plastics consisting of two principal parts: a resinous matrix serving as a structural portion, and an ion-active group serving as a functional portion. The functional group may be acidic or basic. The plastic matrix most often is a copolymer of styrene and divinylbenzene. Acidic ion exchanges are made by sulfonating the plastic beads with, for example, sulfuric acid, chlorosulfonic acid, or sulfur trioxide. Acidic ion exchange plastics are used for softening water. Complete deionization of water is accomplished by use of both acidic and basic plastics, in sequence or in mixed beds. Ion exchanges are also used for other chemical processes such as electrodialysis.

ionic Relating to or characterized by ions.

ionic bonding It provides a moderate form of crosslinking that contributes strength and adhesion to end-use properties. These ionic bonds have proved remarkably fusible and thermoplastic, as compared with the extremely high melting points of inorganic ionic compounds, thus still permitting or even facilitating normal thermoplastic processing.

ionic initiator They are either carbonium ions (cationic) or carbonions (anionic) which attack the reactive double bond of vinyl monomers and add on, regenerating the ion species on the propagating chain.

ionic polymerization A process in which the monomer or mixture of monomers is added to agents containing electrically charged ions, usually conducted in solution with a liquid diluent. Typical plastics produced include polyisobutylene, butyl rubber, polyvinyl ether, and cumarone-idene. Also called cationic polymerization or anionic polymerization. ▷ **radiation-induced reaction**

ionization A chemical change by which ions are formed from a neutral molecule of an inorganic solid, liquid, or gas. ▷ **electroplating**

ionization foaming ▷ **foamed polyethylene ionization**

ionization method A method of X-ray diffraction in which the intensity of the diffracted beam is measured by means of an ionization chamber.

ionization radiation Any electromagnetic or particulate radiation which in its passage through matter is capable of producing ions directly or indirectly. ▷ **radiation-induced reaction**

ionomer plastic IOs are in the polyolefin family. Their interchain ionic bonding distinguishes them from the other polymers. These ionic cross-links occur randomly between long-chain molecules to produce properties usually associated with high-molecular-weight materials. At normal processing temperatures, however, the ionic bonding of these thermoplastics diminishes, allowing them to be processed in conventional extruders and injection-molding machines.

Ionomers are extremely tough, with tensile impact strengths as high as 320 J/cm (600 ft.lb./in.) and tensile strengths as high as 35,000 kPa (5,000 psi), with elongation in the range of 300 to 500%. In addition they have excellent abrasion resistance, with an NBS index as high as 640, and optical clarity, a haze rating as low as 40%. Compounded ionomers are also available that are stiffer and have better heat resistance than standard grades yet retain their excellent impact resistance. This product, intended for semirigid parts, resists many chemicals, solvents, greases, and oils.

The clarity, strength, and good adhesion of ionomer films to metal surfaces are the important properties that have led to its widespread use in food packaging, often as a heat-seal layer in thermoplastic composite structures. Its high impact strength and cut resistance have led to its use in bowling pin and golf ball covers and bumper guards.

iridescence Loss of brilliance in metallized plastics and development of multicolor reflectance. It is caused by the cold flow of plastic or of coating and by excess heat during vacuum metallizing.

iron ingot Highly refined steel with a maximum of 0.15% impurity. Due to high purity, it has excellent ductility and resistance to rusting.

iron ore depletion ▷ **steel resource in U.S. limited**

iron oxide pigment Heat-stable pigments ranging from blacks through yellows are obtained from various iron oxides. Reds are formed from ferric oxide (Fe_2O_3), yellows from hydrated ferric oxide, and blacks from ferroferric oxide (Fe_3O_4).

irradiation With plastics, the bombardment with a variety of subatomic particles, usually alpha-, beta-, or gamma-rays. Used to initiate the polymerization and copolymerization of plastics or in some cases to bring about changes in the physical properties of a plastic such as crosslinking of thermoplastics (polyethylene, etc.).

irreversible Not capable of redissolving or remelting; chemical reactions which proceed in a single direction and are not capable of reversal (as applied to thermoset plastics).

ISO **1.** ISO is the English abbreviation of the worldwide International Organization for Standardization. **2.** A prefix meaning the same as in isomer (the same part), isotope (the same place). In plastics it means having a subordinate chain of one or more carbon atoms attached to a carbon of the straight chain.

ISO 9000 certification Plant with quality-management and quality-assurance processes that meet the industry standards developed by the ISO.

isobar Section at constant pressure through a phase diagram.

isochronous Composed of the same elements, united in the same proportion by weight, and having equal or uniform duration of time, recurring at regular intervals.

isochronous graph ▷ **creep isometric and isochronous graphs** that provides an example of recurring conditions.

isocyanate plastic Based on plastics made by the condensation of organic isocyanates with other compounds. Generally reacted with polyols on a polyester or polyether backbone molecule, with the reactants being joined by the formation of the urethane linkage. ▷ **polyurethane plastic**

isomer A compound, radical, ion, or nuclide that contains the same number of atoms of the same elements but differs in structural arrangements and properties. ▷ **stereoisomer**

isomeric Composed of the same elements united in the same proportion by weight, but differing in one or more properties because of differences in structure.

isometric A form on which the unit dimension on all three axes is the same.

isometric graph ▷ **creep isometric and isochronous graphs** that provides an example of recurring conditions.

isomorphism A state of crystallization characterized by a similar arrangement of geometrically similar structural units. ▷ **polymorphism**

isoprene rubber This elastomer (plastic) is chemistry's nearest approach to synthesizing rubber equal to the natural rubber. It is made from a colorless, volatile liquid derived from propylene or from coal gases or tars. It is chemically similar to the natural rubber molecule.

isotactic A plastic molecular structure containing a sequence of regularly spaced asymmetric atoms arranged in like configuration in a polymer chain (head-to-tail, head-to-tail, etc.). Isotactic (syndiotactic) plastics are crystallizable. It is in contrast to atactic. ▷ **stereospecific (stereoregular) plastic**

isotactic molding/pressing The compressing or pressing of powder material (plastic, etc.) under a gas or liquid so that pressure is transmitted equally in all directions, for example, in sintering, coining, and in an elastomeric mold using hydrostatic pressure. The elastomeric mold system is also called hot isotactic pressing (HIP).

isotensoid ▷ **filament winding geodesic-isotensoid contour**

isotere A plot of equilibrium concentration or pressure against temperature when the quantity adsorbed per unit of adsorbent is held constant.

isotherm Section at constant temperature through a phase diagram.

isothermal 1. Relating to or marked by changes of volume or pressure under conditions of constant temperature. **2.** Relating to or marked by constant or equality of temperature.

isothermal rotor extruder ▷ **extruder screwless**

isotope One of a group of atoms that have the same atomic number (same chemical characteristics) but have a different mass number. The nuclei have the same number of protons but a different number of neutrons, resulting in differing values of atomic mass.

isotropic Having the same value for a property in all directions. ▷ **reinforced plastic, directional properties**

italic The style of letters that slant, in distinction from upright or bold letters. Used for emphasis within the text (printing on plastics, market reports, etc.).

-ite and -ate Compounds with these endings contain oxygen in a negative radical. The -ite represents the lower and the -ate the higher proportion of oxygen. Examples are sodium nitrite ($NaNO_2$) and sodium nitrate ($NaNO_3$).

item 1. An object or quantity of material on which a set of observations can be made. **2.** An observed value or test result obtained from an object or quantity of material.

Izod impact test This is the most widely used impact-resistance test for plastics. It requires specimens 0.318 to 1.270 cm (0.125 to 0.5 in.) thick, molded or cut from test piece. It can be tested unnotched or notched with notched being preferred. A notch of 0.25 mm (0.01 in.) apex radius is then machined across the edge of the specimen to a depth of 0.254 cm (0.1 in.). These specimens are clamped so that the free end may be struck edge-on by a swinging pendulum impactor. Thus, during impact the specimen bends

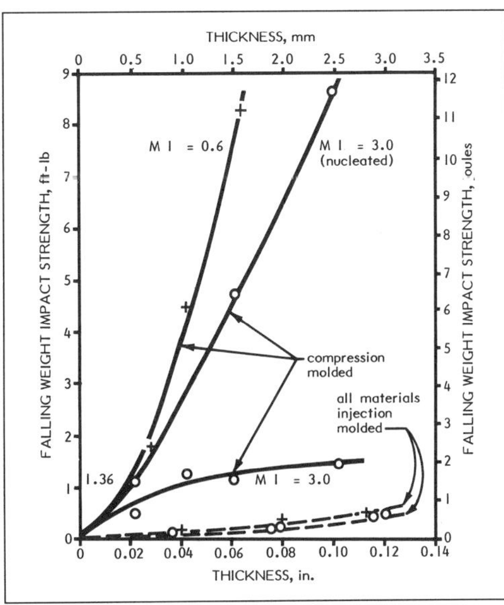

Impact strength versus processing conditions.

with the notch in tension. Energy lost by the pendulum and presumably absorbed by the test specimen during impact is divided by specimen thickness to arrive at the Izod impact energy, expressed as joules per meter (J/m) or foot-pounds per inch (ft-lb/in.). Test specimens of different thickness, method of processing, method of machining, etc, can easily yield different results. The test is very sensitive to relatively small changes in material composition, morphology, and processing such as orientation. As an example one material can have a much higher strength when $\frac{1}{2}$ in. thick compared to an 1/8 in. thick specimen. Another material could be just the reverse of higher strength with the 1/8 in. specimen. Regardless for a specific material, the test is meaningful (useful). It is used widely by material manufacturers and suppliers, as well as processors, for quality control. It can detect contamination with other materials, thermally degraded materials, incompatible regrinds, dirt, and many other situations. The Fig. on p. 403 shows the effect of compression and injection molding on the impact strength of several polypropylene homopolymers.

J

jar mill A small ball mill.

jet engine ▷ **automotive plastic engine**

jet molding ▷ **injection molding, jet method**

jet spinning For most purposes this process is similar to fiber spinning and melt spinning. Hot gas jet spinning uses a directed blast or jet of hot gas to "pull" molten plastic from a die lip and extend it into fine fibers.

jetting ▷ **injection molding, jetting**

jewelry and lost wax process ▷ **soluble core molding**

jig ▷ **machining jig**

job shop ▷ **processor, custom**

joining ▷ **adhesive; assembly/joining; welding; solvent bonding**

joining and bonding Joints using the same or different materials (such as plastic to plastic, plastic to aluminum, etc.) can be classified as having high to low strength test values based on the following configurations (see Fig.): (1a) The *lap shear joint* is perhaps the easiest to make and is quite common. Its shape and mode of loading utilizes most adhesives where they have the greatest strength. (1b) It is easy to calculate the strength of a lap shear joint. Merely figure the lap area and multiply by the nominal lap shear values published by the adhesive manufacturer (or by the use values you have determined). A failure in a lap shear occurs when it degrades into a peel joint as the loads are increased. Increased loads cause the joint to rotate so as to line up the forces. This rotation causes bending in the substrates (plastic, reinforced plastics, etc.) and induces peel conditions at the ends of the lap. If loads increase, then the peel stresses exceed the adhesive's strength and the joint quickly fails. However, if the edges of the lap are tapered, the stiffness is reduced; when the joint rotates to accommodate the tension force, the tapered edges of the lap, being more flexible, do not overstress the adhesive (at the same load). Thus, this simple modification can increase the strength at the failure without increasing the shear area. (1c) By proper preparations, even higher strengths (compared to the lap joint) can be obtained for the same shear area by making a scarf joint. It is a lap shear joint that introduces no rotation when under load. The adhesive is in shear and there are few or no peel effects. Such joints require more labor to prepare and require good jigging or tooling to locate and secure adherends during cure of the adhesive. But they represent the best joints available and often can develop strengths nearly equal to that of the adherends. (2) The *butt joint* is a pure tension joint between rigid adherends. It is usually low to moderate in strength and is easy to calculate, but it represents a type of joint that occurs very seldom in actual products. It must be very carefully prepared and it must be loaded so that the stresses in the joint (under load) are balanced. (3) A *peel joint* represents

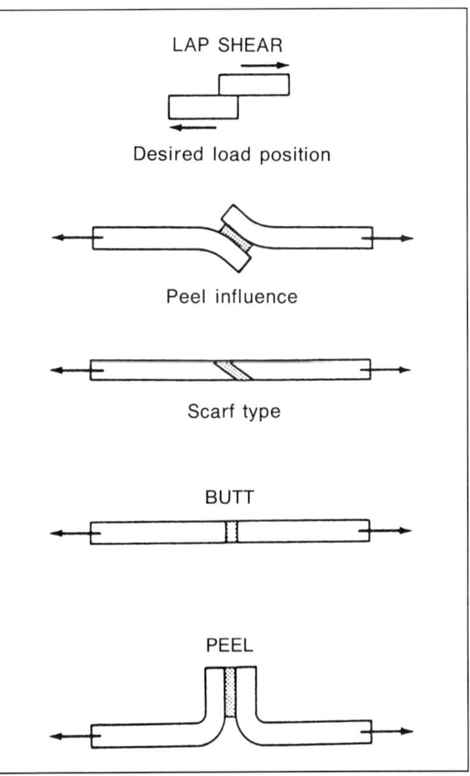

Joining and bonding methods.

a construction wherein the stresses are concentrated in a line where one adherend bends away from the other and puts unbalanced tension stress in the adherend. In this joint, only the adhesive at that point of peel is working; the rest is not loaded until it, too, is stressed at the point of peel as the joint starts to fail.

joint The location at which two adherends are held together with a layer of adhesive; the general area of contact for a bonded structure. Also called *adhesive joint.*

joint, butt A type of edge joint in which the edge faces of the adherends are at right angles to the other faces of the adherends.

joint, conjugate Two sets of faulty joints that formed under the same stress conditions, usually shear pairs.

joint, edge A joint made by bonding the edge faces of two adherends with adhesives.

joint geometry Several types of mechanical joints are successively used, particularly with reinforced plastics. The Fig. on this page shows single and double shear joints. In the double shear butt joints, the bending stresses common to the other joints are avoided, while the tapered butt-plate joint minimizes excessive loads at the joint edges.

joint, lap A joint made by placing one adherend partly over another and bonding together the overlapped portions.

joint, scarf A joint made by cutting away similar angular segments of two adherends and bonding the adherends with the cut area fitted together.

joint, snap ▷ **design snap fit**

joint, starved A joint which has an insufficient amount of adhesive to produce a satisfactory bond. This condition may result from too thin a spread to fill the gap between the adherends, excessive penetration of the adhesive into the adherend, too short an assembly time, or the use of excessive pressure.

joint strength **1.** Tension measured in lb or kg that a tied joint can withstand before the joint slips or breaks. **2.** Regarding adhesive bonded strength joints. ▷ **bond strength**

joint-Y Y-joint also called knuckle area. ▷ **filament winding knuckle area**

joule J is the unit of energy, work, or quantity of heat (Nm). One joule (J) is one wall-second (W · s). ▷ **torque**

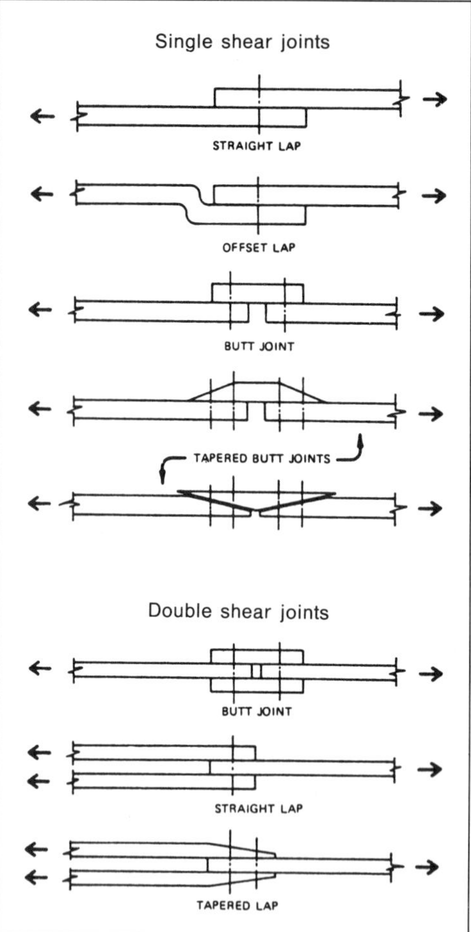

Examples of joint geometries.

just-in-time JIT is a method of inventory control in which materials and/or parts arrive from suppliers just in time to be part of the manufacturing process. It is a process for consistently improving productivity and continuously eliminating waste. Waste is defined as those activities, including time, purchasing, and handling of materials and labor, that do not add value to a product. The process of eliminating waste does not center only on the shop floor, but extends to all areas inside and outside the company. With JIT, engineering, finance, sales, and all other departments within a company come under scrutiny, as do the company's suppliers. With proper handling of JIT the targeted advantages occur. However frequently it results in excess manufacturing capacity, an underutilization of resources, and other situations.

jute ▷ **fiber, jute**

K

kaolin China clay, white-burning aluminum silicate which, due to its great purity, has a high fusion point and is the most refractory of all clays. Uses includes fillers in plastic, coatings, elastomers, and paper.

Kapton Du Pont's trade name for thermoset polyimide film.

Kelvin scale A temperature scale based on the average kinetic energy per molecule of a perfect gas, in which zero is $-273.15°C$ (absolute zero). Thus $K = °C + 273.15$. ▷ **Celsius**

ketone A class of organic compounds possessing a carbonyl group attached to two hydrocarbon groups. Acetone is the first member of this series. Ketones are practically water white liquids with pleasant odors. They possess a high solvent power for vinyl plastics and other plastics, the cellulose esters and ethers, and many substances which are soluble with difficulty in other groups of solvents.

ketone plastic This broad family of crystalline plastics includes polyetherketone (PEK), polyetheretherketone (PEEK), and others (PEKK, PEKEKK, etc.).

Kevlar Du Pont's trade name for an aromatic polyamide fiber of extremely high tensile strength and greater resistance of elongation than steel. Uses include fibers in reinforced plastic. ▷ **reinforcement** and **aromatic polyamide fiber**

keyword A term used for indexing or retrieval purposes, either derivative, keyword-in-context (KWIC) and keyword-out-of-context (KWOC), or assigned usually from a controlled vocabulary or thesaurus.

K-factor ▷ **coefficient of thermal conductivity**

kilogram The kg is the unit of mass; it is equal to the mass of the international prototype of the kg adopted by 1st and 3rd CGPM 1889 and 1901.

kilohertz kHz is equal to 1,000 Hertz (H).

kinetic A branch of dynamics concerned with the relations between the movement of bodies and the forces acting upon them. ▷ **crystallization** and **reactor technology**

kinetic coefficient of friction The friction under conditions of macroscopic relative motion between two bodies.

kinetic energy dissipated Different plastics provide different degrees and excellencies for producing parts which absorb and dissipate energy, usually from impact. Some of the energy absorbing/dissipating flexible to rigid plastics used are made from density foams, solid plastics (unreinforced and reinforced), and their combinations.

kinetic friction Friction developed between two bodies in motion.

kinetic theory A theory of matter based on the mathematical description of the relationship between pressures, volumes, and temperatures of gases (P-V-T phenomena). This relationship is summarized in the laws of (1) Boyle's law, (2) Charle's law, and (3) Avogadro's law.

kink 1. A type of waviness occurring as interior edges, not to be confused with the more abrupt departures as ridges or surface marks. ▷ **waviness 2.** In fabric, a short length of yarn that has spontaneously doubled back on itself to form a loop. Also called curl, looped yarn, and snarl. **3.** ▷ **twisting without kinking**

kirksite ▷ **mold material**

kiss Abbreviation for phrases "Keep it simple and safe" and "Keep it simple, stupid".

kiss roll coating This roll arrangement carries a metered film of very thin plastic coating to a web. At the line of web contact, the film is split, with part of the coating remaining on the roll, and the remainder adhering to the web.

Kling test ▷ **fusion Kling test**

kneader It is the blending of relatively soft plastics and elastomers into a uniform mixture by subjecting them to a rolling pressure exerted by agitators of specific shape rotating in throughlike containers. The action is a combination of turning, folding, and pressing. This operation used with materials such as PVC and sheet molding compounds (SMC) is also used in processing printing inks and bakery doughs. ▷ **extruder compound mixing**

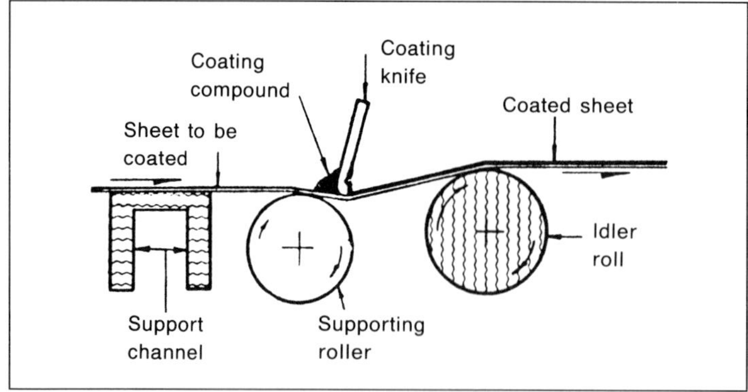

Knife coating.

knife coating A method of coating a substrate such as plastic, paper, fabric and foil in which the substrate, in the form of a continuous moving web, is coated with a plastic whose thickness is controlled by an adjustable knife or bar set at a suitable angle to the substrate (see Fig. above). In the plastic industry PVC formulations are widely used in this system and curing is affected by passing the coated substrate into an oven, usually heated by IR lamps or converted air. There are a number of variations of this basic technique and they vary according to the type of product required.

knit line ▷ **weld line** and **flow line**

knitted fabric This woven fabric has an interlacing (interlooping) yarn or thread in a series of connecting loops with needles. This is a rather compact woven construction used with plastic (reinforced plastics, coating, etc.).

knockout ▷ **mold ejection** and **clamping close preposition**

Knoop hardness Hardness that is measured by calibrated machines that force a rhombic-based pyramidal diamond indenter having specified edge angles under specified conditions into the surface of the test material; the long diagonal is measured after removal of the load. This tester uses a relatively small load to measure surface hardness.

Knoop hardness number The hardness Knoop (HK) number is obtained by dividing the applied load in kg-force by the projected area of the indentation in mm^2, computed from the measurement of the long diagonal of the indentation.

knot **1.** An imperfection or non-homogeneity in materials used in fabric construction, the presence of which causes surface irregularities. **2.** ▷ **yarn, knot tenacity. 3.** A joining by tying together. **4.** In wood, that portion of a branch that has become incorporated in the body of a tree.

knuckle area ▷ **filament winding knuckle area**

kraft A term derived from the German word meaning strength, applied to pulp, paper, or paperboard produced from virgin wood fibers by the sulfate process (unbleached wood pulp).

kraft paper Paper made from sulfate wood pulp; made chiefly from pinewood chips by digestion with a mixture of caustic soda, sodium sulfate, sodium carbonate, and sodium sulfide. Brown in color, it is made on a Fourdinier machine. To provide different properties, such as increased strength, smoother surface, and reduce permeability, different materials such as plastics are incorporated.

Kraton Shell Chemical Co.'s trade name for the first commercial styrenic thermoplastic elastomer (TPE); introduced 1966.

K-Resin ▷ **styrene-butadiene plastic**

Kubelka-Munk theory Provides the basis of virtually all computer-color-matching calculations. It is a phenomenological turbid-medium theory relating the reflectance and transmittance of scattering and absorbing materials to constants and the concentrations of their colorants.

L

label 1. Labeling is the process of affixing a precut, printed, flexible material to the surface of a product. Thus labeling eliminates the need to print on the plastic directly, which may be difficult in the case of irregular parts. Labels are printed in large quantities usually on flat label stock of plastic film, paper, or foil. If the function of a label is purely decorative, it is called a decal; however, both terms are used indiscriminately. Labeling is the least expensive and therefore very widely used method for affixing information messages and decorations to different packages. **2.** Labeling also refers to printing directly on the packages. **3.** A warning notice required by DOT and IATA to be placed on a shipping container of a hazardous material transported by air, highway, rail, or water. **4.** A notice required to appear on food products indicating their composition and nutritional values, or on pharmaceutical as well as household products stating their hazardous properties. **5.** A radioactive isotope or fluorescent dye added to a compound to trace its course and behavior during processing and/or handling.

label panel The plain portion of a decorated container set up for applications of labels; it may be depressed.

label stock Not often mentioned as an important or major application for plastics, label stock is consuming a considerable amount of plastics. Factors that influence their use despite the usual higher cost versus paper are: (1) need to help recycle labeled plastic containers, (2) trend toward post-labeling standard containers like beverage cans to minimize inventories, (3) provides certain attributes aestheticwise, and (4) potential for label to improve package functionality. Labels can contribute to lightweighting by acting as a reinforcement on the package. They can also be constructed to regulate air flow to food products to maintain freshness.

About 50% of plastics used are in pressure sensitive (p/s) label stock and release films. Calender and cast PVC films have the biggest share, due to use in large applications like signs and car trim. PET is the next most widely used film for p/s labels, followed by PS and CA. Polyolefin use is small but growing. Though consumed in small amounts due to their cost, high performance films also find specialty uses. These include PC, PI, fluoropolymer, and special polyolefin-based paper-like films.

laboratory accreditation Formal recognition that a testing laboratory is competent to carry out specific tests.

laboratory condition An ideal set of conditions in which all variant factors except the one under test can be held constant, as for example, rooms provided with constant temperature and humidity conditions, clean room, etc. ▷ **atmosphere standard laboratory**

lac A resinous substance secreted by a scale insect and used chiefly in shellac.

lack of fillout ▷ **reinforced plastic starved area** and **joint, starved**

lacquer A coating formulation based on thermoplastic film-forming material dissolved in organic solvent. The coating dries primarily by evaporation of the solvent. Typical lacquers include those based on nitrocellulose, other cellulose derivatives, vinyl, acrylic, lac, etc.

lacquer, brittle ▷ **brittle lacquer technique**

lacquer, cellulose ▷ **cellulose lacquer**

lactam A cyclic amide produced from amino acids by the removal of one molecule of water.

ladder polymer A polymer with two polymer chains crosslinked at intervals. ▷ **molecule alignment**

lagging molding Process involves the wrapping of plastic impregnated tape (prepreg) around a cylindrical mandrel and applying pressure by shrink tape. Prestretched shrink tape "Tedlar" is the most commonly used; it shrinks upon application of heat. This process is also called tape laying. ▷ **tape placement wrapped molding**

lagoon A scientifically constructed pond 3 to 5 ft (0.9 to 1.5 m) deep in which sewage and other organic wastes are decomposed by action of algae, sunlight, and oxygen thus restoring water to purity equal to that obtained by other types of treatment.

lake dye ▷ **pigment**

lamella A thin, flat scale or part. ▷ **anti-foaming agent** and **Raman spectroscopy**

lamellae Plural of lamella.

lamellar thickness A characteristic morphological parameter, usually estimated from X-ray studies or electron microscopy, that is usually 100 to 500 A (10 to 50 mm). The average thickness of lamellae in a specimen.

lamina A single ply or layer in a laminate, which is made up of a series of layers.

laminae Plural of lamina.

laminar flow 1. The movement of one layer of fluid past or over anotherlayer without the transfer of matter from one to the other; the fluid is in layers or laminae which is maintained as the flow progresses. ▷ **Reynold's number** and **turbulent flow. 2.** Flow of thermoplastic melt in a mold cavity that is accompanied by solidification of the layer in contact with the cooler mold surface that acts as an insulating "tube" through the cavity; in turn melt continues to flow filling the remainder of the cavity. This type of flow is essential to duplication of the mold surface. ▷ **flow model** and **Reynold's number. 3.** Thermodynamically, flow in which the head loss is proportional to the first power of the velocity.

laminate A product made by bonding together two or more layers of material or materials. The types of materials used in a laminate can be endless. Included are: plastic film, sheet, and tape; foils of aluminum, steel, paper, etc.; different types of woven and nonwoven fabrics using synthetic and natural fibers; etc. In the reinforced plastics industry, laminates refer mainly to superimposed layers of plastic impregnated or plastic coated fabrics, or fibrous reinforcements which have been bonded together.

Laminate can have directional lay ups to orient individual layers to meet different performance requirements; materials include oriented film, reinforced plastics, etc. ▷ **orientation** and **reinforced plastic, directional properties.** Methods of processing laminates include coextrusion, coinjection, pressure sensitive adhesive, compression molding, press laminating, etc. Solidification or curing of laminates depends on plastic used; they can be from room temperature with no pressure, through contact or low pressure, to high temperature and high pressure. ▷ **molding pressure, high** and **molding pressure, low**

laminated molding A molded plastic product fabricated by bonding together, under heat and pressure in a mold, layers of materials. Also called laminated pressing.

laminated nested A reinforced plastic laminate in which the plies are placed so that the yarns of one ply lie in the valleys between the yarns in the adjacent ply.

laminated plastic 1. A class of standard structural shapes, plates, sheets, angles, channels, rods, tubes, etc. that are made from reinforced plastics. **2.** ▷ **laminate** since all types of laminated materials can be used as just reviewed.

laminated pulled surface In laminated plastics, imperfections in the surface, ranging from a slight breaking or lifting in localized areas to pronounced separation of the surface from the body.

laminate, high pressure molding ▷ **molding pressure, high**

laminate, high pressure press As shown in the Fig. below, multiple opening platen press is an example of equipment used since the 1920s to mass produce flat laminates (decorative

High pressure laminating press.

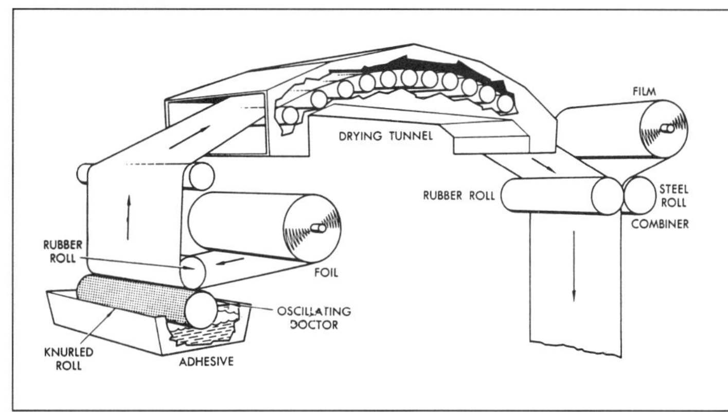

Lamination of a two-ply system.

counter tops, copper clad laminates, etc.) using heat and pressure to cure thermoset laminates. To the right, side loading and unloading elevator is used to speed up production.

laminate, low pressure molding ▷ **molding pressure, low**

laminate, parallel Laminated so that all layers of material are oriented approximately parallel with respect to the strongest direction in tension.

laminate ply One layer that is bonded to adjacent layers.

laminate, single ply A single plastic impregnated sheet of fabric, paper, glass fiber mat, etc. is not considered a laminate. Such a single sheet construction may be called a lamina.

laminate, symmetrical A symmetrical laminate has the stacking sequence of plies below its midplane and is a mirror image of the stacking sequence above the midplane.

laminate, unsymmetric A laminate having an arbitrary stacking sequence without midplane symmetry.

lamination The laying on of layers of materials and bonding them. The Fig. above is an example of a two layer lamination bonding of a plastic film with aluminum foil. Different materials, including reinforced plastics, in two or more plies are laminated to produce different products.

lamination coating ▷ **film coating**

lamination, inverse ▷ **inverse lamination**

lampblack A black or gray pigment made by burning low-grade heavy oils or similar carbonaceous materials with sufficient air and in an enclosed system. Use includes as fillers and pigments in plastic.

land ▷ **mold land**

landfill Usually refers to sanitary landfills, where non-hazardous solid wastes are buried and stored according to federal regulations. A landfill is separated from ground and surface water by plastic lining (usually polyethylene) and not as efficient layer(s) of clay. Waste is buried in layers or cells separated by dirt and clay. Modern landfills also have systems to collect contaminated water, called leachate, which filters through wastes and must be treated to remove heavy metals and other pollutants. ▷ **waste; recycle; incineration; geomembrane liner**

landfill and degradation The idea that products should be made biodegradable to alleviate the solid waste problems is debatable. Studies on landfills reveal that very little in a modern landfill degrades quickly enough to open up free space. Even materials that are completely degradable (grass clippings, food wastes, newspapers, etc.) have been found in a state of mummification after at least 10 to 20 years of burial. Environmentalists, government agenies, and waste experts agree, biodegradability cannot and will not be the solution to the solid waste disposal problem. The solution must lie with an integrated approach that minimizes waste at its source, recycles what is technically and economically feasible, converts to energy through incineration the combustibles that cannot be recycled, and landfills the rest. ▷ **degradable**

language The means by which users describe to the computer the kinds of operations to be performed. Machine language is the set of instructions wired into the computer. Query language is especially designed to aid the user in searching a database.

lap **1.** In filament winding, the amount of overlap between successive windings, usually intended to minimize gapping. **2.** In bonding, the distance between one adherend covering another adherend. **3.** In textile, a matted sheet of cotton wound on a spindle.

lap joint ▷ **joint, lap**

laser The acronym for light amplification by stimulated emission of radiation; an intense light beam with narrow band width.

laser beam welding A welding process wherein coalescence is produced by the heat obtained from the application of a concentrated coherent light beam impinging upon the surface to be bonded. ▷ **welding**

laser disk ▷ **optical data disc**

laser gauge Sensor system based on the use of a laser beam to measure part dimensions; e.g., to measure and control the outer diameter of extruded tubing, pipe, or rod.

latent heat The quantity of energy in calories per gram absorbed or given off as a substance undergoes a change from liquid to solid (freezes), from solid to liquid (melts), from liquid to vapor (boils), or from vapor to liquid (condenses). No change in temperature occurs.

latex A stable dispersion of plastic substance in an essentially aqueous medium. There are different types; milky fluid in certain plants such as milk weeds where it coagulates on exposure to air, rubber tree exudate, and the large market using plastics (synthetics and natural). Examples of synthetic latexes are those made by emulsion polymerization from styrene-butadiene comolymer, acrylate, polyvinyl acetate, etc. A latex is conveniently defined as a stable colloidal dispersion of a plastic substance in an aqueous medium. The plastic particles are usually approximately spherical and of typical colloidal dimensions; diameters range from 30 to 500 mm. The dispersion is relatively concentrated; the volume fraction of contained plastic usually ranges from 0.40 to 0.70. The dispersion medium is usually a dilute aqueous solution containing substances such as electrolytes, surface-active compounds, hydrophilic plastics, and with the synthetic types includes initiator residues.

Latex frequently must be compounded before use. Some compounding ingredients, notable stabilizers and thickeners, are used with almost all types. The stabilizers are either surfactants or water-soluble hydrocolloids. Those of glassy polymers are frequently compounded with additives such as plasticizers, pigments, and fillers. The rubber plastics are often compounded with vulcanizing ingredients that cause the solid phase deposited from the latex to become crosslinked. Different compounding ingredients are used with the different rubbers or elastomers.

Foamed latex rubber is produced by foaming a compounded rubber latex by mechanical or chemical means, and then converting the latex phase to a rubbery continuum. Thin walled articles, such as gloves, condoms, and balloons, are produced by latex dripping.

latexes The preferred plural of latex is lattices, but the alternative latexes is widely used in North America.

latex, mechanical stability The ability of latex to resist coagulation under the influence of mechanical agitation.

lattice **1.** The structural arrangement of substances, such as plastic properties, atoms in a crystal, etc. **2.** The space arrangement of equivalent sites.

lattice, noncubic Crystals with two or more unequal lattice constants and /or non-90° axial angles.

lattice pattern In reinforced plastics, a pattern of filament winding with a fixed arrangement of open voids.

lattices ▷ **latexes**

law, right-to-know ▷ **hazards, Federal Register 29 CFR 1910.1200** and **regulations**

lay **1.** The direction of a predominating surface pattern, usually after a machine operation. **2.** The length of a twist produced by stranding filaments, such as fibers, wires, and rovings; also the angle that such filaments make with the axis of the strand during a stranding operation. The length of twist of a filament is usually measured as the distance parallel to the axis of the strand between successive turns of the filament. **3.** In glass fiber, the spacing of the roving bands on the roving package expressed in the number of bands per inch. **4.** In filament winding, the orientation of the ribbon with some reference usually to the axis of rotation.

lay-flat **1.** The flash area of a mold. **2.** The property of non-warping in laminating adhesives; an adhesive material with good non-curling and non-distension characteristics. **3.** Film which is extruded as a tube, usually blown, cooled, then gathered by rollers, and wound up in flat form.

lay up In reinforced plastics, an assembly of layers of plastic impregnated material (prepreg) ready for processing.

L/D ratio This length-to-diameter (L/D) ratio is commonly used to describe the relative length of a screw. It basically is the length of the screw flights on the screw divided by its diameter. With an injection screw, it does not include the length of the check valve, pressure cone, and tip. The diameter of the ratio is reduced to 1, so the ratio is identified (evenly) as 15 : 1, 24 : 1, etc. The actual value used is an approximate. The L/D ratio is applied to barrels using two different approaches; distance from the forward edge (or rear edge) of the feed opening to the forward end of the barrel bore divided by the barrel bore. Barrel L/D lists how it was measured; with or without the feed opening. Different variables are involved in multiscrew machines so they are generally sized on the basis of output rate (kg/h or lb/h). ▷ **aspect ratio** regarding L/D as it pertains to fibers and other particles.

Regarding L/D of screws, based on plastic melt characteristics, there are general reasons for having short or long L/Ds. Advantages of the short screw are: (1) less residence time in the barrel, keeping heat sensitive plastics at melt temperature for a shorter time, lessening the chance of degradation, (2) occupies less space, (3) requires less torque, making strength of screw and amount of HP less important (particularly in extruder), and (4) less investment cost initially and for replacement parts. Advantages for the long screw are: (1) allows for greater output and recovery rates, (2) screw can be designed for more uniform output and greater mixing, (3) screw can be designed to pump at higher pressures, and (4) screw can be designed for greater melting with less shear and more conductive heat from the barrel.

leach To extract a soluble component from a mixture by the process of using a solvent which will dissolve the component but has no effect on the remaining portions of the mixture. ▷ **silica fiber**

leachate A contaminated liquid that drains from landfills and must be treated before entering the environment. It can contain decomposed wastes, decomposition byproducts, heavy metals, bacteria, etc. ▷ **geomembrane liner**

lead 1. The distance in an axial direction from the center of a screw flight at its outside diameter to the center of the same flight one turn away. **2.** A heavy metal, hazardous to health if inhaled or swallowed. Its use has been restricted by federal law. In plastics, it is found in some pigments and heat stabilizers.

leader pin ▷ **mold pin**

leakage flow ▷ **screw leakage flow**

lease or buy ▷ **capital equipment investment**

leatherlike material ▷ **poromeric**

legionnaire's disease ▷ **antimicrobial agent**

length, full contour The length of a fully extended polymer chain.

length-to-diameter ratio ▷ **L/D ratio**

lengthwise direction Refers to the cutting of specimens and to the application of loads. For rods and tubes, it is the direction of the long axis. For other shapes that are stronger in one direction than in the other, lengthwise is in the direction that is stronger. For materials that are equally strong in both directions, lengthwise is an arbitrary designated direction that may be with the direction of flow in fabrication, longer direction, etc. ▷ **crosswise direction; machine and transverse directions; orientation**

leno weave A locking-type weave in which two or more warp threads cross over each other and interface with one or more filling threads. This fabric is used primarily to prevent the shifting of fibers during molding as could occur in openweave fabrics. ▷ **mock leno weave**

lens ▷ **Fresnel lens, circular; Fresnel lens, linear**

lens, contact ▷ **contact lens**

lens implanted They can follow cataract surgery of the eye. These ultraocular lenses have been made by sheet casting polymethyl methacrylate and shape the lenses using a lathe cut and surface modification process.

letterpress printing Used on plastic films, sheets, etc. using stationary and sheet-fed methods. ▷ **gravure**

leveling-off degree of polymerization LODP is the nearly constant degree of polymerization of cellulose reached after very prolonged mild hydrolysis or short drastic hydrolysis.

level of automation The degree to which a task or process operates automatically. This degree must take into account the ability of the system to diagnose problems in its operation, the ability of a system to recover from an error or fault, the ability of a system to start up and shut down without human intervention, and the like. ▷ **automation**

level of risk ▷ **acceptable risk**

L-glass A glass fiber type used in reinforced plastics to provide radiation protection. ▷ **glass fiber types**

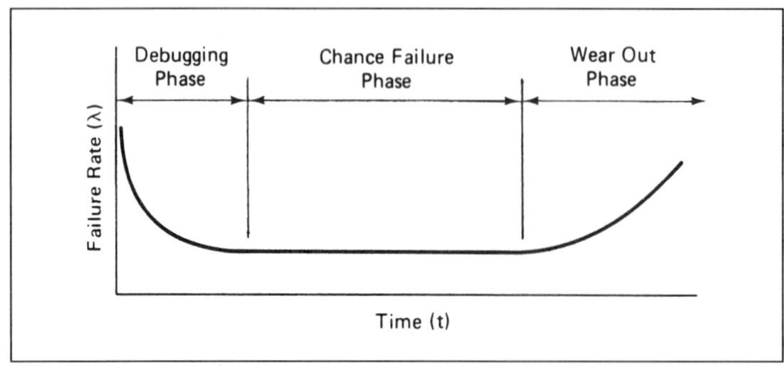

Example of a life-history curve in its basic format.

life-cycle analysis A study of a material, from its manufacture and use through disposal. The period is called "cradle to grave".

life, ecology, waste ▷ **environment, life, plastic, ecology**

life-history curve The Fig. above shows a typical life-history curve of a product for an infinite number of products. It is also called a "bathtub" curve. ▷ **product life cycle**

life of mold ▷ **mold life**

life of plastic ▷ **plastic long life; product life cycle; shelf life**

life on shelf ▷ **shelf life**

life, origin The succession of chemical events that led up to the appearance of living organisms on earth about 3.3 billion years ago (biogenesis).

light Radiant energy in a spectral range visible to the normal human eye, approximately 380 to 780 mm (3,800 to 7,800 A). ▷ **electromagnetic spectrum**

light fastness Satisfactory resistance to light, particularly the colorants or other additives entering into the composition of a plastic material; light resistance.

light frosting A light-scattering surfacing resembling fine crystal can occur on plastics. ▷ **chalking; bloom; haze**

light metal In engineering terminology, a metal of specific gravity less than three that is strong enough for construction use (aluminum, magnesium, beryllium). Most engineering plastics meet this requirement.

light metamerism The phenomenon exhibited by two surfaces which appear to be of the same color when viewed under one light source (daylight), but which do not match in color when viewed under a different light (incandescent lamp). Change in appearance of a colored surface occurs when the viewing angle is changed. Also called geometric metamerism.

light microscopy For illumination of an object, it utilizes a spectrum of electromagnetic radiations that include the visible spectrum from violet to red, and the invisible UV and IR spectra. In the plastic industry, its use includes quality control and problem solving, and to investigate compositions, properties, structures, and morphology. In patent application or litigation, microscopical data are important. In research, data often reveal variations in crystal structure.

light resistance The ability of a plastic to resist fading after exposure to sunlight or UV light (ASTM D 1501). Also called light fastness of color fastness.

light scattering In a dilute polymer solution, light rays are scattered and diminished in intensity by a number of factors including fluctuations in molecular orientation of the polymer solute. Observations of the intensity of light scattered at various angles provide the basis for an important method of measuring molecular weights of high polymers.

light stabilizer An additive to a plastic compound to improve its resistance to light. ▷ **ultraviolet absorber and light stabilizer**

light transmission The percentage of incident light transmitted by the plastic is often time dependent due to the effects of aging and weathering. The reciprocal of light transmissibility is the haze value which increases as the percent transmission decreases. ASTM D 1003 is an adopted procedure for measuring these values. As a general rule, 0% haze relates to complete transparency; up to 30% is translucent, and more than 30% haze is considered opaque.

lignin A naturally occurring resin found in wood and other vegetation as the binding agent for cellulosic structure; denser than cellulose.

lignin plastic Material made by heating lignin or by reaction of lignin with chemicals, the lignin being in greatest amount by mass (ASTM D 883). Use includes as binders or extenders.

lignite A low rank of mined coal between peat and sub-bituminous containing 35% water. Plastics (polyesters and polyamides) can be derived from lignite by oxidation with nitric acid, followed by extraction of the nitro-acid.

lime Fourth highest volume chemical produced in U.S.; various chemical and physical forms exist. Calcium oxide (CaO), noncombustible, is extensively used as a filler in plastics.

limestone ▷ **calcium carbonate**

limiting oxygen index LOI is the concentration of oxygen required to maintain burning and is the basis for evaluating flammability characteristics of plastic. It measures the concentration of oxygen to maintain burning (ASTM D 2863). ▷ **fire retardance**

linear expansion ▷ **coefficient of linear thermal expansion**

linear low density polyethylene plastic ▷ **polyethylene**

linear molecule A long chain molecule as contrasted to one having many side chains or branches.

linear polymer A polymer whose molecular chain is free of branches or side chains formed by polymerization. ▷ **molecular arrangement structure**

linear thermal expansion ▷ **cofficient of linear thermal expansion**

linen Yarn, thread, or fabric made from flax fibers.

linoleum ▷ **flooring material**

linter ▷ **fiber linter**

liquid chromatography This technique separates components of a mixture by differences in their rate of elusion arising from interactions between sample and the column-packing material. ▷ **chromatography**

liquid crystal An organic compound in an intermediate or mesomorphic state between solid and liquid.

liquid crystal polymer plastic LCPs, sometimes called super polymers, which were commercially introduced in 1984, are called self-reinforcing plastics because of their densely packed fibrous polymer chains. LCPs create new design opportunities for plastics with their exceptional range of properties. They have outstanding strength at extreme temperatures, excellent mechanical-property retention after exposure to weathering and radiation, good dielectric strength as well as arc resistance and dimensional stability, a low coefficient of thermal expansion, excellent flame resistance, and easy processability. Their UL continuous-use rating for electrical properties is as high as 240°C (464°F), and for mechanical properties it is 220°C (428°F). LCP's high heat deflection value permits LCP molded parts to be exposed to intermittent temperatures as high as 315°C (600°F) without affecting their properties. Their resistance to high-temperature flexural creep is excellent, as are their fracture-toughness characteristics.

LCPs' ease of processing gives them the ability to fill long, narrow molds, which makes them eminently suitable for such high-performance parts as electronic connectors. They may have 138,000 kPas (20,000 psi) or more in tensile strength, with flexural modulus values up to 5×10^6 psi. They are available in grades with heat deflection temperatures (HDT) of about 357°C (675°F) at 1,820 kPas (264 psi). This family of different LCPs resists most chemicals and weathers oxidation and flame, making them excellent replacements for metals, ceramics, and other plastics.

LCPs are available in both amorphous and crystalline grades. The amorphous types, with their high strength-to-weight ratios, are particularly useful for weight-sensitive items. Most LCPs can be injection molded, extruded, thermoformed and blow molded. The crystalline grades, with glass and other fibers, meet the dimensional requirements and stability at high temperatures required of products for the electrical and electronics markets.

The LCPs are all exceptionally inert and resist stress cracking in the presence of most chemicals at elevated temperatures, including the aromatic and halogenated hydrocarbons as well as strong acids, bases, ketones and other aggressive industrial products. Their hydrolytic stability in boiling water is excellent, but high-temperature steam, concentrated sulfuric acid, and boiling caustic materials will deteriorate LCPs.

In regard to flammability, LCPs have an oxygen index ranging from 35 to 50%. When exposed to open flame they form an intumescent char that prevents dripping and results in an extremely low level of generation of smoke, which contains no toxic by-products. Its resins have UL 94 V-0 and 5V flammability ratings at 1/16 in. and an NBS smoke-chamber rating (NBS--$D_8 - 4$) of 3 to 5. Its compounds are unaffected by high doses of ionizing or cobalt-60 radiation (up to 10 billion rads), can withstand high levels of ultraviolet radiation, and are transparent to microwaves and other radiation at similar wavelengths.

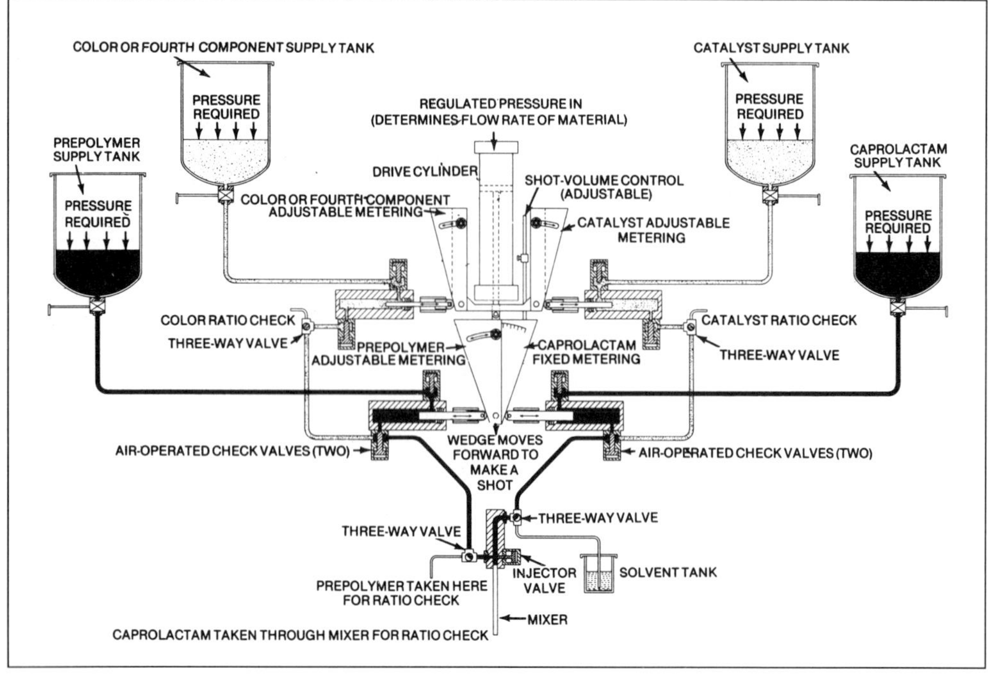

Liquid injection molding machine that can process different liquid plastics. With this "flying wedge" mixing technique, nylon's mixing action is accurate to 0.1 wt%.

LCPs' molecular structure is attributed to their ease of processing. However, molded LCP parts are highly anisotropic, and weld lines in them tend to be much weaker than would normally be expected. Their properties are not affected by minor variations in processing conditions, and no postcuring is required to obtain their outstanding properties.

The major applications of LCPs are in metal and ceramic replacements that require resistance to high temperatures, chemicals, mechanical stress, creep resistance, and so forth. LCP parts include electronic and electrical connectors, sockets and pin-grid arrays exposed to high-temperature manufacturing or service conditions, automotive and aerospace parts that require the ability to withstand high temperatures and flame retardance, and chemical-processing components that exist in aggressive environments.

liquid injection molding LIM is similar to reaction injection molding (RIM). It is a simple way of describing a molding process in which two reactive streams of low viscosity ingredients are mixed and pumped into a mold and the plastic is produced. With RIM, an impingement mixing action combines the reactive streams. LIM principally uses two parts thermosets (silicone, epoxy, etc.) that includes potting and encapsulation (see Fig. above).

liquid penetrant This method is used to identify surface flaws and cracks. Low viscosity fluid containing dye, when placed on the surface of a part, penetrates into the defects. When the surface is washed, the residual penetrants contained in the part reveal the presence of flaws.

liquid plastic An organic, polymeric liquid that becomes a solid when converted to its final state for use.

liter ▷ **meter**

litharge An oxide of lead (PbO) used as an inorganic accelerator, as a vulcanizing agent for neoprene, and as an ingredient of paints.

lithographic resist printing Most commercial printing is accomplished with lithographic materials based on simple inking-noninking systems. A plastic image is formed by masked exposure to light, followed by the dissolution of the unwanted plastic. The plastic adsorbs ink and the substrate rejects it. The ink image is then transferred to product being printed. For many applications, inking selectively is not sufficient for image transfer. A relief image must be created on the plate by etching the uncovered areas of the substrate. The developed plastic image protects underlying areas during etching. These imaging plastics are called resists because of their resistance to etching.

Historically, it has been associated with the printing industry. However, the manufacturing of printed circuit boards, microwave chips, and other prefabricated products also involves the use of photosensitive plastics to form images. Each industrial application requires a specific set of plastics, sensitizers, and developers, but the fundamental concepts of image use remain the same. Image formation involving plastics usually requires changing the solubility of the exposed plastic. ▷ **photopolymer**

litre ▷ **meter**

litter The visible portion of consumer solid waste, predominantly packaging, that is discarded outside the regular disposal system. ▷ **waste**

live feed processing ▷ **extruder melt flow orientation**

living hinge ▷ **hinge, integral**

living polymer system The term living polymer is often used to describe systems in which active centers remain after complete polymerization, so that a new batch of monomer subsequently added to the existing chains increases their degree of polymerization. These systems are documented in anionic polymerization. In living polymerization the mechanism is comprised of chain initiation and chain propagation with no termination reactions (or chain transfer). Living systems have also been produced other than anionic.

load **1.** The force in weight units applied to a body. **2.** The weight of the contents of a container or transportation device. **3.** A qualitative term denoting the contents of a container. **4.** The term load means *mass* or *force* depending on its use. A load that produces a vertically downward force because of the influence of gravity acting on a mass may be expressed in mass units. Any other load is expressed in force units. ▷ **weight**

load amplitude One half of the algebraic difference between the maximum and minimum loads in the load cycle.

load, constant A load that is invariable or unchanging.

load cycle The smallest segment of the load-time function which is repeated periodically.

load, dead A constant load that is due to the weight of the product, the supporting structure, permanent attachments, etc.

load deflection curve A curve in which the increasing flexural loads are plotted on the ordinate axis and the deflections caused by the load are plotted on the abcissae axis.

load, dynamic An imposed force in motion; that is, one that may vary in magnitude, sense, and direction. ▷ **dynamic**

loader Auxiliary equipment used to move material, such as from a simple hopper loader located on a machine (extruder, etc.) using a complex mixing system (color, regrind, filler, and/or others).

load failure mode ▷ **design failure theory**

load, impact ▷ **impact loading**

loading, intermittent behavior ▷ **creep loading, intermittent behavior**

loading, long time behavior ▷ **creep loading, long time behavior**

loading relaxation ▷ **relaxation**

loading, short time behavior There are different short time periods that are based on conditions and/or applications of load, such as short-term stress-strain behavior, impact loading, etc. ▷ **short term behavior**

loading, top ▷ **container top load**

loading tray ▷ **compression molding**

load, live A moving load on a structure, part, etc.

load, static An imposed stationary force, constant magnitude, sense, and direction.

load, uniaxial A condition in which a material is stressed in only one direction along the axis or centerline of component parts. ▷ **reinforced plastic, directional properties**

locating ring ▷ **mold locating ring**

lockout machine ▷ **safety interlock**

log **1.** Roughly cylindrical shaped charge of bulk molding compound which is cut into small sections and placed in the compression mold cavity, fed to the stuffer plunger of an injection molding machine, etc. The glass fiber TS polyester log is extruded from a compound mixer. **2.** In skiving film, a plastic log is used. **3.** Identifies large foamed plastics. ▷ **foamed preform** and **polystyrene foam**

logarithm The exponent that indicates the power to which a number is raised to produce a given number, thus 1,000 to the base 10 is 3.

logarithmic decrement A measure of the mechanical damping. It is measured dynamically using a torsion pendulum, vibrating reed, or some other free vibration instrument, and is calculated from the natural logarithm of the ratio of the amplitudes of any two oscillations (dimensions: unity):

$$\Delta = \frac{1}{n} \ln \frac{A_{(i+n)}}{A_i}$$

where: A_i = amplitude of the ith oscillation; $A_{(i+n)}$ = amplitude of the oscillation n vibrations after the ith oscillation.
For small damping:

$$\Delta \doteq \pi \frac{G''}{G'} = \pi \frac{E''}{E'}$$

logic An action that forces a decision apart from or in opposition to reason; interrelation of sequence of facts or events when seen as inevitable or predictable; a particular mode of reasoning viewed as valid or faulty. ▷ **plastic bad and other myths** and **programmable logic**

logic relay ▷ **relay logic**

logo An identifiable statement or graphic display regarding a product.

London dispersion force It identifies weak intermolecular forces based on transient dipole interactions. As an example, linear hydrocarbon polymers have no polarity, and there is no obvious reason why their molecules should be attached to each other. Nevertheless their mechanical strength and resistance to melt flow show that even here some attractive forces must exist. They are vaguely ascribed to dynamic fluidity and mobility of the valence electron cloud in the polymer molecule, producing transient unsymmetrical states of electrical imbalance and thus momentary polarity. These weak fugative polar attractions draw polymer molecules to within 3 to 5 A of each other with a force of 1 to 2 kcal/mole. While one such attraction would be negligible, the large number of such attractions between large polymer molecules accumulates to produce a large total effect.

For amorphous flexible molecules such as atactic polypropylene, polyisobutylene, and unvulcanized rubber, such attractions produce viscous liquids to tacky gums to soft rubbery solids; when heated, they liquefy and flow easily. For amorphous stiff molecules such as polystyrene, these attractions produce rigidity and strength up to 80 to 90°; but they melt out easily to permit melt processing. In crystalline polymers such as polyethylene and isotactic polypropylene, the same London dispersion forces recur so frequently in the tightly packed crystal lattice that their total is very significant, producing rigidity and strength up to heat deflection temperatures as high as 120°C, and requiring the injection molder to go to melting points as high as 176°C in order to melt out the attractions and produce liquid flow.

These are polymers in which there are no intermolecular attractions other than London dispersion forces. In all other polymers, where there are also polar and hydrogen-bonding attractions, there are still these same London dispersion attractions, and they still form a considerable portion of the total intermolecular attraction in all of them.

long-chain branching A form of molecular branching found in addition polymers as a result of an internal transfer reaction. It primarily influences the melt flow properties.

longos ▷ **filament winding**

long time load behavior ▷ **creep loading, long time behavior**

loop strength ▷ **fiber loop tenacity**

lost core molding ▷ **soluble core molding**

lost wax molding ▷ **soluble core molding**

lot A specific amount of material produced at one time using one process and constant conditions of manufacture, and offered for sale as a unit of quantity. ▷ **batch** and **good manufacturing practice**

low density polyethylene plastic ▷ **polyethylene**

low pressure molding or laminating ▷ **molding, pressure low**

low pressure structural foam molding ▷ **foamed injection molding low pressure**

low-profile plastic Special polyester plastic systems for reinforced plastics that are combinations of thermoset and thermoplastic materials; rather than the usual all thermoset polyester that in certain applications cannot provide a class-A finish (no surface waveness). Although the terms low-profile and low-shrink are sometimes used interchageably, there is a difference. Low-shrink plastics contain up to 30 wt% thermoplastic, while low-profile plastics contain 30 to 50 wt%. Low-shrink offers minimum surface waviness in the molded part (as low as 25 µm or 1 mil/in. mold shrinkage); low-profile offers no surface waviness (from 12.7 to 0 µm or 0.5 to 0 mil/in. mold shrinkage).

low-shrink plastic ▷ **low-profile plastic**

low temperature shrinkage ▷ **coefficient of linear thermal expansion**

lubricant additive Compounded additives which can be classified into two areas: internal and external. The internal lubricants promote plastic flow without affecting fusion properties of the compound. External lubricants promote metal release facilitating the smooth flow of melt over die surfaces, or prevent adhesion of plastics to mold cavities that are also called release agents. There are those, also called slip promoters such as silicones, perfluoroalkyl esters, stearate soaps, and clays, that are effective in reducing blocking by imparting high lubricity to plastic films and sheets causing them to slide easily over each other.

lubricant bloom An irregular, cloudy, greasy film on a plastic (ASTM D 883). Such effects can also be caused by exudation of plasticizers, stabilizers, and other additives, so the term lubricant bloom should be used only when the exudation is caused by a lubricant.

lubricant, solid A solid substance that will reduce the friction or prevent sticking when placed between two moving parts. Materials used include graphite, molybdenum disulfide, etc. ▷ **dusting agent**

lubricating, extruder process ▷ **extruder paste**

lubrication, bearing Bearings made from metals in many applications require some type of lubricant to reduce friction developed between two surfaces moving relative to each other; plastic bearings in most application do not require lubricants since they are self lubricating.

lubrication for processing equipment The plastics fabricating/processing industry (injection, extrusion, etc.) uses hydraulics to provide the energy and force to perform their various operations. Today's hydraulic systems use many different types of hydraulic components, variance displacement pumps, cartridge valves, servos, microprocessors, robots, etc. These newer components provide better system performance with a resulting increase in part quality and production.

The continually new hydraulic environment brings on a need to review existing maintenance practices for hydraulic presses to see what changes or improvements can be made in existing maintenance programs. One of the approaches is the predictive controlled maintenance of hydraulic fluids, through lubrication expertise. This hydraulic environment approach to lubrication expertise must include control of lubrication by analysis and data base. For optimum operation, important areas of operation include: (1) valve analysis and fluid selection, (2) storage and handling of fluids, (3) contamination control, (4) how elevated temperatures affect operations, (5) contaminants introduced during system repair, (6) learning from your breakdowns, (7) leakage control, (8) system design considerations, (9) reclamation procedures, and (10) fluid maintenance procedures.

The greatest underlying factor is contamination control. To be successful in optimum performance of hydraulic components one must understand how contamination of fluids occurs in the shop environment. In the shop, definite maintenance procedures must be understood in order to extend or maximize fluid and increase system performance.

Before choosing a fluid from a performance standpoint, there are several important considerations that must be reviewed and analyzed before the proper fluid choice is made. Thus, one determines what is available for your components that meets the hydraulic fluid specification requirements. An economic impact study should be made for each fluid envolving initial cost, leakage rate, reclamation alternatives, disposal cost, health and safety requirements, maintenance procedures, and availability of fluid now and later. Target is to select a premium grade fluid, minimize leakage on equipment, use conditioning equipment to keep the fluid clean (using filters, magnets, centrifuges, and even reclamation equipment). In the final analysis, the economic realities of system operation (including fluid cost, particularly wasted leakage), disposal cost, and health and safety limitations may be of such magnitude that it is prudent to install a positive maintenance program to control the leaks, modify system components, and analyze the in-process hydraulic fluid.

lubricity It refers to the load bearing characteristics of a plastic under relative motion. Those with good lubricity tend to have low coefficients of friction with themselves or other materials and do not have a tendency to gall.

Lucite Du Pont's trade name for its acrylic plastics.

lug **1.** A type of thread configuration, usually thread segments disposed equidistantly around a bottle neck (finish). The matching closure has matching portions that engage each of the thread segments. **2.** A small indentation or raised portion on the surface of a container, provided as a means of indexing the container for operations such as multi-color decoration, labeling, and/or filling.

lumber The product of the sawmill and planing mill usually not further manufactured other than by sawing, resawing, and matching.

lumber and plastic ▷ **plastic lumber** and **waste and plastic lumber**

lumen ▷ **luminous flux**

luminance The luminous intensity of any surface in a given direction per unit of projected area of the surface as viewed from that direction.

luminescent pigment Special pigments available to produce striking effects in the dark. Basically there are two types: one is activated by UV radiation, producing very strong luminescence and, consequently, very eye catching effects; the other type, known as phosphorescent pigments, does not require any separate source of radiation.

luminous flux The lumen (lm) is the luminous flux emitted in a solid angle of one steradian by a point source having a uniform intensity of one candela (cd · sr). The candela is the luminous intensity, in a given direction, of a source that emits monochromatic radiation of frequency 540×10^{12} H and that has a radiant intensity in that direction of 1/683 watt per steradian.

luminous reflectance The ratio of the light reflected by any test specimen to that incident on it.

luminous transmittance The ratio of the luminous flux transmitted by a body of the flux incident upon it.

luster The appearance of a surface of a substance in reflected light. The term is used particularly in describing minerals. Types of luster are: metallic, vitreous (glass or quartz), adamantine (like diamond), plastic, or dull (like chalk).

lux ▷ **illuminance**

lyophilic Characterizing a material which readily goes into colloidal suspension in a liquid; if into water, it is called hydrophilic. Examples of this material are gelatin and glue.

lyophobic Characterizing a material which exists in the collodial state but with a tendency to repel liquids; lacks affinity for the suspending medium. If the liquid is water, it is called hydrophobic.

lyotropic liquid crystal A type of liquid crystalline plastic that can only be processed from solution.

M

Macbeth A lighting system used for checking color.

macerate **1.** To chop or shred fabric for use as a filler for a plastic molding compound. **2.** To soften or break up a fibrous substance by long soaking in water at or near room temperature, often accompanied by mechanical action, as in the preparation of wood fiber-wood stock.

machine aging To ensure the maximum efficiency performancewise and costwise of plastic products, new machines or auxiliary equipment are always available to meet this target. It requires the processor to keep up to date on fabricating processes and determine when to bring "one" up to date as depicted by the Fig. below. Updating also includes going to another method of fabricating. ▷**capital equipment investment**

You cannot expect a 20-year-old machine to compete with a machine built to today's standards.

machine alignment Incorrect alignment, whether at the time of machine installation or as a consequence of structural settlement, vibration, or machine age, is often the source of product inconsistencies. The problem is due to the lack of awareness of the vital importance of proper alignment in controlling operating and maintenance costs. If the extension of the life of equipment is added, the impact on the bottom line (profit) becomes even more important. ▷**machine precision leveling mounts**

machine and transverse directions Plastic materials, such as sheet being extruded or reinforced plastic being pultruded, basically have a lengthwise (or machine) direction where the direction follows the flow of plastic from the die. At 90° to this direction is the crosswise (or transverse) direction. ▷**orientation** and **reinforced plastic, directional properties**

machine interlock ▷**safety interlock**

machine-performance interfacing In order to fabricate all sizes, shapes and weights of parts that meet all types of performance requirements, the industry has been continuously successful in advancing the state of the art/science throughout the past century. Now more new developments occur to improve the "complete process" ▷**FALLO approach.** With time, significant improvements have been made based on the knowledge gained in understanding the parameters that influence how to best meet part performance requirements. These parameters involve: (1) Set up specific performance requirements; (2) evaluate material requirements and fabricating characteristics; (3) design part based on the material fabricating characteristics; (4) design and manufacture mold or die based on part design; (5) set up and operate the complete fabricating machine line based on meeting mold/die and material processing equipment; (6) test and quality control incoming materials, materials during processing and finished parts; (7) interface all these parameters by available simplified computerized program(s). ▷**equipment**

machine precision leveling mounts Most machines require careful mounting on adjustable mounts to permit accurate leveling and absorption of any shock. ▷**machine alignment**

machine purchase ▷**capital equipment investment**

machinery communication standard ▷**communication protocol**

machinery in use In the U.S. there are about 75,000 injection molders being used in about 7,000 plants, about 12,000 extruders in about 1,500 plants, and about 6,000 blow molders in about 200 plants.

machining Although most plastic parts are usually fabricated into their final shape, there

Examples of machining operations for plastics.

Machining method	Purpose of machining operation
Cutting	
with a single-point tool	Turning, planing, shaping
with a multiple-point tool	Milling, drilling, reaming, threading, engraving
Cutting off	
with a saw	Hack sawing, band sawing, circular sawing
by the aid of abrasives	Bonded abrasives: abrasive cutting off, diamond cutting off Loose abrasives: blasting, ultrasonic cutting off
shearing	Shearing, nibbling
by the aid of heat	Friction cutting off, electrical heated wire cutting off
Finishing	
by the aid of abrasives	Bonded abrasives: grinding, abrasive belt grinding Loose abrasives: barreling, blasting, buffing

are parts that require machining from parts that need supplemental operations (cutting extruded shape, cutting thermoformed scrap, etc.) to taking stock plastics to produce parts via machining. Different machining operations are involved: milling, drilling, cutting, finishing, etc. (see Table above). Different reasons exist for machining such as: (1) Dimensions of fabricated parts may not be sufficiently accurate. Extreme accuracy, particularly when using certain processes or machines with limited capabilities, can be expensive to achieve; (2) fabricated parts can be relatively expensive in small-scale production. It may also be desirable to make parts by machining when the production is not large enough to justify the investment in fabricating equipment; (3) supplementary machining procedures may be required in finishing operations, as shown in the Table below. Examples of machining operations on parts are shown in the Table opposite.

With the many different type plastics, there exist a variety of machining characteristics. Like the different metals, nonmetals, aluminums, woods, glasses, etc., different machining characteristics exist. Thermoplastics (TPs) are relatively resilient compared to metals, and require special cutting procedures. Even within the TPs (PE, PVC, PC, etc.) the cutting characteristic will change, depending on the fillers and reinforcements used. Elastic recovery occurs in plastics both during and after machining; provisions must be made in the tool geometry for sufficient clearance to allow for it. This is so because of the expansion of any compressed material due to elastic recovery causes increased friction between the recovered cut surface and the cutting surface of the tool. In addition to generating heat, this abrasion affects tool wear. Elastic recovery also explains why, without proper precautions, drilled or tapped holes in many plastics often are tapered or become smaller than the diameter of the drills that were used to make them (particularly TPs unfilled or not reinforced).

As the heat of conductivity of plastics is very slow, essentially all the cutting heat generated will be absorbed by the cutting tool. The small amount of heat conducted into the plastic cannot be transferred to the core of the shape, so it causes the heat of surface area to increase significantly. If this heat is kept to a minimum no further action is required; otherwise heat removed by a coolant is used to ensure a proper cut. For many commodity TPs the softening, deformation, and degradation heats are relatively low. Gumming, discoloration, poor tolerance control, and poor finish could occur if frictional heat is generated and allowed to build up. Engineered TPs (PA, PTFE, etc.) have relatively high melting or softening points. Thus,

Supplementary machining.

Processing method	Purpose of machining operation	Types of machining used
Compression, transfer, injection and blow molding	Degating, deflashing, polishing	Cutting off, buffing, tumbling, filing, sanding
Extrusion	Cut lengths of extrudate	Cutting off
Laminating	Cut sheets to size, deflashing edges	Cutting off
Vacuum forming	Polish cut edges, trim parts to size	Cutting off, sanding, filing

Machining examples.

Types of parts	Kinds of machining methods used
Bearing, roller	Turning, milling, drilling, shaping
Button	Turning, drilling
Cam	Turning, copy turning
Dial and scale	Engraving, sand blasting
Gear	Turning, milling, gear shaving, broaching
Liner and brake lining	Cutting off, shaping, planing, milling
Pipe and rod	Cutting off, turning, threading
Plate (ceiling, panel)	Cutting off, drilling, tapping
Tape (mainly for PTFE)	Peeling

they have less tendency to become gummed, melted, burned, or crazed in machining than do plastics with lower melting points.

Thermoset (TS) plastics machining is slightly different than TPs because there is not any great melting distortion from a fast cutting speed. Higher cutting speeds improve machined finishes but tool life can be reduced by the added frictional heat, and the surface of the plastic to be machined can also be distorted in appearance by burning unless precautionary steps are taken, such as spraying a coolant directly on the cutting tool and plastic. Another major difference in machining TSs is the type of chips that are removed by the cutting tool. Almost all of these are in a powder-like form that can be readily removed with the aid of a vacuum hose. This is almost a must in moderate and high production runs due to contamination of the air in the vicinity of the cutting machine. In some machining instances, the dust condition created can be hazardous enough to compel the operator to wear a filtering air mask.

Recognize that all plastics can be properly machined or cut when a few simple rules are observed: (1) use only sharp tools, (2) provide adequate chip clearance, (3) support the work properly, and (4) provide adequate cooling. Dull tools scrape instead of cut and yield a poor surface finish. Because they require greater pressure for cutting, there is unnecessary deflection of the work piece, and excessive frictional heat buildup. Well-sharpened tools scrape properly, leaving a good finish on the work, and remain serviceable for a reasonable length of time.

Adequate chip clearance prevents clogging of the tool and interference with cutting edges. When there is a choice of tools, the one with the greatest provision for chip clearance should be used. As an example, drills with wide flute areas and saw blades with deep gullets are preferred. The work should be properly supported to prevent springing away from the tool under cutting pressure. Excessive deflection of the work by the cutting tool causes chattering or uneven cutting. ▷ **cutter; guillotine; saw**

machining electric discharge EDM is a metal working process applicable to mold and die construction in which controlled sparking is used to erode the workpiece. Also called electrospark machining.

machining jig Mechanism for holding a part and guiding the tool during machining or assembly operation.

machining jig cooling Cooling a fabricated part (after removal from a mold, etc.) in a jig which prevents the part from changing shapes. It can reduce cycle time, such as in injection molding parts particularly those that are large and/or thick. Also called cooling fixture.

macro ▷ **macromechanic**

macrocyclic plastic Macromolecules are commonly represented as long, flexible, randomly coiled chains that may be branched. Some cyclic structures may be present, although in small amounts. Ring-chain equilibria occur, however, in a number of polycondensation systems, implying the presence of functional links in the polymer chain.

macroglycol ▷ **polyurethane plastic**

macromechanic The analysis of the mechanical behavior of reinforced plastics in which the microstructure (the matrix and dispersed phase) is ignored, but in which the material is regarded as being homogeneous. However, allowance can be made for the anisotropic nature of the material. The fibers are used as stapes, strands, or sheets, and such groups of fibers can be used as elements for a macromechanics treatment. A simple example is the derivation of the simple law of mixtures for the modulus of a unidirectional fiber/matrix RP structure in the fiber direction. The properties of an RP structure may be calculated from the properties of the individual elements by assembling them in the appropriate way, including the possibility of arranging them at different orientations. ▷ **reinforced plastic** and **micromechanic**

macromolecular engineering ▷ **designing with model, plastic tailor-made**

macromolecule By definition, it is a very large, usually organic, molecule containing hundreds or thousands of atoms. Most molecules have relatively few atoms and are in the 2- to 100-atom range. For example, regular water (H_2O) contains three atoms, carbon monoxide (CO) contains two atoms, and so forth. A molecule that contains thousands of atoms, such as polystyrene, which has a molecular weight ranging from 60,000 to 1,500,000, in comparison, is out of the ordinary. Plastics have these macromolecules. These large, complex molecules occur both naturally and as synthetically produced substances, and are always the subject of intense study by chemists and the interdisciplinary scientists. ▷ **micromechanic** and **polymer chemistry terminology**

macroscopy Interpretation using only the naked eye, or a magnification no greater than 10×.

macrostrain ▷ **strain, macro-**

magnesium carbonate $MgCO_3$ is a white powder of low density, used as a filler in plastics such as phenolic.

magnesium oxide MgO is a white powder, used as a filler.

magnesium stearate $Mg(C_{18}H_{35}O_2)_2$ is a white, soft powder used as a lubricant and stabilizer.

magnet Magnets of different designs that nest and fit different processing equipment (hoppers, blenders, granulator exits, etc.) are used to catch metallic contaminants in virgin or recycled plastics prior to being processed.

magnetic flux The weber (Wb) is the magnetic flux which, linking a circuit of one turn, produces an electromotive force of one volt as it is reduced to zero at a uniform rate in one second (V · s).

magnetic flux density The tesla (T) is the magnetic flux density given by a magnetic flux of one weber per square meter (Wb/m^2).

magnetic flux field testing This field is developed when an electric current or external magnetic force is applied to a ferritic material that could be adjoining or encapsulated in plastic. Flaws disrupt the magnetic path and set up a field pattern around the flaw. With ferric material, particularly material exposed to the air, when its surface is dusted with finely divided ferritic materials, the area around the flaw is revealed. With encapsulated plastics, this action can occur where thin plastic surface exists. ▷ **nondestructive testing**

magnetic induction That magnetic vector quantity which at any point in a magnetic field is measured either by the mechanical force experienced by an element of electric current at the point, or by the electromotive force induced in an elementary loop during any change in flux linkages with the loop at the point. Also called flux density.

magnetic plastic Ferromagnetism is a well known phenomenon in metallic and inorganic materials. However a rather recent observation shows there are also organic materials (plastics) that are ferromagnetic. As early as 1957, the synthesis of a series of heterocyclic molecules including poly(2,6-pyridinediylmethylidenenitrilohexamethylene nitromethylidene) (PPH) was reported. The origin of ferromagnetism is poorly understood. Two extreme theories proposed by Heisenberg and Block exist, which are synonymous with the valence bond method and the molecular orbital method for the study of molecular electronic structure, respectively. The Heisenberg theory is based on electron exchange between localized electronic systems, and Block's approach is based on collective electron systems. ▷ **superconductivity**

magnetic resonance imaging Uses magnetism, harmless radio waves, and computers. MRI looks through materials (particularly human bones) to examine changes in material density (underlying soft tissues in humans). It then creates detailed images on a computer screen which are transferred to film for study. With bones, images produced are clearer than those of an X-ray or CT scan.

magnetic separation Use of a magnetic field to remove unwanted magnetic particles from plastics.

magnetic tape storage ▷ **computer storage disk and tape**

magneto resistance The change of electrical resistance of a crystal when a magnetic field is applied.

mainframe ▷ **computer mainframe**

maintenance of die ▷ **die maintenance and care**

maintenance of mold ▷ **mold maintenance**

maintenance, preventative ▷ **preventative maintenance**

major axis **1.** In filament winding, the axis in the center of the rotating mandrel. **2.** In rotational molding, the rotation of arm and mold (or molds) about one axis in a horizontal plane.

maleic anhydride Colorless chemical derived from vapor-phase oxidation with atmospheric oxygen and catalyst. Used in producing polyester and alkyd plastics.

male mold ▷**mold cavity, female**

malleability Can be defined as the same as ductility, except that it is applied to compression. Thus, one can say that malleable materials permit high "plastic" deformation in compression without fracture. It can be easily flattened or rolled without preheating. It has plasticity.

management and investment ▷**capital equipment investment**

management and quality ▷**total quality management**

management information system ▷**computer information system**

management risk ▷**risk management**

management, solid waste ▷**solid waste management**

mandrel 1. In blow molding, part of the tooling that forms the inside of the container neck and through which air is forced to form the hot parison to the shape of the mold cavity. **2.** The portion of an extrusion die that forms the hollow center of a profile such as an extruded pipe or tube. **3.** In filament winding of reinforced plastic, the form (usually cylindrical) around which filaments are wound.

mandrel-type die head A die head in which plastic melt is fed into the side of the die head and diverted about the mandrel by flow guides; target is to eliminate or reduce formation of weld line where melt fronts meet on the other side of mandrel from the entrance to the die.

manifold ▷**mold manifold**

manual cycle ▷**operation, manual**

manual tapping test ▷**reinforced plastic tapping test**

manufacturing ▷**fabricating processes** and **standard industrial classification**

manufacturing analysis The Fig. below relates to an approach concerning a manufacturing analysis that is part of the product design. ▷**product design**

manufacturing energy ▷**energy conservation**

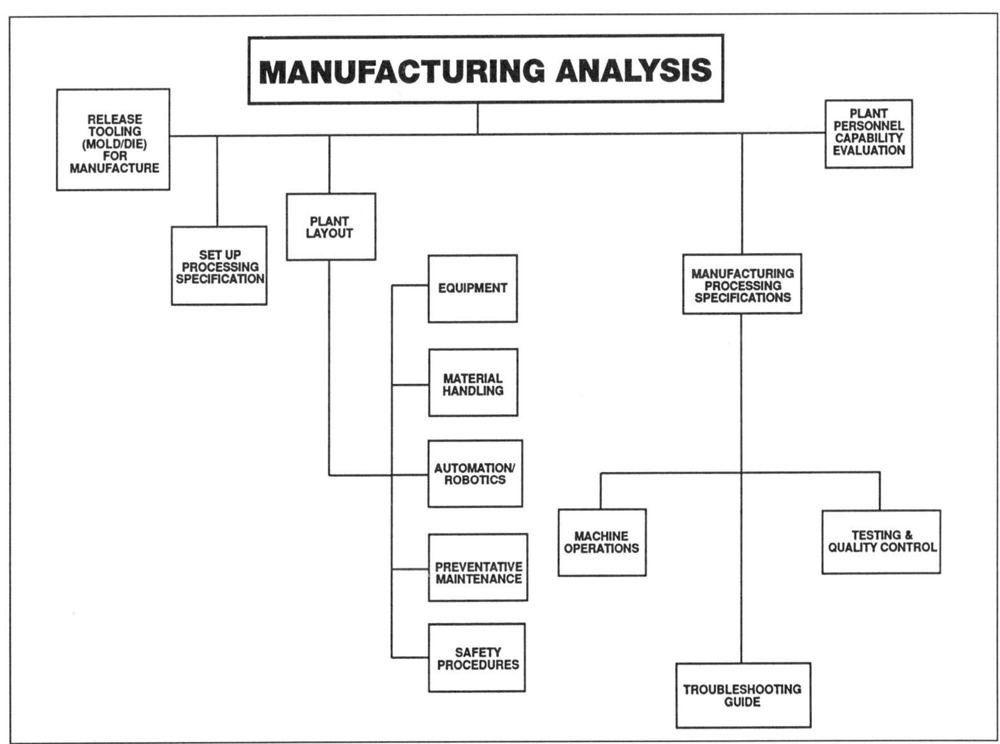

Manufacturing analysis diagram.

manufacturing planning ▷ **perfection**

manufacturing plastic ▷ **plastic** and **polymerization**

manufacturing resources planning ▷ **just-in-time**

manufacturing via computer ▷ **computer-aided manufacturing**

marble melt process ▷ **glass fiber production**

Marco vacuum RP molding method This reinforced plastics process was popular during the 1940s–1950s. Like resin transfer molding (RTM) and bag molding, the reinforcements are laid up in any desired pattern. Low cost matched molds (wood, etc.) confine the reinforcements. A pool of liquid catalyzed TS polyester plastic surrounds the mold above its partially opened parting line. From a central mold opening (hole) a vacuum is applied so that the plastic flows through the reinforcements. With proper melt flow, wet out of fibers occur and voids are eliminated (see Fig.). This method when first used was the reverse of RTM. The Marco method eventually incorporated pressure plugs at parting line with vacuum in addition to just vacuum and also had a push-pull action where pressure was applied in the center (similar to RTM) and vacuum pool. Eventually it was only pressure applied through the center hole; later became known as RTM.

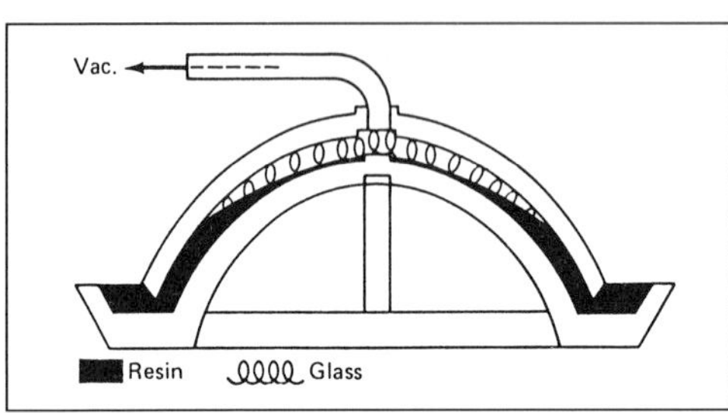

Marco vacuum molding process.

markets emerging The Technology Administration of the U.S. Commerce Department identifies twelve "emerging technologies" that will create markets worth $1 trillion by year 2000. The U.S. share will be roughly a third of the total (usual share based on population of the industrialized countries). There are four areas: (1) advanced materials, such as reinforced plastics, other composites, ceramics, metal alloys, and superconductors; (2) electronics and information systems, including advanced semiconductor microchips and digital imaging technology; (3) manufacturing systems, including artificial intelligence, flexible computer-integrated manufacturing, and sensor technology; and (4) life science applications, including biotechnology, medical devices, and diagnostics. In addition to (1), the others involve the use of plastics.

markets for plastics Within the context of definitions and scope of this book as a mini-encyclopedia, market information is presented based on plastics and reinforced plastics consumption. The different markets include: agriculture, air-ships, appliances, automotive, building and construction (using about 20 wt% plastics), cosmetics, dental, drugs, electricals, electronics, furniture, health care, home security, household, horticulture, industrial, mechanical, medical, microwave, packaging (using about 30 wt% of plastics), pipe, recreation, toys, transportation, and practically any market that exists. ▷ **plastic overview; standard industrial classification; export-import U.S. plastics trade; plastic industry structure**

markets input-ouput data ▷ **standard industrial classification**

markon The amount added to the cost in order to arrive at a selling price. Also referred to as mark-up.

marquardt index In an infrared absorption curve study of the cure advancement of phenolic plastics, the index is the numerical difference in the percent transmission between the absorption peak at 12.2 microns and 13.3 microns. As plastic cure progresses, the intensity of the 13.3 μ absorption changes more readily than that of 12.2 μ peak; thus the marquardt index number decreases as the cure advances.

mar resistance The resistance of glossy plastic surfaces to abrasive action. It is measured by abrading a specimen to a series of degrees, then measuring the gloss of these abraded spots with a glossmeter. Results are compared to an unabraded area of the specimen (ASTM D 673).

masking Spray paint often must be deposited only in selected areas and the areas not to be coated must be protected by masking. The simplest masking method involves employing tape and paper to cover areas of the plastic surface. The choice of tape, usually a crepe paper pressure-sensitive tape, is important. The tape must be resistant to the solvents used in the spray paint, it must be able to withstand the drying conditions, and it should separate cleanly upon removal. The sharpness along the edge of tape largely depends on the tape quality.

Hard masks are reusable metal or plastic parts placed over the object to be painted. Cast polyurethanes and silicone rubbers are often used for plastic masks. Metal types may be fabricated by regular mechanical methods or may be electroformed. Cleaning usually is in a solvent wash tank.

mask, trimetal A mask formed by etching a metal protected in certain areas by a second metal which is itself protected by a third metal in certain areas.

mass The SI unit of mass, or one of the multiples formed by attaching an SI prefix to gram (g), is preferred for all applications. (The kilogram-force should not be used). The megagram (Mg) is the appropriate unit for measuring large masses such as have been expressed in tons (T). However, the name "ton" has been given to several large mass units that are widely used in commerce and technology; the long ton of 2240 lb, the short ton of 2000 lb, and the metric ton of 1000 kg (that is also just called ton). None of these terms are SI. ▷ **load; weight**, and the *Conversion Tables on* pp. xxiii ff.

mass median size A measurement of particle size for samples of particulate plastic filler matter, consisting of that diameter such that the mass of all larger particles is equal to the mass of all smaller particles.

mass polymerization Alternative name for bulk polymerization.

mass production Plastic products continue to be produced more quickly and in larger volumes because of the strides that are continually made in the processing techniques (extrusion, injection molding, blow molding, thermoforming, etc.). Improved mechanization of automatic and semiautomatic machines plus improved processing materials bring about shorter production times (cycles, etc.), improved quality, reduced handling operations, etc.

mass spectrometry MS is a technique for the molecular structural analysis of organic compounds in which a small amount of the compound (a few micrograms) is ionized by electron impact and volatilized ions (including the molecular system ion but mostly fragment ions) are separated according to their mass/charge ratios by passing them through electrostatic and/or magnetic fields (as in a double focusing mass spectrometer). The resultant mass spectrum shows the variation in intensity of the different species and careful interpretation enables fine molecular structural information to be determined.

For plastic analysis, the main difficulty, for other than low molecular weight plastics, is that they are not volatile. Thus, except when the electrospray technique is used, high MWs must be analyzed by a prior degradation to lower MW fragments. The main application of MS to plastics is in the analysis of degradation products. In addition, other structural features, such as stereoregularity, may be examined indirectly.

masterbatch A plastic compound which includes a high concentration of an additive or additives. They are designed for use in appropriate quantities with the basic plastic or mix so that the correct end concentration is achieved. For example, color masterbatches for a variety of plastics are extensively used as they provide a clean and convenient method of obtaining accurate color shades.

mastic A protective finish of relatively thick consistency capable of application to thermal insulation or other surfaces, usually by spray or trowel, in thick coats greater than 30 mils (0.03 in./0.76 mm). It is a natural plastic obtained from the tree *pistacia lentiscus* grown in Chios (Greece). It is alcohol soluble, light color, and is used in spirit varnishes. It softens at about 55°C.

mastication Permanent softening of crude natural rubber and certain other elastomers by application of mechanical energy, as on a roll mill, Banbury mixer, etc. This "breaking down" of a high polymer is essential in preparing it for incorporation of modifying and additive substances. As an example, it is the mechanical shearing of a raw unvulcanized rubber (such as natural rubber) on a mill or mixer in order to reduce its molecular weight and improve its processability. Measurement can be made by a viscometer. At low temperatures, MW reduction is due to mechanochemical degradative chain scission, whereas above 100°C oxidative degradation reduces the MW. A minimum rate of MW reduction occurs at about 100°C. Mastication is often promoted using a peptizer. In the presence of a second monomer, it is a method of graft copolymerization.

mat A nonwoven fabric of fibrous material used as a plastic reinforcement and consisting of randomly oriented chopped filaments, short fibers (with or without a carrier fabric), or swirled filaments loosely held together with a plastic binder. Available in blankets of various widths, weights, and lengths. Also sheet formed by filament winding a single-hoop ply of fiber on a mandrel, cutting across its width and laying out a flat sheet. Mats are usually made up of glass fibers. ▷ **mat needled** and **surface mat**

mat binder Plastic applied to glass fiber and cured during the manufacture of mat, to hold the fibers in place and maintain the shape of the mat.

matched die molding A reinforced plastic manufacturing process in which close-fitting metal matching male and female molds are used (for example, in the telescoping fit of compression molding) to form the part using pressure, temperature, and time cycle. The molds usually provide matched metal shearing area for the cut-off. Sometimes called matched metal molding. ▷ **rubber plunger molding**

material A non-specific term used with various "shades" of meaning in the technical literature. It should not be used as a synonym for substance, but is generally used in the collective expressions such as raw material, material handling, plastic, reinforced plastic, metal, molding compound, mixture, etc. Thus, it is a substance of which anything is composed, such as filled plastics and reinforced plastics.

material and civilization ▷ **civilization and materials**

material and engineering In addition to being a vital contributor to technical products and systems, materials have a direct interaction with nontechnical considerations in modern society. For example, availability of raw materials, materials for energy conservation, and product liability each interface the technology of materials with economic, political, environmental, and consumer considerations. These interactions continue to become more important as time passes when our resources diminish, and if life-quality goals are to be achieved. Technical solutions are required to solve the materials problems that come with resource depletion, increased recycling, materials substitution, more efficient energy conversion, and greater product dependability. Plastics provide these technical solutions. ▷ **design theory and strength of materials**

material cycle The sequence of extraction, refining, manufacturing, use, and discard or eventual recycle of any materials for use including plastics.

material distribution A term which describes the variation in thickness of various parts of a product, i.e., body, wall, shoulder, base, etc.

material engineering problems ▷ **design theory and strength of materials**

material handling In most processes, for either small or large production runs, the cost of the plastics used compared to the total cost of production in the plant may be at least 60%. The proportion might be only 30%, but it is more likely to exceed 60%; so it is important to handle material with "care" and to eliminate unnecessary production problems and waste. Where small-quantity users or expensive engineering plastics are concerned, containers such as bags and gaylords are acceptable; but for large commercial and custom processors, these delivery methods are bulky and costly. Plastic storage in this form is also expensive.

Any large-scale plastic handling system has three basic subsystems: unloading, storage, and transfer. For a complete system to work at peak efficiency, processors need to write specifications that fully account for the unique requirements of each subsystem. The least efficient component, no matter how inconsequential it may seem, limits the overall efficiency of the entire system.

material, organic ▷ **organic material**

material origin Materials engineering, that includes plastics, is based largely on the pure sciences of chemistry and physics. All materials obey the laws of physics and chemistry in their formation, reactions, and combinations. The smallest part of an element that retains the properties of that element is the atom. Atoms are building blocks for engineering materials. All matter is composed of atoms bonded together in different patterns and with different types of bonds. Most substances that we deal with in industry and in everyday life can be categorized as organic and inorganic (includes commodity and engineering plastics). Organics contain the element carbon (and usually hydrogen) as a key part of their structure, and they are usually derived from living things. Petroleum products are organic; crude oil is really the residue of plants that lived millions of years ago and all plants and animals are organic in nature (see petroleum). Inorganics are those substances not derived from living things. Sand, rock, water, metals, and inert gases are inorganic materials. Chemistry as a science is usually separated into two fields based upon these two criteria of organic and inorganic. Metallurgists and ceramists deal primarily with inorganics. Plastic engineers deal principally with organics. The field of materials engineering deals with both areas.

material properties ▷ **plastic properties** where comparisons are made of different materials.

material reclamation ▷ **recycling**

material recovery Separating materials from the waste stream for beneficial purposes, such as recycling and reusing. Can apply to incineration to produce energy.

material recovery facility A MRF plant, often privately owned and operated, receives and processes recyclable materials for resale. A middle person between waste managers and recycling plants. Also called intermediate processing centers. In the past called junk dealers (who did an exceptional job).

material secondary A material (plastic, paper, etc.) other than virgin or raw material that has fulfilled its original function and can be reused, but only after being reprocessed. Can include industrial scrap compromised by the manufacturing process.

material selection Selection of materials (plastics, steel, wood, etc.) can be a highly complex process if not properly approached. Its methodology ranges from a high degree of sophistication in some areas to a high degree of subjective intuition in other areas. It runs the gamut from highly systematic value engineering or failure analysis in aerospace to a telephone call for advice from a material supplier in the decorative houseware business. In order to arrive at the optimum material for a given use with some degree of efficiency and reliability, a systematic approach has to be used. ▷ **design; computer-aided design/computer-aided manufacturing; computer cost modeling; computerized database, plastics; computer modeling; computer processing control; computer tolerance analysis; statistical benefits**

material strength and theory ▷ **design theory and strength of materials**

material types With so many available, it is best to recognize that materials fit into systematic categories. Various groupings, such as plastics, metals, ceramics, glasses, etc. are possible. They in turn are subdivided. With plastics there are thermoplastics and thermosets, unreinforced and reinforced, solid and foam, nonconductive and electrically conductive, weather resistant and non-weather resistant, etc.

material variation, reliability factor Material variation is a very important factor that should not be overlooked by an analyst, statistician, designer, processor, etc. Most conventional and commercial tabulated data and plots such as tensile strength and fatigue strength are mean values and thereby imply 50% survival rate. Target for some level of reliability that will account for material variations, and other variations that can occur in processing.

material, virgin or primary ▷ **virgin plastic**

mathematical model ▷ **designing with model mathematically** and **computer modeling**

mathematical symbols ▷ **symbols and signs**

mat needled A mat formed of strands cut to a short length, then felted together in a needle loom with or without a carrier.

mat, nonwoven ▷ **mat**

matrix The essentially homogeneous plastic in which fiber reinforcement is embedded; both thermoset and thermoplastic materials are used. The fiber can be glass, carbon, ceramic, etc. ▷ **reinforced plastic** and **reinforcement**

matte finish A type of dull, non-reflective finish. ▷ **surface finish**

matter Anything that has mass or occupies space.

Maxwell model A mechanical model of simple linear viscoelastic behavior which consists of a spring of Young's modulus (E) in series with a dash pot of coefficient of viscosity (η). It is an isostress model (with stress σ), the strain (ε) being the sum of the individual strains in the spring and dashpot. This leads to a differential representation of linear viscoelasticity as

$$d\varepsilon/dt = (1/E)\, d\sigma/dt + (\sigma/\eta)$$

This model is useful for the representation of stress relaxation, since when

$$d\varepsilon/dt = 0$$

integration gives

$$\sigma = \sigma_0 \exp(-t/\tau)$$

where τ ($= E/\eta$) is the relaxation time. Such an exponential decay in stress is often observed in practice. However, the model may not be such a good representation since stress does not always decay to zero as $t \to \infty$ as predicted. Often more than one exponential term is required. Also for creep (when $d\sigma/dt = 0$) there is

$$d\varepsilon/dt = \sigma/\eta$$

thus Newtonian flow is predicted which is generally not found for viscoelastic materials (plastics, etc.). The rheological equation for the model is

$$\tau = \eta\dot{v} - (\eta/E)$$

where τ is the shear stress and $\dot{v}$ is the shear rate. Such a model is also often referred to as the Maxwell fluid model since, in contrast to the Voight model, the stress causes the strain to increase continuously, nonrecoverably, and indefinitely.

Maxwell-Wagner effect The effect on dielectric properties caused by discontinuities or inclusions in the dielectric. This results in interfacial polarization and the occurrence of a dielectric relaxation at low frequency. In some

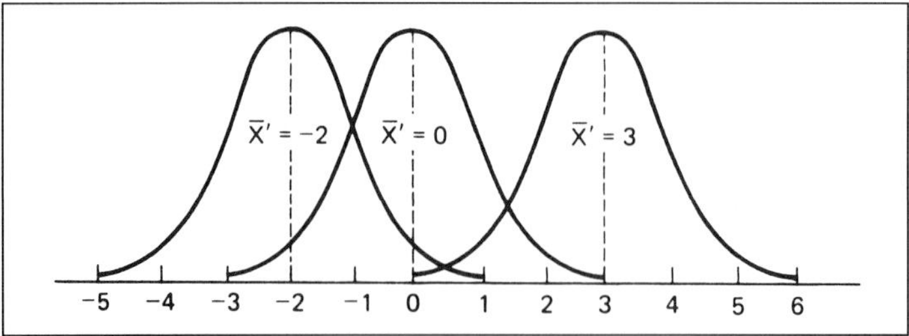

Fig. 1 Normal curve with different means but identical standard deviations.

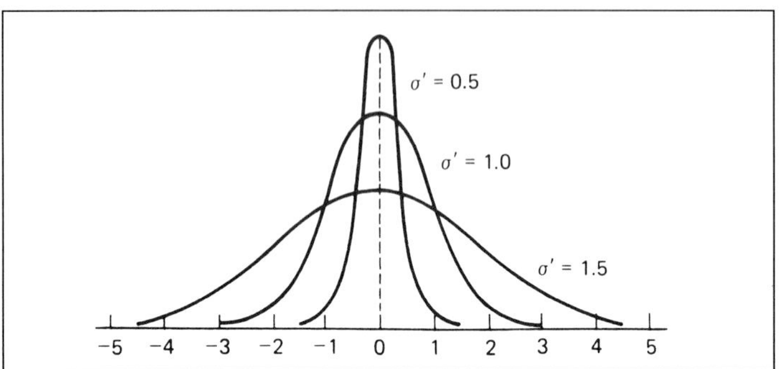

Fig. 2 Normal curve with different standard deviations but identical means.

cases the relaxation may be at a frequency which is high enough to be caused by a dipolar relaxation, so some care must be taken in the interpretation of tear results. The heterogeneity may be a crack or void of a crystalline/amorphous boundary. However, a more serious example is one in which a highly conductive impurity is present in the insulating plastic dielectric.

McDonald's clamshell bombshell
▷ **environment and public opinion**

mean Arithmetical average of a set of numbers.

mean and standard deviation As seen by the formula for the ▷ **statistical normal curve,** there is a definite relationship among the ▷ **mean,** the standard deviation, and normal curve. The normal curve is fully defined by the mean, which locates the normal curve, and the standard deviation which describes the shape of the normal curve. Fig. 1 shows three normal curves with different mean values; it is noted that the only change is in the location. Fig. 2 shows three normal curves with the same mean but different standard deviations. The figure illustrates the principle that the larger the standard deviation, the flatter the curve (data are widely dispersed), and the smaller the standard deviation, the more peaked the curve (data are narrowly dispersed). If the standard deviation is zero, all values are identical to the mean and there is no curve.

A relationship exists between the standard deviation and the area under the normal curve as shown in Fig. 3. The figure shows that in a normal distribution 68.26% of the items are included between the limits of $\overline{X}' + 1\sigma$ and $\overline{X}' + 1\sigma$, 95.46% of the items are included between the limits $\overline{X}' + 2\sigma$ and $\overline{X}' + 2\sigma$, and 99.73% of the items are included between $\overline{X}' + 3\sigma$ and $\overline{X}' + 3\sigma'$. One hundred percent of the items are included between the limits $+\infty$ and $-\infty$. These percentages hold true regardless of the shape of the normal curve. The fact that 99.73% of the items are included between $\pm 3\sigma$ is the basis for control charts.

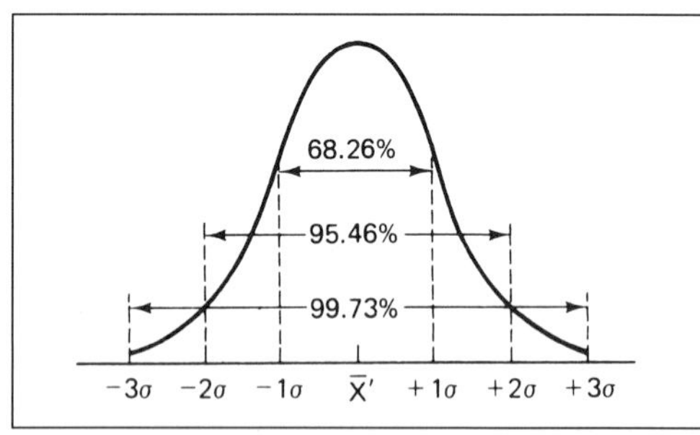

Fig. 3 Percent of items included between certain values of the standard deviation.

mean, arithmetic More simply called the mean, it is the sum of the values in a distribution divided by the number of values. It is the most common measure of central tendency. There are three different techniques available for calculating the mean: (1) raw data or ungrouped, (2) grouped data with a calculator, and (3) grouped data with paper and pencil.

(1) *Raw Data Technique* This technique is used when the amount of data is small or a computer can be used. The mean is represented by the notation $\overline{X}$, which is read as "X bar" and is given by the formula

$$\overline{X} = \frac{\sum_{i=1}^{n} X_i}{n} = \frac{X_1 + X_2 + \ldots + X_n}{n}$$

where $\overline{X}$ = arithmetic mean; n = number of observations; $X_1, X_2, \ldots, X_n$ = value of individual observation identified by the subscript 1, 2, ..., n; Σ = symbol meaning "sum of"; X_i = value of the ith observation identified by the general subscript i.

The first expression is a simplified method of writing the formula whereby $\Sigma_{i=1}^{n} X_i$ is read as "summation from 1 to n of X sub i" and means to add together the values of the observations.

(2) *Grouped Data with a Calculator* When the data have been grouped into a frequency distribution and a calculator or computer is available, the following technique is applicable. The formula for the mean of grouped data is

$$\overline{X} = \frac{\sum_{j=1}^{m} f_j X_j}{n} = \frac{f_1 X_1 + f_2 X_2 + \ldots + f_m X_m}{n}$$

where f_j = frequency of observations in the jth cell; X_j = midpoint of the jth cell; m = number of cells.

The midpoint of each cell is used as the representative value of that cell. Each midpoint is multiplied by its cell frequency; the products are summed; and they are divided by the total number of observations. In the example problem given below, the first three columns are those of a typical frequency distribution. The fourth column is derived from the product of the second column (midpoint) and third column (frequency) and is labeled "fX".

(3) *Grouped Data with Paper and Pencil* When a calculator is not available and the data are grouped, a different technique is used. This technique uses cell deviations from an assumed mean to make the numbers smaller and easier to calculate with a paper and pencil. However, with the advent of the electronic hand calculator, this technique is rapidly becoming extinct. The formula for the mean is

$$\overline{X} = \overline{X}_0 + i\left(\frac{\sum_{j=1}^{m} f_j d_j}{n}\right)$$

where $\overline{X}_0$ = assumed mean; i = cell interval; d_j = deviation in cell units of the j cell from the assumed mean.

mean crossings In fatigue loading, the number of times that the load-time history crosses the mean load level with a positive slope (or a negative slope, or both, as specified) during a given length of the history.

mean deviation The MD is the average deviation of a series of numbers from their mean. In averaging the deviations, no account is taken of signs, and all deviations, whether plus or minus, are treated as positive. The MD is also called the mean absolute deviation (MAD) or average deviation (AD).

mean diameter, arithmetic That diameter located at the centroid of the distribution of size.

mean free path The average distance that a molecule travels between successive collisions with other molecules.

mean modulus The ratio of mean stress to mean strain.

mean square In analysis of variance, a contraction of the expression "mean of the squared deviations from the appropriate average(s)" where the divisor of each sum of squares is the appropriate degree of freedom.

measurement, standard deviation ▷ **standard deviation measurement**

measures and weights units ▷ **decimal system**

mechanical behavior, dynamic ▷ **dynamic mechanical behavior**

mechanical drawing **1.** The stretching of a plastic sheet or film by mechanical devices such as molds and plugs. **2.** Stretching of sheet by differential pressure such as thermoforming. **3.** Stretching film or sheet by orientation in tenter frame. **4.** ▷ **computer graphic** and **design graphics**

mechanical hysteresis ▷ **hysteresis**

mechanical market Plastics are increasingly being used in mechanical applications such as gears, springs, bearings, and snap fits. Plastics offer elimination of parts through design, elimination of finishing operations, simplified assembly, reduced maintenance, obviation of lubrication, weight savings, noise reduction, freedom from corrosion, ease of part identification through use of colors, etc. These advantages must be weighed against the possible limitations imposed by temperature, level and duration of stress, rate of application of stress, nature of environment, etc.

mechanical nonwoven fabric The textile and paper industries are based on two (wet and dry) processes of the oldest arts. Manufacturing of nonwovens for plastics draws on both of these. With the wet process there are two types, the Fourdrinier and cylinder machines. Modifications have been made in these machines so that a satisfactory plastic or matrix situation can be accomplished. The general paper product is highly dense, so that saturation with laminating plastic is difficult. Saturability can be improved by reducing paper thickness, including plastics in the pulp mix, using foaming or dispensing agents in the pulp (so that when paper is dried the fibers are partially separated), air-blowing paper during drying, or increasing hole diameters or porosity in wire screen or felt carriers.

The dry process can be divided into two steps: formation of the web and application of bonding agent. Web, mat, and felt are terms for the nonwoven sheet. The sheet can be formed by mechanical carding of fibers, an air-laying process, or an air-flotation system. The techniques provide latitude in orientation of fibers including continuous swirl fiber patterns. Fibers can be deposited so that they are roughly parallel and in the machine direction. Other patterns include orthotropic and isotropic layups.

The particular equipment and method of operation is influenced by such fiber characteristics as strength, stiffness, length, diameter, flexibility, surface condition, abrasion resistance, softness, ease of fiberizing, tenacity, and resilience. If fibers are used that have the inability to rub without destruction, they can be surface treated or blended with other fibers to permit processing in mechanical equipment. Carding mechanically separates fibers by a combing brush action. Rotating brushes lay down fibers on a conveyer belt. The air flotation process lays down fibers on a large conveyor belt. The fiber deposited by both methods is sprayed with a plastic binder to develop a strong web or sheet. The air flotation process is typical of the methods used to produce the large quantities of nonwoven glass fiber mats for reinforced plastics.

mechanical properties The basic characteristics of the mechanical properties of solids are usually determined by tests resulting in various deformation-vs-stress dependencies, such as stress-strain diagrams. Examination of such dependencies readily brings out characteristics of elasticity, plasticity, and strength; expressed as modulus of elasticity, limit of proportionality, elastic limit, ultimate strength, resistance to failure, etc. The mechanical properties of liquids (plastic melts) are determined by studying the dependence of the rate of strain on the stress applied. One of the most common mechanical characteristics determined in this manner is viscosity. However, all these characteristics are insufficient to describe plastics owing to the specific mechanical properties peculiar to the many different plastics.

The most important of these properties are: (1) highly pronounced mechanical relaxation (creep, stress relaxation, hysteresis, etc.), owing to which mechanical properties of plastics depend largely on the temperature, (2) ability to develop enormous reversible deformations (that caused by axial tension, as an example, may be as high as several hundred percent), this ability being the most pronounced in elastomers, and (3) intimate connection between mechanical and chemical processes, which affect each other substantially. The term mechanical is applied to this category of properties since they are usually used to indicate the suitability of a material for use in mechanical applications, parts that carry a load, absorb shock, resist wear, etc. ▷ **testing; nondestructive testing; physical properties; chemical properties**

mechanical properties and molecular weight ▷ **molecular basic properties effect on product properties**

mechanical properties and morphology ▷ **morphology and mechanical properties**

mechanical properties and orientation ▷ **orientation and mechanical properties**

mechanical properties, superior ▷ **advanced plastic** and **reinforced plastic, advanced**

mechanical properties, theoretical versus actual properties ▷ **data theoretical versus acutal properties**

mechanical properties, thermal ▷ **thermal mechanical properties**

mechanical relaxation ▷ **relaxation**

mechanical, self lubricating ▷ **silicone fluid additives**

mechanical statistics ▷ **statistical mechanics**

mechanical testing The determination of mechanical properties. ▷ **testing**

mechanics, continuum ▷ **Boltzmann super position principle**

mechatronic Integrating electronics with mechanics.

medical biological packaging ▷ **packaging biological substances**

Medical Device Act November 28, 1990 regulation PL 101-629 titled Safe Medical Devices

Act of 1990 provides improvements in FDA's regulation of medical devices. This law is the first major revision of the Medical Device Ammendments of 1976. Although it does not constitute a radical departure from existing medical device regulation, significant new provisions will have far reaching and profound impact upon the U.S. medical device industry regarding user reports on failures, device tracking, substantial equivalence, premarket approval, performance standards, recall authority, etc.

medical device packaging, clarity Clarity is a major functional requirement of medical device packaging. Because a clear package makes a product contained much easier to identify, it consequently can reduce the time hospital personnel and others spend searching for the product as well as the incidence of mistaken identity. A clear package is also cost-effective for manufacturers and purchasers alike. It simplifies product-line standardization; the number of package types and sizes can be minimized and it allows less skilled workers (stock clerks instead of nurses) to retrieve products from storage. Packaging and product quality are also easier to monitor. For example, heat-sealed integrity can be evaluated by looking at the distribution of the coating through the flange.

While clarity has long been an important feature of medical device packaging, there is also a demand for medical procedure kits. They contain multiple components and require simple verification of contents. Clarity is an aesthetic property, not functional.

medical device sterilization ▷ **sterilization, medical devices**

medical health care Health-care professionals depend on plastics for everything from IV bags to wheelchairs, disposable labware to silicone body parts, etc. The diversity of plastics allows them to serve in many ways, improving our lives and sometimes prolonging them (such as a braided, corrugated "Dacron" aorta tube in Rosato). ▷ **absorbable technology; bioplastic-biomedical; sutures; synthetic organs; human implantation; lens implanted**

medical market Many different plastics (PVC, PE, PS, PUR, PA, etc.) are used to meet all types of medical markets ranging from health care to the operating room. Special applications include those shown in the Fig. on p. 434. ▷ **medical health care; human implantation; lens implanted; microencapsulation, coating; suture**

megabyte In computer terminology, 1,000 kilobytes, or 1,024,000 bytes. It is acceptable, though not entirely accurate, to just say a million bytes.

melamine plastic Melamine formaldehyde (MF) is one of two major theormoset resins in the amino family, the other being ureaformaldehyde. Various kinds of fillers are used to make MF compounds to meet different requirements. MF is rigid and possesses a hard surface capable of withstanding continuous handling and wear with negligible effect. Moreover, its surface is unaffected by common organic solvents, greases, and oils, as well as many weak acids and alkalis. When properly molded into food containers and dishes, an MF does not impart odor or taste to solid or liquid foods. There are MF compounds that are insensitive to heat and are highly flame resistant, depending on the fill used. They are recommended for maximum temperatures ranging from 99 to 121°C (210 to 250°F). Low temperatures produce no observable effects on MFs.

MFs are satisfactory for the large majority of electrical applications and are particularly useful where arc resistance is desired. Mineral-filled MFs have one of the highest arc resistances of any plastic plus high dielectric strength and dimensional stability but low moisture absorption. With chopped cotton rags added, an MF has high flexural strength, will absorb considerable shock, and will not support combustion.

An alpha-cellulose-filled MF is inherently colorless, light fast, and translucent. By properly choosing pigments and dyes, an unlimited range of stable, unfading colors can be obtained, as well as a wide range of translucencies. MF moldings have good dimensional stability, high dielectric properties, and are little influenced by high humidity and water. Their strength and shock resistance are also good.

A major use of MFs with alpha cellulose is in heavy-duty dishware. Decorative dinnerware with printed inlays (that is, designs located below the surface) cannot be washed off, abraded, or damaged. Surface glazing can be used to eliminate staining or scratching. Properly designed, they are practically unbreakable.

meld line Line is similar to a weld line except the flow fronts move parallel rather than meeting head on. ▷ **weld line**

melt The plastic material in a molten or plasticized condition.

melt accumulator A cylinder equipped with a ram in which the plastic is stored between shots, such as in certain injection and blow molding machines.

melt-blown nonwoven fabric These fibers are composed of discontinuous filaments and

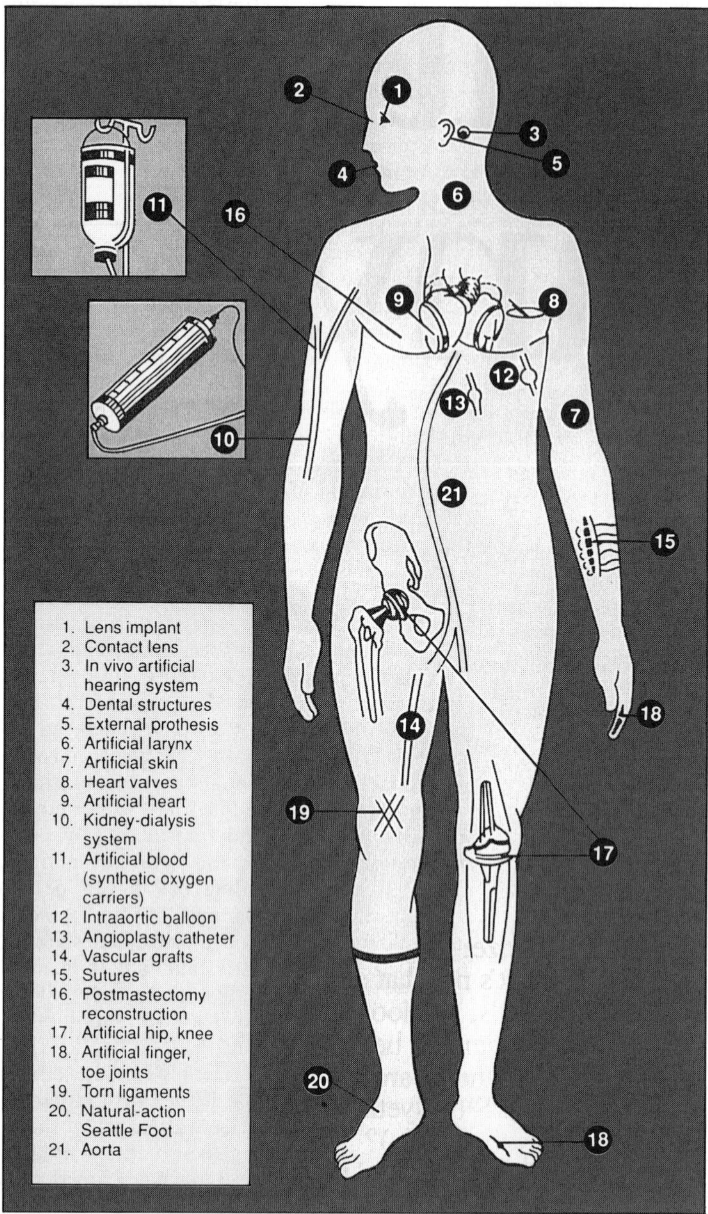

1. Lens implant
2. Contact lens
3. In vivo artificial hearing system
4. Dental structures
5. External prothesis
6. Artificial larynx
7. Artificial skin
8. Heart valves
9. Artificial heart
10. Kidney-dialysis system
11. Artificial blood (synthetic oxygen carriers)
12. Intraaortic balloon
13. Angioplasty catheter
14. Vascular grafts
15. Sutures
16. Postmastectomy reconstruction
17. Artificial hip, knee
18. Artificial finger, toe joints
19. Torn ligaments
20. Natural-action Seattle Foot
21. Aorta

Medical applications.

are smaller than those of spun-bonded fabrics. Although melt-blown fabrics are not generally referred to as spun-bonded because of discontinuous filaments, the integration of spinning, attenuation, laydown, and bonding during production describes a process traditionally defined as spun bonding. Fibers produced by melt blowing are very fine with a typical diameter of 3 µm, which is smaller by an order of magnitude than the smallest traditional spun-bonded fiber. The webs are weak and easily distorted because the fibers are extremely fine and largely unoriented. Most commercial products are made of polyester or high melt-flow polypropylene, but other thermoplastics have been used. ▷ **spun-bonded nonwoven fabric; flash-spun nonwoven fabric; melt-blown nonwoven fabric; fabric nonwoven; mechanical nonwoven fabric**

melt cavity, frozen layer Plastic melt begins to "freeze" as it fills an injection molding mold cavity. The frozen layer can easily vary in thickness as the mold fills, producing different frictional shear forces. As a result, flow (filling) and solidification (cooling of the thermoplastic) should be evaluated together.

melt compressibility ▷ **thermodynamic property**

melt decompression ▷ **injection molding screw decompression**

melt elasticity As a melt is subjected to a fixed stress or strain, the deformation versus time curve will show an initial rapid deformation followed by a continuous flow. The relative importance of elasticity (deformation) and viscosity (flow) depends on the time scale of the deformation. For a short time elasticity dominates, but over a long time the flow becomes purely viscous. This behavior influences processes: when a part is annealed, it will change its shape; or, with postextrusion, swelling occurs. Deformation contributes significantly to process-flow defects. Melts with only small deformation have proportional stress-strain behaviour. As the stress on a melt is increased, the recoverable strain tends to reach a limiting value. It is in the high-stress range, near the elastic limit, that processes operate.

Molecular weight, temperature, and pressure have little effect on elasticity; the main controlling factor is MWD. Practical elasticity phenomena often exhibit little concern for the actual values of the modulus and viscosity. Although the modulus is influenced only slightly by MW and temperature, these parameters have a great effect on viscosity and thus can alter the balance of a process.

melt extensibility ▷ **extruder draw down ratio**

melt extrusion ▷ **extruder**

melt flow behavior In most fluids, flow (the volume pushed through an opening) is directly proportional to the pressure applied. In a plot of flow versus pressure, the flow or rheological behavior of such so-called Newtonian fluids (water is an example) would be described as a straight line. Typical plastic melts are non-Newtonian; their rate of flow increases more rapidly than the pressure exerted. This means that the flow behavior of a highly viscous melt such as polyethylene is greatly affected by machine operating conditions (pressure, temperature, etc.). ▷ **design die; polyethylene; orientation and injection molding melt flow; mold cavity melt flow analysis**

melt flow defects Flow defects affect the appearance of a product; sometimes they are desirable, such as in producing a matte finish. Important types of defects can be identified. The following apply to extrusion: (1) *Nonlaminar flow* The desired flow is a steady, streamlined pattern in and out of the die. The extrudate can be distorted, causing defects identified as melt fracture and elastic turbulence. To reduce or eliminate defects the entry to the die is tapered and streamlined. (2) *Nonplastication* This condition produces uneven stress distribution, with extrudate having lumps. (3) *Volatiles* There are plastics that contain small amounts of material that boil at processing temperatures or they may contain water. These volatiles may cause bubbles, scarred surface, and other defects. Different methods, such as venting during processing and dryers, are used to reduce or eliminate these defects. (4) *Sharkskin* During flow through a die the melt next to the die tends not to move, whereas that in the center flows rapidly. When the melt leaves the die, its flow profile is abruptly changed to a uniform velocity. This change requires a rapid acceleration of the surface layer, resulting in high local stress. If this stress exceeds some critical value, the surface breaks, resulting in a rough appearance called sharkskin. With the rapid acceleration, the deformation is primarily elastic. Thus, the highest surface stress, and worst sharkskin, will occur in plastics with a high modulus and viscosity, or in high molecular weight of narrow MWD at low temperatures and high extrusion rates. The addition of die lip heating, locally reduced viscosity, is an example of reducing the defect. (5) *Shrinkages* The transition from room temperature to a high processing temperature may decrease a plastic's density up to 25%. Cooling causes possible shrinkage of up to 3% and may cause surface distortions or voiding with internal frozen strains. (6) *Melt structure* High shear at a temperature just above the melting point may cause a melt to take on too much molecular order resulting in distortion.

melt flow die instability An instability in the melt flow through a die starting at the land of the die. It leads to the same surface irregularities on the finished product as melt fracture.

melt flow elongation Flow resulting from the stretching of a melt, drawing it from a larger cross sectional area to a smaller one. It occurs in different operations such as when convergent flow occurs in a die or calender, or in the free surface flows of film and fiber drawing, blow molding or blown film causing defects that include parison sagging and draw resonance. It is characterized by the elongational viscosity.

melt flow hinder with additive Different additives such as particulate fillers and especially fibrous reinforcements generally increase viscosity and impede melt flow.

melt flow index ▷ **melt index**

melt flow, laminar ▷ **laminar flow**

melt flow model ▷ **Ellis model; flow model; designing with model, processes**

melt flow mold cavity ▷ **mold cavity melt flow analysis**

melt flow orientation ▷ **orientation**

melt flow performance In any practical deformation there are local stress concentrations. Should the viscosity increase with stress, the deformation at the stress concentration will be less rapid than in the surrounding material; the stress concentration will be smooth, and the deformation will be stable. However, when the viscosity decreases with increased stress, any stress concentration will cause catastrophic failure.

melt flow rate MFR is an alternate name for melt index.

melt flow spiral test A method for finding flow properties of either thermoplastic or thermoset plastics, formulated by the distance it will flow under specified pressure and temperature along a spiral runner in a mold. Test is usually performed using injection molding for TPs. With TSs a compression or transfer molding press is used. Plastic is fed into the center of the mold where the spiral starts.

melt fracture The rupture of the streamlines during melt flow producing a non-laminar flow; also called elastic turbulence. It is most common in extrusion where the extrudate has an uneven appearance, rather than being smooth. There would be a regular or irregular defect of spiralling, rippling, or bambooing. It is the result of the very high tensile stresses that can occur at the entrance to the extrusion die due to the converging flow. If these stresses exceed the rupture stress then irregular flow can occur. The effect occurs above a critical flow (or shear) rate that corresponds to a shear stress of typically about 10^5 to 10^6 Pa, but is also dependent on temperature, increasing with temperature and with widening MWD. The die geometry is also critical; for example, shear rate is increased if the die L/D ratio is increased. Sticking and slippage of plastic at the die wall may also contribute to melt fracture.

melt index The melt indexer (extrusion plastometer) is the most widely used rheological device for examining and studying plastics in many different fabricating processes. It is not a true viscometer, in the sense that a reliable value of the viscosity cannot be calculated from the flow index, which is normally measured. However, it does measure isothermal resistance to flow using an apparatus and test method that are standard throughout the world. Standards used include ASTM D 1238 (U.S.A.), BS 2782-105C (U.K.), DIN 53735 (Germany), JIS K7210 (Japan), ISO R1133/R292 (international), and others.

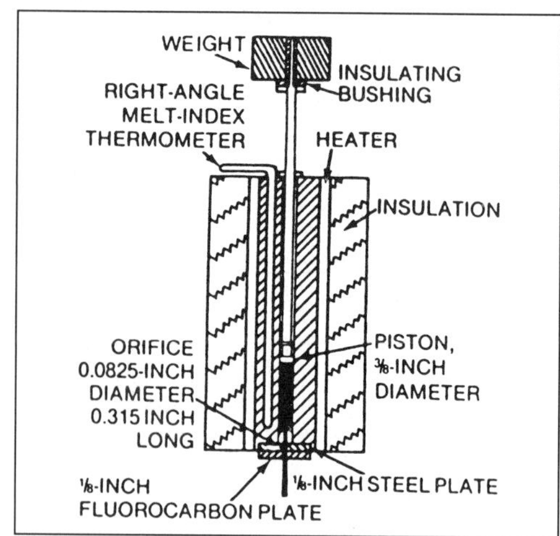

Schematic of the melt index test.

In this instrument (see Fig. above) the plastic is contained in a barrel equipped with a thermometer and surrounded by an electrical heater and an insulating jacket. A weight drives a plunger that forces the melt through the die opening, using a standard opening of 2.095 mm (0.0824 in.) and a length of 8 mm (0.315 in.). The standard procedure involves the determination of the amount of plastic extruded in 10 min. The flow rate (expressed in g/10 min.) is reported. As the flow rate increases, the viscosity decreases. Depending on the flow behavior, changes are made to standard conditions (die opening size, temperature, etc.) in order to obtain certain repeatable and meaningful data applicable to a specific processing operation (see Table).

Examples of melt index for different processes.

Process	MI range
Injection molding	5–100
Rotational molding	5–20
Film extrusion	0.5–6
Blow molding	0.1–1
Profile extrusion	0.1–1

The MI (melt indexer) is easy to operate and relatively low-cost; thus it is widely used for quality control and for distinguishing between members of a single family of plastics. Specifically, this MI makes a single-point test that provides information on resistance to flow only at a single shear rate. Because variations in branching or molecular weight distribution (MWD) can alter the shape of the viscosity curve, the MI may give a false ranking of plastics in terms of their shear rate resistance to flow. To overcome this problem, extrusion rates are sometimes measured for two loads, or other modifications are made.

melt index high load The rate of flow of a melt through a 0.0824 in. orifice when subjected to a high force of 21,600 g at 190°C (374°F).

melt index versus density The Table below provides examples.

melting point An alternate term for melting temperature.

melting temperature T_m is the temperaure at which a plastic liquifies on heating or solidifies on cooling. Some materials have a melting range rather than a single point. Amorphous plastics do not have melting points, but rather softening ranges and undergo only small volume changes when solidifying from the melt, or when the solid softens and becomes fluid. Crystalline plastics have considerable order to the molecules in the solid state, indicating that many of the atoms are regularly spaced, have a true melting point with a latent heat of fusion associated with the melting and freezing process, and a relatively large volume change during the transition from melt to solid.

Melting is a first order transition and occurs with an increase in entropy, volume, and enthalpy. In low molecular weight plastics melting takes over a narrow (about 0.5 to 2°C) range, except in impure substances. With imperfections in the crystallites, melting occurs over a much wider range of 10 to 20°C. However, frequently a precise melting temperature is given. This temperature usually refers to the highest value, when the last and therefore the most perfectly ordered crystals melt. Even this value of T_m is 10 to 20°C below theoretical value quoted for perfect crystals. Plastics may sometimes show a small premelting transition or may exhibit several T_m values, when capable of existing in different crystalline forms (polymorphism).

melting with screw ▷**screw mixing and melting**

melt performance ▷**screw melt performance**

melt pipe The structure manifold containing the flow passage connecting in such machines as an extruder to an accumulator and injection molding two-stage system.

melt polymerization A bulk polymerization in which either, or both, the monomer and polymer are crystalline and which is carried out at a temperature above the melting temperature of both. ▷**bulk polymerization**

melt pressure transducer Different processors, but particularly extrusion processors, employ melt pressure transducers more frequently to help them improve output and melt quality, enhance production safety, and safeguard machinery. To select the right transducer to meet needs, processors must familiarize themselves with the performance characteristics of various transducers. Once a specific type is selected, proper application and maintenance are key factors in ensuring that these instruments provide optimum performance. They can range

MI versus density.

Properties	With increasing melt index	With increasing density
Rigidity	—	Increases
Heat resistance	Decreases	Increases
Stress crack resistance	Decreases	Decreases
Permeation resistance	—	Increases
Abrasion resistance	—	Increases
Clarity	—	Decreases
Flex life	Decreases	Decreases
Impact strength	Decreases	Decreases
Gloss	Increases	Increases
Vertical crush resistance	—	Increases
Cycle	Decreases	Decreases
Flow	Increases	Decreases
Shrinkage	Decreases	Increases
Parison roughness	Decreases	Increases
Parison sag	Increases	Decreases
Pinch quality	Increases	—
Parting line difference	—	Increases

from a single transducer used for indicating a single pressure reading to sophisticated systems that employ a series of transducers and accessories to record data, sound alarms, take corrective action, and relay information to a process control system.

Regardless of a given system's configuration, the key points to be measured in any application are at the die, screen pack, melt pump, and along the barrel. As an example: (1) While most extruder drives and takeoff devices provide almost drift-free operation, variations in material and process conditions occur that affect the flow rate through the die, which results in inconsistent extruder output. A transducer placed at the entrance to the die in conjunction with a pressure–control device helps maintain stable output and melt quality. (2) Dirty or clogged screens cause pressure increases within the barrel, which restricts flow from the screw to the die. (3) A melt pump, when required, helps eliminate fluctuations and deliver precise amounts of melt to the die at a constant flow rate. Processors using melt pumps should measure both the inlet and outlet pressures at the pump to ensure that the melt pressure at the die remains constant and to prevent the possibility of melt-pump equipment damage caused by lack of melt that lubricates the pump. (4) The extruder screw is the single most important piece of equipment in terms of affecting the quality and quantity of melt delivered to the die. Transducers are used in R&D of screw designs, and to evaluate the best plastics and screws to use in specific process lines. Typical measurements in R&D vary within a few psi (Pa).

melt pressure transducer types Pushrod and capillary-fill units are the two most common types used. Each incorporates a strain gauge wired in the form of a bridge that is mounted on a stress member. The strain gauge bridge is mounted on a remote upper diaphragm, while a lower sensing diaphragm comes in contact with the plastic melt. A minute deflection of the stress member causes a change in resistance in the strain gauge and an imbalance in the bridge. The amount of imbalance is proportional to the pressure applied to the sensing diaphragm. When voltage is applied to the bridge, a millivolt output signal is produced that is proportional to the applied pressure. The electrical output generated can be used for data collection, process monitoring and control, and electronic transmission of a pressure reading to a remote display. ▷ **computer-aided manufacturing**

Pushrod transducers use a force rod to isolate the strain gauge from the high temperature sensing diaphragm. Due to its rigid stem design, space and temperature constraints often limit the place where they can be installed.

Capillary-type transducers are filled with mercury or sodium potassium to isolate the strain gauge from the high temperature sensing diaphragm. These units are available in both rigid and flexible stem models. Flexible types allow the strain gauge housing to be mounted away from the high temperature environment and can be used in installations where space limitations are a concern.

Capillary units exhibit greater temperature stability than pushrod types. Temperature gradients along the pushrod stem, particularly during startup, cause different relative expansions between the pushrod and the outer stem. This results in large transient output shifts of up to 25% of full scale pressure. The temperature effect on a capillary type is a predictable 15 to 30 psi (0.1 to 0.2 MPa) per 37.8°C (100°F) of temperature change, which is a small fraction of the effect typically seen with pushrod transducers. Capillary types also exhibit a better combined error specification (the sum of errors due to nonlinearity, hysteresis, and nonrepeatability), usually between 0.5 to 1.0% of full scale. This is a particularly important consideration for transducers used in closed-loop pressure control system.

The most accurate way to calculate combined error is to total all the data deviations from a straight line that passes through zero and the full scale output point. This is known as the terminal method of determining the combined error specification. Mounting torque sensitivity is a potential problem with pushrod units due to their rather rigid design. Overtorquing during installation causes minute dimensional changes in the system, which cause shifts in output. Capillary units are more flexible by design and do not exhibit any significant mounting-torque sensitivity. Be sure to zero any transducer at operating temperatures since this will change with temperature due to thermal expansion. Never handle, unscrew, or tighten a transducer with solidified plastic near the tip, otherwise you will tear the diaphragm. ▷ **strain gauge**

melt pump ▷ **gear pump**

melt roll Usually a two-roll machine that can be used to produce film or sheet, plastic coated fabrics, etc. More precise systems, when required, include roller coating, extruder coating, and calendering.

melt shear rate The speed of shear sliding deformation between melt layers of a plastic body per unit thickness of layers or along the wall in laminar flow. Thus shear rate = velocity (cm/s)/clearance (cm) = s^{-1}.

melt shear sensitivity Most plastic melts are pseudoplastic; at increasing shear rates they become less viscous. However, the relative degree of shear sensitivity varies greatly from one plastic to another. Generally broadening MWD produces increasing shear sensitivity.

melt spinning ▷ **fiber spinning process**

melt stability An instability in the melt flow through a die starting at the land of the die. It leads to the same surface irregularities on the finished part as melt fracture.

melt strength The strength of a plastic while in the molten state; the tensile stress at which a plastic melt fractures when subject to draw-down.

melt structure ▷ **molecular arrangement structure**

melt swell ▷ **design die, basics of flow**

melt temperature The temperature of the melt (stock) as sensed by a thermocouple (T/C) or resistance temperature detector (RTD) and indicated on a compatible meter. The location of measurement must be specified. ▷ **temperature sensor**

melt temperature automatic tuning There is one major disadvantage to using an automatic reset barrel temperature controller: the coefficients of the proportional, the reset, and the rate terms all have to be adjusted properly to obtain desired performance. It is not difficult to do this, but it can be time-consuming. One must follow the manufacturer's instructions.

melt temperature profile Usually the melt temperature only is taken or estimated from the inside of the barrel or the surface of the melt as it moves through the barrel. Various techniques can be used (such as IR sensors) that look at melt temperatures across the entire melt stream, as, for example, when it exits an extruder (or when it exits an injection molding nozzle into space, etc.)

It had been generally accepted by most extrusion processors and suppliers that the melt temperature variance at the end of an extruder was negligible. Stationary thermocouples had been immersed in melts, but very limited useful data could be obtained, as probes tended to disturb the melt flow or be damaged. Obtaining the profile with a standard immersion thermocouple required that an operator position the probe manually, plot the position, and so on. Results were not repeatable, or were tentative at best.

melt temperature timing and sequence Most processes operate more efficiently when functions must occur in a desired time sequence or at prescribed intervals of time. In the past, mechanical timers and logic relays were used. Now electronic logic and timing devices predominate, based on the so-called programmable logic controller. These devices provide sophisticated sequencing and timing, and lend themselves easily to reprogramming if it becomes necessary. Different suppliers provide special consoles that can be plugged in, and logic sequences can be added by means of "ladder diagrams" representing the desired functions and/or timing.

melt viscosity The Fig. below is an example of molecular weight distribution and shear sensitivity in melt processing; pseudoplasticity of polyethylene. ▷ **viscous elasticity** and **mold filling**

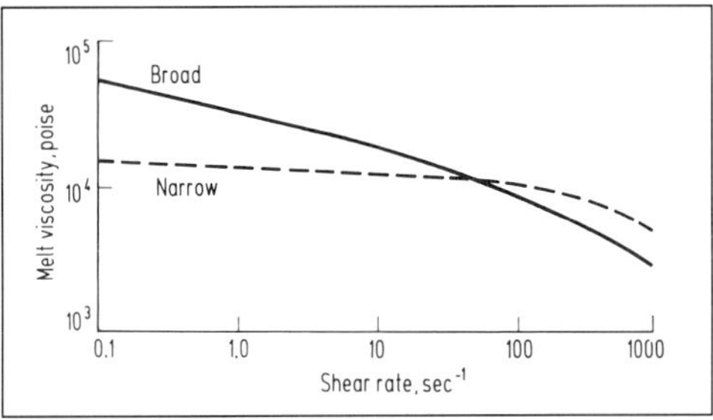

Viscosity vs. shear.

melt zone ▷ **screw melt zone**

membrane A thin barrier that permits selective mass transport. Thus the term permselectivity was coined to distinguish between a thin, nonpermeable film or layer, and a permselective membrane. It can be made of an organic or inorganic, synthetic or biological product. As permselective barriers, synthetic membranes have been employed in a variety of applications and can be classified according to their utilization, configuration, composition, allowable mode of transport, and permselectivity. Synthetic membranes as permselective barriers include dialysis, microfiltration, ultrafiltration, reverse osmosis, osmotic pumping, pervaporation, gaseous separation, electrodialysis, membrane distillation, steam filtration, and thermoosmosis. Special applications include controlled release, tissue-culture growth, biosensors, and ion-specific electrodes. In a membrane reactor they provide immobilization of catalyst and enzyme within the membrane.

Nonporous plastic membranes are used for the separation of gases on a large industrial scale. The separation is based on the observation that gases pass through thin membranes at different rates because their solubilities in the membrane and diffusivity through the membrane differ. Plastics are selected for their permeability and selectivity for the gases to be processed. They must also be processable into practical membranes. Leading plastics include polysulfones, polyimides, silicones, cellulosics, polycarbonates, and others. Expensive plastics can be used because plastic is an extremely small part of the separation equipment.

Separating membranes generally comprise a very thin nonporous separating layer on a non-selective porous membrane. Membranes were first made in the form of flat films, which are now largely supplanted by hollow fibers. Thin hollow fibers, less than 1 mm diameter, offer greater burst strength (which permits higher pressure to be applied as the separation driving force) and higher surface-to-volume ratio (which permits high flow in small equipment). Fibers may be treated or coated to improve their permeability and/or selectivity. Modifications of plastic or the fiber that increase permeability generally decrease selectivity and vice versa. Flat films are spirally wound into modules; hollow fibers are gathered into compact modules of 1,000 ft^2 (155 cm^2) or more.

Membranes are used in four major configurations of sheets, tubes, hollow fibers, and capsules (or microcapsules). However, there is no conceptual limitation for the configuration of a membrane; membranes can be shaped in almost any geometric configuration desired. The membrane morphology dictates the mode of permeation and separation. The basic morphologies are isotropic (dense or porous) and anisotropic with a tight surface extending a highly porous wall structure. ▷**barrier; permeability; hollow fiber; osmosis, reverse**

memory disk ▷**floppy disk** and **hard disk**

memory, elastic ▷**elastic memory**

memory in plastics ▷**plastic memory** and **elastic memory**

meniscus The top surface line of a liquid when enclosed in a container such as a graduate. This surface is always concave, except with mercury, which forms a convex meniscus. When one is measuring liquids, the meniscus should be at eye level.

menu ▷**computer software menu**

mer A unit that repeats itself along the molecular chain. It is the smallest repetitive basic unit of structure in plastics (which literally has many units). One mer is a monomer, two mers form a dimer, three mers a trimer, and a great many mers form the plastic.

Merlon Mobay's tradename for its polycarbonates.

mesh Refers to the number of openings in a lineal inch (cm) measured from the center of one filament to a point 1 in. (2.54 cm) distant.

mesh particle size Particle size is measured with U.S. Standard Sieves. The Table below lists the particle sizes corresponding to mesh sizes. Mesh size indicates the finest U.S. Standard Sieve through which more than 95% of the material will pass. The mesh number is determined by the number of screen openings per linear inch (or 2.54 cm). Therefore, particle size increases with decreasing mesh size. Mesh and particle size are applicable in many different processes such as extrusion (screen pack), expandable polystyrene bead size, coating with powder, rotational molding, compounding and mixing with controlled particle size, etc.

metabolize To change by the chemical and physical processes continuously going on in living organisms and cells.

metal Metals are generally superior to plastics in strength and heat resistance. Though some plastics can withstand high temperatures for short-term exposures, none can match some metals for continuous exposure to high temperatures. Most structures and manufactured products, however, are not required to withstand high heat during use. Most products only have to endure what the human body can endure, thus most plastics can take the heat. As reviewed throughout this book, plastics have certain outstanding properties when compared to metals. Regardless, each material (metal, plastic, ceramic, wood, aluminum, etc.) has its advantages and disadvantages resulting in each having its respective capabilities to produce products that meet cost and performance re-

Guide to converting mesh size into particle size.

Mesh	10	16	20	35	50	120
mil	78.7	46.9	33.1	19.7	11.7	4.9
micron	2,000	1,190	840	500	297	125

quirements. ▷ **nonferrous metal; nonmetal; design**

metal alloy By combining two or more metals into an alloy, materials with different advantages exist. The number of available alloys increases factorially, each with its specific set of properties. ▷ **alloy/blend**

metal deformation Metals under load are stressed; therefore, they are deformed. The resulting strain may be elastic (or recoverable) and/or permanent (plasticity).

metal fiber Metal fibers (with limited use to date in reinforced plastics and as plastic additives) can be grouped into whiskers, metal wools, and filament length fibers. Metals in wire or filament form exhibit high, consistent strength. Beryllium, steel, and tungsten are among the most important ones. Be has extremely low density and high modulus. Tu wires have high density and were originally developed for lamps.

metal fracture Metals fracture in one of two ways: brittle and ductile. Brittle fracture occurs with virtually no plasticity (plastic flow) or reduction of cross sectional area. In ductile failure, there is a plastic flow with separation taking place in the direction of the highest resolved sharing stress.

metal, heavy ▷ **heavy metal**

metal injection molding ▷ **injection molding metal powder; injection molding ceramic; Thixomolding**

metallic core In addition to the usual solid cores in molds, there are also soluble cores.

metallic fiber Generic name for the manufactured fiber composed of metal (or non-metal), plastic-coated metal, metal-coated plastic, or a core completely covered by metal. ▷ **whisker, metallic**

metallic, organo type ▷ **organometallic**

metallic pigment A class of pigments consisting of thin opaque aluminum flakes (made by ball milling either a disintegrated aluminum foil or a rough metal powder and then polishing to obtain a flat, brilliant surface on each particle) or copper alloy flakes (known as bronze pigments). Added to plastics, they produce unusual silvery and other metal-like attractive effects.

metallic "ring" The audible sound emitted when most metals and some plastics are dropped upon a hard surface or sheet.

metallizing plastic Plastic can be coated with metals for decorative and/or functional purposes. Thicknesses can vary at least from 0.01 to 3 mils (0.03 to 0.8 mm). The most important commercial process is electroless plating, which includes use for automobiles, printed circuits, etc. Flame and arc (metal) spraying is mainly used for functional purposes such as electromagnetic interference shielding. Sputtering and vacuum metallizing are often used in continuous coating of plastic films where they are the predominant method used. Plating capability and durability depends on the plastic used; examples are given in the Table below.

metallography ▷ **crystallography**

Guide to plating.

Flame retardants and the concentration level used	Some flame retardants migrate to the surface of the molded part and have a negative effect on the plating process. Certain—but not all—flame retardants can cause adhesion problems during plating.
Mold release (internal and external) used	Certain mold releases can be detrimental to plating adhesion
Fillers used	Even when you use a 'plating' grade, certain fillers and reinforcements can degrade adhesion during plating.
Actual molding conditions	Platers need to know the injection pressures and temperatures used to produce a given part; this gives the plater an indication of molded-in stress.
Stresses	One major problem plating houses confront is internal stresses and surface stresses caused by either molding conditions or part geometry. Platers need to analyze each part in order to generate the best possible plating solutions.
Resin used	Platers require key information such as the resin used in a given application. Handling blends and alloys can be particularly difficult.

metal making and shaping Metals must be extracted from ores, purified, and then shaped into desired products. Refining is primarily a chemical process. Forming is principally a mechanical process using "plastic" deformation or plasticity capabilities of metals. This deformation strain-hardens a metal and makes it less ductile; however, the metal may be softened by annealing. Thus, it is possible to control properties by cold work/annealing operations. Annealing following cold work produces a new generation of grains within the metal. At high temperature, recrystallization occurs almost simultaneously so that there is no strain hardening.

metal matrix composite ▷ **composite metal matrix**

metal shape welding ▷ **shape welding**

metal, single component Metals are materials that have predominantly one kind of atom. These are the commercially pure metals such as aluminum, copper, and iron. Since each of these metals contains only minor amounts of other components, their properties arise from the principal component only.

metal spraying on plastic There are several ways to provide a metal film on a plastic part through the use of atomized metal at atmospheric pressure. The temperature of the part being coated is controlled by the application rate. This process is widely used for RFI or EMI shielding. Environmental pollution is minimal and only vaporized zinc particles need to be removed from the air.

Spray heads using a flame or an electrical arc to melt metal wires or powders directly are much more convenient and are now the only types used on a large scale. The principal metal used is zinc; aluminum and copper are also used. The equipment is relatively simple: a spray head for feeding the metal wire, electrical contacts for maintaining an arc or gas orifices for the flame, compressed air, and fixtures for holding the parts to be coated. A major advantage of zinc is that it can be applied to almost any plastic. It is also suitable for prototypes and small lots of materials. It is less suitable for very small parts and parts with blind holes or complex interior surfaces, or where warpage is a problem. Zn flame spray is normally applied to a thickness of 0.05 to 0.10 mm. Zn arc spray is an inexpenisve process in terms of equipment and raw materials; however, manpower is expensive. ▷ **thermal spraying**

metal vapor synthesis MVS is the use of atoms of the transition metals, lanthanoids, and actinoids as reagents in the preparation of organic, organometallic, coordination, and metal-cluster compounds and catalyst materials. The technique also employs coordinatively unsaturated molecular high temperature gas-phase species, such as metal oxides, halides, and nitrides as reagents. Vapor formed at high temperature is combined under vacuum with a coreactant at a cold surface where products may be formed and isolated. Reduced steric restrictions and the high potential energy for reaction in the free state of the atom often lead to the very low activation-energy requirements for these atom-molecule reactions. With carbon-vapor reactor the use of high temperature species for synthesis is initiated.

Extensive MVS literature recognizes the kinetic and thermodynamic advantages of this technique in providing more direct or higher yield routs to existing compounds and making available new compounds and materials. The methodology is used primarily on a research scale to explore synthesis of organometallic monomers, monomer polymerization induced by high temperature vapors, preparation of organometallic polymers by direct reaction of a polymer with metal atoms, concatenation of organic molecules by metal atoms to give organometallic oligomers, use of polymers as host matrices for metal-atom aggregation or mediation of metal-atom-substrate reactions, and preparation and screening of polymerization catalysts.

metamerism ▷ **light metamerism**

metathesis When two compounds such as aluminum chloride and sodium hydroxide react by the simple interchange of radicals, forming aluminum hydroxide and sodium chloride, this is called double decomposition or metathesis.

meter 1. The basic unit of length of the metric system (39.37 in.) Originally defined as one ten millionth of the distance from the equator to the North Pole. Also defined as 1,650, 763.73 wavelengths of the orange-red line of the isotope krypton 86. The official worldwide SI system identifies the meter as the length of the path traveled by light in a vacuum during a time interval of 1/299 792 458 of a second (adopted by the 17th CGPM 1983). ▷ **SI** **2.** The worldwide international system of units (SI) use the spelling of metre (and litre). The U.S. Department of Defense approved this SI standard with the following exception that DOD has the option to use meter and liter when appropriate in international relations. ▷ **decimal system** and **SI** **3.** A device for measuring the flow rate of liquids, gases, or particulate solids such as flowmeters, proportioning equipment, etc.

metering pump ▷ **gear pump**

metering screw ▷ **screw**

methane A highly volatile, odorless, colorless, and asphyxiating gas produced during ecomposition of solid organic wastes by anaerobic micro-organisms.

methanolysis Complete breakdown in the presence of methanol of reaction or condensation type plastics into polymer, which may be repolymerized.

methylacrylate butadiene styrene plastic ▷ **acrylonitrile-butadiene-styrene plastic**

methylcellulose plastic MC is water-soluble and harmless for external body contact or ingestion (edible). It is used in creams or foods as a thickening agent.

methylene diphenyl diisocyanate ▷ **polyurethane plastic**

methylmethacrylate-butadiene-styrene plastic MBSs are transparent with a structure similar to that of ABS plastics. Some sources appear to give methylacrylate rather than methylmethacrylate as the acrylic component.

methylmethacrylate plastic ▷ **acrylic plastic**

metre ▷ **meter**

metric system ▷ **decimal system; meter; SI**

M-glass A glass fiber type with a high beryllia (BeO_2) content glass designed for high modulus. ▷ **glass fiber types**

MH transparent plastic A new as-yet unnamed transparent plastic from Japan Synthetic Rubber Co. (Tokyo) to compete with polycarbonate and acrylic. It has a heat deflection temperature of 164°C (327°F) and exhibits birefringence of less than 20 nm.

mica Plate-like naturally occurring silicate mineral of varying composition, or synthesized from potassium fluorosilicate and alumina. It is used as a filler with good electric properties and heat resistance, reinforcement in plastic, etc.

micelle A colloidal particle formed by the reversible aggregation of dissolved molecules. Electrically charged micelles form colloidal electrolytes such as soaps and detergents used in emulsion polymerization. The initial stages of polymerization are believed to commence within the soap micelles. ▷ **emulsion polymerization**

micro In relation to reinforced plastics, the properties of the constituents, and interface, and their effects on the properties of the RPs.

microballoons ▷ **microsphere**

microbial ▷ **antimicrobial agent**

microcomputer The generally accepted definition is a computer that can process 8- or 16-bit words. It usually consists of a microprocessor with a control processor unit (CPU) together with memory, input-output circuits, power supply, etc. ▷ **minicomputer** and **computer**

microcracking **1.** Cracks are minute surface flaws on plastics. **2.** Cracks formed in reinforced plastics when local thermal stresses exceed the strength of the matrix. Because most do not penetrate the reinforcing fibers, microcracks in a cross-plied tape or in a laminate made from cloth prepreg are usually limited to the thickness of a single ply. ▷ **stress cracking and crazing**

microcrystalline Minutely crystalline; composed of crystals of microscopic size.

microdynamometer An instrument for measuring mechanical force and observing the change in microscopic appearance of a small specimen.

microencapsulation, coating It is where particulate matter is individually coated for protection against environmental influences. In the broadest sense, it provides a means of packaging, separating, and storing materials on a microscopic scale for later release under controlled conditions. Minute particles or droplets of almost any material can be encased by an impervious capsule wall and thus isolated from reactive, corrosive, or otherwise hostile surroundings. The contents of a capsule can be made available by mechanical rupture of the capsule wall, its disintegration by electrical or chemical means, or by leaching action carried out in an appropriate liquid environment. Since in most applications the particles are very small, the term microencapsulation is appropriate. The term encapsulation refers to the process in which a larger part or assembly is coated, usually by dipping in a highly viscous or thixotropic medium. Both terms have been used loosely. However, microencapsulation involves capsules that start in size of a few microns in diameter to 4,000 μ and even larger. There is no definite industry rule on when it is not micro but the general size is at 200 μ. ▷ **encapsulation** and **embedding**

microfilm copying ▷ **photopolymer**

microgel Small particles, of about 100 nm, of crosslinked and insoluble plastic, which may be considered to consist of single molecules. Microgel of molecular dimensions can dissolve in solvents to give true solutions, even though with reduced solubility due to the presence of the crosslinks, which also reduce the solution viscosity. They can embrittle plastics and reduce tensile strength but may be beneficial such as in having a smoothing action in extrusion of elastomers.

microinch ▷ **mike**

micromechanic The analysis of the mechanical behavior of reinforced plastics by considering the properties, concentration, geometry, and packing of the individual components. This contrasts with macromechanics by recognizing the inhomogeneous nature of the RP. By making various approximations of the packing geometry and stress fields within an element of the matrix, the average properties of the element may be calculated. These average properties may then be used in a subsequent macromechanics treatment of an assembly of such elements. The various methods that have been used differ with respect to the severity of the different assumptions made. They include the mechanics of materials, the self-consistent field, and the variation methods. Numerical methods may also be applied to particular systems, especially when some symmetry exists in the phase geometry. ▷ **reinforced plastic** and **macromechanic**

micrometer ▷ **micron**

micromorphology The shape of structural units whose dimensions are such that they can be observed by electron microscopy but not by optical microscopy.

micron 1 micron = 0.001 mm = 0.00003937 in. The term micron is being replaced by micrometer.

micro penetration hardness ▷ **Knoop hardness**

microphase structure Plastic systems containing two or more components are known as multicomponent plastic materials, alloys, or blends. The following generic terms are examples that include two or more plastics: graft polymers, block copolymers, interpenetrating polymer networks, and AB-cross-linked polymers, as well as various polymer blends. They are an important class of engineering materials applied as impact resistant plastics, knife handles, shoe soles, resilient rugs, etc. They exhibit rather outstanding properties because controlled phase separation frequently leads to synergistic behavior.

The terms compatible and incompatible have been used to indicate a single phase or multiphase mixture of two or more plastics, respectively. However, these terms are also used by polymer technologists and plastic engineers to indicate satisfactory and unsatisfactory behavior on blending, such as good adhesion between the constitutents, improved mechanical behavior, or simply ease of mixing. The terms miscibility and immiscibility are sometimes used to strengthen the thermodynamic implications. ▷ **compatibility** and **miscibility**

microporosity ▷ **polyester reinforced urethane**

microporous Having pores of microscopic dimensions. Some plastic films and fabric coatings are rendered microporous in order to permit breathing, while retaining waterproofness.

microprocessor The basic element of a central processing unit developed on a single integrated chip provides the basic core of a central processing unit, even though it may require additional components to operate as a central processing unit. The center processing unit or "brain" is that part of a personal computer. Sometimes incorrectly used as a synonym for microcomputer. ▷ **computer**

microprocessor basic types **1.** Local control panel is a digital control system programmed to handle all the machine and process control loops of processing machine (extruder, injection, blow, etc.) line to maximize the efficiency of complete operation. **2.** Central control panel is a master control system which coordinates the operation of multiple production lines each of which may have its own control panel. Enables implementation of overall statistical quality control.

microprocessor control It means different things to different people; it can mean anything from a sophisticated temperature controller to a full blown line control. Advantages offered include self-diagnostic capabilities, alarm functions, data printouts, and exports to other plant computers. It can provide preprogrammed setup information by magnetic input card or cassette for virtually fail-safe start up by an operator on any shift.

As a result of the vast range of computer control and monitoring options available there is strong temptation to get "control happy". The key to specifying the right kinds and numbers of microprocessors is their contribution to overall quality of the product and reduction of downtime. The goal is to improve process control and reduce operator involvement and "human error". With need for equipment to provide true process control, selecting the required main and auxiliary equipment is vital to realizing the quickest possible return on investment (ROI). It also helps ensure the best possible product at the end of the line. ▷ **computer microprocessor control**

microorganism ▷ **biodegradable**

microrheology The study of flow in relation to the microstructure of the material undergoing flow. An example is in the study of the effect of dispersed particle shape in a plastic blend or filled plastic on the flow properties.

microsphere Also called microballoons, they are thin walled hollow spheres with diameters in the micron range (20 to 150 μ) and usually made of plastic and glass. Wall thickness is 2 to 3 μ. In appearance, bulk microspheres are a free flowing powder resembling fine sand. Bulk density ranges from 6 to 12 lb/ft^2 (29.5 to 59 kg/m^2). Use includes: (1) a filler in the manufacture of low density filled plastics such as syntactic foams, (2) tiny vinyl spheres used to reduce evaporation of liquids such as oils, by floating a layer of spheres on the surface of storage tanks, and (3) in adhesives, usually 100 μ diameter spheres are occasionally used to control bond line thickness; when the adherends are pressed together the spheres will ensure a bond line thickness of 100 μ (1% spheres is the amount normally used). ▷ **microencapsulation, coating; antibodies and antigens plastic encapsulated; syntactic foam**

microstrain The strain over a gauge length comparable to interatomic distances.

microstructure The possible atomic arrangements within the molecular chains are determined by the polymer production procedures and cannot be modified by further processing. Excess heat or pressure during product processing may produce some degradation and scission of molecules; this is normally negligible. For polymers, from a chemical point of view, microstructure encompasses the molecular structure ural features of single polymer chains, often specifically referring to configurational isomerism (and particularly to tacticity). More broadly, the term also refers to a wider range of structural features, including geometric and positional isomerism, chain branching, and structural irregularities. Copolymer microstructure refers to both composition and, more particularly, to monomer sequence length distribution.

From a materials science viewpoint, it refers to the grosser structural features of the arrangements of polymer chains in aggregates, as may be observed by optical and electron microscopic techniques. This includes the morphological aspects of the crystalline structure of aggregates of crystals (such as spherulites) and of polymer blends and amorphous polymers such as nodules, partially ordered regions and domains. ▷ **molecular arrangement structure**

microtoming, optical analysis In this procedure thin slices of the material are cut from the part and microscopically examined under polarized light transmitted through the sample. Study of the microstructure by this technique enables rapid examination of quality-affecting properties. This kind of approach can provide the molder with information for failure analysis, part and mold design, and processing optimization. Thin sectioning and microscopy are old techniques, having been applied to biological samples for many years. Furthermore, metallurgists have used similar techniques in the microstructural analysis of metals to determine their physical and mechanical properties and to aid in failure analysis.

Microtoming enables slices of plastic to be cut from opaque parts. These slices are so thin (under 30 μm) that light may be transmitted through them. The sample can then be analyzed under a microscope. Another useful technique is to use the microtome to slice down through a specimen until the specific level to be examined is reached. This method reveals a series of sequential levels, each smooth enough for viewing without need for polishing. The usual method is to cut, mount, and polish. Examination can provide different types of evaluation, such as stress patterns that develop in molded corner sections. ▷ **polarized light** and **photoelastic stress analysis**

microwave They are electromagnetic radiations of extremely high frequencies, with a range of about 0.5 to 1,000 GHz (with the higher frequencies widely used in radar).

microwave market The household invasion of microwaves marches on. With it comes the burgeoning use of plastics for microwave cookware and accessories, etc. With this growth, development of new plastics such as polyetheretherketone (PEEK) occur. Plastics in microwave devices are extensive particularly in housings for instrumentation (medical, machine control, aircraft and shipboard control, antennna dish, etc.).

microwave spectroscopy A type of absorption spectroscopy used in instrumental chemical analysis which involves use of that portion of the electromagnetic spectrum having wavelengths in the range of far infrared and the radio frequencies; between 1 mm to 30 cm.

microwave testing ▷ **nondestructive testing**

migration The extraction or bleeding of an ingredient from a material by another material.

migration and additive The surface characteristics of a plastic may be changed by the addition of incompatible additives that migrate to the surface. Additives such as fluorocarbon plastics, low molecular weight fluoroacrylate plastics, polyamides, waxes, silica, and others are used for this purpose. Surface characteristics may also be changed by applying a primer to the surface. Many plastics are useful as primers; an example is polyethylene imide plastic, which is widely used primer for polyolefins.

migration and plasticizer **1.** The exudation of plasticizer from the interior of a thermoplastic product to its surface, where it appears as a greasy or oily film. **2.** Loss of plasticizer from a TP product with subsequent adsorption by an adjacent medium of lower plasticizer concentration.

mike A term adopted by the American Standards Assoc. for a microinch or 10^{-6} inch.

mil One thousandth of an inch; 0.001 in. = 25.4 μm.

milk carton coating ▷ **wax**

mill The term is generally taken to refer to all mechanical devices for transforming raw materials into a condition for use. The equipment (mill) takes two or more individual substances and provides a relatively uniform mixed compound. Examples include a plastic and colorant, plastic with chopped glass fibers and additives (bulk molding compound), etc. The equipment includes: roll mills, attrition mills, ball mills, cage mills, hammer mills, jar mills, tube mills, tumbling agitator, etc. ▷ **mixer**

milled fiber ▷ **fiber, milled**

milling, chemical ▷ **chemical milling**

millitex ▷ **tex**

mineral A widely used general term referring to the nonliving constituents of the earth's crust. It includes natural occurring elements, compounds, and mixtures that have a definite range of chemical compositions and properties that are used in manufacturing plastics to preparing many (thousands) different plastic compounds. ▷ **petroleum**

mineral black Black pigments made by grinding and/or heating slate, shale, or coal.

miniaturization A method for constructing technical components in the smallest possible form; the term is derived from the early use of very reduced scale pictures in the ornamentation of the initial letters of illuminated manuscripts. Plastics provide many different ways to miniaturize and meet different performance requirements.

minicomputer Usually a small computer that can process 16- and 32-bit words. It is an imprecise term that suggests "more powerful than a microcomputer and less than a mainframe".

Minlon Du Pont's tradename for its family of glass fiber reinforced nylon.

miscibility In the search for new plastics, the compounding or mixing together of two or more plastics attracts much interest as a means of arriving at new property combinations without having to synthesize novel structures. A major feature encountered when two plastics are mixed is that in the majority of combinations the components tend to phase-separate to form heterogeneous mixtures that do not exhibit enhanced properties. Only in a limited number of cases do amorphous plastics blend to form one-phase mixtures. The term miscible is used to describe a mixture of two or more plastics that form a single-phase (solid or liquid) solution. ▷ **microphase structure** and **alloy/blend**

mixer Mixers are used to mix materials; mixing is the process of distributing particles of two or more materials (including drops of liquid) so that the lumps, pools, or aggregates of each material are not formed with little or no particle cohesion. Different mixers are available to meet different material requirements such as processing medium to high viscosity formulations, wet-out and disperse solids into a liquid vehicle, solids dispersion, etc. The first Fig. on p. 447 provides examples of mixers that include use on the hopper of machines. The type of mixing equipment required as a function of viscosity and vessel size is summarized in the second Fig. on p. 447. Types of mixers used include the following: ball mill, Banbury, batch, change-can, centrifugal impact, colloid mill, conical dry blender, disc and cone agitator, drum tumbler, extruder compounder, hopper blender, impingement, intensive, kneader, motionless, paddle agitator, propeller, ribbon blender, roll mill, roto mill, screw, sigma blade, static, tumbling agitator, etc. ▷ **mill**

mixing screw ▷ **screw mixing and melting**

mixture A combination of two or more substances intermingled in which each component retains its essential original properties. ▷ **admixture** and **mixer**

mock leno weave An open weave that resembles a leno and is accomplished by a system

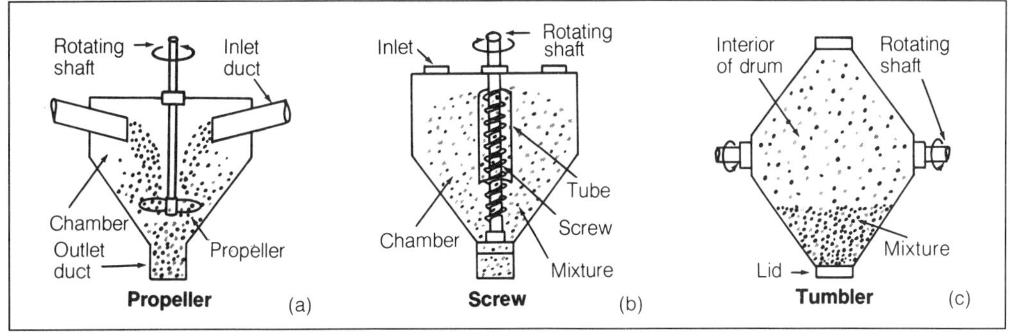

Examples of mixers which receive measured amounts of materials by weight or volume: (*a*) propeller (impeller) is used in many mixer designs, some suitable for continuous operation; (*b*) screw (auger) also has many versions. Type shown is carried to the top of a tube and allowed to fall in clouds to the bottom for recirculation until the desired mix/dispersion has been achieved. In other designs the screws are shaped to mix as well as lift the materials so that the tube is omitted; (*c*) tumblers are batch mixers which receive measured quantities of materials. Type shown is a double-cone mixer/blender.

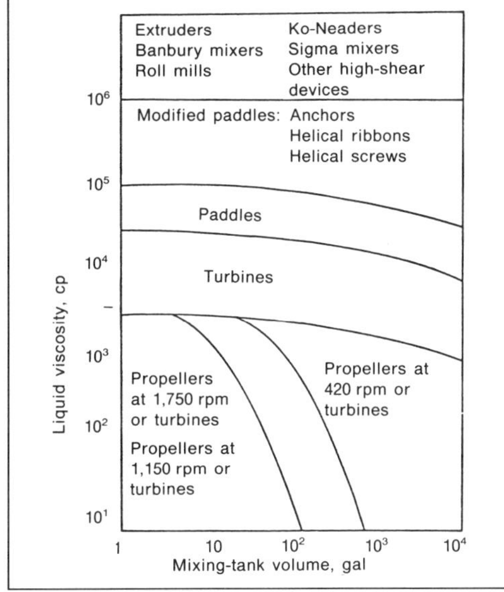

Guide to mixing basics.

of interfacings that draws a group of threads together and leaves a space between that group and the next. The warp threads do not actually cross each other as in a real leno and, therefore, no special attachments are required for the loom. This type of weave is generally used when high thread count is required for strength and the fabric must remain porous and in position during plastic impregnation. ▷ **leno weave**

modacrylic fiber ▷ **fiber modacrylic**

model 1. Overall a representation or prototype, either physical or abstract, of a plastic structure, arrangement, or product which basically cannot be perceived objectively, required to ensure proper fitting of all its parts or subdivisions, required for market/sales promotion, and/or to be used for test and evaluation. ▷ **computer-aided design 2.** A mathematical model is one in which all or most of the parameters of a complex system are assigned symbolic values that can be utilized to given a theoretical approximation of actuality. ▷ **designing with model mathematically; computer arithmetic-logic unit; computer high level language**

modeling ▷ **computer modeling**

modeling cost ▷ **computer cost modeling technically**

modeling crack growth ▷ **fracture, plane stress**

modeling molecules ▷ **computer-aided molecular graphic**

modeling nonlinear viscoelasticity ▷ **Boltzmann superposition principle**

modeling parametric Engineers were previously limited to systems that define parts in terms of exact solid geometry but also have an alternative parametric system. This approach defines other information about an object, including relationships between intent and predictability, and manufacturing constraints. Solid geometry and other outputs are then derived from this information. An engineer can make interactive changes to any design parameters at any time in the evolution of the design model, and allow the parametric system to generate the solid geometry and other outputs, such as detailed drawings.

To the design engineer, parametric systems provide a flexible solid system model that can be used in the early stages of product conceptualization, then modified and evolved into a complete design. To the design manager, it provides the first data base that can correlate information from the design, documentation, analysis, and manufacturing functions to converge on a producible product in the context of a single model.

modeling plastic-chemical structure ▷ **designing with model, plastic-chemical structure**

modeling processes ▷ **designing with model, processes**

modeling, solid A computer model of a part constructed by blending together primitive shapes, including cubes, spheres, cylinders, and wedges. It shows the complete surfacing of the product being designed. ▷ **computer modeling**

modeling stereolithography A process of creating 3-D plastic parts from CAD/CAM/CAE data combining four technologies: laser, optical scanning, chemistry, and software. The net effect is that complex models can be made in hours without tooling. It takes CAD data and automatically produces a hard plastic model in a matter of hours instead of days, weeks, or longer. They are 3-D and include any design features that can be created, defined, and stored by most CAD systems in use. The basic concept starts with a design; the part design created on the CAD system is downloaded to the sterolithography apparatus with its control unit. The control unit then directs a fine laser beam onto the surface of liquid photo curable plastic. An elevator table in the plastic vat rests just below the surface. When the 0.015 in. (0.4 mm) diameter laser hits the liquid plastic suface, it solidifies a layer 0.005 to 0.030 in. (0.1 to 0.8 mm) thick at the point of laser beam impingement.

After a part slice at one depth has been made by scanning the laser beam back and forth in the shape of the model to be developed, the elevator platform upon which the model is being constructed drops the programmed amount. Another layer or "slice" is then created on top of the first in the same manner. The process continues until the complete model has been constructed. Thus, the pattern is built from the bottom up. After laser processing, the model is then raised above the liquid level by the elevator table. The part is stripped from the table and taken to a special "oven" for final curing. The main advantage of this process is the speed at which a computer generated design may be turned into a 3-D model that may be held, viewed, studied, and compared before committing to steps leading to production.

modeling stress loading ▷ **design technology; designing with model analytically; photoelasticity; brittle lacquer technique; microtoming, optical analysis**

modeling surface A computer-aided model of a part that is constructed by utilizing groups of connected surfaces of many types, including swept, mesh, and revolution.

modeling wire frame A computer-aided model that is represented only by its edges.

modem ▷ **computer modem**

modified Containing ingredients such as fillers, pigments, or other additives that help to vary the physical properties of a plastic material. An example is an oil-modified plastic.

modified atmosphere packaging ▷ **packaging via MAP**

modified plastic Synthetic plastics modified by the incorporation of natural plastics, elastomers, or oils, which alter the processing characteristics or physical properties of the basic plastics.

modular structure ▷ **bamboo's modular structure**

module A unit of structure based on a standard pattern of standard dimensions.

modulus Modulus, popular abbreviation used for the modulus of elasticity that also refers to Young's modulus, is the ratio of stress to corresponding strain (stress-strain) below the proportional limit in loadings such as tension, compression, etc. Its symbol is *E*, and expressed in psi (Pa). ▷ **tensile analysis** for diagrams relating to *E* and its other related terms. Stress-strain relationship is proportional (follows a straight line when plotted) for *E* which means it follows Hooke's law ▷ **Hooke's law**. Note that the stress-strain relations of many materials (plastics, steel, wood, etc.) do not conform to Hooke's law throughout the elastic range, but deviate from it even at stresses well below the elastic limit. For such materials the slope of either the tangent to the stress-strain curve at the origin or at a low stress, the secant drawn from the origin to any specified point on the stress-strain curve, or the chord connecting any two specified points on the stress-strain curve is usually taken to be the modulus. In these cases *E* should be designated as tangent modulus, secant modulus, chord modulus, and the point or points on the stress-strain curve, respectively. See Figs in ▷ **stress-strain curve**

modulus, apparent The concept of apparent modulus is a convenient method for expressing creep because it takes into account initial strain for an applied stress plus the amount of deformation or strain that occurs with time.

modulus, bulk The ratio of stress to change in volume (strains) of a material. It is calculated as

$$K = Er/3(1 - 2r),$$

where K = bulk modulus in psi (Pa), E = modulus in psi (Pa), and r = Poisson's ratio.

modulus chord The slope of the chord drawn between any two specified points on the stress-strain curve.

modulus, complex The ratio of stress to strain in which each is a vector that may be represented by a complex number. May be measured in tension or flexure (E^*), compression (K^*), or shear (G^*). Also refers to dynamic modulus and is analogous to complex dielectric constant.

modulus, creep ▷ **creep modulus**

modulus, fiber ▷ **textile modulus**

modulus, initial The slope of the initial straight portion of a stress-strain (or load-elongation) curve. Some materials have a rather brief initial straight line, followed with another straight line which is usually a much longer line and usually is the E used in engineering designs.

modulus, loss A damping term that describes the dissipation of energy into heat when a material is deformed. It is a quantitative measure of energy, defined as the ratio of stress 90° out of phase with oscillating strain to the magnitude of strain. The loss E may be measured in tension of flexural (E''), compression (K''), or shear (G'').

modulus, mean ▷ **mean modulus**

modulus of elasticity ▷ **modulus**

modulus, offset The ratio of the offset yield stress to the extension at the offset point. ▷ **stress, offset yield strength**

modulus, relative The ratio of modulus of rigidity of rubber at a specified low temperature to that at room temperature, as determined in the Gehman torsional test. The temperature at which relative modulus has a specified value may be determined by calculating twist angle corresponding to the specified relative modulus and reading the corresponding temperature from the twist-temperature curve. Twist angle corresponding to a specified relative modulus may be determined from tables listing corresponding values of θ_1 and θ_2 that satisfy the following relationship:

$$\text{R.M.} = \frac{\theta_1(180 - \theta_2)}{\theta_2(180 - \theta_1)}$$

where R.M. = specified Relative Modulus; θ_1 = twist angle at room temperature, deg.; θ_2 = twist angle at unknown temperature, deg.

modulus, resilience The energy that can be absorbed per unit volume without creating a permanent distortion. Calculated by integrating the stress-strain curve from zero to the elastic limit and dividing by the original volume of the specimen.

modulus, rigidity The modulus of rigidity is the ratio of stress to strain within the elastic region for shear or torsional stress. It is also called shear modulus, modulus in shear, torsional modulus, and modulus in torsion. Basically, it is a measure of stiffness of a material subjected to shear loading. Usually the tangent or secant modulus of elasticity of a material in the torsion test. The relationship between torsion stress and torsion strain. The tangent modulus may also be obtained from the torque-twist diagram by dividing slope of the straight-line portion by the polar moment of inertia (in.^{4}) of the specimen. For cast iron, where the specimen has been standardized, modulus of rigidity is calculated by multiplying slope of the torque-twist diagram by 32.2. In the Gehman torsional test, modulus of rigidity is calculated as follows:

$$G = \frac{0.795\,K\,(180 - \theta)}{bh^3\mu\theta}$$

where G = modulus of rigidity, psi; θ = total angular reflection, deg; K = torsional constant of wire, g-cm/deg twist; b = specimen width, in.; h = specimen thickness, in. μ = factor based on b/h. Modulus of rigidity may also be calculated from modulus of elasticity in tension, compression or flexure:

$$G = \frac{H}{2\,(l + r)}$$

where E = modulus of elasticity, psi; r = Poisson's ratio.

An apparent modulus of rigidity is sometimes determined for plastics.

modulus, rupture Modulus of rupture (MOR) is the strength of a material as determined by flexural or torsion test. MOR in flexure is an alternate term for torsional strength.

modulus, rupture in bending The modulus of rupture in bending is the maximum tensile or compressive stress value (whichever causes failure) in the extreme plane of fiber of a beam loaded to failure in bending.

modulus, rupture in torsion The maximum shear stress in the extreme plane or fiber of a member of circular cross section loaded to failure in torsion.

modulus, secant Idealized modulus derived from a secant drawn between the origin and any

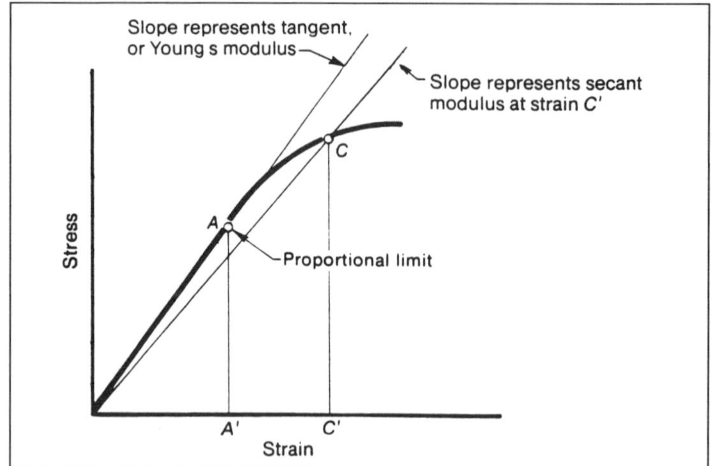

Diagram describing the secant modulus and the tangent modulus.

point on a nonlinear stress-strain curve. It is mainly used on materials for which there is no straight line in the stress-strain curve, such as in the typical elastomer materials. The secant modulus is the line drawn from zero stress point to the curve for a specific designated strain (see Fig. above).

The tangent (also called elastic or Young's) modulus is typically defined as the slope of the stress/strain curve at the origin. When the curve is nonlinear, the use of the tangent modulus predicts the material to be less flexible than it will be in the acutal application. This results in the prediction of low allowable deflections and high actuation forces for a given stress level. The secant modulus represents the actual stiffness of the material at a given stress/strain condition and leads to a more accurate force and deflection calculation. The secant is defined as a given stress divided by its corresponding strain and will vary depending on the value of strain (or stress) chosen, that is, position on the curve.

The secant modulus can be used in different evaluations. As an example, in the beam theory equations it can provide the more accurate results. It can only be determined when stress/strain data is available for the design conditions of the beam. When such data is not available, or straining the material beyond the linear region is not recommended, the published value of elastic modulus or flexural modulus should be used.

modulus, shear ▷ **modulus, rigidity**

modulus, static The ratio of stress to strain under static conditions. It is calculated from static stress-strain tests, in shear, compression, or tension which is the conventional modulus.

modulus, storage A quantitative measure of elastic properties, defined as the ratio of the stress, in-phase with strain, to the magnitude of the strain. The storage modulus may be measured in tension or flexural (E'), compression (K'), or shear (G').

modulus, stress relaxation The ratio of the time-dependent stress to a fixed strain during stress relaxation of a viscoelastic material. Unlike (conventional) modulus, the corresponding compliance is not the inverse of the modulus due to the different time dependencies involved. One of the most frequently determined viscoelastic parameters (especially for rubbers for which measurements are comparatively simple) since it yields useful results for the study of network breakdown. the stress relaxation modulus is an exponentially decreasing function of time. ▷ **stress relaxation**

modulus, tan delta The tan delta ($\tan \delta$) modulus is the ratio of the loss modulus, measured in compression (K), tension or flexural (E), or shear (G). Also, the ratio of the out-of-phase components of the dielectric constant (that is, the loss) to the in-phase component of the dielectric constant (that is, the permittivity).

modulus, tangent The slope of the line at a predefined point on a static stress-strain curve, expressed in force per unit area per unit strain. This is the tangent modulus at that point in shear, tension, or compression. See Fig. in ▷ **modulus, secant**

modulus, tension The ratio of the tension stress to the strain in the material over the range for which this value is constant. ▷ **tension**

modulus, textile ▷ **textile modulus**

modulus, theoretical ▷ **data, theoretical versus actual properties**

modulus, torsion ▷ **modulus, rigidity** and **torsional pendulum**

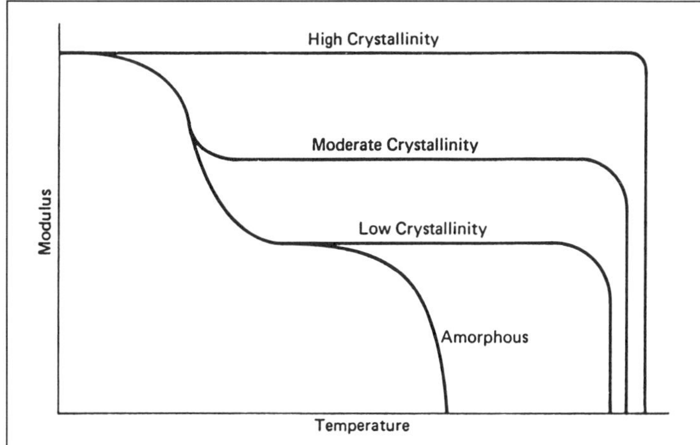

Effect of crystallinity upon modulus versus temperature.

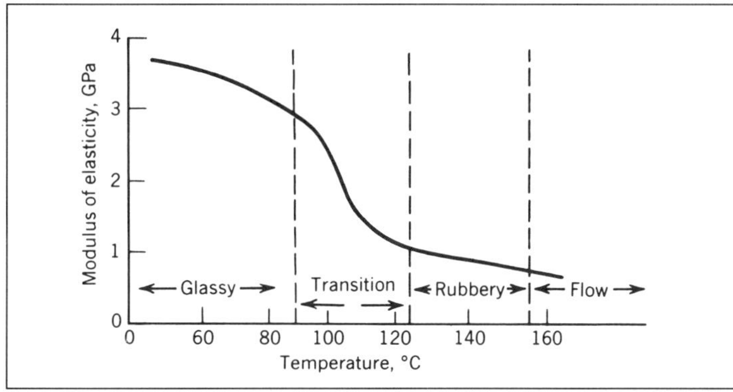

Example of a thermoplastic modulus during different temperature phases.

modulus, toughness Modulus of toughness is the ability of a material to absorb energy and plastically deform before it fractures. Thus, toughness can be calculated by evaluating the size of area under the stress-strain curve; the large the area usually the tougher the material. Toughness is identified in a material to withstand impact or shock load.

modulus, unloading Slope of the tangent to the unloading stress-strain curve at a given stress value.

modulus versus specific gravity See Fig.

modulus versus temperature As shown by the Figs. above, thermoplastics are influenced by their crystallinity. ▷ **molecular arrangement structure**

modulus, vibration ▷ **resonant forced vibration technique**

modulus, Young's ▷ **modulus**

mohair ▷ **fiber mohair**

Mohr circle A graphical representation of the stresses acting on the various planes at a given point.

Mohr circle of stress (strain) A graphical

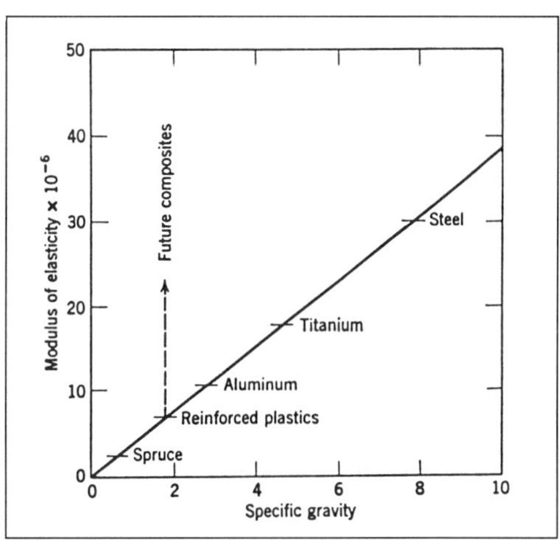

Relationship of modulus versus specific gravity.

representation of the components of stress (and strain) acting across the various planes at a given point, drawn with reference to axes of normal stress (strain) and shear stress (strain).

Mohr envelope The envelope of a sequence of Mohr circles representing conditions at failure for a given material.

Mohs hardness An empirical measure of the scratch resistance of a material. The higher the number, the greater the scratch resistance (number 10 being termed diamond).

Mohs hardness value The following scale was established in 1822 by Frederick Mohs, giving a relative ranking of minerals in the order in which one will scratch another (Mohs scale number-standard material): (1) talc, (2) gypsum, (3) calcite, (4) fluorite, (5) apatite, (6) orthoclase, (7) quartz, (8) topaz, (9) corundum, and (10) diamond.

moire pattern An effect caused by the superimposition of a repetitive design(s) to produce a pattern distinct from that of its components, as in the creation of screening patterns during color separation procedures.

moisture Essentially water, quantitatively determined by definite prescribed methods which may vary according to the nature of the material.

moisture absorption The pickup of water vapor from air by a material, in reference in vapor withdrawn from the air only; as distinguished from water absorption, which is the gain in weight due to the absorption of water by immersion.

moisture adsorption The pickup of moisture from the air by a material on its surface only.

moisture barrier ▷**barrier, moisture**

moisture content 1. The amount of moisture in a material under prescribed conditions and expressed as a percent of the mass of the moist specimen, that is, the mass of the dry substance plus the moisture. **2.** The water in solid waste. Expressed as the percentage of weight lost when a sample is dried at more than 100°C (212°F) until it reaches a constant weight.

moisture content equilibrium Equilibrium moisture content is a steady-state condition obtained by the gain or loss of moisture when a material is exposed to an environment of specific temperature and humidity. This equilibrium condition, independent of drying method or rate, is a material property. Only hygroscopic materials have equilibrium moisture contents.

moisture, frost action Freezing and thawing of moisture in materials and the resultant effects on these materials and on products of which they are a part or with which they are in contact.

moisture, humectant agent Additives which have a pronounced effect on the ability of moisture to adhere to a substance. They are sometimes used in anti-static coatings for plastics.

moisture pick-up The mass of absorbed and adsorbed water that is held by material, compared to the mass of the dried material.

moisture regain The moisture in a material determined under prescribed conditions and expressed as a percent of the weight of the moisture-free specimen. Moisture regain may result from either sorption or desorption, and differs from moisture content only in the basis used for calculation.

moisture vapor transmission MVT is a rate at which water vapour passes through a material at a specified temperature and relative humidity (g/mil/24 h/100 in.^{2}).

molar solution A liquid containing a mole of substance per liter of solution (not per liter of water).

mold A mold is one of the most important pieces of production equipment in the plant. it is a controllable complex device that must be an efficient heat exchanger. If not properly handled and maintained, it will not be an efficient operating device. ▷**design mold** regarding information on molds and Figures that describe different type molds. The Fig. on p. 453 provides additional information.

mold, automatic ▷**mold classification by operation**

mold backing plate 1. In injection molding equipment, a heavy steel plate that is used as a support for the cavity blocks, guide pins, bushings, etc. **2.** In blow molding equipment, it is the steel plate on which the cavities are mounted.

mold base An assembly of precision steel plates that holds or retains the cavities in a mold. Provides a means for melt to be injected into the cavities and provides a means to eject the solidified parts from the mold. It is the assembly of all parts in the mold, other than the cavity, core, and pins. Also called mold frame, mold set, die base, die shoe, or shoe.

mold, blow molding ▷**blow molding mold**

mold bottom plate Part of the mold which contains the heel radius and the push-up (ejecton mechanism). It is used to join the lower section of the mold to the platen of the press.

mold, casting ▷**casting, shell mold type**

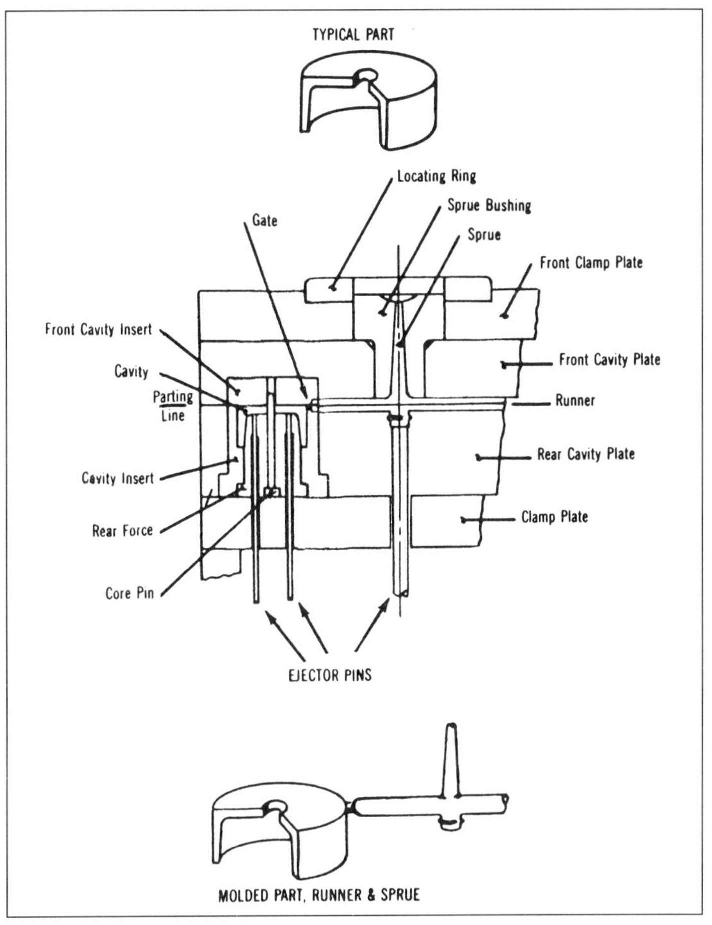

Mold terminology.

mold cavity Depression in mold; the space inside a mold wherein the plastic produces the product; the female portion of a mold; that portion of the mold that encloses the molded product; forms the outer surface of the product (also referred to as the die or tool); also the space between matched molds. Inserted cavities can be used or depression in the mold is made by casting, machining, hobbing, or a combination of these methods. Depending on number of cavities, molds are designated single cavity, double cavity, 32-cavity, multicavity, etc.

mold cavity, blowmold multicavity ▷ **blowmolding, extruder mold multiple/combination cavities**

mold cavity coating A coat of plastic over the bare mold. Used to seal the mold and make a smooth surface on which to mold parts. This is often referred to as a tooling gel coat.

mold cavity, double Double cavity mold is a mold possessing two cavities for simultaneous fabrication of two parts.

mold cavity, duplicate plate Removable plate that retains cavities, used where two-plate operation is necessary for loading inserts, etc.

mold cavity, electroforming A master, sometimes called a mandrel, is an exact reverse of the cavity. On it is plated about 38 mm (0.150 in.) of a nickel cobalt compound at the rate of 0.1 mm/8 h (0.004 in./8 h). On top of this, copper is electroplated, which is harder than mold steel. The rustproof finished cavity has good dimensional stability and high thermal conductivity. It is very precise within 0.0025 mm (0.0001 in.). Electroforming is primarily used when other methods are difficult and expensive such as gears, pen barrels, reflectors, etc.

mold cavity fabricating equipment Toolroom equipment is used for machining mold bases, cores, cavities, pins, blocks, and other parts. Fabrication can be assisted by electronically punched tape and CAM.

mold cavity, female In molding practice, the indented cavity half of a mold designed to receive the male half. The term "halve" is only used as one part of the conventional two part mold; it does not represent a measurement of half.

mold cavity hobbing ▷ **mold hobbing**

mold cavity impression Molds may be designated single-impression or 2-, 3-, 4-, etc. or multi-impression. The term cavity in place of impression has more general use, thus multicavity.

mold cavity, male ▷ **mold cavity, female** and **mold, positive**

mold cavity melt flow analysis The purpose of flow analysis is to gain a comprehensive understanding of the mold-filling process. The most sophisticated models provide detailed information concerning the influence of mold-filling conditions on the distribution of flow patterns and flow vectors, shear stresses, frozen skin, temperatures and pressures, and many other variables. Other, less sophisticated programs that model fewer variables are also available. From these data, conclusions regarding tolerances as well as part quality in terms of strength and appearance can be drawn. The location of weld lines and weld line integrity can be predicted. The likelihood of warping surface blemishes, or strength reductions due to high-shear stress, can be anticipated. On this basis the best mold filling conditions can be selected. ▷ **melt flow behaviour; computer-aided engineering; mold filling**

mold cavity melt flow, multi-live feed ▷ **injection molding, multi-live feed**

mold cavity melt flow, push-pull ▷ **injection molding, push-pull**

mold cavity melt fountain flow The Fig. below shows melt pattern entering the mold cavity from an injection molding machine; a fountain (or balloon) stretching effect results. The stretching melt front oriented outer surface covers the inside wall of the cavity. Melt that follows basically fills within the fountain flow. The result is a nonuniform orientation in the cross section of the molded part (part can still meet performance requirements). Type of plastic and processing conditions of melt and wall cavity (includes speed of melt) can have a significant influence on certain properties of the molded part, such as degree of gloss, warping, impact resistance, and strength. Basically, the degree of ballooning or bubble formation is controllable so that specific desired properties can be obtained.

mold cavity, multiple ▷ **mold cavity**

mold cavity packing Plastic is a compressible fluid. Therefore, it holds pressure and shrinks as it cools requiring decisions to be made about the amount of overpacking necessary to minimize problems that occur when the plastic cools and shrinks, such as developing undue frozen stresses or cause flash (even with thermoset plastics, controlling the amount of flash that will occur). There is a trade off between overpack and shrink arrived at with a certain amount of "guesswork" based on experience. However, computer software provides greater insight into compressibility of plastic materials, so one is able to make better decisions. ▷ **design mold; computer-aided engineering; mold filling**

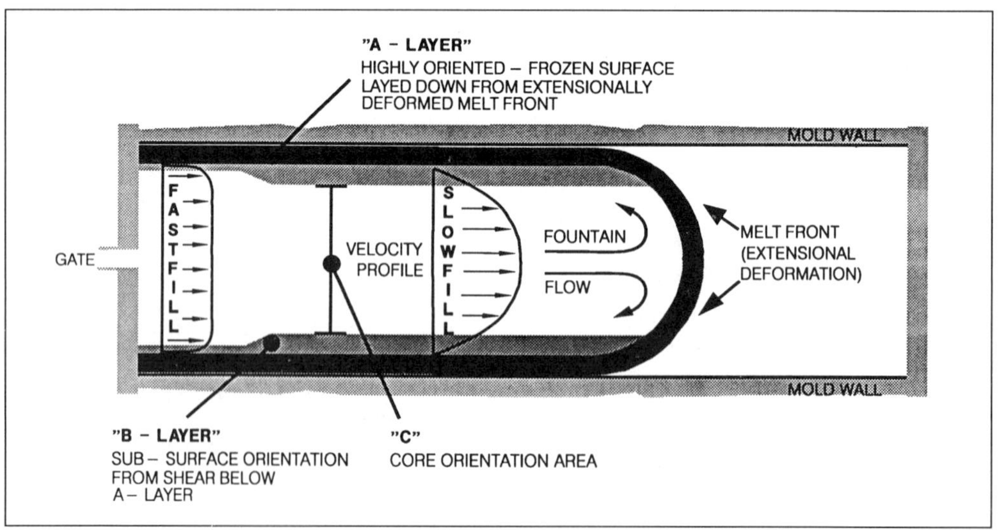

Cavity melt fountain flow; a phenomenon causing flow to deviate from two-dimensional flow between parallel plates.

Mold surface plating and coating treatments.

Process	Material	Applied to	Purpose
Coating by impingement—molecularly bound	Tungsten disulfide	Any metal	Reduce friction and metal-to-metal wear with dry film—nonmigrating
Coating by impingement—organically bound	Graphite	Any metal	Reduce sticking of plastic to mold surface—can migrate
Electrolyte plating	Hard chrome	Steel, nickel copper alloys	Protect polish, reduce wear and corrosion (except for chlorine or fluorine plastics)
	Gold	Nickel, brass	Corrosion only
	Nickel	Steel and copper alloys	Resist corrosion except sulfur-bearing compounds, improve bond under chrome, build up and repair worn or undersized molds
Electroless plating	Nickel	Steel	Protect nonmolding surfaces from rusting
	Phosphor nickel	Steel and copper	Resist wear and corrosion
Nitriding	Nitrogen gas or ammonia	Certain steel alloys	Improve corrosion resistance, reduce wear and galling; alternative to chrome and nickel plating
Liquid nitriding	Patented bath	All ferrous alloys	Improve lubricity and minimize galling
Anodizing	Electrolytic oxidizing	Aluminum	Harden surface, improve wear and corrosion resistance

mold cavity, plating, coating, and heat treatment Molds, and particularly cavities, are generally plated, coated, and/or heat treated to resist wear, corrosion, and melt release problems. Treatments such as those reviewed in the Table above that reduce wear are especially helpful in gates, runners, ejector pins, core pins, inserts, and cavity areas opposite the gate. Other treatments resist the corrosion damage inflected by chemicals such as hydrochloric acid when processing PVC, ammonia with acetals and nylons, and oxidation caused by interaction between molds and moisture in the plant atmosphere. Release problems require treatments that decrease friction and increase lubricity in mold cavities.

No single mold treatment is ideal for solving all problems. The molder must determine which mold problems could occur or be causing the greatest loss of productivity and then select the mold treatments that would be most effective in solving the problems.

Plating and coating affect only the surface of a mold or component, while heat treating generally will affect the mechanical and physical properties of the entire mold. Treatments such as carburizing and nitriding are considered to be surface treatments, and although heat is applied in these processes, they are not considered to be heat treatments. Heat treating is more often the province of the steel manufacturer and moldmaker than the molder. However, stress relieving is a heat treatment that the molder can perform.

Some mold wear cannot be prevented such as processing glass fiber filled compounds. This wear should be acknowledged and/or observed, and in turn dealt with at intervals in the mold's useful life; otherwise the mold could be allowed to wear pass the point of economic repair. Periodic checks of how platings and coatings are wearing will allow the molder to have a mold resurfaced before damage is done to the substrate.

mold cavity register Angled faces on parts of the mold which match when the mold is closed and so ensure correct alignment of the parts.

mold cavity retainer plate Plates in the mold which hold the cavities and forces. These plates are at the mold parting line and usually contain the guide pins and bushings. Also called force retainer plate.

mold cavity side part **1.** The stationary part of an injection mold (U.S). **2.** The side of the injection mold which is adjacent to the nozzle (British).

mold cavity, single or multiple ▷ **mold cavity**

mold cavity, split **1.** Blocks which, when assembled, contain a cavity for molding products having undercuts. **2.** A cavity of a mold that has been designed in sections to permit performing different actions. As an example in blow molding, the two halves of a mold which can open and close during a molding cycle to permit entrance of the parison, forming of the part and ejection of the finished part. Usually, the molds are produced so as to open on some geometric center of the blown part. However, molds are used without a geometric center such as with double wall molded products.

mold cavity surface finish The surface of a cavity affects appearance, ejectability, and cost. It can be specified by comparing it with six different finishes using the SPE/SPI standard that is available from SPI. Companies that provide the service of surfacing generally have more detailed information. Surface finishes include chrome-plated, electroless nickel, etched, sand blasted, and EDM. ▷ **surface finish**

mold cavity texturing ▷ **texture**

mold cavity weld line, part ▷ **weld line**

mold change ▷ **quick mold change**

mold chase The main body of the mold (usually steel) which contains the molding cavity(s), cores, pins, guide pins, or bushings. More specifically, it is an enclosure of any shape used to: (1) shrink-fit parts of a mold cavity in place, (2) prevent spreading or distortion in hobbing, (3) enclose an assembly of two or more parts of a split cavity block. Also called spacer and olster.

mold chase, floating Mold member, free to move vertically, that fits over a lower plug or cavity, and into which an upper plug telescopes.

mold clamping area ▷ **clamping area**

mold clamping operation and mechanisms ▷ **clamping**

mold clamping tonnage ▷ **injection molding clamping tonnage (force)**

mold classification by operation There are basically three modes of operation that the industry uses, namely automatic, semiautomatic, and manual. With automatic once the mold has been set up for production, an operator is no longer needed. Instrumentation control can be very sophisticated. With semiautomatic, the operator will have some limited action to take in order for the machine to operate in production once the mold has been set up. With the so-called manual operation, the operator practically performs all the interface in controlling the machine's operation when changes are required.

mold cleaner Removal of residual plastic from molds by pulling off or mechanical separation with a knife is the easiest method of cleaning a mold. In most cases mechanical cleaning is confined to uncomplicated molds (or screws) and the use of no-problem plastics. As soon as surface conditioning by chemical or thermal post-treatment is necessary, the relevant regulations against air and water pollution and for accident prevention as well as the applicable threshold limit values have to be observed. Basically all plastics, both thermoplastics and thermosets, can be thermally moved. Thermogravimetry provides graphs plotting the decomposition of plastics. TPs disintegrate at temperatures between 300° and 400°C, a 100% loss of weight occurring within a very short period of time. With TSs, too, the weight loss, characteristic of the decomposition process, starts between 300° and 400°C.

A variety of methods are used to carry out thermal decomposition in mold cleaning. The conventional methods of flaming or treatment of the molds in oven chambers have to take into account pollutants that occur. Substantial overheating can occur when flammable components of plastics burn up in an oxygen-containing atmosphere upon reaching their flash point. Mold damage is frequently attributed to these rather uncontrollable reactions of exothermic combustion. Even authentic chrome-nickel steel grades may be at risk under such conditions due to carbonization.

The use of open solvent baths for mold cleaning exists. Solvents used in closed systems are only appropriate under economic aspects where the required cleaning results are not obtainable with any other method. Some molds may justify the use of solvents; however, cleaning in an oil bath yields equally good results in most cases. Solvents should be selected individually for the various plastics. Losses due to evaporation and reprocessing of at least 10% must be expected even with closed systems. Cleaning in the oil bath involves the immersing and heating of the molds within a closed container in an oil bath. The oil used can consist of a synthetic mixture of isomeric dibenzyl toluenes. The equipment used consists of electrically heatable stainless steel tanks adapted to the mold geometries. To reduce the oil oxidation and improve aging behavior, the cleaning process is carried out under a nitrogen blanket.

mold closed process A family of techniques for reinforced thermoset plastics fabrication utilizing a two-piece male and female mold; the processes are usually extensively automated.

mold, coinjection ▷ **coinjection**

mold, cold runner ▷ **mold runner**

mold, cold slug The first thermoplastic melt to enter an injection cold runner mold; so called because in passing through the sprue orifice it is cooled below the effective molding temperature.

mold, cold slug well Space provided directly opposite the sprue opening in an injection mold to trap the cold slug.

mold, collapsible core They provide a means to mold internal threads, undercuts (as in hamper-proof bottle caps, etc.), protrusions, cut-outs, etc. There are more than a dozen patents approved on the design of collapsible cores. Many of these designs will never see the market due to the complexity of the parts or high tooling cost. However, there are two designs in production (U.S.) that are commonly known as a standard collapsible core and a collapsible minicore. The standard type, more often called a collapsible core, is the oldest and most popular (1950s). It is designed to mold circular parts with 360 undercuts. Its assembly consists of three parts: a center pin, a collapsible core, and a sleeve. The center pin is a precision ground shaft with a taper on one end and a flange at the other. It is of D-6 tool steel hardened to 60–62 Rockwell C. The collapsible core is basically a hollow cylinder with twelve matching slots parallel to the cylinder axis changing part of the cylinder into matching segments. These vertical segments are the flexing segments that form the undercut. It is made of 0–1 tool steel that is hardened to 56–58 C. The collapsing sleeve is made of 52100 steel, hardened to 50–54 C. The center pin expands the flexing segments of the core and provides cooling of the molding length. The collapsible core forms the undercut with the expanded flexing segments and releases the part for ejection with segments in a collapsed position. The sleeve functions as a back up unit to collapse the core segments if segments fail to collapse on their own.

The collapsible minicore was designed for less than 1 in. (2.54 cm) closure market. It has a center pin with three narrow, non-collapsing segments, a core body with three wide flexing segments attached to a common base, and a positive collapsible sleeve. The center pin function is to expand the collapsing segments of the core and provide cooling to the core segments. The core function is to form the undercut with the expanded flexing segments and to release the part for ejection with the segments in the collapsed position. The sleeve functions as a back up to collapse the core segments if segments fail to collapse on their own.

mold, combination **1.** A mold which has both positive portions or ridges, and cavity portions such as a refrigerator door liner. **2.** ▷ **mold, family**

mold, compression There are different designs used to provide compression molded parts meeting different processing requirements. Typically used for thermoset plastics molding compounds are the positive, flash, semi-positive, landed plunger, and split-wedge types. The Fig. below illustrates the positive type. The plunger

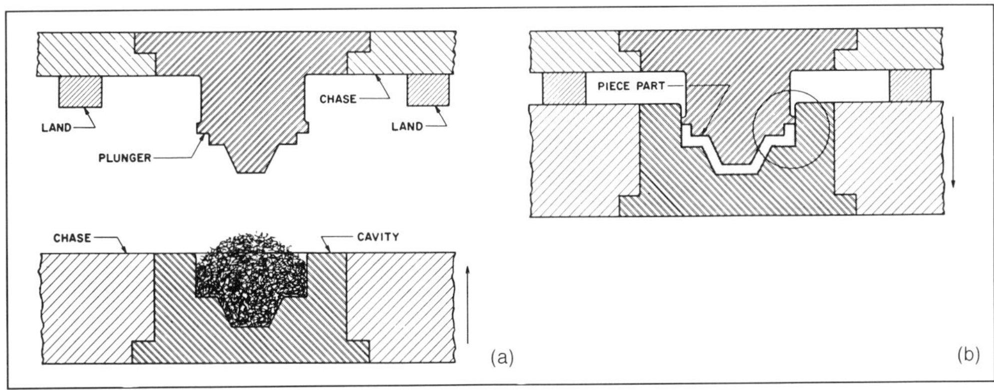

(*a*) Positive mold opened with molding compound in the cavity; (*b*) positive mold closed.

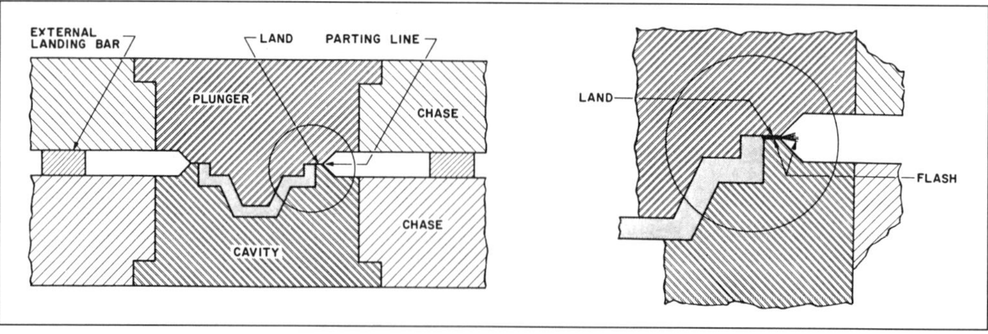

Flash mold.

telescopes within the cavity compressing the material. There is very little clearance between the plunger and cavity wall. Almost all the pressure is exerted on the material and very little material is allowed to escape. The clearance between the plunger and cavity varies from 0.0015 to 0.005 in. (0.04 to 0.13 mm) per side. The amount of material that escapes through the clearance between the plunger and cavity is flash, typical with molding TSs. The disadvantage of this mold with its vertical flash is that after frequent operations the cavity walls become scored and ejection of pieces is difficult. Flash on the part is removed by filling, sanding, tumblers, etc. The positive mold is used primarily with compounds containing coarse fillers. The amount of material placed into the mold cavity must be measured accurately as there is very limited means for the excess material to escape; also required to obtain uniformity in the part's (vertical) thickness.

The Fig. above illustrates a flash type. The cavity is filled with material and the excess is squeezed out over the lands which are about 0.125 in. (3.2 mm) wide. External landing bars are provided so the plunger does not crush the top of the cavity when the mold is completely closed. Clearance between 0.002 and 0.005 in. (0.05 and 0.13 mm) is provided so excess material can escape and the cavity is not damaged. This type mold is not generally used with coarse-filled compounds or for pieces which require a high density. The flash type mold lends itself well to shallow depth parts such as dinnerware plates and saucers.

The Fig. below illustrates the principle of the semi-positive type. As the two halves of the mold begin to close, the mold acts much like a flash mold as the excess material is allowed to escape. As the plunger telescopes into the cavity, full pressure is exerted on the material and piece parts of maximum density are produced. There is very little clearance between the plunger and the side wall of the cavity, which results in a very thin vertical flash being formed. This type mold takes advantage of the free flow of material in a flash mold and the quality of producing dense parts of the positive mold.

The first Fig. on the opposite page illustrates the principle of the land plunger type. This mold has also been called internal landed plunger and landed positive mold. The land is approximately 0.125 in. (3.2 mm) wide. The plunger is not allowed to bear on the land surface in the cavity as the pressure of the press would smash or crush the land surface. This is accomplished by having external landing bars absorb the press pressure before the plunger hits the land. There is a

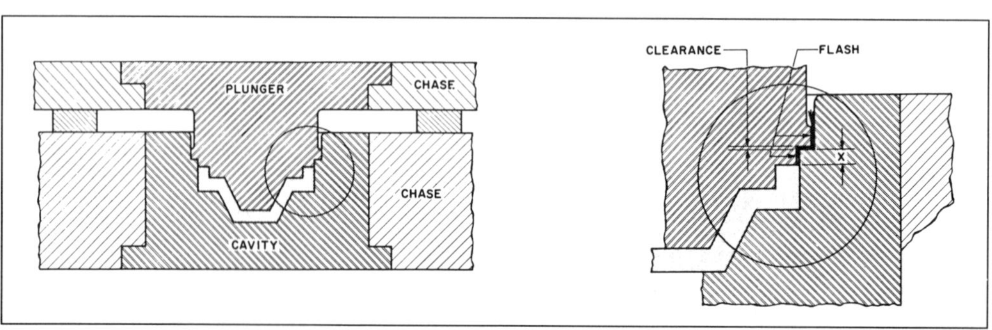

Semi-positive mold.

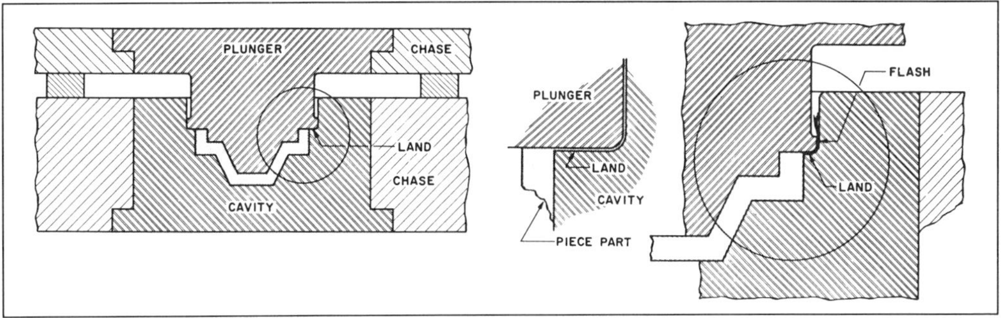

Land plunger mold closed.

clearance of 0.001 in. (0.025 mm) between the plunger and the land to allow excess material to escape. A horizontal flash is formed on the part. Also, some material flows by the plunger.

The Fig. below illustrates the split-wedge or split-cavity type. This mold is used primarily for articles that have undercuts, such as spool-shaped products. Projections or undercuts prevent the part from being removed in the more conventional mold cavity. In order to overcome this difficulty, the cavity is constructed in two or more sections. When these sections are together, the inside surface has the required shape and the exterior of these sections has a wedge-like shape. Different designs are used that include the use of spring loaded pins, T-slots, keys, etc. ▷ **breathing**

mold cooling Cooling of the mold (for thermoplastics) is an essential mold feature and requires special attention in mold design. The cooling system should ensure rapid and uniform cooling of the molding. In the design of mold components and the lay-out of guides and ejectors, allowance should be made for proper size and positioning of the cooling system. Rapid cooling improves process economics, while uniform cooling improves product quality by preventing differential shrinkage, internal stresses and mold release problems. In addition, uniform cooling ensures a shorter molding cycle.

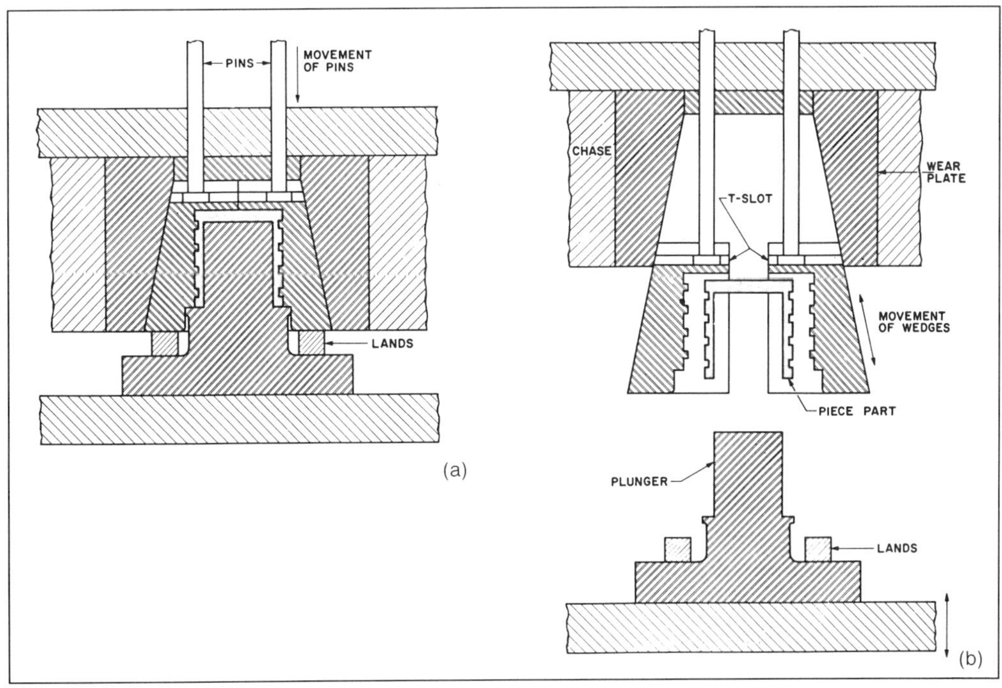

(*a*) Split-wedge mold in the closed position; (*b*) split-wedge mold in the open position.

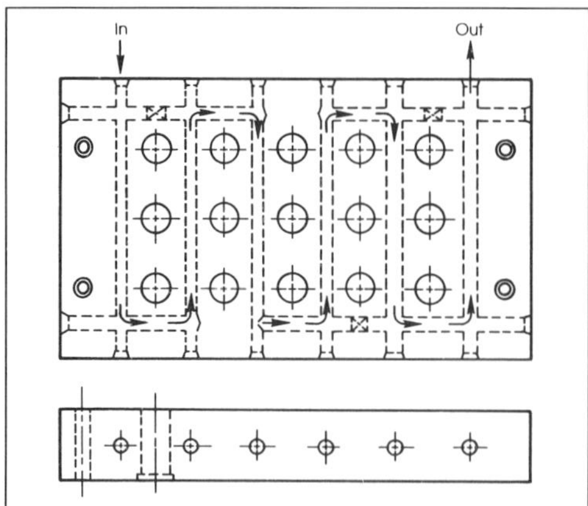

Mold cavity cooling line schematic.

An example of simple mold cooling layout is shown in the Fig. above.

mold cooling analysis ▷**design mold**

mold cooling and heating channel Channels or passageways (usually drilled holes) located within the body of the mold through which a turbulent fluid cooling medium can be circulated to control temperature on the mold cavity surface. May also be used for heating a mold by circulating heated fluids (oil, steam, etc.) through channels as in molding of thermoset and some thermoplastic materials. Heating is also accomplished using electric heaters in the mold body. There are applications where the press platens are heated which in turn heat the mold or are more often used to heat flat plastic laminated material such as thermoset decorative panels, printed circuit board panels, reinforced plastic building panels, etc. ▷**turbulent flow** and **Reynold's number**

mold cooling channel bubbler A device inserted into a mold cavity, such as a rib or core, that allows water to flow deep inside the hole into which it is inserted and to discharge through the open end of the hole. Uniform cooling of the mold and of isolated mold sections can be achieved in this manner.

mold cooling flooding Molds, particularly for blow molding, use a box type enclosure next to the cavity wall rather than using pipe passageways. This flood type turbulent cooling mold system is less expensive and provides adequate cooling.

mold cooling partitioned A large diameter hole drilled into the mold (usually the core) and partitioned by a metal plate extending to near the bottom end of the channel. Water is introduced near the top of one side of the partition and removed on the other side. Like a bubbler.

mold cooling, spiral method A method of cooling injection molds or similar molds in which the cooling medium flows through a spiral cavity in the body of the mold. The cooling medium is introduced at the center of the spiral, near the sprue section, because more heat is localized in this section.

mold cooling time In addition to the mold, plastic material, and machine costs, the final cost to mold a part depends on the molding cycle. A large part of this cycle, up to possibly 80%, is due to time required to cool the molding. This time depends on the heat of the molding. Minimum cycle time, therefore, is governed by the time taken to cool. The injected plastic is cooled rapidly by its contact with the cavity wall, but since plastics are poor heat conductors, the solidified outer layer retards heat transfer from the center of the molding. Most of the cooling time is thus required to cool this center. In principle, the molding may be released from the mold as soon as its outer layer is sufficiently rigid. This temperature is called mold release temperature. The inside of the molding will often still be considerably hotter. Minimum cooling time required to reach mold release temperature is governed by the wall thickness of the molding, difference between polymer and mold temperature and difference between mold release temperature of the article and mold temperature.

mold cooling, vacuum Rather than push liquid coolant through a mold, pulling the coolant can provide advantages such as eliminating water leaks and reaching complicated cavity surface areas to provide cooling action by using water line venting. ▷**mold venting, water transfer**

mold cored A mold incorporating passages for electrical heating elements, water, steam, etc.

mold core pin **1.** Pin used to produce a hole in a mold **2.** In injection blow molding, the internal rod used to hold the inside of the preform. This rod also retains the plastic melt during the injection molding steps as it is transferred through the cycle. The core is also the blowing pin where air or a blowing medium blows through the channels cut in the center of this core rod to expand the preform in the blowing mold. ▷**blow molding, injection**

mold core pin plate Plate holding core pin(s).

mold core pulling sequence The SPI recommended core-pulling sequences are as follows:

(1) sequence A (clamp preposition only required with mechanical ejector): re-set ejector, core-in, clamp close, inject, clamp open (to adjustable stop position), cores-out, clamp open (continue), and eject, (2) sequence B: clamp close, cores-in, inject, cores-out, clamp open, and eject, (3) sequence C (can only be used in hydraulic ejection): clamp close, inject, clamp open, cores-out, eject, and cores-in, and (4) sequence D (requires interlock to ensure cores are in proper position prior to injection or ejection): clamp close during cores-in, inject, clamp open during cores-out, and eject.

mold daylight ▷ **clamping, daylight**

mold, deep draw A mold having a core that is appreciably longer than the wall thickness.

mold deformation After the injection molding stroke and during after-fill, pressure is built up in the mold cavity. This pressure, which depends on the type of molding and plastic, is generally one-third to one-half of the injection pressure set on the machine. The consequences of such pressures must be recognized. They cause elastic deformations, such as bending of cavity retainer plates and cores. The use of a sturdy construction such as thick cavity retainer plates, and support pillars in the open gap for the ejector system, may reduce elastic deformation to a minimum. Such possibilities are often restricted, since light construction is also required for efficient cooling, for the necessary spaces for guide pins and ejector system, side actions, etc. Elastic deformation of weak, or insufficiently solid mold components may result in: (1) differences in wall thickness with consequent excessive dimensional variations as well as insufficient dimensional stability and rigidity of the molding; (2) non-unform melt flow in the mold and in the case of thin-walled moldings, this may give rise to flow lines, weld lines, internal stresses or even trapped air; (3) in weak molds it is possible that the bearing surfaces or other components will be forced apart by the polymer pressure, causing flash formation which may interfere with proper mold release and others.

mold degating Separating the molded part from the runner system automatically or manually in or out of the mold.

mold design Computers are used in many designs. Views, cross sections, projections, changes in size and color, and mechanical and thermal analyses are easily made. ▷ **computer-aided design; computer-aided engineering; computer storage disk and tape; design mold**

mold design errors The Table on p. 462 lists examples of errors in injection mold and product design with possible consequences for process and/or molded part.

mold dowel bushing ▷ **mold leader pin and bushing**

mold, dowel pin ▷ **mold leader pin and bushing**

mold, duplicating A mold made by casting over or duplicating another product by mechanical reproduction using cutting tools that are guided by a master, proportional in size to the desired finished products.

molded edge An edge that is not physically altered after molding (with fiber reinforcements) for use in final form, particularly one that does not have fiber ends along its length.

molded-in hinge ▷ **hinge**

molded insert ▷ **insert**

molded-in stresses ▷ **residual stress**

molded net Description of a molded part that requires no additional processing to meet dimensional requirements.

molded parts buyers guide This guide has been prepared by the Molders Division of the SPI. It contains important points that purchasers have traditionally considered in specifying and purchasing plastic parts. As in every major fabricating industry, various commercial and administrative practices have developed over the years which play an important role in the conduct of day-to-day business. These arrangements, generally expressed in the proposal, acknowledgement, and contract forms of the individual molding companies, have been viewed as constituting "customs of the trade". This informative manual is designed to identify and explain these customs.

mold efficiency In a multimold blowing system, the percentage of the total turn-around time of the mold actually required for forming, cooling, and ejection of the blown part.

mold ejection A device or system fitted to usually the moving platen of a machine for operating the molding ejector(s) to remove molded parts. It may be operated mechanically (including springs), hydraulically, pneumatically, or electrically. It operates in sequence with the clamping close preposition; a provision in the clamping unit that actuates the ejection action. It is available in various designs and qualities, or by systems such as knockout pin(s), stripper plate or ring, unscrewing, cam, removable insert, or bushing. The choice of ejector system is largely governed by article

Errors in mold and part design.

Faults	Possible problems
Wrong location of gate	Cold weld lines, flow lines, jetting, air entrapment, venting problems, warping, stress concentrations, voids and/or sink marks
Gates and/or runners too narrow	Short shots, plastics overheated, premature freezing of runners, sink marks and/or voids and other marks
Runners too large	Longer molding cycle, waste of plastics, and pressure losses
Unbalanced cavity layout in multiple-cavity molds	Unbalanced pressure buildup in mold, mold distortion, dimensional variation between products (shrinkage control poor), poor mold release, flash, and stresses
Nonuniform mold cooling	Longer molding cycle, high after-shrinkage, stresses (warping), poor mold release, irregular surface finish, and distortion of part during ejection
Poor or no venting	Need for higher injection pressure, burned plastic (brown streaks), poor mold release, short shots, and flow lines
Poor or no air injection	Poor mold release for large parts, part distortion, and higher ejection force
Poor ejector system or bad location of ejectors	Poor mold release, distortion or damage in molding, and upsets in molding cycle
Sprue insufficiently tapered	Poor mold release, higher injection pressure, and mold wear
Sprue too long	Poor mold release, pressure losses, longer molding cycle, and premature freezing of sprue
No round edge at end of sprue	Notch sensitivity (cracks, bubbles, etc.) and stress concentrations
Bad alignment and locking of cores and other mold components	Distortion of components, air entrapment, dimensional variations, uneven stresses, and poor mold release
Mold movement due to insufficient mold support	Part flashes, dimensional variations, poor mold release, and pressure losses
Radius of sprue bushing too small	Plastic leakage, poor mold release, and pressure losses
Mold and injection cylinder out of alignment	Poor mold release, plastic leakage, cylinder pushed back, and pressure losses
Draft of molded part too small	Poor mold release, distortion of molded part, and dimensional variations
Sharp transitions in part wall thickness and sharp corners	Parts unevenly stressed, dimensional variations, air entrapment, notch sensitivity, and mold wear

shape, and by the rigidity or flexibility of the plastic used. The mold should preferably be fitted with ejectors at those spots around which the molding is expected to shrink (e.g., around cores). At high mold temperatures allowance must be made for thermal expansion of the mold platens. These platens will expand more than the plates of the ejector mechanism. It is, therefore, recommended that the ejectors be provided with a cylindrical head, and should be mounted with some clearance to allow correction of possible variations in center distances during machine operation. Ejection of articles with large cylindrical or flat surfaces may sometimes be hampered, as such surfaces tend to create a vacuum between article and cavity wall. In such cases, release may be improved and the vacuum broken by an air ejection system.

mold ejection mark A surface mark on the

part caused by the ejector, such as pin, when it pushes the part out of the mold cavity.

mold ejector pin A rod, pin, or sleeve which pushes a molding off a core or out of a cavity mold. It is attached to an ejector bar or plate. Also called knockout pin.

mold ejector plate ▷ **mold ejector pin**

mold ejector ram A small hydraulic, mechanical, or electrical ram fitted to a molding press for the purpose of operating ejector pin(s).

mold ejector retainer plate Retainer in which ejector pin(s) is assembled.

mold ejector return pin Projections that push the ejector assembly back as the mold closes. Also called surface pin, return pin, safety pin, or position pushback.

mold ejector rod and bar Bar that actuates the ejector assembly when mold is opened.

mold ejector sleeve Bushing type ejector.

mold ejector spider A system where part of an ejector mechanism operates the ejector pin(s).

molder, captive ▷ **processor, captive**

molder, custom ▷ **processor, custom**

molder, proprietary ▷ **processor, proprietary**

mold, expandable polystyrene bead type ▷ **expandable polystyrene bead mold**

mold, family A multicavity mold wherein each of the cavities forms one component part of the assembled finished product. The term often applied to molds wherein parts from different customers are grouped together in one mold for economy of production. Sometimes called combination mold.

mold feed bushing The hardened steel bushing in an injection mold which forms a seal between the mold and the injection nozzle.

mold, female ▷ **mold cavity, female**

mold filling The effect of mold dimensions and plastic viscosity on pressure requirements is expressed as follows:

$$Q = \frac{P}{K\eta}$$

or:

$$P = K\eta Q$$

where Q = volumetric rate of mold fill (in.^{3}/sec or cm^3/sec); P = pressure at mold entrance (lbf/in.^{2} or kgf/cm^2); η = resin viscosity (lbf sec/in.^{2}) or kgf sec/cm^2); K = mold flow resistance factor.

For end-gated rectangular cavity section fill out:

$$K = \frac{12L}{W_t^3}$$

For end-gated annular cavity section fill out:

$$K = \frac{12L}{\pi D_m t^3}$$

For end-gated cylindrical cavity section fill out:

$$K = \frac{128(L + 4D_c)}{\pi D_c^4}$$

In these equations, L = mold cavity length (in. or cm); W = mold cavity width (in. or cm); t = mold cavity thickness (in. or cm); D_m = mean diameter of annulus mold cavity (in. or cm); D_c = mean diameter of cylindrical mold cavity (in. or cm).

From the above it may be seen that at constant flow rate and resin viscosity: (1) The pressure required to fill is directly proportional to the mold length. (2) The pressure required to fill is inversely proportional to cavity width or diameter. (3) The pressure required to fill is inversely proportional to the cube of the mold thickness. (4) The pressure required to fill radial fill patterns (i.e., center gated) is exponential.

The pressure required is proportional to the resin viscosity, and is reduced by an increase in temperature and/or shear rate as these equations indicate:

Shear rate for rectangular section

$$= \frac{6Q}{t^3(W + t)} \text{ sec}^{-1}$$

Shear rate for annular section

$$= \frac{6Q}{t^2(\pi D_m + t)} \text{ sec}^{-1}$$

Shear rate for cylindrical section

$$= \frac{32Q}{\pi D_c^3} \text{ sec}^{-1}$$

Thus, shear rate is increased and plastic viscosity decreased by a decrease in mold cavity dimensions; an effect opposite to that which such cavity dimensions have on the mold flow resistance factor K. ▷ **mold cavity packing**

mold finish ▷ **mold cavity surface finish**

mold flash A thin surplus web of plastic material, usually occurring with thermoset plastics, attached to a molding along the parting lines, fins at holes or openings, etc. With most moldings, it would be objectionable and must be removed before the parts are acceptable. ▷ **deflashing** and **mold, compression**

mold flash gate ▷ **mold gate, flash**

mold flash groove A groove ground in the parting line land to allow the escape of excess material during molding operation, particularly compression molding.

mold flash line A raised line appearing on the surface of a molding and formed at the junction of mold faces such as at the parting line.

mold flash ridge That part of a flash compression mold which the excess material escapes until the mold is closed.

mold flash ring, vertical or horizontal The clearance between the force plug and the vertical or horizontal wall of the compression molding cavity in a positive or semi-positive mold; also the ring of excess material which escapes from the cavity into this clearance space.

mold flow analysis ▷ **design mold**

mold flow filling ▷ **mold cavity melt flow analysis**

mold force That portion of the mold which forms the inside. Sometimes called a core or a plunger. In compression molding, the downward acting mold half, usually the male half.

mold force plate The plate that carries the plunger or force plug of a compression mold and guide pins or bushings. Since it is usually driled for hot water or steam lines, it is also called the hot or steam plate.

mold force plug The male half of the compression mold that enters the cavity, exerting pressure on the plastic and causing it to flow. Also called a core, plunger, or ram.

mold, French A two-piece mold for irregular shapes; tall, topheavy, leaning to one side, or with extremely fine detail.

mold gate Basically, it is the orifice through which the melt enters the mold cavity. It can have a variety of configurations, depending on product design.

mold gate blush Associated with melt fracture around the gate from stresses caused by process conditions or mold geometry. It is a blemish or disturbance in the gate area. To eliminate or reduce this problem, raise melt temperature, reduce injection speed, check gate for sharp edges, enlarge gate, and check that runner system has a cold-slug well. ▷ **mold gate strain**

mold gate cosmetic ▷ **mold gate valve**

mold gate, degating ▷ **mold degating**

mold gate, diaphragm A gate used in molding annular or tubular parts. The gate forms a solid web across the opening of the part. Also called disc gate.

mold gate, direct A gate which has the same cross section as that of the runner.

mold gate disc ▷ **mold gate, diaphragm**

mold gate, fan Opening between the runner and the mold cavity which has the shape of a fan. This shape helps reduce stress concentrations in the gate area by spreading the opening over a wider area.

mold gate, flash Usually a long, shallow rectangular gate extending from a runner which runs parallel to an edge of a molded part along the flash or parting line of the mold.

mold gate location The location of the gate must be given careful consideration, if the required properties and appearance of the molding are to be met. In addition, the location of the gate affects mold construction. The gate must be located in such a way that rapid and uniform mold filling is ensured. The gate must be so located that the air present in the mold cavity can escape during injection. If this requirement is not fulfilled, either short shots or burnt spots on the molding will be produced.

The gate should be located at the thickest part of the molding, preferably at a spot where the function and appearance of the molding are not impaired. However, the large diameter gates require mechanical degating after ejection, and always leave a mark on the product. With small or shallow moldings the gate is sometimes located on the inside. However, this necessitates mold release from the direction of the stationary mold half, which interferes with effective cooling and generally increases mold cost. ▷ **design mold**

mold gate mark A surface discontinuity on a molded part caused by the gate through which material enters the cavity. ▷ **mold gate blush**

mold gate, nozzle ▷ **injection molding nozzle gate**

mold gate, pinpoint A restricted orifice of 0.030 in. (3.3 mm) or less in diameter through which melt flows. This small gate minimizes the size of the mark left on the molded part. The gate breaks clean when the part is ejected. Sometimes referred to as a restricted gate.

mold gate, restricted Usually called pinpoint gate.

mold gate, ring Used on cylindrical shapes, this gate encircles the core to permit the melt to first move around the core symmetrically before filling the cavity, preventing weld line. There are external and internal ring gates in respect to the cavity.

mold gate scar Most mold designs start out using a small gate(s). If the gate size is too large, scars in the gate area can occur. However, larger sizes permit faster fill and cycle time.

mold gate size The gate size has a tremendous effect on the success or failure of attempts to produce high quality parts economically. Plastic is a viscous liquid. The cooler the plastic, the more viscous it becomes. The more viscous it becomes, the more difficult it is to move this plastic though very small gates. High injection pressure are then needed to move the material though the gates. The higher the injection pressure, the smaller the total area of the mold must be, otherwise high pressures will result in flash (TP and TS plastics).

Gate size is usually the critical factor that dictates the final mold-filling speed. Reducing melt viscosity by raising the melt temperature increases the mold filling rate since there is less pressure drop across the gate. However, this can increase cycle time, since the heat put into the material must be removed in the mold. While decreasing mold temperature helps achieve faster cycle times, it also requires additional injection pressure, which affects the clamp tonnage (depending on the projected filling area of a mold).

mold gate, spider Multi-gating of a part through a system of radial runners from the sprue.

mold gate strain The Fig. below shows effects of gating methods on molding strains. ▷ **mold gate blush**

mold gate, submarine A type of edge gating where the opening from the runner into the mold is located below the parting line or mold surface. The conventional edge gating (as well as others) is where the opening is machined into the surface of the mold on the parting line. With submarine gates, the molded part is cut (by the mold) from the runner system on ejection from the mold. Also called tunnel gate.

mold gate, tab A small removable tab of approximately the same thickness as the molded part, usually located perpendicular to the item. It is used as a site for edge gating location on parts with large flat sections. Also can be used as a site for gating so that if any unacceptable blemishes appear, they will be in the tab which is cut off. See Figure in ▷ **mold gate strain**

mold gate, tunnel ▷ **mold gate, submarine**

mold gate types The Fig. on p. 466 includes some of the gates described.

mold gate, valve VGs are used in injection molds and provide a wider processing window of operation, better product quality, eliminate gate freezing, and are cost effective. While they have been problematic, VG technology is a matured device providing consistently reliable and productive processing to products ranging from commodity items to highly specialized components. A VR is a type of hot runner gating system that uses a valve, usually a pin, to mechanically open and close the gate orifice. An actuating mechanism coordinates the movement of the pin with the molding cycle. To begin injection, the pin is retracted, opening the valve. After injection, the pin moves forward to close the valve for part cooling and ejection. The pin and its actuation mechanism are usually an integral part of the hot runner nozzle. A wide variety of approaches to actuating the valve have been developed that include springs, adjustable air cushions, mechanical cams, pneumatic and hydraulic pistons, and designs that harness the injection pressure in the melt to actuate the valve(s).

In demanding molding applications that require packing plastic into molds to provide

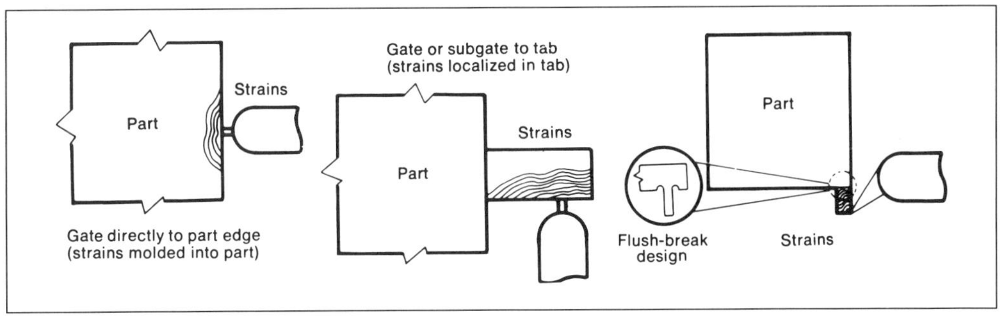

Mold gate strains.

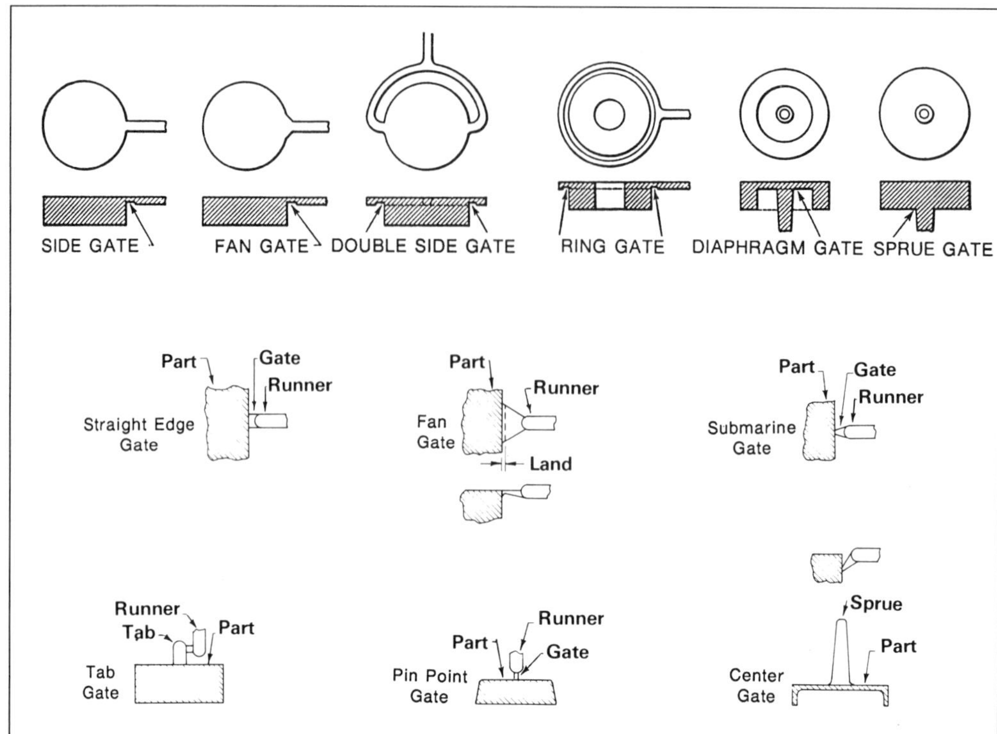

Typical gates in injection molding.

precise part weight and tolerances, the pin is actually driven into semi-solidified gates. As long as the temperature is accurately controlled in the gate area, the gate is properly sized, and the closing is properly timed, the valve will be closed by the action of the pin pushing through the soft core of plastic. This will close the gate precisely, without the risk of pin or gate damage. Regardless of the material used in any VG processing application, the gate must never be allowed to solidify or freeze before the valve is mechanically closed. Otherwise, gate cosmetics will suffer and the gate itself may be damaged. The closing of the pin must always be accomplished above the melting point of a crystalline plastic, or well above the softening point of an amorphous plastic.

mold gate, web ▷ **mold gate, diaphragm**

mold gel coat ▷ **mold cavity, plating, coating, and heat treatment**

mold grid Channel shaped mold supporting members.

mold heating ▷ **mold cooling and heating channel**

mold heat transfer device It transfers localized heat to a heat sink in order to improve mold cooling or transfer heat from a heat source to a localized area such as hot sprue bushings. ▷ **heat pipe**

mold height Overall thickness of the mold as it is located between the platens of the molding machine. Mold height dimension or direction is taken when the mold sits on a table. Thus mold height in the conventional injection molding machine is the horizontal dimension between the platens.

mold hobbing Hobbing is a technique where a master model in hardened steel is used to sink the shape of a mold cavity into heated mild steel such as beryllium copper. The hob is larger than the finished plastic part. After hobbing, the metal shrinks as it cools.

mold hold-down groove A small groove cut into the side wall of the molding surface to assist in holding the molded article in that member while the mold opens.

mold, hot runner ▷ **mold, runner**

mold inching A reduction in the rate of mold closing travel just before the mating mold surfaces touch each other.

molding The forming or shaping of a plastic or reinforced plastic into a solid mass of prescribed shape and size by the application of pressure (zero on up) and in most processes heat for a given time. ▷ **fabricating processes**

molding area diagram By plotting at least injection pressure (ram pressure) with mold temperature, a molding area diagram will provide the best combination of pressure and temperature necessary to produce quality parts (see Fig. below). Developing this MAD approach ends up with a dramatic and easily comprehensive visual aid to analyze the important variables for injection molding. Within the diagram's area, all parts meet the performance requirements. However, rejects can develop at the edge of the diagram because of machine and plastic variations. Other controllable parameters can be added such as temperatures of the melt in the nozzle, rate of injection, etc. ▷ **molding volume diagram**

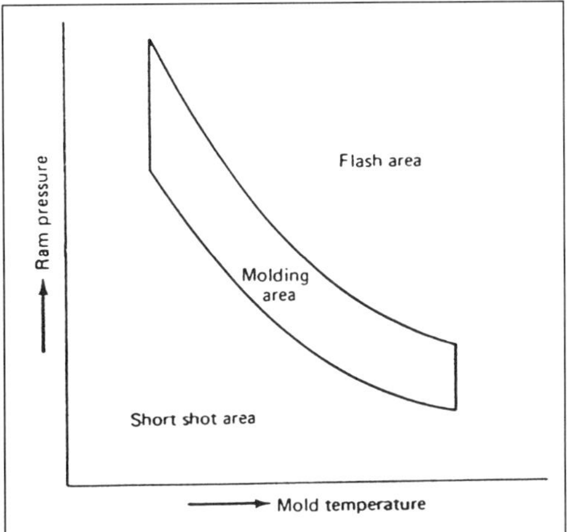

Two-dimensional Molding Area Diagram (MAD) approach.

molding, bag ▷ **bag molding**

molding caul stock ▷ **molding pressure, high** and **caul plate**

molding, centrifugal ▷ **centrifugal casting; casting; rotational molding**

molding clamshell ▷ **thermoforming, clamshell**

molding compound Plastic material in varying stages of pellet form, granulation, or gunk consisting of plastics, filler, pigment, reinforcement, plasticizer, and/or other ingredients ready for use in the molding operations. Also called dry blend, molding powder, bulk molding compound, and sheet molding compound.

molding cycle 1. The period of time required for the complete sequence of operations on a molding press to produce one set of moldings. **2.** The operations necessary to produce a set of moldings without reference to the total time. The sequence of operation (manual, semi-automatic, or automatic) is: (a) close and clamp the mold, (b) inject the mold, (c) hold mold closed under pressure while plastic cools or cures, (d) open the mold, and (e) eject the part.

molding, dip ▷ **dip molding**

molding index A test used with thermoset molding powder where a standard flash type cup mold under prescribed conditions is used. The molding index is the total minimum force required to close the mold (ASTM D 731).

molding material ▷ **molding compound**

molding powder ▷ **molding compound**; not to be confused with ▷ **powder molding process**

molding/pressing, isotactic ▷ **isotactic molding/pressing**

molding pressure The pressure applied either directly or indirectly to the ram action of an injection machine, compression press, transfer press, etc. to force the melt to completely fill the mold cavity.

molding, pressure bag ▷ **pressure bag molding**

molding pressure, contact A method of molding or laminating in which the pressure, usually less than 70 kPa (10 psi), is only slightly more than necessary to hold the materials together during molding to produce an excellent part. Also called contact molding. Usually concerns reinforced plastics.

molding pressure, high A molding or laminating process in which the pressure used is greater than 1,400 kPa (200 psi), but commonly 7 to 13.8 MPa (1 to 2 ksi). Usually concerns reinforced plastics.

molding pressure, low In general, parts molded in the range of pressures from 2,760 kPa (400 psi) down to and including pressure obtained by the mere contact of the plies or material. Usually concerns reinforced plastics.

molding pressure required The unit pressure applied to the molding material in the mold. The area is calculated from the projected area taken at right angles under pressure during complete closing of the mold, including areas of runners that solidify. The unit pressure is calculated by dividing the total force applied by this projected area, and is expressed in psi (Pa).

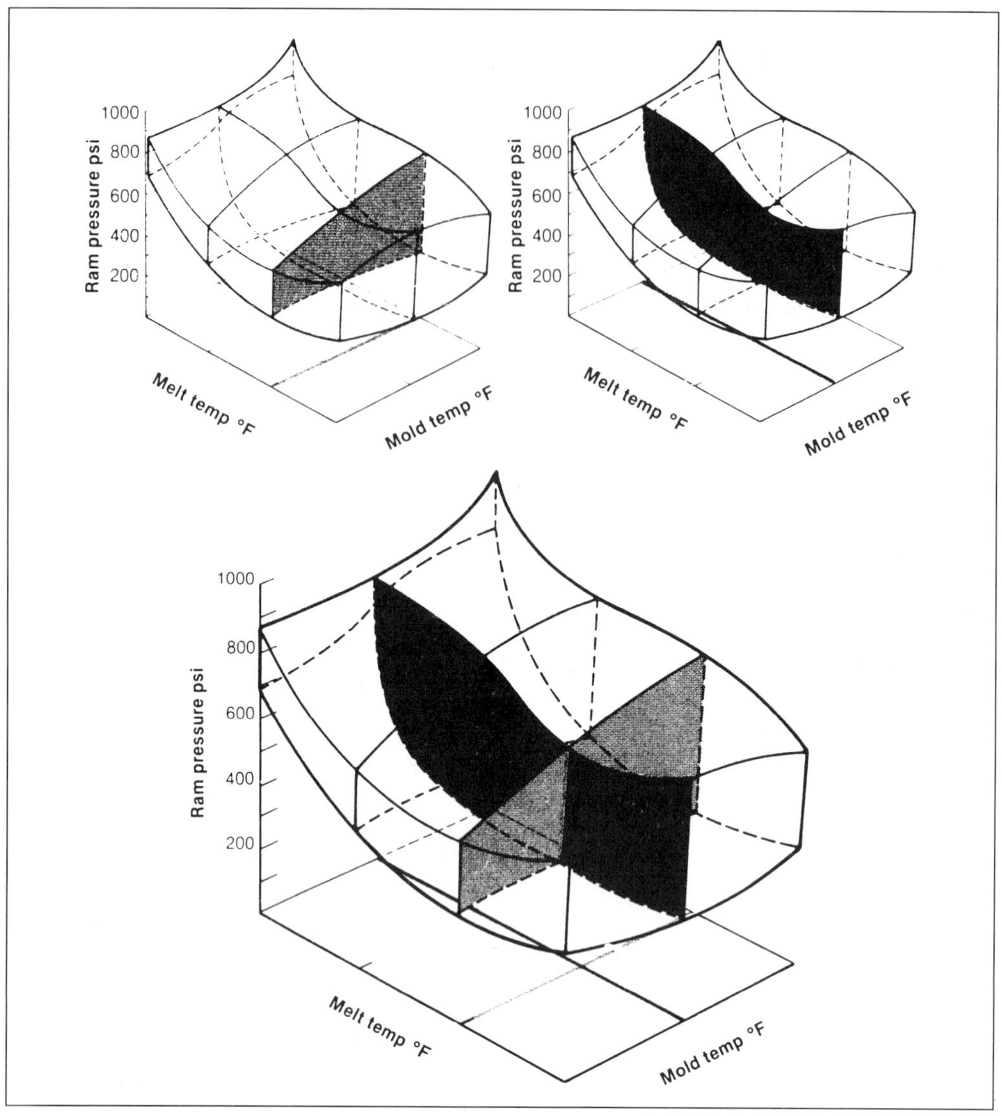

Molding volume diagram for injection molding.

To determine pressure required on a mold that has a specific projected area based on the plastic to be used, the pressure required on the melt is determined (either from past experience, or from the material supplier). This pressure in psi (Pa) is multiplied by the total area. Result is total clamping pressure required. This pressure can be converted to tonnage providing a guide to the clamp tonnage needed in the injection molding machine; to ensure the proper clamp tonnage machine is to be used (or purchased), it is best to provide a safety factor of at least having available another 10% more.

molding processes ▷ **fabricating processes**

molding, short An incomplete molding or a short shot; insufficient plastic to fill the mold. ▷ **short**

molding, squeeze ▷ **squeeze molding**

molding, transfer ▷ **transfer molding**

molding, two-up ▷ **blow molding extruder mold multiple/combination cavities**

molding volume diagram After a three-dimensional molding volume diagram (MVD) is constructed, it can be analyzed to find the optimum combination of melt temperature, mold temperature, and injection or ram pressure (see Fig. above) ▷ **molding area diagram**

Mold for producing pipe L-fitting (located in lower right corner).

molding with rotation ▷ **injection molding with rotation**

molding with soluble core ▷ **soluble core molding**

mold, injection Many different, rather endless, injection molds are used successfully, such as those shown in the Figs. on this page and on p. 470.

mold insert 1. Part of a mold cavity or force which forms undercut or raised portions of a molded product such as with injection or compression molding. ▷ **insert 2.** Part of the mold assembly which forms the neck and finish. Sometimes called neck finish in a blow mold.

mold, insulated runner ▷ **mold runner**

mold, jetting ▷ **injection molding, jetting**

mold knockout bar A bar which holds and actuates ejector pin(s) in a mold. ▷ **mold ejection**

mold land 1. In an extrusion die (sometimes called mold or tool), the surface parallel to the flow of material. **2.** In a two-piece mold, a platform built up to the split line. **3.** The por-

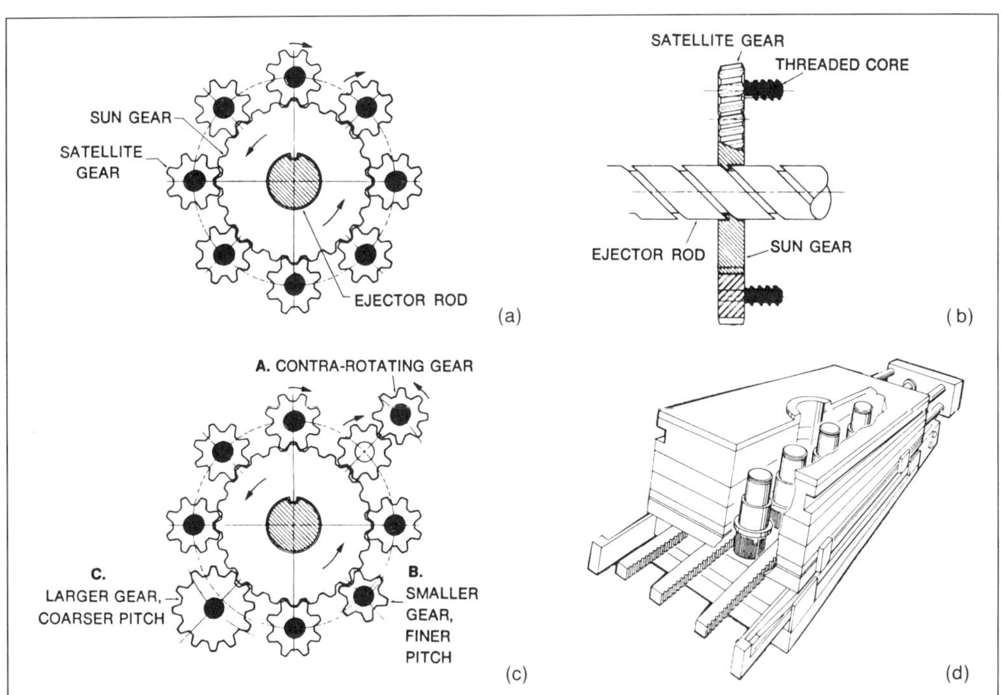

Two different methods for molding threaded caps. (*a*) The sun-and-satellite gear system (front view) provides a simplified method for unscrewing threaded parts from molds. The cores are attached to the satellite gears. (*b*) Side view illustrates gearing relationship between the ejector bar and the two gears used in unscrewing parts. (*c*) Three variations possible with this gear system include (A) inserting an idler gear to permit a contra-rotating thread to be molded with others; (B) creating a finer pitch to one core by reducing the number of teeth in a gear, or (C) having a coarser pitch by using a larger gear. (*d*) Side action mold.

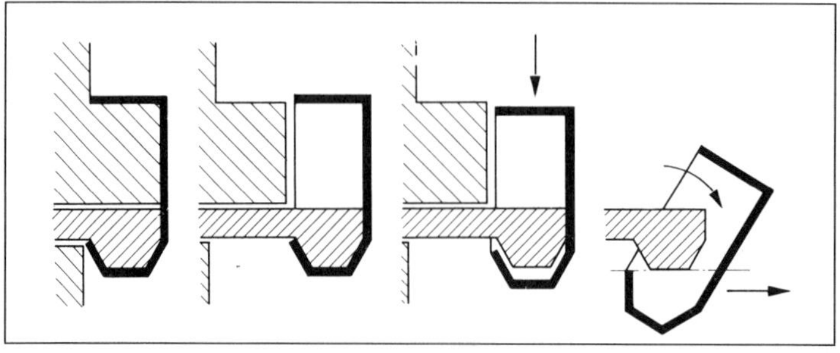

Slide within a slide mold.

tion of a mold which provides the separation or cut-off of the flash from the molded part. **4.** The bearing surface of a mold by which excess material escapes. **5.** In a semipositive or flash mold, the horizontal bearing surface. **6.** The nozzle region of a nozzle used in injection molding. **7.** The parallel parts of a gate. **8.** The bearing surface along the top of the flights of a screw in a plasticator. **9**. The surface of an extrusion die parallel to the direction of melt flow. **10.** ▷ **design mold** and **design die**

mold land area The whole of the area of contact, perpendicular to the direction of application of pressure of the seating faces of a mold; those faces which come in contact when the mold is closed.

mold land force A force with a shoulder which sits on land in a landed positive mold. Also called landed plunger.

mold latch Device to hold together two members of a mold, usually held together mechanically.

mold latch plate A plate used for retaining a removable mold core of relatively large diameter, or for holding insert-carrying pins on the upper part of a mold. Release of the pins or core is effected by moving the latch plate.

mold leader pin and bushing The mating mold components used to align and guide the two halves of the mold as it opens and closes in the machine. Hardened steel leader pins are also called guide pins. The pins fit closely into hardened steel bushings.

mold life and cost The Table below concerns reinforced plastic molding.

For any mold (injection, compression, blow, etc.), the term mold life refers to the number of acceptable piece parts that can be produced in a particular mold. There are molds that only have to produce a relatively few parts (tens of thousands) and others that go up to the millions. Mold life in large measure is determined by a combination of mold design, material used to make all the mold parts, mold fabrication and tolerances held, plastic to be processed, molding process used, and mold maintenance in the plant. Molds containing slides, wedges, and many moving parts generally have shorter production runs than molds with fewer compo-

Mold life and cost.

RP/C process	Approximate number of parts from mold (mold life)	Relative mold cost	Type of mold
Hand lay-up	800–1000	Lowest	RP/C
Spray-up	100–200	Lowest	RP/C
Vacuum-bag molding	100–200	Low	RP/C
Cold-press molding	150–200	Medium	RP/C
Casting, electrical	3500	High	Metal
Casting, marble	300–500+	Lowest	RP/C
Compression molding: BMC	120,000	High	Metal
Matched-die molding: SMC	300,000–400,000	Highest	Metal
Pressure-bag molding	Over 1,000,000	Medium	Metal
Centrifugal casting	Over 1,000,000	Low	Metal
Filament winding	Almost unlimited	Lowest	Metal
Pultrusion	Almost unlimited	Minimal	Metal
Continuous laminating	Almost unlimited	Minimal	Metal
Injection molding: reinforced thermoplastic (RTP)	300,000–1,000,000	Highest	Metal
Rotational molding	100,000	Low	Metal
Cold stamping	1,000,000–3,000,000	Highest	Metal

nents. High clamping and injection pressures, in addition to a wide range of temperature changes to which the mold is subjected, result in greater wear of moving parts. There are plastics used that are abrasive and shorten life. Often mold life is extended by replacement of the various components, regrinding, and repolishing, providing that it is possible to stay within the dimensional tolerances and finish requirements of the piece part. The best way to prolong mold life is through the proper operation and maintenance of the mold.

mold loading well The top area of a compression mold cavity, the size of which is dictated by the bulk factor of the molding compound. High bulk factor materials require deeper wells than do low types.

mold locating ring A ring that serves to align the nozzle of an injection cylinder with the entrance of the sprue bushing and the mold to the machine platen. Also called register ring.

mold locking force The force exerted in the locking mechanism of the machine which keeps the mold closed during injection.

mold locking mechanism A hydraulic cylinder or toggle mechanism which is designed to close the mold and keep it in the closed position during injection.

mold lubricant A substance applied on or into molds to eliminate or reduce friction or prevent adhesion. ▷ **lubrication for processing equipment**

mold maintenance ▷ **die maintenance; mold cleaner; mold life and cost**

mold, male ▷ **mold cavity, female**

mold manifold Configuration of piping in a block of metal that takes a single channel flow of melt from a machine (extruder, injection, etc.) and divides it into various flow channels to feed more than one outlet.

mold manifold heated A mold in which the portion of the mold (the manifold) that contains the runner system has its own heating elements, which keep the molding material in a melt state ready for injection into the cavities, from which the manifold is insulated.

mold manifold, nozzle A series of injection nozzles mounted on a common manifold, each nozzle positioned so as to feed a single cavity in the mold. Such manifolds are used to eliminate runners in molds such as cup shaped articles, when it is desired to gate the cavities at the centers of the bottoms.

mold manifold shut off valve A valve used to shut off plastic flow, usually mounted in a manifold.

mold manufacture, pantograph ▷ **pantographic engraving**

mold manufacturing time schedule The Fig. below provides a guide to the events that usually occur to produce a mold; number columns represent weeks.

mold material Different materials are used for mold construction with various grades of tool steel principally used in order to produce

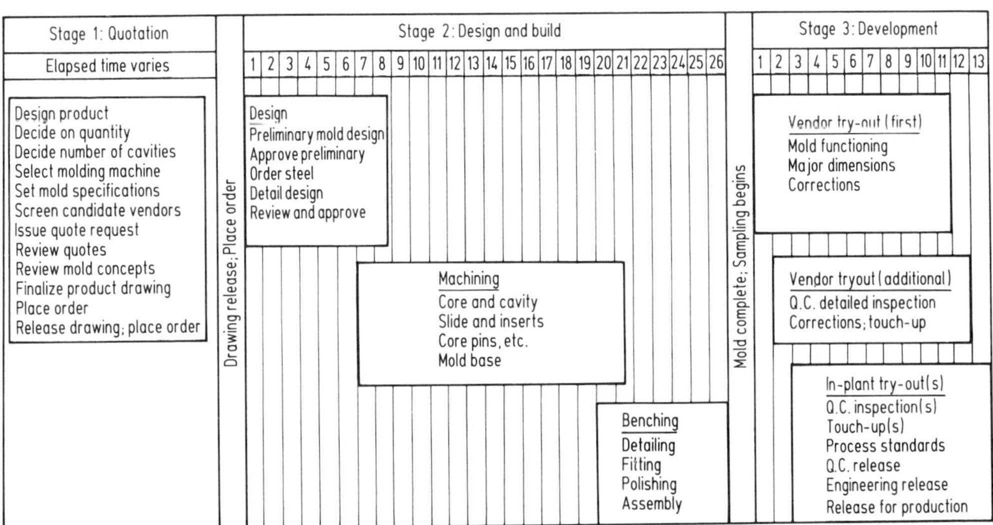

Time guide to produce a mold.

Example of mold materials.[1]

Type	AISI designation	Recommended hardness, Rockwell C	Wear resistance	Toughness	Compressive strength	Hot hardness	Corrosion resistance	Thermal conductivity	Hobbability	Machinability	Polishability	Heat treatability	Weldability	Nitriding ability
Prehardened	4130/ 41040	30–36	2	8	4	3	1	5	1	5	5	10	4	4
	P-20	30–36	2	9	4	3	2	5	1	5	8	10	4	5
Prehardened stainless	414 ss	30–35	3	9	4	3	7	2	1	4	9	10	4	6
	420 ss	30–35	3	9	4	3	6	2	1	4	9	10	4	7
Carburizing	P-5	59–61	8	6	6	5	2	3	9	10	7	6	9	8
	P-6	58–60	8	7	6	5	3	3	8	10	7	6	8	8
Oil hardening	01	58–62	8	3	9	5	1	5	5	8	8	7	2	3
	06	58–60	8	4	8	5	1	5	7	10	5	6	2	3
Air hardening	H-13	50–52	6	7	7	8	3	4	6	9	8	8	5	10
	S7	54–56	7	5	8	8	3	4	6	9	8	8	3	8
	A2	56–60	9	3	9	7	3	4	4	8	7	9	2	8
	A5	56–60	8	4	8	7	2	5	5	10	7	7	4	7
	A10	58–60	9	5	9	7	2	5	5	8	6	7	2	NA[2]
	D2	56–58	10	3	8	8	4	2	4	4	6	9	1	10
Stainless	420 ss	50–52	6	6	6	8	7	2	4	7	10	8	6	8
	440C ss	56–58	8	3	8	7	8	2	3	6	9	7	4	NA
Maraging	250	50–52	5	10	6	7	4	3	4	4	7	9	5	9
	350	52–54	6	10	7	7	4	3	4	4	7	9	5	9
Maraging stainless	455M	46–48	5	10	5	7	10	2	3	4	8	9	5	NA
High-speed	M2	60–62	10	2	10	10	3	3	2	4	6	8	2	10
	ASP	64–66	10	4	10	10	4	3	1	4	7	8	2	NA
Beryllium Copper	Be Cu	28–32	1–2	1	2	4	6	10	10	10	8–9	7	7	NA

[1] Point ratings: 1 to 10 (10 is highest). [2] NA = Not available.

quality molded products; tool steel has its own specific set of properties (see Table above). Molds for large parts are machined from a selection of steels, including AISI 1045 and 4140, as well as a special mold steel P20. Some molds, where slight surface porosity may not be of serious concern, can best be cast of other casting steels, with considerable cost savings over machining from steel billets. For medium to smaller molds, pre-hardened steels (32–35 Rockwell C) are a good choice. They cannot be freely machined and polished to a high finish. For small, high production molds, air hardening tool steels, easy to machine in the annealed state, are readily heat treated to 50–55 Rockwell C with a minimum of distortion. The plastic seal area should be hardened (see Fig. on p. 473). The principal material of construction for molds is steel, followed by beryllium copper alloy. Brass, aluminum, kirksite, and steel-filled epoxy are also used.

mold material, aluminum Aluminum is used in molds for different processes, particularly the production for blow, foam, and certain injection molds, as well as punching tools. Apart from the

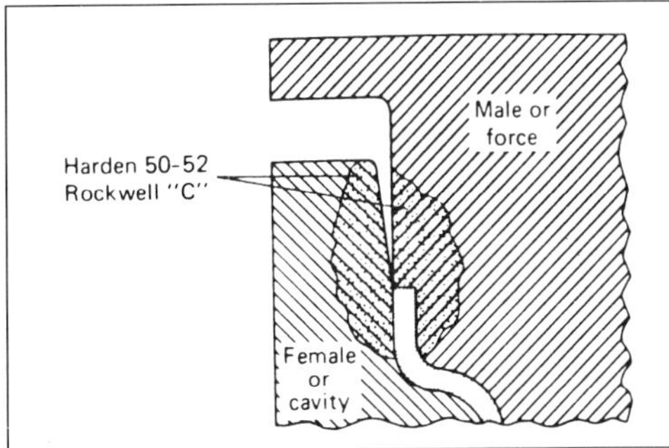

Example of mold hardening in the plastic seal area.

weight advantage of about 50% compared to steel, there are other advantages for its use in certain molds. However, most molds use steels with their overall advantages.

mold material and application The Table below lists a few applications with type of steel.

mold material and hardness The Table on p. 474 lists materials used in molds, arranged in order of hardness.

mold material and heat treatment The Fig. below shows anticipated range of size changes in heat treament of various mold steels.

mold material, beryllium copper There are two basic families of BeCu alloys; high strength alloys and high conductivity alloys. Both are available in wrought and cast forms. High conductivity type has a thermal conductivity that is

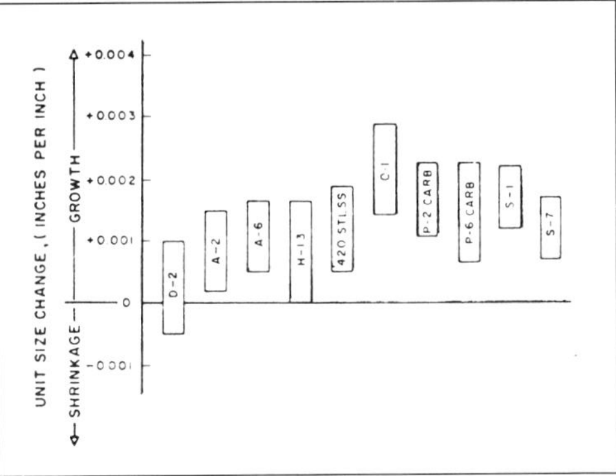

Influence of heat treatment of steels.

Steel and application.

Type of steel	Typical uses in injection molds
4130/4140	General mold base plates
P-20	High-grade mold base plates, hot-runner manifolds, large cavities and cores, gibs, slides, interlocks
4414 SS, 420 SS (prehardened)	Best grade mold base plates (no plating required), large cores, cavities and inserts
P5, P6	Hobbed cavities
01	Gibs, slides, wear plates
06	Gibs, slides, wear plates, stripper rings
H-13	Cavities, cores, inserts, ejector pins and sleeves (nitrided)
S7	Cavities, cores, inserts, stripper rings
A2	Small inserts in high-wear areas
A6	Cavities, cores, inserts for high-wear areas
A10	Excellent for high-wear areas, gibs, interlocks, wedges locks, wedges
D2	Cavities, cores, runner and gate inserts for abrasive plastics
420 SS	Best all-around cavity, core and insert steel; best polishability
440C SS	Small to medium-size cavities, cores, inserts, stripper rings
250, 350	Highest touchness for cavities, cores, small unsupported inserts
455M SS	High toughness for cavities, cores, inserts
M2	Small core pins, ejector pins, ejector blades (up to $\frac{5}{8}$ in. diam)
ASP 30	Best high-strength steel for tall, unsupported cores and core pins

Mold material and hardness.

Material class	Suitable for: Thermoplastics unfilled	Thermoplastics glass filled: Low pressure thermosets SMC, BMC	High pressure thermosets: phenolics, ureas, diallylls, melamines, alkyds	Prototype injection molds, TP resins	Structural foams	Casting of liquid resins	Blow molds	Vacuum forming sheets, TP resins
Carbides		●	●					
Steel, nitriding		●	●					
Steel, carburizing		●	●					
Steel, water hardening	●	●	●					
Steel, oil hardening	●	●	●				●	
Steel, air hardening	●	●	●				●	
Nickel, cobalt alloy	●						●	
Steel, prehardened 44 Rc	●						●	
Beryllium, copper	●						●	
Steel prehardened 28 Rc							●	
Aluminum bronze					●		●	
Steel low alloy & carbon				●	●		●	
Kirksite (zinc alloy)				●	●		●	●
Aluminum, alloy				●	●		●	●
Brass				●		●	●	●
Sprayed metal				●		●		●
Epoxy, metal filled						●		●
Silicone, rubber						●		

about 10 times greater than those of stainless steel and tool steels, double that of aluminum (such as Alloy 7075) and higher than others, and higher hardness and strength than aluminum or any copper alloy of equivalent conductivity, etc. When casting BeCu, the high strength alloys provide very accurate replication of fine detail. Well maintained wrought or cast molds provide a long life, typically 20 to 30 years in use.

mold material, blow mold ▷ **blow molding mold**

mold material, electroformed A mold is made by electroplating metal on the reverse pattern of the cavity. Molten steel may then be sprayed on the back of the mold to increase its strength. ▷ **electroplating**

mold material, flexible Molds made of elastomer plastics, such as silicone rubber, are generally used for prototype or short run production. These molds can be stretched to remove the part.

mold material, foam Low pressure structural foam parts can be molded in jig or cast aluminum (such as 6061-T651 or A356) and kirksite molds. Prototypes can be fabricated on metallized epoxy molds. Parts with complex geometries or those requiring special sliders, core pulls, or ejectors should be fabricated on steel molds. Higher pressure foams require conventional injection molding tool steels (P20, H13). Tool steels are also recommended for SF extrusion dies. ▷ **foamed, structural**

mold material, gravity casting Gravity casting is readily adaptable for injection molds. Any molds can be cast.

mold material, kirksite An alloy of aluminum and zinc used for the construction of molds, such as blow molds. It imparts a high degree of heat conductivity to the mold. Handling and working with kirksite is relatively simple.

mold material, nickel-cobalt alloy For the manufacture, by the electro-deposition process, of complicated mold cavities which would be difficult or impossible to produce by conventional methods.

mold material, reaction injection molding RIM molds may be constructed from epoxy, nickel aluminum, or steel, depending upon the expected life of the mold. They are designed to constrain a foaming pressure of about 30 to 50 psi (0.21 to 0.35 MPa). For molding to obtain a dense outer skin, it is important to use a temperature controlled metal mold.

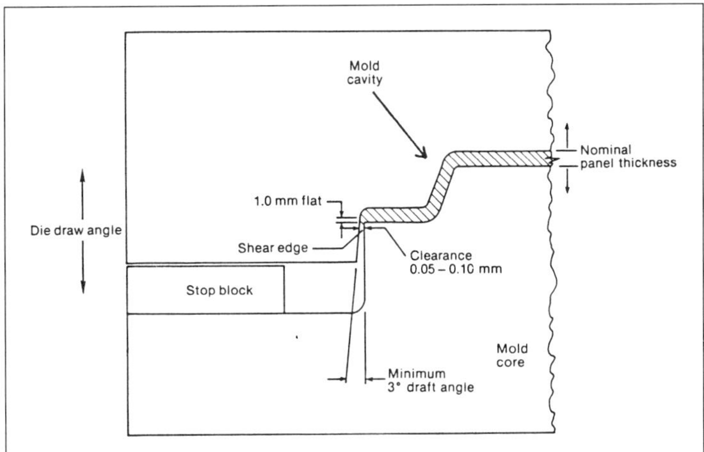

Schematic is an example of a closed mold for glass fiber reinforced plastic using a shear edge around the cavity periphery.

mold material, reinforced plastic See the Fig. above.

mold material sprayed metal Mold made by spraying molten metal onto a master until a shell of predetermined thickness is achieved. The shell is then removed and backed up with plaster, cement, casting plastic, or other suitable material. Used commonly as a mold in sheetforming processes.

mold material, steel Steels are the main building blocks for molds because of the performances that are required (see Table on p. 476). Tool steels for molds have the following characteristics: (1) *Machinability* Molds are usually formed by machining of steel blocks. The steel must possess good machinability. Machinability depends on the composition and structure of the steel as supplied. (2) *Ability to harden* In general, hardening of small molds or mold components does not present problems. However, hardening of large and complicated molds may cause deformation, dimensional variances or even cracks, if in the selection of the tool steel insufficient allowance was made for the hardening treatment, the machining techniques, and the dimensions of the mold components (size and shape). (3) *Ability to take a polish* The surface finish of the molding is first and foremost governed by the mold cavity finish. A cavity polished to a mirror finish produces a glossy molding surface and assists polymer flow in the mold. Polishing ability depends on the hardness, purity, and structure of the tool steel used. High-carbide steel grades are hard to polish to a mirror finish and thus require additional labor. (4) *Corrosion resistance* If corrosive plastics are processed, proper corrosion resistance of the mold steel is a must. Even the slightest corrosion of the mold cavity will interfere with mold release. When molds are not in use, protective, strippable coatings should be used to protect the steel from the humidity in the air.

mold material, texturing ▷ **texture**

mold maximum thickness ▷ **clamping daylight**

mold melt flow ▷ **mold cavity melt flow analysis**

mold model ▷ **modeling stereolithography**

mold, mounting dimensions The SPI Injection Molding Division provides a guideline bulletin that recommends interchangeable mold mounting dimensions for various size injection molding machines. It includes platen bolting patterns, tap hold threads, knockout pin locations, and machine size nozzle and locating rings.

mold, multicavity ▷ **mold cavity**

mold nozzle ▷ **mold manifold, nozzle**

mold nozzle gate ▷ **injection molding nozzle gate**

mold number or mark The number assigned to each mold or set of molds for identification purposes. The number is usually placed in an unobtrusive area such as that part of a container mold that forms the base of the container.

mold orifice groove Small groove used in molds to allow material to flow freely to prevent weld lines and low density, and dispose of excess material.

mold packing ▷ **mold cavity packing**

mold parallel to the draw The axis of the cored position (hole) or insert is parallel to the up and down movement of the mold as it opens and closes.

mold parting line A line established on a three-dimensional model from which a mold is

General characteristics of typical mold steels.

AISI type	Trade designation[1]	General characteristics	Properties rankings[2]				Typical applications
			Toughness	Dimensional stability in heat-treatment	Machinability (annealed)	Polishability (heat-treated)	
P-20	CSM-2	Medium carbon (0.30%) and chrome (1.65%). Available prehardened (300 Bn), or annealed(200 Bn).	10	7	9 (pre-hardened)	8 (pre-hardened)	Excellent balance of properties for injection and compression molds of any size.
H-13	NuDie V	Hot-work die steel; 5% chrome. Hardenable to about 50 Rc.	9	8	9	9	Higher hardness than P-20; good toughness and polishability. Used for abrasion resistance in RP molds and high-finish injection molds.
A-2	Air Kool	Cold-work die steel, high carbon (1.0%) 5% chrome. Hardenable to about 60 Rc.	8	9	8	7	High hardness for abrasion-resistant, long-wearing compression and injection mold. Limited to small sizes.
D-2	Airdi 150	Cold-work die steel; high carbon (1.55%) 11.5% chrome. Hardenable to about 60 Rc.	7	9	5	6	Highest abrasion resistance. Difficult to machine. Susceptible to stress cracking. Small molds only.
414	CSM 414	Stainless steel; 12% chrome, 2% Ni, 1% Mn, low carbon (0.03%). Available pre-hardened (300 Bn).	10	10	9	9	"Stainless version" of P-20; similar properties and uses.
420	CSM 420	Stainless steel; 13% chrome 0.08% Mn, medium carbon (0.30%). Hardenable to about 50 Rc.	9	10	8	10	"Stainless version" of H-13; similar properties and uses. Very stable in heat treatment, takes high polish.
4145	Holder Block	Medium carbon (0.50%) and chrome (0.65%). Available prehardened.	10	10 (pre-hardened)	10 (pre-hardened)	6 (pre-hardened) 7 (fully hardened)	Low cost steel, for mold bases and large molds. Not suited to high quality finish.

[1] Crucible steel designations
[2] On scale of 1 to 10 (10 = best)

to be prepared, to indicate where the mold is to be split into two halves (sections) or several components.

mold, parting line control process ▷ **injection molding processing parting line control**

mold pattern ▷ **pantographic engraving**

mold pillar support The general construction of a mold base usually incorporates the U-shaped ejection housing. If the span betwen the arms of the U is long enough, the forces of molding can cause a sizable deflection in the plates that are supported by the ejector housing. Such a deflection will cause flashing of parts. To overcome this problem, the span between supports is reduced by placing pillar supports at certain spacings so that deflection is eliminated or negligible.

mold pin **1.** Mold dowel pin. **2.** Mold ejector pin. **3.** Mold leader pin. **4.** Mold return pin. **5.** Mold side draw pin. **6.** Mold sprue draw pin.

mold plate-out ▷ **plate-out**

mold polishing Polishing of mold (and die) surfaces is one of the more important phases of mold (die) construction. Although polishing can and does take place during various periods of mold (die) construction, the final finish given to the mold surface generally determines the finish obtained on the molded part. Part surfaces that are visible, or surfaces that will be plated, generally require a rather high polish. The surface finish obtained on the part not only depends on the polishing, but also is determined by the characteristics of the plastic. The surface polish can vary from one finished with a 120 grit emery disc to a very high polish with an 8,000 grit diamond abrasive. The surface finish given to molds varies from a 320 grit stone to a diamond finish. A diamond finish is provided on thc majority of injection, compression, and transfer molds.

Most polishing is done by bench polishers, who employ a wide range of skills to obtain the necessary and desired results. The tools used and the techniques employed vary from shop to shop, as do skills possessed by the individual polishers. Some of the tools and equipment used are any number of files of various shapes and cuts, a large assortment of stones of different grits and shape, various grits of emery cloth, a range of diamond abrasives, wooden dowels, flexible shaft grinders, portable hand grinders, bristle brushes, felt buffing wheels, lubricants, etc. There is always a difference of opinion among polishers as to the methods and procedures to be followed to obtain a particular finish; however, the final results are always the same. For example, if a diamond finish is required, there may be a difference in the intermediate steps, but the final diamond finish is the same.

A common defect is "orange-peel", a wavy effect that results when the metal is stretched beyond its yield point by over-polishing and takes a permanent set. Attempts to improve this situation by further vigorous polishing only make matters worse; eventually the small particles will break away from the surface. The more complicated the mold, the greater the problem. Hard carburized or nitrided surfaces are much less prone to the problem. Orange-peel results from exceeding the yield point of the steel. The harder the steel, the higher the yield point and therefore the less chance of orange-peel.

The surest way to avoid this problem is to polish by hand. With powered polishing equipment, it is easier to exceed the yield point of the metal. If power polishing is done, use light passes to avoid overstressing. Orange-peel surfaces usually can be salvaged. Remove the defective surface with a fine grit stone, stress-relieve the mold, re-stone, and diamond polish. If problem recurs after this treatment, increase the surface hardness by nitriding with a case depth of no more than 0.005 in. (0.13 mm), and repolish the surface.

A large part of mold cost is polishing cost, which can represent from 5 to 30% of the mold cost. Recognize that an experienced polisher can polish from 2 to 5 $in.^2/h$ (13 to 32 cm^2/h). Certain shops can at least double this rate if they have the proper equipment. Polishing is rarely done for appearance alone. It is done to get a desired surface effect on the part, to facilitate the ejection of the part from a mold, or to prepare the mold for another operation such as etching or plating. If a part is to be plated, it is important to remember that plating does not hide any flaws, it accentuates them. Therefore, on critical plated molds, the mold polish must be better than for nonplated parts.

Another purpose of polishing is to remove the weak top layer of metal. It may be weak from the stresses induced by machining or from the annealing effect of the heat generated in cutting. When it is not removed, this layer very often breaks down, showing a pitted surface that looks corroded.

The techniques used to get a good and fast polish are basically simple, but they must be followed carefully to avoid problems. The first rule is to have the part as smooth as possible before polishing. If electrical-discharge machining is used, the final pass should be made with a new electrode at the lowest amperage. If the part is cast or hobbed, the master should have a finish with half the roughness of the desired mold finish.

When the mold is machined, the last cut should be made at twice the normal speed, at the slowest automatic feed, and at a depth of 0.001 in. (0.025 mm). No lubricant should be used in this last machining, but the cutting tool should be freshly sharpened, and the edges should be honed after sharpening. The clearance angle of the tool should be from 6 to 9 degrees, and if a milling cutter or reamer is used, it should have a minimum of four flutes. A steady stream of dry air must be aimed at the cutting tool to move the chips away from the cutting edge.

Polishing a mold begins when the designer puts the finishing information on the drawing. Such terms as "mirror finish" and "high polish" are ambiguous. The only meaningful way is to use an accepted standard to describe what has to be polished and to what level. It is also important that the designer specify a level of polish no higher than is actually needed if one desires to reduce mold cost.

mold, porous Molds that are made up of bonded or fused aggregate (powdered metal, coarse pellets, etc.) such that the resulting mass contains numerous open interstices of regular or irregular size allowing either air or liquids to pass through the mass of the mold. Used in different processes, particularly thermoforming.

mold, positive **1.** Mold designed to trap all the molding material when it closes. **2.** A projecting mold over which the part is thermoformed. This type is often referred to as a male mold. **3.** A compression mold designed with vertical shut-off.

mold pot **1.** To embed a component or assembly in liquid plastic, using a shell, can, or case that remains an integral part of the product after the plastic is cured. **2.** Chamber to hold and heat molding material for a transfer mold.

mold pot plunger A plunger used to force softened molding material into the closed cavity of a transfer mold.

mold, pre-engineered Standardized mold components, such as ejector pins, guide pins, bolts, etc., and complete standardized mold assemblies have been commercially available since 1943. Advantages include: exceptional quality control on materials used, low cost, quick delivery, interchangeability, and promotion of standardization.

mold pressure pad Reinforcements of hardened steel distributed around the dead area in the faces of a mold to help the mold land absorb the final pressure of closing without collapsing.

mold process control As explained in ▷**design mold,** different controls are required as shown in the Fig. below. ▷**injection molding process control** and **process control**

mold production and handling Different standards and practices of plastic molders are reviewed in the SPI Molders Division Guide bulletin. It includes the following: (1) mold maintenance, repair, and/or replacement, (2) molds on consignment, (3) mold drawing, (4) mold usage, (5) mold storage, (6) mold removal, and (7) amortization and insurance.

mold protection A tool that has received all the necessary attention and care from the designer and mold maker should be handled with extreme care so that the expanded effort is fully protected and provides safety of operation. Any protruding parts should be protected against damage in transfer. The mold surfaces, especially cavities and cores, should be covered with

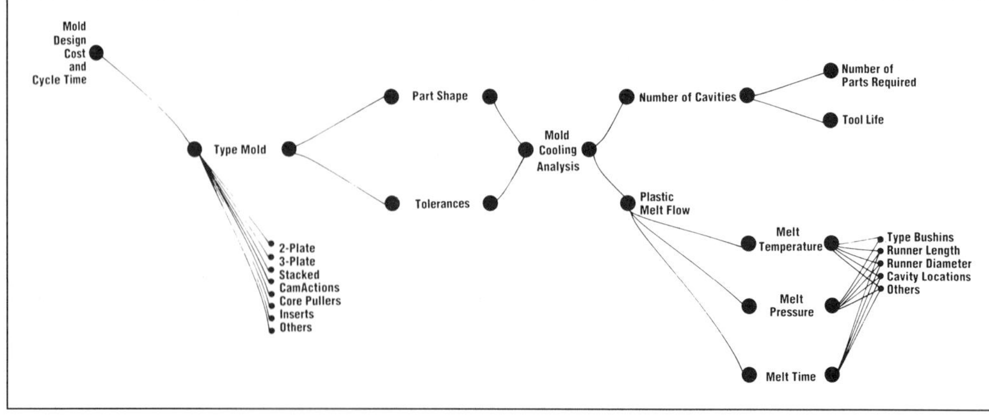

Mold process controls.

THE MOLDMAKERS DIVISION
THE SOCIETY OF THE PLASTICS INDUSTRY, INC.
3150 Des Plaines Avenue (River Road), Des Plaines, Ill. 60018, Telephone: 312/297-6150

TO ______ FROM ______ QUOTE NO. ______
DATE ______
DELIVERY REQ ______

Gentlemen:
Please submit your quotation for a mold as per following specifications and drawings:

COMPANY NAME ______
Name of Part/s 1. ______ B/P No. ______ Rev. No. ______ No. Cav. ______
2. ______ B/P No. ______ Rev. No. ______ No. Cav. ______
3. ______ B/P No. ______ Rev. No. ______ No. Cav. ______

No. of Cavities: ______ **Design Charges:** ______ **Price:** ______ **Delivery:** ______

Type of Mold: ☐ Injection ☐ Compression ☐ Transfer ☐ Other (specify) ______

Mold Construction
☐ Standard
☐ 3 Plate
☐ Stripper
☐ Hot Runner
☐ Insulated Runner
☐ Other (Specify) ______

Mold Base Steel
☐ #1
☐ #2
☐ #3

Special Features
☐ Leader Pins & Bushings in K.O. Bar
☐ Spring Loaded K.O. Bar
☐ Inserts Molded in Place
☐ Spring Loaded Plate
☐ Knockout Bar on Stationary Side
☐ Accelerated K.O.
☐ Positive K.O. Return
☐ Hyd. Operated K.O. Bar
☐ Parting Line Locks
☐ Double Ejection
☐ Other (Specify) ______

Material

Cavities	Cores
☐ Tool Steel	☐
☐ Beryl. Copper	☐
☐ Steel Sinkings	☐
☐ Other (Specify) ______	

Press
Clamp Tons ______
Make/Model ______

Hardness

Cavities	Cores
☐ Hardened	☐
☐ Pre-Hard	☐
☐ Other (Specify) ______	

Ejection

Cavities	Cores
☐ K.O. Pins	☐
☐ Blade K.O.	☐
☐ Sleeve	☐
☐ Stripper	☐
☐ Air	☐
☐ Special Lifts	☐
☐ Unscrewing (Auto)	☐
☐ Removable Inserts (Hand)	☐
☐ Other (Specify) ______	

Finish

Cavities	Cores
☐ SPE/SPI	☐
☐ Mach. Finish	☐
☐ Chrome Plate	☐
☐ Texture	☐
☐ Other (Specify) ______	

Side Action

Cavities	Cores
☐ Angle Pin	☐
☐ Hydraulic Cyl.	☐
☐ Air Cyl.	☐
☐ Positive Lock	☐
☐ Cam	☐
☐ K.O. Activated Spring Ld.	☐
☐ Other (Specify) ______	☐

Cooling

Cavities	Core
☐ Inserts	☐
☐ Retainer Plates	☐
☐ Other Plates	☐
☐ Bubblers	☐
☐ Other (Specify) ______	

Type of Gate
☐ Edge
☐ Center Sprue
☐ Sub-Gate
☐ Pin Point
☐ Other (Specify) ______

Design by: ☐ Moldmaker ☐ Customer
Type of Design: ☐ Detailed Design ☐ Layout Only
Limit Switches: ☐ Supplied by ______ ☐ Mounted by Moldmaker
Engraving: ☐ Yes ☐ No
Approximate Mold Size: ______
Heaters Supplied By: ☐ Moldmaker ☐ Customer
Duplicating Casts By: ☐ Moldmaker ☐ Customer
Mold Function Try-Out By: ☐ Moldmaker ☐ Customer
Tooling Model/s or Master/s By: ☐ Moldmaker ☐ Customer
Try-Out Material Supplied By: ☐ Moldmaker ☐ Customer

Terms subject to Purchase Agreement. This quotation holds for 30 days.

Special Instructions: ______

The prices quoted are on the basis of piece part print, models or designs submitted or supplied. Should there be any change in the final design, prices are subject to change.

By ______ Title ______

Distribution: Use of this 3 part form is recommended as follows: 1) White and yellow - sent with request to quote. Pink - maintained in active file. 2) White original - returned with quotation. Yellow - retained in Moldmaker's active file.

Mold quotation guide.

a protective coating against surface corrosion. The coating should be easily removed before molding.

The protection of mold surface applies equally to the time after a run, when the mold is ready to be removed from the press and to be stored for the next run. In some areas where the atmosphere is highly corrosive, the mold must be protected while in the press for anticipated operation. This is especially important over a long holiday weekend. Commercial coatings are available for this purpose; prior to use however, they should be carefully evaluated for their ability to protect the area involved. Also vacuum containers can be used after molds are properly dried. ▷**mold cavity, plating, coating, and heat treatment**

mold prototype ▷**prototype mold**

mold quotation guide The Fig. above is a guide for mold quotation prepared by the Moldmakers Division of SPI.

mold, re-entrant A mold containing an undercut which tends to resist withdrawal of the molded part.

mold release agent ▷**release agent**

mold release methods There are different release methods such as those listed in the Table on p. 480.

mold restrictor ring A ring-shaped part protruding from the torpedo surface which provides increase of pressure in the mold to improve welding of two melt streams.

mold retainer pin 1. A pin on which an insert is placed in the mold and located prior to molding. **2.** Pins that return the ejector mechanism to molding position.

Mold release methods.

Type	Form	Use
Wax	Paste or liquid (carnuba)	High luster Good detail transfer Multiple runs
PVA	Liquid (usually sprayed)	Water-soluble One-time use Wash off part and mold Excellent release Provides paintable surface
Fluorocarbons silanes and silicones	Liquid or spray	Low coefficient of friction Not very high gloss More expensive
Release papers and release films	Coated paper Cellophane PVA film	One-offs Flat sheet molding
Internal Releases	Liquid (mixed into gel coat)	High luster Good detail transfer Eliminates need for mold waxing Provides paintable surface

mold retainer plate The plate on which demountable pieces, such as mold cavities, ejector pins, guide pins, and bushings are mounted during molding; usually drilled for water or steam.

mold retainer plate nest A retainer plate with a depressed area for cavity blocks used in injection molding.

mold ring ▷ **mold locating ring**

mold rod guide Rods which guide the platens but take no clamp force.

mold, rotational process Molds are manufactured from electroformed nickel, vapor deposited nickel, and cast aluminum. The thickness of the molded parts is controlled by heat sinks fabricated into the tool. The tool must be temperature controlled so it will cure the plastic within it.

mold, rotational process, spherical diameter Distance as a straight line passing though the center of rotation on an angle 45°, from vertical or horizontal to the extremities of the area available for mold swing.

mold runner A groove or channel varying in size, shape, and depth, through which the melt flows to the cavity(s); the channel that connects the sprue to the gate. The term runner system is sometimes applied to all the material in the form of sprues, runners, and gates between the machine nozzle and cavity(s). As shown in the Figs. reviewed in ▷ **design mold,** there are different types of runners. The most popular are cold runners and hot runners used with thermoplastic and thermoset plastics; others include insulated and stacked. With TP, cold runner results in the runner solidifying when the part(s) solidifies, and in the hot runner, its melt remains as a melt without solidifying. TS plastic has a reversal situation where with hot runner the melt in the runner solidifies. With cold runner it remains as a melt. The TP and TS systems are reviewed. ▷ **thermoplastic** and **thermoset plastic**

mold runner, balanced Exists in a multicavity mold when the linear distances of the melt flow from the sprue through the runner network to the gate of each individual cavity are of equal length.

mold runner, cold for thermoplastic Mold in which the sprue, runner(s), and gate(s) of the TP melt, as the melt in the cavity(s), all solidify by the cooling action of the mold. This mold design produces solidified sprue and runner(s) that are usually granulated and recycled.

mold runner, cold for thermoset Provides for injection directly into the cavity(s) from the gate. The runner manifold section is cooled to maintain plastic in a melt stage. The cavity and core plates are heated (to solidify plastic) to normal molding temperature and insulated from the cooler manifold section. This mold design eliminates TS scrap loss from sprue and runner(s) similar to the action in a hot runner system for thermoplastics.

mold runner, hot for thermoplastic Mold in which the sprue and runner(s) are insulated from the chilled cavities and remain hot so that the runner never cools in normal cycle operation. Runners are not ejected with the molded part(s). An insulated runner is a type of hot runner mold. Thus, the next shot is from the gate rather than the machine nozzle.

mold runner, hot for thermoset Mold in which the sprue, runner(s), and gate(s) of the TS melt, as the melt in the cavity(s), all solidify by the heating action of the mold. This mold design produces solidified sprue and runner(s) that can be granulated and recycled at least as plastic filler.

mold runner, insulated Mold has oversized runner passages formed in a conventional cold runner for thermoplastic. The passages in the mold plate are of sufficient size that, under conditions of operation, the insulating effect of the plastic combined with the heat applied with each shot maintains an open path. Runner insulation is provided by a layer of chilled plastic that forms on the runner wall.

mold runner, internal A hidden flow channel to facilitate the filling of a part.

mold, runnerless injection molding Identifies a mold for thermoplastic ▷**mold runner, hot for thermoplastic.** Also identifies a mold for thermoset plastic ▷**mold runner, cold for thermoset**. ▷**mold, sprueless**

mold runner, unbalanced Differs from balanced runner system in a multicavity mold; distances from the sprue through runners are different.

mold seam A line formed by mold construction such as removable members in a cavity, cam slides, etc. The prominence of the line depends on the accuracy with which the mating parts are matched. Usually the line formed by the mold halves is called the mold parting line.

mold, semiautomatic ▷**mold classification by operation**

mold, semipositive As the two halves of a semipositive thermoset compression mold begin to close, the mold acts much like a flash mold. The excess material is allowed to escape around the loose-fitted plunger and cavity. As the plunger telescopes further into the cavity, the mold becomes a positive mold with very little clearance, and full pressure is exerted on the material, producing a part of maximum density. This type of mold uses to advantage the free flow of material in a flash mold and the capability of producing dense parts in a positive mold. ▷**compression molding**

mold, shell tooling ▷**shell molding**

mold shrinkage Refers not to the shrinkage of the mold, but the shrinkage that a molded part undergoes when it is removed from a mold and cooled to room temperature (molded part shrinkage would be a more appropriate phrase to use rather than the usual mold shrinkage phrase used).

mold, shuttle ▷**clamping, shuttle**

mold, siamese blow A colloquial term applied to the technique of blow molding two or more parts of a product in a single blow and then cutting them apart. Multiple cavities are used. ▷**blow molding, extruder mold multiple/combination cavities**

mold side bar Loose pieces used to carry one ot more molding pins, and operated from outside the mold.

mold side coring Projections that are used to core a hole in a direction other than the line of closing of a mold, and that must be withdrawn before the part is ejected from the mold. Also called side draw pin and side action mold. The Fig. on p. 482 shows a cam pin action; it could have other mechanisms such as a hydraulic cylinder. This Figure also shows a puller pin for producing a sprue with a hollow section.

mold size requirements ▷**injection molding clamping tonnage (force)**

mold snap fit ▷**design snap fit**

mold spacer, insulated Insulator sheets placed between mold and platens to restrict heat transfer from mold to platens.

mold spacer, parallel 1. The parallel support spacers placed between the mold and press plate or clamping plate. Also called risers. They take up space to allow a mold that is not wide (short height distance) enough to meet the machine minimum daylight opening. **2.** Spacer(s) placed between the hot plate and press platen to prevent the middle section of the mold from bending under pressure. **3.** Pressure pads or spacers between the hot plates of a mold to control height when closed and to prevent crushing the parts of the mold when land area is inadequate.

mold, split-ring A mold in which a split cavity block is assembled in a chase to permit the forming of undercuts in a molded piece. These

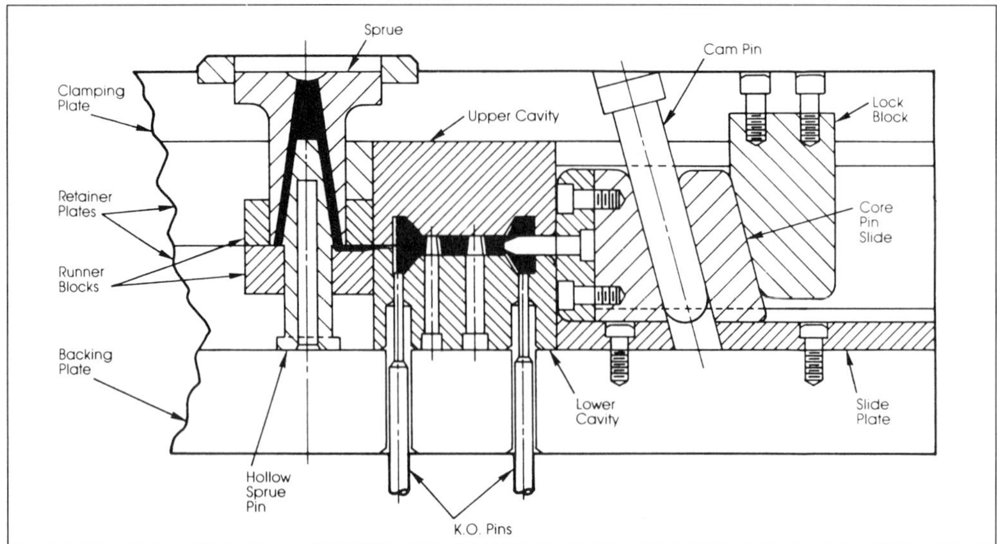

Mold includes side core action.

parts are ejected from the mold and then separated from the molded piece. Also called split mold.

mold, spring box A type of compression mold equipped with a spacing fork which prevents the loss of bottom-loaded inserts or fine details, and which is removed after partial compression.

mold sprue A tapered orifice in an injection or transfer mold through which plastic melt flows from the nozzle to the parting line, molded piece, or runner. The name sprue is also used to identify the plastic formed in this orifice.

mold, sprue break ▷ **injection molding sprue break**

mold sprue bushing A hardened steel insert in an injection mold which contains the tapered sprue hole and has a suitable seat for the nozzle of the injection cylinder. Sometimes called an adapter.

mold sprue bushing heated Mold element that contains a heating element to keep the plastic melt hot within the bushing. The bushing is inserted into the mold to provide a hot channel between the molding machine's nozzle and the mold cavity. As with nozzle thermocouple temperature profile, the temperature profile in a heated sprue is a prerequisite for accurate closed-loop temperature control with thermoplastics and thermosets, particularly TP. ▷ **mold heat transfer device**

mold sprue ejector pin When the undercut occurs on the cavity block retainer plate, this pin is called the sprue ejector pin.

mold sprue gate A passageway through which melt flows from the nozzle of a molding machine to the cavity.

mold sprue, hollow bushing See Fig. above and ▷ **mold side coring**

mold, sprueless Mold design in which the sprue and runner system is insulated from the mold. ▷ **mold runner, cold for thermoset** and **mold runner, hot for thermoplastic**

mold sprue lock or puller In injection molding thermoplastics, a portion of the melt which is held in the cold slug well by an undercut; used to pull the sprue out of the bushing as the mold is opened. The sprue lock itself is pushed out of the mold by an ejector pin. When the undercut occurs on the cavity block retainer plate, this pin is called the sprue ejector pin.

mold sprue puller A slotted pin used to remove a sprue from a sprue bushing.

mold, stack Two level mold, two sets of cavities stacked one above the other, for molding more parts per cycle. Also called three-plate mold since a third or intermediate movable plate is used to make possible center or offset gating of each cavity(s) on the two levels as shown in the Fig. on p. 483.

mold, stacked four level Four-face stack mold, capable of molding parts on four levels.

mold, steam plate Mounting plate for com-

Stack mold or three plate mold.

pression thermoset molds, cored for circulation of steam.

mold stop Metal parts inserted between mold halves used to control the thickness of a press-molded part. Not a recommended practice because the plastic will receive less pressure, which can result in lower density and voids in the part.

mold strength requirements The forces involved with the molding operation are compressive; they are exerted by the clamping ram and the internal melt pressure. Forces exist inside the cavity(s) as a result of injecting the plastic material under pressure. ▷ **injection molding clamping tonnage (force)**

mold stripper plate A plate that strips a molded piece from core pins or force plugs. The stripper plate is set into operation by the opening of the mold.

mold temperature The final mold temperature is usually a byproduct of gate size and the processor's desire to attain short cycles. The smaller the gate, the higher the melt temperature must be in order to get melt through the gate. Therefore, the mold temperature is usually set low to quickly remove the heat from the melt and thus achieve short cycles. However, the colder the mold is, the quicker the plastic that first contacts the mold sets up (hardens). To prevent a part from cooling before the injection cycle has been completed, higher injection speeds and pressures are generally used.

mold texturing ▷ **texture**

mold thickness There are minimum and maximum heights or thicknesses of a mold which can be accommodated by the clamp end. Of the two figures, the maximum is more critical in case there is not sufficient machine clamping daylight opening. If the mold minimum thickness is less than the minimum daylight opening, spacer blocks are used to make up the difference. ▷ **clamping daylight** and **mold height**

mold thread plug, ring, or core A part of a mold that shapes a thread and must be unscrewed from the finished piece to eliminate parting lines across the threads; with a split mold parting lines exist.

mold three plate system ▷ **mold, stack**

mold, two-up ▷ **blow molding, extruder mold multiple/combination cavities**

mold types The mold is identified descriptively by a combination of terms such as the following: injection molding, compression molding, blow molding, reaction injection molding, rotational molding, and mold construction as described in Fig. shown for ▷ **design mold**

mold unit Mold designed for quick changing interchangeable cavity parts.

mold variables Variations in mold conditions have a direct effect on part quality. Important factors are: mold temperature, mold venting, mold closing speed, mold surface condition (wear or damage), and mold accessories (core slides, neck inserts, etc.). The production of defective parts can be greatly reduced by recognizing the interrelationships of process and material variations as well as properly analyzing problems to provide timely, accurate solutions. ▷ **process control** and **FALLO approach**

mold venting In a mold, basically a shallow channel or minute hole cut in the cavity to allow air and other gases to escape as the material enters. Also called breather. With respect to injection molding the air present in the mold cavity must be allowed to escape during injection (see Fig. on p. 484). At high injection speeds, insufficient mold venting may produce a compression of air, with consequent slow mold filling, premature plastic pressure build-up, and, in extreme cases, burning of the plastic (brown streaks on the molding). Venting is done by small gaps or vents provided in the mold parting lines, or by other small channels in the mold, e.g., around ejector pins, cores, vacuum water cooling, etc. Vents must be provided at the end of the flow path(s). A center-gated mold cavity, for instance, must be vented all around, whereas in an edge-gated cavity, the vents must be provided at the cavity end or at the point where the flow path is expected to end. In gate design and even in part design, allowance should be made for mold venting. Direct vacuum venting of molds has not yet

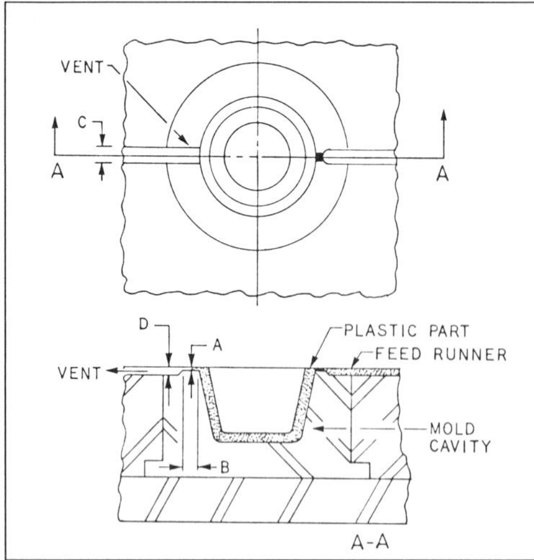

Example of a method of venting thermoplastic injection molds. For most thermoplastics except Nylon and Acetal: A = 0.003 in.; B = 0.125 in.; C = 0.500 in.; D = 0.010 in. For Nylon, Acetal and PET: A = 0.0015 in.; B = 0.125 in.; C = 0.500 in.; D = 0.010 in.

found widespread acceptance in injection molding of thermoplastics. However, view of the present trend towards higher injection speeds, it is most probable that in the future, vacuum molds will be in general use to prevent venting problems. There are molders that use the direction venting system to speed up production, improve quality of parts, etc.

With thermoset plastic, usually gases are formed as the chemical reaction takes place during its cure. Thus, in processes such as compression and transfer molding, provisions are made to remove the gases or poor parts will be the result. One method for removal is to allow the mold to breathe, that is, the mold is closed and then opened again for about 0.125 in. (3.2 mm) to permit gases to escape, and then closed again. Other methods follow the procedure reviewed above in using vent holes or flats. Combinations of these methods are used.

mold venting holes The holes in a thermoforming mold through which the pressurized or vacuum air passes as the plastic sheet or film is forced against the mold.

mold venting, water transfer This technique is based on negative pressure coolant technology. Mold coolant is being pulled, not the more conventional way of being pushed, though the coolant system producing a negative pressure in the coolant system. An easy way to vent into the water is though ejector pins. It requires that the ejector pin(s) run through the waterline. The molding gases vent into the coolant rather than into the atmosphere. Coolant does not leak into the cavity because it is under atmospheric pressure. Porous metal provides another means of venting to the coolant providing a rather large venting area. It can be used at the base of deep cores where gases could be trapped in the adjacent cavity. The water transfer process was designed originally to cool long, thin cores, such as those for pen barrels that have a hole in either end. This technique has been applied many different ways, including molding with a cracked cavity that extends into the coolant.

mold well ▷ **mold, cold slug**

mold width, maximum size ▷ **clamping tie rod distance**

mold wiper In injection molding, a device which enters between the opened mold halves during the ejection cycle, engages the molded piece, and lifts or shoves it from the mold. The wiper movement is interlocked with the mold closing mechanism to prevent closing of the mold until the wiper is retracted.

mole **1.** The molecular weight of a substance in grams. **2.** It is the amount of substance of a system which contains as many elementary entities as there are atoms in 0.012 kg of carbon-12 (adopted by 14th CGPM 1971).

molecular arrangement structure The size and flexibility of the polymer molecule explains how an individual molecule would behave if it were completely isolated from its neighbors. Such isolated molecules are encountered only in theoretical studies on dilute solutions. In actual practice, polymer molecules always occur in a mass, and the behavior of each individual molecule is very greatly affected by its relationship to adjacent polymer molecules in the mass. These intermolecular relationships between adjacent molecules may be divided into two groups: intermolecular order which describes the geometrical arrangement of adjacent molecules in space, and intermolecular bonding which describes the attractive forces between adjacent molecules in the polymeric mass. Together these two relationships modify the simple effects of molecular size and flexibility, and determine the overall behavior of homogeneous plastic materials.

In regard to intermolecular order for thermoplastics, polymer science recognizes three distinctly different states of order, namely amorphous, crystalline, and oriented. When molecules are arranged in completely random, intertwined coils, this completely unordered structure is known as *amorphous* state. When they are neatly arranged so that each of their atoms falls into a precise position in a tight-packed repeating regular structure, this highly ordered structure is described as the *crystalline* state. When molecules are stretched into a rather linear conformation and lie fairly parallel to each other in the mass, this partially ordered structure is described as the *oriented* state.

In practice, some polymers are completely amorphous, others are partly amorphous and partly crystalline, others are partly amorphous and oriented, and still others are partly amorphous, crystalline, and oriented. Each of these basic states has very distinctive effects upon plastics properties, and plastics which contain combinations of these states show their combined effects.

Because of the different molecular geometries, some come closer together than others in which the structure prevents more intimate contact. The structural obstruction to close approach is called steric hindrance. Thus, polymers which can be packed closely or exhibit steric hindrance can ordinarily more easily form crystalline structures. Others, such as polymers which are crosslinked prior to crystallization, are prohibited from aligning themselves in crystals due to the hindrance created by the multiple interconnections and hence tend to be amorphous, or noncrystalline.

When the individual molecules are looked at in terms of how they interact and attract with other molecules, some revealing observations can be drawn. The forces that hold molecules together in the solid state are weaker than the forces that bond the individual atoms together in the molecular structure. These intermolecular forces include van der Waals forces, dipole attractions, and hydrogen bonds. These forces, if high enough, can cause a polymer with a regular structure to crystallize.

Most plastic properties depend largely upon the behavior just reviewed of the individual molecule. There is also the modifying effects of larger structural features. Molecular size and shape includes molecular weight, molecular weight distribution, and branching resulting from intra- or intermolecular chain transfer reactions during polymerizations. Molecular flexibility describes the ability of individual polymer molecules to coil and uncoil in response to external and internal forces, and is determined primarily by freedom or restriction of rotation around the interatomic bonds in the main-chain of the polymer molecule. ▷ **amorphous plastic; crystalline plastic; crosslinking; orientation; microstructure**

molecular basic properties effect on product properties Three basic molecular properties of density, average molecular weight, and molecular weight distribution affect most of the mechanical and thermal properties essential for processing plastics and obtaining required performance of fabricated parts. Small variations in these basics may improve or impair some of these properties considerably. In general, increasing the MW will increase the plastics' tensile and compressive strength (see Fig. below). Similarly, copolymerization and alloying can improve mechanical properties. In some instances, alloys or composite polymers contain a weaker polymer, which has an adverse effect on mechanical properties, but it may be used to increase lubricity or frictional characteristics. The addition of fluorocarbons to various polymers is an example of an alloying agent used for this purpose ▷ **alloy/blend**. The most common factor providing for high strengths and rigidity in plastics is bonding between polymer chains. The simplest thermoplastics have a linear structure. There is a two dimensional array of polymer chain behaving like a chain. That is, there is little breadth of the chain, but significant length. Some properties such as melt processability, hot strength, and solvent resistance depend upon molecular disentanglement, and change continuously with MW up to infinity.

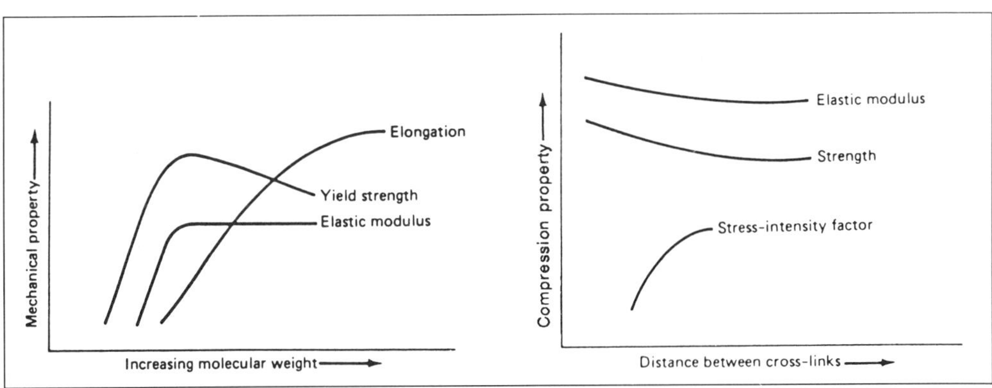

Example of mechanical properties vs. molecular weight and effect of distance between crosslink sites.

The arrangement of the molecules within a structure in many cases are relatively sensitive to temperature. Thus, the structure of any given polymer can be significantly changed by exposure to temperatures and thermal treatments. For example, heating a crystalline-type polymer above its melting point and then quenching it can produce a polymer that is far more amorphous or noncrystalline in structure than the original polymeric sample. Such a quenched material can have properties that are significantly different from the properties of a sample that is cooled slowly and allowed to re-crystallize.

The effects of time on a polymer structure are similar to those of temperature in the sense that any given polymer has a "most preferred" or equilibrium structure in which it would prefer to arrange itself but is prevented from doing so instantaneously on short notice by steric hindrances. However, given enough time, the molecules in a polymer ultimately migrate to arrange themselves in this form. Elevating the temperature and making the molecules more mobile or spreading them apart allows them to accomplish this in a shorter time and vice versa. Thus over an extended period of time, the properties of a polymer can become significantly different from those measured earlier if the structure of the polymer was in an unstable form when the properties were initially evaluated. ▷**modulus versus temperature**

molecular behavior ▷**Boltzmann superposition principle**

molecular bonding Entanglement of amorphous random coils, parallel bundles of oriented molecules, and even neat tight packing in crystallites are not enough to explain the remarkable mechanical and thermal properties of plastics; referred to as intermolecular bonding. It is the attactive forces between polymer molecules, which hold them firmly together and make them able to resist mechanical and thermal stress, that give them their useful properties. However, when processed, such as in injection molding, the molder wants to melt these plastics and make the liquids flow and fill the mold; these same attractive forces can make the IM process much more difficult, requiring accurate process control.

There are a variety of such intermolecular attractive forces. They may be arranged from the weakest to the strongest in the following order: London dispersion forces, polarity, hydrogen-bonding, orientation and crystallinity, ionic bonding, and permanent primary covalent crosslinking. It is useful to consider the effect of each of them individually.

molecular crosslinked The term crosslinked polymer tends to be used for polymers where the individual chains may be distinguished and where the crosslinks are short relative to the chain segments between crosslinks. Such structures may be formed either by crosslinking a preformed linear polymer, or during chain polymerization using a proportion of a multifunctional monomer. However, the accurate characterization of crosslinked polymer networks is among the more difficult tasks of polymer analysis. Yet crosslinks have a major effect on physical properties. Crosslinked materials are difficult to handle by solution techniques due to limited solubility. Solution techniques can be used after a degradative process has been applied. Many of the characterization tests are based on mechanical properties such as stress-strain properties, tensile strength, compression modulus, and hardness.

molecular flexibility The structure of the polymer molecule determines its inherent flexibility/rigidity, and this molecular flexibility in turn effects its processability. The flexibility of the individual polymer molecule is the most general and fundamental factor in its mechanical properties, and is also very important in many of its properties. In addition to its direct effect upon certain properties, it also interacts with the other structural features of the plastic, and thus has further indirect effects on many other properties. It is best analyzed by first examining the effects of molecular structure upon molecular flexibility, and then considering the effects of this action on other properties and applications.

The relationship between molecular structure and molecular flexibility is best understood by first examining the general fundamental concept of a completely flexible chain molecule, as derived from mathematics and physics, and then considering the ways in which chemical structure introduces restriction of rotation, and thus limits the flexibility of actual polymer molecules.

molecular fractionation Concerns different molecular weights of plastics. Common fractionation techniques used to characterize molecular structure include solubility tests [precipitation, fractional dissolution (extraction), coacervate extraction, thin-layer chromatography, countercurrent distribution, and turbidimetry], and measurement of molecular size [size-exclusion (sec) or gel-permeation chromatography (gpc)]. Other fractionation techniques include thin-layer chromatography and field-flow fractionation (fff).

molecular graphic ▷**computer-aided molecular graphic**

molecular level electron microscopy A technique for the observation of individual polymer molecules by electron microscopy. A very dilute polymer solution is sprayed onto a substrate, the solvent is evaporated and the specimen is shadowed. Individual molecules may then be observed, their dimensions can be measured, utilizing the shadow length, and the molecular weight and distribution can be determined.

molecular mass The sum of the atomic mass of all atoms in a molecule. In high polymers, because the molecular masses of individual molecules vary widely, they must be expressed as averages. The average molecular mass of polymers may be expressed as a number-average molecular mass or mass-average molecular map. These averages are the first two moments of the molecular mass (or weight) distribution. Others in common used are (Z) and $(Z+1)$ averages, these being the third and fourth moments. Molecular mass measurement methods include osmotic pressure, light scattering, solution pressure, solution viscosity, and sedimentation equilibrium.

molecular nucleation The process of including a new high polymer molecule in a crystalline phase, by the start of a new crystal, i.e. the earliest stage of primary nucleation, or of a new crystal, as in secondary crystallization.

molecular order Techniques used to characterize molecular order include thermal methods, X-ray diffraction, solid state NMR, Infrared and Raman spectroscopy, microscopy, inverse gas chromatography, neutron scattering, and others such as birefringence, dichroism, and small angle light scattering.

molecular organization Polymer chain interactions may result in an ordering of chains into regions of different supermolecular structure referred to as crystalline or amorphous in terms of the degree of ordering. Relatively small changes in the size and distributions of these ordered regions can be responsible for dramatic differences in the physical and mechanical properties between different samples of the same polymer.

molecular orientation ▷ **orientation**

molecular sieve A microporous structure composed of either crystalline aluminosilicates (chemically similar to clays and feldspars, and belonging to a class of materials known as zeolites) or crystalline aluminophosphates derived from mixtures containing an organic amine or quaternary ammonia salt. Pore size ranges from 5 to 10 A. The outstanding characteristic of these materials is their ability to undergo dehydration with little or no change in crystalline structure. They are used in many fields of technology such as to dry liquids and gases, as catalysts, and as chemical carriers (carriers for blowing agents in plastics so that upon heating, the blowing agents will be released at a desired rate).

molecular sieve chromatography Alternative name for gel permeation chromatography.

molecular size A fundamental question in polymer characterization relates to how large the polymer is. The answer can be expressed as molecular weight or degree of polymerization (DP), hydrodynamic volume, radius of gyration, or some other measure of molecular dimensions. Unlike simple compounds where the molecular weight in the sample is uniform, polymer samples are composed of polymer chains of varying length. Thus, a distribution of molecular weights is present. In the case of copolymers, chemical composition and length of the polymer chain often vary. Therefore, in expressing polymer molecule weights various average expressions are used. ▷ **ultrasonic degradation**

molecular volume Volume occupied by one mole; numerically equal to the molecular weight divided by the density.

molecular weight In most nonpolymeric materials the MW is a fixed constant value. In high polymers (plastics), the MWs of individual molecules vary widely so that they must be expressed as number-average MW ($\overline{M}_n$) or weight-average MW ($\overline{M}_w$). Per ASTM N 310, it is the sum of the atomic weights of all the atoms in a molecule. A measure of the chain length for the molecules that make up the polymer.

molecular weight, air ▷ **altitude chart**

molecular weight and aging Reactivity with oxygen, ozone, and moisture, and UV light sensitization of such reactions; all become important during long-time aging of many neat plastics in use, particularly at high temperature or in outdoor weathering. (Different additive agents are used with different plastics so that long-time aging of at least 25 to 50 years exists, such as acrylic.) Resistance to deterioration should be directly related to MW for three distinct reasons: (1) reactive end groups are inverse to $\overline{M}_n$, (2) reactivity of high MW species of low mobility is much less than for low MW species of high mobility, and (3) degradation of very high MW polymers during aging may still only degrade them to medium MW polymers of almost equivalent properties, whereas degradation of medium MW polymers during aging may degrade them to such small molecules that a significant loss in properties results. Thus, not only does MW affect aging, but aging also affects MW. Aging may either lower the MW by cleavage or may produce crosslinking up to infinite MW. The conclusion is that MW and aging may each be cause and/or effect.

molecular weight and cost ▷**cost and molecular weight**

molecular weight and mechanical properties ▷**molecular basic properties effect on product properties**

molecular weight and theory The ratio of the mass of an individual molecule of a substance to 1/12 the mass of an atom of the ^{12}C isotope. On this basis MW is dimensionless. Alternatively, it is the mass of one mole of the substance in question, which gives the same numerical value but now has the units of $g\,mol^{-1}$ or $kg\,mol^{-1}$. For polymers, although each individual molecule has its own MW, a macroscopic sample contains a distribution of molecules of different MWs, it has a molecular weight distribution (MWD). Thus, an average of the MW (the MW average) must be used. The MW of an individual polymer molecule is given by $M = M_0 \times$ DP, where M_0 is the MW of the repeat unit and DP is the degree of polymerization. Also called molar mass and relative molar mass.

molecular weight and thermal mechanical properties The effect of MW on thermal properties is best understood by examining its effect on the relationship between modulus and temperature. See Fig. under ▷**modulus versus temperature**

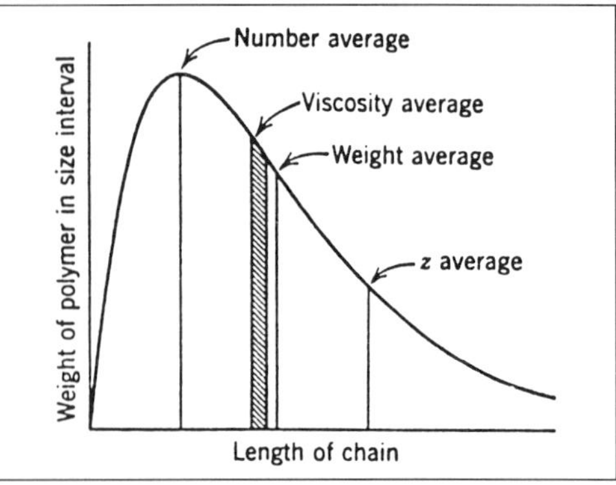

Typical molecular weight averages and distribution.

molecular weight average There are different methods for determining the various molecular weight averages; examples are given in the Table below where $\bar{M}_n$ is number-average MW, $\bar{M}_w$ is weight-average MW, $\bar{M}_z$ is Z-average MW, and $\bar{M}_v$ is viscosity-average MW. The choice of method to be used is often complicated by limitations of the technique as well as by nature of the plastic because most techniques require a sample in solution. The Fig. above is a schematic that shows typical MW averages and distribution. Average MW information is useful. However, characterization of the breadth of the distribution of MW is usually more valuable. For example, two plastics may have exactly the

Examples for determining average molecular weight.

Method	Absolute or relative	Average obtained	Mol wt range, g/mol	Characteristics
Ebulliometry	A	$\bar{M}_n$	up to 10^4	Low sensitivity
Cryoscopy	A	$\bar{M}_n$	up to 10^4	Small samples, fast
Membrane osmometry	A	$\bar{M}_n$	$5 \times 10^3 \sim 10^6$	Suitable membrane required
Vapor-pressure osmometry	R	$\bar{M}_n$	$< 3 \times 10^4$	Suitable standards for accurate calibration required
End-group determination	A	$\bar{M}_n$	$10^2 \sim 3 \times 10^4$	Low sensitivity at higher molecular weight, must assume two ends of same type per molecule
Light scattering	A	$\bar{M}_w$	$3 \times 10^4 \sim 10^7$	Low sensitivity at low molecular weight, expensive equipment, time-consuming
Ultracentrifugation	A	$\bar{M}_w$, $\bar{M}_z$	$2 \times 10^3 \sim 10^7$	Small samples, time-consuming, expensive equipment
Dilute-solution viscosity	R	$\bar{M}_v$	$10^2 \sim 10^7$	Fast, low cost, small samples

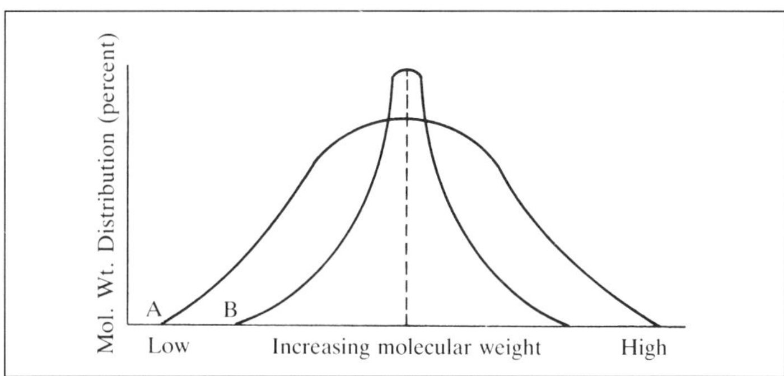

Example of molecular weight distribution.

same or similar average MWs but different molecular weight distribution (MWD). ▷ **molecular weight distribution** and **ultracentrifuge**

molecular weight cryoscopy Technique for determination of the MW of a solute by measurement of its ability to depress the freezing point of the solvent. Used occasionally for the determination of the number-average MW, but less frequently than the closely related colligative property method of ebulliometry. Difficulties restricting its use are precipitation of polymer close to the freezing point and supercooling.

molecular weight determination ▷ **sample standards; thermal analysis; gel chromatography**

molecular weight distribution MWD is the ratio of the weight-average MW (M_w) to the number-average MW (M_n); gives an indication of the distribution. Basically, MWD gives a general picture of the ratio of the large, medium, and small molecular chains in the plastic. It is called narrow if the plastic is made up of chains close to the average length, it is called wide if the plastic is made up of chains of a wide variety of lengths (see Fig. above).

Molecular weight (MW) is a method of defining plastics that refers to the average weight, which is always composed of different weight molecules. These differences are important to the processor, thus uses MWD to evaluate plastics. A narrow MWD enhances the performance of plastic products. Melt flow rates are dependent on MWD. In some cases it has been suggested that the balance of properties may actually be achieved without serious compromise or sacrifice, by choice of an optimum MWD. For example, low weight-average MW ($\overline{M}_w$) may be required for easy melt processing while high $\overline{M}_w$ is desirable for high tensile strength and impact strength; in such a situation a narrow MWD would give the best balance between processability and properties. In the production of polyethylene bottles, wire coating, and monofilaments, broad MWD produces the best combination of melt flow at high shear rates plus melt strength at low shear rates during processing, and also provides high load bearing strength during use.

The exact form of MWD depends upon the details of the polymerization mechanisms, and may also be affected by subsequent treatment of the plastic. Treatment with solvents can selectively remove low MW fractions. Shear induced degradation can preferentially cleave the higher MW components. Chemical reactions such as oxidation can cause either chain scission or crosslinking. Fractionation according to MW can occur during complete precipitation from solution, so that the average MW of a plastic in powder form may depend on the particle size distribution of the powder.

Various physical properties, including rheological properties, have different dependencies on MWD. It is therefore important to be able to describe and measure the MWD. Conversely, the determination of the MWD curve is done by measuring properties that have known dependence on MW. The most commonly used techniques are reviewed in ▷ **molecular weight average.** ▷ **osmometry, dynamic; Poisson distribution; ultracentrifuge**

molecular weight distribution resinography Equilibrium centrifugation, in resinography, is a method for determining the distribution of MWs. It involves spinning a solution of the specimen at a speed such that the molecules of the specimen are not removed from the solvent. They are held at a point where the (centrifugal) force tending to remove them is balanced by the dispersive forces caused by thermal agitation. ▷ **resinography**

molecular weight extraction Extraction is the transfer of a constituent of a plastic mass to a liquid with which the mass is in contact. The process is generally performed by means of a solvent selected to dissolve one or more specific constituents, or it may occur as a result of environmental exposure to a solvent. In a plastic of broad MWD, even though the majority of high MW polymer is solvent resistant, the low MW fraction may provide a significant basis of solubility and extractability. This is a practical approach particularly when the high MW polymer is crosslinked during processing; the low MW fraction is statistically least likely to crosslink, and therefore remains as a highly soluble and extractable fraction in the final polymer.

molecular weight light scattering ▷ **light scattering**

molecular weight, number-average The number-average molecular weight ($\overline{M}_n$) is the average MW of a high polymer expressed as the first moment of a plot of the number of molecules in each MW range against the MW. In effect, this is the total MW of all molecules divided by the number of molecules. ▷ **molecular weight average**

molecular weight, weight-average The weight-average molecular weight ($\overline{M}_w$) is the sum of the total weights of molecules of each size multipled by their respective weights divided by the total weight of all molecules. ▷ **molecular weight average**

molecular weight, Z-average ▷ **molecular mass**

molecule A chemical unit composed of one or more atoms. The simplest molecule contains only one atom. For example, helium (H) molecule with 1 atom/molecule, oxygen (O_2) with 2, and ozone (O_3) with 3. Molecules may have different sorts of atoms. Water contains two different kinds; hydrogen (H) and oxygen (O) that is chemical H_2O. The atoms of a molecule are held together by chemical bonds. Molecules may vary in size from less than 1 to more than 500 millimicrons and in weight from 4 to 40 million (He). Basically a molecule is the smallest quantity of matter which can exist by itself and retain all of the properties of the original substance.

Because there is much diversity among polymer molecules, a number of techniques of defining and quantifying these characteristics are in use by the industry. They are of value to processors and end-users of products as a determinatant of plastic properties. ▷ **molecular weight; molecular weight distribution; degree of polymerization; element; engineering materials, the solid state; polymerization and reactor technology; polymer; plastic; composite; atactic; bifunctional; chain, folded; conformation; conjugated; hydrothermal crystallization; dimer; disproportionation; domain; double bond; epitaxy; habit; head-to-head; head-to-tail; heterogeneous; nonpolar; polar; polyfunctional; properties, colligative; steric hindrance; amorphous plastic; crystalline plastic**

molecule alignment Polymers can form by aligning themselves into long chains of molecules without any side protrusions or branches, or lateral connections, between molecules. Some polymers do largely this and nothering more; however, it is also possible for polymers to form more complex structures. Thus, polymer molecules may form in the shape of branched molecules, in the form of giant 3-dimensional networks, in the form of linear molecules with regular lateral connections to form "ladder-type" polymers. They are in the form of 2-dimensional networks of platelets, and so forth, depending on how many connections or bonds can exist between the mono-disperse monomeric molecules which were used to form the polymer and between sites on the forming or already formed polymer molecule.

molecule and infrared spectrometry ▷ **infrared spectrometry**

molecule chains, geometry Different geometries exist ▷ **linear molecule; branching; crosslinking**. Also these geometries exist in different patterns, namely crystalline, amorphous, and oriented. ▷ **molecular arrangement structure**

molecule modeling ▷ **computer-aided molecular graphic**

molten metal bath extraction Use of a high temperature molten metal bath to break down polymeric chains in plastic waste to produce useful industrial gases. Contaminants in plastics may also be recovered as a metal or synthesized as a chemical.

molybdenum disulfide MoS_2 is a white, shiny crystalline material used as a lubricant in plastics (nylon, fluorocarbons, polystyrene, etc.) to reduce wear and friction. It is also acts as a strength-improving filler. ▷ **lubricant, solid**

moment of inertia The sum of the products formed by multiplying the mass (or sometimes the area) of each element of a figure by the square of its distance from a specified line. Also known as rotational inertia.

Monel ▷ **gasket versus moisture and EMI**

money ▷ **plastic money**

monitoring The continual sampling, measuring, recording, and/or signaling of a material or product.

monoatomic Containing single atom.

monochromatic Radiation of the same wavelength.

monochromatic light Light of a single wave. ▷ **light transmission**

monochromator A device or instrument that with an appropriate energy source, may be used to provide a continuous calibrated series of electromagnetic energy bands of determinable wavelength and frequency range.

monocoque structure A type of engineering construction such as a sandwich structure in which the outer skin carries all or a major part of the stresses (aircraft fuselage, motor bodies etc.) or a type of vehicle construction in which the body is integral with the chassis or main support (motortruck, railroad car, plastic house, etc.).

monodispersity Refers to a polymer system that is homogeneous in molecular weight, i.e., lacks molecular weight distribution.

monofilament A single fiber or filament of indefinite length generally produced by extrusion; a continuous fiber of sufficient size to serve as yarn in normal textile operations. Also called monofil.

monolayer 1. The basic reinforced plastic laminate unit from which cross-plied or other laminate types are constructed. ▷ **reinforced plastic, directional properties** 2. A single layer of atoms or molecules adsorbed on or applied to a surface.

monomer A chemical compound consisting of simple molecules which can be joined together by polymerization to produce a plastic which is composed of much more complex molecules and is the basic material from which plastics are made. It is a simple molecule which is capable of reacting with like or unlike molecules to form the polymer (plastic); the smallest repeating structure of a polymer (mers). For addition polymers, this represents the original unpolymerized compound. Styrene is a monomer for polystyrene plastic, vinyl chloride is a monomer for polyvinyl chloride plastic, etc. ▷ **polymerization reaction** and **mer**

monomer coating ▷ **bulk polymerization**

monomer, residual ▷ **residual monomer**

monomer synthesis ▷ **metal vapor synthesis**

monomolecular layer An adsorbed film, one molecule thick.

Monsanto house ▷ **plastic house**

montage Pictures posted in a pleasing manner; placed at angles, overlap, etc.

Montreal protocol ▷ **chlorofluorocarbon**

Mooney viscosity ▷ **viscosity, Mooney** and **scorch, Mooney**

mordant A substance capable of binding a dye to a textile fiber. The mordant forms an insoluble lake in the fiber; the color depending on the metal of the mordant.

morphology A term borrowed from the biological sciences by physical chemists to denote the shape, structure, or form of substances that in the context of this book refers to plastics and reinforced plastics. It does not have a specific meaning unless given one, such as the overall physical form of the physical structure of a bulk polymer. Common units are lamellae, spherulites, and domains. ▷ **molecular arrangement structure**

morphology, amorphous and crystalline characteristics The Tables below and on p. 492 compare these thermoplastics. ▷ **amorphous plastic** and **crystalline plastic**

morphology, amorphous properties Liquid crystal polymers (LCPs) rheologywise are another form referred to as oriented. There are LCPs supplied as amorphous LCPs. The term amorphous in this case does not relate to its morphology, but to the range of its properties. ▷ **liquid crystal polymer plastic**

morphology and mechanical properties As a results of differences in production, processing, and part design, great differences are found in the mechanical properties of plastics even if based on substances of identical properties. The reason for these differences is to be sought in the different morphologies. Thus the

Examples of thermoplastics.

Crystalline	Amorphous
Acetal (POM)	Acrylonitrile-butadiene-styrene (ABS)
Polyester (PETP, PBTP)	Acrylic (PMMA)
Polyamide (nylon) (PA)	Polycarbonate (PC)
Fluorocarbons (PTFE, etc.)	Modified polyphenylate oxide (PPO)
Polyethylene (PE)	Polystyrene (PS)
Polypropylene (PP)	Polyvinyl chloride (PVC)

Properties of thermoplastics.

Property	Crystalline	Amorphous
Melting or softening	Fairly sharp melting point	Softens over a range of temperature
Density	Increases as crystallinity increases	Lower than for crystalline material
Heat content	Higher	Lower
Volume change upon heating	Higher	Lower
After-molding shrinkage	Higher	Lower
Effect of orientation	Higher	Lower
Compressibility	Often higher	Sometimes lower

knowledge of the morphology of the material can provide an understanding, forecasting, and perhaps specifically changing properties. For use in mechanical engineering, the deformation behaviour and tensile strength are of particular importance in this respect. As the quantitative calculation of the mechanical properties from the structural parameters is not yet possible, the approach remains to correlate between structure and properties.

mortar **1.** A ceramic receptacle used by pharmacists for preparing mixtures of medicinals. **2.** A type of adhesive or bonding agent which may be either organic or inorganic, soft and workable when fresh but sets to hard, infusible solid on standing, either hydraulic action or by chemical crosslinking. Organic types are based on various plastics (epoxy, polyester TS, phenolic, furan, vinyl, etc.); inorganic types are cement, lime, silica, sulfur, and sodium or potassium silicate. All types are resistant to acids. Some are useful up to 870°C (1,600°F).

motion control systems MCSs are the major user of electrical power in the U.S. (and elsewhere). They can be found in practically every aspect of our lives, performing the task of converting electrical energy to mechanical energy in a series of controlled motion activities (to operate plastic fabricating processes, etc.). They permeate a wide cross section of applications. MCS can be found in the factory, office, automobile, home, hospital, and many thousand more applications. One does not usually buy a MCS. It is almost always integrated into the injection molding machine, appliance, etc. that we buy. MCS with its many requirements for plastic parts, can be divided into three major categories: a constant speed, a variable speed, and a positioning motion control systems.

The constant speed system is the simplest system not requiring any control box, power electronic package, or feedback device. It uses ac electric power directly from the power utility. It is the most popular because of its lower cost.

The fastest growing MCS is the variable speed or adjustable speed drive (ASD). It is replacing the constant speed drive in many industrial and factory floor product equipment applications (such as injection molding machines). The emphasis is on eliminating the energy inefficient characteristics of constant speed motor in large horsepower applications. Industrial use converting to the more efficient adjustable speed drive technology includes conveyors, film processing, packaging machines, bottling lines, and crane hoists.

The positioning system can be called a servo system, or a position servo. It uses a feed back device such as an encoder, resolver, or potentiometer. It moves from one position to another, often in milliseconds. Applications include the positioning of plastic film in extrusion lines, coordinated location of a robot hand as it maneuvers to pick up a plastic item, and positioning of a disk drive.

motionless mixer They are also called static mixers; used in melt processing and in mixing liquids to produce a near homogeneous mix. These units are mounted in-line on the input end of the processing machines, such as extruders, injection molding machines, urethane mixing units, etc. The unit consists of a barrel, which houses the mixing elements where a series of welded plates are arranged so that they cause the melt to divide, blend, and redivide numerous times.

They provide effective dispersion of colorants and other additives such as plasticizers, antioxidants, flame retardants, stabilizers, and fillers. They can virtually eliminate melt temperature gradients which, in turn, increase melt quality.

motor-generator MG is a machine that consists of one or more motors mechanically coupled to one or more generators. In plating, it is a machine which delivers dc of appropriate amperage and voltage.

mottle A mixture of colors or shades giving a complicated pattern of specks, spots, and/or streaks of color.

muffle furnace High temperature furnace used primarily to burn off cured plastics for computation of plastic content in such materials as reinforced plastics using reinforcements such as glass fibers. The furnace heat source is kept out of direct contact with the material; combustion being effected by heat reflected from the walls of the furnace. With glass fiber RP the usual plastic decomposition starts at 316°C (600°F) which is lower than the glass melt temperature of 538°C (1,000°F). The plastic disintegrates and the glass remains unaffected and in "position". Since there is no air motion on the RP sample, the direction or layout of fiber pattern can be observed. Weight before and after provides information on RP contents.

mulch, agricultural Polyethylene film is extensively used as a mulch. The beneficial effects of mulching films on many different plants' growth and yield are related to factors such as elimination or reduction of weed problems and better retention of moisture in the soil, avoidance of soil compaction which may choke plant growth, increases in the soil and microclimate temperatures under the film, avoidance of leaching that could deplete nutrient supplies, and the trapping of carbon dioxide under the film. Clear PE is a more effective heat trap than smoke-gray and black films. However, unless the soil is treated, weeds will grow under the clear film. There is no weed growth under black film. Smoke-gray (and other colors) are usually intermediate between clear and black with respect to soil temperature and weed growth. Different colors have different growth effects on crop yields for different crops.

multicomponent injection molding This technique is usually called ▷**coinjection**.

multilayer laminate There are different type materials that are used in multilayer constructions to provide different properties. ▷**laminate**

multilayer woven material ▷**three-dimensional fabric**

multi-live feed molding ▷**injection molding push-pull**

municipal solid waste Residential and light commercial solid waste collected from a selected municipality or geographic area; includes sewage sludge as distinguished from air pollution or waste water.

muscovite ▷**reinforcement, disc**

Mylar A thermoplastic film produced from the polyester of ethylene glycol and terephthalic acid. The fiber made by this method is called *Dacron*. *Mylar* and *Dacron* are tradenames of Du Pont.

myths about plastic ▷**plastic bad and other myths** and **waste myths**

myths about steel ▷**steel resources in U.S. limited**

N

nanosecond One-billionth (10^{-9}) second. Computer data, even long segments, are commonly transmitted in nanoseconds.

National Fire Protection Association ▷ **fire retardance**

National Institute for Science and Technology NIST is in Gathersburgh, MD; was previously called National Bureau of Standards (NBS). ▷ **fire retardance**

Natta catalyst A stereospecific catalyst made from titanium chloride and aluminum alkyl or similar materials by a special process which includes grinding the materials together to produce an active catalyst surface.

Natta, Giulio An Italian chemist (1903–1979) born in Imperia on the Riviera, co-recipient (with Karl Ziegler) of the Nobel prize in 1963 for his fundamental work on catalytic polymerization. In 1954 he developed isotactic polypropylene in his laboratory at the Polytechnic Institute of Milan, which led to the wide application of various stereospecific plastics with organometallic catalysts such as triethylaluminum. The researchers of Natta, together with those of Ziegler, made possible the chemical manipulation of monomers to form specifically ordered 3-dimensional plastics having predetermined properties, to which the term "tailor-made" is often applied. ▷ **Ziegler, Karl**

natural Descriptive of a substance or mixture which occurs in nature such as polysaccharide; the opposite of synthetic or man-made, like practically all plastics.

natural rubber latex The (NR) latex obtained by tapping the bark of the *hevea brasiliensis* tree, containing about 35% natural rubber hydrocarbon as particles about 1 μm in diameter, and about 5% non-rubber components consisting of protein, lipids, sugar, and salts. Most latex is coagulated by the addition of acetic or formic acid to produce solid natural rubber. Some latex is used as the latex itself after concentration to about 60% rubber content by centrifugation or creaming. The stability of concentrated latex is preserved by the addition of about 1.5% ammonia. This releases the fatty acids from the lipids which stabilize the latex after the protein has broken down by natural microbiological attack. ▷ **polyisoprene rubber** and **rubber**

natural, synthesis ▷ **synthetic, natural**

Naval Ordnance Laboratory NOL in MD; name change occurred during the 1980s; now called Naval Surface Weapons Laboratory. ▷ **NOL ring test**

neat plastic Plastic to which nothing has been added, such as additives, fillers, reinforcements, etc. Plastic in its real virgin form (Nothing Else Added To it).

nebs ▷ **fabric nebs**

neck-down ▷ **container neck-down** and **sag**

neck-in In extrusion such as film, sheet, or coating, and flat hot melt adhesive systems, the difference between the width of the extruded or hot web as it leaves the die (or roll) and the width of the cooler web downstream (see Fig. opposite). This shrinkage dimension is used as a guide to ensure that correct processing conditions exist. ▷ **extruder neck-in and beading**

needle blow pin ▷ **blow molding, extruder**

Nemesis racing airplane On its first competitive showing September 1990, the Nemesis plane flashed past the pylons at an average 245.624 mph (395.209 km/h) to win the gold at the Reno (NV, U.S.) National Air Races. It is made almost entirely of carbon fiber reinforced plastics. The plane has a non-detachable wing. Instead of removing the plane's wings for highway trailering, it had a removable tail cone.

neoprene rubber Except for SBR and IR, neoprene (CR) is perhaps the most rubberlike of all materials, particularly with regard to its dynamic response. CRs are a family of elastomers with a property profile that approaches that of NR, but has better resistance to oils, ozone, oxidation, and flame. CRs age better and do not soften up on exposure to heat, although their high-temperature tensile strength may be lower than that of NR. Neoprene comes in grades suitable for service at 250°C (480°F) and has maximal resistance to oils and greases.

Neck-in and beading on an extruder line chill roll. M = hot melt width at the die face, F = coating width on the substrate, M-F = total neck-in at both sides.

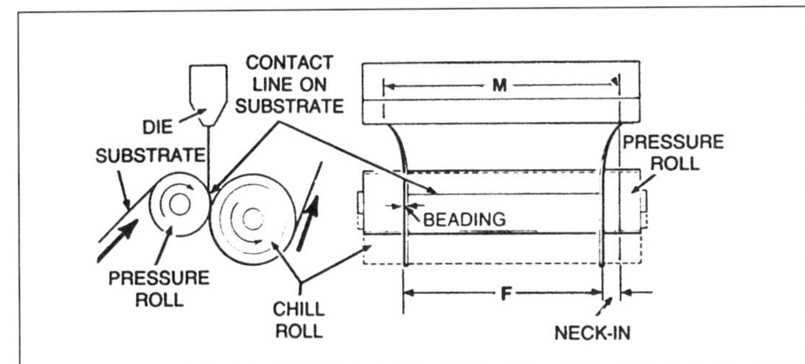

These materials, like NR, can be used to make soft, relatively high-strength compounds. One important difference is that, in addition to neoprene's being more costly by the pound than NR, its density is about 25% greater than NR's. CRs also do not have the low-temperature flexibility of NR, which detracts from their use in low-temperature shock or impact applications. ▷ **polychloroprene rubber**

nep One or more fibers occurring in a tangled and unorganized mass.

nested fabric ▷ **reinforced plastic nesting**

netting analysis ▷ **filament winding netting analysis**

netting, extruded ▷ **die netting**

network parameter M_c is a measure of the crosslink density of a plastic; the molecular weight of the primary chain segment between the crosslinks. It is only readily determined in lightly crosslinked elastomers, either by equilibrium swelling measurements or from measurements of stress-strain behavior.

network polymer A crosslinked polymer where there is a high enough number of crosslinks for all the polymer molecules, or molecular segments, to be joined to each other, thus forming a relatively infinite network. Often the terms network polymer and crosslinked polymer are used synonymously, but the former is often preferred for polymers produced by step-growth polymerization using multi-functional monomers. The latter is used for polymers that have been formed by crosslinking preformed linear polymer molecules.

Polymeric networks, systems of interconnected macromolecular chains, exhibit the property of high extensibility coupled with the capacity for full recovery that is implied by the term "rubber elasticity". Although the constitutional units comprising various networks may differ widely, their mechanical properties have much in common; this is especially evident in their stress-strain relationships. The basic premise of the molecular theory of elasticity in networks states that the stress in a typical strained network originates within the molecular chains of the structure; contributions from interactions between the chains are negligible. This premise provides direct support in elasticity measurements on polymeric networks. The temperature coefficient of the stress at fixed strain and its constancy with dilution are especially significant in this connection.

network structure An atomic or molecular arrangement in which primary bonds form a 3-D network.

neutralization The reaction of acids and alkalies resulting in a neutral compound such as $HCl + LiOH \rightarrow LiCl + H_2O$ (hydrochloric acid plus lithium hydroxide gives lithium chloride plus water).

neutron A fundamental particle of matter having a mass of 1.009 but no electric charge. It is a constituent of the nucleus of all elements except hydrogen; the number of neutrons present being the difference between the mass number and the atomic number of elements.

neutron scattering It has found numerous applications in the fields of polymer science, physical chemistry, materials science, metallurgy, biology, colloids, and solid state physics. In polymer science the majority of these applications involve small angle neutron scattering (SANS), which gives information on the time average molecular structure and conformation of the molecules. It is the interaction of neutrons with a material such that they are deflected. Since neutrons are electrically neutral they are only scattered by collisions with the nuclei of the atoms. As a result the normal optical quantum rules do not apply and all the molecular vibrational frequencies may be excited and observed. At the wavelengths normally used (about 5A), neutrons have velocities of about 10^3 ms^{-1}, and thus, much lower kinetic energies than normal electromagnetic radiation for these wavelengths. Also, owing to the large mass of the neutron, high momentum transfer occurs, giving a very wide range of scattering vectors. Inelastic scattering, i.e., with an exchange of energy, is useful for the study of molecular motions and vibrations in polymers.

Newton The Newton is that force which, when applied to a body having a mass of one kilogram, gives it an acceleration of one meter per second square ($kg \cdot m/s^2$). This is the SI unit of force.

Newtonian ▷ **flow model**

Newtonian flow A flow characteristic where a material (liquid, etc.) flows immediately on application of force and for which the rate of flow is directly proportional to the force applied; it is a flow characteristic evidenced by viscosity that is independent of shear rate. Water and thin mineral oils are examples of fluids that possess Newtonian flow. Plastic melt (liquid) is non-Newtonian ▷ **non-Newtonian flow**

Newtonian viscosity Alternate name for coefficient of viscosity.

Newton's law of viscosity In a simple shearing flow evaluation, it is the shear stress components that are the rate of deformation and the coefficient of viscosity.

nickel Malleable, silvery metal, readily fabricated by hot or cold working, takes high polish, excellent resistance to corrosion. Use includes electroplated protective coatings and electroformed coatings on plastics.

nip The V-shaped gap between a pair of rolls (calender, extruder line, coating line, etc) where incoming material is "nipped" and drawn between the rolls.

nip distance The radial clearance between rolls.

nip rolls ▷ **extruder blown film nip rolls**

nitrate plastic ▷ **cellulose nitrate plastic**

nitration The substitution of the nitro group $-NO_2$ for hydrogen.

nitriding Produces somewhat similar results of steel surface hardening to resist wear and abrasion to those of carbonizing but does not produce the distortion caused by severe quenching of carbonization because no heat treatment is required after the steel is heated to just below its critical temperature. However, nitriding does induce higher residual stresses along with sharp increases in strength, and is more expensive than carbonizing. Not all steels can be nitrided and the process is reserved for certain alloy steels. Process includes treating plasticizing screw surface, interior of barrel, mold surface, etc.

nitrile rubber The nitriles (NBRs) are copolymers of butadiene (B) and acrylonitrile (AN) that are used primarily for parts requiring resistance to petroleum oils and gasoline. Their resistance to aromatic hydrocarbons is better than is neoprene's, but not as good as polysulfide's. NBR has excellent resistance to mineral and vegetable oils, but relatively poor resistance to the swelling action of oxygenated solvents like actone, methyl ethyl ketone, and various other ketones. With its higher AN content its solvent resistance is increased but low-temperature flex decreased.

The low-temperature resistance of NBR is inferior to that of NR and, although it can be compounded to improve its performance in this area, the gain is usually at the expense of its oil and solvent resistance. NBR's tear strength is inferior to NR's, and its electrical insulation rating is also lower. NBR is used instead of NR where increased resistance to petroleum oils, gasoline, or aromatic hydrocarbons is required.

Standard NBR was and still remains, for reasons of price alone, the most important oil, fuel and wear resisting elastomer for numerous applications, including autombiles. However, its growth rate has decreased. Temperatures in car engines now are often 150°C or higher. The maximum long-term service temperature of NBR is only about 120 to 130°C. Thus, in some areas where NBR was formerly dominant, it has been partially or completely replaced by types of elastomers with better heat resistance. Also it is are not always satisfactory with regard to resistance to ozone, the concentrations of which are becoming higher in fully enclosed engine compartments. One of the earliest reasons for NBR failing to meet requirements was the poor resistance to motor oil additives. Other reasons for its replacement are requirements for reduced permeability to fluids in components such as fuel line hoses.

nitrile rubber, hydrogenated Fully hydrogenated nitrile rubber (H-NBR) has considerably better heat resistance than NBR but with some reduced swelling resistance, and is more resistant to chemicals and ozone (no longer contains any double bonds). It is crosslinked by the peroxide process. Partially hydrogenated nitrile rubber, also known as H-NBR, has a slightly lower heat deformation resistance than the fully hydrogenated type (135 to 150°C) and is less resistant to ozone and chemicals. However, as it can be crosslinked using sulphur it has considerably better dynamic properties, which is an important advantage for applications such as drive belts that operate under hot oil. In properties and price, the H-NBR types lie between NBR and their chief competitor, FPM.

nitrile-silicone elastomer NSR is a rubber that combines the characteristic properties of silicones with the oil resistance of nitrile rubber. It is a silicone elastomer based on polydimethylsiloxane in which some methyl groups have been replaced by cyanoethyl or cyanopropyl groups. This improves the solvent resistance.

nitrocellulose ▷ **lacquer**

nitrogen cured XLPE ▷ **extruder wire coating, crosslinkable PE with peroxide** and **radiation crosslinking**

node Point, line, or surface of standing wave system at which the amplitude is zero.

noise **1.** Any undesired signal (electrical or acoustic) that tends to interfere with the normal reception or processing or a desired signal. **2.** In flaw detection, undesired response to dimensional and physical variables (other than flaws) in the test piece is called "part noise".

noise influence on sensor ▷ **sensor, noise effect**

NOL ring test A parallel filament or tape wound hoop test specimen developed by the Naval Ordnance Laboratory (now the Naval Surface Weapons Laboratory), for measuring various mechanical strength properties of the material, such as tension and compression. Also known as parallel fiber reinforced ring.

nomenclature ▷ **plastic nomenclature**

nominal The closest approximate amount. Not exact; may vary somewhat.

nominal value A value assigned for the purpose of a convenient designation. A nominal value exists in name only. In dimensions, it is often an average number with a tolerance in order to fit together with adjacent parts.

nomogram Also called nomograph, where a graph containing several (3 or more) parallel scales is graduated for different variables so that when a straight line connects values of any two, the related value may be read directly from the third at a point intersected by the line. They assist in estimating data that normally would require intricate calculations developed longhand (see Fig. below) or via computer.

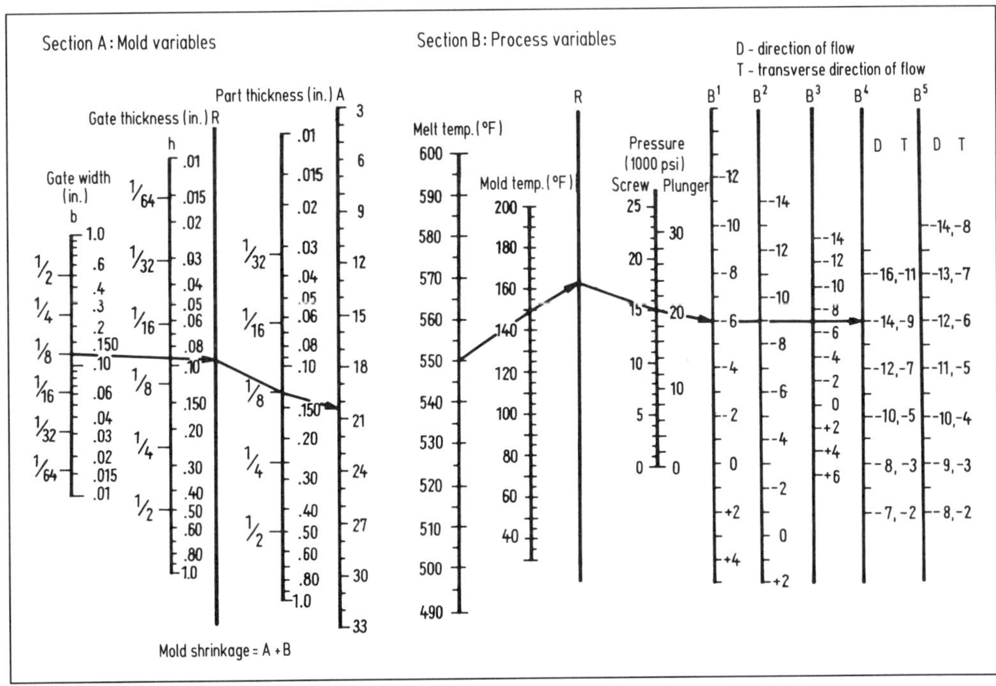

Example of mold shrinkage nomograph for certain type injection molded nylon plastics (B1, B2, B3, B4, and B5).

non-air-inhibited plastic A plastic in which the surface cure will not be inhibited or tacky in the presence of air. If required, a surfacing agent is added to exclude air from the surface of the plastic.

nonaqueous dispersion, organosol ▷ **organosol nonaqueous dispersion**

noncombustible Not combustible. ▷ **combustibles**

non-conducting sensor ▷ **sensor, nuclear**

nonconductive A material that does not conduct thermal or electrical energy such as most plastics. However, there are those that are conductive or can be made conductive by adding appropriate additives and fillers. ▷ **conductivity**

noncrystalline plastic ▷ **amorphous plastic**

nondestructive acoustic holography ▷ **acoustic holography**

nondestructive evaluation NBE is broadly considered synonymous with nondestructive inspection (NDI). More specifically, the analysis of NDI findings to determine whether the material will be acceptable for its function.

nondestructive holography test This technology has been applied to NDI of reinforced plastic and other structures. The structure must be mounted on a very stable platform, and is then subjected to a stress condition, either thermal or mechanical. Holography permits rather precise observation of dimensional deviations from the references configuration, so that anomalies can be located. ▷ **photoelastic strain analysis**

nondestructive inspection NDI is a process or procedure, such as ultrasonic or radiographic inspection, for determining the quality or characteristics of a material, part, or assembly. This procedure takes place without permanently altering the subject or its properties. Used to find internal anomalies in a structure without degrading its properties.

nondestructive photoelastic strain analysis ▷ **photoelastic stress analysis**

nondestructive testing In the familiar form of testing known as destructive testing, the original configuration of a specimen is changed, distorted, or even destroyed for the sake of obtaining such information as the amount of force that the specimen can withstand before it exceeds its elastic limit and permanently distorts (usually called the yield strength) or the amount of force needed to break it (the tensile strength). The data collected in this instance are quantitative and could be used to design structural parts that would withstand a certain oscillating load or heavy traffic usage. However, one could not use the tested specimen in the part. One would have to use another specimen and hope that it would behave exactly the same as the one that was tested.

Nondestructive testing (NDT), on the other hand, examines a specimen without impairing its ultimate usefulness. It does not distort the test specimen's configuration but provides a different type of data. NDT allows suppositions about the shape, severity, extent, configuration, distribution, and location of such internal and subsurface defects as voids and pores, shrinkage, cracks, and the like.

Most materials contain some flaws, which may or may not be cause for concern. Flaws that grow under operating stresses can lead to structural or component failure, whereas other flaws may present no safety or operating hazards. Nondestructive evaluation provides a means for detecting, locating, and characterizing flaws in all types of materials, while the component or structure is in service if necessary, and often before the flaw is large enough to be detected by more conventional means. Nondestructive evaluation methods include the following: acoustic emission, radiography, infrared spectroscopy, X-ray spectroscopy, nuclear magnetic resonance spectroscopy, ultrasonic, liquid penetrant, photoelastic stress analysis, vision system, holography, electrical NDT, magnetic flux field, manual tapping, microwave and birefringence. An example of defects detected by various NDT methods is given in the Table on p. 499.

nondestructive testing, electrical ▷ **electrical nondestructive test** and **magnetic flux field testing**

nondestructive testing method, residual strain A nondestructive test to measure residual strains in transparent thermoplastics uses an automated electro-optical fast system. It can be used as an on-line quality control test. This concept of photoelastic response of transparent material has been known for well over a hundred years. Expressed as Brewster's Law, it states that the index of refraction in a strained material becomes directional, and the change of the index is proportional to the magnitude of strain present. Therefore, a polarized beam of light passing through a strained region in a clear plastic splits into two wavefronts that contain vibrations oriented along the directions

Examples of defects detected by nondestructive testing methods.

Defects	X-ray	Neutron	Gamma ray	Ultrasonic	Sonic	Microwave	Temperature differential	Heat, photosensitive agent	Penetrant
Unbond	●			●	●		●		
Delamination	●			●	●	●	●		●
Undercure				●	●	●		●	
Fiber misalignment	●	●	●						
Damaged filaments	●								●
Variation in resin		●							
Variation in thickness	●		●	●	●	●			
Variation in density	●		●	●	●				
Voids	●		●	●	●	●	●		●
Porosity	●		●	●	●	●			●
Fracture	●		●	●	●				●
Contamination	●		●	●					
Moisture	●	●							

of principal strains. An analyzing filter passes only vibrations parallel to its own transmitting plane. The constructive or destructive interference creates the well-known colorful patterns seen when stressed plastic is placed between two polarized filters. A little information about the strain gradients comes from observation of the patterns, but observations fall far short of quantitatively evaluating birefringence, retardation, or the magnitude of the residual strain.

To solve the measurement problem, a very simple device known as a wedge compensator (described by ASTM D 4093) is placed between the light coming through the sample and the analyzing filter. The compensator reverses the retarding action of the induced strains in the plastic. Strain is calculated in the compensator by multiplying the birefringence (retardation per unit thickness) by a strain-optic response of the plastic being tested. Equal but opposite retardation is established by the compensator and, when superimposed on the retardation caused by induced strain, restores a null. The intensity of the transmitted light becomes zero; revealed by a visible black fringe.

The drawback of a "compensator system" is that it requires a competent technician. Even so, the process is relatively slow because the compensator must be carefully oriented along the strain axis and then moved to make the black fringe appear. This is acceptable in a research atmosphere, but is a quality control situation, an automated system is much preferred. It eliminates the judgement factor and permits fast, on-line inspection. The SCA (Spectral Contents Analysis) permits the on-line inspection.

SCA used in an electro-optical system is the basis for an automated system, yet it works similarly to the original, ordinary visual observation; polarized light is passed through the sample to be inspected. A viewing probe, however, takes the place of a human eye. It channels light through a fiber-optic cable to a spectral analyzer. When digitized, it is compared by a personal computer with a standard photoelastic response, permitting calculation of the strain level. This method, unlike that of a manual compensator, is independent of the direction of stress. The result is a nearly instantaneous readout; the readout can be obtained remotely, and a multichannel or multipoint readout can be easily assembled. Thus, no skilled operator is required to observe and interpret photoelastic response. ▷ **testing residual strain, destructive method; residual strain; residual stress**

nondestructive testing, ultrasonic ▷ **ultrasonic testing**

nondestructive testing, visual ▷ **visual inspection**

non-discriminatory sensor ▷ **sensor, nuclear**

non-durable goods Products with a relatively short useful life, such as newspapers or disposable packaging.

nonferrous metal Metals that are not composed of iron, including aluminum, copper, brass, and bronze.

nonflammable material A gas, liquid, or solid which will not burn under normal conditions. Do not confuse with combustible materials.

nonhygroscopic Lacking the property of absorbing and retaining an appreciable quantity of moisture (water vapor) from the air.

nonisotropic ▷ **reinforced plastic, directional properties**

nonlaminar flow ▷ **melt flow defects** and **non-Newtonian flow**

nonlinear viscoelasticity ▷ **viscoelasticity, nonlinear**

nonmetal Any number of elements whose electronic structure, bonding characteristics, and consequent physical and chemical properties differ markedly from those of metals, particularly in respect to electronegativity as well as thermal and electrical conductivity. In general, they have very low to moderate conductivity and high electronegativity.

non-Newtonian flow Some liquids (plastic melt as an example) have abnormal flow response when force is applied. That is, their viscosity is dependent on the rate of shear. They do not have a straight proportional behavior with application of force and rate of flow; when proportional, the behavior has a Newtonian flow. Deviations from this ideal behavior may be of several different types. One type, called the apparent viscosity, may not be independent of the rate of shear; it may increase with shear rate (shear thickening or dilatancy) or decrease with rate of shear (shear thinning or pseudoplasticity). The latter behavior is usually found with plastic melts and solutions. In general, such a dependency of shear stress on shear rate can be expressed as a power law. Another type is where the viscosity may be time dependent, as for material exhibiting thixotropy or rheopexy. Another usual type found with plastic melts and solutions is where the fluid may exhibit elastic effects, that is it is an elasticoviscous fluid. ▷ **Newtonian flow; flow model; melt flow behavior**

nonplastication ▷ **melt flow defects**

nonpolar Having no concentration of electrical charges on a molecular scale; thus, incapable of significant dielectric loss. Examples among plastics are polystyrene and polypropylene. ▷ **polar**

nonresonant forced and vibration technique A technique for performing dynamic mechanical measurements in which the sample is oscillated mechanically at a fixed frequency. Storage modulus and damping are calculated from the applied strain and the resultant stress and shift in phase angle. ▷ **resonant forced vibration technique**

non-return valve Valve that permits plastic to flow in one direction and closes to prevent back flow in a machine such as the tip of the screw in injection molding ▷ **screw tip, injection.** It is also a one-way valve in a hydraulic system.

nonrigid plastic For purposes of general classification, a plastic that has a modulus of elasticity either in tension or flexure of not over 70 MPa (10,000 psi) at 23°C (70°F) and 50% relative humidity. ▷ **semirigid plastic** and **rigid plastic**

non-staining antioxidant It does not impart color to the plastic which it is protecting, either initially or after degradation (due to its own degradation products being colored). Most hindered and thio-phenols and peroxide destroyers are non-staining.

non-toxic plasticizer The U.S. FDA, per the U.S. Federal Register, has a list of plasticizers that are sanctioned, such as acetyl tributyl citrate, butyl stearate, dibutyl sebacate, diethyl phthalate, triethyl citrate, etc.

nonwoven fabric ▷ **fabric nonwoven** and **mechanical nonwoven fabric**

nonwoven mat ▷ **mat**

nonwoven roving ▷ **roving**

nonwoven spun-bonded ▷ **spun-bonded nonwoven fabric**

normal curve ▷ **statistical normal curve** and **standard and mean deviation**

notch factor Ratio of the resilience determined on a plain specimen to the resilience determined on a notched test specimen. ▷ **impact test** and **fatigue notch factor**

notch sensitivity The extent to which the sensitivity of a material to fracture is increased by the presence of a surface nonhomogeneity, such as a notch, a sudden change in cross section, a crack, a scratch, etc. Low notch sensitivity is usually associated with ductile plastics, and high notch sensitivity is usually associated with brittle plastics.

notched specimen A test specimen that has been deliberately cut or notched, usually in a V-shape, to induce and locate point of failure. The processing conditions and method of preparing the notch (cutting, etc.) can have a significant effect on results. ▷ **impact test**

novalak plastic A thermoplastic phenol-formaldehyde type plastic obtained primarily by the use of acid catalyst and excess phenol. It is a phenolic-aldehyde plastic which, unless a source of methylene groups is added, remains permanently TP. Novalak is a linear TP B-staged phenolic plastic. Used as a molding compound, bonding materials, abrasive grinding wheels, etc. Also called two-stage or two-step plastic. ▷ **epoxy plastic** and **resole plastic**

nozzle ▷ **injection molding nozzle**

nuclear gauge ▷ **sensor, nuclear**

nuclear magnetic resonance spectroscopy NMR relates to the radio frequency induced transitions between magnetic energy levels of atomic nuclei. This instrument consists essentially of a magnet, radio frequency accelerator, sample holder sweep unit, and detector, capable of producing an oscilloscope image or line recording of an NMR spectrum. NMR is a powerful method for elucidating chemical structures such as characterizing material by the number, nature, and environment of the hydrogen atoms present in a molecule. Identification is possible because of the absorptions of radio frequency radiation in a magnetic field as a result of the magnetic properties of nuclei. This technique is used to solve problems of crystallinity, polymer configuration, and chain structure.

nuclear radiation ▷ **radiation**

nucleating agent Chemical substances which when incorporated in certain plastics form nuclei for growth of crystals in the melt. In propylene, for example, a higher degree of crystallinity and more uniform crystalline structure is obtained by adding a nucleating agent such as adipic and benzoic acid, or certain of their metal salts. Colloidal silicas are used in nylon, seeding the material to produce more uniform growth of spherulites.

nucleation, heterogeneous ▷ **heterogeneous nucleation**

nucleation, primary Primary nucleation is the mechanism by which crystallization is initiated, often by an added nucleation agent.

nucleation, secondary Secondary nucleation is the mechanism by which crystals grow.

nucleon Proteins and neutrons are called nucleons; they are in the atomic nucleous per the Periodic table.

number-average, molecular weight ▷ **molecular weight, number-average**

number marker **1.** The recommended U.S. decimal marker is a dot on the line. When writing numbers less than one, a zero should be written before the decimal marker. **2.** Outside the U.S. the comma is often used as a decimal marker. In some applications, therefore, the common practice of using the comma to separate digits into groups of three (as in 40,215) may cause ambiguity. To avoid this potential source of confusion, recommended international practice calls for separating the digits into groups of three, counting from the decimal point toward the left and the right, and using a small space to separate the groups. In numbers of four digits the space is usually not necessary on either side of the decimal point except for uniformity in tables. Examples are: 9 453 611. and 53 611. and 3611. and 611. and 0.5089 and 0.508 945 361 and the width of the space should be narrow, about the width of the letter "i". ▷ **decimal system**

nylon fiber ▷ **fiber, nylon**

nylon plastic Nylon or polyamide (PA) was the first of the so-called thermoplastic engineering plastics in the 1930s. They were originally developed as high-strength textile fibers for stockings. These crystalline plastics—the new developments include amorphous types—are available for processing by different methods. There are different nylons, but as a family their characteristics of strength, stiffness, and toughness have earned them an important place for the designer when compared to such other materials as the die-casting alloys.

Nylon 6/6 is the most widely used, followed by nylon 6, with similar properties except that it absorbs moisture more rapidly and its melting point is 21°C (70°F) lower. Also, its lower processing temperature and less-crystalline structure result in lower mold shrinkage. Nylons 11 and 12 have better dimensional stability and electrical properties than the others, because they absorb less moisture. These more expensive types also are compounded with plasticizers, to increase their flexibility and ductility. With nylon toughening and technology advancements, supertough nylons have become available. Their notched Izod impact values are over 10 J/m (20 ft.lb.in.), and they fail in a ductile manner.

Other important types of nylons include the castable types, liquid monomers (not the usual solid) that polymerize and become solid at atmospheric pressure. From them complex parts several inches thick and weighing hundreds of pounds can be cast. Another castable liquid monomer is a moldable transparent material. This amorphous type offers better chemical resistance than other thermoplastics that are transparent.

Property comparisons among the commercial grades of different nylons vary widely, because so many formulations are available. In general, they all have excellent fatigue resistance, a low coefficient of friction, good toughness (depending on their degree of crystallinity), and resist a wide spectrum of fuels, oils, and chemicals.

Nylon 6/6 has the lowest permeability by gasoline and mineral oil of all the nylons. The 6/10 and 6/12 types are used where lower moisture absorption and better dimensional stability are needed. All nylons are inert to biological attack and have electrical properties adequate for most voltages and frequencies. The crystalline structure of nylons, which can be controlled to some degree by processing, affects their stiffness, strength, and heat resistance. Low crystallinity imparts greater toughness, elongation, and impact resistance—but at the sacrifice of tensile strength and stiffness.

All nylons absorb moisture, if it is present in the application's environment. An increase in moisture content decreases a material's strength and stiffness and increases its elongation and impact resistance. Type 6/6 nylon usually reaches equilibrium at about 2.5% moisture when the relative humidity reaches 50%. The equilibrium moisture at 50 RH in nylon 6 is slightly higher. In general, nylon's dimensions increase by about 0.2 to 0.3% for each 1% of moisture absorbed. However, dimensional changes caused by moisture absorption can be compensated for by performing moisture conditioning prior to putting parts into service. Such formulations as 6/12, 11, and 12 are considerably less sensitive to moisture than others.

When UV stabilizers are compounded in the nylon, they become insensitive to UV light. Carbon black is the most effective stabilizer. UV stabilizers also increase tensile strength and hardness and decrease ductility and toughness slightly.

Nylons have good resistance to creep and cold flow, as compared to many of the less rigid thermoplastics. Usually, creep can be accurately calculated, using apparent modulus values. They also have outstanding resistance to repeated impact. Nylons can withstand a major portion of a breaking load almost indefinitely.

Nylons are used in many different markets, the largest being the automotive. Their performance capabilities make them suitable for different mechanical and electrical hardware, particularly for such under-hood parts as timing sprockets, speedometer gears, cooling fans, wire connectors, windshield-wiper parts, door latches, fender extensions, steering-column-lock housings, brake-fluid reservoirs, and other uses. Their low friction, good abrasion resistance, and ability to operate without lubricants qualify nylons for use in many bearing applications, business machines, and appliances. For extra protection, occasional lubrication can be applied.

Extruded nylon tubing and hoses are used in hydraulic and other fluid systems, because of their reistance to different fluids. The applications for castings are mostly in industrial equipment: large rollers, bearings, gears, cams, sheaves, guide blocks, wear plates, and the like. Nylon powder, which can be applied either electrostatically or by a fluid bed, provides tough, wear-resistant coatings.

nytril fiber ▷ **fiber, nytril**

O

ocean environment ▷ **environment and ocean**

odor An important property of many substances, manifested by a physiological sensation due to contact of their molecules with the olfactory nervous system. Odor and flavor are closely related, and both are profoundly affected by submicrogram amounts of volatile compounds. Many compounds have a characteristic odor that is an effective means of identification. ▷ **plastic identification**

odorant Additives are sometimes incorporated into plastics to give products a specific odor (odorants or fragances) or to control or mask an objectionable odor (deodorants, sanitizers). Sanitizers may have an antimicrobial role.

off-line processing ▷ **processing, off-line**

offset gravure It is used to print different patterns or designs, such as wood grains on different products such as plastic film and wall panels. A converted flexographic press is used. The anilox roller is replaced by a gravure image cylinder and doctor blade for printing the image, and the plate cylinder of the flexographic press is covered with a solid rubber plate. ▷ **gravure**

offset molding ▷ **injection molding, jet method** and **injection molding, offset method**

offset printing/coating Technique in which ink is transferred from a bath (reservoir) onto the raised surface of the printing plate by rollers. Subsequently, the plates transfer the ink to the part being printed (or coated). The distinguishing feature of the printing method is the offset roll. Dry, pasty inks are used. This method is widely used with plastic products. ▷ **gravure**

offset strain ▷ **strain, offset**

offset stress ▷ **stress, offset**

ohm ▷ **electrical resistance**

oil The word "oil" is applied to a wide range of substances that are quite different in chemical nature resulting in different physical characteristics.

oil and gas It would be no exaggeration to characterize oil and natural gas as two of the most important natural resources in use throughout the world. Together, the two materials satisfy more than two-thirds of the world's energy demand. Natural gas accounts for a third of the energy consumed in the U.S. and more than 20% of the energy consumed by the rest of the world. Oil, which in the form of diesel fuel and gasoline, powers most of the world's land, sea, and air vehicles, accounts for even higher percentages of use. In addition, both are important feedstocks for the chemical and plastic industries; about 2% is used for plastics.

Gas, a natural occurring mixture consisting mostly of methane and ethane, with smaller amounts of other hydrocarbons included, and crude oil, or petroleum, occur in underground pockets, which generally are found at depths ranging from 1,500 to 12,000 ft. The reservoirs are made up either of porous, permeable sands and rocks that trap the oil and gas, or in enclosed pools. They are distributed widely over the earth. Known worldwide gas reserves are estimated at 1,500 trillion cu. ft.; world oil reserves are estimated at 1.5×10^{12} barrels.

Although most of the world's attention focuses on oil and gas stores in the Middle East, it should not be forgotten that the North American continent also holds vast deposits. About 25% of natural gas reserves and an almost equal percentage of petroleum reserves are found in Canada, U.S. and Mexico. The Canadian province of Alberta alone has over 60 trillion ft^3 of established natural gas reserves, with another 118 trillion ft^3 potential gas reserves. And counting petroleum from all sources (crude, bitumen, etc.) it would be fair to say that Alberta has as much oil under its earth as does the whole Middle East.

oil canning With flat surfaces fabricated by certain processes (and certain plastics) such as thermoforming, blow molding, and rotational molding, it can bend or flex, rather than remain rigid. ▷ **blow molding, extruder flat surface** to improve stiffness.

oil resistance The ability for a material to withstand contact with an oil without deterioration of properties or geometrical change to a degree which impairs part performance. Different conditions of exposure can exist which in turn can affect the outcome, such as temperature, complete immersion, partial immersion with air, etc.

oil soluble plastic Plastic which at moderate temperature will dissolve in, disperse in, or react with drying oils to give a homogeneous film of modified characteristics.

olefin fiber ▷ **fiber, olefin**

olefinic polymerization ▷ **addition polymerization**

olefinic TPE These are (poly)olefin thermoplastic elastomers (called TPEs or TPOs) that are typically blends of PP, EPDM, or EP rubber, PE, and a variety of fillers and additives. They are formulated to give an extremely wide range of mechanical and physical properties such as a flexural modulus from 2,000 to 300,000 psi. They can be processed in conventional plastic processing equipment. Their low specific gravity and raw material supply base give them advantages on a cost/performance ratio. A major market is automotive since they provide paintability and weatherability. Flexibility remains down to −50°C and they are not brittle at 32°C.

olefin plastic ▷ **polyolefin plastic**

olefin-styrene-acrylonitrile plastic OSA is an SAN polyalloy with an olefinic thermoplastic elastomer.

oleophilic Likes oil; wettable with oils.

oleo plastic Semi-solid mixtures of plastic and essential oil of the agricultural plant from which they exude, and sometimes referred to as balsams. Oleo plastic materials consist of drying oils and natural or synthetic plastics.

oligablock copolymer elastomer ▷ **styrene oligablock copolymers**

oligomer A polymer consisting of only a few monomer units, for example, a dimer, trimer, tetramer, and so forth, or their mixtures. They are simple polymers of relatively small numbers of fundamental repeat molecule. They are differentiated from high polymers (with 1,000 or more repeat units) by the fact that they can be separated in simple manner according to their molecular size.

one-shot molding ▷ **foamed polyurethane molding one-shot**

one-stage plastic ▷ **resole plastic**

one-standard-deviation ▷ **standard deviation measurement**

one-step plastic ▷ **resole plastic**

on-line computer assist ▷ **computer real time or on-line**

opacity/transparency Opacity is the optical density of a material, usually a pigment; the opposite of transparency. A colorant or paint of high opacity is said to have good hiding power or covering power, by which is meant its ability to conceal another tint or shade over which it is applied. Opacity or transparency are important when the amount of light transmitted is a consideration. These properties are usually measured as haze and luminous transmittance. Haze is defined as the percentage of transmitted light through a test specimen which is scattered more than 2.5° from the incident beam. Luminous transmittance is defined as the ratio of transmitted light to incident light. Definitions for terms used in identifying optical conditions are: (1) *Refractive index* The ratio of the velocity of light in free space to the velocity of light in the medium. (2) *Light scattering* The change in direction of a portion of the light transmitted due to refraction or reflection at the surfaces of inclusions in the material. (3) *Birefringence* The property of anisotropic optical media which causes polarized light with one orientation to travel with a different velocity than polarized light with another orientation. (4) *Polarized light* Light which has the electric field vector of all of the energy vibrating in the same plane. Looking into the end of a beam of polarized one would see the electric field vector as parallel or coincident lines. (5) *Dichroism* A property of an optical material which causes light of some wavelengths to be absorbed when the incident light has its electric field vector in a particular orientation and not absorbed when the electric field vector has other orientations. (6) *Light transmissability* The ratio of the light exiting from an optical material to the light entering the material. (7) *Haze* The cloudy appearance in a plastic material caused by inclusions which produce light scattering. (8) *Color* The sum effect of the wavelengths of light transmitted by or reflected from a material. (9) *Dispersion* A property of an optical material which causes some wavelengths of light to be transmitted through the material at different velocities and the velocity is a function of the wavelength. This causes each wavelength of light to have a different refractive index.

opalescence The limited clarity of vision through a sheet of transparent plastic at any angle, because of diffusion within or on the surface of the plastic.

opaque Descriptive of a material or substance which will not transmit light. Opposite of transparent. Materials neither opaque nor transparent are sometimes described as semi-opaque, but are more properly classified as transparent.

open-cell ▷ **foamed open-cell**

open molding This very simple process consumes a considerable amount of vinyl plastisols. It involves pouring the plastisol in the mold cavity. The mold and plastic are heated to gel and fuse the plastisol. The mold is then cooled and the part is stripped from the mold. Inserts can be placed in the liquid plastic before it is fused, and two or more colors can be placed in different parts of the mold. ▷ **contact molding**

operation, automatic A machine operating automatically will perform a complete cycle of programmed molding functions repetitively, and stops only in the event of a malfunction on the part of the machine or mold, or if it is manually interrupted. ▷ **automation**

operation, manual An operation in which each function and the timing of each function is controlled manually by an operator.

operation, secondary After plastic parts are fabricated in their respective basic functional processing machines, secondary operations may be required to produce the final finished product. These operations can occur in-line or off-line during production. Examples include parts handling for finish machining, drilling, reaming, cutting, trimming, etc.

operation, semi-automatic A machine will perform a complete cycle of programmed molding functions automatically and then stop. It will then require an operator to manually start another cycle.

operator's station That position where an operator normally stands to operate or observe the machine.

optical analysis, microtomy ▷ **microtoming, optical analysis**

optical bleach ▷ **optical brightener agent**

optical brightener agent These agents (also called brighteners, whiteners, fluorescent whiteners, or optical bleaches) are a special class of essentially colorless fluorescent organic substances which absorb UV radiation above 3,000 A and emit this as visible radiation below 5,500 A. Usually, the absorption maximum for such substances is near 3,650 A and the emission maximum near 4,350 A. The molecular extinction coefficient for these substances is about $1-6 \times 10^4$, and the quantum efficiency of the fluorescence is generally high.

Brighteners are useful in correcting discoloration and enhancing the whiteness and brightness particularly of plastics. For such purposes, the absorption and emission properties are designed with consideration of the properties of the human visual system, the spectral properties of sunlight, and the nature of the discoloration. In contrast of "blueing agents" which act by removing yellow light, the optical brighteners absorb the visible UV rays and correct their energy into visible blue-violet light; used to increase the luminance factor of a white material, etc. They cannot be used in materials that also contain UV absorbing agents. Use includes in PVC sheet and film, fluorescent lighting fixtures, vinyl floors, nylon fishing lines, PE bottles, etc. Examples of the agents are coumarins, naphthotriazolylstibenes, benzimidazolyl, naphthylimide, etc.

optical character recognition OCR uses optical means to identify graphic characters.

optical data storage ▷ **computer optical data storage**

optical density A measure of image intensity by relectance densitometer; logarithm to the base 10 of the reciprocal of transmittance.

optical disk Data storage device; can be alterable or permanent. More use is being made of erasable plastic optical disks for read/write data storage. Plastics being used in this growth market are highly refined PC, PMMA, PE. It has been predicted that optical disks will eventually replace magnetic and floppy disks as the preferred medium for computer data storage. Oriented TP polyester film is used in the other disks. ▷ **birefringence**

optical distortion Any apparent alteration of the geometric pattern of an object when seen either through a plastic or as a reflection from a plastic surface.

optical emission spectroscopy OES characterizes most of the metallic ions, in addition to certain nonmetals, in terms of the emission spectra produced when electrons are excited by an arc or by other means.

optical fiber ▷ **plastic optical fiber**

optically active plastic Only those molecules in a plastic with dissymmetric or spiral structures, those without inversion and reflection-symmetry elements, possess optical activity.

Both low molecular weight compounds and macromolecules must obey the same symmetry rules, and the preparation of optically active plastics presents problems similar to those encountered in traditional organic chemistry. Optical activity is used as an analytical tool to relate molecular structure to optical properties. In many cases, these properties are very different for macromolecules and low molecular weight compounds resembling the structure of the monomeric residue. Interpretation of these differences allows development of a picture of the conformation in solution, which is difficult to obtain by other techniques.

optical monitoring Used to measure different products such as blown film bubble diameter, film thickness, molded dimensions, etc.

optical properties Transparent plastics offer several advantages in optical applications. Manufacturing costs are low because precision injection molding produces a product that needs no finishing operations and no grinding or polishing. Highly reproducible parts are obtained; linear dimensions can be held to $\pm$ 8 μm for small parts. The ability to design mountings into moldings or to produce multiple-lens arrays reduces the assembly costs. Most plastics have a higher impact strength than silicate glass, and when they fracture, the fragments are less likely to damage the eyes. The density of plastics is about half that of glass, reducing the weight of spectacles. Some plastics are sufficiently flexible, especially when thin, to allow formation of soft contact lenses, flexible mirrors, and other products. Some plastics have a greater transmissibility than silicate glass in IR or UV parts of the spectrum.

However, certain disadvantages prevent plastics from being used in applications such as car windshields (not including plastic interlayer in safety glass). Various coatings can improve scratch resistance, but the yield stress is low. Heat tolerance is low. Even the glass transition temperatures above 250°C are below the range of the T_g of silicate glass (at least 500°C). The temperature coefficients of refractive index are high. Optical plastics are mostly homopolymers; it is not possible to adjust the refractive index or dispersion by adding metal oxides as to silicate glass. The variation in refraction index from point to point is greater than for optical glass by usually an order of magnitude.

The most important plastic is PMMA because of its weathering and scratch resistance. A number of other plastics are transparent and used where transparency is required such as PC, PS and SI. ▷ **refractive index**

optical stress coefficient ▷ **coefficient of optical stress**

optical wave ▷ **wave**

optics, fiber ▷ **fiber optics**

optimum condition The ideal situation; the best possible condition.

orange peel **1.** In injection molding, a part with an undesirable uneven surface somewhat resembling the skin of an orange. **2.** Uneven leveling of coating on RP surfaces, usually because of high viscosity. Simple addition of high boiling point solvent to the coating for a wetter surface is helpful, particularly when spraying. **3.** A term used in the paint industry to refer to a roughened film surface due to too rapid drying. **4.** ▷ **mold polishing**

order of magnitude ▷ **value, order of magnitude**

ordinate direction The vertical direction in a diagram. ▷ **stress-strain curve**

ore An aggregate of valuable minerals and gangue from which one or more metals can be extracted at a profit.

organic Originating in plant and animal life or composed of chemicals of hydro-carbon origin, either natural or synthetic. As used in connection with plastics, it generally refers to material that is of carbon and hydrogen-hydrocarbons, and their derivatives. ▷ **material origin**

organic acid A great many of the organic acids readily found in nature were isolated before chemical nomenclature had been put on a rational basis. For this reason they have acquired names which suggest their natural sources: formic acid from red ants (formicae), acetate acid from vinegar (aceticum), butyric acid from butter (butyrum), and caprotic acid from goats (caper). These acids are members of a homogeneous series known as fatty acids; the name fatty itself arises from the fact that the higher members occur naturally in animal fats. All organic acids contain the animal fats and contain the carboxyl group (COOH). As is true of all acids, the hydrogen atom in this group can be replaced by metals of alkyl radicals with the formation of salts or esters.

organic chemistry ▷ **chemistry**

organic material Materials containing organic carbon and its derivatives, hydrogen and oxygen. Generally made during life processes of plants and animals. They are a source of food for bacteria, decomposable, and usually combustible.

organic peroxide The peroxides useful in the plastics industry are thermally decomposable compounds analogous to hydrogen peroxide (H_2O_2) in which one or both of the hydrogen atoms are replaced by an organic radical. As they decompose, they form free radicals which can initiate polymerization reactions and affect crosslinking. The rate of decomposition can be controlled by means of promoters or accelerators added to the system to increase the decomposition rate; or by inhibitors when it is desired to retard the decomposition. Peroxides are used in curing certain thermoset plastics such as polyesters, and in the polymerization reaction mixtures for many thermoplastics.

organic pigment Characterized by good brightness and brilliance. They are divided into toners and lakes. Toners, in turn, are divided into insoluble organic toners and lake toners. The insoluble organic toners are usually free from salt-forming groups. Lake toners are practically pure, water-insoluble heavy metal salts or dyes without the fillers or substrates of ordinary lakes. Lakes, which are not as strong as lake toners, are water-insoluble heavy metal salts or other dye complexes precipitated upon or admixed with a base or filler.

organoid ▷ **synthetic organs**

organometallic plastic They can be classified into condensation plastics, addition plastics, coordination plastics, and others based on their mode of preparation. Macromolecules generally contain fewer than 10 different elements (carbon, hydrogen, nitrogen, oxygen, sulfur, phosphorus, halides). There are well over 40 additional elements, many metals, which can be built into plastics. Metals often can exist in several different oxidation states. Geometries and reactivities depend on such factors as the nature and extent of substitution. Organometallic plastics are those containing metals either in the backbone chains or pendent to them. The metals may be connected to the plastic by bonds to carbon.

organosol A suspension of a finely divided plastic in a volatile, organic liquid. The most frequently used is PVC. Plastic does not dissolve appreciably in the organic liquid at room temperature, but does at elevated temperatures. The liquid evaporates at an elevated temperature, and the residue upon cooling is a homogeneous plastic mass. Plasticizers may be dissolved in the volatile liquid. In at least a moderate operation, it becomes economically benefical to use a solvent recovery system. ▷ **plastisol**

organosol nonaqueous dispersion Indirect methods for preparing nonaqueous dispersions include grinding bulk or bead type plastic to relatively fine powders that can be dispersed in nonaqueous media; the low practical limit for particle size is 10 μm.

organotin stabilizer These are important for PVC providing high stabilizing efficiency, compatibility, and impartation of clarity. They include dioctyl-tin mercaptides, sulphides and oxides of tin-alkyl or aryl, organotin mercaptides, and maleate compounds.

orientation The process of stretching a hot plastic to realign the molecular configuration, thus improving mechanical properties. A plastic's molecular orientation can be accidental or deliberate. Accidental refers to orientations that occur in processing plastics that may be acceptable. However, excessive frozen-in stress can be extremely damaging if parts are subject to environmental stress cracking or crazing in the presence of chemicals, heat etc. Initially the molecules are relaxed; molecules in amorphous regions are in random coils, those in crystalline regions relatively straight and folded. During processing the molecules tend to be more oriented than relaxed, particularly when sheared, as during injection molding and extrusion. After temperature-time-pressure is applied and the melt goes through restrictions (molds, dies, etc.), the molecules tend to be stretched and aligned in a parallel form. The result is a change in directional properties and dimensions. The amount of change depends on the type of thermoplastic, the amount of restriction, and, most important, its rate of cooling. The faster the rate, the more retention there is of the frozen orientation. After processing, parts could be subject to stress relaxation, with changes in performance and dimensions. With certain plastics and processes there is an insignificant change. If changes are significant, one must take action to change the processing conditions, particularly increasing the cooling rate.

By deliberate stretching (there is a major, big market for stretched film worldwide), the molecular chains of a plastic are drawn in the direction of the stretching, and inherent strengths of the chains are more nearly realized than they are in their naturally relaxed configurations. Stretching can take place with heat during or after processing by blow molding, extruding film, or thermoforming. Products can be drawn in one direction (uniaxially) or in two opposite directions (biaxially), in which case

Effects of orientation of polypropylene films.

Properties	Stretch (%)				
	None	200	400	600	900
Tensile strength, psi (MPa)	5,600 (38.6)	8,400 (58.0)	14,000 (96.6)	22,000 (152.0)	23,000 (159.0)
Elongation at break, %	500	250	115	40	40

Properties	As cast	Uniaxial orientation	Balanced orientation
Tensile strength, psi (MPa)	5,700 (39.3)	150,000 (1,030)	330,000 (2,280)
Tensile strength, psi (MPa)			
MD[1]	5,700 (39.3)	8,000 (55.2)	26,000 (180)
TD[2]	3,200 (22.1)	40,000 (276)	22,000 (152)
Modulus of elasticity, psi (MPa)			
MD	96,000 (660)	150,000 (1,030)	340,000 (2,350)
TD	98,000 (680)	400,000 (2,760)	330,000 (2,280)
Elongation at break, %			
MD	425	300	80
TD	300	40	65

[1] MD = Machine direction.
[2] TD = Transverse direction and direction of uniaxial orientation.

many properties significantly increase uniaxially or biaxially (see Tables above and Fig. on p. 509).

Molecular orientation results in increased stiffness, strength, and toughness as well as liquid resistance to liquid and gas permeation, crazing, microcracks, and others in the direction or plane of the orientation. The orientation of fibers in reinforced plastics causes similar positive influences. Orientation in effect provides a means of tailoring and improving the properties of plastics.

Considering a fiber or thread nylon 6/6, which is an unoriented glassy polymer, its modulus of elasticity is about 2,000 MPa (300,000 psi). Above the T_g its elastic modulus drops even lower, because small stresses will readily straighten the kinked molecular chains. However, once it is extended and has its molecules oriented in the direction of the stress, larger stresses are required to produce added strain. The elastic modulus increases. The next step is to cool the nylon below its T_g without removing the stress, retaining its molecular orientation. The nylon becomes rigid with a much higher elastic modulus in the tension direction (15 to 20 × 10^3 MPa or 2 to 3 × 10^6 psi). This is nearly twenty times the elastic modulus of the unoriented nylon 6/6 glassy polymer. The stress for any elastic extension must work against the rigid backbone of the nylon molecule and not simply unkink molecules. This procedure has been commonly used in the commercial production of man-made fibers since the 1930s.

Another example of the many oriented products is the heat-shrinkable material found in flat or tubular film or sheets. The orientation in this case is terminated downstream of an extrusion-stretching operation when a cold-enough temperature is achieved. Reversing the operation, or shrinkage, occurs when a sufficiently high temperature is introduced. The reheating and subsequent shrinking of these oriented plastics can result in a useful property. It is used, for example, in heat-shrinkable flame-retardant PP tubular or flat communication cable wrap, heat-shrinkable furniture webbing, pipe fittings, medical devices, and many other products. ▷ **extruder film orientation; extruder blown film stretching-orienting; extruder pipe and profile orientation; extruder, sheet orientation; blow molding stretched; stress, plane; residual stress; acrylglass plastic; reinforced plastic, directional properties**

orientation and chemical properties Simple orientation alone increases sorption and solubility; but when it induces crystallization, the overall net effect is a decrease in these properties. Similarly, residual stresses in the structure of foamed plastics make them more susceptible to chemical attack. Orientation of amorphous plastics affects molecular mobility and permeability in similar ways; permeability decreases in the direction of orientation and increases perpendicular to it. Orientation of crystallizable and crystalline plastics decreases permeability

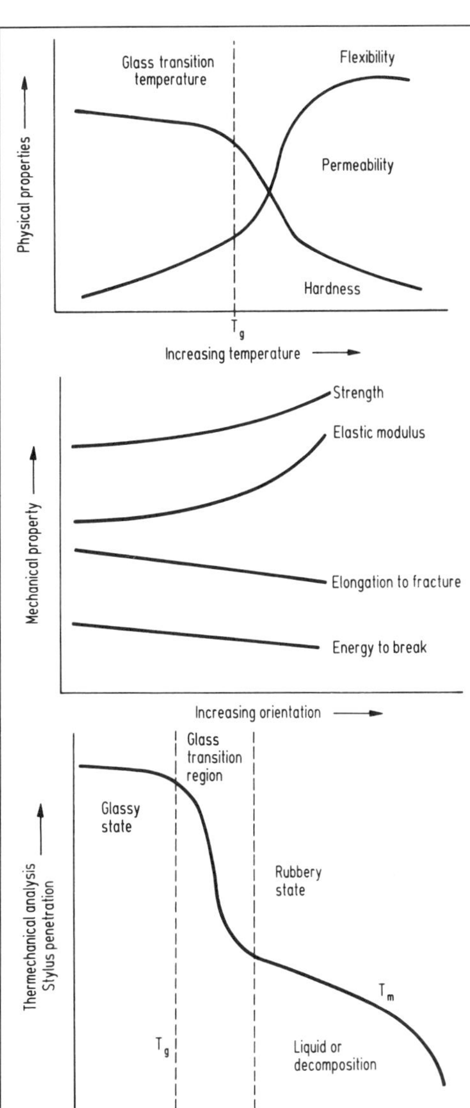

Graphic representations of orientating plastic molecules.

still further. These effects are particularly important in packaging films.

orientation and crystallization When crystallizable plastics have been melted and quenched into the amorphous state, and then are oriented by mechanical stress, such orientation may make their molecules parallel enough to induce crystallization. This is the main reason for the possible confusion between crystallinity and orientation. When crystallites already exist in the amorphous matrix, orientation will make these crystallites parallel. If a plastic crystallizes too far from the melt, it may not contain enough amorphous matrix to permit orientation, and will break during stretching. Most partially crystalline plastics can be drawn 4 to 5 times. A plastic may range from completely amorphous to highly crystalline, with the maximum degree of orientation usually only partial, and only includes a small fraction of the total plastic molecule.

The degree of crystallinity is influenced by the rate at which the melt is cooled. This is utilized in fabrication operations to help control the degree of crystallinity. The balance of properties can be slightly altered in this manner, allowing some control over such parameters as container volume, stiffness, warpage, and brittleness. Nucleating agents are available that can promote more rapid crystallization resulting in faster cycle times.

An important transition occurs in the structure of both crystalline and noncrystalline plastics. This is the point at which they transition out of the so-called glassy state. The glassy state is characterized by rigidity and brittleness. This is because the molecules are too close together to allow extensive slipping motion between each other. When the glass transition (T_g) is above the range of the normal temperatures to which the part is expected to be subjected, it is possible to blend in materials that can produce the T_g of the mix. This yields more flexible, tougher materials.

orientation and directional types ▷ **orientation, uniaxial; orientation, biaxial; orientation, balance**

orientation and electrical properties
Orientation decreases dissipation factor in the direction of orientation, and increases it perpendicular to orientation. Since modulus changes in the opposite way, this indicates that polar vibrations along a stretched plastic molecule are decreased, while transverse vibrations between the stretched molecules become easier. Thus, when PET is extruded and stretched to make film for capacitors, orientation is necessary to produce tough, flexible mechanical properties, but the concomitant increase in dielectric loss across the film is at best a necessary evil.

orientation and fiber reinforced With injection molding (extrusion, etc.) of fiber reinforced plastics, anisotropic mechanical and physical properties usually result from flow induced fiber orientation (see Fig. on p. 510). ▷ **reinforced plastic, directional properties**

orientation and graphite fiber ▷ **oxidation**

orientation and injection molding melt flow
When the plastic melt is injected into the

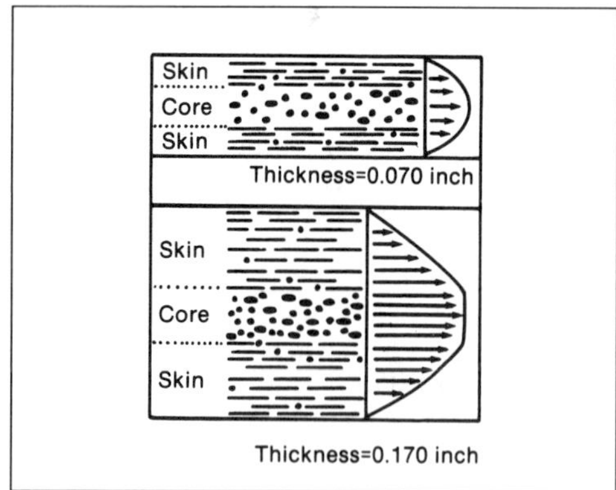

Example that shows fiber orientation varying with thickness and melt velocity across the flow front.

mold, the randomly coiled molecules must disentangle and orient themselves parallel to the flow axis in order to slide past each other easily. This is the mechanism of pseudoplastic and thixotropic rheology typical of a non-Newtonian flow behavior. It is most pronounced when high speed flow through narrow gates and thin wall sections produces the maximum rate of shear and therefore maximum orientation. After entry into the mold, high temperature and thicker volumes permit turbulence and Brownian randomization to reduce or eliminate the orientation with a return toward the random coil isotropic condition. However, oriented molecules flowing along a cold wall will form a film that will solidify so that the orientation is permanently frozen into the final solid product.

orientation and mechanical properties Mechanical properties depend directly upon the relationship between the axis of orientation of the plastic molecules and the axis of mechanical stress upon these molecules. Reversible properties, such as modulus and stiffness, increase in the direction of orientation. In the direction perpendicular to the axis of orientation, modulus decreases and flexibility increases because stress along the axis of the molecules is applied against the strong covalent bonds within the molecules, whereas stress perpendicular is applied only against the weak secondary forces between the molecules. These effects are important to the toughness and flexibility of most films and all fibers.

Ultimate tensile strength generally increases in the direction of stretch and decreases in the perpendicular direction. Changes in strength also relate to possible existing stress concentrators (such as microscopic or submicroscopic flaws) become parallel to the axis of orientation. When stress is applied along the same axis, it no longer tends to pull them apart; perpendicular it pulls them apart. With elongation, variations can develop. Moderate orientation, particularly in rigid amorphous plastics like PS, increases ductility and ultimate elongation in the stretched direction and decreases in the transverse direction. High degrees of orientation of ductile plastics can have the opposite effect. Orientation used up most of its inherent extensibility.

Biaxial orientation increases impact strength significantly; making BO very desirable in most packaging films. With monoaxial (uniaxial) orientation impact strength increases in the direction of stretch; its transverse impact is very weak and usually breaks into bundles of fibers. These impact results can be related to the area under the tensile stress-strain curves; the BO film has a much larger area that can be used as a measure of toughness.

orientation and mobility Orientation requires considerable mobility of large segments of the plastic molecules. It cannot occur below the glass transition temperature (T_g). The plastic temperature is taken to just above T_g.

orientation and optical properties Biaxial orientation of crystalline plastics generally improves clarity of films. This is because stretching breaks up large crystalline structures into smaller than the wavelength of visible light. With uniaxial orientation, the result is an anisotropic refractive index and thus birefringence, especially in crystalline plastics.

orientation and processability Oriented films (and other products such as fibers) may lose some of their orientation because of excess thermal motion during later thermal processing such as thermoforming and heat sealing, and also in the use of solvents for sealing and printing. However, heat shrinkable films and fibers are conveniently made by temporary orientation, which is lost when desired by warming above T_g to produce disorientation and shrinkage back to their original dimensions. In thermoforming film, for example, if the unoriented film tends to sag excessively during warming, preorientation may give it sufficient hot strength for more suitable forming.

orientation, balance Balance in biaxial orientation is the result of the relative degrees of stretching during the orientation process. Balanced biaxial or uniform planar orientation is actually only one special case in a spectrum of many different degrees of combinations. Although a film of balanced stretching is desirable for most markets, there are applications for others involving shrinkage or a greater strength in one direction, in which an unbalanced system is desired.

orientation, biaxial BO occurs when a film or sheet is drawn in more than one direction, commonly along two axes at right angles to one another; also called planar.

orientation, cold stretching Plastic may be oriented by cold stretching, below its glass transition temperature, if there is sufficient internal friction to convert mechanical into thermal energy, thus producing local heating above T_g. This occurs characteristically in the necking of fibers during cold drawing.

orientation, concrete ▷**concrete** and **concrete, reinforced oriented composite**

orientation, fiber ▷**fiber orientation** and **extruder solid-state**

orientation, foam ▷**foamed orientation**

orientation, live feed technique ▷**extruder melt flow orientation; mold cavity melt flow analysis; injection molding multi-live feed**

orientation, monoaxial ▷**orientation, uniaxial**

orientation of an object The angular position of an object described by the angles which a defined set of axes or surfaces of the object make with the frame of reference.

orientation, properties versus cost The process of orientation is fairly expensive, and increases the cost per unit weight of the product. However, the yield increases considerably and the quality improves greatly. Many films, such as PS and PET, are made much stronger, flexible, and highly valuable. The same is true of fibers. Optimum application of coatings from a mixture of low boiling-good solvent and high boiling-poor solvent produces intermediate gelation followed by biaxial orientation producing strength and toughness in the finished coating. Thus on ultimate balance, maximum economic value depends upon the relative cost of stretching versus the increase in yield and properties.

orientation, reinforced plastic ▷**reinforced plastic, directional properties**

orientation release stress The internal stress that remains frozen into the structure of the material after the manufacturing process. It can be relieved by reheating the film, sheet, etc. to a temperature above that at which it was oriented. The release stress is measured by heating the material and determining the force per unit area exerted by the material in returning to its preorientation dimensions.

orientation rules Some general rules for orienting plastic by stretching are: (1) the lowest temperature above its glass transition temperature (T_g) will give the greatest orientation (and tensile strength, etc.) at a given percent and rate of stretch, (2) the highest rate of stretching will give the greatest orientation at a given temperature and percent stretch, (3) the highest percent stretch will give the greatest orientation at a given temperature and rate of stretching, and (4) the greatest quench rate will preserve the most orientation under any stretching condition.

orientation, tentering frame ▷**extruder film orientation**

orientation, theory of stress-induced In stress-induced orientation plastic chains are displaced by hot stretching or drawing the bulk material from a completely random entanglement to a more orderly arrangement parallel to the direction of stress. When chain straightening has occurred, with closer packing that accompanies molecular alignment, mutual attraction between the chains is increased because they are now in a position to exert the greatest possible secondary valence forces on each other. These are particularly large if the chains are symmetrical and/or strongly polar. Since more secondary valence bonds must now be broken, slippage in the direction of alignment is reduced. This, plus the unfolding of the chains, results in increased tensile strength and elastic modulus. With the anisotropic nature of the state, it accounts for the distinctive characteristics.

Molecular orientation during stretching takes place in the following manner. Below glass transition temperature (T_g), polymer chains are rigid. However, at T_g they gain a degree of freedom and become able to unfold as stress is applied. If a mass of randomly coiled and entangled chains is above T_g it may be drawn out. When stress is applied the chains disentangle and straighten as well as slip past one another.

orientation, thermal properties Stretching decreases dimensional stability at higher temperatures. Because the molecules have been stretched into a statistically improbable conformation of thermodynamically high energy level, on rewarming they tend to retract to their original randomly coiled conformation as soon as they acquire sufficient mobility, disorienting to a lower energy and higher entropy level. This makes them deform and distort at lower temperatures than unoriented materials, and causes them to shrink back toward their original size and shape on rewarming. This situation is use-

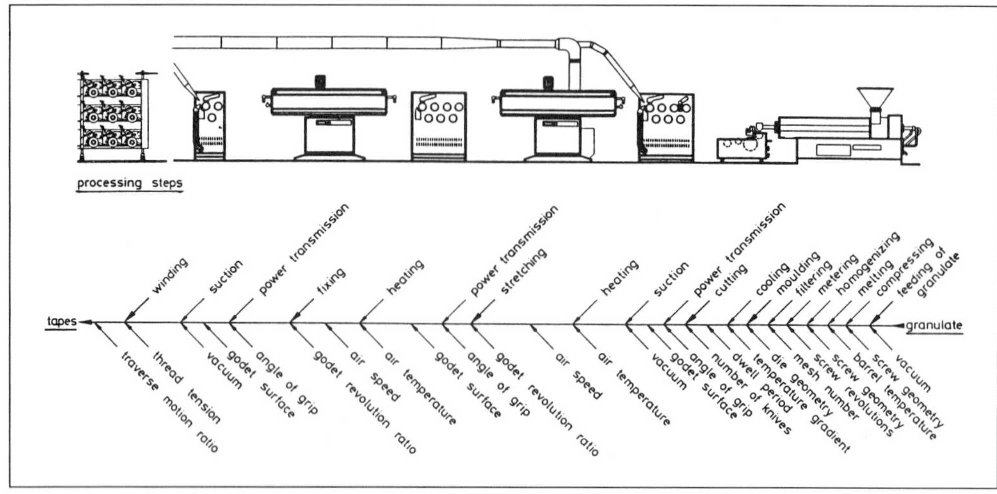

Extruder chill roll process line used to produce uniaxial oriented film tape.

ful in the production of shrink film used in packaging. It is first stretched and oriented, then chilled below the glass transition temperature (T_g), and finally reheated above T_g permitting it to shrink tightly around the object.

Effects of orientation on T_g vary with type of test and test conditions. Generally it restrains molecular mobility and increases T_g slightly. However, disorientation above T_g produces more complex effects on properties than are observed in simple amorphous plastics. Coefficient of linear thermal expansion decreases parallel to the axis of orientation and increases perpendicularly. Consequently their resulting coefficient of volumetric thermal expansion hardly changes at all. Thermal conductivity depends upon transmission of thermal vibrations, and thus travels much more readily along the strong primary covalent bonds within the molecule than across weak secondary bonds between molecules. Consequently it increases parallel to the direction of orientation and decreases in the perpendicular direction.

orientation, uniaxial Takes place when stretched in one direction; the plastic chains are aligned in one dimension. This produces maximum strength in one direction, that of orientation (see Fig. above). Also called axial or monoaxial orientation.

orientation, warm stretching This is the major production method used. For effective orientation, it is best to stretch rapidly somewhat above glass transition temperature (T_g) and then rechill immediately to below T_g. To prevent later thermal rerandomization and loss of orientation, which might occur during use at temperatures above T_g, it may be best to follow the orientation step by a quick high temperature heat-setting by crystallization or by possible vulcanization.

orientation, wet stretching For plastics whose glass transition temperature (T_g) is above their decomposition temperature, orientation can be accomplished by swelling them temporarily with liquids to lower the T_g of the total mass, particularly in solution processing. As an example, cellulose viscose films and fibers can be drawn during coagulation and polyacrylonitrile fibers can be drawn during solution spinning, while they still contain enough fugitive solvent to plasticize them and lower their T_g below the decomposition temperature. Final removal of the plasticizing solvent makes the orientation permanent.

orifice bushing ▷ **die orifice bushing**

origin of material ▷ **material origin**

O-ring A product of precise dimensions molded in one piece to the configuration of a torus with circular cross section, suitable for use in a machined groove for static or dynamic service. Different plastics and elastomers are used to meet many different property requirements.

orthophthalic plastic A TS polyester plastic using phthalic anhydride as one of the chemical constituents. A higher percentage makes a less reactive plastic.

orthotropic direction ▷ **reinforced plastic, directional properties**

oscillating die ▷ **extruder blown film gauge distortion**

oscillating rheometry ▷ **rheometer, dynamic**

osmium A hard brittle blue-gray or blue-black polyvalent metallic element of the platinum group with a high melting point; the heaviest metal known. ▷ **polystyrene plastic, high impact**

osmometer, high speed A modern commercial device which requires only minutes to about half an hour to enable an equilibrium osmotic pressure reading to be obtained. This contrasts with the period of hours to weeks which the traditional osmometer requires and which this type has largely replaced. They sometimes operate in a dynamic equilibrium mode by detecting electrically incipient solvent flow through the membrane. By means of a servomechanism the flow is countered by application of a hydrostatic head of pressure solvent. Some models operate in a static mode, where solvent flow is balanced by the deflection of an attached diaphragm, which also acts as a sensor for pressure, i.e. by means of an attached strain gauge. In either case very little transport of solvent through the membrane is necessary to achieve equilibrium.

osmometry, dynamic Membrane osmometry which is performed with a membrane which is permeable to at least part of the solute (the lower molecular weight species of a plastic sample). Thus the observed osmotic pressure is time dependent. The technique attempts to relate the variation of osmotic pressure with time to reach equilibrium. In osmodialysis, the study of the time dependency can give information on the molecular weight distribution.

osmosis The passage of solvent from a mass of pure solvent into a solution, or from a less to a more concentrated solution, through a membrane which is permeable to the solvent but not to the solute.

osmosis, reverse It is utilized as a method of desalting sea water, recovering waste in pollution control, industrial water treatment, etc. The principles of reverse osmosis are well known ▷ **membrane**. As an example in the desalination of brackish waters, saline water is placed in contact with a suitable membrane (fine hollow plastic fiber structure) at a pressure exceeding the osmotic pressure of the solution. Fresh water, or water with a lower salt content, permeates the membrane and is collected for use. A concentrated brine is discharged from the high pressure side of the membrane as a waste stream. For a membrane with a given specific permeability, the fresh water output or flux of a reverse osmosis device is directly proportional to membrane area and pressure driving force, and inversely proportional to membrane thickness. Membrane area can be maximized and thickness minimized in the hollow fiber form structure. Fine hollow fibers provide a thin, self-supporting membrane with the very high surface-to-volume ratio desirable for reverse osmosis. ▷ **desalination**

osmotic pressure The hydrostatic pressure at which the flow of solvent through the membrane of an osmometer just stops. This pressure is related to the number of plastic molecules in dilute solution, and can be used in calculations of molecular weight.

-ous and -ic endings "Ferrous" indicates a valence of two, whereas "ferric" indicates a valence of three. ▷ **valence**

outgassing The release of a volatile substance from a plastic during heat processing (injection molding, compression molding, etc.) or from a plastic part during vacuum metalizing. Each processing method has techniques such as venting, bumping, for removal of the volatiles.

out of flat The deviation of a surface from a flat plane, usually over a macroscopic area.

out of round Non-uniform radius or diameter.

output Also called throughput; refers to production line output of product.

output rate, percentage variation The maximum measurable difference in output rate expressed as a percentage of average rate.

oven drying ▷ **drying oven**

oven-dry weight ▷ **weight, oven-dry**

oven festooning ▷ **festooning oven**

over aging Continued aging for plastics until softening occurs.

overcapacity In excess of the needs based on existing market conditions.

overcoating In extrusion coating, the difference between the width of the extruded web as it leaves the die and the width of the coating on the substrate.

overcuring The beginning of a thermal decomposition owing to too high a temperature or too long a processing time.

overflow capacity The capacity of a container to the top of the finish or to the point of overflow.

overhead ▷ **capacity overhead rate**

overlap ▷ **adhesive overlap**

overlay sheet ▷ **reinforced plastic surfacing or overlay**

overpack molding ▷ **mold cavity packing**

oxidation Basically the addition of oxygen to a material, reduction of hydrogen, or any chemical reaction in which electrons are transferred. The term oxidation originally meant a reaction in which oxygen combines chemically with another substance, but its usage has long been broadened to include any reaction in which electrons are transferred (such as photo-oxidation). Oxidation and reduction always occur simultaneously and the substance which gains electrons is termed oxidizing agent. Examples of oxidation include: (1) in carbon/graphite fiber processing, the step of reacting the precursor plastic (rayon, PAN, or pitch) with oxygen, resulting in stabilization of the structure for the hot stretching operation, (2) the chemical reaction involving the process of combining with oxygen to form an oxide, (3) the deterioration of an adhesive film due to atmospheric exposure, (4) the breakdown of a hot melt adhensive due to prolonged heating and oxide formation, (5) in general waste management, adding oxygen to break down organic waste or chemicals.

oxidation degradation Plastics tend to be susceptible to thermal oxidative degradation, although there is considerable variation in their degree of stability; some literally cannot degrade. The incorporation of additives is the most common method used to protect against thermal oxidation. Structure modification, usually applied in protection against nonoxidative degradation, can also be effective in protecting against thermal oxidation, but this approach has limited application. ▷ **ultraviolet absorber and light stabilizer**

Plastics degrade because of the presence of weak links or structural defects that are more reactive than the normal segments of the molecules. Oxidative degradation (room temperature and higher) might be expected to be initiated at these sensitive sites. Additives stabilize the plastic by restricting the penetration of oxygen. Another technique produces a densified surface on PE by molding against a noble metal surface. The transcrystalline surface layer that is formed is less permeable than the normal crystalline structure but rapidly reverts to the normal structure. ▷ **strengthening plastics mechanisms**

oxidation, internal The selective oxidation of a dispersed phase which is more reactive than the matrix phase.

oxide A mineral in which metallic atoms are bonded to oxygen atoms.

oxidizing agent Used to inhibit aging caused by natural oxidation. ▷ **oxidation degradation**

oxifluorination ▷ **barrier via chemical modification**

oxirane A synonym for ethylene oxide. An oxirane group is one kind of epoxy group.

oxygen Nonmetallic, noncombustible, gaseous element of atomic number 8, group 4A of the Periodic table. Atmospheric oxygen (O_2) is the result of photosynthesis; it constitutes 20% by volume of air at sea level. Various commercial methods are used to produce O_2. ▷ **atmosphere chart**

oxygen index ▷ **limiting oxygen index**

ozalid Copying process which gives positive prints, dark on white.

ozone A gas (O_3) found in two layers of the atmosphere. In the stratosphere, seven to 10 miles above the earth's surface, O_3 shields the earth from UV radiation. In the troposphere, up to seven miles altitude, ozone is a chemical oxidant and one of the most prevalent air pollutants hazardous to humans. O_3 is produced through chemical reactions of nitrogen oxides, which are among the primary emissions of combustion and the processing of petroleum products (automobile, trucks, manufacturing plants, etc. exhaust). ▷ **electrical corona; antiozonant; antioxidant; atmosphere chart**

ozonolysis 1. Oxidation of an organic material by means of ozone. **2.** The use of ozone as a tool in analytical chemistry.

P

package, bag-in-box ▷ **bag-in-box**

packaging 1. The operation of placing materials in suitable containers or protective covering for purposes of storage, distribution, and sale. Some packages act merely as containers. Others protect perishable materials (especially foodstuffs) from environmental damage, contamination (such as medical devices), and biological deterioration. In this respect, the critical factor is exclusion of moisture vapor, bacteria, and oxygen. Some packages perform both functions. Different types and forms of plastics have provided the means of significantly extending the use and life of packaged materials to the benefit of people worldwide. This market consumes about 30 wt% of all plastics used. ▷ **film** and **barrier material performance** 2. Describes the method of supply of roving or yarn.

packaging and waste ▷ **waste and packaging**

packaging biological substance Years ago, most biological substances, including human body fluids, could be shipped through the mail without much scrutiny. With the advent of AIDS, however, the shipping of blood, urine, medical specimens etc., has become closely regulated and restricted by both governments and private couriers as well as mail handlers. Many of these substances are classified as hazardous and require specialty packaging where plastics play an important role to meet strict requirements.

packaging, blister ▷ **blister package**

packaging, clamshell A container having an integrated lid, usually thermoformed from plastic sheets, that use a living hinge. ▷ **thermoforming, clamshell**

packaging, contour ▷ **contour package**

packaging design Packaging can be designed in such a way that it can be fed into the recycling system. For this reason, producers resort to more economical packaging materials. Usually, the less elaborate the package, the easier it is to recycle.

packaging dual-ovenable tray DOTs for frozen foods have been an upredictable roller-coaster for plastic processors who found they could have a 100-million tray market one day and none the next. That happened to china-like thermoset polyester frozen diner trays, which all but vanished in 1988 (US) after eight years of growth, and with them a slew of big compression molding ventures set up to exploit the burgeoning market for microwavable and ovenable foods. TS lost out to thermoplastic thermoforming of CPET and a few other plastics. Then injection molded nylon appeared on the horizon in 1988, but its death knell was sounded by 1990. Thermoforming appears unchallenged at present, but trends in DOT's future are complicated. Frozen dual-ovenable foods are competing with less expensive fresh refrigerated and shelf stable foods, etc. Price is usually the determinant with DOT.

packaging electronics Plastics' low cost and ease of processing have given them wide application in solving problems of electronic packaging. They range from inexpensive consumer devices to sophisticated computing systems.

packaging, Enviropet ▷ **Enviropet packaging**

packaging, flexible type ▷ **flexible packaging**

packaging form, fill, and seal ▷ **thermoforming, form, fill, and seal**

packaging, hot fill Plastics are used to hot fill (blow molded bottles, thermoformed containers, etc) without sagging or thin-walling during filling and maintain mechanical properties such as impact strength and stiffness in temperatures (-40 to 120°C). Plastics used include special grades of PS, PET, PVC, and PP.

packaging loose-fill plastic Loose-filled plastic using principally PS and PE foam is used in different shapes, with the pretzel and peanut as the most popular. They package all types of products that include sensitive medical devices to complex shaped delicate-large products. Since the 1970s worldwide, their use includes 100% recycled foam. Another popular form is internal bubbled laminated film.

packaging material Any paper, cardboard, ceramic, glass, plastic, metal, or a combination of them used to contain or package products for transportation and sale. ▷**peanut foam packaging material**

packaging, plastic or paper bag ▷**environment and public opinion**

packaging pouch ▷**aseptic liquid pouch**

packaging, shrink ▷**shrink package**

packaging, skin ▷**contour package**

packaging via MAP This is a packaging system called Modified Atmosphere Packaging. Its function is to extend the shelf-life of the product and, in some cases, allow it to be presented in a more palatable manner. Shelf-life is extended by modifying the "atmosphere" inside; generally done by injecting a gas mixture of carbon dioxide, nitrogen, oxygen, or their combinations. Most MAPs use conventional multilayer, high barrier films, such as EVOH/PVDC, LDPE/PA/EVOH, PVDC/coated PET/LDPE, etc. This concept of using a barrier film and a gas flush is not new.

packaging with plastic At least 10 wt% of the U.S. food supply is packaged in plastic.

packaging zipper to film on-line ▷**thermoforming, form, fill, and seal with zipper on-line**

packing 1. Mold packing is filling the mold cavity ▷**mold cavity packing. 2.** A collar or gasket used to seal mechanical devices to prevent leakage of liquids or gases; often made of specialty elastomer compounds. **3.** The operation of placing solid materials or products in shipping containers in such a way to secure maximum space economy and freedom from damage; barrier protectors include plastic foam. **4.** An inert material used in distillation columns.

packing factor Ratio of occupied volume to bulk volume; occupied volume per unit of total volume.

paddle agitator Very simple mixing equipment for plastics in the form of dispersions, pastes, doughs. The most common form is a set of rotating blades driven by a vertical shaft intermeshing with a set of fixed blades.

pad printing Pad transfer printing is basically an offset (or indirect) gravure process. The ink is applied in excess over an engraved steel plate (called a cliche). The excess is removed by a doctor blade, leaving the ink only in the engraved recesses. A soft silicone rubber pad picks up the ink from the plate (cliche) and transfers it to the part to be printed (parts of plastic, etc.) as shown in Fig. on p. 517. This process has been used for a long time, in a limited way, for the printing of watch dials, for which a fragile gelatine pad was used. The method gained wide acceptance only after the introduction of the silicone rubber pad in the late 1960s. Its main advantage is its suitability for printing irregular shaped and rough surfaces as well as soft, flexible products. ▷**decorating**

paint coating For centuries, paints have been used for decorating or protective coatings. Early paints were formulated from natural plastics, dyes, and pigments. The paints used today are similar with the big difference being the range of synthetic plastics that have replaced the natural plastics. A paint is a suspension of pigment in a liquid that dries or cures to form a solid film. Traditional paints contain a vehicle, a solvent, and a pigment. The vehicle forms the film which traps the pigment. The solvent eases application. Some plastic coatings are applied by dipping or spraying parts with a plasticized plastic. Other systems involve heating parts and spraying them with a dry plastic powder that coalesces on the hot part to form a film. The differences between these various coating systems are the mechanism of film formation and the type of plastic that is being applied. Many important details are involved in surface preparation and in application techniques to arrive at a good plastic paint coating.

Both solventborne and aqueous paints are used. Paints are usually classified on the basis of the binder (vehicle) used. The most often used are: (1) acrylics (solventborne enamels, aqueous acrylic emulsions, melamine and other modified acrylic emulsions), (2) polyurethanes (one and two component solventborne urethanes, aqueous PUR emulsions), (3) alkyds and modified alkyds, (4) epoxies and various modifications, (5) polyesters, (6) vinyls and modified vinyls (either solventborne or latex systems), (7) nitrocellulosics (solventborne) and (8) polyamide (solventborne).

Solventborne paints may be ambient air dried or dried with application of some forced air; aqueous latexes require higher drying temperatures; some catalyzed paints (epoxy, polyurethane, some alkyds) dry at room temperature by chemical crosslinking, not by vehicle evaporation. Catalyzed paint has a limited pot life.

paint emulsion This (latex) paint is composed of two dispersions: dry powders (colorants, fillers, extenders) and plastic dispersions. Emulsion paints are characterized by the fact that the binder is in water-dispersed form. Principal types are styrene-butadiene, polyvinyl

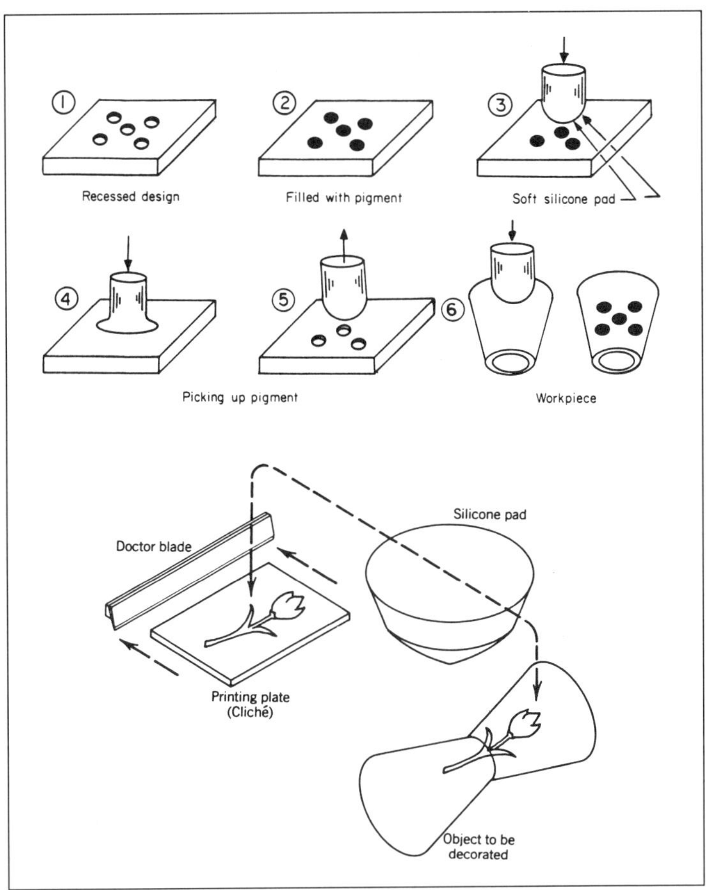

Schematic illustrates pad printing.

acetate, and acrylic plastics. Percentage composition by volume generally is 25 to 30% dry ingredients, 40% latex, and 20 to 30% water, plus stabilizer. Their unique properties are ease of application, absence of disagreeable odor, and nonflammability; used indoor and out-door.

paint fill-and-wipe ▷ **fill-and-wipe**

paint, flame protection coating ▷ **intumescent coating**

painting plastic Some plastic products requiring painting may need special considerations. The Table below lists recommended paints for plastics. Some plastics may be sensitive to certain solvents and care must be taken

Guide to painting plastics.[1]

Plastic	Urethane	Epoxy	Polyester	Acrylic lacquer	Acrylic enamel	Acrylic waterborne
ABS	R[2]	R	NR	R	R	R
Acrylic	NR[2]	NR	NR	R	R	R
PVC	NR	NR	NR	R	R	NR
Styrene	R	R	NR	R	R	R
PPO/PPE	R	R	R	R	R	R
Polycarbonate	R	R	R	R	R	R
Nylon	R	R	R	NR	NR	NR
Polypropylene	R	R	R	NR	NR	NR
Polyethylene	R	R	R	NR	NR	NR
Polyester	R	R	R	NR	NR	NR
RIM	R	NR	NR	NR	R	R

[1] In order to obtain adequate paint adhesion, primers may be required.
[2] R: commended; NR: not recommended.

(when using a solvent system paint) that such a solvent is not used in the formulation in an amount large enough to cause damage to the plastic surface. Such plastic surface solvent should be removed from the surface quickly. As an example, polyolefins and nylon exhibit good solvent resistance; hence, solvent selection is not critical for these plastics.

In painting plastic parts, many different problems can arise in terms of wettability of the plastic surface and paint adhesion. These difficulties are because plastics do not have the rather high surface tension values required for good wetting and adhesion. For good paint adhesion the polar element of surface tension is of great importance. Different pretreatments are used such as solvent etching, flame treatment, plasma treatment, or sulphonation.

paint mask Stencil designed to conform to the shape of the part with the areas to be decorated cut out. The Fig. below is a guide to masking.

pallet 1. In reinforced plastics, usually refers to a number of cartons of roving placed on a wooden skid and strapped together as a shipping unit. Normally a pallet load consists of either 36 or 48 cartons of roving. **2.** A load platform usually of wood (but also metal and plastic used for special use) used for transportation or temporary storage of substances. Plastic pallets are used in "medically clean" operations, etc.

pantographic engraving Technique in which a duplication of a master pattern is cut into steel, plastic, or other materials. It permits use of an oversize master pattern, and the reproduction is a reduced size. Used in mold making.

paper Produced by a wet process. The line of demarcation between specialty papers and nonwoven fabrics is not specific or clear. The term nonwoven fabrics includes nonwoven fibrous sheets made by both textile and paper processes. Paper is a semisynthetic product made

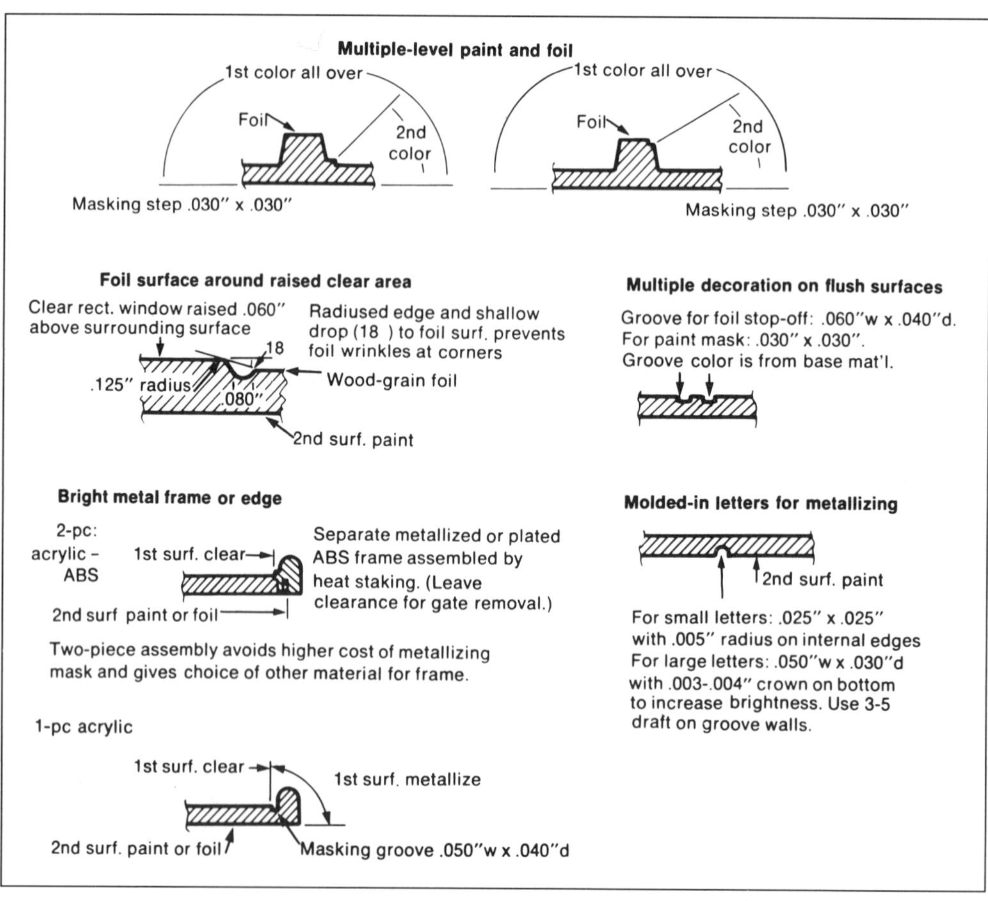

Masking dimensions and stop-off grooves.

by chemical procesing cellulosic fibers; using flax, bagasse, straw, bamboo, jute, and others. By far the largest quantity is made from softwoods such as spruce, hemlock, pine, etc. Some is made from hardwoods of popular oak, etc. And there are plastic fiber papers. Paper-making techniques basically use the Fourdriner machine where the water is screened out of the water liquid fiber stock and the sheet is dried by passing over a series of heated drums.

paper and plastic bags Neither paper nor plastic bags necessarily degrade in landfill. ▷ **grocery bag; environment and public opinion; plastic bad and other myths**

paper coating ▷ **wax**

paper honeycomb, sandwich ▷ **sandwich core material**

paraffin Also called alkane. A class of aliphatic hydrocarbons characterized by a straight or branched chain. It ranges in appearance from a gas (methane) to a waxy solid depending on molecular weight. They have molecular chains with only single bonded carbons. Use includes as a parting agent for plastics.

parameter An arbitary constant, as distinguished from a fixed or absolute constant. Any desired numerical value may be given a parameter.

parametric modeling ▷ **modeling parametric**

parison 1. In blow molding, the hollow tube of melt extruded from the die head which is expanded within the mold cavity by air pressure to produce the molded part. **2.** Refers to the flow of a molten sheet in a thermoforming operation. **3.** An unformed mass of molten glass from which finished products are produced such as glass filaments.

Parkesine plastic Plastic introduced in 1862 by the Englishman Alexander Parkes. It was a product of a mixture of chloroform and castor oil which produced a substance hard as horn, but as flexible as leather, capable of being cast or stamped, painted, dyed, or carved. It could be produced at a lower cost than gutta percha. Unfortunately the material never went into production although a factory was formed in 1866 that went into liquidation in 1868. No further action was taken with this material.

part In its proper literal meaning, a component of an assembly. However, the word is widely used to designate any individual article (cup, box, etc.), even when it is complete in itself (calcium carbonate, silica, talc, carbon black, etc.).

particle Any discrete unit of material structure.

particleboard A generic term for a panel manufactured from lignocellulosic materials (usually wood) primarily in the form of discrete pieces or particles, as distinguished from fibers, combined with a synthetic plastic and bonded together under heat and pressure. When pressure is applied in the direction perpendicular to the faces as in conventional multiplaten hot press, they are defined as flatplaten pressed and when the applied pressure is parallel to the faces, they are defined as extruded.

particle size This term refers chiefly to the solid particles of which industrial materials are composed; carbon black, clays, etc.

particulate matter 1. Solid particle or condensable vapor emissions that result from incomplete combustion. **2.** That nonliquid matter, exclusive of gases, which is heterogeneously dispersed in water.

parting agent ▷ **release agent** and **lubricant**

parting line ▷ **mold parting line** and **die parting line**

parts consolidation The significance of parts consolidation capabilities of plastic has been (and continues to be) demonstrated. Plastic materials and processes permit a wide variation to combine two or more parts into one unit.

parts handling The logic and approach used in materials handling also applies to the use of handling equipment to move processed parts. Parts handling equipment (PHE) does not resemble the humanoids of science fiction. Robots are blind, deaf, dumb, and limited to a few preprogrammed motions; but in many production jobs that is all that is needed. They are solutions looking for a problem. Most plants can use some degree of PHE, and it can substantially increase productivity.

Use of PHE can range from simple operations, to rather complex operations with very sophisticated computer controls. Although the concept of automatic operations is very appealing, the ultimate justification for PHE (like material handling, process controls, etc.) must be made on the basis of economics. At times it may provide the solution to "handling" a part that otherwise would be damaged.

parylene plastic The melting point of these film and coating resins ranges from 290° to

400°C (554 to 752°F), and their glass-transition temperatures range from 60 to 100°C (140 to 212°F). Parylenes' cryogenic properties are excellent. Their physical properties are unaffected by thermal cycles from 2K(−271°C) to room temperature. Their thermal endurance in air is as follows: the short-term (1,000 hr.) exposure is 93 to 129°C (200 to 265°F), the long term (ten years) 60 to 100°C (140 to 212°F). In inert atmospheres or in the absence of air, their properties are maintained up to 216 to 279°C (420 to 535°F).

These thermoplastics are generally insoluble up to 150°C (302°F). At 270°C (518°F) they will dissolve in chlorinated biphenyls, but the solution gels upon cooling below 160°C (320°F). Their weather resistance is poor. Embrittlement is the primary consequence of their exposure to UV radiation.

The first significant commercial application of parylenes was as a dielectric film in high-performance precision electrical capacitors, followed with use in circuitboards and electronic module coatings. These coatings are to protect units from airborne contaminants, moisture, salt spray, and corrosive vapors while maintaining excellent insulator protection. The coatings are also extensively used in the protection of hybrid circuits. Such coatings do not affect parts' dimensions, shapes, or magnetic properties.

Free-standing films can be produced of parylene. These ultrathin (350 A − 3 microns) films, called pellicles, are used as beam splitters in optical instruments, windows for nuclear radiation measuring devices, dielectric supports for planar capacitors, and for extremely fast-responding, low-mass thermistors and thermocouples.

Applying parylene requires special, though not complex or bulky, equipment: essentially a vaporizer, a pyrolysis unit and a deposition chamber. The objects to be coated are placed in the deposition chamber, where the vapor coats them with a polymer. A condensation coating like this does not run off or sag as in conventional coating methods. Neither is it "line of sight," as in vacuum metalizing. In condensation coating the vapor evenly coats edges, points, and internal areas. Although the vapor is all-pervasive, holes can still be coated without bridging. Masking can easily prevent certain areas from being coated, as desired. The objects to be coated can also remain at or near room temperature, thus preventing possible thermal damage. Because of the quantitative nature of this reaction, a coating's thickness can be accurately and simply controlled by manipulating the polymer composition's charge to the vaporizer.

Pascal Pa is the pressure or stress of one Newton per square meter (N/m^2).

Pascal's law ▷ **hydraulic fluid** and **hydraulic press**

passivation The condition in which normal corrosion is impeded by an adsorbed surface film on the electrode.

password for computer ▷ **computer accessibility**

paste A material compound and adhesive composition of semisolid consistency, usually dispersed in water.

paste extrusion ▷ **extruder paste**

paste metering blade ▷ **doctor blade, bar, or knife**

paste plastic A term sometimes used for PVC plastics used in making vinyl dispersions such as plastisols.

patentability The qualifications for obtaining a patent on an invention or a process (U.S.) are: (1) the invention must not have been published in any country or in public use in the U.S. in either case for more than one year prior to date of filing application, (2) it must not have been known in the U.S. before that date of invention by the applicant, (3) it must not be obvious to an expert in the art/technology, (4) it must be useful for a purpose not immoral and not injurious to the public welfare and (5) it must fall within five statutory classes on which only patents may be granted, namely, (a) composition of material, (b) process of manufacture or treatment, (c) machine, (d) design, and (e) a plant produced asexually.

patent information Patents tend to be the literature of technology. A patent is a legal document conferring on its owner the right to exclude others from practicing an invention; making, using, or selling a particular product; or carrying out a parricular process. In return for this monopoly the inventor must fully disclose the details of the invention, and this becomes part of the collective knowledge of human-kind to serve as a spur to further invention and innovation.

patent infringement Generally, ignorance of the patent or *trademark* rights of others is no excuse to an infringing activity. Moreover, an imfringement may give rise to costs and risks in withdrawal or recall of products, ads, or artwork, attorneys' fees, damages, and new product introductions. Together these potential costs will probably outweigh the cost of the initial searches or clearances.

patent, mold Custom molders have traditionally assumed no responsibility for the legality of the design of the customer's product, the design of the molded part as a component of that product, or parts produced to the customers design and specification. In the event a molded part infringes, or is claimed to infringe, any letters of patent, or copyright, the customer has assumed the responsibility involved. Normally most quotation forms include clauses which explicitly detail the indemnification provisions.

patent source The primary source of most patents is the weekly journal/magazine/gazette of countries that announce either granting of legal protection to inventions, as in U.S., or the filling of unexamined patent applications, as in the quick-issue countries, e.g., Germany, France, Japan, etc. These weekly reviews are the earliest records of new technology. As rights of invention apply only to the country issuing the patent, patent applications are usually sent to many countries for legal protection. The huge task of procuring and tracking the immense volume of multilingual records developed commercial patent services that provide a source for abstracts and indexes in English for the weekly patent records reported in the world.

In the plastic (polymer) area, the principal services are: (1) Derwent Publications of London World Patent Index Gazette (WPI), Central Patent Index (CPI), World Patent Abstracts (WPA), Alerting Bulletins, Basic Abstracts Journal, and CPI Section A; PLASDOC; (2) Chemical Abstracts (CA); (3) IFI/plenum Data Co. (IFI Comprehensive Database to United States Chemical Patents, Weekly Patent Profile, Patent Intelligence and Technology Report, and IFI Assignee Index); (4) International Patent Documentation Center in Vienna [INPADOC, Patent-Family Service, and INPADOC Patent Gazette (IPG)]; and (5) American Petroleum Institute (APIPAT). The CPI (1) is the most comprehensive abstracting and indexing system for patents with a broad definition of what constitutes a chemical patent and what constitutes a plastic-related patent. CPI (1) and CA (2) provide both current awareness and retrospective information retrieval, whereas IFI (3) is mainly involved in retrospective retrieval. With INPADOC (4) it includes bibliographic information on all patents from virtually all countries but tends to be limited on subject-base retrieval capability. The API (5) has a specialized plastic retrieval system, but is limited to plastics of direct interest to the petroleum industry.

patent term extension The PTE law of 1984 (U.S.) offers an opportunity to extend the effective life of patents for new medical inventions. This law gives the patent owner a substantial competitive advantage because it allows them to prevent competitors from making, using, or selling an infringing product for up to five years beyond the normal life of the patent. Despite the obvious advantages conferred on the patent owner by law, the law itself is complex and may be underused.

patent terminology Preparing a patent in most cases involves extensive work preparation (time and cost) to ensure it cannot be legally "substituted". With the available technology and the interrelating aspects of "new means" of developing legal products that "do not" compete, proper precautions have to be taken, such as having a patent issue. Preparing a foolproof patent is no problem if done correctly.

pattern making ▷ **pantographic engraving; modeling stereolithography; computer-aided design**

pause timer The process timer which starts the closing of a mold ready for the next cycle to begin. Used when machine is operating fully automatically.

peanut foam packaging material In the past, virgin plastics (PS, PE, etc.) were used along with some recycled plastic. More recently, much more recycled plastics are used that meet solid waste requirements.

pearlescent pigment A class of pigments consisting of particles that are essentially transparent crystals of a high refractive index. The optical effect is one of partial reflection from the two sides of each flake. With reflections from parallel flakes reinforcing each other, a silvery luster results. Effects possible range from brilliant highlighting to moderate enhancement of the normal surface gloss.

peat ▷ **lignite**

pebble A piece of gravel betwen 4 to 8 mm in size.

pebble mill ▷ **ball mill**

peel ply ▷ **reinforced plastic peel ply**

peel strength Bond strength, as in kg/cm (psi), obtained by a stress applied in a peeling mode.

pellet Tablets or granules of uniform size, consisting of plastics or compounded plastics. They are prepared for convenience and aid in controlling feed input to processing machines. They are usually shaped in a pelletizing machine or by extrusion and chopping into short segments.

pelletizer, underwater When using an underwater pelletizer, check the knife sharpness and the screen of the spindryer for fouling. These items can cause fuzzy/poor cut pellets and poor final moisture control.

pelletizing The usual process involves melt flow through an extruder die with many openings conforming to size and shape desired of pellets. The extrudate is cooled to solidification and then cut into pellets, or the molten extrudate is cut as it emerges from the die and the pellets are subsequently cooled. In the latter case, both cutting and cooling may be done in air or water, or cutting may be done in air followed by quenching in water. Pelletizing equipment can be classified as: (1) quenching, solidifying, and cutting by (a) dicers and (b) strand pelletizers, and (2) cutting, quenching, and solidifying die-face pelletizers by (a) dry-face pelletizers, (b) water-ring pelletizers, (c) underwater pelletizers, (d) centrifugal pelletizers, and (e) rotary-knife pelletizers. Each type provides different functions depending on the throughput rate required, the kind of compounding equipment used upstream, the material being processed (unfilled, reinforced, etc.), and the pellet shape required. Uniform pellets offer advantages such as: simpler feeding system with fewer feeders, dust-free handling, and easier cleaning between changes of feedstock; fewer unsatisfactory products because of uniform size and homogeneity of feed; and greater processing capacity with lower shipping costs as a result of higher feed-bulk density. Offsetting these advantages may be a higher heat exposure of plastic (an additional melting step), and pellet's cost increase.

Peltier coefficient The reversible heat which is absorbed or evolved at a thermocouple junction when unit current passes in a unit time.

pencil A rod-like assemblage of fibers in close-packed parallel orientation, of generally uniform diameter that can be fiberized readily.

pendulum impact resistance test ▷ **ball burst test**

pendulum, torsional ▷ **torsional pendulum**

penetrameter Alternate name for image quality indicator. ▷ **quality indicator, image**

penetrant Any agent used to increase the speed and ease with which a bath or liquid permeates a material being processed by effectively reducing the interfacial tension between the solid and liquid. The rate of passage of a permeating species through a plastic matrix is governed by its solubility in the plastic and the relationship between the size of the penetrant molecule and the interstices in the plastic. ▷ **permeability** and **barrier plastic**

penetrant, water-washable A liquid penetrant with a built-in emulsifier.

penetrating agent A material that increases the penetration of a liquid medium into a porous material.

pentane Pentane has been used as a gas blowing agent to produce different foamed plastics or elastomers, particularly in ▷ **expandable polystyrene** (EPS). EPS beads incorporate the pentane and in turn the beads are used during different molding processes to produce different shaped products. Pentane is used to produce certain rigid polyurethane insulation foams as an alternate to CFC blowing agents. As an example during PUR processing, it can be added separately to the mixture bypassing on the high pressure side of the mixing head, thereby bypassing explosive-proof mix chamber and polyol metering pump.

Because of pentane's flammability and chemical makeup, no problems exist when properly processed. It is halogen-free, non-polar, and accepted as non-toxic. The flammability of foam products can be controlled through proper use of flame retardants. It is a hydrocarbon in the methane series occurring in petroleum.

people The recipe for productivity in any company includes a list of ingredients such as research and development, new technologies, updated machinery, required automation systems, and modern facilities. But the one ingredient that ties the recipe together is people. None of the factors has much impact without the right people. If you do not have the people who can do the development, who know the technologies, who can use the machinery, sell the products, and so forth, you are not going to be productive no matter how large you go into capital expenditures, etc. To operate efficiently, one must understand how to obtain the maximum performance for each individual operation and, very important, properly integrate each step through proper planning with proper people. ▷ **design; responsibilities commensurate with abilities**

peptide Low molecular weight plastics of amino acids. Arbitrarily designated as having a molecular weight under 10,000. Higher MW species are called polypeptides. ▷ **mastication**

peptizer A compounding material used in small proportions to accelerate by chemical action the softening of rubber under the influence of mechanical action and/or heat.

percentage point A difference of 1% of a base quantity.

percentile One of the values in a series dividing the distribution of the variable in the series into 100 groups of equal frequency or size.

perception The awareness of the effects of stimuli.

perfection Achievable program plans begin with the recognition that smooth does not mean perfect. Perfection is an unrealistic ideal (except in the eyes of the law; where it is not correct). It is a fact of life that the further someone is removed from a task, the more they are apt to expect perfection from those performing it. The expectation of perfection blocks genuine communication between workers, departments, management, customers, and vendors. Therefore, one can define a smoothly run program as one that creates a product that meets the specifications, is delivered on time, falls within the price guidelines, and stays close to budget. Perfection is never reached; there is always room for more development. As it has been stated, to live is to change and to approach perfection is to have changed often (in the right direction). ▷ **responsibilities commensurate with abilities**

perfluorocarbon plastic PFA is a fluorocarbon plastic. Thermal properties below their melting point [320°C (608°F)] are very similar or somewhat superior to PTFE. It has no room temperature transition, as does PTFE; thus dimensional changes are much less sensitive to small changes in temperature. Mechanical properties are similar to medium density PE. PFA's morphology is such that it does not scatter and reflect light, so essentially water clear film can be made; in contrast to PTFE. In contrast to PTFE, PFAs can be used to make complex injection molded parts and to make long lengths of insulated wire and other extruded shapes by melt extrusion. PFA does not have the stability PTFE exhibits for appreciable periods of time above its melt temperature. A major use is wafer baskets, which are used in automated production of chips for the microcomputers.

perfluoromethylvinyl ether rubber FPM contains about 72% of fluorine resulting in elastomers that are very resistant to alcohol and when crosslinked with peroxide, very resistant to high-peformance oils. Different complex compositions are produced to improve performance in applications such as seals.

perforating Processes by which plastic film or sheeting is provided with holes ranging from relatively large diameters for decorative effects (by means of punching or clicking) to very small, even invisible, sizes. The latter are attained by passing the material between rollers or plates, one of which is equipped with closely spaced fine needles or by spark erosion.

performance influenced by design features ▷ **designing with model, processes** and **design optimized**

performance requirements ▷ **product specification** and **design analysis**

periodic Refers to a system or circuit having repeated beginnings and endings. ▷ **Periodic Table**

Periodic Table Its significance is that the names and chemical symbols for the elements are the building blocks for all engineering materials ▷ **element.** In the Periodic Table on p. 524, the elements exhibit a steady trend in properties from the beginning of each period, where they are metals, to the end, where they are nonmetals. Within each group the elements are quite similar. A given element can be predicted on the basis of its position in a periodic table, to resemble the other elements of its group and be intermediate in properties between its adjacent materials within its period. The chief function of a Periodic Table is to serve as a fundamental framework for the systematic organization of chemistry. Given an understanding of this table with relatively little information, one can predict the properties of many substances, including elements to compounds.

perm ▷ **water vapor transmission**

permanence Resistance of a plastic to appreciable changes in characteristics with time and environment.

permanent set **1.** The deformation remaining after a specimen has been stressed a prescribed amount in tension, compression, or shear for a specified time period and released for a specified time period. **2.** For creep tests, the residual unrecoverable deformation after the load causing the creep has been removed for a substantial and specified period of time. **3.** The increase in length, expressed as a percentage of the original length, by which an elastic material fails to return to its original length after being stressed for a standard period of time.

permeability This term can be applied to any form or shape of a material; the property is most important and most conveniently studied in the passage of matter through a thin film or membrane. The films are generally described as permeable, semipermeable (permeable to some substances but not to others), or permselective

Periodic Table of the elements, symbols based on IUPAC systematic names.

New notation (Group)	1	2	3	4	5	6	7	8	9	10	11	12	13	14	15	16	17	18
Previous IUPAC form	IA	IIA	IIIA	IVA	VA	VIA	VIIA		VIIIA				IIIB	IVB	VB	VIB	VIIB	VIIIA
CAS version			IIIB	IVB	VB	VIB	VIIB		VIII		IB	IIB	IIIA	IVA	VA	VIA	VIIA	
	1 H 1.0079																	2 He 4.00260
	3 Li 6.941	4 Be 9.01218											5 B 10.81	6 C 12.011	7 N 14.0067	8 O 15.9994	9 F 18.9984	10 Ne 20.179
	11 Na 22.9898	12 Mg 24.305											13 Al 26.9815	14 Si 28.0855	15 P 30.9738	16 S 32.06	17 Cl 35.453	18 Ar 39.948
	19 K 39.0983	20 Ca 40.08	21 Sc 44.9559	22 Ti 47.88	23 V 50.9415	24 Cr 51.996	25 Mn 54.9380	26 Fe 55.847	27 Co 58.9332	28 Ni 58.69	29 Cu 63.546	30 Zn 65.39	31 Ga 69.72	32 Ge 72.59	33 As 74.9216	34 Se 78.96	35 Br 79.904	36 Kr 83.80
	37 Rb 85.4678	38 Sr 87.62	39 Y 88.9059	40 Zr 91.224	41 Nb 92.9064	42 Mo 95.94	43 Tc (98)	44 Ru 101.07	45 Rh 102.906	46 Pd 106.42	47 Ag 107.868	48 Cd 112.41	49 In 114.82	50 Sn 118.71	51 Sb 121.75	52 Te 127.60	53 I 126.905	54 Xe 131.29
	55 Cs 132.905	56 Ba 137.33	57 La ★ 138.906	72 Hf 178.49	73 Ta 180.948	74 W 183.85	75 Re 186.207	76 Os 190.2	77 Ir 192.22	78 Pt 195.08	79 Au 196.967	80 Hg 200.59	81 Tl 204.383	82 Pb 207.2	83 Bi 208.980	84 Po (209)	85 At (210)	86 Rn (222)
	87 Fr (223)	88 Ra 226.025	89 Ac ▲ 227.028	104 Unq[a] (261)	105 Unp[a] (262)	106 Unh[a] (263)	107 Uns[a] (262)											

★ Lanthanide series	58 Ce 140.12	59 Pr 140.908	60 Nd 144.24	61 Pm (145)	62 Sm 150.36	63 Eu 151.96	64 Gd 157.25	65 Tb 158.925	66 Dy 162.50	67 Ho 164.930	68 Er 167.26	69 Tm 168.934	70 Yb 173.04	71 Lu 174.967
▲ Actinide series	90 Th 232.038	91 Pa 231.036	92 U 238.029	93 Np 237.048	94 Pu (244)	95 Am (243)	96 Cm (247)	97 Bk (247)	98 Cf (251)	99 Es (252)	100 Fm (257)	101 Md (258)	102 No (259)	103 Lr (260)

(permeable to different extents to different molecular species under equal driving force). A given film, however, may be described by any of these terms depending upon the nature of the penetrant or penetrants being considered.

Permeability is usually referred to as the ease of transmission of penetrants such as gases, vapors, liquid, ions, or solute molecules through some resisting material such as a plastic barrier film. Different processes occur through barrier materials. With paper-based (highly porous) materials, kraft paper to vegetable parchment, woven to nonwoven fabrics, etc., capillary flow or convective flow through macroscopic and microscopic pores and canals is the dominant mechanism. Permeation through metallic foil, with any existing pinholes, also occurs through this mechanism.

With plastic films, the mechanism is of the activated diffusion type: a process in which vapor dissolves in the plastic and then diffuses through and evaporates from the other surface. With plastics, the rate of transmission depends on the solubility of vapor, and on the diffusivity of the dissolved vapor in the plastic medium. Activated diffusion is a highly specific process dependent on the nature of the vapor, whereas capillary flow shows very little difference in the transmission rates of various vapors. The permeability coefficient, diffusion coefficient, and solubility coefficient can all be measured in addition to a gas-transmission rate. Most often the gases or vapors of interest are water vapor, oxygen, carbon dioxide, and nitrogen. Inverse chromatographic and other test methods can be used (ASTM test series exist). ▷**barrier plastic; coefficient of gas permeability; membrane**

permeability, aluminum Bare aluminum foil is impermeable to water vapor and gases if $1\frac{1}{2}$ mil (0.038 mm) and thicker. ▷**aluminum foil**

permeability coefficient ▷**coefficient of permeability**

permeability, coefficient of gas ▷**coefficient of gas permeability**

permeability, gasoline ▷**gasoline tank permeability**

permeability, magnetic Ratio of induction to magnetic field.

permeability tester This term usually identifies an instrument for the measurement of the water vapor transmission rate or gas transmission rate at which these permeate through film (ASTM tests).

permeability, vapor ▷**barrier, vapor**

permeability, water ▷**water vapor permeability**

permeability, water vapor ▷**water vapor permeability**

permeance, water vapor ▷**water vapor transmission**

permittivity, relative The ratio of the capacitance of a particular material to the capacitance of air. The relative permittivity of most insulating materials varies from 2 to 10, air having 1. Higher values indicate greater insulating quality. ▷**electrical permittivity; electrical capacitance**

permselectivity ▷**membrane** and **water vapor transmission**

peroxide cured XLPE ▷**extruder wire coating, crosslinkable PE with peroxide**

peroxy compound Compounds containing O–O linkage.

personal computer PCs are often defined as those that are low cost (relatively mini and small standard hardware systems) based on tiny microcomputer chips; thus portable, personally controllable, and easy to use. There are different classifications such as home, hobbyist, professional, business, appliance, etc. ▷**computer storage disk and tape**

persorption The adsorption of a substance in pores only slightly wider than the diameter of absorbed molecules of the substance.

Petlite This Goodyear Tire & Rubber Co. system is both a plastic and a process for producing foam single-use containers used for food preparation, transported, stored, and heated in either a microwave or conventional oven. The process closely relates to the crystalline PET method of producing trays and other containers. System uses inert gas found naturally in the environment as blowing agents, making it ozone friendly.

petrochemical Chemicals refined from oil and natural gas, primary feedstock materials for the production of plastics (see Fig. below). ▷**material origin**

petroleum Petroleum or crude oil is a highly complex mixture of paraffic, cycloparaffinic (naphthenic), and aromatic hydrocarbons, containing a low percentage of sulfur and trace amounts of nitrogen and oxygen compounds. About 2 wt% of all petroleum (U.S.) is used as feedstock for the plastic industry. ▷**cost, crude oil versus polyethylene**

petroleum and plastic ▷**energy consumption and pollution**

pH The measure of the acidity or alkalinity of a substance, neutrality at pH 7. Acid solutions are less than 7, and alkaline are more than 7.

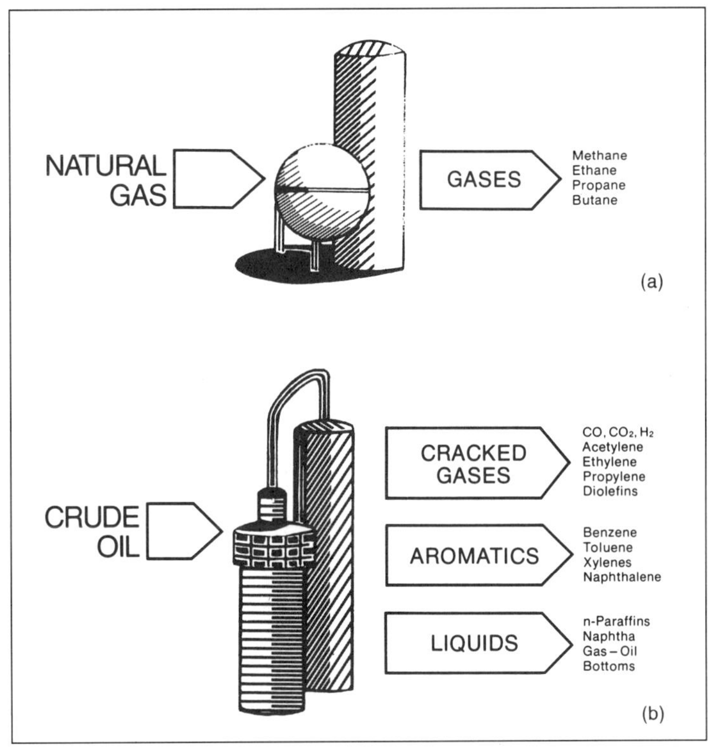

Petroleum feedstock oil and gas processing schematic producing some of the plastic monomers and other products. (*a*) Natural gas processing; (*b*) oil refining.

pharmaceutical ▷**drug application** and **microencapsulation, coating**

phase A physically homogeneous, mechanically separable portion of a material system.

phase angle The angle between a sinusoidally applied perturbation and the resultant sinosoidal reaction. Generally in reference to mechanical and dielectric processes.

phase change The transition from one physical state to another, such as gas to liquid, liquid to solid, gas to solid, or vice versa.

phase diagram ▷**alloy constitutional diagram**

phase material A structurally distinct part of a material system.

phenol A class of aromatic organic compounds in which one or more hydroxy groups are attached directly to the benzene ring. Examples are phenol itself, creosols, xylenols, resorcinols, and naphthols. It is used in producing plastics such as epoxy (bisphenol-A), phenolic, nylon-6 (caprolactum), etc.

phenol-formaldehyde plastic The major class or phenolic plastics. ▷**phenolic**

phenolic Any of several types of thermoset plastics obtained by the condensation of phenol or substituted phenols with aldehydes such as formaldehyde, and furfural. Phenol-formaldehydes are typical and constitute the chief class of phenolics.

Since 1909, phenol-formaldehyde has continued to be generally a low cost general purpose thermoset compound to meet a multitude of applications. There are a wide range of fillers for it, each intended to fulfill the needs of particular end-product service environments. Typical among them is wood flour, for general use in electrical wall plates, industrial switchgears, circuit breakers, handles and knobs for small appliances, and such purposes. For slightly better impact strength, cotton flock is used. Mica, glass, and other minerals provide better electrical properties, heat resistance and dimensional stability, as in automotive powe brakes, industrial electrical terminal strips, and so on.

Compounds are formulated with a one- or two-stage phenolic curing system. In general, one-stage resins are slightly more critical to process. Although phenolics have properties that are somewhat inferior to those of the more expensive TSs, they are usually more easily molded. They can be processed by compression, transfer, and injection molding and to a limited degree by extrusion. The colors of these compounds are limited to black or brown. As is typical of many TSs, they are postcured to obtain maximum performance.

Phenolic molding compounds are generally characterized as being low in cost and having superior heat resistance, a high heat-deflection temperature, good electrical properties and flame resistance, excellent moldability and dimensional stability, and good water and chemical resistance. Specialty compounds can provide high-performance heat resistance, impact strength, electrical properties, and creep resistance. ▷**A-B-C stages** and **novalak**

phenoxy plastic A high molecular weight thermoplastic polyester plastic based on bisphenol-A and epichlorohydrin; outgrowth of the epoxy plastic technology. They have moderately good impact resistance, relatively high strength, and good elongation and creep resistance. They are thermoplastics, but they can also be thermosets, through cross-linking chemical reactions.

As with most of the aromatic polymers, phenoxy resins' color retention, UV resistance, and weatherability are generally poor. They have limited thermal exposure with a recommended operating temperature range from −60 to 80°C (−76 to 176°F). Phenoxy resins are resistant to acids and alkalis, have poor solvent resistance (especially in ketones) but good resistance to aliphatic hydrocarbons, and resist staining from common household agents rather well. Their permeability, particularly to oxygen and other gases, is the lowest of any melt-processable plastic. Their oxygen permeability is one-twentieth that of HDPE and their moisture-vapor transmission is about the same as that of rigid PVC—higher than PE but much lower than the styrenes.

The major use of phenoxies is as a vehicle for coating formulations. They are exceptionally useful in primer applications where drying speed, compatibility with various kinds of top coats, and high adhesive strength are required. Phenoxies are used in automotive and marine primers as well as in heavy-duty maintenance primers.

Phenoxy molding compounds are limited to applications requiring service temperatures not in excess of about 80°C (176°F). Their combination of good impact strength, clarity, and impermeability makes this resin attractive for molding, including blow molding, of cosmetic, foodstuff, and household-chemical bottles.

phenylsilane plastic Thermoset copolymers of silicone and phenolic plastics. Furnished in solution form.

pH indicator A substance that changes color when the pH of the medium is changed. In the case of most useful indicators, the pH range within the color changes is narrow.

phlogopite ▷ **reinforcement, disks**

phosphorescence A type of luminescence in which the emission of radiation resulting from excitation of a crystalline or liquid material occurs after excitation has ceased and may last from a fraction of a second to an hour or more. ▷ **luminescence** and **fluorescence**

photochemistry The absorption of light by plastics can produce noticeable physical and chemical changes. There are commercial plastics that are discolored and lose mechanical strength when exposed to UV light, particularly in the presence of oxygen. Photodegradation and photooxidation can severely limit the usefulness of untreated plastics exposed to sunlight (use is made of appropriate additives based on plastic used). The basic process of photochemistry is that no photochemical reaction can occur unless a photon of light is absorbed. Thus, many commercial plastics transparent in the near UV can undergo photodegradation only as a result of the absorption of light by impurities.

Photoinstability offers advantages in waste disposal. There are the effects of light on plastics that play an important role in a number of specialized technical applications. Plastics insolubilized via photocrosslinking are used as durable coatings and negative-working lithographic resists in printing plates and integrated circuits. Solubilization by light-induced depolymerization or chain scission provides the basis for positive-working lithographic resists. Solventless inks based on UV-curable plastics are used. Photoconductivity is the principle behind photocopying.

photochromic Reversible light sensitivity; darkening with increased intensity and fading with decreased intensity.

photoconductive plastic Plastics that have an increase of conductivity caused by radiation. They are insulating or poorly conductive in the darkness and more conductive when illuminated.

photocurable plastic ▷ **modeling stereolithography**

photodegradable Capable of being decomposed by the action of light, especially UV light. Those plastics that are naturally photodegradable require additives to inhibit degradation by UV light.

This type plastic is used, as an example, to produce photodegradable film for mulch. It enables the farmers to retain moisture on arable land. ▷ **degradable** and **biodegradable**

photoelasticity The property of a transparent material becoming birefingent when subject to stress; changes in optical properties of isotropic, transparent plastics when subjected to stress. The effect of quantitatively described by the stress optical characteristics. The birefringence occurs from the material becoming anisotropic due to micro-orientation of the molecules on stressing. The photoelastic effect is especially useful in the technique of photoelastic stress analysis and also in the examination of residual stress and orientation of transparent plastic products by observing them in polarized light. If white light is used, then a series of colored fringes is observed whose density depends on the amount of stress or orientation, due to interference between two out of phase propagating light rays. For monochromatic light, a series of light and dark fringes is observed. ▷ **polariscope**

photoelastic strain measurement ▷ **nondestructive testing method, residual strain**

photoelastic stress analysis Technique for the determination of the stress components at any point in a stressed product by viewing a transparent model (or the actual plastic part; if not transparent, a plastic coating is used). Loads are applied to the model that are proportional to the loads encountered by the part in service (see Fig. below). Using an optical instrument (polariscope), observed patterns can be interpreted to indicate stress in the part. Stress concentration can be examined at holes, notches, and fillets. In addition, shapes that would be difficult to treat analytically may be studied by photoelasticity methods. Vibrating members and other dynamic problems may be

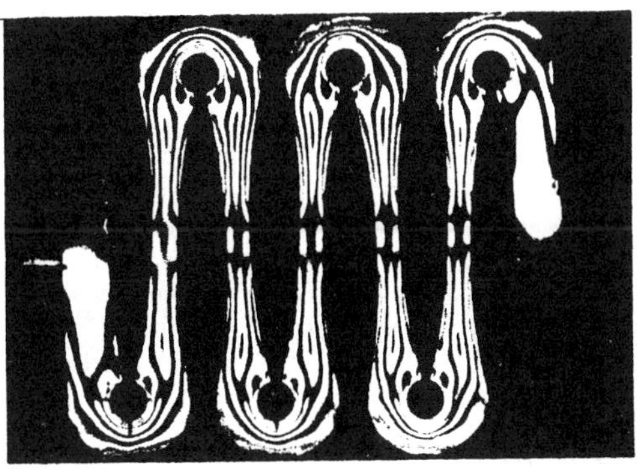

Photoelastic stress pattern of a spring element.

studied by observing a photoelastic pattern using stroboscopic light. Three-dimensional stress patterns may be examined by slicing a "frozen" stress pattern or by using special lateral illumination of the model. Alternatively, in the stress coating technique, the part itself is examined by coating it with a transparent plastic (certain epoxy, PC, and PMMA) and subjecting it to stress systems of interest. The photoelastic stress determination (and strain measurement) is also used in studying fiber reinforced plastics behavior. ▷ **microtoming, optical analysis**

photographic print ▷ **photopolymer**

photography and photomechanics Photography for graphic arts involves the photographic processes and techniques used to produce illustrations and art subjects. Photomechanics or photoplatemaking, like photoengraving, photolithography, photogelatin, photogravure, etc. is the means of using the products of photography like halftones and line films to make plates and cylinders for printing.

photoimage In order to obtain the desired print pattern, parts of the screen must be blocked. As an example, the photoimage process is important for screen printing type stencil making. A photosensitive emulsion is applied over the screen and parts of it are exposed to light through a positive image of the art work. Exposed areas become insoluble and the remainder of the emulsion is removed by washing. Ink can pass through the non-emulsion photoresist areas. With this direct stencil emulsion process, several coats of emulsion may be applied and the coating thickness may vary in the case of stencils prepared by the direct method.

Precast photosensitive films are available and provide a coating of uniform thickness. Such a film is laminated to the screen and processed in a similar way as the direct emulsion coating. Film may be also exposed prior to its lamination to the screen. This is the indirect stencil making process.

A squeegee is used to force ink through the screen. It is a flexible blade made from an elastomer, usually polyurethane because of its durability and good elastomeric properties. The hardness of the rubber used in the squeegee has an effect on the printing. Hard rubber (above 50 Shore A durometer) squeegees produce a cleaner, more crisp definition; softer squeegees deposit more ink and are more suitable for rough surfaces, but print definition is not as good. Textured surfaces will generally be printed by using a squeegee of durometer below 50. The squeegee's blade usually has a rectangular profile and the edge is rubbed against the screen. The edge should be kept sharp. For heavy ink deposits, a rounded profile is used.

photolithographic techniques Lithography in which photographically prepared plates (plastics, etc.) are used.

photolysis Splitting of a molecule through the action of light. There is decomposition into simpler units as a result of absorbing one or more quanta of radiation.

photomechanics The light sensitive coatings used in the photomechanical process change in physical properties after exposure to light. Usually the exposed areas change in solubility in water or other solutions. In the past, natural organic materials (asphalt, shellac, albumin, gum arabic, etc.) were used as ingredients for the coatings. Synthetic plastics such as polyvinyl alcohol and photopolymers are now used.

photon The unit (quantum) of electromagnetic radiation. Light waves, gamma rays, X-ray, etc. consist of photons. They are discrete concentrations of energy that seem to have no rest mass and move at the speed of light.

photooxidation Photodegradation occurring in the presence of oxygen. Since photodegradation is frequently a free radical process, oxygen will also participate, accelerating the degradation process (mainly chain scission) by promoting chain branching via hydroperoxide group formation and causing the incorporation of oxygen-containing groups into the plastic. The main cause of weathering of plastics; alleviated by the use of UV stabilizers in the plastics. ▷ **ultraviolet absorber and light stabilization**

photopolymer A polymer (plastic) so produced that it undergoes a change on exposure to light. Such materials can be used for printing and lithography plates for photographic prints and microfilm copying. The effect of light is to cause further polymerization or crosslinking resulting in degradation and results in providing the printed material. As an example, the use of esters of polyvinyl alcohol which crosslink and so become insoluble, whereas unexposed portions of the plastic remain soluble. ▷ **lithographic resist printing**

photopolymer coating In photomechanics, a plastic plate coating consisting of compounds which polymerize on exposure to light producing tough, abrasion resistant plates capable of long runs especially when baked in an oven after processing.

photopolymerization Free radical, or occasionally ionic, polymerization initiated by the interaction of light, usually of UV wavelengths, with a photosensitive compound, producing free radicals. The compound may be a monomer itself (styrene, etc.) which absorbs a photon to give an excited state, which itself then disassociates to free radicals. ▷ **radiation coating** and **radiation-induced reaction**

photopolymer plate They are easy to process either by hand or on automatic processors; available as negative or positive plates. Photopolymers are different from other sensitizers; they change in molecular size and weight during exposure. This accounts for their many unusual properties such as long runs, resistance of abrasive wear, and increase in wear resistance after baking. Plates have been used for runs exceeding one million impressions.

photoresist A photosensitive plastic system which, when applied as a coating to a substrate, after interaction with UV or visible light undergoes a change in solubility. If the irradiation is performed through a suitable mask, only selected areas are insolubilized and the unexposed areas may be dissolved away leaving a raised image. Such a process is useful in lithography for reprographics and the production of integrated circuits.

photosensitive emulsion ▷ **photoimage**

phthalate ester A main group of plasticizers produced by the direct action of alcohol on phthalic anhydride. The phthalates are the most widely used of all plasticizers and are generally characterized by moderate cost, good stability, and good all-round properties.

phthalic This term was coined from naphthalene, from which phthalic anhydride is made and used principally as a plasticizer for vinyls and cellulosic plastics.

phthalocyanine pigment Organic pigments of extremely stable chemical configuration resulting in very good fastness properties. These properties are enhanced by the formation of the copper complex, which is the phthalocyanine blue most used. The introduction of chlorine atoms into the molecule of blue gives the well-known phthalocyanine green, also usually in the form of copper complex.

physical aging ▷ **annealing** and **aging**

physical blowing agent ▷ **foam and blowing agent**

physical properties They are characteristics of materials that pertain to the interaction of materials with various forms of energy and with other forms of matter. In essence, they pertain to the science of physics. They can usually be measured without destroying or changing the material. Color is a physical property; it can be determined by just looking at it. Density can be determined by weighing and measuring the volume of the object; it is a physical property. ▷ **mechanical properties**

pi Mathematical term; Greek letter $\pi = 3.141593$.

pica Printer's unit of measurement used principally in typesetting. One pica equals about 1/6 in. (4.2 mm). ▷ **printers' measurements**

pick ▷ **fiber pick**

picture-level benchmark ▷ **computer picture-level benchmark**

piezoelectric plastic Plastics (PVDF, etc.) that spontaneously give an electric charge when mechanically stressed or that develop a mechanical response when an electric field is applied. Material's structures are asymmetric so that their centers of positive and negative changes are not coincident. As a result the polarity is sensitive to pressures that change the dipole distance and the polarization. Used as transducers or acoustic sensors. ▷ **ultrasonic sealing**

pigment A coloring agent mixed or applied (spray, dip, print) to achieve color. They are fine, solid particles substantially insoluble in their carrier or vehicle. Pigments may be inorganic (lead chromate, titanium dioxide, chrome yellow, etc.) or organic (azo, phthalocyanine). They can be incorporated directly in plastics, elastomers, fibers, inks, etc. or used as coatings. Colored pigments in water-paste form are called pulp colors; oil-wet pigments are called flush colors. Special effects can be obtained with nacreous and irridescent pigments. Some dyes may be converted to organic pigments called toners and lakes. Toners are generally insoluble heavy metal salts of synthetic dyes. Lakes are pigments consisting of an organic dye precipitated on an inorganic carrier such as hydrated alumina. Lakes are sometimes described as toners which have been extended by the solid substrate. The color of a pigment depends on the spectral composition of the incident light and reflectance. Colors are compared visually and with instruments, which are usually based on trichromaticity principle. Colors are also matched by computers. ▷ **colorant**

pill More often called ▷ **preform**

pilot plant A trial assembly of small scale processing operation which is the intermediate stage between laboratory experiment and full-scale operation in the production of a new product.

pimple An imperfection, such as a small protuberance of varied shape on the surface of a plastic produce.

pin and bushing blank ▷ **die pin and bushing blank**

pinch-off ▷ **blow molding, extruder pinch-off**

pin, ejection ▷ **mold ejection**

pinhole An extremely tiny hole in the surface of, or through, a plastic such as film, coating, molded containers, etc. ▷ **parylene plastic** and **xylyene plastic**

pin mixing screw ▷ **screw mixing and melting**

pinpoint gate ▷ **mold gate**

pipe A hollow cylinder of a plastic material in which the wall thicknesses are usually small when compared to the diameter and in which the inside and outside walls are essentially concentric. Thermoplastic extruded pipe and thermoset reinforced plastic pipe are produced. ▷ **extruded pipe** and **filament winding**

pipe market Thermoplastics were first used for pipe in the 1930s. They were more widely used in the 1950s as a result of advances in materials, formulations, and screw extrusion technology. Since then the industry has grown rapidly with its dollar value ranked second to steel. Plastics have surpassed clay, copper, asbestos-cement, aluminum, iron, and concrete. The material combines strength, stiffness, and toughness with economy, making it the most cost-effective choice for pressure and nonpressure applications.

Although reinforced thermoset plastic pipe represents a small portion of the market, it is the product of choice for many special applications. Corrosion, resistance, toughness and ease of handling and installation contribute to the growing acceptance of plastic piping.

pipe orientation ▷ **orientation** and **reinforced plastic, directional properties**

pit A small, regular or irregular crater in the surface of a plastic, usually of a width about in the same order of magnitude as its depth. ▷ **spalling**

pitch 1. ▷ **screw pitch 2.** ▷ **graphite mesophase 3.** A high molecular weight material that is a residue from the destructive distillation of coal and petroleum products. Pitches are used as base materials for the manufacture of certain high modulus carbon fibers.

plain weave A weaving pattern in which the warp and fill fibers alternate; that is, the repeat pattern is warp/fill/warp/fill, and so on. The two sides, or faces, of a plain weave are identical. It demonstrates the greatest degree of stability with respect to yarn slippage and fabric distortion; however, this stability is also a function of fabric count and yarn count. ▷ **fabric, woven**

planar Lying essentially in a single plane.

planar coating A variety of flexible flat substrates (webs) are coated with plastics for a variety of reasons (appearance, waterroofness, electrical insulation, etc.). Substrates include plastic, aluminum foil, steel foil, paperboard, textiles, etc. ▷ **coating**

planar orientation ▷ **reinforced plastic, directional properties**

planar winding ▷ **filament winding**

plane angle The SI unit for plane angle is the radian. Use of degree and its decimal submultiple is permissible when the radian is not a convenient unit. Use of the minute and second is discouraged by SI except for special fields such as cartography. One degree (°) equals radian (rad) × 0.017 533 or 1° equals $(\pi/180)$ rad.

plane stress ▷ **stress plane**

planetary gear extruder ▷ **extruder, screw multiple type**

planning ▷ **perfection**

plant operation ▷ **economic efficiency and profitability**

plant safety ▷ **safety**

plasma A partially or totally ionized gas or vapor.

plasma coating In this method, a high temperature plasma is established in an inert gas such as nitrogen, and coating powder is introduced at the periphery of the plasma. The particles melt and are propelled at high velocity to the substrate, where they form a film.

plasma treatment A process for modification of plastic surfaces. Results that are more stable and reliable than those of conventional corona discharge processes can be usually be achieved with this technique. Additional advantages include the possibility, relatively simply, of adapting it for use with various reactive gases. These create different chemical structures at the plastic surfaces and deliberately generating specific surface properties.

plastic A material that contains as an essential ingredient an organic substance of large molecular weight, is solid in its finished state, and, at some stage in its manufacture or in its processing into finished articles, can be shaped by flow. The terms plastic, resin, elastomer, and polymer are somewhat synonymous, but the terms resins, elastomers and polymers most often denote only the basic material as polymerized. However, the term plastic encompasses many different products produced including fibers, coating, and adhesives with many diverse properties from rigid to rubbery, poor heat resistance to extremely high heat resistance, poor chemical resistance to extremely high chemical resistance, and so on.

The term preferred much more often worldwide is plastic. Resin, elastomer, polymer (and others) each have their individual descriptions or definitions, but they also identify themselves as plastic. Note that: (1) the plastic industry is identified by the word plastic, (2) by far most people in the industry worldwide use the term plastic, (3) by far most products, materials, shows or exhibitions, technical meetings, advertising, and so on use the term plastic, and (4) practically all people worldwide refer to the 'world of plastics'.

The word plastic, in addition to identifying materials, identifies a flow behavior of all types of materials i.e., plastic, metal, aluminum, and so on. Plastic materials have "plastic" flow when they are processed and, like other materials, also have a "plastic" flow behavior in many of their fabricated products, particularly when subjected to a load or stress.

plastic advantages and disadvantages As a material of construction for all types of products, plastics provide practically unlimited benefits. Unfortunately for plastics (as well as other materials such as steels, aluminum, wood, glass, and so on) no one specific plastic has all the "benefits". The successful applications of their benefits and an understanding of plastics' individual weakness allow useful and successful products to be produced. ▷ **design**

plastic air balloon The Earthwinds balloon project (cost $3.5 million) is to circle the earth November 1992 from Akron, OH, U.S. non-stop with two American and a Russian cosmonaut. They will ride on two LDPE film balloons in a very light weight life support reinforced plastic capsule. One balloon lifts the capsule 6 m (9.7 m) high. Hanging below is an air-filled superstructure balloon called the anchor stability balloon. They will ride the jet stream at 75 mph (125 km/h). Film maintains strength and elongation at temperatures as cold as −90°C (−128°F). The flight balloon is 180 ft (55 m) high by 100 ft (30 m) in diameter filled with a million ft^3 (0.03 M m^3) of helium (that is 10 times the size of a regular hot-air balloon). The lower anchor balloon is 100 ft (30 m) round filled with $\frac{1}{2}$ million ft^3 (0.014 M m^3) of air. It is covered with a fabric woven from PE fibers. Sponsor is the Hilton Hotel Corp.

plastic and civilization ▷ **civilization and materials**

plastic and definition Additional information to what has been presented in ▷ **plastic** is that plastics are a pseudosolid organic material, usually of high molecular weight, that exhibits a tendency to flow when subjected to stress. It usually has a softening or melting range. There are organic and inorganic plastics as well as natural and synthetic plastics; the plastics industry is identified as synthetic using organic and inorganic materials. Very little natural material is used. Most of the plastics used are organic.

There is no one plastic; plastics comprise an extraordinarily large and diverse class of materials of about 15,000 worldwide. They possess a very broad range of properties and processing characteristics. Like other materials (steels, woods, etc.), they can be identified by different terms that relate to different areas or categories within the plastics industry such as resins, polymers, elastomers, foams, reinforced plastics, plastic composites, fibers, adhesives, and more, including just the usual term plastics. There are basically technical differences. The polymer is a pure material (neat) which is usually taken as the family or class name for materials which have no long chain-like molecules (includes rubber). However, most of the polymers (or plastics) have incorporated many different additives, fillers, and/or reinforcements. Even though there are only a couple of hundred basic polymers, about 50 are important marketwise and in turn 5 represent about three quarters of all plastic used. They practically incorporate materials to give them all types of properties and behaviors. See descriptions of the different terms and types as given above. Also ▷ **thermoplastic; thermoset plastic; molecular arrangement structure; engineering materials, the solid state; data, theoretical versus actual properties**

plastic and die cast metal Plastics have several advantages over die-cast metals in many applications that include light weight, resistance to corrosion and chemicals, design flexibility, and lower finishing costs. Die-cast metals, however, have superior temperature resistance, creep resistance, and shielding properties.

plastic and ecology ▷**environment, life, plastic, ecology**

plastic and pollution ▷**pollution**

plastic and public opinion ▷**plastic bad and other myths**

plastic and recycling ▷**recycling**

plastic and rubber printing plates They have the advantage of lightness in weight and low cost, compared to the past metal types. They are made from molds similar to those used for electrotypes. Plastic plates are vinyl type and are used for some types of commercial printing. Rubber plates are from either natural and/or synthetic rubber (elastomer), depending on the solvents used in the inks for printing.

plastic applicator Used in film coating, filament winding, and other processes to deposit the liquid plastic onto the carrier or substrate being coated, impregnated, reinforced, etc.

plasticate To impart flexibility in a plastic through the input of heat and mechanical work as in the plasticating of the plastic in extruding, injection molding, and so on.

plasticating The melting of plastics as it flows during processing, such as in extruders, and so on.

plasticator A device that plasticates or melts platic; many methods are used. By far the most common is the single plasticating screw-barrel system. These systems are used for extrusion compounding, product extrusion, injection molding, blow molding, and so on.

plasticator safety If you pack plastic into a steel pipe with no included air, plug both ends of the pipe, and heat it, you have made a bomb. The damage it can cause depends on the amount of heat applied prior to the pipe or plugs let go. If a small amount of heat has been added (that is a little more than is required to form a melt) before the contents are released, the molten plastic will burst out but little expansion will take place. The pressure generated, which may be large, is caused by the difference between the thermal expansion of the plastic and the steel "container". Although the energy released is not great, the container parts are capable of flying some distance and potentially causing damage. An example of this would be a safety rupture disc failing during processing operations.

If the plugs or pipe let go after heat is applied, the result could be catastrophic. Assume that the heat has caused some or all of the plastic to degrade. Now the pipe is filled with high pressure gas as well as the compressed plastic. A tremendous amount of energy could be stored in the pipe (barrel). If the pipe fails it could explode like a bomb. If the plug let go it could be fired like a cannon. The compressed gas expands when released and pushes plastic and any metal particles ahead of it. In addition, the escaping gas would be flammable and probably above its flash point. Every time you heat up processing equipment (and do not take the proper setup steps) you could cause damage. This is particularly true of multiple processing lines such as coinjection or coextrusion where one plasticator can pack plastic into the metal channel from a non-operating plasticator. The pipe in these examples could be the mold/die adapter, melt transfer tube, nozzle, or the barrel. The plugs could be the cold plastic frozen into the openings at the ends of these "pipes".

There is another potential danger on start-up. If all of the plastic between the screw and the melt path exit is not melted, a frozen plastic plug could form. Most feed screws can generate a pressure in excess of 68.9 GPa (10,000 psi) or even 137.8 GPa (20,000 psi). This pressure buildup can be detected using a pressure gauge(s) in the barrel (pipe). Precautions to be used to eliminate potential problems include: (1) do not heat any of the metal parts enough to degrade the plastic, (2) be sure that the plastic at the ends and joint of melt channels melts as quickly as the plastic in the mid-point of the channel, (3) be sure all the plastic in the system is melted before starting/turning the screw, (4) never be next to unprotected nozzle in contact with the mold bushing, in front of the extruder die opening, transfer tube opening, barrel, and so on during heat-up or start-up, (5) remember that pressure could be building in the equipment and you will not know it unless pressure transducer(s) are used, (6) become familiar with operation of equipment and material prior to start-up (via instruction manuals, supervisor training, and so on), and (7) above all, use common sense. ▷**barrel vented safety**

plasticator throughput check Check the throughput rate periodically. This is especially important when using volumetric feeders and to verify blend ratios.

plastic bad and other myths Imagine our society worldwide magically stripped of plastics' cost-effectiveness and high performance properties, resulting in cars with missing mechanical parts, no interiors, finishes; supermarkets suddenly awash in containerless food and cleaning products; and so on. Indeed, it is difficult to identify any massproduced item of recent decades that is not, at least in part, plastic.

Plastics, like electricity and transportation systems, are fundamental to the functioning of our society. The municipal waste problem (including McDonald's) with its visibility represents the result of our population's throw-away mentality. It includes the myth that landfills work. However, virtually nothing degrades including garbage. The good news is that a steadily increasing level of activity in plastics recycling exists worldwide. So do not use the approach of "don't give me the facts, my mind is made up". ▷**energy conservation; environment and public opinion; oil and gas; steel resources in U.S. limited; polyester thermoplastic and the environment; perfection; polyvinyl chloride plastic and the environment**

plastic card They include credit cards, library cards, promotional cards, identification cards, automatic teller machine cards, etc. Most plastic cards use PVC substrate. Layers of ink, a clear PVC overlay, embossing magnetic stripes, or other features are added in sandwich layup to the substrate.

plastic, ceramic precursor ▷**ceramic precursor plastic**

plastic characterization Plastic characterization is an important step in working with plastics. As a rule, such efforts are directed toward a specific purpose. In newly synthesized material, composition, molecular weight, and physical properties are determined first. Other information may be needed with respect to selection or qualification of plastics for specific properties, analysis of competitive products, or quality control testing. Plastics can be categorized as natural or synthetic and homopolymers or copolymers. Copolymers and terpolymers are further classified according to the method of production and monomer units arrangement.

plastic-cheap Unfortunately, to many consumers, the two words "plastics" and "cheap" remain synonymous. There exist plastics that are relatively low cost; however, others are expensive, even more expensive than metals, aluminum, and ceramic. There are plastics and reinforced plastics with outstanding performances that cost much more than competitive materials. They are used to meet the higher performance requirements, longer life, and so on. Like other materials, there are plastic products that are made to sell for less than competitive plastic products; there are people that will buy the more expensive products, and there are others.

plastic chemical composition ▷**chemical composition and properties of plastic**

plastic, chemical structure ▷**molecular arrangement structure; designing with model, plastic-chemical structure; computer chemometric**

plastic classification ASTM D 4000 A classifying plastic materials standard that can serve all types of industries is available from ASTM, designated D 4000 (ISO 1043) and titled Standard Guide for Identification of Plastic Materials. It provides an easy way to identify for purchasing, quality control, and so on.

plastic classification based on modulus ▷**nonrigid plastic; semirigid plastic; rigid plastic**

plastic commodity types ▷**commodity plastic and engineering plastic**

plastic, computer and design Advances in computer technology have made design engineers quite sophisticated. Math models are used to study stress and strain as well as processing techniques. Computers can make detailed drawings to controlling processes. With all the engineering aids, basic design is intuitive. When a designer is called to design a product to perform some function, the concept of the mechanism that will do the job is arrived at by calling on one's experience and trying many approaches on "paper". Once the design is established and drawings are made, the designer must arrive at the materials of construction for each and every component. The product cannot work for very long if materials cannot carry the loads, if they wear rapidly, and so on. The material selection phase of design (for plastic, steel, wood, etc.), like the concept phase, is based upon accumulated knowledge and/or personal design experiences with performance of materials in previous applications. There are no math models or equations to perform this function for the designer without applicable product history; however, there are aids. The designer must have a basic understanding of material systems and call upon this knowledge to make material selections. Knowledge-based computer selection software systems are available as aids in the selection process, but they can be "dangerous" if the user does not understand the first principles of the material systems that one is using—what do the plastic properties mean and how do they apply to factors such as creep, static and dynamic loads, and so on. ▷**computer-aided design**

plastic-concrete composite ▷**concrete-plastic**

plastic conductivity The basic characteristic of most plastics is their nonconductivity (electrical) where it is very useful in most products.

Plastic conductive coating systems that provide electrical shielding for plastics.

Shielding system	Advantages	Disadvantages
Conductive coatings silver	Highly conductive (0.1 ohm per square or less); applied by conventional sprayequipment; easy application; electrically stable (minimal change in resistance with environmental cycling); easily applied to selected area; field repairable.	High cost.
Nickel	Low cost (15–30 cents per square foot); good conductivity (less than 1.0 ohm per square); applied by conventional spray equipment; easy application; relatively stable (differs with manufacturer); easily applied to selected area; field repairable.	Lesser quality formulations available; some are stable, some are not.
Copper	Highly conductive (less than 0.5 ohm per square); easy application; low cost (15–30 cents per square foot).	Oxidation can reduce conductivity (resistance can change to effectively make copper an insulator); some may be alloys—if layered with silver, cost will rise.
Graphite	Low cost (5–15 cents per square foot); easy application; excellent ESD (electrostatic discharge) performance.	Less conductivity (ranging from 2 ohms to the thousands per square depending upon the amount of graphite); modest shielding capability (up to 30–40 dB).
Arc/flame spray	Highly conductive (less than 0.1 ohm per square); hard dense coating.	Requires grit blasting to promote mechanical bonding to plastic; special applications equipment required; requires special applicator safety procedures for dust and fumes; warps thermoplastic; not suitable for thin-walled designs; not field repairable.
Vacuum metalization/ ion plating	Highly conductive (less than 0.1 ohm per square); controllable film thickness; not limited to simple housing designs.	Requires primer cost; entire part must be done, forcing exterior painting; not field repairable; specialized application equipment; vacuum chamber size a limiting factor; requires specialized knowledge; subject to corrosion in humid atmosphere unless protected.
Electrolysis deposition	Highly conductive (both nickel and copper less than 0.1 ohm per square).	Requires specialized equipment/ knowledge; entire part must be coated, forcing exterior painting; if copper is used it must be protected by a nickel coating or some other coating.
Conductive plastic	Good thermal transfer; elimination of secondary operation for shielding	Requires a secondary operation for grounding.

It can be a major drawback for certain applications. Being electrical insulators, they do not shield electronic equipment generated by outside sources and do not prevent electromagnetic energy from being emitted from equipment housed in a plastic container, etc. However, there are techniques to restrict unwanted transmissions (see Table above) ▷ **electromagnetic interference, conductive plastic.** Certain types of plastics such as melt processable polythiopene derivatives and polyanilines are conductive; there are also conductive additives in the plastic (carbon, steel powder, etc.).

plastic consumption The Fig. on top of p. 535 shows plastic consumption in U.S. ▷ **world consumption of plastics** and **markets for plastics**

plastic contamination ▷ **railcar hopper contamination**

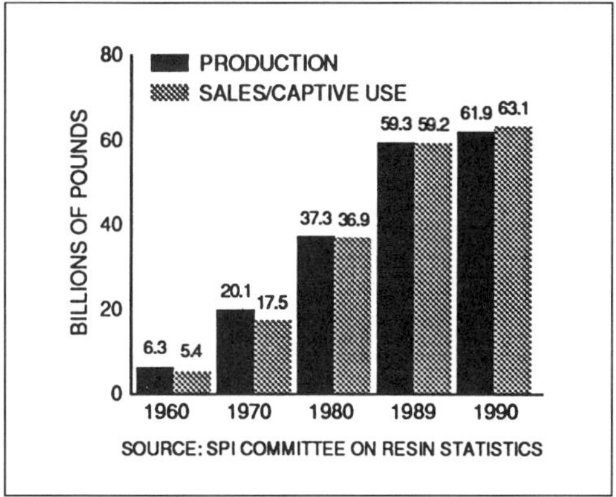

Plastic production versus sales/captive use.

plastic content The amount of plastic in filled or reinforced plastics, expressed as either a percentage of total weight or total volume.

plastic cost ▷ **cost**

plastic database ▷ **computer database**

plastic deformation Change in dimensions of an object under load that is not recovered when the load is removed; opposite to elastic deformation. The term is used to identify (1) solid plastic deformation in products and (2) melt flow deformation that occurs during the fabrication of products.

plastic deformation, nonplastic Many different materials, such as metal, glass, etc., when subjected to a load will deform "plastically"; they have the physical or mechanical behavior of "plastic deformation".

plastic demand Consumer demand for flexibility, safety, convenience, and cost-efficiency continually led to the uprecedented growth of plastics, especially in the packaging industry. However, plastics' popularity has also increased their visibility as a component of municipal solid waste.

plastic elastomer ▷ **elastomer**

plastic energy requirements ▷ **energy**

plastic engineer An engineer with the knowledge of an engineer and knowledgeable in plastics. ▷ **engineer**

plastic fiber ▷ **fiber**

plastic film ▷ **film**

plastic flow **1.** Alternative name for plastic deformation in metals under the action of a force. **2.** In rubber technology, an alternative name for plasticity. **3.** For plastics, the post yield deformation may be recoverable but is often referred to as plastic deformation or plasticity. However, only the permanent, non-recoverable, deformation can be called plastic flow. **4.** Flow of plastic melt during plastic processing. ▷ **melt flow**

plastic future Since the late 19th century fantastic strides have been made with plastics and this growth pattern with its many benefits to people worldwide will continue. This "endless" action of developments will continually occur in development of materials, processes, design concepts, and products. Demand for plastic products will be bolstered by demographic shifts (including aging population, an increasing number of smaller households), more cost-effective products, improvements in plastics performances (see Fig. below), and much more. ▷ **markets emerging**

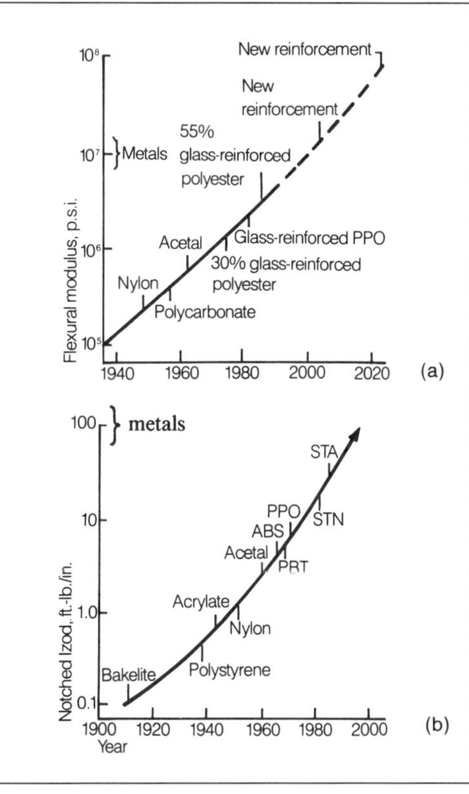

Historical perspective on (*a*) stiffness and (*b*) toughness.

plastic, generic Commodity plastic sold in small quantities (so-called bag and box quantities) often with a private label, broader specification version of a major producer's prime plastic or wide-specification material at discount

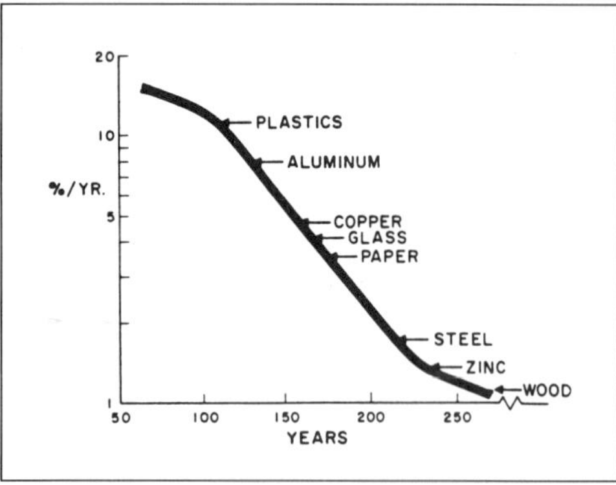

Growth rate versus age.

prices. The distributors, or resellers, provide small lots of plastics.

plastic growth rate The Fig. above provides an estimated pattern.

Plastic Hall of Fame Established in October 1972 by *Modern Plastics* magazine in cooperation with SPI. Its purpose is to honor a small group of industry leaders whose contributions are so significant that without them the industry would not be where it is today. In 1986 it was endorsed by SPI, SPE, PPA, and NPCM.

plastic, heavy type There are so-called heavy plastics. Historically, there have been occasions where light weight has hindered the growth of plastics in certain consumer markets; where the feel of heavier products is associated with quality. To compensate, designers have used highly filled compounds with heavy particles, metal inserts, doubled a part's wall thickness, etc.

plastic history See *Plastics Chronology* on p. xxxvii ff.

plastic house One of the first relatively all plastic houses was the Monsanto House of the Future erected in Disneyland, CA, U.S. in 1957 (see the Fig. below). The key structural components were four 16 ft (4.9 m) U-shaped cantilever (monocoque box girders) reinforced plastic designs by MIT. Different plastics were used throughout the house including different plastic sandwich panels. When this house was pulled down to provide a different scene (a main attraction for almost two decades), it had suffered almost no change in deflection (subjected to winds, earthquakes, subjected to families using it to the equivalent of centuries, etc.). Destruction by conventional techniques (wrecking ball, etc.) was almost impossible; required cutting sections, etc.

plastic hygroscopic ▷ **hygroscopic plastic**

plastic identification To identify a specific plastic, there are detailed techniques of characterization available from different industry tests, as well as the more conventional chemical analysis and synthesis methods routinely performed. To provide a quick way of identification refer to the Fig. opposite. It is only a guide, not foolproof.

Although the chart may appear to be somewhat formidable at first glance, only three simple tests are necessary to identify all of the plastics shown. No special equipment is needed—just water, matches, and a hot surface—and the only sensors required are one's eyes and nose.

The first step is to try to melt the material to determine whether it is a thermoset or a thermoplastic. This is usually done with a soldering iron, but any implement with a temperature of approximately 260°C (500°F) could be used. If the

The Monsanto House Of The Future. An all plastic house built in 1957.

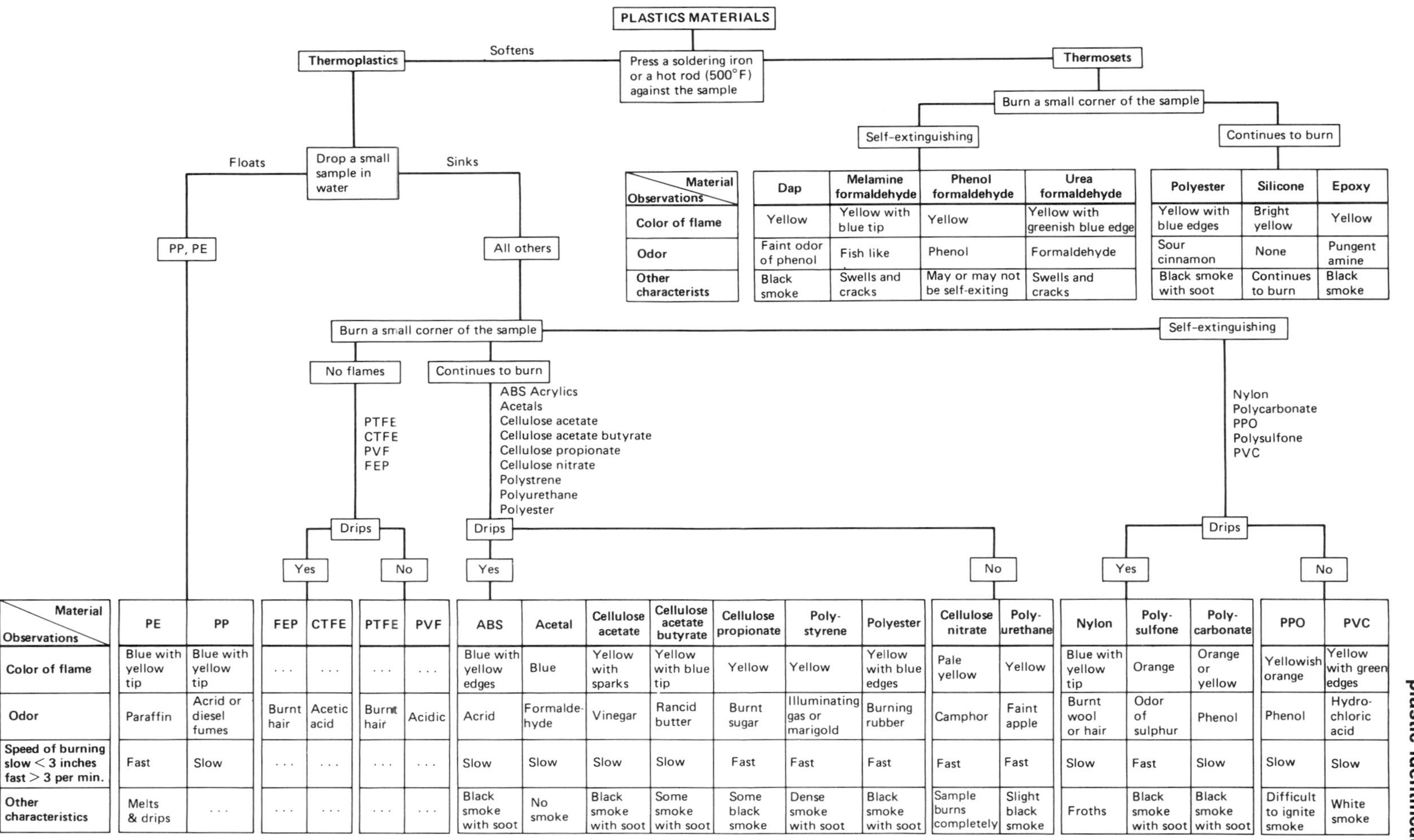

Thermosets – Self-extinguishing:

Observations \ Material	Dap	Melamine formaldehyde	Phenol formaldehyde	Urea formaldehyde
Color of flame	Yellow	Yellow with blue tip	Yellow	Yellow with greenish blue edge
Odor	Faint odor of phenol	Fish like	Phenol	Formaldehyde
Other characterists	Black smoke	Swells and cracks	May or may not be self-exiting	Swells and cracks

Thermosets – Continues to burn:

Observations \ Material	Polyester	Silicone	Epoxy
Color of flame	Yellow with blue edges	Bright yellow	Yellow
Odor	Sour cinnamon	None	Pungent amine
Other characterists	Black smoke with soot	Continues to burn	Black smoke

Thermoplastics:

Observations \ Material	PE	PP	FEP	CTFE	PTFE	PVF
Color of flame	Blue with yellow tip	Blue with yellow tip	. . .	. . .	. . .	. . .
Odor	Paraffin	Acrid or diesel fumes	Burnt hair	Acetic acid	Burnt hair	Acidic
Speed of burning slow < 3 inches fast > 3 per min.	Fast	Slow	. . .	. . .	. . .	. . .
Other characteristics	Melts & drips	. . .	. . .	. . .	. . .	. . .

Observations \ Material	ABS	Acetal	Cellulose acetate	Cellulose acetate butyrate	Cellulose propionate	Poly-styrene	Polyester
Color of flame	Blue with yellow edges	Blue	Yellow with sparks	Yellow with blue tip	Yellow	Yellow	Yellow with blue edges
Odor	Acrid	Formaldehyde	Vinegar	Rancid butter	Burnt sugar	Illuminating gas or marigold	Burning rubber
Speed of burning slow < 3 inches fast > 3 per min.	Slow	Slow	Slow	Slow	Fast	Fast	Fast
Other characteristics	Black smoke with soot	No smoke	Black smoke with soot	Some smoke with soot	Some black smoke	Dense smoke with soot	Black smoke with soot

Observations \ Material	Cellulose nitrate	Poly-urethane	Nylon	Poly-sulfone	Poly-carbonate	PPO	PVC
Color of flame	Pale yellow	Yellow	Blue with yellow tip	Orange	Orange or yellow	Yellowish orange	Yellow with green edges
Odor	Camphor	Faint apple	Burnt wool or hair	Odor of sulphur	Phenol	Phenol	Hydro-chloric acid
Speed of burning slow < 3 inches fast > 3 per min.	Fast	Fast	Slow	Fast	Slow	Slow	Slow
Other characteristics	Sample burns completely	Slight black smoke	Froths	Black smoke with soot	Black smoke with soot	Difficult to ignite smoke	White smoke

Plastic identification guide.

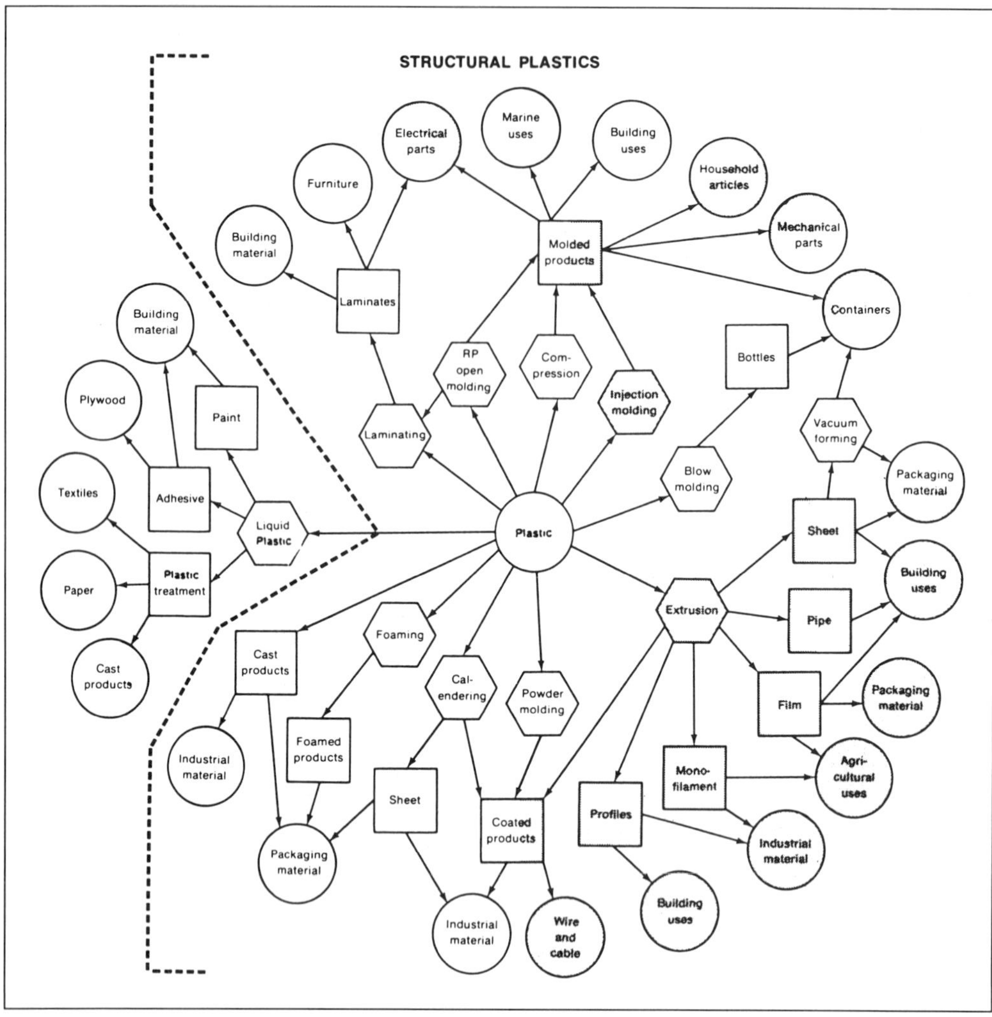

Interrelationship structure between plastics, processing, and markets.

material softens, it is a thermoplastic; if it does not, it is a thermoset.

If the material is found to be a thermoplastic, the next step is to find out whether its specific gravity is greater than or less than 1. This is done simply by dropping a sample in water. If the material floats, its specific gravity is less than 1; if it sinks, its specific gravity is greater than 1. The thermoplastics that have specific gravity of less than 1 are the polyolefins—polypropylene and polyethylene.

The final step for both thermosets and thermoplastics is a burn test, which should, of course, be performed in a well-ventilated area. The material should be held with pliers or clamps, and ignited with long wooden matches or a Bunsen burner. If there is only a small piece of material to test, it is best to break it into several parts, as it might take several tries to identify the odor and to observe the other effects noted on the chart.

The major difficulty in interpreting the burn test is that the burn rate and color of the flame of many plastics are affected by fillers, fire retardants, and other additives. However, in most cases the odor is not affected by these additives. It is recommended that you first perform the tests on a styrene drinking glass, a polyethylene milk bottle, or some other known plastic. This practice will prove invaluable when it is time to identify an unknown material.

plastic impregnated concrete ▷**concrete-plastic**

plastic industry structure The structure is summarized in the Fig. above.

plastic industry wages ▷ **wages, plastic industry** and **plastic processors benefit program**

plastic, inorganic In broad terms, an inorganic plastic may be considered to be any substance containing a large number of repeated units that involve elements other than carbon, connected by any type of chemical bond. Although the definition clearly covers all inorganic solids, including the giant ionic crystals of inorganic salts, based on modern inorganic chemistry the definition also includes compounds which have organic groups apppended in some way to one or more elements (other than carbon) of the plastic backbone. Thus, they are plastics in which all, or a very high proportion, of the chain atoms are not carbon atoms. Most inorganic plastics, in particular the extremely abundant naturally occurring silicate minerals, are highly crosslinked and are therefore hard, strong, but brittle materials, highly insoluble, and with high softening points. In addition, most structures have good heat stability. With the exception of the silicones, and to a lesser extent phosphonitrile plastics, very few synthetic inorganic plastics have achieved any commercial significance.

plastic intermittent load behavior ▷ **creep loading, intermittent behavior**

plasticity **1.** In very general terms, the action of yielding and the subsequent plastic deformation that occurs with increasing stress. It is the ability of a material (plastic, metal, etc.) to be shaped by stressing and to retain its shape after the stress has been removed. It permits the property of plastic which allows it to be deformed continuously and permanently without rupture upon the application of a force that exceeds the yield value of the plastic. This action accounts for the ability of certain plastics to be cold formed. **2.** When a material (plastic, steel, etc.) is subjected to an external load of such magnitude that deformation continues with no apparent further increase in load. ▷ **ductility**

plasticize To impart softness, toughness, and flexibility in a plastic through the incorporation of a plasticizer additive.

plasticizer Its primary role is to reduce the rigidity of a plastic; to render it more flexible. PVC, for which it is widely used, can thus be obtained in a wide range of stiffnesses from rigid and somewhat brittle types to very flexible rubber-like types. Low cost plasticizers, added mainly to reduce the cost of compounds when the level of stiffness is not important, are sometimes called extenders. They usually have a negative effect on strength (see Fig. below). Plasticizers allow the long molecule chains to move more easily relative to each other when a strain is imposed, thus the lower strength; also allows for easier processing. Plasticizers can age or migrate out with time and the plastic can lose its original toughness; this was particularly true up to about the late 1960s. It was rather common to see loss in vinyl in autos, vinyl upholstery, and steering wheels; usually accompanied with a greasy feeling. Most of these instances of loss have disappeared with improved plastic technology, which allowed internal plasticization through the use of blends and copolymerization. A plastic that has adequate flexibility and toughness without the use of plasticizers is always preferred; cost definitely influences choices.

plasticizer extender A substance, which although relatively incompatible with the plastic (only slightly miscible), may be used in conjunction with a primary plasticizer as a lower cost diluent. Also called secondary plasticizer. ▷ **plasticizer**

plasticizer, internal An agent incorporated in a plastic during polymerization, as opposed to a plasticizer added to the plastic during compounding.

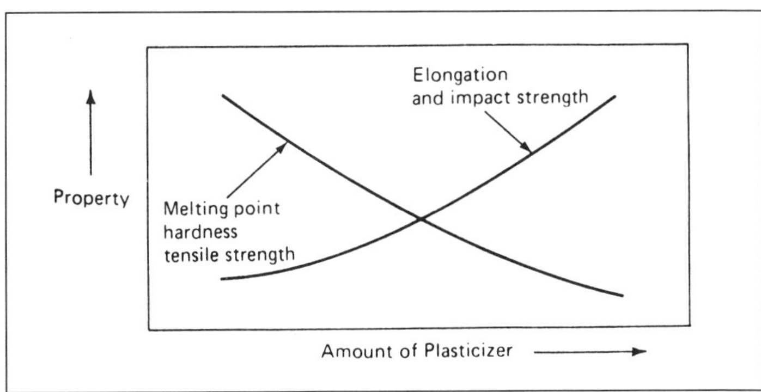

General effect of plasticizers on properties.

plasticizer, iodine value The number (value) of grams of iodine that 100 g of an unsaturated compound will absorb in a given time under arbitrary conditions. It is used to indicate the residual unsaturation in epoxy plasticizers; a low value implies a high degree of saturation.

plasticizer migration ▷ **migration**

plasticizer, polyester They are noted for their permanence and resistance to extraction.

plasticizer, primary Has sufficient affinity to the plastic so that it is considered compatible and therefore it may be used as the sole plasticizer.

plasticizer, secondary Has insufficient affinity for the plastic and must be blended with a primary plasticizer.

plastic, liquid ▷ **liquid plastic**

plastic living system ▷ **living polymer system**

plastic long life In our environmentally oriented system of manufacture one would need to minimize the generation of waste by choosing materials and products with as long a life as possible and with optimal recyclability. Even as early as the design stage one needs to consider the effects of later use. Overall, most plastics meet these conditions. ▷ **energy consumption; recycling; incineration; product life cycle**

plastic long term load behavior ▷ **creep loading, long term behavior**

plastic lumber Recycled plastic that is basically extruded, such as PE, is produced and competes with natural wood lumber in various applications.

plastic lumber and waste ▷ **waste and plastic lumber**

plastic manufacture ▷ **plastic**

plastic market ▷ **markets for plastics**

plastic matrix The plastic portion of a reinforced or filled plastic.

plastic memory The tendency of a thermoplastic which has been stretched while hot to return to its unstretched shape when reheated. ▷ **elastic memory**

plastic misapplication ▷ **plastic product failure**

plastic modeling ▷ **designing with model, plastic-chemical structure**

plastic money Australian researchers have patented a process for producing banknotes made of clear, PP-based film. Note Printing Australia, a Melbourne division of the Reserve Bank of Australia, survey was successful. Result showed the circulation life of plastic notes was far higher than paper notes. A paper $10 would circulate for 10 to 12 months, while the plastic $10 notes were still in circulation after more than two years. While the longer life and the fact that plastic notes did not get as dirty were bonuses, the main reason for their introduction was security. It is very difficult to counterfeit because the security features are incorporated into the plastic substrate.

plastic, natural Vegetable-derived, amorphous mixture of carboxylic acids, essential oils, and terpenes occurring as exudations on the bark of many varieties of trees and shrubs. The best known are rosin and balsam. They are usually transparent or translucent and yellowish to brown, are soluble in organic solvents but not in water, and are electrical nonconductors. Their use in varnishes, adhesives, and printing inks is still rather considerable, though diminishing in favor of synthetic plastics. ▷ **synthetic, natural**

plastic, neat type ▷ **neat plastic**

plastic nomenclature There is no universally accepted system of naming plastics. Yet, there are many ways in which plastics are named; even a cursory glance at any magazine will attest to this situation. Furthermore, the language of the science and that of the technology frequently have too little in common. Fortunately, these problems are generally capable of solution, and several groups continually work diligently at this task. The basic rules of plastic nomenclature were first promulgated in a report by IUPAC in 1952. The report not only covers naming, but also symbology and definitions. The definitions are further refined and extended by a task group in ISO. Naming is also being reviewed by ACS.

Traditionally, plastics have been named by attaching the prefix poly to the name of the real or assumed monomer (the source) from which it was derived. Thus polystyrene is the plastic made from styrene. When a plastic consists of two or more words they are usually without parenthesis: polymethylmethacrylate; with parenthesis they read as poly(methyl methacrylate). Source-based nomenclature can be easily adapted to the naming of copolymers, e.g., polystyrene-co-acrylonitrile. A block copolymer, as an example, containing 75 mass % of polybutadiene and 25 mass % of polystyrene is polybutadiene-block-polystyrene(0.75:0.25 w) or block-copolybutadiene/styrene (75:25 mass %).

For organic plastics that are regular (have only one species of constitutional unit in a single sequential arrangement) and consist only of single strands, the IUPAC has a structure-based system of naming plastics. The steps involved are: (1) identification of the unit, taking into account the kinds of atoms in the main chain and the location of substituents, (2) orientation of the unit, and (3) naming of the unit.

In this book the target has been to use the name predominantly used within the plastics industry worldwide. Thus, the term plastic is more prevalent than polymer. However, cross-references are used (acetal and polyacetal, etc.).

plastic nomenclature abbreviations See *List of Abbreviations* on p. viii ff.

plastic optical fiber POF is increasingly replacing copper wire for carrying computer data and electronic signals. The two biggest application areas are computer networks and automotive. Usage goes beyond light piping. Much of it will be wiring for on-board computers and for controls to powered accessories. Local area networks (LANs), which enable groups of PCs and work stations to communicate with each other, use optical fibers, both glass and plastic, because of their high speed and expansion capabilities over conventional wiring. Glass fibers have a big edge over plastic for speed and transmission distance [thousands versus 200 ft (thousands versus 500 cm)], so they compete only in LANs. But a large market for plastic still exists. POF benefits over glass include: (1) lower cost of cable and espoecially connectors (at 25%), (2) installation savings, connectors can be attached to the cable in about one minute instead of 10 and require less skill, and (3) it is less brittle and bends more easily in tight spaces. The most common fiber materials are acrylics, polystyrene, and polycarbonate. Standard thermoplastics are used for jacketing. ▷ **fiber optics**

plastic or paper grocery bag ▷ **grocery bag** and **environment and public opinion**

plastic overview Before the advent of synthetic plastics, most forms of construction and production were dependent upon the use of natural materials such as metal, wood, rubber, tar, etc. These materials are still very much in evidence today, but in many instances they have been replaced by the materials called plastics. Through the "magic" of the chemist, we now have plastics that can meet almost every nonengineering and engineering requirement.

plastic packing in mold ▷ **mold cavity packing**

plastic pocket ▷ **reinforced plastic pocket**

plastic, porous Different plastics used. Fabricated into a wide variety of shapes, sheets, rods, etc. with different degrees of porosity such as 5 to 20,000 microns. They include use where requirements exist for controlled release venting, aeration, filtration, muffling in different environments (chemical corrosion, abrasion, high and low temperatures, sound, etc.), and others.

plastic processing ▷ **processing** and **fabricating processes**

plastic processors benefit program The SPI issues data, as shown in the Table below. Lists percent of U.S. processors by territory.

Plastic processors benefit program. Percent of U.S. processors by territory.

Benefits		Northeast, %	East North Central, %	Southeast, %	West, %	Total, %
Short-term disability insurance	Hourly	65.9	68.6	65.2	33.3	60.9
	Salaried	64.3	63.0	54.2	35.0	56.5
Long-term disability	Hourly	27.5	18.4	26.7	33.3	24.7
	Salaried	61.9	50.5	47.9	45.0	51.5
Group life insurance	Hourly	90.2	97.0	97.8	70.7	91.3
	Salaried	90.7	97.9	100.0	79.5	93.9
Dental plan	Hourly	57.5	48.0	54.3	59.5	53.4
	Salaried	54.8	53.0	56.3	67.5	56.9
Comprehensive medical	Hourly	48.2	60.2	73.1	45.1	57.7
	Salaried	44.8	59.0	74.5	46.9	57.3
Retirement plan	Hourly	65.0	80.2	76.1	50.0	70.7
	Salaried	67.4	81.8	72.3	59.5	72.8
Deferred profit sharing	Hourly	29.6	44.2	50.0	50.0	43.1
	Salaried	35.7	53.2	54.3	47.6	49.1
Educational reimbursement plan	Hourly	61.1	79.2	63.0	59.5	69.1
	Salaried	65.8	84.5	63.8	65.7	73.5

plastic, process, product interrelation In order to understand designwise potential problems vs solutions, it is helpful to consider the relationships of machine capabilities, plastics processing variables and part performance. A distinction has to be made between machine conditions and processing variables. As an example, machine conditions include operating temperature and presssure, mold and die temperature, machine output rate, etc. Processing variables are more specific, such as the melt condition in the mold or die, flow rate vs temperature, etc. ▷ **design** and **FALLO approach**

plastic product failure Outstanding performance of plastics over long periods of time have been demonstrated in innumerable applications since 1886 in practically all markets. Yet some users of plastics products continue to encounter disappointments in the use of these materials. Practically all incidences of malfunctions are caused by a lack of knowledge of the characteristics and potentials of the plastic, with a resultant misapplication, rather than from any shortcomings in the material itself. In other words, use the correct design, correct material, and properly fabricate it to meet cost-property efficiency. Unfortunately there are cheaply made plastic parts that the public assumes are equal to the more expensive parts that will not fail. Industry standards and specifications are always being developed and used for public awareness of inferior parts. Unfortunately they usually are issued after the problem develops.

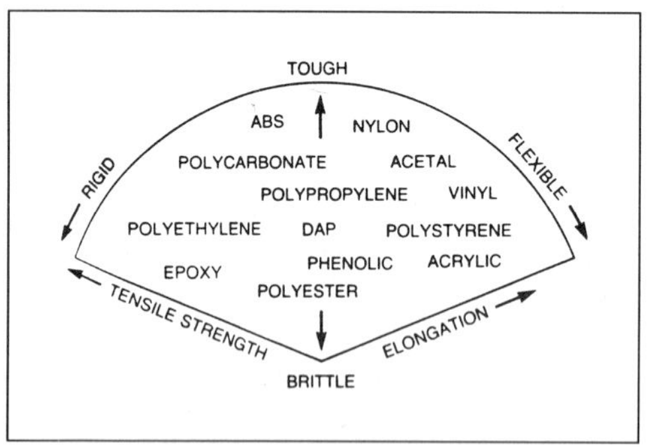

Example of range of mechanical properties.

plastic production ▷ **plastic consumption**

plastic properties The range of properties literally encompasses all types of environmental conditions, static to dynamic loads, etc., each with their broad range of properties. These properties can take into consideration wear resistance, integral color, impact resistance, transparency, ductility, thermal and sound absorption, weight, and others. Unfortunately there is no one plastic that can meet all maximum properties (as with steel, aluminum, wood, etc.) so the user has different options. Usually a compromise is made since many product requirements provide options, particularly if cost is of prime importance. Guide to properties is given in the Table on pp. 544–545 and Figs. here and opposite. ▷ **data, theoretical versus actual properties**

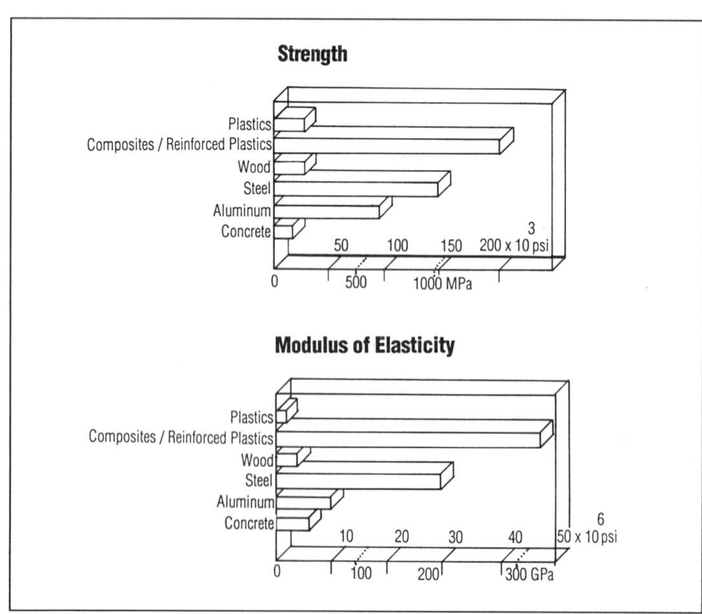

General comparison of different materials.

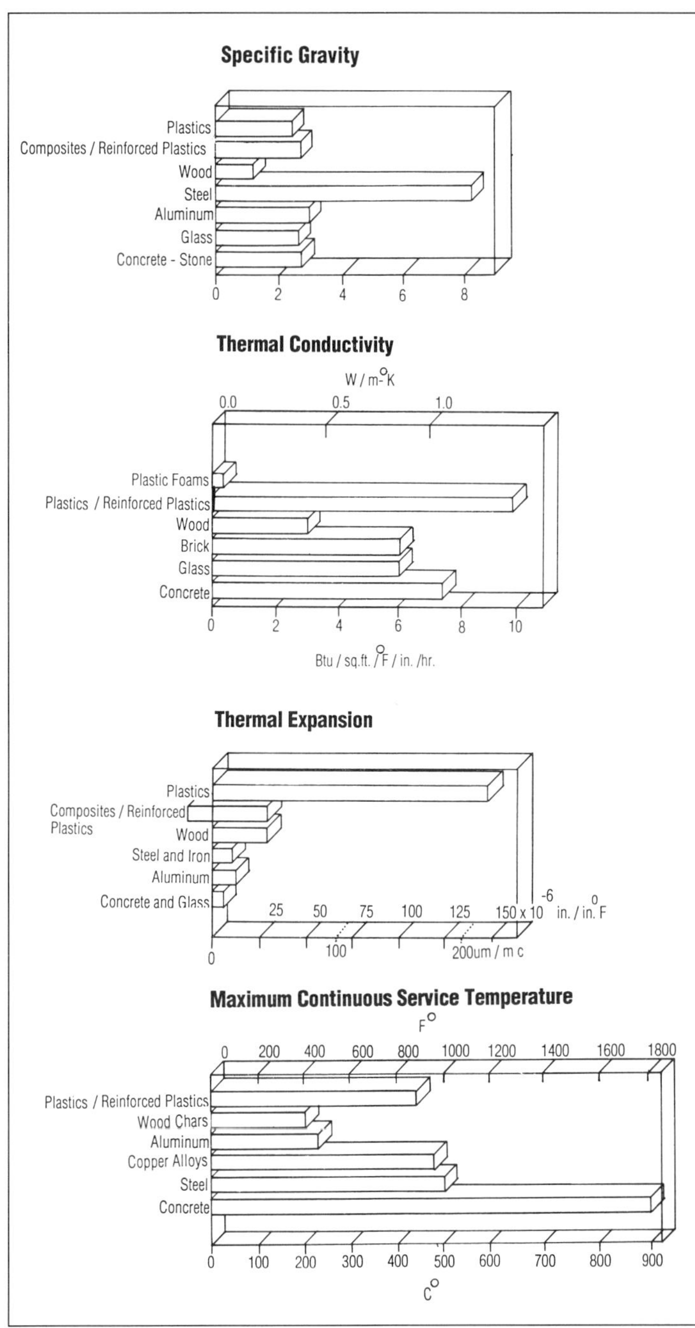

General comparison of different materials (*continued*).

plastic properties, testing procedures ▷ **testing** and **nondestructive testing**

plastic properties, theoretical versus actual ▷ **data, theoretical versus actual properties**

plastic, pseudonym ▷ **plastic definition**

plastic, radiation resistance ▷ **radiation-induced reaction**

plastic received, checking An important factor in the production is that quality control of all types of incoming materials (plastics, additives, etc.) always conform and be checked against specifications. ▷ **quality control** and **quality inspection**

plastic, recycled ▷ **recyclable**

Comparison of relatively high performance plastics.

Material		Polyaryl-sulfone	Polyether sulfone		Polyether-imide	Polyetherketone	
Abbreviation		PAS	PES		PEI	PEEKK	PEKEKK
Commercial grade (Manufacturer)		Radel R 7000 (Amoco)	Ultrason E 3000 (BASF)	Vitrex 3600 G (ICI)	Ultem 1000 (GEP)	Hostatek (Hoechst)	Ultrapek KR 4176 (BASF)
Mechanical properties							
Elastic modulus	N/mm^2	2723	2900	2900	3000	4000	4000
Tensile strength	N/mm^2	76	85	84	105	108	104
Modulus in flexure	N/mm^2	2861	–	2600	3300	3600	3710
Flexural strength	N/mm^2	107	–	129	145	120	135
Ultimate strength	N/mm^2	–	–	–	90	86	~ 100
Elongation at break	%	23	20 to 40	40 to 80	60	36	53
Izod impact resistance	J/m	–	–	–	1300	–	–
Izod impact resistance, notched	J/m	–	80 to 90	76	50	51	52
Thermal properties							
Melt temperature	°C	360	–	–	–	365	375
Glass transition temperature	°C	–	227	225	215	160	175
Heat resistance							
Vicat-procedure B	°C	–	222	222	215	> 300	> 250
F_{ISO} method A, 1.8 N/mm^2	°C	> 204	215	203	200	160	170
Maximum service temperature	°C	–	180	180	170	260	250
Thermal linear-expansion coefficient							
lengthwise	10^{-5} K^{-1}	–	5,5	5,5	5,6	4,5	4,2
crosswise	10^{-5} K^{-1}	–	–	–	5,6	–	–
Thermal conductivity	W/(k · m)	–	0,18	–	0,22	0,21	0,22
Electrical properties							
Electric strength	kV/mm	–	≥ 63	16	33	20	–
Specific breakthrough resistance	10^{16} Ω · cm	–	≥ 1	10 to 100	0,67	1	–
CTI surface leakage	V	–	150-0	–	–	175	150.0
Arc resistance	sec	–	–	20 to 120	128	–	–
Other properties							
Density	g/cm^2	1,28	1,37	1,37	1,27	1,3	1,311
Water absorption							
in 24 h	%	–	–	–	0,25	0,5	0,07
equilibrium value	%	–	2,2	–	1,25	–	0,8
Oxygen index, LOI	%	> 42	41	38 to 41	47	40	37
at specimen thickness	mm	–	3,2	1,6	–	4	3,2
Combustibility (UL), V-0 wall thickness from	mm	–	0,5	0,43	0,41	0,8	1,6
OSU Heat release							
HR	KW · min/m^2	4	18	≈ 65	≈ 65	≈ 60	< 55
HRR	KW/m^2	40	72	≈ 65	≈ 65	≈ 60	< 55
at specimen thickness	mm	–	2	–	–	–	–
Price	DM/kg	60 to 70	35 to 50	≈ 40	30 to 35	≈ 150	≈ 150

plastic, reinforced ▷ **reinforced plastic**

plastic relaxation ▷ **relaxation**

plastic resole ▷ **resole plastic**

plastic, reuse ▷ **recycling capability; waste; reuse of plastic**

plastic-rich area ▷ **reinforced plastic, plastic-rich area**

plastic rigidity ▷ **rigid plastic; semirigid plastic; nonrigid plastic**

plastics Plastics are selected and designed by

Polyetherketone		Liquid crystalline polymers		Polyamide-imide	Polyphenylenesulfide	Polycarbonate		Test Procedure
PEEK	PEKK	LCP		PAI	PPS	PC		
Vitrex 450 G (ICI)	Declar (Du Pont)	KUI-9231 (Bayer)	Vectra A 950 (Hoechst)	Terlon 5030 (Amoco)	Tadur KUI-9511 (Bayer)	Makrolon 6870 (Bayer)	Lexan 950 (GEP)	ASTM/DIN/ISO
3600	4500	1700	9700	14600	19000	2300	2300	D638/53457
92	102	–	–	221	–	> 55	60	D638/53455
3660	–	12000	9000	11700	14000	–	2500	D790/53457
170	–	150	169	338	260	–	100	D790/53452
–	–	160	165	–	200	> 65	70	D638/53455
50	80	1,1	3,0	2,3	1,5	90	–	D638/53455
–	–	560	–	504	–	–	–	D256/ISO 180-IC
83	–	280	520	79	–	> 750	700	D256/ISO 180-1A
334	338	330	280	–	280	–	–	
143	156	–	–	–	–	–	–	
–	–	–	145	–	–	–	145	D1525/53460
140	–	250	180	182	260	126	135	D648/53461
250	–	240	220	220	240	130	–	UL 746B
								D696/52612
4,7	–	−0,4	−0,5	1,62	–	6,5	7	
–	–	8,0	7,5	–	–	–	–	
0,25	–	–	–	0,37	0,29	0,21	0,2	C177/52612
19	–	53	39	–	–	> 30	17	D149/53481
4 to 9	–	1	1	0,2	0,1	> 1	10	D257/53482
–	–	150	175	–	125	200 to 225	–	D3636/53480
–	–	101	137	–	–	–	120	D495
1,32	1,28	1,38	1,4	1,61	1,7	1,2	–	D792/53479
0,5	–	–	0,02	0,24	–	–	0,1	D570/53495
0,5	–	–	–	–	–	0,36	0,35	
35	40	48	35	51	48	36	35	D2865
3,2	–	–	–	–	–	–	–	
1,45	–	0,4	0,8	1,17	1,6	0,8	1,04	UL 94-V
≈ 65	< 20	0	16,8	< 20	4	≈ 140	≈ 140	FAR 25853
≈ 65	< 55	49	57,8	< 20	53	≈ 180	≈ 180	
–	–	2	1,6	–	–	2	2	
≈ 150	> 200	≈ 40	50 to 70	90 to 120	15 to 20	8 to 9	8 to 9	

the same easy and practical method as steel, aluminum, wood, glass, ceramic, and other materials. Many different products have been designed from plastics for over a century; they usually provide a large cost advantage over other materials. New plastics are being made continously to meet new performance or processing requirements, but will never completely replace other materials.

Plastics offer the opportunity to optimize design by focusing on material composition and orientation, as well as structural geometry. The interrelationship between materials selection (including reinforcement orientation), performance, shape, cost, and processing is more important for plastics than for other materials, where the designer is limited to specific forms of profiles that are bent or welded.

Materials selection is based on design process requirements. Data concerning requirements are available from many sources, including manufacturers, or are developed by the materials selector.

As a flow process, plastics fabrication differs from most metals fabrication; furthermore, a one-step process produces a completely finished part. Although this gives the designer great flexibility and provides design freedom not possible in metals, particularly sheet metal, it requires a greater understanding to take advantage of these capabilities. The polymer chemist can rearrange the molecular structure of the plastic or polymer to provide an almost infinite variety of compositions that differ in form, appearance, properties, and characteristics. ▷ **computerized data-base, plastics; material selection; computer cost modeling, technically; statistical benefits; plastic**

Plastics Pioneer Assoc. PPA was established in 1942 to recognize members of the plastics community with long record service.

plastic starved area ▷ **reinforced plastic starved area**

plastic stereoblock plastic A plastic with molecules made up of blocks or long sections of identical stereospecific structure interspaced with sections of another type of structure.

plastic stereograph plastic A plastic consisting of chains of an atactic polymer grafted to chains of an isotactic polymer. For example, atactic PS can be grafted to isotatic PS under suitable conditions to provide different properties.

plastic stereoregular linear plastic According to IUPAC definition, it is a polymer the molecules of which can be described in terms of only one species of stereorepeating unit, in a single sequential arrangement. A stereorepeating unit is a configurational unit having a defined configuration at all sites of isomerism in the main chain of a polymer molecule.

plastic stereospecific ▷ **stereospecific (stereoregular) plastic**

plastic streak A long, narrow surface imperfection on the surface of a laminated or reinforced plastic caused by a local excess of plastic.

plastic strengthened ▷ **strengthening plastic mechanisms** and **oxidation degradation**

plastic structure ▷ **molecular arrangement structure**

plastic, super type ▷ **superplastic**

plastic, synthetic A plastic produced by polymerization of its monomer or monomers by a chemical reaction controlled by people, as opposed to a plastic produced in nature by biosynthesis giving a natural plastic. The most important commercial synthetic type materials are usually called plastics, elastomers or rubbers, fibers, coatings, and adhesives. Natural polymers (plastics) which have been chemically modified to different polymers are identified as synthetic. Alternative names for plastic are polymer and resin.

plastic system A mixture of plastic and additive ingredients such as catalyst, initiator, diluents, fillers, and/or others required for intended processing method and final product.

plastic transition ▷ **transition, first order**

plastic truth and myths ▷ **plastic bad and other myths**

plastic variability Even though equipment operations (extrusion, injection, etc.) have variabilities, the usual most uncontrollable variable in processing is the base plastic. Variations from supplier to supplier of like plastics, and even variations from lot to lot or box to box within a lot from one supplier, can cause havoc. This situation is controllable by proper specification preparation and quality control. It is a fact that there are variables, so required machine process controls should be used.

plastic variation, reliability factor ▷ **material variation, reliability factor**

plastic, virgin type ▷ **virgin plastic**

plastic wages ▷ **wages plastic industry**

plastic, water soluble ▷ **water soluble plastic**

plastic wood treatment ▷ **wood-plastic impregnated**

plastic work energy The energy expended in performing plastic deformation. By an analysis of plastic work, similar to that of thermodynamic theory such as rubber elasticity, the stress-strain relationships for deformation may be derived. However, unlike elasticity, the current state of strain in plasticity theory depends on the strain theory, and the change in plastic work as a function of the change in strain must be considered.

plastify ▷ **plasticate**

plastigel Exhibits putty-like consistency or gel-like flow. It is a plasticol to which a thickening agent has been added.

plastisol A stable dispersion of fine particles (about 1 μm) of emulsion plastic, mainly PVC in a plasticizer, which is a viscous fluid. Upon heating at about 180 to 250°C for a few minutes, the plasticizer is absorbed into the particles and solvates them so that they fuse together to produce a homogenous mass. The fusion process is referred to as gelation. Plastisols and the related organosols, plastigels, and rigisols provide a liquid form of PVC to which special processing techniques may be applied which are often more convenient for producing useful products than conventional melt processing methods. They include dipping, spreading, rotational molding, injection molding, and casting. Materials rheological behavior is important during processing; they can be very complex. Plastisols may be shear thinning or shear thickening, depending mostly on PVC particle size, size distribution, and shape, but also on plasticizer type and other additives used.

plastometer ▷ **rheometer**

platelet ▷ **reinforcement, discs**

plate mark Any imperfection in a pressed plastic sheet resulting from the surface of the pressing plate.

platen ▷ **clamping platen**

platenum spinneret ▷ **spinneret** and **glass fiber production**

plate-out An objectionable coating gradually formed on metal surfaces of molds, calendering and embossing rolls during processing of plastics. Caused by the extraction and depostion of certain components in the plastic such as pigments, lubricants, plasticizers, and/or stabilizers.

plating ▷ **metallizing plastic; polishing; motor-generator**

plexifilament ▷ **flash spun nonwoven fabric**

Plexiglas Rohm & Haas's tradename for acrylic plastics.

plied yarn Yarn made by collecting two or more single yarns. Normally, the yarns are twisted together, though sometimes they are collected without twist (for use in reinforced plastics, etc.)

Pliofilm ▷ **rubber hydrochloride plastic**

plotter Much processing and auxiliary equipment uses graphic displays to obtain immediate updates on their performance. ▷ **computer plotter**

plug thermoforming ▷ **thermoforming, plug**

plunger **1.** The male portion of the mold. **2.** In compression molding, the plunger pushes or forces the material into the opening in the female cavity. Gives the internal shape of the part being molded In injection molding molds, the mold plunger is often referred to as the core. **3.** That part of a transfer or injection molding machine that applies pressure to the unmelted (or melted) plastic to push it into the chamber, which in turn forces the melt at the front of the chamber out of the nozzle. With IM when only a ram (no screw) is used, the unmelted plastic is "pushed"; whereas with the more conventional IM machine that uses a screw plasticator, the melt within the barrel, in front of the screw, when ready to be injected into the cavity is forced by the plunger action of the screw. The screw acts as a ram and normally is not rotating. ▷ **mold compression; injection molding**

plunger, injection molding ▷ **injection molding, plunger**

plunger molding A variation of the transfer molding process in which an auxiliary hydraulic ram is used to assist the main ram. ▷ **injection molding, plunger**

ply **1.** A single layer in a laminate or reinforced plastic. In general, fabrics or felts consisting of one or more layers. **2.** Yarn resulting from a twisting operation; for example, 3-ply yarn consists of three strands of yarn twisted together. **3.** In filament winding, a ply is a single pass; two plies forming one ply.

plywood A wood composite made up of thin wood veneers (with grains placed at right angles to each other; alternate plies laid at 90° to each other) bonded with plastic, usually phenol-formaldehyde or resorcinol-formaldehyde (phenolics). It is actually superior to metals in strength-to-weight comparison and has relatively low thermal expansion, high heat capacity, and low water absorption. It is a form of wood laminated.

plywood head block, retainer board A thick (7 to 12 cm) large piece of laminated lumber, usually with veneer crossings, used for bottom and top of a bale of plywood during pressing and clamping.

pneumatic A system in which energy is transferred by compression flow and expansion of air. ▷ **hydraulic**

pocket-plastic ▷ **reinforced plastic, plastic pocket**

pock mark ▷ **blow molding extruder, pock mark**

point measurement ▷ **printers' measurements**

Poise The metric unit of viscosity, named after the French scientist Poiseuille. One poise (P) is the viscosity of a liquid in which a force of one dyne is necessary to maintain a velocity, differential of one centimeter per second per centimeter over a surface one centimeter square. The centipoise (cP) is one hundredth of a poise. ▷ **dynamic viscosity**

Poiseuille flow ▷ **flow, Poiseuille** and **pressure flow**

Poisson distribution A molecular weight distribution with a differential distribution function as:

$$N(r) = [\exp(-v)^{r-1}v^{r-1}/(r-1)$$

where r is the size of the individual molecular species (such as DP) and $v = \bar{x}_m - 1$, where $\bar{x}_m$ is the number of average degree of polymerization. The corresponding weight function Wr is similar. The weight average degree of polymerization is

$$\bar{x}_w = (1 + 3v + v^2)/(1 + v) \approx 1 + \bar{x}_n,$$

thus this is a very narrow distribution ($\bar{x}_w/\bar{x}_n \rightarrow 1$ at high r). It results when a fixed number of polymerization sites start growing simultaneously and growth is random with no termination. This often happens in the formation of living plastics by anionic polymerization. ▷ **molecular weight distribution**

Poisson probability distribution A discrete probability distribution is referred to as the Poisson, named after Simeon Poisson, who described it in 1837. The distribution is applicable to many situations that involve an observation per unit of time. For example, the number of cars arriving at a highway toll booth in 1-minute intervals; the number of machine breakdowns in 1 day, and the number of shoppers entering a grocery store in 5-minute intervals. The distribution is also applicable to situations involving the number of observasions per unit of amount. For example, the number of weaving defects in 1000 square meters of cloth, the number of defects per lot of product, and the number of rivet defects in a mobile home.

In each of these situations, there are many equal opportunities for the occurrence of an event. Each rivet in a structure has an equal opportunity to be defective; however, there will only be a few defective out of the hundreds of rivets. The Poisson is applicable when n is quite large and p' is small.

The formula for the Poisson distribution is

$$P(c) = \frac{(np')^c}{c!} e^{-np'}$$

where c = number of occurrences per unit time or amount, such as number of defects, cars, customers, or machine breakdowns; np' = average number of occurrences per unit time or amount; $e = 2.718281$.

Poisson ratio Poisson's ratio is the proportion of lateral strain to longitudinal strain under conditions of uniform longitudinal stress within the proportional or elastic limit. When the material's deformation is within the elastic range it results in lateral to longitudinal strains that will always be constant. This ratio is designated by the Greek letter ν. In mathematical terms, Poisson's ratio is the diameter of the test specimen before and after elongation divided by the length of the specimen before and after elongation. Poisson's ratio will have more than one value if the material is not isotropic.

Poisson's ratio always falls within the range of 0 to 0.5. A zero value indicates that the specimen would suffer no reduction in diameter or contraction laterally during elongation but would undergo a reduction in density. A value of 0.5 indicates that the specimen's volume would remain constant during elongation or as the diameter decreases. For most engineering materials the ratio lies between 0.10 and 0.40 (see Table below).

Poisson's ratio is a required constant in engineering analysis for determining the stress and deflection properties of plastic, metal, and other structures such as beams, plates, shells, and rotating discs. Temperature, the magnitude of stresses and strains, and the direction of

An example of the range of Poisson's ratio.

Material	Range of Poisson's ratio
Aluminum	0.33
Carbon steel	0.29
Rubber	0.50
Rigid thermoplastics	
Neat	0.20–0.40
Filled or reinforced	0.10–0.40
Structural foam	0.30–0.40
Rigid thermosets	
Neat	0.20–0.40
Filled or reinforced	0.20–0.40

loading all have their effects on Poisson's ratio. However, these factors usually do not alter the typical range of values enough to affect most practical calculations, where this constant is frequently of only secondary importance.

Poisson ratio, negative Certain engineering factors follow prescribed patterns. However, there are examples where they change because of the type of design applied. One example is Poisson's ratio of lateral strain to axial strain, which always falls within the *positive* range of 0 to 0.5 for any material. There is, however, a basic design configuration using a differently fabricated shaped cell structure that changes a material's strain behavior. When a sample of polyurethane foam is stretched, its cross-section either moves or grows flatter, and when compressed it becomes thinner. Thus, a PUR has a *negative* Poisson ratio.

This "reentrant" foam, as it is called by its inventor Roderic Lakes, a professor of biomedical engineering at the University of Iowa, is the only material thus far to exhibit negative action. The key to this behavior is in its microarchitecture. Whereas conventional foams have a convex cell structure, the ribs of each of the new foam's cells permanently protrude inward. When a tensile force is applied, the ribs push outward, causing this foam to expand laterally. With a compression force the ribs collapse into themselves, causing the material to contract laterally.

Each reentrant foam starts out as a conventional plastic foam with a positive Poisson ratio and a convex, open-celled structure. The conventional foam is then compressed triaxially (that is, in three orthogonal directions) and placed in a mold. The mold is heated to a temperature slightly above its softening temperature, then cooled to room temperature. Any foam subjected to this conditioning that then possesses a permanent volumetric compression factor between 1.4 and 4.0 exhibits a negative Poisson ratio.

When compared to conventional foams, reentrant foams display superior resiliency and toughness. This structure has applications where the redistribution of stresses is desired: in air filters, flexible fasteners, gaskets, sound-absorbing layers, fillers for highway joints, ankle wraps, wheelchair cushions, and many more. An air filter made of reentrant foam would, for example, address the problem of a pressure rise behind a clogged conventional filter. The pore space in the reentrant foam would open rather than close as the pressure increased, to prevent clogging. And if it were used in a flexible fastener, it would expand when the pull-out tension was applied.

polar Description of a molecule in which the positive and negative electrical charges are permanently separated, as opposed to nonpolar molecules in which the charges coincide. Polar molecules ionize in solution and impart electrical conductivity. The formation of emulsions and the action of detergents are dependent on this behavior. ▷ **dielectric properties**

polar diagram A method of graphical representation of directional properties of material by plotting the value of the properties radially against orientation angle. ▷ **reinforced plastic, directional properties**

polarimeter An instrument for determining the amount of rotation of the direction of vibration of polarized light by the specimen; an instrument for determining the amount of polarization of light by the specimen or in the illuminating beam.

polariscope An optical (polarizing) microscope in which the incident light passes through a polarizing filter (polarizer) and the transmitted light through another filter (analyzer); the polarizer for polarizing the beam illuminating the specimen and the analyzer for analyzing the effect, if any, of the specimen on the polarized light. At least one of the polars should be rotatable for obtaining crossed or uncrossed polars. Either the polars should be simultaneously rotatable, or the specimen should be rotatable betweeen polars. As an example, if the direction of polarization of the two filters is perpendicular no light reaches the eyepiece. However, a birefringent sample (crystalline plastic) will cause light to be passed and will form an image. The technique is very useful for the observation of spherulites and crystallite, and in indicating orientation. ▷ **photoelasticity**

polarity The sign of the charge on a molecule or side chain.

polarized light It is easy to tell whether you are dealing with a crystalline or an amorphous plastic by observing the sample using polarized light. Amorphous areas appear black, while crystalline areas can be clearly examined. The explanation for this effect is that in the case of crystalline polymers the molecules crystallize and fold together in a uniformly ordered manner, whereas the amorphous polymers do not produce crystallites and occur randomly positioned. Thus, under polarized lighting crystalline materials exhibit multicolored patterns, whereas amorphous materials appear black. In this way the crystalline microstructure can be examined. Features of the crystalline polymers are readily discerned, whereas those of the amorphous polymers are not. ▷ **polariscope; microtoming, optical analysis; nondestructive test method, residual strain**

polarizing microscope ▷ **polariscope**

polar winding ▷ **filament winding, polar winding**

polepiece ▷ **filament winding, polepiece**

Polimotor Rogers Corp. has exclusive rights to the reinforced plastic automobile engine that has been a reality since 1980. The phenolic-glass fiber RP compound provides excellent performance in dimensional stability, creep resistance, toughness, strength, and heat resistance (120 to 200°C), etc. It weighs 80 kg (175 lb) against the 135 kg (300 lb) of its metal counterpart. ▷ **automotive plastic engine**

polish A solid powder, liquid, or semi-liquid mixture that imparts smoothness, surface protection, and/or decorative finish.

polishing mold ▷ **mold polishing**

polishing roll A roll or series of rolls which have a highly polished chrome plated surface; used to produce smooth surface of products such as film and sheet as they are processed via extruders, coaters, etc.

pollution Introduction of substances into any environment that are not normally present therein and that are potentially toxic or otherwise objectionable. The most serious atmospheric contaminants have been sulfur dioxide (burning fuel in plants) and automobile exhaust gases rich in carbon dioxide, etc. There is also water, land, and other pollution situations. Certain plastics introduce pollutants; recognize that if all plastics in the world did not exist, there would still be enormous pollution problems. The plastics industry has been very successful in eliminating or reducing their relatively small part of the problem. ▷ **chlorofluorocarbon; bottle standard reference material; recyclable; waste; energy consumption and pollution**

polomeric ▷ **polyester reinforced urethane**

poly A prefix denoting many. Thus, the term polymer literally means many mers, a mer being the repeating structural unit of any high polymer (plastics). ▷ **mer**

polyacetal ▷ **acetal plastic**

polyacrolein plastic ▷ **acrolein plastic**

polyacrylamide plastic PAM is strongly polar, water soluble plastic. When high molecular weight PAM is crosslinked, it forms a network plastic. Relatively lightly crosslinked PAM can be swollen with water to form rubber-like gels that are widely used for separation of small molecules (gel chromatography).

polyacrylate plastic ▷ **acrylate plastic**

polyacrylicacid and polymethacrylicacid copolymers PAA and PMAA, respectively, acrylonitrile-based copolymers. Both repeat units are polar and the corresponding plastics are water soluble. They are essential in the formation of ionomers.

polyacrylonitrile plastic **1.** PAN (or polyvinylcyanide) homopolymer is a polar crystallizing polymer that undergoes chemical decomposition before crystalline melting at temperatures above 300°C (572°F). It is therefore not a true thermoplastic material. The almost pure homopolymer, however, can be processed into fiber (acrylic fibers) through its spinning from solutions. **2.** PAN is used as a base material or precursor in the manufacture of certain carbon and graphite fibers. ▷ **carbon fiber** and **graphite fiber**

polyaddition In this method of linkage the reaction partners add together without, as occurs in polycondensation, small molecules in the form of water, etc. being split off. Polyaddition differs from polymerization in that each reaction stage proceeds independently from the previous stage. Linkage occurs with the migration of a hydrogen atom at each reaction step.

polyalkylene terephthalate plastic The thermoplastic polyester plastics PBT and PET, in general can be referred to as PAT.

polyallomer plastic These plastics are block copolymers, and the size of the blocks allows crystallization to take place, although seemingly slower than in either HDPE or PP, which affords an easier control of the crystalline morphology resulting from processing. Properties are quite similar to those of HDPE and PP.

polyalloy ▷ **alloy/blend**

polyalphamethylstyrene plastic PAMS has not achieved much commercial importance as a homopolymer in spite of a relatively high glass transition temperature which gives it much better temperature resistance than PS. It finds significant use in copolymers.

polyamide alloy thermoplastic elastomer TPEs have high elongation with good solvent and abrasion resistance, and low density. They are designed to replace thermoset rubbers such as EPDM, nitrile and neoprene.

polyamide aromatic fiber ▷ **aromatic polyamide fiber** and **Kevlar**

polyamideimide plastic PAIs are engineering thermoplastics characterized by excellent dimensional stability, high strength at high temperatures, and good impact resistance. Molded parts in this material can maintain their structural integrity in continuous use at temperatures of 260°C (500°F). Different grades are available, such as general purpose, injection moldable, PTFE/graphite wear-resistant compounds, 30% graphite-fiber-reinforced compounds, 30% glass-fiber-reinforced components, and so on.

The room-temperature tensile strength of an unfilled PAI is about 192 MPa (28,000 psi), its compressive strength about 220 MPa (32.000 psi). At 232°C (450°F) its tensile strength is about 65 MPa (9,500 psi), or as strong as many engineered plastics at room temperature. Continued exposure at 260°C (500°F) for up to 8,000 hours produces no significant decline in its tensile properties.

PAI's flexural modulus of 5,000 MPa (730,000 psi) in an unfilled grade can be increased with graphite fiber reinforcement, to 2.9×10^6 psi. The degree of retention of its modulus at temperatures to 260°C (500°F) is on the order of 80%. Its creep resistance, even at high temperatures and under load, is among the best of the thermoplastics, and its dimensional stability is extremely good.

The unfilled grade of PAI is rated UL 94 V-0 at thicknesses as low as 0.008 in. and has an oxygen index of 45%. PAIs are extremely resistant to flame and have quite low smoke generation. Some reinforced grades have surpassed the FAA requirements for flammability, smoke density, and toxic gas emission.

PAI's radiation resistance is good, with a tensile strength that drops only about 5% after exposure, to 10^9 rads of gamma radiation. Its chemical resistance is very good, virtually unaffected by the aliphatic and aromatic hydrocarbons as well as halogenated solvents and most acid and base solutions. PAI is attacked, however, by some acids at high temperatures, by steam at high pressure and temperatures, and by strong bases. PAI moldings absorb moisture in humid environments or when immersed in water, but the rate is low and the process reversible. For example, at 50% relative humidity and 23°C (73°F) PAIs absorb about 1% weight in 1,000 hours. Parts can be restored to their original dimensions by drying.

One important area for the use of PAIs is in structural parts requiring high strength at high temperatures: aerospace products, business equipment, industrial chemical plants, heavy-duty trucks, underground environments, and other such markets. Some of the specific parts for which it is used include electrical connectors, switches, relays, gears, ball bearings, marine winches, high-load thrust bearings, and so on. Automotive parts using PAI include power and valve trains, piston skirts, tappets, piston rings, valve stems, and timimg gears. ▷ **polyimide plastics**

polyamide plastic ▷ **nylon plastic**

polyaniline plastic Melt processable electrically conductive plastic.

polyarylate plastic PARs are often defined as copolyesters involving bisphenol-A (BA) and a mixture of terephthalic acid (TA) and isopthalic acid (IA), resulting in two distinct repeat units. This source of irregularity along the chains prevents crystallization, yielding amorphous plastics that are thus naturally transparent. The aryl groups are associated with stiff chains resulting in glass transition temperature of 185°C (365°F). Performance includes good resistance to heat, steam, and radiation; and good weatherability and fire resistance without additives.

polyarylester plastic A number of specialty plastics have repeat units that feature only aromatic-type groups (phenyl, etc.) between ester linkages. Polyarylesters is a general name for this class of plastics that are often referred to as wholly aromatic polyesters.

polyaryletherketone plastic PAEK when compared with the temperature-stable thermo-set plastics and fluoropolymers, clear economic and processing advantages have appeared, particularly for new materials that can be highly stressed thermally and mechanically. PAEK is a leading material among the high-temperature stable thermoplastics. This family of plastics allows continuous operating temperature of 250°C (480°F) and—depending on the type of short-term load—up to 350°C (660°F). The glass transition and melting temperatures are thermodynamic quantities that depend on the ratio of the ketone to the ether groups. Various complicated configurations can be obtained, such as polyetherketoneetherketoneketone (PEKEKK).

The properties of this family of plastics include a tensile strength at break of 85 MPa (12,300 psi), an elongation at break of 56%, a tensile modulus of elasticity of 0.6×10^6 psi, a tensile stress at yield at 23°C (74°F) of 104 MPa (15,100 psi) and at 160°C (320°F) of 37 MPa (5,400 psi), an elongation at yield of 6% at 23°C (74°F) and of 2% at 160°C (320°F), and no break using an unnotched Izod impact test.

The processing flow behavior of PAEK does not differ fundamentally from that of other partially crystalline TPs. The shear rate is similar to Nylon 6 and PBT at 25°C (77°F) above the melting point. Besides having good mechanical and rheological properties, PAEK is characterized by its favorable behavior in fire. Without additives it has a UL 94 V-0 rating down to a test-specimen thickness of 0.030 in. The density of PAEK fumes in a fire is the lowest of the TPs, and it has exceptionally low corrosive and toxic fumes. The quantity of heat released upon the outbreak of a fire is quite low, and it meets aviation regulations for interior use. PAEK has high hydrolysis resistance and good resistance to many different chemicals.

PAEK are plastics in which phenylene rings are linked together via oxygen bridges (ether) and carbonyl groups (ketone) and may be viewed as the family name of this class of plastics; it includes PEEK, PEK, PEEKK, PEKEKK, and PEKK. The various representatives of this class of plastics differ in their chemical composition by the sequence and proportion of ether and ketone units. Since their ratio influences the glass transition temperature (T_g) and the melt temperature of the polyether ketones, they also differ in features which are of such importance to the processor as heat resistance and processing temperature. As an example, a high ketone content leads to a higher T_g and a higher melting point.

polyarylether plastic PAE was introduced in the 1970s and withdrawn around 1980. At the time it appeared to be phenyl(aryl) rings and ether linkages; it turned out to be an ABS/PSU polyalloy. Another similar polyalloy is now offered by another supplier. PAE has a rather high impact strength, with good temperature and chemical resistance.

polyarylsulfone plastic PAS consists mainly of phenyl and biphenyl groups linked by thermally stable ether and sulfone groups. Its most outstanding property is resistance to low and high temperatures from −240 to 260°C (−400 to 500°F). It also has good impact resistance, resistance to chemicals, oils, and most solvents, and good electrical insulating properties. It can be processed by conventional fabricating methods (injection, extrusion, ultrasonic welding, etc.).

polybenzimidazole plastic PBI has no known melting point and a glass-transition temperature of 427°C (800°F). It has an ultrahigh heat-distortion temperature of 435°C (815°F), retards flame, and will not burn in air. The material can withstand steady temperatures up to 427°C (800°F) and short bursts up to 760°C (1,400°F). The material is reported to resist steam at 343°C (650°F) and 15 MPa (2,200 psi) pressure. When exposed to saturated steam, PBI absorbs only 0.4% moisture. It resists a wide range of chemicals, including harsh ones.

This plastic has high mechanical and physical strength properties including a high compression strength. PBE can bear loads for short periods at temperatures up to 650°C (1,200°F). When reinforced with silicon-carbide fibers, it can thwart an attack even from laser weapons. It has a low coefficient both of friction and of thermal expansion (0.000013 in./in./°F).

This wholly aromatic heterocyclic polymer is fabricated by sintering under high pressure. The low-molecular-weight PBI flows better than its high-molecular-weight counterpart. However, HMW PBI outgases less during processing, making it more suitable to mold large parts.

PBI has been targeted to replace metals, ceramics, carbon, and other materials where an industry needs materials that are highly resistant to heat and corrosion, as in chemicals and oil processing, aerospace, and transportation. PBI's main commercial applications include use as valve seats, seals, electrical connections, thrust washers, bearings, and other mechanical components. PBE, the clothing pick of the best-dressed astronauts and firefighters, may become the material of choice for parts that need to resist temperatures up to 400°C (750°F) or more.

polybenzobisoxazole plastic PBZ is a family of high performance liquid crystalline, rigid rod polymer compositions (including polybenzobisoxazole) that are characterized by a unique combination of high molecular weight and concentration resulting in high tensile strength and stiffness, as well as resistance to moisture, heat, and UV exposure. Use includes structural composites for lightweight aircraft, military transportation, industrial parts, and sporting goods.

polybisphenolsulfone plastic ▷ **polysulfone plastic**

polyblend A colloquial term generally used in the styrene field to apply to mechanical mixtures of PS and rubber.

polybutadiene-acrylonitrile copolymer plastic This copolymer with free radical emulsion polymerization gives random copolymers which are important as nitrile rubbers. Ziegler-Natta polymerization can produce highly alternating copolymers.

polybutadiene rubber This general-purpose, crude-oil-based rubber is more resilient than

NR. BR was the material that made the solid golf ball possible. It is superior to NR in its low-temperature flexibility and in having less dynamic heat buildup. However, it lacks NR's toughness, durability, and cut-growth resistance. BR can be used as a blend in NR, SBR, and other materials to improve their low-temperature flexing, but this is achieved at a much higher price and at the sacrifice of other key properties, such as tensile strength, tear resistance, and general durability.

polybutadiene styrene thermoplastic Copolymerization of butadiene gas and styrene liquid. Processed on sheet extrusion, injection molding, blow molding, or thermoforming equipment. Main use is in packaging.

polybutadiene styrene thermoset plastic This high hydrocarbon content has excellent electrical properties and chemical resistance, high thermal distortion temperatures, low water absorption, and ready cure with peroxide catalysts. Use includes in bulk molding compounds, wet and dry friction materials, air drying enamels, baked coatings, laminates for circuit boards, radomes, and other electromagnetic applications.

polybutylene PBS are crystalline thermoplastics in the polyolefin family. Compared to other polyolefins, they have superior resistance to creep and stress cracking. PB films have high tear resistance, toughness, and flexibility. Their chemical and electrical properties are similar to those of the PEs, and PPs, but their degree of crystallinity is much lower. This structure results in a rubberlike, elastomeric material with low molded-in stress.

The main applications of PBS are in pipe, packaging, hot-melt adhesives, and sealants. Piping for cold-water use out of PBS has a higher burst strength than pipe made from any other polyolefin. Large-diameter pipe has been successfully used in mining and power-generation systems to convey abrasive materials. PBS can be alloyed with other polyolefins to provide its inherent advantage. Film made into industrial trash bags gives improved resistance to bursting, puncturing, and tearing.

polybutylene terephthalate plastic PBT is in the class of thermoplastics referred to as the thermoplastic polyesters (TPs); PBT and PET are the most popularly used in production. PBT can crystallize much faster than PET, and PBT is not normally encountered in amorphous solid form. The properties of the highly crystalline PBT (as much as 60%) are fairly similar to those of unoriented crystalline PET. PBT is not as conveniently oriented as PET. It is primarily used in injection molding where fast cycles can be achieved with minimal precautions other than a thorough drying of this hygroscopic plastic (less than 0.005% of water). Suitable grades tend to have a rather sharp melting transition, with a relatively low melt viscosity, allowing for the molding of intricate shapes.

polycaprolactam ▷**caprolactam** and **nylon plastic**

polycarbonate plastic Among the engineering thermoplastics, the amorphous PCs are one of the most exceptional materials, distinguished by their highly versatile combination of properties. Most PCs can exist individually in various other materials, but generally not in their entirety. Different grades of PCs provide specific properties and processing charateristics. These include the flame retardant and reinforced grades, resistance to weather and UV radiation; EMI and RFI shielding, FDA-approved grades for use in food-contact and medical applications, and grades for different processes such as injection, structural foam and blow molding, the extrusion of film and sheet, and others.

PCs are characterized by toughness, heat and flame resistance, and dimensional stability. Thick unreinforced PC resists breakage at temperatures down to −54°C (−65°F). Grades are available to provide high impact strength, based on different thicknesses at room temperature and a notched Izod impact strength of 6.4 to 8.5 J/cm (12 to 16 ft-lb/in. Even in thick sections, a properly designed PC part has more impact strength at −54°C (−65°F) than most plastics generally do at RT. Many plastics are not tough at 18°C (65°F), but there are plastics that are tough even at much lower temperatures. Creep resistance, which is already excellent throughout a broad temperature range, can be further improved by a factor of two to three when PC is reinforced with glass fibers.

Polycarbonates' insulating and other electrical properties are excellent and remain almost unchanged by temperature and humidity conditions. One exception is arc resistance, which in PCs is lower than in many other plastics. They are generally unaffected by greases, oils, and acids. Water at RT has no effect on PCs, but continuous exposure in 65°C (150°F) water causes gradual embrittlement. They are soluble in chlorinated hydrocarbons and attacked by most aromatic solvents, esters, and ketones, which cause crazing and cracking in stressed parts. Grades with improved chemical resistance are available, and special coating systems can be applied to provide additional chemical protection.

PCs are major additions to the group of polymer blends. Their mechanical and thermal properties make them the natural mainstays of the blends. For instance, some PC grades have notched Izod impacts of up to 960 J/m (18 ft-lb/in.), heat-deflection temperatures of 138°C (280°F), and flexural moduli in the 2,067 MPa (300,000 psi) range. Two families of blends dominate: the thermoplastic polyesters PBT and PET and ABS. Many other blends exist to provide specific desirable characteristics. Blending can eliminate one or more shortcomings by the type of blend and the mixture ratio. Trade-offs exist, as might be expected, but with certain blends there are overall net gains and even synergistic gains. The gains include providing for an easier melt flow during processing. In the blending process, the natural water-clearness and transparency of PCs can be reduced or lost.

The applications of PCs are extensive, emanating into all types of markets. Examples would include electronic connectors, switches, terminal blocks, computer disc packs, storage modules and housings, appliance power-tool housings, vacuum cleaner impellers, fan and air-conditioner grills, automotive instrument panels, indoor and outdoor lighting diffusers, medical kidney dialyzers and blood oxygenators, and a host of others.

polycarbonate plastic modified The PC grades used as engineering plastics are based almost exclusively on bisphenol-A (BPA). Smaller quantities of tetrabromo-bisphenol A are used as a comonomer to improve the ignition resistance in flame-retardant grades. The trend towards bromine-free products is causing a marked reduction in the use of this monomeric building block. Other comonomers, like trifunctional phenolic groups used for chain branching to make grades with structure-dependent viscosity, and tetramethyl-bisphenol A used to raise the heat distortion temperature, are used only at very low levels, and should be considered more as modifiers than comonomers. Polycarbonates with thiophenyl, dihydroxydiphenylsulphone and others have been produced.

polychloroprene rubber CR or neoprene was one of the very first synthetic rubbers produced that had desirable properties in many applications in the past. It was a material of choice for exterior applications such as profiles used in vehicles and buildings, and for cables. It has become less important in such applications and is being replaced by products that are more durable and/or contain no halogens. Alternative materials include EP, EVM, EAM, CM, and Q. Major markets are dominated by CR such as open-side drive belts. The continued revitalization and growth of CRs is ensured through the developments of improved CR types, which have the high dynamic load bearing capacity of the sulphur-modified products and good heat resistance of the mercaptan-CR types. ▷ **neoprene rubber**

polychlorotrifluoroethylene plastic The repeat unit of PCTFE differs from that of PTFE by the replacement of a fluorine atom by a chlorine atom, which reduces the flexibility of the chains (higher glass transition temperature), their tendency to crystallize (maximum 40 to 65%) and the melting point. PCTFE can be made optically clear, an amorphous-like characteristic, in thickness as high as 3 mm (1/8 in.). The reduced melting point and a generally lower molecule weight (100,000 to 200,000) make it a true thermoplastic. It has better mechanical properties than PTFE (stiffer, stronger, etc.), but its frictional properties do not come near those of PTFE. Chemical resistance is generally good, although not comparable to PTFE and other fluoroplastics. Chlorinated solvents, in particular, can affect PCTFE, and it can be subjected to stress-cracking at elevated temperatures.

The presence of chlorine atoms, noted to enhance flame retardancy, keeps PCTFE in the nonburning category with PTFE. It causes, however, a serious increase in dielectric losses, particularly at high frequencies. Processsing PCTFE is by the conventional methods (extrusion, injection, etc.); processing temperatures are rather high, and any degradation of PCTFE can cause severe corrosion and environmental problems. It crystallizes on slow cooling, while quenching, for films in particular, and can yield transparent products. Applications include wire and cable insulation, electronic flexible printed circuits (PC). etc. In the chemical industry, used as gaskets, O-rings, valve seats, chemical tank liners, etc. Its extremely low water vapor transmission, even with very thin transparent film, and its thermosealability explains its use as a packaging material, in the pharmaceutical industry in particular (strip and blister packs for tablets and capsules).

polycondensation ▷ **condensation polymerization**

polycycle aromatic hydrocarbon ▷ **bottled standard reference material**

polycyclohexylenedimethylene terephthalate plastic PCT is a high temperature, semicrystalline, thermoplastic polyester. PCT is differentiated from other thermoplastic polyesters by its higher heat deflection temperature. They exhibit low moisture absorption and outstanding chemical resistance to a wide variity of chemicals. They can be flame-retarded to achieve UL 94 V-0 recognition down to a thickness of 1/16 in. (1.6 mm). Different copolyesters of PCT exhibit a wide range of properties depending on particular copolyester.

polyelectrolyte This term denotes a class of macromolecular compounds, which, when dissolved in a suitable polar solvent (generally water), spontaneously acquire or can be made to acquire a large number of elementary charges distributed along the macromolecular chain. In the former case and when the charge that appears spontaneously has its maximum value, these macromolecules are termed low molar-mass (LMM) electrolytes and in other cases, weak polyelectrolytes.

polyester alkyd plastic ▷ **alkyd plastic**

polyester aromatic A polyester derived from monomers in which all the hydroxyl and carboxyl groups are directly linked to aromatic nuclei.

polyester plastic The term polyester is analogous to the term steel in metals. Just as there are many types of steels with widely varying properties, so too are there a multitude of polyesters with a significant range of properties. (This condition is true of the many different families of specific plastics, such as polyurethanes, olefins, vinyls, acrylics, sulfones, imides, ketones, epoxies, phenolics, etc.) In the family of polyesters there are two major groups: (1) the thermoset plastics which are usually typefied by a cross-linked structure and (2) the thermoplastics which are highly crystalline with comparatively high melting points. Thermoplastic polyesters are often called saturated polyesters to distinguish them from unsaturated polyesters that are the thermoset plastics.

polyester plasticizer ▷ **plasticizer, polyester**

polyester reinforced urethane A poromeric, microporous material which may have a urethane impregnation or a silicone coating for shoe uppers and industrial leathers.

polyester thermoplastic This family of plastics includes thermoplastic polyestergeneral (TP-R), polyalkylene terephthalates (PAT), polycyclohexanedimethanol terephthalate (PCT), PCT acid-modified (PCTA), PET glycol-modified (PETG), liquid crystal polymers, and the large production materials polybutylene terephthalate (PBT) and polyethylene terephthalate (PET).

polyester thermoplastic and the environment Environmental compatibility has played a major role in key developments in the field of polyesters. Flame retardancy and disposal problems were the two principal topics on which attention was focused. The conceivable risks involved in the manufacture and use of flame-retarded plastics incorporating brominated diphenylether formed the subject of a report (1990) by the Federal German Office of Environment. Thanks to the development work that many producers had already been engaged in for a long time, it proved possible to record positive progress here. As a result, the full scale substitution of this material in polyester molding compounds, which had commenced as soon as the problem became known, has already been completed.

Despite the fact that it only accounts for a small percentage of plastics refuse in weight terms, the PET bottle, because it is a conspicuous, large-volume polyester application, has attracted much discussion as a form of packaging due to the familar problems of domestic refuse disposal. Large-scale systems are being used to recover and reuse the materials (worldwide).

polyester thermoset plastic These are the unsaturated polyesters (UPs) that are condensation-type plastic principally used with glass fibers as reinforcing material. RPs were developed in the early 1940s in the U.S. for military applications. Styrene, which by far has been the most important monomer, has contributed as a reactive solvent in imparting to UPs a versatile combination of properties. Consequently, a very large number of different applications have been realized since the 1940s. ▷ **styrene monomer emission; alkyd plastic; diallyl phthalate plastic**

polyester, water-extended plastic Special casting polyesters allow the use of water as an extender (filler). Water as an extender offers advantages over conventional fillers such as low density, high temperature control (fast cure), easy mixing, and lower material cost. These plastics form an emulsion with water, providing improved physical properties. They can be thought of as microcellular water-filled foams; they are plastic cellular composite structures. Water acts as a heat sink, facilitating the casting and curing of thick parts without high temperature and cracking problems. A water-in-oil emulsion is prepared where the plastic is the continuous phase, and small diameter (2 mm) water droplets are the discontinuous phase. Before curing, the emulsion is a low viscosity liquid that flows easily into the mold, filling it completely. The emulsion gels and cures quickly.

A wide variation in properties can be readily achieved by changes in polyester formulation, water level, catalysts, and additives. Compressive strengths approaching those of concrete are obtainable at 50 to 60% water. Tensile and flexural strengths correspond to those of wood and related materials of construction. Impact strengths, even at 60% water, are significantly improved over plaster. When substituted for plaster, these polyesters provide significant reduced breakage of decorative art objects during shipping and improved durability for the consumer.

polyester, water-soluble plastic These polyesters (WSPs) have increased significantly in the surface coatings industry. They provide ease of application, ease of cleanup, freedom from toxicity, and freedom from flammability when compared to conventional solvent based paint. These WSPs are obtained by incorporating hydrophilic groups in the polymer backbone during polymerization. WSPs are subsequently diluted in water for application, optionally in the presence of neutralizing agents and water-miscible cosolvents. They can be utilized as hydrophilic plastics in paper-coating and textile-coating. In most surface coatings, clear or pigmented solutions are converted to water-insoluble coatings by condensation or oxidative polymerization. Their largest use is in surface-coating as pigmented electrodeposition and conventional dipping primers. Other applications include sprayed primer-surfacers, semigloss trade-sales paints, coil-coating vehicles, and enamels applied by dip, flow-coat, electrodeposition, and spray methods.

polyether chlorinated plastic Corrosion- and chemical-resistant thermoplastics whose prime use has been to manufacture products and equipment for the chemical and processing industries. It has also found use in molding components for pumps and water meters, pump gears, bearing surfaces, and the like. This plastic resists both organic and inorganic agents, except fuming nitric acid and fuming sulfuric acid, at temperatures up to 121°C (250°F) or higher. Its heat-insulating characteristics, dimensional stability, and outdoor exposure resistance are also excellent.

polyetheretherketone plastic With its flexibility, PEEK behaves like a true thermoplastic (TP), and has the ability to crystallize (25 to 50%). Its high glass transition temperature (T_g) and the high melting point (T_m), combined with high temperature chemical stability, rate this plastic among the most temperature resistant TPs. As with other crystallizing TPs, crystallinity can develop only at temperatures between T_m and T_g, a fact that must be taken into account for processing (extrusion, injection, etc.). PEEK retains good mechanical properties at high temperatures, such as 200°C (392°F) for prolonged periods of time. It is practically insoluble in any solvents and particularly resistant to hydrolysis by steam or high temperature pressurized water, absorbs little moisture, and has excellent resistance to nuclear radiations. As other crystallizing materials, it is resistant to environmental stress-cracking. They have a very low flammability and very low smoke and toxic gas emission. ▷ **polyaryletherketone plastic**

polyetheretherketoneketone plastic The development of PEEKK was the result of selective industrial research for high performance plastics that would meet the growing requirements for thermal stability and mechanical strength in the electronics, automotive, and mechanical engineering industries. The chemical bonds of PAEK rank among the most stable ones in organic chemistry ▷ **polyaryletherketone plastic**. The molecules are closely packed over wide areas, forming crystalline regions. This crystallinity with the chemical nature of PEEKK provides the exceptional performance. Its most important property has been its resistance to dimensional changes (softening) when exposed to high temperatures, and also its resistance to oxidation as it ages.

polyetherimide plastic PEI is an amorphous engineering TP characterized by high heat resistance, high strength and a high modulus, excellent electrical properties that remain stable over a wide range of temperatures and frequencies, and very good processability. Neat (unmodified) PEI is transparent, with inherent flame resistance and low smoke evolution. Its UL continuous-use listing is 170°C (338°F) and its heat-deflection temperature is 200°C (392°F) at 1,820 kPa (264 psi). It has a T_g of 215°C (419°F), a UL rating of 94 V-0 at a thickness of 0.016 in. and of 5V at 0.075 in. without additives. PEI has a limited oxygen index of 47% (one of the highest among the engineering TPs), its smoke evolution as measured in an NBS chamber test per ASTM E 662 is low, and its dielectric constant remains virtually unchanged between frequencies of 60 to 10^9 Hz and temperatures of 28 to 82°C (73 to 180°F). It has a high-volume resistivity of 6.7×10^{17} ohm/cm and a dielectric strength from 830 V/mil at 1/16 in. in air to greater than 6,500 V/mil in submil film thicknesses. Its arc resistance exceeds 120 s, meeting one of the UL electrical requirements for the sole support of "live" parts.

A key feature of PEI is its ability to maintain properties at elevated temperatures. For example, at 180°C (356°F) its tensile strength and flexural modulus are 41 and 2,067 MPa (6,000 and 300,000 psi), respectively. The strength and modulus of the glass-reinforced grades are higher. The modulus at 1.3×10^6 psi with 30% weight of glass to over 80% retained at 180°C (356°F). PEI also has good creep resistance, as indicated by its apparent modulus of 24,115 MPa (350,000 psi) after 1,000 hours at 82°C (180°F) under an initial load of 35 MPa (5,000 psi).

This plastic resists a broad range of chemicals under varied conditions of stress and temperature. PEI's resistance to mineral acids, for example, is outstanding. It is, however, attacked by such partially halogenated solvents as methylene chloride, trichloroethane, and strong acids. Its resistance to UV radiation is good with a change in tensile strength after 1,000 hours of xenon-arc exposure that is negligible. PEI's resistance to gamma-ray radiation is also good, there being a strength loss of less than 6% after 500 megarads' exposure to cobalt 60 at the rate of one Mrad/hr. Hydrolytic stability tests show that more than 85% of PEI's tensile strength is retained after 10,000 hours of immersion in boiling water. This material is suitable for short-term or repeated steam exposure.

polyetherketone plastic PEK is a partially crystalline high-performance aromatic ketone-based thermoplastic that is heat stable and readily processed. As a member of the ketone family it shares with PEEK such properties as good chemical resistance; exceptional toughness, strength, rigidity, and load-bearing capabilities; good radiation resistance; the best firesafety characteristics of any thermoplastic, and the ability to be easily melt processed.

Super PEKs designed for advance composites have a continuous-service temperature rating of 260°C (500°F), a glass-transition temperature (T_g) of 200°C (400°F), and a slow crystallization rate that suits them for processes with slow rates of cooling from the melt. ▷**polyaryletherketone plastic**

polyetherketoneetherketoneketone plastic PEKEKK is one of the various combinations of the repeating monomers of ether groups and ketone groups. It has been designed to have the usual ketone plastic family of properties with a balance of high heat resistance and good processability. ▷**polyaryletherketone plastic**

polyetherketoneketone plastic PEKKs are characterized by good mechanical properties maintained to high temperatures. The modulus drops off at around 150°C (300°F) with a melting point at 345°C (650°F). ▷**polyaryletherketone plastic**

polyether plastic Any plastic containing a number of ether oxygen linkages, –O–, in its main chain or side chains such as polyetherimide plastic.

polyethersulfone plastic PES is a high-temperature engineering TP in the polysulfone family. PES is recommended for load-bearing applications up to 182°C (360°F). Even without flame retardants it offers low flammability, and it has little change in its dimensions of electrical properties in the temperature range from 0 to 200°C (32 to 390°F). At room temperature it behaves like a traditional engineering TP, being rough, rigid, and strong, with outstanding long-term load-bearing properties. Of far greater importance are its high-temperature properties.

PES can be used for tens of thousands of hours at 200°C (390°F) without a significant loss of strength. The UL temperature index is 200°C (390°F) for a PES compound that is 30% glass fiber. Its dimensional changes at 200°C (390°F) are negligible, although small variations occur in its electrical performance from 0 to 200°C (32 to 390°F). Compared with most TPs, PES has low flammability without flame-retardant additives and carries a UL 94 V-0 rating at a thickness of 0.017 in. with glass reinforcement. Its limiting oxygen index is in the range of 34 to 41. Its smoke and gas emissions are very low.

PES possesses good resistance to X rays, beta rays, and gamma rays. Even though it does not have good resistance to outdoor weathering, with a carbon-black filler it is acceptable. Chemical resistance in PES is dependent on the external and molded-in stress levels and the temperature. Its chemical resistance can be improved by annealing it at 200°C (390°F). It has good resistance to aqueous acids, bases, and most inorganic solutions. Most of the common sterilizing solutions and anesthetics can be used with PES safely (many cleaning and degreasing solvents are based on chlorinated and fluorinated hydrocarbons). Unless PES is heavily stressed, it can be cleaned by most of these solvents.

polyethylene Polyethlene (PES) are in the polyolefin family of semicrystalline TPs. The largest volume plastics used worldwide, PEs are available in many varieties with an equally wide range of properties. Some are flexible, others rigid; some have low impact strength, whereas others are nearly unbreakable; some have good clarity, others are opaque, and so on. The service temperatures for PEs range from −40 to 93°C (−40 to 200°F). In general they are characterized by toughness, excellent chemical resistance and electrical properties, a low coefficient of friction, near-zero moisture absorption, and good ease of processing. They are basically classified according to their density (see Tables here and Fig. opposite).

In addition to those PEs listed in the tables, there are others designed to meet different requirements, such as crosslinked PE (XLPE),

Different PE densities.

Type	Density, g/cm(lbs./ft.^{3})
LDPE	0.910–0.925 (56.8–57.7)
MDPE	0.926–0.940 (57.8–58.7)
HDPE	0.941–0.959 (58.7–59.9)
HMWPE	0.960 (59.9) and above

Influences on PEs of increases in density, melt index, and molecular weight.

PE property	Density	Melt index	Molecular weight
Tensile strength (at yield)	Increases	Decreases	
Stiffness	Increases	Decreases slightly	Decreases slightly
Impact strength	Decreases	Decreases	Decreases
Low-temperature brittleness	Increases	Increases	Decreases
Abrasion resistance	Increases	Decreases	
Hardness	Increases	Decreases slightly	
Softening point	Increases		Increases
Stress-crack resistance	Decreases	Decreases	
Permeability	Decreases	Increases slightly	
Chemical resistance	Increases	Decreases	
Melt strength		Decreases	Increases
Gloss	Increases	Increases	Decreases
Haze	Decreases	Decreases	
Shrinkage	Decreases	Decreases	Increases

Effect of intrinsic properties on PEs.

Physical properties	If density increases	If melt index increases	If MWD broadens
Melt viscosity	Higher	Lower	—
Vicat softening point	Much higher	Lower	Lower
Surface hardness	Higher	Slightly lower	Lower
Tensile strength			
Yield	Much higher	Slightly lower	Lower
Break	Slightly higher	Lower	Lower
Elongation	Lower	Lower	Higher
Creep resistance	Higher	Slightly lower	Higher
Flexural stiffness	Much higher	Slightly lower	—
Flexibility	Lower	—	—
Toughness	Lower	Lower	Lower
Low-temperature brittleness	Lower	Lower	Higher
Stress crack resistance	Lower	Lower	Higher
Optical properties			
Transparency	Higher[1]	Higher	—
Freedom from haze	Higher[1]	Higher	—
Gloss	Higher[1]	Higher	—
Barrier properties			
MVT rate	Lower	—	—
Gas and liquid transmission	Much lower	—	—
Greaseproofness	Much higher	Slightly lower	—
Electrical properties	Slightly higher	No effect	—

[1] Not true in the high-density range.

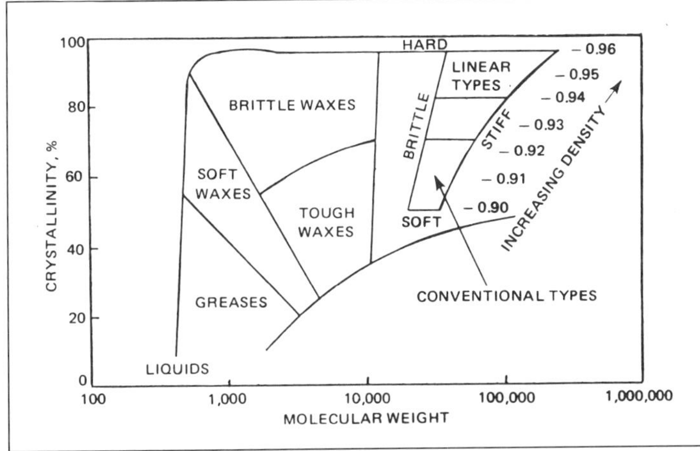

Relationships of PEs between crystallinity, molecular weight, and properties, based on different polymerization reactions.

which by chemical or irradiation treatment becomes essentially a TS with outstanding heat resistance and strength. There is an extra high gloss HDPE, another that retains its toughness at very low temperatures and performs at levels between the commodity and engineering resins, and various others.

Three basic characteristics of PE determines its processing and end-use properties: its density, melt index, and molecular weight distribution. Their range in density, from 0.890 to above 0.96 g/cm^3, is a result of their crystalline structure. This difference accounts for their property variations. As one example, reducing PE's crystallinity increases its impact resistance, cold flow, tackiness, tear strength, environmental stress-crack resistance, and heat-seal range. However, decreases occur in stiffness, shrinkage, brittleness temperature, and chemical resistance. In the following definitions, information and different forms of PEs are provided. ▷ **polyolefin plastic**

polyethylene and the environment PE, in common with other plastics, does not escape attention in discussions on environmental aspects. Requirements with regard to degradability generally still pose problems. Claims of success in this area continue to appear fairly frequently in the press. However, methods generally proposed have been found on closer examination to have flaws which hinder putting them into practice. The problems posed by refuse have led to increased efforts towards reclaiming PE wastes. As an example, the recycling of PE wastes composed of a single type appears straightforward; it is already a long-established practice in many film manufacturing plants. However, difficulties can arise with regard to reclaiming plastic wastes containing different materials or large amounts of impurities. One method of dealing with contaminated PE wastes is by incineration. PE film and in other forms, when combined with other plastics, is recycled to produce manufactured finished products.

polyethylene, branched plastic By contrast with linear PE, branched PE has both short and long chain branches ▷ **polyethylene, linear plastic**. This is one reason properties of LLDPE, for example, differ somewhat from those of its branched analog LDPE. LLDPE is more linear (more crystalline) and thus processes differently and exhibits different product performances. In processing, like blown film, these differences can be significant enough to require equipment modification.

polyethylene, chlorinated plastic ▷ **chlorinated polyethylene plastic**

polyethylene, chlorosulfonated plastic ▷ **chlorosulfonated polyethylene plastic**

polyethylene cost ▷ **cost, crude oil versus polyethylene**

polyethylene, crosslinked plastic ▷ **crosslinked polyethylene plastic**

polyethylene, ethylene acid copolymer plastic ▷ **ethylene acid copolymer plastic**

polyethylene, ethylene-ethyl acrylate plastic ▷ **ethylene-ethyl acrylate plastic**

polyethylene, ethylene-methacrylate plastic ▷ **ethylene-methacrylate plastic**

polyethylene, ethylene-vinyl acetate plastic ▷ **ethylene-vinyl acetate plastic**

polyethylene, ethylene-vinyl alcohol plastic ▷ **ethylene-vinyl alcohol plastic**

polyethylene fiber ▷**solution spinning process**

polyethylene, high density plastic High density polyethylene (HDPE) has rigidity and tensile strength considerably higher than LDPE and medium DPE (MDPE). HDPE's impact strength in slightly lower, as is to be expected in a stiffer material, but its overall values are high, especially at low temperatures, compared to the other TPs.

polyethylene, high molecular weight high density plastic This plastic offers outstanding toughness and durability, particularly at low temperatures. In blow-molding applications HMW-HDPE allows drum manufacturers to meet DOT and OSHA specifications. In pipe production it meets the highest strength rating for PE pipe. Many other products are made of it, using rather conventional processing methods.

polyethylene, linear low density plastic Linear low density polyethylene (LLDPE) is used mainly in film applications but other products using all types of processes as well. Its properties are different from LDPE and HDPE in that its impact, tear, heat-seal strength, and environmental stress-crack resistance are significantly higher. Its major uses at present are for grocery bags, industrial trash bags, liners, and heavy-duty shopping bags.

polyethylene, linear plastic Linear PE (LPE), which includes ultralow density PE (ULDPE), linear low density PE (LLDPE), high density polyethylene (HDPE), high molecular weight-high density polyethylene (HMW-HDPE), and ultra high molecular weight (UHMW-PE), is polymerized in reactors maintained at pressures far lower than those for making branched PE ▷**polyethylene, branched plastic**. In making branched PE, the crucial plastic parameter of density is varied through changes in reactor pressure and heat; which relates to the closeness and regularity (or crystallinity) of the packing of the long polymer backbones. However, linear PE density varies with the quantity of comonomer used with ethylene. The comonomer forms short chain branches along the ethylene backbone; the greater the quantity of comonomer, the lower the density of the plastic.

polyethylene, low density Low-density polyethylene (LDPE), the first of the PEs, has good toughness, flexibility, low temperature resistance, clarity in film, and relatively low heat resistance, as well as good resistance to chemical attack. At room temperature LDPE is insoluble in most organic solvents but attacked by strong oxidizing acids. At high temperatures it becomes increasingly susceptible to attack by aromatic, chlorinated, and aliphatic hydrocarbons.

The LDPEs are susceptible to environmental and some chemical stress cracking. For example, wetting agents such as detergents accelerate stress cracking. Some copolymers of LDPE are available with an improved stress-cracking resistance.

polyethyleneoxide plastic PEO, also called polyoxyethylene or polyethyleneglycol, is similar to polymethyleneoxide except that PEO is water soluble. It is not used as a conventional plastic. It is widely used as a water thickener.

polyethylene terephthalate plastic PET's broad range of mechanical and electrical properties make them ideal replacements in certain applications for such metals as die-cast aluminum or zinc; also in thermoset switches, relays, sensors, etc. To meet specific product requirements such as increased toughness, decreased warpage, or flame retardance, they are specially formulated. PET plastics are hygroscopic so require proper drying before processing. Different PET grades are used in different processes; they are used in applications such as packaging (particularly stretched injection blow molded beverage bottles and film, appliances, electrical/electronics, etc.

There are amorphous (APET), crystalline (CPET) and copolyester plastics. (PET is a thermoplastic polyester.) The name copolyester is applied to those thermoplastic polyesters whose synthesis uses more than one glycol and/or more than one dibasic acid. Its chain is less regular than the monopolyester chain and therefore has reduced tendency to crystallize and provide different properties. An example of a copolyester is PETG, a glycol-modified polyester. After processing, it normally remains amorphous, clear, and virtually colorless even in very thick sections. Recycling all types of PET materials has been easily accomplished.

polyethylene, ultrahigh molecular weight plastic The properties of this high-performance plastic are entirely different and much improved, including outstanding abrasion resistance and a low coefficient of friction. The impact strength of UHMW-PE is high and its chemical resistance excellent. As with most high-performance polymers, the processing of UHMW-PE is not easy. Because of its high melt viscosity—it does not register on a melt-flow index—conventional molding and extrusion would break the long molecular chains that give this plastic its excellent properties. The processing methods used for UHMW-PE are basically compression molding, ram extrusion, and warm forming of extruded slugs. The techniques for using screw melting (that is, injection and extrusion processing) are under development to permit maintaining its UHMW structure.

polyethylene, ultralow density plastic ULDPE is also called very low density PE (VLDPE) that has densities in the range of 0.86 to 0.92 g/cc. ULDPEs offer the flexibility previously available only in generally lower strength materials, such as ethylene-vinyl acetate (EVA), ethylene-ethyl acrylate (EEA), and plasticized PVC, together with the toughness and broad operating temperature range of linear low density PE (LLDPE). In addition, ULDPE exhibits sealing and flexibility characteristics comparable to that of 5 to 20% EVA copolymers, while retaining the physical and mechanical properties of LLDPE.

polyethylene, very low density plastic ▷ **polyethylene, ultralow density plastic**

polyethylene wax PE with a molecular weight in the range of 2,000 to 4,000 has the properties of high molecular weight hydrocarbon wax. These special LDPEs are generally produced by the high pressure polymerization of ethylene. They have a specific gravity of 0.91 to 0.96, depending on operating conditions. Melt index is close to 3.5, tensile strength about 1,500 psi (6.9 MPa), melting point of 99 to 100°C, and needle penetration at 25°C is 1 to 10. Just over 10 wt% of LDPE produced in the U.S. finds use in typical wax applications, such as paper coatings and floor polishes. A major use is coated paperboard for milk cartons.

polyethylmethacrylate plastic This is a special plastic in the acrylic family; PEMA provides the usual properties with flexibility.

polyfluoroalkoxyphosphazene plastic PNF is a very expensive product. It achieved its first mass-production applications in the automobile industry. Although its heat resistance is less than that of FPM, this is offset by its considerably better low temperature flexibility. Thus, it is in competition with FMQ, also an expensive product, and here the better resistance of PNF to fuels is an advantage. ▷ **fluoroplastic**

polyfunctional Molecule with three or more sites at which there can be joining reactions with adjacent molecules.

polyglutarimide acrylic copolymer plastic Family of plastics that can be used in hot fill and retort packaging applications that provide clarity and heat resistance.

polyhexafluoroisobutylene plastic In the family of the fluoropolymers, PHFI has a favorable situation for crystallization. ▷ **fluoroplastic**

polyhexafluoropropylene plastic PHFP is a fluoropolymer that has a repeat unit corresponding to a fully fluorinated polypropylene repeat unit and is significantly more rigid than the PTFE repeat unit with a glass transition temperature about 11°C (52°F).

polyimidazole plastic A variety of polymidazoles can be prepared by aromatic nucleolphilic displacement, from the reactions of bisphenol imidazoles with activated difluoro compounds. These plastics have good mechanical properties that make them suitable for use as films, moldings, and adhesives.

polyimide plastics Polyimides (PIs) were the first so-called high-heat-resistant plastics. They in fact retain a significant portion of their room-temperature mechanical propertes from −240 to 315°C (−400 to +600°F) in air. PIs, which are available in both TPs and TSs, are a family of some of the most heat- and fire-resistant polymers known. As discussed in connection with some of the other plastics, there are others that have heat resistance in the 260°C (500°F) range.

Moldings and laminates are generally based on TSs, though some are made from TPs. PIs are available as laminates and in various shapes, as molded parts, stock shapes, and resins (in powders and solutions). PI parts are fabricated by techniques ranging from powder-metallurgy methods to conventional injection, transfer, and compression molding, and extrusion methods. Porous PI parts are also available. Generally, the compounds that are the most difficult to fabricate are also the ones that have the highest heat resistance. The service temperature for the intermittent exposure of PIs can range from cryogenic to as high as 480°C (900°F). Glass-fiber-reinforced PIs retain 70% of their flexural strength and modulus at 250°C (480°F). Creep in PIs is almost nonexistent, even at high temperatures. Their deformation under a 28 MPa (4,000 psi) load is less than 0.05% at room temperature for twenty-four hours.

These materials have good wear resistance and a low coefficient of friction, both of which are factors that can be further improved by including additives like PTFE and MoS_2. Self-lubricating PI parts containing graphite powders have flexural strengths above 69 MPa (10,000 psi.) Their electrical properties are also outstanding over wide temperature and humidity ranges. They are unaffected by exposure to dilute acids, aromatic and aliphatic hydrocarbons, esters, alcohols, hydraulic fluids, JP-4 fuel, and kerosene. They are, however, attacked by dilute alkalis and concentrated inorganic acids.

PI film has useful mechanical properties, even at cryogenic temperatures. At −269°C

(−453°F) this film can be bent around a $\frac{1}{4}$ in. mandrel without breaking. At 500°C (932°F) its tensile strength is 30 MPa (4,500 psi).

An important class of high temperature matrices is the imide compounds. The early compounds met needs for high temperatures but were brittle and difficult to process. Researchers have since overcome these difficulties. ▷ **polyamideimide plastic**

polyimide plastic, PMR The PMR polyimides are a novel class of high temperature resistant plastics. PMR represents in situ polymerization of monomer reactants.

polyisobutylene butyl rubber PIB is remarkably different from most common rubbers in two respects. It has a very low gas permeability and very high damping properties (energy absorption). Since the molecules do not contain unsaturation (C=C), they cannot be cross-linked by the most conventional methods. However, networks have good weathering, ozone, and heat aging resistance. PIB is capable of strain-crystallization and can have good mechanical resistance. Resistance to oils and fuels is not good.

If isobutylene is copolymerized with a small fraction of isoprene (1 to 2%), the isoprene unsaturations can be used for conventional vulcanization. Such an isobutylene-isoprene copolymer is referred to as butyl rubber (IIR). A major limitation of butyl rubber is its poor compatibility with other common rubbers and generally low adhesion properties. Partial chlorination or bromination brings a marked improvement and also allows faster cure. Such modified butyl rubbers are referred to as chlorobutyl rubber, bromobutyl rubber, or halobutyl rubber.

polyisobutylene plastic The polymerization product of isobutylene. This thermoplastic varies in consistency from a viscous liquid to a rubberlike solid with corresponding variation in molecular weight from 1,000 to 4,000.

polyisoprene rubber The synthetic rubber that comes closest to duplicating the chemical composition of natural rubber (NR) is synthetic polyisoprene (IR, sometimes abbreviated PI). It shares with NR the properties of good uncured tack, high unreinforced strength, good abrasion resistance, and the characteristics that provide good performance in dynamic applications. However, because of having some inherent impurities, NR is somewhat better overall. An IR is distinguished by its low hysteresis and high tensile strength, but it is readily attacked by solvents, gasoline, and ozone. Its tensile strength is in the range of 24 to 31 MPa (3,500 to 4,500 psi), and its elongation is 550 to 650%.

One significant disadvantage of IR is its lack of green strength, which is to say during the time period during processing, prior to curing. An IR can be used interchangeably with NR in all but the most demanding parts. The applications are about the same as for NR.

polyketone-based plastic This family of plastics include polyetherketone, and polyetheretherketone, and polyetherketonether ketone.

polyliner A perforated longitudinally ribbed sleeve that fits inside the cylinder of an injection molding machine plasticator; used as a replacement for conventional injection cylinder torpedos.

Polymat database The German Federalist Ministries of the Economy and of the Research and Technology recognized a situation and during the 1980s launched programs to assist in the development of comprehensive factual databases. Within this framework, the Deutsches Kunststoffinstitut (DKI; German Plastics Institute) established the materials database called Polymat. This program brings greater availability into a plastics market in which a general perspective is becoming increasingly difficult to obtain. This database contains information on plastics, supplying about thirty to fifty properties for each material.

The concept of the Polymat database was based on the following criteria: (1) the database is neutral, independent of raw-material manufacturers; (2) anyone can use the database; (3) all the products on the European market should, if possible, be included; (4) since testing is carried out in accordance with a variety of different international standards, the relevant standard, as well as the testing conditions, should be registered; (5) during the search, all properties should be capable of being linked with one another as desired; and (6) the sources used for the database are the technical data sheets and additional information supplied by raw-material manufacturers, and various lectures, publications, and measured data from different institutes.

In order for such an extensive project to remain manageable, certain requirements were necessary. Initially the data were confined to TPs, TSs, TPEs, and casting resins. To be included in this group were the TSEs, composites, foams, semifinished products, and others. Polymat completed its initial work in 1989. New plastics products on the market and updated additional information on existing products will continue to be added. Data no longer available are still accessible to the user in a memory file.

Each plastic in this database is first characterized by descriptive data such as its trade name, manufacturer, product group, form of supply, or additives. Then follows complex technical information on each material, with details of fields of application, recommended processing techniques, and special features. The central element of this material database is the numerical values it gives on a wide range of mechanical, thermal, electrical, optical, and other properties. All these items can be searched for individually or in the combination of properties that was the subject of the enquiry.

polymer In chemical (or polymer chemical) terms, it is a synthetic or natural compound of high molecular weight, formed by a chain of chemically linked units called monomers. In the field of engineering, processing, design, and other related fields, as well as the plastic industry, worldwide polymer identifies a plastic ▷ **plastic** and **plastic and definition.** The polymer, or plastic, chemistrywise is further identified as having a structure that can be represented by a repeat unit, the mer. In the world of plastics the synthetic polymers are of primary concern since they represent the bulk of development in continually advancing performance and processability and are in very large production producing all types of plastic products. ▷ **polymerization; molecular arrangement structure; morphology; element; mer**

polymer, branched In molecular structure of polymers or plastics (as opposed to linear), basically refers to side chains attached to the main chain. Side chains may be long or short. They form during the polymerization reaction (like tree trunks with their respective limbs). Branching usually causes strengthening and stiffness of plastic, since formation of the polymer requires the movement of chains that are much more entwined than in linear polymers. There are different branching mechanisms; one type permits elastomers to have resilience and can withstand significant stretch without breaking. ▷ **strengthening plastic mechanisms**

polymer, branching **1.** The presence of molecular branches in a polymer. **2.** The generation of branch crystals during crystallization of a polymer.

polymer chain ▷ **chain polymerization**

polymer chemistry terminology The following information is presented only to aid in understanding the composition of plastics. For more complete information ▷ **chemical composition and properties of plastic; chemical characterization of plastics; crosslinking; molecular arrangement structure**

Polymers (plastics) are made up of carbon (C), hydrogen (H), chlorine (CL), fluorine (F), oxygen (O), and nitrogen (N). These six elements, either naturally or synthetically, first form rather simple molecules called monomers. An example of a monomer is the gas ethylene:

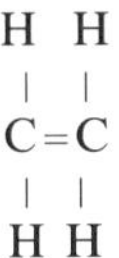

Another example is the gas vinyl chloride:

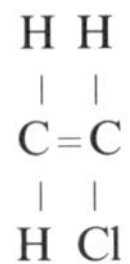

When these monomers are subjected to catalyst, heat, and pressure, the double bonds (or arms) open up and these individual monomer units join arms to form long chains called polymers. This process is called polymerization.

An example of a polymer is polyethylene; the following chemical structure only shows a small segment of a PE chain:

```
 H H H H H H H H H H H H
 | | | | | | | | | | | |
-C-C-C-C-C-C-C-C-C-C-C-C-
 | | | | | | | | | | | |
 H H H H H H H H H H H H
```

Another example of a polymer is polyvinyl chloride; the following chemical structure only shows a small segment of a PVC chain:

```
 H H  H H  H H  H H  H H  H H
 |  | |  | |  | |  | |  | |  |
-C--C-C--C-C--C-C--C-C--C-C--C-
 |  | |  | |  | |  | |  | |  |
 H Cl H Cl H Cl H Cl H Cl H Cl
```

Each of these long chains is an individual molecule; to be specific each is a macromolecule; it is not visible even under a microscope.

The geometry of these chains is just as important as their chemical make-up in determining properties; there are variable chain geometries, namely:

Linear

Branched

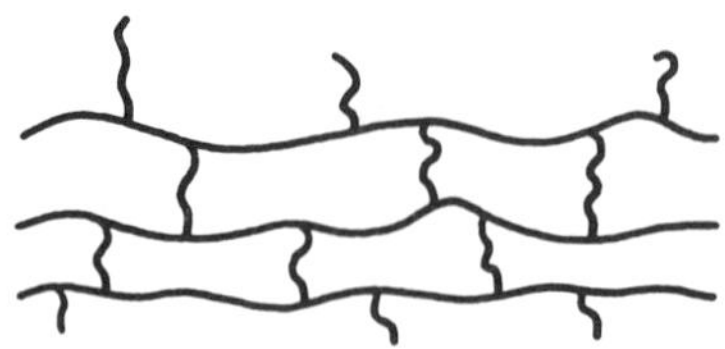

Crosslinked

Also there is the variability in length of chains. Chains can be long, thousands of repeating units, thus molecular weight polymer (plastic); also chains are short, thus the low molecular weight polymer.

Another polymer variable identifies chain patterns. Chains may tend to line with one another and these are called:

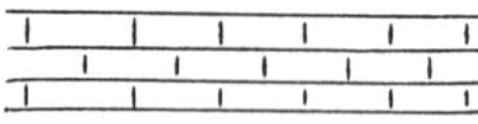

Crystalline (like polyethylene)

but if they form no pattern at all, these polymers are called:

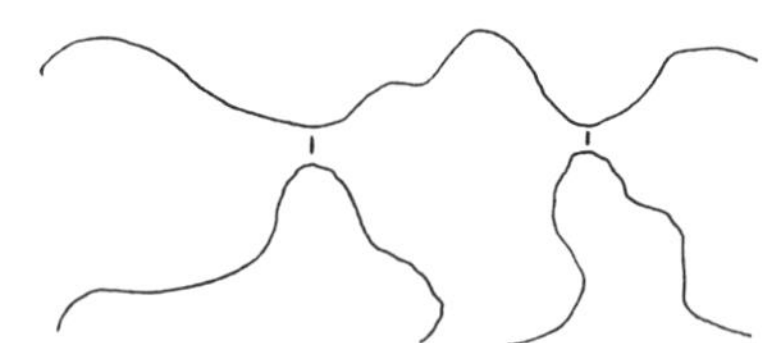

Amorphous (like polystyrene)

Now let us see how these variables affect properties. Linear generally have better mechanical, heat resistance, chemical resistance, and lighter density than branched, and in turn the crosslinked mechanical and physical properties are more rigid as well as more heat resistant than linear or branched. Long chains generally have better mechanical properties, heat resistance, and chemical resistance than short chains. Regarding crystalline or amorphous ▷ **morphology, amorphous and crystalline characteristics**

polymer definition This term comes from the Greek word "poly" which means many, and "meras" which means parts.

polymer dissolution ▷ **solvent fractionation**

polymer, high A high polymer is a macromolecular substance that, as indicated by the polymer by which it is identified, consists of molecules that are multiples of the low molecular unit and have a molecular weight of at least 20,000. It has a high degree of polymerization (DP) that results in high molecular weight plastic. High is often interpreted as meaning a sufficiently high DP so that the effects of end groups may be ignored. In addition, many of the physical properties, e.g. T_m, T_g, and moduli (but not melt or solution viscosity, or strength properties which continue to increase with DP even at very high DP), do not alter significantly with further increase in DP. Typically this means a polymer with DP of more than about 100.

polymer, homo ▷ **homopolymer**

polymeric Composed of or containing polymer units in its chemical structure.

polymeric salt Divalent metal terephthalates that appear to be polymeric exhibit very high decomposition tepmperatures and very low solubilities, offering potential as additives and reinforcements in thermoplastics and thermosets.

polymer, inorganic ▷ **plastic, inorganic**

polymer, isotactic A polymer which contains long blocks of identically oriented monomer units. Each unit has the same steric configuration as each successive unit in its own block; molecular structure containing a sequence of regularly spaced asymmetric groups arranged in like configuration in a polymer chain. Isotactic polymers are crystallizable.

polymerization A chemical reaction in which the molecules of a monomer are linked together to form large molecules with a molecular weight that is a multiple of the molecular weight of the original substance. When two or more monomers are involved, the process is called copolymerization. The molecular structure of a polymer is determined during its formation by polymerization; therefore the conditions (temperature, time, monomer concentration, catalyst or initiator concentration, etc.) must be chosen so that polymer with the desired structure is obtained. The repeat unit structure is determined by the choice of monomer, but the degree of polymerization (DP) depends on

Examples in comparison of polymerization methods.

Method	Advantages	Disadvantages
Bulk (batch)	Homogeneous Minimum contamination; simple equipment for making castings	Strongly exothermic; broadened molecular-weight distribution at high conversion; complex if small particles required
Bulk (continuous)	Lower conversion per pass leading to better heat control and narrower molecular-weight distribution	Requires agitation, material transfer, separation, and recycling
Emulsion	Rapid polymerization to high molecular weight and narrow distribution, with ready heat control; emulsion may be directly usable	Contamination with emulsifier, etc, almost inevitably leading to poor color and color stability; washing, drying, and compacting may be required
Solution	Ready control of heat of polymerization; polymer solution may be directly usable	Not useful for dry polymer because of difficulty of complete solvent removal
Suspension	Heterogeneous Ready control of heat of polymerization; suspension or resulting granular polymer may be directly usable	Continuous agitation required; contamination by stabilizer possible; washing, drying, possibly compacting required

polymerization conditions, as do any structural irregularities formed by side reactions. In addition the polymer may be contaminated by unreacted monomer or other materials, especially solvent, required for polymerization. ▷ **reactor technology**

There are two general types of polymerization reactions, both with many variations: (1) addition polymerization which occurs when reactive monomers unite without forming another product, and (2) condensation polymerization which occurs by condensation of reactive monomers with the elimination of a simple molecule such as water. Examples of condensation polymers are nylon and phenol-formaldehyde plastics. The majority of thermoplastics and some thermosets are made by addition polymerization. Examples of a few of the polymerization methods and their comparisons are listed in the Table above and in the following list of the many different methods:

addition
anionic
block
bulk
cation
chain
charge-transfer
condensation
emulsion
free radical
gas
gas-phase
graft
hetero
interfacial
ion-beam
ionic
isotactic
melt
photo
plasma
radiation
reactive
step-reaction
solution
stereoblock
stereoregular
stereospecific
suspension
syndiotactic
thermal

polymerization catalyst ▷ **metal vapor synthesis**

polymerization chemistry ▷ **alkali metal and derivative**

polymerization, degree of ▷ **degree of polymerization**

polymerization drying ▷ **drying monomer and polymer**

polymerization, living systems ▷ **living polymer system**

polymerization of monomer reactants ▷ **polyimide plastic, PMR**

polymerization, reaction ▷ **polymerization** and **reactor technology**

polymerization, Ziegler-Natta ▷ **Ziegler-Natta polymerization**

polymerize The unit molecule of the same kind to form a compound having elements in the same proportion but possessing much higher molecular weight and different physical properties.

polymer, linear A polymer in which the molecules are linked together in the form of chains, with little or no branching or side links (as with branched polymer).

polymer modeling ▷ **designing with model, plastic tailor-made** and **computer-aided molecular graphic**

polymer portland cement ▷ **concrete-plastic**

polymer structure A general term referring to the relative positions, arrangement in space, and freedom of motion of atoms in a polymer molecule. Such structural details have important effects on plastic properties such as the second-order transition temperature, flexibility, and tensile strength. This characterization is also called morphology or texture. ▷ **chemical composition; designing with model, plastic-chemical structure; molecular arrangement structure**

polymethacrylicacid plastic PMAA is water-soluble and essential in the formation of ionomers (IO).

polymethacrylonitrile plastic PMAN is transparent, is an excellent barrier to carbon dioxide (CO_2), and possesses good creep resistance, making it a suitable material for carbonated beverage containers.

polymethylacrylate plastic PMA is used in adhesives, paints, and other products.

polymethylmethacrylate plastic PMMA is best known for its remarkable property of excellent transparency. For details ▷ **acrylic**

polymethylpentene plastic The major advantages of PMP over other polyolefins are its transparency in thick sections, its short-time heat resistance up to 200°C (400°F), and its lower specific gravity. Unlike the other polyolefins, however, it is transparent, because its crystalline and amorphous phases have the same index of refraction. Almost clear optically, PMP has a light transmission value of 90%, which is just slightly less than that of the acrylics. It retains most of its physical properties under brief exposure to heat at 200°C (400°F), but it is not stable at temperatures for an extended time over 150°C (300°F) without an antioxidant. In a clear form it is not recommended where it will have to undergo long-term exposure to UV environments.

The chemical resistance and electrical properties of PMP are similar to those of the other polyolefins, except that it retains these properties at higher temperatures than do either PE or PP. In this respect PMP tends to compare well with PTFE up to 150°C (300°F). Molded parts made of this resin are hard and shiny, yet their impact strength is high at temperatures down to −29°C (−20°F). Their specific gravity of 0.83 is the lowest of any commercial solid plastic.

polymorphism The ability of an element or compound to exist in different temperatures and pressure ranges in two or more crystalline phases or forms.

polynorbornene plastic PNB has a glass transition temperature of 35°C (95°F). This plastic can easily be plasticized with large amounts of oil, subsequently vulcanized into an elastomer with a low service temperature of 65°C (−85°F). The damping properties of the elastomer can be conveniently adjusted to meet different performance requirements.

polyol An alcohol having many hydroxyl groups. Also known as a polyhydric alcohol. In foam or cellular plastics usage, term includes compounds containing alcoholic hydroxyl groups such as polyethers, glycols, polyesters, and castor oil used in polyurethane foams and other polyurethanes. Polyol is based on ethylene oxide/propylene oxide or propylene oxide; it has molecular weights ranging from 700 to 6,000. Produced to exact specifications for the manufacture of polyurethanes. ▷ **polyurethane**

polyolefinic thermoplastic elastomer TPEs essentially are blends of various amorphous rubbers such as ethylene-propylene and of polyolefin semicrystalline plastics such as polypropylene. Thermoplastic olefins (TPOs) were the second class of TPEs produced commercially in 1974. TPOs are mechanical blends consisting of a hard plastic and softer rubber. They are considered different from blends that are dynamically vulcanized, a process in which the elastomer phase is cured during mixing of the polymers.

polyolefin plastic The family of polyolefins includes polyethylene, polypropylene, ethylene-vinyl acetate, ionomers, polybutylene, polyisobutylene, and polymethylpentene. Because the chemical and electrical properties of the various polyolefins are basically similar, they often compete for the same applications. However, since the different strength and modulus properties vary greatly with the type and degree of crystallinity, the tensile, flexural, and impact strength of each polyolefin may be quite different. Their stress-crack resistance and useful temperature ranges may also vary with their crystalline structure. ▷ **polyethylene; polypropylene; polybutylene; polymethylpentene; ethylene-ethyl acrylate copolymer; ethylene-propylene; ethylene-vinyl acetate; ethylene-vinyl alcohol; ionomer plastic; chlorinated polyethylene**

polyorganophosphazene plastic PPZ is a plastic involving inorganic chains. In this case, atoms of nitrogen (N), and phosphorus (P) form the chain of a variety of organic side groups that can be attached to the phosphorus atom. The resulting high molecular weight chains are often flexible (low glass transition temperature, T_g) and thus are suitable as elastomers. Types with higher T_g and crystallizing types have good applications as coatings, fibers, and biomedical materials. PPZs are inherently fire resistant, offer good weatherability, and water and oil repellency.

polyoxymethylene plastic POM is usually called acetal; also called polyacetal. ▷ **acetal plastic**

polyparamethylstyrene plastic PPMS homopolymer is fairly similar to PS with a slightly higher glass transition temperature. It is becoming a low-cost alternative for styrene in homopolymers and copolymers.

polypeptide ▷ **peptide**

polyperfluoroalkoxy plastic PPFA is a so-called fully fluorinated plastic which has properties quite close to those of PTFE while being a true thermoplastic processwise.

polyphenylene ether plastic PPE is frequently referred to as polyphenylene oxide ▷ **polyphenylene oxide plastic.** Modified PPE products are used in most applications. Their unique compatibility with PS, particularly HIPS, results in a wide range of high temperature, tough, dimensionally stable products. They can be processed by conventional equipment that produces either solid or foam products. PPE compounds are characterized by outstanding dimensional stability, low water absorption in the engineering TPs, broad temperature ranges, excellent mechanical and thermal properties from −46 to 121°C (−50 to 250°F), and excellent dielectric characteristics over a wide range of frequencies and temperatures. They are also reasonably easy to process. Several injection molded and extrusion grades are rated UL 94 V-1 or V-0, including the glass-reinforced compounds. Foamable grades have service-temperature ratings of up to 96°C (205°F) in $\frac{1}{4}$-in. sections.

Because of their hydrolytic stability, both at room and elevated temperatures, blended parts in PPE can be repeatedly steam sterilized with no significant change in their properties. When exposed to aqueous environments their dimensional changes are low and predictable. PPE's resistance to acid, bases, and detergents is excellent. However, it is attacked by many halogenated or aromatic hydrocarbons. ▷ **polystyrene-polyphenylene ether blends**

polyphenylene oxide plastic PPO is a polyether through the –O– group in the repeat unit and thus the term polyethylene ether (PPE) is sometimes used ▷ **polyphenylene ether plastic.** PPO has a high glass transition temperature (T_g). It is capable of crystallizing between T_g and the melting point (T_m) of about 260°C (500°F). Its cost and certain processing difficulties associated with a high melt viscosity originally led to the use of blends (polyalloys) with PS or HIPS resulting in a single T_g about 150°C (302°F) to blends from 100 to 135°C. These lower T_g blends are often referred to as modified PPO (MPPO). The mechanical properties of MPPO are generally good, with high stiffness and low creep over a good temperature range. Good toughness extends to low temperatures. Excellent dimensional stability is associated with the noncrystalline structure, a low coefficient of thermal expansion, and very low moisture absorption. Electrical properties are generally good and unaffected by moisture. Dielectric properties, in particular, are good and stable. It is classified as self-extinguishing and nondripping. Hydrolytic stability is excep tionally high; it is also highly resistant to water, including hot water and steam. It can be repeatedly sterilized in steam autoclaves.

polyphenylene sulfide plastic This crystalline, high-performance engineering TP is characterized by outstanding high-temperature stability, inherent flame resistance, and a broad range of chemical resistance. PPS plastics and compounds provide various combinations of high mechanical strength, impact resistance, and electrical insulation, with its high arc resistance and low arc tracking. The pigmented PPS compounds include several grades that are suitable to support current-carrying parts in electrical components. They are essentially transparent to microwave radiation.

Unreinforced PPS is also available for use in slurry coating and electrostatic spraying. Coatings are suitable for food-contact applications as well as chemical processing equipment.

PPS is also available with long-fiber glass, carbon, or other reinforced forms. The stampable sheet type contains fiber-mat reinforcement and can be processed by compression molding. Other forms can contain predesigned reinforcement patterns for different processes, such as laminating and thermoforming. These cross-linked types of resins are more crystalline than any of the sulfones, which are generally classified as being more amorphous. They are quite stiff, with a flexural modulus ranging from 1.7×10^6 to 2.5×10^6 psi. Their tensile strengths range from 69 to 172 MPa (10,000 to 25,000 psi). Their HDTs are up to 275°C (525°F) at 1,820 kPa (264 psi).

PPS has excellent resistance to a broad range of chemicals, even at high temperatures. In fact, below 200°C (400°F) the resin has no known solvent. PPSs are flame retardant without additives, being rated at UL 94 V-0-V5. The oxygen index of the neat resin is 44, with the indexes of the compounds ranging from 47 to 53. Because flame retardance is inherent in it, a regrind will be as flame resistant as a production in the virgin material.

More recently developed linear PPSs have a far lower proportion of inorganic impurities than the conventional crosslinked material. They are also characterized by higher ultimate strength and an elongation at break of 4 as compared to 1%, as well as higher flexural strength and notched impact strength. However, the cross-linked product is somewhat more rigid. Linear PPS is partially crystalline, with pronounced thermal-transition ranges similar to those of PET that run from 85 to 100°C (185 to 212°F) for the T_g. Its melting point T_m is 280°C to 285°C (535 to 545°F).

polyphenylethersulfone plastic PPESU different formulations include those with a glass transition temperature of 220°C (428°F). Generally, properties are similar to the common polysulfone. Temperature resistance is higher and it is less sensitive to stress-cracking and to oxidative attack.

polyphenyl sulfone plastic PPSU balance of performance includes excellent toughness, excellent hydrolytic stability, excellent creep resistance, high heat deflection temperature [204°C (399°F) at 1.82 MPa (264 psi)], good electrical properties, good environmental stress-crack resistance relative to other amorphous plastics, and low flammability based on standard laboratory tests. ▷ **sulfone plastic**

polyphthalamide plastic Basically a crystalline aromatic nylon, combining the high strength and stiffness of nylon with the thermal stability of polyphenylene sulfide. Molding characteristics are similar to nylon 66, with similar or better chemical resistance, but its 24 hr water absorption is only 0.2 versus 0.7% for nylon 66. A key behavior is high heat resistance.

polypropylene oxide elastomer PPRO has a glass transition temperature of −72°C (−98°F) and melt temperature of 74°C (165°F).

polypropylene plastic PPs are in the polyolefin family of plastics. They are semitranslucent and milky white in color, with excellent colorability. They are produced by a stereoselective catalyst that puts order in their molecular configuration so that the basic resin has a predominantly regular, uniform structure. This means that the molecules crystallize into compact bundles, which makes them stronger than other members of the polyolefin family. PPs are an extremely versatile plastic available in many grades as well as copolymers like ethylene propylene. Neat PP has a low density of 0.90, which, combined with its good balance of moderate cost, strength, and stiffness as well as excellent fatigue, chemical resistance, and thermal and electrical properties, makes PP extremely attractive for many indoor and outdoor applications.

The strength, rigidity, heat resistance, and dimensional-stability properties of PP can be increased significantly with glass-fiber reinforcements. Increased toughness is provided in special, high-molecular-weight rubber-modified grades. The electrical properties of PP moldings are affected to varying degrees by their service temperatures. Its dielectric constant is essentially unchanged, but its dielectric strength increases and its volume resistivity decreases as temperature increases. PPs have limited heat resistance, but heat-stabilized grades are available for applications requiring prolonged use at elevated temperatures. The useful life for parts molded from such grades may be as long as five years at 120°C (250°F), 10 years at 130°C (230°F), and 20 years at 99°C (210°F). Specially stabilized grades are UL rated at 120°C (248°F) for continuous service. Basically, PP is classified as a slow-burning material, but it can also be supplied in flame-retardant grades.

PPs are unstable in the presence of oxidation conditions and UV radiation. Although all its grades are stabilized to some extent, specific stabilization systems are often used to suit a formulation to a particular environment, such as where it must undergo outdoor weathering.

PPs resist chemical attack and staining and are unaffected by aqueous solutions of inorganic salts or mineral acids and bases, even at high temperatures. They are not attacked by most organic chemicals, and there is no solvent for this resin at room temperature. The resins are attacked, however, by halogens, fuming nitric acid and other active oxidizing agents, as well as by aromatic and chlorinated hydrocarbons at high temperatures.

Although PPs retain their strength and stiffness at elevated temperatures, their performance at low temperatures leaves much to be desired. However, copolymers of PP that are available offer as much as two to three times the impact strength of general-purpose PP, even at temperatures as low as −29°C (−20°F).

PP is widely known for its application in the integral "living hinges" that are used in all types of applications; PP's excellent fatigue resistance is utilized in molding these integral hinges. ▷ **rheology, controlled**

polysaccharide Naturally occuring polymers that consist of simple sugars. Examples are starch and cellulose.

polystyrene plastic PS is noted for its sparkling clarity, hardness, extreme ease of processing (at least in the case of general purpose PS, or GPPS), excellent colorability, dimensional stability, and relatively low cost. This amorphous TP often competes favorably with higher-priced resins. It is available in a wide range of grades for all types of processes. Modifications available to the basic GPPS include grades for high heat and for various degrees of impact resistance. Clarity and gloss are reduced, however, in the impact grades. Some examples of members in the PS family are compounds of ABS, SAN, and SMA (styrene maleic anhydride). The structural characteristics of these copolymers are similar, but the SMA one has the highest heat resistance.

Expandable polystyrene (EPS) is a specialized form of plastics ▷ **expandable polystyrene.** Solid PS processed parts have low heat resistance, as compared to most TPs. Their maximum recommended continuous service temperature is below 93°C (200°F). Their electrical properties, which are good at room temperature, are affected only slightly by higher temperatures and varying humidity.

PS is soluble in most aromatic and chlorinated solvents but insoluble in such alcohols as methanol, ethanol, normal heptane, and acetone. Most fluids in households, as well as drinks and foods, have no effect, but PS is attacked by the oil in citrus-fruit rinds, gasoline, turpentine, and lacquer thinner. PSs are available in FDA-approved grades.

polystyrene plastic and environment PS is known to contain small quantities of monomeric styrene. Small traces of styrene migrate from PS packaging into contents of the pack as a function of the duration of storage, the stor age conditions, and the nature of the contents. The styrene content has been steadily reduced through a reduction in the residual monomer content and an alignment of the processing technique. A large number of animal experiments and also a series of studies on humans exposed to high styrene concentrations at the workplace for long periods have so far failed to establish any carcinogenic action on the part of the styrene.

polystyrene plastic and recycling Waste that occurs during the manufacturing and processing of PS has practically always been fed back into the production or processing cycle. The reuse of municipal waste is feasible without any problems with uncontaminated and contaminated materials. Each is used in their respective new market products. ▷ **plastic bad and other myths**

polystyrene plastic bead processing ▷ **expandable polystyrene**

polystyrene plastic copolymer plastic Copolymers of styrene include a large group of radom, graft, and block copolymers; those with a high proportion of acrylonitrile used in barrier films as well as MBS and MBAS plastics used as modifiers in PVC, SAN, ABS, ASA, etc. The styrene-acrylonitrile copolymer (SAN) is the most important when considering volume and number of applications.

polystyrene plastic crystal clear, impact resistance The styrene-butadiene styrene block copolymers with a polybutadiene content of up to 30%, which are referred to as crystal clear, impact-resistant PS, are completely different from standard impact-resistant PS. These are frequently mixed with standard PS on price grounds and also in order to achieve greater rigidity. Only certain defined grades of standard PS will give a mixture that is crystal clear.

polystyrene plastic flame retardant, impact resistant The market for flame retardant PS has been disconcerted by announcements that thermoplastics containing polybrominated diphenyl ethers can release brominated dioxins or furanes under certain conditions. At the same time as investigations were started into the formation of these compounds and their toxicity, a precautionary substitution of the products in question commenced. The advantages of these materials, which also contained halogens, namely an improved flowability and light stability, do not make up for their drawback of a lower temperature stability in a large number of cases. For example, product grades containing polybrominated diphenyl ether are still being used to meet the UL 94 V-0 rating. The manufacturers of these products are not bound by any obligation to find substitutes.

On the basis of the findings regarding the formation and toxicity of brominated dioxins and furanes that have been established to date, the nature, quantity, and toxicity of the substances that develop during the manufacture and processing of PS with additives of brominated diphenyl ether do not present any dangers, providing that the standard industrial safety regulations are respected. As an example, under no circumstances does a running TV set pose a danger to health. However, the debate regarding the potential danger of brominated diphenyl ethers (simply referred to under the general designation of halogen compounds in many cases) led to a call for halogen-free flame retardants for PS. A V-0 product was presented which marked the first of others in this direction. (It is particularly difficult to meet the market requirements on processing and flame retardant performance, physical and mechanical properties, and price.)

polystyrene plastic foam These lightweight foams widely used in packaging and insulation are formed basically by one of two methods. Extruded foam is made by injecting a volatile liquid such as methyl chloride into molten styrene in an extruder. As it emerges from the extruder die, the mass expands to form a low density foam "log" which may be sliced or machined into many varieties of products. In the other basic method, a blowing agent is incorporated in polystyrene beads as they are polymerized. These beads may be molded directly into a closed mold, in which they will expand up to 45 times their original volume; they may be expanded by heating and then molded; or, when combined with nucleating agents, extruded into thick sheets. ▷ **expandable polystyrene** and **foam**

polystyrene plastic heat-sealable film From the viewpoint of recycling, or suitability for recycling, it was particularly important that a substitute be found for the standard heat-sealable film in aluminum or PVC that had been used on thermoformed PS packs. Recycling was not worthwhile unless there was complete compatibility between the material used for the heat-sealable film and that used for the packaging. Material combinations were found for two-layer film that additionally provided good sealing seam strength, tear resistance, and tear propagation strength.

polystyrene plastic high gloss, impact resistance High gloss products with a medium or high impact strength, which incorporate particles of rubber that are several times smaller than for standard impact resistant PS, referred to as capsule or small cell particles, as a function of their structure, have established themselves on the market. With their combination of high gloss, high rigidity, high impact strength, and high heat resistance, which was directed at ABS high gloss products, the products have replaced traditional impact resistant PS in different markets.

polystyrene plastic, high impact PS modified by the incorporation of rubber particles to improve impact strength. A large volume of high impact polystyrene (HIPS) is produced in this form since unmodified PS is rather brittle. It is usually produced by the mass polymerization of styrene containing dissolved rubber. Products obtained merely by milling together rubber and PS or by coagulation of mixed latices of these two materials have inferior impact properties. As the rubber content increases so does the impact strength but correspondingly the softening point and stiffness decrease and the products are no longer transparent. The rubber should have a low T_g value, polybutadiene often being preferred, and it is usually somewhat crosslinked. Some grafting of the rubber to the PS occurs during the polymerization and this action increases interfacial adhesion and impact strength. The rubber is dispersed as particles about 1 to 10 μm in diameter but containing inclusions of PS particles with them. This effectively increases the rubber volume fraction. The study of particle morphology by osmium staining and transmission electron microscopy is a classical application of these techniques to synthetic plastics. ▷ **styrenic plastics**

polystyrene plastic, maleic anhydride Copolymers of styrene with maleic anhydride (SMSA) have become increasingly important because of their high heat resistance under load and good ability to flow.

polystyrene-polyethylene blends Mixing these two is nothing new. The target of combining the lower water vapor permeability and good stress cracking of PE (or PP) with the problem free processing and high rigidity of PS has proven to be unattainable, because of their incompatibility. This situation can be reduced through the use of mixing agents made up of styrene/olefin copolymers, etc. PS-PE blends are primarily used as a substitute for PVC and ABS in the form of monofilm or multilayer film to produce thermoformed packaging for foods such as those that contain fat.

polystyrene-polyphenylene ether blends The good compatibility of PS and PPE has been used for a long time to make blends which, even with a PS content in excess of 50% still count as modified PPE. The addition of PPE results in the increase of PS's heat resistance, which can be raised to the same range as that for ABS. Result is a lower cost plastic.

polysulfide rubber Contains sulfur and carbon linkages, produced from organic dihalides and sodium polysulfide. SR is a thermoset elastomer (TSE). These polymers have outstanding resistance to oils, greases, and solvents but have an unpleasant odor, their resiliency is poor, and their heat resistance is only fair. The abrasion resistance of polysulfides (PTRS) is half that of NR, and its tensile strength runs only from 8.3 to 9.7 MPa (1,200 to 1,400 psi). However, these values are still retained even after extended immersion in oil. Their increased sulfur content improves their solvent and oil resistance but reduces their permeability to gases.

polysulfone plastic PSU are amorphous engineering TPs noted for their high heat-deflection temperatures, outstanding dimensional stability and electrical properties, excellent chemical resistance, and for being biologically inert, rigid, strong, and easily processed by different methods. They are stable and self-extinguishing in their completely natural, unmodified neat form; in most plastics these qualities must be obtained by using chemical modifiers. PSUs are also heat resistant and maintain their properties in a range from −100°C (−150°F) to over 150°C (300°F). These strong, rigid plastics are the only type that will remain transparent at service temperatures as high as 200°C (400°F). The name *polysulfone* has been assigned to polymers with SO_2 groups in their backbone. The basic types are the standard PSUs, polyaryl, polyether, and polyphenyl.

PSUs are available in opaque colors and in mineral-filled and glass- and other reinforced compounds to provide higher strength, stiffness, and thermal stability. For example, reinforced carbon-fiber PSU is used in human hip joints.

The tensile strengths of PSUs go up to 110 MPa (16,000 psi, its flexural modulus to more than 1.0×10^6 psi), and its HDTs to up to 200°C (400°F). A high percentage of its physical, mechanical, and electrical properties is maintained at elevated temperatures. For example, its flexural modulus remains above 0.3×10^6 psi at service temperatures as high as 160°C (320°F). Even after prolonged exposure to such temperatures, its resins do not discolor or degrade. Its thermal stability and oxidation resistance are also excellent at service temperatures well above 150°C (300°F). Heat aging a PSU increases its tensile strength, HDT, and modulus appreciably. However, prolonged heat aging for about a year or so decreases its toughness, tensile strength, and elongation.

PSU's creep, compared with that of other TPs, is exceptionally low at elevated temperatures and under certain continuous loads. For example, its creep at 99°C (210°F) is less than that of acetal or heat-resistant ABS at room temperature.

The hydrolytic stability of these materials makes them resistant to water absorption in aqueous acidic and alkaline environments. Their combination of hydrolytic stability and heat resistance results in their having exceptional resistance to boiling water and steam, even under autoclave pressures and cyclic exposure to hot-to-cold and wet-to-dry repetitions. The PSUs also share the common drawback of absorbing UV rays, which gives them poor weather resistance. Thus, they are not recommended for outdoor service unless they are protected with paint or are plated or UV stabilized.

polyterpene plastic Thermoplastic obtained by the polymerization of turpentine in the presence of catalysts. These plastics are used in the manufacture of adhesives, coatings, and varnishes, and in food packaging. They are compatible with waxes, natural and synthetic rubbers, and polyethylene.

polytetrafluoroethylene plastic PTFE has a unique position in the plastic industry (as well as others) due to its chemical inertness, heat resistance, excellent electrical insulation properties, and low coefficient of friction in a wide temperature range. Polymerization of tetrafluoroethylene (TFE) monomer produces this perfluorinated straight chain high polymer; this white to translucent solid plastic has an extremely high molecular weight, in the 10^6 to 10^7 range, and consequently has a viscosity of about 10 GPa·s (10^{10} to 10^{12} p) at 380°C. It is a highly crystalline plastic. Its high thermal stability is due to the strong carbon-fluorine bond and characterizes PTFE as a very useful high temperature plastic. Even though it is waxy plastic of the general appearance of polyethylene, it has heat resistance up to 288°C (550°F), remarkable lubricity, and is attacked only by sodium and other hot alkali metals. The rheological properties are so different from usual thermoplastics that the common melt processing methods (extrusion, injection, etc.) are not feasible; treated like a ceramic. Basically nearly all PTFEs are processed by forming the plastic to an approximate final shape at or near room temperature, and then completing the operation by heating (sintering) the material at temperatures above the melting point and cooling to adjust the crystalline content. Each individual type of operation has its own specific method, such as billet molding and skiving, sheet molding, automatic preforming and sintering, ram extrusion, etc. ▷ **fluoroplastic** and **skiving**

polythene plastic The British word for polyethylene. In 1937 ICI-England's research produced polythene; original development started by ICI in 1933.

polythiophene plastic Melt processable plastic that is electrically conductive.

polyurethane elastomer A PUR with elastomeric properties. The term covers a very wide range of PURs, classified according to the method of manufacture. The main types are cast PUR, millable PUR elastomer, and thermoplastic PUR elastomer. ▷ **polyurethane plastic**

polyurethane plastic PURs produced by the reaction of polyisocyanates with polyester- or polyester-based resins can be either TPs or TSs. Extremely wide variations in form and physical or mechanical properties are available in PUR, which exhibits an extraordinary range of toughness, flexibility, and abrasion resistance. Its grades can range in density from $\frac{1}{2}$ lb/ft^3 (16 kg/m^3) in its cellular form to 70 lb/ft^3 (1,120 kg/m^3) in a solid form. PUR's hardness runs from rigid, solid forms at 85 Shore D to soft elastomers.

PUR materials are available in three forms: rigid foam, flexible foam, and as an elastomer. They are characterized by high strength and good chemical and abrasion resistance, with superior resistance to ozone, oil gasoline, and many solvents. The rigid foam type is widely used as an insulation material in buildings, appliances, and such applications. The flexible foam is an excellent cushioning material for furniture, and the elastomeric type is used in solid tires, shock absorbers, and so on. It has outstanding flex life, cut resistance, and abrasion resistance. Some formulations are as much as 20 times more resistant to abrasion than are metals.

The T_g of the flexible foams is well below room temperature, and for rigid foams the T_g is actually higher than room temperature. The cells of a rigid foam are about the same size and uniformity as those of a flexible foam, but rigid foams usually consist of 90% of closed cells. For this reason their water absorption is low. Compressing the foam beyond its elastic limit will damage its cellular structure. Rigid foams are blown with either carbon dioxide or fluorocarbons, although the fluoros are now being replaced by a nondamaging ozone-blowing agent. Their thermal conductivity is influenced by the blowing agent used and its density.

PURs are manufactured by reacting a polyfunctional alcohol with an isocyanate in a simple blend-reaction operation. By the proper choice of the alcohol and the isocyanate, polyester or polyether urethanes can be made. Similarly, either thermoplastic or thermoset urethanes can be made by the proper choice of isocyanate. As an example, PURs based on toluene diisocyanate (TDI) continue to hold a large proportion of the market in the soft-foam sector. However, TDI was generally outstripped by methane diisocyanate (MDI), since the more flexible chemistry of these isocyanates as compared to TDI made a wider spectrum of applications possible. MDI offers a highly developed building-block system whose elements allow widely differing materials (soft, semirigid, rigid) to be tailored to specific requirements.

Regarding chlorofluorocarbon (CFC) blowing agent being used in PUR, extensive development and formulation work by the chemical industry has already resulted in a major drop in its use. Complete elimination is targeted to occur within a couple of years. There are different methods that can be used to provide foaming, such as the use of water (creating carbon dioxide) but it has limited use. ▷ **chlorofluorocarbon**

polyurethane plastic foam ▷ **polyurethane plastic** and **foamed polyurethane**

polyurethane rubber Alternative name for polyurethane elastomer.

polyurethane rules, nomenclature The reaction product of an isocyanate with an alcohol is called urethane, according to the rules of chemical nomenclature; but the terms polyurethane and urethane are more widely used in the plastic industry.

polyurethane thermoplastic The first thermoplastic polyurethane (TPU) to become commercialized in 1937 by I.G. Farbenindustrie of Germany (later became Bayer AG). It was targeted to improve the properties of nylon fibers. ▷ **polyurethane plastic**

polyurethane thermoset ▷ **polyurethane plastic**

polyurethane virtually crosslinked A thermoplastic PUR (TPU) that is in a unique physical state. It has the properties of a thermoset elastomer, without being crosslinked. Strong intramolecular forces, such as hydrogen bonds, van der Waals, and London forces, and intramolecular entanglement of chains, all contribute to the virtually crosslinked (VC) state. This state, however, depends on temperature. On heating, the action of these forces disappears, permitting the plastic to be processed by standard methods used for thermoplastic system. On cooling, these forces reappear. The intramolecular forces of TPUs can be temporarily destroyed by solvation, which enables them to be employed in adhesives and coatings. When the solvents are evaporated, the original properties of the TPUs are restored.

polyvinyl The family of vinyl plastics are characterized by a basic molecule having two carbon atoms with three pendant hydrogens and a fourth pendant group that is a unique group of atoms depending on the particular vinyl (as reviewed following this explanation). It is this fourth group of atoms that provides the special qualities of the particular vinyl plastic. The basic molecule repeats in a chain to form the plastic. However, in the plastics literature with all those in the vinyl family, each properly identified by name in their respective classifications, the term vinyl usually identifies the major, very large production of polyvinyl chloride plastic. In addition to reviewing what follows ▷ **vinyl chloride monomer; plastisol**

polyvinyl acetal plastic PVACL, corresponding to acetadehyde, has some use as a coating or as an adhesive.

polyvinyl acetate plastic The PVAC copolymers are odorless, tasteless, nontoxic, slow burning, lightweight, and colorless, with reasonably low water absorption. They are soluble in organic ketones, esters, chlorinated hydrocarbons, aromatic hydrocarbons, and alcohols, but insoluble in water, aliphatic hydrocarbons, fats, and waxes. Water emulsions have extended the use of this resin. Used perhaps most extensively as adhesives, they are also employed as coatings for paper, sizing for textiles, and finishes for leathers, as well as bases for inks and lacquers, for heat-sealing films, and for flashbulb linings.

polyvinyl alcohol plastic PVOH (or tradename PVAL) is crystalline, white powder soluble in water and alcohols. It is the world's largest volume, synthetic, water soluble plastic. In its cast form, it is characterized by water solubility, low gas permeability, high resistance to organic solvents other than alcohol, and crystallinity when stretch oriented. Crystallinity allows the material to polarize light. A series of hydrolysis levels of the plastic are available that range from room temperature solubility to not soluble at all. The major applications of the PVAs are in elastomeric products, adhesives, films, and finishes. Extruded PVA hoses and tubing are excellent for use subjected to contact with oils and other chemicals. PVA is used as a sizing in the manufacture of nylon.

polyvinyl carbazole plastic PVCZ is a thermoplastic, brown in color, obtained by reacting acetylene with carbazole. The plastic has excellent electrical properties and good heat and chemical resistance. Use includes high frequency dielectrics, impregnant for paper capacitors, and photoconductive plastics for xerography.

polyvinyl chloride acetate plastic Copolymer of vinyl chloride and vinyl acetate. It is a colorless thermoplastic solid with good resistance to water as well as concentrated acids and alkalis. It is obtainable in the form of granules, solutions, and emulsions. Compounded with plasticizers, it yields a flexible material superior to rubber in aging properties. It is widely used for cable and wire coverings, in chemical plants, and in protective garments.

polyvinyl chloride chlorinated plastic ▷ **chlorinated polyvinyl chloride**

polyvinyl chloride dispersion plastics They are fine particle-size vinyl homopolymers or copolymers (PVC is the most commercially significant) used in fluid coatings either as plastisols or organosols. ▷ **plastisol**

polyvinyl chloride plastic The PVCs comprise a major volume of the plastics consumed worldwide and are the most commercially significant of the different vinyl polymers and copolymers. Although the vinyls differ in having literally thousands of varying compositions and properties, there are certain general characteristics that are common to nearly all these plastics. For one thing, most materials based on vinyls are inherently TP and heat sealable. The exceptions are the products that have been purposely compounded with TSs or crosslinking agents. For example, PVC can be chlorinated (CPVC) and be alloyed with other polymers like ABS, acrylics, polyurethane, and nitrile rubber to improve its impact resistance, heat deflection, and processability.

In general, vinyls can be plasticized to give them a wide range of hardness ranging from thin, flexible, free films to rigid molded pieces. Most vinyls are naturally clear, with an unlimited color range for most forms of the materials.

They generally have in common excellent water and chemical resistance, strength, abrasion resistance, and self-extinguishability. In their elastomeric form vinyls usually exhibit properties superior to those of natural rubber in their flex life, resistance to acids, alcohols, sunlight, and wear and aging. They are nontoxic, tasteless, odorless, and suitable for use as packaging materials that will come in contact with foods and drugs, as well as for decorative packaging requiring ordinary protection. The vinyl resins can be used in printing inks and be effectively used in coating paper, leather, wood, and, in some cases, plastics. In most forms vinyl can be printed.

Rigid PVC, sometimes called the poor man's engineering plastic, has a wide range of propertries for use in different products. In addition to the noteworthy properties mentioned, it has high resistance to ignition, good corrosion, and stain resistance, and weatherability. However, it is attacked by aromatic solvents, ketones, aldehydes, naphthalenes, and some chloride, acetate, and acrylate esters. In general, the normal impact grades of PVCs have better chemical resistance than the high-impact grades. Most PVCs are not recommended for continuous use above 60°C (140°F). Chlorination to form CPVC increases its heat resistance, flame retardancy, and density, depending on the amount of chlorination introduced. In regard to flammability, note that the vinyls release a limited amount of hydrochloric acid.

polyvinyl chloride plastic and the environment The discussion regarding the environmental compatibility of PVC intensified during the 1980s, affecting public opinion and promoting a negative image. Although no truly new facts have emerged, and certainly no serious risk potential has been established in the life cycle of PVC (or perhaps precisely because of this), the campaign was run at an increasingly ideological level with no bearing on the environmental problems that are of true relevance. Repeated investigations into the flue gases of refuse incineration plants have shown again and again that it is not the percentage of chlorine in the refuse (from PVC products, for example) but solely the incineration conditions that influence the formation of dioxins. The salt circuit has been closed. Flue gas salts are being reused in chlorine production. This means that the chlorine content of the refuse, which is not attributable to PVC but is at least equally high, is also being sensibly recycled. The same also applies for what seems the promising route of a hydrochloric acid circuit. Other factors to analyze include (1) in those cases where use is also made of the energy produced by refuse incineration, no other material can surpass PVC in terms of carbon dioxide emission, (2) a broadly based study of domestic refuse shows no lead or cadmium is introduced into the refuse by short-lived packaging materials, and (3) the considerable progress being made on calcium/zinc stabilization, as an example, will make it possible for cadmium containing stabilizers to be dispensed with, even for long-lived applications, in the foreseeable future.

These factors too will serve to further improve the ecological balance of individual applications and also the overall balance of the life cycle of PVC as a whole. It would be welcomed if greater use could be made of this instrument of ecological balance, with the introduction of a more refined system for the different materials. It is already evident today that a large number of allegedly ecological solutions actually place a greater burden on the environment when all the implications are taken into account. It can be said that the attacks on PVC have become more vehement, while clear progress has been made in improving environmental compatibility and building up a close circuit for PVC. Continuing the work here, and making the public more aware of this work than in the past, is an essential in the future. ▷ **recycling polyvinyl chloride**

polyvinyl chloride plastic recycling ▷ **recycling polyvinyl chloride**

polyvinyl chloride safety issues ▷ **polyvinyl chloride plastic**

polyvinyl chloride ultra high molecular weight plastic UHMW-PVCs are versatile plastics that can provide superior mechanical properties and be formulated to produce a variety of products. Because changes in formulations or equipment conditions may be required to facilitate processing, these plastics are generally used in plasticized applications; it is in highly plasticized uses that they show the greatest advantages in producing compounds with improved properties. They can bring to flexible vinyls improved tensile, modulus, abrasion, and solvent resistance; low and high termperature performance; and retention of properties during aging.

polyvinyl dichloride plastic This is PVC modified by chlorination. ▷ **chlorinated polyvinyl chloride**

polyvinyl ester plastic ▷ **vinyl ester plastic**

polyvinylfluoride plastic PVC products are strong and tough, with good abrasion and staining resistance up to fairly high temperatures of 100 to 150°C (212 to 302°F), and they are classified as slow burning. They are generally less chemical resistant than fully fluorinated plastics but show excellent UV resistance and good color retention, and are not affected by water. Their excellent weatherability has made them a choice material for exterior applications, such as coatings for metals (slidings, gutter, etc.), plywood finishes, architectural sheets, lighting panels, and glazing for solar energy collection. Also for electrical wrapping tape and parting layers for laminates.

polyvinyl formal plastic PVFO, which corresponds to formaldehyde in the presence of PVOH, finds applications as temperature-resistant coatings for containers and electric wires. It is also resistant to greases and oils.

polyvinylidene chloride plastic Molded parts in PVDC have high strength, abrasion resistance, strong welds, dimensional stability, toughness, and durability. This material is especially suited for injection molding at high speed parts that have heavy cross-sections. Molded PVDC fittings and parts are particularly valuable in industries involving the use of chemicals. For example, pipes of this material are superior to iron pipes to dispose of waste acids. Films produced from PVDC exhibit an extremely low water-vapor transmission rate, as well as flexibility over a wide range of temperatures and heat sealability. They are particularly suitable for various types of packaging, including medicinal products, metal parts, and food. Food "packaging" for the home refrigerator uses the highly popular Saran wrap from Dow Chemical.

polyvinylidene fluoride PVDF is a fluorine-containing TP. It is unlike other plastics, being a crystalline, high-molecular-weight polymer of vinylidene fluoride ($CH_2 = CF_2$). Compounds are available that contain 59% fluorine. This nonflammable plastic is mechanically strong and tough, thermally stable, resistant to almost all chemicals and solvents, and is stable to UV and extreme weather conditions. It has a higher strength and abrasion resistance than PTFE; however, it does not match the high chemical and temperature resistance of PTFE.

Where unfavorable combinations of chemical, mechanical, and physical environments may preclude the use of other materials, PVC has been successfully used, as for valve and pump parts, heavy wall pipe fittings, gears, cams, bearings, coatings, and electrical insulation. Its limitations include lower service temperatures than the highly fluorinated fluoropolymers, no antisick qualities, and the fact that it produces toxic products upon thermal decomposition.

polyvinyl plastic The PVBs are soluble in esters, ketones, alcohols, and chlorinated hydrocarbons but insoluble in the aliphatic hydrocarbons. They are stable in dilute alkalis but slowly decompose in dilute acids. PVBs are widely used as safety-glass interlayers and between sheets of acrylic to protect the enclosures of pressurized cabins in aircraft against shattering. Since 1938, PVB film in interlayers from 10 to 40 mils has been an important resource for the glass, automotive, and architectural industries. PVBs are also used as coatings for textiles and paper and as adhesives.

polyvinyl polymerization ▷ **addition polymerization; anionic polymerization; reactivity**

polyvinyl pyridine plastic PVP is primarily used as a constituent in copolymers as adhesives.

polyvinyl pyrrolidone plastic PVPO is highly polar and water soluble, and finds applications in adhesives and as a water thickener. Water solutions can be used as blood plasma substitute or artificial blood.

pony mixer ▷ **change can mixer**

population The totality of products or units of material under considerations; the hypothetical collection of experimental values that would be obtained if a given test were repeated an unlimited number of times, under essentially the same conditions, on a material or on materials having the same true value. From this definition it follows that a given set of data can be considered to belong to many different populations. The choice of population is determined by the specification of the "conditions" under which the repetitive measuring process is conducted.

population parameter A fixed value characterizing a certain aspect of a statistical population. An estimate of the value of a population parameter, derived from a sample, is called a "sample estimate" or "statistic".

poromeric A term coined to describe the microporosity, air permeability, and abrasion resistance of natural and synthetic leather. The pores basically decrease in diameter from the inner surface to the outer and thus permit air and water vapor to leave the material while excluding water from the outside. Since the 1940s PVC, nylon, polyester, polyurethane, and other plastics have been used in different formats as leather imitations in shoes, bags, clothing, and home furnishings. When plasticized, PVC is coated on a fabric substrate and called vinyl-coated fabric. Their applications were limited by the properties of the knit or woven substrates. The real poromerics utilize a nonwoven substrate that is impregnated with a plastic, usually polyurethane (PUR). Fiber as fine as 0.03 tex (0.3 den), and sometimes less, is frequently used to imitate the fibrillated collagen fibers of leather, thereby attaining the soft feel and good appearance essential for clothing applications. The coating layer in poromerics that corresponds to the grain layer of leather is prepared with PUR.

Poromerics are manufactured by combining the technologies of fiber and nonwoven fabrics manufacture with those of PUR preparation and coagulation (immersed in a nonsolvent bath for coagulation). Ordinary PUR coated fabrics are manufactured by drying a cast PUR solution to form a film that is laminated onto the substrate. Significant improvement in appearance, feel, and grain break is achieved by using a brushed fabric as the substrate that is laminated with a cast PUR film. Alternatively, an organic solvent solution of PUR is applied to a brush woven fabric that is coagulated.

Finishing is an important process in the manufacture of poromeric or leatherlike materials. Surfaces are usually grained or sueded. Embossing the coating layer with heated rollers engraved with the desired pattern is a method for graining. The surface is then color-painted with gravure rolls, spraying, or dyeing. Excessive embossing and coloring may damage the porous structure by creating a thick layer that impairs water vapor permeaility, flex endurance, and grain break. The usual two methods to produce sueded leatherlike materials are: (1) coating the material's surface with a porous layer, and (2) napping the substrate's surface before dyeing, producing a fibrous material. The former method gives a suedelike appearance by sanding the surface with a microporous sponge or by embossing or tearing the porous structure at the intermediate stage. Napping PUR impregnated nonwoven fabrics made of fine polyester or nylon fibers, are dyed and used for apparel, shoes, upholstery, and home furnishings.

porosity Existence in a material of very small voids; a condition of trapped pockets of air, gas, or vacuum within a solid material. Usually expressed as a percentage of the total nonsolid volume to the total volume (solid plus nonsolid) or a unit quantity of material.

porosity, apparent Permeable-pore volume divided by total volume.

porosity, total-true Total pore volume divided by total volume.

porous mold ▷**mold, porous**

porous plastic ▷**plastic, porous**

portland cement A hydraulic cement produced by pulverizing clinker consisting of hydraulic calcium silicates, and usually containing one or more of the forms of calcium sulfate as an interground addition. Widely used for reinforced structural concrete.

position control ▷**motion control systems**

postcure Additional elevated temperature cure, usually without tooling or pressure, to improve final properties and/or complete the final cure. This after-baking after part fabrication also can provide decreased volatiles in the part, relieve stresses and/or improve dimensional stability. With certain plastics, particularly certain thermosets, complete cure and ultimate mechanical properties are obtained only by exposure of the plastic to higher temperatures than those of the cure. Property improvements usually include creep resistance and elevated temperatures.

postforming 1. The forming, bending, and/or shaping of fully cured thermoset plastics. C-stage thermoset, as an example, is heated to make it flexible. Upon cooling, the formed material retains the contours and shape of

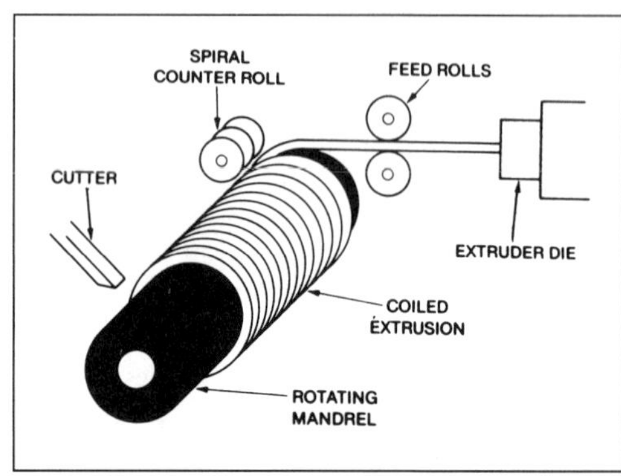

In-line coil former that can produce telephone cords, springs, etc.; extrudate can be round, square, hexagonal, etc.

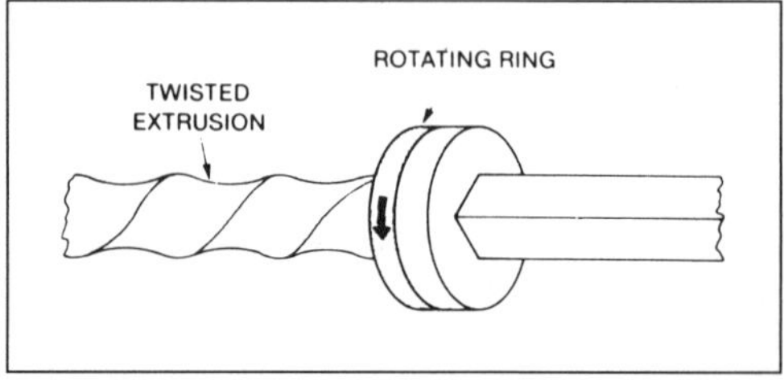

In-line fixed/rotating rings used to twist extrudate.

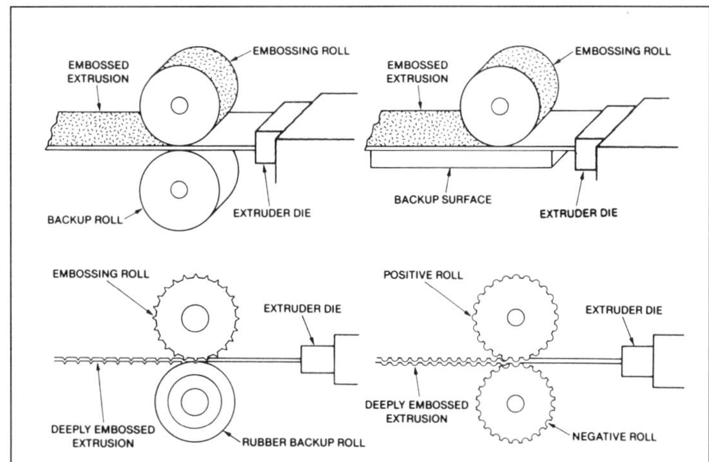

In-line postforming embossing techniques applied after the extruder die.

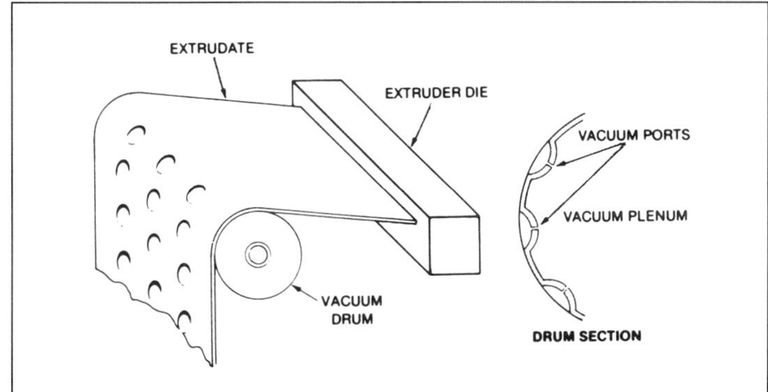

In-line vacuum forming embossing roll with water cooled temperature control.

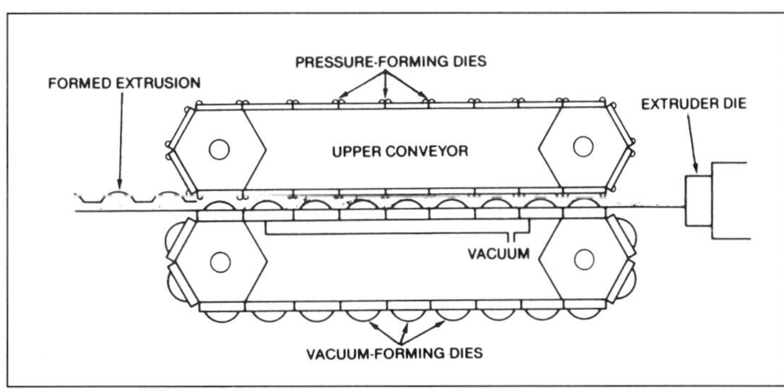

Continuous conveyor system using in-line vacuum/pressure former for plastic sheet with matched, water cooled, forming molds. This system can be used with different profiles, such as small and large tubes producing corrugated tube or pipe.

the mold over which it has been formed. **2.** Postforming is extensively used with thermoplastics. This popular forming technique has provided both performance and cost advantages, principally for long production runs, is applied as the plastic sheet, film, or profile exits an extruder. Upon leaving the die, and retaining heat, the plastic is continuously postformed.

With this type of in-line system the hot plastic is reduced only to the desired heat of forming. All it may require is a fixed distance from the die opening. Cooling can be accelerated with blown air, a water spray, a water bath, or some combination. Examples of some postforming techniques are shown in Figs. above and opposite. This equipment, like others, requires precision tooling with perfect registration. ▷ **thermoforming**

postshrinkage Refers to the difference between the dimensions of a fabricated part at room temperature and the cooled part (immediately after fabricating, such as injection molding), checked usually 24 hr after fabrication. Having an elapsed time is necessary for many thermoplastics, particularly commodity types, to allow parts to complete their inherent shrinkage behavior. The extent of this action can be near zero for certain plastics or may vary considerably. The usual lapse time of 24 hr is ok, but some plastics may take more or less time. Thermosets tend not to have postshrinkage.

post treatment, gasoline tank ▷**gasoline tank permeability**

postulate A study of given rules. ▷**design analysis, pragmatic approach**

potassium compound ▷**ferroelectric**

potentiometer An instrument for the measurement of electromotive force by balancing against it an equal and opposite electromotive force across a calibrated resistance carrying a definite current. Manual or automatic self-balancing versions are available.

pot life The time period during which a plastic remains suitable for the intended use (such as retaining a viscosity low enough to be used in processing), after compounding ingredients such as solvent or catalyst have been added. Also called working life.

potting **1.** Similar to encapsulating except that steps are taken to ensure complete penetration of all the voids in the object before the plastic polymerizes in the container or shell. The container remains an integral part of the finished product. **2.** The terms potting, embedding, casting, molding, impregnation, and encapsulation are often used interchangeably.

pot, transfer mold ▷**mold pot**

pouch ▷**thermoforming, form, fill, and seal** and **aseptic liquid pouch**

pourability The measure of the time required for a standard quantity of material to flow through a funnel of specified dimensions.

pour-in-place-foaming ▷**foamed polyurethane**

pour out finish A container finish with an undercut below the top, designed to facilitate pouring without dripping.

powder Any solid, dry material of extremely small particle size ranging in the colloidal dimensions, prepared either by comminuting larger units (mechanical grinding), by combustion (carbon black, lamp black), or by participation via chemical reaction (calcium carbonate, etc.). Powders that are so fine that they cannot be detected by rubbing between thumb and forefinger are called impalpable. They are handled in equipment such as bag filters.

powder coating Powder coating is a solventless coating—a coating that is not dependent upon a sacrificial medium such as a solvent, but is based on the performance constituents of solid TP or TS plastic. It can be a homogeneous blend of the plastic with fillers and additives in the form of a dry, fine-particle-size compound similar to flour. The advantages of the process include its minimizing air pollution as well as water contamination, and increased part performance when coated, resulting in cost savings. This is basically a chemical coating, so it has many of the same problems as solution painting. If not properly formulated, the coating may sag at high thickness, show poor performance when not completely cured, reveal imperfections such as craters and pinholes, and have poor hiding, with low film thickness.

Plastic powders have proved to be an excellent coating material in a broad range of applications when used as a dry powder. The use of microfine powders expanded coating possibilities even more by making it possible to use powdered plastics (particularly PE) as wet dispersions or paste coatings.

Textiles, paper, and other flexible substrates such as fusible interlining, interlinking, drapery and upholstery fabrics, and carpets (see Fig. opposite) are examples of large volume applications. In addition another important market is with metals and other rigid materials (such as pipes, small difficult to coat parts, large flat surfaces, and metal tanks) can be protectively coated with a variety of processing techniques.

Coating of woven or nonwoven fabric normally involves three steps as it passes from the unwind roll to the rewind stand. Powder is metered onto the fabric, heated in an oven and cooled by a chill roll. The fabric is normally pulled through the system with a set of power driven nip rolls or by constant tension winder. The oven normally has either a gas or electric IR heating system, but hot air convection ovens may also be used. The choice may depend on the relative cost of these utilities in the manufacturing area. Ovens are usually 20 to 30 ft (6 to 9 m) long. They are usually divided into several heating zones,

A number of techniques are available for coating metals and rigid substrates (including plastics). The steps generally involve surface preparation, preheating substrate, powder applications, and postheating. Most metal techniques require that the part be preheated above

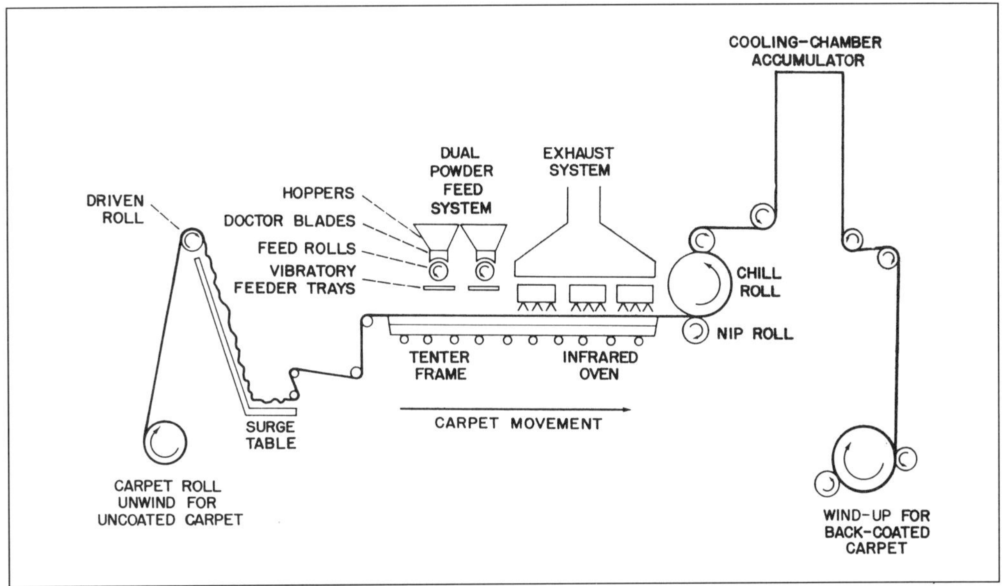

Powder coating schematic of a carpet coating line.

the softening point of the plastic prior to coating ▷ **centrifugal casting; rotational molding; electrostatic spray coating; flame spray coating; flocking or floc spraying; flood coating; plasma coating; fluidized bed coating.** There are combinations and variations of these methods. They are also referred to as fusion coating processes, since at some stage in the process the plastic must be melted and fused to form a continuous coating.

powder compact Molding materials in the form of dry, friable pellets prepared by compacting dry-blend mixtures of plastics (usually PVC) with plasticizers and other ingredients. They offer compounding with low heat history.

powder density ▷ **density, bulk**

powder metallurgy Powder, which was made by the atomization of liquid metals, is compacted in a die by the sintering process.

powder molding material ▷ **molding material**

powder molding process General term used to denote several techniques for producing objects of varying size and shape by melting plastic powder, usually against the inside of a mold. The molds are either stationary (for example, in variations of slush molding) or rotating (for example, in variations of rotational molding).

powder, plastic Material which has been finely pulverized for use in fluidized bed coating, rotational molding, powder coating, sintering, and other techniques requiring powdered plastics.

powder spraying ▷ **flocking or floc spraying**

power, electrical ▷ **electrical power**

practical approach ▷ **engineering approach and practical approach**

practice A definitive procedure for performing one or more specific operations or functions that does not produce a result. Compare to ▷ **testing method.** ▷ **standard deviation**

pragmatic approach ▷ **design analysis, pragmatic approach**

prebillow ▷ **thermoforming, prebillow**

precipitate Small particles that have settled out of liquid or gaseous suspension by gravity, or that result from a chemical reaction.

precision Basically the average deviation from the ideal position as determined from a number of measurements for a given input. Precision as distinguished from accuracy is the degree of mutual agreement between individual measurements, namely repeatability and reproducibility. ▷ **accuracy**

preconditioning Any preliminary exposure of a material to specific atmospheric conditions for the purpose of favorably approaching equilibrium with a prescribed atmosphere.

precure Partial curing of a thermoset plastic prior to final processing where it completely

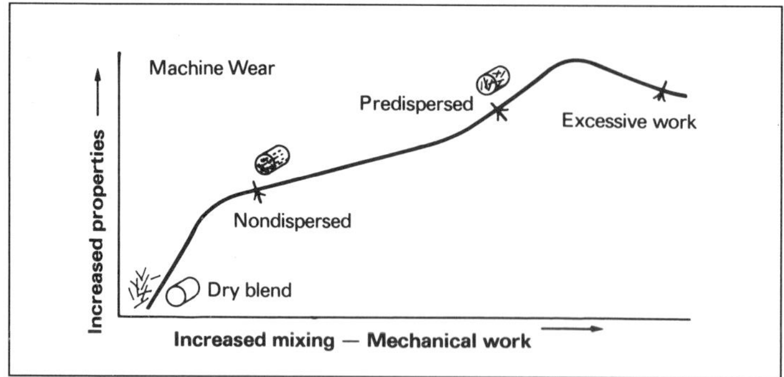

Advantages of properly predispersed plastic compounds.

cures, such as in molding. However, postcuring may also be required.

precursor A material or substance from which another material is produced. With respect to carbon or graphite fiber, precursors PAN or pitch fibers produce carbon and graphite fibers.

predispersed compound The Fig. above provides a guide on how the better mixing/dispersing reinforcements, particularly chopped glass fibers, result in improved properties and less wear on machines such as injection molding.

preengineered mold ▷ **mold, preengineered**

pre-expansion EPS beads ▷ **expandable polystyrene**

prefinish Finishing a processed plastic product such as threads (at the parting line), closures, flash, etc.

prefit A process for checking the fit of mating detail parts in an assembly prior to final assembly.

preform 1. In injection blow molding, the "test tube" shape that is used to form the final blown product. ▷ **blow molding, injection preform 2.** A compressed tablet or biscuit of plastic composition used for efficiency in handling and accuracy in weighing materials, particularly thermosets (see Fig. 1). ▷ **radio frequency preheating 3.** ▷ **foamed preform 4.** In regard to preform packaging ▷ **thermoforming, form, fill, and seal 5.** A preshaped fibrous reinforcement formed by the distribution of chopped fibers or cloth (usually glass) by air, water flotation, or vacuum over the surface of a perforated screen to the approximate contour and thickness desired in the finished part (see Fig. 2). **6.** A preshaped fibrous reinforcement of mat or cloth formed to the desired shape on a mandrel or mock-up before being placed in a mold press.

Fig. 1 Preforms (compressed tablets) are being preheated in a high frequency oven prior to being transferred in a compression mold cavity.

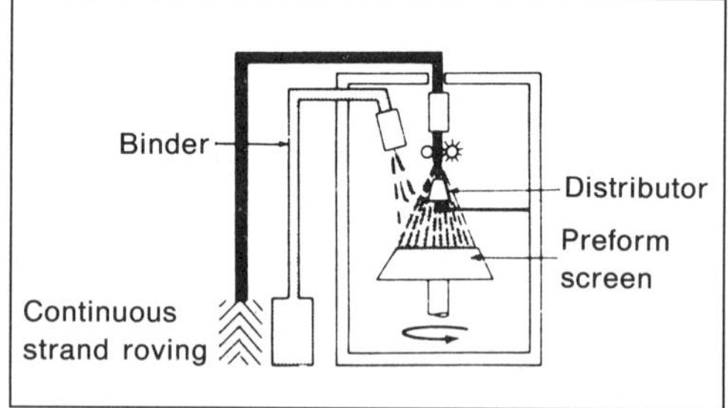

Fig. 2 Schematic of chopped fiber vacuum method over a rotating preform screen. Suction holds the cut fibers, usually glass, to 1 to 2 in. (2.5 to 5 cm) length, while a plastic binder is applied (usually $\frac{1}{2}$% thermoplastic such as polystyrene).

preform binder A plastic applied to the chopped fiber strands of a preform, usually during its formation, and cured so that the preform will retain its shape and can be handled.

preform fiber Fiber formed over a screen shaped like the mold in which the preform will be used; it eliminates the need for over-lapping or mitering the corners in reinforced plastic sheet-type molding materials. Efficiently useful to form complex shapes.

preforming, slurry ▷ **slurry preforming**

preform molding The preshaped fiber preform is placed in a mold (compression, resin transfer, etc.) with the required plastic to produce an RP part.

pregel An unintentional, extra layer of cured plastic on part of the surface of a reinforced plastic. Not a gel coat.

preheating The heating of a plastic material prior to molding or casting in order to facilitate the operation, reduce cycle time, and improve product. ▷ **radio frequency preheating** and **dielectric heating**

preimpregnated ▷ **prepreg**

premix Molding compound prepared prior to and apart from the molding operations and containing all components required for molding; plastic, reinforcement, fillers, release agents, etc.

premolding The lay-up and partial cure at an intermediate thermoset cure temperature of a reinforced plastic detail part to stabilize (fix location) its configuration for handling and assembly with other parts for final cure.

preplastication Technique for premelting molding and extrudable material in a separate chamber, then transferring the melt to the process.

preply ▷ **reinforced plastic preply**

prepolymer A partially polymerized substance, or one polymerized to a low degree of polymerization, for subsequent conversion to a high polymer (plastic); a chemical intermediate with a molecular weight between that of the monomer or monomers and the final plastic.

prepolymer molding ▷ **foamed polyurethane molding prepolymer**

prepreg A term used in reinforced plastics for a reinforcement containing or combined with a thermoset liquid plastic that can be stored under controlled conditions. Reinforcement is in different forms such as woven and nonwoven cloth, filaments, rovings, etc. The TS plastic is completely compounded, which includes the catalyst being impregnated into the reinforcement and partially cured to a tack-free state in the B-stage. The fabricator (molder) uses the prepreg with heat and prssure when a part is to be molded. ▷ **treater**

prepreg basics Basic terminology: *cure methods*—vacuum bagging, oven, autoclave, and press; *manufacturing processes*—solvent, hot melt, and powder; *out time*—length of time prepregs can be handled at room temperature without losing properties (thermoset only); *product forms*—undirectional tape, fabric, and tow; *plastic flow*—movement or bleed of plastic that forces voids out of plies, measured by viscosity (thickness); *shelf life*—length of time prepregs can be freezer stored without losing properties (thermoset only); *voids*—entrapped bubbles of air/gas in laminate plies; and *wetout*—thorough saturation of fiber or fabric by matrix plastic.

prepreg flow control Flow measurements indicate plastic capabilities to fuse successive plies in a molding or laminate, and to bleed out any potential void producing gas reaction by-products. Flow is also an indicator of prepreg age or advancement. It is often desirable to optimize plastic content and tack to attain adequate flows. In some cases, flow is controlled by thickening additives in the plastic.

prepreg gel time An indicator for the degree of prepreg advancement. The useful life of prepregs is limited by the amount of staging or advancement. Most are formulated to attain a useful life of eight days or more at standard atmospheric conditions. The life can usually be prolonged by storage at −40°C (−40°F), but each time the prepreg is brought to equilibrium in the lay-up room temperatures, the useful life is shortened. Gel time measurements are used as quality control assurance verifications. Criteria based on those results determine whether or not to initiate more costly property testing or to dispose of an overage prepreg.

prepreg molding Techniques for locating and orientating them onto a molding surface in accordance with the RP design pattern are adapted to the tack and drape characteristics for the prepreg. The woven fabrics make possible uses of sewn stitches, staples, or clamps. Usually, the lay-ups are enlarged to provide allowances for trimming after the RP has been cured. Sometimes they are draped over male forms with weighted edges to draw the lay-ups snugly onto the molding surface prior to final cure. Very often, successful lay-ups depend on operators' skills to innovate.

prepreg out time The time a prepreg is exposed to ambient temperature, specifically, the amount of time it is out of the freezer. The primary effects of out time are a decrease in the drape and tack, as well as absorption of moisture from the air.

prepreg pucker Local stress on prepreg where the material has blistered and pulled away from the separator film or release paper (used to handle and store prepreg).

prepreg shop life The length of time prepreg remains usable at ambient temperature. A prepreg that has a storage life of 6 months at 0°C (32°F) might have only a 3-day shop life.

prepreg shrink tape ▷ **lagging**

prepreg tack control Tack is the adhesion characteristic which is controlled to facilitate lay-up operations. It is affected by plastic and inert volatiles contents, prepreg advancement, and the lay-up room temperature and humidity. Sometimes tack is increased by increasing plastic and volatile contents, retard prepreg advancement, or a slight increase in the lay-up room temperature. Prepregs with no tack are either excessively advanced or have exceeded their normal storage life, rendering the material useless. Certain plastics, such as silicones and some polyimides, can only be prepared with no tack.

prepeg tack primer Sticky, tacky thermoset plastic used to hold dry or nontack prepreg together during a molding operation.

prepreg tape Unidirectional prepreg tapes for laying onto or around a mold as in filament winding.

prepreg tape laying A fabrication process in which prepreg tape is laid side by side or overlapped to form a structure. ▷ **lagging** and **filament winding, angle wrap**

prepreg thermoplastic From the 1940s to about 1980, the only commercial prepregs were thermoset plastics, primarily TS polyesters. This TS remains the major plastic used now. Thermoplastic prepregs are available and used principally in stamping. ▷ **stamping**

prepreg volatile content Quality control tests do not distinguish inert from reactive volatiles, but are used nevertheless to establish volatile content values. They provide qualitative evaluations of prepreg advancements, degrees of volatilization of solvents, and degree of degradation due to aging. Volatile contents measured prior to lay-up are compared to values when the prepreg was first received. Such comparisons provide indications of excessive aging.

preservative An agent that prolongs the useful life of a material; applicable to plastics, foods, lubricating oils, textiles, etc. ▷ **antioxidant,** used in plastics.

press angle An angle press is a hydraulic molding press equipped with horizontal and vertical rams, and specially designed for the production of complex moldings containing deep undercuts.

press, block 1. A block press is used to mold very large blocks, such as 8 ft^3 (0.2 m^3), of polystyrene foam. **2.** A press used for the agglomeration of laminate squares under heat. The squares are cut from a laminated sheet and are superimposed so that they are perpendicularly crossed in order to reduce the anisotropy caused by laminating.

press clave A simulated autoclave made by using the platens of a press to seal the ends of an open chamber, providing both the force required to prevent loss of the pressurizing medium and the heat required to cure the thermoset laminate inside.

press, cold molding ▷ **cold press molding**

press, double ram A press for injection of transfer molding in which two distinct systems of the same kind (hydraulic or mechanical), or of a different kind, create respectively the injection or transfer force and the clamping force.

press fit Press fit, with its dependency on mechanical interface, provides a fast, clean, and economical assembly. A common usage is with plastic hub or boss accepting either a plastic or metal shaft or pin. The press fit operation tends to expand the hub creating a tensile or hoop stress. If the interference is too great, a very high strain and stress will develop.

press, floating punch A male mold member attached to the head of a press in such a manner that it is free to align itself in the female part of the mold when the mold is closed.

press, gravity closing In a down-stroke press, the closing motion is actuated by the weight of the ram and associated parts only.

press, hydraulic ▷ **hydraulic press**

press, impact ▷ **impact press**

pressing, isotactic ▷ **isotactic molding/pressing**

press platen, "book" opening The more conventional way for a press to operate is having platens that remain parallel from open to close to open positions. Like the way a book opens from its one side, there are presses that use this type action with the platens. Also called tilting press. It is used in different processes, such as compression, reaction injection, injection, etc. molding. It has been very popular since the 1930s in rubber compression molding.

press polish A finish for sheet stock produced by contact, under heat and pressure, with a very smooth metal which gives the plastic a high sheen.

press punching ▷ **punching press**

press, upstroke A hydraulic press in which the main ram is situated below the moving table, pressure being applied by an upward movement of the ram.

pressure Force measured per unit area. The Pascal (Pa) is the pressure or stress of one Newton per square meter (N/m^2) or pounds per square inch (psi). ▷ **pressure gauge**

pressure, absolute Pressure is measured with respect to zero in units of N/m^2 (Pa) (psi).

pressure, air at altitude ▷ **atmosphere chart** and **altitude chart**

pressure, ambient Pressure of the medium surrounding a product or object is at ambient.

pressure and stress unit The SI unit is the Pascal (Newton per square meter). Old gravitational units for *pressure* and *stress* such as kilogram-force per square centimeter (kgf/cm^2) should not be used. Other non-SI units such as bar and torr for pressure also should not be used per SI standards.

pressure bag molding If more pressure is required than what is available with the bag molding, a second envelope (or structure) can be placed around the whole assemblage and air pressure admitted between the inner bag and outer envelope (▷ **bag molding**) or between the inner bag and structure. Application of pressure (air, steam, or water) forces the bag against the part to apply pressure while the part cures. Use of this process includes producing seamless containers, tanks, pipes, etc. The Figs. below and on p. 584 provide examples of techniques used.

pressure blasting A method of deflashing is pressure blasting. This utilizes a stream of small pellets, usually crushed fruit pits, thrown at high speed at the molded parts that are tumbling over a continuous belt. The pellets, although hard, are not as hard as the molded part. This system can remove the flash from the surface of the molded parts, and from holes and other difficult areas to reach. Large parts are usually carried through the stream of pellets on a table which turns inside the unit.

pressure break In laminated plastics, a break in one or more outer sheets of the paper, fabric, or other base, which is visible through the surface layer of plastic that covers it.

pressure fabrication Compacting materials into a product by pressure.

pressure flow Flow brought about by the application of an external pressure to a fluid and in which the boundaries of the fluid are fixed and rigid, as opposed to a drag flow, caused by movement of boundaries. As an example, flow through a circular cross section pipe by the application of a pressure difference across its ends. Analysis of this example for a Newtonian fluid leads to the Poiseuille equation for the volumetric flow rate. For a non-Newtonian fluid, as with most plastic melts and solutions, the power law equation often provides a good model. Pressure flows are frequently found during flow in plastic processing in molds and dies. Also called *Poiseuille flow*.

pressure gauge Pressure is measured with respect to atmospheric pressure in units of N/m^2 (Pag) (psig).

pressure intensifier A layer of flexible material (usually a high temperature rubber) used to ensure the application of sufficient pressure to a

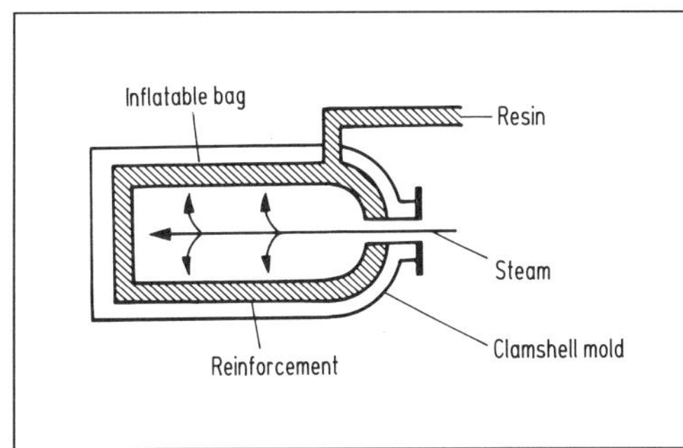

Example of pressure bag molding using an inflatable bag; lining the inside of a tank.

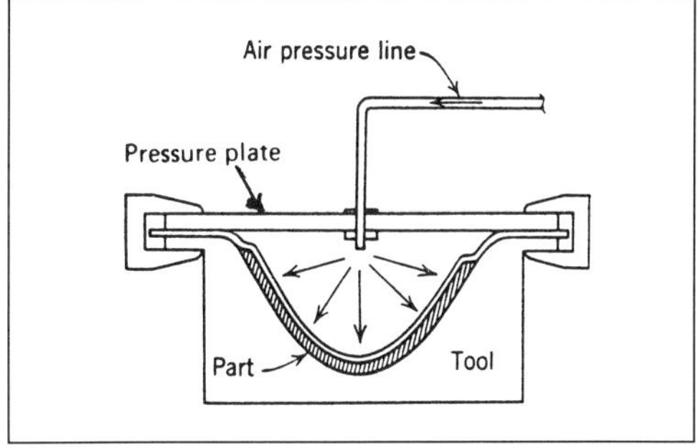

Example of pressure bag molding using an enclosed pressure plate structure.

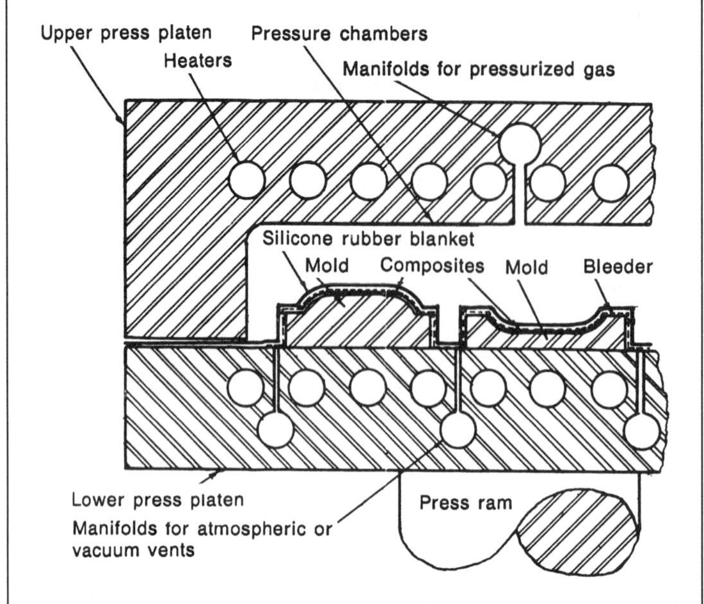

Press modification for pressure bag molding.

location, such as a radius, in a reinforced plastic lay-up being cured.

pressure molding ▷ **molding pressure**

pressure, negative Refers to vacuum pressure.

pressure, proof ▷ **proof pressure**

pressure roll In extrusion coating, a roll used to apply pressure to consolidate the substrate and the plastic film with which it has been coated.

pressure, saturation The pressure, for a pure substance at any given temperature, at which vapor and liquid, or vapor and solid, coexist in stable equilibrium.

pressure sensitive adhesive ▷ **adhesive bonded label**

pressure sensitivity Broadening molecular weight distribution of plastic increases the sensitivity of melt viscosity to changes in pressure. ▷ **molecular weight distribution**

pressure test ▷ **proof pressure**

pressure transducer ▷ **melt pressure transducer**

pressure, vacuum ▷ **vacuum pressure**

press vacuum ▷ **vacuum press**

preventative maintenance It is in your best interest to practice preventative maintenance on the equipment in your plant. Equipment is built to last, but proper maintenance will allow it to perform at its maximum output for the longest length of time. Ultimately, it is less expensive to maintain equipment than it is to replace it. Follow the information given in the machine service manual. Make regular machine checkups and maintenance a habit. A thoroughly carried out machine maintenance program will reduce downtime and operating costs as well as rejects of poor parts by customers. Therefore, periodic machine checkups and regular maintenance should become a habit in every processing plant. The machine operator or attendant will not always be able to do all necessary checking and maintenance steps. For maintenance of equipment such as the drive or instruments an electrician or instrument service people will be needed. Often the manufacturer will prescribe such things as the frequency of lubrication and what types of oil or grease to use. Such instructions should be followed faithfully. ▷ **lubrication**

preventing waste ▷ **recycling**

price ▷ **cost**

primary structure ▷ **structure, primary**

primer A coating applied to a surface, prior to the application of a plastic coating, adhesive, lacquer, enamel, etc. to improve the performance of a bond such as load carrying ability. Also called adhesive promoter.

printed circuit board An electrical or electronic circuit produced mainly from copper clad laminates; copper is etched to produce a circuit pattern on one or both sides. Also called circuit board or printed wiring board.

printer ▷ **computer printer**

printers' measurements The point and the pica are two units of measure universally used in printing in most English-speaking countries. Their use is primarily in typesetting. Type size is measured in points. Line length measure is in picas and points. The pica is used to express overall width or depth as well as the length of a line. ▷ **pica**

printing Methods of printing plastic materials, particularly thermoplastic film and sheet, have developed side by side with the growth of usage of plastics; they are an important part of finishing techniques. There are many different processes and techniques used. ▷ **gravure; flexographic printing; valley printing; silk screen printing; charge couple device; computer assisted makeup; dot; electronic dot generation; electronic printing; halftone photography; offset printing coating; lithographic resist printing; photochemistry; photography and photomechanics; photoimage; photomechanics; photopolymer coating; photopolymer plate; pica; pigment; plastic and rubber printing plates; printers' measurements; quick-setting ink; radiation curing ink; resist; roll leaf stamping; rubber plate printing; screen ruling; signature; spanishing; spectrophotometer; color matching; super quick-set infrared ink; toner; transparent ink; typesetting; vehicle; wysiwyg**

printing and varnish Varnish could be thought of as a variety of ink. It is either clear or tinted, glossy or dull, and it behaves on press much like ordinary ink. From the utilitarian viewpoint, it is a sealer that overprints ink and base sheet, helping to protect them from being scratched and scuffed. For design effects, gloss and dull varnishes are used independently or in combination. Applied overall, it can make a sheet sparkle or give it a smooth and satiny finish. As "spot varnish", it adds crispness to photography, brilliance to color, interest and clarity to charts and diagrams. When tinted, it may be substituted for ink. As a separate element in design, it creates dimensions that are simply not achievable in any other way.

printing, creating new dimension Think for a moment. Is there a particular booklet or container that stands out in your memory? Visualize it and try to recall just what feature or features have kept it with you. Could it be art work; photos; typography or design; unusual format or innovative printing effects? Whatever created that impression, whatever set this one piece apart from all those others that crossed your desk and were forgotten was clearly well worth the thought and effort it required.

printing ink A viscous to semisolid suspension of finely divided pigment in a drying oil such as heat-bodied linseed oil. Alkyd, phenol-formaldehyde, or other plastics are frequently used as binders. Cobalt, manganese, lead soaps, etc. are added to catalyze the oxidative drying reaction. Some types of inks dry by evaporation of a volatile solvent rather than by oxidation and polymerization of a drying oil or plastic. A large number of different plastics, varnishes, solvents, and pigments are now available to the ink makers. Inks may be formulated to give desired performance in the following respects: transparency, opacity, gloss, matte or satin finish, color stability, flexibility, freedom from residual odor, heat block resistance, iridescence, "glow", abrasion resistance, and resistance to alkali and acid, fats and oils, and/or water. Ink companies make special inks for given end uses, and often for specific presses.

printing plates ▷ **photopolymer**

printing surface preparation To develop proper bond with certain plastics, surface treatments, such as flame or electrical corona, are used based on plastic and type of ink used.

printing, thermoformed ▷ **thermoforming, preprinting**

problem solving In order to find unique, creative solutions to difficult challenges that were not resolved by past tried and true techniques, one must get away from the conventional state of mind that is often unimaginative, frustrating, repetitive, and negative. The nature of some problems tends to invite unimaginative suggestions and attempts only to use past approaches.

Problem solving in designing and producing products, as in business and personal problems, generally requires taking a systematic approach, If practical, make rather small changes and allot time to monitor the reaction of result. With whatever time is available, patience and persistence are required.

However, when a problem is particularly difficult or only limited time exists, consider a new and imaginative approach with techniques that previously generated creative ideas. First generate as many ideas as possible that may be even remotely related to the problem. During the idea generating phase it is of critical importance to be totally positive: no ideas are bad. Evaluation comes later, so do not attempt to provide creativity and evaluation at the same time; it could be damaging to your creativity. Look for quantity of ideas, not quality, at this point. Now all ideas are good; the best will become obvious later.

If possible, relate the problem to another situation and look for a similar solution. This approach can stimulate creative thinking towards other ideas. Try humor; do not be afraid to joke about a problem.

The next step is to evaluate all the ideas. Consider categorizing the list, then add new thoughts, select the best, and try them.

After all this action, if nothing satisfactory occurs, rather than give up look for that *really* creative solution—it is out there. You may be too close to the problem. Get away from the trees and look at the forest. Climb up one of the trees and look at things from a different perspective.

Use your creative talents but, again, be positive. You have now creatively worked through the frustrations and negativism that problems seem to generate. Your increasingly creative input will generate future opportunities.

Now let us take the thoughts above and improve on them. In doing so let us avoid saying in effect "My mind is made up—do not give me the facts". Rather, let us use the approach that there is always room for improvement. ▷ **statistical benefits**

process A process characterizes a fabricating method or production line, such as an extrusion blown film line or an injection molding machine.

processability This term does not have the same meaning to all processors. It describes quite generally the ease or difficulty with which a plastic can be handled during its fabrication into film, molded items, pipe, etc. A plastic with good processability is one which possesses the properties necessary to make it easy to process the plastic materials into the desired part. The main characteristics or properties which determine a plastic's processability are molecular weight, uniformity, additive content, and plastic feed rates.

However, it is usually thought of in terms of less tangible properties, which are a result of the basic properties above. In extrusion, for example, these characteristics include: draw-down (hot-melt extensibility), pressure and temperature sensitivity, smoking and odor, product stability during haul-off, and flow rate (which is an operating condition). There are other factors which some processors would add to the list. However, in many instances, it is not the plastic but unfavorable operating conditions which are reasons for inadequate plastic performance.

processability and molecular weight In simplified terms, it is convenient to state that processability is best at low molecular weight (MW), while properties of the finished product are best at high MW. Even though there are exemptions to this simple rule, it is sufficiently important to play a major role in the design for practical use such as: (1) the largest volume of plastic usage is based upon thermoplastic at a constant MW and this MW is chosen to represent the best compromise between processability and final part properties, and (2) on the other hand, the greatest variety of plastics and processes, particularly in thermosets, rubbers, and coatings, start with a low MW for easy processing and convert it into a high MW for best ultimate properties.

Processability in particular requires an optimum MW for each type of process technique being used. Stretching, orientation, and thermoforming involve the ability of a plastic film or fiber to withstand high mechanical stress and permit considerable elongation without failure and are thus best at quite high MW. Extrusion in the form of continuous profile requires sufficient strength so that the molten product coming from the hot die in the unsupported form will be strong enough to retain its shape until it is cooled to the point of substantial strength. In injection molding the melt final product is well supported on all sides by the cold mold and does not require such high melt strength, so all that is required is the lowest MW to provide optimum melt flow in the mold. Coating applications require all of the fluidity of adhesives (that uses a fairly low MW) but place fewer demands upon quick strength, and are therefore generally best carried out with a still lower average MW, most often obtained by the addition of large amounts of monomeric solvents. Thus each type of process technique involves its own optimum MW range for optimum processability. ▷ **molecular weight**

process aid ▷ **plasticizer**

process control Process controls for the individual machines and the complete fabricating line can range from unsophisticated to extremely sophisticated devices. They can have: (1) closed loop control of temperature and/or pressure, (2) maintain preset parameters for process, (3) monitor and/or correct machine operation, (4) constantly fine tune equipment, and (5) provide consistency and repeatability in the operations. Recognize that PC is not a toy or a panacea. PC demands a high level of expertise from the processor.

Examples of controls used with injection molding are seen in Figs. in ▷ **injection molding process control** and **mold process control.**

Based on the process-control settings, different behaviors of the plastic will occur.

Regardless of the type of controls available, the processor setting up a machine uses a systematic approach that should be outlined in the machine or control manuals. Once the machine is operating, the processor methodically makes one change at a time, to determine the result. Two basic examples are presented in Figs. shown with ▷**molding area diagram** and **molding volume diagram** to show a logical approach to evaluating the changes made with any processing machine. These examples refer to IM, as the injection molding machine is very complex with all the controls required to set it up. ▷**computer processing control** and **injection molding computer integrated**

process control and instrumentation Adequate ▷**process control** and its associated instrumentation are essential for product quality control. The goal in some cases is precise adherence to a control point. In other cases, maintaining the temperature within a comparatively small range is all that is necessary. For effortless controller tuning and lowest initial cost, the processor should select the simplest controller (of temperature, time, pressure, melt flow rate, etc.) that will produce the desired results.

process control basics Different degrees in process controls exist such as the open loop, monitor only, monitor and closed loop, and integrated machine and process control (see Figs. below and on p. 588).

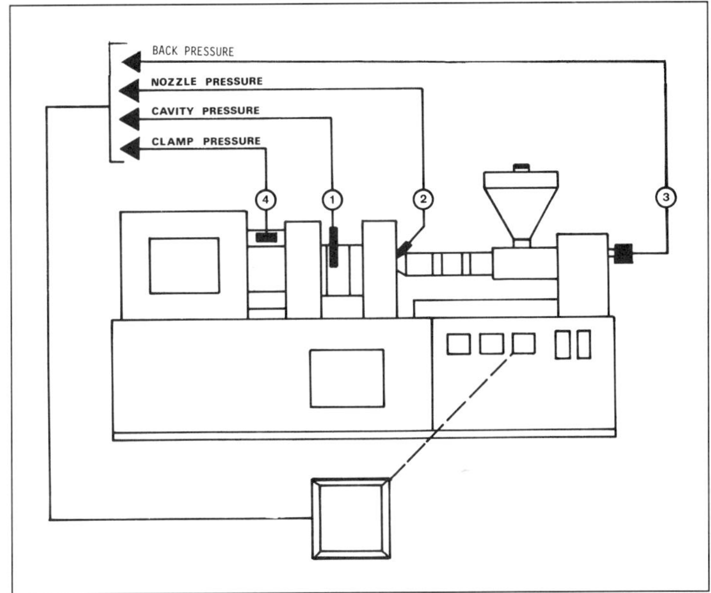

Example of open loop control.

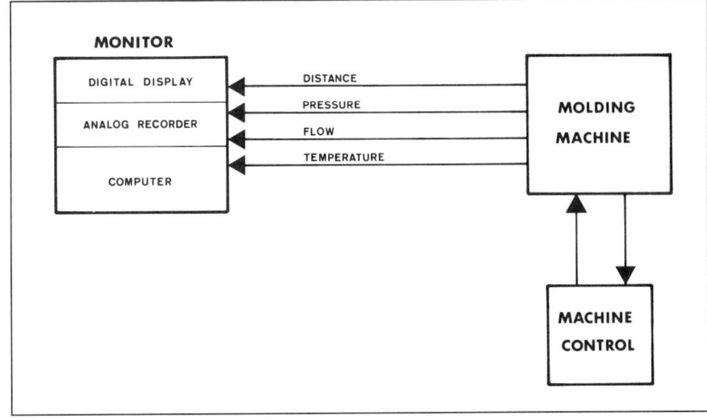

Example of monitor control only.

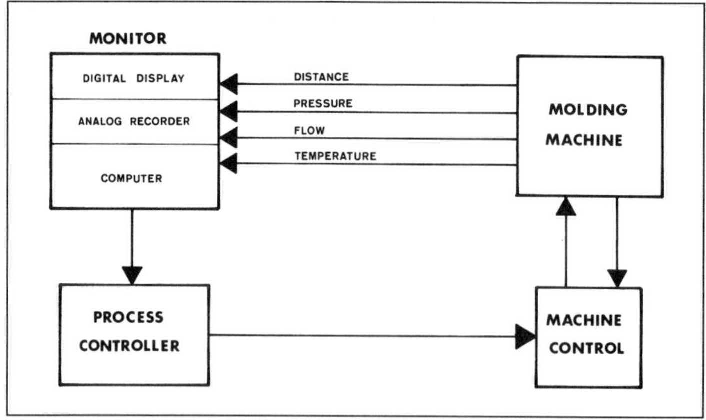

Example of monitor and closed loop control.

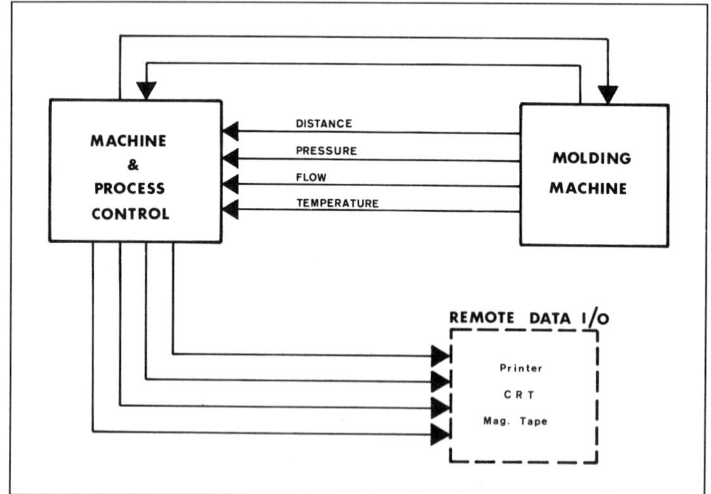

Example of integrated machine and process control.

process control problems Purchasing a sophisticated process control system is not a foolproof solution that will guarantee perfect parts. Solving problems requires a full understanding of their causes, which may not be as obvious as they first appear. Failure to identify contributing factors when problems arise can easily result in the microprocessor not doing its job. The conventional place to start troubleshooting a problem is with the basics—temperature, time, and pressure requirement limits. Often, a problem may be very subtle, such as a faulty control device or an operator making random control adjustments. Process controls cannot usually compensate for such extraneous conditions; however, if desired, they may be included in a program that provides the capability to add functions as needed.

Most controls, particularly the older ones, are the open loop type. They merely set mechanical or electrical devices to some operating temperature, time, and pressure. If this is all that is required, the control may remain in operation. However, this setup is subject to a variety of hard-to-observe disturbances that are not compensated by open loop controls. Thus process control must close the loop to eliminate the effect of process disturbances.

There are two basic approaches to problem solving: (1) find and correct the problem, applying only the controls needed; or (2) overcome the problem with an appropriate process control strategy. The approach one selects depends on the nature of the processing problem, and whether enough time and money are available to correct it. Process controls may, in most cases, provide the most economical solution. To make the right decision, one must systematically measure the magnitude of the disturbances, relate them to product quality, and identify their cause so that proper control action can be taken.

Before investigating in a more expensive system, the processor should methodically determine the exact nature of the problem, to decide whether or not a better control system is available and will solve it. For example, the temperature differential across a mold (for injection molding, etc.) can cause uneven thermal mold growth. The mold growth also can be influenced by uneven heat on tie-bars (uppers can be hotter, causing platens to bend—a change that could be reflected on the mold). Once the cause is determined, appropriate corrective action can be taken. (For example, if the mold heat has varied, perhaps all that is needed is to close a large garage door nearby, to eliminate the flow of air on the mold that has caused the problem; or it may be necessary just to change the direction of flow from an air conditioning duct.)

process control statistically ▷ **statistical process control**

processes ▷ **fabricating processes**

process flow diagram, basics Basically developing a process flow diagram requires a combination of experience (at least familiarity) of the process and a logical approach to meet the objective which has specific target requirements. As an example, to prepare a martini requires a graphic description of the process "road map" to get from one position to another position. The process to prepare a batch of martinis requires: formulation (ingredient ratio), raw materials (gin, vermouth, ice, and olives), equipment (graduated measure), mixer/stirrer, and glasses. A flow diagram is desired that must consider all aspects of the process highlighting gaps, contradictions, and outline on which to build further documentation. Manufacturing equipment requires utilities, space, capacity, special requirements, and size of work crew.

For any parameter that has a number value there must be a reliable determination procedure or "test method". Test methods can be of definite variety, very simple to complex, inaccurate to high accuracy, and unreliable to very reliable. Work done on any process or its output is only as good as the test methods. Test methods consist of procedures, equipment, calibration/standardization, traceability, and precision/accuracy. Fig. 1 summarizes how to make a martini; involves materials, quantities, equipment, and process step. The "finished product" description follows the customer's description, namely, a glass containing a chilled mixture of gin and vermouth with one or two olives. Customer is either satisfied or dissatisfied.

Preparation of flow diagram concerns no absolute technique, wide variety of personal choice, and standardization of layout, symbols (Fig. 2), and terminology. Fig. 3 on p. 590 is the production flow pattern that will meet large scale martini production, ready mixed, bottled martinis, just like mother used to make.

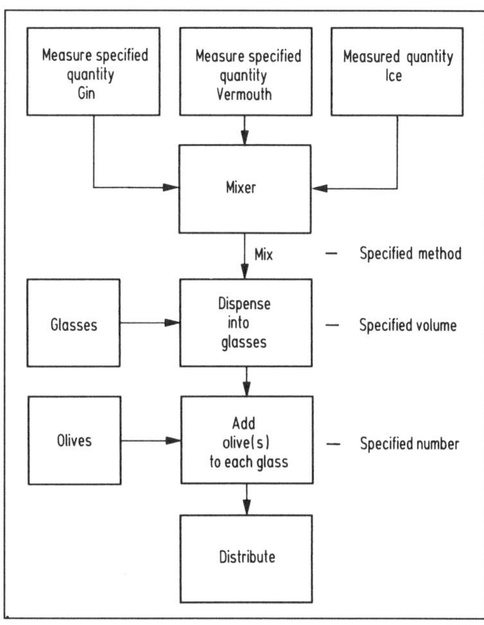

Fig. 1 Process flow.

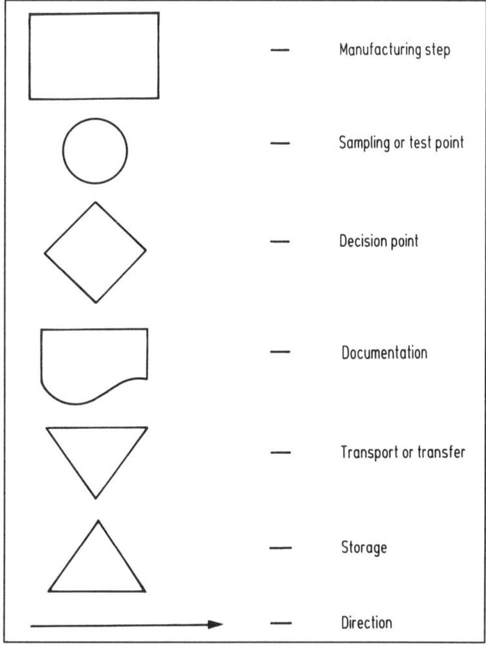

Fig. 2 Typical set of symbols.

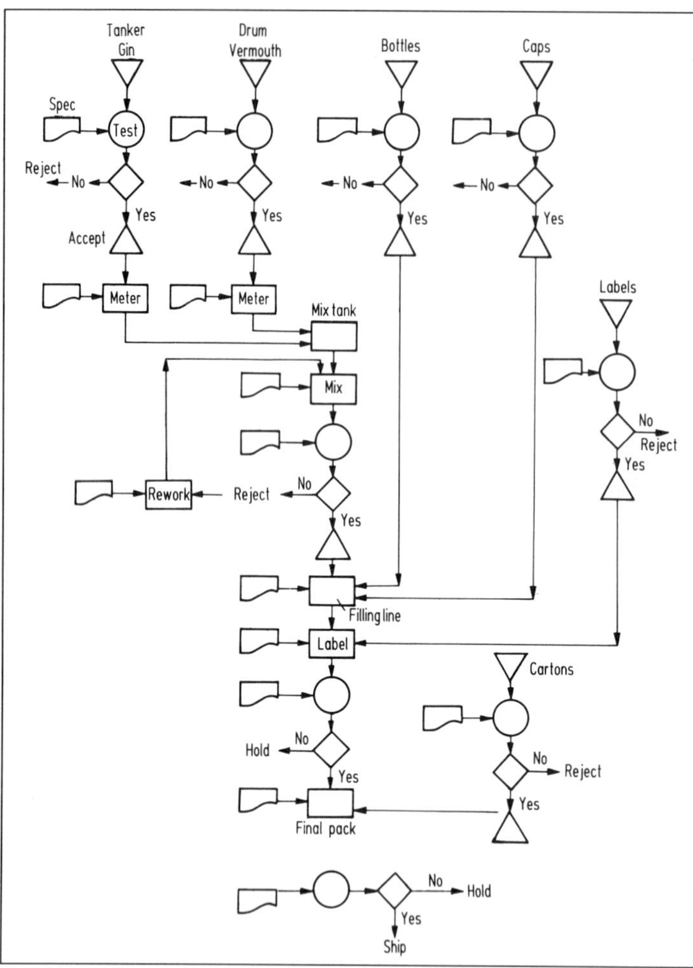

Fig. 3 Production process flow pattern.

Next analyze the process using the "fish bone" diagram (Fig. 4). A capability study is to be run on identifying how much you know about the process that is influenced by the raw materials process parameters. Often answers are not available on factors such as enough time, enough money or equipment needed for production, acceptable product produced, standard

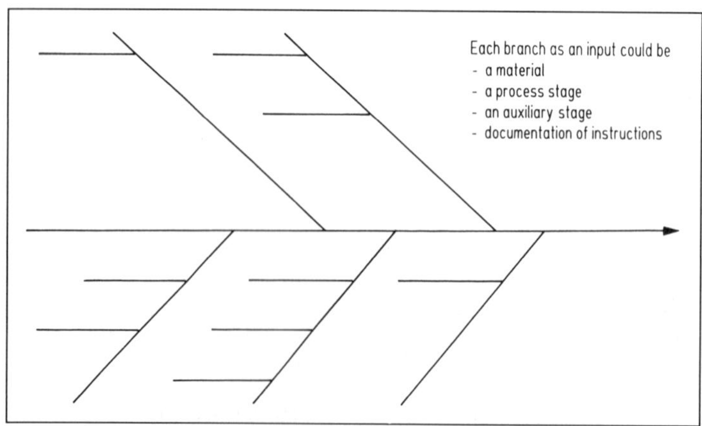

Each branch as an input could be
- a material
- a process stage
- an auxiliary stage
- documentation of instructions

Fig. 4 Typical fishbone diagram.

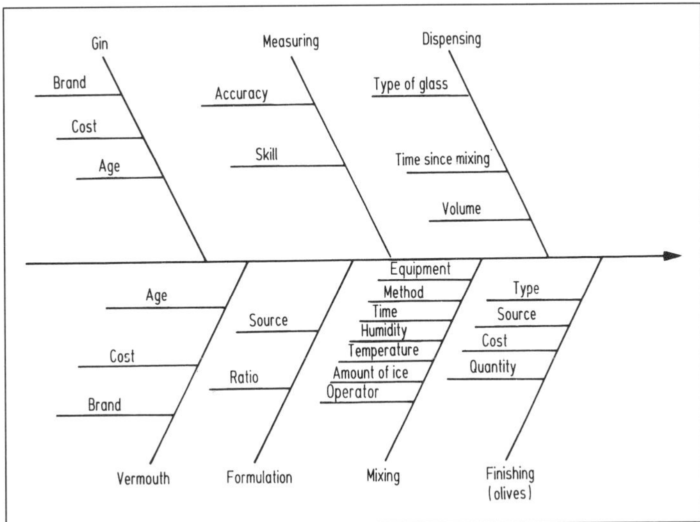

Fig. 5 Home martini mixing fishbone.

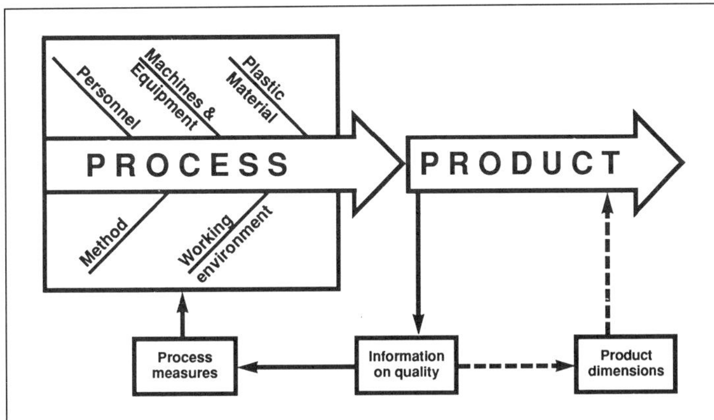

Fig. 6 Example of a simplified fish bone diagram applicable to fabricating an injection molded product.

costs were met, why defective parts were produced, was it important that process parameters shifted, and/or what influence did raw material source have on the process. To analyze the process requires identifying key parameters and determining parameter limits.

Final process analysis requires the complete process flow diagram (Fig. 3) and the completed fishbone diagram (Fig. 5). What one may have thought was a simple process resulted in a multi component diagram. In constructing the fishbone diagram: (1) include all factors, (2) do not prejudge inclusions, and (3) reexamine the diagrams, revise, add or delete ▷ **FALLO approach.** The final fishbone diagram is a cause/effect relationship as known at that time. Fishbone diagrams can be drawn for any process (plastics, etc.) no matter how complex (see Fig. 6). Diagrams will often point out factors or relationships that were unknown or ignored.

Cause/effect relationships can be summarized in a two-dimensional grid or "influence matrix" (see Table on p. 592). Each cause/effect relationship is indicated in the input/output grid as strong (S), moderate (M), weak, (W), none (N), or unknown (?). Variables can be classified as those that have a major influence or intermediates, finished products, yield, and cost. These variable classifications can be used to (1) establish areas for problem resolution, (2) set up control points, and (3) select characteristics to be used for (a) process control, (b) acceptable testing, and (c) capability studies. ▷ **process control; testing; zero defect**

processing The various processes discussed in this book (▷ **fabricating processes**) are used to fabricate all types and shapes of plastic products, ranging from household convenience packages to electronic devices and many others—including the strongest products in the

Martini mix influence matrix.[1]

Variables	Taste	Smoothness	Temperature	Thirst quenching
Gin				
Brand	S	S	N	M
Cost	W	W	N	W
Age	?	?	N	?
Vermouth				
Brand	S	S	N	M
Cost	W	W	N	W
Age	N	N	N	N
Formulation				
Source	S	S	N	S
Ratio	S	S	N	S
Measuring				
Equipment	M	M	N	M
Skill	S	S	N	M
Mixing				
Equipment	W	W	N	N
Method	W	?	N	N
AMT ice	M	W	S	S
Temperature	N	N	S	S
Humidity	N	N	N	N
Time	?	?	M	?
Operator	?	?	?	?
Dispensing				
Glass	W	W	W	W
Time since mix	?	?	S	M
Volume	N	N	W	S
Finishing (olives)				
Type	M	M	N	M
Source	W	W	N	W
Cost	W	W	N	W
Number	M	M	N	W

[1]S = strong; M = moderate; W = weak; N = none; ? = unknown.

world, used in space vehicles, aircraft, building structures, and so on. Proper process selection depends upon the nature and requirements of the plastic, the properties desired in the final product, the cost of the process, its speed, and the product volume. Some materials can be used with many kinds of processes, but others require a specific or specialized machine.

Practically all processing machines can provide useful products with relative ease, and certain machines have the capability of manufacturing products to very tight dimensions and performances. The coordination of plastic and machine facilitates these processes. This inter-facing of product and process requires continual updating because of continuing new developments in manufacturing operations. The information presented throughout this book should make past, present, and future developments understandable in a wide range of applications.

Most products are designed to fit processes of proven reliability and consistent production. Various options may exist for processing different shapes, sizes, and weights. Parameters that will help one to select the right options are (1) setting up specific performance requirements; (2) evaluating materials' requirements and their processing capabilities; (3) designing parts on the basis of material and processing characteristics, considering part complexity and size as well as a product and process cost comparison; (4) designing and manufacturing tools (molds, dies, etc.) to permit ease of processing; (5) setting up the complete line, including auxiliary equipment; (6) testing and providing quality control, from delivery of the plastics through production to the product; and (7) interfacing all these parameters by using logic and experience or obtaining a required update on technology.

processing aid During the conversion of plastic materials into desired parts, various melt-processing procedures are involved ▷ **fabricating processes.** The inherent viscoelastic properties of each plastic type can lead to certain undesirable processing defects, so additives are used to ease these processing related problems. Heat and light stabilizers, antioxidants, and lubricants are well defined, well established additives. Processing aids are another important plastic additive product. Processing aids can be made of small molecules, oligomers, or high molecular weight plastics (mixing).

processing aid, polyvinyl chloride After its initial synthesis in Germany, PVC remained an academic curiosity for a long time until the development of plasticizers in the early 1930s. They permitted PVC processing at temperatures below the degradation temperature, and soft, flexible, rubbery type products rather than rigid glass-like products. It was not until the 1950s and 1960s when the plastic industry was searching for a high temperature solid plasticizer that did not compromise the softening effect on the physical properties of PVC compounds that acrylic processing copolymers with very high molecular weights of from $1 \cdot 10^6$ to $5 \cdot 10^6$ were developed.

The initial efforts to improve the processing of rigid PVC by lowering the molecular weight of the plastic, copolymerizing with vinyl acetate, or the use of low levels of plasticizers were limited in use. Efforts to combine the favorable features of PVC/acrylic and methacrylic ester copolymers were first made in Germany and subsequently in the U.S. This work, however, did not lead to products competitive with vinyl chloride-vinyl acetate copolymers. Today the dominant commercial processing aid compositions are high molecular weight ($1 \cdot 10^6$ to $5 \cdot 10^6$) copolymers of methyl methacrylate (MMA) and alkyl acrylates [preferably ethyl acrylates (EA) or butyl acrylates (BA)] which MMA is the main component. The glass transition temperature of these plastics is generally greater than PVC.

processing and patience When making process changes (screw speed, zone settings, etc.), allow four time constants to achieve a steady state prior to collecting data.

processing, complete operation ▷ **FALLO approach**

processing considerations Basic considerations involve: (1) raw material costs generally exceed contemporary materials, (2) reinforced plastics usually are less dense than metallic materials, (3) optimize design for minimum life cycle costs, and (4) optimize design for minimum manufacturing cost by combining subassemblies into larger, complex single elements.

processing control optimization After the design of a control and the selection of controller types, the control parameters are developed. This can only take place with reference to the process characteristics. The transfer behavior of a circuit must be examined and described. However, only in a few cases can the process action be described from the physical statements with sufficient accuracy. Therefore, experimental methods are used, which produce easily adjusted controllers.

processing control via computer ▷ **computer processing control** and **microprocessor control**

processing equipment communication protocol ▷ **communication protocol**

processing equipment improvements New equipment nearly always offers potential or actual significant improvements in processing capabilities. Designers should always plan for the equipment they use to aid in meeting the goal of zero defects, as well as in reducing production costs. There are many "old" machines in operation, especially in the U.S., so in certain operations there could be ample room to improve and simplify plastics processing. In the U.S. there exist an estimated 80,000 injection-molding machines, 12,000 extruders, and 6,000 blow-molding machines. For each of these types of machines about 30% are under five years old, at least 35% are five to 10 years old, and the rest are more than 10 years old.

processing fundamentals ▷ **rheology; processing; process validation**

processing hygroscopic plastic When running hygroscopic hydrolytically degradable plastics, one way to determine if it is adequately dried is to look at the screw power during processing. If screw power (torque) reduced, then the plastic is being degraded; this reduction in molecular weight can be inferred by a reduction in the drive power.

processing in-line A complete fabricating, production, or fabricating operation that can go from material storage and handling, to produce the part that includes upstream and downstream auxiliary equipment, through inspection and quality control, to packaging, and delivery to destination such as warehouse bins or transportation vehicles. ▷ **computer processing control; FALLO approach; production line**

processing intelligent To remain competitive on a worldwide basic, processors must continue to improve productivity and product quality. What is needed is a way to cut inefficiency and the costs associated with it. One approach that promises to overcome these difficulties is called intelligent processing of materials. This technology utilizes new sensors, expert systems, and process models that control processing conditions as materials are produced, without the need for human control or monitoring.

Sensors and expert systems are not new in themselves. What is novel is the manner in which they are tied together. In intelligent processing, new nondestructive evaluation sensors are used to monitor the development of a material's microstructure as it evolves during production in real time. These sensors can indicate whether the microstructure is developing properly. Poor microstructure will lead to defects in materials. In essence, the sensors are inspecing the material online, before the end product is produced.

Next, the information these sensors gather is communicated, along with data from conventional sensors that monitor temperature, pressure, and other variables, to a computerized decisionmaking system. This "decisionmaker" includes an expert system and a mathematical model of the process. The system then makes any changes necessary in the production process to ensure the material's structure is forming properly. These might include changing temperature or pressure, or altering other variables that will lead to a defect-free end product.

There are a number of significant benefits that can be derived from intelligent processing. There is, for instance, a marked improvement in overall product quality and a reduction in the number of rejected products. And the automation concept that is behind intelligent processing is consistent with the broad, systematic approaches to planning and implementation being undertaken by industries to improve quality.

It is important to note that intelligent processing involves building in quality rather than attempting to obtain it by inspecting a product after it's made. Thus, industry can expect to reduce post-manufacturing inspection costs and time.

Being able to change manufacturing processes or the types of material being produced is another potential benefit of the technique. Also, the technology will help shorten the long lead time needed to bring new materials from R&D to mass production. While much effort has gone into applying this technology to advanced materials, it also holds promise in making such conventional materials as steel and cement.

processing machines ▷ **fabricating processes**

processing methods ▷ **fabricating processes**

processing modeling ▷ **designing with model, processes**

processing off-line Includes use of secondary equipment after product has been fabricated and requires additional work such as painting, inserts, and bonding.

processing optimized ▷ **computer-aided manufacturing**

processing plant, automated The Figs. below and opposite show automotive injection molded part produced at high speed automatically inline; Battenfeld equipment located in Plastimat Produkt plant.

processing plant safety ▷ **safety**

View of an automated processing plant.

Automotive part produced in the automated production line.

processing reinforced plastics ▷**reinforced plastics**

processing residence time ▷**residence time**

processing rules to remember and forget Even though the example that follows concerns injection molding, it can be adapted to other processes.

Rules to Remember: (1) Injection molding is the marriage of machine, mold, material, process, and operator, all working together in a constant cycle. (2) The plastics business is a profit-making business, not a charitable organization. (3) Heat always goes from hot to cold through any substance at a fixed rate. (4) hydraulic fluids are pushed, not pulled, at a rate that depends on pressure and flow. (5) The fastest cycle that produced the most parts uses: (a) minimum melt temperature for fast cooling; (b) minimum pressure for lowest stress; (c) minimum time—fast fill, fast cool, fast and early ejection, minimum delay between cycles. (6) All problems have a logical cause. Understand the problem, solve it, and them allow the machine to equalize its cycle to adjust to the change. (7) If it doesn't fit, don't force it.

Rules to Forget: (1) If a little bit does a little good, a whole lot does a whole lot of good. (2) If you twist enough knobs, the problem will go away. (3) The machine has a mind of its own. (4) It takes a genius to operate a molding machine. (5) All problems are caused by bad part design, bad tooling, or bad setup. (6) My job is secure.

processing salt bath ▷**salt bath**

processing trends Because melts have many different properties and there are many ways to control processes, detailed and factual predictions of final output are difficult. Research and hands-on operation have been directed mainly at explaining the behavior of melts or plastics with other materials (steel, glass, etc.). Modern equipment and controls continue to overcome some of the unpredictability. Ideally, processes and equipment should be designed to take advantage of the novel properties of plastic rather than to overcome them.

processing window The range of processing conditions, such as temperature, pressure, shear rate, etc. within which a particular grade of plastic can be fabricated in a specific machine with optimum or acceptable properties by a particular fabricating process (extrusion, etc.). The processing window for a particular plastic part can vary significantly with the design of the part and the mold or die, with the fabricating machinery used, and with the severity of product performance requirements. The window sets up maximum and minimum limits on the process controls. ▷**molding area diagram** and **molding volume diagram**

process measurement and control ▷**microprocessor control**

processor, captive These are fabricating operations of manufacturers who make their own part rather than have a custom molder produce them. Different reasons exist for this action, such as to improve profit, avoid potential single source supplier, control delivery, etc.

processor, contract Usually considered a subgroup to the custom processor; they have little involvement in the business of their customer. In effect, they just sell machine time.

processor, custom Also called job shops. They make parts for other manufacturers to use in their products. They may be involved, to varying degrees, in the design of the part and mold or die, have a choice in material selection, and in general assume a reasonable level of responsibility for the parts.

processor, proprietary These are operations where the fabricator makes a product for sale directly to the public under their own name.

process, plastic, product interrelation ▷**plastic, process, product interrelation**

process selection Basically for a given part, the most important processing requirements should be determined based on the plastic to be processed, the quantity, and the dimensions of size and tolerances.

process timer A clockwork or electronic timing device for switching an electrical circuit at a predetermined time.

process validation An aspect of early application of GMPs (▷ **good manufacturing practice**) that receives minimal attention is process validation (PV). However, the concept of PV is receiving close attention when existing or planned GMP programs are evaluated or examined by government regulatory agencies and also when sub-contracting any plastics to be processed into end items. FDA definition for PV is a documented program which provides a high degree of assurance that a specific process will consistently produce a product meeting its pre-determined specifications and quality attributes. Elements of validation are product specification, equipment and process qualifications (installation, performance and ranging trials), timely revalidation, and documentation. ▷ **testing; process control; quality control**

product, customized ▷ **custom product**

product design ▷ **computer-aided design/computer-aided manufacturing; design; FALLO approach**

production line The Figs. under ▷ **auxiliary equipment** show production line setup where the first step in planning a plant layup is to set up material flow path from incoming plastic to finished product shipment for each product.

production, mass ▷ **mass production**

production performance A vital step in product design is to determine if it will be capable of performing the task for which it is being designed, and what level of safety factor is available. This requires analysis, testing, or both. The key area on which most analysis is focused is the mechanical load bearing function for both tensile and compressive stresses. Valuable design equations are available in standard texts on designing with plastics and reinforced plastics and the mechanics of materials can often be applied, based on the product geometry. They can yield excellent predictions of short-term (dynamic) loading capabilities, as well as long-term (creep related) approximations. A key factor is to anticipate the extremes of temperature that can be encountered, especially high temperatures. Generous safety factors may be required in order to compensate for a variety of factors that can reduce the allowable load under extreme conditions. ▷ **design safety factor**

production quality level ▷ **quality level, acceptable**

production rate Parts per time, such as hours, produced by the machine.

production scale-up ▷ **scale-up**

production scheduling and control The process of developing one production schedule can be quite simple. All one need do is: (1) determine what needs to be made, (2) assign the orders to the proper work stations, and (3) sequence the orders according to need. However, different factors could have influences, such as those reviewed in ▷ **process flow diagram, basics**

production shake out A condition when producers drop out of a market. It is usually caused by a short interruption of the growth trend in a particular industry. It usually follows a hectic period of production.

productivity The measure of the amount of output, in either goods or services, per unit of input. The higher the productivity, the higher the output versus input.

productivity, set plant in order A manufacturing company is a system made up to the "complete molding operation". Its maximum productivity can only be gained if the whole system works effectively and efficiently. Also, the whole system must be responsive to change, and it must evolve and improve with time. But today's approach to manufacturing automation treats manufacturing as a conglomeration of individual systems like inventory, purchasing. shop control, and accounts payable. Indeed, there are over 50 individual areas of manufacturing that can be profitably automated. The problem is to get everything to play together—to integrate the piece into a whole that is larger than the sum of the pieces.

Across all manufacturing systems, there is only one basic common denominator—data. Planning for manufacturing automation must focus on data as the key to systems integration. Only in this way can manufacturing engineers and management avoid the problems of integration as an after-the-fact phenomenon of almost impossible magnitude. This is especially true if management intends to buy standard software to perform individual system functions. Data requirements definition is indispensable to successful automation planning.

The natural outcome of data requirements planning is a data base definition. This definition—if it is properly developed—can first be implemented on a data-base management system (DBMS) and then interfaced with a multitude of current and future application systems needed by the users. The problem is to get a good data requirement definition first. To do so, it is important to understand the basic business processes that this data must support, and then to extrapolate a precise definition of the data requirements.

Be aware that bringing a new high-tech machine into a poorly managed environment will only guarantee that it too will suffer the same delays and mishandling as the ones already in place.

What makes the difference? It all boils down to management controls. If the machines can achieve an uninterrupted transition from shift to shift and continue to run through rest and lunch breaks, they are indeed in a position to attain their optimum potential. On the other hand, if the machines shut down 15, 20 or even 30 minutes before the end of the shift for report writing, clean-up or lack of incentive with a 15 minute or so delay in getting started on the next one, lost momentum and output can never be regained. Similarly for idle break periods.

Despite the growth and prosperity of the plastics industry many "wrong turns" have been made to produce parts that result in added expenses and usually limited use of the product. There is a tendency to jump from "theory to theory" while supposedly solving each molding problem as it arises rather than evaluating the entire system to see why the problem existed in the first place. There is a practical approach in resolving these problems: a logical back-to-the-basics approach, as reviewed in this book, can be used.

product liability Responsibility assignment for product failure. ▷ **risk management**

product liability law Two types of law are involved in product liability lawsuits, namely contract and tort. A *contract* is an agreement between two or more parties which is enforceable in a court of law. Warranties, either expressed or implied, are a part of the contract of sale of property at the time of sale. Lawsuit for breach of warranty are based on contract law, since there is a contractual relationship between the parties.

A *tort* is a civil wrong committed by the invasion of any personal or private right which each person enjoys by virtue of federal and state laws. The personal or private right affected must be one that is determined by law rather than by contract. In addition to the tortious act, there must also be personal injury or property damage.

Over half of the states have adopted to varying degrees the doctrine of *strict liability tort*, which means that the injured person need only prove that a product was unreasonably dangerous to win his case. Proof that the manufacturer of the product is negligent is no longer required. Under the doctrine of strict liability, *contributory negligence* by the injured party is not an effective defense. Contributory negligence means that the injured party acted in a careless and unreasonable manner while using the product.

While contributory negligence is no longer applicable in most states, some form of *comparative negligence* has been adopted in a majority of states. This concept apportions the award on the basis of the degree of negligence or fault of the parties.

Statutory enactments by some state legislatures declare that if a product does not injure a person within a period of 5 years from the date of manufacture, it is presumed to be free from defect unless the injured party can prove otherwise. The burden of proof that the product was defective lies with the injured party.

It is apparent that product liability law, as with all laws, will vary somewhat from state to state. In all probability the lawsuit will be tried in the state where the injury occurred, which gives the plaintiff's attorney a decided advantage. The Consumer Product Safety Act is a federal law and therefore does not present the same problems of variance from state to state.

product life cycle All products fit into a life cycle, where time periods are estimated by facts, logical evaluation, or both. The Fig. provides an example. ▷ **life-history curve**

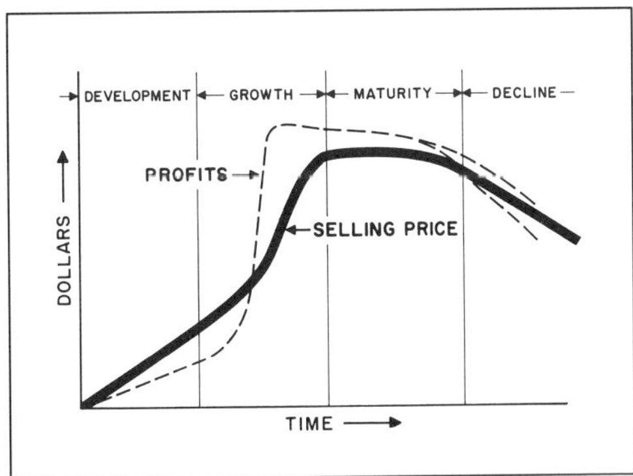

Life of a product.

product, plastic, process interrelation ▷ **plastic, process, product interrelation**

product release The Fig. on p. 598 relates to an appoach concerning product release, which is the final stage in product design.

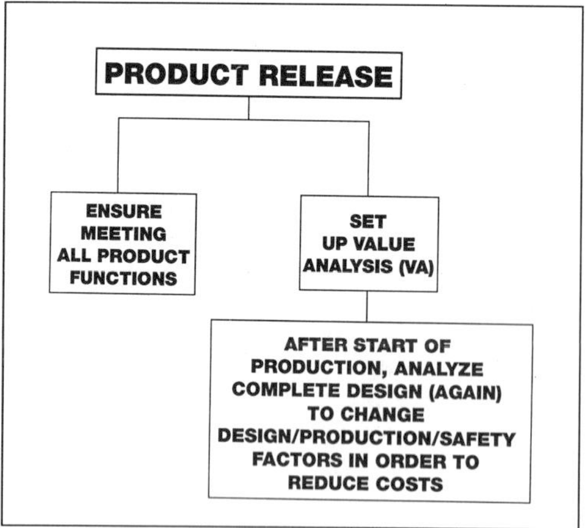

Product release targets.

product shape Both shape and design details are heavily process related. The ability to mold ribs, for example, may depend on material flow during a process or on the flowability of a resin reinforced with glass. The ability to produce hollow shapes depends on the ability to use removable cores, including air, fusible or soluble solids, and even sand. Hollow shapes can be produced using cores that remain in the part, such as foam inserts in RTM or metal inserts in IM.

The geometric symmetry of a part can also influence process selection. For example, an axis of symmetry in a long, narrow part may suggest selecting an extrusion or pultrusion process. Similarly, the need for hollow sections in the part could suggest blow molding or rotational molding. In order to handle materials that melt, flow, and solidify quickly, it is necessary to use a mechanical process such as injection molding, which as a process could still be limited by the time available with the particular machine in question to fill the mold cavity before the melt solidifies; thus, high pressures are used to increase the speed of mold filling.

Each process has certain characteristics that can be summarized by determining whether (1) its ribs and bosses are feasible, depending on whether one or both sides of the part reproduce the tool (mold) surface; (2) the sequence of material injection or some other process and tool closure allows of having deep vertical sections in the surface wall; (3) the material's viscosity is high enough to allow the use of slides and cores in the tool without their being gummed up with material flowing into the slide mechanism; (4) hollow sections or containers are feasible; and, finally, (5) whether hollow or foam-filled box sections can be produced to increase section stiffness.

product size Part size is limited by a process's pressure and the available equipment, whereas the ability to achieve specific shape and design detail is dependent on the way the process operates. Generally, the lower the processing pressure, the larger the part that can be produced. Other restrictions are the size of the equipment that is available, the length of flow, and the material's reaction time. With most labor-intensive methods, such as hand lay-up, slow-reacting TSs can be used and there is virtually no limit on size. With some processes, size is limited only by the size of the equipment that is either available or can be produced. A general guide to practical processing thickness limitations is (in in.): injection molding, 0.02 to 0.5; extrusion, 0.001 to 1.0; blow molding, 0.003 to 0.2; thermoforming, 0.002 to 1.0; compression molding, 0.05 to 4.0; and foam injection molding of 0.1 to 5.0.

The functions and property characteristics of a part will be largely determined by the performance requirements and materials selected for fabrication. The basic requirement of the process is its capability of handling a suitable material. For example, if a major function requirement is for resistance to creep under high loads, it is probable that a long-fiber RP will be necessary, which would immediately eliminate such processes as blow molding and conventional injection molding.

product specification Tolerances on dimensions should be specified only where absolutely necessary. Too many drawings show limits on size when other means of attaining the desired results would be more constructive. For example, if the outside dimensions of certain drill-housing halves were to have a tolerance of ± 0.008 cm (0.003 in.), this would be a tight limit. Yet if half of the housing were to be on the minimum side and the other on the maximum side, there would be a resulting step that would be uncomfortable to the feel of the hand while gripping the drill. A realistic specification would call for matching of halves so as to provide a smooth joint between them, with the highest step not exceeding 0.002 in. The point is that limits should be specified in such a way that those responsible for the manufacture of a product will understand the goal that is to be attained. Thus we may indicate "dimensions for gear centers," "holes as bearing openings for shafts," "guides for cams," and so on. This type of designation would alert a mold maker as well as the molder to the significance of the tolerances in some areas and the need for matching parts in other places and the clearance needed for assembly in still other locations.

product update Tradeoffs exist between coming up with a new design and providing incremental improvements to an existing one to keep a product up to date. A new design usually avoids the constraints imposed by the incremental approach, but it can be costly in terms of time and resources. However, if a company continues the incremental approach too long, the entire concept runs the risk of becoming obsolete.

product weight test Controlling product weight "tightly" permits better control of fabricating the part performancewise and costwise. Both overweight and underweight can pose defect problems specific to variation.

profile ▷ **extruder profile** and **die profile**

profile shape A section other than regular rod, bar, plate, strip, or flat wire; may be oval, half oval, half round, triangular, pentagonal, or of any special cross section furnished in lengths.

profit ▷ **economic efficiency and profitability**

profitability studies, functions They have two functions: the evaluation of alternative investments with the aim of determining the most profitable, and checking of the economic success of investments which have been implemented. The earlier a profitability study is carried out in the planning process, the sooner the prospects for success of a planning alternative or the projected investment as such can be estimated. This makes clear which alternatives are worth pursuing. Unnecessary planning work, because its prospects of success are low, can thus be avoided, and decisions on investments can be taken earlier. ▷ **sales investment turns**

profit plan Formalization of actions leading to the attainment of profit goals. ▷ **product life cycle; FALLO approach; economic efficiency and profitability**

program A set of instructions that "tells" exactly what to do, how to do it, and when. A very popular example is the ▷ **computer software menu**. Also called software.

programmable controller ▷ **computer programmable**

programmable controller safety Guarding of safety circuits are used in programmable controllers (PCs). The purpose is to establish a procedure for the guarding of OEM supplied safety circuits on machines equipped with programmable logic controllers. It is well known that programmable controllers offer substantial freedom and flexibility in the design and modification of logic circuitry. Also, it is imperative that OEM supplied circuitry incorporated for the protection of the machine operators not be subject to modification or deletion by the end user. For this reason programmed safety circuitry must be guarded against access by the end user to prevent inadvertent or intentional safety circuit alterations.

The following two methods can be suggested as a means of accomplishing protection of safety circuits: (1) *External guarding* can be accomplished by supplying all hard wired safety circuits external to the PC in addition to the internal programmed circuits. Thus, the modification of the PC program or failure of the memory cannot compromise the operation of the safety circuits supplied by the manufacturer, and (2) *Internal guarding* of safety circuits could be supplied such that the safety circuit addresses are confined to a non-programmable portion of the memory. Since this memory cannot be accessed by the end user, modification to these circuits is not possible.

Certain design criteria should be followed when using programmable controllers. Applications of PC requires careful consideration of their advantages, disadvantages, and limitations. External guarding of OEM supplied safety circuits should be done in addition to the internally programmed safety logic. PCs are now used as a cost effective means of manipulating inputs while offering an extended degree of reliability in the control system. The following considerations should be observed when utilizing programmable logic controllers: (1) Standards, practices and codes normally observed in the design of electro mechanical systems should also be used in circuit designs for PC. (2) Documentation of logic programs and records must be retained by the equipment manufacturer for future reference and use. (3) The following "sounds and engineering practices" should be observed when using PCs: (a) The motor starting interlock devices should not be subject to a failure of the PC. (b) All pilot devices should be wired from a common bus and fed through a master relay contact. (c) The AC power supply to the PC should give the programmable logic controller sufficient time to stabilize all voltages prior to the pump motor(s) being started. (d) All outputs from the programmable controller should be correctly fused with fast blow rectifier fusing. (e) The AC feed to all output modules should also originate off the incoming bus so that the output solenoids cannot be energized until the master relay contact has been closed. (f) All double solenoids should be interlocked with each other in the logic program. (g) Solenoid suppression may be added as required

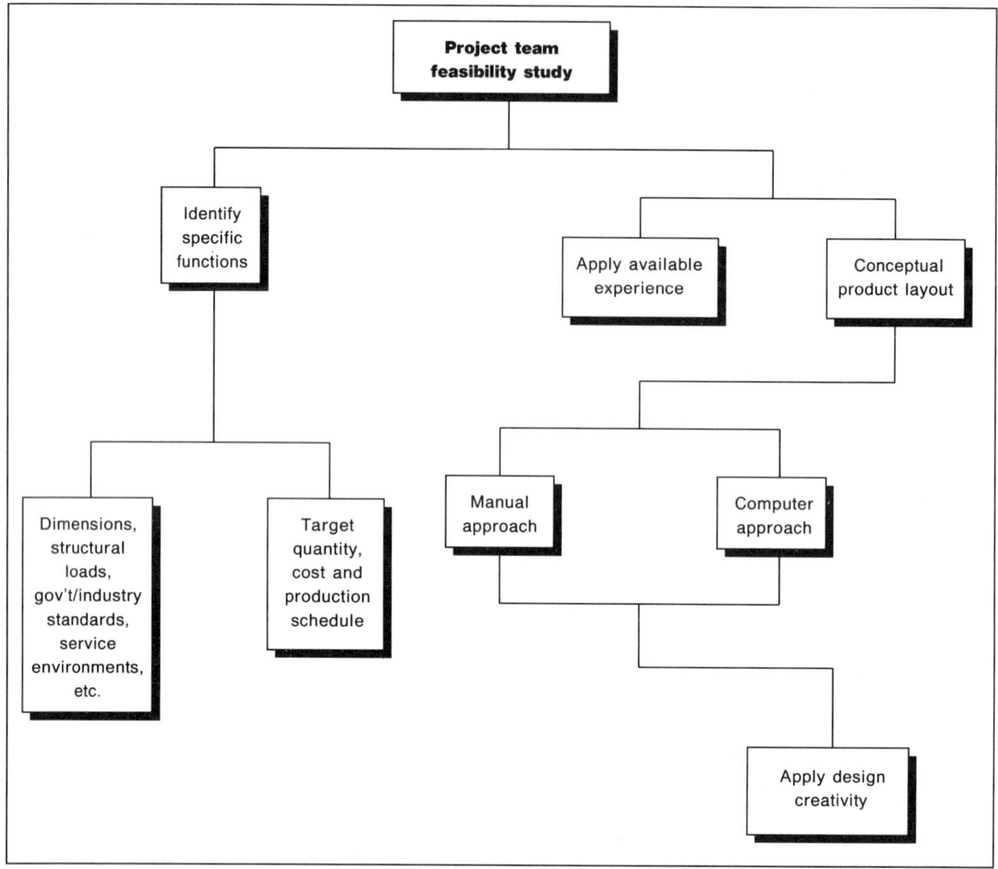

Project team block diagram.

by PC manufacturer. ▷ **safety interlock** and **computer accessibility**

programmable logic Microprocessor controller used on controller fabricating equipment to coordinate various parameters such as temperature, pressure, output rate, and other relationships to maximize quality and efficiency of operation. ▷ **logic**

programmed parison ▷ **blow molding extruder parison programmer**

programmer The person who writes a program.

programming die ▷ **die ring, static and dynamic**

progress ▷ **sales people**

project team The Fig. above relates to an approach concerning a feasibility study for a project team, which is the start of a product design. ▷ **computer-aided design/computer-aided manufacture**

promoter ▷ **accelerator**

promoter, adhesive ▷ **adhesive promoter**

proof To test a component or system at its peak operating load or pressure.

proof pressure The test pressure that components must sustain without detrimental deformation or damage. It is used to give evidence of satisfactory manufacture and/or material quality.

proof stress ▷ **stress, offset yield strength**

propellant **1.** A rocket fuel. **2.** A compressed gas used to expel the contents of containers in the form of aerosols. Chlorofluorocarbons were once widely used because of their nonflammability. The possibility that they contribute to depletion of the ozone layer of the upper atmosphere has resulted in prohibition of their use for this purpose. Other propellants used are hydrocarbon gases such as butane and propane, carbon dioxide, and nitrous oxide. ▷ **chlorofluorocarbon**

propeller mixer Devices comprising a rotating shaft with propellor blades attached. Used for mixing relatively low viscosity dispersions and holding contents of tanks in suspension.

properties, allowables ▷ **A-basis, B-basis, S-basis,** and **typical-basis**

properties and applications The average engineer, chemist, physicist, designer, etc. doing practical work with plastics still must work primarily by trial and error. When organic polymer chemists and chemical engineers synthesize a new plastic, they may predict that it will have properties which will lead to certain applications. But when they actually complete their study, they often find that these properties were obtained from quite different types of polymer structure and led to quite different types of practical applications.

When the product engineer and industrial designer want to make a new product, they may predict that it should have certain properties and that these should be obtained from particular polymer structures; but, when they have finally completed the successful commercial development of the new product, they may find that it ultimately required entirely different properties which were obtained from wholly different structures.

properties and molecular structure ▷ **molecular arrangement structure**

properties, colligative Properties based on the number of molecules present. Most important are certain solution properties extensively used in molecular weight characterization.

properties, specific Material properties divided by material density.

properties versus theoretical ▷ **data, theoretical versus actual properties**

property characterization There are many techniques available to the processor, quality controller, etc. They can be used from the time that materials (plastics, additives, color, etc.) arrive in the plant, during the time that the materials are processed, to control regrind performance, and for quality control from start to finished product. Most of the testing performed continues to be predominantly mechanical rather than analythical. Based on the most pervasive trend in analytical instrumentation with increased computerization, more analytical testing is being conducted.

propionate plastic ▷ **cellulose propionate plastic**

proportional - integral - derivative Pinpoint temperature accuracy is essential to be successful in certain fabricating processes. An example is in runnerless injection molding, particularly with engineering plastics. In order to achieve it, microprocessor-based temperature controllers use a proportional-integral-derivative (PID) control algorithm acknowledged to be the most accurate in tuning gate heaters to process variations. The unit will instantly identify varying thermal behavior and adjust its PID values accordingly. Other benefits include savings in management and maintenance activity and energy savings (eliminates the cycling around setpoint normally associated with ineffectively tuned instruments). ▷ **temperature controller**

proportional law ▷ **definite proportions law**

proportional limit The greatest stress which a material is capable of sustaining without any deviation from proportionality of stress-strain (Hooke's law). These values vary greatly with the sensitivity and accuracy of the testing equipment, eccentricity of loading, the scale to which the stress to strain diagram is plotted, and other factors. When accurate determination is required, the procedure and the sensitivity of the test equipment should be specified.

proportional type temperature controller ▷ **temperature controller**

proportioning pump ▷ **gear pump**

proportioning tolerance interlock A device that prevents continuance of the proportioning cycle when a component quantity varies outside of a preset range.

proprietary molder ▷ **processor, captive**

propyl compound Derivatives in which one hydrogen atom of propane has been replaced.

propyleneoxide rubber PROR does not crystallize in its atactic form and has a low glass transition temperature of −72°C (−98°F). Its copolymer with allylglycidylether (AGE) allows conventional vulcanization. It has excellent dynamic properties (resilience, etc.).

propylene plastic Plastics based on polymers of propylene or copolymers of propylene with other monomers, the propylene being the greatest amount by mass, such as polypropylene plastic.

prostheses Plastics, such as UHMW-PE and other polyethylene compounds, reinforced carbon polysulfone, etc., are important in the growing use of artificial joints such as fingers, wrist joints, elbows, ankles, etc; particularly hips and knees.

protocol The rules of information exchange. ▷ **telecommunication system**

protocol, communication ▷ **communication protocol**

protocol, Montreal ▷ **chlorofluorocarbon**

proton A fundamental unit of matter having a positive charge. They are constituents of all atomic nuclei, their number in each nucleus being the atomic number of the element in the Periodic Table.

prototype A model suitable for use in the complete evaluation of form, design, performance, and material processing. ▷ **model; modeling stereolithography; computer-aided design; computer modeling**

prototype mold A simplified mold (usually a single cavity) routinely used when part quantity requirements are low; used for molding new products for the testing of the product or the mold itself. It may be made from a light metal casting alloy, an epoxy plastic, or an RTV silicone rubber ▷ **design mold**. Prototype die is also applicable within this definition. ▷ **design die**

Prussian blue ▷ **blueing off**

pseudo-elastic design method ▷ **designing with pseudo-elastic method**

pseudonym plastic ▷ **plastic and definition**

pseudoplastic Materials in which viscosity decreases with rate of shear, but the material deforms as soon as shearing stress is applied. This class of materials has the greatest industrial applications, since all high polymers and polymer melt follow this behavior. ▷ **viscoelasticity**

pseudoplasticity ▷ **non-Newtonian flow; dilatancy;** and **extruder melt flow properties**

psychrometer A wet-and-dry bulb type hygrometer. Considered the most accurate instruments practical for industrial plant use for determining relative humidity.

psychrometry drying ▷ **drying, psychrometry**

P-T diagram A two-dimensional graphic representation of phase relationships in a system of any order by means of the pressure and temperature variables.

P-T-X diagram A three-dimensional graphic representation of the phase relationships in a binary system by means of the pressure, temperature, and concentration variables.

public opinion and relations The plastic industry, like other industries, has had the important project to keep the public, government officials, and educational institutions up to date on the facts concerning plastics to beat the unfortunate situation with some of the public who say "Do not give me the facts, my mind is made up". ▷ **environment and public opinion** and **plastic bad and other myths**

pucker ▷ **prepreg**

puckering, film ▷ **extruder film cooling roll versus quench tank**

pug mill A granulating machine whose essential components are a shaft equipped with blades or arms with hardened tips rotating in a trough-like compartment.

pulp A form of cellulose obtained from wood or other vegetable matter by prolonged cooking with chemicals.

pulping Disintegration of wood (mechanically or chemically) into its fibrous components.

pulp molding The process by which a plastic impregnated pulp material is preformed by application of a vacuum and subsequent molding or oven curing.

pulp, paper Processed cellulose fibers into paper. ▷ **mechanical nonwoven fabric**

pultrusion In contrast to extrusion, the process by which a combination of liquid plastic and continuous fibers is pulled continuously through a heated die (also use cellophane or other film wrap) of the shape required for continuous profiles as shown in the Figs. here and on pp. 603 and 604. Reinforced plastic shapes

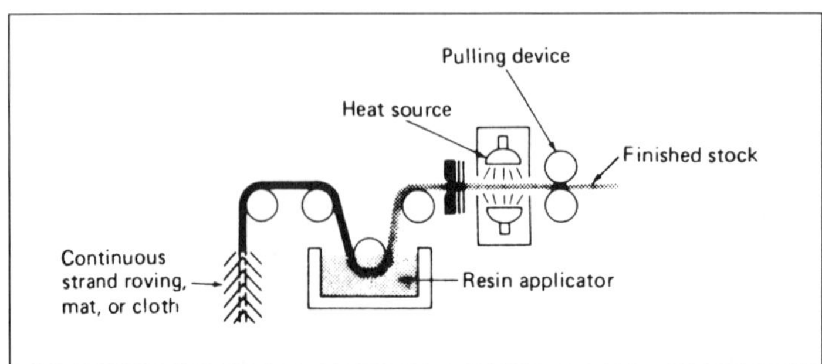

Simplified schematic of continuous pultrusion.

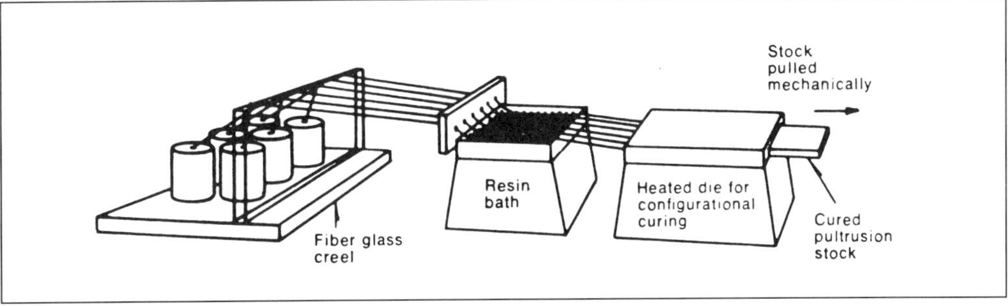

Pultrusion using a die.

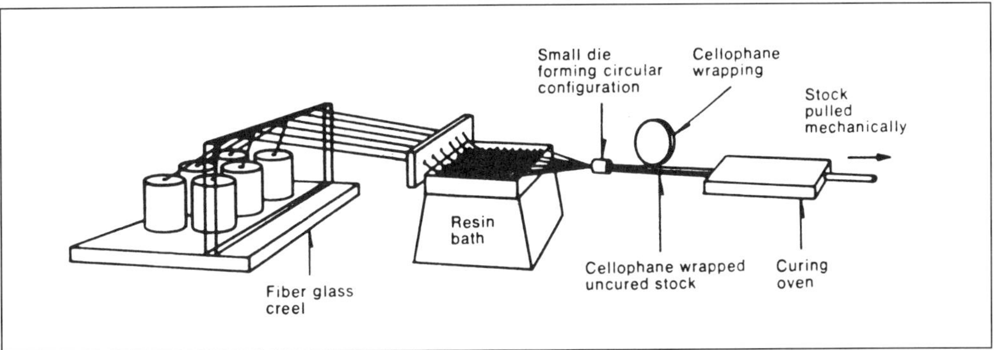

Pultrusion using cellophane.

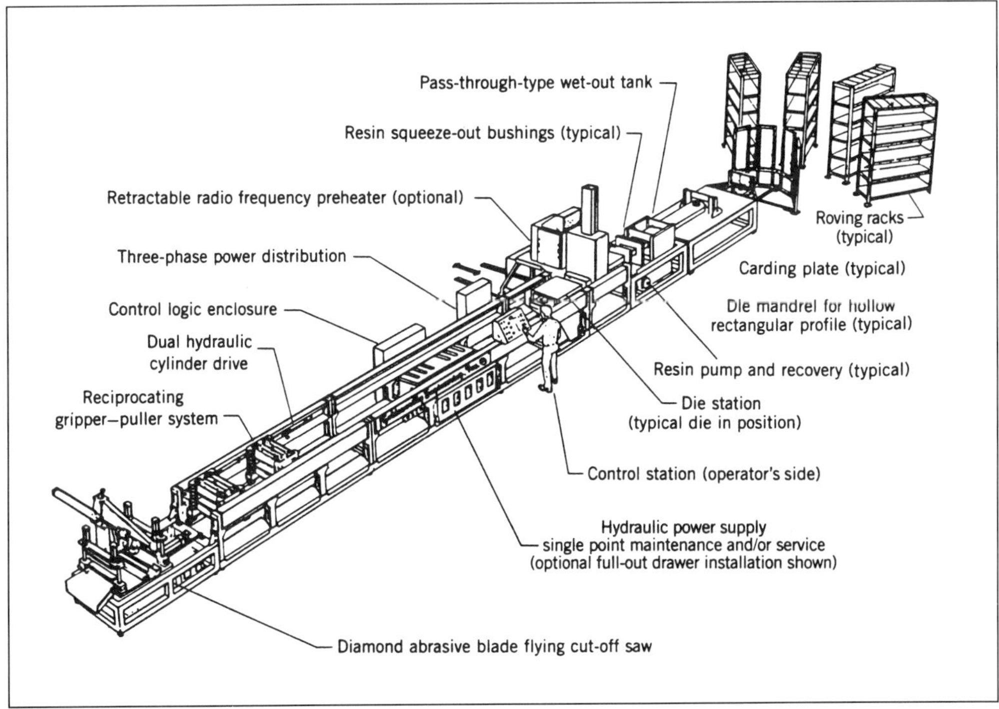

Example of complete pultrusion line.

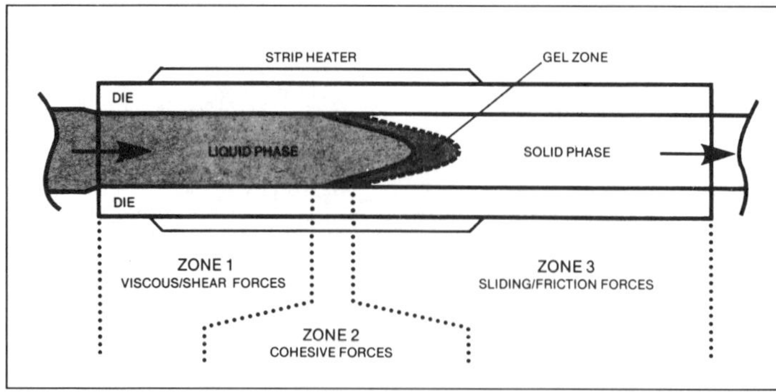

Chemical reaction kinetics in the heated die, represented in this schematic model, are critical in pultrusion of thermoset plastic curing reaction.

include structural I-beams, L-channels, tubes, angles, rods, sheets, etc. The plastic most commonly used is TS polyester with fillers. Other plastics such as epoxy and polyurethane are used where their properties are needed. Longitudinal fibers are generally continuous glass fiber rovings. Glass fiber material in mat or woven form is added for cross-ply properties.

There are six key elements to a pultrusion process, three of which precede the use of the pultrusion machine. The line starts with a reinforcement handling system (referred to as a creel, as used in a textile weaving operation), a plastic impregnation station, and the material forming area. The machine consists of components designed to heat, continuouly pull, and cut the profiles to a desired length. With machines producing profiles, line speeds range at least from 1 to 15 ft/min (with large to small cross sections) (0.005 to 0.075 m/s).

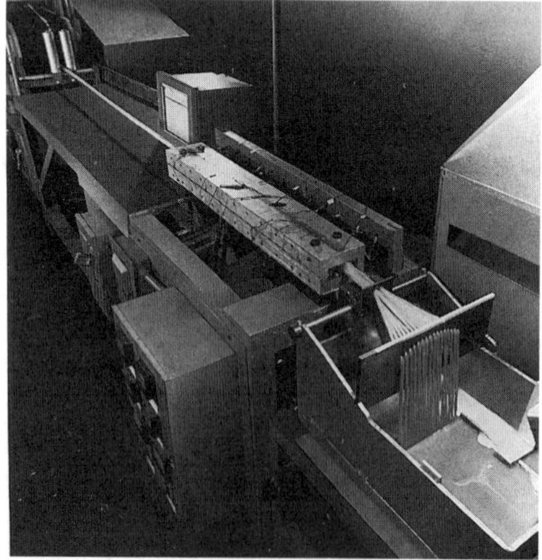

Glass roving reinforcement liquid plastic impregnation station (right side), followed with electrically heated die, and the solid, cured rod exiting through the two guide rolls.

The process starts when reinforcements are pulled from the creels and through a resin bath where they are impregnated with formulated/mixed resin. In some operations, previously resin-impregnated reinforced tapes replace the creel and bath stations. The resin impregnated fibers are usually preformed to the shape of the profile to be produced. This reinforced plastic then enters a heated steel die that has been precision-machined to the final shape of the part. Wheel pullers, clamps, or other devices continuously pull, and when the profile exits the die/mold, it is cured. The profile finishes its cooling in ambient air, water, and/or forced air as it is continuously pulled. The product emerges from the puller mechanism to be cut to the desired length by an automatic device such as a flying cutoff saw.

Control devices must be used to ensure that the proper plastic impregnation occurs and is held within the required limits. Simple devices, such as "doctor" rolls or squeeze rolls, are usually sufficient. It is important to control the plastic viscosity. The most difficult part to set up is the shape of the opening in the die/mold. Experience and/or trial and error are required.

pultrusion, black marking Black smudges on the surface of a pultruded product that result from excessive pressures in the die when the pultrusion is rubbing against it or unchromed die surfaces, and that cannot be removed by cleaning or scrubbing, or by wiping with solvent.

pultrusion bow A condition of longitudinal curvature in pultruded parts.

pultrusion chip Minor damage to a pultruded surface that removes material but does not cause a crack or craze.

pultrusion die parting line ▷**die parting line**

pultrusion dwarf width A condition in which the crosswise (to direction of pultrusion) dimension of a flat surface of the part is less than that which the die would normally yield for a particular reinforced plastic. The condition is usually caused by a partial blockage of the pultrusion die cavity caused by buildup, or particles of the composite adhering to the cavity surface. This condition is also called a lost edge, when the flat surface has a free edge that is altered by the buildup.

pultrusion exposed underlayer The underlayer of mat or roving not covered by surface mat in a pultrusion. This condition can be caused by reinforcement shifting, too narrow a surface mat, too wide an underlying mat, uneven slitting of the surface mat, necking down of the surface mat, or excessive tension in pulling the surface mat off the spindle.

pultrusion fiber bridging Reinforcing fiber material that bridges an inside radius of a pultruded product. This condition is caused by shrinkage stresses around such a radius during cure.

pultrusion fiber prominence A visible and measurable pattern of the reinforcing material on the surface of a pultruded plastic part.

pultrusion flats A longitudinal, flat area on a normally convex surface of a pultrusion, caused by shifting of the reinforcements, lack of sufficient reinforcement, or local fouling of the die surface.

pultrusion glassiness A glassy, marbleized, streaked appearance at the pultruded surface. Although this condition is visually evident, reinforcement is in fact fully encapsulated with the plastic.

pultrusion shrinkage cracks internal Longitudinal cracks in the pultrusion that are found within sections of roving reinforcement. This condition is caused by shrinkage strains during cure that show up in the roving portion of the pultrusion, where transverse strength is low.

pultrusion sluffing An occurrence during the pultrusion process in which scales peel off or become loose, either partially or entirely, from pultrusion. Not to be confused with scraping, prying, or physically removing scale from a pultrusion. Sluffing is sometimes spelt sloughing.

pultrusion star craze Multiple fine pultrusion surface separation cracks that appear to emanate from a central point and that exceed 6.4 mm ($\frac{1}{4}$ in.) in length, but do not penetrate the equivalent depth of a full ply of reinforcement. This condition is often caused by impact damage.

pultrusion wrap seam A depression or step in the surface finish caused by the lap of the flexible mold or carrier strip after it is removed from the cured pultrusion.

pulverizing Utilizing a variety of size reduction or granulating methods to pulverize plastics, including the specialized techniques of cryogenic grinding and air-jet milling. Fine, free-flowing powders can be used in techniques such as rotational molding, plastic compounds, reinforced plastics, adhesives, etc. to improve performance.

pumice A highly porous igneous rock, used in pulverized form as a filler for plastics and an abrasive. It usually contains 67 to 75 wt% of SiO_2 and 10 to 20 wt% of Al_2O_3.

pumicing A finishing method for molded plastic parts, consisting of the rubbing off of traces of tool marks and surface irregularities by means of wet pumice stones.

pump forepressure **1.** In leak testing, the total pressure on the outlet side of a pump measured near the outlet port. Sometimes called back pressure, outlet pressure, or discharge pressure. **2.** In discussing the action of a vapor jet, term forepressure may be used to designate the total pressure of the gas against which the jet impinges.

punch Part of a die or compacting tool set which is used to transmit pressure to the powder in the die cavity.

punched hole burr Jagged edge around a punched hole caused when the punch goes through the material. These jagged edges appear on the bottom side as punched. ▷ **cutting burr-free**

punching press Method of producing parts, such as electrical components, from flat sheets or laminated plastics by punching out shapes by means of a die and punch. Also called clicker press.

puncture test A test for measuring the resistance of a material to puncture; also strength of material, primarily involving tear and stiffness. ▷ **bursting strength; compression test; drop weight test; Elmendorf tear test**

purging Basically the cleaning of one color or type plastic from the cylinder of a plasticator. Purging has always been a necessary evil, consuming substantial amounts of materials, labor, and machine time, all nonproductive. In IM

Guidelines for purging agents.

Material to be purged	Recommended purging agent
Polyolefins	HDPF
Polystyrene	Cast acrylic
PVC	Polystyrene, general-purpose, ABS, cast acrylic
ABS	Cast acrylic, polystyrene
Nylon	Polystyrene, low-melt-index HDPE, cast acrylic
PBT polyester	Next material to be run
PET polyester	Polystyrene, low-melt-index HDPE, cast acrylci
Polycarbonate	Cast acrylic or polycarbonate regrind; follow with polycarbonate regrind; do not purge with ABS or nylon
Acetal	Polystyrene; avoid any contact with PVC
Engineering resins	Polystyrene, low-melt-index, HDPE, cast acrylic
Fluoropolymers	Cast acrylic, followed by polyethylene
Polyphenylene sulfide	Cast acrylic, followed by polyethylene
Polysulfone	Reground polycarbonate, extrusion-grade PP
Polysulfone/ABS	Reground polycarbonate, extrusion-grade PP
PPO	General-purpose polystyrene, cast acrylic
Thermoset polyester	Material of similar composition without catalyst
Filled and reinforced materials	Cast acrylic
Flame-retardant compounds	Immediate purging with natural, non-flame-retardant resin, mixed with 1% sodium stearate

(extrusion, blow molding, etc.), sometimes it is necessary to run hundreds of pounds of plastic to clean out the last traces of a dark color before changing to a lighter one. Sometimes there is no choice but to pull the screw for a thorough cleaning. Although there are few generally accepted rules on how to purge, the following tips should be considered: (1) try to follow less viscous with more viscous resins; (2) try to follow a lighter color with a darker color resin; (3) maintain the equipment; (4) keep the materials handling equipment clean; and (5) use an intermediate resin to bridge the temperature gap (such as that encountered in going from acetal to nylon), and use a PS as a purge.

Ground/cracked cast acrylic and PE-based materials are the main purging agents, but others also are commercially available for certain machines and materials. Cast acrylic, which does not melt completely, is suitable for virtually any plastic. About one pound for each ounce of injection capacity will be needed (5–10 lb/in. of screw diameter in an extruder). With extruders, special conditions and preparations are required, which suppliers of the purging compound can recommend (remove dies, screen packs, etc.).

PE-based compounds usually contain abrasive and release agents. They are used to purge the "softer" TPs (polyolefins, styrenes, some PVCs, etc.). With extruders, many of the requirements/restrictions do not apply.

These purging agents function by mechanically pushing and scouring residue out of the machines. Others also apply chemical means. The Table above provides information on purging.

purification Removal of extraneous materials (impurities) from a substance or mixture by one or more separation techniques. A pure substance is one in which no impurities can be detected by any experimental procedure. Though absolute purity is impossible to attain, a number of standard procedures exist for approaching it to the extent of 1 ppm or impurity of less.

push-pull molding ▷ **injection molding push-pull**

putty A mixture of whiting (chalk) with 12 to 18 wt% of linseed oil, with or without white lead or other pigment. Containers must be air tight. Use includes sealants, glass settings, and caulking agents. Plastic materials such as silicones, vinyls, urethanes, etc. are also prepared and used in these applications. The plastic putties usually provide much more stability, longer life, and permanent color and set, etc.

putty body A paste-like mixture of plastics, usually TS polyester, and a filler such as talc, used to repair surfaces on auto bodies, boats, etc. It is usually called bulk molding compound (BMC), particularly when containing glass fiber reinforcements.

putty, bouncing Bouncing putty is a soft, plastic-like material which is perhaps best known as a novelty item sold commercially as nutty putty, crazy putty, or silly putty; developed during the 1940s. Chemically, it is a boron-containing silicone, and it has the surprising property of rebounding when dropped on a hard surface. In fact there are compositions that bounce under a free-fall higher than the initial height.

P-V diagram A graphical representation of the variation of the specific volume of a substance, with change in pressure.

P-V-T diagram A three-dimensional graphic representation of a surface, describing the variation of the specific volume of a substance, with independent change of pressure and temperature. ▷ **kinetic theory**

P-X diagram A two-dimensional graphic representation of the isothermal phase relationships in a binary system; the coordinates of the graph are pressure and condensation.

pyncometer ▷ **dilatometer**

pyrogenic silica ▷ **silica, synthetic**

pyrolysis **1.** An old technology of decomposing organic materials at high temperatures such as 540 to 1,080°C (1,000 to 2,000°F). **2.** In waste handling combustion facilities, decomposition caused by heat in an oxygen deficient atmosphere. **3.** Produce fibers such as carbon and graphite.

pyrolyzation Chemical change brought about by the action of heat, such as carbonization.

pyrometer Practically speaking, all thermocouple activated devices are called pyrometers. They consist of a readout device and sensor.

pyrophoric material Any liquid or solid that will ignite spontaneously in air at about 54°C (130°F).

pyrrone plastic Polyimidazo-pyrrolones synthesized from dianhydride and tetramines, soluble only in sulfuric acid, resistant to temperatures up to 600°C (1,110°F).

Q

quadruple curve In a P-T diagram, a line representing the sequence of pressure and temperature values along which three conjugate phases occur in univarient equilibrium.

qualification test A series of tests conducted by the procuring activity to determine conformance of materials, or material systems, to the requirements of a specification which normally results in a qualified products list (QPL) under the spec.

qualified products list QPL is a list of commercial products that have been pretested and found to meet the requirements of a specification, especially a government specification.

qualitative analysis An analysis in which some or all of the components of a sample are identified. ▷ **quantitative analysis; chemistry, analytical; infrared spectroscopy**

qualitative chemical analysis Analysis to determine the chemical nature of the constituents of a material, irrespective of their amounts.

quality **1.** A manufacturing term reflecting variation from a norm when the norm represents the absolute specifications (such as weight, size, appearance) of the part being manufactured. **2.** An aspect, attribute, characteristic, or fundamental dimension of experience, which involves variation in kind rather than degree. **3.** The composite of those characteristics that differentiate among individual units of a product and have significance in determining the degree of acceptability of that unit by the user.

quality and control Quality in products begins with good design, which in turn allows for simplifying selection of tests. Unfortunately, so often product design projects start with little appreciation for a good problem statement, an identification of requirements and objectives, and a reasonable schedule that includes all company functions involved. Most of all, what is usually lacking is a complete understanding of the end-user of the product, system, and/or environmental design being considered. ▷ **FALLO approach**

quality and management ▷ **total quality management**

quality and training ▷ **educational information**

quality assurance All planned and systematic actions necessary to provide adequate confidence that a product or facility will perform satisfactorily in service. Note that QA includes quality control, quality evaluation and design assurance. A good quality assurance program is a coordinated system, not a sequence of separate and distinct steps. ▷ **ISO 9000 certification**

quality assurance test A test in a program which is conducted to determine the quality level.

quality auditing There are occasions when organizations have a documented quality assurance program that includes an audit program. A quality assurance program usually contains three tiers of documentation: the quality assurance manual, system-level procedures, and instructions. The purpose of an audit program is to evaluate the existence and adequacy of the QA program and ensure that the manufacturer's operations are in compliance with it.

Putting a program in writing does not ensure that it will be followed, nor does it, in and of itself, provide the feedback necessary to correct and update programs and processes. The audit fills both these gaps. By monitoring porduct, process, and system, and by rat-ing performance against a predetermined scale the auditor determines the need for corrective measures.

quality control Those quality assurance actions which provide a means to control and measure the characteristics of materials, products, processes, and/or facilities to establishd requirements. As an example, although care is taken by materials manufacturers to assure consistency, subtle variations exist in their products. In most general applications, these variations have little effect on finished part properties, but in more stringent cases, these irregularities can present problems. To simplify the task of asssuring that the physical properties of a system are in specification, simple techniques can be used in incoming, on-process, and outgoing quality control. Use of these procedures by companies concerned with maintaining critical properties can keep a tight rein on product quality and provide documented qualification. ▷ **statistical quality control; just-in-time; plastic variability**

quality control and testing ▷ **testing and quality control**

quality control on-line via IR measurement The ability to record IR spectra of plastic melts provides perspectives for process monitoring and control in manufacture and processing. Precise information on quality can be obtained rapidly. Furthermore, it is also possible to make measurements on unstable intermediates of importance. Although spectroscopy on melts is considerably different from that on solid materials, this does not limit the information content. IR has for many years been an important aid to investigating the chemical and physical properties of molecules. It gives qualitative and quantitative information on chemical constituents, functional groups, impurities, etc. As well as its use in studying low molecular weight compounds, it is used with equal success for characterizing plastics. It is a highly informative method for applying testing.

quality control statistically ▷ **statistical quality control**

quality control test An in-plant test that is conducted on a given test frequency to determine whether product is in accordance with the appropriate specification(s).

quality factor 1. The ratio of elastic modulus to loss modulus, measured in tension, compression, flexure, or shear. This is a nondimensional term and is the reciprocal of tan delta. **2.** The reciprocal of the dissipation factor when applied to insulating materials. (This term in the past has been called storage factor).

quality indicator, image In industrial radiology, the image quality indicator (IQI) is a device or combination of devices whose demonstrated image or images provide visual or quantitative data, or both, to determine radiological quality and sensitivity. Also known as a penetrameter. It is not intended for use in judging size nor establishing acceptance limits of discontinuities.

quality level, acceptable Acceptable quality level (AQL) is a quality of product (expressed as percent defective), such that a lot having this percent defective will have a probability of rejection by the purchaser. An ideal sampling and inspection plan would accept all lots of this or better quality and reject all lots of lower quality. Any practical plan can approach this ideal. AQL is the process average at which the risk of rejection is called the producer's risk.

quality management ▷ **ISO 9000 certification**

quantitative analysis A measure in which the amount of one or more components of a sample is determined ▷ **qualitative analysis**

quarter polymer Composed of four different kinds of polymers.

quarter wave plate A device used with a polarizer and analyzer designed to produce circularly polarized light.

quartz Natural crystallized silicon dioxide (SiO_2) which, when ground, is used in plastics as a filler or additive.

quartz fiber The word quartz can denote any high purity glass, but usually are those fibers produced from high purity (99.95% SiO_2) natural quartz crystals. The crystals are formed into rods from which filaments having 1/5th the diameter of human hair are drawn. Up to 240 filaments are combined to form a flexible, high strength fiber that can be made (for reinforced plastics) into yarn and then woven into fabric. All textile forms (including chopped fiber, mat, rovings, cordage, sleeving, tapes, and fabrics) are available (see Fig. on p. 610).

Glass is an amorphous material that is neither solid or liquid; it does not possess either the crystalline structure of solids or the flow characteristics of liquids. Chemically, glass is comprised of a silica (SiO_2) backbone in the form $(SiO_4)_n$ polymer. However, silica by itself, that is quartz, requires an extremely high temperature for liquefaction and drawing. Therefore, modifiers are needed to reduce temperatures to workable levels as well as to obtain molten glass viscosities suitable for drawing. These modifiers are selected for their contribution to both glass properties and manufacturing capability. Quartz fibers retain virtually all of the characteristics and properties of solid quartz; however, they also have many of the properties of glass fibers and are extremely flexible. ▷ **glass; glass fiber production; silica fiber**

quasi-isotropic ▷ **reinforced plastic, directional properties**

quench A method of rapidly (shock) cooling principally thermoplastic fabricated parts as soon as they are removed from the mold, extruder pipe line, etc. This is generally done by submerging the parts in water. To control time of immersion, continuous "open" basket-like filament (wire, etc.) woven type containers move parts through agitated, temperature controlled water rather than just being literally dropped into a container and periodically collected.

Flowchart for the production of quartz textiles.

quench aging Aging induced by rapid cooling after solution heat treatment.

quench annealing Annealing of plastics is sometimes performed to improve properties (stress relieve, etc.). ▷**annealing equipment and method**

quench bath The cooling medium, usually water, used to quench molten TPs to the solid state.

quench tank, extrusion The extruded or calendered film is cooled in a quench water bath.

quer-wave Dispersive surface wave with one horizontal component, generally normal to the direction of propagation velocity with increase in frequency. Also called love wave.

quick burst strength The hoop stress resulting from a quick burst internal pressure in a pipe.

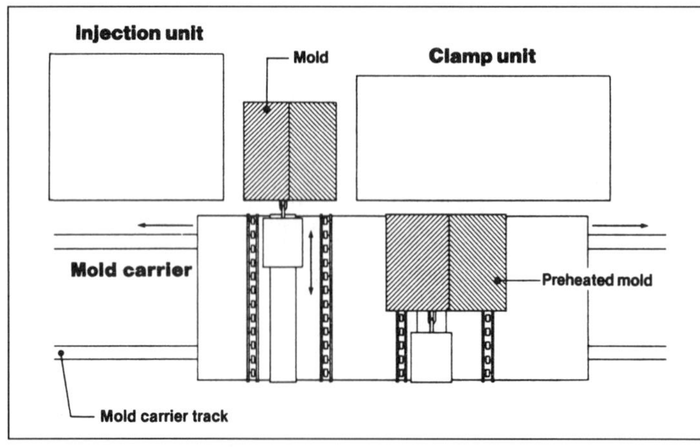

Basic schematic of an automatic quick mold change.

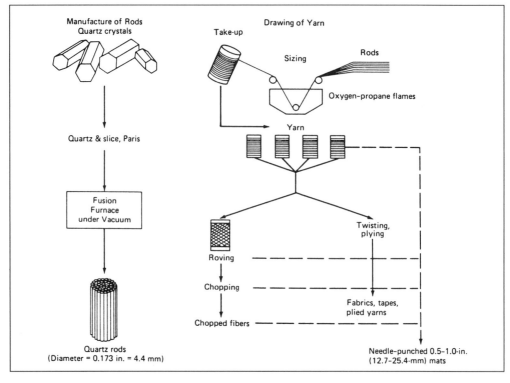

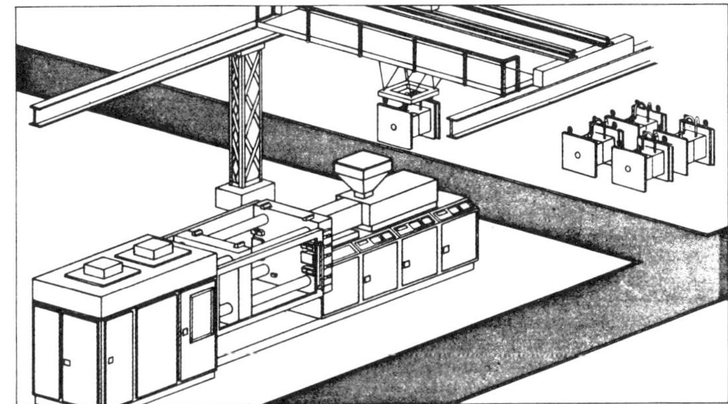

Quick mold change system uses a single robotized overhead crane to service multiple injection molding machines from an inventory of many molds.

quicklime A calcined limestone, the major part of which is calcium oxide or calcium oxide in association with magnesium oxide, capable of slaking with water.

quick mold change QMC systems have the ability to remove, as an example, the mold in different fabricating machines, particularly injection molding, and replace it automatically with another one in minutes. In addition, the microprocessor control of the machine can be programmed to change the mold at a predetermined production point, change the setup of the machine controls, and change the feeding of materials for the new mold (see second Fig. on p. 610 and Fig. above).

quick mold release agent ▷ **mold cleaner**

quick setting ink They are very successful for printing on various substrates, including plastics, in both letterpress and lithography. These inks consist of a delicately balanced oil-plastic-solvent vehicle system. They usually dry with a good gloss.

quotation A document quote that states the selling price and other sales conditions of a product. ▷ **mold quotation guide**

R

rad That quantity of ionizing radiation that results in the absorption of 100 ergs of energy per gram of irradiated material, regardless of the radiation.

radar ▷ **radome**

radar doppler effect ▷ **electronic doppler effect**

radian The plane angle between two radii of a circle which cut off on the circumference arc equal in length to the radius. ▷ **plane angle**

radiance The rate of radiant emission per unit solid angle and per unit projected area of a source in a stated angular direction from the surface (usually the normal).

radiant energy Energy transmitted as electromagnetic waves.

radiation Energy in the form of electromagnetic waves; also called energy or light. It is emitted from matter in the form of photons (quanta), each having an associated electromagnetic wave having frequency and wavelength. The various forms of radiant energy are characterized by their wavelength and together they comprise the electromagnetic spectrum, the components of which are as follows: (1) cosmic rays (highest energy, shortest wavelength), (2) gamma rays from radioactive disintegration of atomic nuclei, (3) X-rays, (4) UV-rays, (5) visible light rays, (6) infrared, (7) microwave, and (8) radio (Hertzian) and electric rays. All these are identical in every way except wavelength, those having the shortest wavelength being the most penetrating. They are not electrically charged and have no mass, their velocity of propagation is the same, all display the properties characteristic of light, and have a dual nature (wave-like and corpuscular). Use includes polymerization of plastics and sterilizing packages.

radiation, absorbed dose The amount of energy imparted by ionizing radiation per unit mass of irradiated matter. Denoted by rad where 1 rad = 0.01 J/kg. SI unit is "gray" (Gy) where 1 gray = 1 J/kg.

radiation coating Since about the 1950s, it was observed that a photosensitive plastic film formed on the walls of a flask containing methyl methacrylate irradiated with UV-light. The mechanism postulated for this transformation involved excitation of the monomer in the gas phase, resulting in addition polymerization. Contact with UV light initiates film formation at rates up to several hundred micrometers per minute. The deposited plastics are generally flexible and contain little crosslinking. However, in some instances extensive side reactions have been observed to yield low molecular weight materials and other by-products.

The polymerization mechanism involves two steps: the gaseous monomers are first attached to the vessel surface by chemisorption or physical adsorption, and then activated with UV light. Substrates can be coated by UV polymerization without the necessity of a mask by using quartz optics to direct the radiation to provide a suitable pattern of UV light at the surface.

Gamma radiation can also be used for formation of thin plastic film coatings via a mechanism of free-radical polymerization similar to UV irradiation and electron-beam polymerization. ▷ **vacuum coating; photopolymerization; coating**

radiation crosslinking The chemistry of radiation crosslinking is similar to peroxide methods except that high frequency electrons, rather than peroxide-free radicals, are used to extract hydrogen atoms from the carbon chain. After hydrogen extraction, the plastic radicals combine in the same way to produce the crosslinked material. This is one of the most common methods of converting thermoplastics to thermosets. ▷ **extruder wire coating, radiation crosslink without peroxide**

radiation curing ink Developed to eliminate spray powder in sheet-fed printing and air pollution from solvents in conventional web heat-set inks. There are two types: ultraviolet (UV) and electron beam (EB) inks. UVs consist of liquid prepolymers and initiators which, on exposure to large doses of UV radiation, release free radicals that polymerize the vehicle to a dry, solid, tough thermoset plastic. Because the active ingredients in these inks are more costly than the solvents they replaced in conventional inks, they are not used much in ordinary web printing. They are used in luxury packaging such as liquor and cosmetic cartons, screen printing, etc.

EBs make a good alternative to UVs since no expensive initiators are needed and some lower cost, less reactive materials can be used. EB's major disadvantage is the high cost of equipping a press to use it. EB uses less energy than UV, which in turn uses about half the energy of gas drying.

radiation damage Structural defects arising from exposure to radiation. ▷ **radiation-induced reaction**

radiation dose equivalent The sievert (Sv) is the dose equivalent when the absorbed dose of ionizing radiation multiplied by the dimensionless factors Q (quality factor) and N (product of any other multiplying factors) stipulated by the International Commission on Radiological Protection is one joule per kilogram (J/kg).

radiation dosimeter A device for measuring radiation-induced signals that can be related to absorbed dose (or energy deposited) by radiation in materials and is calibrated in terms of the appropriate quantities and units. Also called dose meter.

radiation dosimeter, primary standard A system that measures energy deposition directly without the need for conversion factors for interpretation of the radiation absorption process. Examples of such systems are calorimeters and Fricke dosimeters.

radiation dosimeter, secondary standard A system that measures energy deposition indirectly. It requires conversion factors to account for such considerations as geometry, dose rate, relative stopping power, incident energy spectrum, or other effects, in order to interpret the response of the system. Thus, it requires calibration against a primary dosimetry system or by means of a standard radiation source.

radiation dosimeter, solid-phase chemical Apparatus that measures radioactivity by using plastic, dye plastic, or glass with an optical density, usually in the visible range, that changes when exposed to ionizing radiation. Examples used include dyed PMMA, undyed PVC, dyed PA, and dyed polychlorostyrene. This method is also considered to be a secondary-standard dosimetry system.

radiation, electromagnetic ▷ **infrared spectrometry** and **neutron scattering**

radiation, electronic ▷ **electromagnetic interference**

radiation fallout Deposition upon the earth of the radioactive particles resulting from a nuclear explosion. There are certain plastics used that have damage resistance to nuclear fallout. ▷ **radiation resistant plastic**

radiation-induced reaction Deals with reactions induced in monomers and plastics by ionizing radiation and with certain aspects of the photochemistry of plastics. The terms high energy radiation and ionizing radiation are generally used to designate electromagnetic radiation or beams of swiftly moving particles (electrons, atomic nuclei, etc.) which carry enough energy to ionize simple molecules such as the constituents of air (O_2 and N_2). Applications are found along three different lines: radiation-induced polymerization, radiolysis of plastics, and radiation-induced graft copolymerization. Since both ions and free radicals are produced by radiation, the result is either free radicals or ionic processes. In radiation-induced polymerization the free radical or the ionic mechanism prevails, depending on reaction conditions. The chemical transformations occurring in irradiated plastics include chain scissions, crosslinking, and changes in unsaturation. In graft copolymerization the radiation is used as a particularly easy method of activating a plastic. The latter initiates the polymerization of a monomer, giving rise to a graft copolymer.

There exists resistance of common plastics to radiation damage. The most stable are those which contain aromatic groups such as polystyrene and phenolic plastics. Objects molded in such materials can withstand doses of 10^9 rad with only minor losses of mechanical strength. Polyethylene and nylon harden but are not further deteriorated in the same range of doses. Polyvinyl chloride evolves hydrogen chloride and blackens at doses of 10^7 to 10^8 rad. Polymethyl methacrylate, cellulose plastics, and PTFE are severely damaged after 10^7 to 10^8 rad. Most rubbers harden and lose their elastic properties after 10^8 rad. Silicone rubbers are more stable, particularly those which contain phenyl substitutes.

Radiation damage is much more pronounced if the samples are irradiated in air than in an oxygen deficient environment. In air most plastics suffer degradation, which leads to chain rupture and to the formation of carbonyl and carboxyl groups. This reaction may also go on after irradiation as a consequence of the trapped radicals which exist in irradiated plastics. A number of additives have been used to stabilize plastics and rubbers (elastomers) against radiation damage. Such substances, called antirads, either act as antioxidants, thereby reducing the oxidative degradation, or protect the polymer molecule against radiation activation by energy transfer.

Radiation can lead to permanent changes in a variety of ways such as: (1) linear polymers either crosslink or degrade under irradiation, depending on their chemical nature and on the conditions of irradiation, (2) all plastics, as most organic substances, evolve gas under irrradiation with hydrogen usually accounting for a substantial fraction of the gas, and (3) many plastics irradiated in the presence of oxygen suffer oxidation degradation which leads to chain scission.

radiation, monochromatic Radiation at a single wavelength, and by extension, radiation of a very small range of frequencies or wavelengths.

radiation polymerization A polymerization reaction initiated by exposure to radiation such as gamma rays rather than by means of chemical catalysts.

radiation pyrometer An instrument for determining temperatures by measuring the radiance (radiant energy per unit area) from an object.

radiation resistant plastic Ionizing radiation can significantly alter the molecular structure and macroscopic properties of plastics. In numerous applications (space vehicles and nuclear power plants), plastics are specifically needed in environments of ionizing radiation because of various plastic properties such as elasticity, light weight, formability, and others. Such cases require plastics that are as radiation resistant as possible. Plastics exhibit a wide range of radiation stabilities. Radiation resistance is strongly influenced by the basic macromolecular structure, the presence of certain types of additives, and particular environment exposure conditions. ▷ **radiation-induced reaction**

radical When more than two atoms are present in a compound, some of them occasionally group themselves and behave as a unit in a chemical reaction. The SO_4 is a sulfate radical, OH is a hydroxyl radical, etc.

radical polymerization ▷ **free-radical polymerization**

radioactivity Spontaneous nuclear disintegration with emission of corpuscular or electromagnetic radiation, or both.

radio frequency interference ▷ **electrically conductive plastic** and **electromagnetic interference**

radio frequency preheating Basically a method of preheating molding materials to facilitate the molding operation and/or reduce cycle time. RF or electronic preheating has been used with thermosets since the 1930s. Heating is accomplished by taking advantage of the electrical loss factor of the material. Plastic material is heated by using a rapidly oscillating high voltage field to make polar molecules oscillate. This causes increased kinetic molecular activity which is "heat" and the energy absorbed raises the temperature relatively uniformly through the material. All portions of the material heat at the same time, but the outer surfaces of the material (usually as a preform) lose heat to the surroundings. This is why material seemingly heats from the inside out.

RF heaters operate at 20 to 110 megahertz frequency and RF voltages of 5 to 35 kv. The rate of heating is directly proportional to the frequency and varies as the square of the voltage imposed across the material. This is why electrode spacing profoundly affects heating rate. The rate of heating increases as the temperature increases, so a change of a second or two in heating time will significantly affect the temperature attained. Some causes of uneven RF heating include: uneven preform height or electrodes which are not parallel, sharp edges on preforms, varying density in preforms, and slight differences in moisture content in the preforms. ▷ **preform**

radio frequency welding A method of welding thermoplastics using RF field to apply the necessary heat. Also known as high-frequency welding.

With this type process, welding occurs due to the heat created by the application of a strong RF field to the selected joint region on those plastics that are not transparent to RF. The RF is usually applied by a specially formed metal die in the shape of the desired joint, which also applies the clamping pressure needed to complete the weld after plastic melts. This is a very fast process and sensitive to the heat buildup.

This type welding is usually referred to as heat sealing. It is widely used with flexible TP films and sheets such as plasticized PVC and PUR. It can also be used to join film to plastic molded parts.

radiographic contrast The difference in density between an image and its immediate surroundings on a radiograph.

radiographic inspection The use of X-rays or nuclear radiation, or both, to detect discontinuities in material and to present their images on a recording medium.

radiography The most frequently used nondestructive test method. X-rays and gamma rays passing through a structure are absorbed distinctively by flaws or inconsistencies in the material so that cracks, voids, porosity, dimensional changes, and inclusions can be viewed on the resulting radiograph ▷ **brittle lacquer technique**. A permanent, visible image on a recording medium is produced by penetrating radiation passing through the material being tested.

radioisotope An isotopic form of an element (either natural or artificial) that exhibits radioactivity. Use includes as a tracer when melting plastics (through extruder, injection, etc), measurement of thickness (films, profiles, molded wall, etc.), and initiating polymer polymerization.

radiolysis of plastic ▷ **radiation-induced reaction**

radiometer Instrument for measuring radiation in energy or power units.

radionuclide decaying activity The becquerel (Bq) is the activity of a radionuclide decaying at the rate of one spontaneous nuclear transition per second (I/s).

radius of bend The radius of the cylindrical surface of the pin or mandrel that comes in contact with the inside surface of the bend during bending. In the case of free or semiguided bends to 180° in which a shim or block is used, the radius of bend is half the thickness of the shim or block.

radome A radome (radiation dome) is simply a cover for a microwave antenna used to protect the antenna from the environment. Such a dome is basically transparent to electromagnetic radiation and structurally strong. The need for being transparent to radiation rules out metals. The earliest radomes (1942) were of a rubber-coated, air-supported fabric, followed later by an RP made of randomly chopped short glass-fiber, mat-reinforced TS polyester. By 1943 the glass-fiber fabric-TS polyester or epoxy was in use that has been the industry standard worldwide ever since.

The shape of a radome, which is an important factor in its design, is normally chosen on the basis of the optimal electrical characteristics (see Fig. below). For aircraft the ideal shape is a spherical surface with the antenna's gimbal point located at the center of the sphere. Since a spherical radome is virtually impossible to obtain, a simpler configuration of a hemisphere together with a right-circular cylinder are often used, resulting in 95 to 98% efficiency for a relatively low-loss dielectric construction material. Streamlined radomes usually must be a compromise between electrical and aerodynamic considerations. As a result, many of today's aircraft and missile radomes bear a strong resemblance to an icicle, both in terms of having an awkward appearance and in their optical or electrical properties.

The typical all-plastic ground radome is spherical and constructed of a solid RP or an RP in a sandwich construction. All plastic radomes up to 150 ft. in diameter have been built using sandwich construction. Space-frame radomes consist of thin, flat panels of solid laminates in triangular, diamond, rectangular or hexagonal shapes. Each panel is bounded by stiff members to form a polyhedron approximating the shape of a truncated sphere. Although this approach was originally developed for 50- to 150-ft. radomes, it also has economic advantages for use in smaller space-frame radomes.

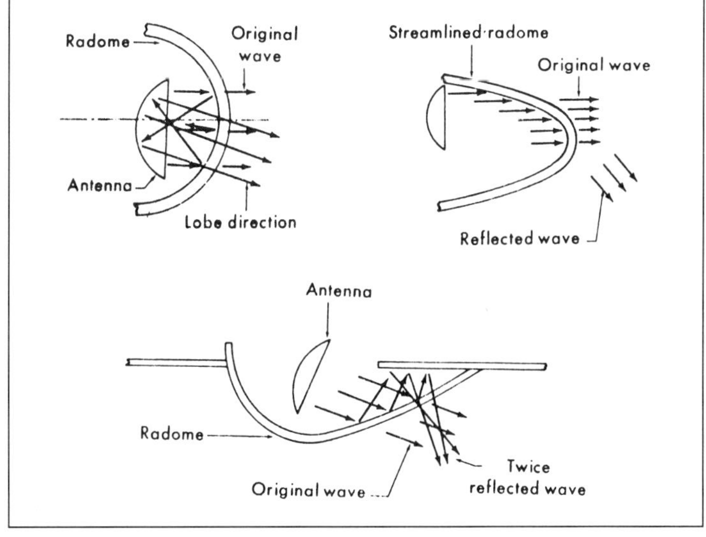

Radome configurations showing their effects on radar waves emanating from the radar reflector or antenna so that the waves are properly focused in the required direction. This is basically the same setup as when optical waves are transmitted through a transparent medium so as not to cause visual distortion.

Ducted radomes are used that are hemispherical domes mounted on a cylindrical base. These consist of several "orange peel" side panels connected by a spherical cap panel. Such an RP structure can include hot-air ducts between the inner and outer skins of the side panels for anti-icing purposes.

railcar hopper The "Glasshopper" (see Fig. opposite), the first hopper railcar using plastics, by Cargill, Inc., Southern Pacific, and ACF Industries. It had two major advantages: lower tare weight (54,000 lb., or 8,000 lb. lighter than steel cars), and corrosion resistance, principally against the contents to be carried, such as fertilizers. The first such car was built and successfully tested in 1973–1976; the second in 1981–1983, the latter successfully meeting or exceeding the guidelines of the American Association of Railroads. The series included static and dynamic tests, coupler tests, ram tests, velocity-impact tests, fully loaded 6,000-mile tests with speeds up to 70 mph, and more. Finite element modeling (FEM) was used throughout the design stages to aid in structural analysis. E-glass rovings with TS polyester resin were used. The car body was filament wound. Other RP or composite parts included outer panels, wide flange beams, stiffeners, a top sill, roof and edge angles, and hatches. The car's capacity was about 5,000 ft^3, its overall length 52 ft., and its height from the rail 15 ft.

This railcar hopper, called the "Glasshopper", is basically an all reinforced plastic, filament wound structure.

railcar hopper contamination Quality conscious customers expect a high degree of purity and consistency in the materials delivered to their loading docks. Plastic producers go to extremes to prevent contamination of their product shipped, but transportation and handling offer numerous possibilities for plastic contamination. Despite the enormous sums invested by plastic producers in making and shipping high quality materials, improper handling of rail cars can defeat their best efforts. Awareness of proper unloading procedures can reduce or eliminate problems attributed to this type contamination.

railcar unloading See Fig. below.

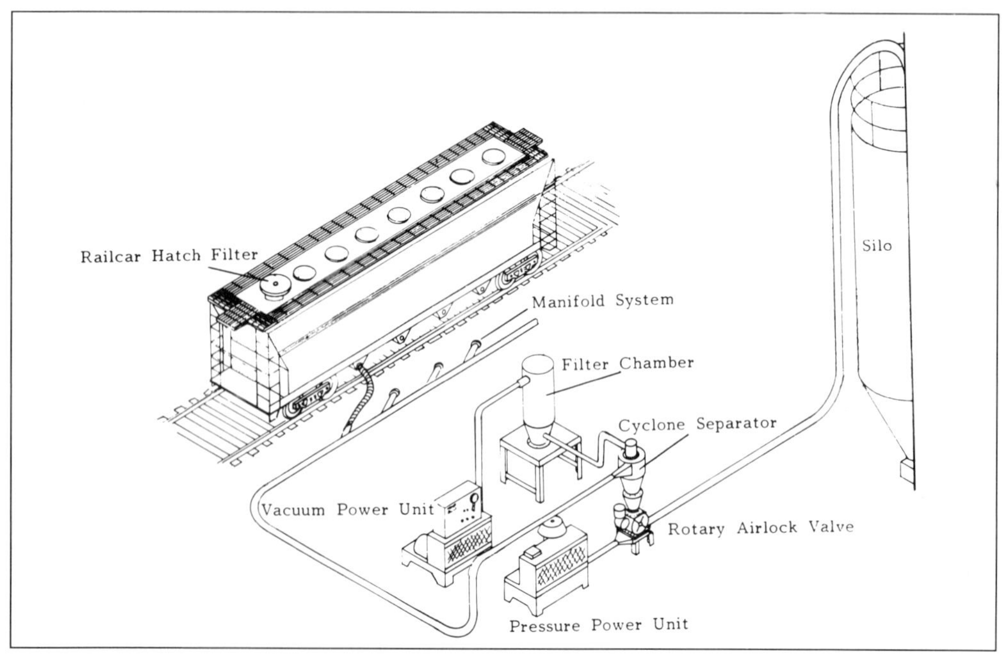

Example of a method for unloading a railcar of plastics.

railroad freight car cost ▷ **demurrage**

rain erosion One who walks through a gentle spring rain seldom considers that raindrops can be small destructive "bullets" when they strike high-speed aircraft. These bulletlike raindrops can erode paint coatings, plastic parts, and even magnesium or aluminum leading edges to such an extent that the surfaces may appear to have been sandblasted. Even the structural integrity of the aircraft may be affected after several hours of flight through rain. This problem is of special interest to aircraft engaged in all-weather flying. It affects commercial aircraft, missiles, high-speed vehicles on the ground, spacecraft before and after a flight when rain is encountered, and even buildings or structures that undergo high-speed rainstorms. The critical situations exist in flight vehicles, since flight performance can be affected to the extent that a vehicle can be destroyed. Research and development concerning rain erosion on aircraft has been extensive.

Erosion by rain of the exterior of high-speed aircraft during flight was observed during World War II on all-weather fighter airplanes capable then of flying at 400 mph. The aluminum edges of wings and particularly of the glass-fiber-reinforced TP polyester-nose radomes (particularly the Eagle Wing on B-29s flying over the Pacific) were particularly susceptible to this form of degradation. The problem continues to exist.

Actual flight tests to determine the severity of this phenomenon of rain erosion carried out in 1943 established that aluminum and RP leading edges of airfoil shapes exhibited serious erosion after exposure to rainfall of only moderate intensity. Inasmuch as this problem originally arose with military aircraft, the U.S. Air Force initiated research studies at the Wright-Patterson Development Center's Materials Laboratory in Dayton. It resulted in applying an elastomeric neoprene coating adhesively bonded to RP radomes. The usual 5-mil coating of elastomeric material used literally bounces off raindrops, even from a supersonic airplane traveling through rain. There is a slight loss of radar transmission of about 1% per mil of thickness, but this is better than losing the radome.

ram **1.** Rod or plunger which forces the plastic through a barrel and into the mold of an injection molding machine or an extruder. **2.** The press member that enters the mold cavity block and exerts pressure on the plastic. It is designated as the top force or bottom force by position of the assembly. **3.** The random computer access memory. **4.** ▷ **extruder ram system** and **extruder, reciprocating ram**

ram accumulator ▷ **accumulator**

Raman spectroscopy Most molecular motions that cause Raman scattering of UV light also produce IR absorption bands. Macromolecular motions that are uniquely accessible to Raman analysis include accordion-like stretchings of chains in lamellar regions. Lamellae are sheetlike regions of crystalline ordering that coexist in many polymers with amorphous regions. Raman spectroscopy thus is important in determining maximum theoretical extents to which plastics may be drawn when high tensile modulus fibers are made.

ram extrusion and injection molding Used to process plastics with very little melt flow ▷ **extruder ram system**. Practically all injection molding machines use the reciprocating screw melt systems; however, prior to the development of screw melting, the original method (patented 1871) was only with the ram (even though melt flow was high). ▷ **injection molding history**

ram force The total applied by a ram, and numerically equal to the product of the line pressure and cross sectional area of the ram. It is normally expressed in tons for injection molding clamping mechanisms.

ramie ▷ **fiber, ramie**

ramping A gradual, programmed increase/decrease in temperature or pressure to control the cure or cooling of plastic parts, such as with reinforced thermoset plastics.

random access memory ▷ **computer random access memory**

random cause One of many factors which contribute to variation but which are not feasible to detect and identify since they are random in origin and usually small in effect.

random copolymer A copolymer consisting of alternating segments of two monomeric units of random lengths, including single molecules. They usually result from the copolymerization of two monomers in the presence of a free-radical initiator.

random error The chance variation encountered in all experimental work despite the closest possible control of variables. It is characterized by the random occurrence of both positive and negative deviations from the mean value for the method, the algebraic average of which will approach zero in a long series of measurements.

randomization The procedure used to allot

treatments of random to the experimental units so as to provide a high degree of independence in the contributions of experimental error to estimates of treatment effects.

randomization statistically ▷ **statistical randomization**

random orientation A condition of a crystalline aggregate in which the constituent crystals have orientations completely random with respect to one another.

random pattern ▷ **fillament winding, random pattern**

range **1.** The absolute value of the algebraic difference between the highest and the lowest values in a set of data. **2.** The range between the limits within which a quantity is measured. It is expressed by stating the lower and upper range-values.

Rankine The Rankine (R) temperature scale is the absolute Fahrenheit (F) scale, that is the sum of absolute zero on the F scale (−459.69) and the F temperature. Approximate R are obtained by subtracting 460 from F. ▷ **Celsius**

rapid loading ▷ **impact loading**

rasp A machine that grinds waste into a manageable material and helps prevent odor.

rate term Feature added to temperature controllers which anticipates and greatly speeds response to changing conditions.

raw material The precursor of processed material into an object; an unprocessed plastic (virgin) material that is used for fabricating or manufacturing. Recycled material is sometimes incorrectly identified as raw material.

ray, light The term applied to the lines perpendicular to the wavefronts of waves of light to indicate their direction of travel in an isotropic medium.

rayon ▷ **fiber, rayon**

R chart The statistical variation over time.

reaction foam molding ▷ **foam and processing method** and **reaction injection molding**

reaction injection molding The RIM process involves the high-pressure impingement mixing of two or more reactive liquid components and injection of the mixture into a closed mold at low pressures (see Fig. below). Large and thick parts can be molded using fast cycles with relatively low-cost materials. Its low energy requirements with relatively low investment costs make RIM attractive.

Different materials can be used such as nylon, polyester (TS), and epoxy, but TS polyurethane (PUR) is predominantly used. Almost no other plastic has the range of properties of PUR—a modulus of elasticity in bending of 200 to 1,400 MPa (29,000–203,000 psi) and heat resistance from 90 to over 200°C (122–392°F), the higher values are for chopped glass-fiber-

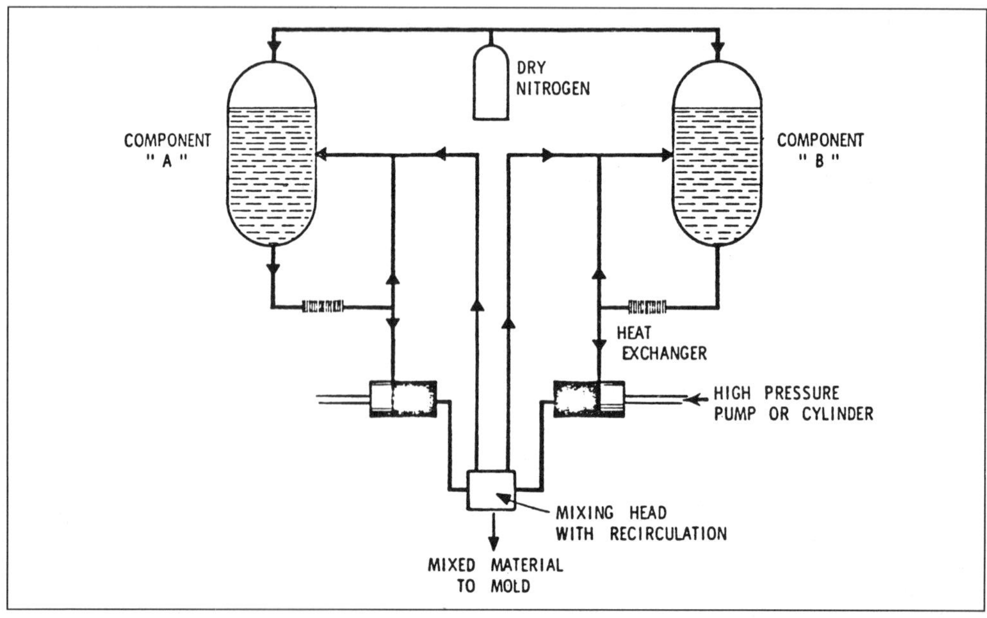

Schematic of the reaction injection molding process.

reinforced RIM, or RRIM. RIM is also comparable to resin transfer molding (RTM) in regard to the processing of TS resins and the molding of large surface areas in that both processes offer the ability to tailor the reinforcement to the application. RRIM generally delivers faster cycles than other processes but needs much more expensive high-pressure dispensing equipment to handle the fast-reacting resin systems.

RIM is very similar to RTM. In the reinforced RIM (RRIM) process a dry reinforcement preform is placed in a closed mold. Next a reactive resin system is mixed under high pressure in a specially designed mix head. Upon mixing, the reacting liquid flows at low pressure through a runner system to fill the mold cavity, impregnating the reinforcement in the process. Once the mold cavity is filled, the resin quickly completes its reaction. The complete cycle time required to produce a molded part can be as little as one minute.

The advantages of RRIM are similar to those listed for RTM. However, RRIM used preforms that are less complex in construction and lower in reinforcement content than those used in RTM. The RRIM resin systems currently available will build up viscosity rapidly, resulting in a higher average viscosity during molding filling. This action follows the initial filling with a low-viscosity resin.

reaction injection molding aftermixer In a RIM system, a section of the runner which creates turbulence within the melt-liquid flow to ensure thorough mixing.

reaction injection molding mold material ▷ **mold material**

reaction injection molding, reinforced ▷ **reaction injection molding** and **reinforced plastic**

reaction spinning A liquid prepolymer is extruded through a spinnerette plate and encounters a chain extending crosslinking component, producing a filament. ▷ **fiber spinning**

reaction viscosity ▷ **viscosity, reaction**

reactive extruder ▷ **extruder, reactive processing**

reactive injection molding Alternative name for reaction injection molding.

reactive polymer A reactive polymer is simply a device to alloy different materials by changing their molecular structure inside a compounding machine. True reactive alloying induces an interaction between different phases of an incompatible mixture and assures the stability of the mixture's morphology. The concept is not new; this technology is now capable of producing thousands of new compounds to meet specific design requirements. The relatively low capital investment associated with compounding machinery (usually less than $1 million for a line, compared with many millions for a conventional reactor), coupled with a processing need for small amounts of tailored materials, now allows small and mid-sized compounding companies to take advantage of it.

There are a variety of reactive alloying techniques available to the compounder today. They typically involve the use of a reactive agent or compatibilizer to bring about a molecular change in one or more of the blend's components, thereby facilitating bonding. They include the grafting process and copolymerization interactions, whereby a functional material is built into the polymer chain of a blend component as a comonomer, with the resultant copolymer then used as a compatibilizer in ternary bonds, such as a PP-acrylic acid copolymer that bonds PP and AA. Another technique is solvent-based interactions, using materials such as polycaprolactone, which is miscible in many materials and exhibits strong polarity, as well as hydrogen bonding, using the simple polarity of alloy components.

reactive processing Traditionally, the manufacture of products made from plastics involved two separate and distinct operations: reaction and processing. Polymerization reactors made monomer molecules into polymer (plastic) molecules, and fabricating processing equipment transformed the plastic molecules into shaped products.

Reactive processing combines these two operations by conducting polymerization and polymer (plastic) modification reactions in processing equipment. This type of processing can be done by reactive extrusion (REX) and injection molding.

reactive system elastomer Materials with good elastomeric properties (rubbers) are also produced in a single step from low molecular weight reactive chemicals. The mechanism is similar to that described for thermoset plastic curings, but since relatively infrequent crosslinking is required for elastomers, chain polymerization is favored over crosslinking in the overall chemical reaction. As an example, certain types of polyurethane and silicone elastomers fall into this category. The starting chemicals are normally in liquid form and thus easy to process into products; the reaction can be triggered by heat, catalysts, or mixing as in the case of thermoset plastics.

reactivity The end group of a polymer is frequently the most reactive point in the entire molecule. Vinyl polymerizations which terminate by disproportionation leave a C = C double bond on the end of the polymer molecule, and it is still quite reactive. Vinyl polymerizations which terminate by transfer to solvent, initiator, monomer, or chain transfer agent, all attach reactive groups to the ends of the polymer molecules. Most condensation polymerization reactions leave a few unreacted polymerizable groups at the ends of the polymer molecules, and these remain quite as reactive as any of those which had entered the polymerization reaction. Thus in most polymer systems, the end group on the polymer molecule is one of the most reactive positions in the entire molecule. Since the number of end groups is exactly inverse to number average molecular weight, it is to be expected that polymer reactivity would be inverse to molecular weight.

It has long been observed that the lower mobility of high molecular weight polymers makes them much less reactive to normal chemical reactions than similar functional groups would be in conventional low molecular weight monomeric structures. To this extent, increasing molecular weight would be expected to decrease reactivity quite rapidly and then taper off at higher molecular weights.

reactor technology It comprises the underlying engineering principles of chemical reaction engineering and the practices used in their applications. It constitutes the evolutionary basis for selecting and designing reactors, their configurations, and their operating characteristics. In addition to stoichiometry and kinetics, it includes requirements for introducing and removing reactants and products, efficiently supplying and withdrawing heat, accommodating phase changes and material transfers, assuring efficient contact among reactants, and providing for catalyst replenishment or regeneration. These issues are taken into account when reaction rates and bench scale data are translated into designs of pilot plants, larger sized units, and commercial plants.

Reactors are employed in polymer manufacture and utilization, from the preparation of feeds and the polymerization reactions through product finishing and upgrading to their ultimate disposal as waste. The basic principles and underlying reactor technology are the same, whether dealing with initiation and propagation of polymer reactions or the production of their feeds.

The type of reactor employed is often determined by the polymerization classification, which includes bulk, solution, emulsion, and suspension polymerizations. If gas-continuous rather than liquid-continuous media are used, the classification is gas-phase polymerization in place of bulk polymerization. For monomers that are homogeneous with their polymers or suspended in solvents during reaction, the polymerization is classified as bulk (gas-phase) or solution polymerization, respectively. However, if the polymerization occurs in a separate phase, e.g., an oil phase after diffusion of the monomer from a water phase, emulsion or suspension polymerization is the designated classification.

reactor volatility Plastics discharged from the reactor sometimes contain a high percentage of volatile components and require purification down to a few parts per million (PPM). The degree of purification is dictated by the ultimate use of the plastic. High purity requirements, for example, are needed to meet health and safety standards for food packaging materials and end use mechanical properties, both of which can be adversely affected even by small amounts of residual contaminants. ▷ **devolatilization**

read only memory ▷ **computer read only memory**

reagent resistance The chemical resistance ability of a plastic to withstand exposure to acids, alkalis, solvents, and other chemicals.

reality versus testing ▷ **testing versus reality**

real time ▷ **computer real time or on-line**

ream **1.** Layers of unhomogeneous material parallel to the surface in a transparent or translucent plastic. **2.** An imperfection; nonhomogeneous layers in flat glass. **3.** Usually 500 sheets, 24 in. by 36 in. (0.6 by 0.9 m) of industrial paper. Sometimes expressed as 3,000 ft^2 (270 m^2). **4.** ▷ **coating weight**

reaming A method used to trim and size different products such as plastic bottle finishes. A special rotating cutting tool trims the sealing surface smooth and simultaneously reams (bores) the bottle opening to desired size.

recalescence The increase in temperature which occurs after undercooling because the rate of liberation of heat during transformation of a material exceeds the rate of dissipation of heat.

recessed letter Letters depressed and produced during plastics processing (injection, thermoforming, etc.).

reciprocal lattice A lattice of points each of which represents a set of planes in the crystal lattice, such that a vector from the origin of the reciprocal lattice to any point is normal to the crystal planes represented by that point and has a length which is the reciprocal of the plane specing.

reciprocating ram ▷ **extruder, reciprocating ram** and **injection molding, plunger**

reciprocating screw ▷ **injection molding, reciprocating**

reciprocity law The statement that in a photochemical reaction a constant effect is produced if the product of time and radiant power is a constant.

reclamation Recovery, recycling, and reuse of scrap materials (plastics, etc.), either in low percentage for new product manufacture or in larger proportions in products where the highest quality is not essential.

recoatability The application characteristics of a polish and the appearance of the film after successive coatings to the surface.

recognition algorithms Computer programs or instruction sets for the recognition of specific phenomena from a processing of data acquired for the system from some external source.

recognition threshold The lowest physical intensity at which a stimulus is correctly identified a specific percent of time.

recommended practice A definitive, standardized set of instructions for performing one or more specific operations or functions other than the identification, measurement, or evaluation of a material.

recoverable resource Materials with physical or chemical properties that allow them to be reused, recycled, or incinerated to produce energy. ▷ **material recovery**

recovery A measure of ability of a material to recover from deformation. A term most commonly applied to properties determined by the compressibility and recovery test, the deformation under load test, and the plastometer test. In the compressibility and recovery tests, it measures the extent to which a gasket material recovers from short time compressive deformation. Recovery (%) is calculated by dividing difference between thickness and thickness under major load by difference between original thickness under preload and thickness under major load and multiplying by 100. It is usually reported in conjunction with compressibility and does not indicate behavior of a material under prolonged load. In the deformation under load test, it measures the extent to which a nonrigid plastic recovers from prolonged compressive deformation occurring at an elevated temperature.

Recovery (%) is calculated by dividing difference between recovered height after 3 hr under load and multiplying by 100. In the plastometer test, it measures the extent to which an elastomer recovers from compressive deformation occurring at an elevated temperature.

recovery, initial The decrease in strain in a specimen resulting from the removal of force, before creep recovery takes place. ▷ **creep**

recovery of plastic ▷ **recycle**

recovery rate ▷ **screw recovery rate**

recreational products Extensive use is made of all type plastics and processes in all types of products (see Fig. below)

Examples of recreational plastic products: inflatable boat, surf boards, and sail-surf board.

recreational surface These surfaces are synthetic, durable areas of consistent properties designed for various recreational activities, including football, soccer, field hockey, cricket, baseball, tennis, track, jumping, golf, wrestling, etc. They include indoor-outdoor carpets, patio surfaces, and similar materials designed for low maintenance in light recreational service. The characteristics of the playing surface may be selected to match natural surfaces under ideal conditions or may have special features. In all cases, the intent is to provide durability for the intended uses.

Recreational surfaces must provide certain performance characteristics at acceptable cost, with a reasonable life time, and with acceptable appearance. For classification, arbitrary but useful distinctions, depending on the primary function of the surface, may be made: a covering intended primarily to provide an attractive surface for private leisure activities such as patio surfaces; a surface designed for service in a specific sport; or a grasslike surface designed for a broad range of heavy duty re-creational activities, including professional athletics, such as artificial turf for outdoor sports. Players and fans alike have accepted the ever changing characteristics of natural playing fields: natural turf's poor durability, erratic influence on traction, variable shock absorbency, ball rebound characteristics, etc. With the availability of plastic recreational surfaces, the uncritical attitude has changed. The plastic turflike surfaces are engineered to have durability, functionality similar to natural turf, and aesthetic appeal based on traditional concepts.

Recreational surfaces have been available since the early 1960s using elastomerics of PVCs, PURS, CRS, PMMAS, PEs, etc. ▷ **flooring**

rectifier Electric "valve" that permits forward current and prevents reverse current.

recyclable Material that can be reprocessed and used again (see Fig below). Controversy surrounds this term, as some local and state regulators contend a material is not recyclable unless it actually is being recycled in a particular area. ▷ **waste**

recyclable buy-back ▷ **buy-back system**

recyclable plastic and scrap Basically all plastics can be recycled by different methods and can be reused in some type of useful products. However, the method and the product are dependent on factors such as type of plastic part to be recycled, environment part exposure, recycled part requirements, and costs involved. Also, scrap does not necessarily connote feedstock that is desirable or is usable as the virgin material from which it was generated. Scrap includes material in a processing plant that generates sprues, flash, excess parison material, runners, rejected parts, etc.; this type scrap can be relatively clean and in most plants since the 1870s has been reused usually by blending with virgin plastics for use in producing the production part (or some other part). Reprocessed plastics may or may not be reformulated by the addition of fillers, reinforcements, plasticizers, stabilizers, pigments, etc. Regarding cost, property performance, and potential metallic contamination of recycled material ▷ **granulating** and **residence time**.

Basically thermoplastics (TP) can be reprocessed by remelting as done with virgin thermo-

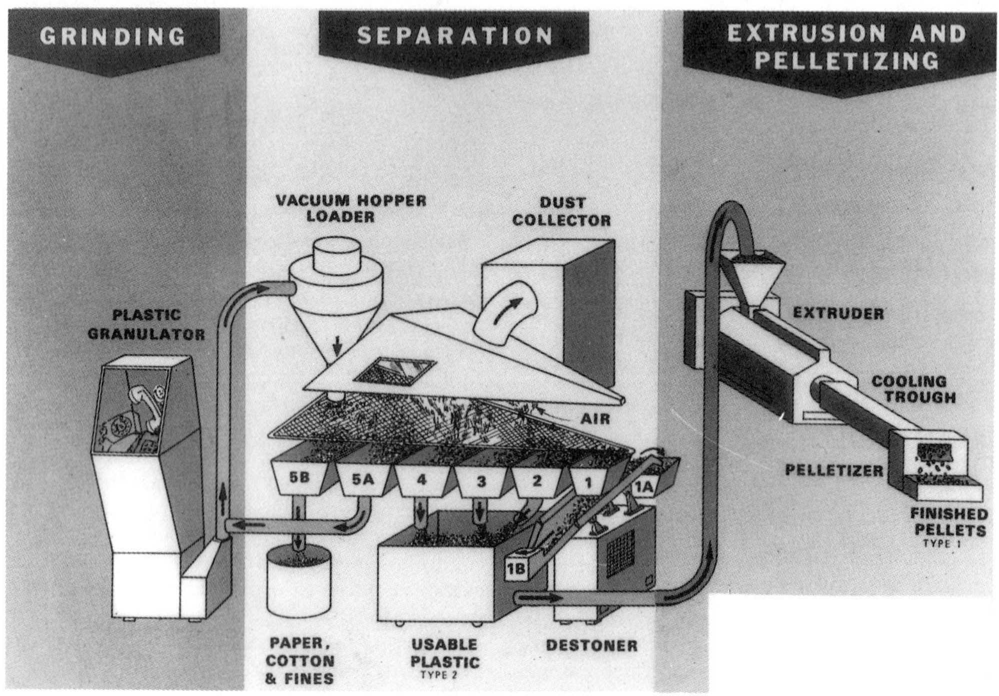

One example of recycling; recycling of electrical parts (can include telephone parts, wiring, etc).

plastics. Thermoset (TS) plastics basically cannot be remelted, but as they have been used since the 1910s, the granulated materials can be used as fillers and reinforcements in TS and TP materials. ▷ **thermoplastic** and **thermoset plastic**

recyclable plastic identified The Society of Automotive Engineers (SAE) has a system for marking plastic parts for recycling. SAE document J-1344/Marking of Plastic Parts, outlines the marking procedure. It lists symbols to be used for easy identification; it also contains information on a plastic's generic (family) name, its common name, previous symbols that may have been used, symbols for commercial blends, how the markings are to be applied, and cross references to common names and trademarks.

recyclable plastic versus others The argument that plastics are especially unsuitable for recycling because of the wide variety of types is a false one. For steels alone there are thousands of known grades; the number of types of paper is far greater and in the order for types of plastics. This means that even for conventional materials, recycling feedstocks cannot be introduced in their original subtly differentiated areas of use, but only in applications where a certain amount of variation in feedstock quality and composition can be tolerated. Alternatively, the waste materials might be laboriously sorted and cleaned, but in that case one would need to take the plastic energy advantage into account. ▷ **energy thermal reclamation**

recyclable reclaim process The Fig. below is a schematic diagram of a plastic reclaim process using a Werner & Pfleiderer ZSK twin screw extruder. The extruder performs moisture removal, addition and blending of stabilizers, contaminant removal, and pelletizing, in one continuous machine operation that also includes on-line measurement and control of diverse parameters.

recycle The return of discarded products to the materials cycle.

recycled Made of or containing material that was used previously and has been reprocessed. There cannot be consensus on the amount of recycled content needed to deem an item recycled; it depends on performance requirements of the item that could range from very little to 100%. There are items that cannot include any recycled material based on performance requirements.

recycled suit Goodyear had a two-piece suit and matching tie made from recycled two-liter polyethylene terephthalate (PET) beverage bottles in 1978 and in 1990 donated it to the new Ripley's Believe It or Not Museum in Wisconsin Dells, Wis. (see Fig. on p. 624). The recycling process that Goodyear developed shreds bottles into small flakes that can then be processed into a reusable TP polyester resin. Goodyear had the suit made to demonstrate the versatility of its recycled PET.

recycle heat history ▷ **residence time**

recycle source reduction ▷ **source reduction, waste**

recycling Separating, processing, and marketing of a component (such as glass, plastic, aluminum, and wood) from the waste stream so it can be reprocessed and used again.

recycling and environment ▷ **environment and public opinion** and **plastic long life**

recycling and plastic The plastic industry worldwide has been committed to significantly

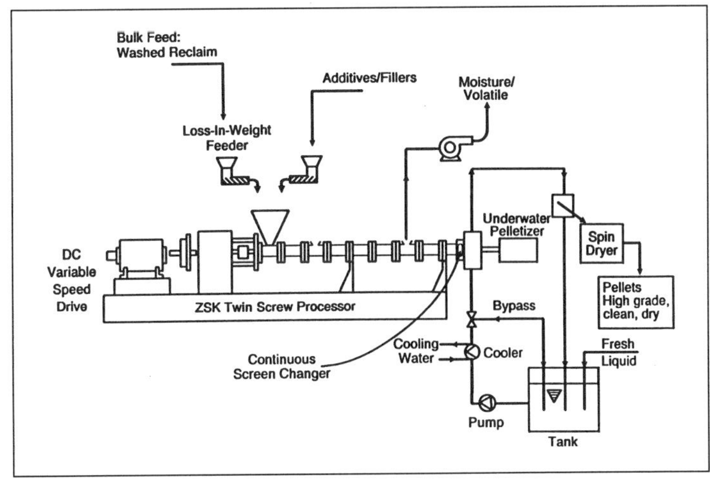

High grade plastic reclaim process configuration.

Suit and tie from reclaimed PET; 1978 vintage, courtesy of Goodyear.

increasing the rate of plastics recycling. Its goal is to make plastics the most recycled part of the waste stream by the year 2000. As an example, the target recycling rate for plastic soft drink bottles, which were introduced in 1979, topped 31% recycled in 1990. Estimated recycling rates for other materials (1988) were (1) paper and paperboard products (which claim a 300-year recycling history) at 26%, (2) glass containers at 12%, and (3) aluminum beer and soft drink cans (introduced in the 1960s) at 55%.

recycling association There are different associations throughout the civilized world both nonprofit and profit to facilitate the collection and recycling of post-consumer plastic products. They have been instrumental in increasing the number of communities in handling plastics using logical and practical approaches. As an example, in the U.S. there is the National Association for Plastic Container Recovery (NAPCOR), which is a non-profit group.

recycling capability Recycling capabilities have always existed for plastics; certain plastic fabricators, material suppliers, and various industries have recycled for over a century.

recycling chemically ▷ **chemical recycling**

recycling clean Of all the possible means of material reclamation, direct recycling of plastic wastes has the most favorable character. The waste is cleaned, comminuted, and fabricated into reprocessed plastic products. Proper material recycling processes are available. The problem is that it becomes more difficult to recycle when uncleaned plastic products from everyday household wastes exist and they are not collected orderly. Regarding contaminated, uncleaned materials, there are basically two means of aiding in resolving the problem: (1) Plastic left in a mixed state can be used to produce products such as garden stakes, garden paving rocks, compost containers, etc. Products that have properties such as resistance to salt water and sewage favor their use; (2) The other recycling option is to reprocess plastics of a single type. One should start with technically simple solutions. Thick walled containers and barrels made of PE should be comminuted, washed, dried, and then processed to a pourable granulate (pellets, etc.).

A difficulty in the processing of these plastic parts is the washing process. They should be washed as large pieces in order to avoid the possibility of water diffusing into the material. Slow running twin-shaft cutting mills are well suited for shredding plastics, since they offer the greatest technical protection against foreign bodies. At times, these processes for waste are scarcely feasible on purely economic grounds. They can be considered, at most, on ecological or environmental policy grounds, but then require the appropriate financial subsidies. ▷ **acceptable risk** and **reuse of plastic**

recycling closed-loop In general, a system to reuse water for non-potable purposes in an enclosed process. In reference to containers, a system to collect and reprocess a specific product back to its original application to reduce reliance on virgin materials, such as recycling PET beverage bottles, instead of lower-grade applications.

recycling code system ▷ **container code system**

recycling communitywise There are three main types of recycling programs: (1) *Curbside collection programs* Residents sort the recyclable materials from their garbage and place them in containers designated for this purpose. They are then left on the curbside for routine pick-up by the local waste hauler or a local recycler. In some communities, participation in residential curbside collection is mandatory. (2) *Drop-off centers* Residents can leave their recyclable materials at local community recycling centers to be recycled. Drop-off centers are most often established in small towns and rural areas. They also tend to be available in urban areas where there is limited or no curbside collection. (3) *Buy-back centers* These differ from drop-off centers in that they are operated as businesses by either local government or private companies. Buy-back centers pay consumers a market rate for their recyclable materials, usually on a per pound or per item basis.

recycling economic balance It can be stated that consideration of waste/refuse treatment (recycling, incineration, waste disposal sites) problems does not lead to a worse ecobalance for plastics compared with other materials, but gives them additional advantages. ▷ **energy conservation** and **recycling, energy consumption**

recycling, electrokinetic ▷ **electrokinetic recycling**

recycling energy balance When compared to other materials, plastics are in a very favorable position based on energy consumption requirements from feedstock to fabricating the finished plastic product.

recycling, energy consumption Plastics have many advantages. They have the lowest consumption in recycling processes, about 2 MJ/kg (2 to 2.5 MJ/I), and the highest recoverable energy content, about 42 MJ/kg. Some comparisons are as follows: (1) Processing waste paper requires 6.7 MJ/kg, and as a general rule about twice as much paper is needed compared with plastics for comparable applications. (2) In glass production, if one uses about 10% of recycled glass, this only reduces the energy consumption of the process by about 2%; thus the use of recycled glass requires about 8 MJ/kg (about 20 MJ/I), but the comparative figure is higher when considered in relation to each product, as one needs about 10 to 20 times as much material compared with plastics. (3) The energy requirement for processing scrap steel and tin-plate is about 6 MJ/kg (about 47 MJ/I), and (4) aluminum recycling requires about 50% of the energy needed to make products from virgin aluminum (about 60 MJ/kg). ▷ **energy conservation**

recycling, energy saver Insulation is the largest single application for plastic foam with building insulation being very significant. The principal heat losses from buildings are through the ceilings, walls, windows, doors, floors, and foundations as well as through air infiltration. A significant reduction in heat loss is realized by insulating attics or ceilings; the improvement by insulating walls is less efficient. Substantial savings can be achieved by insulating basement and perimeter foundation walls.

recycling film and sheet Scrap and product rejects in the production of film accrue both continuously and intermittently in a wide variety of types and forms. Types include PE, PET, or PVC based on sheet (0.5 to 2.5 mm) to PET and PP film (5 to 20 μm) stretched on both sides (bioriented) in the form of edge trims, webs, rolls, and piles. The reuse of such scrap requires the form either of film flakes with high bulk density or regranulated material obtained on plastics compactors, special extruders for film flakes, and direct generating units. With the exception of the direct regenerating units used for special purposes, on which reject rolls or webs of film are respectively paid off and drawn in and regranulated without prior size reduction, any other recycling technique does require a size reduction of the scrap film.

For size reduction of film, maximum demands are made on the efficiency and mechanical strength of the granulators used, for the cutting forces occurring are higher in these applications than in the size reduction of plastics lumps. Suitable granulator screens of small size (often not more than 3 mm in diameter) are required to obtain a high bulk density of the film flakes. Small screen sizes like these, of course, reduce the obtainable throughput, and make the use of granulators with maximum cutting capacity an essential requirement.

Both the throughput of a granulator and the specific energy requirements of size reduction processes depend only on the size of the screen but also decisively on the cutting gap between the stationary and rotating knives. In practice, a cutting gap of between 0.2 and 0.3 mm is used in size reduction of film. ▷ **granulating** and **densifier**

recycling foam plastic ▷ **packaging loose-fill plastic**

recycling history First LDPE bottle molded by Plax Corp., Hartford, CT, that used scrap recycled PE occurred in 1942. ▷ **recycled suit**

recycling packaging material ▷ **environment and public opinion**

recycling packaging via DSD Germany has long been first in many Green Dot issues. The country's Green Party is among the strongest in Europe and the Blue Angel ecology logo was first formalized in Germany in 1978, a decade before other countries even knew what the definition of ecology meant. Devised by the then German Environment Minister, Klaus Töpfer, the Green Dot system was passed in April 1991 to take place by January 1, 1992. The plan was formally called Duales System Deutschland (DSD) and is based on the formation of a private company, DSD, which was a conglomerate of 400 packaging firms.

As a private firm, DSD is sanctioned to operate a curbside program to collect plastics, paper and metal packaging. Glass and various paperboards have been recycled in Germany since 1974. By organizing a private program, the German packaging industry effectively bypasses the mandate to retailers to accept empty packages for recycling.

DSD also has organized a transportation system that ships the used packages to recycling centers. When the center accepts the packages, the government awards a Green Dot to the package meaning that it can be effectively recycled in the commercial stream. In contrast with the Blue Angel, which was devised for the product, the Green Dot is specifically for the recyclability of the package.

Packagers must pay a fee to join the program and receive the Green Dot designation. The entry fees fund the plan. It's estimated that the Green Dot system will cost the industry 1 or 2 pfennigs per package. ▷ **container code system**

recycling polystyrene egg cartons The FDA during 1990 approved egg cartons, meat trays, fast-food containers, school lunch trays, and foam beverage cups made from PS scrap. Until that time, recycled PS had been restricted to VCR tape cases, office accessories, and when combined with other plastics, lumber, traffic sign posts, and car stops. The first processor that received FDA approval to produce recycled egg cartons was Dolco Packaging Corp., Sherman Oaks, CA, the nation's largest producer of PS egg cartons.

recycling polyurethane Recycling and recovering energy from PURs has been a commercially viable technology. A major factor that aids the recycling is the two-thirds of production is used by just four major industries: transportation, furniture, construction, and bedding. Polyurethane Recycle and Recovery Council of SPI can provide information.

recycling polyvinyl chloride Despite its economic and environmental advantages, vinyl continues to come under fire in Europe and the U.S. The controversy is not based on fact, but rather seems to be fueled by lack of knowledge about the ability to recycle and incinerate vinyl and of the economics of its use. Automatic sortation systems have been developed that enable separation of vinyl from other plastics for recycling. Proper incineration and scrubbing techniques reduce the already negligible emissions to near zero. ▷ **polyvinyl chloride plastic and the environment**

redox A contraction of the term oxidation-reduction. Thus, a redox catalyst is one entering into an oxidation-reduction reaction. Plastics formed by such reactions are sometimes called redox polymers.

reference, dimension ▷ **dimension, reference**

references As reviewed in the preface, information contained in this book is a collection from worldwide sources that include many published articles, reports, etc., including the author's personal exposure and experience in the plastics industry since 1939. See *References* on p. lxi.

refinery recycling Introduction of plastic waste into a refining unit so as to snap the polymer chains into lighter fractions comparable to those found in the refinery stream.

reflectance The ratio of the radiant power reflected by the sample to the radiant power incident on the sample. ▷ **gloss**

reforestation ▷ **resource renewable**

refractive ceramic fiber ▷ **ceramic fiber** and **glass fiber**

refractive index Also called the index of refraction. It is the ratio of the velocity of light in a vacuum to its velocity in a material such as a transparent plastic. Light travels at different speeds in transparent materials. This action can be related to inserting a straight pencil into a glass of water; when viewing sideways, it seems to be bent at the surface of the water. This apparent bending is due to the fact that light waves travel one to one-third times faster in air than in water. Since everything we see is through light reflected from the object, the slow down in the light waves reflected from the portion of the pencil under water gives us the visual impression of bending exactly where the water and air meet ▷ **optical properties; light; residual stress; nondestructive testing.** Refractive index values for different plastics follow:

Fluorocarbon (FEP)	1.34
Polytetrafluoroethylene (TFE)	1.35
Chlorotrifluoroethylene (CTFE)	1.42
Cellulose propionate	1.46–1.49
Cellulose acetate butyrate	1.46–1.49
Cellulose acetate	1.46–1.50
Methylpentene polymer	1.465
Ethyl cellulose	1.47
Acetal homopolymer	1.48

Acrylics	1.49
Cellulose nitrate	1.49–1.51
Polypropylene (unmodified)	1.49
Polyallomer	1.492
Polybutylene	1.50
Ionomers	1.51
Polyethylenes (low density)	1.51
Nylons (polyamide) Type II	1.52
Acrylics multipolymer	1.52
Polyethylene (medium density)	1.52
Styrene butadiene thermoplastic elastomers	1.52–1.55
PVC (Rigid)	1.52–1.55
Nylons (Polyamide) Type 6/6	1.53
Urea formaldehyde	1.54–1.56
Polyethylene (high density)	1.54
Styrene acrylonitrile copolymer (unfilled)	1.56–1.57
Polystyrene (heat and chemical)	1.57–1.60
Polycarbonate (unfilled)	1.586
Polystyrene (general purpose)	1.59–1.60
Polysulfone	1.633

refractiveness Relates to light absorption in the surface of material.

refractivity The refractive index minus one. Specific refractivity is given by $(n-1)/d$, where n = refractive index and d = density.

refractory An earthly, ceramic material of low thermal conductivity that is capable of withstanding extremely high temperature (1,650 to 22,000°C) without essential change. Use includes lining furnaces to handle plastics.

refractory furnace ▷ **glass fiber production**

refractory metal Material capable of withstanding extremely high temperatures.

refrigerant ▷ **chlorofluorocarbon**

refuse Alternative name for solid waste.

refuse-derived fuel RDF is organic waste that is converted to fuel pellets which can be stored or transported before combustion.

refuse reclamation ▷ **reclamation**

regenerated cellulose ▷ **cellophane**

regenerated fiber A man-made fiber made from a naturally occurring plastic, which is dissolved in a suitable solvent and wet or dry spun to produce a fiber. Although the natural plastic itself may have been fibrous, and thus the fiber may be said to be regenerated, this is not so with man-made protein fibers. Usually the plastic is cellulose, either cellulose itself, as with viscous and cuprammonium rayon production, or a cellulose derivative, especially cellulose acetate. The earliest man-made fibers were of this type, but synthetic fibers have become much more important technologywise and marketwise.

regeneration Restoration of a material to its original condition after it has undergone chemical modification necessary for its manufacturing purposes. The oldest and most common instance is that of cellulose for rayon production.

register Fitting two or more substances (film, sheet, printing, etc.) in exact alignment with each other or reference media.

regression method Statistical procedures dealing with the study of the association or the relationship between two or more variables.

regrind ▷ **granulating** and **recycling**

regulations The consuming public must assume that the producer of a product has shown reasonable consideration for the safety, correct quantity, proper labeling, and other social aspects of the product. Since the 1960s these types of important concerns have expanded and been reinforced by a recognition of the consumer's right to know as well as by concerns for conservation, ecology, antilittering, and the like. Numerous safety-related and socially responsible laws have been enacted and more are on the way. ▷ **hazards, Federal Register 29 cfr 1910.1200**

regulatory agencies More than 30 federal departments and agencies commissioned by the U.S. Congress currently have significant regulatory responsibilities for interpreting and enforcing public law. These regulatory agencies create the rules and standards that govern our businesses and personal lives, either directly or becaused they are superimposed on state and municipal laws and ordnance.

The laws that have had the greatest impact on the chemical and plastic industries are those related to health, safety, and the environment. For the most part, these laws have evolved only over the past few decades in the wake of a new environmental consciousness that stirred Congress to correct past industrial abuses and forestall future ones. One consequence of the new laws is a dramatic increase in the cost of doing business. The health, safety, and environmental laws of most concern to the plastic industry are FFDCA, TSCA, RCRA, CERLA (or Superfund), CAA, CWA, SDWA, OSHA, and CPSA.

reinforced concrete ▷ **concrete reinforced**

reinforced microcracking ▷ **microcracking**

reinforced molding compound A material reinforced with fillers and/or fibers (glass, minerals, etc.) to meet specific performance and processing requirements such as bulk molding compound (BMC).

reinforced plastic The term RP refers to combinations of plastic material and reinforcing materials that usually come in fiber forms as chopped, continuous, woven and nonwoven fabrics, etc. Composites, when used alone, encompass many different combinations (thousands) of different materials including plastic composites (RPS) ▷ **composite**. Consequently the term reinforced plastic is much more meaningful and is predominantly used worldwide. When using the term composite in reference to plastics, refer to plastic composite (PC).

Both thermoset plastics (TSS) and thermoplastics (TPS) are used in RPS. When the modern RP industry started (1940), glass-fiber-reinforced unsaturated TS polyesters or low-pressure or contact-pressure curing plastics principally were used. Now at least 80% by weight of composites are glass fiber and 60% are polyester (TS) types. Regarding other reinforcements ▷ **reinforcement**. A designer can now produce RP products whose mechanical properties in any direction will be both predictable and controllable. This is done by carefully selecting the plastic and the reinforcement in terms of both their composition and their orientation, and following up with the appropriate process. All types of shapes can be produced: flat and complex, solid and tubular rods or pipes, molded shapes and housings and other complex configurations, such structural shapes as angles, channels, box and I-beams, and so on. The RPS can in fact produce the strongest materials in the world.

The molder has a variety of alternatives to choose from regarding the kind, form, and amount of reinforcement to use. With the many different types and forms (organics, inorganics, fibers, flakes, and more) available, practically any performance requirement can be met, molded into any shape. Possible shapes range from very small to extremely large, and from the simple to the extremely complex.

The reinforcement type and form chosen (woven, braided, chopped, etc.) will depend on the performance requirements and the method of processing the RP. Fibers can be oriented in many different patterns to provide the directional properties desired. Depending on their packing arrangement, different reinforcement-to-resin ratios are obtained. In its simplest presentation, using glass fiber with plastic, if the fibers were packed as closely as possible (like stacked pipe), the glass would occupy 90.6% of the volume (95.6% by weight). With a "square" packing (fibers directly on top of and alongside each other) the glass volume would be 78.5% (88.8% by weight). Glass fibers and most other reinforcements require special treatment to ensure maximum performance, such as selecting materials compatible with the resins used, protecting individual filaments during handling and processing, and so on. ▷ **fiber; finish; sizing**

The acceptance and use of nonwoven fabrics as reinforcements has led to the development of major products. These reinforcements include felts and paper structures, which usually contain a binder that retains these structures and is compatible with the resin matrix. Combinations of different chopped fibers (glass and aramid, and so on) are also used, including long filaments, woven fabrics, and more. The combinations provide unique properties and, in most cases, permit the molding of different shapes that otherwise would not be possible. The longer fibers are best for optimizing mechanical properties. With short, chopped fiber structures, the fiber length can range from extremely short (0.001 in.) to at least 0.5 in., and on up to 2 in. The length used usually depends on the processing and performance requirements. Basically, to obtain the best mechanical performance with fibers in a properly molded part, it is necessary only for them to have an aspect ratio (length over diameter) of about ten.

Practically all TS and TP materials are used in RPS, but a few predominate, with TS polyesters being the major type (60 wt%). The polyester RPS are used in all processes, but their principal use is in the low pressure methods (spray-up, hand lay-up, bag molding, casting, pultrusion, rotational molding, filament winding, and compression molding). ▷ **aircraft**

reinforced plastic, advanced Denotes higher performance RPS principally based on type reinforcements used. Since the 1940s, the fibers that dominated advanced RPS, in chronological development (from the previous wood pulp, sisal, cotton, etc. fibers), have been E-glass, S-glass, boron on tungsten filament core, graphite and carbon, and aromatic polyamide. They possess desirable properties such as low density (1.44 to 2.7 g/cm^3) and extremely high strengths (3 to 4.5 GPa), and moduli (60 to 520 GPa). There are different factors that affect the competition of advanced RPS with traditional engineering materials, such as cost, reliability, and complexity (because RPS are not understood). Fibers exhibit linear elastic behavior to failure at strains of 1 to 3%. Some engineers accustomed to designing to yield with a built-in safety margin of at least 10% strain due to plastic flow can be skeptical about using these materials as primary structures. However, if strains with offsets or secant values are used, safety factors are applied. Recognize that since the 1950s military aircraft have used RPs in primary structures; with some now using up to 60 wt% of primary and secondary structures.

Complexity stems from the anistropy and inhomogeneity (on the microscale) of RPs. In addition to the obvious directional dependence of their thermoelastic properties, RPs exhibit a variety of strengths and failure modes. Thus, direct substitution of an RP for an existing metal using traditional isotropic material design, manufacturing, and joining practices usually has led to unsuccessful designs. This situation is similar to designing with the more popular conventional (unreinforced) plastics ▷**design analysis**. Note that the more advanced high performance fibers became available so that E-glass is not considered in the advanced RP group; however, well over 80 wt% of all RP products use the glass.

reinforced plastic, coin test ▷**reinforced plastic, tapping test**

reinforced plastic continuous laminating An automated technique in which plies of reinforcements such as fabric or mat are continuously passed through a liquid plastic dip tank and are brought together between flexible covering sheets as a lay-up which is cured by passing it through a heating zone.

reinforced plastic, cutting ▷**cutting reinforced plastic**

reinforced plastic, directional properties A major advantage in using RPs by the design engineer is the fact that directional properties can be maximized. As shown in the Fig. on p. 630, they can be isotropic, orthotropic, etc. Basic design theories of combining actions of plastic and reinforcements have been developed and used successfully since the 1940s, based originally on designing with wood-fiber structures.

As an example, woven fabrics that are generally bidirectional in the 0 and 90° angles contribute to the mechanical strength at those angles. The rotation of alternate layers of fabric to a lay-up of 0°, +45°, 90° and −45° alignment reduces maximum properties in the primary directions, but increases in the +45° and −45° directions. Different fabric patterns are used to develop different property performances. ▷**fabric, woven** and **fabric, nonwoven**

Terminology regarding directional properties used with RPs include the following: (1) *Anisotropic construction* One in which the properties are different in different directions along the laminate flat plane; a material that exhibits different properties in response to stresses applied along axes in different directions. (2) *Balanced construction* In woven RPs, equal parts of warp and fill fibers. Construction in which reactions to tension and compression loads result in extension or compression deformations only, and in which flexural loads produce pure bending of equal magnitude in axial and lateral directions. It is an RP in which all laminae at angles other than 0° and 90° occur only in ± pairs (not necessarily adjacent) and are symmetrical around the centerline. (3) *Biaxial load* A loading condition in which a specimen is stressed in two different directions in its plane (i.e., a loading condition of a pressure vessel under internal pressure and with unrestrained ends). (4) *Bidirectional construction* An RP with the fibers oriented in various directions in the plane of the laminate, usually identifies a cross laminate with the directions 90° apart. (5) *Isotropic construction* RPs having uniform properties in all directions. The measured properties of an isotropic material are independent on the axis of testing. The material will react consistently even if stress is applied in different directions; stress-strength ratio is uniform throughout the flat plane of the material. (6) *Isotropic transverse construction* In reference to a material that exhibits a special case of orthotropy in which properties are identical in two orthotropic dimensions but not the third. Having identical properties in both transverse but not in the longitudinal direction. (7) *Non-isotropic construction* A material or product that is not isotropic; it does not have uniform properties in all directions. (8) *Orthotropic construction* Having three mutually perpendicular planes of elastic symmetry. (9) *Quasi-isotropic construction* It approximates isotropy by orientation of plies in several or more directions. (10) *Unidirectional construction* Refers to fibers that are oriented in the same direction, such as unidirectional fabric, tape, or laminate, often called UD. Such parallel alignment is included in pultrusion and filament winding applications. ▷**bamboo's modular structure** (11) *Z-axis construction* In RP, the reference axis normal (perpendicular) to the X–Y plane (so called flat plane) of the RP. Regarding orientation of thermoplastics (unreinforced) ▷**orientation**

reinforced plastic fiber orientation ▷**injection molding push-pull**

reinforced plastic fiber pattern When undesired fiber or fabric patterns occur on the RPs surface different RP surface treatments are used to eliminate them.

reinforced plastic fiber percent by volume The product of the specific gravity of the RP and the percent glass by weight, divided by the specific gravity of the fiber results in the vol%.

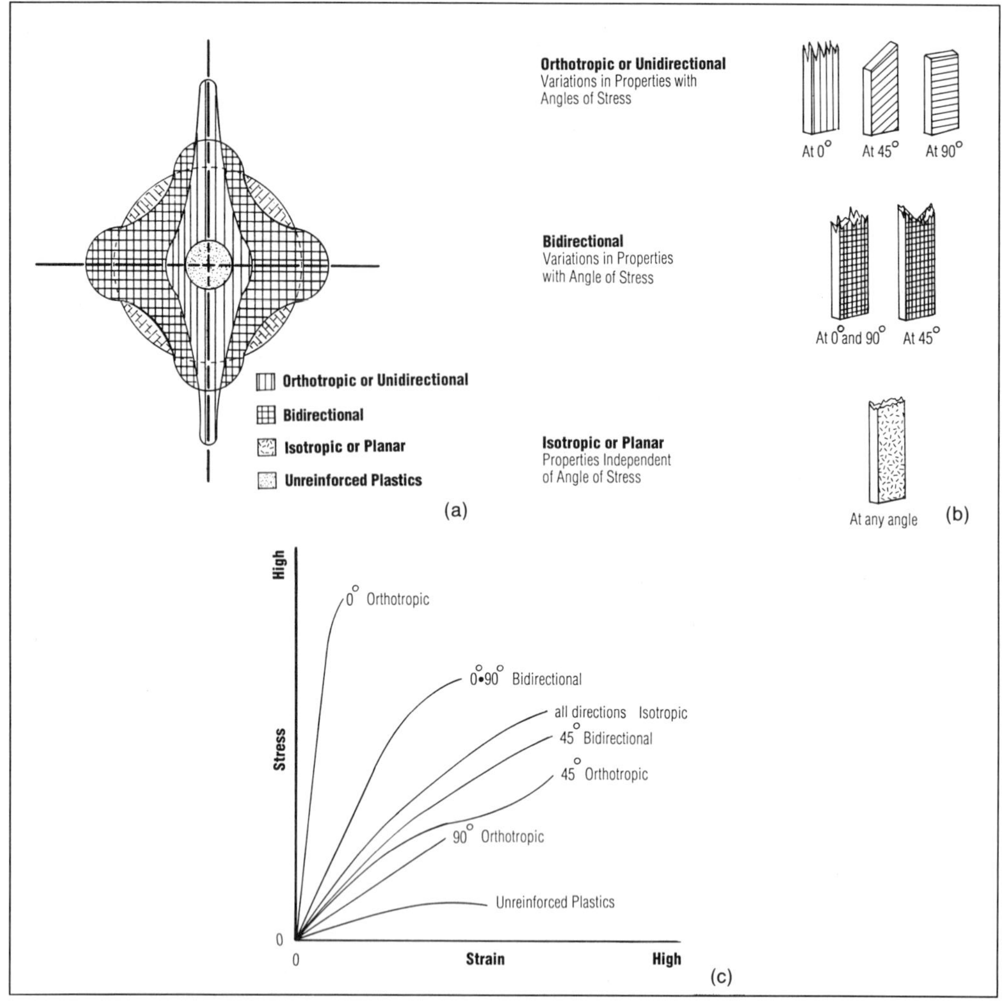

Overview of reinforced plastic's directional properties. (*a*) Polar directional properties; (*b*) different fiber orientations and tensile fracture characteristics; (*c*) stress vs. strain, diagrams at various angles.

Since the weights of fibers, as well as plastics, differ, the amount percentage by volume is not the same percentage amount by weight.

reinforced plastic fiber reinforced ▷ **orientation and fiber reinforced**

reinforced plastic fiber role The first principle, particularly of continuous fiber, in RP is that the fibers must support all main loads and limit deformations acceptably.

reinforced plastic fiber surface treatment ▷ **fiber; finish; sizing**

reinforced plastic filament winding ▷ **filament winding**

reinforced plastic fillers The Table on p. 631 provides examples of fillers used in RPs. ▷ **filler**

reinforced plastic, flexible Non-mechanical high performance features are designed into flexible RPs. Unlike rigid RPs, these flexible, high performance materials represent a class of engineering materials that have been used since the 1940s. As such they have present applications engineers with continually new and exciting challenge; the opportunity to use and exploit flexible materials with many of the structural, chemical, thermal, and electrical properties of metals and ceramics. Examples include permanent structural/architectural fabrics, high temperature cooking sheets and belts, aerospace wire and cable insulation, chemical

Example of a guide for using fillers in RPs; types of fillers, ranges of loading,[1] and typical uses.

Fillers	Plastic extender	Fire retardant	Smoke suppressant	Increase stiffness	Lower exotherm	Reduce shrinkage	Electrical properties	Reduce weight	Syntactic foam	Thixotrope	Improved machinability	Pastes and putties	Chemical resistant coatings	Potting	Hand lay-up	Spray-up
Aluminum trihydrate (ATH)	C	C	C	C	C	C	C								C	C
"Q-Cell"	B,C			C	C		C	C		B	B,C	B	B,C	C	C	C
3M Spheres	B,C			C	C	C		C	C		B	B,C	B	B,C	C	C
Potter's beads	B,C			C	B,C	B,C							B	B,C	B,C	B,C
Suzorite Mica	C			C	C		C						B,C			C
"Micromix"	C			C	C								B,C			C
"Cabosil Aerosil"	A									A		A		A	A	A
Milled fibers					A							A		A	A	
Sand	A				A	A								A	A	
Glass flakes				B		A	A						A,B		A	A
Antimony trioxide		A	A												A	A
Soapstone											A	A				
Clay	A										A	A				

[1] Loading: A = 1–10%; B = 10–30%; C = 30–50%.

protective suits, and domes with its durable and visually attractive roof.

reinforced plastic form and spray ▷ **thermoforming, form and spray**

reinforced plastic future There is always a growing need in many areas of engineering to find alternatives to heavy structures made from iron and steel. The key phrase is "modern lightweight construction". Its aims are to effect savings in raw materials, energy and work costs by the intelligent use of high performance materials of construction in smaller quantities, and also to save energy during their use by reducing the masses of moving parts.

The principle of building into a material anisotopic properties, so as to provide strength and rigidity just where it is needed, is older than the history of engineering. Through innumerable stages of optimization, nature has developed lightweight structures which fulfill the requirements placed on them (such as wood) at the least cost in materials and energy ▷ **bamboo's modular structure.** By using fiber RPs, designers have exploited their built-in directional properties to develop many clever lightweight solutions to particular design projects (like truck springs) and have demonstrated their suitability. Other advantages for the future of RPs also exist as reviewed in this book.

reinforced plastic hairline craze Multiple fine surface separation cracks that exceed 6.4 mm ($\frac{1}{4}$ in.) in length and do not penetrate in depth the equivalent of a full ply of reinforcement. ▷ **hairline crack**

reinforced plastic holography testing ▷ **nondestructive holography test**

reinforced plastic hybrid ▷ **hybrid**

reinforced plastic joining ▷ **joining and bonding** and **joint geometry**

reinforced plastic laminate ▷ **laminate**

reinforced plastic low-profile plastic ▷ **low-profile plastic**

reinforced plastic macromechanic ▷ **macromechanic**

reinforced plastic materials There are many different combinations of the plastic matrix and reinforcements that provide many different product performances. Examples of RP compounds include bulk molding compounds (BMCs), sheet molding compounds (SMCs), and prepregs. The Tables on pp. 632 and 633 provide some information on behavior of matrix in RPs. The Fig. on p. 632 relates matrix to processing behavior.

reinforced plastic micromechanical analysis Even with the simplification afforded by the assumption of isotropy transverse to the

Effect of reinforcements and fillers on thermoplastic RPs.

Reinforcements	Fillers
Amorphous + can more than double tensile strength + can increase flexural modulus four-fold + raise HDT[1] slightly ± toughen brittle resins; embrittle tough resins + can provide 1000 Ω · cm resistivity + reduce shrinkage – reduce melt flow – raise cost	– lower tensile strength + can more than double flexural modulus + raise HDT[1] slightly – embrittle resins + can impart special properties, eg, lubricity, conductivity, flame retardance + reduce and balance shrinkage – reduce melt flow + can lower cost
Crystalline + can more than triple tensile strength + can raise flexural modulus seven-fold + can nearly triple HDT[1] ± toughen brittle resins; embrittle tough resins + can provide 1 Ω · cm resistivity + reduce shrinkage – cause distortion – reduce melt flow – raise cost	– lower tensile strength + can more than triple flexural modulus + raise HDT[1] slightly – embrittle resins + can impart special properties, eg, lubricity, conductivity, magnetic properties, flame retardance + reduce shrinkage + reduce distortion – reduce melt flow + can lower cost

[1] Heat-deflection temperature.

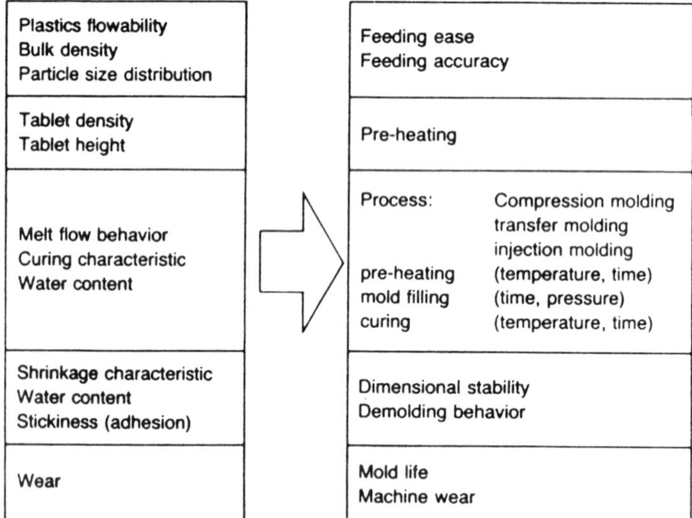

Correlating RP materials processing behavior to product performance.

fiber direction, a formidable array of properties is required to fully characterize a lamina. Because of the large number of measurements needed, techniques for estimating lamina properties from properties of the constituents have been developed. This field, known as reinforced or composite micromechanics, utilizes many of the principles of continuum (macro) mechanics to estimate properties and provide an understanding of RP behavior on the microscale; this enables design and fabrication of RPs having the desired physical properties.

reinforced plastic moisture content In addition to the usual physical moisture content determination tests, electrical systems are used. As an example, in unidirectional RPs, the normalized charge in resistance is measured and found to vary with the square of the moisture content. For multidimensional RPs, a different method is used. A modified, four-terminal method utilizes resistance of the electrical contacts, which eliminates error. Resistance measured across the thickness is linearly proportional to the moisture content.

Examples of properties for the major thermoset plastics used in RPS.

Thermosets	Properties
Polyesters	Simplest, most versatile, economical, and most widely used family of resins; good electrical properties, good chemical resistance, especially to acids.
Epoxies	Excellent mechanical properties, dimensional stability, chemical resistance (especially to alkalis), low water absorption, self-extinguishing (when halogenated), low shrinkage, good abrasion resistance, excellent adhesion properties.
Phenolic resins	Good acid resistance, good electrical properties (except arc resistance), high heat resistance.
Silicones	Highest heat resistance, low water absorption, excellent dielectric properties, high arc resistance.
Melamines	Good heat resistance, high impact strength.
Diallyl *o*-phthalate	Good electrical insulation, low water absorption.

reinforced plastic mold ▷ **tooling, plastic; mold material; design mold**

reinforced plastic, molding with fiber orientation ▷ **orientation and fiber reinforced** and **reinforced plastic, directional properties**

reinforced plastic nesting In RPs, the placing of plies of fabric such that the yarns of one ply lie in the valleys between the yarns of the adjacent ply. Also called nested fabric.

reinforced plastic orientation ▷ **reinforced plastic, directional properties**

reinforced plastic overlay sheet ▷ **reinforced plastic surfacing or overlay**

reinforced plastic peel ply A layer of open-weave material, usually glass fiber or heat set nylon fabric, applied directly to the surface of a prepreg lay-up. The peel ply is removed from the cured laminate immediately before bonding operations, leaving a clean, plastic-rich surface that needs no further preparation for bonding, other than application of a primer if one is required. Also called tear ply.

reinforced plastic, plastic content determination ▷ **muffle furnace**

reinforced plastic, plastic material matrix role The matrix (plastic) maintains the desired fiber orientation and spacings, transmits shear loads between layers of fibers so that they resist bending and compression, and protects the fiber from surface damage. The matrix role is more subtle and complex in the areas of strength and toughness. Glass, graphite, and boron are examples of linear elastic, brittle solids. They fail catastrophically, without plastic flow; however the stress on them is sufficient to cause unstable flaw growth. Flaws are typically surface notches or steps resulting from handling or processing.

Although both fiber and matrix are brittle for high performance RPs, their combination produces a material that is quite tough, indeed much tougher than either of them. This synergism is achieved by a combination of mechanisms that tends to keep cracks small, isolated, and blunted, as well as dissipates energy. These mechanisms, based in part on the heterogeneity of RPs, constitute another difference from structural metals. Toughness in RP is achieved without the large-scale plastic flow seen in tough metals.

reinforced plastic, plastic rich area Localized area filled with plastic and lacking reinforcing material. ▷ **imperfection** and **wash**

reinforced plastic pocket An apparent accumulation of excess plastic in a small, localized section visible on cut edges of molded surfaces, or internal to the structure and nonvisible. ▷ **imperfection**

reinforced plastic preply An RP lamina in the raw material stage, ready to be fabricated into a finished laminate. The lamina is usually combined with other raw laminae before fabrication. A preply includes a fiber system that is placed in position relative to all or part of the required matrix material to constitute the finished lamina. An organic matrix is called a prepreg.

reinforced plastic processes Different fabricating processes are used to produce RP parts. They range from no pressure to high pressure systems. Practically all processes used to fabri-

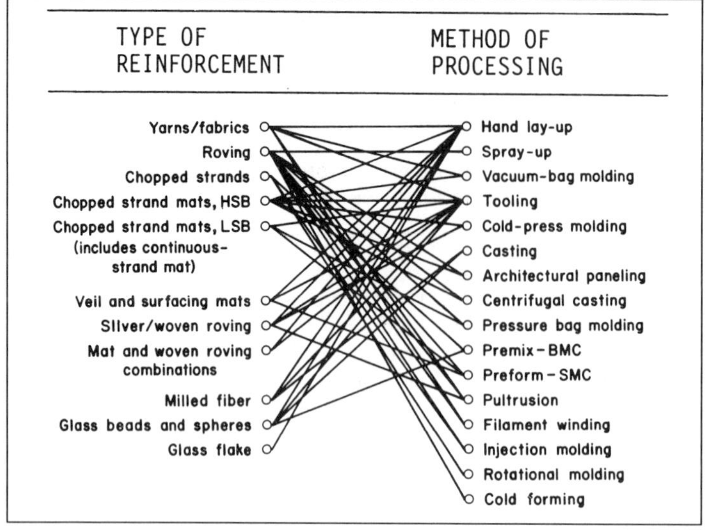

Examples of processes and reinforcements used in RPS.

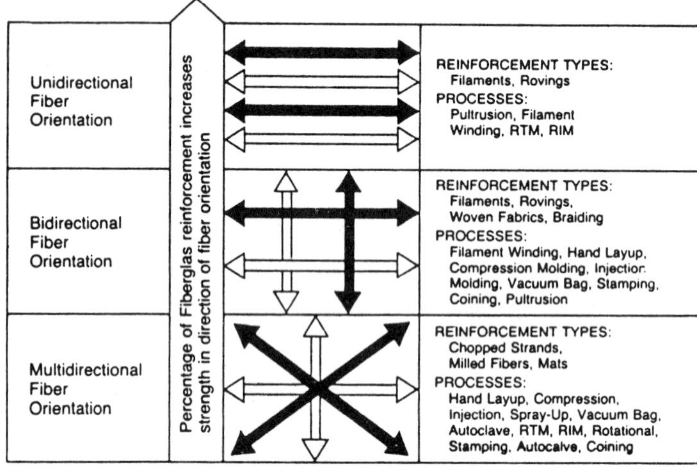

Relating directional properties to processes.

cate any (unreinforced) plastic product can be reinforced, so that they all can be considered applicable to the RP processes, such as those listed in ▷ **fabricating processes** and in the Figs. above. However, the major RP molding processes are hand lay-up, bag, compression, matched die, continuous laminating, pultrusion, resin transfer, spray-up, vacuum bag, filament winding and injection.

reinforced plastic processes automated Different processes are automated such as filament winding, injection molding, and pultrusion: however, to date most are labor intense and not highly automated. The first Fig. on p. 635 shows the start of automated hand lay-up during the 1950s.

reinforced plastic recycling As explained in ▷ **recyclable plastic and scrap,** thermoplastics can be granulated and recycled in the melt processable systems, but thermoset plastics can only be granulated and used as a filler with virgin materials. However, when any reinforced plastic is granulated, the length of the fibers is reduced. This action can affect the expected performance and processabilities of mix with virgin materials.

reinforced plastic reinforcement ▷ **reinforcement**

reinforced plastic, reinforcement mode and percentage Reinforcement may be random or directionally oriented and may vary in length from short milled fibers to chopped strands from 3 mm ($\frac{1}{8}$ in.) to 50 mm (2 in.) or longer. It may also be sold in prepared mats or woven fabrics or as continuous lengths. Mechanical strength is generally favored by increased

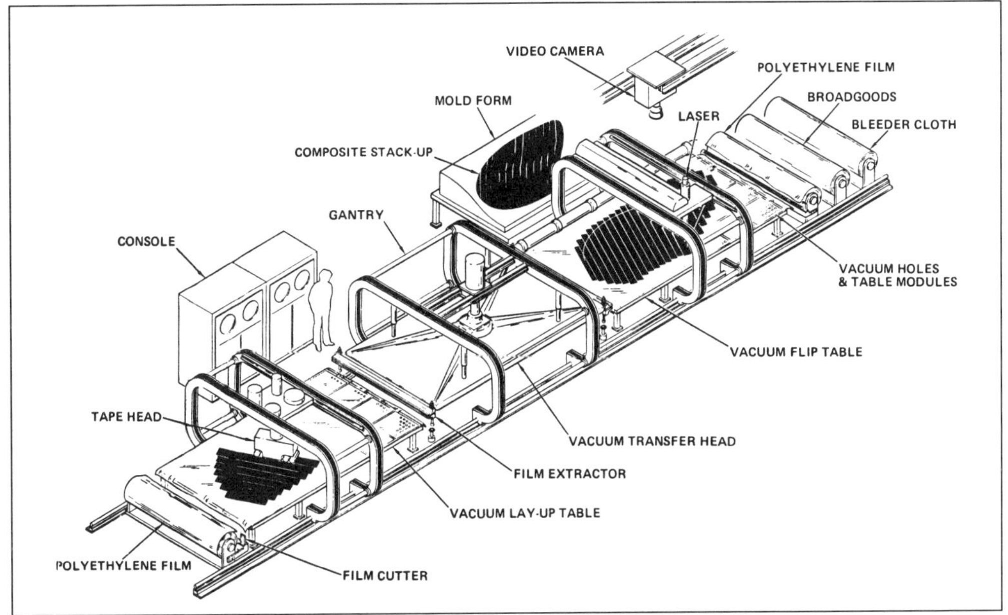

Automated-integrated reinforced plastic lay-up that uses thermoset preimpregnated sheet material; automation includes cutting and providing layout of prepreg in the mold, and final delivery of prepreg lay-up mold to a curing station such as an oven or an autoclave. This is the automated system of a hand lay-up system.

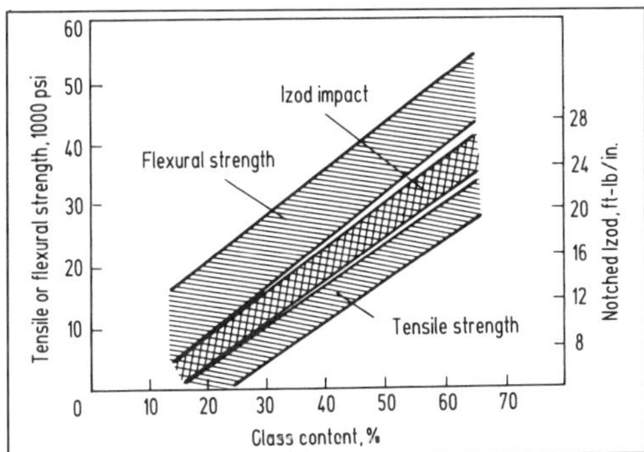

Effect of properties versus glass content.

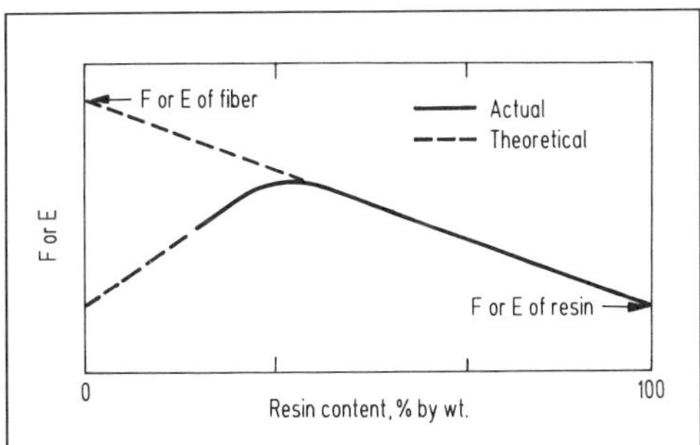

Effect of matrix content on strength and elastic moduli of RP.

amounts of reinforcing agent (see Figs. here), while good electrical properties require a dispersion of the high dielectric glass filaments throughout the molded part. Reinforcement quantities (by weight) for glass-TS polyester vary from a low of 1 to 2% (casting and some

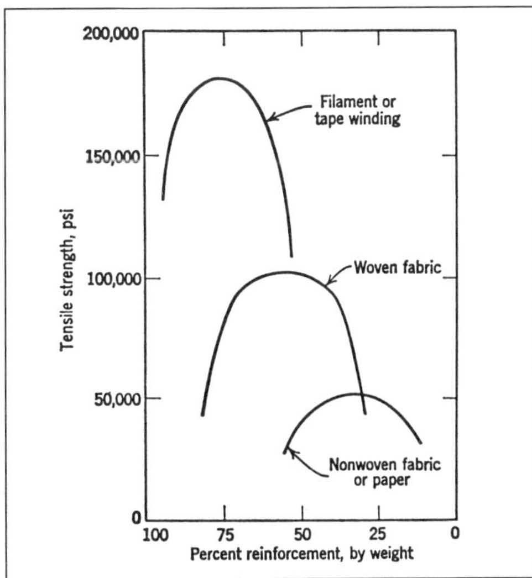

Example of strength versus glass content and type of reinforcement.

rotational molding), through the nominal 20 to 40% for the majority of uses (hand lay-up, compression and injection molding, and rotational molding), to a high of 65 to 85% (for specialty compression molding, pultrusion, and filament winding). Highest physical strengths are provided in the direction of major glass-fiber orientation.

reinforced plastics Plural of reinforced plastic.

reinforced plastic, salt spray process ▷ **salt bath**

reinforced plastic starved area An area in a part that has an insufficient amount of plastic to wet out the reinforcement completely. This condition may be due to improper wetting, impregnation, or plastic flow; excessive molding pressure; or incorrect bleeder cloth thickness. Also called dry laminate and lack of fillout.

reinforced plastic structural delamination ▷ **composite curved bar, delamination analysis**

reinforced plastic, structural integrated An RP structure in which several elements that would conventionally be fabricated separately and assembled by bonding or mechanical fasteners, are instead laid up and cured as a single, complex, continuous structure. The term is sometimes applied more loosely to any structure not assembled by mechanical fasteners. All or some parts of the assembly may be co-cured.

reinforced plastic, surfacing or overlay **1.** Gel coats are surface layers of material not containing reinforcing fibers. Normally 0.25 to 0.30 mm (0.010 to 0.012 in.) thick, they are formed by applying and curing a highly filled plastic layer. They may be designed for a range of characteristics such as improved appearance, chemical resistance, weather and craze resistance, abrasion resistance (see Fig. above). **2.** ▷ **surfacing mat** **3.** Vacuum-formed acrylic or other thermoplastic elements form the outer skin (replacing gel coats) on many RP parts such as sinks and vanities, with good adhering glass fiber-plastic applied as backing for rigidizing. Mold and operating costs are greatly reduced, and some of the defects associated with gel coats are eliminated. **4.** Incorporation of low-profile (low shrink) plastics in bulk moldings (BMCs) and sheet molding compounds (SMCs) greatly enhance acceptance and utilization of RP parts by avoiding the fiber pattern; without the low-profile plastic, fibers are revealed after molding because of plastic contracting around them.

Popular and practically all glass fiber-thermoset polyester hand lay-up RP boat with an exceptional surface finish (class A type) on all surfaces based on use of gel coating.

reinforced plastic tanker ▷ **railcar hopper**

reinforced plastic, tape wrapping ▷ **tape placement wrapped molding** and **lagging**

reinforced plastic tapping test The use of a coin (quarter, or better yet, half dollar) to tap an RP in different spots to detect a change in sound level, which would indicate the presence of a defect, such as a partially or uncured plastic spot. A surprisingly accurate test in the hands of experienced personnel. ▷ **nondestructive testing** and **sonic testing**

reinforced plastic, thermoset cure monitoring Various cure-monitoring methods have been used with the dielectric technique the most widely used. This position of prominence eventually may be usurped by fiber-optic techniques because the microminiature fiber-optic sensors are particularly well-suited for in situ cure monitoring. Other monitoring methods being employed include such sensing devices as frequency-dependent electromagnetic sensors (FDEMS), acoustic-emission transducers, ultrasonic sensors, pressure transducers, and fluorescence. Physical and chemical changes are detected. In general, cure processing sensors are designed to emit a signal that defines the critical material properties responsible for the quality of the manufacturing process being evaluated. In today's manufacturing environment, the sensors most used are thermocouples; there are those that cure without sensors. ▷ **thermoset plastic curing, dielectric monitoring**

reinforced plastic thickness tolerance guide The Table on p. 637 is a guide. ▷ **tolerance** and **shrinkage**

reinforced plastic time-dependent deformation and failures A comprehensive treatment of viscoelastic deformation in RPs shows that for thermorheological materials, creep and

RP wall thickness ranges and tolerances versus process.

Molding method	Thickness range Min., mm (in)	Max., mm (in)	Maximum practicable buildup within individual part	Normal thickness tolerance, mm (in)
Hand lay-up	1.5 (0.060)	30 (1.2)	No limit; use cores	±0.5 (0.020)
Spray-up	1.5 (0.060)	13 (0.5)	No limit; use many cores	±0.5 (0.020)
Vacuum-bag molding	1.5 (0.060)	6.3 (0.25)	No limit; over three cores possible	±0.25 (0.010)
Cold-press molding	1.5 (0.060)	6.3 (0.25)	3–13 mm ($\frac{1}{8}$–$\frac{1}{2}$ in)	±0.5 (0.020)
Casting, electrical	3 ($\frac{1}{8}$)	115 ($4\frac{1}{2}$)	3–115 mm ($\frac{1}{8}$–$4\frac{1}{2}$ in)	±0.4 (0.015)
Casting, marble	10 ($\frac{3}{8}$)	25 (1)	10–13 mm; 19–25 mm ($\frac{3}{8}-\frac{1}{2}$ in; $\frac{3}{4}-1$ in)	±0.8 ($\frac{1}{32}$)
BMC molding	1.5 (0.060)	25 (1)	Min. to max. possible	±0.13 (0.005)
Matched-die molding: SMC	1.5 (0.060)	25 (1)	Min. to max. possible	±0.13 (0.005)
Pressure-bag molding	3 ($\frac{1}{8}$)	6.3 ($\frac{1}{4}$)	2:1 variation possible	±0.25 (0.010)
Centrifugal casting	2.5 (0.100)	$4\frac{1}{2}$% of diameter	5% of diameter	±0.4 mm for 150-mm diameter (0.015 in for 6-in diameter); ±0.8 mm for 750-mm diameter (0.030 in for 30-in diameter)
Filament winding	1.5 (0.060)	25 (1)	Pipe, none; tanks, 3:1 around ports	Pipe, ±5%; tanks, ±1.5 mm (0.060 in)
Pultrusion	1.5 (0.060)	40 (1.6)	None	1.5 mm, ±0.025 mm ($\frac{1}{16}$ in, ±0.001 in); 40 mm, ±0.5 mm ($1\frac{1}{2}$ in, ±0.020 in)
Continuous laminating	0.5 (0.020)	6.3 ($\frac{1}{4}$)	None	±10% by weight
Injection molding	0.9 (0.035)	13 (0.5)	Min. to max. possible	±0.13 (0.005)
Rotational molding	1.3 (0.050)	13 (0.5)	2:1 variation possible	±5%
Cold stamping	1.5 (0.060)	6.3–13 (0.25–0.50)	3:1 possible as required	±6.5% by weight; ±60% for flat parts

stress relaxation can be predicted in RPs if the orthotropic viscoelastic constants are known. Whereas the effect on time on fiber-controlled deformation is not large, its effect on strength is pronounced. Glass fiber is especially susceptible to static fatigue, a loss of strength under sustained load. This effect is accelerated by moisture, which increases the crack-growth rate in stressed glass.

reinforced plastic toughness ▷ **toughness, area under the curve**

reinforced plastic void content Voids are generally the result of the entrapment of air during the construction of a lay-up, particularly with the use of hand lay-up and very low pressure processing methods. It is possible to have void contents of 1 to 3%. Depending on the application, voids can cause a reduction in part performance, particularly in certain environments and after lengthy outdoor exposures. If voids are undesirable, procedures can be used to reduce or eliminate them, such as applying a vacuum during the process. Another preventive method is to squeeze out air during lay-up by a roller or a spatula.

The following method can be used to estimate void content:

$$\text{Percent voids} = 100 - 100a\left(\frac{d}{c} + \frac{e}{b} + \frac{f}{g}\right)$$

where: a = specific gravity of product; b = specific gravity of fiberglass = 2.55; c = specific gravity of cured resin = range 1.18 to 1.24; d = plastic content, by weight; e = glass content, by weight; f = filler content, by weight; g = specific gravity of filler. This method is not exact because the assumption is made that the resin system has the same density with reinforcement as it does in an unreinforced casting. The net result is a possible overstatement of the void content. In addition to air entrapment, entrapment of volatiles can occur with certain plastics that release them during processing.

reinforced plastic weave pattern ▷ **glass fabric designations**

reinforced plastic weight, areal The weight of a fiber reinforcement per unit area (width × length) of tape or fabric.

reinforced railcar hopper ▷ **railcar hopper**

Example of fiber properties.

Property	E-glass	S-glass	HS graphite[1]	HM graphite[1]	Aramid	Boron
Diameter, μm	3–20	9	6–8	7–9	11.9	100, 140, 200
Density, g/cm³	2.54	2.49	1.7–1.8	1.85	1.44	2.65, 2.45, 2.38
Tensile strength, GPa	2.4	4.5	3–4.5	2.4	3.6	3.5
Elastic modulus, GPa	72.4	85.5	234–253	345–520	124	386–400
Thermal expansion, 10^{-6}/°C	5.0	5.6	−0.5(a)[2] 7(r)[2]	−1.2(a)[2] 12(r)[2]	−2(a)[2] 59(r)[2]	5.4
Thermal conductivity, W/(m · K)	1.86	2.55	8–25(a)[2]	105(a)[2]	3.1	2.7

[1] HS = High strength, HM = High modulus.
[2] (a) = axial, (r) = radial.

Comparative fiber and unidirectional RP properties.

Fiber/composite	Elastic modulus, GPa	Tensile strength, GPa	Density, g/cm³	Specific stiffness, MJ/kg	Specific strength, MJ/kg
E-glass fiber	72.4	2.4	2.54	28.5	0.95
Epoxy composite	45	1.1	2.1	21.4	0.52
S-glass fiber	85.5	4.5	2.49	34.3	1.8
Epoxy composite	55	2.0	2.0	27.5	1.0
Boron fiber	400	3.5	2.45	163	1.43
Epoxy composite	207	1.6	2.1	99	0.76
High strength graphite fiber	253	4.5	1.8	140	2.5
Epoxy composite	145	2.3	1.6	90.6	1.42
High modulus graphite fiber	520	2.4	1.85	281	1.3
Epoxy composite	290	1.0	1.63	178	0.61
Aramid fiber	124	3.6	1.44	86	2.5
Epoxy composite	80	2.0	1.38	58	1.45

Comparison of different materials.

Material	Relative price/kg	Density kg/m³	Relative price/m³	Young's modulus, GPa
Carbon steel	1	7800	1	210
E-glass	2	2590	0.7	65
S-glass	8	2590	2.7	90
HS-carbon	55	1800	13	230
MM-carbon	70	1800	16	400
Aramide	40	1450	7.4	130
Polyester	3	1200	0.5	4
Vinyl/ester	4.5	1200	0.7	3.5
Epoxy	4	1200	0.6	3.5
Processed with E-glass				
Filament winding	10	2000	2.6	40
Pultrusion	4	2000	1	38
SMC 50% fibre	7	1900	1.7	18
SMC 25% fibre	5	1800	1.2	10

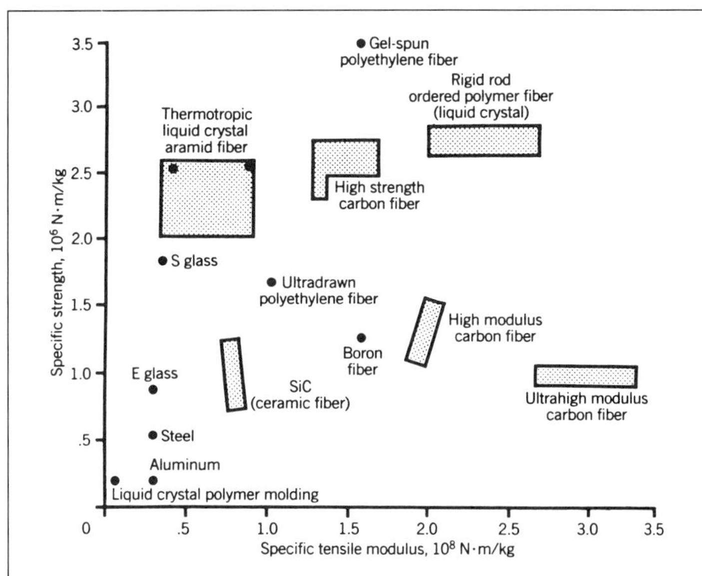

Comparison of specific strength versus specific modulus for a variety of reinforced plastics. Specific properties are normalized by plastic material density (Pa or N/m² divided by kg/m³).

reinforced reaction injection molding RRIM is when reinforcement is added to reaction injection molding (RIM). It is similar in practice to resin transfer molding. Sometimes called structural reaction injection molding. ▷ **reaction injection molding**

reinforcement Reinforcements are used with the plastic matrix to improve properties of the plastics, such as strength, modulus, toughness, and heat resistance. They are usually in fiber form; ▷ **fiber** regarding different forms. The Tables and Figs. on pp. 638–640 review types of fibers and their properties. Reinforcements include constructions other than fibers, such as

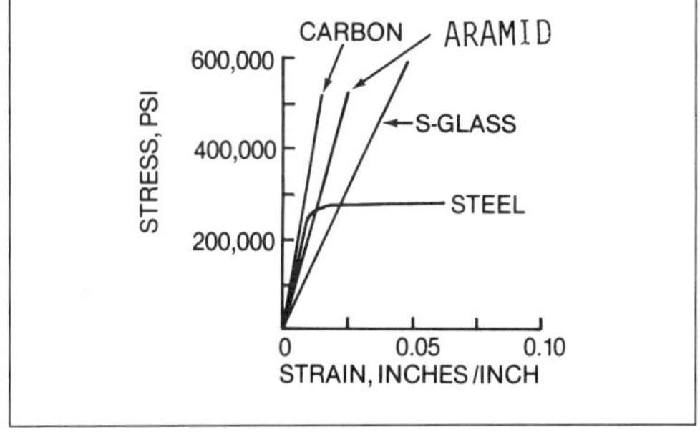

Stress-strain curves for carbon, aramid, S-glass, and ASTM KA-416 seven-wired strand.

Relative price stiffness	Relative weight stiffness	Yield fracture strength, MPa	Relative price strength	Relative weight strength
1	1	300	1	1
2.1	1.1	2000	0.1	0.05
6.2	0.77	2800	0.3	0.04
12	0.21	3400	1.1	0.02
8.5	0.12	2400	2.0	0.03
12	0.30	3000	0.7	0.02
		50		
		80		
		80		
13	1.3	1400	0.55	0.055
5.7	1.4	1100	0.28	0.070
20	2.8	300	1.7	0.24
24	4.8	90	3.8	0.77

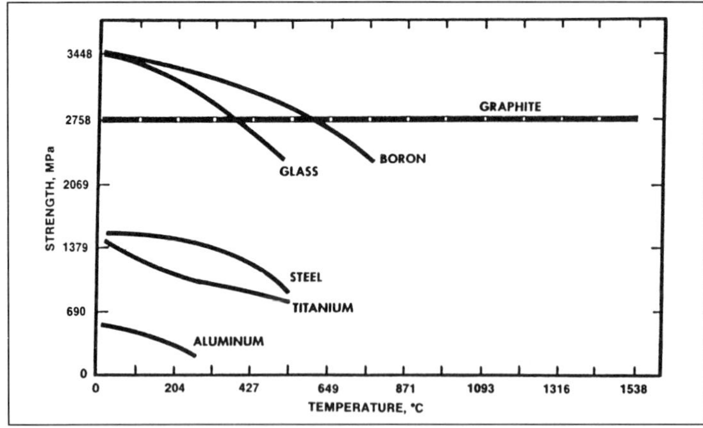

Tensile strength properties versus temperature of fibrous reinforcements used in RPS.

discs/flakes and whiskers. ▷**reinforced plastic; silicon carbide fiber; whisker**

reinforcement, discs Reinforcements and fillers primarily in the disc (also spelled disk) class include mica, glass flakes, and aluminum flakes. Naturally occurring micas have a variety of chemical compositions and morphologies. Three major types are commercially available: wollastonite, muscovite, and phlogopite. Mica particles are sometimes fiber-shaped, but more commonly platelet or flake-shaped, and their aspect ratio (width to thickness ratio ▷**aspect ratio**) plays an important role in reinforcement. The manufacturing process involves delamination of the raw material by wet or dry grinding and possible subsequent separation according to size and shape (aspect ratio). High aspect ratio (HAR of 5 to 10) gives very good reinforcement at reasonable cost, particularly when suitable surface treatments are used.

Glass flakes are formed by different methods such as glass melt literally blown and forced against a steel plate (smashed) and crushing thin glass tubes. Aluminum flakes are intended primarily as conductive filler for electromagnetic interference shielding (EMI). Flakes, particularly glass flakes, have been used in reinforced plastics since the 1950s. Today maximum efficiency in orienting with proper overlapping of flakes has not been achieved; theoretically proper alignment in RP would provide high performance properties. ▷**finish** and **sizing**

reinforcement efficiency The ratio of the amount of fiber contributing to reinforcement of the property under consideration to that not contributing.

reinforcement fabric weave pattern ▷**glass fabric designations**

reinforcement factor The ratio of the modulus of a reinforced plastic to that of its matrix plastic.

reinforcement fibers and sizes The Figs. below and opposite show the ranges of diameters and shapes of different inorganic fibers. The cross sectional shape of fibers affects the flexural rigidity and surface area. The bending stiffness of fibers also relates to cross sectional shape; for example, a triangular shape produces a higher bending stiffness than a circular fiber of the same cross sectional area. Regarding L/D ▷**aspect ratio**

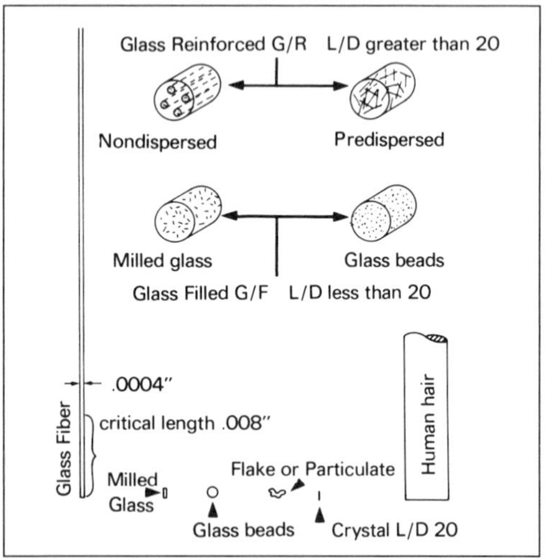

Glass fiber and other glass shapes.

reinforcement, glass fiber The major material used to reinforce plastics. ▷**glass fiber** and **reinforced plastic**

reinforcement metal Metals to date are not widely used as reinforcements. RPs are more often used to achieve weight reductions over metal structures. Metal RPs are too heavy. Other problems to date are bonding of the matric plastic to smooth metal surfaces and machining the RPs. An accurate assessment is that they are not commercially important or readily available. There are some commercial uses of metal powders in thermoplastic matrixes to allow these materials to be used as hot melt adhesives that will respond to heating by induction techniques.

An important technique in the use of metals with RPs is the use of metal skeletal structures such as those in the form of honeycomb panels. These honeycomb form the core of structures with metals or RPs on the facings (skins). These structures have been used (and important) since the 1940s in aircraft, building panels, etc. ▷ **honeycomb reinforced plastic core**

reinforcement, whisker ▷ **whisker**

related rates With problems, one tries to find the rate at which some quantity is changing by relating it to other quantities whose rates of change are known.

relative humidity ▷ **humidity, relative**

relative thermal index ▷ **thermal aging, relative thermal index** and **heat test**

relaxation The time-dependent return to equilibrium of a system, or property of a system, which has been displaced from equilibrium by an applied constraint in the context of plastic relaxation. The constraints may be an electric field (dielectric relaxation), visible or UV radiation (luminescence depolarization or dynamic birefringence), or most importantly the mechanical stress or strain (mechanical relaxation; a decrease in stress under sustained constant strain), or creep and rupture under constant load. A practical example in mechanical relaxation is the gradual "decay" of stress in a specimen which is held stretched. ▷ **dynamic mechanical relaxation**

relaxation stress ▷ **stress relaxation**

relaxation time The time required for a stress under a sustained constant strain to diminish a stated fraction of its initial value.

relaxation, ultrasonic ▷ **ultrasonic relaxation**

relaxation, viscoelastic ▷ **viscoelasticity**

relay A mechanical/electrical device in which a small electrical current is made to switch a large device.

relay logic Technique originally used for

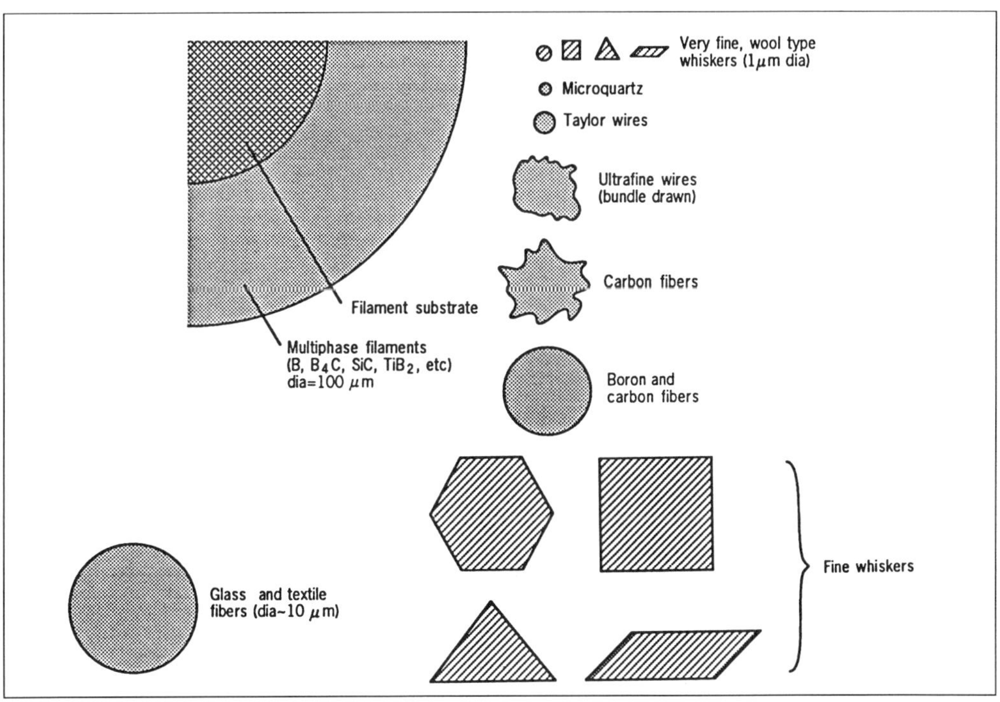

Fiber shapes and sizes.

timing and sequencing operations in processes (extrusion, injection, etc.). It has generally been replaced by electronic logic control.

release agent Also called parting agent, adherent, dusting agent, lubricant dusting agent, and mold release agent depending on type material and/or process involved. **1.** External release agents are lubricating liquids or solids (including dusting powder) substances that are applied to a mold to prevent sticking of the plastic during molding or casting. Examples of products used include silicones, calcium stearate, zinc stearate, sodium dioctylsulfosuccinate, long-chain alkyl quaternary ammonium compounds, talc (soapstone), mica, flour, clay, and, very important, waxes. To improve or ensure satisfactory part release, keep mold cavities clean. Use releases that do not interfere with the plastic or part performance. As an example, using silicone with electrical connectors could cause contamination or corrosion of metal pins; also silicone usually will cause difficulty in bonding or printing on the molded part. **2.** ▷ **lubricant additive** regarding internal release agent. **3.** Environmental concern requires solvent-free agents. They are used to eliminate volatile organic compounds (VOCs).

release agent performance RAs are in different forms (solid, granular, liquid) that reduce or prevent adhesion between two surfaces. They are important in plastic or rubber processing, pressure-sensitive tapes, paper coatings, etc. A number of factors influence adhesion of two materials to each other. The most important ones are penetration, chemical reaction and compatibility, surface tension, surface configuration, and polarity differences between the two materials. Basically two solid surfaces generally do not adhere to each other because wetting does not take place nor does penetration of one into the other. The only exception occurs when one of the surfaces is "tacky" or when chemical reaction takes place between the two surfaces at the interface. Frequently, high static charges can also lead to adhesion ▷ **adhesive**. Two smooth and glossy plastic surfaces adhere to each other also through the creation of a vacuum, which can be prevented by the use of release agents.

Thus, the use of RAs becomes of technical importance when a solid and a liquid, or even more so, when a solid and a paste or dough form an interface and adhere to each other. For many centuries adhesion of a highly viscous material, such as paste or dough, was a problem in home baking and cooking. Abherents in the form of fats, oils, or solids like flour were used in order to prevent the sticking of dough to wooden kneading boards or to various metal baking dishes. With the greater industrial use of plastics, both natural and synthetic, the commercial use of release agents became widespread. Some industries which are of great importance today could not have been developed without the availability of modern abherents ▷ **abherent**. An example is pressure-sensitive tapes, which could not be unwound if the tape backing were not coated with release agent ▷ **adhesive bonded label**.

Since many of the factors causing adhesion are of a chemical nature, one of the first requirements of a good RA is complete chemical inertness toward the two materials whose adhesion is to be prevented ▷ **adhesion**. Adhesion is often due to opposing polarities of the surfaces, therefore the polarity relation of the RA and of one or both of the surfaces in contact with it have to be taken into consideration in the choice of RA. Besides these two factors, a physical property of importance is good spreading ability or low surface tension, so that the RA will form a continuous film between the surfaces and in this way exclude any contact between the two materials. An important factor in this action of RAs is temperature dependence.

release agent use ▷ **mold release methods**

release film An impermeable layer of film that does not bond to the plastic being processed. It is a separator.

release paper A layer of paper which can be separated from the surface of a plastic article to which it has been applied or against which the plastic article has been formed. The term applies to papers used as interleaves between plastic sheets, temporary backings for pressure-sensitive adhesives, and papers used as temporary carriers in film and foam casting processes. These papers may be smooth or embossed, to impart any desired texture to the film or foam cast against them. They may also be preprinted with an ink that is transferred to the cast film.

rennet casein ▷ **casein**

repeatability The ability of a system to bring an object or processing parameter to a desired postion repeatedly. Because of inherent system inaccuracies and plastic material variabilities, it is generally thought of as a range of ideal positions for a series of identical positioning command inputs. Targeting for extreme tight accuracies or repeatabilities is accomplished by using a processing machine that has minimal variation in its mechanical operation with the required specialized process controls. ▷ **process control** and **machine aging**

replication Making a reverse image of a surface by means of an impression on or in a receptive material; usually applied to microscopic techniques for obtaining plastic replicas of observed products.

report In reports and any other type of documentation or written communication, they can include tables, figures, sketches, and/or others. With these type documentations always have them read from the bottom or right side of a page.

reprocessed plastic Thermoplastics that are recycled and either used alone or blended with virgin TPs via a heat meltable process. With thermoset plastics, scrap or used TS is granulated and reused as fillers and/or reinforcements in TSs or TPs.

reprography Copying or duplicating.

research and development expenditures, U.S. R&D in all areas of materials, products, computer softwares, environment, etc. (that includes plastics and plastic related products) are summarized in the Fig. where for the estimated calendar year 1991 total expenditure is $155.2 billion. Industry absorbs most of its own funds, either performing the R&D itself or contracting with other industrial performers. Four government agencies dominate the federal R&D funding authority (only slightly lower than 1990): Department of Defense 56.8%, Health and Human Services 13.1%, NASA 12.1%, and Department of Energy 8.8%.

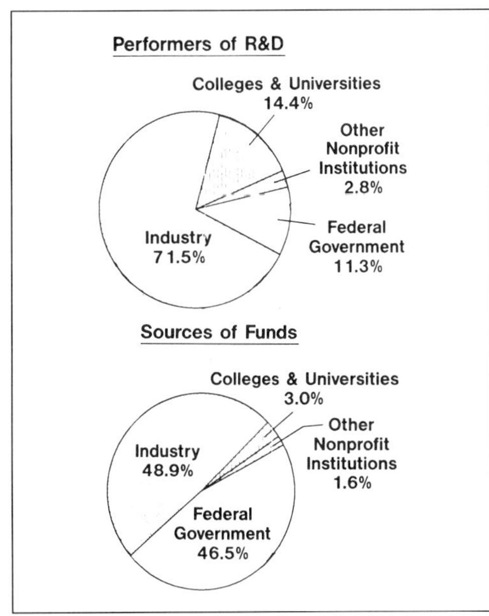

R&D expenditure in U.S. calendar year 1991.

resene The constituents of rosin that cannot be saponified with alcoholic alkali, but that contain carbon, hydrogen, and oxygen in the molecule.

reserves Raw materials identified and capable of economic extraction.

residence time The process of heating and cooling TPs can be repeated indefinitely by granulating scrap, defective parts, and so on. During the heating and cooling cycles of injection, extrusion, and so on, the material develops a "time to heat" history, or residence time. With only limited repeating of the recycling, the properties of certain plastics are not significantly affected by residence time. However, some TPs can significantly lose certain properties. Heat can also develop significantly if improper granulating recycled plastic systems are used; results in quick degradation of plastics. ▷ **granulating**

residual contaminant ▷ **reactor volatility**

residual deflection Permanent deformation after complete or partial removal of applied force on a product, component, structure, etc.

residual error The difference between the observed result and the predicted value.

residual gas analysis RGA is the study of residual gases in vacuum systems using mass spectrometry.

residual monomer The unpolymerized monomer that remains incorporated in a plastic after the polymerization reaction is completed. Plastics are produced with relatively no residual monomer (or technically cannot be determined). Thus for those requiring this type of plastic, order what you require.

residual strain ▷ **nondestructive test method, residual method; testing residual strain, destructive method; orientation; birefringence**

residual stress Such processing-induced residual stresses that influence properties as mechanical, physical, environmental, and aesthetic factors (which also exist in other materials like metals and ceramics) can have favorable or unfavorable effects, depending on the application of the load with respect to the direction of the stresses or orientation. For example, at room temperature an unoriented PS is a brittle, glassy, amorphous polymer, whereas a uniaxial oriented PS is highly anisotropic. High tensile strength, elongation, and resistance to environmental stress crazing and cracking are achieved in the direction of orientation. However, an oriented PS is weaker and more susceptible to stress crazing in its transverse direction than is an unoriented PS. A biaxally oriented PS is strong and tough in all directions.

Residual stresses and molecular orientation play an important role in the toughness enhancement of cold-worked plastics, because toughness is primarily based on the mechanics of craze formation and shear band (crazes and flaws) formation. The shear bands determine the fracture mode and toughness of a polymer when subjected to impact loads. The amount of energy dissipated will depend on whether the material surrounding the flaws deforms plastically. For toughness enhancement the residual stresses play an important role in the suppression of craze formation, by avoiding the stress state that promotes brittle fracture.

The term *residual stresses* identifies the system of stresses that are in effect locked into a part, even without external forces acting on it. For instance, minute stresses may be induced in a material by nonuniform heating and cooling. The production of residual stresses is usually the result of nonhomogeneous plastic deformation occurring during thermal and mechanical actions, arising from changes in either volume or shape. Thermal treatments like quenching (rapid cooling) and annealing (slow cooling) introduce changes in physical and mechanical properties. For example, with sheet plastic the stresses created by quenching are the result of uneven cooling, when the surfaces cool faster than the core. This produces nonuniform volume changes and properties throughout the thickness. The compressive stresses on the surfaces of the quenched plastic produce tensile stresses in the core, which maintain the equilibrium of the forces. ▷ **stress, frozen-in** and **stress relieving**

residual, torsion ▷ **torsional, residual**

residue Any undesirable material remaining on a substrate after any process step, after part is in service, etc.

resilience The ratio of energy returned, on recovery from deformation, to the work input required to produce the deformation, usually expressed as a percentage.

resiliency The ability to quickly regain an original shape after being strained or distorted.

resilient surfacing or flooring ▷ **recreational surface**

resin An alternative term, like polymer, to the predominantly used name of plastic. ▷ **plastic**

resinates, metallic Rosin in which part or all of the rosin acids have been chemically reacted with those metals that give soaps or salts which are water insoluble. Limed rosin, zinc-treated rosin, and the resinates of lead, cobalt, copper, and manganese, are of the greatest industrial importance.

resin binder ▷ **binder**

resin grout A grout system composed of essentially resinous materials such as epoxies, polyester, and polyurethanes.

resinography The science of morphology, structure, and related descriptive characteristics as correlated with composition or conditions and with properties or behavior of plastics, and their products. ▷ **molecular weight distribution resinography**

resinoid Any of the class of thermoset plastics, usually in their initial temporarily fusible state ▷ **thermoset plastic**

resin transfer molding RTM is a closed-mold, low pressure process in which a preplaced dry reinforcement preform is impregnated with a thermoset liquid resin (usually polyesters, although epoxies and phenolics may be used) in an injection or transfer process, through an opening in the center of a mold (see Figs. below and opposite.) The preform is placed in the mold, and the mold is closed. A two-component resin system (including catalyst, hardener, etc.) is then mixed in a static mixer and metered into the mold through a runner system. The air inside the closed mold cavity is displaced by the advancing resin front, and escapes through vents located at the high points or the last areas of the mold to fill. When the mold has filled, the

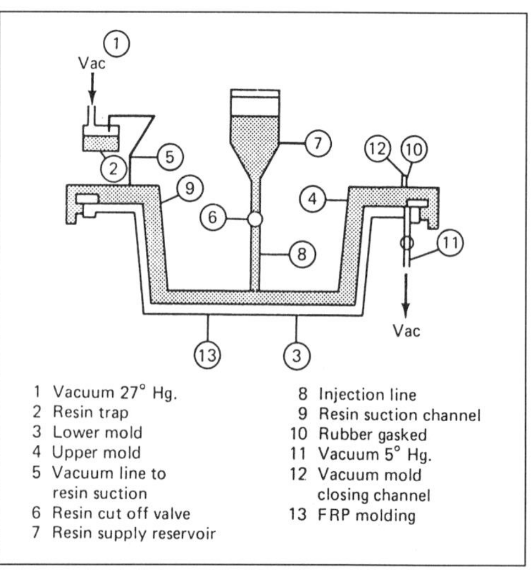

Schematic of RTM with plastic liquid entering from top of mold.

vents and the resin inlets are closed. The resin within the mold cures, and the part can be removed.

During the 1940s and the 1950s a similar system used vacuum. There was a dam around the outside opening of the two-part mold that contained the preform. This dam was filled with the mixed resin, and in the center of the mold, there was an opening that drew a vacuum. Thus resin could be drawn through the reinforcement, producing a cured part subjected to a maximum pressure of up to 14 psi. This type of vacuum at the vents or parting line is sometimes used with RTM to aid resin flow.

Advantages of RTM are that the molded part has two finished surfaces, and the overall process may emit a lower level of styrene vapor if the polyester resin used contains styrene. The mold, unlike a compression or TP stamping mold, is completely closed to defined stops prior to final part formation/curing. This procedure provides a more reproducible part thickness and tends to minimize trimming and deflashing of the final part.

Use of a reinforcement preform allows the preplacement of a variety of reinforcements in precise locations. The preforms remain in position during mold closing and resin injection. If large amounts of random reinforcements are used, consideration must be given to minimizing the washing or movement of the fibers due to resin flow near the resin inlet gates. A low injection pressure is another characteristic. Simple parts with a low proportion (10–20%, by volume) of reinforcement will fill rapidly at pressures of 10 to 20 psi (70–140 kPa). More complex parts, with 30 to 50% reinforcement, may require resin injection pressures in the 100 to 200 psi (700–1,400 kPa) range for rapid mold filling.

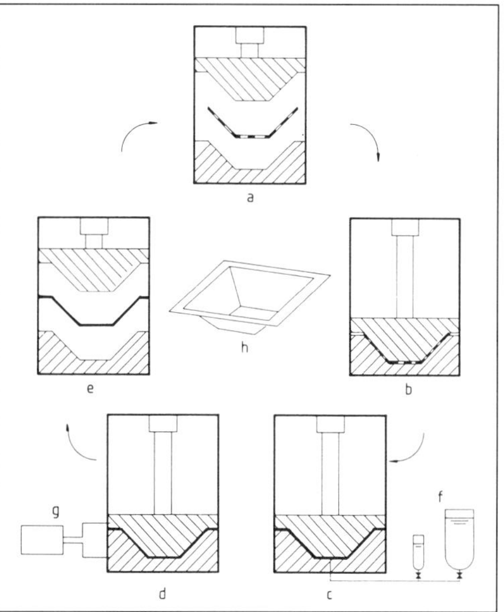

Process cycle in RTM: (*a*) placing reinforcement or preform, (*b*) closing the mold, (*c*) injection of liquid plastic mix, (*d*) heat curing of plastic, (*e*) demolding, (*f*) material storage (view not shown), (*g*) thermal control of mold, and (*h*) molded part removed from RTM process.

If low pressure is a requirement, as with large panels, a low injection pressure generally can be maintained and the fill time extended. In cases where low pressure and a fast fill time are required, the preform construction must be

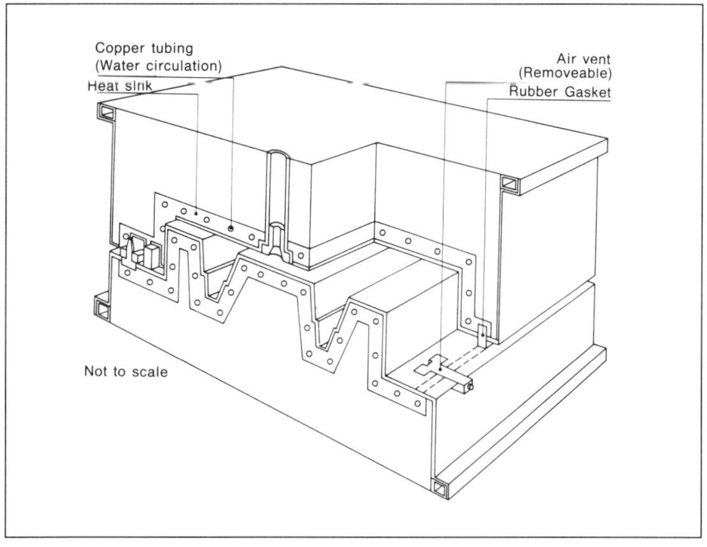

Cross section view of mold used in the RTM process.

carefully tailored to promote a rapid low-pressure fill without fiber movement. For a high volume, the cycle time will vary, depending on the complexity of the part and the degree of part integration achieved. For a simple component, a 1 min. cycle is commercially achievable at a production rate of 1.2 million parts per year. For complex parts, a cycle time of 6 min. or longer could be needed.

resist In photomechanics, a light-hardened stencil to prevent etching or non-printing areas on a printing plate.

resistal Identifies B-stage thermoset plastics. ▷**B-stage**

resistance **1.** Mechanically, an opposing or retarding force. **2.** ▷**electrical resistance**

resistance, abrasion The abilitiy to withstand scuffing, scratching, rubbing, or wind-scouring. ▷**cavitation erosion** and **rain erosion**

resistance strain gauge ▷**strain gauge**

resistance temperature detector ▷**temperature sensor**

resistivity ▷**electrical resistance, plastic**

resole plastic Also called one-step or one-stage plastic. Refers to a phenolic plastic made by adding more than one-to-one mol ratio of formaldehyde to phenol in the presence of a basic acid. This gives a linear phenolic plastic produced by alkaline condensate of phenol and formaldehyde. ▷**novalak**

resolution The minimum controllable motion interval that the system is capable of producing.

resonance **1.** In chemistry, the moving of electrons from one atom of a molecule or ion to another atom of the same molecule or ion. Thus, given atoms may remain in a fixed spatial arrangement with their electrons arranged so as to simultaneously satisfy two or more classical structural formulas. **2.** In the terminology of spectroscopy, resonance is the condition in which the energy state of the incident radiation is identical with the absorbing atoms, molecules, or other chemical entities. **3.** Mechanically, the reinforced vibration of a body exposed to the vibration, at about the frequency of another body.

resonance fluorescence ▷**absorption spectroscopy**

resonant forced vibration technique Technique for performing dynamic mechanical measurements, in which the sample is oscillated mechanically at the natural resonant frequency of the system. The amplitude of oscilllation is maintained constant by the addition of makeup energy. Elastic modulus is calculated from the measured frequency. Damping is calculated from the additional energy required to maintain constant amplitude. ▷**nonresonant forced and vibration technique** and **damping**

resonant frequency A frequency at which resonance exists.

resorcinal-formaldehyde plastic A type of phenol-formaldehyde plastic. Permanently fusible; soluble in water, ketones, and acohols. Adhesive types can be used whenever phenolics are used and where fast or room-temperature cure is desired.

resource Raw materials, including those not yet identified nor currently economical for extraction. ▷**raw material**

resource recovery ▷**material recovery** and **recoverable resource**

resource renewable A natural resource that can be replaced as it is consumed, such as restoring the forest (reforestation) in the lumber industry.

response The motion (or other output) in a device or system resulting from an excitation (stimulus) under specific conditions.

response curve for N cycles, fatigue A curve fitted to observed values of percentage survival at N cycles for several stress levels, where N is the preassigned number such as 10^6, 10^7, etc. It is an estimate of the relationship between applied stress and the percentage of the population that would survive N cycles.

responsibilities commensurate with abilities Now, the method of employing people is to use the avaricious and the stupid, the wise and the brave, and to give responsibilities to each in situations that suit the person. Do not charge people to do what they cannot do. Select them and give them responsibilities commensurate with their abilities. (Quotation from Sun Tzu, *The Art of War*, about 500 B.C.) ▷**people** and **perfection**

restrictor ring ▷**mold restrictor ring**

retainer pin ▷**mold retainer pin**

retardation ▷**inhibition and retardation**

retarder ▷**inhibitor**

retentate ▷**dialysis**

reticulate The formation of a network or net-like structure.

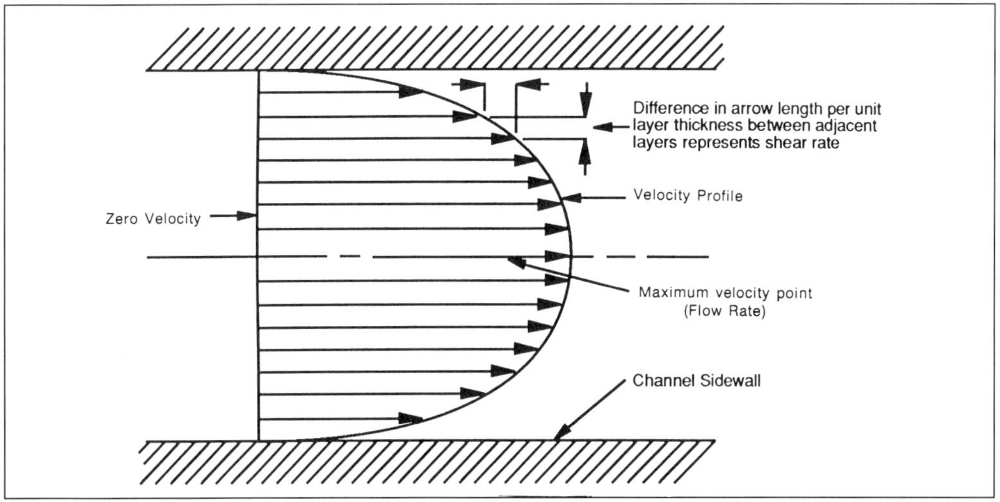

Example of laminar flow in a channel.

retort Refers to the shape of a type of simple distillation unit characterized by a glass neck twisted downward.

retortable pouch ▷ **thermoforming, form, fill, and seal** and **aseptic liquid pouch**

retrosynthesis A computer-assisted analysis of an organic molecule that is to be synthesized.

returnable container ▷ **container, returnable**

return on investment ROI (also called return on capital employed) is the amount of profit expressed as a percentage of the investment in the business. Investment can be stockholders' equity; it can be total assets or it can be limited to some of the assets such as inventories and fixed assets in a manufacturing plant.

reuse of plastic Collecting, cleaning, and marketing a waste component (such as plastic, glass, aluminum container, etc.) for use again. Different from recycling, as the material need not be reprocessed (melted) before reuse. ▷ **recycling**

reverse flighted screw ▷ **screw reverse flight**

reverse osmosis ▷ **osmosis**

reverse roller coating The coating is premetered between rolls and then wiped off on the web (film, sheet, etc.) The amount of coating is controlled by the metering gap and also by the speed of rotation of the coating roll. ▷ **coating**

Reynold's number A ratio used to determine whether the flow of a viscous fluid through a passage (such as a pipe) is laminar (streamlined, see Fig. above) or turbulent. The formula for Reynold's number is:

$$R = \frac{7740\,VD}{n} \text{ or } \frac{3160Q}{Dn}$$

where: V = fluid velocity, ft/s (m/s); D = diameter of passage, in. (cm); n = kinematic viscosity, centistokes (see Table); Q = flow rate, gpm.

Kinematic viscosity, centistokes.

Water temperature °F	Water temperature °C	Viscosity (n)
32	0	1.79
50	10	1.30
68.4	20.2	1.00
100	37.8	0.68
150	66	0.43
212	100	0.28

Values of 2100 or lower represent lamina-flow and those above 3000 denote turbulent flow. This flow information is used in designing water (or liquid) lines in molds and dies where a certain degree of turbulent flow is required to remove heat from plastic melt most efficiently. ▷ **laminar flow; turbulent flow; mold cooling; melt flow defects**

RF heating ▷ **dielectric heating**

R-glass A cross between E-glass and S-glass, that is in limited production. ▷ **glass fiber types**

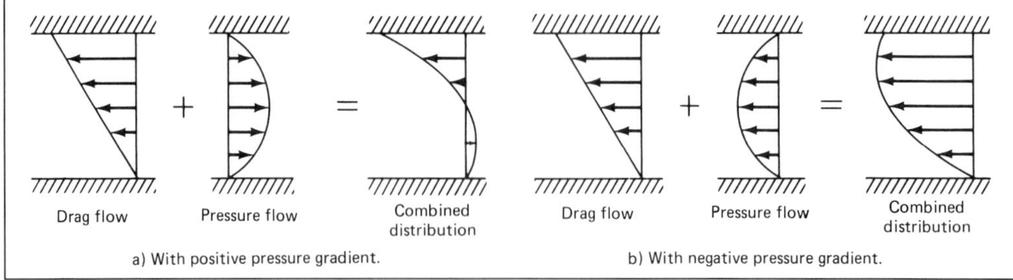

Down channel melt flow velocity during processing.

rheological mechanical spectrometer RMS method relates chemical structure of plastics to physical properties. Measures viscous and elastic response in terms of dynamic viscosity over a wide temperature range (0 to 300°C) and mechanical frequency range. Familiarity with rheology and mechanical properties required.

rheology The science of the deformation and flow of matter. It is concerned with the response of materials to mechanical force (see Fig. above). That response may be irreversible flow, reversible elastic deformation, or a combination of both. An understanding of rheology and the ability to measure rheological properties is necessary before viscous behavior can be controlled. Such control is essential for the manufacture and handling of numerous plastic materials and products. The term is most commonly applied to the study of liquids and liquid-like materials such as blood, paint, catsup, plastic solution, and plastic melt. Concerns materials that flow, although also studies the deformation of solids such as occurs in forming and stretching in different materials. Two key words in defining rheology are deformation and force. To learn about rheological properties of a material, one must either measure the deformation resulting from a given force or measure the force required to produce a given deformation. There are two principal aspects of rheology; quantitative relationships and influencing factors.

One aspect involves the development of quantitative relationships between deformation and force for a material of interest. The information for the development of such a relationship is obtained from experimental measurements. For example, with a plastic foam cushion the force required to compress it a certain distance is proportional to the distance. With a lubricating oil, the speed with which it flows through a small hole in the bottom of a can is proportional to the height of the oil remaining in the can. For a linear elastic material or Newtonian fluid, such simple observations are sufficient to establish a general equation describing how such a material will respond to any type of deformation. Such an equation is called a "constitutive equation" or a "rheological equation of state". However, for more complex materials such as non-Newtonian molten plastics, the development of a constitutive equation is very complex and more difficult to evaluate, requiring many different experiments.

The second aspect of rheology is the development of relationships that show how rheological behavior is influenced by the structure and composition of the material, also the temperature and pressure. Ideally, one would like to know how these parameters affect the constitutive equations that are used on Newtonian materials. With the more complex materials, relationships are developed showing how specific rheological properties such as viscosity and the relaxation modulus are influenced by molecular structure, composition, temperature, and pressure. Since molten plastics are rheologically complex materials that can exhibit both viscous flow and elastic recoil, a truly general constitutive equation has not been developed for these plastics. Present knowledge of their rheological behavior is largely empirical for these viscoelastic materials. ▷ **viscoelasticity**

rheology, controlled Controlled rheology (CR) is the controlled degradation with peroxide in an extruder, and has greatly extended the scope of applications for all types of PP products, whether homopolymers, random copolymers, or block copolymers. The greatest benefits have been in injection molding applications. For example, by using CR products one can injection mold housings that have excellent optical and mechanical properties and are not significantly different from those made of ABS. The extent to which PP has become accepted as an engineering material for IM is largely based on CR technology. Extruded CR products include: (1) high strength yarns, as they make possible a higher draw ratio and increased strength, (2) films, where they offer advantages especially in optical properties (gloss, haze), (3) thermoforming thin-walled items for certain applications.

rheology, melt flow behavior ▷ **melt flow behavior**

rheology, molecular arrangement ▷ **molecular arrangement structure**

rheology, molecular weight ▷ **molecular weight**

rheologhy, molecular weight distribution ▷ **molecular weight distribution**

rheometer A rheological instrument for determining the flow properties of a plastic (usually of high viscosity or in the molten condition of thermoplastic) by forcing the melt through a die or orifice of specific size at a specified temperature and pressure. Also called plastometer or viscometer.

rheometer, capillary A specific type rheometer, comprising a capillary tube of specified diameter and length, means for applying desired pressures to force the molten plastic through the capillary, means for maintaining desired temperatures of the apparatus, and means for measuring differential pressures and flow rates. The data obtained ise usually presented as graphs of shear stress against shear rate at a constant temperature.

rheometer, capillary on-line In on-line systems a slit die or capillary die is fed with a controlled melt volume. The pressure difference between the start and end of the capillary is measured as a function of different flow volumes. The different shear stresses follow Hagen-Poiseulle law regarding the viscosity function. According to the law, the controlled melt flow through the capillaries is directly proportional to the shear rate. It follows that at low shear rates, the melt flows entering the rheometer are small. This results in long measuring system response time. There are two basic on-line in real time concepts, namely, the open system with melt delivery into the open and the closed-loop rheometer with melt feedback.

In the open system, after measurement, the melt is conveyed into the open and scrapped. The compactness of the unit is an advantage. It enables the distances from the melt sampling to the measuring point to be kept short. In a closed-loop system, the melt is recirculated after measurement into the main melt stream of the extruder (or the plasticator). Closed-loops with melt feedback are more complex in design than open rheometers, since in addition to the melt sampling, the problem of feedback of the plastic melt must also be solved. Moreover, at least a second pump is necessary to eliminate process related pressure fluctuations.

rheometer, dynamic A system in which the applied shear or tensile stress (or applied deformation rate) is varied periodically with time, usually sinusoidally. The rheometer may therefore be used to determine the dynamic and complex viscosities of fluids. In general, the sample is deformed by some oscillatory driver, often electromechanically, and the amplitude is measured by a strain transducer (such as a linear variable differential transformer or an optical device). The stress is measured by the small deformation of a relatively rigid spring or torsion bar, to which is attached a stress transducer. Such instruments can operate over a wide frequency range, and therefore a correspondingly wide shear rate range, but only small deformations are possible. In addition to viscosity, elastic modulus may also be determined. Also called oscillating rheometer.

rheometer, extrusion A type of viscometer used for determining the melt index of a plastic. It consists of a vertical cylinder with two longitudinal bored holes, one for measuring temperature and one for containing the melt specimen. This latter hole has a specified orifice diameter at the bottom and a plunger entering from the top. The cylinder is heated by external bands and a weight is placed on the plunger to force the specimen through the orifice. Also called extrusion plastometer.

rheometer, viscometer This term is frequently used for two types of capillary instruments; one used for concentrated solutions or plastic melts (▷ **rheometer, capillary**) and the other used for measuring dilute solution viscosities. The most widely used of the latter types employs a glass capillary tube and means for timing the flow of a measured volume of solution through the tube under the force of gravity. This time is then compared with the time taken for the same volume of pure solvent, or of another liquid of known viscosity, to flow through the same capillary.

rheopecticity The opposite of thixatropy. The viscosity of rheopectic materials increases with time under a constantly applied stress, and decreases upon removal of the stress.

rhombohedral Having three equal axes, with the included angles equal to each other but not equal to 90°.

rib Ribs and gussets are very efficient methods of adding strength and stiffness to any structure since the strength generally increases as the square of the overall height of the section while

This aqua cycle operates most efficiently with its ribbed rotational molded wheels.

the stiffness increases as the cube of the overall height of the section (see Fig. above). Since material furthest from the neutral axis of any section carries the bulk of the load, it is a design goal to have most of the plastic in these outer sections, as in a box section of an I-beam. Ribs (ridges or raised sections) reduce the bulk weight or weight of parts that must meet high strength and rigidity requirements. They provide lateral, longitudinal, or horizontal support. Interconnecting ribs are frequently used to prevent bowing or warpage of large flat surfaces. ▷ **rigidity**

ribbon blender **1.** Mixing devices comprising helical ribbon-shaped blades rotating close to the edge of a U-shaped vessel jacked for temperature control. They are used for relatively high viscosity fluids and plastic dry-blends such as PVC calendering and extrusion compounds. **2.** Agitating devices consisting of two or more metal strips (ribbons) pitched in opposite directions spirally arranged around a central shaft. The curved and reverse-pitch ribbons operate on the principle of a screw; the plastic is moved forward by one ribbon and backward by another, so that efficient mixing results.

rice paper ▷ **straw**

right-angle fold Term used for two or more folds that are at 90° angles to each other.

right-to-know law ▷ **hazards, Federal Register 29 cfr 1910.1200**

rigid electrical insulating material Those having a minimum flexural modulus of 10^5 psi (7,000 kgf/cm^2) as determined by ASTM method D 790, Test for Flexural Properties of Plastics.

rigidity That combination of thickness and inherent stiffness of a material which resists flexure. An example is ribbing, as shown in the Table below. ▷ **rib**

rigidity, flexural ▷ **flexural rigidity**

rigidity, modulus ▷ **modulus, rigidity**

rigidity, relative In dynamic mechanical measurements, the ratio of modulus at any temperature, frequency, or time to the modulus at a reference temperature, frequency, or time.

rigidity, stiffness ▷ **rigidity** and **flexural strength**

rigid plastic For the purpose of general classification, a plastic that has a modulus either in tension or flexural greater than 700 MPa (100,000 psi) at 23°C and 50% relative humidity. ▷ **semirigid plastic** and **nonrigid plastic**

Examples of ways of using ribs to increase rigidity and reduce weight.

Case	Shape	Change	Moment of inertia	Increase in I, %	Increase in weight, %	Ratio I/Wt.
1		Base 2″ × $\frac{1}{4}$″	0.0026			
2		Double height	0.0208	700	100	7
3		Add $\frac{1}{8}$″wx $\frac{1}{4}$″H Rib	0.0048	85	6.25	14
4		Add $\frac{1}{4}$″wx $\frac{1}{4}$″H Rib	0.0064	146	12.5	12
5		Add $\frac{1}{8}$″wx $\frac{1}{2}$″H Rib	0.0118	354	12.5	28
6		Add $\frac{1}{4}$″wx $\frac{1}{2}$″H Rib	0.0194	646	25	26

rigid polyvinyl chloride ▷**polyvinyl chloride, rigid**

rigidsol A term for a plastisol which forms an article of very high durometer hardness. Such hardness is obtained by compounding techniques which permit the use of relatively small amounts of plasticizer, and/or by the incorporation of monomers which serve as diluents at room temperatures but which crosslink or polymerize upon heating.

ring gate ▷**mold gate, ring**

risk level ▷**acceptable risk**

risk management No one would advise, as an example, medical device manufacturers to gamble on their product liability claims. Yet, many state that liability insurance should be the last consideration in a device company's risk management program. One option before considering insurance, or an alternate to it, is retaining the product liability loss exposure, known as risk retention ▷**risk retention**. Insurance is expensive. Policies may be riddled with exclusions. Coverage can be cancelled. Insurers (even banks) can go broke. For the device company with the fortitude to forge its own course, risk retention may be a viable dimension of a sound risk management program. ▷**acceptable risk**

risk retention As reviewed in the example of ▷**risk management**, risk retention is the decision of a device firm to fund its own losses instead of paying them through insurance or other means. Some companies cannot afford insurance. Others can buy it but do not like the terms and conditions offered by the insurers. Still others do not want to delegate the handling of their claims to some insurance company claims adjuster who, a week before, was delivering bread.

Riteflex Tradename of Hoechst-Celanese's copolyester thermoplastic elastomers.

rivet, cold heading ▷**cold forming**

robot A production or laboratory system can use robots to perform automatically simple to complex manual operations that cannot be done manually. Robots can expedite production, ensure consistency of operations, and/or minimize or eliminate human labor. As an example, a simple task for the robot is to extract a part from a mold cavity(s), dropping it onto a conveyor belt, or possibly onto a table for an operator to position, assemble, etc. They can pour materials from drums to hoppers and perform many other simple jobs. They can be programmed for multiple procedures, conduct quality control, work in hazardous environments, and control and operate processing loaders and blenders, chillers and temperature control equipment, granulators, decorating, parts handling, packaging, etc. Glossary of terms applicable to robots follows:

Axes of Motion: The number of moving joints that determine the total movements of which the robot is capable. This is also known as degrees of freedom.

Control—Servo and Nonservo robots: (a) Servo—Point-to-point robots programmed to get from one point to the next without regard for the path they take. Continuous path servo robots follow the path defined by the program. (b) Nonservo—Generally limited sequence robots that move only between pre-difined end points on each axis. They are fast, offer a high degree of repeatability and are generally less expensive than servo controlled robots.

Memory Capacity: Expressed as the number of steps or distinct motions or functions that the robot can perform in one program.

Power Supply: Power supplies are either pneumatic, electric or hydraulic drives, or in some cases combinations therof.

Positioning Accuracy: The accuracy of the tooling on the end of the manipulator in reaching its objective. This is critical for precise unloading of tiny parts.

Programming: There are three basic methods of programming: electronic memory, microprocessor and manual. (a) Electronic Memory—Lead-through is maneuvering the robot's arm from one position to the next from a control console, thereby recording the program. Walk-through is accomplished by the operator physically guiding the robot arm or using a special teaching arm through the desired motions. The robot memorizes these movements and repeats them. (b) Microprocessor—Controls sophisticated robots by using a high level programming language and program that contains identified motions. (c) Manual—Manual programming is accomplished by presetting cams on a rotating stepping drum for example, or by connecting up air logic tubing or in the case of nonservos setting limit switches on each axis.

Weight Carrying Capacity: The maximum amount of weight or payload that can be carried from Point A to Point B at the normal operating speed of the manipulator arm. This weight also includes the weight of the tool (gripper).

Work Envelope: The work envelope is the reach of the robot. It usually has one of three shapes: cylindrical, spherical or spheroidal, depending upon the basic configuration of the arm and on the major axes of motion. Three major parameters give simple descriptions: horizontal arm sweep (degree of rotation around the central axis) vertical motion at minimum and maximum arm extension, and radial arm extension measured from the central axis.

Wrist Movement: Used to orient the gripper or end of manipulator arm tooling that can make a minor contribution to the shape and the size of the work envelope. Pitch is rotation about the transverse axes, (movement in the vertical plane) and roll is rotation about the longitudinal axis and yaw is rotation about the perpendicular axis (movement in the horizontal plant) which is also known as swing.

robot, intelligent A category of robots that have sensory perception, making them capable of performing complex tasks which vary from cycle to cycle. They are capable of making decisions and modifications to each cycle.

robot, material handling A robot designed and programmed so that it can machine, cut, form, or in some way change the shape, function, or properties of the materials it handles between the time they are first grasped and the time they are released in a manufacturing process. ▷ **auxiliary equipment**

robot, mobile A robot mounted on a moving platform. The motions of the robot about the work place are controlled by the robot's control system.

robot, pick and place A simple, point to point, non-servo, limited sequence robot designed primarily to manipulate objects from one place to another.

rock-and-roll processing Similar in some aspects to rotational molding. In this process, the mold is rotated only on the horizontal axis while the mold ends are rocked up and down.

rocker ▷ **container, rocker**

Rockwell hardness A value derived from the increase in depth of an impression as the load on an indenter is increased from a fixed minimum value to a higher value and then returned to the minimum value. Indentors for the test include steel balls of several specific diameters and a diamond cone penetrator having an included angle of 120° with a spherical tip having a radius of 0.2 mm (0.0070 in.). Rockwell hardness numbers are always quoted with a prefix representing the Rockwell Scale corresponding to a given combination of load and indentor, for example, HRC 30. ▷ **hardness**

Rockwell superficial hardness test Same as the Rockwell hardness test except that smaller minor and major loads are used.

rodent resistance additive The ability of a plastic to withstand or repel attacks by rodents. Some plastics require additives to prevent rodents from chewing objects such as cable insulation.

rod mill A closed steel cylinder one-third filled with steel rods of about the same length as the cylinder and 1 to 2 in. (2.5 to 5 cm) in diameter. As the cylinder rotates the rods roll over one another, exerting a combination of impact and grinding action on the material charge. It results in products of 50 to 60 mesh with a minimum of fines. Use includes size reduction of ores, minerals, metal powders, etc.; which in turn includes use as plastic fillers.

roll In a linear stage, an unwanted tendency of a positioned object to rotate about the axis of its translatory motion such as in producing extruded film, etc.

roll bowed ▷ **bowed roll**

roller coating The process of coating substrates with fluid plastics, solution, or dispersions by contacting the substrate with a roller on which the fluid material is spread. The process is often used to apply a contrasting color on raised lettering or markings (see Fig. below). ▷ **coating**

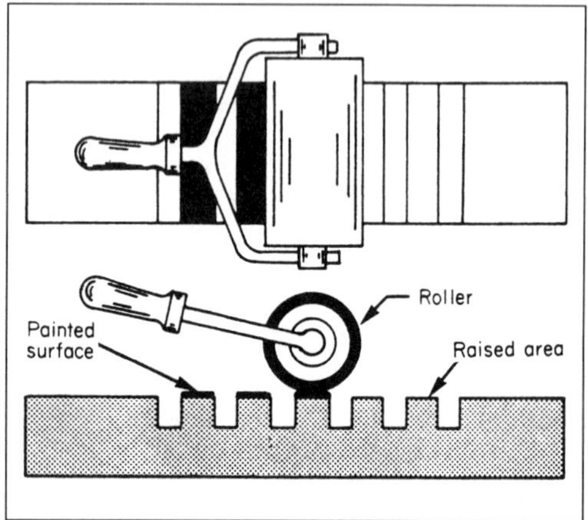

Roller coating decoration on small raised areas of lettering, figures, and other designs.

roll, expander ▷ **expander roll**

roll, heat-transfer adjustment ▷ **extruder web heat transfer roll adjustment**

rolling **1.** Rolling film and sheet is practiced to modify its surface properties and to modify its physical properties by orientation. For example, high and low gloss surfaces can be obtained by using rolls with the appropriate surface. Tensile strength and modulus may be increased by rolling. The rolls are usually chrome-coated steel with carefully prepared surface finishes. ▷ **orientation** **2.** Mechanical working with two or more cylindrical rolls to increase properties of plastic, aluminum foil, steel, etc.

roll leaf stamping Used to produce small designs. It involves the transfer of a dry ink by heat and pressure from a carrier to the film. Also called roll leaf printing or hot stamping.

roll mill Two rolls placed in close relationship to one another used to admix a plastic material with other substances. The rolls turn in opposite directions and different speeds to produce a shearing action to the materials being compounded. The separation or nip between rolls is adjustable (set screws, etc.). With shearing friction generating considerable heat, the rolls are water-cooled temperature controlled.

roll-on machine Roll-on machines are used to advance preprinted heat transfers and conventional hot-stamping foils. ▷ **coating**

roll stand For a sheet line, it usually uses three rolls that are actuated by pneumatic or hydraulic cylinders. Precision stand requires accuracy in flat smooth roll surfaces, temperature control on complete roll surfaces, spacing, and RPM. ▷ **extruder sheet**

room temperature ▷ **temperature, room**

room temperature curing adhesive An adhesive that sets (to handling strength) within an hour at temperatures from 20 to 30°C (68 to 86°F) and later reaches full strength without heating.

room temperature vulcanizing RTV is vulcanization or curing at room temperature by chemical reaction, particularly of silicones and other thermoset elastomers. Use includes producing molds "around" a product model that is used in processes such as: potting; encapsulation; contact, vacuum, or low pressure compression molding; thermoforming, etc. ▷ **silicone elastomer**

root Innermost part of thread, rounded or flattened; joining flanks of adjacent threads.

root-mean-square RMS is a measure of the average size of any measurable item (coiled molecule, film thickness, length of bar, etc.) that relates to the degree of accuracy per standard deviation measurement. ▷ **standard deviation measurement**

root-mean-square difference RMSD is a measure of accuracy determined by the following equation:

$$\text{RMSD} = \left(\frac{1}{n}\sum_{1}^{n} \times e_i^2\right)^{\frac{1}{2}}$$

where n = the number of observations for which the accuracy is determined, and e_i = the difference between a measured value of a property and its accepted value.

root-mean-square strain The square root of the mean value of the square of the strain, averaged over one cycle of deformation. For a symmetrical sinusoidal strain, the RMS strain equals the strain amplitude divided by $\sqrt{2}$.

root-mean-square stress The square root of the mean value of the square of the stress, averaged over one cycle of deformation. For a symmetrical sinusoidal stress, the RMS stress equals the stress amplitude divided by $\sqrt{2}$.

root-mean-square voltage RMS voltage, or "average" voltage, shown on AC test meter.

Rosato Important to provide definitions particularly when words or terms have more than one definition such as: **1.** Rosato is a light red wine, also called rosé. **2.** Rosato is the name of a person, and **3.** See all the definitions for *flaw* listed under ▷ **troubleshooting flaw**

Rosato, Dominick V. (1921–) Involved in working principally with TP and TS plastics, as well as steel, aluminum, wood, etc., since 1939 that includes: R&D in plastics, processes, and product designs; production processing [extrusion (film, sheet, profile, fiber, etc.), molding (injection, blow, compression, etc.), calendering, thermoforming, etc.]; and designing profitable products in different markets (from toys to space vehicles). Honors received include: distinguished SPI Achievements in Machinery, Reinforced Plastics, Safety, etc.; prestigious award for dynamic leadership in Injection Molding (SPE); SPE Fellows (historical first with six other fellows 1984); Extrusion and manufacturing awards (U.S. Gov't); Certificate for Advancing Use of Plastics (National Bureau of Standards); Recognition for Advanced Engineering Design with Plastics (ASME); ASTM Standardization for Plastics Call-Out Achievement; outstanding Editorial Citation of Excellence Presentation; and recognition-involvement in first all plastic airplane 1944 (RP structure). Professional association activities have included SPI Policy Committees (RP, Building, Bottles, etc.); SPE National Executive Committee, Division Boards (Injection, Extrusion), International Conference Committee; Materials Advisory Board of the National Academy of Science; Senior Member of Institute of Electrical

& Electronics Engineers; Licensed Professional Engineer of Massachusetts; etc.

Positions held (worldwide operations) were Chief of Plastics R&D (U.S. Air Force), Chief Engineer/Designer (Raymark), International Marketing Manager (Ingersoll-Rand), Director of Seminars and in-plant programs, and Professor at Rhode Island School of Design and University of Lowell. Worked with thousands of plants worldwide, prepared over 500 technical and marketing articles, and has been involved in publishing over 20 books. See *References* on p. lxi. Received B.S. Mechanical Engineer (Drexel Univ.) with continued education at Yale, Ohio State, and Univ. of Pennsylvania.

rosatte strain gauge ▷ **stress-strain measurements and extensometer**

rosin A translucent amber colored to almost black brittle friable natural plastic. It is obtained by chemical means (distillation) from the oleoresin or dead wood of pine trees or from tall oil, and used in making varnish, paper size, soap, soldering flux, and used on violin bows.

rotary molding A term sometimes used to denote a type of injection, transfer, compression, blow molding, etc. utilizing a plurality of mold cavities mounted on a rotating table or dial. Not to be confused with rotational molding. It is usually called rotary press.

rotary press As the name implies, these presses have a rotary movement of the main moving parts (used in machines listed in ▷ **rotary molding**). In one type, a number of single cavity molds are arranged in a large circle, the lower halves affixed to one platen and the upper halves to another clamping platen. Generally speaking, these platens do not move in relation to one another ▷ **press, platen "book" opening**. A traveling mechanism moves continuously around these two platens at a controlled speed. This mechanism performs, in the appropriate sequence, the functions of causing two individual mold halves to come together, and to remain together while the mechanism completes a controlled position, such as 300° of travel around the platen. The moving mechanism causes the mold to open, the molded parts to be physically ejected, and the cavities cleaned, if required, by an air blast, a new metered charge to enter the open cavity, and the mold halves closed again.

Different processes provide the charge, such as injection, extrusion, or compression drop of plastic or elastomer to mold solid of foamed parts. Each mold is thus actuated individually, and at a uniform sequence after each preceding mold. There can be any number of mold stations such as 10, 20, or 30 on the rotary press. The cavities may all be alike, or they may be different, but the cure or cooling cycle of each must be compatible, as the overall cycle is dependent on the time required for one complete rotation of the moving mechanism.

Also, rotary presses are made in which the mechanism remains stationary and the round platens with the molds rotate about a central axis. In operation, the principle is the same as that described above, except that all molded parts must be of the same size. These rotaries are also called carousal when rotating horizontally and ferris wheel when rotating vertically.

rotary vane feeder Device for conveying and metering dry materials, comprised of a cylindrical housing containing a shaft with blades or flutes attached, rotating at a rate selected to feed at a desired rate.

rotational casting ▷ **rotational molding**

rotational coating ▷ **coating, centrifugal or rotational**

rotational molding Rotational molding is a simple, basic, four-step process that uses a thin-walled mold with good heat-transfer characteristics. This closed mold requires an entrance for insertion of plastic and, most important, the capability to be "opened" so that cured parts can be removed. These requirements are no problem. Liquid or usually dry-powder plastic equal to the weight of the final part is put into the mold, which rotates simultaneously about two axes located perpendicular to each other. With slow rotation about each axis, the material inside the mold tumbles to the bottom, creating a continuous path that covers all mold surfaces equally.

The next step involves heating the mold while it is rotating. Molds can be heated by a heated oven, a direct flame, a heat-transfer liquid (either in a jacket around the mold or sprayed over the mold), or electric-resistance heaters placed around the mold. With uniform heat transfer through the mold, the plastic melts to build up a layer of molten plastic on the mold's inside surface.

After the required heat-time cycle is completed, the mold is ready for cooling, which is accomplished with the mold rotating continually. Cooling is usually done by air from a high-velocity fan or by a fine water spray over the mold. After cooling, the final step is to remove the solid hallow part and reload the mold with plastic (see Figs. 1–3 opposite).

This process is capable of molding small to large hollow items with relatively uniform wall thicknesses, using certain plastics. Its production

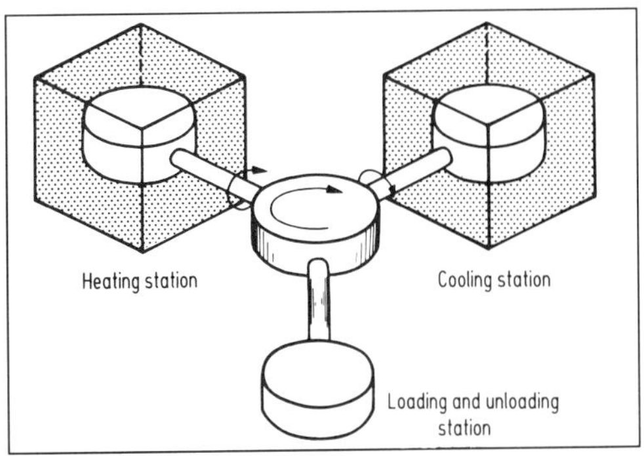

Fig. 1 Basic schematic of rotational molding.

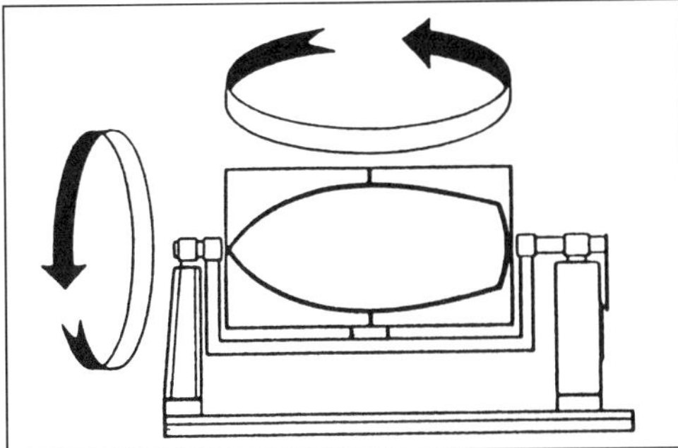

Fig. 2 Illustration of a mold and its two axes rotating mechanism, as used in rotational molding.

rates, compared to those of other processes, can be low. However, the total cost of equipment and the production time for moderate-sized and, especially, large parts are also low. Large parts range up to 85.200 l (22,000 gal.) in size, with a wall thickness of 3.8 cm (1.5 in.). One tank used 2.4 t (5,300 lb.) of XHDPE; the first charge was about 1.5 t (3,300 lb.), followed by 0.45 t (1,000 lb.) and finally another 0.45 t (1,000 lb.).

Molds can be of any shape and can include corrugated or rib constructions to increase their stability and stiffness (if not impossible, large, flat walls can be difficult). The thickness of their walls is limited to allow heat penetration.

Single or multiple arms can be used to one or more molds. Finned thermal pin (heat pipe) can be used to provide heat in areas that may be restrictive such as bosses (see Fig. 4 opposite). This process is particularly suited economically to producing small production runs and large-sized parts, becase molds are not subjected to pressure during molding and relatively inexpensive thin sheet metal molds can thus be used, if the part's shape allows. Lightweight cast aluminum and electroformed or vaporformed nickel molds, which are light in weight and low in cost, can also be used. Large rotational

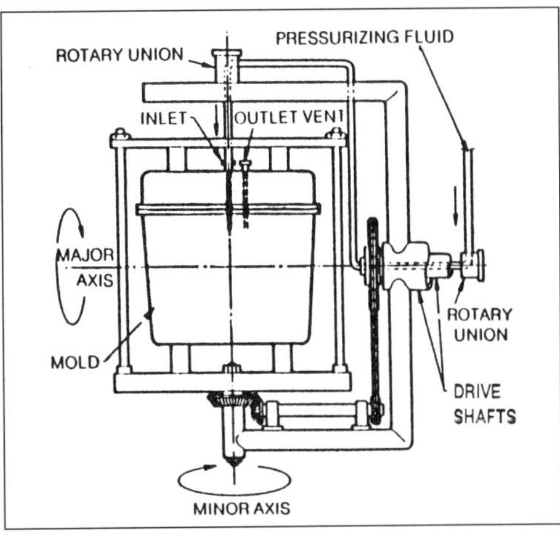

Fig. 3 Diagram shows feeding inlet to form hollow product inside a closed mold while the mold is being rotated about two axes and heat is applied. This system permits molding multiplastic layers of different materials (corotational molding).

molding machines can be built economically, because they can use inexpensive, gas-fired, hot-air ovens and a relatively lightweight mold-rotating mechanism. Also called rotational casting. ▷ **coating, centrifugal or rotational**

rotational molding arm assembly One or more rotating arms; member(s) of a machine which is the whole support or carrier assembly of mold(s).

rotational molding arm minor axis The rotation of mold mounting spindle(s) about one (minor) axis perpendicular to the major axis of rotation.

rotational molding arm offset An arm with one or more vertical members connected to two horizontal members. One member in a lower horizontal plane than the other, with mold mounting spindles located on the lower horizontal plane. The other horizontal plane is the center line of rotation of the offset arm about the major axis.

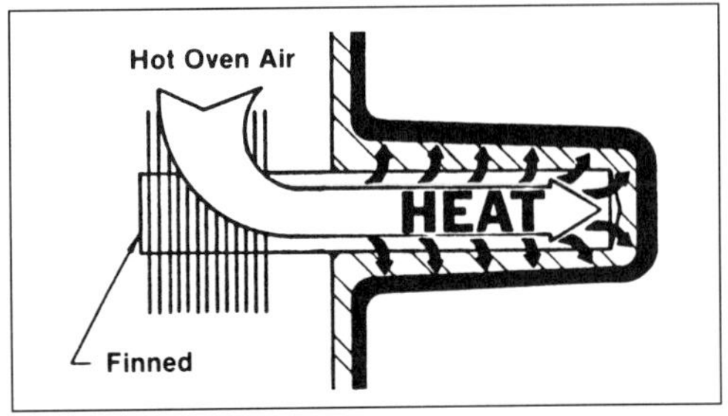

Fig. 4 Finned thermal pin heat conductor used for rotational molding.

rotational molding arm straight That part of the machine by which molds are secured to the machine. Arm extends in a horizontal manner.

rotational molding arm weight Applies to the total weight of mold(s) and material that may be carried on one arm assembly. This weight also includes mold spider and/or frame to which the mold cavity(s) are attached to form a complete mold unit.

rotational molding mold ▷ **mold, rotational process** and **mold material**

rotational molding, venting Venting of molds is often to maintain atmospheric pressure inside the closed mold during the entire molding cycle. A vent will reduce flash and prevent mold distortion as well as lowering the pressure needed to keep the mold closed. It will prevent blowouts caused by pressure and permit use of thinner molds.

The vent can be a thin-walled metal of fluoroplastic (PTFE) tube which extends to near the center of the mold. It must enter the mold at a point where the opening which it will leave will not harm the appearance or utility of the molded part. The vent is filled with glass wool to keep the powder charge from entering the vent during rotation. The end of the vent outside the mold should be protected so that no water will enter it during cooling. Sometimes an oil filler cup or metal cap is used for this purpose.

rotogravure printer It consists of a printing cylinder, an impression cylinder, and an inking system. Ink is applied to the printing cylinder by an ink roll or spray, and the excess is removed by a doctor blade and returned to the ink fountain. The impression cylinder is covered with an elastomer composition that presses the sheet (being printed) into contact with the ink in the tiny cells of the printing surface. Gravure inks are volatile and dry almost instantly. Hot air dryers are used between printing units to speed up drying. Therefore, in color printing ink trapping is not a problem as each succeeding color is printed on a dry color, rather than on one which is still wet as in letterpress and offset. For color printing, presses use electronic systems for automatic register control. Cylinders are chromium plated for press runs of a million or more. When the chromium starts to wear, it is stripped off and the cylinder rechromed. ▷ **gravure printing; off-set gravure; sheet-fed gravure printing**

rotomill A continuous mixing device consisting essentially of a fluted rotor surrounded by a stator.

rotomolding A contraction of the term rotational molding. ▷ **rotational molding**

rotovinyl A printed sheet vinyl flooring in which the pattern is printed by a rotogravure process.

roughness Relatively finely spaced surface irregularities, the height, width, and direction of which establish a definite surface pattern.

roughness, finish ▷ **surface finish**

roving A collection of bundles of continuous filaments either (principally) untwisted strands or lightly twisted yarns. They are a collection of carded fibers rubbed into a single soft and bulky strand without twist or a sliver which has been drawn out and slightly twisted, except that with glass, roving is a collection of continuous filament untwisted yarns into a single bulky strand. The number of strands of fiber is variable (2 to 100) but 60 is usual. Rovings, often comprising 60 strands (or ends), are often used directly in spraying techniques when they are chopped and blown on to a mold with the sprayed plastic. Rovings are also woven into heavy woven roving fabrics.

roving ball The supply package offered to processors, consisting of a number of ends or strands wound onto a length of cardboard tube to a given outside diameter. Usually designated by either fiber or length in yards (meters).

roving catenary A measure of the difference in length of the strands in a specified length of roving caused by unequal tension. The tendency of some strands in a taut, horizontal roving to sag more than others.

roving cloth A textile fabric, coarse in nature, woven from rovings.

roving collimated Roving that has been made using a special process (usually parallel wound), such that the strands are more parallel than in standard roving.

roving constructions See the Table below.

Woven roving constructions.

Count per in. (per cm)	Weight, oz./sq. yd. (g/m^2)	Thickness, in. (mm)	Weave
5 × 8 (2 × 3.2)	18.0 (610)	0.031 (0.787)	Plain
5 × 8 (2 × 3.2)	24.0 (814)	0.038 (0.965)	Plain
5 × 6 (2 × 2.4)	30.0 (1020)	0.049 (1.24)	Plain
5 × 8 (2 × 3.2)	36.0 (1220)	0.052 (1.32)	Plain

roving, continuous Parallel filaments (yarns) coated with sizing, gathered together into single or multiple strands, and wound into a cylindrical package. It may be used to provide continuous reinforcement in woven roving, filament winding, pultrusion, prepregs, or high strength molding compounds, or it may be used chopped.

roving doff Identifies a roving ball or package.

roving, spun A heavy low-cost glass or other fiber strand consisting of filaments that are continuous but doubled back on themselves.

roving, tow ▷ **fiber tow**

roving, woven ▷ **roving cloth**

rub Scratches, close together, or simultaneously produced.

rubber The term elastomer is often used interchangeably with the term rubber, and is often the term preferred when referring to vulcanized material ▷ **elastomer**. Natural rubber (NR) is an amorphous plastic existing somewhat above its glass transition temperature (T_g), so that considerable segmental motion is possible. Rubbers are thus relatively soft (typical modulus about 3 MPa) and deformable. Since linear plastic rubbers are rather too soft and weak to be useful in commercial rubber products the material is crosslinked by vulcanization. This crosslinking raises modulus, softening point, and solvent resistance (the term elastomer is preferred after vulcanization). Although uncrosslinked gum rubbers show considerable elasticity, true elastomer elasticity (high elasticity), with instantaneous recovery from high strain of up to 1,000% elongation, only occurs in vulcanized materials. Some elastomers, notably NR, also have the useful property of crystallizing on stretching which significantly increases the modulus and strength. ▷ **orientation**

Although most amorphous linear plastics exhibit rubbery properties at temperatures well above their T_g values, materials commonly known as rubbers or elastomers are those existing as rubbery at ambient temperatures. Useful elastomers will have a T_g value of well below 0°C (32°F), while useful plastics will have a T_g value well above 60°C (140°F).

In addition to NR, the other general purpose elastomers are styrene-butadiene (the largest tonnage synthetic elastomer), polybutyene, synthetic polyisoprene, ethylene-propylene and EPDM, and butyl elastomers. In addition there are many other lower tonnage special purpose elastomers, which generally have higher heat and solvent resistance. These include nitrile, polychloroprene, acrylic, fluoro- and chlorosulphonated polyethylene, and silicone elastomers. Other specialty types are polyurethane, polyether, and polysulphide. The Fig. on p. 658 compares some of these materials.

rubber cyclized plastic A thermoplastic produced by reacting natural rubber with stannic chloride or chlorostannic acid. One of the few known lacquers for decorating polyolefins without pretreatment is based on a solution of cyclized rubber in toluene. Other uses include films and hot-melt coatings.

rubber elasticity The elastic behavior of plastics well above their glass transition temperatures (the rubbery region of viscoelasticity behavior) where they show elasticity at high strains of up to several hundred percent. If the material is perfectly elastic then all the work done will be stored as strain energy, at least for an isothermal deformation. Molecularly, the phenomenon is due to an uncoiling of the randomly coiled plastic molecules on stressing, and is therefore entropic in origin. A highly successful statistical molecular theory, known as the kinetic theory of rubber elasticity, has been developed which closely describes many of the experimentally determined features of elastomer (rubber) behavior. ▷ **network polymer**

rubber, foamed ▷ **foam**

rubber gel The portion of rubber insoluble in a chosen solvent.

rubber hydrochloride plastic A nonflammable thermoplastic material obtained by treating a solution of natural rubber with anhydrous hydrogen chloride under pressure at low temperatures. The packaging film *Pliofilm* is an example.

rubberize To impregnate and/or coat a substrate with rubber.

rubber, natural The commercial base for natural rubber (NR) is latex, a milklike serum produced by the tropical tree *Hevea braziliensis*. Naturally occurring latex is the rubber that exudes from these trees in an aqueous serum containing various inorganic and organic substances. The rubber precipitated out of this solution can be characterized as a coherent TS elastic solid. It is against NR that all the other rubbers and elastomers are measured. For centuries it was the only rubber available; it was extensively used even prior to the discovery of vulcanization (TS crosslink curing), in 1883. To date no synthetic material has yet equaled the overall depth of engineering characteristics and consequent wide latitude of applications available in NR.

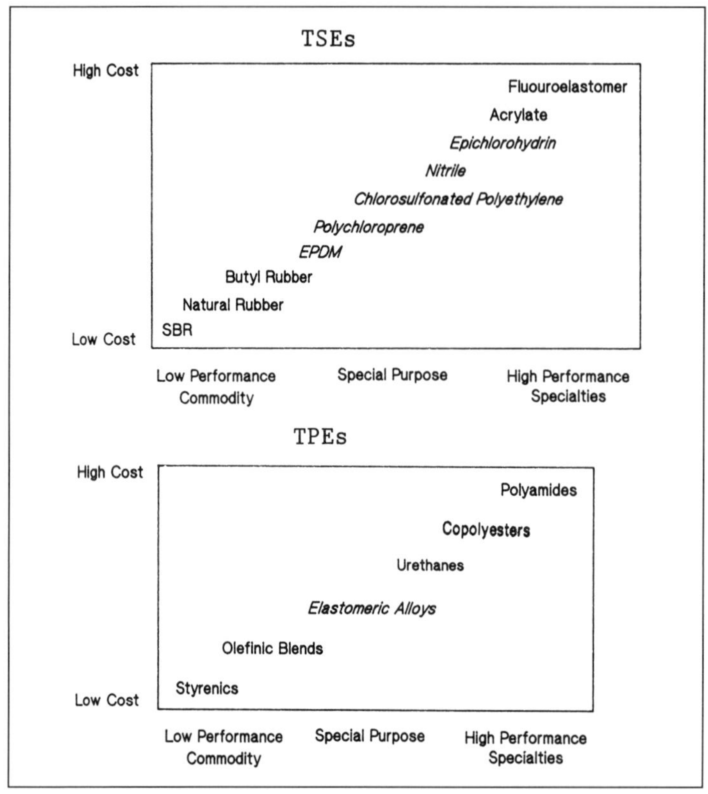

General guide of elastomers versus performances.

As with the other elastomers, many grades and types of NR are available, as produced by varying impurity levels, collection methods, and fillers and processing techniques. NR is generally considered to be the best of the general-purpose rubbers, meaning those with characteristics suitable for broad applications. With NR, compounds can be produced over a wider stiffness range than with any other material. NR could be the best choice, except where an extreme performance or exposure requirement dictates the use of a special-purpose elastomer, which will often occur at the sacrifice of some other, less critical property.

Natural rubber has a great capacity for being deformed. This and its ability to strain crystallize gives it added strength while deformed. Its high resilience, which is responsible for its low heat buildup during flexing, makes it a prime candidate for shock and severe dynamic loads. With its low heat buildup NR is recommended for use in applications where such properties as flexure, cut and abrasion resistance, and general endurance would be adversely affected by heat in less resilient elastomers.

The shortcomings of NR include its service temperature, from −18 to 120°C (−6 to 248°F). Its poor oil, oxidation, and ozone resistance can be minimized either by proper design accommodation or by compounding. Degradation from such environments is essentially a surface effect that can be tolerated or minimized by using thicker cross-sections, shielding, or adding antioxidants and antiozonants. ▷**rubber and elastomer**

rubber peptizer A compounding ingredient used in small proportions to accelerate by chemical reaction the softening of rubber under the influence of mechanical action, or both.

rubber plate printing A marking method sometimes employed for intricate parts such as molded teminal blocks.

rubber plunger molding A variation of matched-die molding, employing a deformable rubber plunger and a heated metal female mold. The process enables the use of high filler and fiber loaded plastic compounds.

rubber, raw Natural or synthetic rubber (elastomer), usually in bales or packages which is the starting material for the manufacture of rubber (elastomer) products.

rubber-toughened polystyrene plastic
▷**polystyrene plastic, high impact**

rubber transition ▷ **glass-transition**

rubbery materials Refers to rubber or elastomer materials.

rubbery plateau For a plastic, the range of temperature between the glass transition temperature and melt temperature, which has a viscoelastic modulus that is relatively con-stant.

rubbish ▷ **waste**

rules to remember and forget ▷ **processing rules to remember and forget**

runner ▷ **mold runner**

runnerless injection molding ▷ **mold, runnerless injection molding**

runout **1.** No failure at a specified number of load cycles. **2.** In a linear stage, any unwanted motion other than pure translation. Thus, runout may include yaw, pitch, and roll.

rupture **1.** The breaking or tearing apart of a material. ▷ **failure** **2.** That stage in the development of a fracture where instability occurs. It is not recommended that the term rupture be used as a synonym for fracture. **3.** A cleavage or break resulting from physical stress. Work of rupture is the integral of the stress-strain curve between the origin and the point of rupture.

rupture disc ▷ **plasticator safety**

rupture envelope ▷ **Mohr envelope**

rupture strength The true value of rupture strength is the stress of a material at failure based on the ruptures cross-sectional area itself. ▷ **strength**

rupture, work The work of rupture is the integral of the stress-strain curve between the origin and the point of rupture. Its dimension is in energy-volume^{-1}.

rust The reddish corrosion product formed by electrochemical interaction between iron and the atmospheric oxygen; no rust forms on plastics. This term is properly applied only to ferrous alloys.

Rynite Du Pont's tradename for glass fiber reinforced thermoplastic polyester reinforced plastic.

Ryton Phillips Petroleum's tradename for polyphenylene sulfide plastics.

S

sabin unit ▷ **sound absorption**

sacrificial ply ▷ **reinforced plastic peel ply**

safe Generally Recognized As Safe (GRAS) ▷ **acceptable risk**

safety Safety in plastic plants and other materials processing industries can be divided into two distinct fields; industry safety and process safety. Industrial safety includes protection of employees and other personnel from the hazards of being struck against, struck by, caught in, falling, slipping, overexertion, contact with temperature extremes, contact with electric current, and inhalation, absorption, or ingestion (see Fig. below). Fire protection also could be included. These hazards usually are confined within the site boundary and do not affect the public.

Very important in the development of safe work practices and a safe work environment are the development of a safety organization and its continuing activities. It should include the highest levels of management to demonstrate that safety has a priority equal to that of production, quality, efficiency, cost control, and employee relations. Only in this way can responsibility and authority be accepted or shared throughout the operation to develop and maintain attitudes essential to safe work practices and conditions.

Other important aspects are inspections of fabrication equipment, molds and dies, audits of work practices, guards on moving equipment, training, accident investigations, record keeping, personal hygiene, personal protective equipment, fire prevention, noise control, and control of thermal radiation, ionizing radiation, and chemical exposures. Process safety includes the safe transportation, handling, and storage of materials (chemicals, plastics, solvents, etc.), the control of reactors and other processing steps, the protection of employees and the public from fires, explosions, and releases of toxic materials, protection of property from the effects of such accidents. ▷ **American National Safety Institute** and **sterilization**

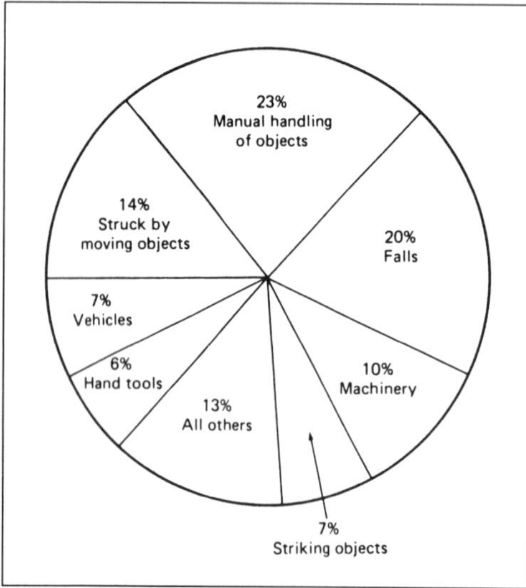

National Safety Council, Chicago, provides updates on where accidents occur in all types of manufacturing plants.

safety and machines To protect operating personnel from recognized hazards, standards have been prepared to assign certain responsibilities to machine manufacturers, remanufacturers, modifiers, and employers. These standards are periodically updated; prepared by the American National Standards Institute with SPI participation. ▷ **processing equipment improvements; programmable controller safety; safety interlock; barrel vented safety**

safety and mold ▷ **mold protection**

safety and processing All processing equipment has standard procedures to operate and meet safety requirements; they are available from equipment suppliers and help to understand how to handle plastics. They include safe start-ups, location of safety devices, etc. (see Table opposite). Processing plastics usually involves high heat melting and pressure; equipment usually generates a lot of force and heat. They are built to run safely, but they must be treated with respect.

Most plastics will decompose if heated too long a time or at too high a temperature. When decomposition produces a gas, there may be a hazard. If gas is trapped in the plasticator (extrusion, injection, etc.) very high pressures may

Example of equipment safety check list; this example pertains to extruder sheet line.

Potential hazard (causes)	Safe practice checks
Tooling change Burns (hot tooling and polymer) Electrical shock (extruder pipes, wiring)	Wear gloves when handling hot tooling. Follow electrical lockout procedures when working on tooling.
Preparation Slipping/falling (materials on floor)	Check housekeeping. Check for any leaks.
Startup Projectiles and burns (excessive head pressure) All hazards (malfunctioning E-stop) Cuts/lacerations (slitter blades)	Check zone temperatures. Monitor head pressure (max. 4000 psi). Check all emergency stops. Keep slitter blades in up position when threading sheet.
Operation Pinch points/burns (heated rollers) Burns (hot sheeting) Cuts/lacerations (utility knife)	Keep hands clear of moving rollers. Wear gloves when handling hot sheeting. Wear gloves when cutting samples.
Shutdown Fire, flooding, etc. (equipment left on)	Make sure all utilities and auxiliary equipment are off.
Cleanup Slipping/falling (materials on floor) Burns (hot polymer)	Check housekeeping. Check for any leaks. Wear gloves when handling hot drool.

develop. Equipment (plasticator parts, molds/dies) may break and fly together with hot, decomposed plastic. Burns and wounds may result. Rather than break metal, hot plastic can shoot out of the die (or mold) or hopper with explosive force. These reactions very rarely occur; they can be prevented by using the right procedures for handling equipment and conditions for the plastic. Part of the responsibility rests with the operator to follow directions and to be alert for unusual conditions. Either overheating caused by a faulty controller or a freeze-off from a burned out heater can be a hazard.

safety assurance ▷ **acceptable risk**

safety coextrusion alarms When running a coextrusion line, make provision to adequately alarm the operators if one of the extruder drives trips out. This will prevent extrudate from back flowing in the stopped machine and creating a blockage in the feed section.

safety, computer accessibility ▷ **computer accessibility**

safety devices All equipment is equipped with (applicable) electrical, hydraulic, and/or mechanical safety devices. Some machines, such as injection molding machines, have all three modes of operation.

safety engineering Application of engineering principles to all facets of plant safety by professionally trained personnel.

safety factor, design ▷ **design safety factor; factor of ignorance; statistical material selection, reliability; design failure theory; service factor**

safety, flammability ▷ **fire** and **flammability**

safety, foamed security system ▷ **foamed security system**

safety gate or screen The movable barriers allowing the operator (of injection, blow molding, etc.) access to the molds and platen area with safety. As an example, a safety device on electrically operated equipment ensures that, upon the opening of a gate, panel, or similar unit, the electrical circuit is broken thereby removing the potential danger from voltages existing within the equipment.

safety glass Shatterproof glass is a composite or laminate consisting of two or more sheets of plate glass (usually tempered glass) with an interlayer of polyvinyl butyral plastic [0.20 to 0.040 in. (0.05 to 0.10 cm) thick] between each adjoining glass plates. The plastic bonded (via air evacuated restricted heat system) to the glass virtually eliminates shattering of the glass upon impact. It is used in car windows, bullet proof glass, trains, etc. This safety construction has been in use since the 1930s.

safety hardener A curing agent which causes only a minimum of toxic effect on the human body, either on contact with the skin or as concentrated vapor in the air.

safety interlock A safety device designed to ensure that equipment will not operate until certain precautions have been taken. As an example ▷ **programmable controller safety**

safety laws ▷ **hazards, Federal Register 29 cfr 1910.1200**

safety machine lockout Procedures are set up for the steps to be taken in proper lockout of machine's operation, such as the electrical, hydraulic, and mechanical circuits (where machines use the circuits). As an example, properly locking out a machine's electrical circuit before starting repairs protects the maintenance worker from accidental start ups which could cause severe injury. The National Safety Council offers the following steps for the proper lockout procedure: (1) shut down all possible switches at the point of operation, then open the main disconnect switch, (2) snap your own lock on the locking device; an ordinary padlock can be used for most electrical lockouts, (3) check the lockout device and safety interlock to make sure the switch cannot be operated, (4) place a name tag on the shank of the lock to indicate that the machine has been locked out, (5) notify the supervisor when repair work has been completed; only a supervisor should give the go ahead to remove your lock, and (6) take off the name tag and remove the lock.

safety manuals and standards The SPI and ANSI are major providers of these manuals and standards on many different aspects in processing plants; includes material handling, material storage, machines as well as upstream and downstream equipment, etc.

safety mechanism A device intended to prevent accidental actuation of tool.

safety, programmable controller ▷ **programmable controller safety**

safety rupture disc ▷ **plasticator safety**

safety stop bar In presses with movable platen (injection, compression, etc.), a mechanical safety stop bar that is not dependent upon electrical switches.

safety, vented barrel ▷ **barrel vented safety**

sag **1.** In blow molding, a local extension (often near the die face) of the parison during extrusion by gravitational forces. This causes necking down of parison. **2.** In thermoforming, the droop of thermoplastic sheet as it is being heated. **3.** ▷ **container neck-down and sag**

sales investment turns The measurement of a cycle. Investment turns are usually measured in terms of how many times the investment is turned over in the annual volume of sales. Example: investment turns = annual sales divided by amount of investment. ▷ **capital equipment investment; economic efficiency and profitability; cost; profitability studies, functions**

sales marginal producers Producers whose sales at existing prices will barely cover the costs of production.

sales people Sales people have an important role in all industries (plastics, etc.) as summarized in the Fig. below.

Sales people's target is to be helpful: "No, I cannot be bothered to see any crazy sales engineer regarding some kind of machine gun—we have a battle to fight."

sales, return on investment The profit expressed as a percentage of sales. ▷ **return on investment**

salt **1.** The compound formed as a result of the reaction of acids and alkalis. **2.** Common salt, sodium chloride, occurs in nature principally on the ocean floor.

salt bath A molten mixture of sodium, potassium, barium, and calcium chlorides or nitrates, to which sodium carbonate and sodium cyanide are sometimes added. Use includes providing a heat "bath" to plastics where uniform heat is required to provide polymerization, cure, heat treatment, and annealing. It is used in certain wire/cable insulation extrusion lines, contact or low pressure curing of reinforced thermoset plastics, etc.

sample ▷ **testing specimen result and processing influence**

sample standard deviation The square root of the sample variance. It is a point estimate of the population standard deviation, a measure of the "spread" of the frequency distribution of a population.

sample standards A variety of plastic samples with stated values of chemical or physical properties and avialable worldwide are widely employed in plastic science and technology from NIST. Such plastic standards, or standard polymers, are used in three ways: (1) to calibrate instruments and techniques that determine physiochemical properties of plastics in a relative sense; chromatographic methods of molecular weight determination are well known examples of relative measurements that require calibration, (2) to check the accuracy of instruments that in principle are absolute but in practice are sufficiently complex to require verification, and (3) often used as well-characterized starting materials for research.

sample variance The use of the squares of the differences between each observed value and the sample average divided by the sample size minus one. It is a point estimate of the population variance.

sampling Obtaining a representative portion of the material or product concerned. The number of samples required generally is specified for each test in order to obtain a reasonably reliable test value. Information on variation test values (sample-to-sample) and other sampling procedures are presented in ASTM D 2188 and D 2188. ▷ **statistic** and **design allowable**

sampling statistically ▷ **statistical benefits**

sand casting ▷ **foundry plastic**

sanding A finishing process employing abrasive belts or discs, sometimes used on parts to remove flash, particularly thick flash on thermoset plastics.

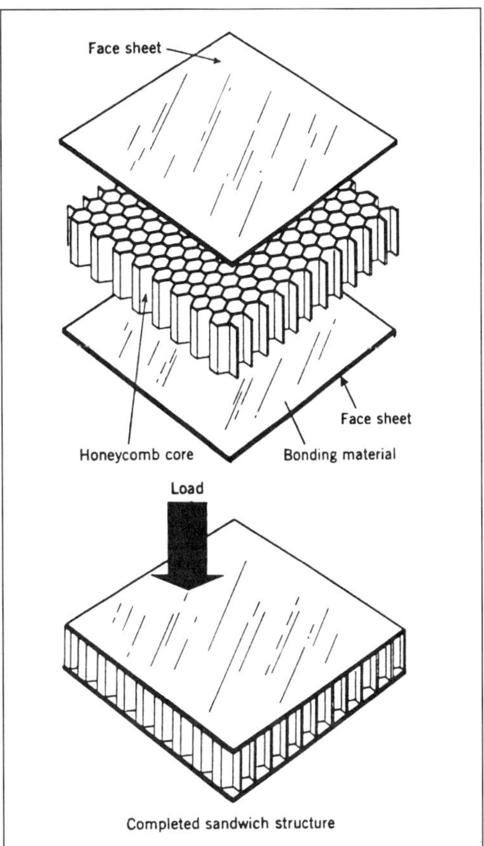

Example of a sandwich structure in which three elements make up the honeycomb sandwich panel.

sandwich construction **1.** A panel or complex structure composed of a lightweight core material surfaced with two relatively thin, dense, high strength or high stiffness facing materials (see Fig. above). **2.** Layup of different materials where skins (surfaces) could be of the same or different materials; also inside there could be one or more materials. The combination of two or more layers provide different properties.

sandwich construction process Different fabricating processes are used. They include: bag molding, compression molding, casting, filament winding, coinjection molding, corotational molding, coextusion, laminating, reaction injection molding, etc.

sandwich core material The primary function of a core in structural sandwich parts is that of stabilizing the facings and carrying most of the shear loads through the thickness. In order to perform this task efficiently, the core must be as rigid and as light as possible, and must deliver uniformly predictable properties in the environment and meet performance requirements. Several different materials are used extensively including: wood, plastic foam, honeycomb, balsa wood, etc. The traditional past advantage of the low cost of wood has progressively eroded. ▷ **foam** and **honeycomb reinforced plastic core**

sandwich design The usual objective of a sandwich design is to save weight, increase stiffness, use less expensive materials, or combinations of these factors in a product. Sometimes other objectives are also involved such as reducing tooling or other costs, achieving aerodynamic smoothness, reducing reflected noise, or increasing durability under exposure to acoustic energy. The designer considers factors such as getting the loads in, getting the loads out, and attaching small or large load carrying members under constraints of deflection, contour, weight, and cost. To design properly, it is important to understand the fabrication sequence and methods, use of the correct materials of construction, important influence of bond between facing materials and core, and allow a safety factor that will be required on original new developments. Use of sandwich, high performance primary structures has been extensive in building panels and aircraft complex shapes since the 1940s.

sandwich facing material The primary function of the face sheets is to provide the required bending and in-plane shear stiffness, and to carry the axial, bending, and in-plane shear loading. In high performance structures, facings most commonly chosen are plastic impregnated fiber reinforced material (usually prepreg), aluminum alloy, titanium, or stainless steel. Even the most economical of these products represents a substantial cost, and customary practice is to choose among them very carefully on a value engineering, or lowest lifetime cost basis.

sanitary landfill ▷ **landfill**

sanltize To make sanitary, such as by cleaning and sterilizing.

Santoprene Monsanto's tradename for its olefinic TPE that contains EPDM.

saran ▷ **fiber, saran**

satin finish A type of finish having a satin or velvety appearance; a surface finish that behaves as a diffuse reflector and which is lustrous but not mirrorlike.

satin weave ▷ **harness satin weave** and **four-harness satin**

saturated compound Organic compounds which do not contain double or triple bonds, and thus cannot add on elements or compounds.

saturated polyester plastic ▷ **polyester thermoplastic**

saturated water vapor ▷ **water vapor, saturated**

saturation **1.** An equilibrium condition in which the net rate of absorption under prescribed conditions falls essentially to zero; the condition of coexistence in stable equilibrium of a vapor and a liquid, or a vapor and solid phase of the same substance at the same temperature. ▷ **fiber saturation point** **2.** In color, in the dimension of color that describes its purity; if highly saturated it appears to be pure hue and free of gray, but if of low saturation it appears to have a great deal of gray mixed with it. ▷ **hue** **3.** Attribute of a visual sensation according to which an area appears to exhibit more or less chromatic color, judged in proportion to its lightness or brightness.

saturation, degree of ▷ **degree of saturation**

saturation pressure ▷ **pressure, saturation**

saw Although a saw can handle fewer cuts per minute than other cutting methods and produces dust and a ragged cut, it is still the only practical way to handle certain products, such as very large, thick plastic parts, including large diameter extruded pipe or profiles. ▷ **machining** and **cutter**

S-basis The S-basis property allowable is the minimum value, specified by the appropriate federal, military, SAE, ASTM, or other recognized and approved specifications for the material. ▷ **A-basis; S-basis; typical-basis**

scale **1.** A condition in which plastic plates or particles are on the surface of a part during processing, such as pultrusion. Scales can often be readily removed, sometimes leaving surface voids or depressions. ▷ **scaling** **2.** A weighing device. **3.** The markings indicating units of measure such as a thermometer. **4.** A graduate standard of measurement. **5.** A type of paraffin or petroleum wax from which all but a few percent of oil has been removed by hydraulic pressing and subsequent processing. **6.** A calcareous deposit in water tubes or lines resulting from deposition of mineral compounds present in water. When scale forms in the cooling lines of molds, for example, the Reynold's number or water flow pattern can go from the required turbulent to laminar flow and cause products to be below product requirements due to incorrect cooling, increasing molding cycle time to compensate for the inefficient cooling action, and/or increase cost to produce parts. **7.** Surface area of oxidized metal. ▷ **corrosion**

scale-up A term used to describe the planning involved in carrying a complete or part of a processing operation from the pilot plant to large scale production.

scaling The process of forming scale with or without acid fumes; sometimes refers to spontaneous detachment of scale. Also called flaking.

scanning Relative movement of the search unit over a test specimen.

scanning computer ▷ **computer scanning**

scanning microscope An electron microscope in which the image is formed by a beam operating in synchronism with an electron probe scanning the object. The intensity of the image forming beam is proprotional to the scattering or secondary emission of the specimen where the probe strikes it.

scarfing The removal of flash or bead by a cutting operation.

scarf joint ▷ **joint, scarf**

scattering The process by which light or other electromagnetic radiant flux passing though matter is redirected over a range of angles. Significant types of scatterings by plastics include scattering of light (both elastic and inelastic), X-ray, neutron, and electron. The elastic scattering of light, called Rayleigh scattering, and of X-ray, usually referred to as simply X-ray scattering. ▷ **coefficient of scatter** and **X-ray diffraction**

scattering loss That part of transmitted energy loss due to roughness of reflecting surface.

scavenger A substance added to a system or mixture to consume or inactivate traces of impurities.

schlieren Regions of varying refraction in a transparent medium often caused by pressure or temperature differences and detectable especially by photographing the passage of a beam of light.

schlieren system An optical system used for visual display of an ultrasonic beam passing through a transparent medium.

science and art ▷ **art and science**

science and experience ▷ **experience and science** and **people**

science, applied ▷ **engineering design**

scientific method The systematic collection and classification of data and, usually, the formulation and testing of hypotheses based on the data.

scission Degradation of plastics by radiation that splits their molecules.

Scleroscope hardness A dynamic indentation hardness test using a calibrated instrument that drops a diamond-tipped hammer from a fixed height onto the surface of the material under test. The height of rebound of the hammer is a measure of the material hardness.

scorch Premature vulcanization of a rubber compound.

scorch, Mooney The time to incipient cure of a compound when tested in the Mooney shearing disc viscometer under specific conditions. ▷ **viscosity, Mooney**

Scorim British Technology Group tradenames *Scorim* and *Scortec* for the process of creating dynamics to molten plastic inside a mold cavity or from a die to minimize or eliminate the usual melt flow problems (internal stress, sink marks, etc.). ▷ **injection molding multi-live feed; injection molding push-pull; extruder melt flow orientation**

scouring A wet process of cleaning by chemical and/or mechanical means.

scrap 1. Any product of a fabrication process that is not part of primary product, such as flash, runners, and trim. ▷ **recyclable plastic and scrap 2.** Industrial wastes that are reusable and usually are separated from other wastes and reprocessed or sold. ▷ **industrial waste**

scrapless forming ▷ **forming scrapless**

scratch Shallow mark, groove, furrow, or channel normally caused by improper handling or storage. ▷ **abrasion resistance** and **mar resistance**

screen A plate, sheet, or woven wire screen (or other device) with regularly spaced square apertures of uniform size, mounted in a suitable frame or holder, for use in separating material according to size. The terms screen or sieve can be used interchangeably. These screens are available in a wide range of sizes or meshes from as coarse as $2\frac{1}{2}$ to as fine as 400 (see Table on p. 666). The mesh is the number of apertures per square inch (cm). A square fabric pattern is used so that the same number of strands per inch are in the warp and fill directions. The mesh number is the square of the number of strands per linear inch. Screens are used as filters to separate fine and coarse fillers and used in an extruder breaker plate. ▷ **extruder screen pack** and **mesh particle size**

screen classification The separation of powder into particle size ranges by the use of a series of graded screens or sieves.

Screen scale sieves classification, adopted by the U.S. Bureau of Standards.

Mesh	Diameter of wire, decimal of an inch	For closer sizing sieves from 0.0015″ to 3,000″ ratio $\sqrt[4]{2}$ or 1.189
$2\frac{1}{2}$	0.099	0.312
3	0.070	0.263
$3\frac{1}{2}$	0.065	0.221
4	0.065	0.185
5	0.044	0.156
6	0.036	0.131
7	0.0328	0.110
8	0.032	0.093
9	0.033	0.078
10	0.035	0.065
12	0.028	0.055
14	0.025	0.046
16	0.0235	0.0390
20	0.0172	0.0328
24	0.0141	0.0276
28	0.0125	0.0232
32	0.0118	0.0195
35	0.0122	0.0134
42	0.0100	0.0168
48	0.0092	0.0116
60	0.0070	0.0097
65	0.0072	0.0082
80	0.0056	0.0069
100	0.0042	0.0058
115	0.0038	0.0049
150	0.0026	0.0041
170	0.0024	0.0035
200	0.0021	0.0029
250	0.0016	0.0024
270	0.0016	0.0021
352	0.0014	0.0017
400	0.001	0.0015

screening A preliminary selection procedure.

screen lens An electrostatic electron lens consisting of a combination of screens or foils at different potentials.

screen pack ▷ **extruder screen pack**

screen printing Some is done by hand with very simple equipment consisting of a table, screen frame, and squeegee. Most commercial screen printing, however, is done with power operated presses of two types. One uses flat screens which require an intermittent motion as each is printed. The other uses rotary screens with the squeegee mounted inside the cylinder, and the ink pumped in automatically. These processes are continuous running, fast, and print continuous patterns with little difficulty (see first Fig. opposite).

The amount of ink applied by screen printing is far greater than in letter-press, lithography, or gravure, which accounts for some of the unusual effects in screen printing. Because of the heavy ink film, the sheets must be racked separately until dry or passed through a heated tunnel or drier before they can be stacked safely without smudging or set-off. UV curing ink has simplified drying and helped to promote greater use of screen printing.

There are many methods of making screens. They consist of a porous material, and the printed image is produced by blocking unwanted holes or pores of the screen. Early screens (prior to about 1940) had the image on silk mounted on a wooden frame, and prints were made manually. (Thus the term silk screening was used; but since silk was no longer used the correct terminology became screen printing.) Masking materials were used to block out unwanted areas. Printing used has been both hand-cut stencils and photomechanical means. In the photomechanical method, the screen is coated with a light-sensitive emulsion; exposure is made through a screened film positive placed in contact with the screen, and the coating in the unexposed areas is developed to form the image through which ink flows to the substrate. The exposed areas form a hardened stencil which prevents the penetration of ink in those areas. ▷ **decal transfer**

screen ruling The number of lines or dots per inch on a halftone screen.

screen ultraviolet ▷ **ultraviolet screen**

screw Basically a geometric-helically flighted hard steel shaft which rotates within a plasticizing barrel to mechanically process and advance a plastic being prepared for processes such as injection molding and extrusion (see second Fig. opposite); explanations will be reviewed on the injection molding screw and the extruder screw. Regarding the conventional single screw, the Fig. on p. 668 explains the melt action of plastics as it travels around the screw inside the barrel. This model is an example for the basis used in most computer simulations of melt flow. ▷ **design screw (for processing plastic)**

Injection: Plastic in the screw channel is subject to changing experiences as the screw operation changes during the cycle. Each operation of the screw, whether it is moving forward, rotating, and retracting during shot preparation or static during an idle period, subjects the plastic to different thermal and shear situations. Consequently, the IM plasticating process becomes rather complex, but it is controllable and repeatable within the limits of equipment capability. At a fixed screw speed, the screw pitch, diameter, and channel depth determine output. A deep-channel screw is much more sensitive to pressure changes than a shallow channel screw.

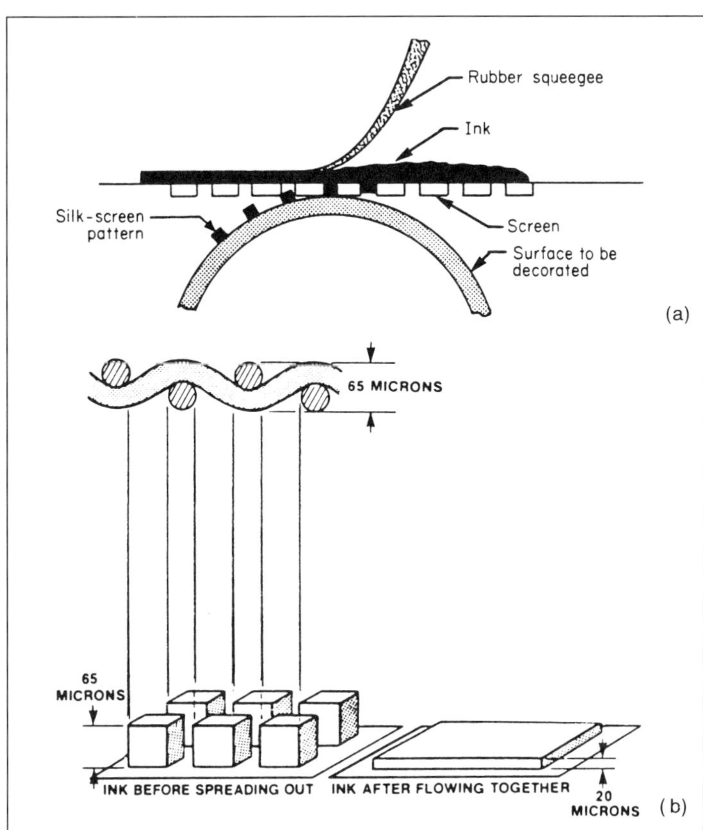

(*a*) The basic concept of screen printing of transferring ink through an open screen onto a flat or rounded surface; (*b*) schematic for the basic principle in the formation of film from ink dots.

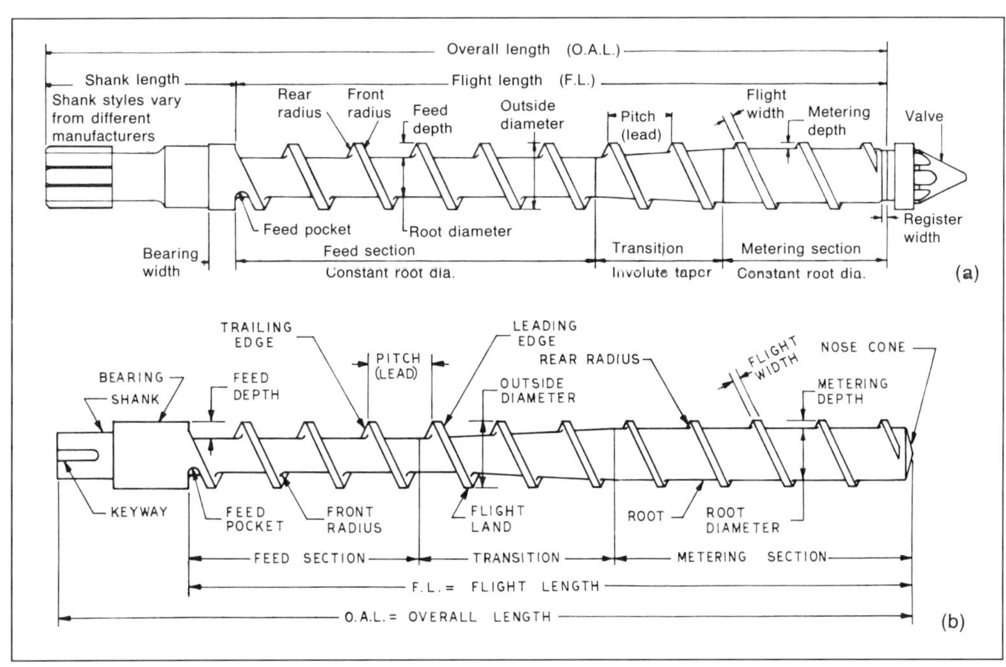

These single conventional screws provide nomenclature where plastic moves from left to right as screw turns. (*a*) Injection screw; (*b*) extrusion screw.

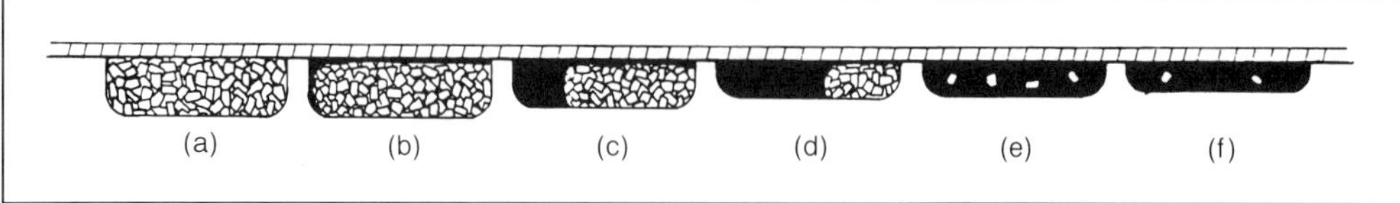

Standard screw melt model.
(*a*) The feed section initiates solids conveying. This is enhanced by sliding on the screw (low friction) and high friction on the barrel. Of course, when the plastic sticks to the screw and slides on the inside surface of the barrel, it just goes around with the screw and never moves forward. In the feed section, there is also some compaction and a little heating of the plastic.
(*b*) At the beginning of the transition, the plastic is further heated and more compression occurs. The solid plastic is forced against the barrel causing a sliding friction. This frictional heat creates a film of melted plastic on the inner barrel surface.
(*c*) As the plastic proceeds down the transition, there is more melting and more compression. Usually most of the melting takes place in the transition. Here the plastic is divided into three parts: a compacted solids bed, a melt film along the barrel surface, and a melt pool. The melt pool is formed as the melt film is collected by the advancing flight. Most of the melting continues to be the result of sliding friction of the solids bed against the heated barrel. This is rapid efficient melting something like melting an ice cube by pushing it against a hot grinding wheel.
(*d*) The channel depth continues to decrease as plastics progress down the transition. Melting continues and the width of the solids bed decreases, while the width of the melt pool increases. As the channel gets shallower, shear rate increases; melt continues to heat.
(*e*) Further down, the solids bed breaks up, and the unmelted pellets are distributed throughout the channel like ice cubes in water. The efficient melting by friction of the solids bed against the barrel stops. Now only less efficient melting remains. This is something like heating the water to melt the ice cubes. It will finally get the job done but it is slow and much less efficient. Overheating of the melt continues in the shallow metering section.
(*f*) The plastic continues down the shallow metering section to the discharge. It is possible that there remains unmelted pellets or portions within the melt having higher or lower temperatures and viscosities. With a situation like this, the melt is nonuniform giving poor properties and color mixing. Great mixing can be achieved by reducing the channel depth, but this must be done at the expense of more overheating and less output per revolution. The constant depth metering section is not a good mixer for thermoplastics, but desired for thermoset plastics. This is because smooth laminar flow patterns are established causing the different portions of melt to continue to move in a fairly constant circular pattern. This does not mix the dissimilar portions of melt.

In the lower pressure range, a deep channel will provide more output; however, the reverse is true at high pressures. Shallower channels tend to give better mixing and flow patterns. Thus, although the screw is usually a simple-looking device, it accomplishes many different operations at the same time with its three sections: (1) solids conveying or feeding; (2) compressing, melting, and pressurizing the melt; and (3) mixing, melt refinement, and pressure-temperature stabilization.

Hypothetical data on screws are given in the Table opposite, which provides some examples of variations on the same length-to-diameter screw processing different plastics. In reality, the L/D ratios (flight length/outside diameter) vary according to the rheology of the resin. Advantages of a short L/D are: less residence times is necessary in the barrel, so heat-sensitive resins are kept at melt heat for a shorter time, lessening the chance of degradation; the design occupies less space; it requires less torque, making the screw strength and amount of horsepower less important; and it requires a smaller investment cost, initially and for replacement parts. Long L/D advantages are: the screw can be designed for a greater output or recovery rate, provided that sufficient torque is available, and it can be designed for more uniform output and greater mixing; also it will pump at higher pressures and give greater melting with less shear, as well as providing more conductive heat from the barrel.

The compression ratio (C/R) relates to compression that occurs on the resin in the transition section; it is the ratio of the volume at the start of the feed section divided by the volume in the metering section (determined by dividing the feed depth by the metering depth). The C/R should be high enough to compress the low bulk unmelted resin into a solid melt without air pockets. A low ratio will tend to entrap air bubbles. High percentages of regrind, powders, and other low bulk materials will be achieved by a high compression ratio. A high C/R can overpump the metering section. A common misconception is that engineering and heat-sensitive resins should use a low C/R. This is true only if it is decreased by deepening the metering section, and not by making the feed section shallower. The problem of overheating is more related to channel depths and shear rates than to C/R. As an example, a high C/R in polyolefins can cause melt blocks in the transition section, leading to rapid wear of the screw and/or barrel. In the processing of TS material, the C/R is usually zero so that accidental overheating does not occur and cause the melt to solidify in the barrel. With overheating, melt solidification occurs, and the zero ratio permits ease of removal—remove the nozzle, and it can be "unscrewed". Zero ratios are also used for TPs when the rheology so requires.

The output of a metering screw is fairly predictable, provided that the melt is under control. With a square pitch screw (conventional screw where distance from flight to flight is equal to the diameter), a simplified formula for output is:

$$R = 2.3D^2hgN$$

where R = rate or output in lb/h, D = screw diameter in inches, h = depth of the metering section in inches (for two-stage screw use the depth of the first metering section), g = gravity of the melt, and N = screw RPM.

This formula does not take into account back flow and leakage flow over the flights. These flows are not usually a significant factor unless the resin has a very low viscosity during processing, or the screw is worn out. The formula assumes pumping against low pressure, giving no consideration to melt quality and leakage flow of severely worn OD screws. With all these and other limitations, the formula can still provide a general guide to output. If the output is significantly greater, that is caused by a high C/R that overpumps the metering section, which sometimes is desirable but can lead to surging and rapid screw wear if it is excessive; and if the output is a lot less than estimated, that usually indicates a feed problem or worn screw and/or barrel. A feeding problem sometimes can be corrected by changes in the barrel heat. More often, the problem is caused by such factors as screw design, shape and bulk density of the feedstock, surface conditions of the screw root, the screw heat, and so forth. The problem of screw/barrel wear can be assessed by measuring the screw/barrel.

An accurate method used to determine output loss due to screw wear is to compare the worn screw's current output with the initial production benchmark, originally determined by shooting into a "bucket" to check the shot weight. Another approach is to measure the worn screw's clearance to the barrel wall (W), which is used along with the original measured screw clearance (O) and the metering depth (M) from the screw root to the barrel wall. Here the approximate percentage output loss (OL), with RPM being constant, is calculated from the formula:

$$OL = (W - O)/M + 100$$

Extrusion: The standard metering extrusion screw with its three zones (conveying, compression, and metering) basically operates like a conventional injection molding (IM) screw. The nomenclature is the same for each, except that no valve is used at the end of the extrusion screw (see Fig. on p. 670). Extrusion screws operate at lower pressures and in a continuous mode (IM is repeatable with abrupt, completely on-off pressure changes and very fast cycles). Even though many variables must be considered, extrusion requires fewer controls and presents fewer problems than IM.

Single screw extruders have changed greatly over the years. Today's functional modular concept developed mainly for reasons of effectiveness and favorable cost comparisons. Their output rates have significantly surpassed those of older designs. The performance of all machines and production lines (film, profile, etc.) will depend on the many factors that have to be controlled and synchronized going from upstream through the extruder and the downstream equipment. The type of screw used has always been a major influence in the complete line.

The blow film extruder has typified the new generation of extruders. The most effective screw design, in most cases, has been an L/D of

Hypothetical screw designs for general types of plastic.

Dimensions, in.	Rigid PVC	Impact polystyrene	Low-density polyethylene	High-density polyethylene	Nylon	Cellulose acet/ butyrate
Diameter	$4\frac{1}{2}$	$4\frac{1}{2}$	$4\frac{1}{2}$	$4\frac{1}{2}$	$4\frac{1}{2}$	$4\frac{1}{2}$
Total length	90	90	90	90	90	90
Feed zone (F)	$13\frac{1}{2}$	27	$22\frac{1}{2}$	36	$67\frac{1}{2}$	0
Compression zone	$76\frac{1}{2}$	18	45	18	$4\frac{1}{2}$	90
Metering zone (M)	0	45	$22\frac{1}{2}$	36	18	0
Depth (M)	0.200	0.140	0.125	0.155	0.125	0.125
Depth (F)	0.600	0.600	0.600	0.650	0.650	0.600

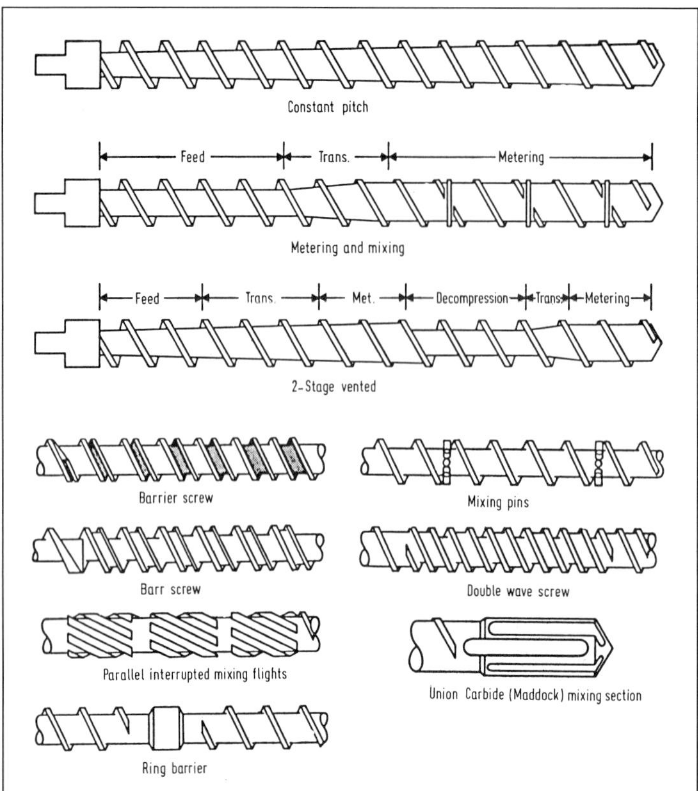

Extruder screw designs with different mixing sections.

25. Longer machines with a 30 to 33 L/D are chosen for venting or special requirements. High outputs are obtained with LDPE blown film or PP cast film extrusion. The 20 L/D machines now are almost always used only for heat-sensitive plastics. The 25 L/D version offers exactly the right compromise for obtaining a high output and preventing overheating and damage of thermally sensitive plastics.

Even in today's high technology world, the art of screw design is still dominated by trial-and-error approaches. However, computer models (based on proper input and experience) play an important role. When new materials are developed or improvements in old materials are required, one must go to the laboratory to obtain rheological and thermal properties before computer modeling can be performed effectively. New screws improve one or more of the basic screw functions of: melt quality, mixing efficiency, melting performance along the screw, melt heat level, output rate, output stability, and power usage or energy efficiency.

Heating can be controlled by using different machine settings, which involve various trade-offs. For example, in choosing the optimum rotation speed, a slow speed places the melt in contact with the barrel and screw for a longer time via heat conduction, and the slower speed produces less shear, so that dissipative heating is reduced, and properties of the plastic (particularly of a film) are enhanced. Sometimes an internal heat control is used with a screw. This type of screw is characterized by deeper channels, steeper helical angles, and an internal heating element. Its internal heating lowers the amount of viscous heating needed to process the material. As a result, the melt heat can be reduced by 50°F.

screw auger Refers to the action of the rotating screw in advancing the plastic going from the unmelted to melted plastic. There are different uses for augers. ▷ **mixer**

screwback Term used during injection molding when the conventional reciprocating screw is preparing the next melt shot size; screw moves backward.

screw/barrel override The screw/barrel combination is a very complex heat transfer system. To understand something that seems as simple as a zone override can require a complete analysis of the system. Just a few of the factors that can cause a zone override are screw design, barrel mass, thermocouple placement, heating and/or cooling jacket fit, barrel/screw wear, head pressure, overall temperature profile, defective temperature controllers, and inadequate cooling. Before assuming that zone override is strictly a screw design problem, analyze the system as a complete heat transfer mechanism. Although the screw is responsible for most of the heat input, it cannot control the heat distribution.

screw, barrier types An important development that occurred in the past was the barrier screw. There are many different patented designs that are useful for the different processed plastics and/or applicable to certain processing lines. They have two channels in the barrier section which are mostly located in the transition section. A secondary flight is started usually at the beginnning of the transition, creating two distinct channels, a solids channel and a melt channel. The barrier flight is undercut below the primary flight allowing melt to pass over it. The basic theory of these screws is summarized in the Fig. below.

screw bridging When an empty hopper is not the cause of failure, plastic might have stopped flowing through the feed throat. An overheated feed throat, or startup followed with a long delay, could build up sticky plastics and stop flow in the hopper throat. Plastics can also stick to the screw at the feed throat or just forward from it. When this happens, plastic just turns around with the screw, effectively sealing off the screw channel from moving plastic forward. As a result, the screw is said to be "bridged" and stops feeding the screw.

The common cure is to use a rod to break up the sticky plastic or to push it down through the hopper and into the screw where its flight may take a piece of the rod and forces it forward. The type of rod fed into the screw should be made of the plastics being processed. Other rods used could be of relatively soft material such as copper.

screw channel With the screw in the barrel, the space bounded by the surfaces of the flights, the root of the screw, and the bore of the barrel. This is the space through which the stock (melt) is conveyed and pumped. ▷ **barrel**

screw channel, axial area The cross section area of the channel measured in a plane through and containing the screw axis. The location of measurement should be specified.

screw channel, axial width The distance across the screw channel in an axial direction measured at the periphery of the flight. The location of measurement should be specified.

screw channel bottom Surface of screw stem or root.

screw channel depth The distance in a radial direction from the bore of the barrel to the root. The location of measurement should be specified.

screw channel depth ratio The factor obtained by dividing the channel depth at the feed opening by the channel depth just prior to

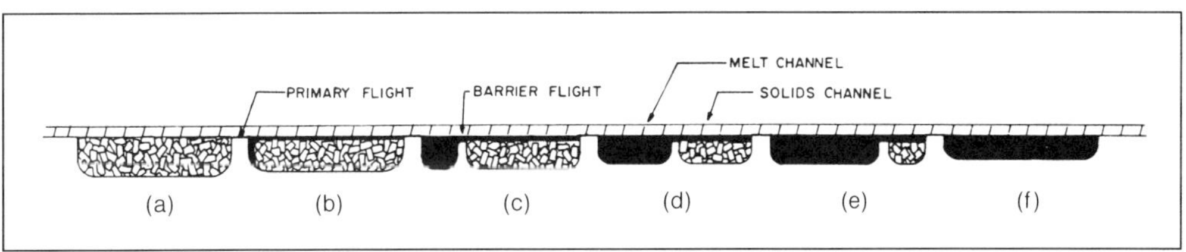

Barrier screw melt model.
(*a*) The feed section establishes the solids conveying in the same way as a conventional screw.
(*b*) At the beginning of the transition (compression), a second flight is started. This flight is called the barrier or intermediate flight, and it is undercut below the primary flight OD. This barrier flight separates the solids channel from the melt channel.
(*c*) As melt progresses down the transition, melting continues as the solids are pressed and sheared against the barrel, forming a melt film. The barrier flight moves under the melt film and the melt is collected in the melt channel. In this manner, the solid pellets and melted polymer are separated and different functions are performed on each.
(*d*) The melt channel is deep, giving low shear and reducing the possibility of overheating the already melted polymer. The solids channel becomes narrower and/or shallower forcing the unmelted pellets against the barrel for efficient frictional melting. Break up of the solids bed does not occur to stop this frictional melting.
(*e*) The solids bed continues to get smaller and finally disappears into the back side of the primary flight.
(*f*) All of the plastic has melted and gone over the barrier flight. Melt refinement can continue in the metering section. In some cases mixing sections are also included downstream of the barrier section. In general, the melted plastic is already fairly uniform upon exit from the barrier section.

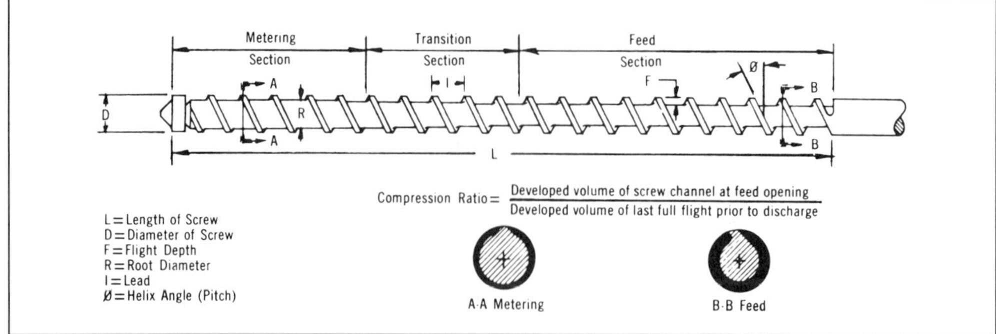

Schematic explaining screw compression ratio.

discharge. In constant lead screws, this value is close to, but greater than, the compression ratio.

screw channel volume developed The volume developed by the axial area of screw channel in one revolution about the screw axis. The location of measurement should be specified.

screw channel volume enclosed The volume of screw channel starting from the forward edge of the feed opening to the discharge end of the screw channel.

screw channel width, normal The distance across the screw channel in a direction perpendicular to the flight measured at the periphery of the flight. The location of measurement should be specified.

screw check up When purchasing new screws, it is important to fully inspect the screw for outside diameter, channel profile, shank dimensions, and overall length.

screw cleaning ▷ **extruder cleaning**

screw coatings Different coating systems are used to meet different requirements of the screw. A few of these coatings are: (1) chrome plating in the flighted area; provides easier cleaning after removal from barrel, feed rate remains more constant over the long run, minimal wear resistance when processing abrasive plastics, and often applied to improve corrosion resistance; (2) nickel plating acts somewhat similarly to chrome; it has some ability to obtain higher hardness by baking but is more costly; (3) other coatings that are usually patented incorporating different materials such as silicone carbide, tungsten carbide, cobalt, etc. ▷ **screw flight land hardened**

screw compression ratio The value obtained by dividing the developed of the screw channel at the feed opening by the developed volume of the last flight prior to discharge (see Fig. above). For thermoplastic, typical values range from 2 to 4, also expressed as 2:1 to 4:1; with thermosets it usually is 1. The value is not carried out to the actual division factor, but rounded off to even or fractions such as $3\frac{1}{2}$, $2\frac{1}{4}$, etc.

screw compression zone This zone or section refers to the screw transition zone. See Fig. with ▷ **screw**

screw constant lead A screw with a flight of constant helix angle; also called uniform pitch screw.

screw constant taper screw ▷ **screw taper**

screw core A hole in the screw for circulation of a heat transfer medium (liquid), or installation of a heater.

screw core plug Plug used in the core to modify the length (or depth) of the core.

screw core tube This inside pipe or tube is used to introduce a heat transfer medium into the screw core and used in conjunction with a rotary union assembly.

screw decompression ▷ **injection molding screw decompression**

screw decompression zone, vented In a vented barrel, the decompression zone exists in between the first and second compression zones and allows venting of volatiles without escape of plastic melt.

screw design ▷ **design screw (for processing plastic)**

screw diameter The diameter developed by the rotating flight land about the screw axis.

screw diametral clearance The difference in diameters between the screw and the barrel bore.

screw drag flow In the metering section, drag flow is the component of total material flow caused by the relative motion between the screw and barrel; the volumetric forward displacement of the plastic in the screw channel. Plasticator output is equal to the drag flow less the sum of the pressure flow and leakage flow.

screw drive The entire electric and mechanical system used to supply mechanical energy to the input shaft.

screw, extruder ▷ **extruder**

screw feed grooved ▷ **extruder grooved feed**

screw feed section The portion of a screw which picks up the material at the feed opening (throat) plus an additional portion downstream. Many screws, particularly for extruders, have an initial constant lead and depth section, all of which is considered the feed section. This section can be an integral part welded onto the barrel or a separate part bolted onto the upstream end of the barrel. The feed section is usually jacked for fluid heating and cooling.

screw feed side opening An opening which feeds the material at an angle into the side of the screw (see Fig.).

screw flight The outer surface of the helical ridge of metal on the screw.

screw flight depth The distance in a radial direction from the periphery of the flight to the root. The location of measurement should be specified.

screw flight front bottom radius The fillet between the front face of the flight and the root.

screw flight front face The face of the flight extending from the root of screw to flight land on side of flight toward the discharge. Same as pushing face of flight or leading edge.

screw flight full length Overall axial length of flighted portion of the screw, excluding non-return valves, smear heads, etc. in injection molding screw.

screw flight helix angle The angle of the flight at its periphery relative to a place perpendicular to the screw axis. The location of measurement should be specified.

screw flight land The surface of the radial extremity of the flight constituting the periphery or outside diameter of the screw.

screw flight land hardened The wear surfaces (primarily of flight lands) are usually protected by welding special wear resistant alloys

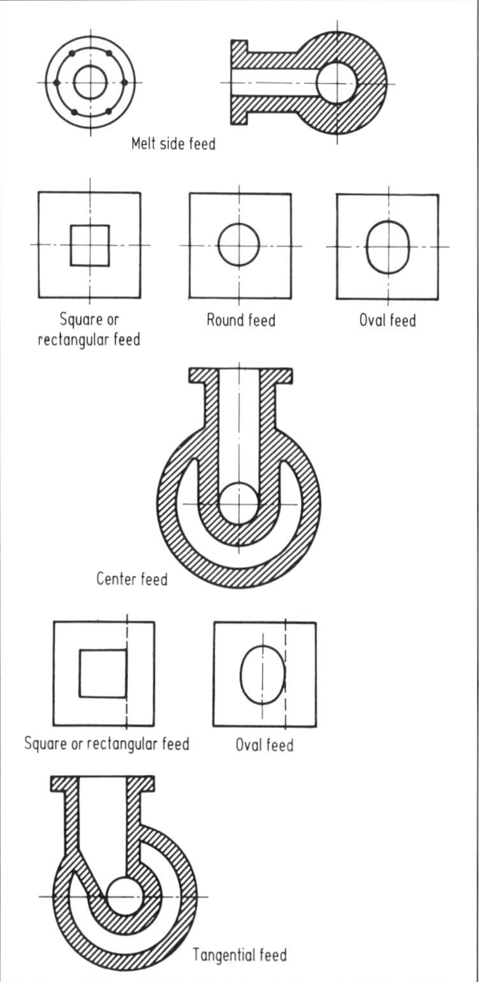

Examples of different feed position openings.

over these surfaces. There are many different types, such as those in the Table on p. 674.

screw flight land width axial The distance in an axial direction across one flight land.

screw flight lead The distance in an axial direction from the center of a flight at its outside diameter to the center of the same flight one turn away. The location of measurement should be specified.

screw flight number of turns Total number of turns of a single flight in an axial direction.

screw flight pitch Distance in an axial direction from the center of a flight at its periphery to the center of the next flight. In a single flighted screw, pitch and lead will be the same, but they will be different in a multiple-flighted screw. The location of measurement should be specified.

Example of hardsurfacing materials.

Product	Base material	Hardness Rc	Cracking tendency	Carbon percent	Chromium percent	Tungsten percent	Boron percent
Stellite No. 1[1]	Cobalt	48–54	4	2.5	30.0	12	—
Stellite No. 6[1]	Cobalt	37–42	3	1.1	28.0	4	—
Stellite No. 12[1]	Cobalt	41–47	3	1.4	29.0	8	—
Colmonoy No. 4[2]	Nickel	35–40	3	0.45	10.0	—	2.0
Colmonoy No. 5[2]	Nickel	45–50	3	0.65	11.5	—	2.5
Colmonoy No. 56[2]	Nickel	50–55	4	0.70	12.5	—	2.7
Colmonoy No. 6[2]	Nickel	56–61	5	0.75	13.5	—	3.0
Colmonoy No. 84[2]	Nickel	40–45	3	1.2	29.0	8	1.8
N-45[3]	Nickel	30–40	3	0.3	11.0	—	2.2
N-50[3]	Nickel	40–45	3	0.4	12.0	—	2.4
N-55[3]	Nickel	45–50	4	0.6	13.5	—	2.8

[1] Trademark of Cabot Corp.
[2] Trademark of Wall Colmonoy Corp.
[3] Trademark of Metallurgical Industries Inc.

screw flight rear face The face of flight extending from root of screw to flight land on side of flight toward the feed opening. Same as trailing edge.

screw heat treatment To improve performance and reduce wear of screws, different heat treatments are used based on screw material of construction and plastics to be processed. Treatments include flame hardening, induction hardening, nitriding, and precipitation hardening.

screw, helical feeder ▷ **feeder, helical screw**

screw helix angle ▷ **screw flight helix angle**

screw hub The portion immediately behind the flight which prevents the escape of the plastic.

screw hub seal A sealing device to prevent leakage of plastic back around screw hub, usually attached to the rear of the feed section.

screw, injection molding ▷ **injection molding**

screw inspection One of the less commonly discussed aspects of maintaining injection and extrusion equipment is the inspection of screws (see Fig. 1) and barrels. From time to time they should be examined to determine whether they are in condition to render the services expected. Screws do not have a continuous outside diameter. This requires special techniques in manufacturing and inspection. The following methods give reliable results and save time.

Inspection Rollers: Proper visual inspection of a screw or barrel requires that it be turned many times in order to see all sides. Screws and barrels are often heavy and difficult to turn when supported by the usual means. Roller supports make the job much easier. The device used two sets of double-conveyor rollers supported by multi-slotted angle irons. These angle irons are mounted on plain wood blocks that can be spaced to accept the screw (see Fig. 2).

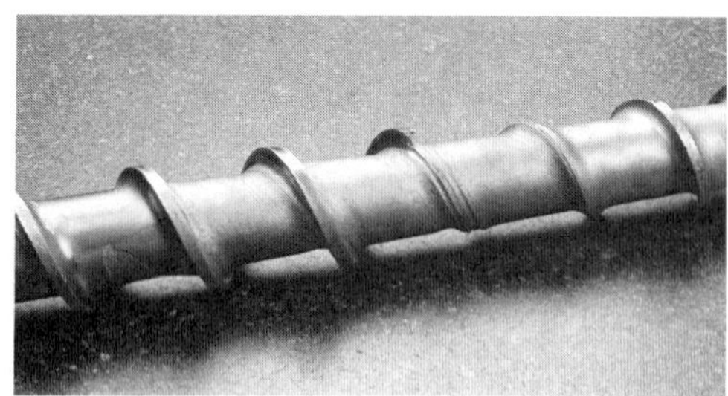

Fig. 1 Abrasive wear on screws (and barrels) is caused by abrasive fillers such as calcium carbonate, talc, glass fibers, titanium dioxide, etc. The mechanism of abrasive wear is much the same as emery cloth on metal such as the wear on these screw flights.

Fig. 2 Inspection rollers make it easy to inspect screws that otherwise would be difficult to handle because of their weight and length.

Diameters: The shank and many other diameters are easy to measure by the usual methods. Other diameters, such as the root diameter or the outside flighted diameter, require special methods. Measuring the root diameter is not always a reliable way to obtain channel depths. Another problem: if the micrometer sits on the radius on both sides, it can give a false reading. If the OD is severely worn, this is still the best method to determine the correct channel depths. Pitches less than square or very deep channels make the problem worse. The best way to obtain root diameter is to find the OD, then substract the channel depths.

The OD is measured with the assistance of a "mike" bar spanning two flights (see Fig. 3). The thickness of the bar is subtracted from the measurement obtained. The usual technique is to place the bar on top and hold the anvil of the micrometer against the slight at the bottom with the left hand. The right hand adjusts the micrometer while making rocking motions along the screw. The bar will rock with the micrometer as the final setting is reached. Of course, it is essential that the bar be straight and of uniform thickness. It is best to check the OD at 90° from the original set of measurements because screws can be manufactured egg-shaped or become worn that way.

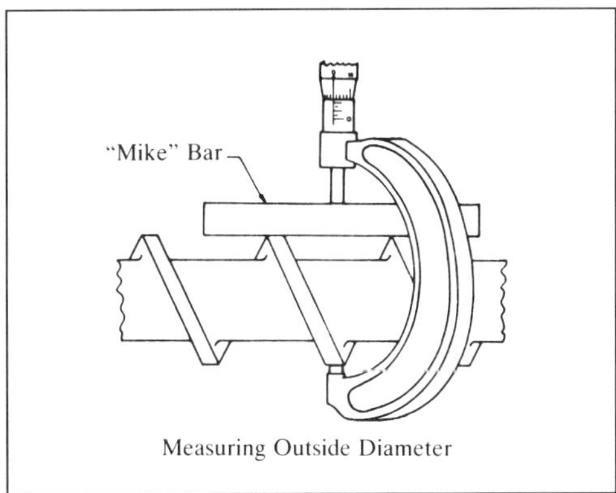

Fig. 3 O.D. measurement.

Depths: The channel depth of small screws can be easily checked with a standard depth micrometer. With larger screws, the depth micrometer will not span from flight to flight. If you intend to check many screws, it is best to make a screw-depth indicator or buy one. The screw-depth indicator consists of a wide angle "V" block with a dial indicator mounted on top and the probe extending down through the center of the V. The indicator is placed with the V resting on top of the screw and the probe on top of the flight. The gauge is then adjusted to zero. When the tip moves down into the root, the dial gives an accurate indication of channel depth. It is also very fast, allowing many measurements to be made very rapidly, and it can give continuous readings as the screw is rotated.

This last feature is also helpful in locating the starting and ending points of the feed, transition, and metering sections of a screw. This is not easy to do without the inspection rollers. The original channel depths of a severely worn screw are difficult to determine by this method. In the case of a severely worn screw, it is best to use the root-diameter method. Sometimes deep-jawed calipers can help if micrometers are running on the radii. A Spirex channel-depth gauge is shown in Fig. 4.

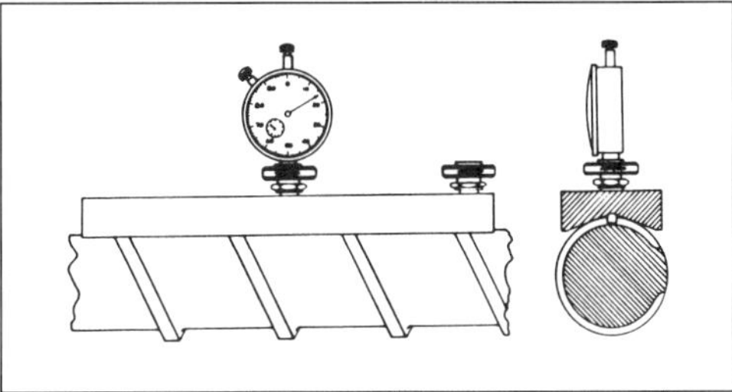

Fig. 4 Channel-depth gauge.

Concentricity and Straightness: The checking for straightness is difficult for the average plastics processor. If a good, long granite inspection table can be found, it will be helpful in checking concentricity and straightness. A preliminary check for straightness is possible just by rolling the screw on the table. If the screw is not straight, it will roll unevenly and show light under the flights in the low areas. The technique is appropriate only if the screw is not worn. The approximate amount that the screw is bent can be determined by feeler gauges. This technique is not completely accurate because the weight of the screw will tend to straighten it against the table. Most injection screws can be mounted between centers on a lathe and checked with an indicator while they are rotated. This requires an accurate center on both ends.

Extrusion screws usually do not have a center on the discharge end, requiring that a center be installed, then rewelded after testing and possible straightening. Checking the runout on the flighted portion is done with a "T" bar that spans at least three flights. The bar leans against the flights and an indicator measures the movement of the bar.

Fig. 5 To obtain a pilot runout measurement at the discharge end of a screw, a sensitive dial indicator as shown here is recommended.

Straightness and concentricity can be determined on screws that don't have centers by rotating them in V blocks on an accurate inspection table. This is done with the help of a height gauge. This method is particularly useful in inspecting the pilot at the discharge end of injection screws. A sensitive dial indicator is best used as shown in Fig. 5 above.

Hardness: The hardness of most portions of a screw is difficult to measure, because the screw is usually too large to test in a Rockwell-type tester. Also, the curved surfaces of the screw present a problem, and it is undesirable to make penetration marks on the surface. A satisfactory method for checking screw hardness is the impact or falling-ball type of tester such as Shore scleroscope (see Fig. 6). It is portable, works on curved surfaces, and can be reliable if checked against calibrated reference samples.

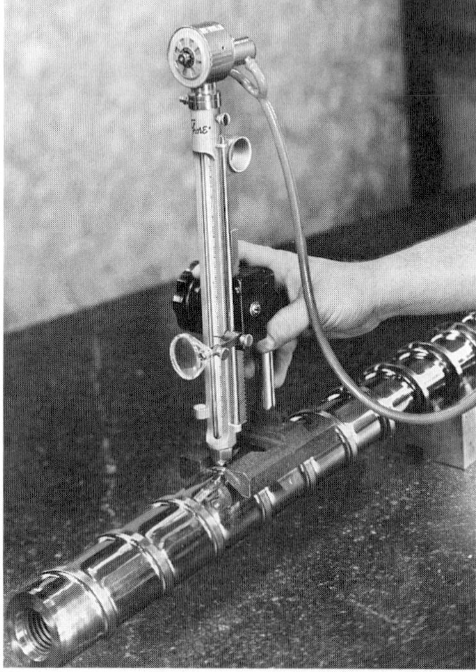

Fig. 6 A Shore scleroscope checks screw hardness using the impact or falling ball technique. The Shore device is portable and works on curved surfaces.

Finish and Coating Thickness: Finishes can be verified by a number of profilometers. A portable thickness tester can be used to test for chrome-plating thickness (see Fig. 7) or, with experience, nickel and other nonmagnetic coatings. Surface profilometer is shown in Fig. 8.

Screw Manufacturing Tolerances: All machined items are manufactured to predetermined dimensional tolerances. For reference, standard screw manufacturing tolerances are published by suppliers and made available on

Fig. 7 This portable thickness tester can be used to test chrome thickness or, in the hands of an expert user, check nickel or other coatings.

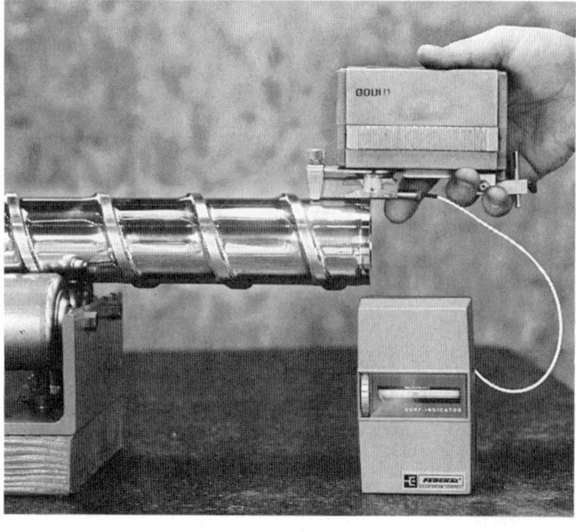

Fig. 8 Finishes can be verified by a profilometer.

request. These tolerances have been established according to practical application requirements and reasonable ease of machining. Some tolerances can be held closer than indicated on the polished list if necessary for a specific application. ▷ **barrel inspection**

screw, kneader type ▷ **kneader**

screw lead constant A screw with a flight of constant helix angle; also called uniform pitch screw.

screw lead decreasing A screw in which the lead decreases over the full flighted length, usually of constant depth.

screw leakage flow In the metering section, leakage flow is the backward flow of plastic through the clearance between the screw flight lands and the barrel. It is usually a very small negative component of total plastic flow.

screw length to diameter ratio ▷ **L/D ratio**

screwless extruder ▷ **extruder, screwless**

screw materials The majority of screws and barrels are made from special steels (see Table on p. 678). Low alloy steels are sometimes used with wear resistant liners.

screw mechanical requirements Screws always run inside a stronger more rigid barrel. For this reason, they are not subjected to high bending forces. The critical strength requirement is resistance to torque. This is particularly true of the smaller screws with diameters of $2\frac{1}{2}''$ and less. Unfortunately, the weakest area of a screw is the portion subjected to the highest torque. This is the feed section which has the smallest root diameter. A rule of thumb is that a screw's ability to resist twisting failure is proportional to the cube of the root diameter in the feed section.

screw melt performance With screws, particularly injection types, melt is not perfect, that is it is not uniform in temperature, consistency or viscosity. With the passing of time, melt performance has always improved via screw designs, such as the barrier screws and different screw mixing actions. Nonuniform melt is also due to the variability in plastic. With certain plastics and conventional screw designs, temperature within the screw channel can vary by 93°C (200°F). This is an extreme case but it explains why selecting the correct (or best) screw for a particular plastic is important. The more uniform the melt output, the better product performances.

screw melt zone The zone or section where the plastic has been plasticized by heat and pressure.

screw metering type A screw which has a metering section.

screw metering zone This zone or section is a relatively shallow portion of the screw at the discharge end with a constant depth and lead, usually having the melt move 3 or 4 runs of the flight in length.

screw mixing and melting A screw without special mixing elements does not do a good mixing job mainly because of the non-uniform shear acting in a conventional screw channel. Mixing is distributive and/or dispersive. Distributive mixing is the mixing of regular fluids, i.e. fluids without a yield point (a plastic with a yield point has the characteristic that it does not deform when the applied stresses are below a critical stress level, the yield stress). Dispersive mixing is the mixing of a fluid with a solid filler, i.e. a plastic with a yield point. The ojective in dispersive mixing is to break down the particle size of solid filler below a certain critical size and to evenly distribute the filler throughout the mixture. An example is in the manufacture of a color concentrate where the breakdown of the pigment agglomerates below a certain critical size is crucial.

Distributive and dispersive mixing are not physically separated. In dispersive mixing, there will always be distributive mixing. However, the reverse is not always true. In distributive mixing, there can be dispersive mixing only if there is a component exhibiting a yield stress and if the stresses acting on this component exceed the yield stress. In order for a dispersive mixing device to be efficient, it should have the following characteristics: (1) mixing section should have a region where the plastic is subjected to high stresses, (2) high stresss region should be designed so that exposure to high stresses occurs only for a short time, and (3) all fluid elements should experience the same high stress level to accomplish uniform mixing. In addition, they should follow the general rules for mixing of minimum pressure drop in the mixing section, streamline flow, complete barrel surface wiping action, and easy to manufacture mixing section.

Examples of mixers are in the Fig. with ▷ **extrusion**. ▷ **static mixer**

screw multiple flighted A screw having more than one helical flight such as: double flighted, double lead, double thread, or two starts, and triple flighted, etc.

screw multiple stage Screws with introduction of special mixing sections such as changes in

Examples of steels used in screw constructions.

Material	Tensile yield strength, psi	Hardness as machined, Rockwell	Availability of case hardness, Rockwell	O.D. wear resistance	Root wear resistance	Corrosion resistance	Material availability	Ease of machining	Approx. cost per pound, $
Alloy steels									
AISI 4140	100,000	28–32Rc[1]	48–55Rc[1]	Fair[1]	Poor	Poor	Excellent	Fair	0.90
AISI 4340	110,000	28–32Rc[1]	48–55Rc[1]	Fair[1]	Poor	Poor	Fair	Fair	1.30
Stressproof[2]	100,000	30Rc	48–55Rc[1]	Fair[1]	Poor	Poor	Fair	Fair	0.90
Nitralloy[3] 135M	85,000	33Rc	60–70Rc[4]	Good[5]	Good	Poor	Poor	Fair	1.65
Stainless steels									
304	335,000	80Rb	90Rb	Poor[5]	Poor	Good	Good	Fair-Poor	3.40
316	35,000	95Rb	90Rb	Poor[5]	Poor	Good	Good	Fair-Poor	4.15
416	115,000	30Rc	30Rc	Poor[5]	Poor	Fair-Good	Poor	Fair-Good	2.95
17-4PH[6]	175,000	38Rc	42Rc[5]	Poor[5]	Fair-Poor	Good	Fair	Fair-Poor	2.90
15-5PH[6]	175,000	38Rc	42Rc[5]	Poor[5]	Fair-Poor	Good	Poor	Fair-Poor	4.40
CPM-10V[7]	275,000	98Rb	56–58Rc	Excellent	Excellent	Fair	Fair	Fair	15.00
D-2	>300,000	96Rb	58–60Rc	Good	Good	Poor	Good	Fair	4.50
H-13	>300,000	96Rb	50–60Rc	Good	Good	Poor	Good	Fair	3.95
Specialty materials									
Duranickel[8] 301	125,000	30–38Rc	32Rc[5]	Poor[5]	Poor	Excellent	Very poor	Poor	25.00
Hastelloy[9] 276	80,000	86Rb	86Rb[5]	Poor[5]	Poor	Excellent	Very poor	Poor	25.00

[1] Flame or induction hardened.
[2] Trademark of La Salle Co.
[3] Trademark of Joseph T. Ryerson & Son Inc.
[4] Nitrided.
[5] Usually improved by hardsurfacing.
[6] Trademark of Armco Steel Corp.
[7] Trademark of Crucible Specialty Metals.
[8] Trademark of Huntington Alloys Inc.
[9] Trademark of Cabot Corp.

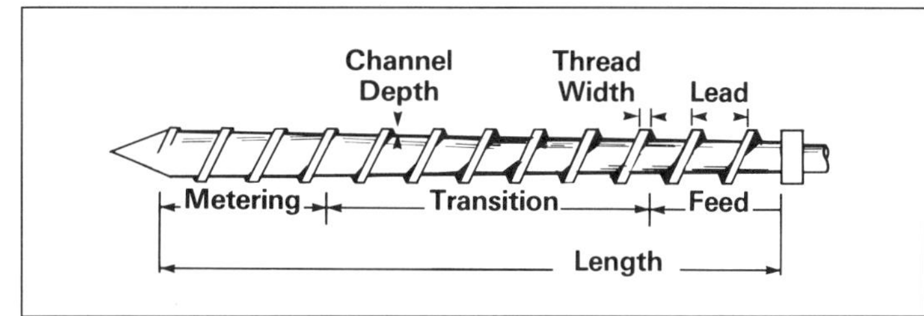

Standard square pitch feed screw.

the flight helix, choke rings, venting, or torpedoes, that combine feeding, mixing, and metering.

screw multiple type ▷ **extruder, screw multiple type**

screw output There is no easy way to calculate the output of screws. A multitude of factors affect this output. Sophisticated computer mathematical models and analysis of screw performance exist; these programs can be of considerable assistance in predicting performance of a certain screw design. The following formula is a simplified approach to output of the metering section of a conventional square pitch (pitch = diameter) screw:

$$R = 2.3D^2hgN$$

where R = rate of output in pounds per hour, D = screw diameter in inches, h = depth of the metering section in inches (for two-stage screws use the depth of the first metering section), g = specific gravity of the resin, N = screw RPM.

This formula does not take into consideration "back flow" or "leakage flow" over the flights. This is not usually a large factor unless the plastic has a very low viscosity at process temperatures and shear rates. Of course, leakage flow becomes a significant factor when screws become severely worn on the OD. The formula also assumes pumping against zero pressure at the heat or die. It is also assumes no over or under pumping from the feed section, and gives no consideration to melt quality. With all these and other limitations, the formula can still give guidance as follows: (1) A general guide to output of the screw. (2) If the actual output of the screw is significantly greater than calculated, it is caused by high compression ratios that overpump the metering section. Sometimes this is desirable, but it can lead to surging and rapid screw wear if it is excessive. (3) If the output is a lot less, it usually indicates a feed problem or a worn screw or barrel. The screw or barrel wear problem can be determined by measurement. A feeding problem can, on occasion, be corrected by changes in barrel temperature settings. More often, the problem is caused by other items such as: screw design, shape and bulk density of the feedstock, surface condition of the screw root and barrel ID in the feed area, feed throat design, screw temperature and other items.

screw pitch ▷ **screw flight pitch**

screw pitch, square A great many screws have a pitch equal to the diameter of the screw (maximum diameter of the flight). This screw is called a "square pitch" with a helix angle of 17.7° (see Fig. above).

screw, planetary ▷ **extruder, planetary screw**

screw plasticating ▷ **plasticating**

screw plunger ▷ **injection molding, plunger**

screw plunger stroke Distance plunger moves.

screw plunger transfer molding This method of molding is a combination of the reciprocating screw injection molding and transfer molding. Plastic is heated just as in a conventional IM machine and the melt is injected into a pot in the mold. As in conventional transfer molding, a transfer ram then forces the melt from the pot through a system of runners into multicavities of the mold (or a sprue into a single cavity mold).

screw pulling ▷ **extruder screw pulling** and **injection molding, screw pulling**

screw pump ratio This is applied to two-stage, vented screws and gives a measure of the ability of the second-stage to pump more than the first stage delivers to it. In extrusion, a high PR will tend to surge and a low compression ratio will tend to cause vent flow.

screw radial clearance One-half the diametral screw clearance.

screw rear bottom radius The fillet between the rear face of the flight and the root.

screw rebuilding and repair Screws and barrels are expensive components. When they are damaged or worn, it is often desirable to repair rather than replace. It is a common practice to rebuild a worn screw with hardsurfacing

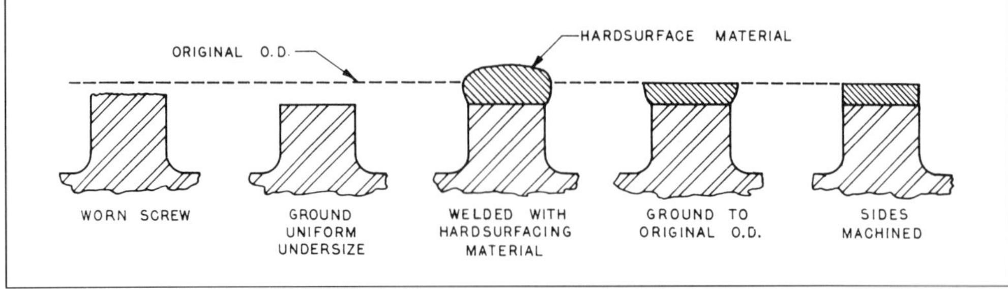

Steps in screw rebuilding.

materials. The various steps in the rebuilding process are shown in the Fig. above. Quite often the rebuilt screw will outlast the original screw. This is always true if the original screw was flame hardened or nitrided. The larger the screw diameter, the more economical screw rebuilding becomes. The rebuilding of a $4\frac{1}{2}''$ diameter 24:1 L/D screw is approximately two thirds the price of a new flame hardened screw and half the price of a new stellited screw. It usually does not pay to rebuild 2″ diameter and smaller screws. Screw repairs are also made on other parts of screws such as internal thread (injection screw), splines, etc.

screw, reciprocating ▷ **injection molding reciprocating screw**

screw recovery rate The volume of weight of a specified processable material discharged from the screw per unit of time, when operating at 50% of injection capacity (not applicable to extrusion). SPI test procedure is used. A high recovery rate can shorten cycle time and eliminate one of the reasons for a nozzle shut-off valve.

screw removal ▷ **extruder screw pulling** and **injection molding screw pulling**

screw restriction or choke ring An intermediate portion of a screw offering a resistance to the forward flow of material.

screw reverse flight A type of extruder screw with left hand flights on one end and right hand flights on the other end, so that material can be fed at both ends of the barrel and extrude from the center.

screw rifled liner A liner whose bore is provided with helical grooves.

screw root or stem The continuous central shaft, usually of cylindrical or conical shape.

screw, self-tapping ▷ **self-tapping screw**

screw shank The rear protruding portion of the screw to which the driving force is applied.

screw shear rate ▷ **melt shear rate**

screw single flighted A screw having a single helical flight.

screw specifications The Machinery Component Manufacturers Division of SPI published "Recommended Dimensional Guideline for Single Screws", and "Recommended Guidelines for Single Barrels". These guidelines were developed by the manufacturers in the industry in order to provide all processors with an authoritative set of standards to insure that they receive a quality part when repairing or replacing a screw or barrel.

screw speed The revolutions per minute (RPM) of a screw.

screw speed control Many processes require speed controls. Performance and reliabilities of these controls are very similar to those of the temperature controls—you get what you purchase. Early speed controllers, like the temperature controllers, were mechanical. Speeds were held within 5%, resulting in poor plastic melt control. Where better speed control is desired, the solution is the same as in temperature control; only the equipment names are changed. A device is added to the motor, and an "integral" characteristic is provided, corresponding to the automatic reset with heat. It brings the speed closer to the set point. A "derivative" characteristic, corresponding to the rate in heat, ensures a prompt response to any upsets.

The arguments for the use of integral or derivative control of speed are the same as for temperature. Different systems are available, including the all-digital speed control on plastic processing machines that require speed control. These speed controls permit accuracies of 0.5% or less. An all-digital phase locked loop system permits all motors in a machine and/or a processing line to be synchronized with each other exactly or in a desired speed ratio, just as if they were mechanically geared together.

screw, square pitch ▷ **screw pitch, square**

screw suck back ▷ **injection molding screw decompression**

screw taper This conical transition section or conical tapered section is a transition section in which the root increases uniformly in diameter so that it is of a conical shape.

screw taper constant Screw of constant lead and a uniformly increasing root diameter over the full flighted length.

screw temperature zone Section of the flow path of the plastic which is controlled to the optimum temperature for that zone. Extruders typically have three to six zones on the barrel and a number of zones down stream in the adapters, screen changer, die, and post-extrusion treatment areas. Injection molding machines typically have two to four zones on the barrel and nozzle, and a number down stream in the mold.

screw, thermoset type The Fig. shows a typical thermoset (with L/D of 1) and water cooled barrel. Heat control of TS plastics is very critical during plasticizing in the screw/barrel; if it goes just slightly too high, it solidifies in the barrel, requiring screw pulling. Thus, temperature control is extremely critical resulting in the usual L/D of 1 and water cooled barrel. ▷ **thermoset plastic** and **injection molding, thermoset machine**

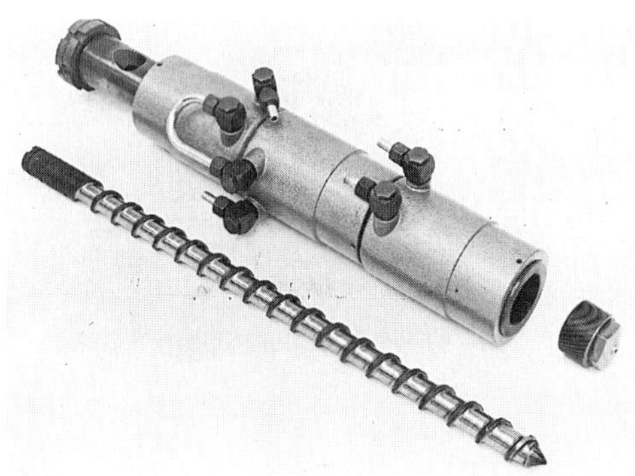

Example of a thermoset screw and water cooled barrel.

screw three-zone melting See Fig. below.

screw thrust The total axial force exerted by the screw on the thrust bearing (screw support). For practical purposes equal to the melt pressure times the cross section of the barrel bore.

screw thrust bearing The bearing used to absorb the thrust force exerted by the screw.

screw thrust bearing rating at 100 RPM The pressure in psi (MPa) that can be sustained under normal operating conditions, for a minimum bearing life (B-10 rating from the Bearing Manufacturers Assoc.) of 20,000 hours.

screw tip, back-flow stop valve ▷ **screw tip, injection**

screw tip, check valve ▷ **screw tip, injection**

screw tip, injection When the melt is forced into the mold, the screw-plunger action could cause the melt to flow back into the screw flights. Generally, with heat-sensitive plastics such as PVC and thermosets, a plain or smearhead screw tip is used. For other plastics this is not adequate, and a number of different check valves are used. These devices work in the same manner as a check valve in a hydraulic system, allowing fluid to pass only in one direction. These check valves, which are basically a sliding ring or ball check design (see Fig. on p. 682) are supplied by many manufacturers. Here are some comparisons (see Table on p. 682). Also see Table in ▷ **injection molding processing temperature**.

screw torpedo An unflighted cylindrical portion of the screw usually located at the discharge end but can be located in other sections, particularly in multiple stage screws.

screw torque The work of melting is done by rotating a screw in a stationary barrel. The rotational force called torque is the product of the tangential force and the distance from the center of the rotating member. For example, if a 1 lb (4.45 N) weight were placed at the end of a 1 ft (0.305 m) bar attached to the center of the screw, the torque would be 1 ft × 1 lb or 1 ft-lb (1.36 N·m). Torque is related to horsepower (HP):

$$\text{power, HP} = \frac{\text{torque (ft-lb)} \times \text{RPM}}{5252}$$

$$\text{kW} = \frac{\text{torque (N·m)} \times \text{RPM}}{7124}$$

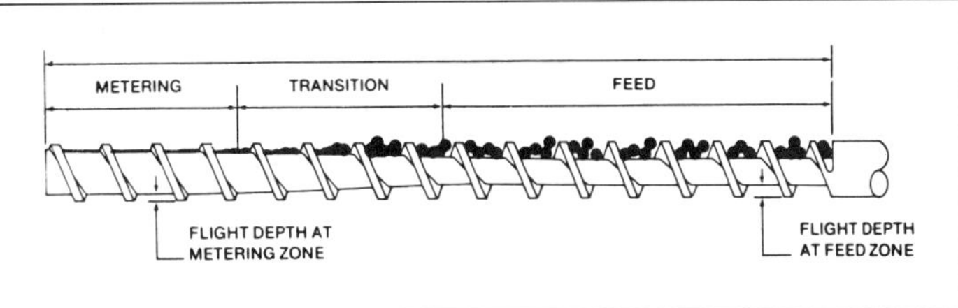

Basic typical three-zone melting screw; flow direction right to left.

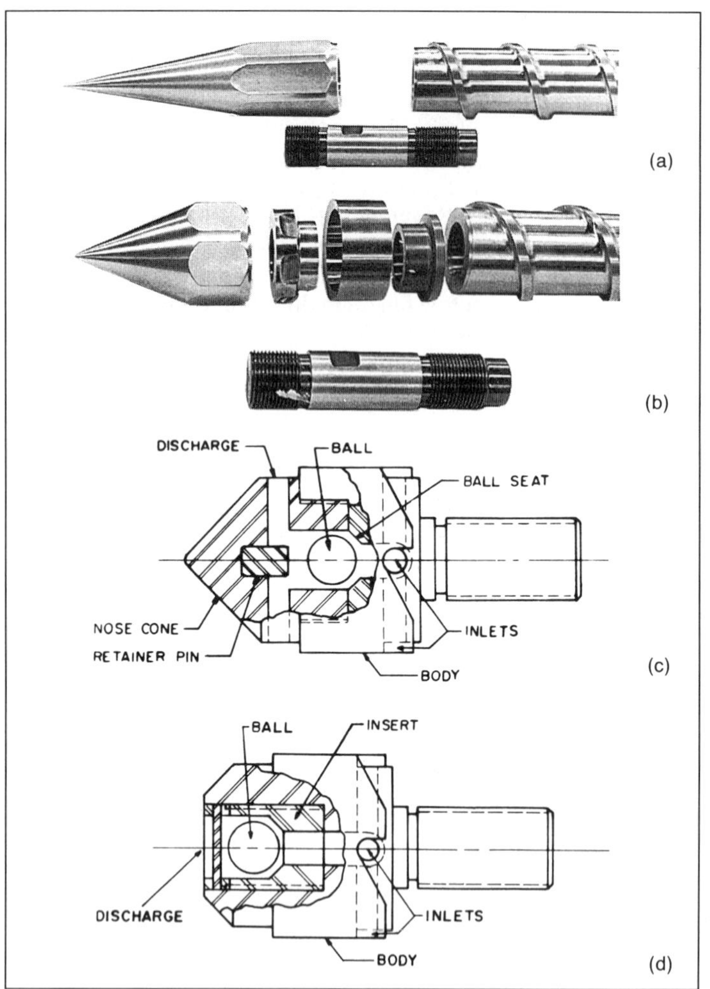

Basic screw tip designs: (*a*) Plain or smearhead (disassembled); (*b*) sliding ring (disassembled); (*c*) side discharge ball check, and (*d*) front discharge ball check valve.

Examples show the influence of check valves on plastic performance.

Type of check valve	Advantages	Disadvantages
Sliding ring valve	Greater streamlining for less degrading of materials. Best for heat-sensitive materials. Less barrel wear. Less pressure drop across valve. Best for vented operation. Easier to clean. Less expensive than side discharge ball check.	Less positive shut off, especially in $4\frac{1}{2}''$ dia. and larger sizes. Less shot control. More expensive than front discharge ball check.
Ball check valve	More positive shutoff. Better shot control. Front discharge ball check less expensive than sliding ring valve.	Less streamlined. More degrading of heat-sensitive materials. More barrel wear. Side discharge type more expensive than sliding ring type. Greater pressure drop, creating more heat. Poor for vented operation. Harder to clean.

The torque output of an electric motor of a given HP depends on its speed. A 30 HP (22 kW) motor has the following torque at various speeds:

Speed, RPM	Torque, ft-lb	N·m[1]
1800	87.5	119
1200	133	181
900	175	238

[1] Newton meter.

The speed of a given HP motor is built into the motor. Changes in speed and torque can also be accomplished by changing the output speed of the motor by using a gear train. The change in torque varies inversely with the speed. AC motors develop a starting torque of almost twice the running torque. The screw has to be protected against overload to prevent screw breakage. This is not a problem with hydraulic drives. The drive must supply enough torque to plasticize at the lowest possible screw speed, but not enough to mechanically shear the metal screw. Changes in torque are needed because of the different processing characteristics of plastics. As an example, much higher torque is required to plastize PC than PS. The strength used limits the input HP. ▷ **extruder torque**

screw transfer molding ▷ **transfer molding; compression molding, screw preplasticizer**

screw transition zone The section of a screw between the feed zone and metering zone in which the flight depth decreases in the direction of discharge; plastic is in both solid and molten state.

screw, twin ▷ **extruder, twin screw**

screw, two-stage venting ▷ **injection molding venting** and **extruder venting**

screw valves ▷ **screw tip, injection**

screw venting ▷ **injection molding venting** and **extruder venting**

screw volumetric efficiency The volume of material discharged from the machine during one revolution of the screw, expressed as a percentage of the developed volume of the last turn of the screw channel.

screw water cooled ▷ **extruder, screw with internal heat control**

screw wear All screws wear, particularly in the flight OD, and in turn influence melt performance that will eventually affect part performance. Some screws wear rapidly and others slowly, depending on factors such as: (1) screw, barrel, and drive alignment, (2) straightness of screw and barrel, (3) screw design, (4) uniformity of barrel heating, (5) material being processed, (6) abrasive fillers, reinforcing agents and pigments, (7) screw surface materials, (8) barrel liner materials, (9) combination of screw surface and barrel liner, (10) improper support of the barrel, (11) excessive loads on barrel discharge end and heavy dies, (12) corrosion caused by polymer degradation, (13) corrosion caused by additives such as flame retardants, and (14) excessive back pressure on injection recovery.

To protect screw and barrel wear, keep a log of output [lb/h/RPM (kg/h/RPM)]. Operators tend to increase RPM to compensate for wear, resulting in higher melt temperatures. A monthly check of specific output will warn about wear.

screw wrap-around transition zone A transition section in which the root is always parallel to the axis of the screw.

scrim cloth **1.** Also cost reinforcing nonwoven fabric made from continuous filament yarn in an open mesh construction. Used in processing of tape or other B-stage material to facilitate handling. **2.** Used as a carrier of adhesives, for use in secondary bonding.

scrubber Equipment to control acid gas emissions at combustion facilities, usually a process involving water.

scrubbing Process for removing one or more components from a mixture of gases and vapors by passing it upward and usually counter current to and in intimate contact with a stream of descending liquid, the latter being chosen so as to dissolve the desired components and not the others.

scuffing Surface marks on the walls of a molding which run in the direction of the mold opening.

seal **1.** A continuous joint of two or more surfaces of sheet material such as made by fusion or adhesion. **2.** In packaging by heat seal; a method of bonding mating surfaces under controlled application of heat, pressure, and dwell time. **3.** Hermetic seal prevents passage of air and other gases. **4.** In products (building, packaging, etc.) requiring a barrier against the passage of liquids, solids, and/or gases.

sealant A material applied to a joint usually in paste or liquid form that hardens or cures (to an elastomeric or rigid state) in place, forming a seal against gas or liquid entry. They also serve to maintain a pressure differential, attenuate mechanical shock, vibration, and sound; protect electronic subcomponents mechanically, electrically, and thermally; and with special formulated conductive sealants, provide electrical continuity. About 75% of this market is in commercial and home construction and repair. Transportation (auto, truck, train, aircraft, marine) is another field using a large volume of sealants. Materials used include silicones, polysulfides, acrylics, polyurethanes, polychloroprenes, and butyls.

sealing diameter That portion of a metal insert that is free of knurl and is allowed to enter the mold to prevent the flow of plastic.

sealing dielectrically ▷ **dielectric heating**

sealing, impulse ▷ **impulse sealing**

sealing, thermal ▷ **thermal sealing**

sealing, ultrasonic ▷ **ultrasonic sealing or welding**

sea water desalination ▷ **desalination**

secant modulus ▷ **modulus, secant**

second The second (s) is the duration of 9 192 631 770 periods of the radiation corresponding to the transition between the two hyperfine levels of the ground state of the cesium-133 atom (adopted by the 13th CGPM, 1967).

secondary bonding The joining together, by the process of adhesive bonding, of two or more already cured plastics (reinforced plastics, etc.) and other material parts, during which the only chemical or thermal reaction occurring is the curing of the adhesive itself.

secondary operation ▷ **operation, secondary**

security device Redesign of devices for securing homes, autos, etc. against intruders, fires, etc. has made them more functional, "intelligent", and attractive. Basic to this effort are cost-effective components.

segregation **1.** With thermoplastics, a close succession of parallel, relatively narrow and sharply defined, wavy lines and color striations on the surface which differ in shade from surrounding areas and create the impression that the components have separated. **2.** In thermoset plastics, usually a separation of plastic and filler on the surface.

Selar Du Pont's patented barrier plastic that is a modified nylon with a compatibilizer or binder applicable to other plastics, such as in gasoline PE fuel tanks.

self-extinguishing A loosely used term describing a material's ability to cease burning when the source of flame is removed. ASTM has ruled that self-extinguishing shall not be used in ASTM standards; it has no meaning except in association with a specific test method or specific conditions of burning.

self-heating A rise in temperature of a material, assemblage, or product caused by internal, exothermic chemical reaction.

self-ignition ▷ **spontaneous ignition**

self-opening style SOS is a common bag shape. ▷ **bag manufacturing**

self-tapping screw If a product requires a secure attachment but may have to be detached and reassembled at some time, different mechanical fasteners are available, such as self-tapping screws. ▷ **assembly/joining**

selvage The narrow edge of woven fabric that runs parallel to the warp. It is made with stronger yarns in a tighter construction than the body of the fabric to prevent raveling. ▷ **fill**

semi-automatic mold ▷ **mold classification by operation**

semi-automatic operation ▷ **operation, semi-automatic**

semiconductive ▷ **plastic, conductivity**

semiconductor **1.** A material with controllable conductivities, intermediate between insulators and conductors. **2.** In pure metals, where electrons are excited across the energy gap.

semicrystalline plastic In plastics, materials that exhibit localized crystallinity, usually just called crystalline plastics.

semi-finished product Plastics stock material usually prepared by extrusion, in the form of pipe, block, sheet, or profile sections, from which it is reworked (cutting, forming, bonding, etc.) for end applications. Other plastics are included such as RP pultrusions.

semipositive mold ▷ **mold, semipositive**

semireinforcement A moderately priced filler added to displace the matrix plastic and promote some improvements in the reinforced plastics properties.

Example of performance guide for different sensors.

Type of sensor	Accuracy	Dimensional range	Transverse measurement	Reflex measurement	Freedom from interference	Material dependency	Sensor-size limitations	Complexity of equipment	Ease of calibration	Sensitivity
Rolling-contact	Good	Wide	Yes	No	Good	No	Low	Low	Easy	Med.
Air	Good	Wide	Yes	No	Good	No	Some	Med.	Easy	High
Magnetic-reluctance	Fair	To $\frac{1}{4}''$	Yes	Poss.	Fair	Some	Some	High	Easy	Med.
Sonic	Good	To 1″	Yes	Yes	Fair	Yes	Some	High	Fair	Med.
Optical	Fair	Wide	Yes	Yes	Good	Some	High	Med.	Fair	Med.
Laser-intercept	Good	Wide	Yes	Yes	Good	Some	High	Med.	Fair	High
Laser-interferometry	Exc.	Ltd.	No	Yes	Good	Yes	Some	High	Easy	High
Capacitance	Good	Med.	Yes	No	Fair	Yes	Low	High	Easy	Med.
Proximity	Good	Wide	Yes	No	Fair	Some	Low	High	Easy	High
Beta-ray	Good	Ltd.	No	Yes	Good	Some	Low	High	Easy	High

semirigid plastic For purposes of general classification, a plastic that has a modulus either in tension or flexure between 70 to 700 MPa (10,000 and 100,000 psi) at 23°C and 50% relative humidity. ▷ **rigid plastic** and **nonrigid plastic**

sensitivity The minimum input capable of producing an output motion.

sensor Basically a device designed to respond to a physical stimulus (temperature, pressure, motion, illumination, etc.) and transmit a resulting signal for interpretation, or measurement, or for operating a control. There is a very broad selection of sensors with extremely different sensitivities, capabilities, and repeatabilities (see Table above).

To select the correct sensor you should know something about how they work, and which is typically used for what application. This is important since not all sensors can measure, as an example, the thickness ranges, not all can measure the same plastics, and not all can measure with the same degree of accuracy or resolution. Some factors to consider are a sensor's measurement range, whether its design is transmission or reflective, whether it is contacting or non-contacting, etc. (see Fig. on next page).

The three most common sensor types are nuclear, infrared, and caliper. There are also specialized types such as microwave, laser, X-ray, and ultrasonic. Sensors are available to sense many different conditions such as color, smoothness, temperature, composition, haze, gloss, moisture, dimensions, speed, etc. Numerous sensors are used to record and/or control process conditions and variables, such as given in the Table opposite.

sensor accuracy When a manufacturer quotes static accuracy, it is essentially referring to how the sensor will perform under the best possible conditions. Although it is composed of a number of factors, it should still be regarded as just one measure of a sensor's performance; it is not indicative of its overall capabilities. To get a truly representative static accuracy rating, a manufacturer will also provide a number of different components or sources of error such as measurement calibration accuracy, long term repeatability, and noise effects.

sensor, acoustic emission Device, generally piezoelectric, that transforms the particle motion produced by an elastic wave into an electrical signal.

sensor, beta gauge Also called a beta-ray gauge; consists of two facing elements, a beta-ray emitting source and a beta-ray detector. As an example, when a film or sheet is passed

Example of process variables and instrument sensors.

Process variables	Instrumentation
Temperature	Thermoelements Resistance elements, PT 100 Radiation recorder
Pressure	Strain gauges Resistance elements
Rotational speed	A-c/d-c-generators Incremental counters
Weight	Strain gauges Piezo elements
Velocity	A-c/d-c-generators Incremental counters Correlators
Torque	Strain gauges Scales
Time	Impulse counters
Logic state (on/off)	Switches

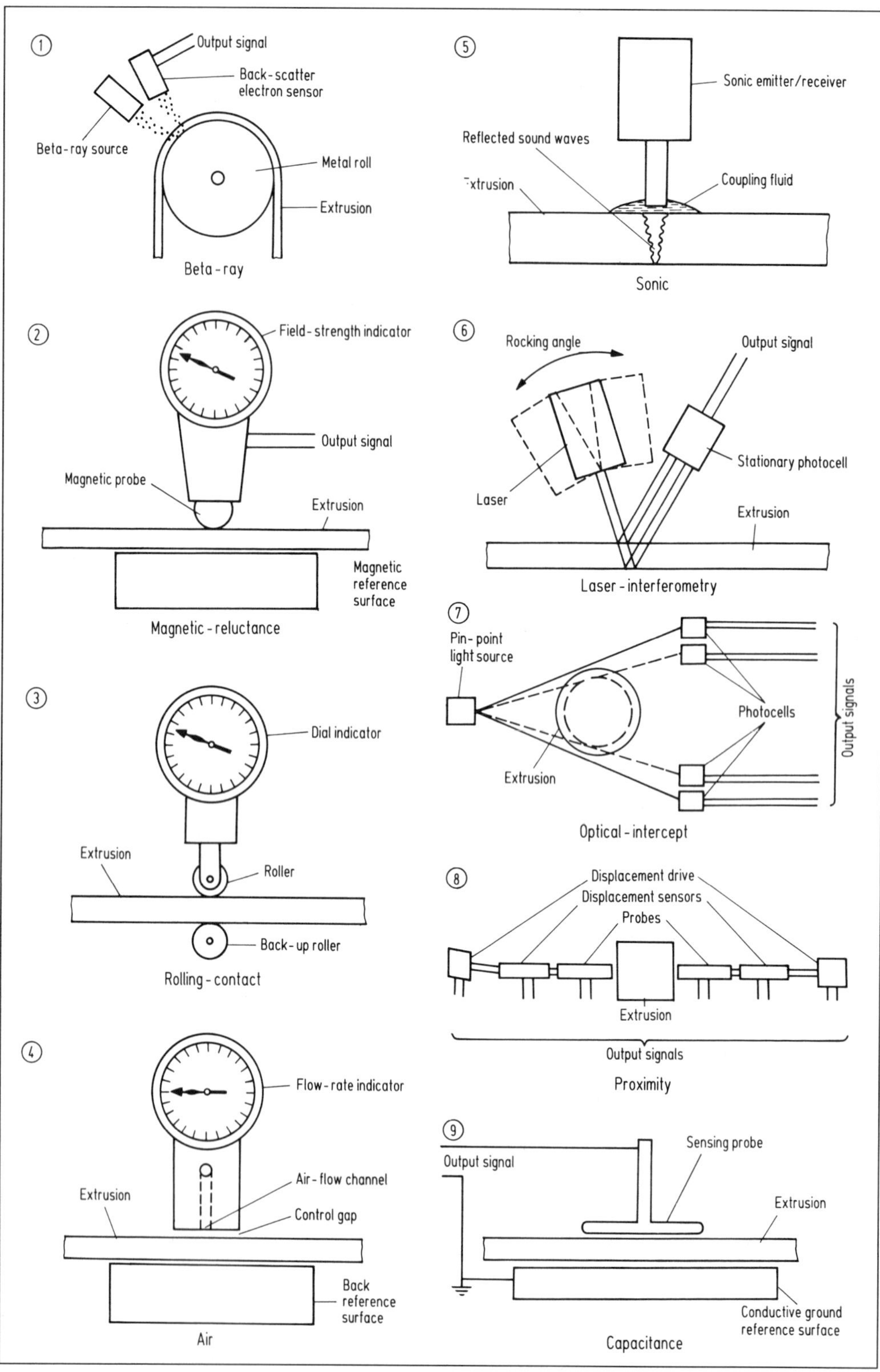

Examples of different performing sensors.

between the gauge elements, some of the rays are absorbed, the percentage absorbed being a measure of areal density or the thickness of the plastic. These gauges are nuclear sensors; different types are available.

sensor, caliper These gauges provide for direct physical measurement of the total thickness. Depending on type, the sensors may contact the product on both sides, or have one or both sides ride on a thin, relatively constant airfilm. They cannot measure individual layers of a composite or laminate.

sensor, computer control ▷ **computer processing control**

sensor, dual laser A double laser beam used, as an example, to measure pipe diameters on two axes during extrusion of pipe.

sensor, dynamic accuracy The dynamic accuracy of a sensor is the indication of how well it will operate in the production environment. It is defined as a comparison of sensor readings on, as an example, sheet with actual samples taken from the sheet and measured. Dynamic accuracy is a function of a number of components, of which sensor static accuracy is one. Others include flutter sensitivity, air gap temperature, mechanical sensor alignment, and sensor response time.

sensor, electron optical Producing and controlling a beam of electrons to produce an image.

sensor, fiber optics ▷ **fiber optic strain gauge**

sensor, film and sheet Sensors for measuring film and sheet thickness usually fall into one of three categories: caliper, nuclear, and infrared. ▷ **extruder web thickness sensor**

sensor, gamma backscatter Nuclear gauge based on the use of gamma-ray emitting source and a gamma-ray detector. Can handle thicker sections than beta gauge techniques.

sensor, inductive and capacitive proximity Sensors detect the presence, or absence, of metallic and non-metallic products without physical contact.

sensor, infrared IR sensors utilize light beams, a form of electromagnetic radiation, in a portion of the spectrum that cannot be seen by the naked eye ▷ **electromagnetic spectrum**. The IR sensors, like nuclear sensors, measure mass per unit area and then convert the measurement to a thickness value. Unlike nuclear types, which measure the total weight of a product, IR can sometimes be tuned to measure different materials independently. However, IR sensors' versatility is not a sign of their universal application. They are best applied to clear films and coatings, and are not particularly well suited to opaque films or films containing certain fillers. The effect of many of the additives can be minimized through a careful selection of the wave lengths measured. There are basically two configurations: transmission and reflective. Each is suited to different applications. The Fig. below an example of transmission.

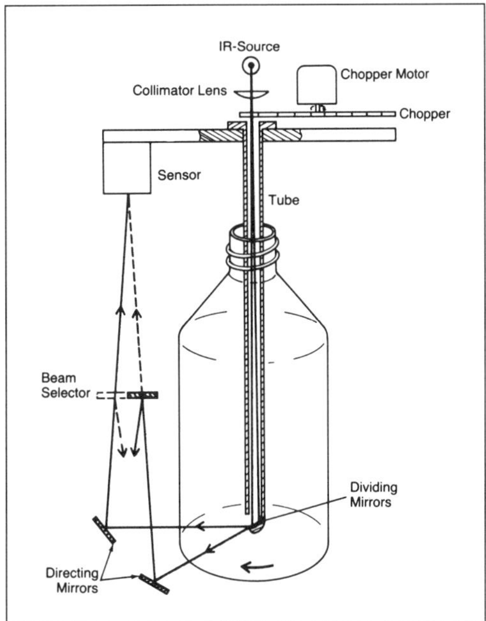

This IR sensor determines wall thickness of the bottle.

sensor, multiaction An advanced technology, many transducer, multipurpose Assembly Test Chip (ATC) senses 13 different parameters (developed by Sandia National Labs., Albuquerque, N.M.). This semiconductor minichip (includes plastic coating and epoxy encapsulation) was developed to monitor packaging of semiconductors. It senses moisture, temperature, mechanical stress, and identifies causes of damage, etc.

sensor, noise effect Noise and its elimination is accomplished through an averaging technique. This can be done because noise typically takes on a random nature, and as a result can be filtered or eliminated over time. The error effect of short-term variation, which is one type of noise, consists of the deviation from the average value during a specified sample time period. Noise can come from a number of sources, but as long as it is random it can be reduced to acceptable limits over sufficient time.

sensor, nuclear A beam of beta or gamma radiation is passed through the material being measured for thickness. The greater the mass of material, the less radiation is able to pass through to the detector. If the material is of constant density, sensor calibration can be in units of thickness. They can only measure total thickness; not individual plies if laminated. Beta provides somewhat faster response; gamma can handle much thicker materials.

sensor, piezoelectric ▷ **piezoelectric plastic**

sensor, pressure ▷ **clamping force measured**

sensor, pressure curing reinforced plastic Failure to apply proper pressure during cure of thermoset RP processing can be as damaging to the quality of the part as poor temperature control. Pressure sensors located in different sections of the RP for prototyping and if possible for production can be used in addition to any press pressure gauges, if used. SR-4 strain gauges are used, etc.

sensor, temperature ▷ **temperature sensor**

sensor, thermoset curing fiber optics ▷ **thermoset plastic curing, fiber optic sensor**

sensor, ultrasonic Used as a measuring technique for blown film bubble diameter or to measure pipe diameter and concentricity in water cooling bath.

sensor, vision ▷ **vision system inspection**

separation of waste ▷ **waste rear-end separation**

separator A permeable layer that also acts as a release film or lubricant. Porous PTFE-coated glass fabric is an example. With bag molding RP, often placed between lay-up and bleeder to facilitate bleeder system removal from the cured RP.

separator, balisic The balisic machine sorts inorganic from organic matter for composting purposes.

sequestering agent They prevent metallic ions from precipitating from solutions by means of reactions which normally would cause precipitation in the absence of a sequestering agent.

serendipity An unexpected engineering and scientific discovery which turns out to be more important than the project being researched or developed. One example is the discovery of the sodium sulfide plastic, latter known as *Thiokol.* White, the researcher, was seeking to develop an improved automotive coolant. Another is the discovery of the reinforcing effect of carbon black on rubber while technologists were using it as a black pigment to counteract the whiting effect of zinc oxide. Many of these "reactions" have occurred in the past, present, and will continue to occur.

service factor A factor which is used to reduce a strength value to obtain an engineering design stress. The factor may vary depending on the service conditions, the hazard, and length of service desired, and the properties of a product. This design factor is generally referred to as a safety factor. ▷ **design safety factor**

servo system ▷ **motion control systems**

set 1. Mechanically, it is the strain remaining after complete release of the load producing deformation. ▷ **permanent set** 2. To convert a liquid plastic or adhesive into a solid state by curing, by evaporation of solvent, by suspending medium, or by gelling.

set at break Elongation measured, such as 10 minutes, after rupture on reassembled tension specimen. ▷ **elongation**

set temperature ▷ **temperature, set**

setting The preparation of a machine ready for processing. It involves fixing the mold or die in place and making all the adjustments necessary to ensure that the machine works properly, safely, and efficiently.

setting time The period of time during which a molded or extruded product, an assembly, etc. is subjected to heat and/or pressure to set or solidify the plastic.

setting up A term sometimes used to denote the hardening of material in the mold prior to removal of the molding. Also called set-up.

sewage solid waste Municipal solid waste sludge materials include garbage, glass, metal, plastic, etc. but not sewage which is identified as municipal waste or sewage solid waste.

S-glass Structural type of glass fiber type of a magnesium aluminosilicate composition that is especially designed to provide very high tensile strength compared to the more conventional E-glass. S-glass and S-2 glass fibers have the same composition but different finishes (coatings).

shape factor A dimensionless ratio of lengths, surface areas, or volumes of the particles, useful for characterizing or comparing particles which otherwise have similar physical properties. It generally defines the ratio of the major to the minor dimensions of a particle.

shape welding Use of only welding to produce parts is called shape welding or shape melting. It is a form of desktop manufacturing (DTM) since a product's design can be programmed into an office computer. The computer then directs a welding machine on the plant floor to produce a hard copy. During the 1960s, Krupp & Thyssen, German steel makers, and Sulzer in Switzerland began developing this process to fabricate pressure vessels for the utilities industry. Strength is greater than traditional casting or forging. Use of plastics has possibilities. ▷ **welding**

shark skin A surface irregularity of a blown container in the form of finely spaced sharp ridges caused by a relaxation effect of the melt at the die exit. ▷ **melt flow defects**

Shaw pot The original (1930s) thermoset transfer molding process. A conventional hydraulic is used, without auxiliary cylinder. The molding material is put in a pot suspended above the mold and when the press is closed the material flows from the pot into mold cavity(s). ▷ **transfer molding**

shear An action or stress, resulting from applied forces, which causes (or tends to cause) two contiguous parts of a body to slide, relative to each other, in a direction parallel to their plane of contact. With a laminated (reinforced plastic, etc.) structure, interlaminar shear (ILS) can occur whereby the plane of contact is composed primarily of plastic.

shear edge The cut-off edge of the mold used in compression molds. ▷ **mold material, reinforced plastic**

shear failure Also called failure by rupture, movement caused by shearing stresses that is sufficient to destroy or seriously endanger a structure.

shear force A force directly parallel to the surface element across which it acts.

shear fracture A mode of fracture in crystalline materials resulting from translation along slip planes that are preferentially oriented in the direction of the shearing stress.

shear heating Heat produced within the plastic melt as the plastic layers slide along each other or along the metal surfaces in the plasticating chamber of the processing machine.

shearing Breaking caused by the action of equal and opposed forces, located in the same plane.

shear, interlaminar ILS is the shearing force tending to produce a relative displacement between two laminae in a laminate along the plane of their interface, usually the weakest element of a reinforced plastic.

shear melt rate ▷ **melt shear rate**

shear modulus The ratio of shearing stress τ to shearing strain γ within the proportional limit of a material.

$$G = \frac{\tau}{\gamma} = \frac{\sigma_s}{\varepsilon_s} \text{ (psi or MPa)}$$

When measured dynamically with a torsion pendulum, the shear modulus of a solid rectangular beam is given by:

$$G = \frac{5.588 \times 10^{-4}\, LI}{CD^3 \mu P^2} \text{ (psi or MPa)}$$

where L = length of specimen between the clamps, in inches (cm), C = width of specimen, in inches (cm), D = thickness of specimen, in inches (cm), I = polar moment of inertia of the oscillating system, in g cm^2, P = period of oscillations, in seconds, μ = a shape factor depending upon the ratio of the width to thickness of the specimen.

The shear modulus for specimens with a circular cross-section is given by:

$$G = \frac{2.22 \times 10^{-5}\, LI}{r^4 P^2} \text{ (psi)}$$

where r = radius of the specimen, in. or cm.

Shear modulus can be determined by a static torsion test or by a dynamic test employing a torsional pendulum or an oscillatory rheometer. ▷ **modulus**

shear plane A plane along which failure of material occurs by shearing.

shear rate The time rate of change of shear strain. For a one-dimension shear flow, it is the velocity gradient.

shear, short beam ▷ **flexural test, short beam shear**

shear strain The tangent of the angular change, due to force, between two lines originally perpendicular to each other through a point in a body. With this strain, there is a change in shape. ▷ **strain**

shear strength The maximum shear stress that a material is capable of sustaining. It is calculated from the maximum load during a shear or torsional test and is based on the original cross sectional area of the specimen. ▷ **strength** and **stress**

shear stress 1. In a plastic fabricated part, stress directly parallel to the plane on which forces act. ▷ **stress** 2. With plastic melt, the force in the melt flow direction per unit area of the layer acting to produce shear sliding deformation between melt layers of the melt. 3. See Fig. below.

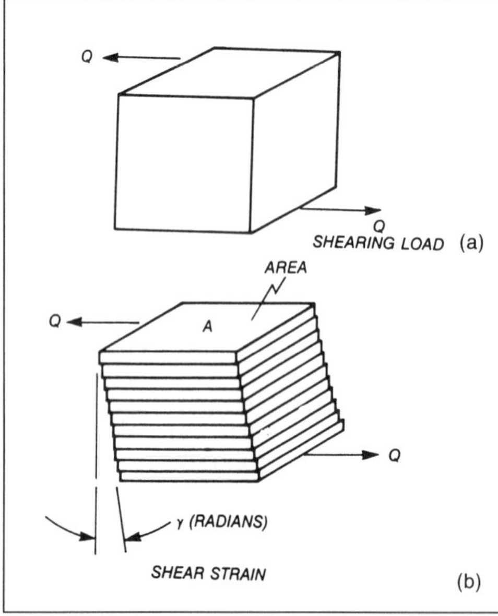

Basic analysis of shear stress: (*a*) Material with equal and opposite shearing forces and (*b*) schematic of infinitesimally thin layers subject to shear stress.

shear stress-strain The shear mode involves the application of a load to a material specimen in such a way that cubic volume elements of the material comprising the specimen become distorted, their volume remaining constant, but with the opposite faces sliding sideways with respect to each other. Shear deformation occurs in structural elements subjected to torsional loads and in short beams subjected to transverse loads. Shear stress-strain data can be generated by twisting a material specimen at a specified rate while measuring the angle of twist between the ends of the specimen and the torque exerted by the specimen on the testing machine. Maximum shear stress at the surface of the specimen can be computed from the measured torque, the maximum shear strain from the measured angle of twist.

shear thinning ▷ **extruder melt flow properties**

shear, torsional test ▷ **torsional shear test**

sheathing Cellulosic fiberboard for use in housing and other building construction, which may be integrally treated, impregnated, or coated (includes plastics) to give it additional water resistance.

sheaves Pulleys and belts connecting extruder motors and gear reducer to rotate screw.

sheen The specular gloss at a large angle of incidence for an otherwise matte specimen; the usual angle of measurement is 85°.

sheer A fabric that is transparently thin or diaphanous.

sheet Any material manufactured in sheet form and cut to suit in further processing or use. Material is considered sheet if it is more than 10 mils (0.01 cm), otherwise it is film below the 10 mils. ▷ **film**

sheet casting ▷ **film casting**

sheeter line Parallel scratches or projecting ridges distributed over a considerable area of a plastic sheet.

sheet-fed gravure printing These presses operate on the same rotary principle as rotogravure. The preparatory work is identical. The image is etched on a cylinder or on a flat flexible sheet of copper which is then clamped around the plate cylinder of the press. Sheet-fed gravure is used primarily for short runs and press proofing. Because of the high quality, it is used for art and photographic reproductions, as well as prestige printing such as annual reports. ▷ **gravure printing**

sheet molding compound An SMC is a reinforced plastic compound in sheet form. Most SMCs combine glass fiber with a polyester (TS) resin. Any combination of reinforcement and resin can be produced (see Fig. *a* opposite). The reinforcements can have continuous long fibers or any size of chopped fibers laid out in a different orientation from that of the resin (see Fig. *b* opposite). The different orientation makes it feasible to use SMCs on flat to complex-shaped molds (see Fig. *c* opposite). These SMCs will contain various additives and fillers to provide a variety of processing and performance properties.

SMCs are made to meet the shelf life required. These B-staged compounds are usually used in a few weeks or months. Some have a shelf life of six months, for example. Suppliers' recommendations should be followed in keeping these compounds at a low temperature, or a curing action will occur.

TPs are also used in sheet form with different reinforcements and resins. They are called

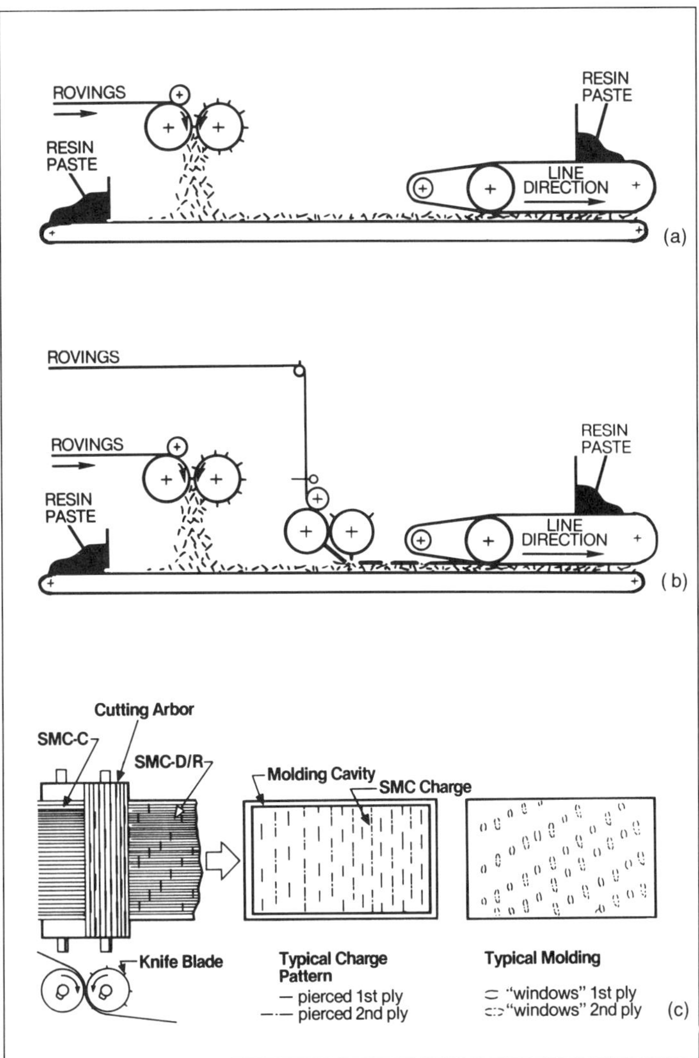

(*a*) Schematic method of manufacturing sheet molding compound (SMC) where continuous roving goes through a chopper (where length of chopped fibers is preset by changing location of blades) at a controlled rate, and resin paste compound is also controlled via a "doctor blade" that provides an opening for paste to move over speed controlled revolving conveyor belt. Not shown is plastic carrier film (PE, etc.) that is fed on both conveyor belts so when the SMC exits, it is "sandwiched" between the carrier films; eliminates sticking problem of B-staged TSS, permits ease of handling for shipment, storage (cool) and lay-up for fabrication. Films are removed prior to fabrication lay-up. (*b*) Schematic production of SMC incorporating long, high performance fiber reinforcements in the machine direction. It can be positioned in any direction using single or multiple fibers to obtain desired orientation. (*c*) Schematic of off-line production process, when required, to cut directional type SMC to conform to a specific mold contour, significantly reducing (or eliminating) unwanted "wrinkles" during lay-up.

stampable sheets rather than SMCs. These compounds provide unique properties with a quick and easy processing capability.

sheet orientation ▷ **orientation**

sheet skiving ▷ **skiving**

sheet train The entire assembly necessary to produce sheet which includes extruder, die, polish rolls, conveyor, draw rolls, cutter, and stacker. ▷ **extruder, sheet**

shelf life The length of time a material, substance, product, or reagent can be stored under specified environmental conditions and continue to meet all applicable specifications requirements and/or remain stable for its intended function.

shellac One of the first natural plastics used for its "plastic behaviors" originally mentioned in very ancient Indian texts. It is secreted by the insect *laccifer lacca* (*coccus lacca*) and deposited on the twigs of trees in India. After collection, washing and purification by melting and filtering, followed with forming into thin sheets, it is fragmented into flakes for use in varnishes, coatings, etc.

shell flour Used as a filler; from walnuts, coconuts, pecans, or peanuts.

shell molding In the foundry industry, a process of casting metal objects in thin molds made from sand or a ceramic powder mixed with a thermoset plastic.

shielding ▷ **electromagnetic interference** and **ablative plastic**

shim Plastic unreinforced and reinforced shims are extensively used particularly in mismatching and repairs (see Fig. below). Also called shim spacers.

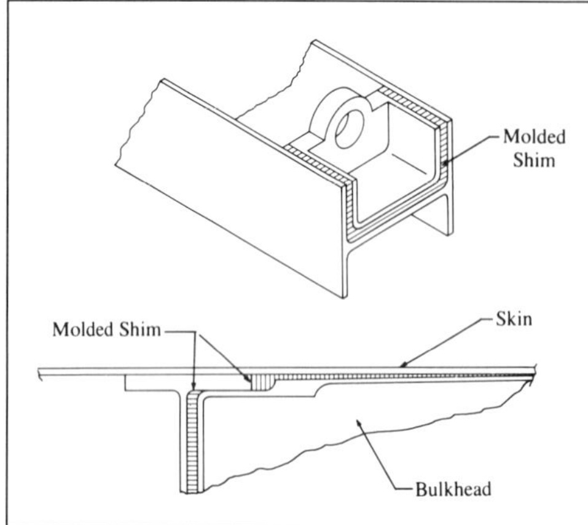

Example in use of plastic shims.

shock pulse A substantial disturbance characterized by a rise of acceleration from a constant value and decay of acceleration to the constant value in a short period of time.

shoe ▷ **filament shoe**

shoe upper ▷ **poromeric**

shop right A "shop right" is a term referring to a non-exclusive royalty-free license given to a employer where an employee uses the employer's time and/or equipment to make an invention. Shop rights usually come into play when there is no assignment agreement.

Shore hardness A method of determining the hardness of plastics using a scleroscope. This device consists of a small conical hammer fitted with a diamond point and acting in a glass tube. The hammer is made to strike the material and the degree of rebound is noted on a graduate scale. Generally, the harder the material, the greater the rebound. Normally used for elastomer/rubber material.

short Refers to processing, where an imperfection in a molded plastic part is due to an incomplete fill. In reinforced plastics, this may be evident either from the absence of surface film in some areas, unfused particles of material showing through a covering surface film, skin blisters, etc. Moldings (injection, compression, etc.) parts surface are obviously not filling the mold; usually called short-shot. ▷ **molding, short**

short-chain branching The dominant form of molecular branching in addition to polymers, usually formed by a "backbiting" transfer reaction and resulting, primarily, in n-butyl side chains, but also other short-pendant groups, such as methyl and amyl. Such branching results in induced levels of crystallinity.

short shot ▷ **molding, short**

short stopper A term used for an agent to a polymerization reaction mixture to inhibit or terminate polymerization.

short time behavior It represents the behavior and response of both unreinforced and reinforced plastics under loads lasting usually only a few seconds or minutes up to a maximum of fifteen minutes. Such short-term tests are used to define the basic or reference designing and engineering stress-strain properties of conventional materials. Such properties as tensile strength, compressive strength, flexural strength (the modulus of rupture), shear strength, and associated elastic moduli are often shown on the data sheets provided by suppliers of plastic materials and are in computerized data banks.

shot The yield from one complete molding cycle, including scrap (runners, etc.). ▷ **injection molding capacity**

shot-short Alternative for the more popular term of short-shot.

shrinkage Basically a reduction in size of a plastic which can occur during processing, particular with hot melts. A certain amount of shrinkage is inevitable in any process that involves cooling of plastic from elevated temperatures. Material behavior and processing influence amount of shrinkage. With certain plastics it may take about 24 hours to stabilize. Then there are plastics, particularly thermoset plastics, that literally have no shrinkage. Reduction can be made by including fillers and/or reinforcement. As shown in the first Table opposite, fillers can have directional influence. Determining shrinkage involves more than just applying the appropriate correction factors from a material's data sheet. ▷ **design die; design mold; injection molding, shrinkage and tolerance; tolerance and shrinkage; coefficient of linear thermal expansion**

shrinkage allowance The additional dimensions that must be added to a mold or die to compensate for shrinkage of plastics during processing.

shrinkage and tolerance ▷ **tolerance and shrinkage**

Reinforcement versus fillers; effect on injection molding shrinkage.

	Crystalline resins (acetal)			Amorphous resins (polycarbonate)		
Orientation	Unfilled	30% glass fiber	30% glass beads	Unfilled	30% glass fiber	30% glass beads
Flow Direction	0.022 in./in.	0.003 in./in.	0.013 in./in.	0.006 in./in.	0.0005 in./in.	0.004 in./in.
Transverse Direction	0.018	0.016	0.011	0.006	0.0010	0.004

shrinkage and warpage Although shrinkage and warpage are related phenomena, the means to prevent one or the other are not always the same; often they are exactly opposite as shown in the Table below, which represents typical thermoplastics such as PE moldings.

shrinkage, concrete ▷ **concrete-plastic**

shrinkage, drying ▷ **drying plastic**

shrinkage index The numerical difference between the plastic and shrinkage limits.

Guide for reducing shrinkage and warpage.

Shrinkage	Warpage
Molding conditions	
Reduced cylinder temperature and low mold temperature	High cylinder temperature and high mold temperature
Low temperatures near mold gating and sprue and entrance to molded item.	Low temperatures near mold gating and sprue and entrance to molded item
Minimum cooling at mold extremities	Minimum cooling at mold extremities
Moderate cylinder temperature and very high injection pressure	Low injection pressure
Fairly high cylinder temperature and moderate injection pressure	High cylinder temperature
High injection pressure and extended injection time	Short injection time
Longer dwell time	Longer dwell time
Mold design	
Proper location of sprue and gating	Proper location of sprue and gating
Resin properties	
Lower density	Lower density (of little importance)
Higher melt index	Higher melt index

shrinkage, plastic fiber ▷ **fiber shrinkage, solvent induced**

shrinkage pool An irregular, slightly depressed area on the surface of a molding caused by uneven shrinkage before complete hardening is attained.

shrinkage prediction ▷ **designing without sink and shrink; nomogram; zero defect**

shrinkage, unrestrained A reduction in size of a material which occurs during its hardening process, curing process, or both, with no external forces applied that can inhibit such reduction.

shrink film A term sometimes used for prestretched or oriented film used in shrink packaging. ▷ **orientation** and **lagging molding**

shrink fit ▷ **lagging molding**

shrink fixture ▷ **cooling fixture**

shrink mark An imperfection, a depression in the surface of a molded material where it has retracted from the mold. Also called sink mark.

shrink packaging ▷ **shrink wrapping**

shrink prepreg tape ▷ **lagging molding**

shrink tunnel An oven in the form of a tunnel mounted over or containing a continuous conveyor belt, used to shrink oriented films in the shrink packaging process.

shrink wrapping A technique of packaging in which the strains in a plastic film are released by raising the temperature of the film, thus causing it to shrink over a package. These shrink characteristics are built into the film during its manufacture by stretching it under controlled temperatures to produce orientation of its molecules ▷ **orientation**. Upon cooling, the film retains its stretched condition, but reverts toward its original dimensions when it is heated. Shrink film gives a good protection to the products packaged and has excellent clarity. ▷ **contour package** and **blister package**

shuttle clamp ▷ **clamping, shuttle**

shuttle mark In woven fabrics, a fine fillingwise line caused by damage to a group of warp yarns by shuttle abrasion.

SI Abbreviation worldwide for the standard prepared by the International System of Units. This standard gives guidance for application of the modernized metric system developed and maintained by the General Conference on Weights and Measures (abbreviated CGPM from the official French name Conférence Générale des Poids et Mesures). The name International System of Units and the international abbreviations SI were adopted by the 11th CGPM in 1960. SI is from the French name Le Système International d'Unités. ▷ **decimal system** and **meter**

SI consists of seven base units, two supplementary units and units that are derived from the base and supplementary units. Derived units are expressed as products and ratios of the base and supplementary units (see *Conversion Tables* on p. xxiii). See Table below as an example for units and symbols.

SI units.

Base units	Unit	SI symbol
Length	meter	m
Mass[1]	kilogram	kg
Time	second	s
Electric current	ampere	A
Temperature[2]	Kelvin	K
Substance	mole	mol
Luminous intensity	candela	cd
Supplementary units	**Unit**	**SI symbol**
Plane angle	radian	rad
Solid plane	steradian	sr

[1] In common usage the term weight is sometimes used instead of the technically correct word mass.
[2] The International Temperature Scale is used in the thermodynamic calculation; the Celsius (C) scale is used for other than thermodynamic applications. The unit Kelvin (K) is written without a degree (°) sign. An interval of one C degree (1°C) is exactly equal to an interval of one K (1 K). Kelvin temperature = 273.15 + Celsius temperature.

siamese blow ▷ **mold, siamese blow**

siemens ▷ **electrical conductance**

sieve ▷ **screen**

sievert ▷ **radiation dose equivalent**

sigma blade mixer A rotating agitator set horizontally in a kneading bowl or chamber used for mixing (plastics, bread doughs, and heavy pastes). The blade or arm is shaped somewhat like a Greek capital sigma (Σ) lying on its side; variations of this shape simulate horizontal letters "S" and "Z". Some kneaders have two such blades which overlap as they turn to provide maximum mixing efficiency.

sigma measurement ▷ **standard deviation measurement**

sigma scale The expression in whole numbers of the number of sigma units covered under the standard curve as determined by the standard error of a percentage.

signature In printing and binding, the name given to a printed sheet after it has been folded.

signs ▷ **symbols and signs**

silane A gas with repulsive odor, solidifies at −200°C, decomposes in water. In a compound, it is used as a binder-finish on glass fibers to provide bonding of glass to thermoset polyester plastic. Used since the 1940s ▷ **glass fiber and fabric surface treatment**. The silane coupling agents or silane finishing compounds of silicon, hydrogen, and other monomeric silicone compounds have the ability to bond inorganic materials such as glass, mineral fillers, metals, and metallic oxides. The adhesion mechanism is due to two groups in the silane structure. The $Si(OR_3)$ portion reacts with the inorganic reinforcement, while the organofunctional (vinyl-, amino-, epoxy-, etc.) group reacts with the plastic. The coupling agent can be applied to the inorganic materials (glass fibers, etc.) as a pre-treatment and/or added to the plastic.

silica Silicon dioxide (SiO_2) is a substance occurring naturally as quartz, sand, flint, chalcedony, opal, agate, etc. In powdered form it is used as a filler, especially in phenolic compounds for ablative nose cones of rockets. These micronsized powders are 99% pure. Their hardness provides both mechanical strength and abrasion resistance. An economical extender/filler which is thermally stable, low in ionic impurities, and hard.

silica fiber The term high silica is used to describe any high-purity glass. For use in reinforced plastics, it is 95%-plus pure SiO_2 produced by a leaching process. High silica fibers and fabrics are flexible materials that are similar in appearance and produced from conventional E-glass fiber. The glass fiber, with a silica content of 65%, is subjected to a hot-acid treatment that removes virtually all the impurities while leaving the silica intact. This treatment is commonly called the leaching process. ▷ **glass fiber**

Quartz, similar to glass and high silica, has 99.95% SiO_2. High silica and quartz are both used in a wide variety of similar products. The selection of what type to use is generally dictated by a combination of performance requirements, manufacturing needs, and cost. Both have higher strength-to-weight ratios than most other high temperature materials. Quartz has about five times the tensile strength of high silica. Both have elongation at break at about 1%. They have similar thermal characteristics. The major difference is the higher melt viscosity of quartz as a result of its higher silica content. Both do not melt or vaporize until the temperature exceeds 1,649°C (3,000°F). At continuous temperature in excess of 982°C (1,800°F), both forms will begin to devitrify into a crystallized form known as cristobalite. This conversion tends to stiffen the materials, but causes no change in their physical form or insulating properties. Both manifest excellent resistance to thermal shock. Their products can be heated to 1,093°C (2,000°F) and rapidly quenched in water without any apparent change. ▷ **quartz fiber**

silica glass Vitreous silicon oxide (SiO_2); quartz glass; pure silicon dioxide (SiO_2) glass.

silica, synthetic They are inorganic white powders having the chemical formula $SiO_2 \cdot XH_2O$, where X is the mols of water associated with the silica compound. They are also called synthetic amorphous silicon dioxide products. The three commercial types are: (1) fumed (also called pyrogenic or anhydrous silica), (2) precipitated (also called hydrated silica), and (3) gel (also called hydrogel, hydrous gel, or hydrated silica). They are characterized by various physical and chemical properties such as surface area, particle size, morphology, silanol group density, percent moisture, pH, oil absorption, bulk density, and percent purity.

Fumed silicas are used in three major application areas: as a reinforcing filler, as thixotropic agents, and as a specialty filler. Precipitated silicas are predominantly used as reinforcing fillers in plastics and rubbers and also as thixotropic agents in vinyl plastisols, thermoset polyester plastics, gel coating, and epoxy plastics. Gel and precipitated silicas are used as flattening or matting agents in plastics and as an antiblocking agent in film and sheeting.

silicate Materials containing SiO_4 tetrahedra plus metallic ions.

silicon A tetravalent nonmetallic element that occurs combined as the most abundant natural element next to oxygen in the earth's crust.

silicon carbide fiber A reinforcing fiber with high strength and modulus; density is equal to that of aluminum. Primary purpose for this development was for the reinforcement of metal matrix and ceramic matrix composite structures used in advanced aerospace applications by the military. SiC fibers were developed to replace boron fibers in metal matrix composites, where boron has drawbacks—principally degradation of mechanical properties at temperatures greater than 540°C (1,000°F) and very high cost. Boron fibers are used in very high performance reinforced plastics in aerospace applications. When SiC fibers are produced commercially, an emphasis will be placed in the area of reinforced plastics, which is currently boron's major area of application. ▷ **boron fiber** and **reinforcement**.

Properties of SiC fibers are: tensile strength = 500,000 psi (3,500 MPa); tensile modulus = 60×10^6 psi (413,000 MPa); density = 187 lb/ft^3 (3.0 g/cm^3); coefficient of linear thermal expansion = 2.7×10^{-6} F (1.5×10^{-6} C); and diameter = 0.0056 in. (0.140 mm). ▷ **chemical vapor deposition**

silicone Any of various polymeric organic silicon compounds obtained as oils, greases, or plastics. Silicone is an alternate name for polyorganosiloxane, being more frequently used when a plastic of this type is used as the basis of useful commercial products. Such products span a diverse range from low molecular weight or branched plastics useful as oils and greases to high molecular weight crosslinkable plastics useful as elastomers (rubbers) to rigid type plastics. The name arises from the assumed, but erroneous, analogy between the structure of silicones (R_2SiO) and ketons ($R_2C=O$).

silicone elastomer Also called silicone rubber, they were first produced in 1940 and have found substantial use ever since in areas where retention of properties at both high and low temperatures is required; temperature range −51 to 316°C (−70 to +600°F) is generally covered with little loss of properties. Silicone elastomer (Q) is a high molecular weight polyorganosiloxane rubber. The basic plastic is polydimethylsiloxane (abbreviated MQ) with a molecular weight in the range of 300,000 to one million. Such plastics are produced by ring-opening polymerization of octamethylcyclotetrasiloxane. Several copolymers are also of interest, notably those containing about 0.5% methylvinylsiloxane groups (the vinylsilicone elastomer VMQ) which are more readily vulcanized and give vulcanizates with better compression set resistance. Copolymers with 5 to 15% of the methyl groups replaced with phenyl groups (phenylsilicone elastomer PMQ) give vulcanizates with better low temperature properties, while related fluorosilicone elastomers (FVMQ) have improved solvent resistance. Nitrilesilicone elastomers have also been of interest.

The unvulcanized polymer (dimethylsilicone gum) is usually crosslinked to a useful elastomer by heating with an organic peroxide, such as benzoyl peroxide or 2,4-dichlorobenzoyl peroxide. Special low molecular weight plastics with reactive end groups are room temperature vulcanized (RTV) silicone elastomers. RTVs are two-component liquids that are important to the plastics and other industries. This system combines the advantages of simple and rapid processing, analogous to that for thermoplastic elastomers, with those of an elastomer that can be chemically crosslinked, and can be used over a wide (low to high) temperature range. The high reactivity allows injection molding with contact times as short as a few seconds, enabling one to produce small elastomer components in large numbers. Molds can quickly and easily be produced, and many other applications exist for RTVs. Despite their relatively high cost, they cost little to process, making them economically viable.

Silicone elastomer vulcanizates have relatively poor mechanical properties compared to other elastomers and plastics (as an example, tensile strength of 600 to 1,350 psi/4 to 9 MPa). However these properties are retained over a very wide temperature range. Typically, they have a useful life of about two years at 150°C (300°F) and retain their flexibility to about −50°C (−60°F) or even lower in the phenyl substituted plastics. They retain excellent electrical properties under extremes of temperature and moisture, but have poor abrasion resistance. They swell moderately in oils, fuels, and in many solvents, although the fluorosilicones are much better in this respect.

silicone fluid additives These additives are clear polydimethylsiloxane liquids which perform two basic functions. At low concentrations, they are used as process improvers, increasing mold flow and providing self release characteristics. At higher concentrations, they are used to form self-lubricating plastics for bearings and other mechanical applications.

silicone molding compound Thermoset material which superficially resembles epoxies, phenolics, and other TSs. However, it has unique heat stability.

silicone plastic Plastics based on the main polymer chains consisting of alternating silicone and oxygen atoms. Basically, their behavior is similar to silicone elastomers except they provide increased mechanical properties. Just with glass fiber-silicone reinforced plastics retention of mechanical and electrical properties up to 316°C (600°F) for relatively long time periods. RPs can be made at vacuum-bag to higher pressure molding techniques. Cure is generally at temperatures in excess of 150°C (300°F), depending on particular thermoset silicone plastic used.

silicone sealant A liquid-applied thermoset curing compound based on polymers of polysiloxane structures.

silk A natural fiber secreted as a continuous filament by the silkworm.

silk screen printing This method of printing or decorating on plastics has been used for the past century. Since about 1940, the silk screen has been replaced by other materials. Since that time the process has been called just screen printing. ▷ **screen printing**

silly putty ▷ **putty, bouncing**

silver spray plating A chemical spray metallizing process based on the glass mirror art. The plastic part is prepared by cleaning and lacquering as in vacuum metalizing, then the lacquer coat is sensitized in an acidic salt solution such as a mixture of sulphuric acid, potassium dichromate, and water. A silver-forming solution, e.g. silver nitrate and an aldehyde, is sprayed on the part, usually with a two-nozzle spray gun so that the components are separated until they reach the surface. A final topcoat of protective lacquer is applied over the silver.

silver streak Silver streaking are silver-white marks or splay usually in the melt flow direction or bubbles in the molded part. Cause could include moisture, entrapped air, decomposition products from overheated plastic, and contaminated plastic.

single-stage plastic ▷ **A-B-C stages**

sinking a mold ▷ **mold hobbing**

sink mark A depression, groove, or dimple that can be extremely shallow on the surface of an injection molded part. It is usually caused by the collapsing of the surface following local internal shrinkage after the gate seals, especially on the face opposite to where the section thickness increases (such as a rib). Also called shrink mark or heat mark. ▷ **designing without sink or shrink**

sinter coating A coating process in which the part to be coated is preheated to sintering temperature and immersed in a plastic powder. Then it is withdrawn and heated to a higher temperature to fuse the sintered plastic coating adhering to the part. ▷ **fluidized bed coating**

sintering The bonding of plastic powders by solid-state diffusion, resulting in the absence of a separate bonding phase. It is the welding together of powdered particles at temperatures below the melting or fusion (sintering) point. Particles are fused together to form a mass, but the mass, as a whole, does not melt. The process is generally accompanied by an increase in strength, ductility, and occasionally density.

SI prefix Prefixes, such as centi, milli, kilo, mega, etc., are used to indicate orders of magnitude, thus eliminating nonsignificant digits and leading zeros in decimal fractions. It provides a convenient alternative to the powers-of-ten notations preferred in computation. See Table 3 on p. xxxvi.

sisal ▷ **fiber, sisal**

size control ▷ **control**

size reduction ▷ **granulating**

sizing 1. Applying a material on a surface in order to fill and thus reduce the absorption of the subsequently applied coating or adhesive, or to otherwise modify the surface properties of the substrate to improve adhesion. Material used is also called size. **2.** Any treatment or dressing consisting of starch (usually dextrinized starch), gelatine, wax, or other suitable ingredient which is applied to fibers (for use in reinforced plastics) at the time of formation to protect the surface and aid the process of handling and fabrication, or to control the fiber characteristics. This binder lubricates the surface and thus prevents the abrasive damage (fiber rubbing fiber) which reduces fiber strength or causes their breakage. It is also usually present to improve packing of the single filaments into strands.

The size treatment contains ingredients which provide surface lubricity and binding action but, unlike a finish, contains no coupling agent. Before final fabrication into a reinforced plastic, the size is removed usually by heat cleaning or burning, and a finish is applied ▷ **glass fiber and fabric surface treatment**. When a finish is not to be applied to the fiber, the size may also contain a coupling agent. Plasticized polyvinyl acetate is often used as a size of this type since it is compatible with plastics such as TS polyesters and epoxies.

sizing content The percent of the total strand weight made up of sizing, usually determined by burning off or dissolving the organic sizing. Also known as loss on ignition.

sizing, extruder ▷ **extruder sizing**

sizing plate, sleeve, or ring ▷ **extruder line cooling and shaping**

skein ▷ **fiber skein**

skeletal Rigid supportive or protective structure of framework.

sketches ▷ **graphic art**

skin 1. The relatively dense material that sometimes forms on the surface of a foamed (cellular) plastic. **2.** A layer of relatively dense material on the surfaces of the core used in a sandwich construction.

skin packaging ▷ **contour package**

skin, synthetic The search goes on for long-lasting artificial skin to cover burned or otherwise damaged areas of a person. Human skin is a stratified bilayered (dermis and epidermis) organ consisting of several cell types intimately colinked and interdigitated, bearing a variety of adnexal structures and performing a variety of functions. The closest approach to duplicating has been the extension of autologous skin-derived cells (fibroblasts and keratinocytes) to sheets in tissue cultured systems. Tissue-cultured cells have been used as skin substitutes. At present there is a limited but growing number of commercially produced or experimentally available skin-substitute wound covers that are classified as synthetics, organics, or composites of synthetic and organic origin. They include methacrylate mixture, PP film over PUR foam, PUR film with adhesive, and porous PUR with polyester.

skiving A specialized process for producing films, skiving is basically cutting off a thin layer of material. It consists of shaving off a thin layer from a large block of solid plastic, specifically a round billet. Continuous film (or sheeting) is obtained by skiving in a lathe type cutting operations; a take-off of producing plywood that is cut from large logs. This process is particularly useful with plastics that cannot be processed by the usual plastic film processes such as extrusion, calendering, or casting. PTFE is an example. PTFE powder is in a mold to make billets. Powder is compressed uniformly (carefully) at pressures of 2,000 to 5,000 psi (14 to 34 MPa). This preform is removed from the mold and sintered by heating unconfined in an oven at temperatures 360 to 380°C (680 to 715°F) for times ranging from a few hours to several days. The time-temperature schedule depends on the size and shape of the billet. Billet sizes go from 2 lb (less than kg) to 1,600 lb (726 kg), among the largest moldings made of any plastics. Time with temperature variation during cure is closely controlled; target is final cure without voids and other defects that could occur internally.

slate A fine grained metamorphic rock of varied composition, used in powdered form as a filler, especially in flooring plastic compounds.

slave A remote controlled mechanism or instrument that repeats the action of an identical mechanism that is controlled by an operator in another location; it may be activated mechanically, electromagnetically and/or electronically.

sleeving 1. Mold bushing type ejector. ▷ **mold ejector** 2. Braided, knitted, or woven fabric of cylindrical form; used with coating applications and in reinforced plastics.

slenderness ratio 1. The ratio of length to the least thickness of a panel is the slenderness ratio. 2. The effective unsupported length of a uniform column divided by the least radius of gyration of the cross sectional area.

slip A slurry containing chemical additives to control rheology.

slip additive A modifier that acts as an internal lubricant which exudes to the surface of the plastic during or immediately after processing; a nonvisible coating blooms to the surface to provide the necessary lubricity to reduce coefficient of friction and thereby improve slip characteristics. ▷ **film blocking**

slip depressant ▷ **antislip agent**

slip forming A sheet-forming technique in which some of the plastic sheet material is allowed to slip through mechanically operated clamping rings during a stretch-forming operation.

slip-plane Plane within transparent material visible in reflected light, due to poor welding and shrinkage on cooling.

slitting Cutting film, sheets, etc. into two or more sections by some means of cutting, such as razor blade or wheels. ▷ **cutter** and **extruder take-off slitting film**

sliver ▷ **fiber sliver**

slot extrusion ▷ **extruder slot**

sludge 1. A water-formed sedimentary deposit, such as waste water. 2. An undesirable residue in a rubber latex.

slug 1. Any nonfibrous glass in a glass fiber product. 2. Unattenuated particles of glass of substantially larger diameter than the average filament diameter, also called bunch, lump, piecing, slough-off, or slub. 3. In raw silk, a thickened place several times the diameter of the yarn, 3 mm (1/8 in.) or over in length.

slump test Standardized test for assessing the workability of a compound mix.

slurry 1. A thin water suspension such as the feed to a filter press. 2. A suspension of solid material in a liquid.

slurry preforming Method of preparing reinforced plastic preforms by wet processing techniques similar to those used in the pulp molding industry. For example, glass fibers suspended in water are passed though a screen that passes the water but retains the fibers in mat form, the shape of the screen.

slush molding Method for casting thermoplastics, in which the plastic in a liquid form is poured into a hot mold where a viscous skin forms. The excess plastic slush is drained off, the mold is cooled, and the molding stripped out. Also called slush casting.

smog A term derived from smoke and fog, applied to extensive atmospheric contamination by aerosols arising partly through natural processes and partly from the activities of people. Now sometimes used loosely for any contamination of the air.

smoke Basically the airborne solid and liquid particulates and gases evolved when a material undergoes pyrolysis or combustion. Several standard tests (UL, ASTM, NBS, etc.) are designed and used to provide quantitative measurement of smoke. Toxic smoke and fumes have became generally recognized as the major cause of fire deaths, making the combustion products released by burning plastics and other materials particularly important. Smoke is recognized by firefighters as being in many ways more dangerous than actual flames because (1) it obscures vision, making it impossible to find safe means of regress, thus often leading to panic; (2) it makes helping or rescuing victims difficult if not impossible; and (3) it leads to physiological reactions such as choking and tearing. Smoke from plastics, wood, and other materials usually contains toxic gases such as carbon monoxide, which has no odor, often accompanied by noxious gases that may lead to nausea and other debilitating effects as well as panic.

Whether a plastic gives off light or heavy smoke and toxic or noxious gases depends on the basic plastic used, its composition of additives and fillers, and the conditions under which its burning occurs. Some plastics burn with a relatively clean flame, but some may give off dense smoke while smoldering. Others are inherently smoke producing. The composition of the smoke depends upon the composition of the plastic and the burning conditions, as with other organic materials.

In a particular application, therefore, careful consideration should be given to the relative importance of smoke and flame, including creating designs favoring the rapid elimination of smoke by venting, for fending off smoke, and other approaches. ▷ **fire retardance**

snap-back forming ▷ **thermoforming, snap-back**

snap fit ▷ **design snap fit**

S–N diagram ▷ **fatigue S–N diagram**

snow, artificial A copolymer of butyl and isobutyl methacrylate often dispersed from an aerosol bomb or other atomizing device. Used in decorative window displays, etc.

soap bubble test A type of pressure testing in which the tracer gas is detected by bubbles formed in a layer of soap solution applied to the surface of the test object.

soap, metallic Products derived by reacting fatty acids with metals, widely used as stabilizers for plastics. The fatty acids commonly used are the lauric, stearic, ricinoleic, naphthenic octoic, or 2-ethylexoic, rosin, and tall oil. Typical metals are aluminum, barium, calcium, cadmium, copper, iron, lead, tin, and zinc.

sodium stearate A white powder used as a non-toxic stabilizer.

soft A non-technical word.

softening point The physical properties of softening points (SPs) are determined by a variety of tests, including deflection temperature under load, Vicat softening temperature, and shear modulus as a function of temperature. ▷ **temperature, softening range**

software A name given to instructions, programs, mathematical formulas, etc. utilized in the computer system, in contrast to the actual physical hardware of the system. Software is a set of instructions that determine what the computer will do and how it will do it. ▷ **computer software**

software, creativity ▷ **biocomputing**

software menu ▷ **computer software menu**

software, part tolerance ▷ **computer tolerance analysis**

softwood Generally, one of the botanical groups of trees that in most cases have needle-like or scalelike leaves; the wood produced by these trees. The term has no reference to the actual hardness of the wood.

soil conditioner An organic material like humus, which can be made from composting certain solid wastes. It helps the soil absorb water, support bacteria, and distribute nutrients and minerals. ▷ **mulch, agricultural** and **agricultural markets**

solar absorptance The ratio of absorbed to incident radiant solar energy (equal to unity minus the reflectance and transmittance).

Solar Challenger airplane The sun-powered airplane made aviation history when it touched down at Manston Air Force Base in England (July 7, 1981) after a flight across the English channel from France. The Du Pont sponsored plane traveled 370 km (230 miles) from Cormeilles-en-Vexin in 5 hr and 23 minutes.

Unlike the wave-skimming trip over the channel by the ▷ **Gossamer Albatross airplane** (June 12, 1979) pedaled by the pilot, the solar soared as high as 3,658 m (12,000 ft) on power from its 16,128 wing-mounted solar cells. This lightweight (98 kg/217 lb), non-polluting source of electric power was an all plastic airplane. Used *Kevlar* aramid fibers in the spars; *Mylar* shrunk polyester film skin for wing, tail and part of fuselage; *Delrin* acetal control pulleys; *Zytel* ST super tough nylon landing gear wheel; and other plastic materials.

solar energy markets The gathering and processing of solar energy is based on large areas that may be in the form of windows, glazings for rooftop collectors, covers for biological reaction ponds, liners for solar ponds, or reflecting surfaces for focusing heliostats or mirrors. In these and other applications, plastics rank high as useful materials. As an example, glazings or cover plates for flat-plate collectors and windows require materials of high transparency. The amount of radiation reflected from the surfaces and thus lost from transmission is controlled by the index of refraction of the material. Index of refraction values are: glass fiber-TS polyester RPs (1.540), acrylic (1.490), PC (1.586), PTFE (1.343), PVF (1.460), TP polyester (1.640), PE (1.500), and glass (1.518).

solar reflectance The percent of solar radiation (watt/unit area) reflected by a material.

solder Metals that melt below 425°C (800°F) and are used for joining. Commonly PB-Sn alloys, but may also be other materials, even glass.

solenoid An electromechanical device in which an electric current causes an electromagnet to move; used in machine controls. ▷ **relay logic**

solid Matter in its most highly concentrated form; the atoms or molecules are much more closely packed than in gases or liquids and thus more resistant to deformation.

solid content The percentage by weight of the nonvolatile matter in a material.

solidification point An empirical constant defined as the temperature at which the liquid phase of a substance is in about equilibrium with a relatively small portion of the solid phase.

solid geometry modeling ▷ **modeling parametric**

solid glass sphere These beads are used as fillers and reinforcements. They are available in a wide range of dimensions (5 to 1,000 μm). Their smooth shapes reduce abrasive and viscosity effects.

solid modeling ▷ **modeling, solid**

solid phase Technique in which a sheet or block of plastic is reshaped under heat and pressure. However, forming temperature is below the melt temperature of the plastic.

solid-phase pressure forming ▷ **forming solid-phase pressure**

solid solution A homogeneous mixture of two or more components, in a solid state, retaining substantially the structure of one of the components.

solid-state extrusion ▷ **extruder solid-state**

solid waste Materials that are discarded after use, as distinguished from air pollution or waste water; includes sewage sludge. ▷ **compaction** and **bulk factor**

solid waste biostabilizer ▷ **biostabilizer**

solid waste, commerical Wastes produced during wholesale, retail, or service business operations. Often collected by private contractors rather than public agencies.

solid waste containment ▷ **geomembrane liner**

solid waste council The Council for Solid Waste Solutions (CSWS) of SPI is an organization that provides help and solutions to the solid waste situation.

solid waste energy ▷ **British thermal unit**

solid waste food The food industry, from the farm, through shipment and storage, to the user, results in rather enormous solid waste that is used in landfills, incinerations, etc.

solid waste management Systematic management of solid waste from the point of generation to final disposal. Can include source reduction, collection, storage, transfer, recycling, recovery, incineration, and landfill.

solid waste source reduction ▷ **source reduction, waste**

solid waste volume reduction Decreasing the volume of solid waste through compaction or incineration. A 50 to 80% reduction is possible through compaction, 90 to 98% through incineration.

solubility The ability or tendency of one substance to blend uniformly with another, e.g. solid in liquid, liquid in liquid, gas in liquid, gas in gas. The solubility of plastics differ both qualitatively and quantitatively from that of nonplastic solids. In general, one or more solvents exist for every plastic. If it is crosslinked or highly crystalline, it will not dissolve, but it may swell.

solubility and molecular weight It is generally accepted that solubility of a plastic in solvents is inverse to its molecular weight. Compatibility of plastics with plasticizers may similarly be inverse to the MW, which affect the latitude available to formulators of plasticized plastics.

solubility limit Maximum solute addition without supersaturation.

soluble core molding The soluble core technology (SCT) also called the lost-wax or lost-core molding. This technique is similar to the lost-wax molding used in jewelry since ancient times. In this process, a core is usually molded of a water soluble thermoplastic, wax formation, low-melting-point alloy (includes zinc alloy and tin-bismuth) etc. The core (thin wall shell to solid) is inserted in a mold, like an injection mold, and plastics injected around the metal core. When the plastic part has solidified, the metal core is removed by melting at a temperature below the melting point of the plastic; core material is poured through an opening that may require drilling a hole. During core installation, it can be supported by the mold (like a standard core pin, etc.). If it is "floating" in mid section, some support is used, such as spiders used in certain pipe or profile extruder die.

With appropriate mold design, including use of foamed core material, all size and shape parts can be molded, particularly complex parts such as auto intake manifolds. The 1944 all plastic airplane used the lost-wax process to bag mold the first prototype glass fiber-TS polyester reinforced plastic skins with the core material also made from this RP to produce sandwich primary structures (including wings, monoque fuselage, etc.). The RP core was individually molded with small box-beams (about 10 mm square); these were made with the wax core. After cores were molded, they formed the layout and followed the contour required with the RP skins (see Fig.

in ▷**aircraft**). ▷**eutectic** and **injection molding fusible core**

solute The material that dissolves in a solvent.

solution Homogeneous mixture of two or more components.

solution casting ▷**film casting**

solution coating Use includes plastic coating of plastic film. Coating compounds (plastics, additives, and fillers needed) are dissolved in appropriate solvents; baths are normally kept at room temperature, but they may require elevated or lower temperatures. Coatings are applied by continuous processing equipment. The thickness of the coating is controlled by various means depending on the coating process. When film is run directly into a coating bath, doctor rolls with controlled openings between the rolls control the thickness after the film leaves the bath. Film speed and bath consistency also influence thickness. Films may be coated on one side by using one roll immersed in the bath and transfering the coating to a second roll which is in contact with the film. The distance between the rolls controls the thickness. Flexographic rolls with controlled engraving patterns will deposit uniform coatings depending on depth of the engraving pattern. In the knife process, coatings are applied in large excess onto the surfaces of films and the excess is removed with a "knife" or "doctor blade".

solution, colloidal A liquid colloidal dispersion is often called a solution. Since colloidal particles are larger than molecules, it is strictly incorrect to call such dispersions solutions.

solution equilibrium with the solid phase The solution will dissolve no more of the solid material.

solution polymerization It is similar to bulk polymerization except that the solvent in solution action is usually a chemically inert medium, whereas the solvent for the forming polymer in bulk is the monomer. The solvents used may be complete, partial, or nonsolvents for growing polymer chains. When monomer and polymer are both soluble in the solvent, initiation and propagation of the growing polymer chains take place in the oil or organic phase. Because of the mass-action law, rates of polymerization in solvents are slower than in bulk and the molecular weight (MW) of the polymers formed is decreased.

In another case when the monomer is soluble in the solvent but the polymer is only partially soluble or completely insoluble in the solvent, initiation of the polymerization takes place in the liquid phase. However, as the polymer molecules grow, some of the propagation of polymers takes place within monomer swollen molecules which are beginning to precipitate from the reaction. When this occurs, it can become possible to build up MW because of the decreased dilution within the polymers. Thus, MWs as high as those possible with bulk can also be achieved in solution polymerizations provided the polymer precipitates out of solution as it is formed and creates a propagation site.

In the third case, in which the polymer is completely insoluble in the solvent and the monomer is only partially soluble in the solvent, rates of reaction are reduced and lower MWs, below those possible in bulk, are formed. However, the formation of relatively high MW polymers is still possible in such a system.

In addition to the relative solubilities of monomer, polymer, and solvent in the system, the way in which the ingredients are fed to the system can also have a significant effect on how polymerization proceeds, and hence affect the structure of the finished polymer. ▷**reactor technology**

solution spinning process Process is used to produce high modulus polyethylene fibers; fibers are called extended-chain PE (ECPE). This development has produced fibers with tensile strengths of 3.75 to 5.60 × 10^5 psi (2,890 to 3,860 MPa) and moduli of 15 to 30 × 10^6 psi (103 to 207 × 10^3 MPa). In this process, a high molecular weight PE is used. The process begins with the dissolution in a suitable solvent of a polymer of about 1 to 5 million molecular weight. The solution serves to disentangle the polymer chains, a key step in achieving an extended chain polymer structure. The solution must be fairly dilute but viscous enough to be spun using conventional melt spinning equipment. The cooling of the extrudate leads to the formation of a fiber that can be continously dried to remove solvent or later extracted by an appropriate solvent. The fibers are generally postdrawn prior to final packaging.

solution viscosity Solution viscosities are measured by flow rate through a capillary. Temperature and concentration are carefully controlled.

solution volumetric analysis This analysis is completed by measuring the volume of a solution of established concentration needed to react completely with the substance being determined. It is customary to divide the reactions of volumetric analysis into four groups: (1) neutralization methods (acidimetry and alkalimetry),

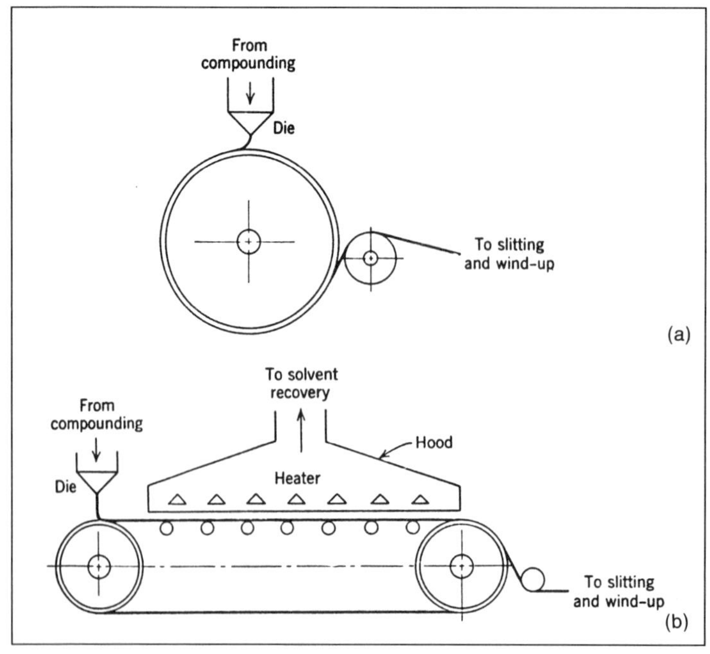

Solvent casting process examples using (*a*) a rotating drum and (*b*) an endless belt.

(2) oxidation and reduction (redox) methods, (3) precipitation methods, and (4) complex formation (ion combination) methods.

solvation The process of swelling, gelling, or dissolving a plastic by a solvent or plasticizer.

solvent Any substance, usually a liquid, which dissolves other substances; it "frees" solids from their confined state.

solvent bonding The process of joining two like or unlike articles made from thermoplastics by applying a solvent capable of softening the bond surfaces. Adhesion comes from evaporation of solvent, absorption of solvent, and/or polymerization of the solvent cement. It works because there is some type of chemical reaction that can literally destroy the plastic. It is important to limit such factors as the length of time and the depth of the plastic soak. The solvent could cause immediate or delayed damage. If the part contains "excessive" internal strains, the solvent could release them and cause cracking, surface defects, etc. The solvent action described does not mean that the solvent system is a problem area, as long as it is properly performed. Process also called solvent welding.

solvent casting Soluble plastics may be formed into film by casting using different methods of application (see Fig. above). The solvent compounded with all its constituents (plasticizers, stabilizers, etc.) is carefully applied at a controlled rate. The solvent is evaporated using controlled heat zones to prevent formation of blisters. The rate of solvent evaporation is inversely proportional to the square of the thickness, thus production decreases with thicker films. To reduce cost and meet regulations, solvent recovery systems are used with explosive hazard safety capabilities. However, water-based solvent solutions are also used, such as with polyvinyl alcohol plastic.

solvent cement An adhesive made by dissolving a thermoplastic (compounded if required) in a suitable solvent or mixture of solvents.

solvent, chlorinated ▷**chlorinated solvent**

solvent cleaning It may consist of wiping, immersion in solvent, spraying, or vapor degreasing. Wiping is the less effective process and may result in distributing the contaminate over the surface rather than removing it (however it is usable, based on what is to be cleaned). Immersion, especially if accompanied by mechanical or ultrasonic scrubbing, is a better process. It is even more effective if followed by either immersion or a spray rinse. Vapor is by solvent vapors condensing on parts; it is the most efficient process because the surfaces do not come in contact with the contaminated solvent bath. Vapor degreasing is carried out in a tank with a solvent reservoir on the bottom. The solvent is heated and vapor condenses on the cool plastic surfaces. The condensate dissolves surface impurities and carries them away.

Cleaning action as fast as a minute occurs. ▷ **sputtered coating** and **water cleaning treatment**

solvent cracking Alternative name for environmental stress cracking.

solvent degreasing ▷ **solvent cleaning**

solvent fractionation Differential dissolving of a mixed plastic stream in selected solvents for latter separation and recovery by plastic type. Also called polymer dissolution.

solvent joint A joint made by using a solvent to unite the components.

solvent molding Process for forming thermoplastic articles by either dipping a male mold in the plastic solution or filling a female mold cavity with the plastic liquid, which may require dispersing it on the cavity wall, followed by emptying it. Thus, a layer of plastic adheres to either mold surface.

solvent polishing A method of improving the gloss of thermoplastic parts by immersion or spraying with a solvent, dissolving surface irregularities, followed by evaporation of the solvent.

solvent removal ▷ **drying equipment for solvent removal**

solvent resistance Ability of a plastic to resist swelling and dissolving in a solution.

solvent stress cracking Environmental stress cracking when a liquid (solvent) causing the cracking also has a solvating effect on the plastic. ▷ **stress crack failure**

solvent stripping ▷ **extruder reactive processing**

solvent welding ▷ **solvent bonding**

sonic nozzle A pneumatic or vibratory atomizer in which energy is imparted at frequencies below 20 kHz to the liquid.

sonic pulse, transverse A sonic pulse in which the deformations involved are at right angles to the direction of propagation.

sonic testing Sound speed and sound absorption measurements in plastics are useful both as a probe of the molecular structure and as a source of engineering design properties. As a molecular probe, acoustic properties are related to such structural factors as the glass transition, crosslink density, morphology, and chemical composition. When the acoustic properties are plotted over broad ranges of frequency and temperature they are usually dominated by the glass transition.

As a source of engineering properties, acoustic measurements are used for applications such as the absorption of unwanted sound and the construction of acoustically transparent windows. As an example from a very basic view, listening to the sound of a 25¢ coin (50¢ better) coin tapping on reinforced glass fiber-TS polyester plastics provides a quantitative analysis on its void-free construction; also indicates cure of the TS plastic. In time, acoustical sounding instruments were developed to provide more accurate data. ▷ **acoustic holography**

sorbent A liquid or solid medium in or upon which materials are retained by absorption or adsorption.

sorption The process of taking up or holding a material by adsorption and/or absorption.

sound absorption **1.** The process of dissipating sound energy. **2.** The property possessed by materials, objects, and structures such as rooms of absorbing sound waves. **3.** The metric unit sabin is a measure of sound absorption; in a specified frequency band, the measure of the magnitude of the absorptive property of a material or object.

sound attenuation The reduction of the intensity of sound as it travels from the source to a receiving location.

source reduction, waste A way to reduce waste is by changing a process or product so that less waste material is generated. Also, source reduction is to garbage what preventative medicine is to health, a means of eliminating a problem before it can happen.

space charge Polarization from conductivity particles in a dielectric.

space environment ▷ **altitude chart** and **atmosphere chart**

spacer ▷ **mold chase**

spalling **1.** Type of wear caused by repetitive contact stress; is a form of stress fatigue. Also known as pitting erosion. **2.** The cracking, breaking, or splintering of material due to heat; thermal stresses occur.

spandex fiber ▷ **fiber, spandex**

spanishing A method of depositing ink in the valleys of embossed plastic films. Scrapers are used.

spark erosion ▷ **electro-erosive cutting and sinking**

spark test An electrical test in which a spark is used to detect discontinuity of coating.

special control ▷ **motion control system**

specification or standard A detailed description of the characteristics of a product and of the criteria which must be used to determine whether the product conforms to the description. Organizations involved in preparing or coordinating specifications, regulations, and/or standards include the following:

ASTM	American Society for Testing and Materials
UL	Underwriters' Laboratories
DIN	Deutsches Institut, Normung, Germany
ACS	American Chemical Society
AMS	Aerospace Material Specification of the Society for Automotive Engineers (SAE)
ANSI	American National Standards Institute
ASCE	American Society of Chemical Engineers
ASM	American Society of Metals
ASME	American Society of Mechanical Engineers
AWS	American Welding Society
BMI	Battele Memorial Institute
BSI	British Standards Institute
CPSC	Consumer Product Safety Commission
CSA	Canadian Standards Association
DOD	Department of Defense
DODISS	Department of Defense Index & Specifications & Standards
DOT	Department of Transportation
EIA	Electronic Industry Association
EPA	Environmental Protection Agency
FMRC	Factory Mutual Research Corporation
FDA	Food and Drug Administration
FMVSS	Federal Motor Vehicle Safety Standards
FTC	Federal Trade Commission
IAPMO	International Association of Plumbing & Mechanicals Officials
IEC	International Electrotechnical Commission
IEEE	Institute of Electrical and Electronic Engineers
IFI	Industrial Fasteners Institute
IPC	Institute of Printed Circuits
ISA	Instrument Society of America
ISO	International Organization for Standardization
JIS	Japanese Industrial Standards
MIL-HDBK	Military Handbook
NADC	Naval Air Development
NACE	National Association of Corrosion Engineers
NAHB	National Association of Home Builders
NEMA	National Electrical Manufacturers' Association
NFPA	National Fire Protection Association
NIST	National Institute of Standards & Technology (previously the National Bureau of Standards).
NIOSH	National Institute for Occupational Safety & Health
NIST	National Institute of Standard Testing
NPFC	Naval Publications & Forms Center
NSF	National Sanitation Foundation
OFR	Office of the Federal Register
OSHA	Occupational Safety & Health Administration
PLASTEC	Plastics Technical Evaluation Center of DOD
PPI	Plastics Pipe Institute of the Society of the Plastics Industry
QPL	Qualified Products List
SAE	Society of Automotive Engineers
SPE	Society of Plastics Engineers
SPI	Society of the Plastics Industry
STP	Special Technical Publications of the ASTM
TAPPI	Technical Association of the Pulp and Paper Industry

▷ **standard** and **standardization**

specification or standard, limited coordination It has not been fully coordinated and accepted by all interested parties. They are issued to cover the need for requirements unique to one particular department or area of interest. Applies primarily to government agency documents.

specific gravity The ratio of the weight in air of any volume of a substance to the weight in air of an equal volume of distilled water at a standard temperature, usually at 23°C (73.4°F). It is a unitless number. When using English units, it can be obtained by dividing a materials density in lb/ft^3 by 62.36. ▷ **density**

specific gravity and density ▷ **density and specific gravity**

specific gravity, apparent The ratio of the weight in air of a given volume of the impermeable portion of a permeable material (that is, the solid matter including its permeable pores or voids) to the weight in air of an equal volume of distilled water at a stated temperature.

specific gravity, bulk The weight in air of a given volume of a permeable material (including both permeable and impermeable voids normal to the material) to the weight in air of an equal volume of distilled water at a stated temperature.

specific gravity versus modulus ▷**modulus versus specific gravity**

specific gravity, wood Ranges from 0.30 to 0.75, depending on type of wood.

specific heat capacity The quantity of heat required to raise the temperature of a unit mass of a substance 1° under specified conditions (see Table).

Specific heats for various plastics.

Type of plastic	cal/g.°C
Polyethylene	0.55
Polypropylene	0.46
Polytetrafluoroethylene	0.25
Polyvinyl chloride	0.25
Polyvinyl fluoride	0.30
Polystyrene	0.32
SBR (Styrene Butadiene Rubber)	0.45
ABS (Acrylonitrile Butadiene Styrene)	0.35
Cellulose acetate	0.40
6-Nylon	0.38
66-Nylon	0.40
Polyester	0.30
Phenol formaldehyde	0.40
Epoxy resins	0.25
Polyimide	0.27

specific humidity ▷**humidity, specific**

specific insulation resistance ▷**electrical volume resistivity**

specific properties ▷**properties, specific**

specimen An individual piece or portion of a sample used to make a specific test; of specific shape and dimensions.

specks Surface imperfections caused by flakes of charred plastic from processing machine melt hangups.

spectrochemical buffer In spectrochemical analysis, a substance which by its addition or presence tends to minimize the effects of one or more of the elements on the emission of other elements.

spectrometer, X-ray fluorescence In plastics, uses of XRF analysis can include quantifying various pigment, flame-resistant, and UV-stabilizer additives that are based on elements such as titanium, copper, zinc, bromide, antimony, and phosphorus. XRF simultaneously measures all the elements in 50 s or less. Examples of use include identifying the amount of manganese and titanium in nylon, amount of zinc in PS, and quantity of calcium stearate in PP. Samples are irradiated by X-rays, which cause electrons in the atoms of the sample to jump to a higher energy level. Upon dropping back to the original energy level, the electrons emit X-rays of precise energy and wavelength that are characteristic of a particular element. This is the process of fluorescence.

spectrometry ▷**infrared spectroscopy**

spectrophotometer Color matching has been done traditionally by visual comparison under standard lighting conditions. Most color matching is now done with spectrophotometers and computer programs. ▷**colorimeter**

spectroscopic analysis Spectroscopic techniques include nuclear magnetic resonance, infrared and Raman spectroscopy, pyrolysis-gas chromatography, mass spectrometry, UV spectroscopy, luminescence spectroscopy, electron spin resonance, and electron spectroscopy for chemical applications.

spectroscopic Fourier transform An analytical method used automatically in advanced forms of spectroscopic analysis.

spectroscopy The study of spectra using an instrument for dispersing radiation. It is for visual observation of the radiation energy emission or absorption by a substance in any wavelength of the electromagnetic spectrum in response to an external energy source. ▷**electromagnetic spectrum**

spectrum 1. The ordered arrangement of electromagnetic radiation according to wavelength, wave number, or frequency. **2.** The radiant energy emitted by a substance as a characteristic band of wavelengths by which it can be identified. **3.** The complete range of colors in the rainbow, from short wavelengths (blue) to long wavelengths (red).

specular transmission The transmission of light across clear and colorless test specimens, within a very narrow angle. The T_s is related to specimen thickness. Expressions, such as transparency, clarity, see-through clarity, and image resolution, are used in this context.

spew line ▷**mold parting line** and **die parting line**

sphere, hollow ▷**microsphere**

Spheripol process This Himont Inc. polymerization process produces polypropylene in "crumb", bead or granular forms, eliminating any pelletizing finishing operation.

spherulite A rounded aggregate of radiating lamellar crystals with appearance of a pom-pom. They contain amorphous material between the crystals and usually impinge on one another, forming polyhedrons. Spherulites are present in most crystalline plastics and may range in diameter from a few tenths of a micron to several mm. ▷**nucleating agent**; **polariscope; chemical composition and properties of plastics**

spice The joining of two ends of glass fiber yarn or strand, usually by means of an air drying adhesive.

spider Assembly of radiating pins, fingerlike rods, etc. to support mechanically a device such as a torpedo in an extruder die. ▷ **design die; die spider; mold gate, spider**

spin axis The axis of rotation of a product, such as a wheel.

spin flow test ▷ **melt flow spiral test**

spinneret A type of extrusion die, that is, a metal plate with many small round or oval holes, through which a melt is forced and/or pulled (rayon, nylon, glass, etc.). For glass, the plate is made of precious metals such as gold, but principally platinum; they provide control of hole size and wear resistance against glass rubbing action. Filaments may be hardened by cooling in air and/or water, or by chemical action. Spinnerets enable extrusion of filaments of one denier or less (denier = 40 micron). For commercial work 12 to 15 denier fiber is generally used. ▷ **fiber spinning process** and **glass fiber production**

spinning **1.** Process of making fibers by forcing melt through spinnerets. **2.** Mechanical working of sheet material on a rotating mandrel.

spinning, flash ▷ **flash spun nonwoven fabric**

spin trimming Trimming method in which a container is revolved into and against a fixed knife.

spin welding Bonds two thermoplastic parts, usually cylindrical, together by frictional heat to produce hollow or solid final assembled parts. The process forces the mating parts together while one is spinning, until frictional heat melts the interface. Spinning is then stopped and pressure held until heat is dissipated. Also known as friction welding. ▷ **vibration welding** and **welding**

SPI-SPE mold finish comparison kit ▷ **mold finish**

splay **1.** A fanlike surface defect or mark near the injection mold gate on a part. **2.** Lines formed in a part after molding, usually due to flow of material in the mold. ▷ **silver streak** **3.** ▷ **foamed injection molding low pressure surface finish**

spline To prepare a surface to its desired contour by working a paste material with a flat-edged tool. The procedure is similar to "screeding" of concrete; also the tool itself.

spontaneous ignition Initiation of combustion caused by internal, chemical exothermic reaction. Also called self-ignition.

spool A term sometimes used to identify a fiber roving ball; roving ball is the preferred term.

sports products ▷ **recreational surface**

spot facing To machine finish a surface such as a small area or top of a container.

spot welding ▷ **ultrasonic welding**

spray-and-wipe ▷ **spray paint, spray-and-wipe**

spray degreasing ▷ **solvent cleaning**

sprayed metal mold ▷ **mold material, sprayed metal**

spray, flame ▷ **flame spray coating**

spraying airless Airless atomization involves pressure forcing a substance, such as paint, through a small nozzle at a sufficiently high velocity, or by impinging the substance stream against a part, causing a sudden change in flow direction. In either case, the fluid stream disintegrates into small particles. The degree of atomization is rather poor, the particle size is large, and the fluid must be of sufficiently low viscosity. This spraying method, however, is more efficient in terms of energy consumption than air atomization, requires less paint, and the transfer efficiency is much better. Paint viscosity may be lowered for airless spraying by heating it. This system can be improved by providing a low pressure air stream to assist atomization and direct the paint to the target. While the transfer efficiency is slightly decreased, the degree of atomization is substantially improved.

spraying, electrostatic ▷ **electrostatic spray coating**

spraying, flocking ▷ **flocking or floc spraying**

spraying, foam ▷ **foamed spray**

spraying, metal ▷ **metal-spraying on plastic**

spraying powder ▷ **flocking or floc spraying**

spraying, reinforced plastic Chipped fibers and plastic are simultaneously deposited in (or on) an open mold. Practically all spray-up processes use glass fiber rovings with a thermoset plastic (which is usually polyester). The glass fiber rovings are fed through a rotating cutter in the spray gun and blown into a plastic stream which is directed at a mold

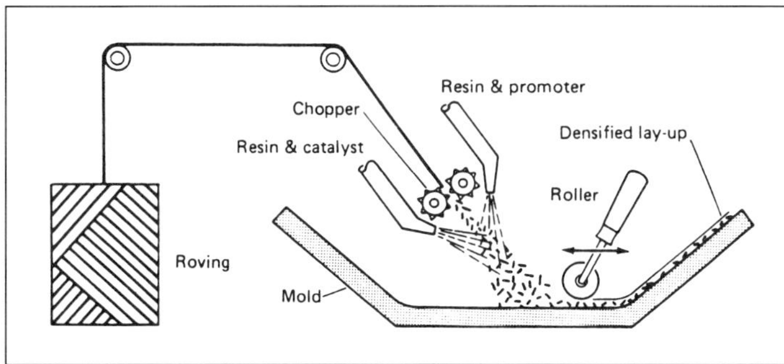

Schematic of two-pot system-airless.

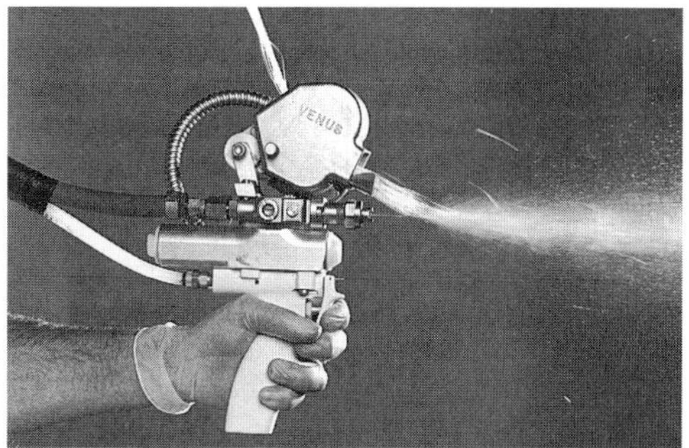

Spray-up gun with two-pot plastic system and fiber chopper.

(see Figs. above). The two-part plastic mix precoats the strands of glass and the merged spray is shot at the mold in an even pattern by the operator (or robot). Different spray-up systems are used that are essentially similar in every aspect but the gun itself. There are many recognized varieties of guns such as: external mix, airless external mix, air internal mix, airless internal mix, and two-pot mix systems. After the fiber-plastic mix is deposited on the mold, it is rolled by hand methods to remove air, to compact the fibers, and to smooth the surface (see Fig. below). Curing system that follows is typically that used for thermoset plastics. As in other RP molding, the first layer on the mold can be a sprayed gel coat and/or final sprayed gel coat on the outside surface. If required, inserts, etc. can be included during the spray-up.

spray paint coating A plastic coating may be applied to products by spraying. This method of application is especially attractive for products that have been assembled, have irregular shapes, and/or curved surfaces. The material applied is frequently in the form of a paint, which is a combination of plastic, solvent, diluent, additives, and pigment. It usually is applied at room temperature, but hot plastic or a plastic completely dissolved in a solvent system can also be used.

Many different types of spray equipment are available; they can be classified in various ways. Typical classifications are the method of atomization (airless, air, rotary, or electrostatic) and the method of deposition assist

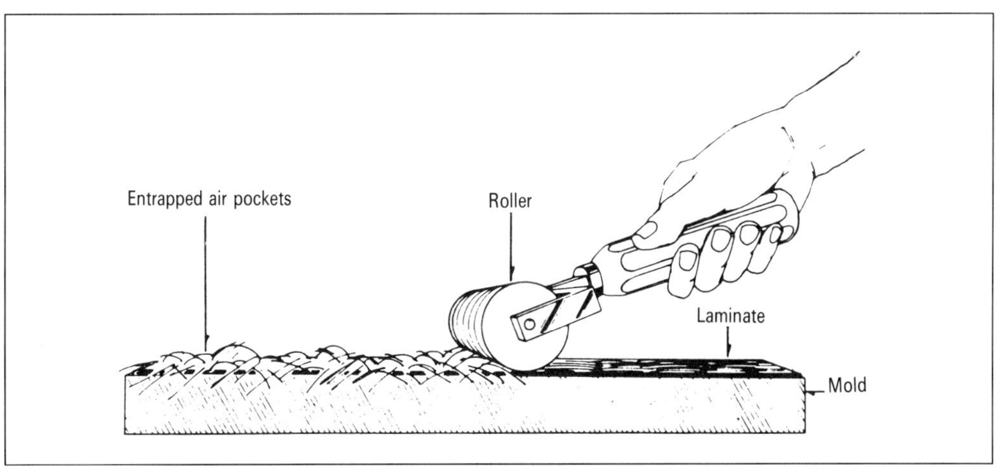

Use of roller to compact spray-up.

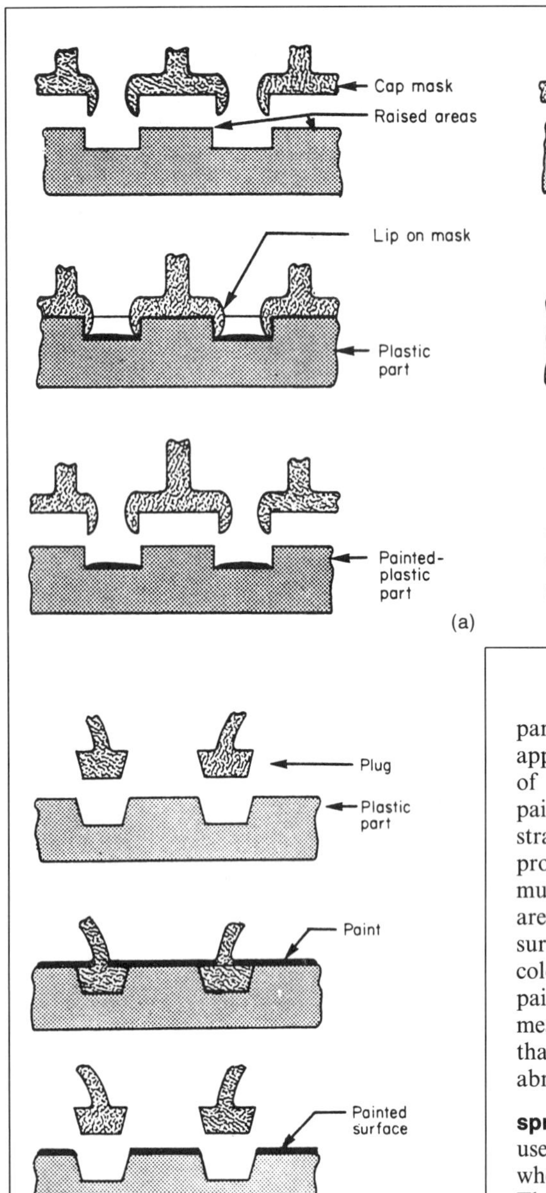

Three types of spray masks: (*a*) cap or lip mask; (*b*) plug-type mask; (*c*) block cut-out mask.

(electrostatic or nonelectrostatic). Different methods can be used in combinations and most can be used for simple one-applicator manual systems to highly complex computer-controlled automatic systems with hundreds of applicators. In an automatic installation, the applicators can be mounted on fixed stands, reciprocating or rotating machines, or robots.

The paint is a very important and critical part of the system because drying rate, ease of application, appearance, and physical properties of the finished coat are all a function of the paint. The choice depends on the plastic substrate and the environment in which the product will be used. Adhesion is critical and must be considered in the choice of paint. There are molded products that can replace painted surfaces on plastics with molded-in textures and colors in an effort to reduce costs. However, painting remains one of the most cost-effective means of producing attractive plastic coating that also serves as protection against excessive abrasion and UV exposure. ▷ **paint coating**

spray paint mask Paint spray masks are used to provide sharp lines of demarcation when different colors are designated (see Fig.). They are generally made of electroformed nickel, but sometimes paper, elastomer, and plastic are used for short runs. If spray masks are to be worthwhile, the molded parts must be held to close tolerances. This calls for good mold design, molding material, and molding technique. Slight variations in dimensions from part to part will allow paint to blow by the mask and cause rejects. Good, consistent molded parts are a must in spray-mask painting.

spray paint, spray-and-wipe In this process paint is sprayed over a recessed area in the plastic part, and excess paint is wiped away.

Wiped-in letters are indented in the part, and either first or second surfaces can be sprayed and wiped. Recess or surface depressions for wipe-in decorations should have a depth-to-width ratio of $1\frac{1}{2}:1$. Recesses are seldom over 0.8 mm (1/32 in.) wide. Indentations or recesses should be sharp and abrupt where they meet the surface of the part. This prevents streaking of the paint across the surface as it is wiped off. Wiped-in letters or decorations will not chip or rub away as easily as stamped letters. This is a more expensive method, but it does improve visibility of letters and decorations. Process can influence results. As an example, an injection molded part that has depressed letters which are to be filled with paint should be gated in such a manner that weld or knit lines do not form between the letters. If lines are present, paint may run into them, resulting in scrap.

spray paint transfer efficiency A measure of the percentage of paint that reaches the target. The Table lists guide values for various methods. This Table takes into account sensitivity to the part geometry. It does not take into account factors such as large flat parts versus small irregular shaped parts, thus values are only guides.

Transfer efficiency for spray methods.

Spray method	Transfer efficiency, %
Air atomization	35
Air atomization with electrostatic charge	55
Airless atomization	50
Airless atomization with electrostatic charge	70
Disk and bell atomization with electrostatic charge	90

spray rinse ▷ **solvent cleaning**

spray-up molding ▷ **spraying, reinforced plastic**

spread coating In this process, the material (film, sheet, etc.) to be coated passes over a roller and under a long blade or knife. The plastic coating compound is placed on the material just in front of the knife and is spread out over the material. The coating thickness is controlled by the speed material travels under the knife, and the positioning with space of the knife from the material. Also called knife spreading.

spreader ▷ **torpedo**

spreader roller ▷ **extruder web wrinkle free**

spring constant The number of pounds required to compress a spring or specimen 25 mm (1 in.) in a prescribed test procedure.

sprue ▷ **mold sprue**

sprue break ▷ **injection molding sprue break**

sprueless molding ▷ **mold, sprueless**

spun-bonded nonwoven fabric Spunbonded fabrics are distinguished from other non-woven fabrics by a one-step manufacturing procedure, which provides a complete chemical to fabric route in some instances and plastic to fabric in others. In either instance the process integrates the spinning, laydown, consolidation, and bonding of continuous filaments to form fabric. The area of largest growth has been disposable diaper coverstock, which counts for about 50% of the U.S. coverstock market.

Regarding structure, spun-bonded fabrics are filament sheets made by an integrated process of spinning, attenuation, deposition, bonding, and winding into rolls. A combination of thickness, fiber denier, and number of fibers per unit area determines the fabric basis weight or weight per unit area, which ranges from 10 to 800 g/m^2, typically 17 to 180 g/m^2. The method of bonding greatly affects the thickness of the sheet and other characteristics. Fiber webs bonded by calendering are thinner than needle-punched webs because calendering compresses the structure through pressure, whereas needle punching moves fibers from the X–Y plane (axis) of the fabric into the Z-direction (thickness).

The method of fabric manufacture determines the sheet characteristics, whereas the plastic determines the intrinsic properties. Properties such as fiber density, temperature resistance, chemical and light stability, ease of coloration, surface energies, and others are a function of the base plastic. Most of these fabrics are based on isotactic polypropylene or polyester (TP). Small quantities are made from nylon 6/6, and an increasing amount from high-density polyethylene. Linear low-densitypoly-ethylene use is on the increase since it gives a softer fabric.

Spun-bonded fabrics are characterized mechanically and physically by tensile, tear, and burst strengths; elongation to break; weight; thickness; porosity; and stability to heat and chemicals. These properties help reflect fabric composition and structure. ▷ **flash spun nonwoven fabric; nonwoven fabric; melt-blown nonwoven fabric**

spun nonwoven fabric These fabrics include spun-bonded, flash-spun, melt-blown, and mechanical nonwoven swirl. The consumption of these fabrics in both durable and disposable areas continues to grow. Uses include: (1) *Consumer disposables*: baby diapers, adult diapers, wipes and roll towels, fabric-in-drier softeners, surgical packs, surgical gowns, surgical masks, caps, shoe covers, hospital bed underpads, medical dressings; (2) *Industrial disposables*: filtration media, wipe cloths, other; (3) *Durables*: interlining-interfacing (apparel), coated and laminated products, home furnishings, carpet backing (primary, secondary), geotextiles, civil engineering, roofing, other.

spun roving ▷ **roving, spun**

spur A term sometimes used for the piece of plastic formed in the sprue of an injection or transfer molding mold.

sputtered coating Like vacuum metalizing, sputtering is a process for depositing permanent metal coatings onto plastic substrates. The term sputtering describes the removal of metal atoms from a base (metal) material utilizing a bombardment action. The bombardment is made of ions from gaseous sources such as argon and controlled within a magnetic field. The energy of the argon ions' bombardment onto the target metal results in metal atoms being dispersed throughout the vacuum atmosphere and impinging on or coating all surfaces exposed to the source material.

Sputtering can be used to coat virtually all thermoplastics and thermoset plastics. When compared to vacuum metalizing, its chief advantage is the ability to deposit a variety of metals on plastics. Metals and alloys such as chromium, stainless steel, copper, brass, titanium, tungsten, and aluminum are used. This makes sputtering very useful for achieving desired decorative effects at reasonable cost. Like other vacuum coating processes, it requires expensive equipment, which can be justified in large scale production or where coating properties are crucial and cost is of secondary importance. However, it is reliable and lends itself to automatic control, permitting economies of scale that make even decorative coatings feasible.

Metal deposition by sputtering is much thicker than that of metalizing. Aluminum films deposited via vacuum metalizing will be in the micron inch range; a thickness of 1.5 microns (1.5×10^{-6} mm) is typical. Attempting to deposit heavier thickness of aluminum results in loss of the bright aluminum finish due to excessive heat and oxidation during the evaporation process. The sputtering process can deposit heavier thicknesses of up to 10 micron (10^{-5} mm) without such impairment; coatings generally have the same composition as the source material (called the target).

Product design considerations for sputtering and vacuum metalizing are identical. Allowance must be made for coating buildups, positioning of the parts during the evaporation process, and all the handling considerations involved in achieving a quality decorative effect. Preparing plastic parts for sputtering requires all the care and consideration involved in vacuum metalizing. Cleanliness must be monitored and maintained at all processing stages, from part production through the final top coating operation. There is also sputter cleaning where sputtering action is used to remove contamination from a material surface. ▷ **vacuum metalizing** and **electroplating**

square mesh Wire cloth screen with mesh count the same in both directions, longitudinal and transverse. ▷ **screen**

squeegee A soft, flexible roll or blade used in wiping operations, especially in screen processing.

squeegee tube ▷ **tube, collapsible squeeze type**

squeeze molding A relatively low pressure reinforced plastic molding process is the squeeze molding technique (see Fig. below).

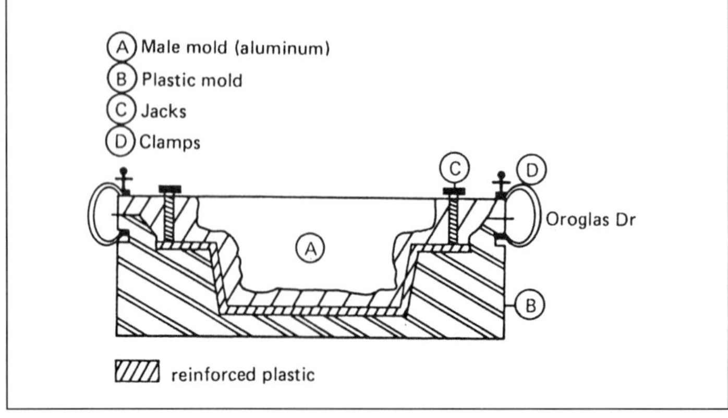

Squeeze molding reinforced plastics.

squirrel-cage reducer ▷ **cage mill**

SR-4 strain gauge ▷ **strain gauge**

stability **1.** The ability of a system to maintain position accuracies with passage of time in a given ambient. It is a function of wear and tear, lubricants (film thickness may contribute to an error), and temperature. **2.** The condition of a structure or a mass of material when it is able to support the applied stress for a long time without suffering any significant deformation or movement that is not reversed by the release of the stress.

stabilization **1.** It denotes the treatments to which plastics are subjected in an effort to control or adjust effectively the deteriorative physiocochemical reactions at work during manufacture, compounding, processing, and/or subsequent life (use) of the plastic product. **2.** In carbon or graphite fiber forming, the process used to render the fiber precursor infusible to carbonization. **3.** Rendering wastes relatively inert, uniform, biologically inactive, nuisance-free, or harmless.

stabilizer Basically materials added to a plastic to impede or retard degradation, usually caused by heat or ultraviolet radiation. They are used in the formulation of some plastics, especially elastomers, to also assist in maintaining the physical and chemical properties of their materials at their initial values throughout the processing and service life of the material. As an example, a specific type of stabilizer known as a UV stabilizer is designed to absorb UV rays and prevent them from attacking the plastic. Other types of stabilizers, such as antioxidant, heat, and viscosity, are used.

stabilizer, internal An agent incorporated in a plastic during polymerization, as opposed to a stabilizer added to the plastic during compounding.

stacked mold ▷ **mold, stacked**

stacked-up tolerances ▷ **tolerance stackup**

stacking sequence A description in reinforced plastic of a laminate that details the orientations of the plies and their sequence in the laminate.

staging Heating a thermoset premixed plastic system, such as in a pregreg, until the chemical reaction (curing) starts, but stopping the reaction before the gel point is reached. Staging is often used to reduce plastic flow.

stain An organic protective coating similar to paint, but with much lower solids content (pigment loading).

staining Areas of a molding (or mold) which take up a dull, discolored appearance.

stainless steel performance SSS fall into four categories: austenitic, ferritic, precipitation hardening, and martensite. Engineering options are available for their composition and processing. However, tradeoffs most commonly made are between maximum mechanical properties and optimum corrosion resistance in specifying these steels for technical products. ▷ **mold materials** and **steel**

stain resistance The ability of a plastic to resist staining caused by many different factors that include spilled food, lipstick, waxing compounds, grease deposits, and nail polish. Different agents and additives are used for different plastics to develop or reduce stain.

staking A term used in fastening. The forming of a head on a protruding stud for the purpose of holding component parts together. Staking (like copper riveting) may be done by cold staking, hot staking, or ultrasonic heating of thermoplastics.

stalk European term for sprue.

stamping In the stamping process, a reinforced thermoplastic sheet material is precut to the required sizes. The precut sheet is preheated in an oven, the heat depending on the TP used (such as PP or nylon, where the heat can range upward from 520°F or 600°F). Dielectric heat is used to ensure that the heat is quick and, most important, to provide uniform heating through the thickness and across the sheet. After heating, the sheet is quickly formed into the desired shape in cooler matched-metal dies, using conventional stamping presses or SMC-type compression presses. Stamping is a highly productive process capable of forming complex shapes with the retention of the fiber orientation in particular locations as required (see Fig. on p. 712). The process can be adapted to a wide variety of configurations, from small components to large box-shaped housings and from flat panels to thick, heavily ribbed parts.

stamping, hot ▷ **hot stamping**

standard **1.** A physical reference used as a basis for comparison or calibration. **2.** A concept that has been established by authority, custom, or agreement to serve as a model or rule in the measurement of quality or the establishment of a practice or procedure. ▷ **specification or standard** and **standardization**

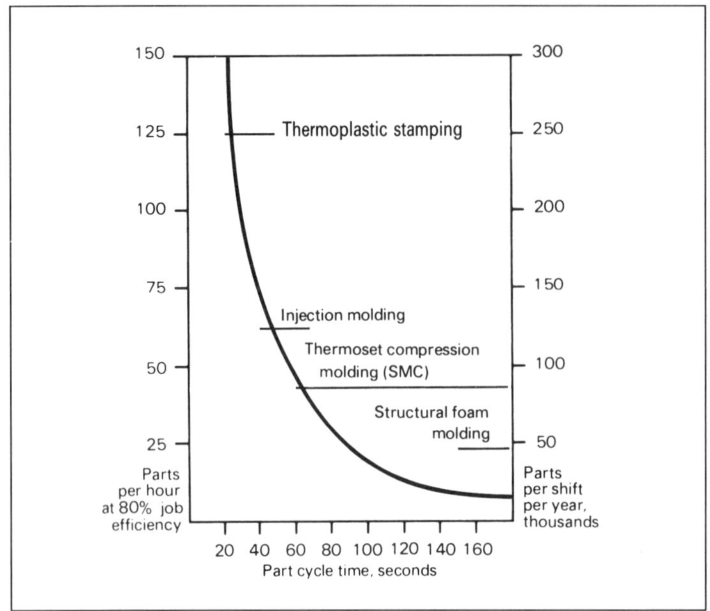

Comparison of thermoplastic stamping versus other processes.

standard air density Atmospheric air density of 0.0750 lb/ft^3 (1.201 kg/m^3). This value of air density corresponds to atmospheric air at a temperature of 20°C (68°F), 14.696 psi (101.32 kPa), and approximately 30% relative humidity. ▷ **atmosphere chart**

standardant A material used for standardization.

standard atmospheric conditions 29.92 in. Hg (101,325 Pa), 20°C (68°F), and 30% relative humidity.

standard depth of penetration The depth at which the eddy current density is reduced to approximately 37% of the density at the surface. Eddy current testing is most effective when the wall thickness does not exceed the SDP or in heavier tube walls when discontinuities of interest are within one SDP.

standard design A published and proven product design. ▷ **design**

standard deviation A measure of the dispersion of a series of results around their mean, computed as the positive square root of the variance. The standard deviation is the basis for most statements of precision and may be obtained from an analysis of variance of results of an interlaboratory test program. ▷ **mean and standard deviation; practice**

standard deviation measurement 1. Basically SDM is a measure of data from the average; the root-mean-square (RMS) of the individual deviation from the average. ▷ **root-mean-square** **2.** SDM expresses a degree of accuracy; the term two-standard-deviation (2 sigma) error can be used. What this means is that if many tests are performed, 95% of the results will have an error of less than ±0.25%. Another standard commonly used in laboratory work is the root-mean-square (RMS) accuracy, which is identical for all practical purposes to one-standard-deviation (1 sigma) on a normal distribution, or 68% of the results. When examining the technical specifications, it is important to know whether they are quoting one- or two-standard deviation accuracies.

standard deviation of sample The sample standard deviation divided by the square root of the number of measurements used in the calculation of the mean. ▷ **sample standard deviation**

standard deviation ratio SDR is the specific ratio of the average specified outside diameter to the minimum specified wall thickness for outside diameter-controlled plastic pipe. This value is derived by adding one to the pertinent number selected from the ANSI Preferred Number Series 10 (Z17.1). As an example: with ANSI Series 10 of 5.0, the SDR is 6.0; 10.0 is 11.0; 31.5 is 32.5; etc.

standard industrial classification The SIC system classifies all manufacturing and services produced in the U.S. (transportation, communication, electronic, sanitary service, construction, etc.). It starts with the broadest industrial aggregations; then, by a series of subdivisions, it identifies more finely detailed classes or groupings right down to the individual product level. Thus at the first level there is the manufacturing sector. At the next level of detail, manufacturing is divided into 20 2-digit major groups, such as SIC 28 on *chemicals*. Those are subdivided into 3-digit *industry groups*, of which there are about 143 (these numbers are subject to change), such as 282 for *plastics and synthetic fibers*. The next level is made up of 4-digit *specific industries*, of which there are about 470, including SIC 2821 on *plastics resins and materials*, and SIC 3079 on *miscellaneous plastics products*.

There is an SIC manual that spells out the complete definitions of all 2-, 3-, and 4-digit industries and their products. A list of 5-, 6-, and 7-digit product classifications can be obtained from the Numerical List of Manufactured Products, Series MC 72-1.2, U.S. Bureau of the Census, Census of Manufacturers. The structure of the SIC makes it easily possible to classify all industry establishments so that input/output data is easily obtained. An example is consumption of plastics in the major group SIC 30 of products such as balloons, bottles, dinnerware, garden hose, insulation, pipe, tile, valves, etc.

I/O in its simplest form is a determination of each industry's dependence on each other; in its more complex format, I/O detail enables creation of complex econometric models and sophisticated computer programs for analyzing inter-industry transactions. I/O studies are published by U.S. Department of Commerce, Bureau of Economic Analysis. I/O analysis has a variety of applications, including such diverse uses as evaluating an individual firm's sales potential and probing the implications of broad economic programs. Basically I/O program determines what each of about 470 "product level" industries consumes of each of the other 370 industries.

standard, internal A compound of known behavior added to a sample to facilitate the analysis.

standardization **1.** Basically the act of adjustment of instrument output to conform to calibration; the process by which a given method, procedure, or protocol is made to conform to prescribed conditions. Standardization can only follow calibration. **2.** Standardization in the field of plastics is a dynamic process that encompasses basic and applied research, design, production, instrumentation, development of test methods, laboratory evaluation of test procedures, and the preparation and promulgation of standards, specifications, and related documents. Basic research usually provides the theoretical and conceptual framework upon which new measurement principles and improved test methods are constructed. Improved test methods permit the properties of materials to be measured more precisely. The test methods find their way into standards; the chemical, physical, mechanical, and other performance characteristics of plastics lead to specifications and related documents. Standards and specifications are components of the overall physical measurement system, which in turn is based on the ability to make accurate, reliable, and compatible measurements. Without this system and the accompanying standardization effort, the more than (probably) 60 billion measurements which are made worldwide each day would lack much of their meaning and importance. ▷ **specification or standard** for a listing of organizations involved in standardization.

standard reference material ▷ **bottle standard reference material**

standard sample ▷ **sample standards**

staple fiber ▷ **fiber, staple**

starch A polysaccharide with the same chemical make-up as cellulose in that it consists of glucose units. It differs from cellulose in the manner in which the glucose units are linked together. It is used with plastics in many different ways.

starch-based plastic ▷ **biodegradable and waste**

starch-oil binder ▷ **sizing**

starved area ▷ **reinforced plastic starved area**

starved feeder ▷ **extruder starved feeder**

starved joint ▷ **joint, starved**

static accuracy ▷ **sensor accuracy**

static charge The electric charge produced by the relative motion of a nonconducting material over a nonconducting plastic material. Charge separation is due to mechanical motion. This charge is a potential problem during processing plastics such as in extrusion, injection and blow molding, and coating. ▷ **film blocking; antistatic agent; destaticization; electrostatic charge**

static coefficient ▷ **coefficient of static**

static electricity control ▷ **antistatic agent**

static eliminator Mechanical devices for removing electrical static charges from plastic articles by creating an ionized atmosphere in close proximity to the surface which neutralizes the static charges. Types of static eliminators include static bars, ionizing blowers and air guns, and radioactive elements. All except the latter operate on the principle that a high voltage discharge from the applicator to ground creates an ionized atmosphere.

static fatigue ▷ **fatigue, static**

static friction Friction developed between two touching bodies at the time one body starts to move relative to another.

static load An imposed stationary force that is constant in magnitude, direction, and sense.

static load measurement ▷ **stress-strain measurements**

static mixer Such a unit is designed to achieve a homogenous mix by flowing two plastic streams through geometric patterns formed by physical elements in a tubular tube or barrel. They can be used to mix different plastics, plastic with its component ingredients (color, additive, etc.), and sometimes inserted at the screw end. Static mixers are successfully installed in the adapters between the barrel and the die for further thermal homogenization of the melt after it leaves the screw (see Fig. below). This causes transitory fluctuations and temperature variations in the melt to decrease considerably. As a result an increased pressure drop occurs and the heat level increases a few degrees, while temperature peaks disappear. Thus in selecting a static mixer, one should be sure that its resistance to flow is as low as possible.

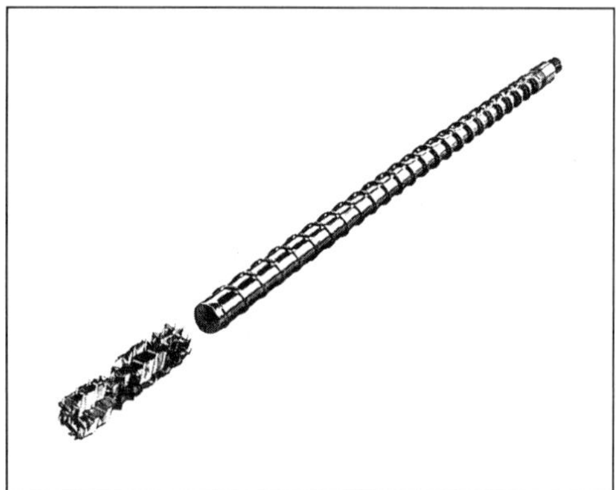

Example of a static mixer located at the end of a screw.

static neutralizer An attachment on an extruder film line (or other applicable processes) to remove static electricity from the substrate (film, etc.) to avoid trouble with wrap-up, etc. ▷ **static eliminator**

statistic A term in a collection of statistics; a summary value calculated from the observed values in a sample. It is a branch of mathematics dealing with the collection, analysis, interpretation, and presentation of masses of numerical data. ▷ **population parameter** and **material variation, reliability factor**

statistical benefits Using statistical methods in the design of experiments and data analysis allows designers, compound formulators, etc. to attain benefits that would otherwise be considered unachievable. Benefits include a 20 to 70% reduction in problem solving time; a minimum 50% reduction in costs due to testing, machine processing time, labor, and materials; and a 200 to 300% increase in value, quality, and reliability of the information generated.

In addition to faster and more cost-effective problem solving, a good test program design and data analysis provides invaluable quantitative information at a very little added cost. This information helps answer such questions as: (1) what is an optimum compound formulation, (2) how does the optimum change, if changes are made, in recipe or process variables, (3) which variables are the machine or process sensitive to, (4) for consistent performance, what are the tolerances for these variables, and (5) how does one design an effective troubleshooting guide or a program.

Test program design or experimental planning is usually carried out to meet, at minimum cost, one or more of the following objectives: (1) maximization of productivity, (2) determination of optimum or preferred conditions for machine settings, (3) optimization of formulations to achieve many product/process characteristics simultaneously, (5) determination of optimum operating conditions for reduced variability in product quality, and (6) determination of stable operating conditions that can be sustained for long production periods and yet provide a product of the desired quality.

Statistical methods are used in many more different analyses that include product needs, process needs, problem objectives in quantitative terms, model form, test design protocol, data collection, data analysis, targets and tolerances, standard operating procedures, documentation, and audit studies. An example is the use of statistical process control (SPC) analysis for injection molding. A condition such as part weight can be used. By simply weighing part potentials, using different time frames and sampling procedures, a wealth of information quickly becomes economically available. This SPC evaluation is also used in actual production. ▷ **injection molding process control; statistical process control; computer and statistics**

People who select any material (plastic, steel, wood, etc.) must understand that they are dealing with substances having variable properties, and people who provide these materials must (and in many cases do) describe materials' properties by taking this variable into account. Failure of parts can be avoided by knowing the variability in strength of a part, and then using the part in an environment where chances of failure are negligible. This same approach is also used in fabricating the part since processes have variabilities. ▷**design safety factor** and **statistical material selection, uncertainties that are nonstatistical**

statistical data collection Data may be collected directly by observation or indirectly through written or verbal questions. The latter technique is used extensively by market research personnel and public opinion pollsters. Data that are collected for *quality control* purposes are obtained by direct observation and are classified as either variables or attributes. *Variables* are those quality characteristics which are measurable, such as a weight measured in grams. *Attributes*, on the other hand, are those quality characteristics which are classified as either conforming or not conforming to specifications. In other words, attributes are either good or bad, while variables indicate the degree of "goodness" or "badness".

A variable that is capable of any degree of subdivision is referred to as *continuous*. Measurements such as meters (feet), liters (gallon), and pascals (pounds per square inch) are examples of continuous data. Variables that exhibit gaps are called *discrete*. The number of defective rivets in a structure, as an example, can be any whole number, such as 0, 3, 5, 10, 96...; however, there cannot be, say, 4.65 defective rivets in a particular trailer. In general, continuous data are measurable, while discrete data are countable.

Sometimes it is convenient for verbal or nonnumerical data to assume the nature of a variable. For example, the quality of the surface finish of a piece of furniture can be classified as poor, average, or good. The poor, average, or good classification can be replaced by the numerical values of 1, 2, or 3, respectively. In a similar manner, educational institutions assign to the letter grades of A, B, C, D, and E the numerical values of 4, 3, 2, 1, and 0, respectively, and use the numerical values as discrete variables for computational purposes.

While many quality characteristics are stated in terms of variables, there are many characteristics which must be stated as attributes. Frequently, those characteristics which are judged by visual observation are classified as attributes. The words on this page are correctly spelled or they are incorrectly spelled; the switch is on or off; and the answer is right or wrong.

statistical effect The response of the process to a change in factor level from low to high.

statistical factor A process or a recipe variable that can be controlled independently, such as temperature and the ratio of filler to plastic.

statistical facts and fiction ▷**plastic bad and other myths**

statistical, F-test A standard statistical test, applied to the ratio of two estimates of variance, to determine whether there is a statistically significant difference between the variances of the distributions from which the estimates are made.

statistical level A specific setting of a factor, such as 50°C (122°F), 20 RPM, and 1:2 ratio.

statistical material selection, reliability Virtually all classical design equations assume single-valued, real numbers. Such numbers can be multiplied, divided, or otherwise subjected to real-number operations to yield a single-valued, real-number solution. On the other hand, statistical materials selection, because it deals with the statistical nature of property values, relies on the algebra of random variables. Property values described by random variables will have a mean value, representing the most typical value, and a standard deviation, which represents the distribution of values around the mean value. This requires treating the mean values and standard deviations of particular property measurements according to a special set of "laws" for the algebra of random variables. Extensive information on this subject can be found in statistical textbooks. The algebra of random variables shares many elements of structure in common with the algebra of real numbers, such as the associative and commutative laws, and the uniqueness of sum and product. In combinations of addition and multiplication, the distributive law holds.

The associative law requires the result of a mathematical operation to be the same regardless of the way the elements are grouped; the commutative law requires the result to be identical without regard to the order of the elements; and the distributive law allows the multiplier to be used separately with each term of the multiplicand.

statistical material selection, uncertainties that are nonstatistical As reviewed in ▷**perfection**, limitations tend to exist. Thus, some engineering random variables carry with them a degree of uncertainty that may be nonstatistical; that is, they cannot be described in terms of mean values and standard deviations.

Examples are: (1) Frequently, a stress analysis may require simplifying assumptions. As a result, uncertainties are introduced of unknown magnitudes. (2) Material properties, such as strength, may be influenced by time, corrosion, and fluctuating thermal environments that are not factored into the analysis. (3) Uncertainties may arise from processing operations assumed to be constant, such as cold working, grinding, and heat treating, as well as assembly operations, such as fastening, welding, and shrink fitting. (4) Uncertainty is always inherent in the definition of system loading, especially when the design environment is complicated. Examples might be shock or overloading and unpredictable variations in the test environments. Also, test results obtained from static loading might not accurately reveal the behavior of a material subjected to the random loading characteristic of many in-service environments.

The statistical approach compels the experimenter to specify accurately and completely those factors that influence the property under examination. Equally important, the technique requires that those factors that cannot be specified accurately are recognized and considered in assessing property values.

statistical measure Statistic or mathematical function of a statistic.

statistical mechanics It is designed to describe systems that have many degrees of freedom and a wide range of possible states. An exact classical or quantum mechanical description of the full system is usually impossible, but a great deal can be understood about the average properties of these systems by using the concepts and methods of statistical mechanics. Plastic systems are naturally adapted to be studied by statistical mechanics and may be used for readily illustrating its general principles.

statistical method They are concerned with deriving maximum information from a given set of data (analysis) to meet product performance requirements as well as solving problems. Conversely it minimizes the amount of data (experimental design) needed to derive specific information.

statistical normal curve Although there are as many different statistical universes as there are conditions, they are usually described by the common types called normal curve or Gaussian distribution. The normal curve or normal universal distribution is a symmetrical, unimodal, bell-shaped distribution with the mean, median, and mode having the same value. A universal curve or distribution is developed from a frequency histogram. As the sample size of a histogram gets larger and larger, the cell interval gets smaller and smaller. When the sample size is quite large and the cell interval is very small, the histogram will take on the appearance of a smooth polygon or a curve representing the universe. A curve of the normal universe is shown in the Fig. below.

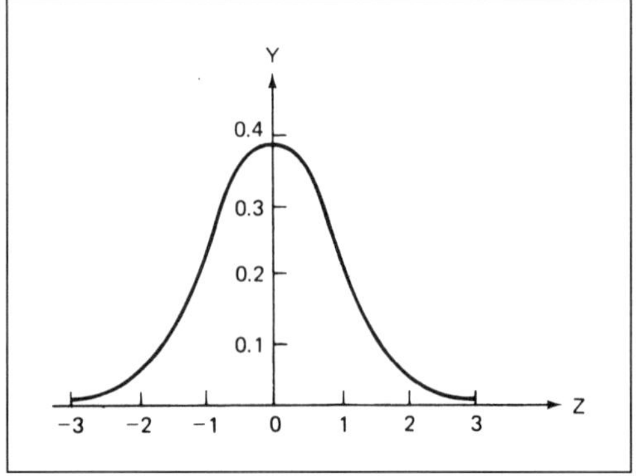

This normal curve has a mean of zero and a standard deviation of 1.

Much of the variation in nature and in industry follows the frequency distribution of the normal curve. Thus, the variations in the weight of people, the speed of horses, and the height of people will follow a normal curve. Also, the variations found in industry, such as the weight of plastic castings, the life of 60-W light bulbs, and the dimensions of a steel piston ring, will be expected to follow the normal curve. When considering the heights of human beings, we can expect a small percentage of them to be extremely tall and a small percentage to be extremely short, with the majority of human heights clustering about the mean value. The normal curve is such a good description of the variations which occur to most quality characteristics in industry that it is the basis for many quality control techniques.

The formula for the normal curve in its standard form is

$$f(Z) = \frac{1}{\sqrt{2\pi}} e^{-Z^2/2} = 0.3989\ e^{-Z^2/2}$$

where $\pi = 3.14159$, $e = 2.71828$, $Z = (X - \overline{X}')/\sigma$.

The variable Z is called the *standardized normal value*. The Fig. above shows the normal curve in its standard form, which is with a mean of zero and a standard deviation of 1. It is noted that the curve is asymptotic at $Z = -3$ and $Z = +3$.

The area under the curve is equal to 1.00 or 100% and therefore can be easily used for probability calculations. ▷**mean and standard deviation**

statistical probability, 6-sigma A statistical probability in manufacturing that greater than 99.9% of all manufactured parts in a lot of 1 billion will fall within specification.

statistical process control SPC seeks to closely control the manufacturing process and permits the manufacture of tighter-tolerance parts by indicating when a process is starting to drift away from the ideal set point. There are basically two possible approaches for real-time SPC. The first, done online, involves the rapid dimensional measurement of a part or a nondimensional "bulk" parameter such as weight, and is the more practical method. In contrast to weight, other dimensional measurements of the precision needed for SPC are generally done off-line, the second approach, and result in a response that is too slow. Also obtaining the final dimensional stability needed to measure a molded part may take time; as an example, amorphous injection molded plastics usually require at least 30 to 60 minutes to cool and stabilize. There are common features of SPC that can be applied to different processes such as raw material characterization, internal handling (drying, blending, etc.), and implementation (including commitment of management). With the use of part or shot weight (injection molding) for SPC, the data developed can go directly into an operator's statistical display or even be used in simple manual plotting. However, weight is a variable property, and confusion over the weight response can lead to the rejection of its use as a reliable indicator of quality. There are two common reasons why the use of weight is rejected. First, it is not likely that an absolute weight correlation will always occur. However, even if it is not perfect, it can still be a useful characteristic unless "absolute perfection" is needed. Second, the weighing method may not be reliable. Modern scales, with powerful internal error reduction algorithms, must be used. The most common error is simply improper selection of the scale's resolution: for a shot weight of 100 g, weigh to 0.001 g; for a shot weight of 100 to 999 g, weigh to 0.01 g. ▷**process control** and **zero defect**

statistical process control computerized ▷**computer processing control, statistically**

statistical quality control SQC measures product quality and provides a tracking mechanism to reveal any shifts in levels of quality. SQC is a derivative practice based on the results of SPC. Conceptually, SQC can reject parts that do not conform to the approved standard sample. In practice, parts are physically rejected and diverted into reclamation systems or review bins for potential reclamation, and alarms are provided at the machine and at the central computer to inform management personnel. The benefit of SQC is in the prevention of defective parts. The savings can be considerable. SQC starts when machine data are compared to the process control limits during production; typically measures a statistical sample of the product run against a set of norms.

statistical randomization A method of sequencing experiments by using a random number table so that each experiment in the proposed plan has an equal chance of being the first, second, or last experiment. This is an extremely effective technique for minimizing errors.

statistical regression method ▷**regression method**

statistical thermodynamic A discipline that tries to compute macroscopic properties of materials from more basic structures of matter. These properties are not necessarily static properties as in conventional mechanics. The problems in statistical thermodynamics fall into two categories. First it involves the study of the structure of phenomenological frameworks and the interrelations among observable macroscopic quantities. The secondary category involves the calculation of the actual values of phenomenological parameters appearing in the phenomenology, such as viscosity or phase transition temperatures, from more microscolic parameters.

With this technique, understanding general relations requires only a model specified by fairly broad and abstract conditions. Realistically detailed models are not needed to understand general properties of a class of materials. Understanding more specific relations requires microscopically detailed models.

steam cured XLPE ▷**crosslinked polyethylene plastic**

steam foam molding ▷**expandable polystyrene**

steam sterilization ▷**sterilization, heat**

steatite Insulating materials made from talc plus clay.

steel An alloy of iron as the principal metal with carbon. It is a very versatile material. The carbon content markedly affects the microstructure and hence, its properties. In steels the carbon content is 0.02 to 1%; in cast irons there is 2 to $3\frac{1}{2}$% carbon. Low carbon or mild steels contain 0.02 to 0.3% carbon. There are many special-purpose types of alloy steels in which one or more alloying metals are used, with or without special heat treatments. The most common additives are chromium and nickel, as in 18-8 stainless steels; they add greatly to corrosion resistance. High speeds and tool steels designed primarily for efficient cutting, contain such alloying metals as tungsten, molybdenum, manganese, and vanadium, as well as chromium. Cobalt and zirconium are used for construction steels.

steel reinforced concrete A composite that combines steel and concrete. ▷ **concrete-plastic**

steel resource in U.S. limited Did you know that it was predicted that U.S. iron ore bodies in the Lake Superior district (U.S.) would be exhausted in the early 1970s? Chances for discoveries of big new ore bodies were nil. That grim forecast made news in 1938 at the annual meeting of a mining and engineering association. It was recalled by Dr. Raymond L. Smith, President, Michigan Technological University, ironically, at the dedication of upper Michigan's Tilden mine, managed by Cleveland-Cliffs Iron Company in 1970. Those forecasters of yesteryear apparently did not consider the role technology would play in meeting the challenge. The existence of the Tilden ore body, and others like it, was known when the forecast was made. However, they were pretty much discounted because no economically feasible process was available to tap low-iron-content ore bodies.

The mining industry, however, was not inclined to believe statements that it was digging its own grave. Pelletizing was perfected, and that development made it feasible to mine low-iron-bearing ores. Concentrating techniques were researched. Cleveland-Cliffs, working with the U.S. Bureau of Mines and steel companies, invested millions of dollars and 25 years in perfecting a chemical technique to concentrate the Tilden's nonmagnetic iron deposits. These pioneering efforts paid off. As Dr. Smith said, "Here we are, not closing shop but celebrating a grand opening". ▷ **plastic bad and other myths**

steel rule die ▷ **die cutting**

steel, stainless Alloy steel containing at least 10 to 25% chromium. There are three groups: (1) austenitic which contains chromium (16% min.) and nickel (7% min.), a stress corrosion resistant type containing 2% silicon; (2) ferritic which contains chromium only and cannot be hardened by heat treatment; and (3) martensitic which contains chromium and can be hardened by heat treatment.

steel wire Steel is the basic metal of modern society. The strongest, most versatile, most economical form of steel is wire. In some sizes, steel wire may be produced with a tensile strength as high as 500,000 psi (3,445 MPa).

stenciling ▷ **photoimage**

step-growth polymerization ▷ **bulk polymerization**

step-reaction polymerization It refers to a mechanism in which the general reaction involves two molecules or molecular fragments of arbitrary size. Their classes include condensation polymerization and rearrangement by skeletal bond interchange.

steradian The solid angle which, having its vertex in the center of a sphere, cuts off an area of the surface of the sphere equal to that of a square with sides of length equal to the radius of the sphere.

stereoisomer An isomer in which atoms are linked in the same order but differ in their arrangement; side changes or side atoms are arranged on the same side of a double bond present in a chain of atoms.

stereoisomer, trans- A trans-stereoisomer is a stereoisomer in which atoms or groups of atoms are arranged on opposite sides of a chain of atoms.

stereolithography modeling ▷ **modeling stereolithography**

stereospecific catalyst An organometallic catalyst, such as the Natta catalyst, which permits control of the molecular geometry of plastic molecules.

stereospecificity A tendency for plastics to form with an ordered spatial three-dimensional arrangement of monomer molecules.

stereospecific (stereoregular) plastic A plastic whose molecular structure has a definite orderly arrangement, i.e., a fixed position in geometrical space for the constituent atoms and atomic groups comprising the molecular chain, rather than the random and varying arrangement that characterizes an amorphous plastic. Achievement of this specific steric (3-dimensional) structure, that is also called tacticity or stereoregular, requires use of special catalysts such as those developed by Ziegler and Natta during the 1950s. Such plastics are wholly or partially crystalline. Synthetic natural rubbers (elastomers), cis-polyisoptenes and polypropylenes are examples of a stereospecific plastic made possible by this means which permits close packing of the molecules and leads to high crystallinity. There are five types of structures: cis, trans, isotactic, sydiotactic, and tritactic. Each of these types have molecules in which groups of atoms that are not part of the backbone structure are located in some symmetrical (each with its own) and recurring fashion above and below the atoms in the backbone chain, when the latter are arranged so as to be in a single plane.

steric hindrance A characteristic of molecular structure in which the molecules have a spatial arrangement of their atoms such that a given reaction with another molecule is prevented or retarded. ▷ **molecular arrangement structure** and **non-staining antioxidant**

sterilization The complete destruction of all bacteria and other infectious organisms in a product such as in industrial, medical, or food products; it usually must be followed by aseptic packaging to prevent recontamination, usually by hermetic sealing. The method of sterilization must not affect material properties, contaminate, or alter the product's geometry. Techniques are categorized as physical or chemical. Physical methods include dry heat, steam, and ionizing radiation. Chemical methods are also widely used. Ethylene oxide (EtO) is effective at relatively low temperatures, with good penetration into porous materials. Other chemical sterilants include ozone, propylene oxide, formaldehyde, glutaraldehyde, phenols, quaternary salts, and hypochlorite. All must be removed completely before use, particularly in medical devices.

sterilization, dry-heat ▷ **sterilization, heat**

sterilization, ethylene oxide Numerous standards, guidelines, and technical publications have been written on the subject of EtO cycle development and validation procedures. One of the most widely accepted is ANSI's Guideline for Industrial EtO Sterilization of Medical Devices: Process Design, Validation, Routine Sterilization, and Contract Sterilization.

sterilization, heat Both steam and dry-heat sterilization are heat methods used extensively in hospitals. Steam is used to sterilize the majority of prefilled syringes, dressings, bandages, and selected products such as sponges, brushes, and swabs. Dry heat is used, although less frequently than steam, for examining gloves, bandages, and dressings.

Steam sterilization, also known as autoclaving, involves exposure of the material to saturated steam at temperatures higher than 100°C (212°F) for a predetermined length of time. The temperature selected for a particular purpose will depend on the thermal stability of the product and its packaging material. Thermal stability is achieved by adjusting the pressure within the autoclave. The limiting factor in the overall growth pattern of steam sterilization is the ability of the product and package to withstand high temperatures. Packaging materials that can withstand steam include plastics (PET, PP, etc.) 40-lb paper, etc. Exposure time required to effect sterilization is in inverse ratio to the heat used. Exposure to steam at 121°C (250°F) for 30 min. or at 132°C (270°F) for 3 min. reduces the bacterial population to almost zero.

Dry-heat sterilization is carried out in a hot-air oven. Because microorganisms are more resistant to dry heat than to wet heat, the temperatures used are higher and the exposure times longer than those used for autoclave. Typical temperatures range from 163°C (325°F) for 2 hr to 177°C (350°F) for 1 hr. Dry-heat for packaging is used only when there is some positive advantage over steam such as better surface accessibility for sterilization or when traces of moisture left in the packages are objectionable. Dry-heat is the least used by the health industry since it has limitations compared to steam, such as packaging materials coupled with a lengthy total processing time.

sterilization, radiation Fundamentally radiation is emission of energy such as light and heat or the transfer of energy through space by electromagnetic waves. Irradiation basically identifies the radiant energy per unit of intercepting area. It affects plastics in different ways, such as degrading them or improving properties and performance. Most nontechnical people only consider that radiation results in degradation; however, irradiation of plastics is an important science for packaging sterilized medical products, curing plastics, converting certain TPs to TSs, etc.

stet A proofreader's mark, written in the margin, signifying that copy marked for corrections should remain as originally prepared.

sticking 1. Moldings tend to stick in the mold by mechanical or vacuum adhesion of the molding to the mold surface, making ejection difficult. Sometimes this fault occurs at the sprue. Different corrective actions can be taken, such as the use of parting agents, mechanical mold ejectors, and compressed air ejection. **2.**

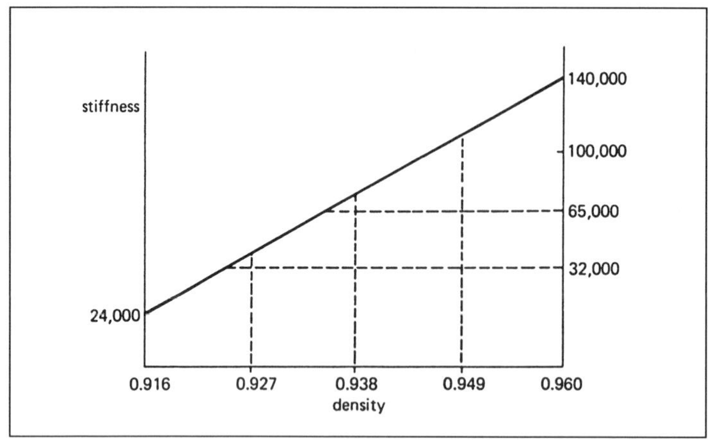

Effect of crystallinity on stiffness of polyethylene.

Extruded film or sheet stacked tend to stick or block without antiblocking additives.

stiffness **1.** A measure of modulus for a particular material; the relationship of load and deformation; the ratio between the applied stress and resulting strain. A term often used when the relationship of stress-strain does not conform to the definition of Young's modulus. **2.** With thermoplastics, crystallinity can influence the plastic's stiffness (see Fig. above).

stiffness constant ▷ **modulus**

stiffness in flexure In a standard ASTM flexural test, the test does not distinguish the plastic and elastic elements involved in the measurement and therefore a true elastic modulus is not calculable. Instead, an apparent value is obtained and sometimes called "stiffness in flexure". It is a measure of the relative stiffness of various plastics and taken with other pertinent property data is useful in material selection.

stir-in plastic A vinyl plastic that does not require grinding to effect dispersion in a plastisol or organisol.

stitching The progressive welding of thermoplastics by successive applications of two small mechanically operated electrodes, connected to the output terminals of an RF generator, using a mechanism similar to that of a normal sewing machine.

stock Another term used for plastic or plastic melt.

stoichiometry The control of tolerances, levels, and amounts in a chemical mix. When exact amounts necessary for reactions are present without excess reactants, the reaction is said to be stoichiometric. ▷ **flame treating** and **reactor technology**

stoke The unit of kinematic viscosity. It is obtained by dividing the absolute viscosity of a fluid by the density of the fluid. A centipoise is 0.01 of a stoke.

Stoke's law **1.** In atomic processes, the wavelength of fluorescent radiation is always longer than that of the exciting radiation. **2.** The rate at which a sperical particle will rise or fall when suspended in a liquid medium varies as the square of its radius; the density of the particle and the density and viscosity of the liquid are essential factors. This law is used in determining sedimentation of solids, etc.

stone Different stone aggregates (pebbles, powder, etc.) are used as a filler and/or reinforcement in plastics, particularly thermosets.

storage **1.** Any method of keeping materials, products, tools, etc. while awaiting use, transportation, or consumption. **2.** It is often applied to various forms of wastes, but the more accurate term is disposal. ▷ **solid waste**

storage life ▷ **shelf life**

straightness The ability of a system to move an object along a perfectly straight path.

strain The per unit change, due to force, in the size or shape of a body referred to its original size or shape. There are six components of strain: three linear and three shear. In the usual tension, compression, and torsion test, it is customary to measure only one component of strain and to refer to this as the strain. In tension and compression, it is the axial component. Strain is a nondimensional quantity, but it is usually expressed in in./in., m/m, or percent. Strain reviewed is sometimes called engineering strain. ▷ **strain, true** and **stress**

strain aging Aging induced by cold working.

strain, alternating amplitude Analogous to ▷ **stress, alternating amplitude;** a sequence of alternating stress amplitude.

strain amplitude The ratio of maximum deformation, measured from the mean deformation to the free length of the unstrained test specimen. Strain amplitude is measured from zero to peak on one side only.

strain, angular ▷ **shear strain**

strain, axial The linear strain in a plane parallel to the longitudinal axis of the specimen.

strain, critical The strain at the yield point.

strain determination in reinforced plastic ▷ **nondestructive testing**

strain, elastic ▷ **photoelastic stress analysis**

strainer Device designed to force a melt through a sieve(s) to remove extraneous matter. ▷ **screen pack** and **calendering**

strain, fiber optic ▷ **fiber optic strain gauge**

strain, flexure of fiber The maximum strain in the outer fiber occurring at mid-span in a reinforced plastic test specimen.

strain, frozen ▷ **residual stress**

strain gauge Device to measure strain, either mechanical or electrical resistance in a stressed material. A resistive element, with or without a carrier, that is attached to a solid body by cementing (such as an SR-4 gauge), welding, or other suitable techniques so that the resistance of the element will vary as the surface to which it is applied is deformed. The measured strain in a stressed material is based on the change in electrical resistance element. ▷ **fiber optic strain gauge** and **melt pressure transducer types**

strain gauge length Length over which deformation is measured, for tensile or compressive test specimen. The deformation over the gauge length divided by the original gauge length determines strain.

strain hardening An increase in hardness and strength caused by plastic deformation at temperatures lower than the recrystallization range.

strain, linear The change per unit length (that is, percent deformation) due to an applied force in an original linear dimension.

strain, macro- Macrostrain is the mean strain over any finite gauge length of measurement large in comparison with interatomic distances.

strain, mean Analogous to **stress, mean.**

strain, natural Also called logarithmic strain or true strain. ▷ **strain, true**

strain, nominal The strain at a point calculated in the net cross section by simple elastic theory without taking into account the effect on strain produced by geometric discontinuities such as holes, grooves, fillets, etc.

strain rate Rate of change with time.

strain ratio The algebraic ratio of two specified strain values in a strain cycle. Two commonly used ratios are that of the strain amplitude to the mean strain and the ratio of the minimum strain to the maximum strain.

strain relaxation Reduction in internal strain over time. Molecular processes are similar to those that occur in creep, except that the body is constrained. ▷ **creep relaxation**

strain relief A dimensional change brought about by subjecting the material to an elevated temperature.

strain, residual The strain associated with residual stress. ▷ **residual stress** and **nondestructive testing method, residual strain**

strain, root-mean-square ▷ **root-mean-square strain**

strain, rupture ▷ **rupture**

strain, shear The tangent of the angular change, caused by a force between two lines originally perpendicular to each other through a point in a body. Also called angular strain. ▷ **shear** and **extensional-shear coupling**

strain, thermal Linear thermal expansion, sometimes called thermal strain (or changes due to the effect of heat). It is not to be considered strain in mechanical testing.

strain, transverse The linear strain in a plane perpendicular to the loading axis of a specimen.

strain, true In a material subjected to axial force, the natural logarithm of the ratio of the gauge length at the moment of observation to the original gauge length. ▷ **fracture strength or stress**

strand Normally, an untwisted bundle or assembly of continuous filaments used as a unit, including slivers, tows, ends, yarn, etc. Sometimes a single fiber or filament is called a strand. The usual strand has 51, 102, or 204 filaments gathered together in the filament forming operations.

strand count The number of strands in a plied yarn, or a roving.

strand integrity The degree to which the individual filaments making up a strand or end are held together by the applied sizing.

strapping tape Extruded strapping tape is an example of a whole family of materials. This basically narrow-width sheeting that is usually oriented to maximize its performance has important uses in packaging applications where only steel strapping had previously been available. Steel and plastic strappings each have their own advantages and disadvantages, so the designer can select the best type based on the product's requirements. For example, when strapping is used where the heat could fluctuate, as in a railroad boxcar or storage room, the steel at high temperature could expand and cause what it contained to become loose. The elastic deformation of plastics lets them retain their tension with temperature change, however.

Some typical strapping properties for PP, nylon, polyester (TP) and low-carbon steel are as follows: the breaking strength of a piece $\frac{1}{2}$ in. wide by 0.020 in. thick is 500, 640, 600, and 1,200 lbs, respectively; the working-range elongation is 5, 7, $2\frac{1}{2}$, and 1/10 percent; the elongation recovery in in. is 5.5, 9, 2, and 1/10; the ratio of retained tension at maximum working range to a time after 24 hours is (in psi) 200/50, 250/175, 300/244, and 700/665; their heat resistance is fair, good, good, and excellent, respectively; and their humidity resistance is excellent, fair, excellent, and excellent. ▷ **orientation**

straw A fibrous, cellulosic component of cereal plants (wheat, rice, etc.). Its fibers are 1 to 1.5 mm long, similar to those of hardwoods. Straw can be pulped by the alkaline process to yield specialty papers of high quality. Use of straw for paper-making is of limited importance in the U.S. due to the abundance of pulpwood.

strength 1. The stress required to break, rupture, or cause a failure. **2.** The property of a material that resists deformation induced by external forces. **3.** Maximum stress which a material can resist without failure for given type of loading. ▷ **stress** and **tensile testing machine test rates**

strength, breaking ▷ **fracture strength or stress**

strength, bursting A measure of the ability of a material to withstand hydrostatic pressure without rupture. It is obtained from a pressure test for rigid materials or a bursting test for flexible materials. For metals it is generally the maximum hoop stress sustained by a material prior to rupture. For glass or rigid plastics it may be the maximum radial stress sustained by a material prior to rupture, in which case bursting strength is valid only for material of the same dimensions. For flexible sheet and film materials, bursting strength is calculated by dividing maximum net pressure observed in the bursting test by cross-section area of the exposed diaphragm portion of the specimen.

strength, cross breaking Alternative name for flexural strength.

strength, dielectric ▷ **dielectric strength**

strength, dry ▷ **dry strength**

strength, electrical ▷ **electrical strength or dielectric strength**

strength, Elmendorf ▷ **Elmendorf tear test** that involves tear strength.

strengthening plastics mechanisms With some exceptions, strengthening of plastics is the job of the polymer chemist. Exceptions include where polyamide-imide and phenolic can be increased in strength by a postmolding thermal treatment (such as heat treating steels). Additives and particularly reinforcing fibers can significantly increase properties. ▷ **polymerization; orientation; chemistry; oxidation degradation; reinforced plastic**

strength, fracture ▷ **fracture strength or stress**

strength, green ▷ **tensile green strength**

strength, melt ▷ **melt strength**

strength of materials ▷ **design theory and strength of materials**

strength ratio The hypothetical ratio of the strength of a product to the strength it would have if no weakening defects are present.

strength, rupture ▷ **rupture strength**

strength, true ▷ **fracture strength or stress**

strength, ultimate The maximum unit stress a material will withstand when subjected to an applied load in a tension, compression, or shear test.

strength, wet ▷ **wet strength**

strength, yield Also called yield point. The stress (strength) on the stress-strain curve where the test specimen experiences a relatively large increase in deformation with no increase in load. This is the ideal situation based on what is considered a perfectly elastic material. Actually the usual stress-strain curves show (for neat plastics) that the stresses are actually reduced while the strains continue. After a period of strain, the material can recover and continue to increase in stress (at a much reduced rate) with increasing strain. Where confusion might result in specifying the yield strength, usually an offset is used ▷ **stress, offset yield strength**. Basically the yield strength is the lowest stress at which a material undergoes plastic deformation. Below this stress, the material is considered elastic; above it is viscous.

stress 1. The intensity at a point in a body (product, material, etc.) of the forces or components of force that act on a given plane through the point. Stress is expressed in force per unit area (psi, kPa, MPa, or others). As used in tension, compression, or shear tests as prescribed in product specifications, stress is calculated on the basis of the original dimensions of the cross section of the specimen. This stress is sometimes called engineering stress; it is different from ▷ **stress, true**. **2.** Internal force exerted by either of two adjacent parts of a body upon the other across an imagined plane of separation. When the forces are parallel to the plane, the stress is called shear stress; when the forces are normal to the plane, the stress is called normal stress; when the normal stress is directed toward the part on which it acts, it is called tensile stress. Shear, compressive, and tensile stresses, respectively, resist the tendency of the parts to mutually slide, approach, or separate under the action of applied force.

stress, alternating amplitude A stress varying between two maximum values that are equal but of opposite signs (+ and −); test parameter of a dynamic fatigue test with one half of the algebraic difference between the maximum and minimum stress in one cycle.

stress amplitude The ratio of the maximum applied force, measured from the mean force to the cross sectional area of the unstressed test specimen.

stress analysis, photoelastic ▷ **photoelastic stress analysis**

stress concentration On a macromechanical level, the magnification of the level of an applied stress in the region of a notch, void, hole, or inclusion.

stress concentration factor The ratio of the maximum stress in the region of a stress concentrator to the stress in a similarly strained area without a stress concentrator.

stress corrosion Preferential attack of areas under stress in a corrosive environment, where such an environment alone would not have caused corrosion. ▷ **corrosion**

stress corrosion crack A crack which may be intergranular or transgranular depending on the material, resulting from the combined action of corrosion and stress, either external (applied) or internal (residual) or both.

stress corrosion cracking Alternative name for ▷ **environmental stress cracking**

stress crack An external or internal crack in a plastic caused by tensile stresses less than its short time mechanical strength.

stress crack failure Failure of a material by cracking or crazing some time after it has been placed under load. Time-to-failure may range from minutes to many years. Causes include internal processing frozen stresses, postfabrication shrinkage or warpage, and hostile environment.

stress crack model ▷ **fracture, plane stress**

stress, crystallization induced The production of crystals in a plastic by the action of stress, usually in the form of an elongation. It occurs in rubber elongation, fiber spinning, etc. and results in improved mechanical properties.

stress, cure Cure stress is a residual internal stress produced during the thermoset curing cycle of reinforced plastics. Normally these stresses originate when different components of a processing lay-up, particularly wet lay-up, have different thermal coefficients of expansion.

stress decay ▷ **stress relaxation**

stress deflection ▷ **deflection**

stress determination in reinforced plastic ▷ **photoelastic stress analysis**

stress, elastic limit The greatest stress which a material is capable of sustaining without permanent strain remaining upon the complete release of the stress. A material is said to have passed its elastic limit when the load is sufficient to initiate "plastic" or nonrecoverable deformation.

stress, elastic limit, apparent An arbitrary approximation of elastic limit for a material that does not exhibit a significant proportional limit. It is obtained from a stress-strain diagram and is equal to the stress at which the rate of strain is 50% greater than at zero stress. It is determined as the stress at a point of tangency between the S–S curve and a line having a slope with respect to the stress axis 50% greater than the slope of the curve at the origin.

stress, engineering The stress calculated on the basis of the original dimensions of test specimen. This value of stress is used in material specifications, quality control, etc. ▷ **stress, true**

stresses, cooling During melt processing, plastic melts are subjected to processing forces. They can remain in the plastic during cooling as frozen stresses. Usually they are not a problem in the finished product; however, with excess stresses, the product could be damaged quickly or from a short to long-time. ▷**residual stress** and **stress, frozen-in**

stress, fracture The true normal stress on the minimum cross sectional area at the beginning of fracture; usually applies to tension tests of unnotched specimens.

stress, frozen-in Undesirable "frozen-in" or residual stresses are often the result of non-uniform cooling of the part while in the mold or overpacking of the mold cavity during injection-mold stage. Thermally-induced stresses occur when one region of the part cools more rapidly than adjacent areas. The residual stresses may show up as non-uniform shrinkage. The degree of shrinkage is influenced by mold and melt temperature, injection pressure and part design. Since shrinkage is temperature dependent, cooler regions shrink sooner than hotter areas. Non-uniform cooling in a part of complex geometry can create a complicated stress distribution throughout its volume. In order to minimize residual stress, part wall thickness should be uniform to prevent even cooling. The substantial frictional forces developed between part and mold surfaces during ejection can also contribute to residual stress. In most cases, good mold design can eliminate this potential hazard. The inclusion of a sufficient draft angle on deep-reaching walls and minimization or elimination of undercuts are just a few ways to reduce ejection resistance. ▷**orientation** and **residual stress**

stress-induced, orientation ▷**orientation, theory of stress induced**

stress, initial The stresses introduced into a specimen by imposing the given constraint conditions before stress relaxation takes place. Sometimes referred to as instantaneous stress.

stress intensity factor A constant that relates the design limit for the normal stress to the depth of a propagating crack; applies to a given steel.

stress, internal for adhesive Stress created within a material, such as an adhesive layer, by the movement of the adherends at differential rates or by the contraction or expansion of the adhesive layer.

stress, mean A dynamic fatigue parameter. The algebraic mean of the maximum and minimum stress in one cycle (psi or MPa) thus:

$$\text{mean stress or } \bar{\sigma} = \tfrac{1}{2}(\sigma_1 + \sigma_2)$$

where σ_1 = maximum stress, σ_2 = minimum stress.

stress, molded-in ▷**stress, frozen-in**

stress, nominal The stress at a point calculated on the net cross section without taking into consideration the effect on stress of geometric discontinuities, such as holes, grooves, fillets, etc. The calculations are made using simple elastic theory.

stress, normal The stress component that is perpendicular to the plane on which the forces act. They may be either: normal tensile stress due to forces directed away from the plane on which they act, or normal compressive stress due to the forces directed toward the plane on which they act.

stress-number of cycles ▷**fatigue S-N diagram**

stress, offset yield strength The stress at which the strain exceeds by a specified amount (the offset) an extension of the initial proportional portion of the stress strain curve. It is expressed in force per unit area, usually kPa, MPa, or psi. This measurement is useful for materials whose stress-strain curve in the yield range is of gradual curvature. The offset yield strength can be derived from the stress-strain curve (see Fig. below) by a specified strain offset (O–M) called by the percent of strain (such as the usual 0.01%, 0.1%, or 0.2%; how-

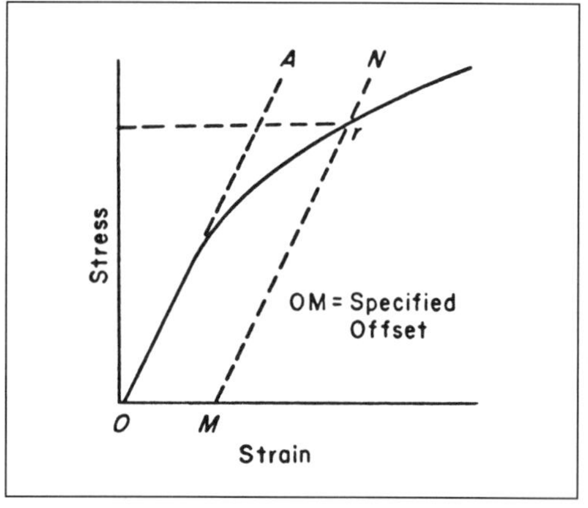

Example of determining from the stress-strain curve the offset yield strength (the stress at which the strain exceeds by a specified percentage).

ever, any amount can be used). From point M, a straight line (M–N) is drawn parallel to the straight line (O–A) portion of the stress-strain curve. Where line M–N intersects the stress-strain curve (r) is the offset yield strength.

stress, optical coefficient ▷ **coefficient of optical stress**

stress orientation ▷ **orientation** and **crystallization**

stress, plane Plane stress or biaxial stress is a state of stress in which the normal stress to the plane under consideration is zero. Thus a thin sheet parallel to this plane has stress-free surfaces. If the Z-direction is that of the normal to the plane, then it is a principal direction, because the shear stresses are zero.

stress, principal (normal) The maximum or minimum value of the normal stress at a point in a plane considered with respect to all possible orientations of the considered plane. On such principal planes the shear stress is zero.

There are three principal stresses on three mutually perpendicular planes. The states of stress at a point may be: (1) uniaxial—a state of stress in which two of the three principal stresses are zero, (2) biaxial—a state of stress in which only one of the three principal stresses is zero, or (3) triaxial—a state of stress in which none of the principal stresses is zero. There is also a multiaxial condition that refers to either biaxial or triaxial. ▷ **orientation**

stress ratio The algebraic ratio of two specified stress values in a stress cycle. Two commonly used stress ratios are: (1) the ratio of the stress amplitude to the mean stress and (2) the ratio of the minimum stress to the maximum stress.

stress relaxation Basically the decrease in stress under sustained, constant strain; also called stress decay. It is the relatively slow decay of the stress when a viscoelastic material (plastic) is held at a constant strain after being rapidly stressed initially. Characterized by the time-dependent stress relaxation modulus, defined as the ratio of the stress to the fixed strain. Usually the stress decays exponentially and at sufficiently long times may become zero if viscous flow takes place. However, if the material retains some rigidity, eventually a constant finite stress level is reached, corresponding to an equilibrium or relaxed stress relaxation modulus. Like creep, stress relaxation is one of the most commonly performed types of viscoelastic experiment. Quantitatively, the stress decays in a similar manner to the increase in creep strain with time and shows similar temperature dependence and time-temperature superposition. The rate of the stress decay is determined by the relaxation time, which is similar, but not identical to, the retardation time of creep.

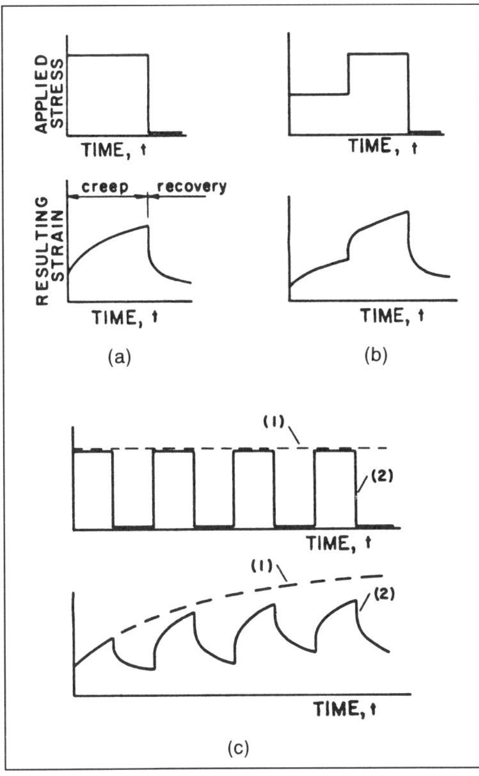

Examples of stress relaxation behavior under various intermittent and cyclic loads: (*a*) recovery after creep, (*b*) strain increment due to stress step function, and (*c*) strain with the same stress applied (1) continuously and (2) intermittently.

Stress relaxation behaviour is often presented in the form of graphs (see Fig. above). The simplest graph is a plot of stress versus time. From the graph, stress relaxation is the difference between stress at the specified time and initial stress. Such curves can be plotted for several different temperatures at one constant strain, or both. From such curves can be determined, for example, the loss in bolting pressure that would be caused by stress relaxation over a period of several days at high temperature. Stress relaxation rate can also be determined. ▷ **relaxation** and **viscoelasticity**

stress relieving Heating to a suitable temperature, holding long enough to reduce residual stresses and then cooling slowly enough to minimize the development of new residual stresses.

stress, remaining The stress remaining at a given time during stress relaxation test.

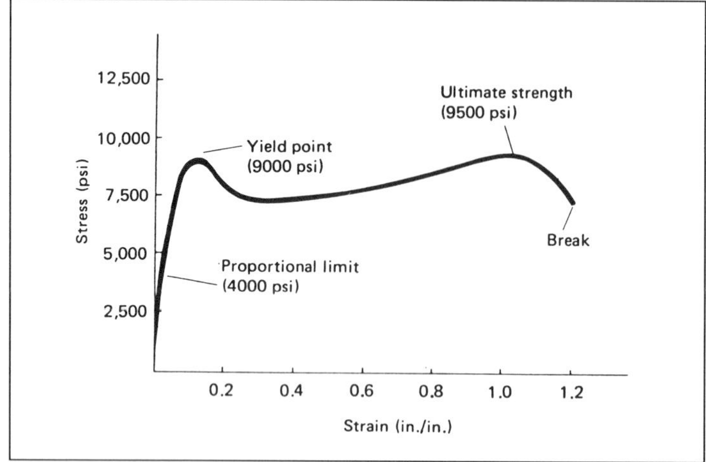

Example of a commodity plastic's stress-strain diagram.

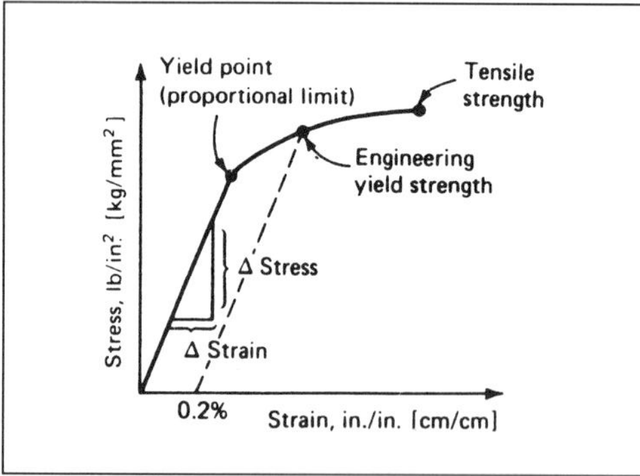

Example of modulus determined on the initial straight portion of the stress-strain diagram.

stress, residual The stress existing in a body at rest, in equilibrium, at uniform temperature, and not subjected to external forces. Often caused by the processing of plastics. ▷ **residual stress; thermal stress; crazing**

stress riser ▷ **stress concentration**

stress, shear The stress component tangential to a given plane. ▷ **shear stress**

stress softening The smaller stress required to strain a material to a certain strain, after a prior cycle of stressing to the same strain followed by removal of the stress. Mostly observed in filled elastomers or rubbers (when it is known as the Mullins effect), where it results from the detachment of some plastic molecules from filler particles in the first cycle and which therefore cannot support the stress on subsequent straining to the same strain.

stress, static A stress in which the force is constant or slowly increasing with time.

stress-strain curve or diagram A curve or graphical representation of the stress and strain relationship of a material under test conditions of tension, compression, shear, or torsion. It is presented in a diagram where values of stress are usually plotted as ordinates (vertical) and values of strain as abscissas (horizontal) as shown in the Figs.

stress-strain measurements Testing machines can provide and develop stress-strain curves. Different types of extensometers are used on test specimens to record and plot strain measurements with stress loadings. ▷ **extensometer**

stress-strain ratio The ratio of stress to strain in a material at a specified stress or strain. Below the elastic limit it is also known as the secant modulus.

stress-strain, shear ▷ **shear stress-strain**

stress, thermal ▷ **thermal stress**

stress, torsional The shear stress on a transverse cross section resulting from a twisting action.

stress, true The stress along the axis calculated on the actual cross section at the time of observation instead of the original cross sectional area. Applicable to tension and compression testing. ▷ **stress, engineering**

stress whitening The appearance of white regions in a material when it is stressed. Stress whitening or crazing is damage that can occur when a TP is stretched near its yield point. The surface takes on a whitish appearance in regions that are under high stress. Crazing is usually associated with yielding. For practical purposes stress whitening is the result of the formation of microcracks or crazes, which is another form of damage. Crazes are not true fractures, because they contain strings of highly oriented plastic that connect the two flat faces of the crack. These fibrils are surrounded by air voids. Because they are filled with highly oriented fibrils, crazes are capable of carrying stress, unlike true fractures. As a result, a heavily crazed part can still carry significant stress, even though the part may appear to be fractured.

It is important to note that crazes, microcracking, and stress whitening represent irreversible first damage to a material, which could ultimately cause failure. This damage usually lowers the impact strength and other properties of a material compared to those of undamaged plastics. One reason is that it exposes the interior of the plastic to attack and subsequent deterioration by aggressive fluids. In the total design evaluation, the formation of stress cracking or crazing damage should be a criterion for failure, based on the stress applied. ▷ **environmental stress cracking** and **crazing**

stress wrinkle Distortions in the face of a bonded laminate caused by uneven web tensions, slowness of adhesive setting or curing, selective absorption of the adherends, and/or by reaction of the adherends with material in the adhesive.

stretch 1. An increase or elongation in dimension. **2.** ▷ **orientation**

stretch blow molding ▷ **blow molding, stretched**

striae Surface or internal thread-like inhomogeneities in transparent plastics.

striation 1. A separation of colors resulting in a linear effect of color variation. **2.** A rippling of thick extruded blow molded parisons caused by a local orientation effect in the melt by uneven temperature of melt, spider legs in die, etc. **3.** ▷ **flow line 4.** A fracture surface marking consisting of a separation of the advancing crack front into separate fracture planes. Also known as coarse hackle, step fractures, or lances. They may also be known as shark's teeth and whiskers.

strip 1. Plastic parts can incorporate a transparent or color view striping during processing such as extrusion, blow molding, and injection molding. Similar or dissimilar plastics can be used. ▷ **blow molding stripping 2.** Removal of relatively volatile components from plastics by distillation or evaporation. ▷ **barrel, vent 3.** Rapid removal of color from an improperly dyed fiber or fabric by a chemical reaction. Used in vat dyeing or in discharge printing. Commonly used strippers are sodium hydrosulfide, titanous sulfate, sodium and zinc formaldehyde sulfoxylates.

strippable coating Temporary coatings applied to finished products to protect them from abrasion or corrosion during shipment and storage, and which can be removed when desired without damage to the product.

stripper plate ▷ **mold stripper plate**

stripping fork A tool, usually of brass or laminated sheet, used to remove parts from a mold. Also called comb.

stroboscope An instrument for determining speeds of rotation or frequencies of vibration made in the form of a revolving disk with holes around the edge through which an object is viewed or a rapidly flashing light that illuminates an object intermittently. ▷ **photoelasticity**

stroke 1. ▷ **screw plunger stroke 2.** ▷ **clamping stroke, maximum**

structural adhesive Adhesive used for transferring required loads between adherends exposed to service environments typical for the structure involved. They are available in different forms including paste, film, foam, water-based, solvent-based, and hot melt. Plastics used include acrylic, bismaleimide, cyanoacrylate, epoxy, nylon, polyimide, silicone, and polyurethane. The different forms and materials meet different requirements.

structural fairing A secondary structure, such as in airframes and ship hulls, the major function of which is to streamline the airflow or flow of fluid by producing a smooth outline and reducing drag.

structural foam ▷ **foamed, structural**

structural frame ▷ **design architectural space frame**

structural modeling plastic ▷ **designing with model, plastic-chemical structure**

structural modification ▷ **oxidation degradation** and **strengthening plastics mechanisms**

structural reaction injection molding ▷ **reinforced reaction injection molding**

structure Something made up of interdependent part(s) in a definite pattern of organization.

structure, integral ▷ **reinforced plastic, structural integrated**

structure, monocoque sandwich ▷ **aircraft**

structure, primary Mainframe of a product is the primary structure. Examples include aircraft main supports, building main beams, and automobile frame. If the primary structure fails, it would be damaging or catastrophic to the product and/or people.

structure, secondary The parts of a product that are not primary structures, so if they fail no major problem would develop and the product could still function. As an example, a structure in aircraft that is not critical to flight safety.

stuffing, injection molding ▷ **injection molding, plunger**

stuffing, mold ▷ **injection molding, plunger prepack**

St. Venant's principle In effect, it states that the stress and deflection of a member (such as handle and gear) at points sufficiently distant from points of load application may be determined on the basis of a statistical equivalent loading system.

S-twist fiber ▷ **twist, direction of yarn**

styrenated alkyd plastic ▷ **alkyd molding compound**

styrene A colorless liquid, easily polymerized by exposure to light, heat, or a peroxide catalyst. It is the monomer from which polystyrene is produced.

styrene-acrylonitrile copolymer SAN are amorphous, transparent plastics which are prepared by emulsion, suspension, or bulk polymerization processes. They differ from standard polystyrene in important properties such as toughness, heat resistance under load, chemical resistance, and resistance to stress cracking (crazing). SAN's properties are determined by the amount of acrylonitrile (AN), its molecular weight, and its molecular distribution. With the increased MW, toughness and long-term mechanical properties are improved, at the expense of good flow properties during processing. Increase in AN leads to improved chemical resistance, an increased hardness, and an increased heat resistance under load; at the same time the natural color changes.

styrene-acrylonitrile, olefin-modified plastic OSA (olefin-modified styrene-acrylonitrile) is a tough specialty engineering thermoplastic that resists changes in physical properties and color when exposed to weather. Use includes as a protective cap layer over a less costly substrate to enable cost-effective products.

styrene-alphamethylstyrene plastic P(S-AMS) is a styrene base plastic with a very high glass transition providing improved heat resistance.

styrene-based copolymer plastics The low cost of styrene monomer and the good processability of the plastic make it an attractive major (dominant) component for a wide range of copolymers that are relatively easy to polymerize.

styrene-butadiene elastomer This elastomer, SBR, emerged as a high-volume substitute for natural rubber (NR) during World War II because of its suitability for use in tires, belts, hoses, rubber floor tiles, and the like. Its tensile strength after compounding it with carbon black and vulcanizing it is 17 to 24 MPa (2,500 to 3,500 psi), which is less than NR's, but it has an elongation of 500 to 600%. In abrasion and skid resistance it is superior to NR, but has better resistance to solvents and weathering.

This general-purpose rubber continues to be used in many applications where it has replaced NR, even though it does not have NR's overall versatility, because it meets its performance requirements but has a cost advantage over NR. For most uses SBR must be reinforced to have acceptable strength, tear resistance, and general durability. It is significantly less resilient than NR, so it has higher heat buildup upon flexing. It also lacks NR's green strength and tack.

styrene-maleic anhydride plastic SMA copolymers of styrene and maleic anhydride result in higher heat resistance than the parent styrenic and ABS families.

styrene-methylmethacrylate plastic P(S-MMA) or SMMA has improved weatherability and impact properties of polystyrene for transparent applications.

styrene monomer Styrene with purity of 99.6 wt.% minimum. This water-thin liquid is used to produce plastics and to thin thermoset polyester plastics (and acts as its crosslinking agent).

styrene monomer emission A potential workplace hazard in regard to toxic or carcinogenic properties of styrene. Legal limits are set up by regulations in the workplace. Solutions to this problem have been developing with more use of other reactive monomers (that have been used). They include para-methylstyrene (PMS), vinyl toluene (VT), and diallyl phthlate (DAP).

styrene oligablock copolymers The thermoplastic elastomer-styrenic (TPE-S) is the oldest and most rubber-like of the TPE types. They are relatively low in cost. Their present use has been extending through improved compounding, including the addition of polyimides, polyesters, etc. modifiers. They are made from "living polymers" using bioorganic catalysts. By this means it is possible to produce linear or star-shaped block copolymers. Such plastics can be designed and tailored to give desired properties. The morphology of these block copolymers determines whether their properties are predominantly elastomeric or rigid plastic. Their heat deformation temperatures are relatively low, from 80 to 120°C (176 to 248°F) depending on type plastic used. The main market growth is likely to be in non-elastomer products.

styrene-paramethylstyrene plastic This general purpose plastic [P(S-PMS)] has commercial success because of its low cost.

styrene plastic ▷ **polystyrene plastic**

styrene-rubber plastic Identifies different plastics based on styrene polymers and rubbers, styrene being the greatest by mass.

styrenic plastics The family of styrenics includes: acrylonitrile-butadiene-styrene, acrylonitrile-chlorinated polyethylene-styrene, acrylic-styrene-acrylonitrile, crystal clear, impact resistant polystyrene, expandable polystyrene, high impact polystyrene, olefin-modified SAN, polyparamethylstyrene, polyalphamethylstyrene, styrene-acrylonitrile, styrene-butadiene, and styrene-maleic anhydride.

Styrofoam Dow Chemical's tradename for its expandable polystyrene.

styrol The name given to styrene by the chemist who first observed the monomer in 1839. The name was changed to styrene by German researchers in about 1925.

sublimable dye transfer Dye transfer resembles hot stamping, but instead of a foil, a paper liner printed with sublimable dyes is used. These dyes sublime upon the application of heat and are transferred to the plastic. The pattern is not deposited on the plastic surface, but diffuses into the plastic, thus providing a considerably more abrasive resistant image. The diffusing dye, however, gives a slightly blurred image. The usual operating temperature range is from 150 to 230°C (300 to 450°F); the dwell time is between 15 to 30 s. Thus, the plastic used should have a sufficiently high temperature resistance. It is limited to only a few selected plastics.

Sublimable dye transfer is an adaptation of a similar process developed for textile printing, especially for the printing of polyester fabrics. Its use for plastics has never developed to a large volume business because the process is rather slow compared to hot stamping or decal transfer, and the processing temperature is high.

sublimation The direct passage of a substance from solid to vapor without appearing in the intermediate (liquid) state.

submarine gate ▷ **mold gate**

substance Any chemical element or compound. All substances are characterized by a unique and identical constitution and are thus homogeneous materials.

substrate Any material which provides a supporting surface for other materials.

suck back ▷ **injection molding screw decompression**

sulfonation The introduction into an organic molecule of the sulfuric ester group where the sulfur is linked through an oxygen atom to the parent molecule. This chemical reaction changes properties of plastics. ▷ **barrier via chemical modification**

sulfone plastics These plastics emerged during the 1960s. They have the characteristic sulphone ($-SO_2$) groups with chain backbone of two phenyl groups. The expression diphenysulfone (DPSU) characterizes the complete grouping. It contributes to material rigidity, and thermal, oxidative, and hydrolysis resistance. The sulfone base plastics differ through the types of other groups completing the repeat units that include the phenyl rings, as well as carbon atoms or oxygen atoms (ether) in the backbone; the latter two contribute to the chain flexibility. Plastics in this family include polysulfone, polyarylsulfone, polyethersulfone, polyphenylsulfone, poly-phenylethersulfone, and polyarylether.

superalloy An iron-base, cobalt-base, or nickel-base alloy which combines high temperature-mechanical properties, oxidation resistance, and creep resistance to an unusually high degree.

superconductivity The phenomenon in which certain materials at temperatures usually near absolute zero (0 K) lose both electrical resistance and magnetic permeability; have infinite electrical conductivity. ▷ **cryogenic service; Kelvin scale; conductivity; magnetic plastic**

supercooling The rapid cooling of a normally crystalline plastic through its crystallization temperature, so it does not get a chance to crystallize and it remains in the amorphous state.

superfund The program that funds and carries out EPA's solid waste emergency and long-term removal activities. These activities include establishing a National Priorities List, investigating sites to be included in the list, and conducting or supervising clean-up and other remedial actions.

superplastic 1. This term is used to designate plastics (polymers) of very high molecular weight. **2.** ▷ **data, theoretical versus actual properties 3.** ▷ **commodity plastic and engineering plastic** and **reinforced plastic**

superplastic forming SPF is a strain rate sensitive forming process that uses characteristics of materials exhibiting high elongation to failure.

superplastic forming/diffusion bonding process The combination of SPF with DB permits the molding of complex reinforced plastic parts; process is abbreviated SPF/DB. ▷ **isotactic molding/pressing**

super quick-set infrared ink These inks are a modification of quick-set inks using plastics with controlled solubility properties in combination with special blended solvent systems and a minimal amount of drying oils. The setting of these inks is greatly accelerated by the application of heat energy, and IR radiation is a convenient way to apply the energy on a sheet fed press. Even without heat, they set almost 10 times faster than conventional quick-set inks which they are gradually replacing.

supersaturation The condition in which a solvent contains more dissolved matter (solute) than is present in a saturated solution of the same components at equivalent temperature; most commonly achieved by supercooling.

surface coating They are applied to materials of all types. Two basic purposes are common to their usage, namely protection and decorating the substrate. ▷ **coating**

surface conductivity ▷ **electrical surface conductance**

surface faying The surfaces of materials in contact with each other and joined or about to be joined.

surface finish Most manufactured parts do not require any special quality of surface finish other than that obtained by the method of fabrication. However, there are component parts (such as bearings, gears, and machine feed rolls) and certain fit requirements (for example running and sliding fits) that make it necessary to accurately specify the quality of surface finish required in mold cavities or dies. Different guides can be used to specify the finish. A common method is the SPE/SPI kit ▷ **mold cavity surface finish**. Very accurate system is provided in ANSI Standard B46.1 titled *Surface Texture*. Terms used and defined include degree of roughness (width and height), waviness (width and height) etc.

surface glass fiber treatment ▷ **glass fiber and fabric surface treatment**

surface mat A very thin, usually nonwoven, mat or veil from 180 to 510 μm (7 to 20 mil) thick of highly filamentized glass fiber (usually glass). In reinforced plastic molding it provides a smoother finish, minimizes the appearance of the fibrous pattern, and/or permits machining or grinding to a precise dimension. Also called overlay sheet and surface veil. ▷ **mat**

surface modeling, computer ▷ **computer modeling**

surface-modifying additives A number of additives are used to modify surface (or interface) properties in a desirable manner. Examples include external mold release agent, internal mold release agent, slip agent, antistatic agent, and antifogging agent.

surface mounted technology SMT is an alternative name for through-hole mounting on printed wiring board.

surface resistivity ▷ **electrical surface resistivity**

surface skin The smooth surface on the material formed during fabrication by contact with the molds.

surface tension The force existing in a liquid-vapor phase interface that tends to diminish the area of the interface. This force acts at each point on the interface to the plane tangent to that point; different tests used such as capillary tube.

surface tension, critical That value of surface tension of a liquid below which the liquid will spread on a solid.

surface treatment 1. Any method of treating a material to alter the surface and render it receptive to inks, paints, lacquers, adhesives, etc.; methods include the more popular chemical, flame, and electronic treatments, and water-wash, mechanical abrasion, and buffing. **2.** To enhance bonding and performance requirements of plastics used in reinforced plastics, different fiber size and finish operations are sometimes required. ▷ **glass fiber and fabric surface treatment**

surfactant Chemicals which modify the surface properties of plastics to influence the wetting and flow properties of liquids allowing formation of emulsion or intimate mixtures of normally incompatible substances.

surgical implant ▷ **absorbable technology; bioplastic-biomedical; human implantation; lens implanted; microencapsulation, coating; suture**

surging Unstable pressure build-up in an extruder leading to variable throughput (output) and waveness of extrudate. Performance properties can be influenced.

Surlyn Du Pont's tradename for its ionomer plastics.

susceptibility When not otherwise qualified, the degree of change in viscosity with temperature.

suspension A mixture of fine particles (solid, semisolid, or liquid). The particles are called the disperse phase, the suspending medium is called the continuous phase.

suspension polymerization Often called "pearl" polymerization, this technique is normally used only for catalyst-initiated or free-radical addition polymerizations. The monomer is mechanically dispersed in a liquid, usually water, which is a nonsolvent for the monomer as well as for sizes of polymer molecules which form during the reaction. The catalyst initiator is dissolved in the monomer and it is preferable that it does not dissolve in the water so that it remains with the monomer. The monomer and polymer being formed from it remain within the beads of organic material dispersed in the phase. Actually suspension polymerization is essentially a finely divided form of bulk polymerization.

The advantage of the suspension system over bulk is that it allows the operator to effectively cool exothermic polymerization reactions and thus maintain closer control over the chain building process. Other behavior is the same as bulk. By controlling the degree of agitation, monomer-to-water ratios, and other variables, it is also possible to control the particle size of the finished polymer, thus eliminating the need for reforming the material into pellets from a melt such as is usually necessary with bulk polymerization. ▷ **reactor technology**

suture Surgical sutures are medically sterile filaments used to hold tissues together until they heal adequately for self-support or to join tissues with implanted prosthetic devices. They are normally attached to needles for coaptation of the edges of wounds or surgical incisions. As ligatures, they are generally used without a needle, to tie off ends of severed tubular structures such as blood vessels and ducts to prevent bleeding or other fluid leakage.

Sutures are characterized according to type material, physical form, biodegradability, size, surgical use, and other criteria. The materials utilized are natural products, such as gut or silk, many common (synthetic) plastic fibers, and some fibers from synthetic plastics which have been synthesized specifically for use as sutures. Sutures may be fabricated as monofilaments or multifilaments; the latter are usually braided, but sometimes twisted or spun, and may be coated with waxes, silicones, fluorocarbons, or other plastics to reduce capillarity and improve handling or functional properties.

Suva Du Pont's tradename for a family of environmentally acceptable refrigerants (hydrochlorofluorocarbons) that is replacing its *Freon* (chlorofluorocarbon).

sweating Exudation of small drops of liquid, usually a plasticizer or softener, on the surface of a plastic part.

swelling 1. The increase in volume of a material. It can be caused by water vapor, water solution, chemicals, heat, etc. **2.** ▷ **design die, basics of flow**

swelling, absorption, and permeability It is usually reported that molecular weight (MW) does not affect diffusion and permeation by liquids and gases. There have been reports that MW has inverse effects on swelling, absorption, and permeability. Increasing MW in polyethylene, for example, produces increased grease-proofness and slightly lower gas permeability. A more detailed examination of absorption in glassy polymers suggests that when such polymers absorb solvent, it results in plasticization, which lowers the glass transition temperature, increases mobility, and therefore produces even higher absorption.

swept volume The volume of material which is displaced as the plasticator screw (or plunger) moves forward. It is the effective area of the screw multiplied by the distance of travel. ▷ **shot**

symbols and signs Examples are in the Table on p. 732.

syndiotactic stereoisomerism A polymer molecule in which side atoms or side groups alternate regularly on opposite sides of the chain.

syneresis The contraction of a gel, accompanied by the separation of a liquid.

synergism Mixture or arrangement of substances in which the total resulting performance is greater than the sum of the effects taken independently. A substance that causes this result when added to another substance is called a synergist.

Symbols and signs.

Symbols/signs	Meaning	Symbols/signs	Meaning
+	plus (addition)	(),[],{}	parentheses, brackets, braces
−	minus (subtraction)	∠ ⊥	angle, perpendicular to
± ∓	plus or minus (minus or plus)	a^2, a^3	a-square, a-cube
×	times, by (multiplication)	a^{-1}, a^{-2}	$\frac{1}{a}$, $\frac{1}{a^2}$
÷, /	divided by	$\sin^{-1}a$	the angle whose sine is
:	is to (ratio)	π	pi = 3.141593 +
: :	equals, as, so is	μ	microns = 0.001 millimeter
∴	therefore	mμ	micromillimeter = 0.000001 m
=	equals	Σ	summation of
≡	identical with	ε, e	base of hyperbolic, natural or Napierian logs = 2.71828 +
~ ≈	approximately equals	Δ	difference
>	greater than	g	acceleration due to gravity (32.16 feet/sec. per sec.)
≫	much greater than	E	coefficient of elasticity
<	less than	v	velocity
≧	greater than or equals	f	coefficient of friction
≦	less than or equals	P	pressure of load
⇄	direction of reaction	HP	horsepower
≠	not equal to	RPM	revolutions per minute
≐	approaches	ρ	density
∝	varies as	σ	tensile stress
∞	infinity	τ	shear stress
‖	parallel to	θ	angle
√	square root, cube root	α	coefficient of thermal expansion
□	square	ω	frequency
○	circle	η	viscosity
°	degrees (arc or thermometer)	ε	strain
′	minutes or feet	γ	shear strain
″	seconds or inches	μin.	microinch
a', a''	*a*-prime, *a*-second	μm	micrometer (micron)
a_1, a_2	*a*-sub one, *a*-sub two	ν	Poisson's ratio

syntactic foam In syntactic foams, instead of employing a blowing agent to form bubbles in the plastic mass, preformed bubbles of glass, ceramics, plastics, etc. are embedded in the thermoset matrix mass. These bubbles are microspheres (also called spheres and microballoons) and of extremely small size and uniformity ▷**microsphere**. These lightweight materials have been used since the 1940s as buoyant, energy absorbants, electrical/electronic waveguides, core for high performance sandwich structures, etc. These foams will have isotropic mechanical properties and are not affected by impact angle. If directional properties are desired, reinforcements can be included such as fibers or fabrics. They can be formulated into a moldable mass that can be shaped, or pressed into cavities of a mold(s).

synthesis Creation of a substance which either duplicates a natural product (material) or is a unique material not found in nature. This occurs by means of one or more chemical reactions, or (for elements) by a nuclear change. Though syntheses are more readily achieved with organic compounds because of the great versatility of the carbon atom, extremely important syntheses of other atoms also exist, such as inorganic silicones.

synthetic elastomer surface ▷**recreational surface**

synthetic fiber ▷**fiber**

synthetic, natural This term is often applied to synthesized compounds that are relatively identical with the natural substance, such as synthetic natural gas and synthetic natural rubber.

synthetic plastic ▷**plastic, synthetic**

synthetic rubber Any of a group of synthetic elastomers which approximate one or more of the properties of natural rubber (NR). Their properties are widely different. ▷**rubber** and **elastomer**

T

tab gate ▷ **mold gate, tab**

tablet ▷ **pellet**

tachometer An instrument that measures rotational motion. When the pointer touches the center of a shaft, readout is in RPM. With a wheel-like attachment touching a roll or belt, readout is surface speed in ft/min. (m/min).

tack **1.** The ability of a material to adhere to itself, such as prepregs, self-adhesives, and unvulcanized rubber that frequently show high tack. Tack is commonly assessed simply by applying finger pressure; test methods also are used. High tack is useful in building up products from several layers (or plies) which must adhere to each other. **2.** Sticky, gummy character of a polish film, rendering polish surface conductive to dust accumulation, fingerprints, etc.

tackifier A substance which is added to a plastic or elastomer to improve or provide tack.

tack range The period of time in which an adhesive will remain in the tacky-dry condition after application to the adherend, under specified conditions of temperature and humidity.

tack stage ▷ **adhesive tack stage**

tack weld An initial and brief weld (such as spot or button-like welds) made to hold parts of a weldment in proper alignment until the final complete welding is performed.

tailing **1.** Impurities remaining after extraction of useful minerals from ore. **2.** Any residue from a mechanical refining or separation process.

take-off The mechanism for drawing extruded or calendered material away from the output of the machines. The most common form of take-off is a pair of endless caterpillar belts with resilient grip pads conforming to the section being drawn, driven at a speed synchronized with the basic machine output rate.

talc Refined mineral product (hydrated magnesium silicate) that is a reinforcing filler-extender. Because of its platy configuration, it tends to add stiffness to the plastic, while its low cost categorizes it as an extender. Similar to talc is ▷ **vermiculite**

tall Derived from the Swedish word for pine, to distinguish tall oil from the U.S. meaning of pine oil.

tampo printing ▷ **pad printing**

tape ▷ **extruder web wrinkle free** and **film and tape**

tape, computer storage ▷ **computer storage, disc and tape**

tape placement wrapped molding Wrapping of heated preimpregnated tape onto a rotating mandrel, which is subsequently cooled to form the surface for the next tape layer application. These processes are usually automatic. ▷ **lagging molding**

taper, back The back taper is the reverse draft or undercut used in a mold to prevent molded parts from drawing freely.

tapping Cutting threads in the walls of a circular hole.

tare The weight of a container (railroad tanker, etc.) which is deducted in determining the net weight of the material in the container.

tear, Elmendorf test ▷ **Elmendorf tear test**

tear failure A tensile failure characterized by fracture initiating at one edge of the specimen and progressing across the specimen at a rate slow enough to produce an anomalous load-deformation.

tear ply ▷ **reinforced plastic tear ply**

tear resistance Resistance of a material to a force acting to initiate and then propagate a failure at the edge of a test specimen.

tear strength The maximum force required to tear a specified specimen, the force acting substantially parallel to the major axis of the test specimen.

technical cost modeling ▷ **computer cost modeling, technically**

technology The practice and description of any or all of the applied sciences which have commercial value. ▷ **design technology** and **markets emerging**

Tedlar Du Pont's tradename for its family of fluoroplastics (FEP, etc.).

Telcothene In 1937, when polyethylene was developed and produced by ICI-England, it was identified very quickly as the best electrical insulator known. However, it had low and variable molecular weight, as well as being brittle. To improve performance and make it extrudable, it was blended with polyisobutylene. This blend was named *Telcothene*. By 1938 it was used in a submarine cable that operated in a high frequency range. At that time, radar was developed and *Telcothene* was required.

telecommunication system Ties the user and terminal, processing equipment, and other peripherals to the computer as well as the databases to be searched. Information stored in most electronic text systems may be communicated over telephone lines. Modems convert signals from these systems into telephone signals and then reconvert them at the other end. Transmission requirements are called protocols, allowing transmission in one direction (asynchronous) or in both directions simultaneously (synchronous) for error correction. All word processors and personal computers telecommunicate, but only with like models.

telomer A polymer composed of molecules having terminal groups incapable of reacting with additional monomers, under the conditions of the synthesis, to form larger polymer molecules of the same chemical type. ▷**chain transfer**

temper To reheat after hardening to some temperature below the critical temperature, followed by air cooling to obtain desired mechanical properties and to relieve hardening strains.

temperature The thermal state of matter as measured on a definite scale. The SI unit of thermodynamic temperature is the kelvin (K), and this unit is properly used for expressing thermodynamic temperature and temperature intervals. Wide use is also made of the degree Celsius (°C), which is the SI unit used for expressing Celsius temperature and temperature intervals. The Celsius scale (formerly called centigrade) is related directly to thermodynamic temperature kelvin as follows: $°C = K + 273.15$ or $K = °C - 273.15$. ▷**Celsius; Kelvin; Fahrenheit; Centigrade; Rankine**

temperature, absolute The fundamental temperature scale used in theoretical engineering, chemistry, physics, etc. It is expressed either in kelvin (K) or corresponding to Celsius (°C), formerly Centigrade (°C).

temperature, aging ▷**aging at elevated temperature**

temperature, ambient Temperature of the medium surrounding an object.

temperature at atmospheric altitude ▷**altitude chart**

temperature, autoignition ▷**autoignition point**

temperature, brittleness ▷**brittleness temperature**

temperature controller Heat is usually applied in various amounts and in different locations, whether in a metal plasticating barrel (extrusion, injection molding, etc.) or in a metal mold/die (compression, injection, thermoforming, extrusion, etc.). With barrels a thermocouple is usually embedded in the metal to send a signal to a temperature controller. In turn, it controls the electric power output device regulating the power to the heater bands in different zones of the barrel. The placement of the thermocouple temperature sensor is extremely important. The heat flow in any medium sets up a temperature gradient in that medium, just as the flow of water in a pipe sets up a pressure drop, and the flow of electricity in a wire causes a voltage drop.

Barrels are made of steel, which is not a particularly good conductor of heat (being ten times worse than copper). Thus there is a gradient in the steel barrel from the outside of the barrel to the inside next to the plastic. In $3\frac{1}{2}$ in. (88.9 mm) and $4\frac{1}{2}$ in. (114.3 mm) extruder barrels, these gradients or differences in temperature can routinely be 23.9 to 32.8°C (75 to 100°F) or more, as the zone heaters pump in heat or zone coolers take excess heat out. Yet, for past years users routinely accepted extruders with sensors mounted in very shallow wells, or, even worse, mounted in the heating/cooling jacket.

Consider a barrel with a shallow well for its sensor. Assume a perfect temperature controller set at 204°C (400°F). There is a 75°F gradient from the outside to the inside of the barrel; thus the actual temperature down near the plastic would be 325°F with the sensor set at 400°F. If the extruder started to generate too much heat, the temperature could reach 475°F before the sensor detected the increase. With this on-off control action, even with the controller set at 400°F the plastic temperature variation is 150°F. The result could be poor product performance and increased cost to process the plastic.

A deep well sensor will respond much more quickly than a shallow one to changes in the plastic's temperature. However, it responds slowly to changes, for example, in the heater line voltage or in the cooling water heat. The time constant for heat to propagate from the

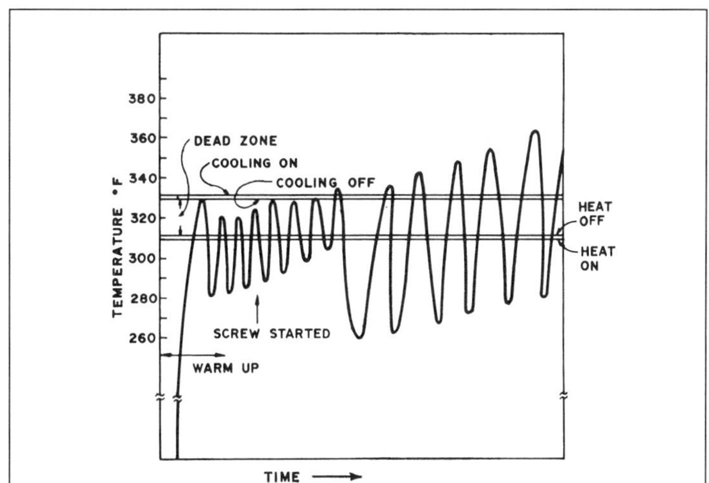

Temperature variations with time in a typical extruder barrel using on-off controls.

heater down to a deep well location is about 6 minutes in a $3\frac{1}{2}$ in. barrel. Thus an upset due to a cooling water temperature change might take 20 minutes or more to settle out. This system does respond to ambient conditions rapidly, but it retains part of the temperature error inherent in the use of shallow wells. In the example just given for a shallow well with 150°F variation, the variation would be only half as great, or 75°F, if two sensors were used, one deep and one shallow.

A dual-well system was developed to solve this problem, retaining the advantages of both deep and shallow wells by using a cascade control loop. The primary temperature loop is a shallow well, and a secondary loop sensed the deep well temperature, using it to adjust the set point of the shallow well. This system offers such advantages as preventing the temperature of the heater from rising as high as it otherwise would, greatly extending the heater band life, and so on.

These on-off controllers are unsatisfactory for a loading having a long time constant, such as an extruder barrel, a die adapter, a die, and so forth. The temperature will oscillate violently at an amplitude that is set not by the characteristic of the controller, but by the delay in the load, as reviewed in the Fig. above. To reduce this variation, a proportional control was developed. It is similar to the on-off, but operates in between full on and off, with its output proportional to the deviation of temperature from the set point value (see Fig. below). Variations still exist with this system, but they are less than those of the on-off control.

This type of temperature controller has three characteristics: (1) the actual temperature

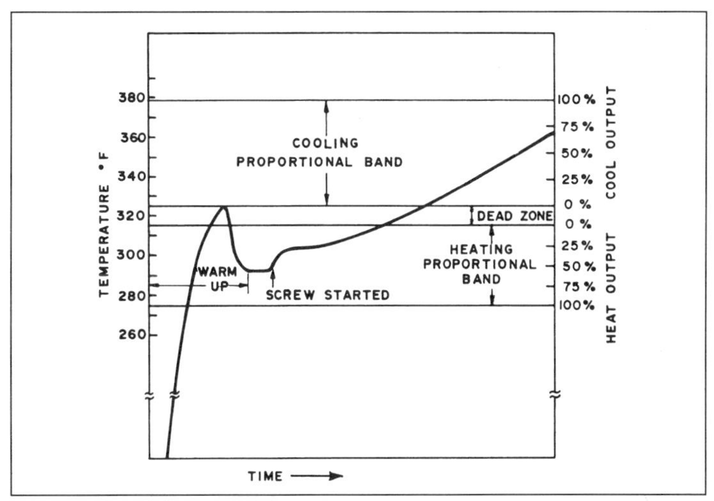

Example of temperature variation with proportional control of an extruder barrel (no automatic reset).

of a single proportional controller will never be at the set point; (2) the error in temperature, or droop, of a proportional controller, will vary over a considerable portion of a proportional band as the process varies; and (3) in the case of a large time lag, the proportional band of a simple proportional controller will have to be quite large. A considerable portion of the proportional band will normally be used; so the temperature will vary considerably during normal operation of the extruder. Thus a simple proportional controller is better than an on-off control but does not do the best job of controlling temperature.

The introduction of automatic reset into controllers for the plastic processor made it possible to hold the temperature constant even in the presence of extremely long lags. Automatic reset is a characteristic added to a proportional controller that functions as an integrating, or averaging, system, looking at the droop, or temperature error, over a period of time and adjusting the output so that the droop goes to zero. As a result, the actual temperature goes to the set point (see Fig. below). Automatic reset is almost always used with an additional "rate" term, which adds an anticipatory characteristic that does not affect steady state performance but does speed up the response to changes in operating conditions. A modern proportional plus automatic reset plus rate—a three-mode controller— is capable of controlling within 1°F (0.6°C) of the set point all the way from full heating to full cooling, even when controlling from a deep well sensor. ▷**proportional-integral-derivative** and **computer microprocessor control**

temperature curing ▷**curing temperature** and **electrical cure monitoring**

temperature decomposition ▷**decomposition** and **plastic long life**

temperature differential by infrared In this method, heat is applied to a part and the surface is scanned to determine the amount of infrared radiation emitted. Heat may be applied continuously from a controlled source, or the part may be heated prior to inspection. The rate at which radiant energy is diffused or transmitted to the surface reveals defects within the part. Delaminations, unbonds, and voids have been detected in this manner. This nondestructive test method is particularly useful with reinforced plastics.

temperature, dry-bulb The temperature of the air as indicated by an accurate thermometer, corrected for radiation if significant.

temperature electrical resistance detector Contains temperature sensor made from high purity platinum wire; resistance of the wire changes rapidly with temperature. RTD (resistance temperature detector) sensors are about 60 times more sensitive than thermocouples. ▷**temperature sensor**

temperature, eutectic ▷**eutectic temperature**

temperature flexibility of plastic All plastics which are flexible at room temperature become less flexible as they are cooled, finally becoming brittle at some temperature. This property is often measured by torsional test over a wide range of temperatures.

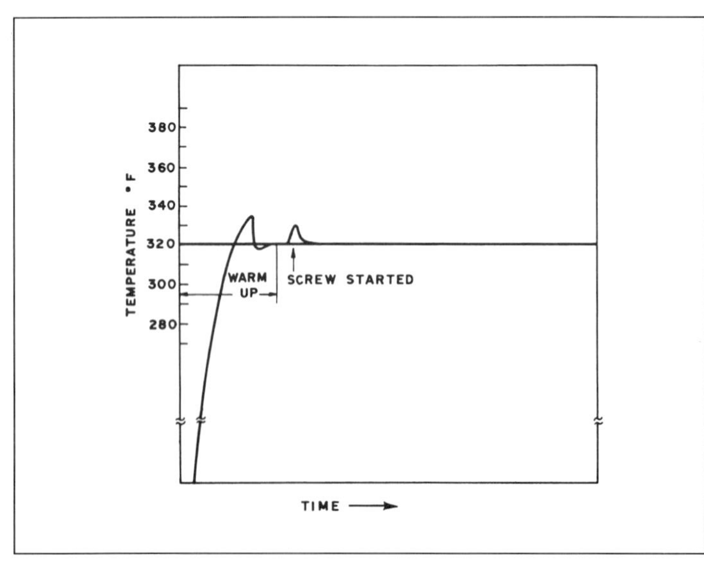

Variations of temperature in an extruder barrel with time, using proportional plus automatic reset control.

temperature, glass transition ▷ **glass transition temperature**

temperature, heat distortion ▷ **deflection temperature under load**

temperature, homologous The ratio of the absolute temperature of a material to its absolute melting temperature. Here temperatures are measured in Celsius.

temperature index ▷ **fire retardance**

temperature, liquids The maximum temperature at which equilibrium exists between the molten glass (during glass filament manufacture) and its primary crystalline phase.

temperature, low ▷ **cryogenic**

temperature, Martens A measure of the softening temperature of a plastic. The temperature at which a standard test specimen, heated at a determined rate, bends to a certain extent under a defined load. A similar measurement to the heat distortion temperature, but giving a somewhat different result. For an amorphous plastic the value is about 20°C below the glass transition temperature. In the Martens test, it is the temperature at which a flexural bar specimen deflects by a specified amount under four-point bending, when subjected to a specified bending stress (see Fig. under ▷ **flexural properties**). The bending is magnified by the loading arm attached to the upper end of the vertically mounted sample.

temperature, melt ▷ **melt temperature**

temperature properties of plastics Plastics can be affected in different ways by temperature. Among other things, it can influence short- and long-time static and dynamic mechanical properties (see Fig. below), aesthetics, dimensions, electronic properties, and other characteristics. Some plastics cannot take boiling water, others can operate up to 149°C (300°F) and the so-called high-temperature types can take various degrees of continuous use above 149°C (300°F). Then there are the plastic composites used as heat-shield ablative materials on the nose cones of space vehicles that reach temperatures of about 1,370°C (2,500°F) for fractions of a second upon reentering the atmosphere. Practically all plastics can take heat up to at least what the human body can endure, which is one important reason they are used so extensively.

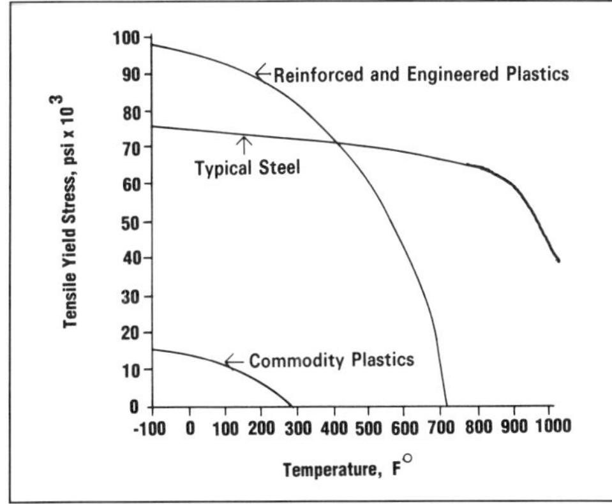

Guide to maximum short term tensile stress versus temperature.

Thermoplastics soften to varying degrees at elevated temperatures, but thermosets are much less affected. In fact, a few plastics even reach 538°C (1,000°F). The maximum temperatures under which plastics can be employed are generally higher than the temperatures found in buildings, including walls and roofs, but some such as LDFPE are marginal and others cannot carry appreciable stresses at moderately elevated temperatures without undergoing noticeable creep. Many plastics can take shipping conditions that are more severe than their service conditions, as in an automobile trunk or railroad boxcar that might reach 52°C (126°F).

The response of a plastic to an applied stress depends on the temperature and the time at that temperature to a much greater extent than does that of a metal or ceramic. The variation of an amorphous TP over an extended temperature range can be exemplified by the behavior of its elastic modulus as a function of temperature.

temperature ramping ▷ **ramping**

temperature, room A temperature in the range of 20 to 30°C (68 to 85°F). The term RT is usually applied to an atmosphere of unspecified relative humidity.

temperature scale, international ▷ **temperature** and **Celsius**

temperature, self-ignition ▷ **spontaneous ignition**

temperature sensor Two common sensors are used for temperatures in the ranges experienced in plastic processing equipment; the thermocouple (TC) and the resistance temperature detector (RTD). The TC is by far the more common type. It depends on the fact that every type of metallic conductor has a characteristic electrical barrier potential, and whenever two different metals are joined together, there will be a net electrical potential at the junction. This electrical potential changes with temperature.

The RTD sensor is based on the fact that the resistance of some metals changes markedly with temperature, whereas the resistance of platinum, the metal most commonly used in RTDs, is extremely stable. Its variation in temperature is both repeatable and predictable to a high degree of accuracy. In the past, TCs offered major cost advantages; but with the advent of low cost solid state dc amplifiers, the use of RTDs has become more realistic.

RTDs have about 60 times more sensitivity than TCs, their amplifiers are less expensive and much less sensitive to electrical noise disturbance, they offer better linearity (are twice as linear as TCs), and they are twice as interchangeable. The RTD does not have the TC's compensating cold junction; so only the desired temperature is involved. With TCs both ends of the wire are sensitive to temperature changes; there is no way of distinguishing between a change in the process and a change in the ambient temperature, so there is some residual drift. Although the RTD itself costs more than a TC, an RTD system that includes the sensor plus an amplifier is almost always less expensive for an equivalent quality level. Processors should be aware of the availability and superiority of RTDs. ▷ **Peltier coefficient**

temperature, set The temperature to which a plastic or adhesive is used to produce a product or assembly that is subjected to set (solidify or cure) the plastic or adhesive.

temperature shallow well Location of temperature sensor which is more responsive to changes in ambient temperature, line voltage, and cooling water. Usually coordinated with temperature measurements at deep well. ▷ **temperature controller**

temperature shrinkage of plastics ▷ **coefficient of linear thermal expansion**

temperature softening range The range of temperature in which a plastic changes from a rigid to a soft state. Actual values will depend on the method of test ▷ **softening point**. The SP (softening point) for normally flexible thermoplastics can relate to the temperature in which a rather sudden and substantial decrease in hardness occurs.

temperature solidification point An empirical constant defined as the temperature at which the liquid phase of a substance is in approximate equilibrium with a relatively small portion of the solid phase.

temperature stability The percent change in tensile strength or in percent elongation as measured at a specified temperature and compared to values obtained at the standard conditions of testing.

temperature timing and sequencing Most processes operate more efficiently when functions must occur in a desired time sequence or at prescribed intervals of time. In the past, mechanical timers and logic relays were used. Now electronic logic and timing devices predominate. These devices, based on so-called programmable logic control, provide sophisticated sequencing and timing, and lend themselves easily to reprogramming. Logic sequences can be added by means of a ladder diagram (circuit diagram) representing the desired functions and/or timing.

temperature, transition The temperature at which the properties of a material change. Depending on the material, the transition change may or may not be reversible.

temperature versus modulus ▷ **modulus versus temperature** and **molecular basic properties effect on product properties**

temperature, wet-bulb The equilibrium temperature of a liquid vaporizing into a gas. With water and air, wet-bulb and dry-bulb temperatures give a measure of the relative humidity. It is the temperature indicated by a wet-bulb thermometer of a psychrometer. ▷ **drying, psychrometry**

temperature zone, plasticator ▷ **screw temperature zone**

tempered glass Glass with surface compressive stresses induced by heat treatment, resulting in toughened glass. ▷ **safety glass**

template A pattern used as a guide for cutting and laying plies of plastics or reinforced plastics.

tenacity The term generally used in yarn manufacture and textile engineering to denote the strength of a yarn or of a filament for its given size. Numerically, it is the grams of breaking force per denier unit of yarn or filament size; expressed as grams per denier (gpd), gram-force per tex (gf/tex), gram-force per denier (gf/d), millinewton per tex (mN/tex), or millinewton per denier (mN/d), with gpd the most common. The yarn is usually pulled at the rate of 12 in./min (30 cm/min). Tenacity equals breaking strength (g) divided by denier (d). To obtain pound per square inch (psi), multiply tenacity (gpd) with the fiber's specific gravity and 12,800, or (gpd)(sg)(12,800) = tensile strength, psi. ▷ **fiber loop tenacity**

tensile analysis The tensile test is the experimental stress-strain test method most widely employed to characterize the mechanical properties of materials like plastics, metals, and

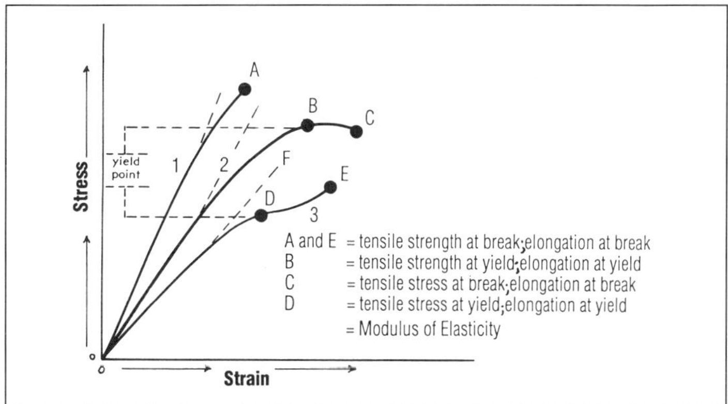

Tensile designations per ASTM D 638.

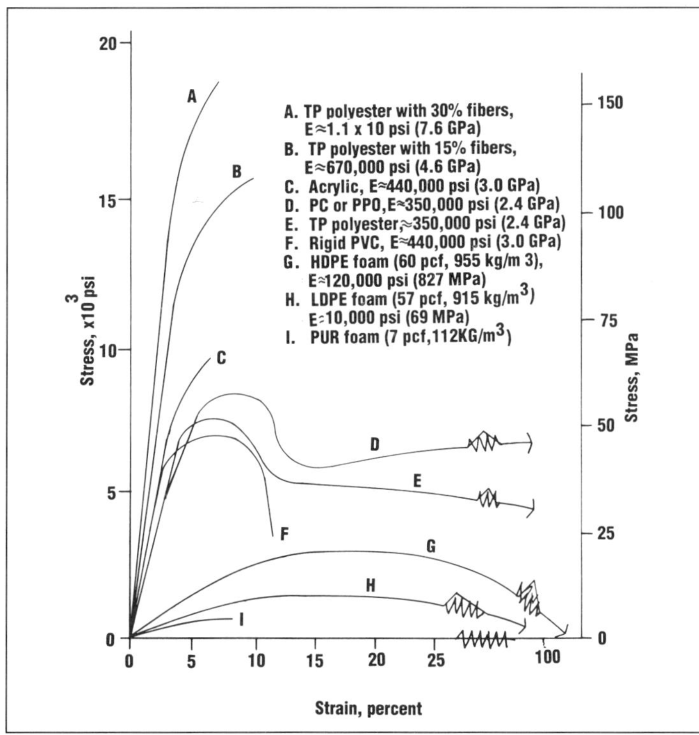

Examples of range in tensile strength, modulus (E), and elongation (% strain) of a few thermoplastics with and without chopped glass fibers (wt%) reinforcements.

wood. From any complete test record one can obtain important information concerning a material's elastic properties, the character and extent of its plastic deformation, and its yield and tensile strengths and toughness. That so much information can be obtained from one test of a material justifies its extensive use. To provide a framework for the varied responses to tensile loading in load-bearing materials that occur, several stress-strain plots, reflecting different deformation characteristics, will be examined. Examples of tensile stress-strain curves are shown in the Figs. above. See also those for ▷ **stress-strain curve or diagram** and **orientation**

tensile, elastic limit ▷ **stress, elastic limit**

tensile elongation ▷ **elongation**

tensile extensometer ▷ **extensometer**

tensile green strength Green strength is the tensile strength of a raw unvulcanized rubber or elastomer compound. Natural rubber has one of the highest values. A high green strength is desirable in those processing operations in which the integrity of a shaped piece of rubber needs to be maintained. While cure is not complete, it allows removal from the mold and handling without tearing or permanent distortion.

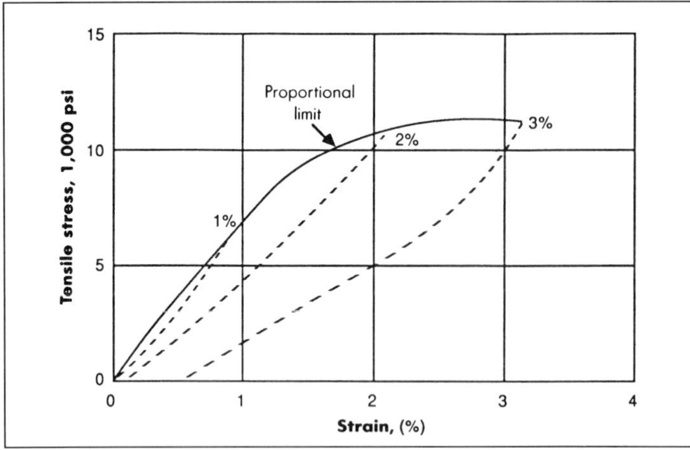

Example of recovery to near zero strain shows material can withstand stresses beyond the proportional limit for a short period of time, resulting in different degrees of hysteresis effect.

tensile heat distortion temperature ▷ **deflection temperature under load**

tensile hysteresis The hysteresis effect is a retardation of the strain when a material is subjected to a force or load (see Fig. above). ▷ **hysteresis**

tensile impact test The tensile impact test subjects a tensile test bar to a rapid pulling force. The speciment is clamped at one end to a pendulum and at the other to a weighted crosshead. The pendulum is let go from a height of about 2 ft (5 cm). At the bottom of its travel, the cross head is stopped by two anvils. The shock breaks the specimen, but the pendulum continues to travel upward. The apparatus has a scale that indicates in ft-lb (J) how much energy has been expended in breaking the specimen. Like the Izod impact test, it has its advantages and disadvantages. It can be used for materials either too flexible or too brittle for Izod or Charpy tests. The primary limitation of this test is that, like any uninstrumented impact test, it does not distinguish between two qualitatively different materials that may absorb the same amount of energy. For example, a strong, yet brittle, material may absorb the same amount of energy as a weak, but ductile, material. ▷ **impact test**

tensile modulus Also called modulus of elasticity or Young's modulus. It is the ration of stress to strain for a given material within its proportional limit ▷ **modulus**. Using these parameters, if a tensile stress of 13.8 MPa (2.0 ksi) results in an elongation of 0.01 cm/cm (in./in.) or 1%, the modulus is 1,380 MPa (200 ksi).

tensile modulus secant ▷ **modulus, secant**

tensile, Poisson's ratio ▷ **Poisson's ratio**

tensile proportional limit ▷ **proportional limit**

tensile strain ▷ **strain**

tensile strain recovery The percent of recoverable extension of the total extension that occurs in a material. It includes both immediate elastic recovery and delayed recovery.

tensile strength The maximum or ultimate tensile load per unit area of original cross section area of the test specimen, within the gauge boundaries, sustained by the specimen during the test. For the usual material and product evaluations, area used in computing strength is the original, rather than the neck-down area. ▷ **strength**

tensile strength, theoretical ▷ **data, theoretical versus actual properties**

tensile strength, yield ▷ **strength, yield**

tensile stress ▷ **stress**

tensile stress necking Necking is the localized reduction in a cross section that may occur in a material under tensile stress.

tensile stress-strain ▷ **stress-strain curve or diagram**

tensile stress-strain area under the curve Generally, the area under the stress-strain curve is proportional to the energy required to break the plastic. It is thus sometimes referred to as the toughness of the plastic (see Fig on top of p. 741). However, there are types, particularly among the many fiber-reinforced TSs, that are hard, strong, and tough, even though their area is extremely small. ▷ **modulus, toughness**

tensile testing machine An apparatus designed to impart or transmit force/extension or stress-strain to a material; the machine measures the effect of the action on test specimens. Machines are available from rather simple (rather

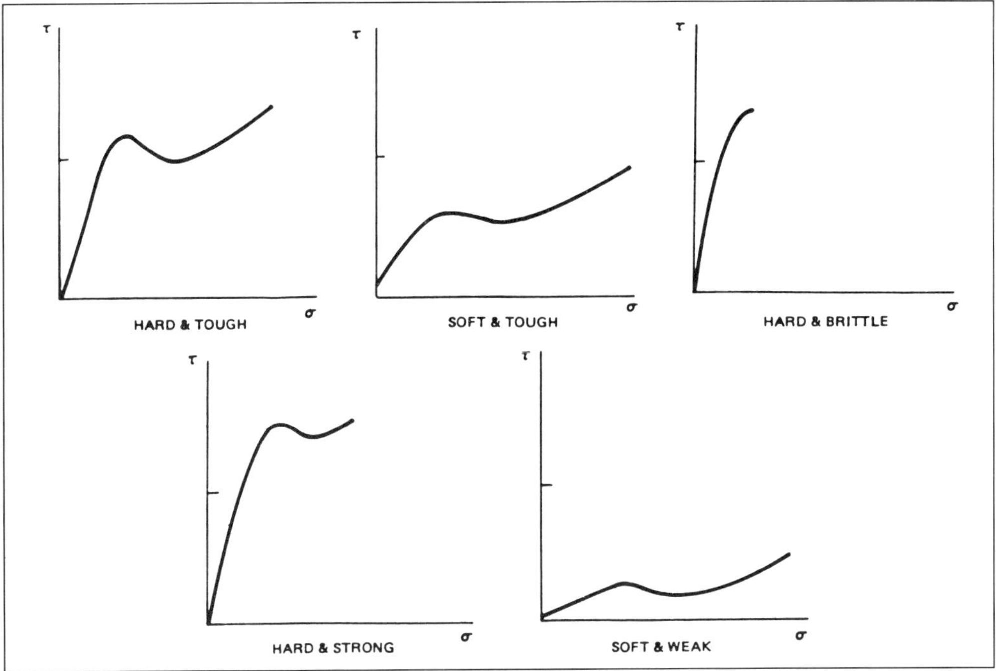

Tensile stress-strain curves for different plastics that relate the area under the curves to toughness or other properties.

manual operation) to extremely highly sophisticated computerized systems that meet the many different requirements throughout the industry. They can be programmed to be extremely useful in quality control. The Fig. shows the basic machine.

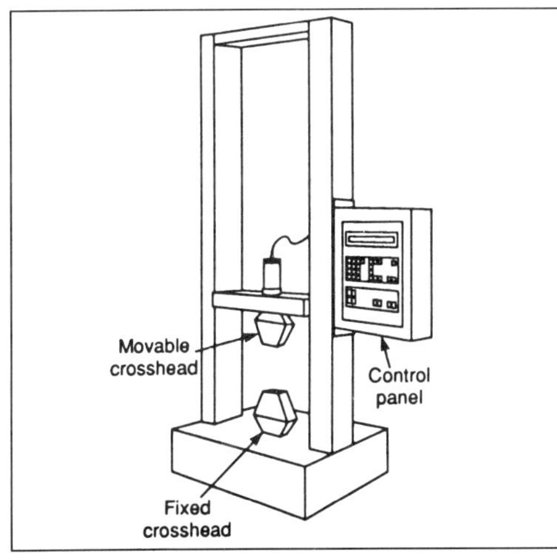

Schematic of a tensile testing machine. The specimen is held between the fixed and movable crossheads. The stress-strain results are displayed on the control panel or downloaded to a computer or strip-chart recorder.

tensile testing machine test rates The test rate or cross-head rate is the speed at which the movable crosshead moves. An increase in strain rate typically results in an increasing yield point and ultimate strength (see Fig. 1 on p. 742 and Fig. 2 on p. 743). For most rigid plastics the modulus (the initial tangent to the stress-strain curve) does not change significantly with the strain rate. For softer TPs, such as polyethylenes, the theoretical elastic or initial tangent modulus is usually independent of the strain rate. The significant time-dependent effects associated with such materials, and the practical difficulties of obtaining a true initial tangent modulus near the origin of a nonlinear stress-strain curve, render it difficult to resolve the true elastic modulus of the softer TPs in respect to actual data. Thus, the observed effect of increasing strain is to increase the slope of the early portions of the stress-strain curve (see Fig. 1*b* on p. 742), which differs from that at the origin. The elastic modulus and strength of both the rigid and the softer plastics each decrease with an increase in temperature. While in many respects the effects of a change in temperature are similar to those resulting from a change in the strain rate, the effects of temperature are relatively much greater.

Test rate of machines can be classified as (1) CRE: The constant-rate-of-extension is a

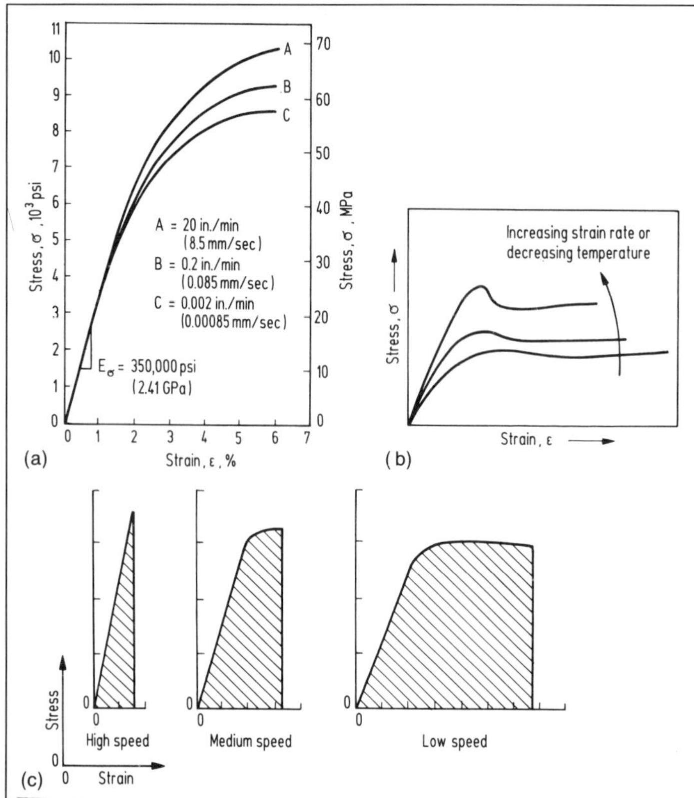

Fig. 1 Example of influence of test rate and temperatures on basic stress-strain behavior of plastics: (*a*) different testing rates per ASTM D 638 are shown for a polycarbonate; (*b*) effects of tensile testing speeds on the shape of stress-strain diagrams; (*c*) simplfied version of effect on curves with changes in test rate and temperatures.

machine in which the rate of increase of specimen length is uniform with time, (2) CRL: The constant-rate-of-load is a machine in which the rate of increase of the load being applied to the specimen is uniform with time after the first 3 s, and (3) CRT: The constant-rate-of-traverse is a machine in which the pulling clamp moves at a uniform rate and the load is applied through the other clamp which moves appreciably to actuate a weighing mechanism, so that the rate of increase of load or elongation is dependent upon the extension characteristics of the specimen.

tensile test specimen The Fig. shows a typical $\frac{1}{2}$ in.-thick (12.7 cm) dogbone shaped specimen, also called bar. Different shapes and sizes exist to meet different material performance requirements. ▷ **testing**

tensile thermoelastic inversion The decrease in tensile force with increase in temperature necessary to maintain a constant length of a plastic, such as elastomer, sample under tension. It occurs only at low (less than 10%) elongation; at higher elongations, thermoelasticity occurs. Caused by thermal expansion of the elastomer, which increases the length in the unstrained state, and thereby reduces the effective elongation.

tensile viscoelasticity Plastics respond to stress with elastic strain. In this material, strain increases with longer times and higher temperatures.

tensile yield strength ▷ **strength, yield**

tension A uniaxial force tending to cause the

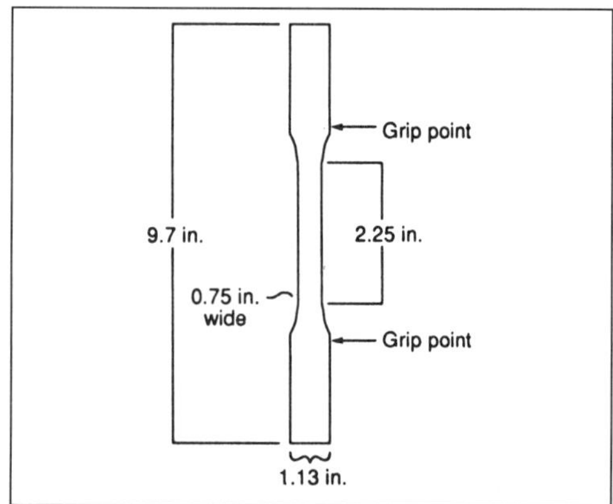

Example of a tensile test specimen.

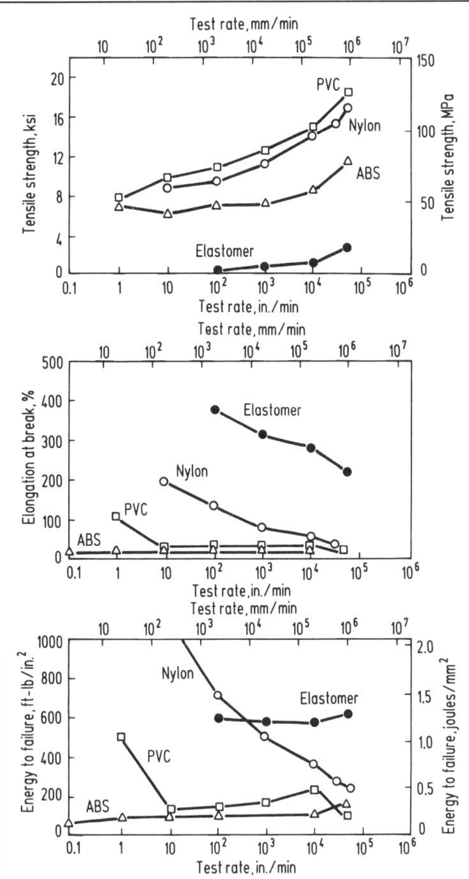

Fig. 2 Behavior of different plastics during high speed tests.

extension of a body or the balancing force within that body resisting the extension.

tension fatigue Fracture, through crack growth of a component or test specimen subjected to repeated tensile deformation. ▷ **fatigue**

tension member Any component which carries horizontal tension loads.

tension parallel The imposition of a tensile stress which acts in a direction parallel to the fiber direction of a material (wood, reinforced plastic, etc.).

tension-recovery chart In tension testing, a continuously plotted graph of tension versus extension resulting from a tension-recovery cycle.

tension set The strain remaining after a test piece or product has been stretched and allowed to retract.

tension, shrink film The force per original average cross sectional area developed by a film in a specified direction and at a specific temperature in its attempt to shrink while under restrain. ▷ **orientation** and **shrink wrapping**

tension tie Strapping applied with mechanical tools. ▷ **strapping tape**

tension winding ▷ **filament winding**

tentering 1. In the plastic industry, tenter frame is used for film orientation in one or both directions. The tenter frame is located inside a closely controlled temperature and air flow oven. (For orientation in the machine direction, the tenter frame is not the only technique; an in-line series of temperature controlled rolls can be used where each successive roll rotates faster.) ▷ **extruder film orientation** and **orientation 2.** For centuries past, the name tenter frame was derived from housewives that stretched curtains and the like on frames with pins. **3.** A machine used for holding a processed fabric taut (in one or two directions) as it is fed into a wind-up or to a cutter. It consists of a frame along the inner sides of which travel continuous moving chains to which gripping hooks or clamps are attached at intervals of a few inches (cm). As the fabric moves into the machine, the edges are engaged by the grippers automatically and are automatically released at the end of the frame.

tenter mark A visible deformation on the side edge of a material due to the pressure from clips or clamps; this trim is cut.

tenth-value-layer TVL is the thickness of the layer of a specified substance which, when introduced into the path of a given narrow beam of radiation, reduces the intensity of this radiation by a factor of ten.

tera Because billion means a thousand billion (prefix giga) in U.S. but a million million (prefix tera) in most other countries, this term and others, such as trillion, should be avoided in U.S. technical writing.

terephthalate A compound used in the manufacture of linear crystalline polyester plastics, fibers, and films by combination with glycols.

ternary Three components.

terpolymer A copolymer, such as ABS, made from three monomers. ABS is made from acrylonitrile, butadiene, and styrene. Three different monomers can be simultaneously polymerized, or there can be grafting of one monomer to the copolymer of two different monomers.

tertiary recycling Recovery of reuseable chemical products by chemical modification of plastic waste.

tesla ▷ **magnetic flux density**

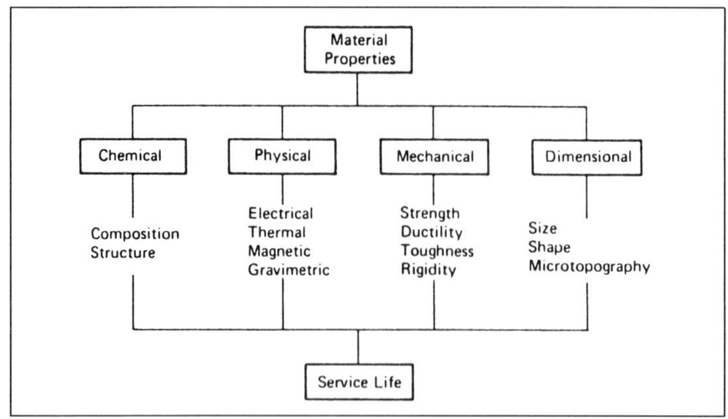

General guide to material property tests.

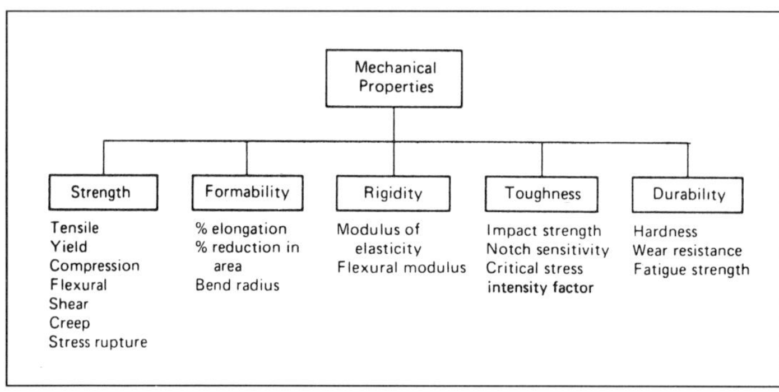

General guide to mechanical property tests.

testing The determination, by technical means, of properties, performance, or elements of materials, products, services, systems, or environments. This action, when possible, should involve application of established scientific principles and procedures. Testing requires specifying what requirements are to be met (see Fig. in ▷**design**). The Table below provides a guide to types of tests that can be performed. There are many different tests that can be conducted that relate to practically any requirement (see Figs. above) ▷**specification or standard** for a listing of those that prepare them.

The properties of plastics are directly dependent on temperature, time, and environmental conditions, and these conditions can be related to raw material, processing, and part performance. The most important testing is that done on the finished part. In turn, tests done on materials and during processing all must be related to part performance.

Unfortunately there is no single set of rules designating which tests are to be conducted in order to manufacture a part repeatedly with zero defects. The tests depend on the required performance. For example, if a part is to operate where

Example of tests: ASTM test methods by subject.

ASTM No.	Subject
Mechanical testing	
D 638	Tensile properties of plastics
D 695	Compressive properties of rigid plastics
D 2344	Apparent horizontal shear strength of reinforced plastics by short beam method
D 3039	Tensile properties of oriented fiber composites
D 3518	In-plane shear stress-strain response of unidirectional reinforced plastics
D 732	In-plane shear
D 785	Rockwell hardness
D 790	Flexural properties of plastics and electrical insulating materials
D 953	Bearing strength
D 2344	Short beam shear
D 3410	Test for compressive properties of oriented fiber composites

Example of tests: ASTM *test methods by subject* (*continued*).

ASTM No.	Subject
Fatigue	
D 3479	Tension-tension fatigue of oriented fiber resin matrix composites
D 671	Flexural fatigue of plastics by constant-amplitude-of-force
Impact	
D 256	Impact resistance of plastics and electrical insulating materials
D 1822	Tensile-impact energy to break plastics and electrical insulating materials
D 3029	Impact resistance of rigid plastic sheeting or parts by means of tup (falling weight)
Creep	
D 2990	Tensile, compressive, and flexural creep and creep-rupture of plastics
D 2991	Stress relaxation of plastics
Physical properties	
D 570	Water absorption
D 792	Specific gravity and density of plastics by displacement
D 1505	Density of plastics by the density-gradient technique
D 2734	Void content of reinforced plastics
D 3355	Fiber content of undirectional fiber/polymer composites
Thermal properties	
D 648	Deflection temperature of plastics under flexural load (HDT)
D 746	Brittleness temperature
D 3417	Heats of fusion and crystallization
D 3418	Transition temperatures
Thermal expansion	
D 696	Coefficient of linear thermal expansion of plastics
E 228	Linear thermal expansion of rigid solids with a vitreous silica dilatometer
Thermal conductivity	
C 117	Steady-state thermal transmission properties by means of the guarded hot plate
Electrical properties	
D 149	Dielectric breakdown voltage and dielectric strength of electrical insulating materials at commercial power frequencies
D 257	Electrical resistance
D 495	Arc resistance
D 150	A–C loss characteristics and permittivity (dielectric constant) of solid electrical insulating materials
Wear resistance	
D 673	Mar resistance of plastics
D 1242	Resistance of plastic materials to abrasion
Chemical resistance	
C 581	Chemical resistance of thermosetting resins used in glass fiber reinforced structures
D 543	Resistance of plastics to chemical reagents
Flammability tests	
D 635	Rate of burning
D 2843	Smoke density
D 2863	Oxygen index
E 662	Smoke emission
Weatherability tests	
D 1499	Operating light- and water-exposure apparatus (carbon-arc type) for exposure of plastics
D 2565	Operating xenon-arc type (water-cooled) light- and water-exposure apparatus for exposure of plastics
D 4141	Conducting accelerated outdoor exposure testing of coatings
E 838	Performing accelerated outdoor weathering using concentrated natural sunlight
G 23	Operating light-exposure apparatus (carbon-arc type) with and without water for exposure of nonmetallic materials
G 26	Operating light-exposure apparatus (xenon-arc type) with and without water for exposure of nonmetallic materials
G 53	Operating light- and water-exposure apparatus (fluorescent UV-condensation type) for exposure of nonmetallic materials

Characterizing plastic instruments.[1]

Characterization of instrument[2]	Capability				
	Cost	Material incoming QC	In-process QC	Finished product QC	Sample time and interpretive time
DMA	4	3	3	3	5
DSC	5	6	6	6	2
IR	7	7	7	7	4
LC	6	5	5	5	1
MI	1	8	8	8	8
RMS	8	1	1	1	7
TGA	3	6	6	6	2
TMA	3	6	6	6	2
TR	4	4	4	4	3

[1] No. 1 indicates lowest cost or best capability.
[2] See *List of Abbreviations* on p. viii and ▷**thermal analysis**

any type of failure could be catastrophic to life, then extensive and usually expensive testing is necessary. How deeply one gets involved depends on the performance requirements. If all that is required is to weigh the part, that is all that needs to be performed. It usually is not this simple.

testing analysis, micromechanical In order to determine the strength and endurance of a material under stress, it is necessary to characterize its mechanical behavior. Moduli, strain, strength, and toughness, in addition to the conventional methods (▷**testing**) are measured microscopically. These parameters are useful for material selection, process evaluation, and design. They have to be understood as to applying their mechanisms of deformation and fracture because of the viscoelastic behavior of plastics. The fracture behavior of materials, expecially macroscopically brittle materials, is governed by the microscopic mechanisms operating in a heterogeneous zone at the crack tip or stress raising flow. In order to supplement macromechanical investigations and advance knowledge of the fracture process, micromechanical measurements of the deformation zone are required to determine local stresses and strains. The required measurements depend, to a large extent, on the complexity of the model used in the subsequent analysis.

In thermoplastics, craze zones can develop that are important microscopic features around a crack tip governing strength behavior. Fracture is preceded by the formation of a craze zone, which is a wedge shaped region spanned by oriented microfibrils. The investigation of craze properties on the micromechanical level covers orders of sizes between 10 nm to several hundred μm, thus situated between the macromechanical and the molecular levels. Measurements in this microregion are adequate for analyses using craze-micromechanics models, which include the elastic properties of the continuum. Methods of craze zone measurement include optical emission spectroscopy, diffraction techniques, scanning electron microscopy, and transmission electron microscopy.

testing and classification The physical, mechanical, and chemical properties of plastics are governed by the molecular weight, molecular weight distribution, structure, composition, and other molecular parameters of plastic as well as by the nonplastic additives such as stabilizers, antioxidants, plasticizers, flame retardants, colors, fillers, etc. that are added to enhance certain processing and/or performance characteristics. Properties are also affected by their previous history, since the transformation of plastics into products is through the application of heat and pressure involving all types of fabricating processes (extrusion, injection, etc.). Thus, definite variations in properties of products can occur even with the same material and processing machine. Thermal type tests usually requiring samples as small as grams are used; some of these tests are included in the Table above.

testing and computer The Fig. opposite shows some equipment. ▷**computer-aided testing**

testing and design ▷**design failure theory**

testing and meaning **1.** A single observation made on one (test) specimen. **2.** A series of observations of which the average, or some other function, is considered a significant result for a sample.

testing and quality control Testing and QC are the most discussed but often the least understood facets of business and manufacturing. Many companies spend a high percentage of each sales dollar on QC. Usually it involves the inspection of components and parts as they complete

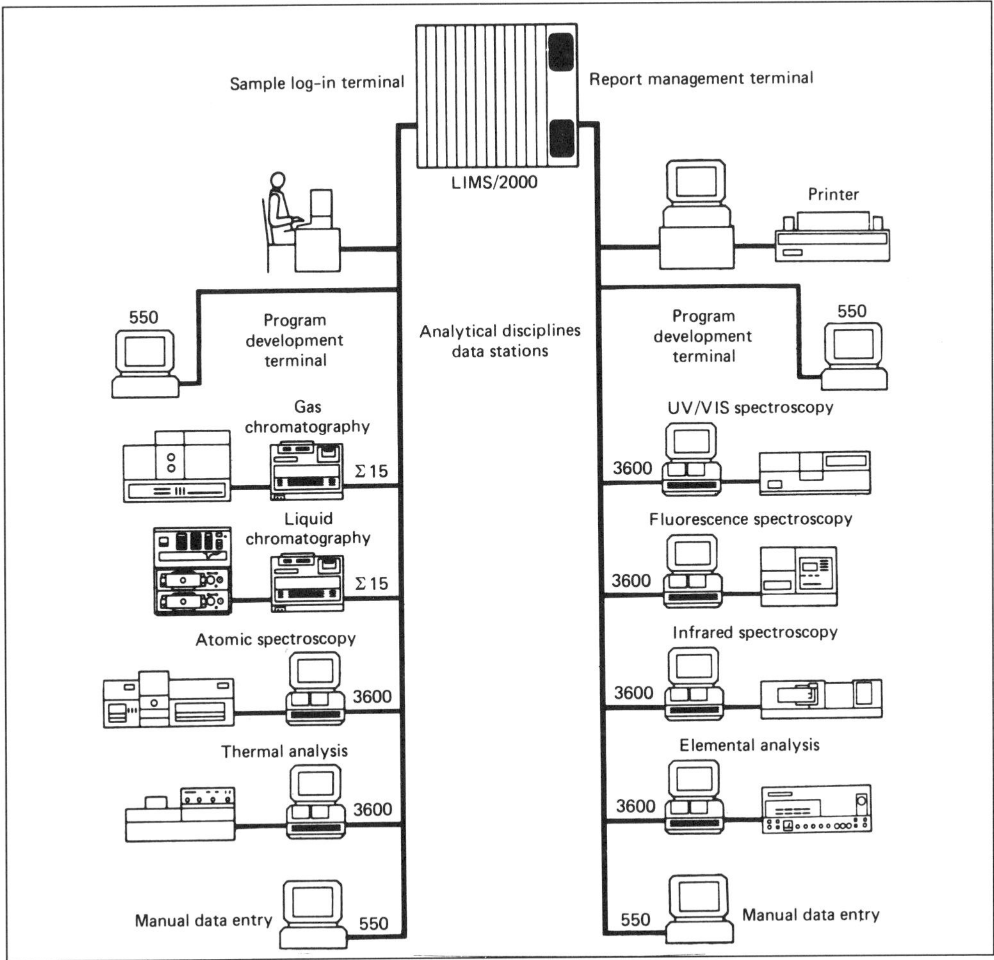

Examples for plastics evaluation in a computer-aided chemistry laboratory.

different phases of processing. Parts that are within specifications proceed, while those that are out of spec are either repaired or scrapped. The workers who made the out-of-spec parts are notified that they produced defective parts, and that they should correct "their" mistakes.

The approach just outlined is after-the-fact QC; all defects caught in this manner are already present in the part being processed. This type of QC will usually catch defects, and it is necessary, but it does little to correct basic problems in production. One of the problems with add-on QC of this type is that it constitutes one of the least cost-effective ways of obtaining a high-quality part. Quality must be built into a product from the beginning (as illustrated in Fig. for ▷**FALLO approach**); it cannot be "inspected" into the process. The closest any add-on, after-the-fact quality control can come to improving the quality built into a part is to point out processing defects to the departments or persons responsible for them. The object instead should be to control quality before a part becomes defective.

testing certification A written, printed, or signed document attesting to the validity of the test performed.

testing inadequacies ▷**testing versus reality**

testing jaws The elements of a clamp which grip the test specimen; type of grip design and grip load applied to sample can have a direct influence on repeatability of test results, outcome of test data, etc. Simple rules exist on how to eliminate any major problems.

testing laboratory Lab that measures, examines, tests, calibrates, or otherwise determines the characteristics or performance of materials or products.

testing laboratory, worldwide approval A U.S. government directory lists about 900 countries endorsed by the national Voluntary Accreditation Program (NVLAP) for various forms of testing that includes plastics. Available from NIST, NVLAP Directory, A124 Bldg., Gaithersburg, MD, U.S. 20899 or via computer modem at 301-975-2762.

testing, least count In mechanical testing, the smallest change in indication that can customarily be determined and reported.

testing, mechanical properties ▷ **mechanical properties**

testing method A definitive, standardized set of instructions for the identification, measurement, or evaluation of one or more qualities, characteristics, or properties of a material. ▷ **practice**

testing method conformance Agreement of the properties of a sample, or lot, with specification requirements.

testing, microtoming ▷ **microtoming**

testing, nondestructive ▷ **nondestructive testing**

testing residual strain, destructive method There are nondestructive and destructive methods ▷ **nondestructive testing method, residual strain**. The following destructive methods are used: *Layer removal:* It is used to evaluate stresses in flat sheets. A thin surface layer is chemically removed. Relieved of the strains in that layer, the remaining sample curves proportionately so that the residual stress in the removed layer can be calculated. *Section removal:* The sample is sectioned into small elements, thus freeing them from balancing stresses. Residual stresses can be evaluated from the relieved strains. *Hole drilling:* A 1/16 in. hole is drilled at the center of a rosette composed of three strain gauges cemented to the desired area. From measurement of the relieved strains around the hole, the residual strain at the center of the gauge can be calculated. *Stress corrosion:* A tensile stress generates surface crazing in certain plastics exposed to chemical agents. A sample or part exposed to a carefully selected chemical will craze in areas of sizable strains (popular method).

testing residual strain, nondestructive method ▷ **nondestructive testing method, residual strain**

testing specimen, moisture and drying The presence of water in a test sample represents a common problem that frequently can distort test results or produce unreliable or unrepeatable results. Water may exist as a contaminant from the atmosphere or from the solution in which the substance was formed, or it may be bonded as a chemical compound, a hydrate. Regardless of its origin, water plays an important part in determining the composition of the sample. Unfortunately, particularly with solids, the water content is a variable quantity that depends upon such things as humidity, temperature, and the state of subdivisions. Thus, the constitution of a sample may change significantly with environment and method of handling. In order to cope with these variables, there are specifications and standards on procedures to follow to stabilize this situation. They include removal of water (where possible), exposing specimens to temperature and humidity conditions for prescribed time periods, etc.

testing specimen result and processing influence Test specimens are prepared based on requirements for the specific test to be conducted. Result of test can differ or be influenced by melt flow during fabrication. To illustrate the influence of processing on mechanical properties, the test specimens in the Fig. below can be analyzed and related to what can happen in a fabricated part. It shows three sets of injection-molded specimens where the same plastic is processed in all specimens. There are three sets of similar specimens: a tensile one on top, a

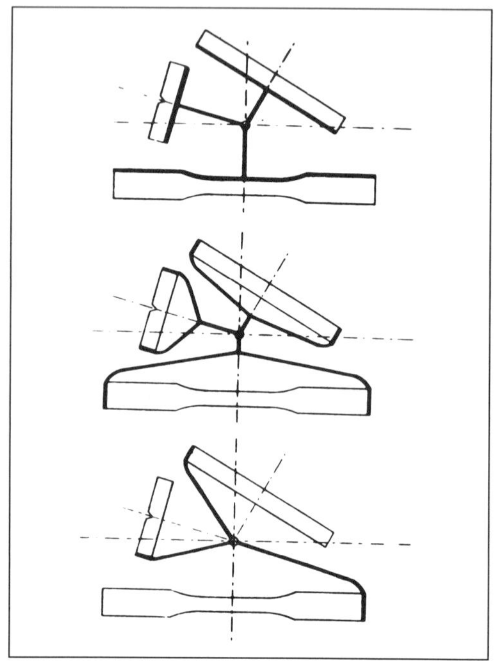

Injection molded test specimens that can be related to melt flow orientation and weld lines.

a notched Izod impact one on the right side, and a flexural one on the left. The top set has a single gate for each specimen, the center set has double gates that are opposite each other for each specimen, and the bottom set has fan gates on the side of each specimen. The highest mechanical properties come with the top set of specimens, because of its melt orientation being in the most beneficial direction. The bottom set of specimens, with its flow direction being limited insofar as the test method is concerned, results in lower test data performance. With the double-gated specimens (the center set) weld lines develop in the critical testing area that usually result in this set's having the lowest performance of any of the specimens in this figure. Fabricating techniques can be used to reduce the potential problems in a product. However, the approach used in designing the product and its mold or die is most important to target, to eliminate unwanted orientation or weld lines. If potential problems exist, the design can incorporate the necessary changes, or make them later. This approach is no different from that of designing with other materials like steel, aluminum, or glass.

testing speed ▷ **tensile testing machine test rates**

testing standard and specifications Test procedures are subject to change and it is essential that one keeps up to date on the changes.

testing statistically A function of the observed values in a sample that is used in a test of significance. ▷ **statistical material selection, reliability**

testing versus reality It should be kept in mind that most standardized laboratory tests are at best a simplification or approximation of what may happen to a finished plastic part in use. Shape and dimensions of the test specimens and the procedure by which they are made practical never duplicate those of extruded, molded, blown, etc. end product. The test results can at best approximate reality. However, when properly analyzed and applied, tests are exceptionally functional in relating test results with product service or environmental performance. The usual problem is that there are cases and organizations that do not put them to proper use. Recognize that testing has been the backbone to producing successful parts for centuries. Today and tomorrow is different in that more precise and reliable data is available than during prehistoric times.

tetrafluoroethylene/hexafluoropropylene copolymer FEP with a heat deflection resistance of about 95°C (205°F) has a lower thermal stability than PFA but otherwise has similar properties to it and is also melt processable. For price reasons, it is the most widely used fluoroplastic in the cable and wire coating market as an insulating and sheathing material. Other uses include electric underfloor heating system, and coaxial insulation.

tetrafluoroethylene/perfluoroalkylvinylether copolymer This thermoplastic (PFA) has a melting range of 305 to 310°C (580 to 590°F). PFA is largely similar to PTFE in its other properties, such as all-round chemical resistance, UV resistance, dielectric characteristics, non-stick and sliding properties, and flame retardancy. Since PF may be melt processed by all conventional methods used for thermoplastics, it considerably extends the range of applications for fluoroplastics. Many uses exist such as chemical resistant lined pumps, fittings, and pipelines; flue gas desulphurization plants; compensators and heat exchangers; thick coating for heavy duty corrosion protection; semi-conductors; containers for highly pure aggressive chemicals; cable and wire insulation; and foamed non-conductor in high-power signal transmission lines.

tetrafluoroethylene plastic ▷ **polytetrafluoroethylene plastic**

tetragonal Having three mutually perpendicular axes, two equal in length and unequal to the third.

tetramer A molecule formed by uniting four different simple molecules.

tex A unit for expressing linear density equal to the mass of weight in grams per kilometer (g/km) or micrograms per millimeter or in millitex units. Thus, basic textile unit of linear density is the weight in g of a fiber 1 km in length that = g/km = g/cm × 10^{-5} or millitex (mtex) = tex × 10^{-3}.

textile fiber ▷ **fiber textile**

textile materials A general term for fibers, yarns, fabrics, and products made from fabrics which retain approximately the strength, flexibility, and other typical properties of the original fibers or filaments.

textile modulus The ratio of change in strain in the initial straight line portion of a stress-strain curve following the removal of any crimp. ▷ **modulus**

textile tenacity ▷ **tenacity**

textile, three-dimensional ▷ **three-dimensional fabric**

textile woven and nonwoven ▷ **fabric nonwoven** and **fabric woven**

texture The surface appearance or structure of a solid or semisolid (flexible, elastomeric) material.

texturizing ▷ **glass fiber texturizing**

theoretical versus actual properties ▷ **data, theoretical versus actual properties**

theory and practice ▷ **experience and science** and **design theory and strength of materials**

therimage A decorating process for plastic which transfers the image of a label of decoration to the object under the influence of heat and light pressure.

thermal aging, relative thermal index The Underwriters' Laboratory UL 746B test provides a basis for selecting high-temperature plastics and provides a long-term thermal-aging index, the RTI or relative thermal index. The testing procedure calls for test specimens in selected thicknesses to be oven aged at certain elevated temperatures (usually higher than the expected operating temperature, to accelerate the test), then be removed at various intervals and tested at room temperature. Another reason for using higher temperatures is that for an application requiring long-term exposure a candidate plastic is often required to have an RTI value higher than the maximum application temperature. The properties tested can include mechanical strength, impact resistance, and electrical characteristics. A plastic's position in a test's RTI is based on the temperature at which it still retains 50% of its original properties.

The time required to produce a 50% reduction in properties is selected as an arbitrary failure point. These times can be gathered and used to make a linear Arrhenius plot of log time versus the reciprocal of the absolute exposure temperature. An Arrhenius relationship is a rate equation followed by many chemical reactions.

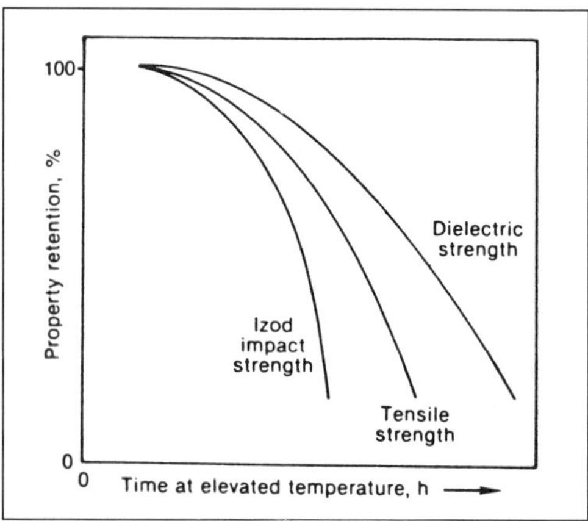

Fig. 1 Example of physical property loss due to long term heat aging (UL 746B).

A linear Arrhenius plot is extrapolated from this equation to predict the temperature at which failure is to be expected at an arbitrary time that depends on the plastic's heat-aging behavior, which is usually 11,000 hours, with a minimum of 5,000 hours. This value is the RTI.

As practiced by the UL, the procedure for selecting an RTI from Arrhenius plots usually involves making comparisons to a control standard material and other such steps to correct for random variations, oven temperature variation, the condition of the specimens, and others. The stress-strain and impact and electrical properties frequently do not degrade at the same rate (see Fig. 1 above), each having their own separated RTIs. Also, since thicker specimens usually take longer to fail, each thickness will require a separate RTI.

The UL uses RTIs as a guideline to qualify materials for many of the standard appliances and other electrical products it regulates. This testing is done in a conservative manner qualified by judgements based on long experience with such devices; UL does not apply indexes automat-

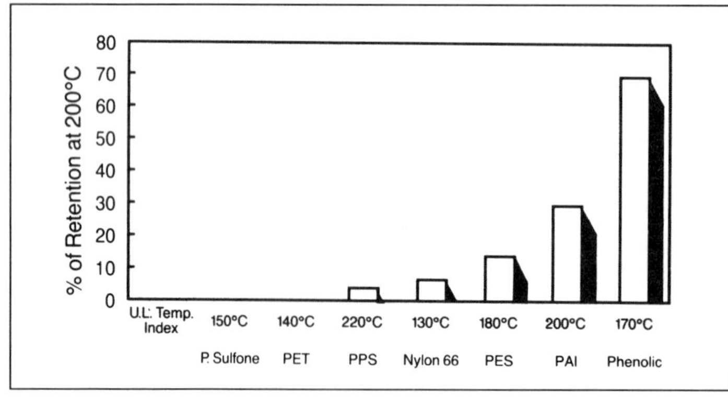

Fig. 2 Example of room temperature tensile strength retention at 200°C (392°F) based on UL's relative thermal index (RTI) test.

Guide for thermal analysis and gel chromatography.

Information	Process	Data obtainable
Composition		
Plastic modifiers	DSC	Types present, plus ratio if copolymer, blend or mixture
	GC	Polymers, oligomers, and residual monomer; amounts present
Additives	DSC	Deduce presence and amount from thermal effects (stabilizers, antioxidants, blowing agents, plasticizers, etc.)
	GC	Detect any organic additive (by MW)
Reinforcement, fillers	TGA	Amount (from weight of ash)
Moisture, volatiles	TGA	Amounts (from weight loss)
	DSC	Amounts (if sufficient heat absorbed)
Regrind level	DSC	Deduce amount from melting-point shift
	GC	Deduce amount from shift in MW distribution
Processability		
Melting behavior	DSC	Melt point and range (each resin, if blend); melt-energy requirements
Flow characteristics	GC	Deduce from balance of high and low MW polymer in MW distribution
Physical, mechanical		
Glass transition temperature	DSC	Shown by step-up in energy-absorption as resin heats (marginal for some semicrystalline resins)
	TM	Detected by sample's expansion
Crystallinity	DSC	Calculate percentage from heat of fusion during melting; also can find time-temperature conditions for desired percent crystallinity
Tensile, flexibility, impact	GC	Deduce from balance of high and low MW polymer in MW distribution
	DSC	Deduce from overall composition
Cure characteristics, thermosets		
Reactive systems	DSC	Shows gel time, cure temperature and cure time
Prepreg	DSC	Measures unreacted resin in B-stage prepreg or after cure (by volatiles)
	GC	As above, but checks by MW analysis of composite residue

ically. In general, these RTIs are very conservative and can be used as safe continuous-use temperatures for low-load mechanical products (see Fig. 2 opposite).

thermal agitation Thermally induced movements of atoms and molecules.

thermal analysis Thermal analysis (TA) includes a group of techniques in which specific properties of plastics are measured as a function of temperature. The techniques include the measurement of temperatures at which changes may occur, the measurement of the energy absorbed (endothermic transition) or evolved (exothermic transition) during a phase transition or a chemical reaction, and the assessment of physical changes resulting from changes in temperature. Examples of TA techniques include: (1) *differential scanning calorimeter* (DSC) involves measurement of heat and temperature changes; (2) *thermogravimetric analysis* (TGA) involves measurement of weight change; (3) *thermomechanical analysis* (TMA) involves measurement of dimensional change; (4) *dynamic mechanical analysis* (DMA) involves measurement of mechanical change; (5) *dielectric analysis* (DEA) involves measurement of dielectrical change; (6) *enthalpimetric analysis* (EPA) involves thermal energy release, and (7) *dynamic mechanical analysis* (DMA) involves viscoelastic changes. The Table above provides guidelines on use of a few of the TAs; includes ▷ **gel chromatography** (GC).

Various environments (vacuum, inert or controlled gas composition) and heating rates from 0.1 to 500°C·min^{-1} are available for temperatures ranging from −190 to 1,400°C. The analysis of gas(es) released by the specimen as a function of temperature is possible. The versatility of TA is thereby increased.

thermal black ▷ **carbon black**

thermal capacity The amount of thermal energy that can be stored in a storage device during a period of time and for a specific set of values (that is, initial temperature of the storage device, the temperature of the entering fluid, and the mass flow rate of fluid through the storage system).

thermal coefficient ▷ **coefficient of thermal conductivity**

thermal conductance Time rate of heat flow through a unit of a body induced by a unit temperature difference between two body surfaces.

thermal conductivity The ability of a material to conduct heat; the quantity of heat conducted per unit of time through unit area of a material of unit thickness having unit temperature differences between its faces. For purposes of comparison it is reduced to elementary units. A calorie is a standard unit of heat; it is the volume of heat necessary to raise the temperature of one gram of water 1°C. Hence, the figures given for thermal conductivity show a number of calories conducted through a cm^3 of the sample material in each second under a difference in temperature of 1°C. The result is usually in the fourth decimal place, such as 0.0003, and is shown in tables as 3×10^{-4}.

K factor is used to compare coefficient of thermal conductivity when difference in temperature of two faces is 1°C. Metals have very high thermal conductivities; their K factors lie between 100 to 3,000. Most plastics are below a K factor of 1.0 particularly foamed plastics. Plastics filled with heat conductive material (carbon, aluminum, etc.) have an increased K factor. ▷ **orientation, thermal properties**

thermal contraction ▷ **coefficient of linear thermal expansion**

thermal decomposition It results from the action of heat. It occurs at a temperature for which some components of the material are separating or associating together, with a modification of the macro or microstructure. ▷ **decomposition; degradation; mold cleaner**

thermal degradation ▷ **degradation**

thermal diffusivity The ratio of thermal conductivity to the volumetric heat capacity (product of density and specific heat). Plastics have not only the lowest conductivity, but also the highest specific heat of any structural material. ▷ **ablative plastic**

thermal endurance Property of a material to resist changes in mechanical, physical, chemical, and/or electrical properties upon exposure to temperatures for prescribed extended periods of time.

thermal expansion ▷ **coefficient of linear thermal expansion**

thermal expansion molding A process in which elastomeric tooling details are constrained within a rigid frame to generate consolidation pressure by thermal expansion during curing cycle of the autoclave molding (or other) process.

thermal index ▷ **heat test**

thermal oxidation ▷ **oxidation degradation**

thermal oxidation, recuperative ▷ **incineration fume system**

thermal oxidizer ▷ **incineration fume system**

Examples of thermal properties of plastics and other materials.

Plastics (morphology)	Density, g/cm³ (lb./ft.³)	Melt temperature T_m, °C (°F)	Glass transition temperature T_s, °C (°F)
PP (C)[1]	0.9 (56)	168 (334)	5 (41)
HDPE (C)	0.96 (60)	134 (273)	−110 (−166)
PTFE (C)	2.2 (137)	330 (626)	−115 (−175)
PA (C)	1.13 (71)	260 (500)	50 (122)
PET (C)	1.35 (84)	250 (490)	70 (158)
ABS (A)	1.05 (66)	105 (221)	102 (215)
PS (A)	1.05 (66)	100 (212)	90 (194)
PMMA (A)	1.20 (75)	95 (203)	100 (212)
PC (A)	1.20 (75)	266 (510)	150 (300)
PVC (A)	1.35 (84)	199 (390)	90 (194)
Other materials			
Aluminum	2.68 (167)	537 (1,000)	
Copper/bronze	8.8 (549)	982 (1,800)	
Steel	7.9 (493)	1510 (2,750)	
Maple wood	0.45 (28.1)	204 (400) (burns)	
Zinc alloy	6.7 (418)	427 (800)	

[1] C = Crystalline resin. A = Amorphous resin.

thermal pin ▷**heat pipe** and **mold heat transfer device**

thermal polymerization Refers to polymerization induced by heat alone (in the absence of catalyst(s)).

thermal properties In order to select materials that will maintain acceptable mechanical properties and dimensional stability, one must be aware of both the normal and extreme operating environment to which the product will be subjected. Properties and processes are influenced by thermal characteristics of plastics, such as melt temperature (T_m), glass transition temperature (T_g), dimensional stability, thermal conductivity, thermal diffusivity, heat capacity, coefficient of thermal expansion and decomposition (T_d). The Table below provides some of these data on different plastics. All these properties relate to the determination of the most useful processing conditions to meet product performance requirements. There is a maximum temperature, or to be more precise a maximum time to temperature relationship for all materials prior to loss of performance or their decomposition.

The Table on p. 754 provides additional detailed guides to thermal properties. Some of the values from this Table may differ from the previous Table because a particular family of plastics does vary. ▷**plastic properties** and **plastic variability**

thermal reclamation ▷**energy thermal reclamation**

thermal resistance Under steady-state conditions, the temperature difference required to produce a unit of heat flux through a specimen.

thermal resistivity The reciprocal of thermal conductivity.

thermal sealing Also called thermal heat sealing and heat sealing. ▷**heat sealing**

thermal spectrometry ▷**differential thermal analysis**

thermal spraying A group of processes wherein finely divided metallic and nonmetallic materials are deposited in a molten or semimolten condition to form a coating. Coating material may be in the form of powder, ceramic rod, wire, or molten material. ▷**metal spraying on plastic**

thermal stability Resistance to permanent changes in properties caused solely by heat.

thermal stress The stress produced by a temperature differential within a body. When a product is heated to above room temperature, it will tend to expand. If the temperature change is uniform, if the product is made of a single material, and if there are no external restraints, then the unit dimension change (or true strain) will be constant throughout the product. With these conditions, there will be no stress due to temperature change. However, stresses may be induced when temperature varies with location within a product, or by a temperature change in a product made of dissimilar materials, or

Thermal conductivity, 10^{-4} cal/s · cm °C (BTU/lb. °F)	Heat capacity, cal/g °C (BTU/lb. °F)	Thermal diffusivity, 10^{-4} cm²/s (10^{-3} ft.²/hr)	Thermal expansion, 10^{-6} cm/cm °C (10^{-6} in./in. °F)
2.8 (0.068)	0.9 (0.004)	3.5 (1.36)	81 (45.0)
12 (0.290)	0.9 (0.004)	13.9 (5.4)	59 (33)
6 (0.145)	0.3 (0.001)	9.1 (3.53)	70 (39)
5.8 (0.140)	0.075 (0.003)	6.8 (2.64)	80 (44)
3.6 (0.087)	0.45 (0.002)	5.9 (2.29)	65 (36)
3 (0.073)	0.5 (0.002)	3.8 (1.47)	60 (33)
3 (0.073)	0.5 (0.002)	5.7 (2.2)	50 (28)
6 (0.145)	0.56 (0.002)	8.9 (3.45)	50 (28)
4.7 (0.114)	0.5 (0.002)	7.8 (3.0)	68 (38)
5 (0.121)	0.6 (0.002)	6.2 (2.4)	50 (128)
3000 (72.5)	0.23 (0.0009)	4900 (1900)	19 (10.6)
4500 (109)	0.09 (0.0003)	5700 (2200)	18 (10)
800 (21.3)	0.11 (0.0004)	1000 (338)	11 (6.1)
3 (0.073)	0.25 (0.0010)	27 (10.5)	60 (33)
2500 (60.4)	0.10 (0.0004)	3700 (1430)	27 (15)

Thermal data guide to materials; includes maximum operating temperatures.

Material	Density (kg/m³)	Specific heat (cal/g °C)	Thermal conductivity (W/m/K)	Coeff. of therm. exp. (μm/m/K)	Thermal diffusivity (m²/s) × 10^{-7}	Max. operating temp. (°C)
ABS (high impact)	1040	0.35	0.3	90	1.7	70
Acetal (homopolymer)	1420	0.35	0.2	80	0.7	85
Acetal (copolymer)	1410	0.35	0.2	95	0.72	90
Acrylic	1180	0.35	0.2	70	1.09	50
Cellulose acetate	1280	0.36	0.15	100	1.04	60
CAB	1190	0.35	0.14	100	1.27	60
Epoxy	1200	—	0.23	70	—	130
Modified PPO	1060	—	0.22	60	—	120
Nylon 66	1140	0.4	0.24	90	1.01	90
Nylon 66 (33% glass)	1380	0.3	0.52	30	1.33	100
PEEK	1300	—	—	48	—	204
PEEK (30% carbon)	1400	—	—	14	—	255
PET	1360	—	0.14	90	—	110
PET (36% glass)	1630	—	—	40	—	150
Phenolic (mineral filled)	1690	—	—	22	—	185
Polyamide-imide	1400	—	—	36	—	260
Polycarbonate	1150	0.3	0.2	65	1.47	125
Polyester (TP)	1200	—	0.2	100	—	—
Polyetherimide	1270	—	0.22	56	—	170
Polyethersulphane	1370	—	1.18	55	—	180
Polyimide	1420	—	—	45	—	260
Polyphenylene sulfide (30% carbon)	1460	—	—	16	—	200
Polypropylene	905	0.46	0.24	100	0.65	100
Polysulphane	1240	—	—	56	—	170
Polystyrene	1050	0.32	0.15	80	0.6	50
Polythene (LD)	920	0.55	0.33	200	1.17	50
Polythene (HD)	950	0.55	0.63	120	1.57	55
PTFE	2100	—	0.25	140	0.7	50
PVC (rigid)	1400	0.24	0.16	70	1.16	50
PVC (flexible)	1300	0.4	0.14	140	0.7	50
SAN	1080	0.33	0.17	70	0.81	60
DMC (polyester) (TS)	1800	—	0.2	20	—	130
SMC (polyester) (TS)	1800	—	0.2	20	—	130
Polystyrene foam	32	—	0.032	—	—	—
Stainless steel	7855	—	90	10	—	800
Nickel chrome alloy						900
Molybdenum						1000

nonuniform wall thickness of the same material, or by a temperature change in a product with external restrains. Since fabricating processes (such as molding and welding) can involve nonuniform heating and cooling, they can result in unacceptable stresses at room temperature. ▷ **stress** and **residual stress**

thermal stress cracking TSC is crazing and/ or cracking of some plastics, paricularly thermoplastics, which results in overexposure to elevated temperatures. ▷ **crazing; crack growth; stress-crack failure**

thermister Semiconductor device with a high resistance dependence on temperature. It may be calibrated as a thermometer.

thermoanalytical method TA methods characterize a system, either single or multicomponent, in terms of the temperature dependencies of its thermodynamic properties and its physiochemical reaction kinetics. ▷ **thermal analysis**

thermobalance The instrument used for thermogravimetric analysis (TGA). Consists of an analytical balance, one arm of which is attached to the sample container by a quartz rod such that the sample is situated in an oven remote from the balance. Alternatively, the sample may be suspended in an oven from a quartz spring balance. The oven may be operated isothermally or at a programmed heating rate.

thermoband welding A variation of the hot plate welding method. A metallic tape acting as an electrical resistance element is adhered to the material to be welded. Low voltage is applied to heat the material to softening temperature. ▷ **welding**

thermocompression bonding The joining together of two materials without an intermediate material by the application of pressure and heat in the absence of an electric current.

thermocouple A device for measuring temperature, consisting of two pieces of electrical resistance wire of different types welded together at one end. The wires are insulated from each other and connected to a sensitive millivoltmeter. A small current is generated in the system and this is proportional to the temperature. ▷ **temperature sensor**

thermocouple depth in barrel ▷ **temperature controller**

thermodilatometery A technique in which a dimension of a material under negligible load is measured as a function of temperature while it is subjected to a controlled temperature program.

thermodynamic property With the heat exchange that occurs during heat processing, thermodynamics becomes important. It is the heat content of melts (about 100 cal/g) combined with the low rate of thermal diffusion (10^{-3} cm^2/s) that limits the cycle time of many processes. Also important are density changes, which for crystalline plastics, may exceed 25% as melts cool. Melts are highly compressible; a 10% volume change for 10,000 psi (69 MPa) force is typical. Surface tension of about 20 g/cm may be typical for film and fiber processing when there is a large surface-to-volume ratio.

Thermodynamic properties provide a means of working out the flow of energy from one system to another, the transformation of energy and matter from one form to another, and the utilization of energy for useful mechanical work. These properties also govern the process in which one molecular, free-radical, or ionic species changes to another, as in a chemical reaction. Any substance of specified chemical composition, perpetually in electrical, magnetic, and gravitational fields, has five fundamental thermodynamic properties, namely, pressure, temperature, volume, internal energy, and ▷ **entropy**. All changes in these properties must fulfill the requirements of the first and second laws of thermodynamics. The third law provides a reference point, the absolute zero temperature, for all these properties although such reference state is unattainable experimentally. The proper modes of applying these laws to the above five fundamental properties of an isolated system constitute the well-established subject of thermodynamics. ▷ **plastic work** and **statistical thermodynamic**

thermoelastic effect The related effects of temperature (▷ **enthalpy**) and elasticity of a material. In the case of rubber the effects are anomalous compared with other materials. The temperature of the rubber increases on stretching and decreases on retraction. Also, if the temperature of a stretched rubber is increased, the rubber contracts, whereas expansion occurs if the rubber is cooled; the linear coefficient expansion is negative except at low elongation, where thermoelastic inversion is said to occur.

thermoelastic inversion ▷ **tensile thermoelastic inversion**

thermoelasticity Rubber-like elasticity exhibited by a rigid plastic and resulting from an increase of temperature.

thermoelement One of two dissimilar electrical conductors comprising a thermocouple.

thermoforming The process usually consists of heating thermoplastic (TP) sheet, film, and profile to its softening heat and forcing the hot and flexible material against the contours of a mold by pneumatic means (differentials in air pressure are created by pulling a vacuum between the plastic and the mold, or the pressure of compressed air is used to force the material against the mold), mechanical means (plug, matched mold, etc.), or combinations of pneumatic and mechanical means.

The process involves (1) heating the sheet (film, etc.) in a separate oven and then transferring the hot sheet to a forming press, (2) using automatic machinery to combine heating and forming in a single unit, or (3) a continuous operation feeding off a roll of plastic or directly from the exit of an extruder die (postforming). Practically all the materials used are extruded TPs; very small amounts are calendered or cast. To date very few thermosets (TSs) are used, as the markets have not developed for them. These TSs can be either unreinforced or reinforced. Practically any TP can be used, but certain types are easier to use, permitting deep draws without tearing or excessive thinning in certain areas such as corners. The ease of forming depends on material characteristics; it is influenced by minimum and maximum thickness, pinholes, ability of the material to retain heat profile gradients across the surface and the thickness, the controllability of applied stress, the rate and depth of draw, the mold geometry, the stabilizing of uniaxial or biaxial deformation, and, most important, minimizing the thickness variation of the sheet.

One of the oldest thermoforming techniques is bending, which is relatively easy to handle.

The production of finished parts made by bending often also involves joining (adhesive or welding) or mechanical operations (milling, drilling, polishing). If the sheet is heated only locally in the bending operation, no special forming tools are needed. The width of the heating zone and the thickness of the sheet determine the bending radius. Limitations are related to the softening point of the sheet and the intrinsic rigidity of the heated sheet (sag should be minimized). Extensive use of the method is made in bending transparent plastics (such as PMMA and PC) up to $3\frac{1}{2}$ in. (90 mm) thick, for use in store displays, staircases, partitions in banks, aircraft windows, and so on. With this type of plastic, if restrictions in the bending area are minimized, the thickness at the bend can remain unchanged.

In many applications of conventional thermoforming, low-cost tooling is used compared to that of other processes, particularly in cases of limited production and/or the forming of very large parts. Thermoforming of thin parts has an advantage over most other processes, where very thin "walls" cannot be produced. An example of its use is in skin and blister packaging.

To improve the strength or structural performance of formed plastics, the processor can utilize design features such as corrugations, box shapes, and so on. These features are very easily incorporated with thermoforming. One example of minimizing the thickness of a product and improving its strength is a formed drinking cup with a rolled edge (which also eliminates cutting lips).

With most forming (not including bending) there can be up to 50% scrap trim or web. This material could be wasted, but it is usually recycled and blended with virgin resin. Individual sheet stock formed into round shapes could have 50% or more scrap. With square forms, there could be up to 25% scrap.

The various thermoforming techniques are generally described in terms of the means used to form the sheet, such as bending, vacuum forming, pressure forming, plug-assist forming, matched mold forming, and so on. The different methods enable the processor to form different-shaped products to meet various performance requirements. Most of these techniques are reviewed in the Figs. on pp. 757–759. An evaluation of these methods shows that simple to very complex shapes can be formed, and the shape as well as the surface condition can be accurately controlled outside, inside, or on both sides.

Compressed air thermoforming is a technique "borrowed" from sheet steel processing; its main use in plastics processing is in plastic cup production. Machines are also coming into use for the production of engineering components, such as computer covers. A flexible-pressure pad is used to press the hot sheet into the mold cavity, with the aid of an air cushion maintained under pressure. Compared with vacuum forming, this method has the considerable advantage that depressions and protrusions of the molding tool are very accurately reproduced. Even undercuts can be molded with very high precision, as well as surface features with different degrees of roughness.

A compressed air thermoforming machine is essentially a deep drawing machine with a controlled heat shield, except that, in place of an upper ram, a pressure bell is used. The heated rubbery material is pressed into the molding tool using a differential pressure of up to 100 psi. After cooling and demolding, the formed part is precisely shaped. ▷ **blister package; contour package; shrink wrapping; postforming**

thermoforming, air-assist Methods in which air flow or air pressure is employed to preform the sheet partially before the final pull-down onto the mold using vacuum.

thermoforming, air-slip A variation of snap-back thermoforming in which the male mold is enclosed in a box in such a way that when the mold moves forward toward the hot plastic, air is trapped between the mold and the plastic sheet. As the mold advances, the plastic is kept away from it by the air cushion formed as described, until the full travel of the mold is reached, at which point a vacuum is applied, removing the air cushion and forming the part against the plug.

thermoforming, billow Heated sheet is clamped over a billow chamber. Air pressure in the chamber is increased causing the sheet to billow upward against a descending male mold.

thermoforming, bubble Sheet is clamped into a frame suspended above a mold, heated, blown into a blister shape by air, then molded to shape by means of a descending plug applied to the blister, forcing it downward into the mold.

thermoforming, clamshell A variation of blow molding and thermoforming in which two preheated sheets are clamped between halves of a split mold (like the two-part mold used to form the final blow molded part). Each sheet is drawn into the individual mold cavity by vacuum and simultaneously injecting air between the sheets. An end contact surface could include an integral hinge.

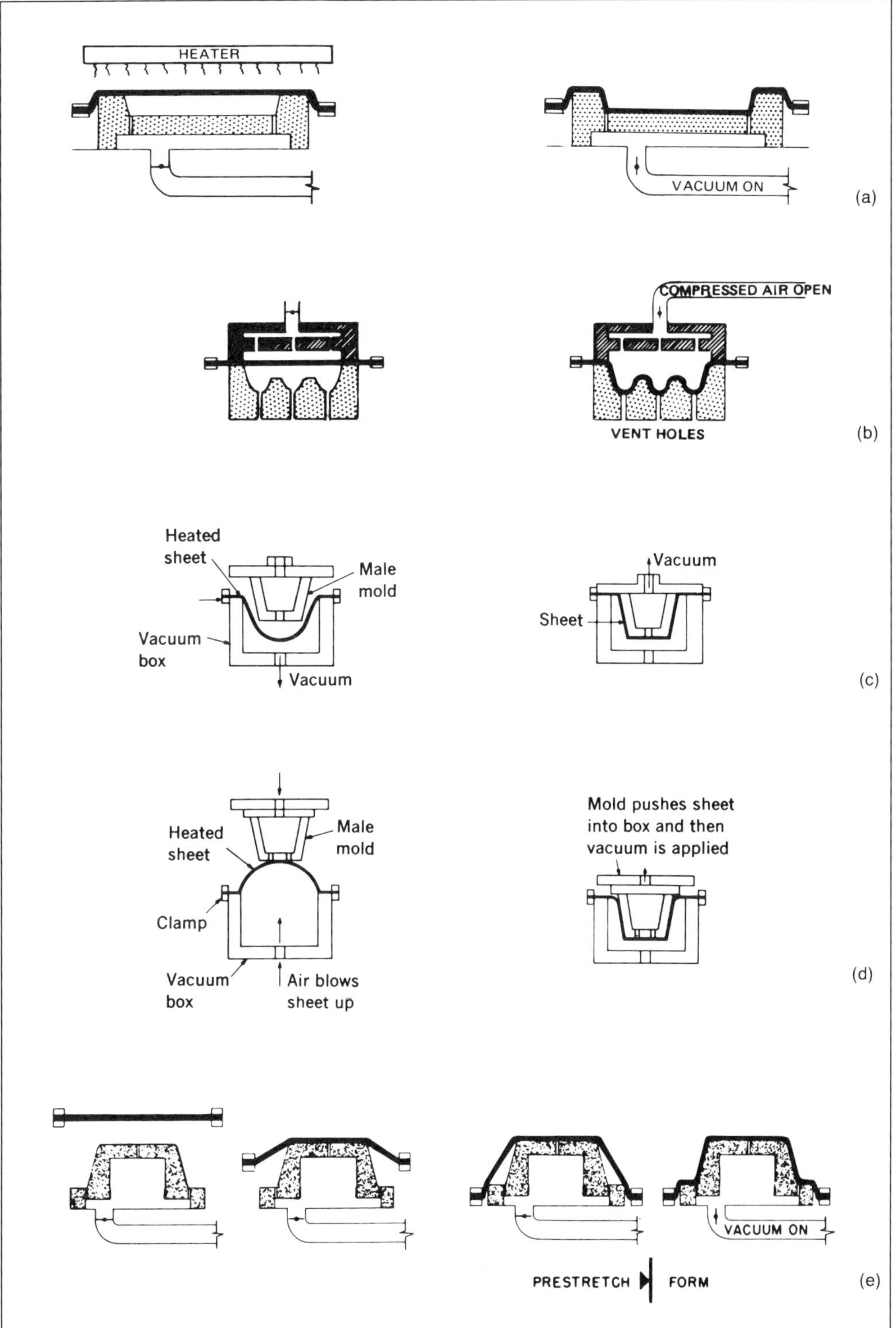

Examples of the different thermoforming techniques. (*a*) Straight forming: vacuum; (*b*) straight forming: pressure; (*c*) snapback forming; (*d*) forming with a billow snapback is recommended for parts requiring a uniform controllable wall thickness; (*e*) drape forming.

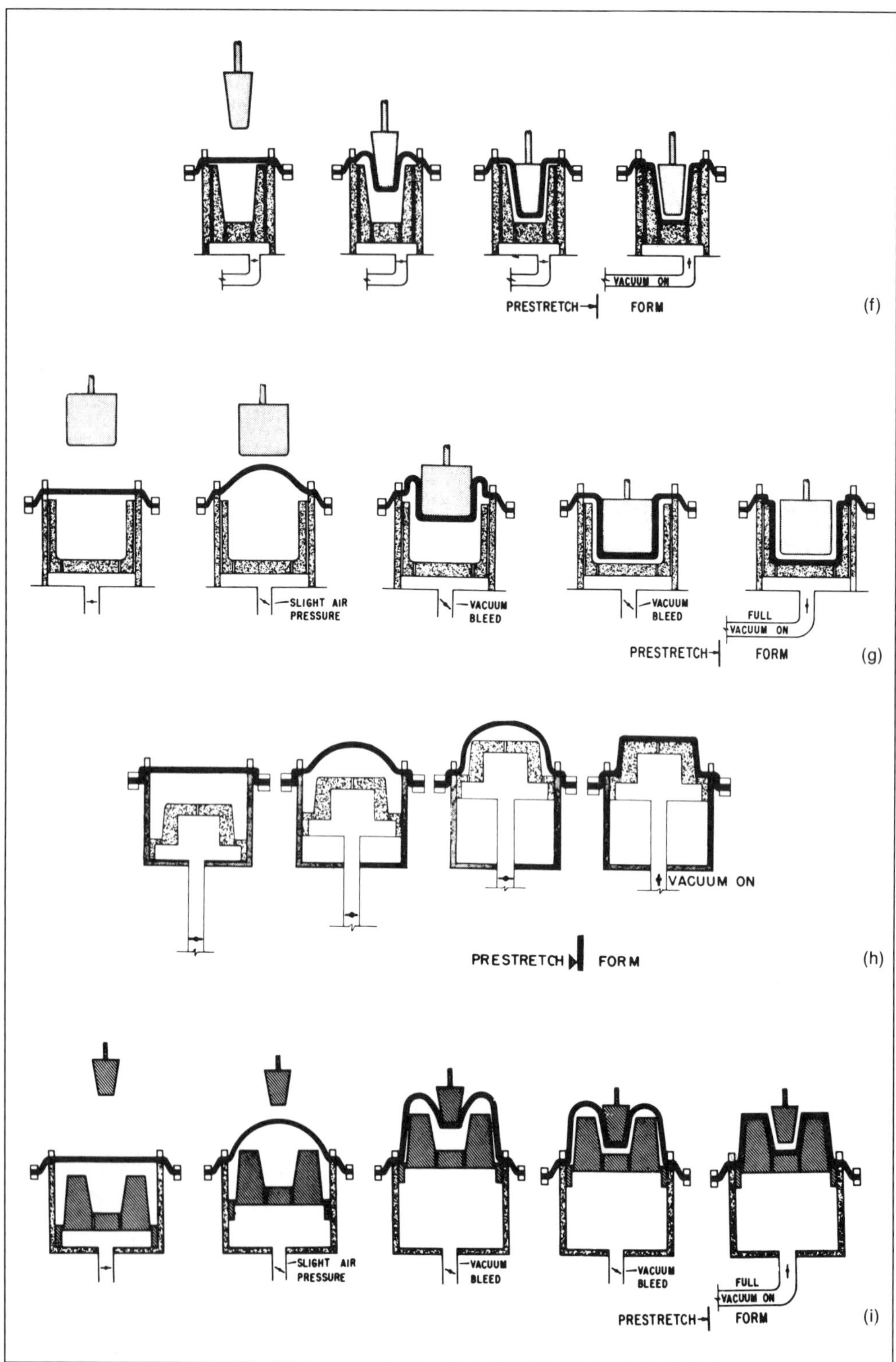

Examples of the different thermoforming techniques (*continued*): (*f*) Plug-assist forming; (*g*) plug-assist, reverse-draw forming; (*h*) air-slip forming; (*i*) plug-assist, air-slip forming.

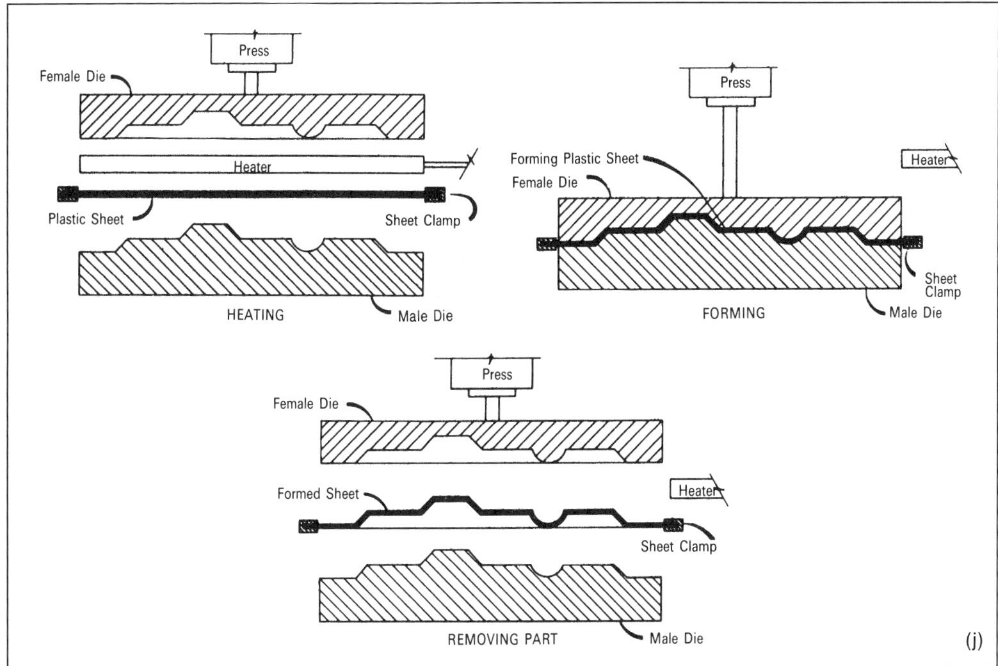

Examples of the different thermoforming techniques (*continued*): (*j*) Matched-die forming.

thermoforming, cold ▷ **cold forming**

thermoforming, comoform cold molding An extension of the cold molding process which utilizes a thermoformed plastic skin to impart excellent surface and other characteristics (weather resistance, etc.) to a cold molded reinforced plastic or laminate.

thermoforming disadvantages Like any material, product, etc. nothing reaches perfection, so it is best to recognize "limitations". (They become disadvantages when the limitations are not "recognized".) Thermoforming requires trimming either within the forming line or after being removed from the machine. All types of machines trim all kinds of materials and shapes at many different speeds, including quick cutting knife changes. Making glossy products may be a problem.

thermoforming, drape Sheet is clamped into a frame, heated, and draped over the mold. A vacuum can be used to pull the sheet into conformity with the mold.

thermoforming, drape assist frame or drape forming A frame, made up of anything from thin wires to thick bars, is shaped to the peripheries of the depressed areas of the mold and suspended above the sheet to be formed. During forming, the assist frame drops down, drawing the sheet tightly into the mold and thereby preventing webbing between high areas of the mold and permitting closer spacing in multiple molds.

thermoforming, form and spray Technique to strengthen thermoformed sheets by applying on one side spray-up of reinforced plastics.

thermoforming, form, fill, and seal FFS pouch, extensively used in packaging, involves inline thermoforming film or sheet, inserting product being packaged, and sealing the package which is closed by heat sealing, adhesive, etc. As shown in the Fig. on p. 760, there are basically three types of pouches used. Each has many variations. ▷ **medical device packaging, clarity**

thermoforming, form, fill, and seal versus preform FFS packages based on present technology present different concerns regarding clarity. Preforms are typically thick walled and rigid, to protect expensive, heavy, and/or sharp devices, to accommodate intricate shapes and compartments, and to prevent corner thinning. Thickness, however, is often accomplished by haze. FFAs are usually less thick and rigid than preforms. While thinness aids clarity, it limits depth of draw. Hence, FFS is well suited for packaging inexpensive, high volume products such as syringes, gloves, etc. that do not require much physical (as opposed to microbiological) protection. When deeper draw and clarity are

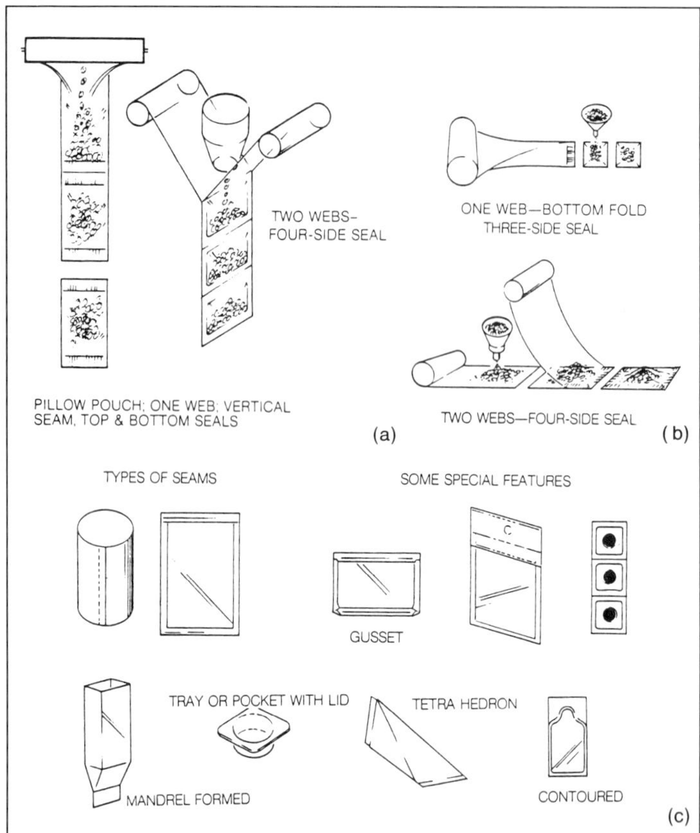

Basic features and constructions of form, fill, and seal pouches. (*a*) Vertical formed; (*b*) horizontal formed; (*c*) mandrel or shape formed.

required, co-extrusions are an option. There are combinations that are flexible yet tough enough for deeper draws. Nylon is an example.

thermoforming, form, fill, and seal with zipper on-line The zipper is usually put in the film by a secondary operation, which adds cost and tends to be wasteful (up to 30% becomes scrap). Solutions to this problem were developed during 1990 (by both Bodolay Pratt Division of Package Machinery Co., Stafford Springs, CT and Klockner-Bartelt Co., Sarasota, FL). Both systems essentially combine the pouch web and zipper strip from a supply roll and pass them through a strip-seal station, where the zipper is heat sealed to the web. The system basically has two zipper sealing stations, plus an ultrasonic spot-seal station for packages that are hermetically sealed or gas-flushed. There is no effect on the machine speed line when compared to conventional FFS lines.

thermoforming gasoline tank These automobile, truck, etc. tanks are usually blow-molded. However, thermoforming techniques are applicable. ▷ **gasoline tank permeability** and **sulfonation**

thermoforming machines The machines range from a "home-made", simple single-stage operation to multistage computerized process-controlled equipment. With single-stage machines, precut sheets are loaded individually into a clamping frame, moved into a heating chamber, and moved back to their original position where the forming takes place. The first Fig. on p. 761 shows a single-stage plug-assist former. A two-stage unit consists of two forming stations with one heating chamber.

Another type of machine uses three or more stages. They are usually built on a horizontal circular frame that rotates (see second Fig. on p. 761). The rotary table operates like a merry-go-round, indexing through the various stations. A three-stage machine would have stations for loading and unloading, heating and forming, and cooling; stations would be indexed 120 degrees apart.

To speed up output, in-line sheet-fed machines are used. Two parallel continually moving tracks hold and move a clamped sheet through the required stations of heat and forming. All movements are indexed so all actions are repeatable. To further increase the output,

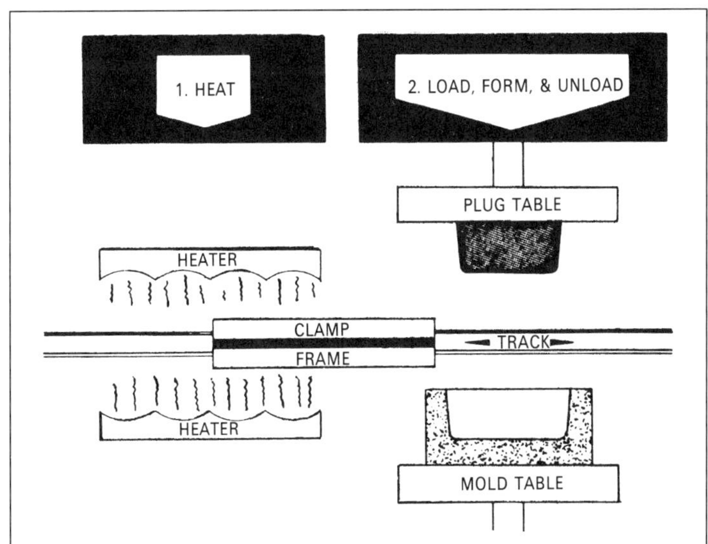

Schematic of a single-stage thermoforming machine.

continuous rolls of sheet or sheet material are fed directly from an extruder. A set of continuously conveying chains/tracks indexes the sheet as it moves accurately through the heating, forming, trimming, and packaging stations.

Other stations can be included, such as decorating. Multicavity molds are used extensively. As is typical of injection molding and extrusion machines, they can have sophisticated computer controls to ensure proper operation of all machine and material functions.

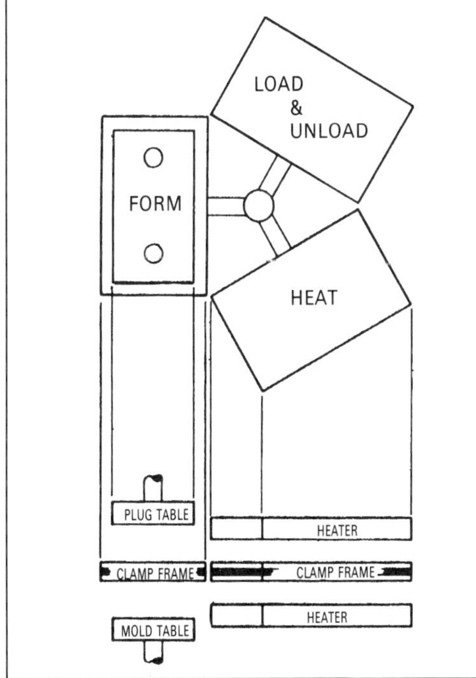

Three-stage thermoforming machine schematic.

Trimming of plastics, if not performed correctly, can be damaging to formed parts and slow down or stop the output. Tools for trimming include shear discs, steel rule dies, and saws. The cutting action can be done with the usual punch press, as well as press brakes and other devices. Punch and die clearances should be held to a minimum. The generally acceptable rules that are applied to metals are not applicable to plastics. Also, what is good for one plastic may not work on another. Plastics have different cutting habits—some tend to be brittle, rubbery, and so on. Material suppliers and tool manufacturers can provide useful information about trimming.

In-line thermoforming production lines, particularly those being fed directly from an extruder, have to be completely synchronized, or inferior parts result, and/or the cost of the operation goes up. For example, if the trimmer operation has to be slowed down, the extruder output has to be reduced. In fact, a slowdown can result in a shutdown if the extruder cannot operate at the slower speed required. All functions and stations have to be properly interrelated.

thermoforming mold Tools (molds) for forming are of all sizes and shapes. Generally made from aluminum, either cast or machined, and include many holes (or the equivalent) to allow for air movement from between the heated sheet and contact mold surface. Other materials of mold construction are used, such as wood, reinforced plastics, steel, etc. depending on various factors such as heat transfer desired, part quantity, cost, etc. ▷**mold material**

thermoforming, orientation ▷**orientation**

thermoforming, plug Also called plug-assist. Process in which a plug, male mold, or male stretching device is used to partially preform the part before forming is completed using vacuum and/or pressure.

thermoforming, plug-and-ring Plug functioning as a male mold is forced into a heated plastic sheet held in place by a clamping ring.

thermoforming, pneumatic control This review on vacuum thermoforming can be related to most of the other forming processes. With a vacuum system a sheet is subjected to heat to meet its required processing temperature, or technique that forces it against the shape of a mold. The hot, pliable material is moved rapidly to the mold (for example, by gear drives) and/or is moved by an air pressure differential, which holds it in place as it cools. When the proper set temperature is reached, the formed part can be removed and still retain its shape.

Two important needs in this cycle are to sustain the pressure and to maintain uniform heating of the plastic. Generally, the faster a vacuum is created, the higher the part quality. It is important that the mold be at the proper heat so the fast vacuum will produce a part with no internal stress (or very little). During forming the vacuum gauge should never fall below 20 in. of mercury (Hg), which at sea level is 9.82 psi of atmospheric pressure on the part. As a TP cools, this pressure cannot provide sufficient force to form the part and will not hold the plastic tight against the mold (see Table).

A vacuum under 20 in. Hg is not satisfactory; at least 25 in. Hg is required. For proper pressure regulation, a vacuum storage or surge tank is necessary to retain a minimal even vacuum. For long forming cycles, a surge tank will permit the use of a smaller vacuum pump than would otherwise be required. To determine the vacuum surge tank size in cubic feet, use the following formula (229):

$$V_0 \times P_0 + V_m \times P_m = V_1 \times P_1$$

where: $V_0 =$ surge tank volume, including piping to vacuum control valve, $V_m =$ mold area volume, $V_1 = V_0 + V_m$, $P_0 =$ absolute pressure in surge tank (0.5 psi), $P_m =$ initial pressure in the mold (at sea level 14.7 psi; or with prestretched forming, use 17.7 psi), $P_1 =$ desired atmospheric working pressure.

In an example where the volume of the mold and piping is 4 ft³, the vacuum pump can pull about 29 in. Hg, so the surge tank pressure is 0.5 psi. The desired working pressure is 2.42 psi in the tank, and the initial mold pressure is 14.7 psi. Thus:

$$V_0 \times 0.5 + 4 \times 14.7 = (V_0 + 4) \times 2.42$$

$$0.5\ V_0 + 58.8 = 2.42\ V_0 + 9.68$$

$$V_0 = 25.58\ \text{ft}^3\ (191\ \text{gal or}\ 723\ \text{L})$$

When a lower pressure of 20 in. Hg is used, which is 4.88 psi in the tank:

$$V_0 \times 0.5 + 4 \times 14.7 = (V_0 + 4) \times 4.88$$

$$0.5\ V_0 + 58.8 = 4.88\ V_0 + 19.52$$

$$V_0 = 8.97\ \text{ft}^3\ (671\ \text{gal or}\ 2540\ \text{L})$$

In thermoforming it is sometimes necessary to prestretch (or preblow) the hot sheet before final forming. Usually 3 to 5 psi compressed air is used, which results in a greater amount of air being at atmospheric pressure than in the processing of nonprestretched parts. In the above formula add the volume of the prestretched bubble to the volume of the mold and the pressure differential needed for blowing the bubble to the initial atmospheric pressure in the mold.

The objective is to have the vacuum surge tank as close as possible to the forming station and the vacuum control valve. Use of flexible vacuum hose with connections eliminates el-

Vacuum pressure measurements.

Pressure, psi		
Gauge[1]	Absolute[2]	pressure, in. Hg
0.0	14.7	0.0
−1.0	13.7	2.04
−2.0	12.7	4.07
−4.0	10.7	8.14
−6.0	8.7	12.20
−8.0	6.7	16.30
−9.0	5.7	18.32
−9.9	4.9	20.00
−10.0	4.7	20.36
−11.0	3.7	22.40
−12.0	2.7	24.43
−12.3	2.4	25.00
−13.0	2.7	26.47
−13.7	1.0	27.89
−14.0	0.7	28.50
−14.2	0.5	28.91
−14.3	0.4	29.00
−14.6	0.1	29.73
−14.7	0.0	29.92

[1] Amount of pressure exceeding atmospheric pressure.
[2] Measured with respect to zero (absolute) vacuum; in a vacuum system, absolute pressure (psia) is equal to the negative gauge pressure (psig) subtracted from the atmospheric pressure.

bows, tees, and tubing reducers. All valves must be capable of operation at the full open position. To utilize fully the rapid vacuum capability provided by the surge tank, the mold must be able to take advantage of all vacuum pressure available. Vacuum holes should be drilled as large as possible, and a maximum number should be used.

Back drilling of large holes (to 0.125 in.) on the underside can be used when smaller holes are required on the part side. Male molds can be mounted on a vacuum plate with thin washers or shims, and large vacuum holes can be drilled under the mold. Narrow slots also can be used, and they offer much less resistance than holes when air is evacuated through the mold. Flat areas, segmented sections, or male portions of a mold can be joined with shims, providing long slots.

thermoforming, postforming ▷ **postforming**

thermoforming, prebillow Prestretching of the heated plastic sheet by differential air pressure prior to thermoforming.

thermoforming, preprinting Printing of a distorted pattern on a plastic sheet which is then thermoformed to the desired shape bringing the printed pattern into the proper undistorted shape.

thermoforming, pressure Application of air pressure onto the sheet to force it into the cavity to form the part rather than using vacuum to draw the sheet against the mold cavity.

thermoforming, prestretched Stretching of heated sheet either by mechanical means or by differential air pressure prior to the final shaping by differential air pressure.

thermoforming, rigidizing ▷ **thermoforming, form and spray**

thermoforming, sandwich heating The usual method of heating the sheet, prior to forming, that consists of heating both sides of the sheet simultaneously.

thermoforming, scrapless ▷ **forming scrapless**

thermoforming, sheet The forming of heated sheet into some definite shape by pneumatic and/or mechanical means.

thermoforming, snap-back A variation of vacuum forming. Heated sheet is pulled to a concave form by the vacuum box underneath, then is snapped upward against a male plug by vacuum through the plug. The process can extend deep drawing.

thermoforming, stretch Heated sheet is stretched over a male mold and then drawn to the mold form by vacuum and/or pressure.

thermoforming, temperature control Even though TPs have specific processing heats, forming requires thorough , fast, and uniform radiant heat from the surface to the core to the surface. To achieve these conditions, sheet plastics over 0.040 in. (1.02 mm) should use sandwich-type (bottom and top) heater banks. To ensure that sufficient heat is used, heaters should have capacities of at least 4 to 6 kW/sq ft. Various type of radiant heating elements and their performances are shown in the Table below.

Types of radiant heating elements.[1]

Element	Efficiency, %		Average life, hours	Performance
	When new	After 6 months		
Ceramic panel	65	55	12,000–15,000	Best buy; heats uniformly and is efficient and capable for profiling heat.
Quartz panel	58	50	8,000–10,000	Same as ceramic heaters.
Coiled nichrome wire	18–20	8 –10	1,500	Initially lowest cost; is very inefficient, and heats non-uniformly with use.
Tubular rods[2]	45	20	3,000	Inexpensive; heats nonuniformly with use and is difficult to screen or mask for profiling heat.
Gas-fired infrared	40–45	25	5,000–6,000	Lowest cost to operate; has many disadvantages including wavelength variations and frequency maintenance.

[1] Steel clamping frames should be nickel-copper-chrome-plated to reflect heat to sheet edges. After 6 months' use, consider replacing side and back reflectors in order to regain 4 to 8 percent efficiency.
[2] Sanding and polishing oxidized tubular heaters can improve their efficiency 10 to 15 percent.

Guide to thermoforming temperatures (°F).

Plastic	Mold heat[1]	Lower processing limit[2]	Normal forming heat[3]	Upper limit[4]	Set heat[5]
HDPE	160	260	295	330	180
ABS	180	260	325	380	200
PMMA	190	300	350	380	200
PS	185	260	295	360	200
PC	265	335	375	400	280
PVC	140	210	275	300	160
PSU	320	390	475	575	360

[1] The mold temperature is important in the forming process. High mold heats provide high-quality parts with high impact strength, low internal stress, and good detail, material distribution, and optics (clarity and lack of distortion). However, thin gauge materials frequently can be thermoformed on molds at lower heat, such as 35–90°F, as the additional stresses produced are not pronounced in the thin gauges and do not interfere with product performance.
[2] The lower processing limit represents the lowest heat at which the sheet can be formed without undue stresses. This means that the sheet should touch every corner of the mold prior to reaching this lower limit; otherwise problems develop such as stresses/strains that can cause warpage, brittleness, or other physical changes in the part.
[3] The normal forming temperature is the heat at which the sheet should be formed under normal operation. This temperature should be reached throughout the sheet. Shallow draws with fast vacuum and/or pressure forming will allow somewhat lower sheet heat and thus a faster cycle. Higher heats are required for deep draws, prestretching, detailed mold decorations, etc.
[4] The upper limit is the heat point where the sheet begins to degrade or becomes too fluid and pliable to form. These temperatures normally can be exceeded only with an impairment of the plastic's physical properties (higher heats obtain for IM and extrusion).
[5] The set temperature is the heat at which the part may be removed from the mold without warpage. Sometimes parts can be removed at higher heats if postcooling fixtures are used.

The cycle time is controlled by the heating and cooling rates, which in turn depend on the following factors: the temperature of heaters and the cooling medium, the initial temperature of the sheet, the effective heat transfer coefficient, the sheet thickness, and thermal properties of the sheet material. Different materials absorb radiant heat most efficiently at various wavelengths, which in turn are affected by the temperature of the emitting heater. The most appropriate wavelengths for TPs fall within the infrared spectrum of 6 μm (400°F) to 3.2 μm (1,200°F). For example, ABS, PE, and HIPS absorb radiant heat most efficiently when the heating elements emit 3.5 to 3.3 μm, whereas PC requires 3.4 μm.

Typical material and process heats for a variety of plastics are given in the Table above. The normal forming heat should be attained throughout the sheet, and should be measured just before the mold and sheet come together. Shallow draw projects with fast vacuum and/or pressure forming allow somewhat lower sheet heats and thus a faster cycle. Slightly higher heats may be required for deep draws, prestretching, and highly detailed molds.

When extrusion and thermoforming are separate operations, the heat energy supplied for extrusion is completely lost by chilling the sheet. Reheating for thermoforming requires additional heat energy. The in-line process offers the advantage of using a high percentage of the energy contained in the sheet to condition it to the forming heat. Actual savings of about 30 to 40% can be obtained. The in-line process provides a more even heat distribution, and weight distributions can be reduced without changing physical properties. At equal output rates, an in-line process needs only half the floor space of separate operations.

thermoforming thermotropic liquid crystal A liquid crystal polymer (LCP) that can be processed using thermoforming techniques.

thermoforming troubleshooting The Table opposite is a guide.

thermoforming, twin-sheet ▷ **thermoforming, clamshell**

thermoforming, unequal stretch With constant suction created by the vacuum across the face of the sheet, the major portion of the sheet is pulled down until it contacts the mold. But, the sheeting at the edges of the mold or close to the clamp is stretched most and thus becomes the thinnest portion of the formed item. A number of methods are used which partially correct this situation. One of them is vacuum forming into a female mold with a helper (plug-assist). A helper is a plug shaped device, roughly designed like the formed piece, which pushes the hot sheet downward in the center of the mold cavity and stretches it before the vacuum is applied. The amount of stretch can be

Guide to thermoforming problems.

Problem	Probable cause(s)	Solution(s)
Blisters or bubbles in part	Moisture in sheet Heating too rapidly	Predry sheet, heating from both sides. Lower heater temperatures.
Webbing, wrinkling in parts	Sheet is too hot	Shorten heat cycle or lower temperature. Increase heater distance.
Chill marks on parts	Inadequate mold temperature control	Increase number of water cooling channels.
Part corners and bottoms too thin	Variation in sheet or mold temperatures	Adjust oven heating pattern and mold temperature control system for uniformity. Adjust timing of forming functions.
Shrink marks on part especially in corners	Inadequate vacuum	Check for vacuum leaks or plugged vacuum holes. Add vacuum surge capacity or vacuum holes.
Parts sticking to mold after forming	Part temperature too high	Lower mold temperature slightly. Increase cooling cycle.
Poor part detail	Insufficient vacuum Forming air pressure too low, timing off	Clear clogged vacuum holes. Increase number or size of vacuum holes. Enlarge vacuum line and valves. Increase air pressure. Adjust air-on timing.
Pock marked parts	Air entrapped over smooth mold surface	Grit blast mold surface. Add vacuum holes.
Drag lines on parts	Excessive material drag over lip of mold cavity	Reduce plug assist travel to half-way point in cavity.
Shiny streaks on parts	Sheet overheated in this area	Lower heater temperature. Slow heating cycle or increase distance between heater and sheet.
Sheet sticking to plug assist	Plug temperature too high	Reduce plug temperature. Spray with mold release.
Poor wall thickness distribution in parts	Hot or cold spots in oven Excessive sheet sag	Adjust oven profile. Screen or otherwise control temperature of center areas of heater banks.
Splits and tears in parts	Incorrect timing of sheet indexing Too high or low eject air pressure	Adjust indexing timing. Adjust eject air pressure.
Too much detail in parts	Sheet too hot Form air pressure too high	Cut heating time. Reduce air pressure.
Sheet tears during forming	Sheet temperature too high or too cold Poor mold design	Reduce or increase heating time or temperature. Increase radius of mold corners.
Poor part surface clarity	Mold and/or plug assist too hot	Reduce mold and/or plug assist temperature.
Part warpage	Insufficient cooling Mold temperature too low	Cool to below set temperature. Raise mold temperature to just below material set temperature.
Excessive part shrinkage after forming	Erratic mold temperatures Forming cycle speed is off	Adjust mold temperature. Adjust forming cycle speed.
Inconsistent forming	Heater elements out Drafts in oven	Replace malfunctioning heater elements. Enclose heating and forming areas.

controlled by means of the plug temperature. Thus, the sheet is deformed in its central portion before the vacuum pulls it down at the edges. This results in a much more uniform wall thickness and allows a higher depth-to-diameter ratio. But there may be two drawbacks: the plug may leave a mark on the sheeting, and the clarity or the gloss on the inside surface of the formed article may be reduced.

There is less danger of thinning the sheet at the edges with drape forming procedures with a male mold, which works in principle similarly to plug-assisted vacuum forming. The proper temperature of both the mold and sheeting will govern the amount of stretch of the sheet on the mold and at the edges. ▷ **thermoforming, temperature control**

thermoforming, vacuum Vacuum is an important aspect with thermoforming. It provides and is adapted to many (most) of the forming techniques. ▷ **thermoforming pneumatic control**

thermoforming, web or bridge An excess fold of plastic which sometimes occurs during forming, particularly drape forming. It is caused by the plastic not being able to shrink as rapidly as it is being forced to conform to the shape of the mold by differential air pressure.

thermoforms The product that results from a thermoforming operation.

thermogram ▷ **differential thermal analysis**

thermographic transfer process A modification of the hot stamping process wherein the design to be transferred is first printed on a film, from which it is transferred to the plastic part by means of heat and pressure.

thermogravimetric analysis This method measures the weight of a substance heated at a controlled rate as a function of time or temperature. To perform the test, a sample is hung from a balance and heated in the small furnace on the TGA unit according to a predetermined temperature program. As all materials ultimately decompose on heating, and the decomposition temperature is a characteristic property of each material, TGA is an excellent technique for the characterization and quality control of materials (see Fig below and on top of p. 767).

Properties measured include thermal decomposition temperatures, relative thermal stability, chemical composition, and the effectiveness of flame retardants. TGA also is commonly used to determine the filler content of many thermoplastics.

A typical application of TGA is in compositional analysis. For example, a particular polyethylene part contained carbon black and a mineral filler. The electrical properties were important in the use of this product and could be affected by the carbon black content. TGA was used to determine the carbon black content and mineral-filler content for various lots, which were considered either acceptable or unacceptable. The samples were heated in nitrogen to volatilize the PE, leaving carbon black and a mineral-filler residue. The carbon content was then determined by switching to an air environment to burn off the carbon black. The weight loss was a direct measure of the carbon black content.

thermomechanical analysis TMA measures the dimensional changes as a function of temperature. The dimensional behavior of a material can be determined precisely and rapidly with small samples in any form—powder, pellet, film,

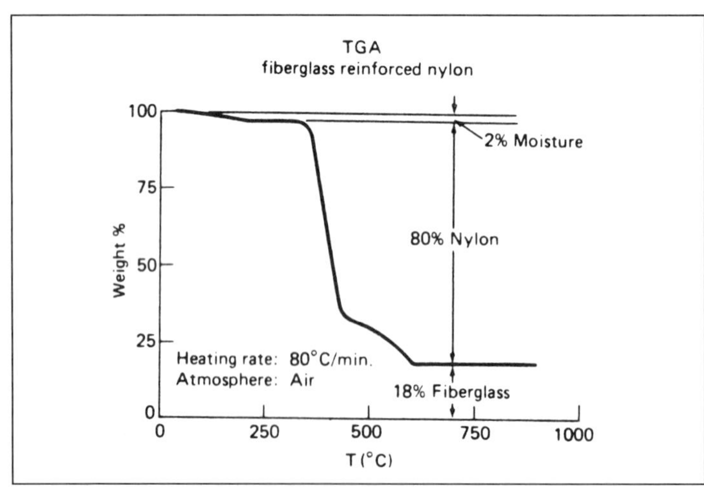

TGA determines the amount of glass fiber reinforcement in nylon plastic matrix.

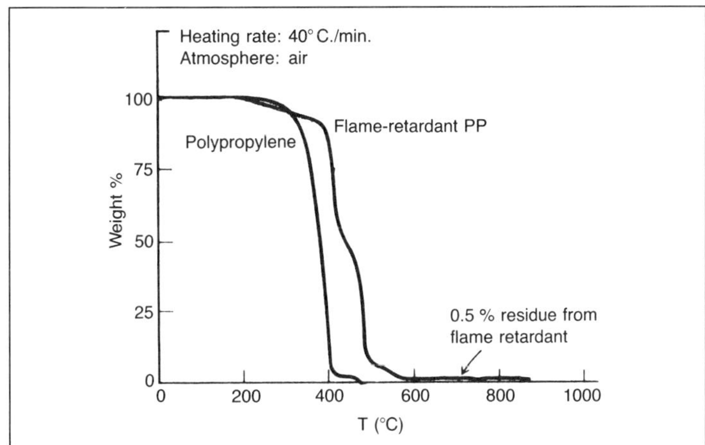

Characterizing the flame retardant in polypropylene using TGA.

fiber, or molded part. The parameters measured by thermomechanical analysis are the coefficient of linear thermal expansion, the glass-transition temperature (see Fig. below), softening characteristics, and the degree of cure. Other applications of TMA include the taking of compliance and modulus measurements and the determination of deflection temperature under load.

Tensile-elongation properties and the melt index can be determined by using small samples such as those cut directly from a part. Part uniformity can be determined by using samples taken from several areas of the molded part. Samples also can be taken from an area where failure has occurred or continues to occur. This permits comparisons of material properties in a failed area with properties measured either at an unfailed section or from a sample of new material. Samples also may be taken from within a material blend to ensure that a uniform blend is being supplied. The results of such testing can be used either for evaluation of part failure or in the acceptance testing of incoming materials or parts.

thermomechanical spectrum A plot of the variation of a mechanical property against temperature. If the temperature range includes the transition zone of viscoelastic behavior, then the term viscoelastic spectrum may be used. Since it is frequently the dynamical mechanical behavior which is determined as a function of temperature, plots are often of storage or loss moduli or of tangent of the loss angle against temperature, although any mechanical property can be plotted.

thermometer An instrument for measuring temperature. There are several types: (1) gas in which either the pressure at constant volume or the volume at constant pressure measures the temperature, used for extremely accurate thermodynamic determinations, (2) bimetallic in which the sensing element consists of two strips of metals having different heat expansion coefficients providing a range from −185 to 425°C (−300 to 800°F), (3) thermoelectric or thermocouple in which measurement is made by the electromotive force generated by two dis-

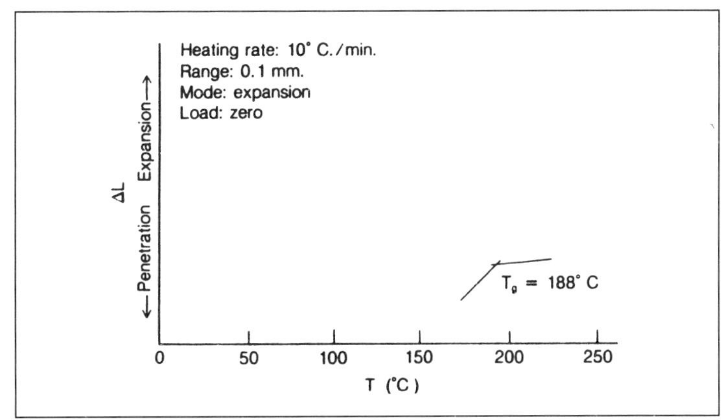

TMA determines the coefficient of expansion and the glass transition temperature of epoxy plastic-graphite fiber reinforced plastic.

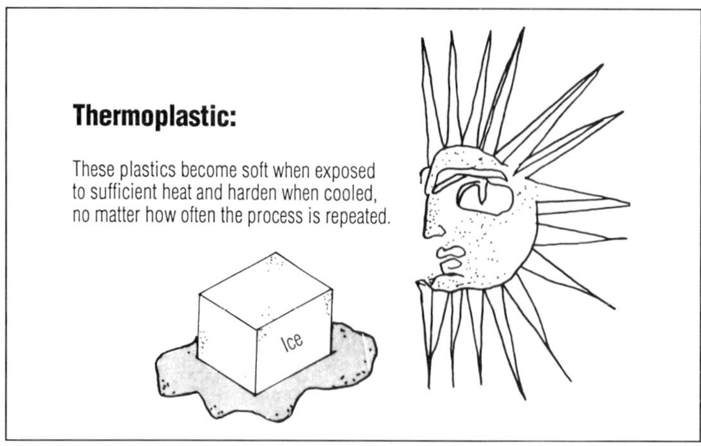

Thermoplastic:
These plastics become soft when exposed to sufficient heat and harden when cooled, no matter how often the process is repeated.
Ice

Characteristic of thermoplastics.

similar metals providing a range from −200 to 1,800°C (−328 to 3,270°F), (4) resistance in which temperature is measured by change in the electrical resistance of a metal, usually platinum providing a range from −163 to 660°C (−260 to 1,220°F), and (5) optical fiber developed by NIST that has a very accurate range up to 2,000°C (3,632°F).

thermometer, partial-immersion Designed to indicate temperatures correctly when the bulb and a specified part of the stem are exposed to the temperature being measured. The remainder of the stem containing the liquid index will be exposed to temperatures which may or may not be different. For measurements of greatest accuracy the temperatures of the exposed portion should be specified.

thermoplastic Thermoplastics (TP) are plastics that repeatedly soften when heated and harden when cooled (see Figs. above and below). Many are soluble in specific solvents and burn to some degree. Their softening temperatures vary with the polymer type and grade. Care must be taken to avoid degrading, decomposing, or igniting these materials. Generally, no chemical changes take place during processing. An analogy would be a block of ice that can be softened (turned back to a liquid), poured into any shape mold or die, then cooled to become a solid again. TPs generally offer higher impact strength, easier processing, and better adaptability to complex designs than do TSs.

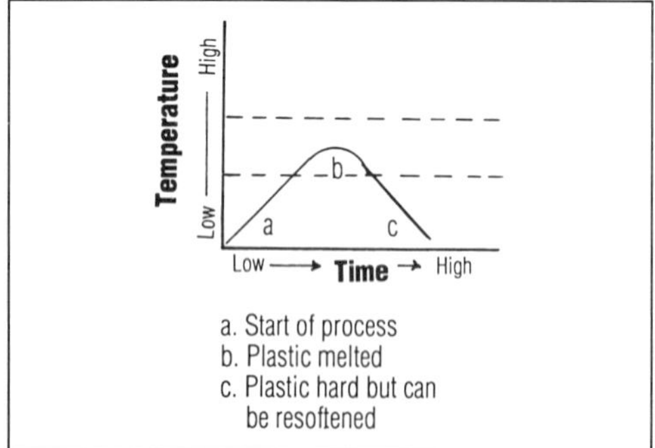

Example of a thermoplastic processing heat-time profile cycle.

Most TP molecular chains can be thought of as independent, intertwined strings resembling spaghetti. When heated, the individual chains slip, causing a plastic flow. Upon cooling, the chains of atoms and molecules are once again held firmly. With subsequent heating the slippage again takes place. There are practical limitations to the number of heating and cooling cycles before appearance or mechanical properties are affected. ▷ **plastic**

thermoplastic elastomer Since there exists, in principle, a whole continuum of materials between elastomers and thermoplastics (TPs), it is necessary to define what is meant by thermoplastic elastomers (TPEs). According to morphological considerations the characteristics that define TPEs are not their chemical compositions but rather the structure of the materials. On this definition they consist of hard, meltable, and soft. The thermodynamically incompatible phases may be present in the form of block copolymers of three or more components in the same molecule, or in the form of elastomer blends. The latter class includes blends of crosslinked rubbers such as EPM, EPDM, NBR or NR, etc. dispersed in TPs such as PP or PE. Although simple blends of uncrosslinked rubbers in TPs are usually included in statistics on the consumption of TPEs, they are not true TPEs, according to a strict definition (DIN 7724), and are usually far removed from TPEs in terms of mechanical properties.

The curves of modulus versus temperature for TPEs are characterized by two melting regions: the lowest glass transition temperature (T_g) and the highest melting temperature (T_m). The further apart these are, the greater the range of working temperatures and therefore of potential applications of the TPE. A further criterion for identifying TPE is a short relaxation time; after stretching to 100% elongation or more and then releasing the load, the TPE should recover very quickly to its original length with no appreciable residual strain. However, only a few TPEs satisfy this condition completely, and in some cases it is necessary to limit their use to situations where the strains are small. To design an ideal TPE one must first look for a group of materials whose T_g and T_m values are as far apart as possible.

In practice, there are just a small number of extensive groups of materials that are used as TPEs, as these unquestionably fulfill the morphological conditions reviewed. The important TPEs include: (1) oligablock copolymers based on styrene (TPE-S), (2) olefin types (TPE-O), although may not be true TPEs, (3) polyurethane types (TPE-U), (4) copolyester types (TPE-E), and (5) copolyamide types (TPE-A). ▷ **elastomer**

thermoplastic elastomer copolyamide The various TPE-A types cover a range of hardness from 60 Shore A to 75 Shore D, and they can directly replace softer elastomers where more hardness is desired. They do not contain any plasticizers and have excellent resistance to flexural cracking (they are able to withstand over 60 million flexings). Other characteristics include low hysteresis, high tear strength, and good resistance to oil and fuels. Despite their rather limited usable temperature range [−40 to 80°C (−40 to 176°F)], they have applications in the areas of hoses, seals, and joint-protecting boots.

thermoplastic elastomer copolyester With a hardness of about 88 Shore A to 82 Shore D, TPE-E occupies a place between conventional elastomers and thermoplastics. They can fill the roles either of hard elastomers or of thermoplastics with elastic properties. However, where they are used as alternatives to elastomers, one must take into account higher elongation with less residual deformation than for most elastomers. The maximum strain limit that this imposes for replacing elastomer components varies from about 7 to 25% depending on hardness. If the strain were allowed to exceed this limit the flow effect would be great enough to cause the component to fail in a short period of use. In cases where this would occur, the design of the component must be altered so that the limiting strain is not exceeded.

thermoplastic elastomer polyolefin TPE-O are polyolefins from crosslinked EPM or EPDM, but also simple blends of EPM or EPDM with PP or PE. Also called thermoplastic olefins (TPO) that can be compounded (CTPO) and reactor-made (RTPO). EPDM-PP blends have high compression set values, low strength at elevated temperatures, long relaxation times, and high swelling factors in oils. It is different with crosslinked rubbers such as EPM or EPDM with olefins (which are true TPE-OS). These types of TPEs consist of finely dispersed mixtures of a rubber vulcanizate in a thermoplastic matrix. TPE-O properties depend critically on the particle size of the rubber. Their usable temperature range is 80 to 100°C (176 to 212°F), which tends to restrict their applications. Uses include filters for washers, bellows-type joint protectors or boots, headlamp seals, electrical plugs, and hoses.

thermoplastic elastomer polyurethane ▷ **polyurethane plastic**

thermoplastic elastomer styrene copolymer TPE-Ss are the oldest and most rubber-like of the TPEs. Range of use is likely to be still further extended in the future through improved compounding, including, for example, the addition of polyamides and polyesters as modifiers. TPE-S copolymers are made from "living polymers" using bioorganic catalysts. By this means it is possible to produce linear or star-shaped block copolymers (the latter have 3, 4, or more branches radiating from one or more central atoms). Such copolymers can be designed and tailored to give desired properties. The morphology of these block copolymers determines whether their properties are predominantly elastomeric or thermoplastic; the product is a TPE-S only if there are styrene blocks at the ends of the molecules, and if the copolymer consists of at least three blocks with elastomer segments between the stryrene blocks. All this action leads to commercial TPE-S products that can be processed directly using conventional rubber processing machines, with properties optimized for special applications and with hardness values from less than 30 Shore A to over 65 Shore D. Uses include footwear soles, bottle seals, adhesives, etc. The main market growth is likely to be in the nonelastomer sector. Within their usable range of temperatures, the strengths of finished articles are similar to those of covalently crosslinked elastomers.

thermoplasticity The ability of a material to be deformed without breaking.

thermoplastic polyester This is a family of plastics and elastomers. ▷ **polybutylene terephthalate plastic** and **polyethylene terephthalate plastic**

thermoset elastomer ▷ **elastomer**

thermoset molding Compression and transfer molding (CM and TM) are the two main methods used to produce molded parts from thermoset (TS) resins. Compression molding (CM) was the major method of processing plastics during the first half of this century because of the development of a phenolic resin (TS) in 1909 and its extensive use at that time. By the 1940s this situation began to change with the development and use of thermoplastics (TPs) in extrusion and injection molding (IM) processes. CM originally processed about 70% (by weight) of all plastics, but by the 1950s its share of total production was below 25%, and now that figure is about 3%. This change does not mean that CM is not a viable process; it just does not provide the much lower cost to performance of TPs, particularly at high production rates. In the early 1900s resins were almost entirely TS (by weight); that proportion had fallen to about 40% by the mid-1940s, and now is about 3%.

During this century, TSs experienced an extremely low total growth rate, whereas TPs expanded at an unbelievably high rate. Regardless of the present situation, CM and TM are still important, particularly in the production of certain low-cost parts as well as heat-resistant and dimensionally precise parts. CM and TM are classified as high pressure processes, requiring 2,000 to 10,000 psi molding pressures. Some TSs, however, require only lower pressures of down to 50 psi or even just contact (zero pressure). CM is the most common method of molding TSs. In this process, material is compressed into the desired shape using a press containing a two-part closed mold, and is cured with heat and pressure. This process is not generally used with TPs. ▷ **compression molding; transfer molding; reinforced plastic processes; preform molding**

thermoset plastic TSs are plastics that undergo chemical change during processing to become permanently insoluble and infusible (see Figs.). Such natural and synthetic rubbers (elastomers) as latex, nitrile, millable polyurethanes, silicone butyl, and neoprene, which attain their properties through the process of vulcanization, are also in the TS family. The best analogy with TSs is that of a hard-boiled egg whose yolk has turned from a liquid to a solid and cannot be converted back to a liquid. In general, with their tightly crosslinked structure TSs resist higher temperatures and provide greater dimensional stability than do most TPs.

Thermosetting:

The plastics materials belonging to this group are set into permanent shape when heat and pressure are applied to them during forming. Reheating will not soften these materials.

Egg

Characteristic of thermoset plastics.

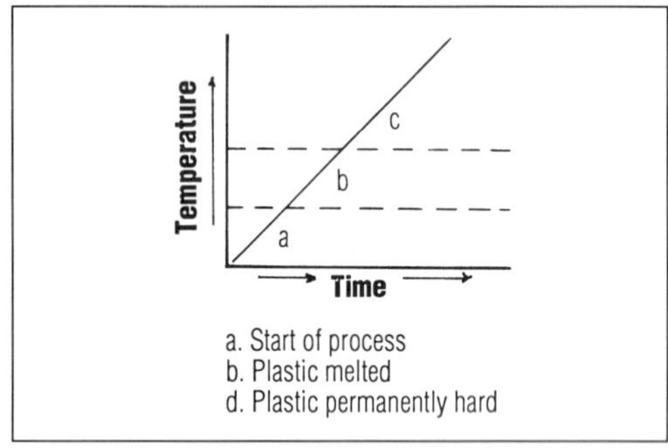

Example of a thermoset plastic processing heat-time profile cycle.

The structure of TSs, as of TPs, is also chainlike. Prior to molding, TSs are similar to TPs. Crosslinking is the principal difference between TSs and TPs. In TSs, during curing or hardening the cross-links are formed between adjacent molecules, resulting in a complex, interconnected network that can be related to its viscosity and performance (see Fig. in ▷ **gel point**). These cross-bonds prevent the slippage of individual chains, thus preventing plastic flow under the addition of heat. If excessive heat is added after crosslinking has been completed, degradation rather than melting will occur.

TSs generally cannot be used alone structurally and must be filled or reinforced with materials such as calcium carbonate, talc, or glass fiber. The most common reinforcement is glass fiber, but others are also used. ▷ **plastic** and **A-B-C-stages.**

thermoset plastic curing, dielectric monitoring Monitoring the cure of TSs is done by tracking the changes in their electrical properties during the processing, particularly with reinforced plastics. In a typical application, the sensor is placed at the location where the cure is to be monitored. During cure the capacitance and conductance of the material are recorded; measurements are taken at several frequencies over several orders of magnitude (0.1 Hz to 100 kHz). From these data, the value of the ionic conductivity is deduced. Research has provided information about the relationship between the ionic conductivity and the viscosity and degree of cure of TS RPs (since 1940s). Results show correlation with fluidity before gelation and with flexibility after gelation. Rugged computer-controlled dielectric monitoring systems are used. ▷ **reinforced plastic, thermoset curing monitoring**

thermoset plastic curing, fiber optic sensor With some of the methods used to mold or cure thermosets, the hostility of the environment both within and around the reinforced plastics may preclude the use of conventional styles of sensors. This situation can potentially be handled by employing in situ fiber-optic sensors to monitor RPs curing. Because of their hair-like size, fiber-optic sensors can be embedded within the RP prior to the cure process, and allowed to remain as a part of the product after curing. They have been extensively used in pultrusion lines.

thermoset polyester plastic ▷ **polyester thermoset plastic**

thermoset polyurethane plastic ▷ **polyurethane plastic**

thermostat metal A composite material, usually in the form of sheet or strip, comprising two or more materials of any appropriate nature, metallic or otherwise which by virtue of the differing expansivities of the components tends to alter its curvature when its temperature is changed.

thermotropic material Where a temperature gradient determines the orientation, it exhibits thermotropism.

thesaurus The vocabulary and associated terms to be used in indexing to ensure retrieval. Tight vocabulary control with continual updating is essential to retrieval of pertinent information.

thickening agent Also called anti-sag agent. Material added to a plastic to thicken it or raise the viscosity index so that it will not flow as readily; they impart thixotropy. Use includes molding compounds and coatings.

thick molding compound TMC is similar to sheet molding compound except it is two to three times thicker. The Fig. shows its manufacturing process.

thickness control ▷ **injection molding thickness adjustment** and **control**

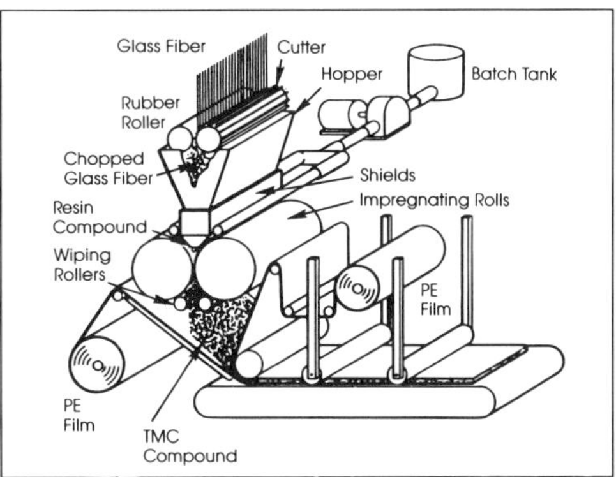

Schematic of the thick molding process.

thickness gauge ▷ **sensor** and **extruder web thickness gauging**

thin-layer chromatography TLC is a microtype of chromatography in which a thin layer of special absorbent is applied to a glass plate, a drop of a solution of the material being investigated is applied to an edge, and that side of the plate is then dipped in an appropriate solvent. The solvent travels up the thin layer of absorbent, which selectively separates the molecules present in the material being investigated.

thinner Material added to plastic to thin or lower the viscosity. They may also be crosslinking agents.

thinning Refers to the finished wall of a blow molded container or the corners of a thermoformed part. The wall thickness has thinned out in some areas due to improper blowing or excessive stretching.

thin-wall tubing cut ▷ **cutting large diameter, thin-walled tubing**

thixatropy Opposite to ▷ **rheopecticity**

Thixomolding Thixomat Inc's tradename for metal powders that can be made injection moldable without mixing with a thermoplastic binder; materials injected include magnesium, aluminum, or zinc. This one-step process produces a finished part out of the mold with no need for subsequent sintering. It uses what resembles a standard horizontal reciprocating screw injection molding machine though built to withstand temperatures of 594°C (1,100°F) or higher and provide very short injection times around 20 millisec. Combined induction and resistance barrel heating melts 1/8 in. (0.3 cm) metal granules into half-solids/half-molten slurry. This slurry has the thixotropic (shear thinning) rheological characteristic of a plastic melt. The screw injects this slurry into a standard die-cast mold at a total cycle time of about 20 s. ▷ **injection molding metal powder**

thixotropic In respect to materials, gel-like at rest, but fluid or liquified when agitated (such as during molding). Having high static shear strength and low dynamic shear strength at the same time. Losing viscosity under stress. It describes a filled plastic (like BMC) that has little or no movement when applied to a vertical plane. Powdered silica and other fillers are used as thickening agents.

thixotropy ▷ **non-Newtonian flow**

thread 1. ▷ **fiber** 2. Universally one of the most common means of attachment and assembly. Integral, or molded-in threads can easily be obtained during fabrication with practically all processes or machined in secondary operations. ▷ **mold thread plug, ring, or core** 3. In plasticating (extrusion, injection, etc.), there is a screw inside a barrel; screw thread is not uniform like an assembly screw. ▷ **screw**

thread, blunt start A detail of thread design in which the start of the thread has been squared off, i.e., there is no gradual thread "fade-in". The blunt thread start is used as a means of orienting a container in a printing machine or labeling machine.

thread, buttress A type used for transmitting power in only one direction. It has the efficiency of the square thread and the strength of the V-thread.

thread, chainstitch A single thread stitch, characterized by the fact that the entire thread may be pulled out when one stitch is cut or broken.

thread, continuous A spiral, protruding finish on the neck of a container to hold a screw-type closure.

thread count The number of yarns (threads) per inch (cm) in either the lengthwise (warp) or crosswise (fill or weft) direction of woven fabrics.

thread, effective turns The number of full 360° turns on a threaded closure that are actually in contact with the neck thread.

thread torque ▷ **torque, cap and thread**

thread, V Thread with leading flank of the thread intersecting with flowing flank of adjacent thread at thread root.

three-dimensional fabric Multiaxial (3-D) textile reinforcement materials are used in reinforced plastic products such as gears and support pads. These materials include multilayer woven mats, woven or knitted spacing fabrics, and multiaxial layered materials. The weaving process permits combining several materials having different properties. Whereas most woven reinforcement materials consist of orthotropic fiber systems in two directions (2-D along the X- and Y-axes), the 3-Ds have fibers also in the third dimension (Z-axis). In reinforced plastics, modulus for 3-Ds is greater than that for ordinary 2-Ds with the same fiber mass distribution and the same fiber content. Based on how the 3-Ds are manufactured, a variety of three-dimensional properties are obtained that include high shear strengths in all directions.

three-dimensional in-mold ▷ **injection molding circuit board**

three-dimensional network polymer ▷ **crosslinking**

three-dimensional stress pattern measurement ▷ **photoelasticity; brittle lacquer technique; microtoming**

three-plate mold ▷ **mold, stack**

throughput Refers to machine or production output.

thrust The total force exerted by the extruder screw on the thrust bearing. For practical purposes, equal to the extrusion pressure times the cross sectional area of the bore.

tie layer Material used when required for providing adhesion between layers such as coextrusion, coinjection, and laminating.

tie rod ▷ **clamping tie rod**

time profile The plot of characteristics versus time such as modulus, damping, or both of a material.

time sharing ▷ **computer time sharing system**

tint Various even tone areas (strengths) of a solid color.

tire, non-pneumatic These rather solid, lightweight, no-maintenance vehicle tires are used industrially (factories, airports, agricultural, etc.). Different processing methods are used, primarily casting and injection molding.

titanium dioxide TiO_2 is a white powder available in two crystalline forms, the anatase and rutile types. Both are widely used as opacifying pigments in different plastics; used alone when whites are desired or in conjunction with other pigments when tints are desired. They are essentially chemical inert, light-fast, resistant to migration, and resistant to heat. The rutile type has the higher refractive index (2.75 versus 2.55 for antase), and thus has the greater opacifying power.

titration In chemical analysis, the determination of the reactive capacity, usually a solution. The analytical process of successively adding measured amounts of a reagent (as a standard solution) to a known volume or weight of a sample or sample solution until a desired end point is reached.

T-manifold ▷ **die, T-type**

toggle clamp ▷ **clamping, toggle**

tole-in A small reduction of the outside diameter at the cut end of a length of thermoplastic pipe.

tolerance The allowable deviation from a value or standard; especially the total range of variation permitted in maintaining a specified dimension in machining, fabricating, and/or constructing a member or assembly. The specific dimensions that can be obtained on a finished, processed plastic product basically depend on the performance and control of the plastic material, the fabrication process and, in many cases, upon properly integrating the materials with the process. In turn, a number of variable characteristics exist with the material itself. Unfortunately, many designers tend to consider dimensional tolerances on plastic products to be complex, unpredictable, and not susceptible to control. This is simply not true, though they can be complex. Plastics are no different in this respect than other materials. If steel, aluminum, and ceramics were to be made into complex shapes but no prior history on their behavior during processing existed, a period of trial and error would be required to ensure their meeting the required measurements. If relevant processing information or experience did exist, it would be possible for these metallic products to meet the requirements with the first part produced. This same situation exists with plastics. To be successful with this material requires experience with its melt behavior, melt-flow behavior during processing, and the process controls needed to ensure meeting the dimensions that can be achieved in a complete processing operation. Based on the plastic to be used and the equipment available for processing, certain combinations will make it possible to meet extremely tight tolerances, but others will perform with no tight tolerances or any degree of repeatability.

Fortunately, there are many different types of plastics that can provide all kinds of properties, including specific dimensional tolerances. It can thus be said that the real problem is not with the different plastics or processes but rather with the designer, who requires knowledge and experience to create products to meet the desired requirements. The designer with no knowledge or experience has to become familiar with the plastic-design concepts expressed throughout this book and work with capable people such as the suppliers of plastic materials.

Some plastics, such as the TSs and in particular the TS-RP composites, can produce parts with exceptionally tight tolerances. In the compression molding of relatively thin to thick and complex shapes, tolerances can be held to less than 0.001 in. or to even zero, as can also be done using hand layup fabricating techniques. At the other extreme are the unfilled, unreinforced extruded TPs. Generally, unless a very thin uniform wall is to be extruded, it is impossible to hold to such tight tolerances as just given. The thicker and more complex an extruded shape is, the more difficult it becomes to meet tight tolerances. (This situation is also true with most other nonplastic materials) What is important is to determine the tolerances that can be met and then design around them. ▷ **computer tolerance analysis; shrinkage; reinforced plastic thickness tolerance guide**

tolerance and computer software ▷ **computer tolerance analysis**

tolerance and reinforced plastic ▷ **reinforced plastic thickness tolerance guide**

tolerance and shrinkage Two different forms of shrinkage must be considered when designing to meet tolerances: the initial shrinkage that occurs while a part is cooling, called the mold or die shrinkage, and that which occurs after as many as twenty-four hours, called the after-shrinkage or after-swell. Some plastics are more stable than others after aging, regardless of their initial shrinkage. In many cases low shrinkage may indicate greater stability. As noted earlier, some plastics have zero shrinkage, with others having little or a high degree of shrinkage. ▷ **shrinkage**

Large, unpredictable shrinkages can make close-tolerance designing almost impossible, so these must be indicated on the drawings. If it has been determined in advance that a part must be postcured, stress relieved, or baked, allowance must be made for probable additional shrinkage. These requirements must be specified on the drawings.

Especially for long runs, mold or die design is an important factor. The metals that will be used, particularly in mold cavities, and the forces required will largely be determined by the complexity of the product design. This complexity will, of course, dictate in turn the intricacy of the tool design that will eventually be used. In general, pack hardening, oil hardening, and prehardened steels are used, with materials such as beryllium copper and electroformed cavities finding use in applications for specialized purposes. Chrome plating is frequently used to protect parts from the corrosive effect of volatiles present in some materials. Plating not only produces high luster and prevents tool staining but also eliminates the sticking of parts on removal from a mold or die. However, plating will only duplicate an existing surface, so the tool itself must be highly polished before being plated. The intricacy required in tool design, and the commensurate costs, may be leading factors when choosing a plastic.

If the material must flow around pins, spiders, and projections, it must have suitable flow properties and weld properly, leaving only minimal flow marks. Thus, the availability of the proper material becomes an important consideration. ▷ **injection molding, shrinkage and tolerance**

tolerance and thermal properties ▷ **orientation, thermal properties**

tolerance, damage measured ▷ **damage tolerance**

tolerance, geometric ▷ **dimensioning and tolerancing, geometric**

tolerance selection It is not a random process, but requires careful judgement based on logical calculations, material behavior, processing capabilities, and cost. As a general rule, tolerances should be as large as possible because they generally simplify fabricating method. However, tighter tolerances usually result in lower part cost for high production quantities. ▷ **zero defect**

tolerance stackup It is possible for an accumulation (that is, stackup) of tolerances to cause an inoperable or malfunctioning assembly.

toluene A colorless, flammable liquid with a benzene-like odor, used as a solvent for various plastics. It is also used as an intermediate for polyurethanes and polyesters.

toluene diisocyanate ▷ **polyurethane plastic**

tomography ▷ **computer-aided tomography**

ton ▷ **mass**

toner Any of several dyes used to develop a particular color characteristic (blueness, whiteness, etc.) to either clear or pigmented plastic. Used in imaging material in electrophotography and some off-press proofing printing systems; in inks or dyes used to tone printing inks, especially black. They are organic pigments which do not contain inorganics. ▷ **pigment** and **dye**

tooling All types of tools exist in the plastics and other industries. Plasticwise, the terms tool, mold, and die are virtually synonymous or interchangeable. Tooling represents materials, equipment, or forms onto which (or into which) the product is made, assembled, cast, cut, etc. Choice of tooling is based upon several interacting inputs such as plastic to be used, process to be used, quantity of parts, value of the part to be made, size of part, tolerances of part, part appearance, and part complexity.

tooling, plastic Plastic made tools are used in the plastic and other industries. It includes construction of master models, patterns, trim tools, drill jigs, dies, prototypes, checking and assembly fixtures, and other tools required to produce the final product. Plastics are used in tooling to the best advantage when complex contours and fine details are required. Their ability to be cured in the desired shape accounts for significant savings compared to the costs of machining metal. They are fabricated usually by surface casting, mass casting, lamination, and machined blocks. For most applications, thermoset plastics are used to construct plastic tooling. They are generally applied as liquid two-component systems except for modeling blocks and prepregs. For rigid tool construction the most common types are epoxy and polyester (thermoset). The flexible tools use modified versions of these and silicone or polyurethane elastomers. Although in many cases the plastic is used in conjunction with wood, plaster, or metal, the finished product is usually classed as a plastic tool. Materials used include different types but principally those listed as well as phenolics.

tooling, shell A mold or bonding fixture consisting of a contoured surface shell supported by a substructure to provide dimensional stability. ▷ **shell molding**

tooling, static ▷ **die ring, static and dynamic**

tools, brass When a tool is used to clear or remove melted plastic during processing (injection, extrusion, etc.) such as hopper throat when melt bridges, a steel is not used because it damages the machine surface, etc. Beryllium tools are sometimes used, but they are hard. However, brass tools do not damage equipment.

tool steel ▷ **mold material**

top load ▷ **container, top load**

torpedo 1. ▷ **screw torpedo 2.** In an injection molding plunger machine, the solid metal block of streamlined form fitted inside the barrel which causes the molten material to flow near to the barrel wall. Also called spreader. See Fig. under ▷ **injection molding, plunger**. Also ▷ **injection molding melt extractor**

torpedo, mixing ▷ **screw torpedo**

torque A moment (or force) which produces or tends to produce rotation or torsion ▷ **screw torque**. The determination of the SI units for torque and other related quantities depends on whether the radian is omitted or used in expressions for derived units. The radian is omitted when torque is defined as a vector product; it is used when torque is defined as a component of an energy integral. With radian omitted the unit of torque and bending moment is N·m; the unit for moment of inertia is $kg{\cdot}m^2$; and the unit for moment of momentum is $kg{\cdot}m^2/s$. The unit N·m is convenient to use in the solution of problems in statics.

When the radian is used, the unit for torque is N·m/rad or J/rad; the unit for moment of inertia is $kg{\cdot}m^2/rad^2$; and the unit for moment of momentum is $kg{\cdot}m^2/(rad{\cdot}s)$. In the solution of problems that involve rotation, the use of radian in these units will retain all advantages of dimensional analysis.

The use of the unit N·m for torque and bending moment may result in confusion with the use of the unit N·m for mechanical energy. If vectors were shown, the distinction between mechanical energy and torque would be obvious since torque is the product of moment arm and force perpendicular to the moment arm, while mechanical energy is the product of force and displacement in the direction of the force. It is important to recognize this difference when N·m is used as the unit for torque. The joule, which is a special name for energy, should not be used for the torque unit N·m but may be used in the torque unit J/rad when rotation is involved and work occurs.

torque, cap and thread It can be measured as application torque, removal torque, or given torque.

torque rheometer It provides a standardization in extrusion and particularly high-intensity compounded material. This quantitative data output instrument measures temperature of fusion, time of fusion, and torque (work) required. Auxiliary capability allows for gas evolution measurements (cc/g) useful in chemical blowing agent studies, pollution control emission measurements, etc. Samples used range from 5 to 30 g.

torr A unit of pressure equal to 1/760th of an atmosphere.

torsional braid analysis A method of performing torsional tests on small amounts of materials in forms where they cannot support their own weight, such as liquid thermoset plastics. A glass braid is impregnated with a solution of the material to be tested. After evaporation of the solvent, the impregnated braid is used as a specimen in an apparatus which measures motions of the oscillating braid as it is being heated at a programmed rate in a controlled atmosphere.

torsional coefficient ▷ **torque**

torsional deformation The angular twist of a specimen produced by a specified torque in the torsion test. Torsional deformation (radian/in.) is calculated by dividing observed total angular twist (the twist of one end of the gauge length with respect to the other) by original gauge length.

torsional modulus of rupture ▷ **modulus, rigidity** and **modulus, rupture in torsion**

torsional pendulum A device for performing dynamic mechanical analysis, in which a sample is deformed torsionally and allowed to oscillate in free vibration. Modulus is determined by the frequency of the resultant oscillation, and damping is determined by the decreasing amplitude of the oscillation.

torsional property A moment that tends to twist a bar about its own axis is called a torsional moment, or simply a torque. The same force system may cause bending in one member of a product and torque in another. Stress is caused by twisting a material.

torsional, residual Revolutions made by a specified length of cord when one end is held in a flexed position and the other allowed to turn freely.

torsional rigidity The torque required to produce an angular deflection of 1 degree.

torsional shear modulus Commonly designated as modulus of rigidity, shear modulus, or torsional modulus.

torsional shear test Test in which a relatively thin specimen of solid circular or annular cross section, usually confined between rings, is subjected to an axial load and to shear in torsion.

torsional strain The strain corresponding to a specified torque or torsional stress in the torsion test. It is calculated by multiplying torsional deformation by the specimen radius. ▷ **strain**

torsional strength Also called modulus of

rupture in torsion and sometimes shear strength. A measure of the ability of a material to withstand a twisting load. ▷ **strength**

torsional stress It is calculated as follows:

$$S = \frac{Tc}{J}$$

where S = torsional stress, psi, T = torque, in.-lb., c = distance from axis of twist to outermost fiber of specimen, in., J = polar moment of inertia, in.^{4}. For solid cylindrical specimens, $J = \frac{1}{32}\pi d^4$, where d is diameter (in.) and the formula is:

$$S = \frac{16T}{\pi d^3}$$

For tubular specimens, $J = \frac{1}{32}\pi(d_2^4 - d_1^4)$, where d_2 is outer diameter and d_1 is inner diameter, and the formula is:

$$S = \frac{16Td_2}{\pi(d_2^4 - d_1^4)}$$

Torsional stress as calculated above is not a true stress above the proportional limit, since the formula assumes proportionality of stress and strain, but it is accepted as practical and convenient. ▷ **stress**

torsional test A method of determining behavior of a material subjected to twisting loads. A cylindrical specimen with a straight reduced section and longitudinal gauge mark is twisted axially to rupture. A torque-twist diagram may be plotted or an analogous stress-strain diagram derived from these measurements. Properties that can be determined from the torsion test include elastic limit, maximum torsional deformation, modulus of elasticity (or modulus of rigidity), proportional limit, torsional strength, yield point and yield strength. The torsion test is sometimes used in preference to the tension test for brittle materials. It is required by few specifications. For large strains, torsion data are considered more valid than tension data and are often used in the solution of certain mechanical design problems involving shear loading. A special limited torsion test may be used to determine an apparent modulus of rigidity for plastics.

tort law ▷ **product liability law**

total quality management TQM is a principle of manufacturing associated with the adage "do it right the first time". The term is not associated with any product; it reflects a philosophy and its implementation.

toughness That property of a material by virtue of which it can absorb energy; the actual work per unit volume or unit mass of material that is required to rupture it. ▷ **impact test; extruder film impact strength; bag drop test; dart drop test; ball burst test; Tyvek**

toughness, area under the curve Toughness is usually proportional to the area under the load-elongation curve such as the tensile stress-strain curve. However, there are exceptions, primarily with many thermoset reinforced plastics where its area is extremely small but toughness is extremely high. ▷ **stress-strain curve or diagram**

toughness, breaking ▷ **toughness**

toughness, film ▷ **ball burst test**

toughness, fracture ▷ **fracture toughness**

toughness modulus ▷ **modulus, toughness**

tow ▷ **fiber tow** and **filament placement process**

toxicity The propensity of a substance to produce adverse biochemical or physiological effects. Although most neat plastics are relatively nontoxic, compounding additives such as plasticizers, colorants, and stabilizers could change this condition. So where there is a requirement for nontoxic materials to be used, select the appropriate plastic or compound.

toxicity containment ▷ **geomembrane liner**

toxicology The precise definition of toxicology varies among different industries and people's interests depending on background, specialization, and breadth of interest and knowledge. Meaningful definition is the concept that toxicology is concerned with the potential of chemicals, plastics, etc., or mixtures of them, to produce harmful effects in living organisms. Adverse effects are taken to mean those that are detrimental to the survival or normal functioning of the individual. ▷ **acceptable risk** and **perfection**

toy market Plastics have been used in toys or games from the beginning of the plastics industry, since 1868 when John Hyatt developed cellulose nitrate plastic to produce billiard balls. The acceptable cost for high volume production of realistic looking, and to an ever increasing degree, functional, participatory, and interactive products was the driving force that put plastics into the toy business. In addition to the wide use of plastics in conventional toys (dolls, games, etc.) an important effect of the advent of plastics has been to facilitate the use of toys as a part of the educational process. All types of plastic materials and processes are used to meet all types of requirements. The major materials are PEs, PSs, PVCs, and PPs. Special plastics include PAs, ABSs, PCs, PMMAs, and PURs. The principal processes used are injection, blow and rotational moldings.

TPX Mitsui Petrochemical Industries Ltd.'s trademark for polymethylpentene plastic.

traceability The capability for ascertaining quantitatively the total measurement uncertainty in a datum relative to a national or other recognized standard through an unbroken chain of comparisons. Also, the capability to trace the ancestry of a particular batch of material back to an earlier point in the general materials cycle.

tracer **1.** A fiber, tow, or yarn added to a prepreg for verifying fiber alignment and, in the case of woven materials, for distinguishing warp fibers from fill fibers. **2.** A chemical entity, almost invariably radioactive and usually an isotope, added to a compound in a process so that it can be traced through the process by appropriate detection methods such as a geiger counter.

tracking ▷ **electrical tracking**

trademark TM is a word, symbol, or insignia designating one or more proprietary products or the manufacture of such products, which has been officially registered and approved by the U.S. Patent & Trademark Office (PTO). The acceptable designation is a superior capital R enclosed in a circle. However, quotation marks may be used.

trade name TN is the name or style under which a concern does business (e.g. Du Pont). The TN alone or with a device such as a surrounding oval may be registered by the government concerned. In this book only a few TNs have been included; the many thousands that exist are in appropriate books, publication, software, etc.

training in Germany In Germany, the training process has been different throughout the 20th century than in most countries. The country has an apprenticeship system that develops skilled people for all sorts of industries, from plastics to baking. It is administered by government, but companies provide the apprentice positions and do the training. Plastics-related programs might involve becoming molding technicians, CNC machine tool operators, or moldmakers. This is not a giveaway system. For two years, apprentices receive a fraction of what other full-time workers are paid. No one without a career commitment endures such a program. On the other hand, this is also not indentured servitude. A company may train someone who then goes to work for the competition.

transducer Broadly used term for any device that is actuated by an input signal from one source to supply an output signal to another. Device converts some form of energy to another; usually electrical energy to or from mechanical energy. In regard to force measuring device, it has characteristics of providing an output, usually electrical, which serves as the measurement of load, force, pressure, etc., when placed along the sensitive axis of the force cell.

transducer, melt pressure ▷ **melt pressure transducer**

transducer, piezoelectric ▷ **piezoelectric plastic**

transference, thermal The steady-state heat flow from (or to) a body through applied thermal insulation and to (or from) the external surroundings by conduction, convection, and radiation. It is expressed as the time rate of heat flow per unit area of the body per unit temperature difference between the body surface and the external surroundings.

transfer molding In TM the mold halves are brought together under pressure as in CM ▷ **compression molding**. The charge of molding compound [usually thermoset (TS)] is then put into a pot, and is driven from the pot through runners and gates into the mold cavities by means of a plunger. Its basic construction, driving system, and controls are similar to those of CM except for the additional action required by the transfer pot (see Figs. below and on p. 778).

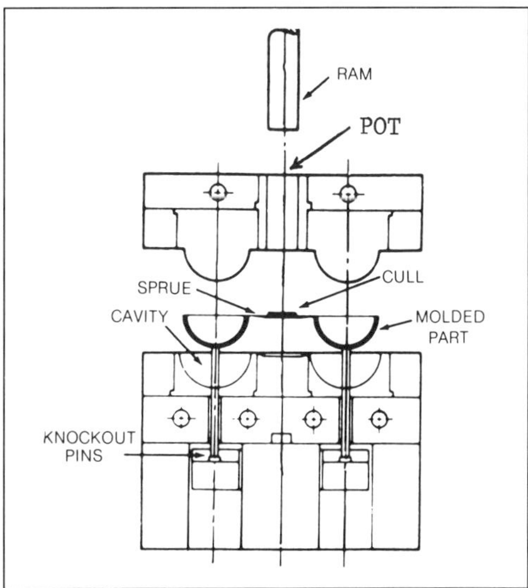

In transfer molding the plastic "transfers" from a "pot" through runners and gates into cavities retained in a closed heated mold.

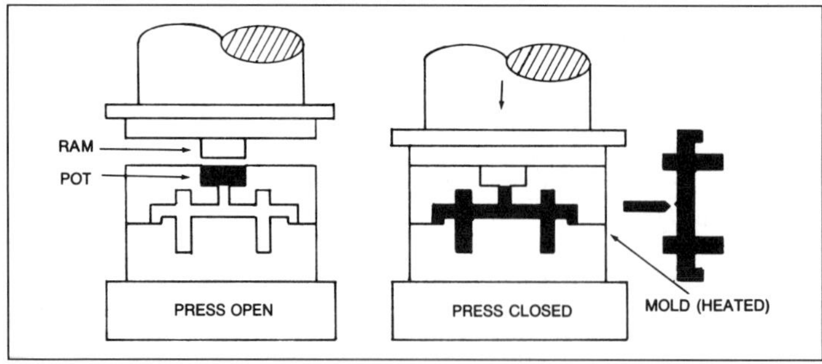

Schematic of transfer molding.

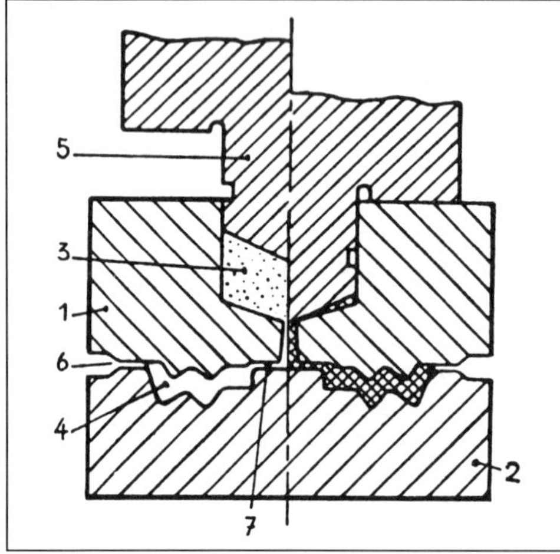

Molding with transfer mold. Left half has plastic in the fill space or pot (No.3) and right side melt is transferred into the cavity. Parts of molds are: (1) center part of mold, (2) lower part of mold (die), (3) fill space or "pot", (4) finished molding volume, (5) upper part of mold (transfer plunger), (6) venting channel, and (7) transfer channel.

This process differs from CM in that the plastic is heated to a point of plasticity in the pot before it reaches and is forced into the closed mold.

This procedure facilitates the molding of intricate parts with small holes, numerous metal inserts, and so on. Less force is used, and less melt action occurs in the cavity.

Automation of the transfer/plunger concept is accomplished by the addition of a hopper-fed screw plasticator, in a system called screw transfer, which can replace the preform and preheat operations and automatically load the pot in CM (and is used to load a CM mold cavity). Conventional screw injection molding (IM) is another so-called transfer system; for TSs the processor uses a screw with a compression ratio of one, the barrel heat is kept relatively low (below the curing/hardening heat), and the mold is at the higher heat to permit final cure.

▷ **screw, thermoset type; thermoset plastic; outgassing; preform; preheating**

transfer molding, cull Material remaining in a transfer chamber after the mold has been filled. Unless there is a slight excess in the charge, the operator cannot be sure cavity is filled. Charge in chamber is generally regulated to control thickness of cull.

transfer molding, flash ▷ **mold flash**

transfer molding molds Examples of molds are shown in the Figs. on p. 779.

transfer molding pressure The pressure applied to the cross sectional area of the material pot or cylinder, expressed in psi (MPa).

transfer molding, screw transfer Automation of TM includes this concept. The screw plasticizer replaced the preform/preheat operations (see Fig. below). It provides a hopper-fed screw that is targeted to develop a mixing action of the TS molding compound as it moves through a heated barrel. With the mixing action, there is more heating action on material (the action that a dielectric heater provides with preforms). This screw action does not occur in the conventional screw plasti-

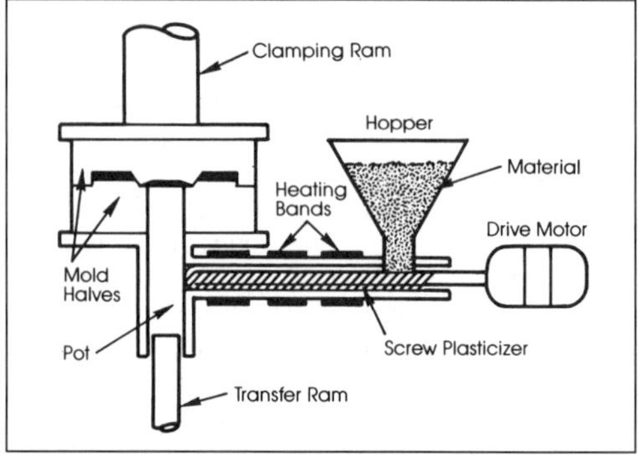

Screw transfer schematic; material travels from the hopper to screw to pot to mold halves.

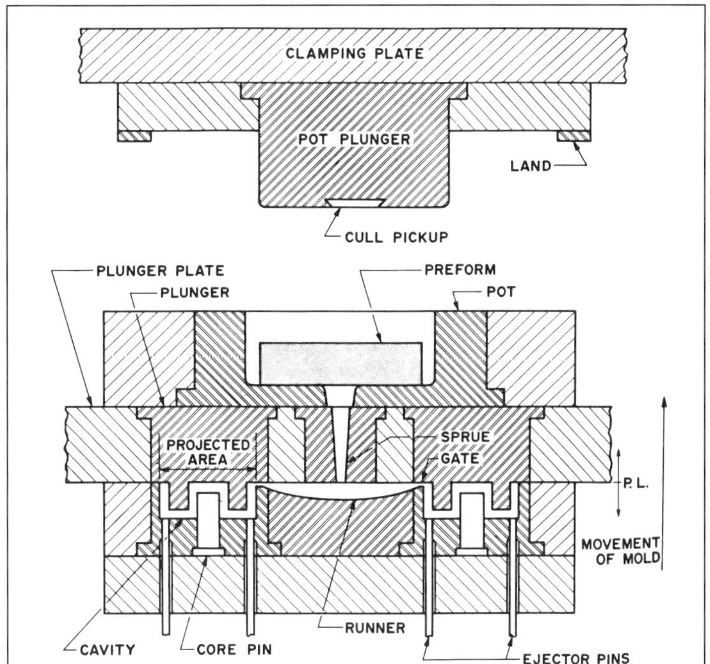

Schematic of transfer molding shows the mold (opened) in the position in which the preform is loaded into the pot or loading chamber.

A 64-cavity mold showing unmolded IC in workloading frame about to be placed in mold for transfer molding; pot can be seen in center of mold. For high production, this system is automated.

cators, such as injection molding and extrusion. ▷ **screw**

transfer molding, venting All closed molds, as in TM, CM, IM, BM, etc., require a means by which air and/or volatiles (for certain TSs and TPs) are evacuated from the cavities. Bumping can be used ▷ **breathing**. However, the usual technique is to incorporate "openings," usually located at the mold parting line. Their size depends on the plastic compound's viscosity, but they are usually 0.25 in. wide × 0.001 to 0.003 in. deep, located where the cavity will be filled last. The vent-opening location also depends on the heating pattern of the mold, particularly if the heat flow pattern was not logically planned. CAD programs are available to provide the proper heating pattern. With excessive heat in one section of the mold, the viscosity of the compound could be low enough to require a vent opening in that area. Knockout pins often provide a means for venting, and they may require recessed sections, such as "flats" ground on the OD, that will allow venting. ▷ **vent hole**

transfer molding versus compression molding ▷ **compression molding versus transfer molding**

transfer point control ▷ **injection molding processing parting line control**

transfer pot A heating cylinder; transfer chamber in a transfer mold.

transfer time ▷ **molding cycle**

transfinite algebra A branch of higher mathematics dealing with the algebra of infinity.

transition curve In a P-T diagram, the focus of the temperature and pressure values at which a congruent equilibrium between two solid phases exists.

transition, first order A reversible change in phase of a material; in the case of plastics, usually crystallization or melting.

transition section ▷ **screw transition zone**

transitor Semiconductor device for the amplification of current. There are two principal types, namely field-effect and junction.

translucent Transmitting light diffusely, but not permitting a clear view of objects beyond the specimen and not in contact with it.

transmission electron microscopy TEM is a technique to greatly magnify images of objects by means of electrons: (1) they permit the visual examination of structures too fine to be resolved with light microscopes, and (2) they permit the study of surfaces that omit electrons. In its simplest form, a TEM consists of a source supplying a beam of electrons of uniform velocity, a condenser lens for concentrating the electrons on the specimen, a specimen stage for displacing the specimen that transmits the electron beam, an objective lens, a projector lens, and a fluorescent screen on which the final image is observed.

transmission haze When a parallel beam of light impinges normally (90°) on a test specimen of a material which is not highly transparent and clear, significant fraction of the transmitted light is deviated in directions between 0° and 90° to the normal. This is often referred to as forward diffusion; the expression scattering tends to be reserved for polarized light.

transmission, water vapor ▷ **water vapor transmission**

transmittance The ratio of the transmitted radiant flux to the incident flux.

transmittance of light That fraction of the emitted light of a given wavelength which is not reflected or absorbed, but passes through a substance.

transmittance, regular Ratio of undiffused transmitted flux to incident flux.

transparent Descriptive of a material or substance capable of a high degree of light transmission; the degree of regular transmission, thus the property of a material by which the objects may be seen clearly through a sheet of it. ▷ **schlieren** and **opacity/transparency**

transparent conductor ▷ **electrical transparent conductor**

transparent ink A printing ink which does not conceal the color beneath. Plastic inks are transparent so that they will blend to form other colors.

transparent plastics The Table opposite compares transparent plastics for optical properties.

transparent UV coverings ▷ **solar energy markets**

transportation markets For today's and tomorrow's vehicles (automobiles, trucks, boats, airplanes, etc.) plastics offer a wide variety of benefits. Included are durability, lightweight, corrosion resistance, fuel savings, recyclability, aids safety glass, etc.

transverse direction ▷ **machine and transverse directions**

treater Equipment for preparing plastic-impregnated reinforcements including means for delivery of a continuous web or strand to a plastic tank, controlling the amount of plastic pickup, drying and/or partially curing the plastic (B-stage), and rewinding the impregnated reinforcement. ▷ **prepreg**

triacetate fiber ▷ **acetate**

triallyl cyanurate A colorless liquid or solid, highly reactive, used in copolymerizations with vinyl-type monomers to form plastics of the allyl family. Since the 1940s, they have been used as copolymers to produce exceptionally high heat resistant plastics. Also used to crosslink unsaturated polyester plastics.

trickle impregnation A related process to thermoset casting, potting, and encapsulation, it also uses low viscosity liquid reactive plastics to provide trickle impregnation. As an example, the catalyzed plastic is allowed to drip on an electrical transformer coil (or other objects) with small openings. Capillary action draws the liquid into the openings at a rate slow enough to enable air to escape as it is displaced by the liquid. When fully impregnated, the object is exposed to heat to cure the plastic.

trim To remove flash from a part or process in some manner appropriate. ▷ **mold flash**

trimer ▷ **mer**

trim nest A jig or form used to hold a part to be trimmed.

Trommsdorff effect ▷ **free-radical polymerization**

Optical properties for typical transparent plastics; specimen thickness 1/8 in. (0.3 cm) unless otherwise listed.

Polymer generic family	Optical properties		
	Refractive index	Light transmission, %	Haze, %
Transparent ABS	1.536	72 to 88	5 to 7
Acrylic (PMMA)	1.49	88 to 92	1 to 3
Allyl diglycol carbonate	1.5	89 to 90	1 to 1.5
Cellulosics	1.46 to 150	88	>1 (thin film)
Nylon, amorphous	1.566	85 to 90	7.00
PET	1.64	90 (10 mils)	0.5 (10 mils)
PETG	1.567	90 (10 mils)	0.5 (10 mils)
Polyarylate	1.61	80 to 84	1 to 2
Polycarbonate	1.586	87 to 91	0.7 to 1.5
Polyetherimide	1.658		
Polyester carbonate (polyphthalate)	1.6	85 to 90	1 to 2
Polyethersulfone	1.65	76	8
Polymethylpentene	1.463	90	1.5
Polyphenylsulfone		50	15
Polystyrene	1.57	87 to 92	0.1 to 3
Polysulfone	1.633	75	7.5 to 8
PVC, rigid	1.52 to 1.57	74 to 76	8 to 18
Styrene acrylonitrile (SAN)	1.56 to 1.57	78 to 88	0.4 to 1
Styrene butadiene	1.571	89 to 95	1 to 3
Styrene maleic anhydride (SMA)	1.60	86 to 91	1 to 2
Styrene methyl-methacrylate (SMMA)	1.56	90	2.2
Thermoplastic urethane, rigid	1.65	88	2

troubleshooting With all types of processes, materials, and products, troubleshooting guides are set up (usually required) to take fast, corrective action when products do not meet their performance requirements. This problem solving approach fits into the overall fabricating-design interface ▷**FALLO approach** and Fig. in ▷**design**. Brief examples of troubleshooting are given in the Tables on p. 782. ▷**thermoforming troubleshooting**. A simplified approach to troubleshooting is to develop a checklist that incorporates the basic rules of problem solving such as (1) have a plan, and keep updating it, based on the experience gained; (2) watch the processing conditions; (3) change only one condition or control at a time; (4) allow sufficient time for each change, keeping an accurate log of each; (5) check housekeeping, storage areas, granulators, etc; and (6) narrow the range of areas in which the problem belongs—that is, machine, molds-dies, operating controls, materials, part design, and management.

troubleshooting by remote control To aid the manufacturing plants, "remote troubleshooting" has been available from different equipment manufacturers and service facilities. Users of certain microprocessed equipment need not be concerned about their plant personnel's ability to service and maintain the equipment. Via telephone link from your controller to a central service computer, a specialist at the controls supplier's office can immediately check out conditions in your controller and in the entire processing line or machine.

Different techniques are used but basically the equipment has installed, or one can add, an interfacing link that goes from the machines to the telephone. The adaptor (or modem) provides a remote diagnostic link so that the machine manufacturer's service personnel could directly provide corrective action to the equipment with no interference in production; no down time. When required, instructors will be provided. This diagnostic link can be used to set-up preventative maintenance programs.

troubleshooting flaw When setting up troubleshooting, it is important that the terms used to identify a problem be understandable, clear, and properly defined. As an example, the word "flaw" could have any of the following meanings:

Troubleshooting RP processes.

Problem	Possible cause	Solution
Nonfills	Air entrapment Gel and/or plastic time too short	Additional air vents and/or vacuum required Adjust plastic mix to lengthen time cycle
Excessive thickness variation	Improper clamping and/or lay-up	Check weight and lay-up and/or check clamping mechanisms such as alignment of platens
Blistering	Demolded too soon Improper catalytic action	Extend molding cycle Check plastic mix for accurate catalyst content and dispersion
Extended curing cycle	Improper catalytic action	Check equipment, if used, for proper catalyst metering Remix plastic and contents; agitate mix to provide even dispersion

Troubleshooting—simplified approach for "cause due to plastic material".

	Possible causes												
Problems	Too high a moisture content	Too little lubricant	Too much monomer	Contaminated granules	Too high a proportion of material to be ground	Too long preheating	Too high a drying temperature	Uneven addition of colorant	Uneven granule size	Too much fines	Uneven granule feed	Variations in granule preheating temperature	Variations in moisture content
Sink marks	●	●	●								●		
Flow marks	●			●									
Brittleness	●			●	●								
Discoloration	●					●	●	●					
Surface blemishes				●					●	●	●	●	
Varying shrinkage	●								●		●		
Varying dimensional stability	●								●		●		
Sticking to the mold	●		●										
Varying strength												●	●

Blush	Discoloration caused by plastic flow during molding.
Burn	Discoloration caused by thermal decomposition.
Discoloration	Any change from original color or unintended, inconsistent part color.
Fill-in	An excess of ink that alters the form of a screened feature, affecting clarity and legibility.
Flow marks (plastic)	Wavy or streaked appearance of a surface.
Flow marks (silk screen)	Waviness of edge or excessive linear surface texture of screened areas.
Glossiness	An area of excessive or deficient gloss.
Gouge	Indentation that can be felt (dents).
Haze	Cloudiness of an otherwise transparent part.
Inconsistency	Variation of gloss, thickness of line, or surface texture not called for by master artwork.
Marks	Pits, sanding, machining, or other marks on part surface that are unacceptable.
Misalignment	The failure of the screened graphics to align with the part or its features.
Nonadhesion	Lack of proper sticking of the coating to the surface (chipping, orange peel).
Nonuniform (coverage)	Areas that have an insufficient or excessive coating.
Pit	Small crater on a surface.
Porosity	Holes or voids (blow holes, pits, or underfills).
Protrusion	A raised area on a surface (blister, bump, ridge).
Runs	Excessive coating that causes drips.
Scratches	Shallow grooves.
Sink	A depression on a surface (shrink mark).
Smearing	The presence of ink on areas not called for by master artwork.
Speck	An included substance that is foreign to its intended composition (bubble, inclusion).
Void	Failure of a plastic to completely fill a cavity.
Weld line	A visible line or mark on a surface, caused by plastic flow molding.

This is "stretching" the term *flaw*. However, it reviews what could be a normal operating procedure.

T-shirt bag ▷ **grocery bag**

tube, collapsible squeeze type These tubes, traditionally an impact-extruded aluminum, lead, or tin product, were first used as an oil paint container. September 11, 1841 is the date of the first patent. It is now very big business worldwide. Tubes (see Fig. below) are big business with 30% made of aluminum, 30% of plastics, and 40% laminated of plastic, paper, aluminum, and more plastics (as the TCNA reports). Some of the aluminum tubes must be coated on the inside with a barrier material to protect the Al. PE and PP are predominantly used with coextruded plastic tubes.

tube mill A fine grinding machine that will finish-grind particulates; it is usually fed 20-mesh material which is reduced to 325-mesh. It has a rotating steel chamber which may be from 15 to 50 ft. ($4\frac{1}{2}$ to 15 m) long and 6 to 8 ft. (2 to $2\frac{1}{2}$ m) diameter. Within the chamber are steel

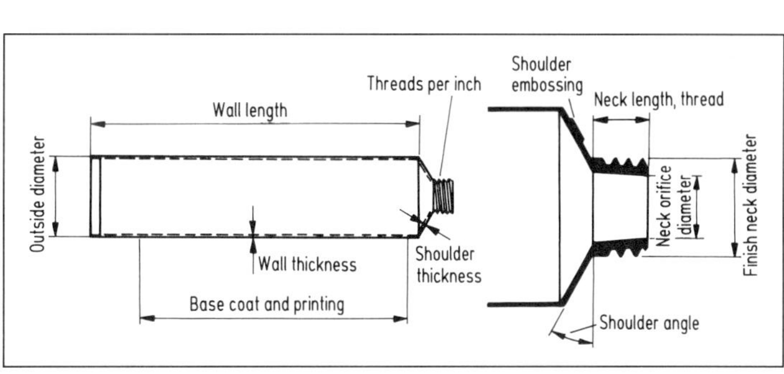

Collapsible tube nomenclature.

balls from 1 to 5 in. ($2\frac{1}{2}$ to 13 cm) in diameter. There are batch and continuous types used. ▷ **mesh particle size**

tub impact test ▷ **impact, tub**

tubing Plastic tubings were introduced during the 1930s as replacements for natural rubber tubing and hose. Now used are natural and synthetic rubbers, silicone rubbers, and fluoroelastomers; growth has been in thermoplastics that can be extruded into long lengths without the need for postcuring. Choice of TPs depends on application.

tubing, heat-shrinkable Tubing usually made of TFE or TFE copolymer plastics whose inside diameter may be reduced to a predetermined size by the application of heat.

tub test ▷ **dart drop test**

tumbling Finishing and/or deflashing machine operation for relatively small plastic parts by which gates, flash, fins, etc. are removed and/or surfaces are polished by rotating them in a barrel together with wooden pegs, sawdust, and polishing compounds. There are batch and continuous systems.

tumbling agitator Cylindrical or cone-shaped vessels rotating about a horizontal or inclined axis, with internal ribs which lift the material and then let it tumble back into the charge. They are used mainly for dry blending operations such as adding color concentrates to molding powders.

tunnel fire test Also called the Steiner tunnel test (ASTM E 84), it is intended to provide a comparative assessment of the surface burning characteristics of materials on a relatively large scale. Different results are reported. Important data is the flame spread distance versus time on materials to determine a flame spread index (FSI). It is 0 for incombustible cement-asbestos board and 100 for red oak. FSI values below 25 correspond to materials normally rated as incombustible; 25 to 50 fire resistant; 50 to 75 slow burning; 75 to 200 combustible; and over 200 highly combustible.

turbostratic A type of crystalline structure where the basal planes have slipped sideways relative to each other, causing the spacing between planes to be greater than ideal.

turbulent flow The opposite to laminar flow, where a fluid moves in all different directions, such as desired in mold cooling lines. With turbulence, more heat will be removed from the mold cavity. With laminar flow the liquid heat buildup on the wall of the mold tubular line would act as an insulator so that inside laminar flow would be an inefficient heat remover. ▷ **Reynold's number** and **laminar flow**

turflike surface ▷ **recreational surface**

turnkey operation A complete plastic fabrication line or system, such as an extruder line with its upstream and downstream equipment. Controls that interface the complete line require and initial startup run to set the line producing products that meet all requirements. After initial startup, it is a true turnkey operation. Startup could be by equipment and/or material suppliers, or the plant personnel.

turns per inch TPI is a measure of the amount of twist produced on a yarn, tow, or roving during its processing cycle. It represents the lead rate of a hoop layer at a specified band width. ▷ **twist, direction of yarn**

turret Table or indexing head associated with equipment to repeat certain actions. Example is to move molds in an orderly manner, as designed into the system.

twill weave ▷ **fabric, twill weave**

twin screw ▷ **extruder, twin screw**

twin screw change After changing the configuration of the screws of a twin screw machine, before reinstalling, roll them on a flat surface (together) to make sure configuration and element orientation are identical on both shafts.

twin screw extruder, chemical reactor ▷ **extruder reactive processing**

twin sheet thermoforming ▷ **thermoforming, clamshell**

twist, direction of yarn In yarn or other textile strand, it is the spiral turns about its axis per unit of length. Twist may be expressed as turns per inch (TPI). The letters S and Z indicate direction of twist, in reference to whether the twist direction conforms to the middle-section slope of the particular letter (see Fig. opposite).

A yarn or strand has what is known as an "S" twist if, when held in a vertical position, the spirals conform in slope to the central position of the letter S; it has a "Z" twist if the spirals conform in slope to the central portion of the letter Z. Strands that are simply twisted (greater than 1 turn/in. = 40 turns/m) will kink, corkscrew, and unravel because of their twist in one direction only. The plying operation normally eliminates this problem by countering the twist in the twisted "singles" yarn with an opposite twist in the plied yarn. For example,

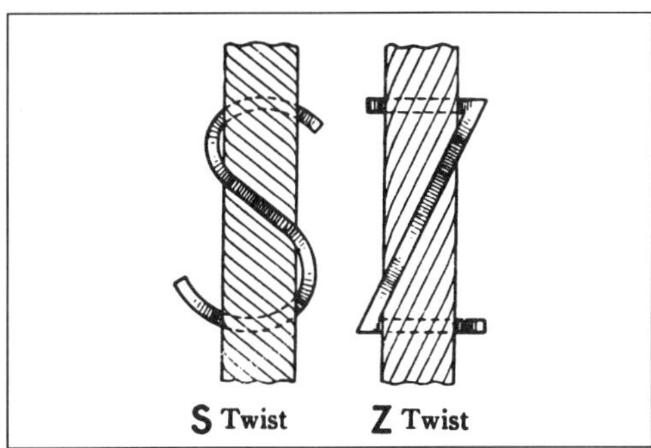

Twist directions (S and Z) in a yarn or other textile strand.

"singles" yarns having a "Z" twist are plied with an "S" twist, thus resulting in a "balanced" yarn. The twisting and plying operations permit the yarn strength, diameter, and flexibility to be varied, and are important steps in producing the variety of fabrics which reinforced plastic designers and fabricators require.

twist, hawser The construction of cabled yarn, cord or rope in which the single and first-ply twist are in the same direction and the second-ply twist is in the opposite direction and in the S/S/Z or Z/Z/S construction.

twisting without kinking A balanced arrangement of twists in a combination of two or more strands which does not cause kinking or twisting on themselves when the yarn produced is held in the form of an open loop.

two-color molding ▷ **injection molding, two-color**

two-level mold Another name for stacked mold. ▷ **mold stacked**

two-roll mill ▷ **mill**

two-stage molding ▷ **injection molding, two-stage unit**

two-stage plastic ▷ **Novalak plastic**

two-stage screw molding ▷ **injection molding venting**

two-standard-deviation ▷ **standard deviation measurement**

two-step plastic ▷ **Novalak plastic**

two-up molding ▷ **blow molding, extruder mold multiple/combination cavities**

typesetting After the different characteristics and typestyles are known, it is important to be familiar with the various methods of typesetting. There are four basic methods of producing type: cast metal or hot type composition, typewriter or strike-on composition (sometimes called "cold type"), photographic typesetting, and electronic printing. Hot type refers to cast metal type whether it is set by hand or machine. Each has its advantages and limitations. ▷ **printers' measurements**

typical-basis The typical property value is an average value. No statistical assurance is associated with this basis. ▷ **A-basis; B-basis; S-basis**

Tyrin Dow Chemical's tradename for its family of chlorinated polyethylenes.

Tyvek Du Pont's trademark for a spun bonded, tough, strong, high density polyethylene fiber sheet product. Its use includes mailing envelopes (protects contents), wrapping around buildings to completely seal off cracks and seams to prevent drafts and cut airflow penetration between the outside and inside (allow moisture to escape from walls, eliminating or minimizing the prospect of harmful condensation damage) etc.

U

ultimate strength ▷ **tensile strength**

ultracentrifuge A centrifuge capable of rotating from 20,000 to 60,000 RPM, creating forces of 250,000 times gravity. Sedimentation studies of high polymers performed are used for determining weight-average molecular weights and molecular weight distributions.

ultrahigh molecular weight polyethylene plastic ▷ **polyethylene, ultrahigh molecular weight plastic**

ultrahigh molecular weight polyvinyl chloride plastic ▷ **polyvinyl chloride, ultrahigh molecular weight plastic**

ultralow density polyethylene plastic ▷ **polyethylene, ultralow density plastic**

ultramicroscopic Below the resolution of the microscope.

ultrasonic The science of effects of mechanical or sound vibrations beyond the limit of audible frequencies (greater than approximately 20,000 Hz). Use includes friction welding, drilling hard materials, nondestructive testing, cleaning of tools, etc.

ultrasonic cavitation test device A device whose driving frequency is in the ultrasonic range (greater than 20,000 Hz). ▷ **cavitation erosion**

ultrasonic cleaning A method used for thoroughly cleaning plastic parts, including electrical and mechanical parts. A transducer mounted on the side or bottom of a cleaning tank is excited by a frequency generator to produce high frequency vibrations in the cleaning medium. These vibrations dislodge contaminants from crevices and blind holes that normal cleaning methods would not affect.

ultrasonic degradation A type of mechanochemical degradation occurring when a plastic solution is irradiated with ultrasonic radiation. Cavitation (rapid collapse of regions of low pressure) occurs and the resulting very high local shearing forces can cause mechanochemical chain scisson of the plastic, thus reducing molecular weight.

ultrasonic distance-amplitude response curve A curve showing the relationship between the different distances and the amplitudes of ultrasonic indication from targets of equal size in an ultrasonic transmitting medium.

ultrasonic fabrication Methods of ultrasonic assembly of plastic parts include plastic welding, metal inserting, staking, spot welding, and sewing. In each application ultrasonic vibrations above the audible range generate localized heat by vibrating one surface against another. Sufficient heat is released, usually within a fraction of a second, to cause most thermoplastics to melt, flow, and fuse. Ultrasonic assembly can be cleaner, faster, and more economical than conventional bonding methods. It eliminates the application of heat, solvents, or adhesives, and does not require any curing time. Therefore it permits higher production rates.

ultrasonic insertion The inserting of a metal insert into a thermoplastic part by the application of vibratory mechanical pressure at ultrasonic frequencies.

ultrasonic nozzle A pneumatic or vibratory atomizer in which energy is imparted, at high frequency, to the liquid.

ultrasonic penetration A relative term denoting the ability of an ultrasonic testing system to inspect material exhibiting high absorption or scattering.

ultrasonic relaxation Relaxation occurring as a result of ultrasonic irradiation. Irradiation results in a periodic longitudinal compression and rarefaction (a pressure fluctuation) of the material. This may be resolved into an isotropic and a shear component. The response of a sample to the two components may be evaluated so that effectively such measurements amount to the determination of the moduli at higher frequencies than in other mechanical relaxation methods. Usually measurements are made at a fixed frequency over a temperature range, so that transitions may be observed at higher frequencies than is normal. In addition, the passage of a wave may cause adiabatic heating and cooling with consequent effects on wave propagation. Monitoring of this response

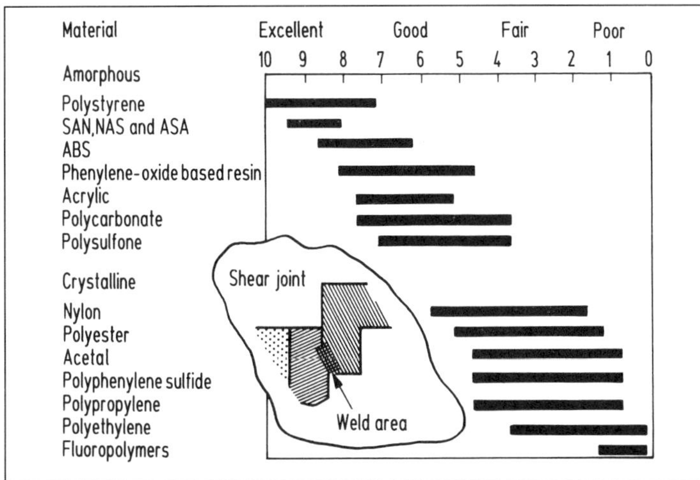

Ultrasonic welding of various thermoplastics.

yields thermodynamic data which can be related to specific conformational changes in the plastic. In practice the explanation of the rates and energies of these changes is restricted to dilute solutions.

ultrasonic sealing or welding Sealing accomplished through the application of vibratory mechanical pressure at ultrasonic frequencies (20 to 40 kc). Electrical energy is converted to ultrasonic vibrations through the use of either magnetostrictive or piezoelectric transducer. The vibratory pressures at the interface in the sealing area generate frictional heat, melting the thermoplastics and allowing them to bond. As shown in the Fig. above, the amorphous plastics have better bond action than the crystalline plastics with their tightly packed molecules. However, any of these plastics may not weld if they contain nonmelting fillers, such as glass fibers, if they are of high concentration.

ultrasonic testing In ultrasonic testing the sound waves from a high-frequency ultrasonic transducer are beamed into a material. Discontinuities in the material interrupt the sound beam and reflect energy back to the transducer, providing data that can be used to detect and characterize flaws.

When an electromagnetic field is introduced into an electrical conductor, eddy currents flow in the material. Any variations in material conductivity due to cracks, voids, or thickness changes can alter the path of the eddy current. Probes are used to detect the current movement and thus describe the flaws.

When flaws or cracks grow, minute amounts of elastic energy are released that propagate in the material as an acoustic wave. Sensors placed on the surface of the material can detect these waves, providing information about the location and rate of flaw growth. These principles form the basis for the acoustic emission test method.

Although they have been commercially available since the 1940s, ultrasonic detectors never really caught on as a diagnostic or maintenance tool. The biggest problem with ultrasonic detectors was their inability to produce measurements as accurately or consistently as could many competing devices used for nondestructive testing. The advent of microprocessing is dramatically improving the ability of ultrasonics to detect the wall thickness of metals and plastics, to determine particle dispersion in suspensions, and to detect potential leakage and faulty parts.

ultraviolet Pertaining to the region of the invisible electromagnetic spectrum from about 10 to 400 nm (nanometer). The term UV without further qualification usually refers to the region from 200 to 400 nm. ▷ **electromagnetic spectrum**

ultraviolet absorber and light stabilizer Light itself does not directly harm plastics, but the radiations and particularly UVs tend to initiate or catalyze chemical degradation. Result is oxidation, a process often globally referred to as photooxidation ▷ **oxidation degradation**. Various plastics are susceptible to photooxidation (PMMA, PE, PP, PS, PVC, etc.). Absorbers and/or stabilizers are used to provide long outdoor exposure, such as at least 40 years with PMMA, etc. Chemists attempting to elucidate the mechanisms of photooxidation, and its reduction by suitable additives often distinguish between UV absorber (UA), which reduces the essential factor of degradation, and light (or photooxidation) stabilizers (LS), which control its progress; although the distinction appears sometimes subtle. There are many classes of UAs and LSs for the different plastics. Amount use ranges from 0.1 to 0.6%. UAs also called UV inhibitors (UVIs).

ultraviolet light scatter ▷ **Raman spectroscopy**

ultraviolet radiation Radiation for which the wavelengths of the monochromatic components are smaller than those for visible radiation, and more than 1 nm.

ultraviolet screen A type of UV stabilizer that is insoluble in the plastic and therefore renders a transparent material opaque. Carbon black, especially if of small particle size, is the most effective screen. Other pigments (such as zinc oxide and the rutile, but not the anatase, form of titanium dioxide) have lesser screening power and act by reflecting rather than absorbing UV.

ultraviolet spectrophotometry A method of analysis similar to IR spectrophotometry except that the spectrum is obtained with UV light. It is somewhat less sensitive than the IR method analysis, but is useful for detecting some plasticizers and antioxidants.

ultraviolet stabilizer Another name for ultraviolet absorbers.

unary system Composed of one component.

unbond Area of a bonded surface in which bonding of plastics or adherends has failed to occur.

unbonded batting A textile filling material which is neither needle-punched, plastic bonded, or thermal bonded.

uncertainties An estimate of potential inaccuracies in a measured or derived quantity based on an explicit evaluation and combination of all sources of error. Quantitative uncertainty estimates are typically given in a form of variances (or standard deviations) and co-variances (or correlations) derived from statistical procedures combining random, and calculational (modeling) uncertainties. ▷ **design safety factor** and **designing with model**

undamped natural frequency The frequency of free vibrations resulting from only elastic and inertial forces of a mechanical system.

undercure An undesirable condition of a fabricated part due to little time, temperature and/or pressure for adequate hardening of the part.

undercut Having a protuberance or indentation that impedes withdrawal from a two-piece rigid mold; flexible plastics usually can be ejected intact with slight undercuts; flexible mold can provide for ejection of rigid plastic. Undercuts should be avoided whenever possible. ▷ **mold**

undertone The color of a thin layer of pigment-vehicle mixture applied on a white background.

underwater and ocean ▷ **environment and ocean**

underwater pelletizing ▷ **pelletizing**

Underwriters' Laboratory classified product A product which has been produced under UL's Classification and Follow-Up Service and which bears the authorized Classification Marking of UL as the manufacturer's declaration that the product complies with UL's requirements in accordance with the terms of the Classification and Follow-Up Service Agreement.

Underwriters' Laboratory cone and lift tests ▷ **fire tests, cone and lift** and **flammability**

Underwriters' Laboratory consumer advisor council A group of individuals selected by UL as representatives of organized consumer groups, large mail order and department stores who have knowledge of and reflect a close concern for consumers, representatives of the government who have responsibilities involving consumers, persons formerly associated with public safety activities, and persons associated with consumer related groupings within the American National Standards Institute to advise UL in establishing levels of safety for consumer products, provide additional user field experience and failure information in the area of product safety and assist in educating the general public in the limitations and safe use of specific consumer products.

Underwriters' Laboratory factory inspection Visits by UL's representatives to a factory or other facility where listed, classified, or recognized products are made for the purpose of conducting examination and/or tests of such products and for checking the means which the manufacturer exercises to determine compliance with UL's requirements.

Underwriters' Laboratory fire resistance index A summary of classified fire resistance product cards and building construction design fire resistance ratings published in booklet form for general distribution.

Underwriters' Laboratory flammability UL-94 test ▷ **fire retardance**

Underwriters' Laboratory listing service A system whereby UL determines that a manufacturer has demonstrated the ability to produce a product that complies with UL's requirements with respect to reasonable foreseeable hazards associated with the product; and, by the terms of the Listing and Follow-Up Service Agreement, authorizes the manufacturer to use the UL Listing Mark on products that comply with UL's requirements and establishes a Follow-Up Service conducted by UL as a check on the means which the manufacture exercises to determine compliance with UL's requirements.

Underwriters' Laboratory thermal index ▷ **heat test**

Underwriters' Laboratory V-0 ratings ▷ **fire retardance**

uniaxial load A condition where a material is stressed in only one direction.

uniaxial orientation A method of orientation in which the orienting is applied only in one direction. ▷ **orientation**

uniaxial state of stress State of stress in which two of the three principal stresses are zero.

Unicarb Union Carbide's tradename for their finish systems that compete with solvent organic systems. ▷ **finish system, reduce solvent**

unicellular plastic Term sometimes used for closed cell foamed plastics.

unidirectional fabric ▷ **fabric woven**

unidirectional orientation **1.** Alignment of the plastic molecules in one direction, much more than in any other direction. **2.** ▷ **reinforced plastic, directional properties**

unimeric Pertaining to a single molecule that is not monomeric, oligomeric, or polymeric, such as saturated hydrocarbons.

Unipol Union Carbide's tradename for its low pressure process that made possible the large volume utilization of linear low density polyethylene and other plastics.

unit **1.** A part on which a measurement or observation may be made. **2.** Measurement-wise, a precisely specified quantity in terms of which magnitudes of other quantities of the same kind can be stated.

unit, coherent system A system of units of measurement in which a small number of base units, defined as dimensionally independent, are used to derive all other units in the system by rules of multiplication and division with no numerical factors other than unity.

unit elongation In a tensile test, the ratio of the elongation to the original length of the specimen, that is, the change in length per unit of original length.

unitization The assembled group of containers or items in a single load that can be handled as a unit throughout the distribution system.

unit mold ▷ **mold unit**

unit weight Weight per unit volume.

unsaturated compound Any compound having more than one bond between two adjacent atoms, usually carbon atoms, and being capable of adding other atoms at that point to reduce it to a single bond.

unsaturated polyester ▷ **polyester, thermoset plastic**

unsaturation Implies a condition of partially filled. In terms of a compound, it denotes a condition of being able to take up or react with more atoms.

upstream Refers to material movement and auxiliary equipment (dryer, blender, storage bin, etc.) that exists prior to plastic entering the main processing equipment such as extruder and blow molder ▷ **downstream**

urban waste Solid waste material including garbage, glass, plastic, metal, etc., but not including air pollution or waste water materials.

urea formaldehyde plastic UF thermoset plastic compounds are in the amino family of plastics. They are available in a wide range of colors, from translucent colorless and white through to a lustrous black. Unlike the colored phenolic compounds, the molded UFs can be made with a considerable degree of translucency, giving them a brightness and depth of color somewhat similar to, although better than, opal glass. Although the UF's appearance can be duplicated in some TPs, the fact that they are not affected by heat within their range of operating temperatures makes their use necessary in many cases. These noninflammable (self-extinguishing), odorless, and tasteless materials char at about 200°C (395°F). Temperatures from −21°C (−70°F) to 80°C (175°F) have no effect on them, but higher temperatures over prolonged periods will cause fading and eventual blistering.

When used within their temperature limitations, UFs have good electrical properties. They have high dielectric strength, high arc resistance, no tendency to track after arcing, and a low order-power factor. Their electrical properties are not greatly influenced by high humidity, and they resist static electricity buildup.

Under dry conditions, UF moldings are remarkable resistant to corrosive fumes and have no effect on organic solvents in terms of absorption, swelling, or changes in appearance. However, their water absorption is relatively high. For this reason they are not recommended for applications involving continuous or intermittent exposure to water, although occasional exposure will have little effect if the material has been well cured. The UF intermediate water-soluble products are starting materials for the production of adhesives, surface coatings, paper conditioners, and other such special items that require heat and catalysts for their final curing. They are used to bond laminated sheets, sometimes only on the surface, for color effects.

The applications of UFs include sanitary wares such as toilet seats, and knobs, closures, buttons, electrical accessories like housings and switches, laminates, and so on. Compounds of UFs use different additives, fillers, and reinforcements to provide different characteristics and permit processing in different equipment, principally by compression, transfer, and injection molding. Like many other TSs, such as the phenolics and melamines, they are easily preformed and preheated, either by RF preheaters or with screw plasticators. The higher bulk-factor grades of the melamine compounds require using special equipment for these operations, because of their lack of easy pourability.

urethane coating plastic Coatings based upon vehicles containing a minimum of 10 wt% (nonvolatile vehicle basis) of a polyisocyanate monomer reacting in such a manner as to yield plastics containing any ratio, proportion, or combination of urethane linkages, active isocyanate groups, or polyisocyanate monomer. The reaction products may contain excess isocyanate groups available for further reaction at time of application or may contain essentially no free isocyanate as supplied.

urethane foam plastic ▷**foamed polyurethane**

urethane plastic ▷**polyurethane plastic**

U.S. Post Office Abbreviations for the states are as follows:

Alabama	AL
Alaska	AK
Arizona	AZ
Arkansas	AR
California	CA
Colorado	CO
Conneticut	CT
Delaware	DE
District of Colombia	DC
Florida	FL
Georgia	GA
Hawaii	HI
Idaho	ID
Illinois	IL
Indiana	IN
Kansas	KS
Kentucky	KY
Louisiana	LA
Maine	ME
Maryland	MD
Massachusetts	MA
Michigan	MI
Minnesota	MN
Mississippi	MS
Missouri	MO
Montana	MT
Nebraska	NE
Nevada	NV
New Hampshire	NH
New Jersey	NJ
New Mexico	NM
New York	NY
North Carolina	NC
North Dakota	ND
Ohio	OH
Oklahoma	OK
Oregon	OR
Pennsylvania	PA
Puerto Rico	PR
Rhode Island	RI
South Carolina	SC
South Dakota	SD
Tennessee	TN
Texas	TX
Utah	UT
Vermont	VT
Virginia	VA
Washington	WA
West Virginia	WV
Wisconsin	WI
Wyoming	WY

Avenue	AVE
Boulevard	BLVD
Circle	CIR
Court	CT
Expressway	EXPY
Freeway	PWY
Lane	LN
Parkway	PKY
Road	RD
Square	SQ
Street	ST
Turnpike	TPKE

UV absorber ▷**ultraviolet absorber and light stabilizer**

vacuum In vacuum technology a given space filled with gas at pressures below atmospheric pressure. ▷**torr**

vacuum bag molding A reinforced plastic molded part made by hand lay-up or spray-up is allowed to cure without the application of external pressure. For many applications this approach is sufficient, but maximum consolidation usually is not achieved with its use. There is some porosity, fibers may not fit closely into internal corners with sharp radii but tend to spring back, and resin-rich or resin-starved areas may occur because of drainage, even with thixotropic agents. With moderate pressure these defects can be overcome, with an improvement in mechanical properties and better quality control of parts.

One way to apply such moderate pressure is to enclose the "wet-liquid resin" composite and mold in a flexible membrane or bag, and draw a vacuum inside the enclosure (see Fig.). Atmospheric pressure on the outside then presses the bag or membrane uniformly against the wet composite. Pressures commonly range from 69 to 283 kPa (10–14 psi). ▷**bag molding** and **vent cloth**

vacuum bag molding, bag side The side of a part that is cured against the vacuum bag.

vacuum casting Vacuum casting is primarily used to encapsulate high-voltage components in a void-free, dielectric compound based on a plastic casting material such as principally epoxy, and also polyurethane, silicone, or polyester (TS). The objective of the process is to have: (1) homogeneous structure of the plastic and thus high mechanical strength of the casting, (2) blister-free surface requiring only little post-casting treatment, (3) consistent quality of castings, and (4) reliable protection of the encapsulated components from environmental influences. ▷**casting**

vacuum chamber A chamber connecting the vent holes with the main vacuum line.

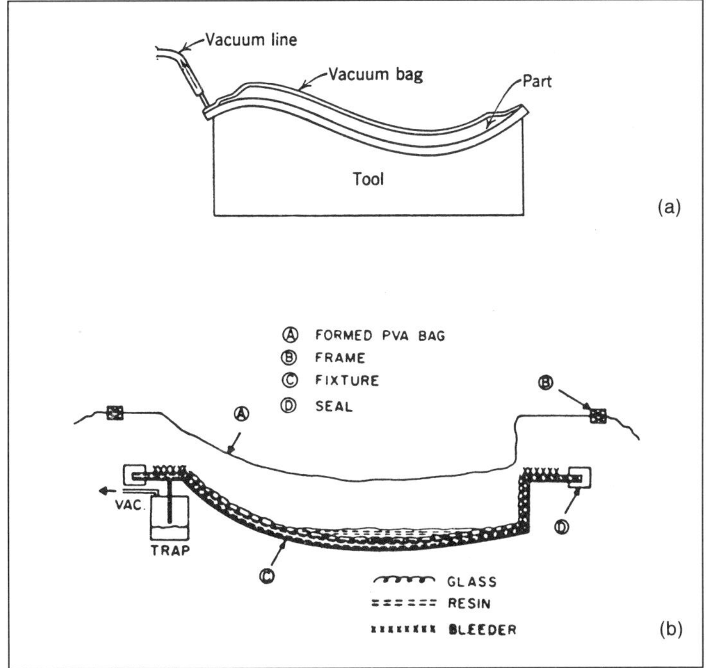

Bag molding schematics reviewing (*a*) a simplified view and (*b*) examples of details shown in a partial section. Also see Fig. on p. 30 in ▷**autoclave**

vacuum coating This technology and use is important in different industries, particularly in advanced applications such as microelectronics. Coatings for these high technology parts are employed to maintain certain desirable surface properties that differ from those of bulk material for protection of the underlying product. Good coatings can be deposited using vacuum techniques, either by physical or chemical vapor-deposition methods. Physical methods include evaporation and sputtering; chemical method includes polymerization through pyrolysis and glow discharge (plasma). The starting materials may be either solid or gas, and the type of energy applied either plasma or thermal. Sputtering employs a solid target and a plasma energy source.

vacuum deposition The process of coating a base material by evaporating a metal under high vacuum and condensing it on the surface of the substrate to be coated.

vacuum forming ▷ **thermoforming, vacuum**

vacuum gauge, Knudsen An absolute manometer based on the principle of the transfer of momentum from a hot to a cold surface by gas molecules as in a radiometer.

vacuum holes ▷ **mold venting holes** and **thermoforming mold**

vacuum hot pressing VHP is a method of processing materials (especially powders) at elevated temperatures, consolidation pressures, and low atmospheric pressures.

vacuum impregnation ▷ **impregnation**

vacuum metallizing The thermal evaporation and subsequent condensation of a metal onto the substrate in a vacuum. Base and topcoats can be applied by a simple tool such as a hand sprayer, an elaborate automated spray robot, or a flow coater. Although dipping and spraying are common coating techniques, flow is predominantly used. Coating materials in decorative metallizing are usually called lacquers; they are usually dried in convection ovens. Typical lacquers are based on nitrocellulose or other cellulosics, as well as acrylic and vinyl plastics.

Requirements for brightwork, specifically second surface decorative techniques on plastics such as PMMA and PC, are routinely fulfilled by vacuum metalization. Formerly the dominant method for the first surface brightwork, vacuum metallization has lost ground to electroplating.

The common methods of depositing metals are chemical reduction, electroplating, spraying, and vacuum metallizing. Chemical reduction requires stringent temperature control, generally produces noxious fumes, and does not compete economically with the other deposition processes where they are compatible. The quality of chemically reduced deposits is inferior to either electrodeposits or vacuum method with respect to dimensional control, durability, and reflectivity. The processing temperatures involved generally exceed the heat distortion point of most plastics, thereby eliminating this process from consideration. Electroplating has the distinct disadvantage of requiring a conductive substrate; also requires buffing to produce a brilliant finish. Electroplating may be disregarded for plastic coating where steps to provide a conductive substrate are not available. For applications suitable to both electroplating and vacuum metallizing, economics generally favor metallizing. Spraying is applicable primarily for heavy deposits. However, a sprayed coating is porous, dimensionally nonuniform, and usually requires thermal treatment to improve adherence.

vacuum mold cooling ▷ **mold cooling, vacuum**

vacuum molding processes Includes vacuum bag, vacuum pressure, vacuum pressure bag, and vacuum thermoforming.

vacuum press Molding presses, such as compression molding presses, can include a vacuum chamber or system that is used with the mold; provides removal of air from the cavity(s). ▷ **breathing**

vacuum pressure Refers to negative pressure.

vacuum sizing and calibration, profile ▷ **extruder line cooling and shaping**

vacuum snap-back forming ▷ **thermoforming, snap-back**

vacuum wood impregnation ▷ **wood-plastic impregnated**

valence A whole number which represents the combining power of one element with another. By balancing these integral valence numbers in a given compound, the relative proportions of the elements present are accountable. If hydrogen and chloride both have a valence of 1, oxygen a valence of 2, and nitrogen of 3, the valence-balancing principle gives the formulas HCl, NH_3, H_2O, Cl_2O, NCl_3, and N_2O_3, which indicate the relative numbers of atoms of these elements in compounds.

valence band Highest energy band normally occupied by electrons.

valence electron Electrons which are gained, lost, or shared in a chemical reaction.

valley printing It provides three-dimensional texturing with surface coloring. In the process, embossing and printing are accomplished simultaneously on preheated plastic. It is usually done in only one color on a material of contrasting color to create two-color, three-dimensional effects. Ink is applied to the high points of an embossing roll and subsequently deposited in what becomes the valleys of the embossed plastic material. Also called inlay printing.

value An amount regarded as a fair equivalent for something; that which is desirable or worthy of esteem; thing of quality having intrinsic worth.

value analysis While there are many definitions of VA, the most basic is the following formula:

$$\text{VA} = \frac{\text{Function of the part}}{\text{Cost of the part}}$$

value, approximate A value that is nearly, but not exactly correct or accurate.

value, normal A value assigned for the purpose of convenient designation, existing in name only.

value, order of magnitude A range of values applied to numbers, distances, dimensions, etc. which begins at any value and extends to 10 times that value, i.e., 2 is of the same order of magnitude as any number between itself and 20 or 5 miles is of the same order of magnitude as any distance between 5 and 50 miles. The expression usually applies to extremely large or extremely small units.

valve gating ▷ **mold gate, valve**

valve screw ▷ **screw tip, injection**

van der Waals' forces Weak attractive forces acting between molecules. They are somewhat weaker than hydrogen bonds and far weaker than interatomic valences. Information regarding the numerical values of van der Waals' forces is mostly semiempirical, derived with the aid of theory from an analysis of physical or chemical data. Also called secondary valence forces or intermolecular forces.

vapor The gaseous form of substances that are normally in the solid or liquid state, and that can be changed to these states either by increasing the pressure or decreasing the temperature.

vapor barrier ▷ **barrier, vapor**

vapor degreasing ▷ **solvent cleaning**

vapor deposition, chemical ▷ **chemical vapor deposition** and **xylylene plastic**

vapor diffusion ▷ **water vapor diffusion**

vaporization point At a given pressure, the temperature at which the vapor pressure of the liquid is equal to the external pressure or at a stated temperature the external pressure on the liquid that is equal to its vapor pressure.

vapor-liquid chromatography ▷ **chromatography**

vapor-liquid-solid process The VLS process of Carborundum Co. (Niagara Falls, NY) produces high quality, rather large quantity of silicon carbide whiskers. ▷ **whisker reinforcement; ceramic matrix composite; silicon carbide fiber; reinforced plastic, advanced**

vapor pressure The pressure exerted by the vapor of a solid or liquid when in equilibrium with the solid or liquid.

vapor transmission ▷ **water vapor transmission**

vapor vacuum deposition The condensation and solidification of the metal or metal containing vapors, under high vacuum, to form deposits on a substrate.

variable A quantity to which any of the values in a given set may be assigned.

variable, independent An experimental factor that can be controlled (temperature, pressure, order of test, etc.) or independently measured (hours of sunshine, specimen thickness, etc.). Independent variables may be qualitative (such as a qualitative difference in operating technique) or quantitative (such as temperature, pressure, or duration).

variable speed control ▷ **motion control systems**

variable statistic ▷ **statistical data collection**

variance The mean square of deviations (or errors) of a set of observations; the sum of square deviations (or errors) of individual observations with respect to their arithmetic mean divided by the number of observations less one (degree of freedom); the square of the standard deviation (or standard error).

varnish A liquid formulation that is converted to a transparent or translucent, solid film after application as a thin layer. Oil is a typical varnish which contains plastic and drying oil as the chief film-forming ingredients and is converted to a solid film primarily by chemical reaction.

vector Mathematical term completely specified by a magnitude and a direction; a one-dimensional array.

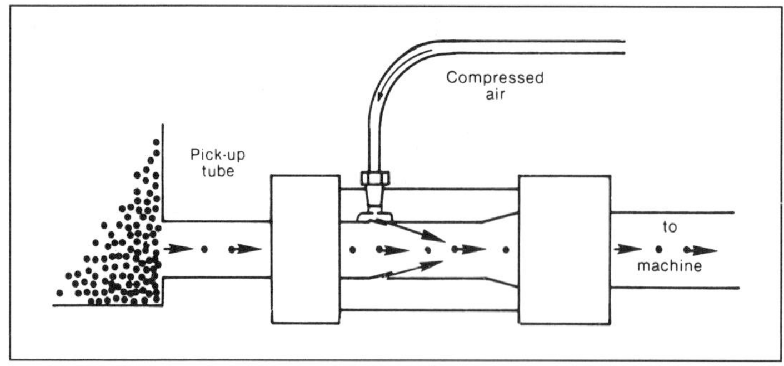

Pneumatic venturi flow diagram.

vehicle The liquid medium in which pigments, etc. are dispersed in coatings such as paint and which enable the coating to be applied.

veil A mat used to improve plastic surface characteristics particularly for reinforced plastics. ▷ **surface mat** and **mat**

velocity-pressure-transfer molding control ▷ **injection molding process control, compensation approach**

veneer Thinly cut wood (usually premium wood) applied as a surface laminate to various materials, such as wood, plastic, etc. Thin sheets are also used to produce plywood (of low to premium grade); also referred to as glued panel.

vent cloth A layer or layers of open-weave cloth used to provide a path for vacuum to reach the area in which a reinforced plastic is being cured, such that volatiles and air can be removed. It causes the pressure differential that results in the application of pressure to the part being cured. Also called breather cloth. Used in processes such as bag molding, autoclave molding, and vacuum bag molding. ▷ **bleeder cloth**

vented barrel ▷ **barrel vent**

vent hole An opening for the escape of gases for relief of pressure, often required in fabricating plastics. ▷ **mold venting** and **thermoforming mold**

venting, plasticator ▷ **injection molding venting; extruder venting; transfer molding venting; blow molding venting; compression molding venting; rotational molding venting; mold venting; barrel vent; autoclave venting; screw decompression zone, vented; breathing; bleeder cloth; barrel vented safety**

vent purifier The exhaust from vented barrels (extruders, injection molders, etc.) can show a dramatic cloud of swirling white gas; almost all of it is condensed steam proving that the vent is doing its job. However, a small portion of the vent exhaust can be other materials such as by-products released by certain plastics and/or additives and could be of concern to plant personnel and/or plant equipment. Purifiers can be attached (with or without vacuum hoods located over the vent opening) to remove and collect steam and other products. The purifiers include electronic precipitators.

venturi A type of flow meter. It is basically a tube-like device having broad, flaring ends and a narrow central portion (or throat). This shape constricts the passage of the "fluid" so that its rate of flow increases while the pressure decreases. The difference in pressure creates a measure of the flow. It is used in many different types of processing equipment such as scrubbers, liquid and solid conveying systems, and pipelines (see Fig. above).

venturi dispersion plug In injection molding, a plate having an orifice with a conical relief drilled therein which is fitted into the nozzle to aid in the dispersion of colorants in a plastic melt.

vermiculite A crystalline layer silicate mineral of similar structure to talc. However, some silicon atoms are replaced with aluminum, producing a negative charge that is neutralized by the interlayer cations, mostly magnesium. The ionic forces bind the layers together strongly. Water molecules in the layers are hydrogen bonded to oxygens of the silicates. On rapid heating to about 300°C the steam produced causes separation of the layers, giving an expansion (exfoliation) of up to 30 times. Use as a speciality type filler, as an example, mixed with plastic to form a filler compound of relatively high compression strength.

vertical extruder An extruder arranged so that the barrel is vertical and extrusion is downward; however, most have the barrels horizontal.

vertical flash ring The clearance between the force plug and the vertical wall of the cavity in a positive or semi-positive compression mold; also the ring of excess material which escapes from the cavity into the clearance space. ▷ **mold, compression**

very low density polyethylene plastic ▷ **polyethylene, ultralow density plastic**

vessel, closed end Parts in filament winding that have much smaller diameters or totally closed domes at the ends. ▷ **filament winding**

vibration An oscillation wherein the quantity is a parameter that defines the motion of a mechanical system.

vibration damping ▷ **dash pot**

vibration dynamic mechanical measurement ▷ **resonant forced vibration technique**

vibration feeder ▷ **feeder, vibratory**

vibration, forced Vibration that occurs if the response is imposed by the excitation. If the excitation is periodic and continuing, the oscillation is steady-state.

vibration, free A technique for performing dynamic mechanical measurements in which the sample is deformed, released, and allowed to oscillate freely at the natural resonant frequency of the system. Elastic modulus is calculated from measured resonant frequency, and damping is calculated from the rate at which the amplitude of the oscillation decays.

vibration welding In vibration welding, two plastic parts are rubbed together in either linear or angular displacement, producing frictional heat that results in a melt at the interface of the two parts. Different bonding joints can be used to eliminate having flash that is visible at the joints; basically, recesses within the bond exist. The vibration is in the form of high-amplitude, low-frequency, reciprocating motion. With circular parts a rotary motion is used. When the vibration stops, the melt cools and the parts become permanently welded in the alignment that is held. Typical frequencies are 120 and 240 Hz, with amplitudes ranging from 0.10 to 0.20 in. of linear displacement.

Vibration welding, like ultrasonic welding, produces high-strength joints for materials that can be melted. However, it is much better suited to large parts and irregular joint interfaces. Moisture in materials does not usually have an adverse effect on the weld as it does with ultrasonics.

vibratory cavitation test device ▷ **ultrasonic testing**

Vicat hardness A determination of the softening point for thermoplastics which have no definite melting point. The softening point is taken as the temperature at which the specimen is penetrated to a depth of 1 mm by a flat-ended needle with a 1 mm^2 (0.0015 in.^{2}) circular or square cross section, under a 1,000 g load.

vinal fiber ▷ **fiber vinal**

vinylchloride-based polyalloy There are several classes of such polyalloys. One corresponds primarily to the desire to improve the impact resistance of PVC and is achieved by blending with compatible rubbery plastics, such as ethylene/vinyl-acetate (EVA), nitrile rubber (NBR), and chlorinated PVC (CPVC).

vinyl chloride monomer VCM was first prepared by Regnault in 1835. Activity by others occurred with the 1921 discovery of how to polymerize PVC by Plausen. Commercial production started in 1931. Many new developments occurred thereafter. ▷ **polyvinyl chloride plastic and the environment**

vinyl dispersion ▷ **plastisol**

vinyl ester plastic These thermoset plastics are stiff, brittle, and tough; major use is as the matrix in glass fiber reinforced plastics. They have exceptional high strength properties in highly corrosive or chemical environments when compared to other RPs such as glass fiber-TS polyesters.

vinyl plastic ▷ **polyvinyl chloride plastic**

vinyl plastisol ▷ **plastisol**

vinyl polymerization ▷ **addition polymerization; anionic polymerization; reactivity**

vinyon fiber ▷ **fiber vinyon**

virgin plastic A plastic material in a form such as pellets, granules, powder, flock, or liquid that has not been subjected to use, recycled, or processed other than that required for its initial manufacture. ▷ **recyclable plastic and scrap** and **fiber, virgin**

viscoelastic creep When a viscoelastic (plastic) material is subjected to a constant stress, it undergoes a time-dependent increase in strain. This behavior is called creep.

viscoelasticity A property involving a combination of elastic and viscous behavior. A material having this property is considered to combine the features of a perfectly elastic solid and a perfect fluid. A phenomenon of time-dependent, in addition to elastic, deformation (or recovery) in response to load (see Fig. on p. 796). This property, possessed by all plastics to some degree, dictates that while plastics have solid-like characteristics such as elasticity,

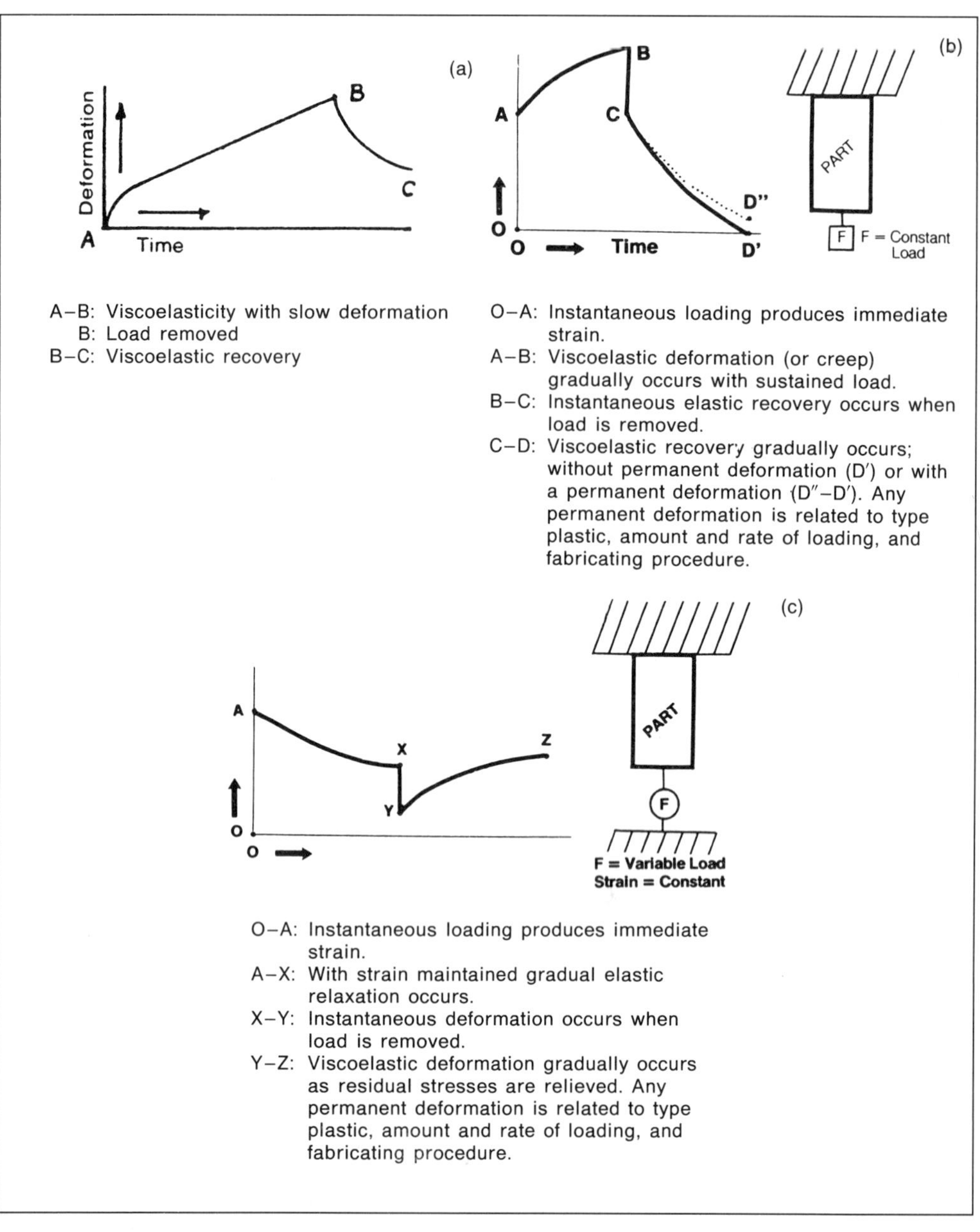

(a)
Deformation
B
C
A
Time
A–B: Viscoelasticity with slow deformation
B: Load removed
B–C: Viscoelastic recovery
(b)
A
B
C
D''
D'
O
O
Time
PART
F
F = Constant Load
O–A: Instantaneous loading produces immediate strain.
A–B: Viscoelastic deformation (or creep) gradually occurs with sustained load.
B–C: Instantaneous elastic recovery occurs when load is removed.
C–D: Viscoelastic recovery gradually occurs; without permanent deformation (D′) or with a permanent deformation (D″–D′). Any permanent deformation is related to type plastic, amount and rate of loading, and fabricating procedure.
(c)
A
X
Y
Z
O
O
PART
F
F = Variable Load
Strain = Constant
O–A: Instantaneous loading produces immediate strain.
A–X: With strain maintained gradual elastic relaxation occurs.
X–Y: Instantaneous deformation occurs when load is removed.
Y–Z: Viscoelastic deformation gradually occurs as residual stresses are relieved. Any permanent deformation is related to type plastic, amount and rate of loading, and fabricating procedure.

Examples of time-dependent viscoelasticity characteristics of plastics: (*a*) simplified deformation versus time behavior; (*b*) stress-strain deformation versus time (creep), and (*c*) stress-strain deformation versus time (stress-relaxation).

strength, and form-stability, they also have liquid-like characteristics such as flow depending on time, temperature, rate, and amount of loading. ▷ **elasticity; rheology; pseudoplastic; melt elasticity; Boltzmann superposition principle**

viscoelastic modulus ▷ **modulus, stress relaxation**

viscometer Also called a viscosimeter. An instrument used for measuring the viscosity and flow properties of fluids. A commonly used type is the Brookfield that measures the force required to rotate a disc or hollow cup immersed in the specimen fluid at a predetermined speed. Of the many other types, some employ rising bubbles, falling or rolling balls, and cups with orifices through which the fluid flows by gravity.

Instruments for measuring flow properties of highly viscous fluids and molten plastics are more often called rheometers or plastometers.

viscometer, capillary This term is used for two types of capillary instruments: one used for concentrated solutions or plastic melts described under capillary rheometer, and the other used for measuring dilute solution viscosities. The most widely used of the latter types employ a glass capillary tube and means for timing the flow of a measured volume of solution through the tube under the force of gravity. This time is then compared with the time taken for the same volume of pure solvent, or of another liquid of known viscosity, to flow through the same capillary.

viscometry The viscosity of a fluid is a measure of its resistance to flow. Induced motion, such as flow, requires a force to initiate the motion and to sustain it against frictional forces. Solids, when placed under a stress beyond their elastic limits, can maintain a strain, whereas fluids must have a sustaining force (stress) to maintain strain; otherwise, the motion and relaxation of the molecules in the fluid dissipate the stress. When flow exhibits a smooth response to the force in the direction in which it is applied, the flow is said to be laminar (Newtonian flow); an uneven response characterizes turbulent flow (non-Newtonian flow). Two basic models to define viscosity generally evolve, the Newtonian and the Maxwell models; it is not unusual to find the nomenclature intermixing them.

viscosity The property of resistance of flow exhibited within the body of a material. In testing, the ratio of the shearing stress to the rate of shear of a fluid. Viscosity is usually taken to mean Newtonian viscosity in which case the ratio of shearing stress to rate of shearing is constant. In non-Newtonian behavior which is the usual case with plastics, the ratio varies with shearing rate. Such ratios are often called the apparent viscosities at the corresponding shear rates.

viscosity, absolute The ratio of shear stress to shear rate; it is the property of internal resistance of a fluid that opposes the relative motion of adjacent layers.

viscosity, apparent ▷ **viscosity**

viscosity-average molecular weight ▷ **molecular weight average**

viscosity, coefficient The shearing stress necessary to induce a unit velocity gradient in a material. In actual measurement, the viscosity coefficient of a material is obtained from the ratio of shearing stress to shearing rate. This assumes the ratio to be constant and independent of the shearing stress, a condition satisfied only by Newtonian fluids. Consequently, in all other cases that includes plastics, values obtained are apparent and represent one point in the flow curve.

viscosity depressant A substance which, when added in a relatively minor amount to a liquid, lowers its viscosity. Such materials are often incorporated in vinyl plastisols to lower their viscosities without increasing plasticizer levels.

viscosity, dilute solution The viscosity of a dilute solution of a plastic, measured under prescribed conditions, is an indication of the molecular weight of the plastic.

viscosity, Hagen-Poiseuille law ▷ **Hagen-Poiseuille law**

viscosity, inherent In dilute solution viscosity measurements, inherent viscosity is the ratio of the natural logarithm of the relative viscosity to the concentration of the plastic in grams per 100 ml of solvent.

viscosity, intrinsic (Abbreviation IV = intrinsic viscosity) IV is a measure of the capability of a polymer in solution to enhance the viscosity of the solution. IV increases with increasing polymer molecular weight (see Fig. on p. 798).

viscosity, kinematic The ratio of viscosity to density, both at the same temperature.

viscosity, K-value A number calculated from dilute solution viscosity measurement of a plastic, used to denote degree of polymerization or molecular size.

viscosity, melt ▷ **melt viscosity**

viscosity, melt flow ▷ **mold filling**

viscosity, Mooney A measure of the viscosity of a rubber or elastomer determined in a Mooney shearing rotation disc viscometer (ASTM D 1646). Viscosity values depend on the size and configuration of the polymer molecule. With proper interpretation, the viscosity and the molecular weight or molecule size can be correlated. ▷ **scorch, Mooney**

viscosity, Newtonian An alternative name for coefficient of viscosity.

viscosity, number The IUPAC term for reduced viscosity.

viscosity, ratio The IUPAC term for relative viscosity.

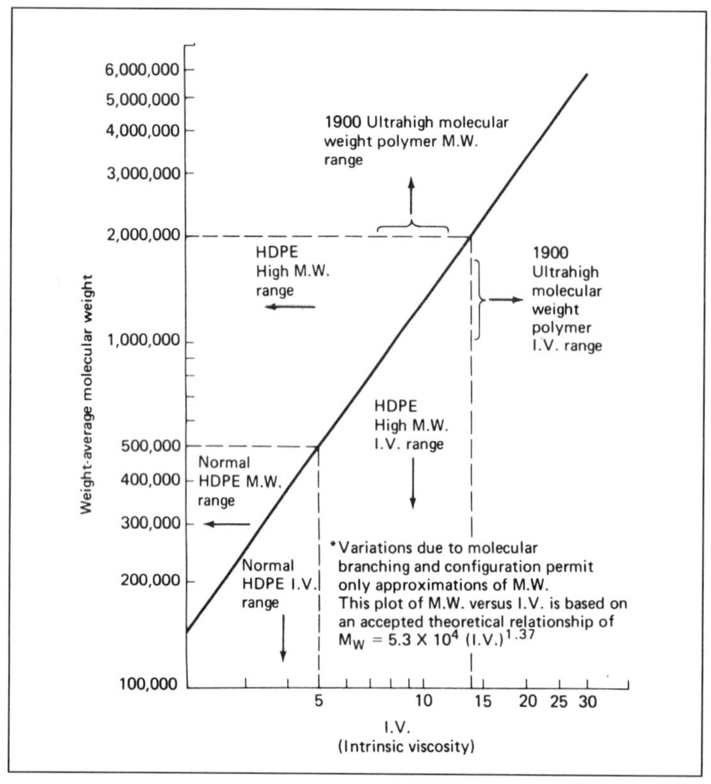

Relationship of intrinsic viscosity and molecular weight of UHMWPE.

viscosity, reaction The design of conventional (nonreactive) polymer processing equipment is complicated by the non-Newtonian nature of polymer melt viscosity. When attempting to design equipment to process reacting fluids, one is faced with an even more formidable task; accounting for changes in viscosities with conversions, temperature, and molecular weight, as well as nonuniformities within equipment. Difficulties can be experienced when attempting to mix or pump polymerizing fluids with rapidly rising viscosities that accompany reaction. To understand the associated flow phenomena, it is necessary to deal with the coupling between extent of reaction and viscosity. Reaction viscosity is much more sensitive to concentration and molecular weight than to temperature and shear rate.

viscosity, reduced Ratio of the specific viscosity to the concentration. Reduced viscosity is a measure of the specific capacity of the plastic to increase the relative viscostiy. The IUPAC term is viscosity number.

viscosity, relative The ratio of the viscosity of a solution to that of the pure solvent at the same temperature. IUPAC uses the term viscosity ratio.

viscosity, Saybolt The efflux time in seconds of 60 ml of sample flowing through a calibrated Saybolt universal orifice under specified conditions (ASTM D 1695).

viscosity, solution ▷ **solution viscosity**

viscosity, specific The difference between the viscosity of a solution and that of a solvent, divided by the latter.

viscosity, susceptibility ▷ **susceptibility**

viscous A term used to loosely denote that a material is thick and sluggish in flow rather than thin and free flowing.

viscous damping The dissipation of energy that occurs when a particle in a vibrating system is resisted by a force that has a magnitude proportional to the magnitude of the velocity of the particle and direction opposite to the direction of the particle.

viscous deformation Any portion of the total deformation of a body that occurs as a function of time when load is applied but that remains permanently when the load is removed. The term anelastic deformation is also used. ▷ **elastic deformation**

viscous elasticity A degree of elasticity in which the time necessary to recover initial dimensions is longer than a stated time such as 5%.

viscous flow A type of fluid in which all particles of the fluid flow in a straight line parallel to the axis of a container pipe or channel, with little or no mixing or turbidity.

viscous heating Heat generated within the stock (melt) due to friction as a result of mechanical working when screw rotates in a barrel.

viscous modulus ▷ **creep modulus, apparent**

viscous process The best and most well known process for making regenerated cellulose (rayon) is by converting cellulose to the soluble xanthate, which can be spun into fibers and then reconverted to cellulose by treatment with acid. The process starts with wood pulp in a 17–20% caustic soda. ▷ **fiber, rayon; cellophane**

vision system inspection There are many opportunities for automatic vision systems in controlling quality and productivity of molded containers, such as inspection, gauging flaw detection, verification, counting, character reading, identification, sorting, robot guidance, location analysis, and adaptive control. The inspection covers the feed rate of materials into equipment, parison shape/drop distance, preform shape/neck geometry/molded-in specks or flaws, container shape/neck geometry/size, and so on.

As an example, equipment is available to detect minute flaws at line speeds of up to 51,000 preforms/hr (see Fig. below) for an on-line system diagram to check PET injection blow mold bottle preforms' neck geometry and specks or flaws at rates up to 850/min. The system inspects each product with video cameras containing 180,000 photoelectric cells, using stroboscopic lighting to eliminate motion blur. The image is then analyzed by a gray-scale image processor that recognizes 256 different shades of gray and compares it to a standard image preset by the user. The system reportedly can detect flaws as small as 0.04 mm ($\frac{1}{625}$ of a sq. in.).

visual inspection Visual and optical inspections should not be overlooked as important nondestructive test techniques. Low power magnification lenses and microscopes can be used to advantage in improving visual inspection. Continuous on-line inspection and imaging systems are used for specific applications, and are used successfully. Surface defects, voids, porosity, delaminations, plastic rich or starved areas, and contaminants may be detected, particularly with transparent plastics and reinforced plastics. ▷ **nondestructive testing**

vitreous Glassy or glasslike.

void Air or gas pockets that have been trapped in the plastic during processing. ▷ **air entrapment**

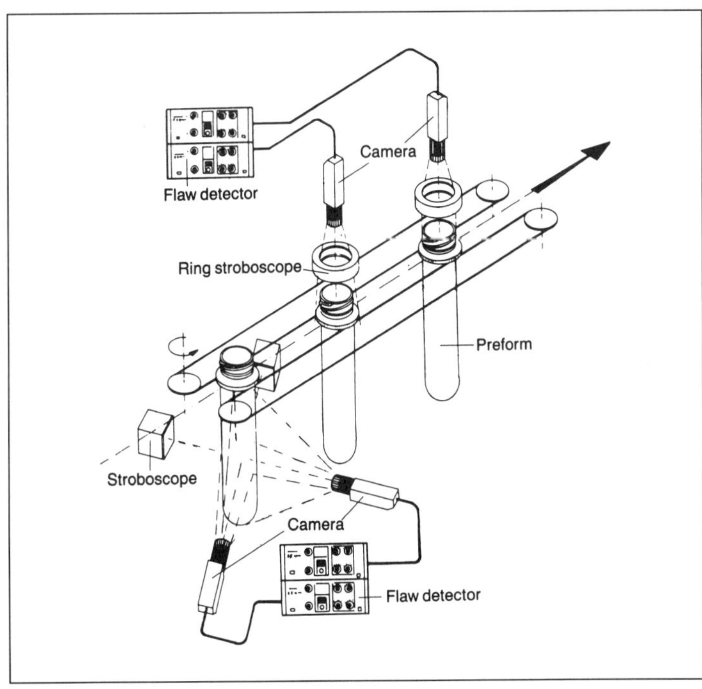

Example of an on-line vision inspection system.

volatile Materials readily vaporizable at relatively low temperatures; materials such as water and alcohol, in a sizing or plastic formulation, that are capable of being driven off as a vapor at room temperature or slightly higher.

volatile content The percent of volatiles that are driven off as a vapor from a plastic or reinforced plastic. ▷**prepreg volatile content**

volatile extraction or removal ▷**striping; vent hole; devolatilization, basics; reactor volatility**

volatile loss Weight loss by vaporization.

volatile organic compound VOCs reduction involves different plastic processing techniques, such as paint systems that use carbon dioxide finishing systems. ▷**drying equipment for solvent removal; finish system, reduce solvent; incineration fume system; release agent**

volt ▷**electrical volt**

volume adjustment, blown container It is important for sales purposes that, as an example, a milk container looks full and contains a specific quantity. The level of the milk could differ at times and appear that the contents are not equal; problem is due to shrinkage differentials that can occur after being blown. Thus, the molds could have a movable plug set to control contents of bottle. The bottle's side wall has a depression (small, usually circular) that is adjusted based on performance of the blown bottles.

volume fraction Fraction of a constituent material based on its volume.

volume reduction ▷**solid waste volume reduction**

volume resistivity ▷**electrical volume resistivity**

volume, specific **1.** The reciprocal of the density. **2.** The volume of a unit weight of a substance, as ft^3/lb, m^3/kg, etc.

volumeter An apparatus for the measurement of the volume of a known mass of powder for the purpose of determining its density.

volumetric Chemical analysis based upon the reaction of a volume of standard solution with the material being analyzed.

volumetrically Refers to the measuring of components by volume rather than weight.

volumetric feeder ▷**feed volumetric**

Vought model ▷**Maxwell model**

V-0, UL flammability test ▷**fire retardance**

vulcanizate The product of vulcanization; a crosslinked rubber or elastomer.

vulcanization An irreversible process, usually accomplished through the application of heat, during which a rubber or elastomer compound through a change in its chemical structure (cross linking) becomes less plastic in behavior and more resistant to swelling by organic liquids, and elastic properties are conferred, improved, or extended over a greater range of temperature.

vulcanization, dynamic ▷**dynamic vulcanization**

vulcanization reclaiming ▷**devulcanization**

vulcanize To subject to vulcanization.

vulcanized elastomer Method of producing a material with good elastomeric properties (rubber) involves the formation of chemical crosslinks between high molecular weight linear molecules. The starting polymer must be of the noncrystallizing type, and its glass transition temperature must be well below room temperature to ensure a rubbery behavior. This formation of chemical crosslinks is commonly referred to as vulcanization or curing.

vulcanized fiber ▷**fiber, vulcanized**

vulcanizing agent Compounding material that produces crosslinking in rubber or elastomers.

vulcanizing, room temperature ▷**room temperature vulcanizing**

vulcanizing system The combination of vulcanizing agent and, as required, accelerators, activators, and retarders used to produce the desired degree of vulcanization characteristics or vulcanizate characteristics.

V-X diagram A graphical representation of the isothermal or isobaric phase relationships in a binary system, the coordinates of the graph being specific volume and concentration.

wadding ▷ **fiber wadding**

wafer A thin disc-like section of a semiconductor crystal used for the fabrication of semiconductor devices.

wafer basket Usually injection molded PFA fluorocarbon plastic used in automated production of chips for the microcomputer industry.

wages, plastic industry The Table below reflects weighted average hourly rates in U.S. (1990).

warehousing There is a wide variety of tasks for warehousing. Raw materials, additives, auxiliary equipment, spare parts, molds, tools, processed plastic parts, etc. that require proper handling and storage procedures that are stored economically. Various systems are used very successfully such as the unit warehouse, which makes use of pallets, cages, and similar equipment. It employs a certain organizational scheme for integrating order-picking and transportation. The system is perfected by integration of the inward and outward flow (input-output matrix) of goods, the factory administration, process control, etc.

warmware Refers to people in the computer industry.

warp 1. Dimensional distortion in a plastic part after fabrication. **2.** The yarn running lengthwise in a woven fabric. **3.** A group of yarns in long lengths and approximately parallel, put on beams or warp reels for further textile processing including weaving, knitting, dyeing, etc.

warpage Curvature or dimensional distortion in a plastic part after being processed, particularly when molded. It is directly related to material shrinkage and the relieving of unwanted stresses forced upon it while being shaped in the mold in a viscous state. Warpage is primarily affected by processing conditions that will require changes to eliminate the problem, and also the type of plastic being processed which may require very tight processing control to produce warp-free parts. ▷ **residual stress**

warp face ▷ **fabric warp face**

wash An area where reinforcement has moved during the closing of the molding of reinforced plastic, resulting in a plastic rich area. ▷ **reinforced plastic, plastic rich area**

waste The waste-management problems of the U.S. and the rest of the world continually threaten to reach crisis proportions. The U.S. takes top billing, with each person producing at least $3\frac{1}{2}$ lb./day of waste. Such other countries as Germany and Japan generate about 2 lb./day/person.

Industrialized countries have generated a lot of garbage for a long time but now are rapidly running out of environmentally acceptable landfills. Unfortunately, this problem expands with the world population. At present, more than 2 billion lb. of solid waste are pouring into waste streams annually worldwide.

There is no single, simple answer to this problem. Different, limited approaches have been used successfully, and much more action has begun occurring here and internationally to

Wages by job title (1990).

Job title	Highest wage	Lowest wage	National average
Injection molding foreman	$12.54	$6.17	$9.47
Injection molding operator	6.87	4.69	5.91
Extrusion foreman	13.67	10.12	12.15
Extrusion operator	9.61	7.63	8.82
Reinforced plastics foreman	11.16	9.07	9.93
Reinforced plastics operator	8.73	7.54	8.25
Assembler	7.40	5.62	6.24
Mold maker	17.81	10.77	13.36
All positions	8.30	7.01	7.75

Plastic waste management summation.

Reduction at source	
Re-use of materials	
Collection, segregation	
• Material recycling	• Generic material reclamation • Mixed plastics waste recycling
• Chemical recycling	• Hydrolysis • Pyrolysis • Hydro cracking } Recovery as monomers
Incineration	• Energy recovery • Volume reduction
Landfilling	

integrate environmentally secure landfills, recycling, advanced waste-to-energy incineration, degradability, product design, waste-source reduction, industry support, public education and support, regulation support, and various economic considerations (see Table above). We now should stop merely living with past problems and start solving them. Waste is a widespread, but solvable, problem; there is an abundance of possible cures and fixes, some good, others not so good. There are nevertheless logical approaches and facilities to check their reliability, rather than just criticizing them.

This overview includes information and positive actions being now taken to provide solutions that will affect all materials. Because plastics usually receive the biggest emphasis, they are the main focus here. Plastics as well as other materials must all definitely be seen as problems (see second Table). Practically all plastics can be made recyclable, incinerable, or degradable, but the conflict of product-performance requirements as against economics in most past applications has prevented these factors from being viable. Actions have thus been taken by the plastics industry here and abroad to make positive steps toward helping to reduce plastics waste by recycling, incineration, and so on.

Unfortunately, generalizations that "plastics are bad" and "burning plastics always generate toxic products" are too often heard from customers and media representatives. More unfortunately, plastics packaging is a highly visible element in the waste stream. And the negative public perceptions about plastics sometimes lead to negative opinions about the companies that use them. These companies must then respond to consumer opinions to maintain their reputations.

The plastics industry has fallen victim to an unrelenting international smear campaign, particularly in the U.S.. Discriminatory measures have been taken in a number of countries against plastic packaging, although scientific investigations have proven that certain products in fact have nothing to do with the rise in the amount of domestic refuse. On the other hand, the demand for plastics products among customers, who readily appreciate the advantages of this material in day-to-day living, has risen so much that there is now a distinct possibility of disposal bottlenecks arising.

Estimated Contributors to Solid Waste.[1]

Waste material	% by weight	% by volume
Paper[2]	37	40
Yard	18	18
Metal	10	2
Glass	9	3
Food	8	8
Plastic	7	9–12[3]
Others	11	13

[1] Total annual solid U.S. waste is estimated to be more than 300 billion lb. (136 billion kg).
[2] Includes, by volume, 12% in packaging, 12% in newspaper, 4% in cardboard, 2% in magazine, and 10% in others.
[3] By some reports, up to 16%.
Note: Seven percent of 300 billion lb. is 21 billion lb. of plastics. Annual U.S. plastics consumption is about 67 billion lb. (30 billion kg), with domestic products at about 61 billion lb. (28 billion kg) (including about 33 percent, or 20 billion lb. [9 billion kg], in packaging) and imported products at about 6 billion lb. (2.7 billion kg) (contained in electronics, autos, appliances, packaging, medical products, and so on). Waste, like computer programming and nuclear physics, tends to be a subject shrouded in mystery and reportedly understood by only the few. The annual U.S. Control and Service Environment Business is estimated at $80 billion or larger than the total computer business of all hardware and software, plus the telecommunications and airline businesses.

The throwaway aspect, particularly with regard to fast-food packaging, of today's society has resulted in what has been billed in the press and by legislative bodies as the nation's solid-waste crisis. Ironically, in many modern composite landfills a high-density polyethylene (HDPE) liner is used to reinforce the conventional clay layers, as a way of minimizing leaching. The matter has become a crisis simply because many cities are facing the dilemma of how to dispose of their municipal waste. Many municipalities have filled existing landfills and establishing new ones is becoming more and more difficult.

The plastics industry's response has been to commit itself more firmly to recycling and to reaffirm its earlier position that waste-to-energy incineration is critical. ▷ **plastic bad and other myths**

waste, agricultural ▷ **agricultural solid waste**

waste and biodegradable ▷ **biodegradable**

waste and ecology ▷ **environment, life, plastic, ecology**

waste and environment ▷ **plastic long life** and **polyvinyl chloride plastic and the environment**

waste and packaging Packaging plays an important role worldwide and will continue to do so, but the packaging industry has (unfortunately) certainly taken much abuse. Studies show that 75% of the new materials to be used in the future packaging will be based on various plastic combinations. The benefits that packaging gains with plastics (as well as aluminum, glass, etc) will continue to provide factors such as containment, protection, visual information, and utility of use. They improve public health and standard of living. Without packaging, much of our food would be lost to spoilage, insects, and other vermin. While packaging provides a great deal to the economy, it represents less than 7% of the cost of goods. Many packaging decisions have obscure rationales for the average consumer, but they serve to solve social problems, such as pilferage and product tampering. Food packaging reduces rather than increases total solid waste.

waste and plastic lumber About 9,000 lb (4,080 kg) of plastic "lumber" during 1989 were made just from used polystyrene foam cups, food containers, and others were used in US to construct park benches, wildlife signs, wetland walkways, etc. Plastic wood is handled (drilling, cutting, etc.) in much the same way as real wood. Yet, unlike real wood, it is impervious to weather, insects, and the decaying effects of time.

waste and public education ▷ **plastic bad and other myths** and **environment and public opinion**

waste buy-back ▷ **buy-back system**

waste control Waste materials can be classified by type (gaseous, liquid, solid, radioactive, etc.) and by source (municipal, chemical, agriculture, packaging, urban, nuclear, etc.). Many methods of treating waste, either by converting it to useful byproducts (economically) or by disposing of it, are in operation (recycling, incineration, landfill, etc.).

waste dump ▷ **landfill**

waste energy and pollution ▷ **energy conservation; pollution; British thermal unit**

waste, hazardous ▷ **hazardous material; hazardous warning signs; geomembrane liner**

waste incineration ▷ **incineration**

waste, invisible Weight loss due to dust, moisture, loose fibers, etc. carried away by the atmosphere.

waste, landfill ▷ **landfill**

waste nostalgia trap As some consider restrictions on certain plastic consumer products, the appeal is often connected to a romantic image of a simpler, purer past, a time when good old-fashioned materials packaged good old-fashioned products. But in many instances, this image simply is not consistent with the facts of modern life.

waste per capita generation The quantity of solid waste produced by each person in an area.

waste prevention The prevention of waste should be at the top of the list of priorities. This is the most efficient way of reducing the amount of dumped plastics (glass, steel, etc.). More efficient plastics, materials oriented design, and improved processing techniques considerably reduce the amount of materials for problem solutions. ▷ **design**

waste rear-end separation A chemical, thermal, or biological system and facilities used to convert pre-processed wastes into useful products.

waste reclamation ▷ **recycling** and **chemical reclamation**

waste recoverable resource ▷ **material recovery** and **recoverable resource**

waste reduction ▷ **source reduction, waste**

waste-to-energy Recovery or generation of energy through incineration of waste. ▷ **energy thermal reclamation**

waste water ▷ **lagoon; osmosis**

water Colorless, odorless, tasteless liquid.

water absorption **1.** The amount of water absorbed by a material under specified test conditions (such as 24 hr in water) commonly expressed as weight percent of the test specimen. **2.** The increase in mass of a product during immersion in water under specified conditions of time and temperature, expressed as a percentage of its dry weight.

water adsorbed Water bonded to a solid surface.

water beading Surface property that causes the formation of discrete water droplets on the polished surface.

water, brackish ▷ **brackish water**

water break The appearance of a discontinuous film of water on a surface signifying non-uniform wetting and usually associated with a surface contamination.

waterborne coating ▷ **coating, waterborne system**

water cleaning treatment Water washing removes various surface impurities, such as release agents, electrostatically or otherwise attracted dust particles, and additives that have migrated to the surface. A typical cleaning cycle may consist of several steps: treatment with a cleaner followed by several rinses and finished by deionized water. ▷ **solvent cleaning**

waterfall coating ▷ **curtain coating**

water glass Sodium silicate that is soluble in water.

water, industrial Water, including its impurities, used directly in industrial processes.

water jet cutting Water emitted from a nozzle under high pressure of 70 to 420 MPa (10 to 60 ksi) or higher at mach 2 speed. It can cut through most plastics, including reinforced plastics, without creating heat or dust and without exerting lateral force on the material being cut. This action eliminates deformation of the cut edge. No other cutting method, including lasers, offers these advantages. Applications are many including trimming diapers, auto dashboard panels, and slitting a glass fiber construction. Add abrasives, such as garnet powder, to the jet and it will cut through virtually any material that includes aramid fibers, titanium, etc. Water jets are created by converting the potential energy of high pressure water into kinetic energy by passing it through a small orifice usually 0.004 to 0.020 in. (0.01 to 0.05 cm) diameter.

water of crystallization ▷ **hydrate**

water of hydration Water released by thermal decomposition. ▷ **hydrate**

water of suspension Water supporting colloidal particles in a slip (or slurry).

water pollution ▷ **acceptable risk**

waterproofing Treatment of a surface or structure to prevent the passage of liquid water under hydrostatic, dynamic, or static pressure.

water, properties of General information follows: One gallon of water weighs 8.3356 lbs at 62°F (air free weighed in vacuum.) One gallon of water occupies 231 cubic inches or 0.13368 cubic feet. One cubic foot of water equals 7.4805 gallons. A cylinder 7″ in diameter and 6″ high contains one gallon. One cubic inch of water weighs 0.576 oz. Maximum density of water at 39.1°F. Freezing point at sea level, 32°F. One cubic foot of water at 39.1°F exerts 0.4335 lbs per sq. inch. Boiling point of water at normal pressure, 212°F.

water purification ▷ **geomembrane liner** and **ion exchange plastic**

water repellant A material (or treatment) for surfaces to provide resistance to penetration of water.

water resistance 1. Measured ability to retard both penetration and wetting by water in liquid form. **2.** Ability of part to resist deformation or change in color with immersion in water.

watershed All lands enclosed by a continuous hydrologic-surface drainage divided and lying upslope from a specified point on the stream.

water soluble plastic Any plastic of high molecular weight that swells or dissolves in water at normal room temperature. The principal members of this class are certain polyvinyl alcohols, ethylene oxides, polyvinyl pyrrolidones, and polyethyleneimides.

water solubility The amount of material that is miscible or will dissolve in water at a given temperature.

water vapor barrier ▷ **water vapor retarder**

water vapor diffusion The process by which water vapor spreads or moves through permeable materials caused by a difference in water vapor pressure.

water vapor permeability The time rate of water vapor transmission through unit area of flat material of unit thickness induced by unit vapor pressure difference between two specific surfaces, under specified temperature and humidity conditions.

water vapor pressure The pressure of water vapor at a given temperature; also the component of atmospheric pressure contributed by the presence of water vapor.

water vapor resistance Measured ability to retard penetration and permeation by water vapor.

water vapor resistivity The steady vapor pressure difference that induces unit time rate of vapor flow through unit area and unit thickness of a flat material (or construction that acts like a homogeneous body), for specific conditions of temperature and relative humidity at each surface.

water vapor retarder A material (such as a plastic barrier) or system that adequately impedes the transmission of water vapor under specified conditions.

water vapor, saturated Water vapor that is in equilibrium with pure liquid water at the existing pressure. The weight of saturated water vapor in lb/ft^3 (kg/m^3) of gaseous mixture (including water vapor) equals the weight per ft^3 (m^3) of water vapor in equilibrium with water at the existing temperature and pressure.

water vapor transmission WVT is the rate of water vapor flow, under steady specified conditions, through a unit area of material, between its two parallel surfaces and normal to the surfaces. Metric unit of measurement is 1 g/24 h·m^2. (Perm is a unit of measurement of water vapor permeance; a metric perm is 1 g/24 h·m^2·mm Hg or in U.S. unit of 1 grain/h·ft^2·Hg.) ▷ **barrier material performance** and **permeability**

water-white Having the clarity and appearance of water.

watt ▷ **electrical power**

wave An optical effect due to uneven transparent material distribution, or striae; disturbance propagated in medium in such a manner that at any point in medium the amplitude is a function of time, while at any instant the displacement at point is a function of position of point.

wave front A continuous surface drawn through the most forward points in a wave disturbance which have the same phase.

wavelength 1. The distance, measured along the line of propagation of a wave, between two points that are in phase on adjacent waves. **2.** A measure of the nature of incident electromagnetic radiation.

wave number The number of waves per unit length.

waviness A wavelike variation from a perfect surface; generally much wider in spacing and higher amplitude than surface roughness.

waviness, finish ▷ **surface finish**

wax Any substance physically resembling beeswax; a dull, crystalline-solid plastic when warm; composed of a mixture of esters, cerotic acid, and hydrocarbons. Other waxes are from various animal, vegetable, mineral, or synthetic sources. Waxes differ from fats in being less greasy, harder, more polishable by rubbing, and containing esters of higher fatty acids and higher alcohols, free higher acids or higher alcohols, and/or saturated hydrocarbons. Waxes are used with plastics as an additive to improve processing and/or part performance. They are used extensively in milk cardboard cartons, mold release agent, etc.

wear The cumulative and integrative action of all the deleterious mechanical influences encountered in use which tend to impair a material's serviceability. As an example, it is the damage to a solid surface, generally involving progressive loss of material, due to relative motion between that surface and a contacting substances(s). Wear can be classified in categories. ▷ **abrasion; cavitation erosion; rain erosion; frettage; galling; pit; ablation; spalling**

wear resistance ▷ **abrasion resistance**

weather conditions, normal The range (actual or anticipated) of environmental conditions (rain, temperature, pollution, etc.) that will typically occur in a local climatic region over several years.

weathering The process of disintegration and decomposition as a consequence of exposure to the atmosphere, to chemical action, and the action of frost, water, and heat. Term normally refers to the effect on materials of prolonged outdoor exposure.

weathering, artificial The exposure of material to simulated and/or accelerated laboratory-produced environmental conditions. Since natural weather is unpredictable with extreme variations in most regions of the world, laboratory tests are usually intensified beyond those expected to be encountered in actual outdoor exposure. Many different weatherability tests are available from industry.

weathering factors responsible for deterioration The components of the weather responsible for the deterioration of certain plastics are radiation, atmospheric temperature and its cycles, moisture in various forms, wind, and the normal constituents and contaminants.

Although the UV portion of solar radiation is mainly responsible for initiating weathering effects, the visible and near-infrared portions also contribute to the degradative processes ▷ **electromagnetic spectrum**. Colored materials are susceptible to visible radiation, and near-IR radiation can accelerate chemical reactions by raising the temperature. The other factors act synergistically with solar radiation to significantly influence the weathering processes.

In condensation type plastics (certain thermosets), moisture alone can be a major cause of degradation by promoting hydrolysis. All weathering factors, including the quality and quantity of sunlight, vary with geographic location, time of year, time of day, and climatological conditions. Therefore, in order to understand and predict the effect of weather on materials, data are required on each factor that may contribute to degradation.

weatherometer An instrument that is utilized to subject articles to accelerated weathering conditions using UV source and water spray.

weave The particular manner in which a fabric is formed by interlacing yarns. Usually assigned a style number. ▷ **fabric woven**

web **1.** Continuous sheet or film of plastic. In flat extrusion, as an example, the extrudate leaving the sheet die. **2.** In blown film extrusion, the film leaving the collapsing rolls. ▷ **extruder, blown film** **3.** In thermoforming, the continuous roll stock fed to the former. **4.** In web coating, the substrate on which the coating is applied.

web coating ▷ **spread coating** and **extruder coating**

weber ▷ **magnetic flux**

web gate ▷ **mold gate**

web guide A device for positioning, centering, and/or controlling one or both edges of any material used in different processing lines, such as calendering, extrusion, and fabric impregnation. ▷ **extruder web guide control**

web heat transfer roll adjustment ▷ **extruder web heat transfer roll adjustment**

web tension control ▷ **extruder web tension control**

weeping Slow leakage manifest by the appearance of water (or other product depending on plastic, such as plasticizer) on a surface.

weft ▷ **yarn, filling**

weight Confusion usually exists in the use of the term weight as a quantity to mean either *force* or *mass*. In commercial and everyday use, the term weight nearly always means mass; a person's weight is a quantity referred to as mass. This is a nontechnical term. In science and technology, the term weight of a body has usually meant the force that, if applied to the body, would give it an acceleration equal to the local acceleration of free fall on the surface of the earth. Because of the dual use of the term weight as a quantity, it should be avoided. When used the units of kilograms (kg) refer to mass or newtons (N) refer to force per SI standard.

weight and measure units ▷ **decimal system**

weight, areal ▷ **reinforced plastic weight, areal**

weight, molecular ▷ **molecular weight**

weight, oven-dry The constant weight obtained by drying at a specified temperature (such as $105 \pm 3°C$) for the time required.

weight, plastic ▷ **density and specific gravity**

weight, specific The weight per unit volume of a substance.

Weissenberg effect A phenomenon encountered sometimes in rotational viscometric studies at high speeds, particularly when the alignment between the cups is not perfect, characterized by a tendency of the plastic solution to climb the wall of the cylinder or cup which is rotating.

welding Welding is one of the most commonly used methods of joining thermoplastics. As with metals, welding is accomplished by application of heat sufficient to produce fusion of the areas to be joined. The major differences among the various techniques are in the methods of applying heat to the materials. Other differences include tooling sizes and shapes, output rates, quality of bond, and economics (see Tables on p. 807 and 808). ▷ **dielectric heating; electromagnetic adhesive; electromagnetic-induction weld; electron beam welding; friction welding; hot-gas welding; hot wire welding; induction welding; laser beam welding; radio frequency welding; solvent bonding; spin welding; thermoband welding; ultrasonic sealing or welding; vibration welding**

welding ability factors Weldability using different techniques is influenced by factors such as type plastic and its composition and moisture content. Certain fillers, particularly in high concentrations, that do not melt can cause parts to have weak or disastrous joints. Lubricating agents and release agents can interfere.

Characteristic welding examples.[1]

Thermoplastics	Mechanical fasteners	Adhesives	Spin and vibration welding	Thermal welding	Ultrasonic welding	Induction welding	Remarks
ABS	G	G	G	G	G	G	Body type adhesive recommended
Acetal	E	P	G	G	G	G	Surface treatment for adhesives
Acrylic	G	G	F–G	G	G	G	Body type adhesive recommended
Nylon	G	P	G	G	G	G	
Polycarbonate	G	G	G	G	G	G	
Polyester TP	G	F	G	G	G	G	
Polyethylene	P	NR	G	G	G–P	G	Surface treatment for adhesives
Polypropylene	P	P	E	G	G–P	G	Surface treatment for adhesives
Polystyrene	F	G	E	G	E–P	G	Impact grades difficult to bond
Polysulfone	G	G	G	E	E	G	
Polyurethane TP	NR	G	NR	NR	NR	G	
PPO modified	G	G	E	G	G	G	
PVC rigid	F	G	F	G	F	G	

[1] E = Excellent, G = Good, F = Fair, P = Poor, NR = Not recommended.

welding processes, economic data guide See Table on p. 809.

weld line With molding specifically injection molding, parts that include openings and/or multiple gating can develop problems. (See Fig. in ▷**design mold, basics of flow**). In the process of filling a cavity the hot melt is obstructed by the core, and by the meeting of two or more melt streams. With a core the melt splits and surrounds the core. The split stream then reunites and continues flowing until the cavity is filled. The rejoining of the split streams forms a weld line that lacks the strength properties that exist in an area without a weld line because the flowing material tends to wipe air, moisture, and lubricant into the area where the joining of the stream takes place and introduces foreign substances into the welding surface. Furthermore, since the plastic material has lost some of its heat, the temperature for self-welding is not conducive to the most favorable results. A surface that is to be subjected to loadbearing should not contain weld lines. If this is not possible, the allowable working stress should be reduced by at least 15%.

well ▷**mold, cold slug** and **compression molding, plastic material well**

wet abrasive ▷**abrasion cleaning**

wet-bulb temperature ▷**temperature, wet-bulb**

wet felting Forming of a fibrous mat from a water suspension. They can be flat or shaped to fit cavities or molds to provide the reinforcement in reinforced plastics.

wet layup molding A method of making a reinforced plastic product by applying the plastic liquid system when the dry reinforcement is put in place prior to cure via techniques such as bag molding and compression molding.

wet-out In reinforced plastic, this condition occurs during the soaking of porous materials with liquid plastic when all voids between filaments become filled with the plastic.

wet-out rate Time required for the plastic to fill the interstices of the reinforcement material and wet the surfaces of the fibers.

wet process, nonwoven ▷**mechanical nonwoven fabric**

wet spinning ▷**fiber spinning process**

wet strength **1.** The strength of a material determined immediately after removal from a liquid in which it has been immersed under specified conditions of time, temperature, and pressure. **2.** The strength of paper when saturated with water, especially used with plastic treated paper during manufacture to increase wet strength.

wet stretching ▷**orientation, wet stretching**

wet system Reinforced plastic fabrication processes and equipment that incorporates reinforcement impregnation as part of the process prior to entering the die or mold, such as with pultrusion.

Tensile strength retention with different welding methods.

Plastics	Original tensile strength, psi	Hot-air welding, %	Friction welding, %	Hot-plate welding, %	Dielectric welding, %	Solvent welding, %	Adhesive bonding, %	Polymerization welding, %
Thermosetting plastics								
Epoxy	7,000–13,000	—	10–50	10–50	—	—	50–80	60–100
Melamine	7,000–13,000	—	—	—	—	—	50–80	60–100
Phenolic	6,000–9,000	—	—	—	—	—	50–80	60–100
Polyester	6,000–13,000	—	—	—	—	—	50–80	60–100
Thermoplastics								
Acrylonitrile butadiene styrene	2,400–9,000	50–70	50–70	50–70	50–80	30–60	40–60	—
Acetal	8,000–10,000	20–30	50–70	20–30	—	—	—	—
Cellulose acetate	2,400–8,500	60–75	65–80	65–80	—	90–100	50–60	—
Cellulose acetate butyrate	3,000–7,000	60–75	65–80	65–80	—	90–100	50–80	—
Ethyl cellulose	2,000–8,000	50–70	50–70	50–70	—	80–90	50–80	—
Methyl methacrylate	8,000–11,000	30–70	30–50	20–50	—	40–60	40–60	60–90
Nylon	7,000–12,000	50–70	50–70	50–70	—	—	20–40	—
Polycarbonate	8,000–9,500	35–50	40–50	40–50	—	40–60	5–15	—
Polyethylene	800–6,000	60–80	70–90	60–80	—	—	10–30	—
Polypropylene	3,000–6,000	60–80	70–90	60–80	—	—	20–40	—
Polystyrene	3,500–8,000	20–50	30–60	20–50	—	25–50	20–50	—
Polystyrene acrylonitrile	8,000–11,000	20–60	20–50	20–50	30–50	25–60	20–50	—
Polyvinyl chloride	5,000–9,000	60–70	50–70	60–70	60–70	50–70	50–70	—
Saran	3,000–5,000	60–70	50–70	60–70	60–70	50–70	50–70	—

Welding processes, economic data guide.

Process	Equipment cost	Tooling cost	Typical output rates	Normal economic production quantities	Remarks
Ultrasonic welding	Moderately low to high	Moderate to high	1000 pieces per hour, manually loaded	High	Automatic operation possible
Vibration welding	Moderate	Moderate	240 pieces per hour from single cavity, manually loaded	Medium and high	Setup time 10 min; multiple cavities and mechanized loading possible
Spin welding	Moderate	Moderate	640 pieces per hour, manually loaded	High	Setup time $\frac{1}{2}$ h; mechanization possible
Hot-plate welding	Moderately low to high	Moderate to high	120 pieces per hour per fixture cavity	Medium and high	Setup time 1 h or less
Induction welding	Low to moderate	Low	900 pieces per hour, manually loaded	High	Setup time 1 h or less
Hot-gas welding	Very low	Low (holding fixture only)	0.3 to 1.5 m (12 to 60 in) of weld seam per minute	Very low	Manual operation

Properties of high performance whiskers in reinforced plastics.

Whisker composition	Diameter, µm	Density, g/cm	Tensile strength, MPa	Elastic modulus, GPa	Cost, $/kg
Al_2O_3	1–10	3.97	4,138–24,138	552–1,034	16,500
Al_2O_3	0.5–2.0	3.97	6,897–20,690	414–483	18,700
SiC	1–10	3.22	13,793–41,379	552–1,034	25,300
SiC	0.5–0.3	3.22	20,690	483	440
Si_3N_4	1–10	3.19	4,828–10,345	276	22,600
Al_2O_3	38–500	3.97	2,552–4,310	462	14,100

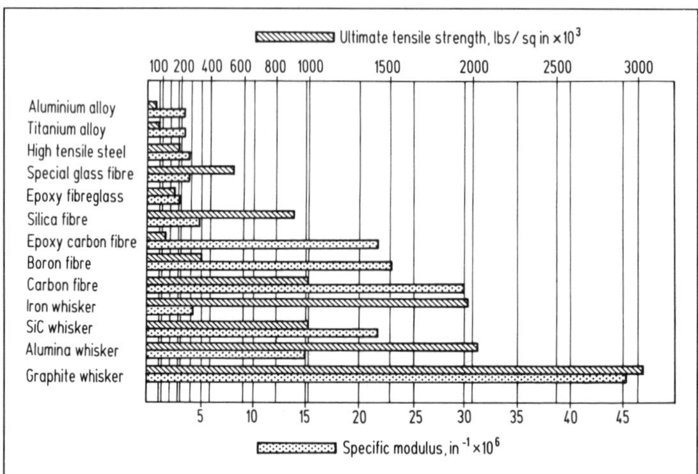

Tensile strengths and specific modulus (E divided by density) of different type plastics and other type composites compared to whisker types.

wettability The rate at which particles, fibers, etc. can be made wet under specified conditions.

wetting agent A substance capable of lowering the surface tension of liquids, facilitating the wetting of solid surfaces, and facilitating the penetration of liquids into the capillaries. It is a phenomenon involving a solid and a liquid in such intimate contact that the adhesive force between the two phases is greater than the cohesive force within the liquid. Thus, a solid is wet, and on being removed from the liquid bath, will have a thin continuous layer of liquid adhering to it.

wetware In computer industry, it refers to the person's brain.

wet winding ▷ **filament winding, wet**

wheelabrating Deflashing molded parts by bombarding them with small particles at a high velocity.

whisker reinforcement Whiskers are metallic and nonmetallic single crystals of ultrahigh strength and modulus (see Table and Fig. above) and micrometer size diameters. Their extremely high strength is attributed to a near perfect crystal structure, chemically pure nature, and fine diameters that minimize defects. With their high modulus, elongation is 1 to 4% range. They exhibit a much higher resistance to fracture (toughness) than all other types of reinforcing fibers. Many different materials have been used (literally hundreds) with diameters ranging from 1 to 25 µm (40 to 980 µin.) and having aspect ratios between .100 to 15,000. Because of their extreme high cost (for these high performance types), use has been in specialty reinforced plastic markets such as aerospace and medical (dental). Matrices include plastics, as well as other materials such as different ceramics and metals. ▷ **reinforced plastic; reinforcement; composite metal matrix; ceramic matrix composite**

white metal Any of a group of alloys having relatively low melting points other than copper-base alloys. They usually contain tin, lead, antimony, cadmium, and/or zinc as the chief component. Use includes as a soluble core. ▷ **soluble core molding**

whitener ▷ **optical brightener agent**

whitening ▷ **calcium carbonate** and **stress whitening**

wicking Passage of liquid and/or air in a filled plastic, particularly reinforced plastics. With RPs, penetration is longitudinally along or through fibers that have been encased in plastic during fabrication. This action could be damaging to the performance of the plastic.

Wiegand pendulum An apparatus that demonstrates the Gough-Joule effect. It comprises a pendulum so that an elastomer material is under stretch. Heat from the lamp causes material to contract and swing the pendulum. This pulls the material into a shaded area where it extends and moves the pendulum back to the original position, whereupon the cycle repeats.

Windecker Eagle airplane The first all reinforced plastic commercial airplane to receive FAA certification (1967) (see Fig. below).

window 1. ▷ **processing window** 2. ▷ **fish eye**

window glass, laminated ▷ **safety glass**

wind-up, torsional An effect whereby a torque applied to the drive end of a lead-screw rotates it further than the output end.

wipe-in ▷ **fill-and-wipe** and **spray paint, spray-and-wipe**

wire and cable From the very beginning of the electrical industry plastics have been used for their insulation. Different plastics are used to meet different performance requirements that include: electrical, mechanical, chemical, and/or thermal. Different conditions exist for each of these categories such as operating at different frequencies, underground or ocean depths, etc. ▷ **extruder, wire and cable; extruder coating**

wire frame modeling ▷ **modeling wire frame**

wire train The entire extruder line assembly which is utilized to produce plastic coated wire/cable. See the figure in ▷ **extruder, wire and cable** that will show what can be included in a line.

witness mark A mark or line on a molding where different parts of the mold come together or "mate".

wollastonite A calcium metasilicate $CaSiO_3$, containing theoretically 48.3% lime (CaO) and 51.7% silica (SiO_2) occurring in acicular masses of elongated triclinic crystals, usually white or pale gray. Use includes as a filler or reinforcement for plastics.

wood Industrial timber products represent about 23wt% of all industrial raw materials consumed. The largest single use of wood in the U.S. is sawnwood or lumber (about 55% of total consumed). Veneer logs consume about 10%. At 30% is pulpwood. Smaller quantities are consumed as cooperage logs; posts, poles, and piling; chemical wood; etc. ▷ **compreg**

wood cellulose, purified Chemical cellulose from wood.

wood, compreg ▷ **compreg**

wood, compressed Wood which has been subjected to high pressure to increase its density without and with plastics. It is usually supplied in the form of a laminate in which plastics have been incorporated by drying the wood and using a vacuum. Also called densified wood.

wood, cord A cord of wood is a unit volume of cut wood stacked in a pile measuring 4 × 4 × 8 ft (1 × 1 × 2 m) that contains 128 ft^3 (3.6 m^3).

wood flour Finely divided dried wood, used as a filler principally in thermosets (phenolics and ureas). Particle size is such that they usually pass through a 40 mesh screen. All types of wood are used.

wood formulation and composition Wood is a cellular form of cellulose; cellulose is the most abundant of all naturally occurring organic compounds. It makes up at least one-third of all vegetable matter in the world. Conventional wood has been extensively used for centuries. The high strength to weight of wood, good insulating properties (cork and balsa), and cushioning properties (cork and

The all-plastic (glass fiber-thermoset polyester reinforced plastic) Eagle airplane.

straw) have contributed to a broad range of cellular synthetic plastics in use today.

woodgraining A group of processes used to impart wood-like appearance to sheets or shaped parts. The substrates may be of plastic, wood, steel, etc. Processes used to apply plastics include laminating and coating.

wood, petrified Wood in which the original chemical components have been replaced by silica. The change occurs in such a way that the original form and structure of the wood are preserved. A famous location for them is the Petrified Forest of Arizona.

wood-plastic impregnated Also called compreg. Process (WPI) started in the early part of this century after phenolic was developed (1909). Dry wood has unique properties; its tensile strength, bending strength, compression strength, impact strength, and hardness per unit weight are actually the highest of all construction materials. Plastic loaded wood (impregnated) results in significant increased performances plus gaining hardness, rot resistance, long life, etc. with a slight increase in weight. Originally most of the plastics used were phenolics. By the 1960s a new class of materials containing one or more double bonds was used to treat wood. They consisted of vinyl type monomers that could be polymerized into solid plastics by means of free radicals. Vinyl polymerization was an improvement over condensation polymerization with no residue, such as water, left behind that had to be removed from the final WPC (wood-plastic composite).

Processing starts by first evacuating the air from the wood. Any type of mechanical vacuum pump is adequate that can reduce the pressure to 133 Pa (1 mm Hg) or less. The catalyzed monomer containing crosslinking agents, and possibly dyes, is introduced into the evacuated chamber through a reservoir at atmospheric pressure. The wood must be weighted down so that it does not float in the monomer solution. After the wood is covered with the monomer solution, air is admitted at atmospheric pressure, or dry nitrogen with the radiation process. Immediately the solution begins to flow into the evacuated wood structure to fill the void spaces. The soaking period, like the evacuation period, depends on the structure of the wood. Maple, birch, and other open-cell woods are filled in about 30 minutes; other woods require more time. WPI using a radiation process rather than regular polymerization reaction results in increased hardness and abrasion resistance.

wood pulp ▷ **pulp, paper**

wood veneer A thin sheet of wood, generally within the thickness range from 0.01 to 0.25 in. (0.3 to 6.3 mm) to be used in laminates.

woof ▷ **yarn, filling**

word processing In business, engineering, etc. offices, the WPs are typewriters connected to some form of a video recorder.

workability Flowability for a material to fill forms, molds, etc. without the presence of large voids.

working capital ▷ **capital equipment investment**

working life ▷ **pot life**

workplace ▷ **ergonomic**

world consumption of plastics Plastics are widely used throughout the world, about one third in U.S. and one third in Europe. In the early 1980s, more plastics were used than steel on a volume basis (see Fig. *a* opposite); at about the turn of this century plastics should surpass steel on a weight basis (see Fig. *b* opposite). These figures do not include the two major and important materials consumed, namely wood (paper, etc.) and construction (concrete, bricks, etc.). Each of these of the total materials volumewise (possibly about 70 billion ft^3/2 billion m^3) represents about 43% of total consumption. The remaining (about) 14% are shown in Fig. *a* opposite on volume.

world without plastics When one examines the facts (as contained in this book), it would not make sense to consider such a world. This does not mean that plastics are perfect. They have their drawbacks and unfortunately problems develop when they are not used correctly by people starting from the design through processing and to its use by people. With the proper requirements initially taken care of during the design phase, there literally should be very few problems when put into service. In fact the few problems that would exist would have to be related to an error by someone (from design, etc.). This philosophy is true for any material (steel, etc.). ▷ **design; plastic bad and other myths; acceptable risk; perfection**

woven fabric ▷ **fabric woven**

woven roving ▷ **roving cloth**

wrap-around bend The bend obtained when a specimen is wrapped in a close helix around a cylindrical mandrel.

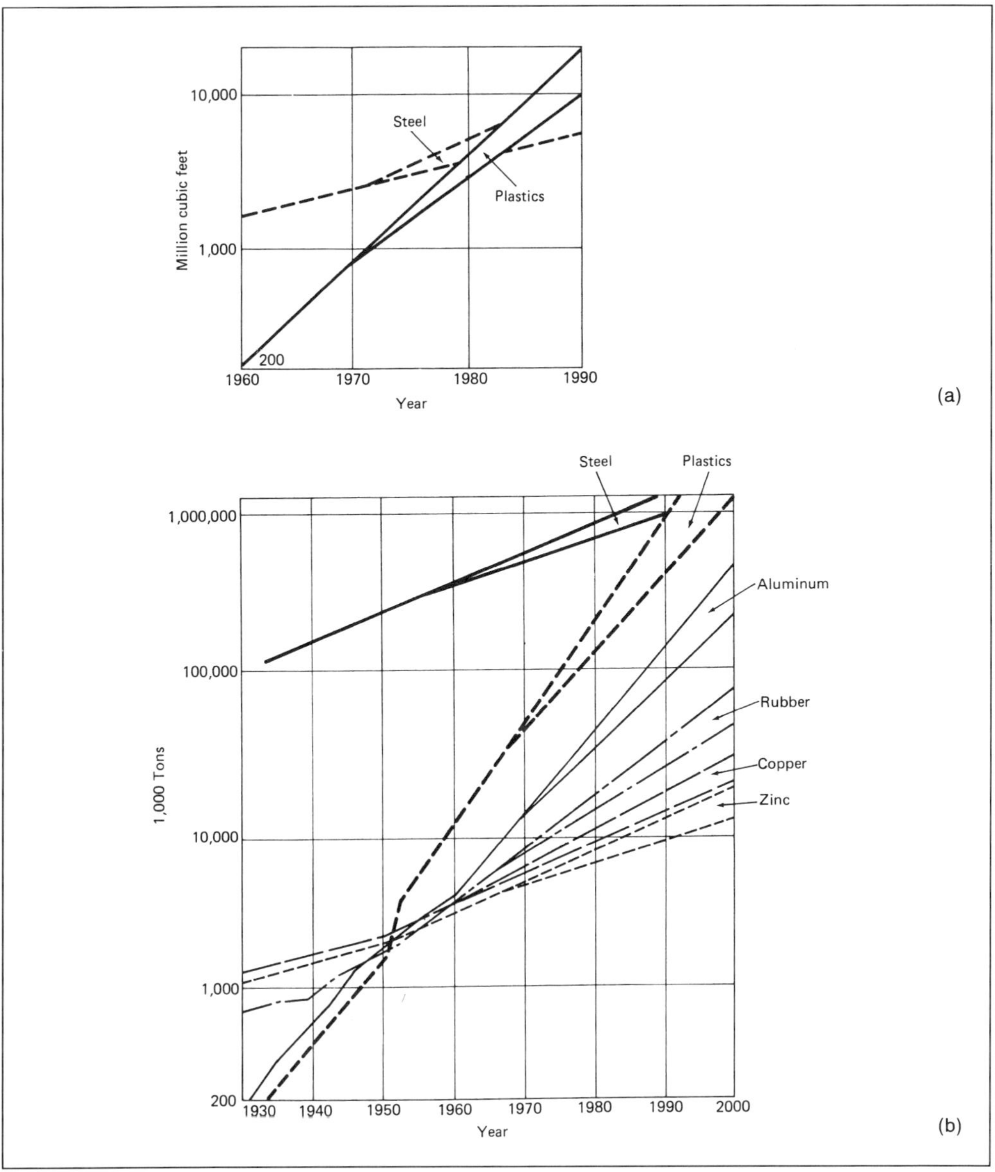

World consumption of plastics and other materials by (*a*) volume and (*b*) weight.

Wright-Patterson AFB, Materials Laboratory Since 1940, very active in advancing all kinds of materials for advanced products, particularly reinforced plastics. In the meantime, its name was changed to Wright Research & Development Center or WRDC.

wrinkle Plastic, such as film or sheet, produced with an undesirable surface can also have creases. With reinforced plastics, an imperfection on the surface that has the appearance of a wave molded into one or more plies of fabric or other reinforcing material.

wrinkle depression An undulation or series of undulations or waves on the surface of a pultrude RP part.

wysiwyg An acronym for "what you see is what you get".

X-axis The axis in the plane of a material used as 0° reference; thus the Y-axis is the axis in the plane of the material perpendicular to the X-axis; thus the Z-axis is the reference axis normal to the X-Y plane (see Fig.). The terms plane or direction are also used in place of axis, thus the X-plane or X-axis is also the X-direction. ▷ **reinforced plastic, directional properties** and **orientation**

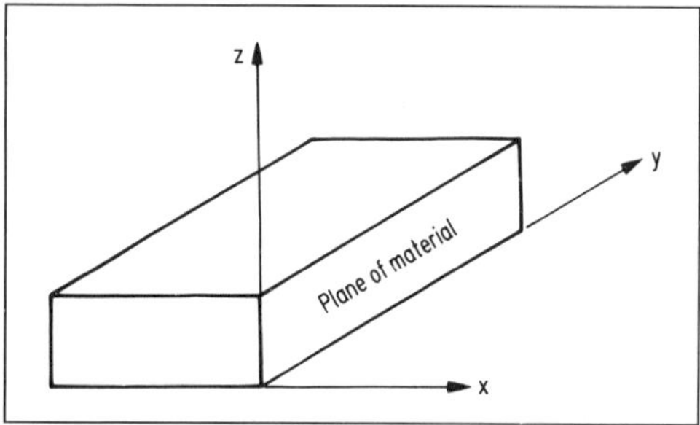

Schematic of X-Y-Z axes.

X-ray diffraction It is used to determine crystallinity in polymers and the polymer structure. It makes possible the determination of detailed information on the state of order or disorder of the polymer system. Data obtained includes: (1) the identification of the material, (2) its crystallinity, (3) the relative disposition and geometry of the crystallites, and (4) the relative disposition of the atoms in the crystallites. The crystallinity and texture of the crystals in the polymeric material may be studied as functions of the preparative procedure and the thermal and mechanical treatment that the material has undergone. ▷ **scattering**

X-ray fluorescence ▷ **spectrometer, X-ray fluorescence**

X-ray microscopy The technique of examining X-rays by means of a microscope. In a variation called point projection, an enlarged image is obtained from X-rays emitted from a pinhole point source. It is useful for studying the structure of materials such as reinforced plastics, plastic foams, and fibers.

X-ray radiograph An X-ray film, plate, or paper that is placed at the image plane and is used for recording an X-ray image of the object being examined.

X-ray scatter, long period A morphological parameter obtained from small-angle X-ray scattering. It is usually equated to the sum of the lamellar thickness and the amorphous thickness.

X-ray sensor ▷ **sensor, nuclear**

X-ray spectroscopy This method identifies crystalline compounds by the characteristic X-ray spectrums produced when a sample is irradiated with a beam of sufficiently short-wave-length X radiation. Diffraction techniques produce a fingerprint of the atomic and molecular structure of a compound and are used for identification. Fluorescence techniques are used for quantitative elemental analysis.

XT plastic A member of the family variously called impact acrylics or multipolymers. It was introduced in 1963 by a team of researchers at American Cyanamid, which later formed a joint venture company, Cyro Industries, with Rohm GmbH. "XT Polymer" is Cyro's tradename for this family of plastics. It's naturally pale transparent yellow; however, its production materials have a glass tint permitting a wide range of transparent or opaque colors. Natural grade's light transmission is 87% and haze is 9% (ASTM D 1003). This terpolymer yields products that are tough and rigid, having several times the notched Izod impact strength of many of the familiar transparent, glassy plastics such as PMMA, PS, and SAN.

X-X axis The horizontal axis, or axis in the left to right direction, in a plane Cartesian coordinate system along which a row of functional patterns is nominally arranged of by stepping and repeating.

Xydar Amoco Performance Products Inc.'s tradename for its liquid crystal polymer.

xylene A mixture of hydrocarbons used as a solvent for alkyd plastics.

xylenol plastic A phenolic-type plastic produced by condensing xylenol (a coal tar derivative) with aldehyde.

xylylene plastic In a coating process capable of producing pinhole-free coatings of outstanding conformality and thickness uniformity by the chemistry of the xylylene monomer, a substrate is exposed to a controlled atmosphere of pure gaseous monomer, p-xylylene (PX). The coating process is a vapor deposition polymerization (VDP). The monomer itself is thermally stable but kinetically unstable. Although it is stable as a gas at low pressure, on condensation it spontaneously polymerizes to produce a coating of a high molecular weight, linear poly(p-xylylene) (PPX).

X-Y plane The reference plane to the plane of the material, such as a reinforced plastic. ▷ **X-axis**

X-Y-Z axes ▷ **X-axis**

yarn A generic term for a continuous strand of textile fibers, filaments, or material in a form suitable for weaving, knitting, braiding, or otherwise intertwining to form a textile fabric. Use includes plastic coated materials and reinforced plastics.

yarn, carded Yarns made from fibers that have been carded but not combed in the manufacturing process. Most spun yarns are of this type. ▷ **carding**

yarn, combed Yarns made from fibers that have been carded and combed in the manufacturing process. Combed yarns are generally cleaner, smoother, and more lustrous than carded yarns.

yarn, combination A ply yarn twisted from single yarns of different fibers, for example, glass and rayon.

yarn construction number A system designed to show the construction, namely, the cut of the single yarn, the number of plies, and whether reinforcements are present. Yarns up to 9-cut, inclusive, have 3-digit construction numbers; the first digit indicates the cut, the second digit the number of plies, and the third digit the number of reinforcements. Yarns containing reinforcement are designated by the yarn construction number followed by the description of the reinforcing strands. Examples are: (1) No. 1420 yarn has 14-cut, 2 ply, and no reinforcement, and (2) No. 931 has 9-cut, 3 ply, and 1 reinforcement. ▷ **glass fabric designations**

yarn distortion In woven fabrics, a condition in which the symmetrical surface appearance of a fabric is altered by the shifting or sliding of warp or filling yarns.

yarn, filling The transverse threads or fibers in a woven fabric; those fibers running perpendicular to the warp. Also called weft or woof.

yarn, final twist The number of turns per unit length in a single yarn component of a plied yarn or the plied yarn component of a cabled yarn as the component lies in the more complex structure. Also called "as-is" twist.

yarn, knot tenacity The tenacity or knot strength in grams per denier (g/den) of a yarn where an overhand knot is put into the filament or yarn being pulled to show sensitivity to compressive or shearing forces.

yarn, multifilament A large number (500 to 2,000) of fine, continuous filaments (often 5 to 100 individual filaments), usually with some twist in the yarn to facilitate handling.

yarn package A length or parallel lengths of yarn in a form suitable for handling, storing, or shipping.

yaw In a linear system, an unwanted tendency of a positioned object to move left and right tilt from the motion axis.

Y-axis ▷ **X-axis**

yellowness Attribute by which an object color is judged to depart from colorless or a preferred white toward yellow. Negative values denote blueness.

yellowness index A number, computed by a given procedure from calorimetric or spectrophotometric data, that indicates the degree of departure of an object color from colorless, or from a preferred white toward yellow.

yield point In engineering terms for tensile, compression, or shear type test, the first stress in a material (less than the maximum attainable stress) at which the strain increases at a higher rate than the stress. The point at which permanent deformation of a stressed specimen starts to take place. Only materials that exhibit yielding have a yield point. For materials that do not exhibit a yield point, yield strength serves the same purpose as yield point. ▷ **strength, yield; stress-strain curve or diagram; tensile analysis**

yield point elongation In materials that exhibit a yield point, the difference between the elongation at the completion and at the start of discontinuous yielding.

yield strength ▷ **strength, yield**

yield value The stress (either normal or shear) at which a marked increase in deformation occurs without an increase in stress (load).

Young's modulus ▷ **modulus**

Y-point ▷ **filament winding knuckle area**

Y-Y axis The vertical axis orthogonal to the X-X axis in a plane Cartesian coordinate system along which a column of functional patterns is normally arranged of by stepping and repeating.

Z

Z-average, molecular weight ▷ **molecular mass**

Z-axis The axis to the plane of the X-Y axes. ▷ **X-axis**

Z-calender A calender with four rolls arranged so that the material being processed passes through them in the form of the letter Z. ▷ **calender**

zein plastic A naturally occurring, high molecular weight copolymer of amino acids linked by peptide bonds, derived from corn. It is considered a member of the protein family of plastics, the main member is casein plastic. Zein plastic is rarely used; has been used for fibers, films, and coatings.

zero air void curve This saturation curve shows the zero air voids unit weight as a function of water content. Unit weight is weight per unit volume.

zero bleed **1.** A reinforced plastic fabrication procedure that does not allow loss of plastic during cure. **2.** Describes a prepreg made with the amount of plastic desired in the final product, such that no plastic has to be removed during cure.

zero crossing In fatigue loading, the number of times that the load-time history crosses zero load level with a positive slope (or negative slope, or both, as specified) during a given length of the history.

zero defect All targets in any area of the business world, particularly in fabricating products, are for zero defects. From the concept of a product through design and product release, proper action can be taken (see Fig. with ▷ **design** and **FALLO approach**). The approach as shown in the Fig. here is, of course, not the way to go, but unfortunately it does exist. ▷ **design safety factor**

zero numbers When writing numbers less than one, a zero should be located before the decimal point to eliminate possible confusion, thus 0.02 is used instead of .02.

zero time The time when the given loading or constraint conditions are initially obtained in creep and stress-relaxation tests, respectively.

zero twist Twistless; devoid of twist.

Ziegler, Karl (1898–1973) A German scientist who was co-recipient (with Giulio Natta) of the Nobel prize in 1963. A great deal of his work was concerned with the chemistry of carbon compounds and development of plastics. A recipient of the Swinburne medal from the Plastics Institute of London in 1964. After studying at Marburg, he was a professor at Heidelberg.

Ziegler-Natta catalyst Z-N catalysts are named after their originators, Karl Ziegler of the Max Planck Institut für Kohlenforschung in Mülheim and Giulio Natta of the Instituto di Chimica Industriale del Politecnico di Milano. Initially, they consisted essentially of an alkylaluminum compound together with a compound of the titanium group of the periodic table; a typical combination being triethylaluminum and either titanium tetrachloride or titanium trichloride. Subsequently, an enormous variety of mixtures of this general type were prepared and used in polymerization, and these are commonly referred to as catalysts of the Ziegler-Natta type.

The interest in these catalysts is in their remarkable stereospecificity. Their discovery by Ziegler and subsequent utilization by Natta opened entirely new vistas in polymer chemistry and technology. The monumental contributions of Ziegler and Natta received recognition when they were jointly awarded the Nobel Prize in chemistry in 1963.

This is not the way to achieve zero defects.

Ziegler-Natta polymerization Chain polymerizations using the Z-N catalyst are remarkable in that olefins may be polymerized under mild conditions to high molecular weight polymer and also high stereo-regulating effects are possible. Polymerizations are usually carried out in hydrocarbon solvents, with the strict absence of moisture, air, carbon dioxide, and other impurities which react with the catalyst or with the active centers and thus kill the polymerization.

A wide variety of monomers may be polymerized by the Z-N catalysts. However, their importance is largely due to their ability to polymerize x-olefins, especially propylene, to high molecular weight isotactic polymers, and to polymerize dienes, especially butadiene and isoprene, to stereoregular forms. ▷ **inhibition and retardation**

zinc borate White, amorphous powders of different compositions containing various amounts of zinc oxide and boric oxide. They are used as fire retardants in PVC, PVDC, polyesters, and polyolefins, usually in combination with antimony oxide.

zinc oxide An amorphous, white or yellowish powder, used as a pigment in plastics. It has a high UV light absorbing power of all commercially available pigments.

zinc stearate A white powder used as a lubricant.

zipper In 1851 Elias Howe, Jr. patented a device composed of a series of clasps and ribs that would join two pieces of material. Even though the concept had merit, he abandoned it to concentrate on the sewing machine. Howe's invention remained forgotten until the turn of the century, when it evolved into the zipper. Used at first to close money belts and tobacco pouches, it was not widely accepted by the apparel industry until the 1940s. This delay occurred because of complaints over snags, jams, and slipping in the relatively complex design. These problems translated into opportunities for Elie Gut, an immigrant (to the U.S.) who had helped his father manage the family textile mill in Switzerland. Gut had grown up watching master Swiss watchmakers at work, thus he made zippers to the standards of those watchmakers. He opened in 1939 in New York City the Ideal Fasteners Co. making zippers which at that time had 45 separate inspections to ensure quality products. Zippers now come in a variety of compositions, ranging through brass, aluminum, and plastic. Thermoplastic polyesters and acetal are the popular plastics with the usual plastics advantages that include corrosion resistance and light weight.

zipper added to film on-line ▷ **thermoforming, form, fill, and seal with zipper on-line**

zipper, chain An assemblage formed by interlocking several elements of two stringers.

zirconium oxide A white, amorphous powder used as a pigment when good electrical properties are required.

zone Any group of crystal planes which are all parallel to one line, called the zone axis.

zone fusion Procedure for growing single crystals by moving a molten zone along a rod of the material.